TREASURY EDITION

The McGraw-Hill Literature Series

Focus

Perception

Insights

Encounters

American Literature:
A Chronological Approach

English Literature:
A Chronological Approach

American Literature:
A Thematic Approach

British and Western Literature:
A Thematic Approach

G. Robert Carlsen
General Editor

Editors

Anthony Tovatt
Muncie, Indiana

Patricia O. Tovatt
Muncie, Indiana

CONTRIBUTORS AND SPECIAL CONSULTANTS

Sandra E. Bowen, New York, New York
Lee Davis, Westhampton, New York
Kathy Donahue, South Orange, New Jersey
Eleanor Hardt, Portland, Oregon
Nancy Icenogle, Milwaukie, Oregon
Lorraine Labate, Stamford, Connecticut
Brian K. McLaughlin, Lexington, Massachusetts
Bea Rockstroh, Clayton, Missouri
Eleanor Wier, St. Johns, Missouri

ADVISORS

John Olsen, Scottsdale, Arizona
Gay Tanner, Chino, California
Helen Fontaine, Manchester, Connecticut
Michael Bannigan, Waterbury, Connecticut
Peggy Ealum, Ft. Walton Beach, Florida
Mary Baltzelle, Plantation, Florida
Bonnie Crawford, Smyrna, Georgia
Roger Hines, Marietta, Georgia
Karen Fenton, Notus, Idaho
Mary Ann Ranells, Nampa, Idaho
Joseph Weaver, Converse, Indiana
Caroline Craeton, Topeka, Kansas
Blanche Back, Jackson, Kentucky
Francis Blair, Elizabethtown, Kentucky
Greg Reed, Lincoln, Maine
M. Davis, Park Ridge, Illinois
Thomas Freeling, Waterville, Maine
Patricia Hawkes, Berwich, Maine
Frances West, Baltimore, Maryland
Ellen Oberfelder, Baltimore, Maryland
Joan I. Brennan, New Bedford, Massachusetts

Eileen K. Shofield, Westwood, Massachusetts
Doris Cook, Detroit, Michigan
Josephine Hosey, Jackson, Mississippi
Patricia Hemeyer, Herman, Missouri
Tom Sharp, Richmond, Missouri
John J. Betunjar, Sutton, Nebraska
Meredith Berman, Plymouth, New Hampshire
Jane Lambert, Charlotte, North Carolina
Evelyn Stanton, Charlotte, North Carolina
Bonnie Cook, Winston-Salem, North Carolina
Marietta Hickman, Wake Forest, North Carolina
Brenda McClary, Charlotte, North Carolina
Jane Leigh, Dayton, Ohio
Susan Cummins, Claremore, Oklahoma
Laura MacManus, Albany, Oregon
Andy Anderson, Gladstone, Oregon
Sheila Webb, Dover, Pennsylvania

Robert Bell, McClennanville, South Carolina
Pansy Carter, Murfreesboro, Tennessee
Peggy Leeman, Dallas, Texas
Janet Molina, Bedford, Texas
Virginia Fields, Dallas, Texas
Sandra Wartell, San Antonio, Texas
Gail Olsen, San Antonio, Texas
Caryl Green, San Antonio, Texas
Ann Sochat, El Paso, Texas
Anita Arnold, San Antonio, Texas
Clair Murphy, El Paso, Texas
James Jacobson, Salt Lake City, Utah
Paul Dewanne, Sheboygan, Wisconsin
Marsha Hubbard, Mechanicsville, Virginia
Barbara Bowles, Richmond, Virginia
Sue Critzer, Charlottesville, Virginia
Cynthia Masincup, Woodstock, Virginia

INSIGHTS

G. Robert Carlsen • Anthony Tovatt • Patricia O. Tovatt

TREASURY
EDITION

WEBSTER DIVISION, MCGRAW-HILL BOOK COMPANY
New York, St. Louis, San Francisco, Dallas, Atlanta

Cover Art:

THE DUCK POND
Claude Monet
Sterling and Francine Clark Art Institute
Williamstown, Mass.

Editorial Direction: John A. Rothermich
Editor: Steven Griffel
Editing and Styling: Sue McCormick
Design Supervision: Valerie Greco
Production: Salvador Gonzales

Photo Editor: Alan Forman
Text and Cover Design: Blaise Zito Associates, Inc.
Cover Concept: Alan Forman

This book was set in Baskerville with Avant Garde Gothic by York Graphic Services, Inc. The color separation was done by York Graphic Services, Inc.

Library of Congress Cataloging in Publication Data
Main entry under title:

Insights.

(The McGraw-Hill literature series)
Summary: An anthology of poems, short stories, plays, and novels arranged by themes and by genre for ninth-grade readers.
1. Children's literature. [1. Literature—Collections]
I. Carlsen, G. Robert, 1917–   . II. Tovatt, Anthony.
III. Tovatt, Patricia O., 1916–   . IV. Series.
PZ5.I54 1985   808.8   83-17489
ISBN 0-07-009809-3

2 3 4 5 6 7 8 9 10   VNH VNH   93 92 91 90 89 88 87 86 85

Call to Adventure

With What You Have

The Inner Circle

The Ways of a Poet

The Poet Sees

The Poet Feels

The Poet Tells a Story

Identity

The Strange and Eerie

Once Upon a Midnight

Moments of Decision

How many a man
has dated a new era in his life
from the reading of a book.
The book exists for us, perchance,
which will explain our miracles and reveal new ones.
The, at present, unutterable things
we may find somewhere uttered.
These same questions that disturb and puzzle and confound us
have in their turn
occurred to all the wise men: not one has been omitted;
and each has answered them according to his ability,
by his word,
and his life.

HENRY DAVID THOREAU

MONARCH OF THE GLEN
Sir Edwin Landseer

John Dewar & Sons Ltd.

Call to Adventure

Kansas Boy

This Kansas boy who never saw the sea
Walks through the young corn rippling at his knee
As sailors walk; and when the grain grows higher
Watches the dark waves leap with greener fire
Than ever oceans hold. He follows ships,   5
Tasting the bitter spray upon his lips,
For in his blood up-stirs the salty ghost
Of one who sailed a storm-bound English coast.
Across wide fields he hears the sea winds crying,
Shouts at the crows—and dreams of white gulls flying.   10

RUTH LECHLITNER

A young man stands on a high and desolate cliff; his face is
ruddy in the setting sun of an England 1000 years ago. His
rough cloak flies outward from his shoulders in the whipping sea wind. With restless eyes he searches the distant
horizons of the sea and sky, like the modern day "Kansas
Boy" who never saw the sea, but "follows ships,/Tasting the
bitter spray. . ."

The sound of the angry waters crashing and tumbling
on the rocky coast fills the young man with an intense
yearning. He dreams of testing himself in a crude sailing
ship against the strength of the endless seas.

"Kansas Boy" first appeared in *Poetry*, November 1931. Was copyrighted
1931 by the Modern Poetry Association, and is reprinted by permission of
the author, Ruth Lechlitner.

The youth asks himself, What lies beyond the sunset?
He dreams of adventure:

> Oh, wildly my heart
> Beats in my bosom and bids me to try
> The tumble and surge of seas tumultuous,
> Breeze and brine and the breaker's roar.
> Daily, hourly, drives me my spirit   5
> Outward to sail, far countries to see.
> Liveth no man so large in his soul,
> So gracious in giving, so gay in his youth,
> In deeds so daring, so dear to his lord,
> But frets his soul for his sea adventure,   10
> Fain to try what fortune shall send.

The call to adventure is an old one. It comes from deep within. In every age, both the great and unknown have heard it and have answered. Odysseus heard it on the shores of the Aegean Sea over 3000 years ago, before he set sail for the war at Troy. Columbus heard it when he struck out across uncharted waters in search of new lands and riches. The men and women who pioneered the American wilderness heard it. Matthew Henson heard it when he wrote "The lure of the Arctic is tugging at my heart; to me the trail is calling!" Fourteen-year-old John Wise heard it when he first went up in a balloon he had made of old shirts and his mother's laundry basket. And today our astronauts continue to hear it as they explore the universe.

But travel is only one of the many dimensions of adventure. Adventure can be found in all kinds of experiences and situations. Adventure is all around you if the spirit of adventure is within you. It is as near as the book you hold in your hand.

From OLD ENGLISH POETRY, "Seafarer," p. 145, by J. Duncan Spaeth.
Copyright 1921 by Princeton University Press.

UNIT TECHNIQUES

The Reading for Appreciation sections of the study notes focus on techniques of good writing featured in the unit.

SUSPENSE

Suspense is a state of excited uncertainty. The reader intensely wants to know *what* is going to happen. *Who* is going to appear? *How* will the hero escape? Adventure writers deliberately withhold the answers as long as they can.

One moment of high suspense in the story you are about to read, "The Most Dangerous Game," comes on page 18, when Rainsford is hiding in a tree. General Zaroff is standing directly beneath him: "The general's eyes had left the ground and were traveling inch by inch up the tree. . . ."

FORESHADOWING

Foreshadowing is one of the chief means of creating suspense. The writer plants hints of dangers and perils that lie ahead. In "The Most Dangerous Game," even the title foreshadows the excitement. The mood of the story is set immediately by the name of the mysterious island (Ship-Trap Island) and by the description of the "dank tropical night that was palpable as it pressed its thick, warm blackness in upon the yacht."

CONFLICT

Conflict is the struggle between opposing forces. Without conflict there is no drama, no interest, no suspense—no story. The conflicting action may be between an individual and—

1. another individual or an animal
2. forces of nature, such as a storm or a flood
3. society
4. herself or himself

The last item, the conflict *within* an individual, is the basis for much of the world's best literature.

In real life, a person usually has more than one problem or conflict to handle. So it is in most stories. There is more than one conflict involved. Usually, however, there is a central conflict that is the most important. It is the unraveling of this main conflict that makes for the *plot*.

PLOT

Plot is the series of related incidents put together in a planned order so that a solution to the conflict is reached. If the plot is closely knit, no incident can be removed or changed in position without destroying the story's unity.

Many modern stories are simply a series of incidents loosely held together by a central character. These are stories without plot. They simply begin at one place and end at another without any sort of satisfactory solution, however interesting the story may be.

The tightly plotted story, then, has a beginning, a middle, and an end. Somewhere near the end, the action builds to a high point of interest. At this point the reader can see that the conflict must be resolved. This high point is called the *climax*.

IMAGINATIVE LANGUAGE

In *imaginative language,* words are used so that they arouse the reader's feelings. One sees, hears, smells, touches, tastes with the author. A word picture can be as vivid as a photograph or drawing. Sometimes a vivid image appeals to more than one sense at a time. An example of this is Rainsford's description of the tropical night: "moist black velvet."

THE
SHORT STORY

Opening with that classic of suspense, "The Most Danger-ous Game," *Insights* offers a panorama of short stories that demonstrate the variety in form and content to be found in short fiction.

The short story has no set pattern nor exact definition. It utilizes the same basic literary elements that are found in the novel, in drama, and in some poetry and nonfiction. The short stories in CALL TO ADVENTURE demonstrate particularly the elements that make good adventure writing exciting: *suspense, foreshadowing, conflict, plot,* and *imaginative language.*

In the short story section of WITH WHAT YOU HAVE, you will find O. Henry's "The Gift of the Magi." This classic story is well known for its artful plot and sur-prise ending. Study emphasis throughout this unit is on *characterization* and *significant detail.*

Morley Callaghan's "All the Years of Her Life," which opens the short story portion of THE INNER CIRCLE, is preceded by an overview of short story elements with em-phasis on *theme, narrative viewpoint,* and *symbolism.* Succeed-ing units, which consider *style* as well as *beginnings* and *end-ings,* contain stories as diabolical as Poe's "The Cask of Amontillado" and as suspenseful and thoughtful as Frank Stockton's "The Lady, or the Tiger?"

As you explore the techniques authors use to write short stories, you gain insight that increases your appreciation and enjoyment of this literary genre.

A mysterious island looms to the right of the ship—
an island whose very name suggests evil! What adventure lies
ahead? What will prove to be "the most dangerous game"?

THE MOST DANGEROUS GAME
Richard Connell

"Off there to the right—somewhere—is a large island," said Whitney. "It's rather a mystery. . . ."

"What island is it?" Rainsford asked.

"The old charts call it 'Ship-Trap Island,'" Whitney replied. "A suggestive name, isn't it? Sailors have a curious dread of the place. I don't know why. Some superstition . . ."

"Can't see it," remarked Rainsford, trying to peer through the dank tropical night that was palpable as it pressed its thick, warm blackness in upon the yacht.

"You have good eyes," said Whitney, with a laugh, "and I've seen you pick off a moose moving in the brown fall bush at four hundred yards; but even you can't see four miles or so through a moonless Caribbean[1] night."

"Nor four yards," admitted Rainsford. "Ugh! It's like moist black velvet."

"It will be light enough in Rio,"[2] promised Whitney. "We should make it in a few days. I hope the jaguar guns have come. We'll have some good hunting up the Amazon.[3] Great sport, hunting."

"The best sport in the world," agreed Rainsford.

"For the hunter," amended Whitney. "Not for the jaguar."

"Don't talk rot, Whitney," said Rainsford. "You're a big-game hunter, not a philosopher. Who cares how the jaguar feels?"

"Perhaps the jaguar does," observed Whitney.

"Bah! They've no understanding."

"Even so, I rather think they understand one thing—fear. The fear of pain and the fear of death."

"Nonsense," laughed Rainsford. "This hot weather is making you soft, Whitney. Be a realist. The world is made up of two classes—the hunters and the hunted. Luckily, you and I are hunters. Do you think we've passed that island yet?"

"I can't tell in the dark. I hope so."

"Why?" asked Rainsford.

"The place has a reputation—a bad one. It's gotten into sailor lore, somehow. Didn't you notice that the crew's nerves seemed a bit jumpy today?"

"They were a bit strange, now you mention it. Even Captain Nielsen . . ."

1. **Caribbean** (kaȧ′ə bē′ən, kə rib′ē ən), of or pertaining to the arm of the Atlantic Ocean between the West Indies islands and the American mainland.
2. **Rio,** short for **Rio de Janeiro** (rē′ō dā zhə ner′ō), the large seaport in southeast Brazil.
3. **Amazon** (am′ə zon), the huge river flowing in an easterly direction through Brazil, called the largest river in the world.

"Yes, even that tough-minded old Swede, who'd go up to the devil himself and ask him for a light. All I could get out of him was: 'This place has an evil name among seafaring men, sir.' Then he said to me, very gravely: 'Don't you feel anything?'—as if the air about us was actually poisonous. Now, you mustn't laugh when I tell you this—I did feel something like a sudden chill.

"There was no breeze. The sea was as flat as a plate-glass window. We were drawing near the island then. What I felt was a—a mental chill; a sort of sudden dread."

"Pure imagination," said Rainsford. "One superstitious sailor can taint the whole ship's company with his fear."

"Maybe. But sometimes I think sailors have an extra sense that tells them when they are in danger. Sometimes I think evil is a tangible thing—with wave lengths, just as sound and light have. An evil place can, so to speak, broadcast vibrations of evil. Anyhow, I'm glad we're getting out of this zone. Well, I think I'll turn in now, Rainsford."

"I'm not sleepy," said Rainsford. "I'm going to smoke another pipe up on the afterdeck."

"Good night, then, Rainsford. See you at breakfast."

"Right. Good night, Whitney."

There was no sound in the night as Rainsford sat there but the muffled throb of the engine that drove the yacht swiftly through the darkness, and the swish and ripple of the wash of the propeller.

Rainsford, reclining in a steamer

chair, indolently puffed on his favorite brier. The sensuous drowsiness of the night was on him. "It's so dark," he thought, "that I could sleep without closing my eyes; the night would be my eyelids. . . ."

An abrupt sound startled him. Off to the right he had heard it, and his ears, expert in such matters, could not be mistaken. Again he heard the sound and again. Somewhere, off in the blackness, someone had fired a gun three times.

Rainsford sprang up and moved quickly to the rail, mystified. He strained his eyes in the direction from which the reports had come, but it was like trying to see through a blanket. He leaped upon the rail and balanced himself there, to get greater elevation; his pipe, striking a rope, was knocked from his mouth. He lunged for it; a short, hoarse cry came from his lips as he realized he had reached too far and had lost his balance. The cry was pinched off short as the blood-warm waters of the Caribbean Sea closed over his head.

He struggled up to the surface and tried to cry out, but the wash from the speeding yacht made him gag and strangle. Desperately he struck out with strong strokes after the receding lights of the yacht, but he stopped before he had swum fifty feet. A certain cool-headedness had come to him; it was not the first time he had been in a tight place. There was a chance that his cries could be heard by someone aboard the yacht, but that chance was slender, and grew more slender as the yacht raced on. He wrestled himself out of some of his clothes, and shouted with all his power. The lights of the yacht became faint and ever-vanishing fireflies; then they were blotted out entirely by the night.

Rainsford remembered that the shots had come from the right; and doggedly he swam in that direction, swimming with slow, deliberate strokes, conserving his strength. For a seemingly endless time he fought the sea. He began to count his strokes; he could do possibly a hundred more and then . . .

Rainsford heard a sound. It came out of the darkness, a high, screaming sound, the sound of an animal in an extremity of anguish and terror.

He did not recognize the animal that made the sound; he did not try to; with fresh vitality he swam toward the sound. He heard it again; then it was cut short by another noise, crisp, staccato.

"Pistol shot," muttered Rainsford, swimming on.

Ten minutes of determined effort brought another sound to his ears—the most welcome he had ever heard—the muttering and growling of the sea breaking on a rocky shore. He was almost on the rocks before he saw them; on a night less calm he would have been shattered against them. With his remaining strength he dragged himself from the swirling waters. Jagged crags appeared to jut up into the opaqueness; he forced himself upward, hand over hand. Gasping, his hands raw, he reached a flat place at the top. Dense jungle came down to the very edge of the cliffs. What perils that tangle of trees and underbrush might hold for him did not concern Rainsford just then. All he knew was that he was safe from his enemy, the sea, and that utter weariness was on him. He flung himself down and tumbled headlong into the deepest sleep of his life.

When he opened his eyes, he knew from the position of the sun that it was late in the afternoon. Sleep had given him new vigor; a sharp hunger was picking at him. He looked about him, almost cheerfully.

"Where there are pistol shots, there are men. Where there are men, there is food," he thought. But what kind of men, he wondered, in so forbidding a place? An unbroken front of snarled and ragged jungle fringed the shore. He saw no sign of a trail through the closely knit web of weeds and trees; it was easier to go along the shore, and he floundered along by the water. Not far from where he had landed, he stopped.

Some wounded thing, by the evidence a large animal, had thrashed about in the underbrush; the jungle weeds were crushed down and the moss was lacerated; one patch of weeds was stained crimson. A small, glittering object not far away caught Rainsford's eye and he picked it up. It was an empty cartridge.

"A twenty-two," he remarked. "That's odd. It must have been a fairly large animal, too. The hunter had his nerve with him to tackle it with a light gun. It's clear that the brute put up a fight. I suppose the first three shots I heard was when the hunter flushed his quarry and wounded it. The last shot was when he trailed it here and finished it."

He examined the ground closely and found what he had hoped to find—the print of hunting boots. They pointed along the cliff in the direction he had been going. Eagerly he hurried along, now slipping on a rotten log or a loose stone, but making headway; night was beginning to settle down on the island.

Bleak darkness was blacking out the sea and jungle when Rainsford sighted the lights. He came upon them as he turned a crook in the coast line, and his first thought was that he had come upon a village, for there were many lights. But as he forged along he saw to his great astonishment that all the lights were in one enormous building—a lofty structure with pointed towers plunging upward into the gloom. His eyes made out the shadowy outlines of a palatial château;[4] it was set on a high bluff, and on three sides of it cliffs dived down to where the sea licked greedy lips in the shadows.

"Mirage," thought Rainsford. But it was no mirage, he found, when he opened the tall spiked iron gate. The stone steps were real enough; the massive door with a leering gargoyle[5] for a knocker was real enough; yet about it all hung an air of unreality.

He lifted the knocker; and it creaked up stiffly, as if it had never before been used. He let it fall, and it startled him with its booming loudness. He thought ıe heard steps within; the door remained closed. Again Rainsford lifted the heavy knocker, and let it fall. The door opened then, opened as suddenly as if it were on a spring, and Rainsford stood blinking in the river of glaring gold light that poured out. The first thing his eyes discerned was the largest man he had ever seen—a gigantic creature, solidly made and black-bearded to the waist. In his hand the man held a long-barreled revolver, and he was pointing it straight at Rainsford's heart. Out of the snarl of beard two small eyes regarded Rainsford.

"Don't be alarmed," said Rainsford, with a smile which he hoped was disarming. "I'm no robber. I fell off a yacht. My name is Sanger Rainsford of New York City."

The menacing look in the eyes did not change. The revolver pointed as rigidly as if the giant were a statue. He gave no sign that he understood Rainsford's words, or that he had even heard them. He was dressed in uniform, a black uniform trimmed with gray astrakhan.[6]

"I'm Sanger Rainsford of New York," Rainsford began again. "I fell off a yacht. I am hungry."

The man's only answer was to raise with his thumb the hammer of his revolver. Then Rainsford saw the man's free hand go to his forehead in a military salute, and he saw him click his heels together and stand at attention. Another man was coming down the broad marble steps, an erect, slender man in evening clothes. He advanced to Rainsford and held out his hand.

In a cultivated voice marked by a slight accent that gave it added precision and deliberateness, he said: "It is a very great pleasure and honor to welcome Mr. Sanger Rainsford, the celebrated hunter, to my home."

Automatically Rainsford shook the man's hand.

"I've read your book about hunting snow leopards in Tibet,[7] you see," explained the man. "I am General Zaroff."

---

4. **château** (sha tō'), the French word for castle; also a large country house.
5. **gargoyle** (gär'goil), a protruding ornament in the shape of a fantastic animal.
6. **astrakhan** (as'trə kən), curly, fur-like wool of caracul lambs from Astrakhan.
7. **Tibet** (ti bet'), central Asian country between China and India.

Rainsford's first impression was that the man was singularly handsome; his second was that there was an original, almost bizarre quality about the general's face. He was a tall man past middle age, for his hair was a vivid white; but his thick eyebrows and pointed military mustache were as black as the night from which Rainsford had come. His eyes, too, were black and very bright. He had high cheekbones, a sharp-cut nose, a spare, dark face, the face of a man used to giving orders, the face of an aristocrat. Turning to the giant in uniform, the general made a sign. The giant put away his pistol, saluted, withdrew.

"Ivan is an incredibly strong fellow," remarked the general, "but he has the misfortune to be deaf and dumb. A simple fellow, but I'm afraid, like all his race, a bit of a savage."

"Is he Russian?"

"He is a Cossack,"[8] said the general, and his smile showed red lips and pointed teeth. "So am I."

"Come," he said, "we shouldn't be chatting here. We can talk later. Now you want clothes, food, rest. You shall have them. This is a most restful spot."

Ivan had reappeared, and the general spoke to him with lips that moved but gave forth no sound.

"Follow Ivan, if you please, Mr. Rainsford," said the general. "I was about to have my dinner when you came. I'll wait for you. You'll find that my clothes will fit you, I think."

It was to a huge, beam-ceilinged bedroom with a canopied bed big enough for six men that Rainsford followed the silent giant. Ivan laid out an evening suit, and Rainsford, as he put it on, noticed that it came from a London tailor who ordinarily cut and sewed for none below the rank of duke.

The dining room to which Ivan conducted him was in many ways remarkable. There was a medieval magnificence about it; it suggested a baronial hall of feudal times with its oaken panels, its high ceiling, its vast refectory table where two score men could sit down to eat. About the hall were the mounted heads of many animals—lions, tigers, elephants, moose, bears; larger or more perfect specimens Rainsford had never seen. At the great table the general was sitting alone.

Rainsford noted the table appointments were of the finest—the linen, the crystal, the silver, the china.

They were eating *borsch,* the rich, red soup with sour cream so dear to Russian palates. Half apologetically General Zaroff said: "We do our best to preserve the amenities of civilization here. Please forgive any lapses. We are well off the beaten track, you know. Do you think the champagne has suffered from its long ocean trip?"

"Not in the least," declared Rainsford. He was finding the general a most thoughtful and affable host, a true cosmopolite.[9] But there was one small trait of the general's that made Rainsford uncomfortable. Whenever he looked up from his plate he found the general studying him, appraising him narrowly.

"Perhaps," said General Zaroff, "you were surprised that I recognized your name. You see, I read all books on hunt-

8. **Cossack** (kos'ak), one of a warlike people from the plains of southeast Russia. They were noted for their horsemanship.
9. **cosmopolite** (koz mop'ə līt), a person with wide international sophistication.

ing published in English, French, and Russian. I have but one passion in my life, Mr. Rainsford, and that is the hunt."

"You have some wonderful heads here," said Rainsford as he ate a particularly well-cooked filet mignon. "That Cape buffalo is the largest I ever saw."

"Oh, that fellow. Yes, he was a monster."

"Did he charge you?"

"Hurled me against a tree," said the general. "Fractured my skull. But I got the brute."

"I've always thought," said Rainsford, "that Cape buffalo is the most dangerous of all big game."

For a moment the general did not reply; he was smiling his curious red-lipped smile. Then he said slowly: "No. You are wrong, sir. The Cape buffalo is not the most dangerous big game." He sipped his wine. "Here in my preserve on this island," he said in the same slow tone, "I hunt more dangerous game."

Rainsford expressed his surprise. "Is there big game on this island?"

The general nodded. "The biggest."

"Really?"

"Oh, it isn't here naturally, of course. I have to stock the island."

"What have you imported, general?" Rainsford asked. "Tigers?"

The general smiled. "No," he said. "Hunting tigers ceased to interest me some years ago. I exhausted their possibilities, you see. No thrill left in tigers, no real danger. I live for danger, Mr. Rainsford."

The general took from his pocket a gold cigarette case and offered his guest a long black cigarette with a silver tip; it was perfumed and gave off a smell like incense.

"We will have some capital hunting, you and I," said the general. "I shall be most glad to have your society."

"But what game——" began Rainsford.

"I'll tell you," said the general. "You will be amused, I know. I think I may say, in all modesty, that I have done a rare thing. I have invented a new sensation. May I pour you another glass of port, Mr. Rainsford?"

"Thank you, general."

The general filled both glasses, and said: "God makes some men poets. Some He makes kings, some beggars. Me He made a hunter. My hand was made for the trigger, my father said. He was a very rich man with a quarter of a million acres in the Crimea,[10] and he was an ardent sportsman. When I was only five years old, he gave me a little gun to shoot sparrows with. When I shot some of his prize turkeys with it, he did not punish me; he complimented me on my marksmanship. I killed my first bear when I was ten. My whole life has been one prolonged hunt. I went into the army—it was expected of noblemen's sons—and for a time commanded a division of Cossack cavalry, but my real interest was always the hunt. I have hunted every kind of game in every land. It would be impossible for me to tell you how many animals I have killed."

The general puffed at his cigarette.

"After the debacle[11] in Russia I left the country, for it was imprudent for an officer of the Czar[12] to stay there. Many

---

10. **Crimea** (krī mē′ə), a peninsula jutting into the Black Sea from southwestern Russia.
11. **debacle** (dā bä′kel, di bak′əl), sudden collapse or overthrow.
12. The general here refers to the overthrow of the **Czar's** (Tsar's) government in Russia, 1917, with confiscation of the estates of the old Russian nobility.

noble Russians had lost everything. Luck-ily, I had invested heavily in American securities, so I shall never have to open a tea room in Monte Carlo or drive a taxi in Paris. Naturally, I continued to hunt—grizzlies in your Rockies, crocodiles in the Ganges,[13] rhinoceroses in East Af-rica. It was in Africa that the Cape buf-falo hit me and laid me up for six months. As soon as I recovered I started for the Amazon to hunt jaguars, for I had heard they were unusually cunning. They weren't." The Cossack sighed. "They were no match at all for a hunter with his wits about him, and a high-pow-ered rifle. I was bitterly disappointed. I was lying in my tent with a splitting head-ache one night when a terrible thought pushed its way into my mind. Hunting was beginning to bore me! And hunting, remember, had been my life. I have heard that in America businessmen often go to pieces when they give up the busi-ness that has been their life."

"Yes, that's so," said Rainsford.

The general smiled. "I had no wish to go to pieces," he said. "I must do some-thing. Now, mine is an analytical mind, Mr. Rainsford. Doubtless that is why I enjoy the problems of the chase."

"No doubt, General Zaroff."

"So," continued the general, "I asked myself why the hunt no longer fascinated me. You are much younger than I am, Mr. Rainsford, and have not hunted as much; but you perhaps can guess the answer."

"What was it?"

"Simply this; hunting had ceased to be what you call 'a sporting proposition.' It had become too easy. I always got my quarry. Always. There is no greater bore than perfection."

The general lit a fresh cigarette.

"No animal had a chance with me any more. That is no boast; it is a mathemati-cal certainty. The animal had nothing but his legs and his instinct. Instinct is no match for reason. When I thought of this it was a tragic moment for me, I can tell you."

Rainsford leaned across the table, absorbed in what his host was saying.

"It came to me as an inspiration what I must do," the general went on.

"And that was?"

The general smiled the quiet smile of one who has faced an obstacle and sur-mounted it with success. "I had to invent a new animal to hunt," he said.

"A new animal? You're joking."

"Not at all," said the general. "I never joke about hunting. I needed a new ani-mal. I found one. So I bought this island, built this house, and here I do my hunt-ing. The island is perfect for my pur-poses—there are jungles with a maze of trails in them, hills, swamps——"

"But the animal, General Zaroff?"

"Oh," said the general, "it supplies me with the most exciting hunting in the world. No other hunting compares with it for an instant. Every day I hunt, and I never grow bored now, for I have a quarry with which I can match my wits."

Rainsford's bewilderment showed in his face.

"I wanted the ideal animal to hunt," explained the general. "So I said: 'What are the attributes of an ideal quarry?' And the answer was, of course: 'It must have courage, cunning, and, above all, it must be able to reason.'"

13. **the Ganges** (gan′jēz), the great river flowing south in northern and northeastern India.

"But no animal can reason," objected Rainsford.

"My dear fellow," said the general, "there is one that can."

"But you can't mean——" gasped Rainsford.

"And why not?"

"I can't believe you are serious, General Zaroff. This is a grisly joke."

"Why should I not be serious? I am speaking of hunting."

"Hunting? General Zaroff, what you speak of is murder."

The general laughed with entire good nature. He regarded Rainsford quizzically. "I refuse to believe that so modern and civilized a young man as you seem to be harbors romantic ideas about the value of human life. Surely your experiences in the war——"

"Did not make me condone cold-blooded murder," finished Rainsford stiffly.

Laughter shook the general. "How extraordinarily droll you are!" he said. "One does not expect nowadays to find a young man of the educated class, even in America, with such a naïve, and, if I may say so, mid-Victorian[14] point of view. Ah, well, doubtless you had Puritan ancestors. So many Americans appear to have had. I'll wager you'll forget your notions when you go hunting with me. You've a genuine new thrill in store for you, Mr. Rainsford."

"Thank you, I'm a hunter, not a murderer."

"Dear me," said the general, quite unruffled, "again that unpleasant word. But I think I can show you that your scruples are quite ill-founded."

"Yes?"

"Life is for the strong, to be lived by the strong, and, if needs be, taken by the strong. The weak of the world were put here to give the strong pleasure. I am strong. Why should I not use my gift? If I wish to hunt, why should I not? I hunt the scum of the earth—sailors from tramp ships—lascars,[15] blacks, Chinese, whites, mongrels—a thoroughbred horse or hound is worth more than a score of them."

"But they are men," said Rainsford hotly.

"Precisely," said the general. "That is why I use them. It gives me pleasure. They can reason, after a fashion. So they are dangerous."

"But where do you get them?"

The general's left eyelid fluttered down in a wink. "This island is called Ship-Trap," he answered. "Sometimes an angry god of the high seas sends them to me. Sometimes, when Providence is not so kind, I help Providence a bit. Come to the window with me."

Rainsford went to the window and looked out toward the sea.

"Watch! Out there!" exclaimed the general, pointing into the night. Rainsford's eyes saw only blackness, and then, as the general pressed a button, far out to sea Rainsford saw the flash of lights.

The general chuckled. "They indicate a channel," he said, "where there's none: giant rocks with razor edges crouch like a sea monster with wide-open jaws. They can crush a ship as easily as I crush this nut." He dropped a walnut on the hard-

14. **mid-Victorian** (mid vik tôr′ē ən), suitable to the times of Queen Victoria of England, whose reign (1837–1901) was marked by ideas now regarded as narrow and limited.
15. **lascar** (las′kər), a native East Indian sailor.

wood floor and brought his heel grinding down on it. "Oh, yes," he said, casually, as if in answer to a question, "I have electricity. We try to be civilized here."

"Civilized? And you shoot down men?"

A trace of anger was in the general's black eyes, but it was there for but a second; then he said, in his most pleasant manner: "Dear me, what a righteous young man you are! I assure you I do not do the thing you suggest. That would be barbarous. I treat these visitors with every consideration. They get plenty of good food and exercise. They get into splendid physical condition. You shall see for yourself tomorrow."

"What do you mean?"

"We shall visit my training school," smiled the general. "It's in the cellar. I have about a dozen pupils down there now. They're from the Spanish bark *San Lucar*[16] that had the bad luck to go on the rocks out there. A very inferior lot, I regret to say. Poor specimens and more accustomed to the deck than to the jungle."

He raised his hand, and Ivan brought thick Turkish coffee. Rainsford, with an effort, held his tongue in check.

"It's a game, you see," pursued the general blandly, "I suggest to one of them that we go hunting. I give him a supply of food and an excellent hunting knife. I give him three hours' start. I am to follow, armed only with a pistol of the smallest caliber and range. If my quarry eludes me for three whole days, he wins the game. If I find him"—the general smiled—"he loses."

"Suppose he refuses to be hunted?"

"Oh," said the general, "I give him his option, of course. He need not play that game if he doesn't wish to. If he does not wish to hunt, I turn him over to Ivan. Ivan once had the honor of serving as official knouter to the Great White Czar,[17] and he has his own ideas of sport. Invariably, Mr. Rainsford, invariably they choose the hunt."

"And if they win?"

The smile on the general's face widened. "To date I have not lost," he said.

Then he added, hastily: "I don't wish you to think me a braggart, Mr. Rainsford. Many of them afford only the most elementary sort of problem. Occasionally I strike a tartar.[18] One almost did win. I eventually had to use the dogs."

"The dogs?"

"This way, please. I'll show you."

The general steered Rainsford to a window. The lights from the windows sent a flickering illumination that made grotesque patterns on the courtyard below, and Rainsford could see moving about there a dozen or so huge black shapes; as they turned toward him, their eyes glittered greenly.

"A rather good lot, I think," observed the general. "They are let out at seven every night. If anyone should try to get into my house—or out of it—something extremely regrettable would occur to him." He hummed a snatch of a gay French song.

"And now," said the general, "I want to show you my new collection of heads. Will you come with me to the library?"

16. **San Lucar** (san lü kär').
17. The **Great White Czar** was Alexander III, who reigned from 1881 to 1894. Ivan punished criminals and opponents of the Czar by flogging them with the **knout**, a leather and metal whip.
18. **to strike a tartar** is to meet with an opponent who shows unexpected strength or resistance.

"I hope," said Rainsford, "that you will excuse me tonight, General Zaroff. I'm really not feeling at all well."

"Ah, indeed?" the general inquired solicitously. "Well, I suppose that's only natural after your long swim. You need a good, restful night's sleep. Tomorrow you'll feel like a new man, I'll wager. Then we'll hunt, eh? I've one rather promising prospect. . . ."

Rainsford was hurrying from the room.

"Sorry you can't go with me tonight," called the general. "I expect rather fair sport—a big, strong black. He looks resourceful. . . . Well, good night, Mr. Rainsford; I hope you have a good night's rest."

The bed was good, and the pajamas of the softest silk, and he was tired in every fiber of his being; nevertheless Rainsford could not quiet his brain with the opiate[19] of sleep. He lay, eyes wide open. Once he thought he heard stealthy steps in the corridor outside his room. He sought to throw open the door; it would not open. He went to the window and looked out. His room was high up in one of the towers. The lights of the château were out now, and it was dark and silent, but there was a fragment of sallow moon, and by its wan light he could see, dimly, the courtyard; there, weaving in and out in the pattern of shadow, were black, noiseless forms; the hounds heard him at the window and looked up, expectantly, with their green eyes. Rainsford went back to the bed and lay down. By many methods he tried to put himself to sleep. He had achieved a doze when, just as morning began to come, he heard, far off in the jungle, the faint report of a pistol.

General Zaroff did not appear until luncheon. He was dressed faultlessly in the tweeds of a country squire. He was solicitous about the state of Rainsford's health.

"As for me," sighed the general, "I do not feel so well. I am worried, Mr. Rainsford. Last night I detected traces of my old complaint."

To Rainsford's questioning glance the general said: "Ennui. Boredom."

Then, taking a second helping of crêpes suzette,[20] the general explained: "The hunting was not good last night. The fellow lost his head. He made a straight trail that offered no problems at all. That's the trouble with these sailors; they have dull brains to begin with, and they do not know how to get about in the woods. They do excessively stupid and obvious things. It's most annoying. Will you have another glass of Chablis, Mr. Rainsford?"

"General," said Rainsford firmly, "I wish to leave this island at once."

The general raised his eyebrows; he seemed hurt. "But, my dear fellow," he protested, "you've only just come. You've had no hunting——"

"I wish to go today," said Rainsford. He saw the dead black eyes of the general on him, studying him. General Zaroff's face suddenly brightened.

He filled Rainsford's glass with venerable Chablis from a dusty bottle.

"Tonight," said the general, "we will hunt—you and I."

Rainsford shook his head. "No, general," he said. "I will not hunt."

---

19. **opiate** (ō′pē it, ō′pē āt), anything that quiets or soothes.
20. **crêpes suzette** (krāp′sü zet′), thin, sweet pancakes rolled with various sauces.

The general shrugged his shoulders and delicately ate a hothouse grape. "As you wish, my friend." he said. "The choice rests entirely with you. But may I not venture to suggest that you will find my idea of sport more diverting than Ivan's?"

He nodded toward the corner to where the giant stood, scowling, his thick arms crossed on his hogshead of a chest.

"You don't mean——" cried Rainsford.

"My dear fellow," said the general, "have I not told you I always mean what I say about hunting? This is really an inspiration. I drink to a foeman worthy of my steel—at last."

The general raised his glass, but Rainsford sat staring at him.

"You'll find this game worth playing," the general said enthusiastically. "Your brain against mine. Your woodcraft against mine. Your strength and stamina against mine. Outdoor chess! And the stake is not without value, eh?"

"And if I win——" began Rainsford huskily.

"I'll cheerfully acknowledge myself defeated if I do not find you by midnight of the third day," said General Zaroff. "My sloop will place you on the mainland near a town."

The general read what Rainsford was thinking.

"Oh, you can trust me," said the Cossack. "I will give you my word as a gentleman and a sportsman. Of course, you in turn must agree to say nothing of your visit here."

"I'll agree to nothing of the kind," said Rainsford.

"Oh," said the general, "in that case——But why discuss that now? Three days hence we can discuss it over a bottle of wine, unless——"

The general sipped his wine.

Then a businesslike air animated him. "Ivan," he said to Rainsford, "will supply you with hunting clothes, food, a knife. I suggest you wear moccasins; they leave a poorer trail. I suggest, too, that you avoid the big swamp in the southeast corner of the island. We call it Death Swamp. There's quicksand there. One foolish fellow tried it. The deplorable part of it was that Lazarus followed him. You can imagine my feelings, Mr. Rainsford. I loved Lazarus; he was the finest hound in my pack. Well, I must beg you to excuse me now. I always take a siesta after lunch. You'll hardly have time for a nap, I fear. You'll want to start, no doubt. I shall not follow till dusk. Hunting at night is so much more exciting, don't you think? *Au revoir,*[21] Mr. Rainsford, *au revoir.*"

General Zaroff, with a deep, courtly bow, strolled from the room. From another door came Ivan. Under one arm he carried khaki hunting clothes, a haversack of food, a leather sheath containing a long-bladed hunting knife; his right hand rested on a cocked revolver thrust in the crimson sash about his waist. . . .

Rainsford had fought his way through the bush for two hours. "I must keep my nerve. I must keep my nerve," he said through tight teeth.

He had not been entirely clear-headed when the château gates snapped shut behind him. His whole idea at first was to put distance between himself and

---

21. **au revoir** (ō rə vwàr′), French for "good-bye; till I see you again."

General Zaroff; and, to this end, he had plunged along, spurred on by something very much like panic. Now he had got a grip on himself, had stopped, and was taking stock of himself and the situation.

He saw that straight flight was futile; inevitably it would bring him face to face with the sea. He was in a picture with a frame of water, and his operations, clearly, must take place within that frame.

"I'll give him a trail to follow," muttered Rainsford, and he struck off from the rude path he had been following into the trackless wilderness. He executed a series of intricate loops; he doubled on his trail again and again, recalling all the lore of the fox hunt, and all the dodges of the fox. Night found him leg-weary, with hands and face lashed by the branches, on a thickly wooded ridge. He knew it would be insane to blunder on through the dark, even if he had the strength. His need for rest was imperative and he thought: "I have played the fox, now I must play the cat of the fable."[22] A big tree with a thick trunk and outspread branches was nearby, and, taking care to leave not the slightest mark, he climbed up, and stretching out on one of the broad limbs, after a fashion, rested. Rest brought him new confidence and almost a feeling of security. Even so zealous a hunter as General Zaroff could not trace him there, he told himself; only the devil himself could follow that complicated trail through the jungle after dark. But, perhaps, the general was a devil. . . .

An apprehensive night crawled slowly by like a wounded snake, and sleep did not visit Rainsford, although the silence of a dead world was on the jungle. Toward morning when a dingy gray was

varnishing the sky, the cry of some startled bird focused Rainsford's attention in that direction. Something was coming through the bush, coming slowly, carefully, coming by the same winding way Rainsford had come. He flattened himself down on the limb, and through a screen of leaves almost as thick as tapestry, he watched. The thing that was approaching was a man.

It was General Zaroff. He made his way along with his eyes fixed in utmost concentration on the ground before him. He paused, almost beneath the tree, dropped to his knees and studied the ground. Rainsford's impulse was to hurl himself down like a panther, but he saw that the general's right hand held something metallic—a small automatic pistol.

The hunter shook his head several times, as if he were puzzled. Then he straightened up and took from his case one of his black cigarettes; its pungent incenselike smoke floated up to Rainsford's nostrils.

Rainsford held his breath. The general's eyes had left the ground and were traveling inch by inch up the tree. Rainsford froze there, every muscle tensed for a spring. But the sharp eyes of the hunter stopped before they reached the limb where Rainsford lay; a smile spread over his brown face. Very deliberately he blew a smoke ring into the air; then he turned his back on the tree and walked carelessly away, back along the trail he had come. The swish of the underbrush against his hunting boots grew fainter and fainter.

22. **the cat of the fable,** Rainsford has used the craft of a fox and now he must watch patiently like a cat at a mousehole.

The pent-up air burst hotly from Rainsford's lungs. His first thought made him feel sick and numb. The general could follow a trail through the woods at night; he could follow an extremely difficult trail; he must have uncanny powers; only by the merest chance had the Cossack failed to see his quarry.

Rainsford's second thought was even more terrible. It sent a shudder of cold horror through his whole being. Why had the general smiled? Why had he turned back?

Rainsford did not want to believe what his reason told him was true, but the truth was as evident as the sun that by now had pushed through the morning mists. The general was playing with him! The general was saving him for another day's sport! The Cossack was the cat; *he* was the mouse. Then it was that Rainsford knew the full meaning of terror.

"I will not lose my nerve. I will not."

He slid down from the tree, and struck off again into the woods. His face was set and he forced the machinery of his mind to function. Three hundred yards from his hiding place he stopped where a huge dead tree leaned precariously on a smaller, living one. Throwing off his sack of food, Rainsford took his knife from its sheath and began to work with all his energy.

The job was finished at last, and he threw himself down behind a fallen log a hundred feet away. He did not have to wait long. The cat was coming again to play with the mouse.

Following the trail with the sureness of a bloodhound, came General Zaroff. Nothing escaped those searching black eyes, no crushed blade of grass, no bent twig, no mark, no matter how faint, in the moss. So intent was the Cossack on his stalking that he was upon the thing Rainsford had made before he saw it. His foot touched the protruding bough that was the trigger. Even as he touched it, the general sensed his danger and leaped back with the agility of an ape. But he was not quite quick enough; the dead tree, delicately adjusted to rest on the cut living one, crashed down and struck the general a glancing blow on the shoulder as it fell; but for his alertness, he must have been smashed beneath it. He staggered, but he did not fall; nor did he drop his revolver. He stood there, rubbing his injured shoulder; and Rainsford, with fear again gripping his heart, heard the general's mocking laugh ring through the jungle.

"Rainsford," called the general, "if you are within sound of my voice, as I suppose you are, let me congratulate you. Not many men know how to make a Malay man-catcher. Luckily, for me, I, too, have hunted in Malacca.[23] You are proving interesting, Mr. Rainsford. I am going now to have my wound dressed; it's only a slight one. But I shall be back. I shall be back."

When the general, nursing his bruised shoulder, had gone, Rainsford took up his flight again. It was flight now, a desperate, hopeless flight that carried him on for some hours. Dusk came, then darkness, and still he pressed on. The ground grew softer under his moccasins; the vegetation grew ranker, denser; insects bit him savagely. Then, as he stepped forward, his foot sank into the ooze. He tried to wrench it back, but the

23. **Malacca** (mə lok′ə), an area on the southwestern coast of Malaya in extreme southeastern Asia.

muck sucked viciously at his foot as if it were a giant leech. With a violent effort, he tore his foot loose. He knew where he was now. Death Swamp and its quicksand.

His hands were tight closed as if his nerve were something tangible that someone in the darkness was trying to tear from his grip. The softness of the earth had given him an idea. He stepped back from the quicksand a dozen feet or so and, like some huge prehistoric beaver, he began to dig.

Rainsford had dug himself in in France when a second's delay meant death. That had been a placid pastime compared to his digging now. The pit grew deeper; when it was above his shoulders, he climbed out and from some hard saplings cut stakes and sharpened them to a fine point. These stakes he planted in the bottom of the pit with the points sticking up. With flying fingers he wove a rough carpet of weeds and branches, and with it he covered the mouth of the pit. Then, wet with sweat and aching with tiredness, he crouched behind the stump of a lightning-charred tree.

He knew his pursuer was coming; he heard the padding sound of feet on the soft earth, and the night breeze brought him the perfume of the general's cigarette. It seemed to Rainsford that the general was coming with unusual swiftness; he was not feeling his way along, foot by foot. Rainsford, crouching there, could not see the general, nor could he see the pit. He lived a year in a minute. Then he felt an impulse to cry aloud with joy, for he heard the sharp crackle of the breaking branches as the cover of the pit gave way; he heard the sharp scream of

pain as the pointed stakes found their mark. He leaped up from his place of concealment. Then he cowered back. Three feet from the pit a man was standing, with an electric torch in his hand.

"You've done well, Rainsford," the voice of the general called. "Your Burmese tiger pit[24] has claimed one of my best dogs. Again you score. I think, Mr. Rainsford, I'll see what you can do against my whole pack. I'm going home for a rest now. Thank you for a most amusing evening."

At daybreak Rainsford, lying near the swamp, was awakened by a sound that made him know that he had new things to learn about fear. It was a distant sound, faint and wavering; but he knew it. It was the baying of a pack of hounds.

Rainsford knew he could do one of two things. He could stay where he was and wait. That was suicide. He could flee. That was postponing the inevitable. For a moment he stood there, thinking. An idea that held a wild chance came to him, and, tightening his belt, he headed away from the swamp. The baying of the hounds drew nearer, then still nearer, nearer, ever nearer. On a ridge Rainsford climbed a tree. Down a watercourse, not a quarter of a mile away, he could see the bush moving. Straining his eyes, he saw the lean figure of General Zaroff; just ahead of him Rainsford made out another figure whose wide shoulders surged through the tall jungle weeds; it was the giant Ivan, and he seemed pulled forward by some unseen force; Rainsford

---

24. **The Burmese** (bér'mēz') **tiger pit** is a deep pit covered over with light brush wood and used to trap tigers in **Burma** (bér'mə), the country in southeastern Asia between India and Thailand.

knew that Ivan must be holding the pack in leash.

They would be on him any minute now. His mind worked frantically. He thought of a native trick he had learned in Uganda.[25] He slid down the tree. He caught hold of a springy young sapling and to it he fastened his hunting knife, with the blade pointing down the trail; with a bit of wild grapevine he tied back the sapling. Then he ran for his life. The hounds raised their voices as they hit the fresh scent. Rainsford knew now how an animal at bay feels.

He had to stop to get his breath. The baying of the hounds stopped abruptly; and Rainsford's heart stopped, too. They must have reached the knife.

He shinned excitedly up a tree and looked back. His pursuers had stopped. But the hope that was in Rainsford's brain when he climbed died, for he saw in the shallow valley that General Zaroff was still on his feet. But Ivan was not. The knife, driven by the recoil of the springing tree, had not wholly failed.

Rainsford had hardly tumbled to the ground when the pack took up the cry again.

"Nerve, nerve, nerve!" he panted, as he dashed along. A blue gap showed between the trees dead ahead. Ever nearer drew the hounds. Rainsford forced himself on toward that gap. He reached it. It was the shore of the sea. Across a cove he could see the gloomy gray stone of the château. Twenty feet below him the sea rumbled and hissed. Rainsford hesitated. He heard the hounds. Then he leaped far out into the sea.

When the general and his pack reached the place by the sea, the Cossack stopped. For some minutes he stood regarding the blue-green expanse of water. He shrugged his shoulders. Then he sat down, took a drink of brandy from a silver flask, lit a perfumed cigarette, and hummed a bit from *Madame Butterfly*.[26]

General Zaroff had an exceedingly good dinner in his great paneled dining hall that evening. With it he had a bottle of his rarest wine. Two slight annoyances kept him from perfect enjoyment. One was the thought that it would be difficult to replace Ivan; the other was that his quarry had escaped him; of course the American hadn't played the game—so thought the general as he tasted his after-dinner liqueur. In his library he read, to soothe himself, from the works of Marcus Aurelius.[27] At ten he went up to his bedroom. He was deliciously tired, he said to himself, as he locked himself in. There was a little moonlight; so, before turning on his light, he went to the window and looked down at the courtyard. He could see the great hounds, and he called: "Better luck another time," to them. Then he switched on the light.

A man, who had been hiding in the curtains of the bed, was standing there.

"Rainsford!" screamed the general. "How did you get here?"

"Swam," said Rainsford. "I found it quicker than walking through the jungle."

25. **Uganda** (ü gan′də), an area in East Africa north of Lake Victoria.
26. **Madame Butterfly,** famous Italian opera by Giacomo Puccini. It is ironic that the Cossack should hum a bit of this tragic love story.
27. **Marcus Aurelius** (mär′kəs ô rē′lē əs), a Roman emperor (A.D. 161–180) and famous Stoic philosopher, who attempted to govern Rome and himself by stern standards and indifference to pleasure and pain.

The general sucked in his breath and smiled. "I congratulate you," he said. "You have won the game."

Rainsford did not smile. "I am still a beast at bay," he said, in a low, hoarse voice. "Get ready, General Zaroff."

The general made one of his deepest bows. "I see," he said. "Splendid! One of us is to furnish a repast for the hounds. The other will sleep in this very excellent bed. On guard, Rainsford."

He had never slept in a better bed, Rainsford decided.

READING FOR DETAILS

The Hunter Becomes the Hunted

1. In what ways are Rainsford and Whitney different from each other? How does the author reveal Rainsford's attitude toward the animals he hunted? In what two situations does Rainsford feel that Whitney is not a "realist"—one who sees things as they really are? How is Whitney proved right in both cases?

2. Why does General Zaroff recognize Rainsford's name? The author establishes Zaroff as an evil man by a series of clues and revealing statements. What convinces us of this beyond question?

3. Authors often take advantage of the fact that a word can have more than one meaning. An excellent example of this is the title of this story. What two meanings of "game" make sense in this title?

4. How does Rainsford show his wide knowledge of hunting tactics? Although you are not told how Rainsford disposed of General Zaroff, you do know that he gave him a chance to fight for his life. Why do you think Rainsford gave him this chance? What might Rainsford have done instead?

READING FOR MEANING

Many times, after you have read a story, play, or poem, you realize that it suggests some puzzling or debatable ideas about how people act and think. Throughout this book you will find these implied ideas set forth in statements for you to consider and discuss in light of the selection you have just read. Whatever your opinion of the statement as it relates to the selection, it is important that you support your position with evidence from the selection. You may agree or disagree. You may even decide that you do not have enough evidence to make any decision at all.

Now that you have read "The Most Dangerous Game," consider and discuss these propositions:

1. General Zaroff is a coward who is used to getting his own way.

2. The author is against hunting as a sport.

READING FOR APPRECIATION

Suspense and Foreshadowing

1. Even before General Zaroff and Ivan appear, Rainsford has seen and heard a number of things that arouse apprehension in the reader. Discuss what these things are.

2. The introduction of Ivan and his master increases concern for Rainsford's safety. Describe Zaroff and Ivan. When do you first suspect that Zaroff is evil? What feature of his face makes him seem like a beast of prey?

3. Why is suspense increased when Rainsford indicates that if he returned to the mainland he would not remain silent about the general's activities?

Conflict

1. What is the main conflict in "The Most Dangerous Game"? Are the two opposing forces evenly matched? Is there a conflict of ideas or beliefs in this story? What is it?

THE MOST DANGEROUS GAME

2. Conflict cannot be resolved or settled without *action*. The moment of most crucial action is usually the high point of interest and suspense. This moment is called the *climax* of the story. "The Most Dangerous Game" has several episodes, and each episode has its own climax. What is the most important climax, or turning point, in the story? Which moment of action finally settles the conflict?

Imaginative Language

Much of the imagery in this short story is made up of *similes* and *metaphors*. Both simile and metaphor are used to suggest a likeness or resemblance in things which are unlike or dissimilar. While the simile compares one thing with another and uses the words *like* or *as*, the metaphor states directly that one thing is another. Thus, from "The Most Dangerous Game" an example of simile would be: ". . . giant rocks with razor edges crouch *like* a sea monster with wide-open jaws. They can crush a ship *as* easily as I crush this nut."

Metaphor is used in the sentence: ". . . the sea licked greedy lips in the shadows."

1. Locate five examples of imagery expressed in simile or metaphor in the selection you have just read.

2. Richard Connell's choice of verbs in combination with other descriptive words makes his imagery especially vivid. Locate and discuss those word combinations in the following quotations which appeal most strongly to the senses.

  a. The cry was pinched off short as the blood-warm waters of the Caribbean Sea closed over his head.

  b. . . . the dank tropical night . . . pressed its thick, warm blackness in upon the yacht.

  c. . . . and on three sides of it cliffs dived down to where the sea licked greedy lips in the shadows.

  d. Twenty feet below him the sea rumbled and hissed.

COMPOSITION

When an author writes how he or she agrees or disagrees with an idea, the *essay* is most often the writing form used.

The essay may be defined as *a composition presenting the opinion or personal views of its author*. Three sections, an *introduction*, a *body*, and a *conclusion*, make up the basic essay. The introduction, usually a paragraph or two in length, contains the *thesis statement*, which is the opinion statement of the writer. The body is made up of a varying number of paragraphs in which the author explores arguments for and against the thesis statement. The conclusion restates the writer's thesis in a more general way.

Choose one of these ideas and write an essay that argues *for* the thesis:

1. Hunting any bird or animal for sport should be outlawed.

2. Few people in today's society hold General Zaroff's point of view.

BIOGRAPHICAL NOTE

Richard Connell (1893–1949), son of a New York newspaper editor and congressman, was born in Poughkeepsie, New York. City editor of the *Poughkeepsie News Press* at sixteen, Connell further pursued his interest in writing at Harvard University. He was editor of two Harvard student publications, the *Daily Crimson* and the *Lampoon*. After graduation from Harvard in 1915, Connell served stints as a newspaperman, advertising copy editor, and soldier in World War I. In 1919, he became a free-lance fiction writer, concentrating chiefly on short stories, with an occasional novel, motion picture story, or screenplay. By the time of his death, more than three hundred of his short stories had been published in American and English magazines.

He was terrified,
but he would not give up, would not turn back.

THE WOODS-DEVIL
Paul Annixter

For the four days since his father's accident, it had snowed intermittently. The slate-black clouds of winter had banked up in the north and west. They were motionless, changeless, remote, and ridged like banks of corrugated metal. For days during this north Maine winter, the only sun the family had seen had been a yellowish filter at midday that came in the cabin window like a thin sifting of sulphur dust.

Nathan was just bringing the night's wood, enough short logs to burn till morning; with another pile of wood chunks beside the daubed clay fireplace they would last the following day if need be. His face and ears burned from laboring in a temperature of thirty below. He was dressed in brown linsey-woolsey[1]; on his feet were shoes of heavy felt, stuffed with coarse, gray socks against the cold. A cap of worn coonskin crowned his shagbark hair that had not been cut in many weeks. He had reached the gangling age of fifteen and a half, when the joints are all loose and clumsy. His lean face was drawn and pinched, the dark eyes sullen from overwork.

His mother sat darning a sock over an egg, rising now and then to stir the pot of mush or turn the cooking rabbit. His father lay in the cord bunk in the corner of the cabin, his injured leg raised high beneath the blankets. His gaunt, unshaven face was etched with the memory of the pain he had endured before the settlement doctor had come to set the broken bone. Worry showed in his black eyes turned up to the ceiling poles. Little food was left for the family—a bit of jerked venison in the smokehouse, a side of bacon, some beans, and meal. The Stemlines were true woodsies.[2] They'd been eking along, waiting for the fur season. All that they ate, spent, and wore came from their traps and rifles.

Nathan went out for the final log, and the door creaked behind him on its crude hinges. The snow in the clearing was almost knee-deep. The forest surrounded it on all sides broken only where a road cut a black tunnel through the balsams[3] toward the settlement down to the south.

A sudden wind rose with the darkness. Nathan could hear it far off and high, a growing roar above the forest. Abruptly it snatched at the clearing, whirling the snow in eddies; the serried[4] pine tops bent in rhythm. Because his

1. **linsey-woolsey** (lin′zē wŭl′zē), a strong, coarse fabric made of wool and linen or cotton.
2. **woodsies** (wŭd′zez), people whose lives are built around the woods.
3. **balsams** (bôl′səmz), evergreen trees having small needles and cones more than two inches long.
4. **serried** (ser′ēd), pressed together in rows.

impulse was to hurry in and close the door against it, Nathan stood for several minutes, his face straight into it, letting the cold and darkness and emptiness sink into him.

Indoors, he eased down his log and took off his sheepskin coat and cap, baring his mop of brown hair. He sat down beside Viney, his eight-year-old sister, playing with the endless paper people she cut out of the mail order catalogue. The wind made hollow bottle noises down the chimney, and the driven snow made a dry *shish-shish* against the log walls.

"Listen to that," said Nathan's mother. "The Almanac was right. We're due for another cold spell. 'A stormy new moon. Keep a good fire,' Father Richard says for the ninth. 'Colder. Expect snow,' it says for the tenth."

Nathan's voice had a manly note. "It's getting colder all right, but it won't snow. It's too darned cold to snow. A fellow'd soon be stiff if he didn't keep working."

"Is the ax in?" his father asked.

"Yes," Nathan fetched it and put a keen, shining edge on it with the whetstone. Then he ran a greased rag through each of the rifle barrels. He could feel his father's approving gaze on his back as he sighted through each barrel into the firelight. "Bright's a bugle," he copied his father's invariable comment.

Then he sat waiting, his hands clasped tightly between his knees, for what he knew must come.

"Nathan," his father said presently, and the boy went over and stood dutifully by the bunk. "Do you think you can cover the trapline tomorrow, son?"

"Yes, I guess I can."

He was prickling with trepidation. The wind shook the cabin door as he spoke, and he thought of all that lay up in the far pine valley—things to be felt, if not seen or heard.

"It's a long ways, I know, and it's mortal cold. . . ." His father's voice was drained and tired, and for a moment Nathan glimpsed the naked misery and worry in his mind. "But money's scarce, son. We've got to do what can be done."

"I don't mind the cold or the snow." Nathan stared down at his feet until that look should leave his father's face.

"I'll be laid up three, four weeks, maybe more. It's four days since we laid out the line. Varmints may have got most of our catch by now. You've got to go, Nathan. If you start at daylight you can make the rounds and be back by night."

"Shucks, yes." Nathan forced a smile.

When he dared lift his eyes, he saw his father's face had hardened again in coping with the problem.

"You needn't try to bring in the catch," he said. "You can hang some of it on high boughs, then reset the traps. Main thing's to find what kind of range we got in there. Later on, you may have to spend a night in the valley. Think you'll be a-scairt to sleep alone in the deep woods?"

"Not me." Nathan's tone discounted all concern, but misgivings quickly crowded in. "Anyhow I'd have an ax and a rifle and plenty cartridges," he said.

His father managed a smile. "Might have to sleep in there once every week till I'm up again. So you'd best look at that log cache[5] we built to store traps in. It's plenty big enough to sleep a man."

Pride filled Nathan. This was real man's work he was detailed to do.

"You'd best eat now and turn in early," his father said, "so's you can start at dawn."

"All right."

"You're a brave boy, Nathan," his mother said. "You're the provider for this family now. What a blessing it is you're big enough to cover the line while your father's down. Last year you could never have done it."

"He's near about as good as any man now," his father said. "Knows the woods and critters as well as I."

Young Nathan grew more stolid than usual, holding himself against the rushing tide of feeling. He wished he were all they said of him. Inside he was fright-

---

5. **log cache** (kash),   a hiding place built of logs, used for storing things necessary for life in the wilderness.

ened whenever he thought of the Little Jackpine Valley where their trapline had been laid out. For three days the vision of the valley and what he had felt there had lurked before his mind's eye, filling him with dread, even when he tried to put his mind to something else.

Methodically, Nathan ate the man's share of food his mother set before him on the hewn-log table. Soon after, he climbed the sapling ladder to the small quarter loft where he slept. He lay quiet, pretending to sleep, but long after the lamp went out he was still grappling with his thoughts. Storm gripped the cabin. The snow crept up against the walls and the night was full of voices. Once far in the forest a wolf howled. Nathan's skin prickled and his two hands made fists underneath the blankets.

Now and again he could hear his father stirring and knew that he, too, was thinking the same thoughts.

Dawn had not yet come when Nathan descended the ladder. He built up the fire, made coffee, and ate a hurried breakfast. He took down his old wool sweater to wear under his sheepskin coat.

"Make sure you don't forget anything," his father said. "Have you got plenty cartridges . . . matches? Belt ax? Bait?"

"Yes, Pa."

"Best take my rifle," his father said.

Nathan took down his father's finely balanced rifle with its curly walnut stock and held it proudly in his hands. It was a far better weapon than the old Sharps Nathan usually carried.

"I wouldn't take the sled," his father was saying. "It's heavy, and I want you should be back by night. Be right careful, won't you, son?" he called as Nathan lifted the latch.

The cold bit deep. It was scarcely light yet in the clearing. The storm had died down in the night, and there was no wind now, but the air cut Nathan's cheeks like a razor. It was colder than anything he had ever known.

After twenty minutes of tramping he thought of turning back. His face and hands were numbing; his joints seemed to be stiffening. Each breath was agony. He snatched up some of the hard, dry snow and rubbed it against his stiffened face till a faint glow of feeling came. Then he ran for a long way—beating his arms, one, then the other, against his body, shifting the rifle, till his thin chest was heaving. Again his face was like wood. He was terrified, but he would not give up, would not turn back.

He covered the three miles to the mouth of the Little Jackpine in a daze. He did not know what he could do with his numbed hands if he did find a catch in the traps; he could not even use the rifle if the occasion arose. He would have cried had he been a year younger, but at fifteen you do not cry. He started into the valley.

The Little Jackpine lay at the foot of old Shakehammer Mountain, and through it a small stream rushed and snarled like a wildcat, its bed choked with almost inaccessible jungles of windfalls. It was an appalling wilderness.

Both Nathan and his father could read the silent speech of place and time in the outdoors, and what the valley had said to them had been vaguely antagonistic from the first—almost a warning. Nathan remembered how they had threaded the valley bottom, in single file, silent. The breeze had droned its ancient dirge in the treetops, but not a breath of it had stirred along the stream bed. The hiss of the water had created an intense hush.

He remembered how he had spat in the boiling waters to show his unconcern, but it hadn't done much good. Several times as they headed homeward, Nathan's father had stopped abruptly in his tracks to look behind and to all sides. "Queer," he had muttered. "A full hour past I had a right smart feelin' we were bein' watched and followed. I still got it."

"I had it, too, Pa," Nathan had said. "It's mighty fearsome back yonder, ain't it?"

"It ain't a bear." His father had evaded the question. "May be some young lynx cat, figurin' he'd like to play with us. A lynx is a tomfool for followin' humans."

They had backtracked to the top of a rise to look, but they saw nothing. Then the valley struck its first blow. A perfectly placed boulder that had lain poised for untold years had toppled at that exact moment to crush the older Nathan's leg as he scrambled down a rocky ledge. . . .

Nathan passed the spot, but he did not pause. Something seemed to listen behind each tree and rock, and something seemed to wait among the taller trees ahead, blue-black in the shadows. After a while it felt warmer, perhaps because he was climbing. Then he came to the first trap and forgot wind, cold, and even fear.

A marten, caught perhaps two days before, lay in the set. Its carcass had been partially devoured, its prime pelt torn to ribbons as if in malice. Roundabout in the snow were broad, splayed tracks, but wind and sleet had partly covered them, so that their identity was not plain. But they told Nathan enough. Neither fox nor wolf had molested this trap, nor was it a bear. Nathan knew what it was, but he wasn't admitting it yet—even to himself.

He stood up, his eyes searching for a glimpse of a secret enemy, but the valley gave back nothing. Except for the soughing of the balsam boughs far overhead, the stillness was complete.

He moved on between the endless ranks of trees and again had the feeling of being watched. At intervals he stopped to glance back along his trail, but saw nothing. The trunks of the dark trees seemed to watch him as he approached, slipping furtively behind him as he passed.

The next trap had been uncovered and sprung, the bait—a frozen fish— eaten, and the trap itself dragged off into the brush and buried in the snow. It took nearly half an hour of floundering and digging to uncover trap and clog. Hard by was another set, and there Nathan saw a thing that made his skin crawl. The remains of a porcupine lay in the trap, and the creature had been eaten—quills, barb, and all. Blood from the jaws of the eater was spattered all around. Only a devil could have done that! Beneath a spruce he saw clearly the despoiler's trail—splayed, hand-shaped tracks like those of a small bear, each print peaked with fierce claw marks.

These were the tracks of a giant wolverine, the woods-devil, bane of all hunters and trappers.

For long minutes Nathan stood in the dusky shadows, fighting down his fear. He had heard about the evil fortune that fastens upon trappers molested by a wolverine. Then he thought of what awaited him at home—that stricken look on his father's face. His fear of that was greater than his fear of the valley.

He hung his sack of frozen bait on a high bough. Useless to reset any of the traps now, for the creature he was pitted against could smell cold steel, unbaited, through two feet of snow, and, in sheer deviltry, would rob and destroy wherever it prowled.

Nathan plodded on again, his chest hollow with hopelessness, not knowing what he could do.

The snow became deeper. One after another he came upon six more sets that had been robbed. Each had held a catch, and each ravaged pelt meant the loss of food and clothing to his family.

Then Nathan gave a whimpering cry. He had come to the seventh trap and that one had contained treasure, a pelt worth a whole season's work to the Stemlines. This was a black fisher marten, always a trapper's prize. If only he could have carried home such a pelt on this first day of his rounds! How smoothed and eased his father's worried face would have become! But the woods-devil had destroyed it—an even more thorough job than on any of the others, as if he had sensed the value of this catch.

The boy whimpered again as he crouched there in the snow. Then anger flooded him, fought back the tears. He rose and began the endless plodding again, peering into every covert for the dark, skulking shape. He did not know the size of a wolverine. He'd never seen one. He recalled old Laban Knowles's tale of the wolverine that had gnawed his walnut rifle stock in two and scored the very rifle barrel. And Granther Bates told of a woods-devil that had killed his

two dogs, then gnawed through a log wall to rob him of his grub cache.[6]

It was afternoon when Nathan neared the farthest limit of the trapline. Of twenty-odd traps, only two had been unmolested. Abruptly he came upon a fresh trail in the snow: the same hand-shaped tracks and demon claws, no more than an hour old. Grimly he turned aside to follow their twisting course.

He was descending a steep wooded slope, when on a sudden impulse he doubled back on his own tracks and plunged up the grade through deep snow. As he reached the crest, a dark, humped shape took form beneath the drooping boughs of a spruce—a ragged, sooty-black and brown beast, some three and a half feet long, that lumbered like a small bear; it was lighter colored along its back and darker underneath, in direct contrast to all other forest beings. It saw him, and its green-shadowed eyes fixed on those of the boy beneath a tree some hundred feet away. The black jaw dropped open, and a harsh grating snarl cut the stillness. The utter savagery of this challenge sent a shiver through Nathan's body. His rifle flew up, and without removing his mitten he fired. The whole valley roared. In the same instant, the wolverine disappeared.

Nathan rushed forward, reloading as he ran. Under the spruce were several drops of blood in the snow, but the wolverine had vanished completely. Because of his haste and the clumsiness of his mittened hand, Nathan had only grazed the animal; he'd lost his one big chance.

Panting, stumbling, sobbing, the boy plunged along the trail, bent low, duck-

6. **grub cache,** hidden food.

ing under the drooping limbs of the trees, sometimes crawling on hands and knees. He saw other drops of blood. They gave him heart. He had a lynx eye, his father had often said. He would follow on to the very Circle[7] if need be; he would not miss a second time. His one hope now was to settle with the beast for good and all.

The trail led down along the stream bed, twisting through tangles of windfalls, writhing masses of frost-whitened roots, and branches that seemed caught in a permanent hysteria. Twice he fell, but each time he thrust high the rifle as he went down to keep the snow from jamming its snout. He plunged on again; he did not know for how long or how far, but he was aware at last of the beginning of twilight. And the end of light meant the end of the trail. Victory for the enemy.

The way had grown steeper. He was coming to the narrow throatlatch of the valley's head, a place where hundreds of great trees, snapped off by storm and snowslide from the slopes above, had collected in a mighty log jam, a tangle of timber, rock, and snow that choked the stream bed from bank to bank. Countless logs lay crisscrossed helter-skelter with two- and three-foot gaps between. The great pile was acre large, fifty feet high, rank with the odor of rotted logs and old snow.

Into this maze led the trail of the woods-devil. Nathan skirted the pile. The trail did not come out!

Trembling, he squeezed his way between two logs into the great jam. The wolverine might be fifty yards inside, but somehow it must be ferreted out. In and in Nathan wormed his body, pausing to

watch, to listen, his rifle thrust carefully before him. Then down and down into the twisting chaos of dead and dying trunks, led by his nose, for the rank odor of the devil's den now filled the air. Coming upward from the very bottom of the jam, it was fouler than any skunk taint.

Nathan stopped short, his body tensing like a spring. To his ears came a harsh and menacing growl, but from which direction he could not tell. He waited but could see nothing. He loosened the safety on his rifle and wriggled forward again, and again the air was filled with that ominous challenge. This time it seemed to come from behind him. He whirled in panic, but there was nothing. His terror mounted. The creature must be watching him, and he could not see it. And might not there be *two* of them? Then a movement caught his eye, and he glimpsed a soot-dark shape in the lower shadows.

The boy wriggled on his belly along a slanting log, maneuvering for a shot through the intervening timbers. He braced himself, craning far downward. . . . Then in the very instant he took aim, he slipped on the snow-sheathed log. The gun roared; the shot went wild; and, as Nathan caught himself, the rifle slid from his ice-slick grasp. It clattered downward, striking against log after log before it lodged at the bottom of the jam, snout down in snow, its barrel clogged and useless.

In that instant all the craft that has made man master of the wild fell away, and Nathan was reduced to first principles. The wolverine clambered slowly upward. Inexorably it advanced upon him. He screamed at it, but there was no

7. **Circle,** that is, the Arctic Circle.

vestige of fear in the beast. Nathan's hand went to his light belt ax; he gave no ground.

With a panicking shout he leaned and swung at the low flat head, but missed because of hindering logs. He swung again and again, and the blade struck, but with no apparent effect, for the creature's advance never checked. Its small, implacable eyes shone blue-green.

It lunged suddenly for Nathan's dangling legs. He flung himself up and over the log, then slipped on the icy sheath, grasped desperately for another log, and slipped again to a point eight feet below. He flung around with a cry of desperation, expecting to meet open jaws, as the demon was almost upon him. But the animal was logy. Its power lay in its indomitability—a slow, irresistible power.

In it came again, above him now. He stood upright, braced on two logs, to meet it. He was crying now, sobbing and unashamed.

He struck again, yelling with each blow of the belt ax, but hack and cut as he would, the beast bore in and in, maneuvering along the undersides of logs to avoid the ax blows.

Then as Nathan slipped again, he avoided the traplike jaws. He fell to the bottom of the jam, biting snow as he screamed. He was on his feet again before the creature above released its claw hold and dropped upon him like a giant slug.

Flinging an arm up over his throat, he jerked back blindly. Spread saber claws tore open his heavy coat. Then the ax fell again, blow after blow with all his strength; he shouted with every blow. No longer cries of terror, but of war.

The thing would not die. The jaws clamped on Nathan's leg above the knee, and he felt his own warm blood. Then his hand found the skinning knife at his belt, and the blade sank into the corded neck—turned till the clamp of jaws released.

Nathan climbed up out of the abatis[8] till half his body emerged from the top of the great jam, and there he rested— panting, spent. He whimpered once, but there were no tears now. Instinctively, his eyes lifted skyward. Overhead, as night drew on, a great rift appeared in the leaden canopy of cloud, and a few stars shone through. He fixed his eyes on the brightest star until chaos left him; then his vision steadied, as if his head were higher than ever it had been before, in a realm of pure air. His brain was almost frighteningly clear.

The trickle of warm blood down his leg roused him. He pressed his heavy pants leg around his wound till he felt the bleeding stop. Painfully, he turned down into the maze of logs again and brought up the rifle. Then down again to struggle upward, dragging the woods-devil by its short and ragged scut.[9] He laid it out on the snow and pulled out his bloody knife. He wasn't tired now, he wasn't cold, he wasn't afraid. His hands were quick and sure at the skinning; even his father had never lifted a pelt with smoother, defter hand. Darkness shut down, but he needed no light. There was no hurry. The head he cut from the body, leaving it attached to the hide.

He thought of the proud fancy that made the far northern Indians covet a

---

8. **abatis** (ab′ə tis), a defensive obstacle formed by felled trees with sharpened branches facing the enemy.
9. **scut** (skut), a short erect tail, as of a hare, rabbit, or deer.

garment made of a wolverine's skin. Oh, there would be talk in the cabin tonight; they would sit at the table long after their eating was done, as great folk were supposed to do. He'd recount all the details of the day and the fight before he brought his trophy in to show.

He rose at last and rolled up his grisly bundle, fur side out, and moved away through the blackness of the trees, sure of tread, for he had the still hunter's "eyes in the feet." Reflection from the snow gave a faint light. He was limping a bit.

Off in the black woods, a wolf howled dismally, and Nathan smiled. Never again would the night dogs make his skin crawl. Never again would he be afraid of anything above ground.

READING FOR DETAILS

Nathan Conquers His Fear

1. What traits does the wolverine have that would cause people to think of it as a "woods-devil"?
2. Why doesn't Nathan go back home when he realizes the kind of animal that is destroying his furs?

READING FOR MEANING

Agree or disagree with the following:
1. Nathan would not have feared the wolverine if he had known what it looked like.
2. Skinning the wolverine is an act of revenge.

READING FOR APPRECIATION

Conflict

Three of the four kinds of conflict between opposing forces can be seen in this story. Discuss what they are.

Suspense and Foreshadowing

Find and discuss two illustrations of foreshadowing early in the story.

COMPOSITION

Using language imaginatively is one mark of the skilled writer. Reread the information on Imaginative Language in Unit Techniques, page 3. Now write a paragraph describing a familiar place at a particular time of day. Tell what you see, hear, smell, and/or taste. Create a word picture that appeals to the senses.

BIOGRAPHICAL NOTE

Paul Annixter (1894–   ) is the pseudonym of Howard A. Sturtzel, who lives in Pasadena, California. At 18 he left school and took to the open road, roaming over much of the United States and Canada. Drawing on his experiences, he has written over 500 short stories published in magazines in the United States, Canada, and England. He believes that the head and hands should work together and "that the best ideas that come to a writer are apt to drip off the end of a shovel or trowel." Mr. Annixter does not confine himself to short stories. One of his most popular novels is *Swiftwater*. He often collaborates with his wife, Jane. Their latest book is *The Last Monster*.

Supposing he died there, trapped?

THROUGH THE TUNNEL
Doris Lessing

Going to the shore on the first morning of the holiday, the young English boy stopped at a turning of the path and looked down at a wild and rocky bay, and then over to the crowded beach he knew so well from other years. His mother walked on in front of him, carrying a bright striped bag in one hand. Her other arm, swinging loose, was very white in the sun.

The boy watched that white, naked arm, and turned his eyes, which had a frown behind them, toward the bay and back again to his mother. When she felt he was not with her, she swung around.

"Oh, there you are Jerry!" she said. She looked impatient, then smiled. "Why, darling, would you rather not come with me? Would you rather . . ." she frowned, conscientiously worrying over what amusements he might secretly be longing for which she had been too busy to imagine.

He was very familiar with that anxious, apologetic smile. Contrition sent him running after her. And yet, as he ran, he looked back over his shoulder at the wild bay; and all morning, as he played on the safe beach, he was thinking of it.

"Through the Tunnel," by Doris Lessing. Originally published in *The New Yorker*. Copyright © 1955 by Doris Lessing; from *THE HABIT OF LOVING*, Thomas Y. Crowell Company, New York. (Copyright © 1957 by Doris Lessing.)

Next morning, when it was time for the routine of swimming and sunbathing, his mother said, "Are you tired of the usual beach, Jerry? Would you like to go somewhere else?"

"Oh, no!" he said quickly, smiling at her out of that unfailing impulse of contrition—a sort of chivalry. Yet, walking down the path with her, he blurted out, "I'd like to go and have a look at those rocks down there."

She gave the idea her attention. It was a wild-looking place, and there was no one there, but she said, "Of course, Jerry. When you've had enough, come to the big beach. Or just go straight back to the villa, if you like."

She walked away, that bare arm, now slightly reddened from yesterday's sun, swinging. And he almost ran after her again, feeling it unbearable that she should go by herself, but he did not.

She was thinking. Of course he's old enough to be safe without me. Have I been keeping him too close? He mustn't feel he ought to be with me. I must be careful.

He was an only child. . . . She was a widow. She was determined to be neither possessive nor lacking in devotion. She went worrying off to her beach.

As for Jerry, once he saw that his mother had gained her beach, he began the steep descent to the bay. From where he was, high up among red-brown rocks, it was a scoop of moving bluish green fringed with white.

As he went lower, he saw that it spread among small promontories and inlets of rough, sharp rock, and the crisping, lapping surface showed stains of purple and darker blue. Finally, as he ran sliding and scraping down the last few yards, he saw an edge of white surf, and the shallow, luminous movement of water over white sand, and, beyond that, a solid, heavy blue.

He ran straight into the water and began swimming. He was a good swimmer. He went out fast over the gleaming sand, over a middle region where rocks lay like discolored monsters under the surface, and then he was in the real sea—a warm sea where irregular cold currents from the deep water shocked his limbs.

When he was so far out that he could look back not only on the little bay but past the promontory that was between it and the big beach, he floated on the buoyant surface and looked for his mother. There she was, a speck of yellow under an umbrella that looked like a slice of orange peel. He swam back to shore, relieved at being sure she was there, but all at once very lonely.

On the edge of a small cape that marked the side of the bay away from the promontory was a loose scatter of rocks. Above them, some boys were stripping off their clothes. They came running, naked, down to the rocks.

The English boy swam toward them, and kept his distance at a stone's throw. They were of that coast, all of them burned smooth dark brown, and speaking a language he did not understand. To be with them, of them, was a craving that

filled his whole body. He swam a little closer; they turned and watched him with narrowed, alert dark eyes.

Then one smiled and waved. It was enough. In a minute, he had swum in and was on the rocks beside them, smiling with a desperate, nervous supplication. They shouted cheerful greetings at him, and then, as he preserved his nervous, uncomprehending smile, they understood that he was a foreigner strayed from his own beach, and they proceeded to forget him. But he was happy. He was with them.

They began diving again and again from a high point into a well of blue sea between rough, pointed rocks. After they had dived and come up, they swam around, hauled themselves up, and waited their turn to dive again.

They were big boys—men to Jerry. He dived, and they watched him, and when he swam around to take his place, they made way for him. He felt he was accepted, and he dived again, carefully, proud of himself.

Soon the biggest of the boys poised himself, shot down into the water, and did not come up. The others stood about watching. Jerry, after waiting for the sleek brown head to appear, let out a yell of warning; they looked at him idly and turned their eyes back toward the water.

After a long time, the boy came up on the other side of a big dark rock, letting the air out of his lungs in a sputtering gasp and a shout of triumph. Immediately, the rest of them dived in. One moment, the morning seemed full of chattering boys; the next, the air and the surface of the water were empty. But through the heavy blue, dark shapes could be seen moving and groping.

Jerry dived, shot past the school of underwater swimmers, saw a black wall of rock looming at him, touched it, and bobbed up at once to the surface, where the wall was a low barrier he could see across. There was no one visible; under him, in the water, the dim shapes of the swimmers had disappeared. Then one, and then another of the boys came up on the far side of the barrier of rock, and he understood that they had swum through some gap or hole in it. He plunged down again.

He could see nothing through the stinging salt water but the blank rock. When he came up, the boys were all on the diving rock, preparing to attempt the feat again. And now, in a panic of failure, he yelled up, in English, "Look at me! Look!" and he began splashing and kicking in the water like a foolish dog.

They looked down gravely, frowning. He knew the frown. At moments of failure, when he clowned to claim his mother's attention, it was with just this grave embarrassed inspection that she rewarded him.

Through his hot shame, feeling the pleading grin on his face like a scar that he could never remove, he looked up at the group of big brown boys on the rock and shouted *"Bonjour! Merci! Au revoir! Monsieur, monsieur!"*[1] while he hooked his fingers round his ears and waggled them.

1. Commonplace French phrases: **bonjour** (bôn zhür′), "good day"; **merci** (mār sē′), "thank you"; **au revoir** (ō rə vwàr′), "good-bye"; **monsieur** (mə syœ′), "mister," "sir."

Water surged into his mouth; he choked, sank, came up. The rock, lately weighted with the boys, seemed to rear up out of the water as their weight was removed. They were flying down past him, now, into the water; the air was full of falling bodies. Then the rock was empty in the hot sunlight. He counted one, two, three. . . .

At fifty, he was terrified. They must all be drowning beneath him, in the watery caves of the rock! At a hundred, he stared around him at the empty hillside, wondering if he should yell for help.

He counted faster, faster, to hurry them up, to bring them to the surface quickly, to drown them quickly—anything rather than the terror of counting on and on into the blue emptiness of the morning. And then, at a hundred and sixty, the water beyond the rock was full of boys blowing like brown whales. They swam back to the shore without a look at him.

He climbed back to the diving rock and sat down, feeling the hot roughness of it under his thighs. The boys were gathering up their bits of clothing and running off along the shore to another promontory.

They were leaving to get away from him. He cried openly, fists in his eyes. There was no one to see him, and he cried himself out.

It seemed to him that a long time had passed and he swam out to where he could see his mother. Yes, she was still there, a yellow spot under an orange umbrella. He swam back to the big rock, climbed up, and dived into the blue pool among the fanged and angry boulders. Down he went, until he touched the wall of rock again. But the salt was so painful in his eyes that he could not see.

He came to the surface, swam to shore and went back to the villa to wait for his mother. Soon she walked slowly up the path, swinging her striped bag, the flushed, naked arm dangling beside her. "I want some swimming goggles," he panted, defiant and beseeching.

She gave him a patient, inquisitive look as she said casually, "Well, of course, darling."

But now, now, now! He must have them this minute, and no other time. He nagged and pestered until she went with him to a shop. As soon as she had bought the goggles, he grabbed them from her hand as if she were going to claim them for herself, and was off, running down the steep path to the bay.

Jerry swam out to the big barrier rock, adjusted the goggles, and dived. The impact of the water broke the rubber-enclosed vacuum, and the goggles came loose.

He understood that he must swim down to the base of the rock from the surface of the water. He fixed the goggles tight and firm, filled his lungs, and floated, face down on the water.

Now he could see. It was as if he had eyes of a different kind—fish-eyes that showed everything clear and delicate and wavering in the bright water.

Under him, six or seven feet down, was a floor of perfectly clean, shining white sand, rippled firm and hard by the tides. Two grayish shapes steered there, like long, rounded pieces of wood or slate.

They were fish. He saw them nose toward each other, poise motionless, make a dart forward, swerve off, and come around again. It was like a water dance. A few inches above them, the water sparkled as if sequins were dropping

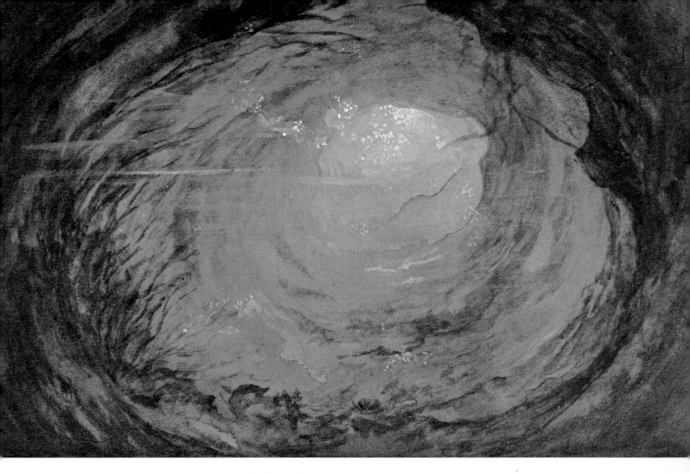

through it. Fish again—myriads of minute[2] fish, the length of his fingernail, were drifting through the water, and in a moment he could feel the innumerable tiny touches of them, against his limbs. It was like swimming in flaked silver.

The great rock the big boys had swum through rose sheer out of the white sand, black, tufted lightly with greenish weed. He could see no gap in it. He swam down to its base.

Again and again he rose, took a big chestful of air, and went down. Again and again he groped over the surface of the rock, feeling it, almost hugging it in the desperate need to find the entrance.

And then, once, while he was clinging to the black wall, his knees came up and he shot his feet out forward and they met no obstacle. He had found the hole.

He gained the surface, clambered about the stones that littered the barrier rock until he found a big one, and, with this in his arms, let himself down over the side of the rock. He dropped, with the weight, to the sandy floor.

Clinging tight to the anchor of the stone, he lay on his side and looked in under the dark shelf at the place where his feet had gone. He could see the hole.

It was an irregular, dark gap, but he could not see deep into it. He let go of his anchor, clung with his hands to the edges of the hole, and tried to push himself in.

He got his head in, found his shoulders jammed, moved them in sidewise, and was inside as far as his waist. He could see nothing ahead.

2. **minute** (mī nüt′), very small.

Something soft and clammy touched his mouth. He saw a dark frond moving against the grayish rock, and panic filled him. He thought of octopuses, or clinging weed.

He pushed himself out backward and caught a glimpse, as he retreated, of a harmless tentacle of seaweed drifting in the mouth of the tunnel. But it was enough.

He reached the sunlight, swam to shore, and lay on the diving rock. He looked down into the blue well of water. He knew he must find his way through that cave, or hole, or tunnel, and out the other side.

First, he thought, he must learn to control his breathing. He let himself down into the water with another big stone in his arms, so that he could lie effortlessly on the bottom.

One, two, three. He counted steadily. He could hear the movement of blood in his head. Fifty-one, fifty-two . . .

His chest was hurting. He let go of the rock and went up into the air. He saw that the sun was low. He rushed to the villa and found his mother at her supper. She said only, "Did you enjoy yourself?" and he said, "Yes."

All night, the boy dreamed of the water-filled cave in the rock, and as soon as breakfast was over he went to the bay.

That night, his nose bled badly. For hours he had been underwater, learning to hold his breath, and now he felt weak and dizzy. His mother said, "I shouldn't overdo things, darling, if I were you."

That day and the next, Jerry exercised his lungs as if everything, the whole of his life, all that he would become, depended upon it. Again his nose bled at night, and his mother insisted on his coming with her the next day.

It was a torment to him to waste a day of his careful self-training, but he stayed with her on that other beach, which now seemed a place for small children, a place where his mother might lie safe in the sun. It was not his beach.

He did not ask for permission, on the following day, to go to his beach. He went, before his mother could consider the complicated rights and wrongs of the matter.

A day's rest, he discovered, had improved his count by ten. The big boys had made the passage while he counted a hundred and sixty. He had been counting fast, in his fright. Probably now, if he tried, he could get through that long tunnel, but he was not going to try yet.

A curious, most unchildlike persistence, a controlled impatience, made him wait. In the meantime, he lay underwater on the white sand, littered now by stones he had brought down from the upper air, and studied the entrance to the tunnel. He knew every jut and corner of it, as far as it was possible to see. It was as if he already felt its sharpness about his shoulders.

He sat by the clock in the villa, when his mother was not near, and checked his time. He was incredulous and then proud to find he could hold his breath without strain for two minutes. The words "two minutes," authorized by the clock, brought the adventure that was so necessary to him close.

In another four days, his mother said casually one morning, they must go home. On the day before they left, he would do it. He would do it if it killed him, he said defiantly to himself. But two days before they were to leave—a day of triumph when he increased his count by fifteen—his nose bled so badly that he turned dizzy and had to lie limply over the big rock like a bit of seaweed, watching the thick red blood flow onto the rock and trickle slowly down to the sea. He was frightened.

Supposing he turned dizzy in the tunnel? Supposing he died there, trapped? Supposing—His head went around in the hot sun, and he almost gave up. He thought he would return to the house and lie down, and next summer, perhaps, when he had another year's growth in him—then he would go through the hole.

But even after he had made the decision, or thought he had, he found himself sitting up on the rock and looking down into the water, and he knew that now, this moment, when his nose had only just stopped bleeding, when his head was still sore and throbbing—this was the moment when he would try. If he did not do it now, he never would.

He was trembling with fear that he would not go, and he was trembling with horror at that long, long tunnel under the rock, under the sea. Even in the open sunlight, the barrier rock seemed very wide and very heavy; tons of rock pressed down on where he would go. If he died there he would lie until one day—perhaps not before next year—those big boys would swim into it and find it blocked.

He put on his goggles, fitted them tight, tested the vacuum. His hands were shaking. Then he chose the biggest stone he could carry and slipped over the edge of the rock until half of him was in the cool, enclosing water and half in the hot sun.

He looked up once at the empty sky, filled his lungs once, twice, and then sank fast to the bottom with the stone. He let it go and began to count. He took the edges of the hole in his hands and drew himself into it, wriggling his shoulders in sidewise as he remembered he must.

Soon he was clear inside. He was in a small rock-bound hole filled with yellowish-gray water. The water was pushing him up against the roof. The roof was sharp and pained his back. He pulled himself along with his hands—fast, fast—and used his legs as levers.

His head knocked against something; a sharp pain dizzied him. Fifty, fifty-one, fifty-two . . . He was without light, and the water seemed to press upon him with the weight of rock. Seventy-one, seventy-two . . . There was no strain on his lungs. He felt like an inflated balloon, his lungs were so light and easy, but his head was pulsing.

He was being continually pressed against the sharp roof, which felt slimy as well as sharp. Again he thought of octopuses, and wondered if the tunnel might be filled with weed that could tangle him. He gave himself a panicky, convulsive kick forward, ducked his head, and swam.

His feet and hands moved freely, as if in open water. The hole must have widened out. He thought he must be swimming fast, and he was frightened of banging his head if the tunnel narrowed.

A hundred, a hundred and one . . . The water paled. Victory filled him. His lungs were beginning to hurt. A few more strokes and he would be out. He was counting wildly; he said a hundred and fifteen, and then, a long time later, a hundred and fifteen again. The water was a clear jewel-green all around him. Then he saw, above his head, a crack running up through the rock. Sunlight was falling through it, showing the clean dark rock of the tunnel, a single mussel shell, and darkness ahead.

He was at the end of what he could do. He looked up at the crack as if it were filled with air and not water, as if he could put his mouth to it to draw in air. A hundred and fifteen, he heard himself say inside his head—but he had said that long ago.

He must go on into the blackness ahead, or he would drown. His head was swelling, his lungs cracking. A hundred and fifteen, a hundred and fifteen pounded through his head, and he feebly clutched at rocks in the dark, pulling himself forward, leaving the brief space of sunlit water behind.

He felt he was dying. He was no longer quite conscious. He struggled on in the darkness between lapses into unconsciousness. An immense, swelling pain filled his head, and then the darkness cracked with an explosion of green light. His hands, groping forward, met nothing, and his feet, kicking back, propelled him out into the open sea.

He drifted to the surface, his face turned up to the air. He was gasping like a fish. He felt he would sink now and drown; he could not swim the few feet back to the rock. Then he was clutching it and pulling himself up onto it.

He lay face down, gasping. He could see nothing but a red-veined clotted dark. His eyes must have burst, he thought; they were full of blood. He tore off his goggles and a gout of blood went into the sea. His nose was bleeding, and the blood had filled the goggles.

He scooped up handfuls of water from the cool, salty sea, to splash on his face, and did not know whether it was blood or salt water he tasted. After a time, his heart quieted, his eyes cleared, and he sat up.

He could see the local boys diving and playing half a mile away. He did not want them. He wanted nothing but to get back home and lie down.

In a short while, Jerry swam to shore and climbed slowly up the path to the villa. He flung himself on his bed and slept, waking at the sound of feet on the path outside. His mother was coming back. He rushed to the bathroom, thinking she must not see his face with bloodstains, or tearstains, on it. He came out of the bathroom and met her as she walked into the villa.

"Have a nice morning?" she asked, laying her hand on his warm brown shoulder a moment.

"Oh, yes, thank you," he said.

"You look a bit pale." And then, sharp and anxious, "How did you bang your head?"

"Oh, just banged it," he told her.

She looked at him closely. He was stained. His eyes were glazed-looking. She was worried. And then she said to herself, "Oh, don't fuss! Nothing can happen. He can swim like a fish."

They sat down to lunch together.

"Mummy," he said, "I can stay under water for two minutes—three minutes, at least." It came bursting out of him.

"Can you, darling?" she said. "Well, I shouldn't overdo it. I don't think you ought to swim any more today."

She was ready for a battle of wills, but he gave in at once. It was no longer of the least importance to go to the bay.

READING FOR DETAILS

A Boy Proves Himself

1. Jerry's relationship to his mother has great influence on his actions at the seashore. What kind of mother is she? Does she really understand Jerry?
2. Why doesn't Jerry wish to stay and swim with his mother? With whom does he wish to swim and make friends? How does he discover the existence of the underwater tunnel?
3. How did Jerry prepare himself for the ordeal of swimming through the hole? Why did he need goggles? How did he make use of the large stones?
4. What gave him a sense of false victory before he really reached the end of the tunnel? What psychological effect did this have on Jerry?

READING FOR MEANING

The directions for these propositions will usually ask you to "consider and discuss." Remember that the *considering* is just as important as the *discussing*—perhaps even more so. It is pointless to speak or write before you have decided *what* you want to say and *how* you want to say it. Before you begin to speak, make a mental note of three or four points you want to make, and arrange your points in a logical order. *Consider*, then discuss:

1. Does the author imply that people benefit from any test they force on themselves?
2. Find evidence in the story to support the following statement: Often after a person works hard to achieve something, it no longer seems important to him or her.

READING FOR APPRECIATION

Suspense

By the time the boy has made the decision that the moment has come when he will try to swim through the tunnel, the author has carefully acquainted the reader with the dangers involved.

1. What two dangerous possibilities particularly frightened Jerry?
2. List other possibilities of danger which the author mentioned earlier in the story.

Conflict

This story is rich in elements of conflict. Jerry's desire to test himself results from conflicting feelings which struggle within him. He loves his mother, but he is in rebellion against the restraint and "safeness" she represents.

1. Jerry takes action to prove his own worth. What is the opposing force against which he chooses to struggle?
2. The notes above suggest that the main conflict of the action (the boy against the dangers beneath the sea) may not be the story's most important conflict. Where is the climax, or turning point, of the action? How is the conflict inside the boy settled?

COMPOSITION

Choose one of the ideas in Reading for Meaning to use as a topic sentence, or thesis statement, and expand it into an essay. Relate the topic to your personal experience.

BIOGRAPHICAL NOTE

Doris Lessing (1919–   ), whose parents were English, was born in Kermanshah, Persia. When her father tired of the graft and corruption in Persia at the time, he moved the family to southern Rhodesia where he bought a corn farm. *In Pursuit of the English,* her autobiography, *Children of Violence,* and *The Golden Notebook* are her best-known works. Many of her stories center on South Africa; in fact, she has recently published a book entitled *African Stories.* She is considered one of Britain's foremost writers.

 Gallery

A dventure calls to everyone, but not all of us listen. For one good reason or another, we avoid the excitement, bypass the danger, and waste the riches that can come only from an investment in adventure. But the arts save us. If we let our imagination be excited by the artist, we can almost live the danger, feel the thrill, and—for a moment at least—experience the risk and reward and richness of adventure.

Leroy Neiman
BENGAL TIGER

Winslow Homer, **BREEZING UP**
National Gallery of Art, Washington, D.C.
Gift of W. T. and May T. Mellon Foundation

American artist Winslow Homer relives a boyhood adventure off the coast of Maine. It's a classic confrontation—boy against blustering breeze—and contained in it is an even *more* classic conflict—human being versus nature. Anyone who has lived near the sea knows that for all of the wonderful luminosity of a summer afternoon, there is always danger lurking in wind and water. It makes the fun all the more adventurous. The jungle scene at the left, by contemporary artist Leroy Neiman, contains the same kind of conflict. There are really two figures in the painting, and one of them is you. The agitated brush strokes of the artist have set the tiger in motion. Let your imagination go—and run for your life!

Persian, **SHAH-NAMA OR BOOK OF KINGS** by Firdausi, XV Century
Metropolitan Museum of Art, New York City, Bequest of William M. Grinell

The pent-up power and grace of horses is as exciting as it is beautiful. Try to guess the story behind the ancient Persian myth, the barely tethered turmoil of horses at a fair by the nineteenth-century artist Rosa Bonheur, and the onslaught of racehorses charging directly at you through dust and sunlight by the French painter Edouard Manet.

Rosa Bonheur, **THE HORSE FAIR**
Metropolitan Museum of Art, New York City, Gift of Cornelius Vanderbilt

Edouard Manet, **AT THE RACES**
National Gallery of Art, Washington, D.C., Widener Collection

Albert Gleizes, **FOOTBALL PLAYERS**
National Gallery of Art, Washington, D.C., Ailsa Mellon Bruce Fund

A writer makes us experience adventure by exciting us with words. An artist can involve us by creating exciting visual effects. A cubist painter doesn't represent experience as a unified whole, but in fragments, and we're drawn into that experience by putting the fragments together. Let your eyes piece together the cubistic football game above. Then experience the impact of the fiery red splash of the Royal Guard's uniform at the right. Red is the most thrilling of all colors. Like the trumpeter in the painting, it sounds its own call to adventure.

Théodor Géricault, **TRUMPETER OF NAPOLEON'S IMPERIAL GUARD**
National Gallery of Art, Washington, D.C., Chester Dale Collection

NONFICTION

The term *nonfiction* is generally used to describe any work of literature that deals with real people and events. The forms of nonfiction in *Insights* include the *biography,* in which a writer tells of the life of another person; the *autobiography,* in which the writer tells of his or her own life; and the *essay,* a relatively short composition, usually prose, in which a writer presents a particular opinion or point of view.

In this unit, "The Wild Flight of John Wise" and "Woman of Iron" are two entertaining examples of biography. "The Pole," Matthew Henson's personal account of his adventures with Commander Peary, is an exciting and informative example of autobiography. In "A Boy Who Was Traded for a Horse" (WITH WHAT YOU HAVE) and "Nathan Hale" (IDENTITY), biographers James Saxon Childers and Nancy Hale present their viewpoints of George Washington Carver and Nathan Hale, respectively. Each of these biographical sketches could also be classified as an essay. Also in WITH WHAT YOU HAVE, you will read three very stimulating autobiographical stories: "Best Foot Forward," "A Little Mudhole in the Road," and "Why Don't You Wear Shoes?"

You will find that the nonfiction selections in *Insights* make use of many of the same literary elements found in the short story. These stimulating accounts of real people and events provide reading experiences that are enjoyable and informative.

Some people look out over the water and wish for a ship. Johnny Wise looked up into the sky and wished for a way to sail among the clouds.

THE WILD FLIGHT OF JOHN WISE

Lyman M. Nash

On a warm day in the summer of 1822, a housewife on the outskirts of Lancaster, Pennsylvania, straightened up from her gardening and very nearly swooned. Floating 100 feet in the air was a large wicker basket.

She shut her eyes, shook her head, and took a second look. The basket was still there, all right, and now she could see it contained young Johnny Wise, busily engaged in shoving straw into a small stove. Above the stove was a cloth bag, inflated with hot air, and the entire assemblage was proceeding leisurely toward Lancaster.

Midway over the city Johnny ran out of straw. The hot air in his homemade fire balloon began to cool. Down it came, slowly at first, and then more rapidly.

It was Johnny's misfortune to land with a thud on the roof of a house highly susceptible to ignition. Hot coals, still in the stove, spilled out, and in moments the roof was ablaze. Fortunately, Johnny escaped. Unfortunately, the house did not.

After that ill-fated jaunt, there were some who said Johnny's ingenious flight showed promise of a great future in ballooning. Others swore he would come to no good end. In a way both factions were correct.

Almost from the moment of his birth in 1808, it seemed John Wise was destined to take to the air. He scarcely learned to walk before he was flying kites. When he learned to read, he ignored children's stories, instead poring over his father's technical magazines, devouring every article on ballooning. At night he dreamed of the time he would be old enough to soar aloft. That day came sooner than anyone expected.

At fourteen he collected all the old shirts he could find and sewed them into a balloon. With a small stove to provide hot air and his mother's laundry basket to ride in, Johnny sailed off to burn down that house.

When nothing but ashes remained, an irate Lancasterian stormed up to the boy. Shaking his finger under Johnny's nose, he thundered, "A little more wind and the whole town might have gone up in flames."

"But if there had been more wind," the boy aeronaut[1] answered, "I would have been carried beyond town, and this wouldn't have happened."

Sound as Johnny's reasoning was, it failed to save him from getting a good tanning and grounded him for thirteen years. Meanwhile, he finished school,

Reprinted by permission of Lyman M. Nash and *Boy's Life*, published by the Boy Scouts of America.

1. **aeronaut** (er′ə nôt), navigator of a balloon.

Crawling into the wicker car to check the progress of his hydrogen generating machine, John was about to announce that the balloon needed another hour's inflating. He didn't get a chance to open his mouth. The ground crew, fully as inexperienced as he, let go of the mooring lines. With a mighty shove, they sent balloon and balloonist shooting high into the sky.

Weighted down with sandbags, picnic lunch, and John Wise, and only partially inflated, the balloon reached housetop level. There it began a swift horizontal journey, bumping into roofs, knocking over chimneys, and scaring late sleepers out of their wits. Finally, it came to earth half a dozen blocks away.

An excited crowd bore down on the hapless adventurer, expecting to find him more dead than alive. But rounding a corner, they saw him tossing ballast, lunch, hat, and topcoat out of the basket. Considerably lighter, the balloon resumed its flight, rising to an altitude of 1,000 feet.

On a gentler wind, it soared off over Philadelphia, continued on to New Jersey, and landed in the middle of a forest. Late that night John Wise returned to civilization with a tremendous appetite and an even greater enthusiasm for ballooning.

His third flight, a few weeks later, nearly ended his career and his life at the same time. Twenty-five hundred feet in the air, the lower portion of his balloon burst. Down he plunged. Luckily,

becoming an apprentice pianoforte[2] tuner. Since pianofortes were considered racy instruments in those days, they were in short supply, and pianoforte tuners were in even shorter demand.

He pursued his profession diligently, but with little zeal, saving every cent he could. By 1835 he had enough money to build another balloon.

His second flight began as disastrously as the first had ended. Early on the morning of May 2, he rose from the corner of Ninth and Green streets, in Philadelphia, not far from where Jean Blanchard[3] made the first balloon flight in American history. John's takeoff was completely unintended.

---

2. **pianoforte** (pē an'ə fôr'tē), piano.
3. **Jean Blanchard** (1753–1809), a French aviation pioneer. He made the first balloon flight in the United States in 1793.

enough gas remained trapped in the upper half to avert complete disaster. Not wishing to land ignominiously on the heads of spectators, he waited until the last moment before dumping his sand. With renewed lift, he was able to swoop off and crash in privacy.

Undismayed, John Wise kept right on ballooning. In the course of some 200 flights, he experienced explosions, storms, accidents, and animosity in about equal proportions. Frequently, he was forced to tune pianofortes for months before earning enough to invest in another balloon. Then he would take to the air again.

With each new flight, he became more convinced that man's destiny lay in the air. More important, John Wise discovered a river of air, flowing constantly west to east, thousands of feet above earth. Prior to this discovery, a balloonist could control only his rise and descent. Where he went depended pretty much on luck.

By making use of this aerial river, a balloonist could virtually bank on traveling eastward. Sailing over the countryside one sunny afternoon, Wise asked himself: Why not build large commercial balloons, capable of carrying passengers and freight cross-country to the Atlantic seaboard or across the ocean to Europe? Once arrived at their destinations, the balloons could be deflated and shipped back to their starting point by fast freight.

The more he pondered the question, the fewer objections he could find. Thus was born his magnificent idea, the wonderful Trans-Atlantic Balloon Company.

It is, however, a long way from idea to reality. The money he made passing the hat at ascensions would never be enough to put his dream into action. So John Wise set out to find a backer.

Prospect after prospect listened bemusedly. Prospect after prospect turned him down.

Dejected, but not discouraged, Wise took off on an exhibition tour through New England. In Vermont he met a shrewd businessman named Oliver A. Gager. Bowled over by Wise's fiery oratory, Gager reluctantly agreed to discuss financing the proposed company while going for a balloon ride.

Up they went. At 5,000 feet Gager said, "The idea sounds feasible." At 6,000 feet he said, "Yes, it sounds fine." At 7,000 feet he said, "Count me in." Wise lost no time in valving out hydrogen and returning his benefactor to earth.

Back on the ground, Gager coerced three friends into investing in what he called "this momentous undertaking." With the matter of financing solved, Wise turned his attention to publicizing the newly formed company.

At a meeting with Gager, he suggested placing ads in the large newspapers.

"No," Gager said, exercising his Yankee know-how, "what we need is something spectacular, like an exploit. And it has to be so breathtaking, the name of our company will be on everyone's lips."

"Spectacular, eh?" Wise answered. "Well, suppose we make a flight from St. Louis to New York. On our way we could pass over Chicago, Cleveland, maybe even Pittsburgh, and shout greetings to the folks below. That should be spectacular enough for anybody."

It was so ridiculously simple. You merely ascended in St. Louis and came down in New York, letting the west-east

wind do the work. Struck by the excellence of his inspiration, Wise turned immediately to making plans.

The balloon would be the most advanced ever designed and carry the latest meteorological instruments, navigational aids, and scientific doodads. It would be so huge that all previous balloons would look like children's playthings. With a stroke of pure genius, he decided to name it *Atlantic*.

The voyage would commence from Washington Square, St. Louis, on the afternoon of July 1, 1859. That much was certain. Wise wished he could set a time of arrival in New York, but that, of course, depended on the wind.

As the great day approached, Wise began to worry. Newspapers might look on the flight as just another balloonist's harebrained scheme. There had been enough stunts recently—men going up hanging by their teeth or going up to set off fireworks. One even went up sitting astride a horse. Such foolishness gave ballooning a bad name. Wise wanted no part of it.

This flight, Wise determined, would demonstrate ballooning's practical side and, at the same time, blaze a trail for the company's regularly scheduled passenger flights later.

To keep it out of the silly category, Wise announced that Oliver Gager would accompany him as scientific observer. Another investor, John LaMountane, would accompany them as cosmical[4] navigator, although exactly what he would navigate remained obscure, for the bal-

---

4. cosmical (koz'mik əl), having to do with the universe.

loon, floating free, could go only where the wind directed.

July 1, 1859, was a perfect day. The St. Louis Gaslight Company honored the occasion by laying a special pipeline to the scene, and inflating began in mid-morning. But long before that time Washington Square was swarming with spectators. Whole families had driven in from surrounding farms during the night and now stood agog as the great balloon took form.

By late afternoon it was fully inflated with 60,000 cubic feet of illuminating gas. Large enough to envelop a five-story building, *Atlantic* stood 60 feet high and had a 50-foot diameter. Thirty-six shroud lines were needed to distribute the giant's lift. These were secured to the concentrating ring, from which a dozen heavier ropes descended to support the car, 10 feet below. And a dozen feet below the car hung a wooden lifeboat.

Originally, the lifeboat was intended only as a safety precaution, in the event the balloon was forced down over the Great Lakes. But by the time all the provisions, ballast, instruments, and suitcases had been stowed in the car it was discovered that the only way the three men would fit in was by sitting on each other's shoulders. Gager and LaMountane, therefore, were assigned to the boat with some of the ballast.

Shortly before takeoff time the boat also became a cargo hold. An American Express wagon fought its way through the crowd, bringing bundles of newspapers, packages, and letters to be carried to New York as airmail.

Promptly at 6:30, John Wise climbed to the basket and squeezed in amid the sandwiches, sandbags, thermometers, ba-rometers, compasses, sextants, transits, and telescopes. Gager and LaMountane boarded the lifeboat. At the last moment a young reporter, eager for a firsthand story, volunteered to join the adventurers. Wise motioned him aboard as publicity director. Then ground lines were cast off, and with a gentle lurch the *Atlantic* struggled aloft.

Almost from the beginning nothing went right. Rising upward, with the crowd cheering wildly below, Wise noticed the balloon was dangerously out of trim. The extra man and unexpected mail had shifted its center of gravity. Instead of thirty-six shroud lines sharing the weight, only six were doing the job. The other thirty hung loose.

Wise considered landing, correcting the trim, and starting off again. Rather than create a needless stir, he decided to carry on as if nothing were wrong. When safely out of sight, the trim could be corrected.

Over Illinois the *Atlantic's* condition grew worse. Something had to be done immediately. Wise called to Gager. Gager took one glance at the fast fading landscape below, looked up at the threatening bulges in the balloon above, gulped twice, and proceeded to climb, hand over hand, to the basket. Then he and Wise crawled over the network of retaining ropes, pushing and shoving the varnished silk back into place. This done, with the *Atlantic* in good trim, Gager returned to the lifeboat, his hands raw and bloodied.

At nightfall the cosmical navigator, LaMountane, glanced at the setting sun, surveyed the heavens, and called out, "Right on course." Presumably he meant they were headed for Chicago, as planned. He was wrong; they were far to the south and whipping briskly along.

A little later Wise called down to the men below that since all was in order, he was going to sleep. Hours passed. Near Lafayette, Indiana, the balloon started descending. Alarmed, Gager ordered some ballast dumped. As Wise slept, the *Atlantic* shot upward, much faster and much higher than expected.

The cooling air distended the balloon, so much so that the gas escape nozzle worked out of position, dropped inside the car, and hung a few inches above Wise's nose.

Sound asleep, Wise could not hear the steady hiss of escaping illuminating gas. In the boat the three men were frightened by the alarming increase in altitude and chilled by the corresponding drop in temperature. Through chattering teeth they called to Wise but got no answer.

For the second time Gager climbed to the basket, his bleeding hands pulling him up inch by inch. He found Wise not only asleep but unconscious and very close to asphyxiation. Working fast, Gager got the nozzle back in place and slapped Wise into consciousness. Somewhat groggily, the commander valved out sufficient gas to bring them down to a comfortable altitude. Then Gager rejoined the lifeboat.

Dawn found the trailblazers starting out over Lake Erie. In his log Wise noted that he could see Toledo on his left and Sandusky on his right. He also noted that they were barreling along at 60 miles an hour and heading into a hurricane.

Any other man would have landed immediately. Not John Wise. If they could tag on to that hurricane, he figured, there'd be no reason to stop at New York. They could sail on to Europe and be there in a day's time.

Elated by this sudden change in plans and wanting the world to know, he valved out more gas and dropped low to pass the word to a fishing trawler. At 60 miles per hour his stirring message was lost to the winds, and watching the speed at which the vessel disappeared behind, he raised his estimate of their speed to 80 miles an hour.

Oddly enough, the only indication of their breakneck pace was the waves slipping by below. Since they were moving as fast as the wind, there was utter silence, with not a breeze to flutter the pages of Wise's log.

While Wise thoroughly enjoyed their rapid progress, the three men below had entirely opposite feelings. They were not only terrified, but also seasick. At that low altitude there was a violent turbulence, and the balloon would zoom up 150 feet, shoot down 100, then zoom up again.

They begged Wise to ascend to quieter air. Leery of valving out any more gas lest they not have enough to make Europe, he ordered them to dump more ballast. They were so pleased at the prospect of rising above the turbulence that they dumped every bag of sand. A few minutes later they were zipping over Niagara Falls, 10,000 feet high and traveling 90 miles an hour.

Leaving Niagara far behind, they whipped along, dropping closer and closer to the ground. The gas escape valve had jammed, and they were losing gas. Soon they were low enough to hear earth sounds. They heard the crash of uprooted trees, saw small buildings bowled over, but felt not the slightest breeze.

Aware of their perilous position, Wise called down, "Toss out everything you can."

Turning to with a gusto not expected of the desperately ill, the hapless aerial mariners gleefully jettisoned newspapers, packages, and letters. Then they threw the oars overboard. Still not satisfied, they ripped out the seats.

The *Atlantic* climbed rapidly and streaked out across Lake Ontario. "Next shoreline a hundred miles ahead," Wise yelled down. "We're making good time. Should be there in little over an hour." Somehow his voice had lost the ring of enthusiasm.

Again the balloon started sinking. Wise tossed out his suitcase, his cigars, and the expensive instruments. The lifeboat crew started ripping up the floorboards. The *Atlantic* regained a little lost altitude.

With the shoreline coming up fast, Wise faced an important decision. Should he valve out gas and attempt a landing on the lake or take a chance on coming down over dry land? One look at the foaming waves gave him his answer. "Join me in the basket," he shouted. "We'll cut the boat loose." Reaching Europe was now out of the question.

Their strength stemming from pure panic, the scientific observer, cosmical navigator, and publicity director scrambled up to the chief balloonist. Free of the boat, the *Atlantic* bounced upward, but not for long.

Careening through the storm-darkened sky, dropping steadily, the four aeronauts could hear the wind ripping into the forest and growing ominously louder. All they could do was hang on for dear life, which they were certain wouldn't be with them long.

Eyes shut, they flinched at the sickening sound of a tree limb scraping the bottom of the car.

"To the rigging, men," Wise shouted. "We'll be safer there." Hardly had they clambered out before a branch slashed through the wickerwork. Caught for an instant, the *Atlantic* suddenly jerked free, tossing them back into the shattered remains of the wicker gondola.[5]

The climax came moments later. Whipping along nearly horizontally, the gas bag impaled itself on a tree. The car plunged to earth, tumbling its human contents like dice from a cup.

They landed in a heap at precisely 2:20 in the afternoon, July 2, 1859, not far from Henderson, New York. They had been aloft nineteen hours and fifty minutes and had traveled 1,200 miles.

Newspapers said it was the greatest balloon flight ever made. In 100 years there has been no reason to challenge that label. Not until 1910 did a balloon fly farther, but none has ever flown faster.

The ride was so wild, so dangerous, and proved such a fiasco, it was a miracle anyone survived. The only casualty, however, was the Trans-Atlantic Balloon Company, which couldn't weather the publicity and had to suspend operations.

As soon as the young reporter returned to St. Louis, he asked to be transferred to the society beat. Gager, convinced that ballooning was not conducive to longevity, withdrew his backing and

---

5. **gondola** (gon'dl ə), a basket or enclosure attached to and carried aloft by a balloon.

never again climbed higher than the top of his stepladder. LaMountane made one more ascension, landing in the wilds of Canada, and had to walk 300 miles, putting an end to his desire to fly.

Wise alone remained a staunch advocate of balloons. In 1879, aged seventy-one, he made his four hundred and forty-sixth ascension, which was one too many. Rising from Chicago, he sailed over Lake Michigan and vanished forever.

READING FOR DETAILS

An Early Aeronaut

1. How old is Johnny when he builds his first balloon? Describe it and the flight he makes.
2. What is funny about Johnny's second balloon venture? Why does it increase his enthusiasm for ballooning?
3. What happens to him in his third flight? Does this discourage him? What important discovery does he make in later flights? What wonderful idea does he get from this?
4. Why do he and Gager plan the trip from St. Louis to New York? Why are Gager and LaMountane assigned to the lifeboat?

READING FOR MEANING

Can you find support in the story for the following generalizations? Discuss each.

1. Things that seem ridiculously simple in the planning usually turn out to be much more complicated in the doing.
2. A hasty judgment is seldom an accurate one.
3. Even the most serious predicaments of people can be very funny.

READING FOR APPRECIATION

Foreshadowing

1. What two things about Johnny's future are foreshadowed in the fifth paragraph of the story?
2. On page 51, the author states: "It was so ridiculously simple." What is your immediate reaction?
3. In what way does the author's mention of the cargo and passengers aboard the *Atlantic* foreshadow the success or failure of the venture?

COMPOSITION

How often a project begun in a glorious dream ends in disappointment and frustration! It might be the "elegant" cabinet built in shop that ends up in the garage or the "svelte" skirt designed in sewing class that comes to rest in the rag bag.

Using the personal essay form, write a lively composition about a real or imagined project. In your introductory paragraph, foreshadow the project's disappointing conclusion. Then, strive to deepen the reader's humorous appreciation with the use of details, as Nash does when he lists the many items in Wise's basket (bottom of column 1, page 53). In your concluding section, try for as dramatic an effect as the author achieves in his last sentence.

BIOGRAPHICAL NOTE

Lyman M. Nash (1926–   ) was born in Wisconsin and moved to Minnesota at an early age. He went to sea and later served in the Army. After his discharge from the Army he married. Since then he has twice lived in Madrid, Spain and is now living in Chicago where he is a free-lance writer.

Introduction to THE POLE

Inside the warm igloos of the Eskimos of North Greenland at feast time, the name *Miy Paluk,* which means "brother," is still heard in song and story. It stands for a man whose warm, hearty laughter and skill at hunting and fishing made him a hero these people like to remember. *Miy Paluk's* formal name was Matthew Alexander Henson. He was the black man who accompanied Navy Commander Robert E. Peary on all but one of his hazard-filled expeditions to the Arctic.

Had it not been for *Miy Paluk's* extraordinary intelligence, ingenuity, and dependability, it is quite possible that Peary might never have achieved his goal. It was Henson who quickly learned the language of the Eskimos and acted as trader and hunter for the expeditions; Henson who designed and built the sledges used for the final dash to the Pole; Henson who trained the dogs to pull the sledges; and Henson whose unfailing good humor and quiet courage served as a continuing source of inspiration for the other expedition members.

Left an orphan at seven, Matthew Henson was only thirteen when the desire for adventure became so strong within him that he could no longer resist it. He left his job in Washington, D.C., and walked to Baltimore to ship aboard the towering three-masted merchantman *Katie Hines* as cabin boy. After his first voyage he became a seaman and for the next four years sailed all over the world.

When Captain Childs died, Henson took a job ashore as a stock clerk in a clothing store in the nation's capital. After his years at sea, he did not find this work to be very exciting. When a young civil engineer named Peary came into the store one day and offered Henson the chance to go with him to Nicaragua on a surveying expedition for the Navy, Henson accepted eagerly.

Between 1891 and 1909, Peary led eight expeditions to the frozen North, each of the last ones bringing him a little closer to finding out what lay at the uppermost axis of the earth. On July 8, 1908, the final expedition left New York on the specially built icebreaker, the *S.S. Roosevelt.* Struggling through ice-filled Arctic waters, the *Roosevelt* made it to Cape Sheridan, a base where the party spent the long winter of continuous darkness. From there they embarked by sled on February 18, 1909, across the ever-moving and drifting ice of the Arctic Ocean, to make their last attempt to reach the North Pole.

At this time Arctic night still prevailed, but to the south a thin band of twilight was beginning to show. Each day the period of light would lengthen. Every minute counted if the trip to the North Pole were to be accomplished and the return to land made before the ice floes became impassable. And, if the ship were to be able to take advantage of the breakup of the ice to make the voyage back to the states, the party had to return to the *Roosevelt* by midsummer.

In their race against time, designated support teams moved ahead to break trail and carry supplies. On a planned schedule, the teams turned back, eventually to reassemble at the ship to await Peary's return. By March 30, all of the teams had turned back except for the two headed by Bartlett, captain of the *Roosevelt,* and Matthew Henson. They awoke that morning to find open water all around them, and it was not until 5 P.M., with the temperature at 43 degrees below zero, that they were able to move ahead. The ice was so thin in places that it undulated beneath them. As this account begins it is April 1, and Captain Bartlett, who has broken trail ahead to a point 87° 48′ north latitude,* the farthest north thus far reached by man, has just turned back.

*87° 48′ **north latitude.** Latitude measures distance north and south of the Equator.

THE POLE
Matthew A. Henson

Day and night were the same. My thoughts were on the going and getting forward, and on nothing else. The wind was from the southeast, and seemed to push us on, and the sun was at our backs, a ball of livid fire, rolling his way above the horizon in never-ending day.

Captain Bartlett had gone. Commander Peary and I were alone (save for the four Eskimos, Ootah, Egingwah, Seegloo and Ooquah), the same as we had been so often in the past years. As we looked at each other, we realized our position and we knew without speaking that the time had come for us to demonstrate that we were the men who, it had been ordained, should unlock the door which held the mystery of the Arctic. Without an instant's hesitation, the order to push on was given, and we started off in the trail made by the captain to cover the Farthest North he had made and to push on over one hundred and thirty miles to our final destination.

The captain had had rough going, but, owing to the fact that his trail was our track for a short time, and that we came to good going shortly after leaving his turning point, we made excellent distance without any trouble, and only stopped when we came to a lead[1] barely frozen over, a full twenty-five miles beyond. We camped and waited for the strong southeast wind to force the sides of the lead together. The Eskimos had eaten a meal of stewed dog, cooked over a fire of wood from a discarded sledge, and, owing to their wonderful powers of recuperation, were in good condition. Commander Peary and myself, rested and invigorated by our thirty hours in the last camp, waiting for the return and departure of Captain Bartlett, were also in fine fettle,[2] and accordingly the accomplishment of twenty-five miles of northward progress was not exceptional. With my proven ability in gauging distances, Commander Peary was ready to take the reckoning as I made it and he did not resort to solar[3] observations until we were within a hand's grasp of the Pole.

The memory of those last five marches, from the Farthest North of Captain Bartlett to the arrival of our party at the Pole, is a memory of toil, fatigue, and exhaustion, but we were urged on and encouraged by our relentless commander, who was himself being scourged by the final lashings of the dominating influence that had controlled his life. From the land to 87° 48′ north, Commander Peary had had the best of the going, for he had brought up the rear and had utilized the trail made by the preceding parties, and thus he had kept

1. **lead** (lēd), a narrow channel of water through a field of ice.
2. **fettle** (fet′əl), good spirits.
3. **solar** (sō′lər), pertaining to the sun.

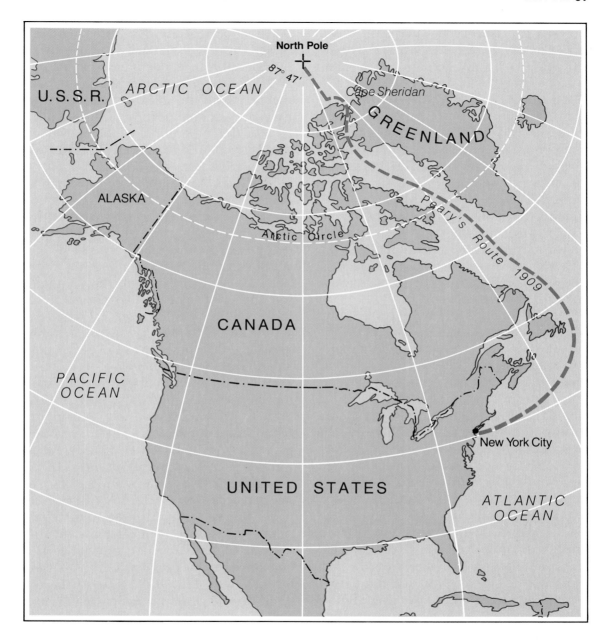

himself in the best of condition for the time when he made the spurt that brought him to the end of the race. From 87° 48′ north, he kept in the lead and did his work in such a way as to convince me that he was still as good a man as he had ever been. We marched and marched, falling down in our tracks repeatedly, until it was impossible to go on. We were forced to camp, in spite of the impatience of the commander, who found himself unable to rest, and who only waited long enough for us to relax into sound sleep, when he would wake us up and start us off again. I do not believe that he slept for one hour from April 2 until after he had loaded us up and ordered us to go back over our old trail, and I often think that from the instant when the order to return was given until the land was again sighted, he was in a continual daze.

Onward we forced our weary way. Commander Peary took his sights from the time our chronometer watches[4] gave, and I, knowing that we had kept on going in practically a straight line, was sure that we had more than covered the necessary distance to insure our arrival at the top of the earth.

It was during the march of the third of April that I endured an instant of hideous horror. We were crossing a lane of moving ice. Commander Peary was in the lead setting the pace, and a half hour later the four boys and myself followed in single file. They had all gone before, and I was standing and pushing at the upstanders of my sledge when the block of ice I was using as a support slipped from underneath my feet, and before I knew it the sledge was out of my grasp, and I was floundering in the water of the lead. I did the best I could. I tore my hood from off my head and struggled frantically. My hands were gloved and I could not take hold of the ice, but before I could give the "Grand Hailing Sign of Distress," faithful old Ootah had grabbed me by the nape of the neck, the same as he would have grabbed a dog, and with one hand he pulled me out of the water and with the other hurried the team across.

He had saved my life, but I did not tell him so, for such occurrences are taken as part of the day's work, and the sledge he safe-guarded was of much more importance, for it held, as part of its load, the commander's sextant,[5] the mercury, and the coils of piano wire that were the essential portion of the scientific part of the expedition. My *kamiks* (boots of sealskin) were stripped off, and the congealed water was beaten out of my bearskin trousers, and with a dry pair of *kamiks* we hurried on to overtake the column. When we caught up, we found the boys gathered around the commander, doing their best to relieve him of his discomfort, for he had fallen into the water also, and while he was not complaining, I was sure that his bath had not been any more voluntary than mine had been.

When we halted on April 6, 1909, and started to build the igloos, the dogs and sledges having been secured, I noticed Commander Peary at work unloading his sledge and unpacking several bundles of equipment. He pulled out from under his *kooletah* (thick, fur outer garment) a small folded package and unfolded it. I recognized his old silk flag, and realized that this was to be a camp of importance. Our different camps had been known as Camp Number One, Number Two, etc., but after the turning back of Captain Bartlett, the camps had been given names such as Camp Nansen, Camp Cagni, etc., and I asked what the name of this camp was to be—"Camp Peary"? "This, Matthew, is to be Camp Morris K. Jesup, the last and most northerly camp on the earth." He fastened the

---

4. **chronometer** (krə nom′ə tər) **watches,** exceptionally precise timepieces.
5. **sextant** (sek′stənt), an instrument for measuring altitudes of celestial bodies from a moving ship or airplane in order to determine longitude and latitude.

MATHEW HENSON
Celine Tabary
Anacostia Neighborhood Museum, Washington, D.C.
Barnett Aden Collection

flag to a staff and planted it firmly on the top of his igloo. For a few minutes it hung limp and lifeless in the dead calm of the haze, and then a slight breeze, increasing in strength, caused the folds to straighten out, and soon it was rippling out in sparkling color. The stars and stripes were "nailed to the Pole."

A thrill of patriotism ran through me and I raised my voice to cheer the starry emblem of my native land. The Eskimos gathered around and, taking the time from Commander Peary, three hearty cheers rang out on the still, frosty air, our dumb dogs looking on in puzzled surprise. As prospects for getting a sight of the sun were not good, we turned in and slept, leaving the flag proudly floating above us.

This was a thin silk flag that Commander Peary had carried on all of his Arctic journeys, and he had always flown it at his last camps. It was as glorious and as inspiring a banner as any battle-scarred, bloodstained standard of the world—and this badge of honor and courage was also bloodstained and battle scarred, for at several places there were blank squares marking the spots where pieces had been cut out at each of the "farthests" of its brave bearer and left with the records in the cairns[6] as mute but eloquent witnesses of his achievements. At the North Pole a diagonal strip running from the upper left to the lower right corner was cut, and this precious strip, together with a brief record, was placed in an empty tin, sealed up and buried in the ice as a record for all time.

Commander Peary also had another American flag, sewn on a white ground, and it was the emblem of the "Daughters of the Revolution Peace Society." He also had and flew the emblem of the Navy League and the emblems of a couple of college fraternities of which he was a member.

It was about 10 or 10:30 A.M., on the seventh of April, 1909, that the commander gave the order to build a snow shield to protect him from the flying drift of the surface snow. I knew that he was about to take an observation, and while we worked I was nervously apprehensive, for I felt that the end of our journey had come. When we handed him the pan of mercury the hour was within a very few minutes of noon. Lying flat on his stomach, he took the elevation and made the notes on a piece of tissue paper at his head. With sun-blinded eyes, he snapped shut the *vernier* (a graduated scale that subdivides the smallest divisions on the sector of the circular scale of the sextant) and with the resolute squaring of his jaws, I was sure that he was satisfied, and I was confident that the journey had ended. Feeling that the time had come, I ungloved my right hand and went forward to congratulate him on the success of our eighteen years of effort, but a gust of wind blew something into his eye, or else the burning pain caused by his prolonged look at the reflection of the limb of the sun forced him to turn aside; and with both hands covering his eyes, he gave us orders to not let him sleep for more than four hours. Six hours later he purposed to take another sight about four miles beyond, and he wanted at least two hours to make the trip and get everything in readiness.

---

6. **cairns** (kārnz), piles of stone erected as memorials or landmarks.

I unloaded a sledge, and reloaded it with a couple of skins, the instruments, and a cooker with enough alcohol and food for one meal for three, and then I turned into the igloo where my boys were already sound asleep. The thermometer registered 29 degrees below zero. I fell into a dreamless sleep and slept for about a minute, so I thought, when I was awakened by the clatter and noise made by the return of Peary and his boys.

The commander gave the word, "We will plant the stars and stripes—*at the North Pole!*" and it was done. On the peak of a huge paleocrystic floeberg[7] the glorious banner was unfurled to the breeze, and as it snapped and crackled with the wind, I felt a savage joy and exultation.

READING FOR DETAILS

The Unknown Beckons

In the opening years of this century, when Peary made up his mind that he was going to be the man to discover the North Pole, most people thought he was foolhardy. At this time aviation had not developed to the point where aerial surveys or rescues could be made. No one even knew whether there was land at the North Pole or only shifting ice floes. There wasn't even radio to keep in touch with the outside world. But even though the danger was great, Matthew Henson said that Peary semed to inspire confidence in all who worked with him.

1. What evidence do you find in the account you have read to show that Peary, in turn, places great confidence in Matthew Henson?
2. Describe Matthew Henson's instant of "hideous horror."

---

7. **paleocrystic floeberg** (pā lē ō kris′tik flō′bėrg), a massive slab of ice of ancient origin formed on the surface of a body of water.

READING FOR MEANING

Consider and discuss the following:
1. Matthew Henson ended his book, first published in 1912, with the words: ". . . the lure of the Arctic is tugging at my heart; to me the trail is calling." From this the conclusion could be drawn that a real adventurer, such as Henson, continues to feel a desire for adventure throughout life and that the ordinary person does not have this feeling.
2. The selection suggests that the achievements of most great explorers are built on the labors of those who accompany and aid them.

READING FOR APPRECIATION

Conflict

In the concluding chapters of *A Black Explorer at the North Pole* are found the words: "Commander Peary had taken the North Pole by conquest, in the face of almost insuperable natural difficulties. . . . The winning of the North Pole was a fight with nature." From your reading, discuss at least three illustrations of the explorers fighting nature in order to achieve their purpose.

BIOGRAPHICAL NOTE

Matthew A. Henson (1866–1955) was born in Charles County, Maryland. His book, *A Black Explorer at the North Pole,* touches only lightly on the hardships of his childhood. Although he did not have the advantage of many years of formal schooling, he had an active, inquiring mind, and he became well educated. In the years after he and Peary had reached the North Pole, Henson was made a member of the famous Explorer's Club, was granted honorary Master of Science degrees from Howard University and Morgan College, and, in his eighty-eighth year, was invited to the White House to be honored by President Eisenhower.

It's a killing journey
and at your age you'll never have a chance.

WOMAN OF IRON
Louis Wolfe

Strong-willed Tabitha Brown sat beside the fireplace, moving back and forth in her rocking chair. Her determined brain was working as furiously as the knitting needles in her firm, bony hands. Sitting there in her neatly ironed gingham dress and trim lace cap, she weighed a serious problem. Her children and some of the folks of St. Charles, Missouri, were getting ready to start out on a dangerous journey to Oregon. Should she go, too?

This was not the first time she had had to decide whether to pull up stakes and go West. Ever since her husband had died thirty years before, she had taught school and raised and supported her children all by herself. She had taught in Maryland, then moved on to Virginia and later to Missouri. Now, in the year 1846, she was a widow, sixty-six years old and lame in one foot.

Tabitha stopped knitting, rested her hands in her lap and gazed into the fireplace. Her thin, strong face looked as if it had been carved from granite. Suddenly, she rocked back and forth faster and once more the knitting needles were moving very rapidly. Her mind was made up. And nobody was going to change it—not even her own son, Orus.

Late that evening a March wind whistled through the nearby hickory grove as Orus walked in. A few years before he

By permission of the author, Louis Wolfe.

had gone out to look things over in Salem, Oregon. He was so impressed by what he saw that he had come back to organize a wagon train of pioneers to return and settle there. His plans were almost complete now. In a few weeks they would start out on the long, hard trek.

Orus kissed his mother, then sat on the buffalo robe that was spread out before the fireplace. As he gazed at the flames he talked about his wife and children. He also asked about his sister, Pherne Pringle, her husband and their children. Tabitha pretended she did not know the real purpose of his visit. She answered his questions and kept on rocking back and forth.

Just then snoring was heard in the bedroom. "Is Captain John sleeping?" Orus asked.

"Yes," Tabitha answered. "Let the old man rest his weary bones. He will need his strength."

Captain John Brown was a seventy-seven-year-old sea captain, the brother of Tabitha's husband. She had been taking care of him for many years.

Orus turned a log in the fireplace. His brow was wrinkled. "What do you mean, Captain John will need his strength?"

Tabitha's clear blue eyes took on a wise look. "For the journey to Oregon, of course."

Orus slowly shook his head and gazed at the musket hanging on the wall. "Maw, do we have to go over this again? You know you can't go with us. It's a killing journey and at your age you'll never have a chance. The West is for young men and . . ."

"Tut, tut, that's the trouble with you young 'uns. You think us old folks can't . . ."

"But it's two thousand miles to Oregon, and the journey will take eight or nine months. There are hostile Indians, mountains and deserts to cross and all kinds of hardships. . . ."

"Look here, Son. When I came out west years ago we had all that and a lot more. So don't tell me about hardships."

"But you're settled here now. You have a job, a house and friends. Stay here with Captain John and enjoy the rest of your . . ."

Tabitha reached to the floor for her cane and hobbled over to her son. "Orus, don't talk to me as if my days were numbered. I'm younger in spirit than a lot of you young folks. I want to stay with my children. I want to go West." Her face lost its hardness and broke into a soft smile as she added, "Son, don't ever worry about me. I'll take good care of myself and Captain John. We'll be no bother."

Orus shrugged his shoulders. He knew his mother. Once she made up her mind, there was no use arguing. On the way home he admired her spunk, but he was still sure she was too old to make the journey.

In a few weeks preparations were completed, and on April 15 the handful of pioneers and their wagons rolled out of St. Charles. While passing through the Kansas Territory, they were joined by others, making a total of sixty-nine wagons and one hundred fifty-six men, women and children. In the party were Orus Brown, his wife and eight children, Pherne and Virgil Pringle and their six children, and scores of other families.

Captain John and Tabitha, of course, were there too. After selling her house and most of her belongings, Tabitha had bought a covered wagon, an ox team and some provisions, and hired a driver. She was the oldest woman in the party. Everyone was sure she would never live to see Oregon.

The first part of the journey went along smoothly. The Indians were friendly, the weather clear and the trails in good shape for travel. For weeks, the wagon train snaked its way across the plains and over the hills of Nebraska and Wyoming. Captain John and Tabitha, instead of proving a burden, managed nicely by themselves. The Captain rode horseback and stood up surprisingly well in the saddle. As for Tabitha, she not only took care of herself but she helped the young mothers with their children and did other chores. Her covered wagon was the neatest and most comfortable in the whole train. It was furnished with a carpet, a bed, two chairs, a small mirror, books, a water barrel and her cherished rocking chair. At night, when the wagons were drawn in a huge circle around the campfire as a defense against Indian attack, Tabitha would sit in her rocker knitting, her cane by her side. The lonely young men and the frightened girls gathered around each night and talked to her. Tabitha's calm face, her cheery smile gave them new strength and courage. Her gray hair and motherliness reminded them of the folks they had left behind. Somehow, home did not seem so far away, nor the vast plains and rugged mountains so dark and forbidding.

By early August the pioneers had covered fourteen hundred miles and had reached Fort Hall in Idaho. There they stocked up on supplies and made ready to push on again, hoping their good luck would hold out on the last leg of the journey. But their luck did not hold out—not for some of them anyway.

At Fort Hall a smooth-talking guide told them of a new route, a short cut he had blazed. It went through Utah, California, and then on up into Oregon, skirting the desert, the Cascades and the Columbia Gorge. With his glib tongue he claimed the trail would get them to Oregon much sooner. He would gladly act as guide for the payment of two dollars from each family.

Orus Brown and most of the other pioneers scorned the idea. The old route had been used several times and had proved successful. So they pushed on.

The Pringles and the men of several other wagons, however, took a vote and decided to risk the short cut. Tabitha did not like the idea at all. That guide sounded *too* good. But since she was traveling with the Pringles, she had no choice but to go along with them. Rolling out of Fort Hall, she sat glumly on the front seat of her wagon and stared straight ahead. "I don't like it," she snapped to Captain John, riding alongside. "I just don't like it."

The little party of fourteen wagons and sixty-two pioneers was out of Fort Hall no more than a couple of weeks when they discovered their tragic mistake. The trail was no trail at all. It had never been traveled over by wagon train.

The pioneers had to cut and chop their way through the tangled forests. And one night the guide deserted them, so they were left completely on their own. From then on trouble clung to them like an ugly shadow.

Each day the Utah hills grew steeper and more rugged. Riders were forced to dismount and walk their horses. Drivers were forced to get out and help their oxen haul the wagons up steep grades. Furniture, stoves and farm tools were thrown away to make the wagons lighter. Swollen streams rose higher by the hour, becoming almost impossible to ford.* Two wagons were overturned and smashed while crossing swift-flowing current. The women and children in them barely escaped drowning. Tabitha let several mothers and their children ride in her wagon, even though it already was dangerously overloaded.

By September the battered party reached the southern part of the Oregon Territory and wearily started across the burning desert. The blistering sun, the dust, the killing thirst added to their misery. For miles they traveled without finding a water hole. Water was rationed. Horses and oxen slowed down. Some stopped altogether. Four dropped dead from exhaustion and thirst. Tabitha drank very little and shared her water with Captain John, her driver and others in her wagon.

Leaving the burning sands behind them at last, the pioneers began the long climb up the mountains of northern California, where they were harried by Indians. The redskins stuck to their trail day and night, stealing their horses, shooting

* **ford** (fôrd, fōrd), to cross a body of water at a shallow place.

LAKE, WIND RIVER, CHAIN OF MOUNTAINS Alfred J. Miller
Joslyn Art Museum, Omaha, Nebraska
Northern Natural Gas Company Collection

their cattle and wounding three men. All day Tabitha sat alertly on the front seat of her wagon, her cane by her side and musket in her lap.

Now it was October and the winds had turned raw and it rained without let up. Wagons plowed through axle-deep mud. Horses slipped and fell. Oxen got stuck in the mud. Another wagon cracked up and others had to be emptied of beds and clothing to make them as light as possible. Exhausted pioneers fell by the wayside, some never to rise again. Behind the wagon train, the trail was strewn with rotting wagons, tools, clothing and unmarked graves. Swaying from side to side and bouncing over the rough trail, Tabitha's driver predicted gloomily, "*None* of us will get there alive."

Tabitha just stared straight ahead.

"We'll get there," she said. "Don't worry. Just keep driving."

By now all the remaining pioneers were discouraged or exhausted or sick. For the first time Captain John showed signs of cracking up. He could barely sit in the saddle while climbing the steep twisting grades. Tabitha was not spared either. While crossing the Rogue River, her wagon was overturned. She lost her ox team, her wagon and all her belongings, including her cherished rocker. Considering herself lucky to be alive, however, she refused to crowd into any of the already overloaded wagons. She insisted on riding horseback, even though she had to be helped into the saddle each time she mounted.

With three hundred miles still to go, the ragged band was haunted by a new terror—hunger. Game was scarce, and besides, the men were too weak to aim a musket. From day to day their food supply dwindled. Rations had to be cut repeatedly. The instant an ox dropped dead in his tracks, his skeleton-like carcass was stripped of every ounce of flesh and devoured. Finally, the little band could go on no longer. The wagon train groaned to a halt. The men held a meeting. Their situation was desperate. Drastic measures were necessary. Someone had to ride on ahead and try to get help. Fourteen-year-old Octavius Pringle volunteered and rode off. The pioneers also decided that the five wagons with teams still strong enough to carry on should continue their journey. Maybe they would find food and send back relief. After the wagons were made as light as possible, the drivers pulled out and rolled northward. The Pringles, the Browns and two other families decided to remain where they were and rest for the night before carrying on the next morning.

As the rising sun broke through the gray December sky, these twenty-four pioneers started out. They forged ahead in their wagons for days and by the time they reached the foothills of the wild Umpqua Mountains their meager food supply was nearly exhausted. Tabitha watched her daughter, her son-in-law, her grandchildren grow weaker and thinner by the day. They were doomed to die of starvation unless something was done. She would not just stand idly by and watch this happen.

One morning she beckoned Virgil and Pherne aside. "We can't go on this way," she said. "I'll ride on with Captain John. Maybe I'll catch up to the other wagons. Maybe I'll get to a settlement."

Virgil gruffly brushed the idea aside. "How can you two old folks get through this wilderness? It's a miracle you've lasted this long."

"Mother," Pherne pleaded, "this is rough country. You wouldn't have a chance."

Nobody could stop Tabitha, however. She knew it. So did they. "Lift me up into the saddle," she ordered. "We'll leave right away."

In a short while the two old people were ready. Captain John sat astride his roan, while Tabitha was mounted on a black mare, reins in one hand and cane and bundle of clothes in the other. Under her saddle were a blanket and the canvas cover she had salvaged when her wagon cracked up. For food she refused to take any more than three slices of bacon and some tea. As the sun moved behind the clouds the gallant old lady and old man, completely unarmed, bade farewell to their loved ones and were soon swallowed up in the wilderness. Pherne waved good-by, trying to hold back the tears. She was sure she would never see her mother again.

Leading the way, Tabitha sat straight in the saddle and followed the wagon tracks on the trail. For hours she and Captain John pushed their way through the forest and across swift-flowing streams. Along the trail they saw flocks of geese overhead, winging southward, and spotted some deer drinking in a creek. They also saw two Indians off in the distance. Captain John valiantly rode along behind and tried not to show the effects of the killing journey, but his face was ashen, his back bent, his hands trembling. For the first time he looked like the old man he was. Now and then Tabitha spoke an encouraging word to him, but she knew that at any moment he might drop from the saddle. At dusk they overtook two of the wagons from their train, but the pioneers had found no food and were still on low rations. Tabitha and Captain John spent the night with them in an oak grove.

At dawn she shared some of her food with the pioneers and then carried on again. One behind the other, the forlorn couple rode through the wilderness, with Tabitha keeping close watch on the wagon tracks and on the feeble old man who now was failing fast. By afternoon he complained of dizziness in his head and pains in his stomach. His face twisted in agony, he sometimes stopped his horse and rested. Later, a chipmunk scampered across the trail and frightened his horse, making him rear. The old man toppled from his saddle and lay on the ground, writhing in pain. When Tabitha rode back to him, he moaned, "I can't . . . go on. . . ."

Not daring to dismount, Tabitha gazed down at him. "Lie still . . . rest for a while."

"Go on . . . leave me. . . ."

"Rubbish!" she snapped. "Don't let me hear that kind of talk."

As the old man lay sprawled out on the trail, Tabitha fastened the bundle to her saddle and took a firm grip on her cane. Then she leaned far down and thrust the tip of the cane into the ground beside the old man. "Now, take hold," she ordered, "and pull up."

The old man wrapped his trembling fingers around the cane. "Pull up . . . pull up," Tabitha urged.

Slowly, agonizingly, he raised himself to his knees. Tabitha steadied her horse, held the cane in place and let him rest a while. "Now try again."

The old man huffed and puffed and finally got to his feet. Tabitha waited to make sure he could stand by himself, then rode over to get his horse. He tried to mount but could not lift his foot into the stirrup. "No use," he wheezed. "Leave me. . . We both don't have to die . . ."

A biting wind wailed through the forest. Tabitha looked about and thought. She dared not dismount. She would not leave him alone to die. Just then her eye fell on a sunken spot up ahead, about two feet deep. "I have it," she muttered to herself.

Taking the Captain's horse by the bridle, she led it over to the spot, then maneuvered her horse alongside, but on a higher level. With both horses in position, the old man tottered over and stood between them. Tabitha told him to grab the pommel of his saddle with one hand and the cantle with the other. As he put his foot in the stirrup, she reached down with both hands and took him under the armpits. "Now up . . . up," she grunted. The old man struggled with all his might. Tabitha shoved with all the strength left in her body and finally got him into his saddle. He wobbled from side to side and was much too weak to ride by himself, so Tabitha told him to hold onto his horse's mane while she took the roan by the bridle, and once more they started along the trail.

Tabitha continued the journey for the rest of the day, always fearful that Captain John might topple to the ground at any moment and never rise again. At dusk they rode over the crest of the mountain and entered a beautiful, tremendous valley. But not a single wagon was in sight. The two old people could

ENCAMPMENT OF THE PLAINS Worthington Whittredge
Joslyn Art Museum, Omaha, Nebraska
Northern Natural Gas Company Collection

not carry on any longer. They just had to pitch camp and rest, even though it meant Tabitha would have to dismount. But it had to be done.

Soon Tabitha was out of the saddle and busily hobbling here and there with the help of her cane. She eased the old man down from his horse and made him comfortable at the foot of a huge oak tree. She removed the blankets and canvas cover from under the saddles. Finding a low limb that jutted out from an ash tree, she threw the canvas over it to make an improvised tent. Then she piled up a soft bed of hazel rods, helped Captain John into the tent and wrapped him snugly in a blanket. Finally, she dragged the bundle, the food and the bridles under the tent. Everything in order, she tried to get the old man to eat the last strip of smoked bacon, but by now he was almost unconscious. It seemed as though he could not live through the night.

As the dreary hours passed, the sky darkened to an inky blackness and an eerie wind whistled through the trees of the wilderness. Sitting in the tent, Tabitha heard the bloodcurdling squeals, squawks and growls of birds and animals. There was the *hoo—oosh—oosh* of the big owl, the piercing *ka—ze—azz—ear* of the screech owl. Now and then a lonely coyote wailed or a wolf howled in the blackness. At times the ghastly noises ceased and the silence that followed was broken by the cracking of twigs in the woods. Tabitha sat alert and tense. Was it a prowling bear? Or an Indian? Suddenly, the forest came alive again with those nightmarish squeals, squawks and growls.

The loneliness and blackness were enough to terrify even a hardy frontiersman. Yet Tabitha, though cold and hungry and weary, sat calmly beside Captain John and kept vigil. She listened to his breathing. She wiped his brow. She covered him each time he moved. All through the night, except when she dozed off for a few minutes, she kept constant watch. And as the hours passed, she was rewarded for her tenderness and care. The old man's breathing became more regular, less harsh. When dawn came and the first streaks of light stole into the tent, her hard-fought battle had been won. The Captain would live. What's more, he would be able to carry on. Tabitha gazed upward, clasped her hands and thanked God.

But as the bright morning sun cast its light over the valley, she was faced with a new problem. How would she mount her horse? She had not been able to get into the saddle by herself for many a year. And now. . . .

Just then she heard footsteps in a nearby oak grove. They came closer . . . closer. Cautiously, she lifted the flap of the tent and peered out. She could hardly believe her eyes. It was a white man, hunting game. He was one of the men from the party she was trying to overtake.

Tabitha called to him and he ran over to the tent. He explained that the wagons were up ahead, just around the bend, with plenty of venison. In no time Tabitha broke up camp and all three of them pushed on to the wagons. There was laughter and weeping at the unexpected reunion. Captain John was placed in a covered wagon and cared for as the women and children gathered around Tabitha and hugged her. She greeted them joyously, praying meanwhile that the Pringles, too, might be safe.

And before long her prayers were answered. That very morning the Pringle party was spotted, not far back on the trail. Another happy reunion followed. Tabitha listened eagerly as Pherne told how they had just about given up all hope when Octavius returned with the provisions he had set out for.

Together again, the brave little party of pioneers once more traveled northward. Again they fought their way over mountains, again they suffered from exhaustion and hunger. But, luckily, on the fifth day they met Orus Brown, who had taken the other trail out of Fort Hall and had reached Salem, Oregon, without any trouble. After waiting in vain for his mother and the others, he had loaded down four pack horses and started searching for them.

With Orus leading the way, the rag-ged and weary settlers finally staggered into Salem on Christmas Day. They went to the home of a Methodist minister. It was the first roof they had had over them in nine months. Most of the survivors, young and old alike, had to be helped or even carried into the house. But sixty-seven-year-old Tabitha, who had lost all her life's savings and belongings, walked as resolutely as ever. Her bundle in one hand, her cane in the other, she stepped across the threshold unaided.

The next day Orus reluctantly told his mother that he and the Pringles must be off. They had to find homes for themselves and families. What about her and the Captain?

Tabitha patted her son on the back. "Orus, I did not need your help back in Missouri. I managed without you on the journey. I can get along by myself now."

"But, Maw, this is not Missouri. This is rough country . . . only fit for young men."

"Be on your way, Son, and bless you." Tabitha smiled serenely. "I will manage to take care of myself and Captain John. Don't bother your head about me."

And manage she did. In fact, better than most of the settlers. She started her new life with the only money she had left, a picayune, a coin worth about six cents. With it she bought two knitting needles. Then she traded her dress to a squaw for some buckskin. Out of the buckskin she made several pairs of gloves and sold them for thirty dollars. With that as a start, she went on to support herself and Captain John by cooking and sewing and caring for the pioneer children. Things were going along fine, just fine.

Several months later she found a place in Salem for Captain John to stay while she went to visit Orus in Forest

Grove, in what is today the state of Oregon. There she met Reverend and Mrs. Harvey Clark, who liked her so much they coaxed her to live with them that winter of 1848. As usual, she made herself useful, doing all kinds of work, but when Spring came she felt restless. There were a lot of orphans and pioneer children who needed care and schooling. She made a bargain with the villagers that she would do this work for nothing if they would build a log cabin school. Of course the pioneers were delighted with the idea, and within a short time Tabitha Brown was teaching school again.

At first the charge was one dollar a week for each child for board, food and washing. Children who just went to school, or could not afford to pay, attended free. By the end of the year the school had thirty pupils and was a tremendous success. And as the years rolled by, the school grew and grew and things happened. It was given the high-sounding name of Tualatin Academy. Nine trustees were appointed. More buildings went up. New teachers were hired. And now Tabitha was allowed to keep whatever profits she had left over after paying expenses.

One evening Orus came over to see his mother. He wanted to talk to her about Captain John, who had died recently. Orus had something else on his mind, too. Wearing a neat calico dress, Tabitha sat in her new rocker and knitted. At first Orus strutted around the room, talking about his children, the Pringles and other things. Then he stood before his mother, proudly folded his arms and said, "Maw, I own my own house now. I want you to come and live with us."

Tabitha smiled, shook her gray head and went on with her knitting. "No, thanks, Orus."

"But I'm well off," he boasted. "I can take good care of you now. I have my own cabin, some land, one cow and three horses."

Tabitha nodded her head. "That's fine, my boy. You've done well and I'm proud of you. But I don't need your help. *I* own eight cows, six calves, four horses, this log cabin and the frame house across the way." A glint came into her eye as she added, "I also own eight lots and have about one thousand dollars saved up."

Orus stood motionless, his mouth wide open. Then he slapped his thigh and exclaimed, "Doggone it, Maw, you beat us all. How did you do it?"

"Just as always . . . by working and keeping my spirit up. Now you'd better be on your way. It's getting late. Thanks, Orus, for your kind offer, and give my love to your family and the Pringles."

As Orus walked down through the village that night, he pushed his hands deep into his pockets and chuckled to himself. He just could not get over it. That mother of his! What a woman!

If Orus Brown could only have looked ahead, he would have admired his mother all the more. The Tualatin Academy grew larger and larger, and in 1854 Tabitha's pluck and work and vision were crowned with a glory she had never dared dream of. The Academy was granted a charter by the legislature and became a real university, Pacific University!

Yes, Tabitha Brown did do pretty well in a country—"fit only for young men."

READING FOR DETAILS

An Adventurer at Sixty-six

When our country was first being settled there were many hardy pioneers—persons who dared to challenge the wilderness to find land of their own or a better place to live. Do you think someone of Tabitha's spirit would find challenge in the America around her today?

1. For what reasons does Orus try to discourage his mother from going to Oregon? What is Tabitha's principal reason for wanting to go?
2. How many wagons and persons make up the wagon train when it leaves Kansas Territory?
3. Why does Tabitha take the new route when the wagons leave Fort Hall, Idaho? Why is taking this route a mistake?
4. How does Tabitha lose all her possessions? What new terror haunts the party on the last 300 miles of their journey?
5. When does Tabitha reach Salem? How does she prove she is truly an adventurous spirit in the way she makes a new life for herself after she gets there?
6. What was Tabitha's final and perhaps greatest achievement?

READING FOR MEANING

Find evidence in the story to support the following statements:

1. Success depends upon an adventurous spirit.
2. Where there's a will, there's a way.
3. It is important to go through life with a positive self-image.

READING FOR APPRECIATION

Suspense and Foreshadowing

The early part of the journey goes smoothly with Tabitha's calm cheer a comfort to the younger members of the party. When they leave Fort Hall in Idaho, however, the reader knows that their good fortune is not to continue much longer.

1. What statement forewarns readers that trouble lies ahead?
2. By October, when the trail behind them has become strewn with graves and abandoned wagons, what gloomy prediction does Tabitha's driver make?
3. What is the reader told about Pherne's feelings as she waves good-by to Tabitha and Captain John as they set off by themselves to try to find help?

Imaginative Language

If Tabitha's true experiences had been told without any effort to make them interesting, "Woman of Iron" would be very dull reading. Instead, the author has used imaginative details to make the story vivid. A good example can be found in the paragraph that describes the night Tabitha spends in the makeshift tent watching over Captain John. This is the paragraph on page 70 beginning, "As the dreary hours passed . . ."

1. Discuss the descriptive words used in this passage.
2. Find and discuss other examples of the use of imaginative language elsewhere in the account.

BIOGRAPHICAL NOTE

Louis Wolfe (1905–   ) was born in Bound Brook, New Jersey. Following work in history at Rutgers, New York, and Columbia Universities, he spent much time in travel and research in all parts of the United States, Canada, the Caribbean, South America, and Europe. His exciting adventure stories, based on historical research, have appeared in many magazines, and he has produced and directed radio and television programs.

Can you see in this poem
another kind of adventure . . .

I Am A

Cosmonaut
Cradled in dangers
Orbiting a garden universe
Snipping cosmos, probing Venus,   5
Sighting summer's end blindly,
Weightily weightless
Spinning out of reach,
            out
                of   10
                    reach
Signaling strangers.

LENORE MARSHALL

SUMMING UP: CALL TO ADVENTURE

Adventure can be found anywhere if you have an adventurous spirit. Its call can be heard in the roar of the sea, the whistle of a train, or the silence of a classroom. Adventure is where you find it!

READING FOR MEANING

Consider each of the following statements before you decide whether you agree or disagree. Most of these statements would make a good topic for a brief essay or talk. If you choose to use one of them for this purpose, remember that your talk or essay will be more interesting and convincing if you refer as often as possible to *specific* points in the selections in CALL TO ADVENTURE.

1. Reading stories of adventure satisfies the basic human need to have some variety in the pattern of everyday existence.
2. To hear the call to adventure you must be an original and independent thinker.
3. People's actions are largely determined by the way they think about themselves.
4. A hero is simply a person who happens to be in the right place at the right time.
5. A person dares all in achieving some objective. Once achieved, however, the objective is no longer of interest. Thus one could conclude that the effort was not worth it.
6. In making up the true image of a hero, honor should be the first qualification, courage and daring being secondary considerations.

READING FOR APPRECIATION

In many respects, fiction and nonfiction are alike. Explain this statement after considering the following questions:

1. What makes fictional, or imaginary, adventure seem real?
2. Do you understand characters in stories better if they talk and act like people you know?

Conflict

Discuss the following statements, and tell why you think they are true or untrue.

1. "The Most Dangerous Game" centers on the conflict of individual against individual; it also shows inner conflict, where one idea struggles against another; and there is a third kind of conflict, the individual against nature.
2. "Through the Tunnel" shows only one type of conflict.

Suspense and Foreshadowing

Foreshadowing is one of the many ways an author has of building the suspense that makes an audience or reader wonder what is going to happen.

1. How does the title "The Woods-Devil" help create suspense?
2. In the third paragraph of "Woman of Iron," what is foreshadowed?

Imaginative Language

1. Think back to "The Most Dangerous Game." In this story, author Richard Connell imprints imaginative images on the reader's mind that allow the reader to experience the story as if through his or her own senses. What character or characters described by Connell return to you most vividly?
2. Think back over the selections in this section. Write down at least three images you can recall immediately. For example, from "The Most Dangerous Game," do you see, feel, or hear the "apprehensive night" that "crawled slowly by like a wounded snake"? Give reasons why the three images you chose have stayed with you.

COMPOSITION WORKSHOP

THE BRIEF REPORT

The process of writing a brief report is almost identical to the process of writing a single paragraph. You begin by identifying a topic and then gathering information on the topic. You then examine all of the gathered information and arrange it into related groups. Each group of related information will form one of the paragraphs in the report. You then decide the most effective order for the arrangement of the paragraphs. In the final step of the process, you write an introductory paragraph that introduces the report to the reader and announces your main idea. Let's take a closer look at the process.

Let's say that when reading Paul Annixter's short story "The Woods-Devil" you become curious about the wolverine. You decide to write a report with the wolverine as the general topic. The story provides some information about the wolverine, but Annixter's main purpose is not to provide information about the animal but to show how the young boy in the story answers adventure's call. So you must go to the library to dig out the needed information.

Using a number of resources in the library, you accumulate a lot of information about the wolverine in the form of notes. These notes are taken first from a general encyclopedia and later from these three books: *Wild Animals of North America, Mammals of North America,* and *Wild Animals of the World.* After two hours or so of research, you have collected a lot of information about the animal's external features, its hunting methods, its eating habits, and its attitude toward the humans it encounters. You realize that running through all of this information is the clear suggestion that the animal is rather unpopular and hateful. You now are in a position to make a more careful statement of the topic. Having seen that the information groups itself under a number of headings, you are also ready to do what all experienced report writers do. You take note of the topic and develop the following rough outline:

Topic: The Unpopular Wolverine

I. External appearance
II. Method of hunting
III. Eating habits
IV. Attitude toward humans

With the rough outline as a guide and using the gathered and sorted information, you are now ready to develop the four paragraphs that will make up the body of the report. Here are the paragraphs that could result. Notice that each main idea, or topic, sentence has something to do with the animal's unpleasantness and lack of popularity.

The wolverine's lack of popularity might have something to do with its external appearance. The animal is between three and four feet long from the tip of its snout to the tip of its bushy tail. Its chunky body, which can weigh anywhere from 17 to 50 pounds, is covered with thick brown fur. Stout bowlegs and large feet tipped with long, needle-sharp claws carry it slowly along. Its most memorable feature is a large head that very much resembles the head of a bear. Many people familiar with the wolverine call it "Skunk-Bear," since it resembles both of these animals.

The wolverine's method of hunting does not endear it to many people. The creature is a cunning strategist. It uses its cleverness to hunt animals many times its own size. It will track a caribou herd for hours, waiting patiently for a young calf or an old and weak animal to wander away from the main group. It will climb a tree and wait quietly for a deer, a mountain sheep, a coyote, or even a mountain lion to pass beneath. It has even been known to attack elk and moose when they are bogged down in deep snow. One of its favorite tactics is to allow another animal to do the killing. Bears, coyotes, and mountain lions are often frightened away by a snarling wolverine.

The wolverine's eating habits do not help the animal gain a good reputation. It earns its Latin name *Gulo luscus* or "one-eyed gullet." It

focuses continually upon feeding itself and eats just about anything. If larger animals that can furnish many a meal are not to be found, the wolverine will satisfy itself with frogs, fish, birds, rabbits, or squirrels. It will even devour long-dead carcasses. When it kills a larger animal or steals it from another hunter, it will stay with the prize until it is gone. It will camp nearby and eat until it is exhausted. After a restful sleep, it will return for another hearty meal. The wolverine has even been known to drag a kill three times its own size for a mile or more to a safe dining area.

The testimony of trappers and fur hunters has helped to build the wolverine's bad reputation. The gluttonous animal can drive the human hunter to madness and ruin. It can cleverly remove the bait from any human trap ever devised. It will boldly remove and devour every trapped animal that it finds. It has even been known to hide and destroy traps, never getting caught itself in the process. Its destruction extends beyond the trapline to the trapper's own cabin. It can climb, dig, or chew its way into any building. It can eat an entire winter's supply of food in just a few days. What it won't eat it will destroy by spraying it with a foul-smelling musk. In a final act of pure deviltry, the wolverine will scatter pots, plates, kitchen utensils, dishes, and canned goods in the surrounding woods. Perhaps worst of all, the woods-devil is too busy eating and destroying to hibernate and therefore harasses the human hunter all year long.

A report's introductory paragraph is to the body of the report what the topic sentence in a paragraph is to the paragraph's supporting sentences. A topic sentence in a paragraph tells the reader what it is that holds all of the supporting sentences together. The introductory paragraph in a report tells the reader what it is that holds the paragraphs in the body of the report together. One sentence in the introductory paragraph—called the thesis statement or controlling idea—summarizes the writer's major point of view.

In addition to announcing the main idea of the report, the introductory paragraph also tries to stimulate the reader's interest in the topic. As a result, the introductory paragraph is usually made up of three or more sentences. The thesis statement announces what the writer will try to prove in the report. The other sentences provide some additional information about the overall topic or try to get the reader's attention. Here is a possible introductory paragraph for the report on the wolverine. Which sentence is the thesis statement? What role is played by the other sentences in the introductory paragraph?

The wolverine is an animal with few admirers. Like the much-sought-after mink, the wolverine is a member of the weasel family. But as far as popularity goes, it has much more in common with the skunk, another member of the same family.

ACTIVITY 1

Find a topic for a brief report of between four to six paragraphs. Try to find a topic that is suggested by one of the selections in this unit. Select a topic that you believe you can gather enough information about to deal with in a brief report. Gather the information by consulting standard references and books on the topic.

ACTIVITY 2

Sort through the information that you gathered for Activity 1. Arrange the information into three or four groups. Find an idea that relates to all of the groups to identify your topic more exactly. Prepare a rough outline of the body of your report. Write each of the paragraphs that will make up the report's body.

ACTIVITY 3

Write an introductory paragraph for your report. Include a thesis statement that will explain to the reader what main idea the paragraphs in the body of the report will support. Add two or three sentences to the thesis statement which more fully explain the point to be made in the report or which attempt to develop the reader's interest in the report's topic.

INTRODUCTION TO
Homer's Odyssey

Nearly thirty centuries ago (roughly 800 B.C.), Homer, a blind minstrel in ancient Greece, is thought to have put together two of the world's great adventure stories. One story, the *Iliad*,[1] tells of the war between Greece and Troy.[2] It was a war which dragged on for ten long years, until finally a crafty Greek warrior named Odysseus[3] thought of a plan which brought victory to his people. The other story, the *Odyssey*,[4] tells of the many adventures of this same hero, Odysseus, as he struggles to sail home to Greece after the war is over.

The Epic

These ancient adventure tales, the *Iliad* and the *Odyssey*, are called *epics*. One of the oldest of literary forms, the *epic* is a story-poem about some great hero who performs daring deeds that require superhuman courage. In the Greek epics, the gods take an active part in helping or hindering the hero. For example, in the *Odyssey,* the god of the sea, Poseidon,[5] is Odysseus' enemy; while Athene,[6] the goddess of wisdom, helps the courageous Greek.

Recited from memory by minstrels who wandered from one lord's banquet hall to another, epics were passed along from minstrel to minstrel for many centuries.

Every epic took one hero, a man anyone could be proud to claim as an ancestor, through a series of separate adventures. When all of these separate stories were strung together into a long story-poem, they became an epic. The fate of the hero is usually bound up with the fate of a whole nation or race. Like most ancient peoples, the Greeks of Homer's time and later believed that their ancestors had been supermen, great in physical strength and unusually keen in mind. These superbeings supposedly found their greatest glory in battle.

By the time the *Odyssey* was written, the pattern of the Greek epic was well established. The verse form used was the hexameter. The prefix *hexa* indicated that there were six poetic measures to a line.

The Epic Poet

The epic poet did not "create" his story in the same way as a modern writer. The Greeks called an epic singer a *rhapsode*. This means "song-stitcher," which describes a minstrel very well. He felt free to borrow from legends and epics which were already well known to him and to his audience, but characters and places might be changed to suit a particular story. Since the epics were sung or told aloud, they had to be clear and readily understood. The minstrel-poet drew from a large store of

1. **Iliad** (il′ē əd).
2. **Troy** (troi), an ancient city of northwest Asia Minor south of the mouth of the **Dardanelles** (därd′n elz′) straits connecting the **Aegean** (ī jē′ən) **Sea** with the Sea of Marmara.
3. **Odysseus** (ō dis′ē əs, ō dis′yüs).
4. **Odyssey** (od′ə sē).
5. **Poseidon** (pə sīd′n), the Earth-Shaker, called **Neptune** (nep′tün, nep′tyün) by the Romans.
6. **Athene** (ə thē′nə), the goddess of wisdom, industry, and arts, and protector of civilized life. She has always helped Odysseus. Called **Minerva** by the Romans.

phrases and descriptions from familiar epics, all of which had been repeated so often they were quickly recognized by his listeners. Above all, the epic singer had to make his stories as uncomplicated for his listeners as possible. Thus he dealt with only one thing at a time.

Homer

Within the set epic pattern there was still opportunity for the poet-singer to display originality of idea, expression, and effect. Here Homer outshone the other epic singers. He had the ability to bring his heroes alive. His epics were the ones which the Greeks valued enough to save for future generations.

Reading the Odyssey

The lines of the following poem flow smoothly, much as a person would speak. This, however, is an English translation of the original Greek poetry. It does not use the hexameter verse form which fit the Greek language perfectly but which usually seems heavy and clumsy when attempted in English. To allow the action to move ahead rapidly, this translation is written in a verse form which has four measures to the line, is unrhymed, and has a certain marked rhythm. If it is read aloud, as it was meant to be, readers can avoid the singsong, which robs any poetry of its vitality, if they will *pause only briefly* at the end of each line in which the thought runs into the line following.

In this abridgement of Bates's translation of *The Odyssey of Homer*, many episodes and details have necessarily been omitted. If you enjoy these adventures of Odysseus, you will probably be interested in reading the whole book.

The War at Troy

No one really knows the reasons the Trojan War was fought. Some classical scholars believe that it came about when the Greeks decided to control the trade route between the Aegean Sea and the Black Sea, and thus spent many years both blockading and attacking Troy and towns along the coast of Asia Minor that were friendly to the Trojans.

According to ancient myth, however, the bitter fighting at Troy all began when the Trojan prince, Paris, kidnapped Helen, the beautiful queen of Sparta, and carried her across the sea to Troy.

Gathering a huge army and a thousand ships, the angry Greeks sailed over the Aegean Sea. There they anchored their vast fleet by the shore before Troy and prepared to assault the forbidding walls of the city. However, the Trojans had prepared for the coming of the Greeks and they put up a stiff resistance. The result was that instead of the quick victory the Greeks had expected there was a long, drawn-out war in which the gods and goddesses took sides.

For nine long years the struggle went on with fortune favoring first one side, then the other. The Greeks could not batter down the Trojan walls; the Trojans could not destroy the Greek fortifications or their ships along the shore.

In the tenth year of the war, Odysseus, who was famous for his craftiness, devised a plan which brought about the fall of the Trojan stronghold. The Greeks built a huge, hollow wooden horse and left it in view of Troy. Odysseus and a picked band of men were hidden inside the horse. Then the Greek armies, pretending to give up the long struggle, sailed off to a hiding place down the coast to await the coming of the night.

An Adventure in Archaeology

The search for and the eventual discovery of the ruins of Troy was in itself a thrilling adventure. The man who made the first great excavation, Heinrich Schliemann,* had become so intrigued with Homer's stories that, as a boy in a small German village, he vowed some day to find the great ruins. Schliemann amassed a fortune before he was forty and began his search for the ancient Greeks in earnest. In 1868, he went to what is now Turkey to dig.

Using the descriptions of Troy which Homer gives in the *Iliad,* Schliemann located a vast mound of earth on the shore of the Dardanelles. There he began his excavation.

Within the mound he found many levels of cities which over the centuries had been built one atop the ruins of another. He also unearthed a great store of priceless gold and silver ornaments. Most important of all, he established that there was a historical basis to the *Iliad.*

The Unlikely Hero, a book by Alan Honour, is an especially interesting account of Schliemann's life and discoveries.

Overjoyed that their enemies had gone at last, the Trojans poured from the city. They surrounded the great horse, and thinking it their spoils of battle, pushed the great wooden structure inside the walls of their city. In the darkest hour of night, Odysseus and his men slipped from the horse and opened the gates to the returning Greek armies.

Caught off guard and hopelessly outnumbered, the Trojans were slaughtered and their beautiful city sacked and burned.

With the ruins of Troy smoking behind them, the Greeks sailed for home rejoicing that the ten years of war were over. But many were never to reach their homelands, for in destroying the Trojan city they had offended many of the most powerful gods. Not only had the victorious Greeks violated certain of the Trojan temples, but they also had failed to make suitable offerings to the gods after the fighting was ended.

These angry gods caused great storms to wreck many Greek ships. Scores of men were drowned. Great numbers were killed in other ways. Since Odysseus was the one who had suggested the plan for taking Troy, the gods decreed that he should spend ten more years wandering before he reached his home.

Homer begins the *Odyssey* with a traditional plea to the muse of poetry. He begs her to help him tell the story of the hero whom the gods sent wandering over the seas and who found that even after he reached his homeland and his loved ones his struggles were not over.

To make certain that his audience knows what story he is to tell, Homer also sings in the opening lines about some of the places Odysseus visited and of the gods and people the hero met. The modern reader might think this strange and repetitious, but the ancient Greeks never tired of the story. Here was a Greek to make every Greek proud. Where, indeed, could one find a hero as handsome, as courageous, and as clever as Odysseus? Where could one hope to match such a clear-voiced poet as Homer to tell the story of The Great Adventure!

Homer need not be afraid of "giving away" his story in the opening lines by telling what will happen. The audience already knew the tale of Odysseus. They were more interested in *how* Homer told the ancient stories than in *what* the plot would be.

---

*__Heinrich Schliemann__ (hīn´rik shlē´män).

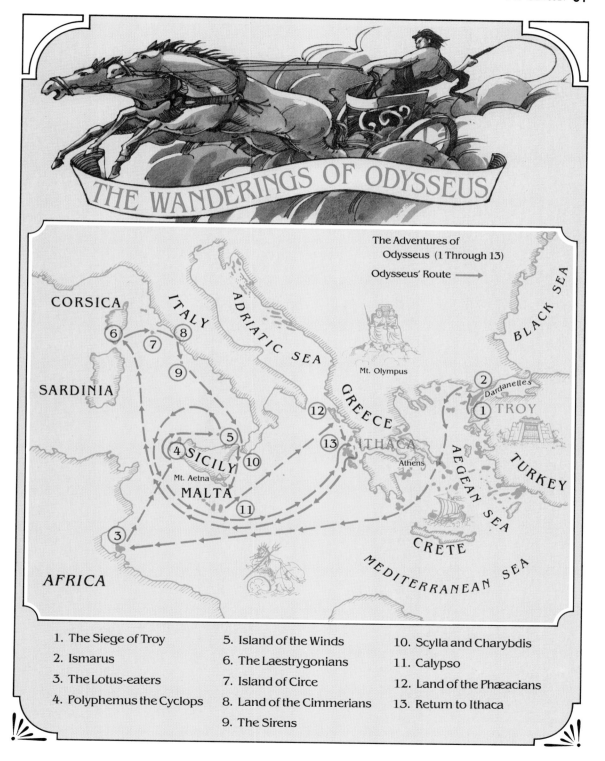

THE WANDERINGS OF ODYSSEUS

The Adventures of
Odysseus (1 Through 13)

Odysseus' Route ⟶

CORSICA

ITALY

ADRIATIC SEA

BLACK SEA

⑥ ⑦ ⑧

⑨

SARDINIA

Mt. Olympus

② Dardanelles
① TROY

⑫

GREECE

⑤

④ SICILY ⑩

⑬ ITHACA

Athens

TURKEY

Mt. Aetna

MALTA

AEGEAN SEA

⑪

③

CRETE

AFRICA

MEDITERRANEAN SEA

1. The Siege of Troy
2. Ismarus
3. The Lotus-eaters
4. Polyphemus the Cyclops
5. Island of the Winds
6. The Laestrygonians
7. Island of Circe
8. Land of the Cimmerians
9. The Sirens
10. Scylla and Charybdis
11. Calypso
12. Land of the Phæacians
13. Return to Ithaca

Portrait bust of Homer.

THE ODYSSEY OF HOMER

Translated into English Verse by Herbert Bates

Part I, Books I–IX: The Wanderings of Odysseus

Prologue

Tell me the tale, Muse, of that man
Of many changes, he who went
Wandering so far when he had plundered
Troy's sacred citadel. And many
The men whose cities he beheld,   5
Whose minds he learned to know, and many
The sorrows that his soul endured
Upon the deep the while he strove
To save himself from death and bring
His comrades home.
                    Of these things now,   10
Daughter of Zeus,[1] O goddess, tell us,
Even as thou wilt, the tale.
                    Ere this
Those others who escaped death's stroke
Had reached their homes at last, delivered
From battle and the sea. But him   15
And him alone—though still he longed
For home and wife—the nymph Calypso,[2]
A mighty goddess, kept imprisoned
Within her hollow caves, and longed
To make him there her husband. No,   20
Not when the day came when the gods
Granted, as circling seasons passed,
That he might once again return
To Ithaca[3]—not even then,
With those that loved him, might he find   25
A rest from strife. And all the gods
Felt pity for him, all but one—
Poseidon. Still, with wrath unceasing,

He strove against the good Odysseus
Until he reached his home.   30

Odysseus Tells His Story

[Ten years have passed since the Greeks destroyed Troy. At this point in the story, Odysseus has been shipwrecked and has made his way to shore half-drowned. He has been taken in as a guest at the palace of King Alcinoüs. At a feast in the palace, he sits among the guests as a stranger. The King and his lords do not know he is the famous hero, Odysseus.

The feasting is ended. The minstrel has sung so vividly of the ruin and death at Troy that Odysseus is greatly moved. The King notices this and asks the handsome stranger to tell his story. Odysseus answers:]

          "Mighty Alcinoüs,[4]
Honored of all men, good indeed
It is to hear the minstrelsy
Of such a singer, for he sings
Even as a god. Never, I think,
Can man attain a fairer goal   35
Than this:—when all a people meet
In joy and friendship. Side by side
They sit in the great hall at feast
And hear the minstrel's song. Beside them
Stand tables heaped with meat and bread.   40
While ever he who serves the wine
Dips from the mixing-bowl and fills

---

1. **Zeus** (züs), god of the sky, wielder of the thunderbolt, and leader of all the gods, called **Jupiter** (jü′pə tər) by the Romans.
2. **Calypso** (kə lip′sō), sea nymph of the island Ogygia.
3. **Ithaca** (ith′ək ə), one of the Ionian islands off the coast of northwestern Greece, Odysseus' homeland.
4. **Alcinoüs** (al sī′nō əs), king of the Phæcians (fē ā′shənz), an island or coastal people who help the shipwrecked Odysseus.

The feasters' cups. Such scenes I deem
Of all scenes, sweetest.
     But your heart
Now urges you to ask what sorrow   45
Brings forth these sighs—though this but
  leads me
To sigh and weep the more. Nay, then—
What shall I tell you first, and what
Leave to the last? For many a sorrow
The gods that dwell on high have given   50
To be my lot.
     And first of all
I will tell forth my name that you,
Like all, may know it; and at last,
When I have shunned death's cruel day,[5]
We may be friends still, host and guest,   55
Though I dwell far away.
      I am
Odysseus, great Laërtes'[6] son,
For cunning plans of every kind
Known among men; and even to heaven
Has spread my fame. My native land   60
Is Ithaca, a sun-bright island
Where rises Neriton,[7] a mountain
Far-seen, with wind-stirred woods. About it
Lie many an island, close together—
Doulichium, wooded Zacynthus,[8]   65
And Same.[9] Ithaca itself
Is low of shore and lies far out
To sea and toward the west: the others
Lie toward the dawn and sunrise. Rugged
It is, this land of mine, yet breeds   70
A sturdy youth, and I can find
No land more sweet to me than this,
My native land.
     But come,
For I will tell the many sorrows
Zeus sent upon me as I traveled   75
Homeward from Troy.

Adventure of the Lotus-Eaters

Great Zeus, who guides the clouds, sent forth
Against our ships a wild north wind,
A raging tempest, and enshrouded
In dark clouds land and sea. Deep night   80
Came rolling from on high. Our ships
Drove headlong, while their sails were riven
Asunder by that gale; but these
We stored beneath the decks, still toiling
In dread of death, and striving ever,   85
Rowed on and reached the land
Where dwell the Lotus-eaters,[10] men
Whose food is flowers. And we all
Here went ashore and drew us water,
And by the sides of their swift ships   90
My men prepared their meal. And now
When we at last had had our fill
Of meat and drink, I sent forth men
To learn what manner of mankind
That live by bread might dwell here. Two   95
I chose to go and sent with them
A third, a herald. And these quickly
Went forth into that land and mingled
Among the Lotus-eaters. Never
Did these men, eaters of the lotus,   100
Plan evil to my men, and yet
They gave them of the lotus flower
And bade them eat of it, and lo,
Whatever man of them but tasted
That blossom strange and honey-sweet,   105
Naught cared he then to hasten back
With tidings to the ships, or ever
Turn homeward any more, but longed
To dwell there with the Lotus-eaters,
And pluck and eat the lotus blossoms   110
And think no more of home.
      But these
I brought back to the ships by force,
Though they lamented, and I dragged them
Aboard the hollow ships and bound them
Beneath the benches. Then I bade   115

5. Escaped death by reaching home.
6. **Laërtes** (lā ar′tēz).
7. **Neriton** (nā′rə tən).
8. **Doulichium** (dü li′kē əm), **Zacynthus** (zə kin′thəs).
9. **Same** (sa mā′).
10. **Lotus** (lō′tus), the Lotus-eaters ate the fruit of the lotus tree, which supposedly had magical properties.

The rest, my true companions, hasten
Aboard the ships, lest one of them
Taste of the lotus, too, and lose
All memory of home. So straightway
They came aboard and sat them down   120
In order on the thwarts and smote
The foaming sea with oars.
                              So thence
We sailed upon our way sad-hearted.

Adventure of the Cyclops

And now we came unto the land
Where dwell the Cyclops[11]—arrogant   125
And lawless beings, who, with trust
In the undying gods, plough not
Nor plant with hands a single plant.
Yet crops spring up for them unsown
On fields untended—wheat and barley   130
And vines that bear full-clustered grapes
To make them wine. The rain of Zeus
Still brings increase in all. These men
Have neither meeting-place for council
Nor settled laws. They live apart   135
On lofty mountain ridges, dwelling
In hollow caverns. Each makes laws
For wife and child, and gives no heed
To any save himself.

                    There lies,
Facing the Cyclops' land, an island,   140
Sheltering the haven's outer side,
Not near, nor yet far out.
                         Thither we sailed
Seeking the land. Surely it was
Some god that gave us guidance thither
Through the dense night, for we could
    see   145
Nothing before our eyes: the mist
Shut close about the ships; no moon
Showed forth in heaven, for clouds en-
    closed it.
So no man with his eyes beheld
That isle or saw the long seas rolling   150

Bronze helmeted warrior.

Against the land till we had beached
Our well-benched ships.
                        We drew our ships
Forth on the sands and lowered sail,
And we ourselves went up beyond
The breaking of the seas, and there   155
We fell asleep, and lay awaiting
The sacred dawn.

11. **Cyclops** (sī'klops), a legendary giant having only
one eye in the center of his forehead.

But when the dawn
Came, early-born and rosy-fingered,
We went forth, roaming through the island,
Gazing in wonder.
          Now we looked   160
And saw not far away the mainland
Where dwelt the Cyclops. And we saw
Smoke rise, and heard the speech of men
And bleat of sheep and goats.
Then I called together   165
My men and spoke to all:
             'Rest here,
Dear comrades, while with my own ship
And my own men I go to learn
What men these are—if wild and cruel
And ignorant of right, or kind   170
To every stranger and with hearts
That fear the gods.'
          I spoke and went
Aboard my ship and bade my men
Embark and loose the cables. Quickly
They came aboard and sat them down   175
Each in his place and smote with oars
The whitening sea.

          Now when we reached
That land that lay hard by, we saw
Upon its utmost point a cave
Close to the sea: high-roofed it was,   180
With laurel overhung, and many
The flocks of sheep and goats that there
Found shelter in the night. Around it
A courtyard lay, high-walled with stones
Set deep in earth, with lofty pines   185
And high-leaved oaks.
          Within this lair
A man was wont to sleep, a monster
Who grazed his sheep far off, alone,
Nor ever mingled with his kind,
But lonely dwelt—lawless and evil.   190
And marvelously was he shapen—
This monstrous being, not like mortals
That live by bread, but like a peak
That rising rough with woods stands forth
Apart from other hills.

          And I   195
Now bade my trusty men to bide
Close by the ship and guard the ship,
But twelve I chose, the best of all,
And we set forth.
          I bore with me
A goatskin filled with dark sweet wine,   200
Which Maron, priest of Phœbus,[12] gave me,
Sweet and unmixed, a drink for gods.
As I set forth, I bore besides
Food in a leathern sack. For now
My fearless heart foresaw a meeting   205
With a strange man of monstrous might—
A savage, scornful of the gods
And of man's law.
          Straightway we reached
His cave and entered, but we found not
The man within. For far away   210
He herded, while they grazed at pasture,
His goodly flock. So on we passed
Far into that great cave and marveled
At all we saw within. Here stood
Crates heaped with cheese and here were
     pens   215
Crowded with lambs and kids; all these
Were penned in pens apart; in one
Were kept the eldest, in another,
The younger; in a third, the youngest;
And all the well-wrought vessels used   220
For milking—pails and bowls—stood full,
Brimming with whey.
          And now my men
Besought me eagerly to carry
The cheeses thence, and come again
And loose the kids and lambs and drive
     them   225
In haste to our swift ship, then sail
Away o'er the salt sea. But this
I would not grant, though better far
Had I but done so! For I hoped
To look upon this man—he might   230
Give gifts of friendship. But, alas,

12. **Maron** (mā′rən). **Phœbus** (fē′bəs), or **Phœbus Apollo** (fē′bəs ə pol′ō), the god of the sun.

When he appeared, he was to bring
My poor men little joy!
           So there
We kindled fire and of that cheese
We made an offering, and ate   235
Ourselves thereof, and sat and waited
Until at last he entered, driving
His flock before him.
           He bore in
Dry wood to cook his meal, a load
Of wondrous weight, and down he
       flung it   240
Within the cave, with such a crash
We cowered back with fear and crouched
In the cave's corner. Then he drove
Into that spacious cave the sheep
That he must milk, and left the others—   245
The rams and goats—without, to roam
The high-walled court.
           Then in its place
He set the massive rock that closed
The doorway of the cave; he raised it
Lightly aloft, a weight so vast   250
That never two and twenty wagons,
Four-wheeled and firmly built, might stir it
From where it lay on earth—so great
That towering crag was that he set
To close his door.
           Now sat he down   255
And milked his sheep and bleating goats
All in due order, and he set
Her young by each. Half the white milk
He curdled and then gathered it
And set it by in wicker baskets;   260
And half he left there in the bowls
That he might sup thereon. And now,
When he had labored busily
And finished every task, he stayed
And kindled up the fire and saw us   265
And asked us:
           'Strangers, who are you,
And whence do you come sailing hither
Over the sea's wet ways? What errand
Can bring you hither? Or perchance
You wander purposeless, like robbers   270

Who rove the seas and venture life
To bring to strangers in far lands
An evil fortune.'
           So he spoke,
And at his words our hearts within us
Were crushed and broken, for we feared   275
The man's deep voice and monstrous body.
Yet I spoke up and answered, saying:
'We are Achæans[13] come from Troy;
We wander blown by every wind
Over the sea's great gulf, still striving   280
To reach our homes, yet ever go
On alien ways, by paths we never
Have willed to travel—so it pleases
Zeus to decree. We boast we once
Were warriors under Atreus' son,   285
Great Agamemnon,[14] he whose fame
Is highest under heaven—so great
A city he laid low, so many
The men he slew there. Now we come
Hither before your knees to pray you   290
Give welcome to your guests and grant us
Such gifts as guests should have. Respect,
O mighty one, the gods, for we
Are suppliants, and Zeus avenges
The suppliant and stranger: he   295
Is god of strangers, watching over
Each worthy wanderer.'
           So I spoke,
And pitiless of heart, he answered:
'Stranger, you either are a fool
Or come from a far land, to bid me   300
Fear or beware the gods! We Cyclops
Fear not your ægis-wielding[15] Zeus
Nor any god above. For we
Are mightier far than they. I would not
Show mercy to your men or you   305

---

13. **Achæans** (ə kē′ ənz), a people thought to have migrated down into Greece from Danube regions in the thirteenth century B.C.; in Homer's works, any people living in what is now Greece.
14. **Atreus** (ā′trē əs), father of **Agamemnon** (a gə mem′non), a Greek leader in the Trojan War.
15. **ægis-wielding** (ē′jis), shield-handling; the Cyclops claim not to fear the power of Zeus' protection.

To shun the wrath of Zeus, nay, never
Unless my own heart bade. But come,
Tell me, where left you your good ship
When you came hither? Was it near
Or at the land's far end? Nay, tell me,   310
For I would know.'
        So asked he, striving
To trap the truth from me, but caught not
My tried mind unaware. So thus
With crafty words I spoke:
        'The god
Who shakes the earth, Poseidon, broke   315
My ship asunder, for he drove her
Upon the cliffs that line your land
And dashed her on the rocks. A tempest
Had blown us in from sea and I
And these my comrades here but barely   320
Escaped sheer death.'
        So I replied.
He, cruel-hearted, made no answer,
But springing up, reached forth his hands
And seized my comrades. Two at once
He snatched up in his grasp and dashed
    them   325
To earth like helpless puppies. Forth
The brains flowed, moistening the ground.
Then limb from limb he tore their bodies
And made his meal, devouring them
Savagely as a lion bred   330
Among the mountains. Naught of them
He left uneaten—flesh or entrails
Or marrowy bones. And we cried out
In lamentation and uplifted
Our hands to Zeus, to see a deed   335
So horrible. Numb terror laid
Hold on our hearts.
        And now the Cyclops,
When he had filled that monstrous belly
With flesh of men, and followed this
With draughts of unmixed milk, lay
    stretched   340
Full length upon the cavern floor
Among his flock.
        And now I formed
This plan within my daring heart—

To venture nearer and to draw
My keen sword from my thigh and
    thrust it   345
Deep in his breast, straight to the spot
Where lay his liver, feeling first
To seek the place; and yet a thought
Withheld me, for we all, each man,
Must then have met sheer death; for
    never   350
Could our strength stir from that high
    door
The massive stone he set there. So
Lamenting there we sat and waited
The sacred dawn.
        And when the dawn
Came, rosy-fingered, then once more   355
He kindled fire and milked his flock
Of wondrous sheep, in order due,
Setting her young by each; and now
When he had labored busily
And finished every task, he seized   360
Once more upon two men and made
His morning meal. And after this,
His breakfast done, he drove away
His goodly flock, moving with ease
The mighty door-stone thence, then
    set it   365
In place as lightly as a man
Would set the lid upon a quiver.
So with a mighty whoop the Cyclops
Went driving his fat flock away
Off to the mountains.
        There he left me   370
Pondering evil—how I best
Might find revenge, if but Athene
Would hear my prayer. And this plan
    seemed
Best to my mind at last:
        There lay
Close by the pens, a mighty staff   375
Cut by the Cyclops. Olive wood
It was, still green, for he had cut it
To use when it had dried: it seemed,
As we stood gazing, the great mast
Of some broad ship of twenty oars,   380

Laden with cargo, a black ship
That sails the great gulf of the sea,
So long and thick it seemed. So there
I took my stand by it and cut
A fathom's length away, and this   385
I gave my men and bade them shape it.
They made it smooth, while I stood by
And brought it to a point and charred it
In glowing fire; and then I took it
And hid it in the dung that lay   390
In heaps about the cave.
                    I bade then
My company cast lots to see
Which men of them would dare to join me
And lift that stake and bore it deep
Into his eye when gentle slumber   395
Should come upon him. And the lot
Fell on the four I should have chosen,
And I myself became the fifth
To share the venture.
                    And now came
The Cyclops home at evening, herding   400
His well-fleeced flocks. Straightaway he
  drove
Into that cavern, one and all,
His goodly flocks, nor left he any
In the wide court without. He felt,
Perhaps, some sense of coming evil;   405
Perhaps some god had warned him. Next
He set in place the massive door-stone,
Lifting it lightly, and sat down
And milked his sheep and bleating goats
All in due order, and he set   410
Her young by each; and when at last
With busy labor he had finished
His every task, then once again
He seized on two of my companions
And made his evening meal.
                    And now   415
I stood before him, and thus spoke,
The while I held forth in my hands
An ivy bowl, filled with dark wine:
'Here, Cyclops, take this wine, and drink
After your feast of human flesh,   420
And learn how good a drink we kept

Hidden within our ship. I brought it
An offering to you, in hope
You might have pity on my sorrows
And help me home. But you, alas,   425
In rage exceed all patience! Madman!
How shall there ever come hereafter
Another stranger here to seek you
From any land on earth, if you
Thus scorn all human laws!'
                    So said I.   430
He took the wine and drank it. Vastly
That sweet drink pleased him. And again
He begged of me:
                    'In goodness give me
Yet more, I pray. And tell me now
Your name, and quickly! I will give you   435
A gift to make your heart rejoice.
Indeed the Cyclops' fertile fields
Yield noble wine from mighty clusters,
And Zeus sends rain to speed their
  growing,
But this you give me is a cup   440
Of nectar and ambrosia[16] mingled.'
So spoke he, and once more I bore him
That glowing wine. Aye, thrice I bore it
And gave it him, and thrice in folly
He drained it off. Then when the wine   445
Had stolen round his wits, I spoke
And said in honeyed words:
                    'O Cyclops,
You ask my far-famed name, and this
I now will tell you. Give me therefore
The stranger's gift, as you have promised. 450
My name is Noman; aye, and Noman
My father and my mother called me
And all my comrades.'
                    So I spoke,
And he with cruel heart replied:
'Noman, of all his company,   455
I shall eat last; and all the others
I'll eat before him. This shall be
My gift to you—my guest.'

16. **nectar and ambrosia** (nek′tər, am brō′zhə),   the
drink of the gods, the food of the gods.

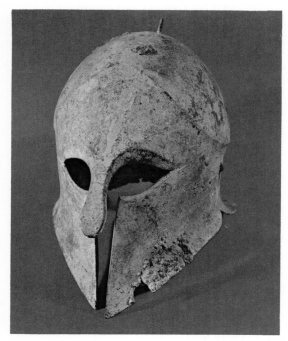

Bronze helmet.

So spoke he,
Then down he sank and on his back
Lay flat, his thick neck bent aside,   460
And from his throat there poured forth
    wine
And fragments of men's flesh.

And now
Deep under heaped-up coals I thrust
That stake till it grew hot, and stirred
The courage of my men with speech   465
Lest one of them should shrink with fear
And fail my need.
And now that stake
Of olive wood, green as it was,
Was ready to burst forth in flame,
All glowing with fierce heat. I drew it   470
Forth from the fire, while round about me
My men stood ready. Then—for surely
Some god had breathed into our hearts
High courage—they laid hold upon
That sharpened olive stake and thrust it   475

Deep in his eye, the while above them
I leaned upon its top and turned it
As one who with an auger bores
A great ship timber. Those below him
Twist it by thongs on either side,   480
And still it ever turns unceasing.
So holding that huge stake of wood
Deep in his eye, we kept it turning.
Round that hot brand, forth poured the
    blood;
And round it all his brows and lashes   485
Were singed off by the blast that came
Out of that burning eye. Its roots
Seethed in the fire. As when a smith
Dips a great axe or adz in water
To temper it, and loud it hisses—   490
For so steel gets its strength—even so
His eye hissed round that olive stake.
And loud his cry and terrible
Till the rocks echoed and we fled
Away in fear. Then from his eye   495
He wrenched away that stake, thick
    clotted
With his own blood and raging hurled it
Out of his hands. Then loud he shouted
To all the Cyclops who dwelt round him
In caves upon the windy heights.   500

They heard his shout and straggling
    gathered,
One here, one there, from every side,
And standing all about his cave
They asked what grieved him.
'What can ail you,
O Polyphemus,[17] that so loudly   505
You cry out in the heavenly night
And keep us sleepless? Is some man,
Some mortal, driving off your flocks
Against your will; or is some man
Now slaying you by force or cunning?'   510
And thus in answer from his cave
Spoke mighty Polyphemus:

17. **Polyphemus** (pol'ə fē'məs), son of Poseidon.

'Friends,
Noman is slaying me by cunning,
Nor uses force at all!'
                    And they
With wing'd words thus replied:
                              'Since no man   515
Now does you violence, while you
Are there alone, this illness sent
By mighty Zeus, no man may shun
In any way. But pray you now
To your great father, Lord Poseidon.'   520
So said they and then went their way.
And in my heart I laughed to think
How with that name and my shrewd plan
I had deceived them.
                    But the Cyclops,
Groaning in agony and anguish,   525
Went groping with his hands, and lifted
The great rock from the door and there
He sat athwart the doorway, stretching
His hands, to catch, if it might be,
Any who sought to pass the door   530
Among the sheep; for in his heart
He hoped that I might prove so foolish
As thus to venture. But I still
Sat planning how to bring this peril
To a good end and win us all—   535
My men and me—escape. Full many
The plan and trick I fashioned, striving
For life itself, for great the peril
And close at hand. And at the last
This, as I deemed, was of them all   540
The wisest plan.
                There in the cave
Were well-grown rams of thickest wool,
Fair beasts and great, and dark of fleece.
These silently I bound together
With twisted willow withes, whereon   545
The Cyclops slept, that savage monster
Who knew no law nor right. I bound them
By threes together and the midmost
Bore under him a man; the others,
One on each side, were to conceal   550
And save my comrades: so there went
A man to each three sheep. And I,

Myself, now seized upon a ram,
The best of all that flock, and grasped
His back from underneath, and lay   555
Beneath his shaggy belly; there
Twisting my fingers deep within
That wondrous fleece, I hung, face
    upward,
With steadfast heart. And so, lamenting,
We waited sacred dawn.
                      And now,   560
When earliest dawn came rosy-fingered,
Then forth the rams went to the pasture,
But all the unmilked ewes went bleating
About their pens with swollen udders.
Their lord, though torn by cruel pain,   565
Yet, ere each ram passed, made him stand
And felt along his back. He guessed not
In his dull mind, that there beneath
Those fleecy breasts, were bound my men.

Now to the door, last of them all,   570
The great ram slowly came, weighed down
With heavy fleece and with the burden
Of me and my shrewd plans. Upon him
The mighty Polyphemus then
Laid searching hands, and said:
                              'Dear ram,   575
Why do you cross the cave so slowly,
Last of the flock? Till now, you never
Lagged thus, but ever first of all
Sped forth with mighty strides to crop
The soft bloom of the grass, and ever   580
Were first to reach the running waters,
And first, when evening came, to long
To turn back home. And yet you now
Come last of all. Surely you sorrow
Over your lord's lost eye! A villain   585
Has quenched its sight—he and his crew
Of wretched fellows, mastering
My wits with wine, this fellow Noman!
Not yet, I say, has he escaped
The death that waits him. Would but you   590
Could know my thought and had the power
To speak in words and let me know
Where he is skulking from my wrath!

For I should smite him down and dash
His brains about the cave—here, there,   595
Aye, on the ground! By such a deed
My heart might find some ease from all
The evils that this worthless Noman
Has brought upon me.'

            So he spoke,
And sent the ram forth through the
    doorway.   600

And now, when we were safe outside
That cavern and its yard, I loosed
My grip upon the great ram's fleece
And then unbound my men in turn,
Setting them free. And then in haste   605
We drove that flock before us—sheep
Most rich in fat, most long of stride—
And yet we often turned our heads
To glance behind us ere we came
Safe to our ship. Welcome indeed   610
We were to our dear comrades, snatched
From death itself; and yet they wept
Lamenting those we lost. But this
I would not suffer, but forbade,
With lifted brows, all lamentation,   615
And bade them quickly bear aboard
Into the ship those many sheep
So fine of fleece, and sail away
Across the salt sea waves. And they
Went then aboard and took their seats   620
Each in his place, and smote with oars
The whitening sea.

         And now, when yet
A shout might reach the land, I called
To Cyclops, taunting him:

            'O Cyclops,
You were not, then, to find that man   625
A helpless weakling—him whose men
You ate there in your hollow cave
With might and cruel strength. For surely
These evil deeds of yours are doomed
To overtake you. O mad fool   630
Who felt no shame, but must devour
Your guests in your own home! May Zeus
And all the other gods send vengeance

Upon you for such deeds!'

            So spoke I,
And he in heart grew angrier yet   635
And tearing off a hill's great summit,
He hurled it. And it fell beyond
Our dark-bowed ship: the sea surged high
As that great rock crashed down. A wave
Came rolling back, a mighty billow   640
Out of the deep, and swept our ship
In toward the land. Swiftly I grasped
A great pole in my hands and thrust
The ship from shore and bade my men,
Nodding my brows, fall to and pull   645
Their best upon the oars and flee
Out of that danger; and they all
Bent to their oars.

         But when we now
Were twice as far from shore as we
Had been before, once more I called   650
Unto the Cyclops, but my men
With pleading words came all about me
And begged me stay:

          'Why, like a madman,
Will you enrage this savage monster
Who made but now so great a cast   655
He drove our ship, then far at sea,
Back to the land. We thought that we
Were lost indeed there. Had he heard
A man of us but stir or speak,
He would have shattered all our heads   660
And our ship's timbers, too, so rugged
A rock he would have cast, so strongly
He sends it on its way!'

           So spoke they.
But did not move my lordly spirit,
And once again with angry heart   665
I called back, saying:

           'If, O Cyclops,
A mortal man shall ever ask you
How it befell your eye was blinded
So hideously, then answer thus:
It was Odysseus blinded you,   670
Taker of Troy, Laërtes' son,
Who dwells in Ithaca.'

           So spoke I,

And with a groan he spoke and answered:
'Alas, for now are come upon me
The ancient oracles.[18] A prophet   675
Once dwelt here, a great man and good,
And he foretold me everything
That time should bring to pass—that I
Should lose my sight here at the hand
Of one Odysseus. But I ever   680
Watched for the coming of a man
Tall, handsome, armed with wondrous
    strength;
And now this little worthless fellow
Has robbed me of my eye by craft,
First mastering me with wine. Yet now   685
Come hither, O Odysseus, come!
For I would give my guest his gifts
And would implore the far-famed god
Who shakes the shores to give you help
Upon your way. I am his son: 690
He owns himself my father. He,
And he alone, can make me whole
If so he will, but this no other
Can do, no other of the gods
On high or mortal men who perish.'   695

So spoke he and I answered thus:
'Would I could be as sure that I
Could strip you bare of soul and being,
And send you to Death's house, as I
Am sure of this:—that none shall ever   700
Restore your eye, not even he
Who makes earth tremble!'[19]
        So I spoke,
And he with hands upraised in prayer
To starry heaven, thus besought
The lord Poseidon:
        'Hear me now,   705
Thou dark-haired god who mak'st earth
    tremble!
If I be verily[20] thy son
And thou wilt own thyself my father,
Grant that Odysseus, he who took
The towers of Troy, come never home.   710
Yet, should it be his fate to see
His friends once more and come at last

Zeus

To his good house and native land,
Late may he come, in evil fortune,
With loss of all his men, and borne   715
Within a stranger's ship, and meet
In his own home affliction.'
        So
He spoke in prayer, and to his words
The dark-haired god gave ear.
        Once more
He stooped and lifted up a rock   720
Far greater than before, and swung it
And summoned all his monstrous strength
And hurled it. And it fell behind
Our dark-bowed ship and barely missed
The rudder's end. Up surged the sea   725
As that huge rock came down: the wave
Drove us upon our way and toward
The farther shore.
        And so we came
Back to the isle where our good ships
Were lying side by side, and here   730
Beside them sat our comrades weeping
And watching for our coming.

18. **oracles** (ôr′ə kəlz, or′ə kəlz), messages of advice
from the gods.
19. **Poseidon,** the father of Polyphemus, was called the
"Earth-Shaker."
20. **verily,** truly.

> So all that day
> Until the sun went down, we sat
> And feasted there on meat in plenty
> And pleasant wine; and when the sun   735
> Went down and darkness came upon us,
> There slept we by the breaking sea.
> But when the earliest dawn appeared
> Rose-fingered, then I roused my men
> And bade embark and loose the cables.   740
> Then quickly they embarked and took
> Their seats upon the thwarts, in order,
> And smote with oars the whitening sea.
> So sailed we on with aching hearts,
> Glad we were saved from death, yet sad   745
> To think how our dear comrades perished."

READING FOR DETAILS

The Greek Hero

Homer's listeners must have found Odysseus an ideal figure—a hero. Odysseus was daring, strong, intelligent, decisive.

1. The Greeks looked upon Odysseus' ideas and actions as fitting and proper to a leader. And they *were* fitting and proper—in Homer's day. Today, however, we might regard some of Odysseus' actions in a different light. Recall the following sections of the poem and discuss whether you would consider Odysseus' behavior proper for a hero today:
   a. The way Odysseus introduced himself to Alcinoüs (ll. 56–60).
   b. Odysseus' first thought on entering the Cyclops' cave (ll. 229–231).
   c. His taking of the Cyclops' sheep (ll. 541–607).
   d. His taunting the blind Polyphemus (ll. 624–634).
2. How does Polyphemus reply to Odysseus when the latter says the Greeks are suppliants and are thus protected by Zeus?
3. What does Odysseus gain by not telling Polyphemus the location of his ship and by giving a false name?
4. How do you feel toward the blinded Polyphemus as he talks to his prized ram before sending it to the pasture?
5. How did the coming of Odysseus fulfill the prophecy given to Polyphemus through the oracle?

READING FOR APPRECIATION

Conflict

1. The *Odyssey* is a tale of conflict: Odysseus struggles against one foe after another in his effort to reach his home and family. Who is his chief enemy? Why?
2. What conflict did Odysseus have to face in the land of the Lotus-eaters?

Foreshadowing

1. Discuss the foreshadowing in the Prologue (ll. 21–26). Which lines foreshadow continued trouble after Odysseus reaches Ithaca?
2. Polyphemus prays to his father, Poseidon, the dark-haired god of the sea, to curse Odysseus. What punishment does the Cyclops ask for the Greek? Which line indicates that this prayer will be answered?

Imaginative Language

A noteworthy feature of Greek epic poetry is the use of word combinations known as *epithets*. These are names or descriptions applied to persons or things over and over again. Homer uses epithets when he speaks of "ægis-wielding Zeus" or "wing'd words." Sometimes an epithet can provide a particularly vivid image. The famous Homeric epithet "rosy-fingered dawn" paints a picture of the morning sky streaked with lines of crimson fire.

Locate and discuss other epithets found in the *Odyssey* so far. Be on the lookout for this type of imagery as you continue reading of Odysseus' adventures.

Part II, Books X—XII: The Odyssey
Adventure of the Winds

"And now we came unto the isle
Æolia. Here Æolus,[1]
Dear to the deathless gods was dwelling.
His island floated on the deep,   750
And round it rose on every side
A brazen wall unbreakable,
In sheerest cliff. And here were born
Twelve children to him; six were
    daughters,
And six, grown sons. And these beside   755
Their father and their honored mother
Sit at unending feast. Before them
Are set fine foods innumerable,
And all day long the house is fragrant
With steam of feasting, and reëchoes   760
With music to its gates. At night
They sleep beneath soft coverings
In smooth-strung beds.
               And now we came
To this their city and fair mansion,
And here a month he made me welcome   765
And questioned me of all: he asked
Of Ilium and the Argive[2] ships,
And the Achæans sailing homeward,
And I of each, in order due,
Told him the tale. But when I asked him   770
Which way to sail for home, and prayed him
To aid me on my road, naught then
Did he refuse me, but was ready
To help me onward. For he gave me
A sack, the whole hide of an ox   775
Nine winters old. In this he tied
The roaring winds from every quarter,
For mighty Zeus had made him keeper
Of all the winds, to still or rouse them,
Even as he would.
             This sack he gave me   780
To carry in my hollow ship:
A shining cord of silver bound it
That not a breath could pass. And with me

He sent a fair west wind to bear
My ships and men along. Far other   785
Must be our journey's end, alas,
For through our own rash deed we came
To utter ruin.
           Thence we sailed
Nine days, both day and night, and spied
On the tenth morning, plain before us,   790
The fields of our own land, so near
We saw men tending fires.
              That instant
Upon me, worn with weariness,
Sweet sleep seized suddenly, for ever
In my own hand I had held fast   795
The corner of the sail, nor dared
Entrust this charge to any other
Of all my men, for I would quickly
Come to my own dear land.
              But now
As I lay slumbering, my men   800
One with another spoke, and whispered
That what I homeward bore was treasure,
Silver and gold, gifts given me
By noble Æolus. For one,
With meaning glances to his neighbor,   805
Would say:
          'Ah me, how strange it is
That wheresoever this man wanders,
In every land and every city
He gets from all men love and honor!
A fine big treasure this he carries   810
From plundered Troy, while we, alas,
Who labored on the same hard road
Sail home with empty hands. Nay, come
   now
And quickly! Let us see what lies
Hid in this sack—what gold, what silver!'   815
So spoke they, and their evil plotting

---

1. **Æolia** (ē ō′lē ə), **Æolus** (ē′ə lus), the god of the wind.
Since the ancient Greeks believed that all the land rested
on the sea, it was not hard for them to imagine that
Æolus' domain was a floating island.
2. **Ilium** (il′ē əm), another name for Troy. **Argive**
(ar′jīv, ar′gīv), Greek.

At last prevailed. They loosed the cord;
The sack was opened. From it burst
The bound winds, all, at once. Down
    swirled
A swooping gust and swept them seaward   820
Far from their own dear land, lamenting.

Then I awakened. In my heart,
Though free from blame, I wondered
    whether
It were not best at once to leap
Forth in the sea and so to perish,   825
Or whether I should yet remain
Among the living and endure.
Yet I remained there and endured,
Laying me down within my ship,
My mantle round my head.
                    So we   830
And all our ships once more were driven,
Swept back by stormy blasts, the while
My men lamented, to the island
Of Æolus.
          Thither we came
And went ashore, and here my men   835
Drew water, and they made them ready
By the swift ships a hasty meal.
And then, when we had satisfied
Our need of food and wine, I chose me
A herald and a man to follow,   840
And forth we went to seek the famed
Palace of Æolus. We found him
Sitting at feast, and there beside him
His wife and children. And we entered
Into his house, and by the pillars,   845
We sat us down as suppliants
Upon his threshold.
             In amazement
They saw us, and they asked:
                'How came you
Thus here again, Odysseus? Tell us
What evil power of the gods   850
Has wrought against you? For we sent you
Safe on your way with every care
That you might reach your land, wherever
Your heart's desire might lead.'

              So said they,
And I with sorrowing heart replied: 855
'My men turned utterly to evil,
And cruel sleep betrayed me. Friends,
Help now, for you have power!'
                So said I,
Beseeching with soft words. But they
All sat in silence. Then the father   860
Answering, spoke:
            'Hence quickly! Get you
Out of this island, man most luckless
Of all men living. Heaven itself
Forbids we shelter here or help
Upon his way a man so hated   865
By the blest gods. Hence! for it was
The hatred of the gods that brought you
Back to this island!'
             So he spoke,
And sent me from his house lamenting.
Thence on we sailed with aching hearts,   870
And each man's soul was spent with toiling
Hard at the oar, a toil we owed
To our own folly, but no wind
Now came to help us."

[After this disheartening adventure, Odysseus
and his men go to another land where even
greater disaster comes to them. There gigantic
cannibals destroy the ships and kill the men.
Only Odysseus and the crew of the one ship
escape. They make their way to the island of
the goddess Circe. Circe turns one group of
Odysseus' men into swine by feeding them
drugged food. Through using an herb called
moly, which was given him by Hermes, Odysseus
is able to counteract the drug and gain power
over Circe. She restores his men to human form
and entertains them all with feasting for a year.
At the end of the year Circe sends Odysseus to
the Land of the Dead where he learns what he
must do to reach his home. After this adventure,
he returns briefly to Circe's island before
sailing on.

    Just before he leaves, Circe takes Odysseus
aside and warns him of some of the dangers he
will meet in his journey. She tells him what pre-

The land of the Laestrygoni.

cautions to take so that he and his men will not
fall prey to the sweet-singing Sirens, whose marvelous voices have lured so many to their deaths
on the rocky shores. She describes the dreadful
Clashing Rocks and the horrible monsters, Scylla
and Charybdis, that will rob him of more of his
men. Finally, she tells him that he must at all
costs avoid harming the sacred cattle of the
Sungod.]

Adventure of the Sirens

              "And now I said,
Sad-hearted, to my men:
               'Unfitting   875
It is, friends, that but one or two
Should hear the sacred prophecies
Of that dread goddess, Circe.[3] These
I now shall tell you, for then either

We die foreknowing what shall fall,   880
Or we escape and shun the death
And doom that wait us.
                  This she first
Bids us:—to shun the wondrous Sirens,[4]
With their sweet voices and their meadows
Abloom with flowers. For she bade   885
That I alone should hear their song.
So bind me fast in bonds—aye, lash me
Upright against the mast, that thence
I may not stir, and cast strong ropes
About me, too. If I entreat you   890
And bid you set me free, then bind me
Yet tighter than before.'

---

3. **Circe** (sẻr′sē), an island sorceress whose magic
turned men into beasts.
4. **Sirens** (sī′rənz), womanlike creatures whose en-
chanting songs lured sailors to their deaths.

And so
I told them all she said. And ever
Our good ship sailed on swiftly, nearing
The Sirens' island, for the wind   895
Blew fair and drove her on. And now
The wind ceased suddenly; there came
A calm without a breath: some god
Laid all the sea to sleep. So now
My men rose, furled the sail, and stowed it   900
Within the hollow ship, and sitting
In order on the thwarts, they smote
With polished oars the whitening sea
But I, with my keen blade, now cut
A great round lump of wax, and kneaded   905
The fragments with my hands, till swiftly
The wax was softened, for my strength
Had warmed it and the shining rays
Of the great Sun, the mighty lord
Who rides on high. With this, I stopped   910
The ears of all my crew, in turn;
Then fast they bound me, hand and foot
Upright in my swift ship, my back
Against the mast, with ropes cast round me.
Then once again they sat and smote   915
The foaming sea with oars.

                        And now,
When we were but so far away
As a man's cry may reach, and lightly
Went driving on—our ship's swift flight,
As close to land she sped, escaped not   920
The Sirens' sight, and they upraised
At once their clear, sweet song:
                          'Come hither,
O famed Odysseus, mighty glory
Of the Achæans. Turn your ship
But hither to the shore and hearken   925
The song we sing, for no man ever
Has steered his black ship hence till he
Has heard the honey-sweet delight
Of music from our lips; then forth
He went upon his way with joy   930
And fuller wisdom. For we know
All that the Argives and the Trojans
Endured on Troy's wide plains; we know
All that befalls mankind on earth;

The nourisher of all.'
                        So sang they,   935
Uttering their sweet song. My heart
Yearned to hear further, and I bade
My men to loose me, and I frowned
My bidding with my brows, but they
Bent busier to their oars, and two,   940
Eurylochus and Perimedes,[5]
Arose and bound me ever faster
With double lashings. But at last,
When we had passed them and no more
Might hear the song those Sirens sang   945
And their sweet voices, then my men
Took quickly from their ears the wax
Wherewith I stopped them, and they loosed
The bonds that bound me.

Adventure of Scylla and Charybdis

                        And we now
Had left that isle behind, but soon   950
I saw the smoke of flying spray,
And huge seas rolling, and I heard
The boom of breakers. From the hands
Of my affrighted men the oars
Fell and trailed idle, roaring through   955
The running sea beside us. Quickly
The ship lost way and stopped, for now
My men no longer toiled, with hands
Upon the tapered oars. Now swiftly
I passed through all the ship and paused 960
By each in passing, cheering him
With gentle words:
                        'We are not, friends,
Untried in danger. This new peril
That lies before us is no greater
Than when the Cyclops caught and
          held us   965
Fast in his hollow cave. Yet thence
We found escape—all through my valor

---

5. **Eurylochus** (yü rī′lə kəs), **Perimedes** (pə rī′məd ēz), sailors.

And wit and shrewdness; and I think
That we shall live to tell the tale
Of this day too. But rouse you now.   970
Do as I bid you. Take your seats
Upon the thwarts and drive your oars
Deep in the sea whose billows roll
So steep against us. We shall see
If Zeus will grant us to escape   975
Out of this place of death. And you,
Helmsman, I charge you, fix my words
Fast in your heart, for you alone
Hold in your hand the helm that guides
Our hollow ship. Steer boldly forth   980
Out of these smoking seas and head her
Straight for yon crag, and take good heed
Lest she swing wide and sweep us all
Into sore peril!'
        So I spoke,
And they obeyed my order quickly,   985
And yet I did not speak of Scylla,[6]
That monster none may face, in fear
Lest they from terror drop their oars
And hide within the hold.
          Slight heed
I gave to Circe's hard command   990
I should not arm me. I put on
My glorious armor and I grasped
Two spears in hand and took my station
On the decked prow, for there I thought
I first should see appear this Scylla   995
That dwelt within the rock, to bring
My men destruction.
          And yet nowhere
Could I behold her, and my eyes
Wearied with wandering up and down
That shadowy wall of stone.
          So onward   1000
Into that strait we sailed lamenting—
On one side Scylla, on the other
Dreadful Charybdis.[7] Terribly
She swallowed down the salt sea-water
Then spewed it forth till all   1005
Was tossed and whirling like a caldron
Above a raging fire; and spray
Flew high and fell upon the tops

Of the tall crags. But when once more
She sucked the salt sea down, we saw   1010
The whirl's wild depths laid bare; the waters
Roared loud about the rocks; far down
We saw the bottom of the deep
Blackened with sand.
          Pale terror then
Laid hold on us: we saw the monster   1015
And feared death near.
          And on that instant
Scylla reached forth and snatched my men
Out of my hollow ship—six men,
My best in strength and courage. Lo,
Even as I looked along the ship   1020
To seek them, there I saw, above me,
Their hands and feet as up she swung them
Aloft in air. And loud they cried,
Calling, for the last time, my name,
In agony of heart. And even   1025
As one who fishes from a rock
That juts far out to sea, casts down
His bait to lure small fish and tosses
Into the deep a bit of horn
From kine[8] of his own field—aye, even   1030
As he, if then he takes a fish,
Flings it aloft out of the sea
All quivering, even so she swung them
All quivering up to her high crag.
There she devoured them, one and all,   1035
Before her doorway, while they shrieked
And still stretched out their hands to me
In dying agony. That sight
Was saddest of all sights my eyes
Have ever seen, while through sore trials   1040
I wandered the sea's ways.
          So now
We had escaped the Clashing Rocks,
And Scylla and the dread Charybdis,

---

6. **Scylla** (sil′ə), a hazardous rock on the Italian coast mythically thought of as a female monster.
7. **Charybdis** (kə rib′dis), a whirlpool opposite Scylla; passage between the two "monsters" was very treacherous.
8. **kine** (kīn), cows or cattle.

Greek warships from a Roman fresco.

And quickly came to the fair isle
Of the great Sun."

[On the island of the Sungod, Odysseus' men disobeyed him and killed some of the sacred cattle for a feast. Odysseus knew that the gods would punish them. He tells how that punishment came.]

The Shipwreck

    "And now,   1045
When we had left the isle behind us,
And yet no other land appeared—
Nothing but sea and sky, then Zeus,
The son of Cronus,[9] set in heaven
Over our hollow ship, a cloud   1050
Of sullen blue which darkened all
The deep below. And now our ship
Sped on, yet not for long; for swiftly

Out of the west there burst a gale
Shrieking in raging blasts. A gust   1055
Snapped the two forestays[10] of the mast.
Back fell the mast upon the stern,
And all its tackle lay entangled
In the ship's hold. And as it fell,
Striking the stern, it struck the
   helmsman[11]   1060
Upon the head and broke and shattered
Each bone within. Down he fell headlong,
As falls a diver, from the deck:
His proud soul left his body. Zeus
Now thundered from on high and hurled 1065
His bolt upon the ship. She quivered

---

 9. **Cronus** (krō′nus), a Titan who had dethroned his father Uranus. Uranus was the primary god of the sky and husband to the Earth.
10. **forestays,** oxhide ropes supporting the mast. The Greek ship had one large square sail attached to the mast.
11. **helmsman,** the one who steered the ship.

Through all her length, struck by the bolt
Of Zeus: a smoke of sulphur filled her;
And straightway from the ship my men
Fell to the sea, and breakers swept them   1070
On past the black ship's side, like sea-birds.
And so now God forever ended
Their hopes of home.

                Still to and fro
I hastened through the ship. At last
A great wave tore her keel away   1075
Out of her frame, and on the billows
It floated bare. The mast had broken
Clear from the keel, but still the backstay
Kept it close by. And with this stay,
Twisted of oxhide, I made fast   1080

Athena

The two together, mast and keel.
And seated on them both, I drifted
Before that deadly storm."

[Odysseus goes on to tell King Alcinoüs and
the banquet guests how he had been cast ashore
on an island where the goddess Calypso held
him prisoner seven long years. At the end of
that time the goddess Athene persuaded Zeus to
order Calypso to free the lonely wanderer. But
Poseidon wrecked the raft Calypso gave Odysseus,
and he nearly drowned before he swam
ashore and came to the palace of Alcinoüs.
Thus Odysseus completes the telling of his adventures up to this time.

All are moved by Odysseus' story, and the
good king not only orders a swift ship to carry
Odysseus to his homeland, but he also presents
the weary wanderer with many valuable gifts.]

READING FOR DETAILS

A Man Who Wouldn't Give Up

After escaping the Cyclops, Odysseus and his
men continue to suffer misfortune. Gradually the noble Greek loses his followers.

1. While Æolus is happy to help Odysseus
   the first time, he fears to give him aid
   the second time. Why? Of what dangers
   does Circe warn Odysseus? How did
   Odysseus bring his ship safely by the Sirens?
2. Although Circe has warned Odysseus of
   Scylla, he does not tell his men what to
   expect. Why? What do we mean when
   we say that someone is caught between
   Scylla and Charybdis?
3. What final act of folly brings destruction
   to Odysseus' men? How does Odysseus
   manage to save himself? How long does
   the goddess Calypso hold him prisoner?
   What goddess intervenes to force Calypso to release him so that he can start
   homeward once more?
4. Homer shows his understanding of
   human nature in the naturalness of the
   actions and words of his characters. Re-

read (ll. 806–15) the words spoken by Odysseus' men before they loosed the bag of winds. What common traits of men make these words natural in such a situation?

5. Odysseus often reproaches himself for actions that are too hasty. Does this make him seem to be less of a hero? How would it affect his appeal to the ordinary listener or reader? Should a hero be less than perfect? Discuss.

READING FOR APPRECIATION

Conflict and Foreshadowing

As you continue reading, you realize that although Odysseus struggles valiantly, he is also at the mercy of the gods. He accepts their whims and punishment with little complaint and continues to battle toward his objective.

1. Which of the gods sent the destruction which took the last of Odysseus' men? Is there any indication thus far in the story that this god does not hold a permanent grudge?

2. After Odysseus tells how Æolus tied the roaring winds (the storm winds) into a bag which he gave to him, he says:

    And with me
    He sent a fair west wind to bear
    My ships and men along. (ll. 783–85)

    How do the lines immediately following these foreshadow disaster?

Imaginative Language

1. There is an exceptionally sharp piece of imagery in lines 1025–34 beginning: "And even/As one who fishes . . ." Discuss the picture it contains by rephrasing it in your own words. What is the literary term used to identify this kind of comparison?

2. Look back over the episodes you have read thus far. What epithets and word combinations have you found repeated often enough that you have become familiar with them?

Part III, Books XIII–XX: The Homecoming of Odysseus
Arrival in Ithaca

[Swiftly and safely the ship brings Odysseus to his homeland from which he has been gone for twenty years. He rejoices to be back in Ithaca. But his joy is short-lived, for on the shore he is met by Athene who warns him he cannot go at once to his home because he would surely be murdered. Three years ago, she tells him, many suitors came to his great house. They came to convince Odysseus' wife, Penelope (pə nel′ō pē), that her husband is dead and that she should marry one of them. The faithful Penelope still hopes for her husband's return and has constantly refused the suitors. However, she has been unable to get rid of them because the men loyal to Odysseus had gone with him to war. Her servants are mostly women and a few men advanced in age. Even now, Athene says, the suitors sit in Odysseus' banquet hall drinking, feasting, wasting his wealth, and plotting to kill his son Telemachus (tə lem′ə kəs), who is just growing into manhood. With Telemachus dead, the suitor who married Penelope would gain all of Odysseus' wealth.]

        And then spoke
Keen-eyed Athene:
        "Think now well,
Noble Odysseus, shrewd in counsel,   1085
How you may lay your hands in vengeance
Upon these shameless wooers, men
Who for three years have ruled as masters
Here in your hall, the while they wooed
Your noble wife, with proffered gifts,   1090
While she, her heart still sorrowing
Because you come not, holds forth hope
To every one and gives her promise
To each in turn and sends to each
Her messages; though all her mind   1095
Is set on other hopes."

Then answered
Crafty Odysseus:
       "Come, fashion now
Some crafty plot that I may take
My vengeance on them. Stand you now
Yourself beside me! Fill my heart   1100
With courage to dare all—aye, even
As once you did of old, when we
Brought low Troy's shining crown.[1] If you,
O keen-eyed goddess, stand beside me
Eager as then, I could do battle   1105
Against three hundred men—would you,
O mighty goddess, but vouchsafe
To be my helper!"
       Then thus answered
Keen-eyed Athene:
       "Surely I
Will be beside you. You shall never   1110
Be from my mind when we begin
This mighty task. Aye, some, I think,
Of these same wooers that devour
Your substance now, with blood and brains
Shall spatter the broad earth. But come,   1115
For I will change you now, that mortals
Shall know you not. For I will wither
The fair flesh from your pliant limbs,
And pluck from off your head the locks
That now shine yellow, and will clothe
      you   1120
In such a wretched garb that he
Who sees shall shrink away in loathing
From him that wears it. I will dim
The luster of your eyes that once
Were beautiful to see, till you   1125
Shall seem most foul to all the wooers,
Aye, even to your own wife's sight
And to the son you left behind you,
An infant in your hall.
       Now first
Seek out the swineherd who keeps watch   1130
Over your swine, for he is loyal,
True to your son and steadfast wife,
Penelope. And you will find him
Sitting beside his swine that pasture
Close by the Raven Rock.[2]

       There   1135
Stay you awhile and sit beside him
And question him of all. And I
Will go, meanwhile, my way to Sparta,[3]
Land of fair women, and will summon
Telemachus—your own dear son,   1140
Odysseus!—home again, for he
Went forth to wide-wayed Lacedæmon,[4]
To Menelaüs'[5] house, to seek
Tidings of you, to learn if you
Were yet alive."
       So spoke she,   1145
And with her wand clothed him
In a vile cloak and tunic—tattered,
Unclean, stained foul with smoke, and o'er
      them
A great hide, a swift stag's, its hair
All worn away. A staff she gave him   1150
And a poor beggar's scrip[6] with many
A rent therein, its only strap
A wretched cord.
       So the two made
Their plans and parted. Off she sped
Hasting to sacred Lacedæmon   1155
To find Odysseus' son.

Telemachus Meets His Father

[In Sparta, Athene finds Telemachus and warns
him that some of the wooers lie in wait for his
ship in order to murder him on his voyage
home. She tells him where to steer his vessel in
order to avoid the suitors and advises him that
as soon as he reaches Ithaca he should go to the
hut of the faithful swineherd, Eumæus
(yü mā′əs).

---

1. Athene had helped Odysseus in the Trojan War.
2. **Raven Rock.** A great jutting rock in Ithaca still bears this name.
3. **Sparta** (spär′tə), an ancient city-state in southern Greece.
4. **Lacedæmon** (las′ə dē′mən), another name for Sparta.
5. **Menelaüs** (men′ə lā′əs), king of Sparta; Helen of Troy had been his queen.
6. **scrip,** a bag or wallet carried by beggars.

Meanwhile Odysseus has already met the swineherd and has been given food and lodging. He is very careful not to reveal his identity. Instead, he tells Eumæus and the other swineherds that he is a wanderer who had fought at Troy and had known Odysseus.]

Odysseus and the goodly swineherd
Together in the hut at dawn
Prepared their breakfast, kindling fire,
When they had sent the men away   1160
To drive the swine afield. And now
Telemachus drew near. The dogs,
Though wont to bark, now wagged their
    tails
Nor barked at all; and great Odysseus
Saw how they wagged their tails, and
    heard   1165
The sound of footsteps, and spoke quickly
With wing'd words to Eumæus:
                        "Surely,
Eumæus, there comes hither now
A friend or one you know! The dogs
Bark not, but wag their tails, and faintly   1170
I hear the fall of steps."
                    And scarcely
Had he thus said, when his dear son
Stood in the doorway. Then the swineherd
Sprang up surprised, and from his hands
Let fall the bowl with which he labored   1175
Mingling the glowing wine. He hastened
To greet his master. . . .
                    And said:
"So you are come, Telemachus,
Sweeter than light. I thought I never
Should see you more when you went
    sailing   1180
Away to Pylus.[7] Come, come in!"
                    So he spoke,
And took the young man's brazen spear.
So in now stepped Telemachus
Over the sill of stone. His father
Rose from his seat to give him place,   1185
But this he would not have, and stayed
    him,
And said:

"Nay, stranger, sit. For we,
Here on this farm of ours, with ease
Shall find a seat, and this man here
Will soon provide one."
                    So he spoke.   1190
Back to his seat then turned Odysseus,
And the good swineherd heaped fresh
    bushes
And spread a fleecy skin upon them
And here now sat Telemachus.
                        And now,
When food and drink had stayed their
    hunger,   1195
He said to the good swineherd:
                    "Whence,
Good father, comes this stranger? . . ."
                        Then,
Swineherd Eumæus, thus you[8] answered:
"From Crete,[9] he told me, but through
    many
A city of mankind he passed   1200
In wandering hither. . . . He has come
To my own house, and to your charge
I give him now. Do with him, then,
Whate'er you will. He is, he says,
Your suppliant."
                    Then thus replied   1205
Prudent Telemachus:
                    "Eumæus,
Your words pierce to my heart. How can I
Receive a guest at home? . . . And yet,
Since he has come here to your house,
I'll give him garments, cloak and tunic,   1210
Besides a two-edged sword and sandals
To bind upon his feet, and send him
Where he would go. Or keep him here
With you upon your farm, and I

7. **Pylus** (pī'ləs), a city at which Telemachus stopped on his way to Sparta.
8. Homer uses the second person pronoun, the form for direct address, to show an especially kindly feeling toward the old and faithful servant.
9. **Crete** (krēt), a large island in the eastern Mediterranean. Odysseus had made up a story to tell the swineherd.

Will send him clothing, aye, and food 1215
Of every kind, lest he prove costly
To you and yours. But to my house
Among the wooers, he shall never
Go by my will, for they are filled
With sin and insolence. . . . But go, 1220
Quickly, my good old friend—go tell
Prudent Penelope that I
Am safe here, come from Pylus. . . ."
                                    So
Then spoke Telemachus, and sent
The swineherd on his way. He took 1225
His sandals and he bound them on,
And set off for the town. And yet
He did not go his way unseen
By great Athene, for she came,
In form a woman, fair and tall, 1230
And skilled in dainty crafts, and stood
Close by the door. Odysseus saw her;
His son beheld her not, though standing
Before his face, nor knew her presence,
For not to all men do the gods 1235
Appear in open sight. Odysseus
Saw, and the dogs saw too; they barked
    not,
But whimpering slunk off in fear
Across the farmland. With her brows
She signed to him. Odysseus saw 1240
And understood, and forth he came
By the great courtyard wall and there
He stood before her. Then to him
Thus spoke Athene:
                "Shrewd Odysseus,
Laërtes' son, now you shall tell 1245
Your son your secret; now no longer
Need you keep silence. And you twain
Shall plan together death and doom
For the proud wooers. Then go forth
Together to your glorious city. 1250
I shall not be far off. My soul
Looks forward to the battle."[10]
                        So
Athene spoke, and upon his body
She put a fresh new cloak and tunic,
And mightier she made him seem 1255

Odysseus and the Sirens.

And fairer, and the deeper hue
Of youth came back; his cheeks once more
Were rounded, and upon his chin 1260
His beard was darkened. This she did,
Then went her way.
                And now Odysseus 1260
Entered the lodge, and his son marveled
Beholding him, and turned his eyes
Away in awe, lest this might be
A god before him, and he spoke
In wing'd words:
                "You are changed, O stranger, 1265
From what you seemed but now. Your
    garments
Are not the same; your very flesh
Is altered. Surely you are one
Of the immortal gods that have
Wide heaven for home. Then look
    upon us 1270
In kindness while we offer you
A welcome offering and bring you
Gifts finely wrought of gold. Show, now,
Compassion on us!"

10. Athene is a warlike goddess often found in the thick
of battle.

Then replied
Noble, long-tried Odysseus:
                     "Nay,   1275
I am no god! Why liken me
To those that die not! I am he
Whom you so long have wept, for whom
You bore men's violence."
                     But his son,
Who could not yet believe that this   1280
Could be his father, answered him
And said:
             "No, you are not Odysseus;
My own dear father!
                A moment past
You were an old man, meanly clad,
Now you are like the gods who dwell   1285
In the wide heavens."
               Then Odysseus
Answered and said:
              "Telemachus,
It is unworthy of you thus
To stare and marvel beyond measure
At your own father, when at last   1290
He stands before you! No Odysseus
But I will ever come! For I

It is, I that you see before you,
Who have borne perils and have wandered
In many lands, and now at last   1295
Come, after twenty years, again
To my own native land."
             So said he,
And sat him down. Then round his neck
His son cast both his arms and sobbed
And poured forth tears. Upon them both 1300
Came longing and wild weeping.
            At last thus spoke
Noble Odysseus:
          . . . "Hither now
I come at counsel of Athene,
That you and I may plan the slaying
Of all our enemies. But tell me   1305
The number of these wooers—tell me
That I may know how many men
They are and of what sort. I then
May ponder in my heart, and find

Whether we two may fight them here   1310
With no man's aid, or needs must call
For aid on others."
           Then thus answered
Discreet Telemachus:
            "Dear father,
Long have I heard of your great name—
A warrior strong of arm, and wise   1315
When men hold council. But this thing
You speak of—this is far too great!
Awe takes me at the thought, for never
Could two men fight against so many,
All mighty warriors. They number   1320
Not ten, nay, not twice ten, but more.
Bitter for us and terrible
May prove this vengeance that you seek,
Now you are come. Nay, rather think
As best you may, what men will fight   1325
Upon our side, or will in friendship
Give us their help."

            Then thus replied
Noble, long-tried Odysseus:
               "Nay,
But I will tell you of such helpers.
Heed then and listen! Think you, now,   1330
That Father Zeus and great Athene
Are aid enough, or must I seek
For more to help us!"
           Then replied
Telemachus:
          "Strong helpers truly
Are these you name, who sit on high   1335
Among the clouds and rule there ever
O'er men and deathless gods."
            Then spoke
Noble Odysseus thus:
          "Not long
Will those two keep them from that battle
And its wild tumult, when we two   1340
In our own hall shall meet those wooers
In the dread strife of war. But go you
Tomorrow morning home; there join
The haughty wooers. And the swineherd
Shall bring me in, an aged beggar.   1345
Then, if they treat me with foul insult

In my own home, still let your breast
Endure it all. Nay, though they drag me
About the hall, and hurl their missiles,
Look on in patience: speak smooth words 1350
And bid them cease, but they will heed
   not,
For on them comes their fated day.
And this I say now: mark it well:
If you are truly mine, the son
Of my own ancient blood, let no one   1355
Learn that Odysseus is returned—
No, not Laërtes, not the swineherd
Nor any of the house, nay, not
Penelope herself!"

          And now, at evening,
Back came the swineherd to Odysseus   1360
And his brave son, and there they made
Their supper ready. But Athene
Had first drawn near.

          And once again
She made him agèd to behold
And meanly clad, lest the good swineherd 1365
Should look upon his face and know him,
And go to wise Penelope
And tell his tidings.

         Now they turned them
From toil and feasted, and when hunger
Was stayed with food and drink, their
   hearts   1370
Then thought of rest, and so upon them
There came the gift of sleep.

Odysseus Comes to His Own Home

And now Telemachus went forth
Across the farmland. Fast he walked
With hurrying feet, still planning evil   1375
Against the wooers.

         And at last
He reached the stately house and set
The spear he carried in its place
By a great pillar. Then he entered
O'er the stone threshold. First of all   1380

To see him was old Eurycleia,[11]
His nurse, as she was spreading fleeces
Upon the carven chairs. And swiftly
She came with flowing tears to meet him.
And now there came forth from her
   room   1385
Penelope, like Artemis,[12]
Or golden Aphrodite.[13] Weeping,
She cast her arms about her son
And kissed his face and his fair eyes,
And then amid her sobs she spoke   1390
And said, in wing'd words:

         "Now at last
You come, Telemachus, more welcome
Than the sun's light. I thought my eyes
Should never see you more, when you
Went off so secretly to Pylus   1395
Aboard your ship, to seek for tidings
Of your dear father."

         But meanwhile
Before Odysseus' door the wooers
Were all at play: on level ground
They hurled their spears and cast the
   discus   1400
As they had done before, so great
Their reckless insolence. Now came
The time for supper, and the flocks,
Driven by those whose wont it was,
Came home from pasture. Then up
   spoke   1405
Before them Medon,[14] the good herald
Who ever pleased them most, and ever
Was present at their feasts:

         "Come, now,
Young masters, since you all have taken
Your pleasure in the sports, come hither 1410
Within the house, and we shall make
Our good meal ready. Naught is better
Than food at feasting-time!"

---

11. **Eurycleia** (yü rə klē′ə).
12. **Artemis** (ar′tə mis), goddess of the moon and hunting, called **Diana** (dī a′nə) by the Romans.
13. **Aphrodite** (af′rə dī′tē), goddess of love and beauty, called **Venus** (vē′nəs) by the Romans.
14. **Medon** (mē′dən).

So spoke he,
And up they sprang and hastened in,
Heeding his words. So they all came   1415
Into that stately house and cast
Their cloaks upon the chairs and couches,
And slew great sheep and fatted goats
And killed a fat hog and a heifer
And so prepared their feast.
Meanwhile   1420
The herdsman guided toward the city
His lord and master, like a beggar
Wretched and old, and leaning ever
Upon a staff, his body clad
In wretched garments.
At last Odysseus   1425
And the good swineherd stayed their steps
As they drew near, for all about them
Came music of the hollow lyre,
For Phemius[15] within was singing
And struck the strings. And now
Odysseus   1430
Took the good swineherd by the hand
And said:
"This is, indeed, Eumæus,
Odysseus' house. Aye, easily
A man might tell it, though full many
Stood all about. For building here   1435
Is joined to building, and the courtyard
Is closed about with walls and coping,
And double gates protect it. None
Could capture it by force. And this
I see, moreover: many a man   1440
Is gathering for a feast. The savor
Of roast fat rises. In the hall
I hear the lyre, a gift the gods
Have given us, the fit companion
Of the glad feast."
And thus you answered,   1445
Swineherd Eumæus:
"Aye, you know it,
And readily. You are in nowise
Of sluggish wit. But come, consider
How we shall best contrive! Will you
Go first into the stately dwelling   1450
And join the wooers, while I wait

Without the door? Or, if you will,
Wait here, while I go first. Yet linger
Not overlong, lest some one spy you
Lingering without, and hurl things at you   1455
Or drive you hence with blows. I bid you
Think warily of this."
Then answered
Long-tried Odysseus:
"Nay, I know;
I see your meaning, for you speak
To one who understands. Go first   1460
And I will wait behind. For I
Am not unused to blows and missiles.
I have a sturdy spirit: many
The cruel hardships I have suffered
From war and wave; be this but added   1465
To swell the tale."
So spoke they
One to another.

Now a dog
Lay near, and heard, and straightway lifted
His head and ears. For this was Argos,[16]
Steadfast Odysseus' dog—a dog   1470
He reared long since, but never used,
For ere he used him, he went thence
To sacred Ilium. Young men,
In days now gone, would take the dog
To chase wild goats and deer and hares,   1475
But now, his master far away,
He lay despised upon the dung
Left by the cattle and the mules
Heaped high before the doors.
There
Argos, this dog, now lay, all foul   1480
With vermin. Yet when he beheld
Weak though he was, Odysseus near him,
He wagged his tail and dropped both ears,
Though he had now no strength to move
Nearer his master.
And Odysseus   1485
Saw him, but drew not near. He wiped

---

15. **Phemius** (fē′mi əs), a minstrel.
16. **Argos** (är′gōs, är′gəs).

A tear away before Eumæus
Might see he wept; then thus he spoke
And said:
      "Now this is strange, Eumæus,
Why should a dog like this lie here   1490
Upon a dunghill? For this dog
Is finely formed: I cannot say
Whether his speed can match his beauty,
Or if he be but of those dogs
That masters keep for show at table."   1495
Then, good Eumæus, you replied:
"Aye, he who owned this dog has perished
In a far land. Were this dog now
What he was once, in grace of form
And feats of hunting—on the day   1500
His master went to Ilium
And left him here—you would be seized
With sudden wonder did you see
His swiftness and his strength. No beast
That he once started from his lair   1505
In the dense forest depths escaped him;
Keenly he followed scent. But now
His evil days have come. His master
Has perished far away; the women
Care not and let him lie untended.   1510
For slaves, when masters pass from power,
Give no more heed to toil. When once
Ill fortune brings a man to bondage
Far-thundering Zeus then takes from him
Full half his worth."
      So spoke Eumæus,   1515
Then entered that fair house and passed
Straight down the hall and through the
    midst
Of those proud wooers. Then on Argos
Death's dark end came, when he had seen
Odysseus, gone for twenty years.   1520

Noble Telemachus first saw,
Long ere the rest, the swineherd coming
Across the hall, and nodded to him
And called him thither. And the swine-
    herd,
Glancing about him, took a chair   1525
That stood hard by, the chair from which

The carver sent forth meat in plenty
Among the wooers when they feasted
There in the hall. This chair the swineherd
Borne to the table where he faced   1530
Telemachus, and sat him down.
A herald brought him food and served it
With bread out of the basket.
        Now,
A little after him, Odysseus
Entered the house. He seemed a beggar   1535
Wretched and old, and wretched too
The clothing that he wore. And there
He sat him on the ashen threshold
Within the doorposts. . . .

Penelope Meets Odysseus in Disguise

[The haughty and treacherous suitors treat the
"beggar" roughly. One hits him with a stool.
Others curse him. Odysseus holds his anger in
check and plans how he will deal with these evil
men. Penelope treats the beggar graciously and,
since she believes he has some news of her
husband, takes him aside and says:]

      "Alas,
O stranger, but now all wherein   1540
I once excelled, in form or face,
The gods laid waste that day the Argives
Embarked for Ilium; for with them
My husband went away, Odysseus!
Would he might come again to watch   1545
Over my life here: better far
Would be my fame, and fairer. Now
I can but suffer. Such the evil
Some power from on high has sent
For my affliction. So I give   1550
But little heed to wanderers
Or suppliants or heralds serving
The people's need, but ever long
After Odysseus, wasting ever
My heart away.
      These men would hasten   1555

Odysseus returning to Penelope, disguised as a beggar.

My marriage day, so I must spin
A skein[17] of trickery. And first
Some power whispered to my heart
That I should build me in my hall
A great loom, and should weave me here   1560
A robe, a garment rich and wide.
So then I said to all:

                    'Young men
Who come to woo me—this I pray you:
Though great Odysseus now lie dead,
Forbear to urge this marriage. Wait   1565
But till this robe I weave is finished—

I would not have its threads all wasted!
This is a shroud for lord Laërtes[18]
When the dread doom of death shall take
    him
And leave long sorrow. I must do this   1570
Lest some Achæan woman blame me
In my own land, if he should lie

17. **skein** (skān), a quantity of spun yarn wound off the reel in a twisted loop; a metaphor for any twisted arrangement.
18. **shroud for lord Laërtes,** a corpse wrapping for Odysseus' aged father.

Without a shroud, who once was lord
Of wealth so great.'
          So then I spoke,
And their proud hearts agreed. And so   1575
Each day I wove at my great web,
But every night I bade them bring
Torches to light me, and unraveled

All I had wrought by day. And thus
Three years I did, unseen, and ever   1580
Deceived the wooers. But at length,
When the fourth year came round, my
    maids,
Ungrateful, like base dogs, betrayed me.
The wooers came and caught me. Harshly
They railed against me. So, compelled,   1585
And through no will of mine, I brought
That weaving to its end. And now
I can no longer put off marriage
Or shape me a new plan. My son
Grows angry that these men devour   1590
His very livelihood, for now
He knows what passes: he is now
A man indeed, and fit to watch
The fortunes of his house, a man
Whom Zeus grants honor."
          And then indeed   1595
Odysseus' heart was filled with pity
At his wife's weeping. But now,
When she with many a tear had taken
Her fill of sorrow, once again
She spoke and told him:
          "Now I mean   1600
To try you, stranger. I would know
If you in truth[19] received my husband
As guest in your own hall, and all
His noble comrades with him there
As you have said. So come now—tell me   1605
What clothing did he wear? How looked
    he?
And tell me too of his companions
Who followed after."
         Thus then answered
The wise Odysseus:
         "Noble lady,

This is a hard thing to tell rightly   1610
After so long a time, for now
Full twenty years have gone their way
Since he set forth and left my land.
Yet I will tell you how my heart
Still sees his picture. Great Odysseus   1615
Then wore a cloak of purple wool
In double fold. Upon it shone
A brooch of gold: two clasps it had,
And thus its front was carved:—a dog
Held with its paws a dappled fawn   1620
Struggling, and gripped it in its jaws;
And all who saw it marveled how,
Though wrought of lifeless gold, that dog
Held the fawn gripped, and strangled it,
While, striving to escape, the fawn   1625
Still struggled with its feet. I marked
His tunic, too, that shone as bright
Upon his body as the skin
That gleams upon a sun-dried onion,
So smooth it was, and shining like   1630
The sun itself. And many a woman
Gazed at him wondering. And this
I say besides; mark well: I know not
If he was wont to wear this clothing
At home, or if some comrade gave it   1635
When he embarked in his swift ship,
Or if some host had given it him,
For he was loved by many, few
So loved as he. And I myself
Gave him a sword of bronze, a cloak   1640
With double fold, of fairest purple,
And a fringed tunic, and so sent him,
With love and honor, on his way
In his good ship."
         So he spoke,
And once again he waked in her   1645
The need of weeping, for she knew
So well each token that Odysseus
Told her so clearly. But at length

---

19. **in truth,** actually; Odysseus has told Penelope the story he told the swineherd: that he was of the noble family of Crete who had played host to Odysseus years ago.

She answered:
                    "From this moment, stranger,
You who have been a sight for pity,   1650
Shall be beloved and honored. I
It was, with my own hand, who gave him
Those garments you have told of. First
In my own room, I folded them
And fixed upon them the bright brooch,   1655
That precious jewel. Yet I never
Shall greet him now, returning hither
To his own land."
                    And thus Odysseus
Answered her saying:
                    "Honored wife
Of great Odysseus, mar no more   1660
Your lovely flesh, nor waste away
Your heart with weeping for your husband,
And yet I blame you not. No woman
But weeps to lose her lord, the man
She loved, whose children she has
          borne—   1665
Aye, even though he were far other
Than was Odysseus who, men say,
Is like the gods. But cease your weeping
And heed my words, for I will speak
Truth only and will hold back naught   1670
Of all I lately heard: Odysseus,
They say, is near at hand and safe.
I say that he is safe. Already
He is at hand: no longer now
Will he delay and linger far   1675
From friends and native land. Nay, more,
I add my oath. Be witness, now,
Zeus, highest of the gods and best,
And let this hearth of good Odysseus,
Where I now stand, be witness too   1680
That now, this very year, Odysseus
Shall come here, aye, as this moon passes
And the new moon begins."
                    Then spoke
Prudent Penelope:
                    "Alas,
I would, O stranger, that your words   1685
Might but be true. Then you would learn
My kindness to the full, and many

The gifts that I should give, and all
You met would call you happy. Yet
This thought is ever in my heart: 1690
That thus it all must end—that he
Will nevermore come home.
                    But come,
I have an aged woman here.
Her heart is prudent. It was she
Who in his childhood nursed and tended   1695
My luckless lord and took him up
In her own arms the very day
His mother bore him. And this woman,
Though weak with years, shall wash your
          feet.
So rise now, trusty Eurycleia,   1700
And wash this stranger's feet—a man
Old as your master. Aye, Odysseus
May be already as this man,
With aged hands and feet: men soon
Grow old in evil fortune."
                    So said she.   1705
Therewith the aged woman took
The shining bowl they ever used
To wash the feet. First into it
She poured cold water freely, then
She added hot.
                    Meanwhile Odysseus   1710
Was sitting by the hearth, but quickly
Turned toward the darkness, for the
          thought
Now rose within his mind, she might
When she should lift his foot, behold
The scar and know it, and then all   1715
Would come to light.
                    And now she drew
Nearer her master and made ready
To wash his feet. And straightway then
She knew the scar. It was the scar
A boar's white tusk made long ago   1720
Upon a day Odysseus went
To far Parnassus.[20] And now

---

20. **Parnassus** (pär nas′əs),   a mountain in central
Greece.

As the old woman put her hand
Upon his leg, and laid the palm
Upon the scar, at once she felt it   1725
And knew it well. She let the leg
Fall as it would. Down dropped the foot
Into the basin, and the bowl
Of copper rang aloud and tilted
Upon its side till all the water   1730
Ran on the ground. Joy suddenly,
And sorrow, both together, seized
Upon her heart. And her two eyes
Were filled with tears. Her eager voice
Faltered, and on Odysseus' beard   1735
She laid her hand, and said:
                         "Yes, truly,
You are Odysseus, my dear child,
And yet I knew not it was you
Until I felt the wound that told me
It was my master."
                    Swiftly Odysseus   1740
Drew her close to him and said:
"Good mother, why are you so eager
To bring me ruin? It was you
Who nursed me long ago and held me
To your own breast. And now I come,   1745
When twenty years are past, far struggling
Through many perils, once again
To my own land. Be silent,
Nor let one person here be wiser."

And then answered   1750
The prudent Eurycleia:
                         "Child, you know
How steadfast is my soul, a spirit
That naught can shake. I shall stand firm
As stubborn rock or iron!"

                         And now,
When she had washed him and anointed   1755
His body with smooth oil, once more
Odysseus moved his bench and sat
Still nearer to the fire, but covered
The scar beneath his rags. Then thus
Prudent Penelope began: 1760
"Already there draws near that morning

Of evil omen that shall part me
From my Odysseus' home. Today
I hold a contest for the wooers,
The contest with the axes. These,   1765
He used, when he was here, to set
All in a row, twelve axes, ranged
Like frames to build a ship, and then,
Standing far off, he shot an arrow
Straight through them all.[21] This is the
     trial   1770
That I have set before the wooers.
He who most easily shall bend
The bow with his two hands and shoot
His shaft through those twelve axes—him
I then will follow, and forsake   1775
This house to which I came a bride,
A house so beautiful, so filled
With all that makes life good. I know
That oft hereafter, in my dreams,
I shall remember it."

                         And thus   1780
Odysseus spoke:
                         "Delay no longer,
O honored wife of great Odysseus,
But hold here straightway in your hall
This trial with the bow. For here
Odysseus, with his ready counsel,   1785
Will be at hand before the wooers
Can take the polished bow in hand,
And stretch the string and speed an arrow
Straight through the iron."
                         Then again
Prudent Penelope replied: 1790
"If you were only willing, stranger,
To sit here in my hall and give me
Delight like this,[22] then sleep would never
Fall on my eyes again. And yet
No man can live on without sleep   1795

---

21. **an arrow . . . through them all.** Many ancient Greek axes had a large round opening in their iron blades.
22. **delight like this.** Penelope enjoys the "beggar's" talk of Odysseus' return, but she thinks it idle chatter.

So spread your bed here on the ground
Or let the maids bring bedding."
                                        So
She spoke and to her shining room
She went her way.

So there Odysseus laid him down   1800
To slumber in the porch. He spread
A rough hide on the ground, and on it
Laid many a fleece stripped from the sheep
The wooers slew. But Odysseus
Lay sleepless, ever pondering   1805
Evil against the wooers.

READING FOR DETAILS

Home in Ithaca

Even though Odysseus, with the ship and crew furnished him by Alcinoüs, is at last able to reach his beloved Ithaca after twenty years away, he finds many problems.

1. Why does Athene warn Odysseus not to go to his home? Where does she instruct him to go instead?
2. Why had Telemachus gone to Sparta? Why is he in danger from the suitors?
3. To whom does Odysseus first reveal his identity? Why is Telemachus doubtful that they can slay all of the suitors? What two helpers does Odysseus tell him that they can depend upon? How does Odysseus describe his home to Eumæus?
4. Describe Argos. How had he changed in appearance during the absence of Odysseus? What happens to him after he has once again looked upon his master?
5. What treatment does Odysseus receive at the hands of the suitors? What reception is given him by Penelope? How had she deceived the suitors for three years? What ended her deception?
6. Odysseus is now approaching the most personal and dramatic conflict of his adventurous life. Soon he and Telemachus will face some three hundred enemies in hand-to-hand combat. This seems like terrific odds until you consider that he has the guidance and aid of Athene and now, surprisingly enough, of her father Zeus.

   Locate the passage in lines 1097–1108 which indicates that through all his experiences, even the fighting at Troy, Odysseus has depended greatly on Athene. Discuss how the request which Odysseus makes of Athene as he plans for the coming conflict does not make him any the less of a hero to his admirers.

READING FOR APPRECIATION

Suspense

To quicken the pulses of his listeners, Homer, the master storyteller, resorts to a trick which has always increased anticipation of coming action. His hero is disguised so that his enemies fail to recognize him until that dramatic moment when he chooses to reveal his identity.

1. Describe how Athene changes Odysseus in appearance. Even though the goddess ages the Greek hero, what is the one identifying sign which might betray him that she does not erase? Does anyone recognize him from this mark, and does it place him in danger?
2. What test does Odysseus encourage Penelope to demand of her suitors? Why does this increase interest as to what *may* happen?

Part IV, Book XXI: The Contest with the Bow

[When morning comes, Penelope sets about preparing for the contest with the great bow.]

So she came,
This noble lady, to the wooers,
And took her stand close by a pillar
Of that great hall. Before her face
She held a fair-wrought veil, and thus   1810
She spoke to the proud wooers:
"Come, then, you wooers,
Here stands your prize! And here before
    you
I now set forth the mighty bow
Of great Odysseus, and the man   1815
Who with his hands most readily
Shall bend it, and shall send an arrow
Through the twelve axes, he shall be
The man I follow; for I then
Will leave this house of my first bridal,   1820
So beautiful, so filled with all
That makes life good! Always in dreams
I shall remember it."
         So spoke she,
And bade Eumæus, the good swineherd,
Set forth the bow and the grey iron   1825
Before the wooers. He with tears
Took them and set them down; the
    herdsman[1]
Wept too, in his own place, to see
His master's bow.
Now spoke Telemachus before them   1830
In might and honor:
         "Come, you wooers,
Here stands your prize, and such a woman
As is not found in all Achæa,[2]
In holy Pylus—not in Argus
Nor in Mycenæ.[3] But all this   1835
You know already. Why should I
Thus praise my mother? Hold not back
With vain excuse, but bend the bow
And learn how this will end. I too

Would try the bow, for if I bend it   1840
And send my arrow through the iron,
I need not suffer shame that now
My honored mother leaves our house
To follow a new lord, while I
Remain behind; for I should be   1845
A man, then, able to perform
My father's glorious feats."
         So said he,
And up he sprung full height and cast
His scarlet mantle from his shoulders,
And from his shoulders laid aside   1850
His keen-edged sword. And first of all
He set the axes: one long furrow
He dug for all and laid it straight
With a stretched line, and stamped the
    earth
About them on both sides. And wonder   1855
Laid hold on all who saw, so fitly
He set them up, though ne'er before
Had he beheld them. Then he went
And took his stand upon the threshold
And tried the bow. And as he strove   1860
To bend and string it, thrice indeed
He made it tremble, and thrice stayed
To rest his strength, but still he hoped
To stretch the string and send the arrow
Straight through the axes. And he yet,   1865
Straining the fourth time, might have
    strung it,
But now Odysseus shook his head
And staved his eager strength. Then thus
Spoke the great lord Telemachus:
"Alas, must I, then, ever be   1870
Worthless and weak! Or am I yet
Too young to trust these hands of mine
To win me justice if a man
Assails me unprovoked! But come,
You who are stronger; try the bow   1875
And end the contest!"

---

1. The herdsman **Philœtius** (fĭ lē′ti əs) is loyal to Odysseus.
2. **Achæa** (ə kē′ə), ancient Greece.
3. **Argus . . . Mycenæ** (mī sē′nē), cities in ancient Greece.

[One by one the suitors try vainly to string the great bow. At last they decide to let the contest go until the next day when they will hold a great feast in honor of Apollo, the god of archery. They believe Apollo will thus allow one of them to string the bow and send an arrow through the axes. While they are thus engaged, Odysseus goes out of the hall and tells Eumæus and the faithful herdsman who he is. He convinces them by showing them the great scar on his leg. Eumæus and the herdsman are overjoyed their master has returned and agree to help him fight the suitors. They return to the hall where the suitors are drinking wine.]

           Now
When each man to his heart's desire
Had poured and drunken, wise Odysseus,
With crafty purpose spoke:
                  "Now hearken,
Wooers of our famed queen! A boon   1880
I beg now of Eurymachus
And great Antinoüs[4]—for rightly
He counseled that we now lay by
The bow and leave the gods to settle
The issue of the strife. Tomorrow   1885
Let God grant mastery as he will!
But give me now the polished bow
And let me try before you here
My skill and strength—whether there yet
Dwells in these supple limbs the might   1890
That once was theirs, or if already
With wandering and want it now
Is brought to nothing."
             So he spoke,
But when they heard him, all broke out
In furious anger, for they feared   1895
That he might bend the polished bow.
Then thus Antinoüs rebuked him
And said:
        "O wretched stranger, surely
Your wits have left you! Are you not
Content to eat at ease among us,   1900
Men rightly proud, here where you miss
Naught of our feast, but hear our words

And noble speech? No other beggars
Or strangers—you alone—can listen
To all we say. It is the wine   1905
Distracts you thus, the honeyed wine,
That often has brought grief to others
Drunk greedily and out of measure! . . .
And this I prophesy: if you
Shall bend that bow, then sore indeed 1910
Shall be your sufferings, for no one
In all this land will ever hail you
With friendly greeting: we will send you
In a black ship to Echetus,[5]
The king who murders all mankind;   1915
Thence you shall not escape. So sit
And drink in peace, and do not try
To strive with younger men."
           Then answered
Prudent Penelope:
             "Unfitting
It is, Antinoüs, and unjust   1920
Thus to deny the right of strangers,
Guests of Telemachus, who come
Here to this house. What, do you think
That if this stranger proves he rightly
Trusts his arms' strength and power, and
    bends   1925
Odysseus' mighty bow—that he
Would lead me straightway to his home
And take me for his wife! The man
Has never in his inmost bosom
Had such a thought. Let none of you 1930
Who sit at feast here vex your spirit
With thoughts like these. Never, I say—
Never could that befall."
           Then spoke
Polybus'[6] son, Eurymachus,
And answered:

---

4. **Eurymachus** (yŭ ri′ma kəs) and **Antinoüs** (an tin′ō əs) were the two chief suitors who had plotted to kill Telemachus (Book XV); Athene had saved him with a warning.
5. **Echetus** (ē′kə təs), a Greek king who had ordered a dreadful punishment for his daughter and her lover. Here Antinoüs belittles Odysseus as if he were a small child—threatening to send him to the hobgoblins.
6. **Polybus** (pō′le bəs).

     "Wise Penelope,   1935
Icarius'[7] daughter, we have never
Once thought this stranger here would
    wed you,
For that could never be. And yet
We shame to think what might be said
By men and women—how some fellow,   1940
One of the baser sort among us,
Should say: 'These men who came to woo
That great lord's wife were all too weak:
They could not bend his polished bow.
And yet another came, a beggar,   1945
A vagabond—and he with ease
Bent the great bow and sent an arrow
Straight through the iron.' Even so
The tale will run, and this will bring us
Reproach forever!"
             Then replied   1950
Prudent Penelope:
              "You cannot,
Eurymachus, win any honor
Here in this land by eating all
A great man's wealth the while you bring

Dishonor to his house. Why lay, then,   1955
Such weight on the reproach! This stranger
Is big of body and well-built,
And is, he says himself, the son
Of a good father. Come, then, give him
The polished bow, and let us see   1960
What he can do! For this I say,
And as I say, so shall it be:
If great Apollo grant his prayer
And let him bend the bow, I then
Will give him clothing—cloak and
    tunic—   1965
And a sharp spear to ward away
Both dogs and men, and a good sword,
Two-edged, besides; and I will give him
Sandals upon his feet; and hence
I then will send him wheresoever   1970
His heart and soul may wish."
                  Then spoke
The wise Telemachus and answered:
"Mother, no man of the Achæans

7. **Icarius** (ī kā′rē əs).

Has greater right than I to give
This bow or hold it back.
                    But go   1975
Now to your room. There busy you
With woman's proper work, the loom
And distaff; give your maids commands
And let them ply their tasks. A bow
Is matter fit for men—for all men—   1980
But most of all for me, for I
Am master in this house."
                    And she,
Astonished at his words, went thence
Up to her room, and laid to heart
Her son's wise words. So she ascended   1985
To her own room, among her maidens,
And wept her own dear lord Odysseus
Until at last keen-eyed Athene
Sent on her eyes sweet sleep.

                    And now
The swineherd took the bow in hand   1990
To bear it to his lord. The wooers,
Beholding, each and all broke out
With clamor in the hall, and one
Of the proud youths thus spoke:
                    "Now where,
You worthless swineherd, are you taking   1995
That curved bow? O you idle rascal,
I wish that those swift dogs you breed
Might eat you, off there all alone
Among your swine! Would but Apollo
Might grant us this!"
                    These words he spoke,   2000
And in his fear the swineherd quickly
Laid the bow down where he was
          standing,
For many a man, through all the hall,
Cried out against him. Loudly then
From where he sat, Telemachus   2005
Called, threatening:
                    "Go on, good father,
Take him the bow! But I shall teach you,
And soon, you must not take your orders
From every man.

          Ah, would I were
As surely, stronger than these men,   2010
These wooers in this house! For soon
Would I send some of them in sorrow
Off home, out of our house! Their deeds
Are all of evil!"
          So he spoke,
And all the wooers laughed thereat   2015
With merry laughter, and forgot
The bitter wrath they felt before
Against Telemachus. And now
Down through the hall the swineherd
          came
Bearing the bow, and by Odysseus   2020
He halted, and he gave the bow
Into his hand. And then he called
Nurse Eurycleia from within
And said:
          "Telemachus thus bids you,
Wise Eurycleia. Lock you now   2025
The close-set doors between the chambers
And the great hall. If any woman
Hear there within the sound of groans
Or combat from the men without
In the great hall, let her not look   2030
Forth from the door, but bide within
And ply her task in silence."
          So
He spoke to her. His words unwing'd
Rested unanswered and she fastened
The doors of that fair hall. And softly   2035
Philœtius sped forth from the house
And barred the gates of the walled court.
Then back he went and sat him down
Where he had sat before; and ever
He fixed his eyes upon Odysseus.   2040
And now Odysseus held the bow
And turned it, side to side, and tried it
In every part, lest worms, the while
Its lord was far away, had eaten
Into the horn. And one who watched   2045
Would say, quick glancing at his neighbor:
"This fellow must be used to bows,
A clever rascal. He may have

A bow like this laid by at home
Or studies how to make one. Look: 2050
See how the idle beggar turns it
This way and that with ready hands,
Well tried in mischief!"

        And another
Of the proud youths would say:
               "May he
Meet ever such good luck as now 2055
Will be his lot, when he shall fail
To bend the bow!"

           So spoke the wooers.
But wise Odysseus, who had handled
That mighty bow, testing each part,
At once as easily as a man, 2060
A singer, skillful with the lyre,
Stretches a string in place and fits it
To its new peg, and at each end
Makes fast the twisted gut—even so
With ready ease Odysseus bent 2065
And strung that mighty bow.

          He took it
In his right hand and tried the bowstring,
And at his touch it rang out loud,
Clear as a swallow's cry.

        Then fell
A deadly dread on all the wooers, 2070
And every face turned pale. Zeus sent
His sign from heaven in loud thunder,
And great Odysseus, who so long
Had suffered and endured, rejoiced
To hear this signal from the son 2075
Of artful Cronus.

       Now he took
A swift shaft in his hand: it lay
Before him, drawn, upon the table;
For in the hollow quiver yet
The rest lay waiting—as the Achæans 2080
Ere long should learn.

      And now he laid
The arrow in the rest, and seated
There on the bench, he drew the string

And the notched arrow. Straight he aimed,
And loosed the shaft.

      And not one axe 2085
Of all it missed. Through every one
From the first axe, that bronze-tipped
   arrow
Went speeding to the very last
And out beyond. Then thus Odysseus
Spoke to Telemachus:

       "This stranger, 2090
Telemachus, who as your guest
Sits in your hall, has not, you see,
Brought shame on you. I have not missed
The mark nor made a mighty labor
Of stringing the great bow. My strength 2095
Is even as of old, nor fails me now
As these in insult deemed.

     At last
The time is come, the destined hour
To bid these wooers sup with us,
Though yet it is full day! And we 2100
Have sport for them besides—the dance
And twanging of the lyre, to crown
This coming feast!"

       So spoke Odysseus,
And gave, with bended brows, the signal.
And, on the instant, his dear son 2105
Telemachus girt by his side
His keen-edged sword and took his stand
Beside his father's seat, all armed
In glittering bronze.

READING FOR DETAILS

The Contest

1. Prudent and beauteous Penelope promises to leave the home she loves and follow the suitor who can string Odysseus' bow and send a shaft through the center holes of the twelve axes. Before any of the suitors can try, however, Telemachus announces that he wishes to test himself and see if he can perform the feat. What reason does he give?

2. Even though Telemachus does not complete the test, his subsequent actions show that he is eager to assume the responsibilities of a grown man. Give two illustrations of such actions which show this.

READING FOR APPRECIATION

Suspense

After Penelope first announces the contest of the bow, Homer arranges the action which follows so that it builds toward the moment when Odysseus reveals his identity.

1. Discuss those incidents which, taking place between the time the contest is announced and the moment Odysseus has the fateful bow in his hands, prolong the coming of the awaited moment and increase the listeners' suspense.

2. Authors sometimes make use of what is known as *irony* to draw their audience or readers closer to them and increase the interest in what is going to happen. After all, anything is more fun if you feel that you're "in the know" or "on the inside" as to what is taking place. Irony occurs when what appears to be true really isn't so at all. For example, when Penelope says to the suitors that even if the stranger strings the bow and sends an arrow through the axes, he has no thought of making her his wife, this is ironical. Explain.

Conflict

Finally, after a fitting build-up, the moment arrives! Odysseus "who so long had suffered and endured" is at last to get revenge.

What sign from a god does the courageous hero get to show him that the time has come for taking action? What precautions had been taken to see that the suitors did not flee from the hall? Who took his stand beside Odysseus to fight along with him? How many other men could he count upon to help him in the fighting?

Part V, Book XXII: The Battle in the Great Hall

Now wise Odysseus stripped away   2110
His ragged garments. Up he sprang
To the great threshold with the bow
And the full quiver, and poured forth
The swift shafts at his feet. Then thus
Before the wooers he spoke:
         "So now   2115
Ends this dread contest. And again
I aim, at a new mark, a mark
No man has hit before. And may
My aim be true, and great Apollo
Grant me the glory!"
         So he spoke,   2120
And at Antinoüs he aimed
His piercing arrow. Now this man
Was just then lifting to his lips
A fair gold cup of double handle
And held it high in both his hands   2125
Ready to drink the wine. Of death
No thought was in his heart. For who
Could think that here among these men,
Sitting at feast, one man, alone
Among so many, though his strength   2130
Were great indeed, could bring upon him
Dread death and fate's black end?
         Odysseus
Took steady aim and drove the arrow
Straight to the throat: the keen point sped
Through the soft neck. The man sank
     down: 2135
Sidelong he bent: out of his hand
As he fell smitten, dropped the cup;
Forth from his nostrils sprang the blood
In a thick stream.
         And when the wooers
Saw the man fall, they rose in tumult   2140
Through all the hall. Up sprang each man
Out of his place and ran about
Searching in terror every side
Of those strong walls; but there they found

No shield or warlike spear.[1] And thus 2145
They spoke, then, and in angry words
Rebuked Odysseus:
              "This, O stranger,
Will bring you evil, thus to turn
Your shafts on men!
                You have slain
The first and foremost man of all 2150
The youth of Ithaca!"
              But Odysseus
Spoke, frowning sternly on them:
                 "Dogs,
You told yourselves that I should never
Come back again to my own home
Out of the land of Troy. And so 2155
You have devoured my house,
             And though I
Myself was living, sought like traitors
To woo my wife. You neither fear
The gods that dwell in the high heavens
Nor yet the wrath of man that ever 2160
Follows with vengeance. Round you all
Death's cords are tightening!"
              So spoke he,
And at his words their knees grew weak,
And weak their hearts within. And then
Eurymachus at once spoke out 2165
Before them all:
           "Never, my friends,
Will this man stay his ruthless hand
Now that he holds the polished bow
And quivered arrows; but will stand there
On that bright threshold and will
      smite us 2170
Till he has slain us all. So summon
Your spirit to the fight. Draw swords!
Hold up the tables as a shield
Against these shafts of death, and rush
Upon him swiftly, all at once, 2175
Locked close together. So perhaps
We yet may thrust him from the threshold
And from the door, and so flee forth
And reach the town and there raise quickly
Our cry for aid. And then this man 2180
Will soon shoot his last shaft!"

              So said he,
And with these words he drew his sword,
Keen, double-edged, and rushed upon him,
Shouting a dreadful shout!
             That instant
Noble Odysseus loosed his arrow. 2185
It struck him in the breast.
             Out of his hand
His sword flew. Lifeless, limp, he sank
Across the table, and fell headlong,
O'erturning food and cup. His head
Beat on the ground in agony; 2190
He writhed, and thrusting with both feet
Spurned back the chair and threw it over,
And dark upon his eyes then fell
The mists of death.
          Telemachus sped
To his dear father's side, and there 2195
He stood and with wing'd words he said:
"Now, father, I will bring you hither
A shield, and I will bring two spears
And a good helmet all of bronze
Fitting your brows, and I myself 2200
Will get me armor, and will arm
The swineherd and the herdsman; armor
Will make us safer."
          Then replied
The wise Odysseus:
           "Run, then, fetch them,
While I have arrows yet remaining 2205
To hold our foemen off, or they,
When I am left alone, may drive me
Out of the doorway."
          So he spoke,
And good Telemachus obeyed
His father's bidding. Forth he hastened 2210
Up to the room wherein lay hidden
Those glorious arms, and thence he took
Four shields, eight spears, and four good
      helmets
Brazen, with horsehair crests. And these
He bore with him, and quickly came 2215

1. **no shield or warlike spear.** Earlier, Telemachus had
locked their weapons in a room off the banquet hall.

Back to his father's side. And first
Round his own body he girt on
The brazen mail, and then those two,
His servants, armed them like himself
In that fair armor. There they stood   2220
Beside their lord, the wise Odysseus,
Ready of counsel.
          Now so long
As he had shafts wherewith to hold
His foes afar, he still smote down
A wooer with each shaft; they fell there   2225
One by another. But at length
The mighty archer's arrows failed him.
Then he set down his bow and leaned it
Close by a pillar of the hall
Against the shining wall's bright surface,   2230
Then round his shoulders slung a shield
Of four-fold hide and on his head
He set a helmet, finely fashioned,
And terribly its horsehair crest
Nodded above it; and he took   2235
Two bronze-tipped spears in hand.
            There was,
It chanced, a postern door that pierced
The massive wall, just at the level
Of the great threshold of the hall.
Through this a man might reach the
     passage   2240
That ran without, but this was barred
By well-joined doors. And here Odysseus
Bade the good swineherd take his stand
And keep good watch, for here alone
Might those within pass forth. And now   2245
Thus to his comrades Agelaüs[2]
Made plain his thought:
          "Friends, might not one
Climb up and reach that little door,
And so pass forth and tell our people
And raise the cry for help? This man   2250
Would soon shoot his last shaft."
            Then answered
Melanthius[3] the goatherd:
             "Never
Can that be done, great Agelaüs.
It lies too near the fine great doors

That lead forth to the court, and hard   2255
It is to pass these; for one man,
If stout of heart, might hold the passage
Against us all. But look, now—I
Will bring you from the upper room
Arms for each man, for there, I think,   2260
Odysseus and his valiant son
Have stored the arms away."
             So spoke
Melanthius the goatherd; straightway
He clambered up and through the holes
That aired the hall, slipped forth and
     reached   2265
Odysseus' inner room. And thence
He chose out twelve good shields and
     spears
And helmets with high crests of horsehair,
And back he brought them all in haste
And gave them to the wooers.
           So they stood   2270
Breathing fierce breath of battle, ready
Upon the threshold, four alone
While those who faced them in the hall
Were many, tried in arms.
           And Agelaüs,
Son of Damastor,[4] now urged forward   2275
The wooers to the fight, and with him
Eurynomous, Amphimedon,[5]
And Demoptolemus: Peisander,
Polyctor's[6] son, and Polybus,
Famed for his wisdom. These men stood   2280
Highest in worth among the wooers
Who yet were left alive and battled
For life itself. The rest, the bow
And those thick-flying shafts already
Had struck with death.
           And Agelaüs,   2285
Son of Damastor, now spoke out

---

2. **Agelaüs** (ā jə lā′əs),   one of the wooers.
3. **Melanthius** (mə lan′thi əs),   one of the household servants who threw in his lot with the wooers.
4. **Damastor** (də mas′tər).
5. **Eurynomous** (yū rin′ə məs), **Amphimedon** (am fī′mə dən).
6. **Demoptolemus** (də mop tō′lə məs), **Peisander** (pī san′dər), **Polyctor** (pō′līk tər).

Before the wooers, and made clear
His thought to all:
        "Now cast
All your long spears, yet not together.
Come, let six cast at once and learn   2290
If Zeus will let us now lay low
Odysseus and win glory. Heed not
The others, so he fall!"

        So said he,
And at his word all cast their spears

And mightily. But great Athene   2295
Made them of no avail. One struck
A pillar that upheld the roof
Of the great hall; another smote
The firm-set door, and a third spear,
With ashen shaft and brazen head,   2300
Drove deep into the wall. So now
When every spear the wooers hurled
Had missed its mark, then spoke Odysseus,
So sorely tried:
        "Now, friends, I tell you

We too must cast our spears and aim
    them   2305
All at that throng of wooers, men
Who madly long to strip our bodies
And add to their foul score."
                    He spoke,
And each of them took aim and cast
His keen spear at the man who faced
    him.   2310
Odysseus with his flying spear
Struck Demoptolemus; his son
Smote down Euryades;[7] the swineherd
Slew Elatus;[8] and the good herdsman
Struck down Peisander. And they all   2315
Fell there together and their teeth
Bit the broad earth. Back up the hall
Shrank all the wooers to the far
Sheltered recesses, and those others
Sprang forward and plucked forth the
    spears   2320
From those that lay there slain.
                      Once more
The wooers then all hurled together
Their pointed spears, and mightily,
But great Athene made them all
Of no avail. For one but struck   2325
A pillar that upheld the roof
Of the great hall; another smote
The firm-set door; and a third spear,
With ashen shaft and brazen head,
Drove deep into the wall. But one,   2330
Amphimedon's long spear, struck lightly
Telemachus upon the wrist,
Grazing the skin; and now Ctesippus,[9]
Sending his spear above the shield,
Just touched Eumæus' shoulder: onward 2335
It sped and fell to earth.
                    Once more
The men who fought beside their wise
And crafty lord Odysseus, cast
Their keen spears all together, aiming
Into the throng. And now Odysseus,   2340
Taker of Troy, struck with his spear
Eurydamas;[10] Telemachus
Smote down Amphimedon; the swineherd

Slew Polybus, and the good herdsman
Struck, full upon the breast, Ctesippus.   2345
             Then on their hearts
Came panic; through the hall they fled
Like kine some darting gadfly follows
And stings to madness in the springtime
When days grow long. And as the
    vultures   2350
Come down from mountain heights and
    swoop
Upon the lesser birds that cower
Beneath the clouds and flit their way
Upon the levels, as they pounce
Upon them, slaying, where no help   2355
Or hope of flight is found, while men
Look on and see the sport with gladness—
Even so these men came rushing down
Upon the wooers, and they drove them
Through all the house on every side   2360
And smote them down. And horrible
Arose the groans of men who fell
With shattered heads, and all the floor
Was red with blood.
              And now
The son of Terpes,[11] Phemius,   2365
The minstrel whom the wooers forced
To sing before them, still was seeking
How he might shun black death. He stood
Close by the postern door; his hands
Held his clear lyre. . . .
           And now he set   2370
His hollow lyre upon the floor . . .
And he himself sprang forth and clasped
Odysseus' knees, and with wing'd words
Besought him thus:
          "A suppliant,
I clasp your knees, Odysseus. Honor   2375
And pity a poor minstrel. Sorrow
May seize you later if you slay

---

7. **Euryades** (yü rē'ə dēz).
8. **Elatus** (ē'lə təs).
9. **Ctesippus** (tē'sə pəs).
10. **Eurydamas** (yü rid'ə məs).
11. **Terpes** (tẻr'pēz).

A singer who has made sweet music
For gods and men.
                    So do not seek
To smite my head from me. Your son,   2380
Your own Telemachus, will tell you
That not of my own will, nor seeking
For gain thereby, did I come hither
To sing my songs here in your house
While these men sat at feast. For they   2385
Were mightier than I and many,
And forced me to their will."
                    So said he,
And the great prince Telemachus
Heard him and by his father's side
Thus quickly spoke:
                    "Nay, hold your hand,   2390
Nor slay this man with your bronze blade,
For he is blameless. Let us spare, too,
Medon, the herald. For when I
Was still a child, here in our home
He had me ever in his keeping.   2395
Spare him, unless Philœtius slew him
Or the good swineherd, or he fell
Before your hand as you swept raging
Through all the house."
                    He spoke, and Medon,
A man of wisdom, heard, for crouching   2400
He lay beneath a chair, all hidden
In a raw oxhide, so escaping
From fate's black end. And now he quickly
Came from beneath the chair, and rose,
And cast the hide aside, and ran   2405
Straight to Telemachus and clasped
His hands about his knees and spoke
Beseeching in wing'd words:
                    "Yes, friend,
Here I am now! So stay your hand,
And speak, I pray you to your father,   2410
Lest in his strength he smite me dead
With his sharp sword in his great anger
Against these wooers—these who wasted
His wealth here in his halls, too foolish
To heed your words."
                    Then smiling spoke   2415
The wise Odysseus:

                    "Have good courage,
For he has snatched you from your peril
And saved you. Lay this truth to heart:
Aye, and tell others: he who does
Good deeds will find far better fortune   2420
Than he whose deeds are evil. Go you
Forth from the hall now. Sit you down
Out in the court, far from this slaughter,
You and yon minstrel, rich in music,
While in the house I do the work   2425
I yet must do."
                    He spoke, and they
Passed quickly from the hall and sat them
Beside the altar of great Zeus,
Peering about on every side
In dread of death.

                    And now Odysseus   2430
Went through the house and searched about
To see if anywhere remained
A man yet left alive and hiding
To shun black death. But he beheld
Them one and all, each man, all lying   2435
In blood and dust.

[Odysseus now sends for Eurycleia to help in
placing the hall back in order.]

                    And Eurycleia,
When she beheld those bodies there,
And that dread flow of blood, was ready
To cry aloud for joy, beholding
How great a deed was done. But he   2440
Stayed her and bade her to refrain
Her eager longing, speaking thus
In wing'd words:
                    "Let your heart rejoice,
Old woman, but refrain, nor cry
Aloud in triumph. It is evil   2445
To glory o'er the slain. Their fate
Has brought them to this end, the fate
The gods have shaped them, and their own
Foul deeds of sin. These men respected
No man on earth, or good or evil,   2450
Who came among them. So they now,

Through their own evil deeds, are fallen
A prey to dreadful death."
                              And now
He called to him Telemachus
And called the swineherd and the herds-
      man,   2455
And in wing'd words he said:
                              "Begin, now
The work of bearing out the dead."
                              Now Odysseus
Spoke to his good nurse Eurycleia:
"Bring hither brimstone now, old woman,
To keep off harm; bring fire besides   2460
To purify the hall, then go
And bid Penelope come hither
With all her maids: bid all the women
Within the house to come."
                              So said he,
And Eurycleia, his dear nurse,   2465
Failed not to heed his words. She brought
      him
Brimstone and fire besides; with these
Odysseus purified the hall,
The buildings and the court.
                              And now
Up through the fair house the old
      woman   2470
Went hastening to tell the women
And speed them on. And forth they came
Out of their room, and in their hands
They all bore torches, and they thronged
About Odysseus and with joy   2475
Welcomed him home.

READING FOR DETAILS

The Great Battle

1. The suitors seemed unable to organize themselves effectively to fight Odysseus, Telemachus, and the two loyal servants. Discuss how the following factors contributed to their confusion:
   a. shock effect of the "beggar's" true identity
   b. suitors' lack of shields and spears
   c. suitors' lack of physical fitness and battle experience
   d. suitors' indifference to the gods
   e. early deaths of Antinoüs and Eurymachus
2. How do the suitors later obtain spears, shields, and helmets?
3. What reasons does Phemius the minstrel give that Odysseus should spare his life? What insight does this give you into the regard with which the minstrel was held in Odysseus' time?
4. The Greeks looked upon arrogance or insolence toward gods and men as lawlessness, and the word they had for such conduct was *hubris*. Those guilty of hubris were bound to be punished or destroyed. Discuss in what ways the suitors were guilty of hubris.

READING FOR APPRECIATION

Conflict

In considering conflict in the other selections in this unit, you have been concerned with the four basic types: (1) a person struggles against another person or an animal; (2) a person struggles against the forces of nature; (3) a person struggles against society or groups of people who represent certain ideas or beliefs; (4) a person is torn by an inner conflict. There is a fifth type of conflict. This is the struggle of people against fate or destiny. When the gods enter into a conflict, the odds are heavily weighted against the people they oppose. These people are fated to be punished. This type of conflict is seen throughout the *Odyssey,* and it is especially notable in this episode, which brings to a high point the conflict between Odysseus and the suitors.

1. How does Athene aid Odysseus each time the suitors cast their spears?
2. Describe how Medon escaped "fate's black end." What grim humor can be seen in this incident? How does it help the story?

Part VI, Book XXIII: The Reunion of Odysseus and Penelope

Now the old woman went her way,
Laughing for joy, up to the room
Where lay her mistress, with the tidings
That her dear lord was come. Her knees   2480
Grew strong with joy; her feeble feet
Ran faster than their wont. She halted
There by her lady's head and thus
She spoke to her:
        "Awake, dear child,
Penelope, and see at last   2485
With your own eyes what you have hoped
   for
Day after day. For now Odysseus
Is come again, to his own home;
Long looked for, he has come at last,
And he has slain the haughty wooers   2490
Who troubled all his house and wasted
His wealth away and threatened evil
To his dear son."
       Then thus replied
The wise Penelope:
         "Dear nurse,
The gods have made you mad: 2495
Your mind, till now, was ever steady.
Why do you mock me, now my spirit
Is heavy with its grief, to tell me
Such tales as this?"
       Then replied
Her dear nurse Eurycleia:
         "Nay,   2500
Dear child, I do not mock you. Here
In very truth, Odysseus now
Is with us, he himself. For he
Was the poor stranger every man
Insulted in the hall. Long since   2505
Telemachus knew well that he
Was here among us, but with foresight
He hid his knowledge, that his father
Might all the better take his vengeance
For all the cruel wrongs these men   2510

Have wrought in arrogance."
       Then replied
Prudent Penelope:
        "Dear nurse,
Now be not over-quick to boast
And laugh with joy. You know indeed
How welcome he would be to all   2515
In his own house, and most to me
And to the son I bore him. Yet
This tale you tell cannot be true:
Alas, it is some god came hither
And slew those haughty wooers, angered   2520
At the rash insults of their pride
And all their evil deeds.
         So for their crimes
They met this end. But far away
Odysseus now has lost forever
All hope of his returning hither—   2525
Nay, he himself is lost!"
        Then answered
Her dear nurse Eurycleia:
        "Child,
What words are these that now have
   passed
The portal of your teeth! To say
That your own husband, he who now   2530
Stands here upon his hearth, will never
Come home again. Your heart is ever
Slow to believe. Yet I can tell you
Another sign, a sign yet surer,
The scar of the deep wound the boar   2535
Once gave with his bright tusk. I spied it
That day I washed his feet, and longed
To tell you what I saw. But he
Laid hand upon my mouth and so
With his wise foresight, stopped my
   speech.   2540
But come, now, follow me."
Then wise Penelope replied:
"Dear nurse, wise as you are, 'tis hard
To guard against the secret purpose
Of the eternal gods. And yet   2545
Let us go down and seek my son
And see these wooers who lie slain
And him that slew them."

So she spoke,
And down she passed then from her room,
And sorely was her heart divided   2550
Whether to stand far off and question
Her own dear lord, or stand beside him
And kiss his face and clasp his hand.
But when she entered and passed over
The threshold of carved stone, she went   2555
And sat her down, facing Odysseus,
In firelight, by the farther wall.
And he still sat with downcast eyes
By the tall pillar and awaited
In wonder if his stately wife   2560
Would speak to him when she should turn
Her eyes and see him. A long time
She sat in silence, and amazement
Was in her heart; then for a time
She gazed upon him face to face,   2565
And then again she knew him not,
For he still wore upon his body
A beggar's raiment.
              And her son,
Telemachus, now spoke, and said,
Reproaching her:
              "Mother of mine,   2570
Unmotherly, why is your heart
So hard? Why do you ever keep
Far from my father?
             Your heart is ever
Harder than stone!"
             Then thus replied
Prudent Penelope:
             "My son,   2575
My spirit is amazed within me.
I have no power to speak or question
Or look upon his face. And yet,
If this can be Odysseus' self,
And he has now come home, we two   2580
May know each other far more surely
Than any other may, for we
Have secret tokens known to us,
Hidden from all besides."
             So said she,
And great Odysseus smiled and quickly   2585
Thus to Telemachus he spoke

In wing'd words:
             "Go, Telemachus,
And leave your mother in the hall
To test me. She shall learn ere long
More surely what I am. But now,   2590
Because I am unclean to see,
And wear base garments on my body,
She holds me in dishonor, saying
That I am not her lord!"

[Odysseus leaves to bathe and to dress in more
fitting clothing. At that time Athene restores his
handsome appearance.]

             So he came
Forth from the bath, and seemed in
       presence   2595
Like the immortal gods. And thus
He came once more back to the seat
Whence he had risen, and there sat
Facing his wife, and spoke to her
And said:
             "O most perplexing woman,   2600
Surely the dwellers on Olympus
Have given you a harder heart
Than other tender women. Nay,
There is no other woman living
Would stand aside thus, hardening   2605
A stubborn heart against her husband
Who after many a peril past
Comes, in the twentieth year, once more
To his own land."
             And thus answered
The wise Penelope:
             "O man   2610
Perplexing to my soul—nay, I
Am not held off by pride, nor scorn you,
But I am lost in wonder. Well
I know what you were once when, sailing
Away in your oared ship, you left   2615
Your home in Ithaca. But come
Now, Eurycleia, and make ready
His firm-built bed. Make it outside
The room he built him himself. Aye, move
His firm-built bedstead forth and strew   2620

Upon it bedding—fleeces, covers,
And bright-hued rugs."

                 All this she said
To try her husband. But Odysseus
Was angered at her words, and thus
He spoke to his true wife:
                 "What, woman!   2625
What words are these you now have said
To pierce my heart! Who can have set
My bed in a new place?
               No mortal man
Of living men, in his full strength,
Could ever move it easily   2630
Out of its present place. For in it,
Wrought in its very frame, is hidden
A secret token, and no other
Wrought this, but I alone.
               There grew
Within our yard an olive tree,   2635
Long-leaved and thriving, strong of
   growth,
Thick as a pillar. Round its trunk
I shaped my room and built it thus
Till all was finished, walling it
With massive stone, and well I
   fashioned   2640
The roof to cover it and hung
And fitted its joined doors. And then,
From that long-leaved tall olive tree
I cut the crown away and squared,
Using my axe, the stem remaining   2645
Above the roots; then with the adz
I smoothed it and made true the line,
And thus I made my bed-post. Next
I bored it all with a keen auger
And, so beginning, ever worked   2650
On to the end, and it stood finished.
I decked it all with gold and silver
And ivory, and across it stretched
Long strips of oxhide bright and red.
This is the token that I mean.   2655
Now, wife, I do not know if still
That bed is standing there, or whether
Some one has cut that olive stem
And moved it elsewhere."

               So he spoke,
And at his words her knees grew weak   2660
And all her soul within, for well
She knew this token that Odysseus
Had told so plainly. And she wept,
And straight to him she ran, and cast
Her arms about her husband's neck   2665
And kissed his face and said:
               "Odysseus,
Pray be not angry with me. You
Have ever been, through every fortune,
Wisest of men. The gods have sent
Sore grief upon us, for they grudged us   2670
That we should side by side together
Share the delight of youth and cross
The threshold of old age. Yet be not,
I pray you, wroth with me or blame me,
Because I did not when I saw you,   2675
Run thus to greet you! For my heart
Within my breast was shuddering ever
Lest some strange man should come and
   cheat me
With lying words. For many a man
Will plot base deeds for gain. But now,   2680
Since you have made so plain the secret
Of this our bed
               —lo, now
You quite convince this heart of mine,
Stubborn what though it be!"

               So spoke she,
And stronger still there came upon him   2685
A yearning need of tears, and there,
Holding his wise and faithful wife,
He wept with joy. And she beside him,
Like men that see the land with gladness—
Seamen whose sturdy ship Poseidon   2690
Has smitten on the deep and shattered
With storm and mighty seas, and few
Are they who from the foaming waters
Escape to swim to shore: their skin
Is crusted with the brine, but happy   2695
They step to land once more, delivered
Out of their danger—with such gladness
She gazed upon her husband.

READING FOR DETAILS

An Adventure for All Times

For Homer, life was filled with many hazards, but it was still a heroic adventure to be undertaken with joy and courage. The Homeric hero was not discouraged by the fact that he could unknowingly be condemned to destruction by the gods or by fate. His joy of living was apparent in the way he faced each new experience.

The poetry of Homer has continued to appeal to readers through the years because his characters are true to the fundamentals of human nature.

1. Think over this last statement carefully, then list what you feel to be some of the fundamental characteristics of human nature.
2. Discuss, with specific illustrations from the *Odyssey*, whether or not you feel Homer's characters to be basically true to life.

READING FOR MEANING

Reflect on the following statements, then discuss each as it applies to the *Odyssey*.

1. The person who really mattered in the ancient Greek world was the king or chief.
2. Men were not considered unmanly if they cried when moved by joy or grief.
3. The position of Penelope was similar in many ways to that of women today.

READING FOR APPRECIATION

The Homeric story-poems, or epics, continue to be admired for three reasons: (a) The action moves rapidly. (b) The language is simple. (c) Noble actions or deeds are glorified.

What relationship can you see between these three characteristics and the fact that the epic was first sung as entertainment?

LANGUAGE AND VOCABULARY

A. The procedure of using context clues to find the meaning of unfamiliar words may be applied to any kind of writing—poetry or prose, narrative or exposition, new styles or old, simple or difficult. When ancient Homer says, "Good indeed it is to hear the minstrelsy of such a singer," we have a fair idea of what *minstrelsy* means. Guess at the meanings of the italicized words in the following contexts; then look up the words in your dictionary.

1. Within this lair a man was *wont* to sleep. . . .
2. And we cried out in *lamentation*. . . .
3. As one who with an *auger* bores a great ship timber.
4. Groaning in agony and *anguish*. . .
5. If I *entreat* you and bid you set me free. . .
6. ". . . would you, O mighty goddess, but *vouchsafe* to be my helper!"

However, the method of context clues—like anything else—has its limitations. Sometimes there will be no adequate context clue to help you unlock the meaning of an unknown word. Consider the lines "But this you give me is a cup of nectar and ambrosia mingled." Guess at the meaning of *nectar* and *ambrosia* and then look them up in your dictionary.

B. The English language has, of course, many prefixes that are not negative. A second group of prefixes might be labeled *situational* prefixes, in that they suggest situation, location, or direction. Perhaps the simplest prefixes of this kind are *a-*, as in *abed*, which suggests the meaning of *up, in, on, to*; *be-*, as in *beset*, roughly meaning *around, about*; and *for-*, as in *forsake*, suggesting *away, off, from*. But prefixes are often general and unstable in their meanings. To what extent do the comments made above apply to these words from the Homer selection: *await, arise, amid, aloud, athwart, aloft, asunder; beseech, befall, behold; forbid, forbear?*

COMPOSITION

Characterization is of great importance in the epic. In various ways, Homer told his listeners enough about each of the important persons appearing in his songs that his audience was interested in hearing what happened to them.

Write a brief essay on one of the following topics:
1. the character of Penelope
2. my opinion of Odysseus
3. Telemachus as the ideal son

BIOGRAPHICAL NOTE

Homer may have lived about 800 B.C. There is actually very little known about Homer. There are no facts to prove that such a person even existed. However, the ancient Greeks believed that an old, blind, wandering poet named Homer composed the two great Greek epics, the *Iliad* and the *Odyssey,* and that he went about from place to place reciting these stirring tales.

So great was the honor accorded these stories that no fewer than seven cities of the ancient Greek world claimed to be Homer's birthplace. For centuries Greek schoolboys learned by heart some version of these Homeric poems. Groups of men devoted their lives to preserving, reshaping, and reciting these verses of the deeds and legends of the men who fought at Troy.

Some scholars, probing the mists of antiquity, believe that the two epics were the works of many men. Other scholars simply accept the legend that such a person as Homer did exist. The question of the authorship is really not too important. What is important is the fact that we have these great stories that are still the basis of Western classical education in every part of the world.

With
What You Have

Phizzog

This face you got,
This here phizzog you carry around,
You never picked it out for yourself, at all, at all—did
    you?
This here phizzog—somebody handed it to you—am I
    right?
Somebody said, "Here's yours, now go see what you can
    do with it."   5
Somebody slipped it to you and it was like a package
    marked:
"No goods exchanged after being taken away"—
This face you got.

CARL SANDBURG

From GOOD MORNING, AMERICA, copyright 1928, 1956, by Carl
Sandburg. Reprinted by permission of Harcourt Brace Jovanovich, Inc.

L'EDITION DELUXE
Lillian Westcott Hale
Courtesy, Museum of Fine Arts, Boston
Gift of Miss Mary C. Wheelwright

We all have the ability to think and imagine.
This woman, reading, is using what she has
to transcend her immediate surroundings.

"Make the most of yourself,
for that is all there is of you."—Ralph Waldo Emerson

A boy in a segregated high school in Hawaii is shamed by snobbish classmates because he doesn't wear shoes. An infant girl is left blind and deaf by a searing fever. A small slave child, ruthlessly kidnapped, is redeemed for a broken-down racehorse.

When he grows older, Daniel Ken Inouye, the boy rejected by snobbish classmates, becomes the first American of Japanese descent to serve in both the U.S. House of Representatives and the Senate. The infant girl, Helen Keller, grows into an outstanding woman who "sees" and "hears" with more perception than many persons who have perfect sight and hearing. The kidnapped child, George Washington Carver, acquires a great knowledge about growing things and uses his ability to "make something from nothing" to become one of America's foremost scientists.

Each of us is born with particular physical characteristics. Each of us is born into a particular environment. We must accept what we have and go from there.

Some people seem to be able to do everything quite easily. They never seem to have any real problems. They are popular and good-looking. They are good in sports or smart in class or both. Others do not seem to be that fortunate. Many people have handicaps, real or imagined, which they believe prevent their natural abilities from being developed. But these handicaps can become assets if they force people to work harder to find a place for themselves—a place where they feel useful and secure.

The lives of individuals who accept what they have and manage to achieve some triumph, great or small, are found in biographies, short stories, plays, and poems. Young people who read of the longings, hopes, fears, frustrations, and triumphs of such people know that they have feelings in common with others—in dreaming their dreams, they are not alone.

UNIT TECHNIQUES

CHARACTERIZATION

A person who appears in a piece of literature, whether it be fiction or nonfiction, is referred to as a character. A writer who wants to tell you what a character is like has five commonly used ways to do this. She or he may tell you:

1. what the character looks like
2. what the character says and thinks
3. what others say and think about the character
4. the way the character acts in a given situation
5. the way others act toward the character

Some of the most vivid characterizations are found in fiction (made-up stories), poems, and plays. Usually, when a character in fiction seems real and alive, it is because he or she is like someone the reader knows or knows about in real life.

The first selection in this unit, "Why Don't You Wear Shoes?", is a nonfiction, autobiographical account. In such a selection the writer has the task of showing his or her own character. Daniel Inouye does this by making frequent use of the second and fourth characterization techniques listed above. For example, note what Dan thinks about the young women who came to Hawaii as teachers. Note too his conduct when Miss Dolton catches him eating in the classroom. Dan's conduct in the Japanese language classroom illustrates a different facet of Dan's character.

SIGNIFICANT DETAIL

A character cannot be developed into a memorable person, nor can a story be written so that it seems real, without the use of details. However, writers, either of fiction or nonfiction, cannot tell every real or imagined event in the lives of their characters. They must select only those details that will have the most meaning or give the best insight. For example, Daniel Inouye chooses to tell about what was happening in the Japanese government and Southeast Asia in 1939. You will discover why these details are of significance to the reader.

Dan's confrontation with the priest gives one picture of the Japanese people as narrow fanatics. But details in the account of Dan's mother's interview with the principal of the language school give another view of Japanese character.

How autobiographers handle their material is a matter of personal choice. Since they are writing about their own lives, they may be very selective and share with their readers only those things they wish known about themselves. They may fictionalize their stories to the extent that they re-create scenes by recalling conversations, thoughts, and actions as accurately as possible, or they may use an entirely factual approach and include documents to substantiate the information they give.

Biographers also have a choice in the way they handle their materials. They may limit themselves to facts alone—actual records, diaries, letters, interviews, authentic documents. Factual biographers never put words into their characters' mouths unless they have evidence the words were really spoken. Factual biography, however, is less popular than biography that is fictionalized to some extent. In fictionalizing biography, authors do painstaking research about their subjects and then put their information together with imagination. They may invent possible incidents and make up conversations in order to have their biographies read like stories. A skilled biographer can offer much insight into the character of the individuals about whom they have written.

In World War II, "Go for broke" was the battle cry of the legendary 442nd Regiment, which was made up of young Japanese-Americans. They fought so courageously for their country that they were called the most decorated outfit in the U.S. Army. One member of this outfit to be awarded the Distinguished Service Cross was Daniel Ken Inouye, whose heroism in action resulted in the loss of his right arm. When Hawaii attained statehood in 1959, he was sent to Congress as the first representative of the new state. He was at the same time the first American of Japanese descent to serve in either house of Congress. One of Dan Inouye's stories about his boyhood is of his mother dividing a single breakfast egg among a family of six. Although the Inouyes were poor and lived in a climate of racial prejudice and discrimination, Dan never wasted any time feeling sorry for himself—not even when he was taunted because he didn't wear shoes.

WHY DON'T YOU WEAR SHOES?
Daniel K. Inouye

I didn't wear shoes regularly until I was in high school—none of us *nisei*[1] kids did—and it was as much a matter of comfort as money. After all, this was Hawaii, a truly blessed place for a boy to grow up in.

We were a trial to our teachers, I'm sure. Many of them were *haoles*[2] from the Mainland, properly reared and educated young ladies, and they must have been disconcerted, to say the least, to be suddenly confronted with a ragtag crew of barefooted, sport-shirted kids whose English was liberally larded with Japanese, Chinese, Hawaiian and some exotic combinations of each. But they were a wonderfully dedicated group and they did their best to make educated Americans out of us young savages. And even more important, they accepted us on our own terms—they didn't despair over us, or patronize us, or slough us off as inferiors and hopeless delinquents. They treated us as exactly what we were, a bunch of kids from poor homes with hard-working parents, with a sort of built-in eagerness to become part of the mainstream of American life, and there is no way in which I can adequately express my thanks to them.

I loved school. Each day brought its own separate reward and learning became a constantly intriguing challenge. Of course when you're a boy there is always a danger of being tagged a bookworm and, in natural consequence, a sissy.

From the book JOURNEY TO WASHINGTON by Senator Daniel K. Inouye with Lawrence Elliott. © 1967 by Prentice-Hall, Inc. Published by Prentice-Hall, Inc., Englewood Cliffs, New Jersey 07632.

1. **nisei** (nē'sā'), one born in the United States of immigrant Japanese parents.
2. **haoles** (hou'lās, hou'lēs), Hawaiian for "white persons."

And so I was careful not to be caught studying or doing more homework than was absolutely necessary, and I warily cultivated a manner of dress and classroom manner that, even by our group's casual standard, was pretty flamboyant.

By this time we had returned to Coyne Street, in an area officially known as Bingham Tract but more readily recognizable by its popular name: Chinese Hollywood. Here Chinese families clustered together, and here came aspiring Americans from China with every new ship bound east from the Orient. The Inouyes were one of only two Japanese families in Bingham and, perhaps inevitably, we were soon virtually adopted by our sweet-natured neighbors. To this day I am known by our old neighbors as Ah-Danny-Jai, affectionate Chinese for little Danny.

As for me, I acquired a highly-cultivated taste for Chinese delicacies, not the least of which was dried water beetles. When these were roasted, the tails could be pulled from the body and made a delicious snack, like peanuts. One day, hungry as usual, I took a whole bagful of these morsels to school with me and whiled away the afternoon cracking them and stuffing the tasty tails into my mouth. So long as there was activity in the classroom I was safe, the teacher couldn't hear me and I took care that she didn't see me. But toward the end of the day, with all of us hushed in assigned study, the sharp crack of a beetle back sounded through the silent room like a rifle shot. Miss Dolton, who was blond and beautiful, looked up and I looked down. Miss Dolton looked down and—CRACK—went another beetle.

"Dan!"

"Gmmm?" I mumbled, my mouth stuffed with tails.

"Are you *eating* something?"

I nodded, trying to express an apology with my eyes alone.

"Well!" said the proper young lady indignantly. "You know the rule about eating in class. Now you may bring whatever it is you have there up to me and I will take my share and pass it around to the class."

Now, as you can see, this was truly punishment to fit the crime—forcing any of us kids to give up food was like shredding a tobacco addict's last cigarette. Crushed and contrite, and still unable to speak a word in my defense, I carried my precious bag up front and deposited it on Miss Dolton's desk. Whereupon she righteously reached in, produced a beetle and, on the verge of popping it into her mouth, caught sight of what she was holding and delivered herself of a shriek that, they say, was heard on the far side of Diamond Head.[3] Into the wastebasket went my bag—punishment enough!—and back to my seat I marched, directed by Miss Dolton's quivering finger. Years later, when I went back to see her, we had many laughs over my school days. But when I brought up the matter of the Chinese water beetles, the same look of dread crossed her face, and she said, "Oh, Dan, how could you!"

The trouble I got into at Japanese language school was something more serious and crystallized for me, once and for all, the matter of who I was and where in this cultural melting pot I was headed. Most of my contemporaries quit at the end of the tenth year, by which

3. **Diamond Head,** a famous, inactive volcano.

time they had a fair grounding in Japanese history and tradition. In deference to my grandparents, I suppose, I was enrolled for the eleventh grade and sat through excruciatingly long afternoons listening to lectures on the sacredness of the royal family and being admonished to preserve the centuries-old customs of my people. Then, all in one cataclysmic afternoon, I unburdened myself of my smoldering resentment and, in consequence, was flung bodily from the classroom, never to return.

The year was 1939 and already times had turned tense in the Far East. The Japanese government was in the iron grip of fanatic warlords and the Imperial Army was waging aggressive war in China and menacing all of Southeast Asia. Day after day, the priest who taught us ethics and Japanese history hammered away at the divine prerogatives of the Emperor, and at the grand destiny that called on the Japanese people to extend their sway over the yellow race, and on the madness that was inducing the American government to oppose them. He would tilt his menacing crew-cut skull at us and solemnly proclaim, "You must remember that only a trick of fate has brought you so far from your homeland, but there must be no question of your loyalty. When Japan calls, you must know that it is Japanese blood that flows in your veins."

I had heard his jingoistic[4] little speeches so many times that I suppose they no longer really registered on me. He was an old man, to be respected for his station, but when he began spouting nonsense I could easily tune him out. But one day he shifted his scorn to the Bible and I reacted by instinct—and violently.

He had been discussing the inadequacy of Christianity compared to Shintoism, the state religion of Japan, and already my hackles were up. Then he favored us with an elaborate grin and, mockery dripping from his every word, he said, "I give you the Bible itself as the best evidence of this Christian foolishness. Their God made the world in seven days, it says. Ha! Then he made a man and from a rib of that man—a rib, mark you!—he made a woman. Ha! Anyone with only part of a brain can see that this is the wildest nonsense!"

I never realized that I was on my feet and shouting until I saw the grin on his face twist, first into astonishment, and then into fury. Then my words echoed in my head:

"That's not right! That's not fair! I am a Christian, a lot of us here are, and you mustn't talk that way! I respect your faith. You must respect mine."

"How dare you!" he roared.

"I do. I do dare! You have no right to make fun of my beliefs."

"You are a Japanese! You will believe what I. . . ."

"I am an American!"

He flinched, exactly as though I had struck him. With a single compulsive jerk, he threw the book he had been holding through the open window, and we watched the pages flutter in the wind for a moment. Then he started toward me, and the class watched in silent terror, and his face was black as a thunderhead and his mouth worked violently as he cried, "You are a Japanese!" Now his fin-

---

4. **jingoistic** (jing′gō is′tik), supporting a warlike policy against other nations.

gers clutched at my open collar and he was shaking me back and forth. "Say it!" he screamed into my face. "You are a Japanese!"

And barely able to bring my voice up out of my tortured throat, I muttered, "I—am—an—American."

With that, he lifted me from my feet and half-dragged, half-carried me to the door, and he threw me with full force into the schoolyard. "You are a faithless dog!" he screamed, and slammed the door closed.

Dazed and trembling, I stumbled to my feet. My trousers were torn and one knee was scraped and bleeding. Crazily, my first thought was how to hide this from my mother. But I had only taken a few steps toward home when I realized that I didn't want to hide it. I had had all I could take of that Japanese teacher and if it took this catastrophe—and the punishment I was sure to get for it—to free me, well, so be it.

But, of course, I had underestimated my mother again. She took one look at my tattered pants and the mutinous expression I wore, and she demanded the whole story. And I told it to her, and all the time I spoke she was washing and bandaging my skinned knee, so that I could not see her face and could not gauge how she was reacting to this great crisis in my life. But when I was all finished, she got to her feet and said, "Come, we are going back there."

This was something more than I had bargained for. Maybe I had used up my day's supply of bravery, but the fact is that I had no desire to face the priest's wrath again. "Mama," I began hesitantly. . . .

She shushed me. "You have nothing to fear or to be ashamed of," she said crisply. "But there is a matter of honor to be settled."

Nor did she waste any time on the teacher. Instead, she went directly to the office of the principal, a gentle and distinguished Japanese. And Mother stood before his desk, a tiny figure whose massive indignation strengthened her words, and she told him exactly what happened. "I do not send him here to become a Shintoist or a samurai.[5] I want him to learn the language and traditions of his ancestors, but we are Americans and shall always remain so."

Amazingly, he nodded his agreement. He would speak to the priest, he assured my mother. There would be no more such authoritarian teaching, and I could return to my class without fear of retribution.

"That is up to Ken," my mother said looking straight at me and using, as she almost always did, my Japanese name. "He is old enough now to decide this for himself."

And I said, "I don't want to go back. I've learned enough about the old ways." My mother thanked the principal for hearing her out, and we left, and for the first time, I suppose, I knew what it was to *feel* like an American. . . .

It was in my sophomore year in high school that I first came under the warm and rewarding spell of Mrs. Ruth King, a teacher whose influence in my young life ranked just behind that of my mother

---

5. **Shintoist or a samurai** (sam′ů rī′). A **Shintoist** is a member of the Shinto religion, the native faith of Japan. A **samurai** is a soldier belonging to the hereditary military class in Japan.

and father. She certainly didn't look inspiring, a short, plump lady in her middle forties with graying hair and eyes that seemed to look vaguely out from behind a pair of rimless glasses and to see practically nothing. But the truth was that she saw practically everything, surely nothing of any real importance that happened in her classroom escaped her notice.

Hers was the top tenth-grade class at McKinley High. I don't know how I got into it and, from the very first day, I wanted out. In place of all my old live-and-let-live buddies from Moiliili and McCully, I found myself rubbing shoulders with a breed of kids who kept trying to pretend that their skin was white and their eyes were blue. And there in the midst of this pretense, surrounded by all those starched white shirts and shined shoes, was rough-and-tumble Dan Inouye, to whom a necktie was a garrote on the spirit, and shoes an encumbrance to be suffered through at funerals and in church.

In those days, McKinley High School was jokingly referred to as Tokyo High. Thanks to an ingenious system of segregation, nearly all of us there were of Japanese ancestry, and from the least affluent *nisei* families, at that. It worked through a device known as the English Standard School and neatly sidestepped the law that, theoretically, opened all the public schools to everyone regardless of race, color or creed. To be admitted to an English Standard School—which by invariable coincidence had better facilities and better faculties—one had to pass an examination. The written part was fair enough since everyone had an equal chance. But the oral test served as an automatic weeding-out factor, for rare indeed was the student of Asian parentage who could properly pronounce the "th" sound, the "r" and the "l." The obvious result was that the English Standard Schools became almost the exclusive province of Caucasian youngsters, and that handful of Japanese and Chinese whose parents could afford to give them private tutoring. Not until 1955 was the last of this subtle segregation eliminated from Hawaii's public school system.

I was too young and unknowing then to be troubled by the concept of "Tokyo High." Only my stiff-necked classmates bothered me and sometimes it seemed that the only person who ever talked to me in that grade was Mrs. King. "Your grammar leaves something to be desired, Dan," she would say to me privately. "Why don't you stay after school today and we'll work on it?" And I would, happily, because to be in her presence was suddenly to glimpse something beyond the narrow horizons of the life I'd known, to sense that being a clerk, or even a beach boy, was not the ultimate and only hope for a kid like me. She took me seriously, which is something that no one, not even I myself, had ever done.

All at once literature was exciting and history was real. Washington and Jefferson and Lincoln suddenly stepped out of some mythical haze and became men of flesh and blood, men with great problems and the great courage to face them. I felt the bitter cold and despair of that winter at Valley Forge. I felt a sharp sense of personal loss at the death of Lincoln, the lost opportunity to bind up the nation's wounds. Whereas Japanese history had always sounded like some great impersonal pageant, the story of America had the ring of an adventure in human progress, troubles and setbacks and the inexorable march down to the present.

But most important of all, I came to believe that the giants who made American history were *my* forefathers. Always before, I had been a little embarrassed singing about the "land where my fathers died," and I always spoke of *the* fathers of *the* country. It was Mrs. King who, in some wonderfully subtle way, convinced me of the essential relationship between America's founding fathers and all of America's people.

In midyear, Mrs. King recommended me for membership in McKinley's two junior honor societies, the Torch Society and the McKinley Citizenship Club. My mother and father glowed with pride and although I tried to pretend that it didn't

matter to me one way or the other, the truth is that I was really excited by the prospect. On the appointed afternoon, beaming with good fellowship, I strode up before the Student Council for my interview. They sat behind a long table, four seniors trying to look as stern as bankers. They didn't ask me to sit down.

"Why do you think you belong in an honor society?" one of them asked.

I shrugged. "It was Mrs. King's idea. I . . . ."

"Why don't you wear shoes?" another suddenly shot at me, a Japanese kid I'd known for at least five years.

"Because I only have one pair," I said to him. "They have to last." It was a silly question, he knew I only had one pair. He probably even knew that they'd been

bought two years ago, and bought two sizes too large so I wouldn't grow out of them, and that until only recently I'd had to stuff the toes with paper to keep them on.

But the silly questions were only beginning. "Why don't you wear a white shirt?" they asked. "Why don't you wear a tie?"

I didn't know what to say. I looked from one to the other, a gathering fear inside me, like dirty fingers squeezing my stomach. What was this all about? I thought they were going to interview me about my interests and ideas, about my schoolwork maybe. Why did they care what I wore?

"Are you going to answer the question?"

"I don't know," I said. "My shirt is for church. . . ."

"Don't you care how you look in school?"

Not wanting to, I looked down at my sports shirt and my denim pants and bare feet. "My clothes are clean," I mumbled. "I don't know what's wrong."

"What about your friends?" one of them barked, and rattled off a list of kids from my neighborhood. "Are *they* your friends?"

"Yes," I said, and all at once I knew that they were going to turn me down. "What's the matter with them?"

"Delinquents!"

"Because they don't wear shoes?" I said, and it was not a question. "Because they're poor? They're no more delinquents than I am. Or you are." All the disappointment, all the fear had suddenly boiled up in anger, and when they tried to interrupt me I shouted them down: "Hey, listen, I thought this was an honor society—honor, scholarship. But if all you're looking for is guys who wear white shirts and shoes, you don't want me and I for sure don't want you. I wouldn't trade one of my friends for . . . for both your honor societies and all four of you, so just forget the whole thing!"

For a long, long time afterward I would stiffen with an inner fury every time I remembered those moments of humiliation, and I remembered them often. Nor was that the end of it. Somehow I had to explain to my parents that I had not been accepted into the honor societies without telling them the real reasons, for they would then have blamed themselves. So I stammered and stuttered through some lame explanation that fooled them not a bit, and their eyes grew sad and there was no more for any of us to say. As for Mrs. King, who seemed to know everything there was to know about my unhappy encounter with the Council without my saying a word, she was so deeply hurt by their behavior that not once in my next year at McKinley High did she recommend another candidate for the Torch Society or the McKinley Citizenship Club.

But the most important effect of the entire episode was to convince me of the essential truth of that old saw about it being an ill wind that blows no good. It left me enraged and a little confused, but most of all it left me with a fiery resolve to "show those guys!" Never before had I felt so challenged, nor so determined to make something of myself. As a matter of fact, I don't think it's unfair to say that those four snobbish seniors are at least partly responsible for whatever successes I subsequently enjoyed. Their faces stuck in my mind, and do to this day, and for years afterward I charged at every obstacle in my path as though those four had personally put it there and it was absolutely essential for me to overcome it to prove that shoes and neckties were no measure of a man.

READING FOR DETAILS

An Insult Long Remembered

Whatever Daniel Inouye has set out to do over the years, he has brought honor to himself and to his family. One wonders just how much of his success can be credited to those four snobbish seniors who refused him admittance to the junior honor societies.

1. What is the name given people of Japanese descent born in the United States? What racial mixtures were predominant in Dan's school and home associations?
2. Why did Dan get into trouble at the Japanese language school?
3. How did Mrs. King show her interest in Dan? What happened when she recommended him for membership in McKinley's two junior honor societies?
4. How did Mrs. King feel about Dan's experience at the hands of the students on the council?

READING FOR MEANING

Find evidence in the selection to support the following statements:

1. It is better to be an individualist than a conformist.
2. What you become is up to you.
3. A negative experience can have positive results.

READING FOR APPRECIATION

Characterization

1. Paragraph three gives insight into Daniel Inouye's way of thinking that shows why he later became a very good politician. Discuss.
2. What trait of character does Dan strongly display in both the episode in the Japanese language school and the honor society interview?
3. Which characterization technique does the author employ most heavily in giving the reader an idea of what Dan's mother is like?

Significant Detail

1. What ingenious system made McKinley into a segregated high school? How did the students in the top tenth-grade class here differ from those Dan was used to associating with in Moiliili and McCully?
2. How did Dan feel about the statesmen he read about in American history? Why is this information significant?

COMPOSITION

Select one of the three statements in Reading for Meaning and argue *for* or *against* the statement in a brief essay. Be certain to include sufficient details to support your point of view.

BIOGRAPHICAL NOTE

Daniel K. Inouye (1924–   ) was born in Honolulu. As a boy he dreamed of becoming a physician and had begun medical studies at the University of Hawaii when World War II interrupted his work. Following rehabilitation from war wounds, he completed his law degree at George Washington University. His career in national public life began in 1959 when he was elected to Congress.

When she was eight, Louise had to have her right leg amputated above the knee because she took "an unauthorized spin" on a neighbor's red bicycle and collided with a car. Grandma has unusual concerns about Louise's future. It may have been the strenuous lesson Louise learned at fifteen that kept Grandma's fears from being realized.

BEST FOOT FORWARD

Louise Baker

Grandma said it was an outrage. "One of two terrible things will happen," she predicted. "She'll either kill herself, or worse yet, she'll get along fine and end up in vaudeville. We've had six clergymen, a smattering of lawyers and doctors and a raft of school teachers and good honest farmers in this family. We've never had a show girl!"

"What about our Great-great-great-cousin Thaddeus?" Bernice demanded, just to keep things interesting.

"Hah! That was on your mother's side." Grandmother nodded her head with satisfaction. "And even that rascal wasn't a show girl."

"But he was a perfectly marvelous outlaw and shot a man in cold blood," I bragged. "That's just as bad."

"It's not just as bad," Grandma stated with finality.

"Now, listen to me, Mother." On rare occasions Father was bold enough to stand up to Grandma. "We're off the subject. Louise is nine years old and she wants some roller skates for her birthday. Is there anything so strange in that? Bernice[1] had roller skates when she was nine."

"That's different. Bernice didn't make an unnatural spectacle of herself using them. Everyone will stare, and first thing you know, Louise will become a disgusting little exhibitionist and skate off with a carnival or something and you'll never see her again. It's a pity she isn't a little lady, content to learn to sew and do water colors and read good literature. I never skated when I was her age, and I had both my limbs."

When Grandmother spoke of her own legs, she called them limbs, as if they were slightly more refined than ordinary appendages.

In reality Grandmother wasn't the sharp-bladed battle-ax she pretended. She was really fond of me and every new hurdle I wanted to leap seemed twice as hazardous to her as the last one.

But Father bought me the skates. I had already experimented with Barbara Bradley's and knew I could manage. With a skate on my one foot and a crutch on each side, I propelled myself. My balance was exceptional—as is most every uniped's. This is a natural physical compensation that develops quickly—as do strong shoulders and arms. After a few

From OUT ON A LIMB by Louise Baker, McGraw-Hill. Copyright © 1946 Louise Baker. By permission of the author, Louise Baker.

1. **Bernice,** Louise's older sister.

good shoves, I could lift up my crutches and coast along easily on the one skate, pushing with my sticks only when I needed fresh momentum. For a child of nine, supposedly sentenced to a plodding pedestrianism, getting back on wheels was sheer ecstasy.

Of course, I fell frequently while developing skill on roller skates. Every child sprawls when learning to skate. I am not convinced that I spread myself out on the sidewalk any more often than a normal child does. But this is the curious fact: my playmates, wise in their childhood, accepted my spills as inevitable to the process of learning—but adults didn't. No army of rescuers advanced double-quick time to pick up any other youngster on the block when he came a cropper.[2] But whenever I took a header, for all the turmoil the minor catastrophe created, it might have been a four-car smashup at a busy intersection. All the women in our neighborhood must have squandered their days with their eyes glued to a crack in the window blind while I learned to roller skate. For a brief time, I was as prominent as a lurid scandal.

Whenever I fell, out swarmed the women in droves, clucking and fretting like a bunch of bereft mother hens. It was kind of them, and in retrospect I appreciate their solicitude, but at the time I resented and was greatly embarrassed by their interference. It set me apart and emphasized my difference. For they assumed that no routine hazard to skating—no stick or stone—upset my flying wheels. It was a foregone conclusion that *I* fell because I was a poor, helpless cripple.

"What must her mother *think!*" was a phrase with which I became very familiar. I know now what my mother thought. Inside our house, she too kept her eye on the crack in the blind, and she wrung her hands and took to biting her fingernails while she developed a lot of fortitude. For Mother differed from the other women in only one particular. She never ran out and picked me up. I believe that Father, a normally devoted husband, threatened homicide if she did.

Eventually, of course, nobody paid any attention to me. The women abandoned their watchful vigils at windows and went back to more pressing problems—their baking and dishwashing. I rolled up and down the street unheeded and was no longer good box office.

However, the roller-skating incident left its mark on me, and consciously or unconsciously, it influenced my future approach to physical activity. I was by nature energetic and athletic. I wanted to engage in all sorts of "inappropriate" games and sports, but I became overly sensitive to failure—foolishly so. I had a stubborn pride that was wounded by any hint that my handicap was a "handicap." It really wasn't much of one, compared to the frustrating handicaps many less fortunate people carry. Still I was practically neurotic over The Word.[3] My feathers ruffled at the drop of it. A wise psychologist friend of mine has since put a name on this attitude of mind. She called it a tendency to overcompensate.[4]

When I learned to swim, I insisted that Father drive me out to the country to

---

2. **came a cropper,** fell.
3. **The Word:** "handicap."
4. **a tendency to overcompensate.** Louise was so overly sensitive about failing at anything because of her handicap that she outdid herself to prove she could do as well as a normal person.

a friend's ranch where, in guarded privacy, I went through my dog-paddling period in a muddy irrigation ditch. I forewent the greater comfort and the companionship of the public swimming pool until I not only swam as well as other eleven-year-olds (the age at which I took to the water), but better. Then, when I made a public appearance, no one even noticed my handicap—I falsely deduced.

My swimming ability, in point of fact, probably was more conspicuous than utter ineptitude would have been. But blissfully, I had no such realization. In the water, my arms and shoulders, disciplined into extra strength by my crutches, compensated in the Australian crawl for my one-cylinder flutter kick. I felt completely anonymous—happy moron, me! Actually, I wasn't the least bit anonymous, although my family encouraged me in this wild surmise. My sister tells me that my red bathing cap, bobbing about in the water, was invariably pointed out to bystanders. "See the little girl in the red cap? Would you believe it, she only has one leg!"

The same was true of tennis, which I learned in semisecrecy. Father taught me in the early morning hours when the courts were unpopular. My father didn't permit me to luxuriate in a lot of fancy complexes, but he was sympathetic with my reluctance to display physical clumsiness. Tennis presents more limitations for an amputee than swimming. The basic constraint is the necessity of holding one crutch with just the upper arm, leaving a hand free to manipulate a racket. I heard of a man with a left leg amputation who played tennis with only one crutch. I always used two since I am both right-handed and right-crutched and could

not control both a racket and a completely weight-bearing crutch with one arm.

In spite of restrictions, I did fairly well at tennis as a child. I even competed, with average success, in a few junior tournaments. This brief period of minor distinction was not the result of exceptional skill, however. It was rather the happy aftermath of the advantage of earlier and better instruction than my contemporaries. Father was a very able tennis amateur. He was infinitely patient in developing in me a good serve and a strong, deep-court drive to offset my inadequate technique at the net. In playing tennis, I discovered that it is essential to hug the serving line. It is easy to run forward, but not backward, on crutches. I am completely vulnerable at the net or even mid-court where a lob over my head spells defeat. I can't readily retreat to get it on the bounce, and the alternative, a high aerial stroke, invariably makes me drop a crutch.

I enjoy tennis very much, but stacking up all the good points of my game against the poor ones, I come out a mediocre performer. "A good, average housewife tennis player," someone dubbed me— and that is no enviable distinction. I usually compete with people who are better than I, so am rarely victorious—which is perhaps just as well.

Friends who know me, and with whom I play frequently, don't care whether I win or lose. We just play tennis. Some of them avoid cutting and lobs because it keeps our game more rallying, but they are in no way offensively patronizing to me.

Pit a stranger against me, however— especially a male stranger—and he will methodically do one of two things, according to his basic character. He will make the gallant gesture and let me win—which is easily detected and humiliating. Or, he will kill himself before admitting defeat by a one-legged woman.

I once confronted across a net, by the conniving conspiracy of some school friends, a boy who was notoriously cocky on the tennis court. The essence of the cunning plot was that I must defeat this self-advertising fire-eater so ignominiously and completely that he would never again hold up his arrogant head. I had no confidence in my ability to do this and, frankly, neither did my conspiring boy friends. It was such a superb scheme, however, that they were all willing to co-operate on its success. They concluded that if I won, it would be magnificent irony—a baby stealing candy from a man, for a change.

Two boys were assigned to pound away at my backhand for a week, and spies reported my unsuspecting enemy's weaknesses and strengths. He was definitely not the ball of fire he advertised, but he was better than I, it was mournfully agreed. However, everyone hoped that I could at least give him enough competition to make him feel foolish. I was pledged to outplay myself, even if I folded in complete collapse.

I didn't even know Charlie, the victim, but it all seemed solemnly important to me at the time. I was fifteen, and the prime-mover in the plot was a very handsome muscular gent of seventeen for whose smallest favor I would gladly have given my last leg.

By the most contrived casualness, I was introduced to Charlie at the tennis courts, where he was loudly quoting what Bill Tilden[5] said to him and what smart repartee he handed Bill. The game was arranged. We had decided to contract for only one set, as my well-wishers, in their wildest dreams, didn't hope I'd last longer than that.

In analyzing mine and my opponent's weaknesses, one great big one was overlooked. The outcome of that game was not traceable to technique and tenacity and my newly polished backhand, although all these helped, no doubt. The game was won on temper—both mine and Charlie's. To start with, Charlie's first sentence contained fighting words, as far as I was concerned. He said, with a patronizing air, "Sure, I'll take her on if you guys don't want to bother. I don't mind a bit."

I let this go by unchallenged. I merely seethed. Then he suggested that he should be handicapped[6] if he played me. "I'll give you fifteen," he offered pompously. This was red flag to my bull!

"Pooh! I'll give *you* thirty," I counter-offered. This was red flag to his bull!

We marched out on the court as mad as if we'd just blacked each other's eyes. Temper warms up my reflexes, but it completely melted Charlie's. He belonged to the racket-throwing persuasion.[7]

I must have been dropped on my head as a baby. I can't imagine any other explanation for squandering exertion as extravagantly as I did on that occasion. I

---

5. **Bill Tilden** (1893–1953), outstanding tennis player through the 1920s and into the 1940s.
6. **handicapped.** Charlie suggested that he give Louise the first point, scored 15, in each game of the set. Louise, in a huff, offers to give *him* double that.
7. **racket-throwing persuasion.** Charlie threw his racket when upset.

wouldn't work that hard today if I were promised the Davis Cup[8] for keeps. Somehow, I got the psychotic notion embedded in my half-a-mind that nothing mattered so much as beating Charlie.

As soon as Charlie and I spun for serve,[9] all the tennis games in progress on the other courts stopped immediately, and the players became our spectators. They all belonged in my camp and they helped me by none-too-sporting maneuvers. They worked poor Charlie into impotent fury by catcalls and other impertinences.

When he missed a shot or netted a serve, they'd all yell, "What's s'matter, got a Charlie—*Horse?*" This was regarded in our high school intellectual circles as overpoweringly witty. Everyone hooted and howled.

"Maybe *you* need some crutches, Charlie!"

8. **Davis Cup,** the cup awarded the team winning the international tennis championship.
9. **spun for serve.** Players spin a racket to determine who will first hit the ball (serve) to an opponent. In the spin the player calls for either the rough or smooth side of the spinning racket, much as other players call for one side of a flipped coin.

"Fault!"[10] they'd yell before Charlie's serves even bounced. To ensure a modicum of fair play, I had to call all the shots[11] myself.

In spite of the tremendous nuisance value of my audience and the demoralizing effect on Charlie of his own temper, I had a desperate time beating him. We ran the set, most of the games long deuce-score ordeals, to twelve-ten before I won.[12]

When it was over, my breath was coming in rattling gasps and I looked like a dripping hot beet just out of a stew pot and dragged home by an insensitive cat. Charlie walked off the court and broke up his racket by bashing it against a steel post. He wasn't a very lofty character.

I rode a brief wave of delirious ecstasy while a crowd of what I regarded as exceedingly smooth boys banged me on my aching back and shouted my praises. Then I staggered home to soak my weary heroic bones in a hot tub.

Father peered at me over his paper as I came in and collapsed on the davenport.[13]

"Good heavens!" he gasped. Father did not ordinarily use such expressions so I must have resembled a sister of Grim Death.

"What in a holy name have you been doing?"

"I beat Charlie," I puffed proudly. "Been practicing for over a week to do it."

"Well—you look as if *you'd* been beaten—by a bunch of strong-armed thugs. Why was it so important to beat Charlie?"

"Because he's so cocky—that's why. Jerry and Frazier and Donald Manker and some other kids thought it up and planned the whole thing."

"Why didn't Frazier beat him?" Father asked with deliberate denseness. "Frazier's the best player in high school."

"Father!" I groaned. "That wouldn't have meant anything. It had to be me."

"Oh—because you're a girl. I see." Father again used his annoying simpleminded ruse. "Why didn't Helen Fitzgerald take on this Charlie? She's twice the tennis player you are. She could have beaten him without getting apoplexy."[14]

"Oh, for goodness' sake, Father, are you dumb or something? Can't you see how much worse this dope would feel having *me* beat him?"

"I get it." Father sighed deeply. "Well, all I can say is that I'm disappointed in you."

"Disappointed in me! Every single person in this whole town thinks I'm wonderful, that's all!"

"Well, I don't!" Father snapped. "I thought you'd long since decided it wasn't sporting to take advantage of people because of your crutches."

"Father—for heaven's sake, what's the matter with you? I didn't take advantage of him. I beat him fair and square. He played just as hard as he could. The score was twelve-ten—that shows you. The kids called a lot of the shots wrong but I corrected every time in Charlie's favor. And he offered me a fifteen hand-

10. **Fault,** term used when a player fails to serve the ball into the proper court area.
11. **call . . . shots.** Louise announced whether Charlie's shots landed in or out of bounds.
12. **We ran the set . . . won.** The players were so evenly matched that the score was often tied (deuce), thus the game was continued until one player won by getting two points in succession.
13. **davenport,** a long sofa.
14. **apoplexy,** a stroke, caused by injury to the brain when a blood vessel breaks or the blood supply becomes obstructed.

icap but I threw it right back in his face."

"You certainly salted his wounds, didn't you?"

I stared, incredulous, at Father.

"You know . . ." Father paused to frown at me. "You present a very complex moral problem and I don't have any good precedents to follow in rearing you properly. But of *this* I am convinced: you took greater advantage of that boy today than if you'd frankly cheated him. You had a physical and personality advantage over him that must have made his defeat insufferable. If he'd beaten you twelve-ten, you'd have walked off the court the victor, just the same."

"That's absolutely silly!" I protested, although this was true and I knew it. We'd counted on just that in our ingenious plot.

"It's complicated, I grant you, but not silly. This isn't complicated, however. I'm glad you can swim and play tennis and ride a horse, but the only reason I'm glad is because these things are fun. That's why you and everyone else is supposed to do them. When you play a game just to demonstrate what hot stuff you are on your crutches, it's time you quit and took up china painting, as your grandmother would have you do. Remember Grandma and your first roller skates? She was afraid you'd join a carnival if you learned to skate. Well—for my money, you were too close to the carnival for comfort today."

"Honestly, Father, you *surprise* me!" I protested even as my mind touched the peculiarly devious truth toward which he was leading me. "I suppose you just never want me to win anything," I continued perversely.

"Of course, I want you to win—but only the game. Now, beat it! Take a bath and go to bed. Get out of my sight. I can't stand you."

I started to cry as I left the room.

"By the way, you must have played inspired tennis today," Father called after me.

"I was hot, all right. I played much better than I am able to play."

"Hum . . ." Father sighed with what seemed almost wistfulness. "I wouldn't have minded seeing that game."

"You'd have put a stop to it though, I suppose—You and your ideas!"

"That's right," agreed Father, "I would have."

He was furious enough with me to cheerfully shake out my molars. But at the same time, reluctantly and in spite of himself, he was proud. The ethics of being crippled were, I decided, exceedingly complicated and obscure. But clear enough, nevertheless, that I never bragged to anyone about beating Charlie.

READING FOR DETAILS

A Questionable Victory

Louise Baker was so determined not to be a "poor, helpless cripple" that she learned to do with one leg what many people are unable to do with two. She wanted no pity.

1. Why did Louise learn to swim and play tennis in semisecrecy? Why was tennis more difficult for her than swimming or skating?

2. In a tennis match, what two kinds of behavior had she come to expect from boys she didn't know well? Why did her friends arrange to have her play Charlie?

3. Why was she able to beat Charlie?

READING FOR MEANING

Discuss whether you find support for all of the following concepts in "Best Foot Forward."

1. Pity breeds weakness.
2. The human body compensates for its inadequacies.
3. Children show more natural wisdom than adults.
4. There is the danger of using a handicap to satisfy one's ego.

READING FOR APPRECIATION

Significant Detail

Reader interest in the tennis match is increased greatly by the author's use of specific detail.

1. What was Charlie bragging about when the match was arranged?
2. What patronizing statement does he make about playing Louise?
3. What exchange puts them both into a bad temper?
4. When Charlie plays badly, what does the crowd yell?
5. How does Louise say she looked at the end of the match? What was Charlie's characteristic action?

COMPOSITION

Now sharpen your biographical writing skill. Think of a particular situation in which you and your family were involved that caused discussion and differences of opinion. Perhaps the situation developed outside of your immediate family, involving an aunt, an uncle, or a cousin.

As you recall what transpired, try to recapture what the various characters said. Be sure you enter the conversation as the first-person narrator, the *I* of your sketch.

As you write, try to use at least three of the characterization techniques given. In your concluding paragraph let your reader know how you felt about the situation and the principal character, or characters, involved.

BIOGRAPHICAL NOTE

Louise Baker (1909–   ) was born in California, attended schools there, and later studied at Columbia University. She has been a newspaper reporter, a teacher in a boys' school, and a staff member of the Fels Research Foundation at Antioch College in Ohio. She has also served on the executive board of the National Society for Crippled Children. Her short stories have appeared in many magazines and her books have been widely read.

When George Washington Carver arrived at Tuskegee
Institute in 1896, the laboratory was a barren room and there
was no equipment and no money to buy any. But the quiet
scientist, who had learned early in life to make something
from nothing, set about constructing laboratory equipment
from the scrap heaps and junk piles in the community.
He had something more important than money and shining
equipment. Discover what he had and what he did with it.
This account was written a few years before Dr. Carver's death.

A BOY WHO WAS TRADED
FOR A HORSE

James Saxon Childers

The stooped old Negro trudged along through the dust of an Alabama road at a curiously rapid rate. He was carrying an armful of sticks and wild flowers.

The sticks I could understand—he would use them for kindling—but I had never before seen an old black man ambling along a road at nine o'clock in the morning with swamp roses, wild geranium, and creeping buttercups mingled with a lot of dry sticks.

When I got a little closer to him I saw that he was wearing a saggy coat which originally might have been a green alpaca, but which the sun had faded until I couldn't be sure about the color; there were so many patches that I couldn't even be certain about the material.

The old man was walking towards a large brick building, one of the buildings of Tuskegee Institute, the famous school for Negroes at Tuskegee, Alabama.[1] His thin body bent by the years, his hair white beneath a ragged cap, he seemed pathetically lost on the campus of a great modern educational institution.

At the entrance of the building toward which we were both walking, the old Negro turned in. "He's probably the janitor," I told myself, "and I'm sincerely glad that they've given him a job of some kind."

I stepped into the hallway. I saw a trim little secretary hurry toward the bent old Negro. I heard her say to him, "That delegation from Washington is waiting for you, Doctor Carver."

Dr. George Washington Carver, the very man I had come to see! Fantastic and unbelievable as it seemed, this old man with his armful of sticks and wild flowers was none other than the distinguished Negro scientist of Tuskegee Institute. A discoverer renowned far and wide for his chemical wizardry in creating useful new products from such stuff as peanut shells and fallen leaves which most of us waste and throw away. An in-

---

Reprinted by permission of James Saxon Childers.

1. **Tuskegee** (təs kē′gē) **Institute** is in the city of Tuskegee in eastern Alabama.

ventor acclaimed for his genius in transforming such common things as peanuts, sweet potatoes, and even the clay of the earth, into things of uncommon value for our everyday needs.

That saggy alpaca coat covered a Bachelor of Science, Master of Science, Honorary Doctor of Science, winner of the Spingarn Medal for Negro achievement, member of the Royal Society for the Encouragement of Arts, Manufactures and Commerce of Great Britain.

Yet as I looked at him, studied his kindly face, and recalled what I had heard of the story of his life, I saw that the figure of the man himself was not half so fantastic or unbelievable as is the record of his achievement.

Dr. George Washington Carver started with nothing. He never had anything. Yet out of nothing he has created inestimable wealth for fellow human beings to whom he has devoted his life.

Born a slave child, he began life without even so much as a name. He never knew his father. He never knew his mother. To this day he doesn't know just when he was born, though he figures his age at somewhere close to seventy. Without a red cent he worked out his own early schooling, then his higher college education, then the postgraduate work for his Master of Science degree. All his life he has been joyously at work with common, everyday things, making something out of nothing, or next to nothing. During the thirty-six years in which he has been Director of Agricultural Research at Tuskegee Institute, that has been his work. And out of it have come scientific marvels:

From wood shavings he has made synthetic marble.

From peanut shells he has made insulating walls for houses.

From the muck of swamps and the leaves of the forest floor he has made valuable fertilizers.

From cow dung he has made paint.

From the common, ordinary peanut he has made 285 useful products, including milk, butter, cheese, candies, instant coffee, pickles, sauces, oils, shaving lotions, wood stains, dyes, lard, linoleum, flour, breakfast foods, soap, stock foods, face powder, tan remover, shampoo, printer's ink, and even axle grease!

From the lowly sweet potato he has made 118 products, among them flour, meal, starch, library paste, vinegar, shoe blacking, ginger, ink, rubber compound, chocolate compound, dyes, molasses, wood filler, caramels.

From clays of the earth he has made nonfading paints and pigments.

From worn-out sandy soil he has produced paying crops.

Something from nothing. And this is only a portion of his work. Experts say that he has probably done more than any other living man to rehabilitate agriculture in the South.

And more still. Doctor Carver is also an artist, especially skilled in painting flowers. His paintings have been exhibited at world fairs, and at least one is going to the Luxembourg Gallery in Paris after his death. He makes all his own paints, using Alabama clays. The paper he paints on he makes from peanut shells, and the frames for his pictures he makes out of corn husks. His work in embroidery and crochet has won prizes in various exhibits. He has woven gorgeous rugs with fibers he had made from cotton stalks. He is a skilled musician, too—once he toured the Middle West as a concert pianist. And last, but not least, he is an expert cook. His recipes are used today in some of the leading hotels of the country.

All this does sound a bit incredible, doesn't it? I confess that when I set out for Tuskegee to see and talk with Doctor Carver, I was more than skeptical of many of the stories I had heard about him. And so, after he had entertained the visiting delegation from Washington, I returned to see him, in his office in the big brick building, with many doubts lingering in my mind.

He was sitting behind a desk cluttered inches high with letters and papers. On top of the papers were the sticks and wild flowers that I had seen him carrying that morning. As I went in, he was looking through a microscope at the stems of a wild rose.

"I beg your pardon," I said.

The old man raised his head and looked at me; then, taking hold of the edge of the desk to steady himself, he pushed himself up from his squeaky swivel chair. He wore a long canvas apron that was splotched and stained. His gold-rimmed spectacles rested far down on his nose. Standing there so tall despite his noticeable stoop, he peered over the tops of his spectacles and smiled at me.

"Good morning," he said, and the quiet tone of his voice blended with the gentle sincerity of his smile.

In slight confusion, then, I explained why I had called on him. "People tell me that I couldn't possibly write a story about Tuskegee unless I wrote a lot about you," I added.

The old Negro grinned with the genuine shyness that has kept him so long

hidden from the public. "People are too kind to me," he insisted. "I'm really a very small part of this institution. Won't you sit down?"

I was touched by his gentleness, and by an unmistakable spiritual quality in the glow of his face. Frankly, I was confused. To open the conversation, I remarked on the numerous Maxfield Parrish[2] paintings that hang on his office walls. "Somehow they seem a little out of place in the office of a scientist," I said lamely.

"But can't a scientist be a lover of the beautiful?" he asked. "There is no one of the moderns who uses blue half so well as Maxfield Parrish uses it."

And then he was off. For forty-five minutes he walked about his office, showing me how Maxfield Parrish uses blue, and telling how the ancients used the color. Quietly he told how the Egyptians loved it, how they had adorned their homes and tombs with it.

Then he led me from his office across the hall into his laboratory, a room about thirty by twenty feet. It was filled with racks and shelves and tables, bottles and tubes and retorts. He picked up a jar and carried it to the window. "See"—and he held it to the sun.

And I saw the richest, the purest blue that I have ever seen.

Doctor Carver was talking quietly as he tilted the jar one way and the other, giving the sun its full chance to mate with the glorious color. "I believe," he went on, "that it's a rediscovery of the old Egyptian blue. A number of chemists have come to see it, and they agree with

2. **Maxfield Parrish** (1870–1966), American illustrator and muralist.

me. At present I'm working on the Egyptian purple; I believe that soon we shall have that, too.

"I get my dyes," the old man continued, "from Alabama clays. You remember what the Bible says"—Doctor Carver has built his life on what the Bible says—"you remember that the Bible says, 'Look to the hills from whence cometh your help.'[3] I did it; I looked to these Alabama hills, and I made these dyes from the clays that I found there. All these dyes and paints"—he waved toward thirty-six boards, each of which was colored differently—"all of them were made from Alabama clay—all," he added, "except this one; it was made from rotten sweet potatoes; and this one, which was made from cow dung; and this one, a much finer paint, was made from horse dung."

After I had been an hour in Doctor Carver's laboratory, after I had seen rope made from okra fiber, baskets from wistaria, and dyes from dandelion, black oak, wood ashes, sweet gum, swamp maple, sweet potato, pomegranate, peanut, Osage orange, muscadine grape, onion, velvet bean, and tomato vine—after I had seen those discoveries, among a few hundred others, I was willing to believe almost anything possible to this kindly man to whom apparently brick without straw would be a simple problem.

"When you do the common things of life in an uncommon way," Doctor Carver once said to his students, "you will command the attention of the world." In that sentence lies the secret of his own achievement.

He was born in a rude slave cabin on the farm of Moses Carver near Diamond Grove, Missouri. Moses Carver owned his mother, and a neighbor owned his father. When he was a baby six months old, night riders swooped down on his master's plantation and carried away a number of slaves, among them the baby and his mother.

In their flight, the raiders took no care of the child; he developed whooping cough and was dying when emissaries sent out by Moses Carver arrived from Missouri to buy back the stolen slaves.

But the mother had already been disposed of; no one ever learned what became of her. Indeed, there is only one thing of hers that is left: In Doctor Carver's room in one of the dormitories at Tuskegee is a battered old spinning wheel on which his mother spun flax when she was a slave. A friend of Doctor Carver's said to me, "I've seen him touch that wheel; he touches it like a priest reverently touching an altar. I sometimes feel that if I could be in his room when he retires, I should hear the old man say 'Good night' to that wheel."

The emissaries sent to ransom the stolen slaves finally struck a bargain with the night riders. The baby was evaluated and traded back to his owner; he was traded for a broken-down racehorse worth about $300!

The Carvers reared the sickly child, and from them he took his surname, according to the practice common among slaves. It is told that they bestowed the given name "George Washington" upon him because of his youthful honesty and industry. Because he was a frail and undersized lad and could do no heavy work, he performed household chores, getting

3. . . . **from whence cometh your help,** paraphrased from Psalms 121:1.

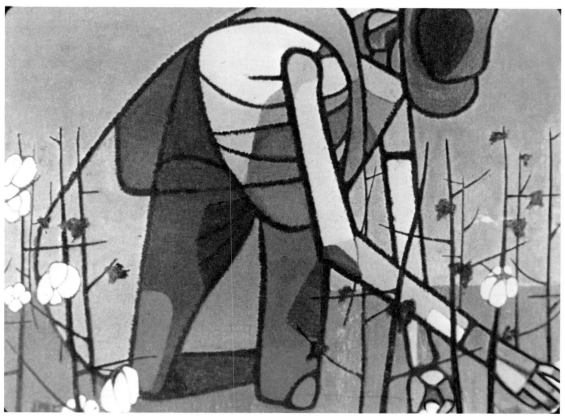

THE COTTON PICKER Robert Gwathmey
Anacostia Neighborhood Museum, The Barnett Aden Collection

in the wood, tending the fires, and helping Mrs. Carver with the meals. He became an excellent cook and also learned to sew and mend clothes.

When the chores were done, his favorite playground was in the woods nearby, where his companions were the birds, the flowers, the trees, and the small animals.

As a boy he had only one book. It was Webster's blue-back speller.

"With that book," he said to me, "I began my education. Even as a boy I realized that life requires a thorough preparation; there is no shortcut to achievement; veneer isn't worth anything. And so I studied that book until I knew every word of it."

When he was about ten years old, having mastered the speller, he determined to get further schooling. He heard of a school in the village of Neosho, Missouri, eight miles away. The Carvers wanted him to have an education, but offered him no money. So, without a cent in his pockets, he set out over the hills for Neosho. Arriving there, alone among strangers, he slept at first in an old horse barn. Soon he picked up odd jobs about the village and entered the school. It wasn't much of a school—an old log cabin equipped with hard, high benches for the pupils. Within a year he had mastered all that the teacher could tell him and more. But he had learned enough to be eager for more knowledge.

One day, while walking along the road, he met a mule-team outfit headed for Fort Scott, Kansas. In true hitchhike fashion, he asked the travelers if he could go along with them. After several days' journey they reached Fort Scott, where he got a job in a home as cook, dishwasher, and all-round housekeeper.

In this way, and by washing clothes, he earned his keep while he attended classes in high school. Still frail in physique and small for his age, he was continuing to make something out of nothing. Seven years passed, and he completed his high school course. He was now in his early twenties. And, almost miraculously, he began suddenly to grow in body. Within a year or so he developed from a weakling into a strapping six-footer.

Without accepting financial aid, he had struggled through his schooling; now he determined to make his way through college. But first he paid a summer visit to his old home with the Carvers back in Missouri. They gave him his mother's spinning wheel, which he carried back with him to Fort Scott.

In the fall he mailed an application to a college in Iowa, and by mail he was accepted. But when he arrived at the college, they refused to admit him because he was a Negro. He had spent most of his money for railway fare, and there was not enough left to take him out of town. But he was undismayed. Again he worked at odd jobs—cooking, cleaning carpets, and doing other chores. Before long he had accumulated enough money to open a small laundry, which was pa-tronized by college students and townspeople. For a time he worked as a hotel cook.

The next year he entered Simpson College at Indianola, Iowa. After he had paid his entrance fee he had ten cents left, which he invested in five cents' worth of cornmeal and five cents' worth of suet. On this fare he lived for nearly a week. For three years he worked his way at Simpson; then in 1890 he enrolled at Iowa State College. Four years later he was graduated, taking his degree in agriculture, having earned every penny of his expenses.

Two years after graduation he won his Master of Science degree. His work in agricultural chemistry so impressed the authorities of the college that they appointed him to a place on the college faculty—this boy who only a few years before had been traded for a horse!

While Carver was teaching at Iowa State College, the late Booker T. Washington, the great Negro educator, heard of him and asked him to come to Tuskegee.

"He asked me to come here and to let down my bucket,"[4] Doctor Carver told me one day as I watched him busy in his laboratory. Turning from his work, he looked out of the window, and I saw that he was looking back through the years. "I did come here. I did let down my bucket. And every time I've pulled it up, it has

---

4. **". . . let down my bucket."** Dr. Carver is referring to one of Booker T. Washington's favorite stories: A ship lost at sea for several days signaled another ship that the crew was out of water and the men were dying of thirst. The other vessel responded: "Cast down your bucket where you are." When the captain of the vessel in distress finally cast down his bucket, it came up full of fresh water. His ship was in the mouth of the Amazon River.

been brimful and running over—running over," he repeated.

In accepting Doctor Washington's call, Carver saw a great opportunity to serve his own people in the South, an opportunity for which he had fully prepared himself by his work in agriculture and chemistry. He saw that the valuable cotton lands of the South, where for years cotton had been the chief paying crop, were wearing out through neglect of simple scientific methods of farming, such as proper fertilizing and rotation of crops. He saw small farmers overburdened by debt and facing poverty. He saw a way to help lift their burden.

Carver's first job when he arrived at Tuskegee in 1896 was to create an efficient department of agriculture, which had barely been started in the school. The department was housed in an old building and was almost entirely lacking in laboratory equipment. At once he put into practice what he had learned about making something out of nothing. He and his students went out into back alleys and searched trash piles, collecting old bottles and jars, bits of rubber and wire and other odds and ends. Out of these he built laboratory apparatus—later to be replaced by new equipment.

His next big job was to take over and work nineteen acres of the worst land in Alabama. He used this plot of ground as an experiment station, where he proceeded to prove to the Alabama farmers that coarse sand, fine sandy loam, and clay loam could be worked profitably. If crops could be developed successfully on this patch of land, he argued, they certainly could be grown in any part of the South.

In 1897, when Carver began this work, the best methods of farming, combined with abundant use of fertilizer, had produced a net loss of $16.25 an acre on this land. Within a year he had treated the soil until it showed a net gain of $4 an acre. Seven years later he produced eighty bushels of sweet potatoes on an acre of sandy loam; and that same year he produced another crop on the same acre. The profit was $75. The next year he raised a 500-pound bale of cotton on that acre, and in Alabama there aren't many acres that will bear a 500-pound bale.

Profits out of barren soil. In these experiments in crop rotation during his first twelve years at Tuskegee Institute, Doctor Carver demonstrated something of inestimable value to the farmers—that by intelligence and industry and simple understanding of the ways of Nature it was possible to make a great deal out of nothing and turn waste and loss into gain. One of the incidental results of the experiments, he pointed out, was to prove that the world allows to go to waste an almost unlimited supply of valuable fertilizer that most soils need—the muck from swamps and the leaves from forests.

Carver's third big job, which continues unceasingly to this day, was to serve as a scientific pilot to the Southern farmers in the face of disaster. That disaster was the coming of the boll weevil, the insect pest which attacked and devastated the cotton fields.

Thirty years ago Carver witnessed the arrival of the boll weevil in Alabama. He saw the almost total destruction of the cotton crop. He set himself to two tasks: He would assist in fighting the pest, and he would preach a gospel of native money crops other than cotton.

After study, and thought, and experiment, he decided that the Southern farmer could get his money with more surety, and with less damage to his soil, by growing peanuts and sweet potatoes than by attempting any other crop. Doctor Carver began to write bulletins proving his contentions. He made speeches arguing his beliefs. After a time, a number of Southern farmers increased their peanut and sweet potato acreage. And then, suddenly, and sadly, Doctor Carver awoke to what he had done. He had increased the supply without increasing the demand. The peanut and the sweet potato were rotting; the Southern farmer was not only losing the money that he had hoped to make, but he was losing the cost of production and the cost of labor as well.

Almost fiercely the Negro scientist set about the work that the centuries will probably declare to be his greatest contribution to knowledge. He had made a great mistake. He felt that he had done a great personal injustice. Days and nights he spent in his laboratory, seeking to develop new commercial uses for the peanut and for the sweet potato. Slowly, one product at a time, this man forced Nature to give up her secrets; and as each of them was learned, Doctor Carver gave them freely to the world, asking only that they be used for the benefit of mankind.

"He cares nothing about marketing his products," I was told. "He merely discovers them, then gives them away to anyone who wants them."

Inevitably Doctor Carver's work in agriculture, in chemistry, and in other sciences brought him offers to leave Tuskegee and go elsewhere. One of these offers was made by Thomas A. Edison.

On the walls of Doctor Carver's office are two autographed pictures from Edison.

"He sent me one of them when he asked me to come to his laboratory and work with him," Doctor Carver explained. "He sent me the other, the larger one, when I told him that my work was here in the South, and that I didn't think God wanted me to leave it."

Another offer tempted the old Negro—him who once had been valued and traded for $300—tempted him with an annual salary of $100,000. He refused it. He stayed in Tuskegee, where his meager salary is quickly consumed in anonymously paying the bills of worthy boys, both white and black, who are trying to get an education. He stayed in Tuskegee and continued to wear the old alpaca coat which he himself has so often mended, the black trousers which he has so frequently patched, the old shoes which are just a little too large for him, and which he has patched until the patches overlap. Neckties, too, are expensive: so he knits his own out of fibers that he makes himself.

"Money means nothing to him," a friend told me. "Some wealthy peanut growers in Florida were suffering terribly from a diseased crop. They sent Doctor Carver some specimens. He told them what was wrong and how to cure it. After his diagnosis and treatment had proved correct, they sent him a check for $100, promising that they would send him the same amount monthly as a retainer's fee. He sent back the check, telling them that God didn't charge them anything for growing the peanut and that he shouldn't charge them anything for curing it."

I had known Doctor Carver for two

PORTRAIT OF GEORGE WASHINGTON CARVER
E. H. Bischoff
Schomberg Center, New York Public Library

days when, at ten o'clock one morning, he took off his spectacles, put the cover on his microscope, and said, "I should be greatly honored if you would come to my rooms with me. I should like you to see some of my pictures."

On the morning that Doctor Carver and I started out to walk to his rooms, we were interrupted by an eight-year-old boy who had caught a fluffy young wood thrush and brought it to Doctor Carver. The old man took the bird, soothed it, and with long black fingers stilled its feeble fluttering. Once the bird no longer darted its little yellow-marked head about, Doctor Carver began to describe its habits, telling the lad how the bird lived, the things it ate, where it loved best to sit and sing; the old man softly whistled the song of the bird. "And now take it back and turn it loose, my boy; take it back to its mother. It's terrible when a young bird is taken from its mother. You wouldn't want to be taken from your mother, would you?"

The lad shook his head.

"That's right"—Doctor Carver looked away—"of course you wouldn't—none of us would."

When at last we arrived at Doctor Carver's rooms, he unlocked the outer door and bowed me in. "I'm just a little crowded here," he admitted, waving his arm toward a living room that is in reality a confused combination of library, picture gallery, hothouse, and museum.

There are bookshelves from the floor almost to the ceiling—books on geology, agriculture, botany, chemistry, physics, astronomy, butterflies, mushrooms, and frogs; books in English, German, and other languages. In the corners are stacks of scientific journals.

In the center of the room and almost filling the place is a table on which are piled rocks and stones and stalactites and stalagmites[5] and scores of other formations known only to the trained geologist. Outside the window is a great shelf on which stand fifty pots of plants and flowers with which Doctor Carver is constantly experimenting.

On one wall of the room is a glass case four feet wide and six feet high. It is filled with embroidery, tatting, and crochet work. Even an absolute layman can recognize their exceeding delicacy and beauty.

"But how do you find time to do it all?" I asked.

"Chiefly because I've made it a rule of my life to get up every morning at four o'clock. Winter and summer, I wake at that hour; and I get up. I go out into the woods. Alone there with the things I love most, I gather specimens and study the great lessons that Nature is so eager to teach me. I return to my laboratory at nine o'clock, and I work there all day. Every night, and regardless of what kind of entertainment or celebration is going on, I go to bed at nine o'clock."

He hesitated a moment, then went on: "But don't talk as if I had accomplished very much. What I've done may seem a lot, though I"—he shook his head sorrowfully as he turned away—"though I know that it's mighty little when compared to all that I should have done, all that I want to do."

Doctor Carver's belittlement of his own achievements is an unobtrusive indi-

---

5. **stalactite,** a rock formation, shaped like an icicle, hanging from the roof of a cave; **stalagmite,** a rock formation, shaped like a cone, built up on the floor of a cave, formed by water dripping from a stalactite.

cation of his sincere humility. A few years ago he made a trip to Washington. After he returned to Tuskegee, he said nothing about what had happened.

"A week passed before we learned what he had done," an official of the institute told me. "We heard about it first from some newspaper clippings that were sent us."

When the Hawley-Smoot tariff bill[6] was being considered, Southern farmers sent plea after plea to Congress asking that the peanut be named as an article on which import duty was to be charged. Congress saw no reason for acceding to the pleas; but the Ways and Means Committee granted a hearing, and named a day.

On that day, a dozen men appeared before the committee, each man in his turn consuming his allotted ten minutes. In the background, standing alone, Doctor Carver, with his trembling hands, awaited his time to speak. Last on the list of speakers, he finally came forward to address congressmen who were thoroughly tired of harangues about the peanut.

The old man took his place behind the table, where stood scores of bottles and cases containing products that he had made from the peanut. Smiling his humble smile, he explained that he had been brought to Washington by a group of Southern peanut growers; he apologized for taking up the time of his hearers; he thanked them for listening. Then simply, and with an occasional reference to God, he told the tired congressmen the story of the peanut. He told the congressmen merely of how he had asked, "God, what is a peanut and why did you make it?" Then he told how he had sought the answer to his question, and how in his searching he had discovered products ranging from face powder to chocolate wafers. As he talked, he pointed to each product that he had made in his Alabama laboratory.

Exactly at the end of ten minutes, Doctor Carver thanked the committee for allowing him to appear before them. But the congressmen would not let him go; they demanded that he continue his story.

He spoke for one hour and forty-five minutes before the most important committee of Congress. And when he finished, the committee adjourned to the next room and wrote the peanut into the tariff bill of the United States.

No one can adequately report the strange feeling of spiritual betterment that one constantly feels while with this unusual man; nor can one even intimate one's regret at the time of saying good-by—when Doctor Carver, his smile itself a God-speed, places his trembling hand on your shoulder and says, "Good-by, my boy, good-by. And may God bless you". . . . It is a benediction from a simple, a kindly, a noble heart.

---

6. **Hawley-Smoot tariff bill,** passed in 1930, was the last general tariff. It had the highest rates ever enacted into a United States tariff bill. Four years later, legislation brought about the gradual reduction of many of these tariffs.

READING FOR DETAILS

He Blazed New Trails

Few lives so exactly illustrate the central theme of this group of selections, WITH WHAT YOU HAVE, as does that of George Washington Carver. His was an amazing ability to overcome obstacles and to make use of what he had. Over and over in his life, he quietly moved forward when the path seemed closed to him.

In building the department of agriculture at Tuskegee Institute from a bare room to a widely respected research laboratory, Dr. Carver discovered many ways to put to use things most people wasted. Recognition came from all over the world. He was sought after by foreign governments for help with their agricultural problems. He was made a consultant to the United States Department of Agriculture. He was elected a member of the British Royal Society of Arts. He was given medals and honors and degrees. A ship and several schools were named for him. Active until the end, the scientist died quietly at Tuskegee in 1943.

1. Under what kinds of handicaps did Dr. Carver work at Tuskegee?
2. By what means did he win the respect of others?

READING FOR MEANING

Find evidence in the selection that supports the following statements:

1. A scientist can be a lover of beauty.
2. There is no shortcut to achievement.

READING FOR APPRECIATION

Characterization

Writers are well aware that people judge others by what they say, as well as by the way they act. Think about each of the following quotations carefully and tell what each reveals about Dr. Carver's character:

1. "He's probably the janitor," I told myself, "and I'm sincerely glad that they've given him a job of some kind."
2. "People are too kind to me," he insisted. "I'm really a very small part of this institution."
3. When you do the common things of life in an uncommon way . . . you will command the attention of the world.
4. He sent back the check, telling them that God didn't charge them anything for growing the peanut and that he shouldn't charge them anything for curing it.

COMPOSITION

George Washington Carver was a genius at turning scrap materials into useful tools, common plants into tasty and nutritious foods. At some time or other, many of us have tried to transform junkyard scrap or leftover foods into something more useful or appetizing.

Think back to your most memorable effort in working with "throw-away" materials and describe in some detail the undertaking and the result.

BIOGRAPHICAL NOTE

James Saxon Childers (1899–1965) was born in Birmingham, Alabama. He held degrees from Oberlin College, Oxford University, and Oglethorpe University, and was a Rhodes Scholar in 1923. He served in both World War I and World War II, and was a columnist, feature writer, newspaper editor, college English professor, and lecturer for the U.S. State Department in the Far and Middle East. His last work was *Nation on the Fighting Trapeze*.

We were a united little group.
We were small, but we were powerful.

A LITTLE MUDHOLE IN THE ROAD
Jesse Stuart

When I told my pupils about a scholastic contest with Landsburgh High School, I watched their expressions. They were willing and ready for the challenge. The competitive spirit was in them.

"We must review everything we have covered in our textbooks," I told them. "We must cover more territory in our textbooks too. Hold up your right hands if you are willing!"

Every pupil raised his hand.

Right then we started to work. In addition to regular assignments, my pupils began reviewing all of the old assignments we had covered.

Despite the challenge ahead and all the reviewing and study we planned to do, we never stopped play. The Tiber River was frozen over. The ring of skates and merry laughter broke the stillness of the winter nights. We skated on the white winding ribbon of ice beneath the high, cold winter moon. Often we'd skate until midnight. We'd hear the wind blow mournfully over the great white silence that surrounded us and sing lonesome songs without words in the barren branches of the bankside trees. And we'd hear the foxes' barking, high upon the walls of sheltering cliffs, mocking the music of our ringing skates.

Over the weekends we'd go to Tiber where we'd cut holes in the ice and gig fish.* The boys and I would rabbit-hunt up and down the Tiber Valley in the old stubble fields now covered with snow and swept by wind. We'd track minks, possums, raccoons, weasels, and foxes to their dens. We'd climb the mountains and get spills over the rocks into the deep snow. This took our minds from books and taught us another kind of education. It was as much fun as reading books. Now that a big contest was before us, we needed diversion. And we got it. Our state was not usually cold enough for winter sports. This winter was an exception, and we took full advantage of it.

When we hunted, the girls didn't go with us, but when we skated, fished, and rode sleighs they went along. There was a long, gentle slope not far from the schoolhouse we found ideal for our sleighs. It was almost a mile to the end of our sleigh run. We went over the riverbank and downstream for many yards on the Tiber ice. We rode sleighs during the noon hour, before and after school.

On winter days when the snow had melted, leaving the dark earth a sea of sloppy mud, we designed floor games for our little one-room school. They were

*__gig fish,__ to spear fish in schools with a series of hooks attached to a kind of fishing rake called a gig.

simple games, such as throwing bolts in small boxes. And we played darts. We also played a game called "fox and goose." We made our fox-and-goose boards, and we played with white, yellow, and red grains of corn. We had to make our own recreation. I never saw a distracted look on a pupil's face. I never heard one complain that the short, dark winter days were boresome because there wasn't anything to do. I think each pupil silently prayed for the days to be longer. We were a united little group. We were small, but we were powerful. We played hard, and we studied hard. We studied and played while the December days passed.

That day in early January, we dismissed school. This was the first time we had dismissed for anything. We had never lost an hour. I had actually taught more hours than required. This was the big day for us. It was too bad that another blizzard had swept our rugged land and that a stinging wind was smiting the valleys and the hills. But this didn't stop the boys and me from going. Leona Maddox, my best Latin pupil, couldn't go along. Her father, Alex Maddox, wouldn't let her ride a mule seventeen miles to Landsburgh to compete in a contest on a day like this. I couldn't persuade him to let her go.

On that cold, blizzardy morning, Budge Waters rode his mule to school very early and built a fire in the potbellied stove. When the rest of us arrived on our mules at approximately seven o'clock, Budge had the schoolroom warm. We tied our mules to the fence, stood before the fire, and warmed ourselves before we started on our journey. Then we unhitched our mules from the

fence and climbed into the saddles. Little clouds of frozen snow in powdery puffs arose from the mules' hoofs as six pupils and their teacher rode down the road.

Though the force of wind in the Tiber Valley was powerful, it was at our backs. The wind was strong enough to give our mules more momentum. We made good time until we left the valley and climbed the big hill. Here, we faced the wind. It was a whipping wind—stinging, biting wind on this mountain—that made the water run from our eyes and our mules' eyes, but for us there was no turning back. We were going to Landsburgh High School. That was that. We were determined to meet this big school; big to us, for they outnumbered us twenty-six to one. Soon we were down in Hinton Valley. Then we rode to the top of the Raccoon Hill, where we faced the stinging wind again.

"Mr. Stuart, I have been thinking," Budge Waters said, as we rode along together, "if you can sleep in a fodder shock when it's twelve degrees below zero, we can take this contest from Landsburgh High School! I've not forgotten how you walked seventeen miles to carry us books. All of your pupils remember. We'll never let you down!"

Budge Waters thought of this because we were riding down the mountain where I had slept that night. Then we rode down into the Raccoon Valley, and Billie Leonard, only thirteen years old, complained of numbness in his hands, feet, and lips. He said he felt as if he was going to sleep. I knew what he was talking about. I had had the same feeling the day Ottis Baylor had put my hands and feet in cold water. We stopped at a home, tied our mules to the fence, and went in and asked to warm. Bert Patton, a stranger to us, piled more wood on the open fire until we were as warm as when we had left the schoolhouse. We told him who we were and where we were going.

"On a day like this!" he said, shaking his head sadly.

We climbed into the saddles again. We were over halfway now. The second hitch would put us at Landsburgh High School. We had valley all the way to Landsburgh, with walls of rugged hills on each side for windbreaks.

At eleven o'clock we rode across the Landsburgh High School yard, and hitched our mules to the fence around the athletic field. There were faces against the windowpanes watching us. Then we walked inside the high school, where Principal Ernest Charters met and welcomed us. He told us that he was surprised we had come on a day like this and that we had been able to arrive so soon.

In the principal's office my pupils and I huddled around the gas stove while we heard much laughter in the high-school corridors. The Landsburgh High School pupils thought we were a strange-looking lot. Many came inside their principal's office to take a look at us. We were regarded with curiosity, strangeness, and wonder. Never before had these pupils seen seven mules hitched to their schoolyard fence. Never

before had they competed scholastically with so few in number—competitors who had reached them by muleback. The Landsburgh High School principal didn't feel about the contest the way we felt. To him, this was just a "setup" to test his pupils for the district contest which would soon be held. He told me this when he went after the sealed envelopes that held the questions. We warmed before the gas stove while he made arrangements for the contest.

"These questions were made out by the state department of education," he said when he returned. "I don't know how hard they are."

My pupils stood silently by the stove and looked at each other. We were asked to go to one of the largest classrooms. A Landsburgh High School teacher had charge of giving the tests. When the Landsburgh High School pupils came through the door to compete against my pupils, we knew why Principal Charters had selected this large classroom. My pupils looked at each other, then at their competitors.

I entered redheaded Jesse Jarvis to compete with ten of their plane-geometry pupils. I entered Billie Leonard against twenty-one of their selected algebra pupils.

"Budge, you'll have to represent us in grammar, English literature, and history," I said. "And I believe I'll put you in civil government. Is that all right?"

"Yes," he agreed. Budge had never had a course in civil government. All he knew about it was what he had read in connection with history.

"Robert Batson, you enter in history and grammar.

"Robin Baylor, you enter in algebra.

"Snookie Baylor, you enter in algebra and plane geometry.

"Sorry, Mr. Charters," I said, "we don't have anyone to enter in Latin. My best Latin pupil, Leona Maddox, couldn't make this trip."

After the contest had begun, I left the room. Miss Bertha Madden was in charge. I took our mules to Walter Scott's barn on the east end of Landsburgh, where I fed and watered them.

With the exception of an interval when the contestants ate a quick lunch, the contest lasted until 2:30 P.M. I had one pupil, Budge Waters, in four contests. I had planned to enter him in two. Just as soon as Budge finished with civil government, we started grading the papers. All the pupils were requested to leave the room.

We graded the papers with keys. Mr. Charters, Miss Madden, and two other teachers, and I did the grading. Mr. Charters read the answers on the keys, and we checked the answers. Once or twice we stopped long enough to discuss what stiff questions these were. We wondered how far we would have gotten if we—all of us college graduates—had taken the same test. One of the teachers asked me, while we graded these papers, if Budge Waters had ever seen these questions before.

When we were through grading the papers, Mr. Charters called the contestants into the classroom.

"I want to read you the scores of this contest," Principal Charters said. His voice was nervous.

"Budge Waters, winner in English literature.

"Budge Waters, winner in grammar.

"Budge Waters, winner in history with almost a perfect score.

"Budge Waters, winner in civil government.

"Why didn't you bring just this one boy?" Principal Charters asked me.

"Because I've got other good pupils," I quickly retorted.

"Billie Leonard, winner in algebra, with plenty of points to spare.

"Jesse Jarvis, second in plane geometry, lost by one point.

"Snookie Baylor and Robin Baylor tied for second place in algebra.

"Congratulations," said Principal Charters, "to your pupils and to you, on your success. It looks as though Winston High will represent this county in the district scholastic contest. I've never heard of such a remarkable thing."

When we left the Landsburgh High School we heard defeated pupils crying because "a little mudhole in the road like Winston beat us."

In a few minutes our mule cavalcade passed the Landsburgh High School. Faces were against the windowpanes, and many pupils waved jubilantly to us as we rode by, our coat tails riding the wind behind our saddles, and the ends of our scarfs bright banners on the wind. We rode victoriously down the main street of Landsburgh on our way home.

READING FOR DETAILS

Twenty-Six to One

1. What evidence is there that Jesse Stuart inspired his students to do their best?
2. In what way were the odds against them? What "advantages" did they have over students in the larger schools?
3. How did the pupils of Landsburgh High

feel when the Winston students arrived and when they left?

READING FOR MEANING

Can you find evidence in the selection to support these propositions?
1. Appearances can be deceiving.
2. The outcome of a contest depends on the contestants, not the odds.

READING FOR APPRECIATION

Characterization

Although in this autobiographical account attention is centered upon what the students did, much is revealed indirectly about the author. You know, for example, that while he is matter-of-fact, he has poetic feelings. What other traits of character are suggested? Do you think he has determination, concern for the feelings of others, and ambition? Support all claims of character traits with evidence taken from the selection. In what traits does he resemble George Washington Carver? How does his character differ? How are their problems similar?

BIOGRAPHICAL NOTE

Jesse Stuart (1907–1984), short story writer, novelist, poet, and teacher, was born in Greenup County, Kentucky, where he now lives. The first of his family to go to high school, he taught in a country school at seventeen and worked his way through Lincoln Memorial University. One of America's most popular writers, Stuart says that he has been writing for as long as he can remember. Many of the stories and poems he wrote in high school and college were later published. His best-known books are *Man with a Bull-Tongue Plow*, *Taps for Private Tussie*, *Hie to the Hunters*, and *The Year of My Rebirth*, the last written while he was recovering from a heart attack. A recent collection of his essays is entitled *If I Were Seventeen Again, and Other Essays* (1980).

We do with what we have. Given much, some of us do little. Given nothing, some of us do wonders. Consider the children below, for instance. Ravaged as the buildings behind them, their spirited youth and imagination still renders them airborne.

Ben Shahn, **LIBERATION**
James Thrall Soby Collection

Consider how imagination can become the key in the door of what you have. In the painting at the left, the tattered boys are made richer by the shared imagination of the equally tattered teller of tales. And below, an abandoned stagecoach grows wheels and is set in motion by the imagination of a group of young children.

Philip Evergood, **HER WORLD**
Metropolitan Museum of Art
New York City
Arthur H. Hearne Fund

Ejnar Nielsen, **THE BLIND GIRL**
Hirsprung Collection, Copenhagen

At the right, Paul Gauguin uses minimal detail, simple lines, and simple patterns to create a sensitive study of two Tahitian women. The women are simply clothed, have only a little food before them, and appear very content. A little bit has gone a long way for both the artist and his subject.

Paul Gauguin
WOMEN FROM TAHITI
Musée du Jeu de Paume, Paris

The three solitary figures on these pages have time to think about what they have—or don't have. Philip Evergood's black girl leans on the limits of her world so far. It recedes behind her, but she looks beyond it. Nielsen's blind girl must create her own world, and its scope and depth depend upon the limits of her inner vision. Homer's young boy is reaping a multitude of harvests, not the least of which is freedom.

Winslow Homer, **THE REAPER**
Sotheby Parke Bernet/Art Resource, Inc.

Suzuki Harunobu, **TWO WOMEN PLAYING CAT'S CRADLE**
Metropolitan Museum of Art, New York City
Bequest of Mrs. H.O. Havemeyer
The H.O. Havemeyer Collection

Pedro Figari, **DANCE IN THE COURTYARD**
Sotheby Parke Bernet/Art Resource, Inc.

It often happens that a social relationship or a shared experience means as much or more than what we have by ourselves. The two young Japanese girls in the tranquil Harunobu woodcut at the left have created a universe of serenity out of two pieces of string. The cat's cradle of the title implies that what they have is complex and fragile. The family group, caught in a courtyard dance by the Uruguayan artist Pedro Figari, has created its own whirling world of bright motion. The brilliance of the costumes, in contrast to the plainness of the walls, suggests that color and light and brilliance come not from where we live but how we live.

The Wise Men, or Magi, who long ago brought gifts to the Child in the manger, started the custom of Christmas giving. In this famous O. Henry story, two young people demonstrate that they have wisdom to match that of the Magi when it comes to providing gifts for one another.

THE GIFT OF THE MAGI
O. Henry

One dollar and eighty-seven cents. That was all. And sixty cents of it was in pennies. Pennies saved one and two at a time by bulldozing the grocer and the vegetable man and the butcher until one's cheeks burned with the silent imputation of parsimony[1] that such close dealing implied. Three times Della counted it. One dollar and eighty-seven cents. And the next day would be Christmas.

There was clearly nothing to do but flop down on the shabby little couch and howl. So Della did it. Which instigates the moral reflection that life is made up of sobs, sniffles, and smiles, with sniffles predominating.

While the mistress of the home is gradually subsiding from the first stage to the second, take a look at the home. A furnished flat at eight dollars per week. It did not exactly beggar description,[2] but it certainly had that word on the lookout for the mendicancy squad.[3]

In the vestibule below was a letter box into which no letter would go, and an electric button from which no mortal finger could coax a ring. Also appertaining thereunto was a card bearing the name "Mr. James Dillingham Young."

The "Dillingham" had been flung to the breeze during a former period of prosperity when its possessor was being paid thirty dollars per week. Now, when the income was shrunk to twenty dollars, the letters of "Dillingham" looked blurred, as though they were thinking seriously of contracting to a modest and unassuming D. But whenever Mr. James Dillingham Young came home and reached his flat above, he was called "Jim" and greatly hugged by Mrs. James Dillingham Young, already introduced to you as Della. Which is all very good.

Della finished her cry and attended to her cheeks with the powder rag. She stood by the window and looked out dully at a gray cat walking a gray fence in a gray back yard. Tomorrow would be Christmas Day, and she had only $1.87 with which to buy Jim a present. She had been saving every penny she could for months, with this result. Twenty dollars a week doesn't go far. Expenses had been greater than she had calculated. They always are. Only $1.87 to buy a present for Jim. Her Jim. Many a happy hour she had spent planning something nice for

---

1. **imputation of parsimony** (pär′sə mō′nē), charge of stinginess.
2. **beggar description,** exhaust the powers of description.
3. **mendicancy** (men′də kən sē) **squad,** police unit assigned to arrest those illegally begging. The reference is to the word *beggar*.

him. Something fine and rare and sterling—something just a little bit near to being worthy of the honor of being owned by Jim.

There was a pier glass[4] between the windows of the room. Perhaps you have seen a pier glass in an eight-dollar flat. A very thin and very agile person may, by observing his reflection in a rapid sequence of longitudinal strips, obtain a fairly accurate conception of his looks. Della, being slender, had mastered the art.

Suddenly she whirled from the window and stood before the glass. Her eyes were shining brilliantly, but her face had lost its color within twenty seconds. Rapidly she pulled down her hair and let it fall to its full length.

Now, there were two possessions of the James Dillingham Youngs in which they both took a mighty pride. One was Jim's gold watch that had been his father's and his grandfather's. The other was Della's hair. Had the Queen of Sheba lived in the flat across the air shaft, Della would have let her hair hang out the window some day to dry just to depreciate Her Majesty's jewels and gifts. Had King Solomon been the janitor, with all his treasures piled up in the basement, Jim would have pulled out his watch every time he passed, just to see him pluck at his beard from envy.

So now Della's beautiful hair fell about her, rippling and shining like a cascade of brown waters. It reached below her knee and made itself almost a garment for her. And then she did it up again nervously and quickly. Once she faltered for a minute and stood still while a tear or two splashed on the worn red carpet.

On went her old brown jacket; on went her old brown hat. With a whirl of skirts and with the brilliant sparkle still in her eyes she fluttered out the door and down the stairs to the street.

Where she stopped, the sign read, "Mme Sofronie. Hair Goods of All Kinds." One flight up Della ran and collected herself, panting. Madame, large, too white, chilly, hardly looked the "Sofronie."

"Will you buy my hair?" asked Della.

"I buy hair," said Madame. "Take yer hat off and let's have a sight at the looks of it."

Down rippled the brown cascade.

"Twenty dollars," said Madame, lifting the mass with a practiced hand.

"Give it to me quick," said Della.

Oh, and the next two hours tripped by on rosy wings. Forget the hashed metaphor. She was ransacking the stores for Jim's present.

She found it at last. It surely had been made for Jim and no one else. There was no other like it in any of the stores, and she had turned all of them inside out. It was a platinum fob chain, simple and chaste in design, properly proclaiming its value by substance alone and not by meretricious[5] ornamentation—as all good things should do. It was even worthy of The Watch. As soon as she saw it, she knew that it must be Jim's. It was like him. Quietness and value—the description applied to both. Twenty-one dollars they took from her for it, and she hurried home with the eighty-seven cents. With that chain on his watch Jim might

---

4. **pier glass,** tall, narrow mirror.
5. **meretricious** (mer′ə trish′əs), gaudy, cheap looking.

be properly anxious about the time in any company. Grand as the watch was, he sometimes looked at it on the sly on account of the old leather strap that he used in place of a chain.

When Della reached home her intoxication gave way a little to prudence and reason. She got out her curling irons and lighted the gas and went to work repairing the ravages made by generosity added to love. Which is always a tremendous task, dear friends—a mammoth task.

Within forty minutes her head was covered with tiny, close-lying curls that made her look wonderfully like a truant schoolboy. She looked at her reflection in the mirror long, carefully, and critically.

"If Jim doesn't kill me," she said to herself, "before he takes a second look at me, he'll say I look like a Coney Island chorus girl. But what could I do—oh! what could I do with a dollar and eighty-seven cents?"

At seven o'clock the coffee was made and the frying pan was on the back of the stove, hot and ready to cook the chops.

Jim was never late. Della doubled the fob chain in her hand and sat on the corner of the table near the door that he always entered. Then she heard his step on the stair away down on the first flight, and she turned white for just a moment. She had a habit of saying little prayers about the simplest everyday things, and now she whispered, "Please, God, make him think I am still pretty."

The door opened, and Jim stepped in and closed it. He looked thin and very serious. Poor fellow, he was only twenty-two—and to be burdened with a family! He needed a new overcoat, and he was without gloves.

Jim stopped inside the door, as immovable as a setter at the scent of quail. His eyes were fixed upon Della, and there was an expression in them that she could not read, and it terrified her. It was not anger, nor surprise, nor disapproval, nor horror, nor any of the sentiments that she had been prepared for. He simply stared at her fixedly with that peculiar expression on his face.

Della wriggled off the table and went for him.

"Jim, darling," she cried, "don't look at me that way. I had my hair cut off and sold it because I couldn't have lived through Christmas without giving you a present. It'll grow out again—you won't mind, will you? I just had to do it. My hair grows awfully fast. Say 'Merry Christmas!' Jim, and let's be happy. You don't know what a nice—what a beautiful, nice gift I've got for you."

"You've cut off your hair?" asked Jim, laboriously, as if he had not arrived at that patent fact yet even after the hardest mental labor.

"Cut it off and sold it," said Della. "Don't you like me just as well, anyhow? I'm me without my hair, ain't I?"

Jim looked about the room curiously.

"You say your hair is gone?" he said, with an air almost of idiocy.

"You needn't look for it," said Della. "It's sold, I tell you—sold and gone, too. It's Christmas Eve, boy. Be good to me, for it went for you. Maybe the hairs of my head were numbered," she went on with a sudden serious sweetness, "but nobody could ever count my love for you. Shall I put the chops on, Jim?"

Out of his trance Jim seemed quickly to wake. He enfolded his Della. For ten

seconds let us regard with discreet scrutiny some inconsequential object in the other direction. Eight dollars a week or a million a year—what is the difference? A mathematician or a wit would give you the wrong answer. The Magi brought valuable gifts, but that was not among them. This dark assertion will be illuminated later on.

Jim drew a package from his overcoat pocket and threw it upon the table.

"Don't make any mistake, Dell," he said, "about me. I don't think there's anything in the way of a haircut or a shave or a shampoo that could make me like my girl any less. But if you'll unwrap that package, you may see why you had me going a while at first."

White fingers and nimble tore at the string and paper. And then an ecstatic scream of joy; and then, alas! a quick feminine change to hysterical tears and wails, necessitating the immediate employment of all the comforting powers of the lord of the flat.

For there lay The Combs—the set of combs, side and back, that Della had worshiped for long in a Broadway window. Beautiful combs, pure tortoise shell, with jeweled rims—just the shade to wear in the beautiful vanished hair. They were expensive combs, she knew, and her heart had simply craved and yearned over them without the least hope of possession. And now they were hers, but the tresses that should have adorned the coveted adornments were gone.

But she hugged them to her bosom, and at length she was able to look up with dim eyes and a smile and say, "My hair grows so fast, Jim!" And then Della leaped up like a little singed cat and cried, "Oh, oh!"

Jim had not yet seen his beautiful present. She held it out to him eagerly upon her open palm. The dull precious metal seemed to flash with a reflection of her bright and ardent spirit.

"Isn't it a dandy, Jim? I hunted all over town to find it. You'll have to look at the time a hundred times a day now. Give me your watch. I want to see how it looks on it."

Instead of obeying, Jim tumbled down on the couch and put his hands under the back of his head and smiled.

"Dell," said he, "let's put our Christmas presents away and keep 'em a while. They're too nice to use just at present. I sold the watch to get the money to buy your combs. And now suppose you put the chops on."

The Magi, as you know, were wise men, wonderfully wise men, who brought gifts to the Babe in the manger. They invented the art of giving Christmas presents. Being wise, their gifts were no doubt wise ones, possibly bearing the privilege of exchange in case of duplication. And here I have lamely related to you the uneventful chronicle of two foolish children in a flat who most unwisely sacrificed for each other the greatest treasures of their house. But in a last word to the wise of these days let it be said that of all who give gifts these two were the wisest. Of all who give and receive gifts, such as they are wisest. Everywhere they are wisest. They are the Magi.

READING FOR DETAILS

An Exchange of Love

Paradoxically, people willing to sacrifice their greatest treasure to show their love for another person may be unwise, but they are at the same time extremely wise. This would seem to be the theme, or central idea, of "The Gift of the Magi."

1. Although the theme remains ageless, there are many indications to show that the story took place a number of years ago. Discuss details that date the account.
2. How much money had Della saved? How much does Mme Sofronie pay her for her hair? What does she buy for Jim?
3. How does Jim act when he first sees Della? Why is he so completely at a loss? What does he say when Della shows him the present she bought for him?

READING FOR MEANING

Discuss the following quotations as they relate to the O. Henry story:

1. "It is more blessed to give than to receive"—Acts 20:35.

2. "One must be poor to know the luxury of giving"—George Eliot, *Middlemarch*.
3. "A man there was, though some did count him mad,
   The more he cast away, the more he had"—John Bunyan, *Pilgrim's Progress*.

READING FOR APPRECIATION

Characterization

1. What does the following quotation reveal about Della's character?

   "But what could I do—oh! what could I do with a dollar and eighty-seven cents?"

2. Although O. Henry wrote "The Gift of the Magi" in third person—that is, using "he," "she," or the names of the characters—he did not confine himself simply to the thoughts and actions of the characters themselves. He allowed himself to be present on the scene as an observer who communicated directly with the reader. This was a literary device (known as "Dear Reader") commonly used by writers of a century ago but rarely used now.

   Which of the character techniques does the observer/narrator use to tell the reader about Della and Jim?

Significant Detail

The action in most O. Henry stories had to be tightly organized, or contrived, in order to allow for the surprise ending. What significant details does O. Henry use to prepare the reader for the surprise ending?

COMPOSITION

Although now out-of-date, the "Dear Reader" technique utilized by O. Henry and other authors of his time allowed those writers great liberty in revealing information about their characters directly to the reader. After you have read the short narrative passage below, use the lead-in: "Dear Reader, what you do not know is . . . ." and write a paragraph or more in which you reveal the circumstances that lie behind the behavior of Seth and Sadie. Use as many significant details as possible to increase the interest of the reader in this dramatic situation.

Seth and Sadie stood in front of the fresh produce section of the busy supermarket. Sadie was clutching a package of parsnips in her hand, and Seth had just shoved his billfold into his back pocket. Sadie's eyes blazed with an anger that was matched by the pugnacious set of Seth's jaw. As Seth moved toward her, Sadie whirled and threw the parsnips to the floor and ran headlong from the store, bumping incoming shoppers in her flight. The package of vegetables skidded in front of a police officer's cart as Seth stood, one arm extended in embarrassed appeal. As the eyes of all who witnessed the scene focused upon him, he swung round and followed Sadie from the store.

BIOGRAPHICAL NOTE

O. Henry (1862–1910) is the pen name of William Sydney Porter. Born in Greensboro, North Carolina, he was a school dropout at fifteen, working first in a drugstore, then as a teller in a bank in Austin, Texas. When a shortage was discovered in his accounts at the bank, Porter foolishly fled to Honduras. However, he soon returned and was tried and sentenced to prison. Ironically, it was later determined almost conclusively that he was not an embezzler, but simply the victim of a poor bookkeeping system. It was in prison that he began writing stories, and after his release he went to New York City to write for the *New York World*. His stories were very popular and have been widely imitated.

Have you ever thought
what a wonderful world this would be if everyone were equal?
See if you still think this way after reading this story.

HARRISON BERGERON

Kurt Vonnegut, Jr.

The year was 2081, and everybody was finally equal. They weren't only equal before God and the law. They were equal every which way. Nobody was smarter than anybody else. Nobody was better looking than anybody else. Nobody was stronger or quicker than anybody else. All this equality was due to the 211th, 212th, and 213th Amendments to the Constitution, and to the unceasing vigilance of agents of the United States Handicapper General.

Some things about living still weren't quite right, though. April, for instance, still drove people crazy by not being springtime. And it was in that clammy month that the H-G men took George and Hazel Bergeron's fourteen-year-old son, Harrison, away.

It was tragic, all right, but George and Hazel couldn't think about it very hard. Hazel had a perfectly average intelligence, which meant she couldn't think about anything except in short bursts. And George, while his intelligence was way above normal, had a little mental handicap radio in his ear. He was required by law to wear it at all times. It was tuned to a government transmitter. Every twenty seconds or so, the transmitter would send out some sharp noise to keep people like George from taking unfair advantage of their brains.

George and Hazel were watching television. There were tears on Hazel's cheeks, but she'd forgotten for the moment what they were about.

On the television screen were ballerinas.

A buzzer sounded in George's head. His thoughts fled in panic, like bandits from a burglar alarm.

"That was a real pretty dance, that dance they just did," said Hazel.

"Huh?" said George.

"That dance—it was nice," said Hazel.

"Yup," said George. He tried to think a little about the ballerinas. They weren't really very good—no better than anybody else would have been, anyway. They were burdened with sash weights and bags of birdshot, and their faces were masked, so that no one, seeing a free and graceful gesture or a pretty face, would feel like something the cat drug in. George was toying with the vague notion that maybe dancers shouldn't be handicapped. But he didn't get very far with it before another noise in his ear radio scattered his thoughts.

George winced. So did two out of the eight ballerinas.

Hazel saw him wince. Having no mental handicap herself, she had to ask George what the latest sound had been.

"Sounded like somebody hitting a milk bottle with a ball peen hammer," said George.

"I'd think it would be real interesting, hearing all the different sounds," said Hazel, a little envious. "All the things they think up."

"Um," said George.

"Only, if I was Handicapper General, you know what I would do?" said Hazel. Hazel, as a matter of fact, bore a strong resemblance to the Handicapper General, a woman named Diana Moon Glampers. "If I was Diana Moon Glampers," said Hazel, "I'd have chimes on Sunday—just chimes. Kind of in honor of religion."

"I could think, if it was just chimes," said George.

"Well—maybe make 'em real loud," said Hazel. "I think I'd make a good Handicapper General."

"Good as anybody else," said George.

"Who knows better'n I do what normal is?" said Hazel.

"Right," said George. He began to think glimmeringly about his abnormal son who was now in jail, about Harrison, but a twenty-one-gun salute in his head stopped that.

"Boy!" said Hazel, "that was a doozy, wasn't it?"

It was such a doozy that George was white and trembling, and tears stood on the rims of his red eyes. Two of the eight ballerinas had collapsed to the studio floor, were holding their temples.

"All of a sudden you look so tired," said Hazel. "Why don't you stretch out on the sofa, so's you can rest your handicap bag on the pillows, honeybunch." She was referring to the forty-seven pounds of birdshot in a canvas bag, which was padlocked around George's neck. "Go on

and rest the bag for a little while," she said. "I don't care if you're not equal to me for a while."

George weighed the bag with his hands. "I don't mind it," he said. "I don't notice it any more. It's just a part of me."

"You been so tired lately—kind of wore out," said Hazel. "If there was just some way we could make a little hole in the bottom of the bag, and just take out a few of them lead balls. Just a few."

"Two years in prison and two thousand dollars fine for every ball I took out," said George. "I don't call that a bargain."

"If you could just take a few out when you came home from work," said Hazel. "I mean—you don't compete with anybody around here. You just set around."

"If I tried to get away with it," said George, "then other people'd get away with it—and pretty soon we'd be right back to the dark ages again, with everybody competing against everybody else. You wouldn't like that, would you?"

"I'd hate it," said Hazel.

"There you are," said George. "The minute people start cheating on laws, what do you think happens to society?"

If Hazel hadn't been able to come up with an answer to this question, George couldn't have supplied one. A siren was going off in his head.

"Reckon it'd fall all apart," said Hazel.

"What would?" said George blankly.

"Society," said Hazel uncertainly. "Wasn't that what you just said?"

"Who knows?" said George.

The television program was suddenly interrupted for a news bulletin. It wasn't clear at first as to what the bulletin was about, since the announcer, like all announcers, had a serious speech impediment. For about half a minute, and in a state of high excitement, the announcer tried to say, "Ladies and gentlemen—"

He finally gave up, handed the bulletin to a ballerina to read.

"That's all right—" Hazel said of the announcer, "he tried. That's the big thing. He tried to do the best he could with what God gave him. He should get a nice raise for trying so hard."

"Ladies and gentlemen—" said the ballerina, reading the bulletin. She must have been extraordinarily beautiful, because the mask she wore was hideous. And it was easy to see that she was the strongest and most graceful of all the dancers, for her handicap bags were as big as those worn by two-hundred-pound men.

And she had to apologize at once for her voice, which was a very unfair voice for a woman to use. Her voice was a warm, luminous, timeless melody. "Excuse me—" she said, and she began again, making her voice absolutely uncompetitive.

"Harrison Bergeron, age fourteen," she said in a grackle squawk, "has just escaped from jail, where he was held on suspicion of plotting to overthrow the government. He is a genius and an athlete, is under-handicapped, and should be regarded as extremely dangerous."

A police photograph of Harrison Bergeron was flashed on the screen—upside down, then sideways, upside down again, then right side up. The picture showed the full length of Harrison against a background calibrated in feet and inches. He was exactly seven feet tall.

The rest of Harrison's appearance was Halloween and hardware. Nobody had ever borne heavier handicaps. He had outgrown hindrances faster than the H-G men could think them up. Instead

of a little ear radio for a mental handicap, he wore a tremendous pair of earphones, and spectacles with thick wavy lenses. The spectacles were intended to make him not only half blind, but to give him whanging headaches besides.

Scrap metal was hung all over him. Ordinarily, there was a certain symmetry, a military neatness to the handicaps issued to strong people, but Harrison looked like a walking junkyard. In the race of life, Harrison carried three hundred pounds.

And to offset his good looks, the H-G men required that he wear at all times a red rubber ball for a nose, keep his eyebrows shaved off, and cover his even white teeth with black caps at snaggletooth random.

"If you see this boy," said the ballerina, "do not—I repeat, do not—try to reason with him."

There was the shriek of a door being torn from its hinges.

Screams and barking cries of consternation came from the television set. The photograph of Harrison Bergeron on the screen jumped again and again, as though dancing to the tune of an earthquake.

George Bergeron correctly identified the earthquake, and well he might have—for many was the time his own home had danced to the same crashing tune. "My goodness," said George, "that must be Harrison!"

The realization was blasted from his mind instantly by the sound of an automobile collision in his head.

When George could open his eyes again, the photograph of Harrison was gone. A living, breathing Harrison filled the screen.

Clanking, clownish, and huge, Harri-

son stood in the center of the studio. The knob of the uprooted studio door was still in his hand. Ballerinas, technicians, musicians, and announcers cowered on their knees before him, expecting to die.

"I am the Emperor!" cried Harrison. "Do you hear? I am the Emperor! Everybody must do what I say at once!" He stamped his foot and the studio shook.

"Even as I stand here—" he bellowed, "crippled, hobbled, sickened—I am a greater ruler than any man who ever lived! Now watch me become what I *can* become!"

Harrison tore the straps of his handicap harness like wet tissue paper, tore straps guaranteed to support five thousand pounds.

Harrison's scrap-iron handicaps crashed to the floor.

Harrison thrust his thumbs under the bar of the padlock that secured his head harness. The bar snapped like celery. Harrison smashed his headphones and spectacles against the wall.

He flung away his rubber-ball nose, revealed a man that would have awed Thor, the god of thunder.

"I shall now select my Empress!" he said, looking down on the cowering people. "Let the first woman who dares rise to her feet claim her mate and her throne!"

A moment passed, and then a ballerina arose, swaying like a willow.

Harrison plucked the mental handicap from her ear, snapped off her physical handicaps with marvelous delicacy. Last of all, he removed her mask.

She was blindingly beautiful.

"Now—" said Harrison, taking her hand, "shall we show the people the meaning of the word dance? Music!" he commanded.

The musicians scrambled back into their chairs, and Harrison stripped them of their handicaps, too. "Play your best," he told them, "and I'll make you barons and dukes and earls."

The music began. It was normal at first—cheap, silly, false. But Harrison snatched two musicians from their chairs, waved them like batons as he sang the music as he wanted it played. He slammed them back into their chairs.

The music began again and was much improved.

Harrison and his Empress merely listened to the music for a while—listened gravely, as though synchronizing their heartbeats with it.

They shifted their weights to their toes.

Harrison placed his big hands on the girl's tiny waist, letting her sense the weightlessness that would soon be hers.

And then, in an explosion of joy and grace, into the air they sprang!

Not only were the laws of the land abandoned, but the law of gravity and the laws of motion as well.

They reeled, whirled, swiveled, flounced, capered, gamboled, and spun.

They leaped like deer on the moon.

The studio ceiling was thirty feet high, but each leap brought the dancers nearer to it.

It became their obvious intention to kiss the ceiling.

They kissed it.

And then, neutralizing gravity with love and pure will, they remained suspended in air inches below the ceiling, and they kissed each other for a long, long time.

It was then that Diana Moon Glampers, the Handicapper General, came into the studio with a double-barreled ten-gauge shotgun. She fired twice, and the Emperor and the Empress were dead before they hit the floor.

Diana Moon Glampers loaded the gun again. She aimed it at the musicians and told them they had ten seconds to get their handicaps back on.

It was then that the Bergerons' television tube burned out.

Hazel turned to comment about the blackout to George. But George had gone out into the kitchen for a can of beer.

George came back in with the beer, paused while a handicap signal shook him up. And then he sat down again. "You been crying?" he said to Hazel.

"Yup," she said.

"What about?" he said.

"I forget," she said. "Something real sad on television."

"What was it?" he said.

"It's all kind of mixed up in my mind," said Hazel.

"Forget sad things," said George.

"I always do," said Hazel.

"That's my girl," said George. He winced. There was the sound of a riveting gun in his head.

"Gee—I could tell that one was a doozy," said Hazel.

"You can say that again," said George.

"Gee—" said Hazel, "I could tell that one was a doozy."

READING FOR DETAILS

A World of Equals

1. What year is it when the story opens? How has equality been brought about?
2. How have George and Hazel been made equal in intelligence? How are the ballerinas handicapped?

3. Why had Harrison Bergeron been taken from his parents and put in jail? How was he handicapped?
4. Where and how does Harrison proclaim himself Emperor? Who becomes his Empress? What three kinds of laws do they disobey when they dance?

READING FOR MEANING

The author gives support to all of these generalizations in the story. Discuss.

1. Because complete equality is impossible, people should stop thinking and talking about equality.
2. All disagreeable things about living can be eliminated.

READING FOR APPRECIATION

Characterization

1. Discuss the ways Vonnegut makes Hazel seem ridiculous as a "normal" woman.
2. Because George is much above average intelligence, he is an even more pathetic figure than Hazel. When he and Hazel are talking, what does he reveal about his way of thinking?
3. How do Harrison's actions and words, when he first appears on television, show that for all his size he is still like a little boy?

BIOGRAPHICAL NOTE

Kurt Vonnegut, Jr. (1922–   ) was born in Indianapolis. During World War II he served as an army combat intelligence scout, was captured, and spent 5 months as a prisoner of war in Dresden, Germany. Widely read and much in demand as a speaker, Vonnegut first published in such magazines as *Cosmopolitan, Ladies' Home Journal, Playboy,* and the *Saturday Evening Post.* Among his most popular books are *The Sirens of Titan; Mother Night; God Bless You, Mr. Rosewater; Slaughterhouse Five;* and *Cat's Cradle.* His most recent novel is *Deadeye Dick* (1982).

What does he have—
this old black man—that raises him above
the miseries and pain of living?

Jazz Poem Two

there he stands. see?
like a black Ancient Mariner* his
wrinkled old face so
full of the wearies of living is
turned downward with   5
closed eyes. his frayed-collar
faded-blue old shirt turn
dark with sweat & the old
necktie undone drops
loosely about the worn   10
old jacket see? just
barely holding his
sagging stomach in. yeah.
his run-down shoes have
paper in them & his   15
rough unshaven face shows
pain
in each wrinkle

but there he stands. in
self-brought solitude head   20
still down eyes
still closed ears
perked & trained upon
the bass line for
across his chest lies an old   25
alto saxophone—
supported from his neck by
a wire coat hanger.
gently he lifts it now
to parted lips. see? to   30
tell all the world that

*Ancient Mariner, a reference to a poem, "The Rime
of the Ancient Mariner," by Samuel Taylor Coleridge, in
which a seaman shoots an albatross, a bird of good omen,
and suffers supernatural punishment. The seaman is
compelled to tell his story repeatedly.

he is a Black Man. that
he was sent here to preach
the Black Gospel of Jazz.

now preaching it with words of   35
screaming notes & chords he
is no longer a man. no not even
a Black Man. but (yeah!)
a Bird—
one that gathers his wings & flies   40
   high
      high
         higher
until he flies away! or
comes back to find himself   45
a Black Man
again.

CARL WENDELL HINES, JR.

Originally appeared in AMERICAN NEGRO POETRY, edited by Arna
Bontemps. Hill and Wang, Inc. Copyright © 1963. By permission of the
author, Carl Wendell Hines, Jr.
© 1965 by The New York Times Company. Reprinted by permission.

A GOSPEL WITHOUT WORDS

Like the ancient mariner in Coleridge's poem, the old jazz musician feels he has a message for the people of the world. He is a pitiable figure, but he is also a commanding one. He has the power to speak in a way that makes men listen—a gift that many people richer in worldly goods do not possess. He speaks eloquently through his music; it is this act of creation that lifts him above the squalor of his surroundings.

Coleridge's ancient mariner felt compelled to travel from land to land to preach love and reverence for all forms of life, great and small. Discuss whether you think this message might also be found in the "preaching" of the old jazz musician.

Characterization

Carl Wendell Hines, Jr. wants the reader to "see" the old man clearly, and he manages to give a vivid picture without waste of words.

1. What are you told about the old man's face, his clothing, his shoes? How do you know he isn't much interested in talking to those around him? What instrument is his "voice"?

2. Why are the last ten words of the poem significant?

BIOGRAPHICAL NOTE

Carl Wendell Hines, Jr. (1940–   ), was born in North Carolina. He was graduated from Tennessee Agricultural and Industrial University in 1962. His verses have been hailed as some of the best by contemporary black writers.

Do you have pictures in your memory?
For example, have you ever seen . . .

A Clown at Ten

We should have guessed—
When he pounced home in a flailing
    dance,
Clucking like a hen possessed,
Elbows flapping in a sidelong prance,
Grinning grimly,   5
Mocking primly
A saucy schoolmate's slur—
The deepdown bite of her.
We should have known
His pull-ups on the closet pole,   10
His swimming in the kitchen zone,
His pugilistic body roll

On the church pew
And museum queue
Were ways to storm the pass   15
For the smallest in his class.
Each noon he licked his silly grin
And ate beyond our discipline.
We called him fool
And fed him shame,   20
This little giant
With our name.

JAMES A. EMANUEL

A COMIC WITH A PURPOSE

It is easy to see this "clown at ten" when you read the poet's words and make an effort to picture, in your mind's eye, a boy going through all the antics described in order to establish his importance. His handicap is his size.

1. How do you imitate a hen? Discuss.
2. What did he do to try to build up his chest and general physique?
3. The poet uses the expression, "he licked his silly grin." What common association is made with the gesture of licking the lips?

COMPOSITION

Think about a young child in your own family or neighborhood who plays a role or assumes a kind of character to make himself or herself seem important in the eyes of others. Better still, recall what *you* did as a child to gain stature among your peers or elders. Then write a couple of paragraphs or a poem in which you picture this child.

BIOGRAPHICAL NOTE

James A. Emanuel (1921–   ), born and raised in Alliance, Nebraska, attended Howard, Northwestern, and Columbia universities where he received, respectively, his B.A. (1950), M.A. (1953), and Ph.D. (1962) degrees. Emanuel's poetry was first published in college periodicals. By 1958 his work began to appear in *Midwest Quarterly*, the *New York Times*, *Negro Digest*, *Freedomways*, and other periodicals. His poetry has been anthologized in several collections and textbooks. Two volumes of his poetry are *The Treehouse and Other Poems*, published in 1968, and *A Chisel in the Dark*, published in 1980.

SUMMING UP: WITH WHAT YOU HAVE

If you look around at school or in your community at the people who are successful, you will discover that they spend little time envying others or complaining about what they do not have. They are people like Daniel Inouye or Jesse Stuart who use what they have and make it count.

READING FOR MEANING

Discuss the following statements as they relate to your reading in this unit:
1. It's an ill wind that blows no good.
2. Many commonly accepted customs reflect hypocrisy and discrimination.
3. Taking on a seemingly impossible task strengthens character.
4. Humility is one sign of greatness.
5. All people should be equally endowed.

READING FOR APPRECIATION

Characterization

In your daily contact with others, perhaps you have noticed that at times a few chance words or a gesture will reveal something significant about someone's personality or character. If a friend loses the contest for the class presidency, does this friend laugh and say, "Better luck next time," snarl that dirty tactics were used, or refuse to comment? Such reactions can be revealing.

Writers of fiction or nonfiction whose principal interest is setting forth clearly and vividly the personalities of their subjects, know the value of such character indicators. They use five common ways to tell you what an individual is really like. In review, these are:
1. what the character looks like
2. what the character says and thinks
3. what others say and think about the character
4. the way the character acts in a given situation
5. the way others act toward the character

Consider the following and discuss what is revealed about the character of the person whose name precedes the quotation.
1. Daniel Inouye: It left me enraged and a little confused, but most of all it left me with a fiery resolve to "show those guys!" Never before had I felt so challenged, nor so determined to make something of myself.
2. Jesse Stuart: We had never lost an hour. I had actually taught more hours than required. . . . It was too bad that another blizzard had swept our rugged land. . . . But this didn't stop the boys and me from going.

Significant Detail

The following are statements which the author might have used if he or she had omitted the significant details. Supply three details, in each case, with which the author added reality and vividness. Do not look up the incident in the selection until after you have tried to supply the details from memory.
1. Dr. Carver made many products from plants ("A Boy Who Was Traded for a Horse," p. 153).
2. Louise Baker learned to roller-skate well ("Best Foot Forward," p. 145).
3. Della and Jim each sold a personal possession to buy the other a Christmas gift ("The Gift of the Magi," p. 176).
4. Jesse Stuart's students took part in a scholarship contest ("A Little Mudhole in the Road," p. 165).

COMPOSITION WORKSHOP

THE BIOGRAPHICAL REPORT

In this unit are included several forms of biographical writing: "Best Foot Forward," "A Boy Who Was Traded for a Horse," and *The Miracle Worker*. While imaginative writers will often use a variety of forms to communicate biographical or autobiographical information, the practical writer will almost always choose the brief biographical report to present the highlights of a person's life. Such a report will usually be made up of from four to six paragraphs. The report will be designed to do two things. First, it will give basic details about the person's life. A reader always wants to know when and where the person lived, for example. Second, the report will usually focus on two or three important things that the person did.

Study the following brief biographical report. Notice that it both sketches out the life of its subject and also zeroes in on two important achievements.

Maria Mitchell made full use of her talents and opportunities to become a leading American scientist and educator. Her achievement is especially great because she managed to have two successful careers at a time when women were expected to remain quietly in the home.

Maria Mitchell was born in 1818 on the island of Nantucket off the coast of Massachusetts. In the early nineteenth century, Nantucket was the center of the whaling industry in the United States. Maria's father served that industry by repairing and checking the nautical instruments used by the whaling captains. In her early years Maria showed signs of an ability that was rarely encouraged in young girls. By the time she was seven years old, Maria was fascinated by the mathematical calculations that her father had to use to set the instruments. After she enrolled in the local school, her interest in mathematics became obvious to all, and her ability in the subject far exceeded that of her teacher.

After graduating from the Nantucket grammar school, Maria Mitchell wanted very much to further her natural interest in mathematics and science. But opportunities for girls did not exist in mathematics and science, and formal education never extended beyond grade school. Fortunately, her father was fascinated by astronomy, and Maria became deeply involved in his nightly observations. A tremendous opportunity presented itself when the island's town officers placed her in charge of the local library. Her librarian's duties did not take the entire day, so Maria had plenty of time to further her own scientific interests through daily reading and study. She would then spend most of her evenings studying the heavens through her father's crude telescope located in a small observatory built on the roof of the family's house.

An event occurred on October 1, 1847, that brought Maria Mitchell to the attention of the scientific world. While her family entertained guests, Maria was in the rooftop observatory as usual. As the family and its guests called out to Maria to join them, she excitedly asked her father to come to the telescope to check an observation she had made. She explained to her father that she had seen what she believed to be a previously unknown comet. Rather skeptically, her father looked through the instrument's eyepiece and saw at once a comet where no known comet should have been. On the very next day Maria wrote to the observatory at Harvard University to announce her discovery. Skilled astronomers throughout the world confirmed her discovery shortly afterwards. She received for her achievement a gold medal from the king of Denmark, who had established prizes to encourage the growth of the science of astronomy. Her successful discovery, accomplished with a primitive instrument and without the benefit of formal training in astronomy, led to her election as a fellow of the American Academy of Arts and Sciences. By the middle of the nineteenth century, Maria Mitchell was hailed as one of the world's leading astronomers.

Maria Mitchell's scientific reputation led to an additional career that was to occupy her until shortly before her death in 1889. In 1865, Mr. Matthew Vassar was attempting to found in Poughkeepsie, New York, the woman's college that today bears his name. He invited Maria Mitchell to become the college's first professor of astronomy. After a great deal of thought she accepted his invitation, although somewhat reluctantly. Self-taught herself, she wasn't sure she had either the background or the ability to teach others. But she became one of the new college's most inspired and gifted teachers and introduced two generations of women to a science that was previously beyond their reach. During her years on the college's faculty, she and her students conducted important studies and observations of the sun and of the planets Jupiter and Saturn. Maria Mitchell died in 1889, known throughout the country and a large part of the world as an important pioneer in both science and education.

Note the following things about this brief biographical report:

1. The writer had to gather the factual information about the subject of the report. People rarely carry such information around in their minds. It must be collected from basic information sources.

2. The brief biographical report has a definite structure. The first or introductory paragraph announces what the report will be about. The first sentence of this paragraph is the thesis sentence for the entire report. It summarizes the major areas that the report will cover. It promises that the paragraphs in the body of the report will show that Maria Mitchell did indeed make full use of her talents and opportunities in becoming an important American scientist and educator.

3. The paragraphs that make up the body of the report are arranged in a sensible order. The paragraphs are in chronological, or time, order. The first paragraph in the body of the report notes when and where Maria Mitchell was born and tells about the young girl's interest in mathematics. The second paragraph explains how she further developed that interest by making the most of her opportunities. The third paragraph focuses on her scientific achievement. The fourth paragraph shows how she succeeded in yet another field. This rough outline of the body of the report shows the structure clearly:

   I. Ability in youth
   II. Takes opportunity for further study
   III. Scientific achievement
   IV. Educational career

4. Notice that the topic sentences of these paragraphs relate to the thesis sentence. The second and final sentence of the introductory paragraph notes the overall importance of Maria Mitchell's achievement and helps get the reader interested in the report.

A good biographical report is not merely a listing of events in a person's life. A good report does more than supply basic information about what the person did and where and when it was done. It identifies and presents to the reader the significant things that a person has done, and it explains why those things make the person's life worth knowing about.

ACTIVITY

Select a famous person to be the subject of a brief biographical report. Gather information on the person in the form of notes. Arrange the notes into three or four groups that will eventually become the paragraphs in the body of the report. Write a topic sentence for each group. Finally, write each of the paragraphs. Study the paragraphs and then write an introductory paragraph of two or three sentences. Make sure that the first sentence is a thesis sentence that identifies the report's topic and is related to the topic sentences of the paragraphs in the body of the report.

Homeless Annie Sullivan spent a good part of her childhood in a state almshouse, playing with rats instead of toys. It might seem that there would be little she could give to a pampered child surrounded with comfort. Yet Annie had courage, compassion, and a fighting spirit. With "what she had," she worked a miracle.

INTRODUCTION TO
The Miracle Worker

In the evening of October 19, 1959, an opening night audience at the Playhouse on New York's Broadway watched in fascination as the talented cast of William Gibson's play, *The Miracle Worker,* brought to life a stirring chapter from the early life of Helen Keller. When the final curtain came down, the audience responded with thunderous applause. They had been through a moving and memorable experience. Their emotions had been drawn taut as they witnessed the mind and soul of the deaf, blind, and mute seven-year-old Helen being pulled from an animal-like existence into a world she could at last understand.

Mark Twain, who met Helen Keller when she was still quite young, said that she was one of the two outstanding personalities of the nineteenth century. (The other was Napoleon.) She had traveled to all parts of the globe, lectured to thousands, written books, and made friends with most of the leading figures of her time. Yet had it not been for the efforts of Annie Sullivan, her teacher and her constant companion for nearly fifty years, the brilliant mind of Helen Keller might have remained forever isolated on an island of darkness.

Two years before she graduated from Radcliffe College with honors, Miss Keller completed an autobiography, *The Story of My Life.* The story of her early life was an immediate success and became required reading for students at various colleges and high schools over the United States. This story of her triumph has inspired millions of people, among them playwright William Gibson, who was moved to write *The Miracle Worker.*

In the beginning, Mr. Gibson wrote *The Miracle Worker* for television. Following its presentation in February of 1957, the response from viewers was so enthusiastic that he was asked to rewrite it for the Broadway stage. It appeared later as a successful motion picture.

When he had completed the original script, Mr. Gibson had it typed in Braille and sent to Miss Keller for corrections. She returned it with four pages of notes to aid him in avoiding factual errors. While the incidents in the play are basically accurate, the writer was forced to use imaginative devices introducing background information to explain the actions of the characters. The offstage voices which Anne Sullivan hears during the play are part of such a device.

The most persistent of these voices out of Annie's past is that of her little brother Jimmie. Since there is a flesh-and-blood Jimmie in the play, as Helen's half-brother James is sometimes called, the reader will need to be alert not to confuse the two.

As you read the first act of *The Miracle Worker,* watch for lines that give you clues to the personality of each character.

On Reading a Play

Plays are written primarily to be translated by actors into speech and action on a stage. When we read a play, then, we obviously miss certain dimensions. We cannot actually hear the voices of the actors speaking the lines. We do not see the movements, the gestures, the costumes, the color—all of the reality of a performance. Too, we miss the shared dramatic experience of being in a darkened theater, the hurry and scurry of our everyday lives shut out for a time, our attention focused on the stage where trained performers are bringing a written script to life.

In order to make up for the things in a live production that we miss, we must make special demands on our imaginations as we read a play. One of the best ways to get the most from reading drama is to "stage" the play in our minds. In this way, we take the script, or the blueprint, of the playwright and build our own production. From their descriptions, we picture the characters and we visualize the sets. We imagine the movements, the gestures, the tone of voice of each actor. Actually, there is an advantage in doing this. We can avoid some of the disappointments we have in the theater when the sets and lighting are poor, or when some actors are stiff or weak in their parts. Too, we can halt the action of the play any time that we wish to reflect over the significance of a speech or action, something impossible at a real performance.

However, in order to stage our own ideal production as we read, we must follow carefully the blueprint of the playwright's stage directions.

A spoon went flying over the footlights and into the audience on opening night during the breakfast-room struggle between Anne Bancroft (Annie Sullivan) and Patty Duke (Helen) on Broadway. Director Arthur Penn gave these versatile performers free reign in the interpretation of this episode, and it was never played exactly the same way twice. The pantomime siege was of such sustained length and violence that some theatergoers conjectured wryly whether or not understudies might be needed for the rest of the performance.

When the show opened, both Miss Bancroft and Patty Duke were fitted with knee pads and elbow pads. Before many performances had been given, they realized that they needed even more protection: shin guards, arm guards, and pads for the fronts and backs of their legs were added, along with padding sewed to the insides of their dresses. For this very real battle, Patty Duke found the high button shoes of her costume were a decided help.

THE MIRACLE WORKER
William Gibson

At another time she asked, "What is a soul?" "No one knows," I replied; "but we know it is not the body, and it is that part of us which thinks and loves and hopes.... [and] is invisible."... "But if I write what my soul thinks," she said, "then it will be visible, and the words will be its body."

—ANNIE SULLIVAN, 1891

CHARACTERS
In Order of Appearance

A DOCTOR

KATE

KELLER

HELEN

MARTHA

PERCY

AUNT EV

JAMES

ANAGNOS

ANNIE SULLIVAN

BLIND GIRLS

VINEY

A SERVANT

OFFSTAGE VOICES

William Gibson, THE MIRACLE WORKER. Copyright © 1956, 1957 by William Gibson; copyright © 1959, 1960 by Tamarack Productions, Ltd., and George S. Klein and Leo Garel as Trustees under three separate deeds of trust (New York: Atheneum, 1960). Reprinted with the permission of Atheneum Publishers.

Time: The 1880's.

Place: In and around the Keller homestead in Tuscumbia, Alabama; also, briefly, the Perkins Institution for the Blind in Boston.

The playing space is divided into two areas by a more or less diagonal line, which runs from downstage right to upstage left.

The area behind this diagonal is on platforms and represents the Keller house; inside we see, down right, a family room, and up center, elevated, a bedroom. On stage level near center, outside a porch, there is a water pump.

The other area, in front of the diagonal, is neutral ground; it accommodates various places as designated at various times—the yard before the Keller home, the Perkins Institution for the Blind, the garden house, and so forth.

The convention of the staging is one of cutting through time and place, and its essential qualities are fluidity and spatial counterpoint. To this end, the less set there is, the better; in a literal set, the fluidity will seem merely episodic. The stage therefore should be free, airy, unencumbered by walls. Apart from certain practical items—such as the pump, a window to climb out of, doors to be locked—locales should be only skeletal suggestions, and the movement from one to another should be accomplishable by little more than lights.

Act I

It is night over the Keller homestead.

Inside, three adults in the bedroom are grouped around a crib, in lamplight. They have been through a long vigil, and it shows in their tired bearing and disarranged clothing. One is a

young gentlewoman with a sweet girlish face, KATE KELLER; *the second is an elderly* DOCTOR, *stethoscope at neck, thermometer in fingers; the third is a hearty gentleman in his forties with chin whiskers,* CAPTAIN ARTHUR KELLER.

DOCTOR. She'll live.
KATE. Thank God.

[*The* DOCTOR *leaves them together over the crib, packs his bag.*]

DOCTOR. You're a pair of lucky parents. I can tell you now, I thought she wouldn't.
KELLER. Nonsense, the child's a Keller, she has the constitution of a goat. She'll outlive us all.
DOCTOR (*amiably*). Yes, especially if some of you Kellers don't get a night's sleep. I mean you, Mrs. Keller.
KELLER. You hear, Katie?
KATE. I hear.
KELLER (*indulgent*). I've brought up two of them, but this is my wife's first, she isn't battle-scarred yet.
KATE. Doctor, don't be merely considerate, will my girl be all right?
DOCTOR. Oh, by morning she'll be knocking down Captain Keller's fences again.
KATE. And isn't there anything we should do?
KELLER (*jovial*). Put up stronger fencing, ha?
DOCTOR. Just let her get well, she knows how to do it better than we do.

[*He is packed, ready to leave.*]

Main thing is the fever's gone, these things come and go in infants, never know why. Call it acute congestion of the stomach and brain.
KELLER. I'll see you to your buggy, Doctor.
DOCTOR. I've never seen a baby with more vitality, that's the truth.

[*He beams a good night at the baby and* KATE, *and* KELLER *leads him downstairs with a lamp. They go down the porch steps, and across the yard, where the* DOCTOR *goes off left;* KELLER *stands with the lamp aloft.* KATE *meanwhile is bent lovingly over the crib, which emits a bleat; her finger is playful with the baby's face.*]

KATE. Hush. Don't you cry now, you've been trouble enough. Call it acute congestion, indeed, I don't see what's so cute about a congestion, just because it's yours? We'll have your father run an editorial in his paper, the wonders of modern medicine, they don't know what they're curing even when they cure it. Men, men and their battle scars, we women will have to—

[*But she breaks off, puzzled, moves her finger before the baby's eyes.*]

Will have to—Helen?

[*Now she moves her hand, quickly.*]

Helen.

[*She snaps her fingers at the baby's eyes twice, and her hand falters; after a moment she calls out, loudly.*]

Captain. Captain, will you come—

[*But she stares at the baby, and her next call is directly at her ears.*]

Captain!

[*And now, still staring,* KATE *screams.* KELLER *in the yard hears it, and runs with the lamp back to the house.* KATE *screams again, her look intent on the baby and terrible.* KELLER *hurries in and up.*]

KELLER. Katie? What's wrong?
KATE. Look.

[*She makes a pass with her hand in the crib, at the baby's eyes.*]

KELLER. What, Katie? She's well, she needs only time to—
KATE. She can't see. Look at her eyes.

[*She takes the lamp from him, moves it before the child's face.*]

She can't *see!*
KELLER (*hoarsely*). Helen.
KATE. Or hear. When I screamed she didn't blink. Not an eyelash—
KELLER. Helen. Helen!
KATE. She can't *hear* you!
KELLER. *Helen!*

[*His face has something like fury in it, crying the child's name;* KATE *almost fainting presses her knuckles to her mouth, to stop her own cry.*

The room dims out quickly.

Time, in the form of a slow tune of distant belfry chimes which approaches in a crescendo and then fades, passes; the light comes up again on a day five years later, on three kneeling children and an old dog outside around the pump.

The dog is a setter named Belle, and she is sleeping. Two of the children are Negroes, MARTHA *and* PERCY. *The third child is* HELEN, *six and a half years old, quite unkempt, in body a vivacious little person with a fine head, attractive, but noticeably blind, one eye larger and protruding; her gestures are abrupt, insistent, lacking in human restraint, and her face never smiles. She is flanked by the other two, in a litter of paper-doll cutouts, and while they speak* HELEN'S *hands thrust at their faces in turn, feeling baffledly at the movements of their lips.*]

MARTHA (*snipping*). First I'm gonna cut off this doctor's legs, one, two, now then—
PERCY. Why you cuttin' off that doctor's legs?
MARTHA. I'm gonna give him a operation. Now I'm gonna cut off his arms, one, two. Now I'm gonna fix up—

[*She pushes* HELEN'S *hand away from her mouth.*]

You stop that.
PERCY. Cut off his stomach, that's a good operation.
MARTHA. No, I'm gonna cut off his head first, he got a bad cold.
PERCY. Ain't gonna be much of that doctor left to fix up, time you finish all them opera—

[*But* HELEN *is poking her fingers inside his mouth, to feel his tongue; he bites at them, annoyed, and she jerks them away.* HELEN *now fingers her own lips, moving them in imitation, but soundlessly.*]

MARTHA. What you do, bite her hand?
PERCY. That's how I do, she keep pokin' her fingers in my mouth, I just bite 'em off.
MARTHA. What she tryin' do now?
PERCY. She tryin' *talk.* She gonna get mad. Looka her tryin' talk.

[HELEN *is scowling, the lips under her fingertips moving in ghostly silence, growing more and more frantic, until in a bizarre rage she bites at her own fingers. This sends* PERCY *off into laughter, but alarms* MARTHA.]

MARTHA. Hey, you stop now.

[*She pulls* HELEN'S *hand down.*]

You just sit quiet and—

[*But at once* HELEN *topples* MARTHA *on her back, knees pinning her shoulders down, and grabs the scissors.* MARTHA *screams.* PERCY *darts to the bell string on the porch, yanks it, and the bell rings.*

Inside, the lights have been gradually coming up on the main room, where we see the family informally gathered, talking, but in pantomime: KATE *sits darning socks near a cradle, occasionally rocking it;* CAPTAIN KELLER *in spectacles is working over newspaper pages at a table; a benign visitor in a hat,* AUNT EV, *is sharing the sewing basket, putting the finishing touches on a big shapeless doll made out of towels; an indolent young man, JAMES KELLER, is at the window watching the children.*

With the ring of the bell, KATE is instantly on her feet and out the door onto the porch, to take in the scene; now we see what these five years have done to her, the girlish playfulness is gone, she is a woman steeled in grief.]

KATE (*for the thousandth time*). Helen.

[*She is down the steps at once to them, seizing HELEN'S wrists and lifting her off MARTHA; MARTHA runs off in tears and screams for momma, with PERCY after her.*]

Let me have those scissors.

[*Meanwhile the family inside is alerted, AUNT EV joining JAMES at the window; CAPTAIN KELLER resumes work.*]

JAMES (*blandly*). She only dug Martha's eyes out. Almost dug. It's always almost, no point worrying till it happens, is there?

[*They gaze out, while KATE reaches for the scissors in HELEN'S hand. But HELEN pulls the scissors back, they struggle for them a moment, then KATE gives up, lets HELEN keep them. She tries to draw HELEN into the house. HELEN jerks away. KATE next goes down on her knees, takes HELEN'S hands gently, and using the scissors like a doll, makes HELEN caress and cradle them; she points HELEN'S finger housewards. HELEN'S whole body now becomes eager; she surrenders the scissors, KATE turns her toward the door and gives her a little push. HELEN scrambles up and toward the house, and KATE rising follows her.*]

AUNT EV. How does she stand it? Why haven't you seen this Baltimore man? It's not a thing you can let go on and on, like the weather.

JAMES. The weather here doesn't ask permission of me, Aunt Ev. Speak to my father.

AUNT EV. Arthur. Something ought to be done for that child.

KELLER. A refreshing suggestion. What?

[*KATE entering turns HELEN to AUNT EV, who gives her the towel doll.*]

AUNT EV. Why, this very famous oculist in Baltimore I wrote you about, what was his name?

KATE. Dr. Chisholm.

AUNT EV. Yes, I heard lots of cases of blindness people thought couldn't be cured he's cured, he just does wonders. Why don't you write to him?

KELLER. I've stopped believing in wonders.

KATE (*rocks the cradle*). I think the Captain will write to him soon. Won't you, Captain?

KELLER. No.

JAMES (*lightly*). Good money after bad, or bad after good. Or bad after bad—

AUNT EV. Well, if it's just a question of money, Arthur, now you're marshal you have this Yankee money. Might as well—

KELLER. Not money. The child's been to specialists all over Alabama and Tennessee, if I thought it would do good I'd have her to every fool doctor in the country.

KATE. I think the Captain will write to him soon.

KELLER. Katie. How many times can you let them break your heart?

KATE. Any number of times.

[*HELEN meanwhile sits on the floor to explore the doll with her fingers, and her hand pauses over the face: this is no face, a blank area of towel, and it troubles her. Her hand searches for features, and taps questioningly for eyes, but no one notices. She then yanks at her AUNT'S dress, and taps again vigorously for eyes.*]

AUNT EV. What, child?

[*Obviously not hearing, HELEN commences to go around, from person to person, tapping for eyes, but no one attends or understands.*]

KATE (*no break*). As long as there's the least chance. For her to see. Or hear, or—

KELLER. There isn't. Now I must finish here.

KATE. I think, with your permission, Captain, I'd like to write.

KELLER. I said no, Katie.

AUNT EV. Why, writing does no harm, Arthur, only a little bitty letter. To see if he can help her.

KELLER. He can't.

KATE. We won't know that to be a fact, Captain, until after you write.

KELLER (*rising, emphatic*). Katie, he can't.

[*He collects his papers.*]

JAMES (*facetiously*). Father stands up, that makes it a fact.

KELLER. You be quiet! I'm badgered enough here by females without your impudence.

[JAMES *shuts up, makes himself scarce.* HELEN *now is groping among things on* KELLER'S *desk, and paws his papers to the floor.* KELLER *is exasperated.*]

Katie.

[KATE *quickly turns* HELEN *away, and retrieves the papers.*]

I might as well try to work in a henyard as in this house—

JAMES (*placating*). You really ought to put her away, Father.

KATE (*staring up*). What?

JAMES. Some asylum. It's the kindest thing.

AUNT EV. Why, she's your sister, James, not a nobody—

JAMES. Half sister, and half—mentally defective, she can't even keep herself clean. It's not pleasant to see her about all the time.

KATE. Do you dare? Complain of what you *can* see?

KELLER (*very annoyed*). This discussion is at an end! I'll thank you not to broach it again, Ev.

[*Silence descends at once.* HELEN *gropes her way with the doll, and* KELLER *turns back for a final word, explosive.*]

I've done as much as I can bear, I can't give my whole life to it! The house is at sixes and sevens[1] from morning till night over the child, it's time some attention was paid to Mildred here instead!

KATE (*gently dry*). You'll wake her up, Captain.

KELLER. I want some peace in the house, I don't care how, but one way we won't have it is by rushing up and down the country every time someone hears of a new quack. I'm as sensible to this affliction as anyone else, it hurts me to look at the girl.

KATE. It was not our affliction I meant you to write about, Captain.

[HELEN *is back at* AUNT EV, *fingering her dress, and yanks two buttons from it.*]

AUNT EV. Helen! My buttons.

[HELEN *pushes the buttons into the doll's face.* KATE *now sees, comes swiftly to kneel, lifts* HELEN'S *hand to her own eyes in question.*]

KATE. Eyes?

[HELEN *nods energetically.*]

She wants the doll to have eyes.

[*Another kind of silence now, while* KATE *takes pins and buttons from the sewing basket and attaches them to the doll as eyes.* KELLER *stands, caught, and watches morosely.* AUNT EV *blinks, and conceals her emotion by inspecting her dress.*]

AUNT EV. My goodness me, I'm not decent.

KATE. She doesn't know better, Aunt Ev. I'll sew them on again.

---

1. **at sixes and sevens,** in a state of neglect and confusion.

JAMES. Never learn with everyone letting her do anything she takes it into her mind to—

KELLER. You be quiet!

JAMES. What did I say now?

KELLER. You talk too much.

JAMES. I was agreeing with you!

KELLER. Whatever it was. Deprived child, the least she can have are the little things she wants.

[JAMES, *very wounded, stalks out of the room onto the porch; he remains here, sulking.*]

AUNT EV (*indulgently*). It's worth a couple of buttons, Kate, look.

[HELEN *now has the doll with eyes, and cannot contain herself for joy; she rocks the doll, pats it vigorously, kisses it.*]

This child has more sense than all these men Kellers, if there's ever any way to reach that mind of hers.

[*But* HELEN *suddenly has come upon the cradle, and unhesitatingly overturns it; the swaddled baby tumbles out, and* CAPTAIN KELLER *barely manages to dive and catch it in time.*]

KELLER. Helen!

[*All are in commotion, the baby screams, but* HELEN *unperturbed is laying her doll in its place.* KATE *on her knees pulls her hands off the cradle, wringing them;* HELEN *is bewildered.*]

KATE. Helen, Helen, you're not to do such things, how can I make you understand—

KELLER (*hoarsely*). Katie.

KATE. How can I get it into your head, my darling, my poor—

KELLER. Katie, some way of teaching her an iota of discipline has to be—

KATE (*flaring*). How can you discipline an afflicted child? Is it her fault?

[HELEN'S *fingers have fluttered to her mother's lips, vainly trying to comprehend their movements.*]

KELLER. I didn't say it was her fault.

KATE. Then whose? I don't know what to do! How can I teach her, beat her—until she's black and blue?

KELLER. It's not safe to let her run around loose. Now there must be a way of confining her, somehow, so she can't—

KATE. Where, in a cage? She's a growing child, she has to use her limbs!

KELLER. Answer me one thing, is it fair to Mildred here?

KATE (*inexorably*). Are you willing to put her away?

[*Now* HELEN'S *face darkens in the same rage as at herself earlier, and her hand strikes at* KATE'S *lips.* KATE *catches her hand again, and* HELEN *begins to kick, struggle, twist.*]

KELLER. Now what?

KATE. She wants to talk, like—*be* like you and me.

[*She holds* HELEN *struggling until we hear from the child her first sound so far, an inarticulate weird noise in her throat such as an animal in a trap might make; and* KATE *releases her. The second she is free* HELEN *blunders away, collides violently with a chair, falls, and sits weeping.* KATE *comes to her, embraces, caresses, soothes her, and buries her own face in her hair, until she can control her voice.*]

Every day she slips further away. And I don't know how to call her back.

AUNT EV. Oh, I've a mind to take her up to Baltimore myself. If that doctor can't help her, maybe he'll know who can.

KELLER (*presently, heavily*). I'll write the man, Katie.

[*He stands with the baby in his clasp, staring at* HELEN'S *head, hanging down on* KATE'S *arm.*

ANAGNOS: "It will no doubt be difficult for you there, Annie."

The lights dim out, except the one on KATE *and* HELEN. *In the twilight,* JAMES, AUNT EV, *and* KELLER *move off slowly, formally, in separate direction;* KATE *with* HELEN *in her arms remains, motionless, in an image which overlaps into the next scene and fades only when it is well under way.*

Without pause, from the dark down left we hear a man's voice with a Greek accent speaking:]

ANAGNOS. —who could do nothing for the girl, of course. It was Dr. Bell[2] who thought she might somehow be taught. I have written the family only that a suitable governess, Miss Annie Sullivan, has been found here in Boston—

[*The lights begin to come up, down left, on a long table and chair. The table contains equipment for teaching the blind by touch—a small replica of the human skeleton, stuffed animals, models of flowers and plants, piles of books. The chair contains a girl of 20,* ANNIE SULLIVAN, *with a face which in repose is grave and rather obstinate, and when active is impudent, combative, twinkling with all the life that is lacking in* HELEN'S, *and handsome; there is a crude vitality to her. Her suitcase is at her knee.* ANAGNOS, *a stocky bearded man, comes into the light only towards the end of his speech.*]

ANAGNOS. —and will come. It will no doubt be difficult for you there, Annie. But it has been difficult for you at our school too, hm? Gratifying, yes, when you came to us and could not spell your name, to accomplish so much here in a few years, but always an Irish battle. For independence.

[*He studies* ANNIE, *humorously; she does not open her eyes.*]

This is my last time to counsel you, Annie, and you do lack some—by some I mean *all*—what, tact or talent to bend. To others. And what has saved you on more than one occasion here at Perkins is that there was nowhere to expel you to. Your eyes hurt?

ANNIE. My ears, Mr. Anagnos.

[*And now she has opened her eyes; they are inflamed, vague, slightly crossed, clouded by the granular growth of trachoma, and she often keeps them closed to shut out the pain of light.*]

---

2. Captain Keller appealed to Alexander Graham Bell (1847–1922), who became famous as developer of the telephone but who had come to America from Scotland as a teacher of speech to the deaf. Bell referred Captain Keller to Mr. Anagnos, Director of Perkins Institution for the Blind in Boston.

ANAGNOS (*severely*). Nowhere but back to Tewksbury,[3] where children learn to be saucy. Annie, I know how dreadful it was there, but that battle is dead and done with, why not let it stay buried?

ANNIE (*cheerily*). I think God must owe me a resurrection.

ANAGNOS (*a bit shocked*). What?

ANNIE (*taps her brow*). Well, He keeps digging up that battle!

ANAGNOS. That is not a proper thing to say, Annie. It is what I mean.

ANNIE (*meekly*). Yes. But I know what I'm like, what's this child like?

ANAGNOS. Like?

ANNIE. Well—Bright or dull, to start off.

ANAGNOS. No one knows. And if she is dull, you have no patience with this?

ANNIE. Oh, in grownups you have to, Mr. Anagnos. I mean in children it just seems a little—precocious, can I use that word?

ANAGNOS. Only if you can spell it.

ANNIE. Premature. So I hope at least she's a bright one.

ANAGNOS. Deaf, blind, mute—who knows? She is like a little safe, locked, that no one can open. Perhaps there is a treasure inside.

ANNIE. Maybe it's empty, too?

ANAGNOS. Possible. I should warn you, she is much given to tantrums.

ANNIE. Means something is inside. Well, so am I, if I believe all I hear. Maybe you should warn *them*.

ANAGNOS (*frowns*). Annie. I wrote them no word of your history. You will find yourself among strangers now, who know nothing of it.

ANNIE. Well, we'll keep them in a state of blessed ignorance.

ANAGNOS. Perhaps *you* should tell it?

ANNIE (*bristling*). Why? I have enough trouble with people who don't know.

ANAGNOS. So they will understand. When you have trouble.

ANNIE. The only time I have trouble is when I'm right.

[*But she is amused at herself, as is* ANAGNOS.]

Is it my fault it's so often? I won't give them trouble, Mr. Anagnos, I'll be so ladylike they won't notice I've come.

ANAGNOS. Annie, be—humble. It is not as if you have so many offers to pick and choose. You will need their affection, working with this child.

ANNIE (*humorously*). I hope I won't need their pity.

ANAGNOS. Oh, we can all use some pity.

[*Crisply*]

So. You are no longer our pupil, we throw you into the world, a teacher. *If* the child can be taught. No one expects you to work miracles, even for twenty-five dollars a month. Now, in this envelope a loan, for the railroad, which you will repay me when you have a bank account. But in this box, a gift. With our love.

[ANNIE *opens the small box he extends, and sees a garnet ring. She looks up, blinking, and down.*]

I think other friends are ready to say goodbye.

[*He moves as though to open doors.*]

ANNIE. Mr. Anagnos.

[*Her voice is trembling.*]

Dear Mr. Anagnos, I—

[*But she swallows over getting the ring on her finger, and cannot continue until she finds a woe-begone joke.*]

---

3. **Tewksbury** (tüks′be′rē), location of the state (Massachusetts) almshouse where Annie and her brother were sent as young children after her mother died and her father became an alcoholic.

Well, what should I say, I'm an ignorant opinionated girl, and everything I am I owe to you?

ANAGNOS (*smiles*). That is only half true, Annie.

ANNIE. Which half? I crawled in here like a drowned rat, I thought I died when Jimmie died, that I'd never again—come alive. Well, you say with love so easy, and I haven't *loved* a soul since and I never will, I suppose, but this place gave me more than my eyes back. Or taught me how to spell, which I'll never learn anyway, but with all the fights and the trouble I've been here it taught me what help is, and how to live again, and I don't want to say goodbye. Don't open the door, I'm crying.

ANAGNOS (*gently*). They will not see.

[*He moves again as though opening doors, and in comes a group of girls, 8-year-olds to 17-year-olds; as they walk we see they are blind.[4] ANAGNOS shepherds them in with a hand.*]

A CHILD. Annie?

ANNIE (*her voice cheerful*). Here, Beatrice.

[*As soon as they locate her voice they throng joyfully to her, speaking all at once; ANNIE is down on her knees to the smallest, and the following are the more intelligible fragments in the general hubbub.*]

CHILDREN. There's a present. We brought you a going-away present, Annie!

ANNIE. Oh, now you shouldn't have—

CHILDREN. We did, we did, where's the present?

SMALLEST CHILD (*mournfully*). Don't go, Annie, away.

CHILDREN. Alice has it. Alice! Where's Alice? Here I am! Where? Here!

[*An arm is aloft out of the group, waving a present; ANNIE reaches for it.*]

ANNIE. I have it. I have it, everybody, should I open it?

CHILDREN. Open it! Everyone be quiet! Do, Annie! She's opening it. Ssh!

[*A settling of silence while ANNIE unwraps it. The present is a pair of smoked glasses, and she stands still.*]

Is it open, Annie?

ANNIE. It's open.

CHILDREN. It's for your eyes, Annie. Put them on, Annie! 'Cause Mrs. Hopkins said your eyes hurt since the operation. And she said you're going where the sun is *fierce*.

ANNIE. I'm putting them on now.

SMALLEST CHILD (*mournfully*). Don't go, Annie, where the sun is fierce.

CHILDREN. Do they fit all right?

ANNIE. Oh, they fit just fine.

CHILDREN. Did you put them on? Are they pretty, Annie?

ANNIE. Oh, my eyes feel hundreds of percent better already, and pretty, why, do you know how I look in them? Splendiloquent.[5] Like a racehorse!

CHILDREN (*delighted*). There's another present! Beatrice! We have a present for Helen, too! Give it to her, Beatrice. Here, Annie!

[*This present is an elegant doll, with movable eyelids and a momma sound.*]

It's for Helen. And we took up a collection to buy it. And Laura[6] dressed it.

ANNIE. It's beautiful!

---

4. In order to lend reality to this scene, these children in the original cast of the play were actually blind.

5. **splendiloquent** (splen'di′ lə kwənt). a made-up word meaning something like splendid and excellent.

6. Laura Bridgman, a blind deaf-mute who had been taught to communicate with those about her by Dr. Samuel Gridley Howe, former Director of Perkins Institution. She remained at Perkins Institution because she was never able to adapt herself to any other kind of life. Annie first learned the manual alphabet in order to talk with Laura.

CHILDREN. So don't forget, you be sure to give it to Helen from us, Annie!

ANNIE. I promise it will be the first thing I give her. If I don't keep it for myself, that is, you know I can't be trusted with dolls!

SMALLEST CHILD (*mournfully*). Don't go, Annie, to her.

ANNIE (*her arm around her*). Sarah, dear. I don't *want* to go.

SMALLEST CHILD. Then why are you going?

ANNIE (*gently*). Because I'm a big girl now, and big girls have to earn a living. It's the only way I can. But if you don't smile for me first, what I'll just have to do is—

[*She pauses, inviting it.*]

SMALLEST CHILD. What?

ANNIE. Put *you* in my suitcase, instead of this doll. And take *you* to Helen in Alabama!

[*This strikes the children as very funny, and they begin to laugh and tease the smallest child, who after a moment does smile for* ANNIE.]

ANAGNOS (*then*). Come, children. We must get the trunk into the carriage and Annie into her train, or no one will go to Alabama. Come, come.

[*He shepherds them out and* ANNIE *is left alone on her knees with the doll in her lap. She reaches for her suitcase, and by a subtle change in the color of the light, we go with her thoughts into another time. We hear a boy's voice whispering; perhaps we see shadowy intimations of these speakers in the background.*]

BOY'S VOICE. Where we goin', Annie?

ANNIE (*in dread*). Jimmie.

BOY'S VOICE. Where we goin'?

ANNIE. I said—I'm takin' care of you—

BOY'S VOICE. Forever and ever?

MAN'S VOICE (*impersonal*). Annie Sullivan, aged nine, virtually blind. James Sullivan, aged seven—What's the matter with your leg, Sonny?[7]

ANNIE. Forever and ever.

MAN'S VOICE. Can't he walk without that crutch?

[ANNIE *shakes her head, and does not stop shaking it.*]

Girl goes to the women's ward. Boy to the men's.

BOY'S VOICE (*in terror*). Annie! Annie, don't let them take me—Annie!

ANAGNOS (*offstage*). Annie! Annie?

[*But this voice is real, in the present, and* ANNIE *comes up out of her horror, clearing her head with a final shake; the lights begin to pick out* KATE *in the* KELLER *house, as* ANNIE *in a bright tone calls back.*]

ANNIE. Coming!

[*This word catches* KATE, *who stands half turned and attentive to it, almost as though hearing it. Meanwhile* ANNIE *turns and hurries out, lugging the suitcase.*

The room dims out; the sound of railroad wheels begins from off left, and maintains itself in a constant rhythm underneath the following scene; the remaining lights have come up on the KELLER *homestead.* JAMES *is lounging on the porch, waiting. In the upper bedroom which is to be* ANNIE'S, HELEN *is alone, puzzledly exploring, fingering and smelling things, the curtains, empty drawers in the bureau, water in the pitcher by the washbasin, fresh towels on the bedstead. Downstairs in the family room* KATE *turning to a mirror hastily adjusts her bonnet, watched by a Negro servant in an apron,* VINEY.]

VINEY. Let Mr. Jimmie go by hisself, you been pokin' that garden all day, you ought to rest your feet.

KATE. I can't wait to see her, Viney.

---

7. Jimmy suffered from a tubercular hip and died in agony four months after he and Annie were sent to the State Infirmary at Tewksbury.

VINEY. Maybe she ain't gone be on this train neither.

KATE. Maybe she is.

VINEY. And maybe she ain't.

KATE. And maybe she is. Where's Helen?

VINEY. She upstairs, smellin' around. She know somethin' funny's goin' on.

KATE. Let her have her supper as soon as Mildred's in bed, and tell Captain Keller when he comes that we'll be delayed tonight.

VINEY. Again.

KATE. I don't think we need say *again.* Simply delayed will do.

[*She runs upstairs to* ANNIE'S *room,* VINEY *speaking after her.*]

VINEY. I mean that's what he gone say. "What, again?"

[VINEY *works at setting the table. Upstairs* KATE *stands in the doorway, watching* HELEN'S *groping explorations.*]

KATE. Yes, we're expecting someone. Someone for my Helen.

[HELEN *happens upon her skirt, clutches her leg;* KATE *in a tired dismay kneels to tidy her hair and soiled pinafore.*]

Oh, dear, this was clean not an hour ago.

[HELEN *feels her bonnet, shakes her head darkly, and tugs to get it off.* KATE *retains it with one hand, diverts* HELEN *by opening her other hand under her nose.*]

Here. For while I'm gone.

[HELEN *sniffs, reaches, and pops something into her mouth, while* KATE *speaks a bit guiltily.*]

I don't think one peppermint drop will spoil your supper.

[*She gives* HELEN *a quick kiss, evades her hands, and hurries downstairs again. Meanwhile*

CAPTAIN KELLER *has entered the yard from around the rear of the house, newspaper under arm, cleaning off and munching on some radishes; he sees* JAMES *lounging at the porch post.*]

KELLER. Jimmie?

JAMES (*unmoving*). Sir?

KELLER (*eyes him*). You don't look dressed for anything useful, boy.

JAMES. I'm not. It's for Miss Sullivan.

KELLER. Needn't keep holding up that porch, we have wooden posts for that. I asked you to see that those strawberry plants were moved this evening.

JAMES. I'm moving your—Mrs. Keller, instead. To the station.

KELLER (*heavily*). Mrs. Keller. Must you always speak of her as though you haven't met the lady?

[KATE *comes out on the porch, and* JAMES *inclines his head.*]

JAMES (*ironic*). Mother.

[*He starts off the porch, but sidesteps* KELLER'S *glare like a blow.*]

I said mother!

KATE. Captain.

KELLER. Evening, my dear.

KATE. We're off to meet the train, Captain. Supper will be a trifle delayed tonight.

KELLER. What, again?

KATE (*backing out*). With your permission, Captain?

[*And they are gone.* KELLER *watches them offstage, morosely.*

Upstairs HELEN *meanwhile has groped for her mother, touched her cheek in a meaningful gesture, waited, touched her cheek, waited, then found the open door, and made her way down. Now she comes into the family room, touches her cheek again;* VINEY *regards her.*]

VINEY. What you want, honey, your momma?

[HELEN *touches her cheek again.* VINEY *goes to the sideboard, gets a tea-cake, gives it into* HELEN'S *hand;* HELEN *pops it into her mouth.*]

Guess one little tea-cake ain't gone ruin your appetite.

[*She turns* HELEN *toward the door.* HELEN *wanders out onto the porch, as* KELLER *comes up the steps. Her hands encounter him, and she touches her cheek again, waits.*]

KELLER. She's gone.

[*He is awkward with her; when he puts his hand on her head, she pulls away.* KELLER *stands regarding her, heavily.*]

She's gone, my son and I don't get along, you don't know I'm your father, no one likes me, and supper's delayed.

[HELEN *touches her cheek, waits.* KELLER *fishes in his pocket.*]

Here. I brought you some stick candy, one nibble of sweets can't do any harm.

[*He gives her a large stick candy;* HELEN *falls to it.* VINEY *peers out the window.*]

VINEY (*reproachfully*). Cap'n Keller, now how'm I gone get her to eat her supper you fill her up with that trash?

KELLER (*roars*). Tend to your work!

[VINEY *beats a rapid retreat.* KELLER *thinks better of it, and tries to get the candy away from* HELEN, *but* HELEN *hangs on to it; and when* KELLER *pulls, she gives his leg a kick.* KELLER *hops about,* HELEN *takes refuge with the candy down behind the pump, and* KELLER *then irately flings his newspaper on the porch floor, stamps into the house past* VINEY *and disappears.*

The lights half dim on the homestead, where VINEY *and* HELEN *going about their business*

soon find their way off. Meanwhile, the railroad sounds off left have mounted in a crescendo to a climax typical of a depot at arrival time, the lights come up on stage left, and we see a suggestion of a station. Here ANNIE *in her smoked glasses and disarrayed by travel is waiting with her suitcase, while* JAMES *walks to meet her; she has a battered paperbound book, which is a Perkins report,[8] under her arm.*]

JAMES (*coolly*). Miss Sullivan?

ANNIE (*cheerily*). Here! At last, I've been on trains so many days I thought they must be backing up every time I dozed off—

JAMES. I'm James Keller.

ANNIE. James?

[*The name stops her.*]

I had a brother Jimmie. Are you Helen's?

JAMES. I'm only half a brother. You're to be her governess?

ANNIE (*lightly*). Well. Try!

JAMES (*eyeing her*). You look like a half a governess.

[KATE *enters.* ANNIE *stands moveless, while* JAMES *takes her suitcase.* KATE'S *gaze on her is doubtful, troubled.*]

Mrs. Keller, Miss Sullivan.

[KATE *takes her hand.*]

KATE (*simply*). We've met every train for two days.

[ANNIE *looks at* KATE'S *face, and her good humor comes back.*]

ANNIE. I changed trains every time they stopped, the man who sold me that ticket ought to be tied to the tracks—

JAMES. You have a trunk, Miss Sullivan?

ANNIE. Yes.

---

8. **Perkins report,** a report of work done by the Perkins Institution for the Blind in Boston.

[*She passes* JAMES *a claim check, and he bears the suitcase out behind them.* ANNIE *holds the battered book.* KATE *is studying her face, and* ANNIE *returns the gaze; this is a mutual appraisal, southern gentlewoman and working-class Irish girl, and* ANNIE *is not quite comfortable under it.*]

You didn't bring Helen, I was hoping you would.

KATE. No, she's home.

[*A pause.* ANNIE *tries to make ladylike small talk, though her energy now and then erupts; she catches herself up whenever she hears it.*]

ANNIE. You—live far from town, Mrs. Keller?

KATE. Only a mile.

ANNIE. Well. I suppose I can wait one more mile. But don't be surprised if I get out to push the horse!

KATE. Helen's waiting for you, too. There's been such a bustle in the house, she expects something, heaven knows what.

[*Now she voices part of her doubt, not as such, but* ANNIE *understands it.*]

I expected—a desiccated spinster. You're very young.

ANNIE (*resolutely*). Oh, you should have seen me when I left Boston. I got much older on this trip.

KATE. I mean, to teach anyone as difficult as Helen.

ANNIE. I mean to try. They can't put you in jail for trying!

KATE. Is it possible, even? To teach a deaf-blind child *half* of what an ordinary child learns—has that ever been done?

ANNIE. Half?

KATE. A tenth.

ANNIE (*reluctantly*). No.

[KATE'S *face loses its remaining hope, still appraising her youth.*]

ANNIE: *"Language is to the mind more than light is to the eye."*

Dr. Howe did wonders, but—an ordinary child? No, never. But then I thought when I was going over his reports—

[*She indicates the one in her hand.*]

—he never treated them like ordinary children. More like—eggs everyone was afraid would break.

KATE (*a pause*). May I ask how old you are?

ANNIE. Well, I'm not in my teens, you know! I'm twenty.

KATE. All of twenty.

[ANNIE *takes the bull by the horns, valiantly.*]

ANNIE. Mrs. Keller, don't lose heart just because I'm not on my last legs. I have three big advantages over Dr. Howe that money couldn't buy for you. One is his work behind me, I've read every word he wrote about it and he wasn't exactly what you'd call a man of few words. Another is to *be* young, why, I've got energy to do anything. The third is, I've been blind.

[*But it costs her something to say this.*]

KATE (*quietly*). Advantages.
ANNIE (*wry*). Well, some have the luck of the Irish, some do not.

[KATE *smiles; she likes her.*]

KATE. What will you try to teach her first?
ANNIE. First, last, and—in between, language.
KATE. Language.
ANNIE. Language is to the mind more than light is to the eye. Dr. Howe said that.
KATE. Language

[*She shakes her head.*]

We can't get through to teach her to sit still. You *are* young, despite your years, to have such—confidence. Do you, inside?

[ANNIE *studies her face; she likes her, too.*]

ANNIE. No, to tell you the truth I'm as shaky inside as a baby's rattle!

[*They smile at each other, and* KATE *pats her hand.*]

KATE. Don't be.

[JAMES *returns to usher them off.*]

We'll do all we can to help, and to make you feel at home. Don't think of us as strangers, Miss Annie.
ANNIE (*cheerily*). Oh, strangers aren't so strange to me. I've known them all my life!

[KATE *smiles again,* ANNIE *smiles back, and they precede* JAMES *offstage.*

The lights dim on them, having simultaneously risen full on the house; VINEY *has already entered the family room, taken a water pitcher, and come out and down to the pump. She pumps real water. As she looks offstage, we hear the clop of hoofs, a carriage stopping, and voices.*]

VINEY. Cap'n Keller! Cap'n Keller, they comin'!

[*She goes back into the house, as* KELLER *comes out on the porch to gaze.*]

She sure 'nuff came, Cap'n.

[KELLER *descends, and crosses toward the carriage; this conversation begins offstage and moves on.*]

KELLER (*very courtly*). Welcome to Ivy Green, Miss Sullivan. I take it you are Miss Sullivan—
KATE. My husband, Miss Annie, Captain Keller.
ANNIE (*her best behavior*). Captain, how do you do.
KELLER. A pleasure to see you, at last, I trust you had an agreeable journey?
ANNIE. Oh, I had several! When did this country get so big?
JAMES. Where would you like the trunk, father?
KELLER. Where Miss Sullivan can get at it, I imagine.
ANNIE. Yes, please. Where's Helen?
KELLER. In the hall, Jimmie—
KATE. We've put you in the upstairs corner room, Miss Annie, if there's any breeze at all this summer, you'll feel it—

[*In the house the setter Belle flees into the family room, pursued by* HELEN *with groping hands; the dog doubles back out the same door, and* HELEN *still groping for her makes her way out to the porch; she is messy, her hair tumbled, her pinafore now ripped, her shoelaces untied.*

KELLER *acquires the suitcase, and* ANNIE *gets her hands on it too, though still endeavoring to live up to the general air of propertied manners.*]

KELLER. And the suitcase—

ANNIE (*pleasantly*). I'll take the suitcase, thanks.

KELLER. Not at all, I have it, Miss Sullivan.

ANNIE. I'd like it.

KELLER (*gallantly*). I couldn't think of it, Miss Sullivan. You'll find in the south we—

ANNIE. Let me.

KELLER. —view women as the flowers of civiliza—

ANNIE (*impatiently*). I've got something in it for Helen!

[*She tugs it free;* KELLER *stares.*]

Thank you. When do I see her?

KATE. There. There is Helen.

[ANNIE *turns, and sees* HELEN *on the porch. A moment of silence. Then* ANNIE *begins across the yard to her, lugging her suitcase.*]

KELLER (*sotto voce*). Katie—

[KATE *silences him with a hand on his arm. When* ANNIE *finally reaches the porch steps she stops, contemplating* HELEN *for a last moment before entering her world. Then she drops the suitcase on the porch with intentional heaviness,* HELEN *starts with the jar, and comes to grope over it.* ANNIE *puts forth her hand, and touches* HELEN'S. HELEN *at once grasps it, and commences to explore it, like reading a face. She moves her hand on to* ANNIE'S *forearm, and dress; and* ANNIE *brings her face within reach of* HELEN'S *fingers, which travel over it, quite without timidity, until they encounter and push aside the smoked glasses.* ANNIE'S *gaze is grave, unpitying, very attentive. She puts her hands on* HELEN'S *arms, but* HELEN *at once pulls away, and they confront each other with a distance between. Then* HELEN *returns to the suitcase,*

tries to open it, cannot. ANNIE *points* HELEN'S *hand overhead.* HELEN *pulls away, tries to open the suitcase again;* ANNIE *points her hand overhead again.* HELEN *points overhead, a question, and* ANNIE, *drawing* HELEN'S *hand to her own face, nods.* HELEN *now begins tugging the suitcase toward the door; when* ANNIE *tries to take it from her, she fights her off and backs through the doorway with it.* ANNIE *stands a moment, then follows her in, and together they get the suitcase up the steps into* ANNIE'S *room.*]

KATE. Well?

KELLER. She's very rough, Katie.

KATE. I like her, Captain.

KELLER. Certainly rear a peculiar kind of young woman in the north. How old is she?

KATE (*vaguely*). Ohh— Well, she's not in her teens, you know.

KELLER. She's only a child. What's her family like, shipping her off alone this far?

KATE. I couldn't learn. She's very close-mouthed about some things.

KELLER. Why does she wear those glasses? I like to see a person's eyes when I talk to—

KATE. For the sun. She was blind.

KELLER. Blind.

KATE. She's had nine operations on her eyes. One just before she left.

KELLER. Blind, good heavens, do they expect one blind child to teach another? Has she experience at least, how long did she teach there?

KATE. She was a pupil.

KELLER (*heavily*). Katie, Katie. This is her first position?

KATE (*bright voice*). She was valedictorian—

KELLER. Here's a houseful of grownups can't cope with the child, how can an inexperienced half-blind Yankee schoolgirl manage her?

[JAMES *moves in with the trunk on his shoulder.*]

JAMES (*easily*). Great improvement. Now we have two of them to look after.

KELLER. You look after those strawberry plants!

[JAMES *stops with the trunk.* KELLER *turns from him without another word, and marches off.*]

JAMES. Nothing I say is right.

KATE. Why say anything?

[*She calls.*]

Don't be long, Captain, we'll have supper right away—

[*She goes into the house, and through the rear door of the family room.* JAMES *trudges in with the trunk, takes it up the steps to* ANNIE'S *room, and sets it down outside the door. The lights elsewhere dim somewhat.*

Meanwhile, inside, ANNIE *has given* HELEN *a key; while* ANNIE *removes her bonnet,* HELEN *unlocks and opens the suitcase. The first thing she pulls out is a voluminous shawl. She fingers it until she perceives what it is; then she wraps it around her, and acquiring* ANNIE'S *bonnet and smoked glasses as well, dons the lot: the shawl swamps her, and the bonnet settles down upon the glasses, but she stands before a mirror cocking her head to one side, then to the other, in a mockery of adult action.* ANNIE *is amused, and talks to her as one might to a kitten, with no trace of company manners.*]

ANNIE. All the trouble I went to and that's how I look?

[HELEN *then comes back to the suitcase, gropes for more, lifts out a pair of female drawers.*]

Oh, no. Not the drawers!

[*But* HELEN *discarding them comes to the elegant doll. Her fingers explore its features, and when she raises it and finds its eyes open and close, she is at first startled, then delighted. She*

picks it up, taps its head vigorously, taps her own chest, and nods questioningly. ANNIE *takes her finger, points it to the doll, points it to* HELEN, *and touching it to her own face, also nods.* HELEN *sits back on her heels, clasps the doll to herself, and rocks it.* ANNIE *studies her, still in bonnet and smoked glasses like a caricature of herself, and addresses her humorously.*]

All right, Miss O'Sullivan. Let's begin with doll.

[*She takes* HELEN'S *hand; in her palm* ANNIE'S *forefinger points, thumb holding her other fingers clenched.*]

D.

[*Her thumb next holds all her fingers clenched, touching* HELEN'S *palm.*]

O.

[*Her thumb and forefinger extend.*]

L.

[*Same contact repeated.*]

L.

[*She puts* HELEN'S *hand to the doll.*]

Doll.

JAMES. You spell pretty well.

[ANNIE *in one hurried move gets the drawers swiftly back into the suitcase, the lid banged shut, and her head turned, to see* JAMES *leaning in the doorway.*]

Finding out if she's ticklish? She is.

[ANNIE *regards him stonily, but* HELEN *after a scowling moment tugs at her hand again, imperious.* ANNIE *repeats the letters, and* HELEN *interrupts her fingers in the middle, feeling each of them, puzzled.* ANNIE *touches* HELEN'S *hand to the doll, and begins spelling into it again.*]

JAMES. What is it, a game?

ANNIE (*curtly*). An alphabet.

JAMES. Alphabet?

ANNIE. For the deaf.

[HELEN *now repeats the finger movements in air, exactly, her head cocked to her own hand, and* ANNIE'S *eyes suddenly gleam.*]

Ho. How *bright* she is!

JAMES. You think she knows what she's doing?

[*He takes* HELEN'S *hand, to throw a meaningless gesture into it; she repeats this one too.*]

She imitates everything, she's a monkey.

ANNIE (*very pleased*). Yes, she's a bright little monkey, all right.

[*She takes the doll from* HELEN, *and reaches for her hand;* HELEN *instantly grabs the doll back.* ANNIE *takes it again, and* HELEN'S *hand next, but* HELEN *is incensed now; when* ANNIE *draws her hand to her face to shake her head no, then tries to spell to her,* HELEN *slaps at* ANNIE'S *face.* ANNIE *grasps* HELEN *by both arms, and swings her into a chair, holding her pinned there, kicking, while glasses, doll, bonnet fly in various directions.* JAMES *laughs.*]

JAMES. She wants her doll back.

ANNIE. When she spells it.

JAMES. Spell, she doesn't know the thing has a name, even.

ANNIE. Of course not, who expects her to, now? All I want is her fingers to learn the letters.

JAMES. Won't mean anything to her.

[ANNIE *gives him a look. She then tries to form* HELEN'S *fingers into the letters, but* HELEN *swings a haymaker instead, which* ANNIE *barely ducks, at once pinning her down again.*]

Doesn't like that alphabet, Miss Sullivan. You invent it yourself?

[HELEN *is now in a rage, fighting tooth and nail to get out of the chair, and* ANNIE *answers while struggling and dodging her kicks.*]

ANNIE. Spanish monks under a—vow of silence. Which I wish *you'd* take!

[*And suddenly releasing* HELEN'S *hands, she comes and shuts the door in* JAMES'S *face.* HELEN *drops to the floor, groping around for the doll.* ANNIE *looks around desperately, sees her purse on the bed, rummages in it, and comes up with a battered piece of cake wrapped in newspaper; with her foot she moves the doll deftly out of the way of* HELEN'S *groping, and going on her knee she lets* HELEN *smell the cake. When* HELEN *grabs for it,* ANNIE *removes the cake and spells quickly into the reaching hand.*]

Cake. From Washington up north, it's the best I can do.

[HELEN'S *hand waits, baffled.* ANNIE *repeats it.*]

C, a, k, e. Do what my fingers do, never mind what it means.

[*She touches the cake briefly to* HELEN'S *nose, pats her hand, presents her own hand.* HELEN *spells the letters rapidly back.* ANNIE *pats her hand enthusiastically, and gives her the cake;* HELEN *crams it into her mouth with both hands.* ANNIE *watches her, with humor.*]

Get it down fast, maybe I'll steal that back too. Now.

[*She takes the doll, touches it to* HELEN'S *nose, and spells again into her hand.*]

D, o, l, l. Think it over.

[HELEN *thinks it over, while* ANNIE *presents her own hand. Then* HELEN *spells three letters.* ANNIE *waits a second, then completes the word for* HELEN *in her palm.*]

L.

[*She hands over the doll, and* HELEN *gets a good grip on its leg.*]

Imitate now, understand later. End of the first les—

[*She never finishes, because* HELEN *swings the doll with a furious energy, it hits* ANNIE *squarely in the face, and she falls back with a cry of pain, her knuckles up to her mouth.* HELEN *waits, tensed for further combat. When* ANNIE *lowers her knuckles she looks at blood on them; she works her lips, gets to her feet, finds the mirror, and bares her teeth at herself. Now she is furious herself.*]

You little wretch, no one's taught you *any* manners? I'll—

[*But rounding from the mirror she sees the door slam,* HELEN *and the doll are on the outside, and* HELEN *is turning the key in the lock.* ANNIE *darts over, to pull the knob; the door is locked fast. She yanks it again.*]

Helen! Helen, let me out of—

[*She bats her brow at the folly of speaking, but* JAMES, *now downstairs, hears her and turns to see* HELEN *with the key and doll groping her way down the steps;* JAMES *takes in the whole situation, makes a move to intercept* HELEN, *but then changes his mind, lets her pass, and amusedly follows her out onto the porch. Upstairs* ANNIE *meanwhile rattles the knob, kneels, peers through the keyhole, gets up. She goes to the window, looks down, frowns.* JAMES *from the yard sings gaily up to her.*]

JAMES.
Buffalo girl, are you coming out tonight,
Coming out tonight,
Coming out—

[*He drifts back into the house.* ANNIE *takes a handkerchief, nurses her mouth, stands in the middle of the room, staring at door and window in turn, and so catches sight of herself in the*

mirror, *her cheek scratched, her hair dishevelled, her handkerchief bloody, her face disgusted with herself. She addresses the mirror, with some irony.*]

ANNIE. Don't worry. They'll find you, you're not lost. Only out of place.

[*But she coughs, spits something into her palm, and stares at it, outraged.*]

And toothless.

[*She winces.*]

Oo! It hurts.

[*She pours some water into the basin, dips the handkerchief, and presses it to her mouth. Standing there, bent over the basin in pain— with the rest of the set dim and unreal, and the lights upon her taking on the subtle color of the past—she hears again, as do we, the faraway voices, and slowly she lifts her head to them; the boy's voice is the same, the others are cracked old crones in a nightmare, and perhaps we see their shadows.*]

BOY'S VOICE. It hurts. Annie, it hurts.
FIRST CRONE'S VOICE.[9] Keep that brat shut up, can't you, girlie, how's a body to get any sleep in this damn ward?
BOY'S VOICE. It hurts. It hurts.
SECOND CRONE'S VOICE. Shut up, you!
BOY'S VOICE. Annie, when are we goin' home? You promised!
ANNIE. Jimmie—
BOY'S VOICE. Forever and ever, you said forever—

[ANNIE *drops the handkerchief, averts to the window, and is arrested there by the next cry.*]

Annie? Annie, you there? Annie! It *hurts!*
THIRD CRONE'S VOICE. Grab him, he's fallin'!

9. **crones,** old women, inmates of the State Infirmary at Tewksbury.

BOY'S VOICE. Annie!

DOCTOR'S VOICE (*a pause, slowly*). Little girl. Little girl, I must tell you your brother will be going on a—

[*But* ANNIE *claps her hands to her ears, to shut this out; there is instant silence.*

As the lights bring the other areas in again, JAMES *goes to the steps to listen for any sound from upstairs.* KELLER *reentering from left crosses toward the house; he passes* HELEN *en route to her retreat under the pump.* KATE *reenters the rear door of the family room, with flowers for the table.*]

KATE. Supper is ready, Jimmie, will you call your father?

JAMES. Certainly.

[*But he calls up the stairs, for* ANNIE'S *benefit:*]

Father! Supper!

KELLER (*at the door*). No need to shout, I've been cooling my heels for an hour. Sit down.

JAMES. Certainly.

KELLER. Viney!

[VINEY *backs in with a roast, while they get settled around the table.*]

VINEY. Yes, Cap'n, right here.

KATE. Mildred went directly to sleep, Viney?

VINEY. Oh yes, that babe's a angel.

KATE. And Helen had a good supper?

VINEY (*vaguely*). I dunno, Miss Kate, somehow she didn't have much of a appetite tonight—

KATE (*a bit guilty*). Oh. Dear.

KELLER (*hastily*). Well, now. Couldn't say the same for my part, I'm famished. Katie, your plate.

KATE (*looking*). But where is Miss Annie?

[*A silence.*]

JAMES (*pleasantly*). In her room.

KELLER. In her room? Doesn't she know hot food must be eaten hot? Go bring her down at once, Jimmie.

JAMES (*rises*). Certainly. I'll get a ladder.

KELLER (*stares*). What?

JAMES. I'll need a ladder. Shouldn't take me long.

KATE (*stares*). What shouldn't take you—

KELLER. Jimmie, do as I say! Go upstairs at once and tell Miss Sullivan supper is getting cold—

JAMES. She's locked in her room.

KELLER. Locked in her—

KATE. What on earth are you—

JAMES. Helen locked her in and made off with the key.

KATE (*rising*). And you sit here and say nothing?

JAMES. Well, everyone's been telling me not to say anything.

[*He goes serenely out and across the yard, whistling.* KELLER *thrusting up from his chair makes for the stairs.*]

KATE. Viney, look out in back for Helen. See if she has that key.

VINEY. Yes, Miss Kate.

[VINEY *goes out the rear door.*]

KELLER (*calling down*). She's out by the pump!

[KATE *goes out on the porch after* HELEN, *while* KELLER *knocks on* ANNIE'S *door, then rattles the knob, imperiously.*]

Miss Sullivan! Are you in there!

ANNIE. Oh, I'm in here, all right.

KELLER. Is there no key on your side?

ANNIE (*with some asperity*). Well, if there was a key in here, I wouldn't be in here. Helen took it, the only thing on my side is me.

KELLER. Miss Sullivan. I—

[*He tries, but cannot hold it back.*]

Not in the house ten minutes, I don't see *how* you managed it!

[*He stomps downstairs again, while* ANNIE *mutters to herself.*]

ANNIE. And even I'm not on my side.

KELLER (*roaring*). Viney!

VINEY (*reappearing*). Yes, Cap'n?

KELLER. Put that meat back in the oven!

[VINEY *bears the roast off again, while* KELLER *strides out onto the porch.* KATE *is with* HELEN *at the pump, opening her hands.*]

KATE. She has no key.

KELLER. Nonsense, she must have the key. Have you searched in her pockets?

KATE. Yes. She doesn't have it.

KELLER. Katie, she must have the key.

KATE. Would you prefer to search her yourself, Captain?

KELLER. No, I would not prefer to search her! She almost took my kneecap off this evening, when I tried merely to—

[JAMES *reappears carrying a long ladder, with* PERCY *running after him to be in on things.*]

Take that ladder back!

JAMES. Certainly.

[*He turns around with it.* MARTHA *comes skipping around the upstage corner of the house to be in on things, accompanied by the setter* Belle.]

KATE. She could have hidden the key.

KELLER. Where?

KATE. Anywhere. Under a stone. In the flower beds. In the grass—

KELLER. Well, I can't plow up the entire grounds to find a missing key! Jimmie!

JAMES. Sir?

KELLER. Bring me a ladder!

JAMES. Certainly.

[VINEY *comes around the downstage side of the house to be in on things; she has Mildred over her shoulder, bleating.* KELLER *places the ladder against* ANNIE'S *window and mounts.* ANNIE

meanwhile is running about making herself presentable, washing the blood off her mouth, straightening her clothes, tidying her hair. Another Negro servant enters to gaze in wonder, increasing the gathering ring of spectators.]

KATE (*sharply*). What is Mildred doing up?

VINEY. Cap'n woke her, ma'am, all that hollerin'.

KELLER. Miss Sullivan!

[ANNIE *comes to the window, with as much air of gracious normality as she can manage;* KELLER *is at the window.*]

ANNIE (*brightly*). Yes, Captain Keller?

KELLER. Come out!

ANNIE. I don't see how I can. There isn't room.

KELLER. I intend to carry you. Climb onto my shoulder and hold tight.

ANNIE. Oh, no. It's—very chivalrous of you, but I'd really prefer to—

KELLER. Miss Sullivan, follow instructions! I will not have you also tumbling out of our windows.

[ANNIE *obeys, with some misgivings.*]

I hope this is not a sample of what we may expect from you. In the way of simplifying the work of looking after Helen.

ANNIE. Captain Keller, I'm perfectly able to go down a ladder under my own—

KELLER. I doubt it, Miss Sullivan. Simply hold onto my neck.

[*He begins down with her, while the spectators stand in a wide and somewhat awestricken circle, watching.* KELLER *half-misses a rung, and* ANNIE *grabs at his whiskers.*]

My *neck*, Miss Sullivan!

ANNIE. I'm sorry to inconvenience you this way—

KELLER. No inconvenience, other than having

that door taken down and the lock replaced, if we fail to find that key.

ANNIE. Oh, I'll look everywhere for it.

KELLER. Thank you. Do not look in any rooms that can be locked. There.

[*He stands her on the ground.* JAMES *applauds.*]

ANNIE. Thank you very much.

[*She smooths her skirt, looking as composed and ladylike as possible.* KELLER *stares around at the spectators.*]

KELLER. Go, go, back to your work. What are you looking at here? There's nothing here to look at.

[*They break up, move off.*]

Now would it be possible for us to have supper, like other people?

[*He marches into the house.*]

KATE. Viney, serve supper. I'll put Mildred to sleep.

[*They all go in.* JAMES *is the last to leave, murmuring to* ANNIE *with a gesture.*]

JAMES. Might as well leave the l, a, d, d, e, r, hm?

[ANNIE *ignores him, looking at* HELEN; JAMES *goes in too. Imperceptibly the lights commence to narrow down.* ANNIE *and* HELEN *are now alone in the yard,* HELEN *seated at the pump, where she has been oblivious to it all, a battered little savage, playing with the doll in a picture of innocent contentment.* ANNIE *comes near, leans against the house, and taking off her smoked glasses, studies her, not without awe. Presently* HELEN *rises, gropes around to see if anyone is present;* ANNIE *evades her hand, and when* HELEN *is satisfied she is alone, the key suddenly protrudes out of her mouth. She takes it in her*

Annie learns what happened to the lost key in this scene from the film version of The Miracle Worker.

fingers, stands thinking, gropes to the pump, lifts a loose board, drops the key into the well, and hugs herself gleefully. ANNIE *stares. But after a moment she shakes her head to herself, she cannot keep the smile from her lips.*]

ANNIE. You *devil.*

[*Her tone is one of great respect, humor, and acceptance of challenge.*]

You think I'm so easily gotten rid of? You have a thing or two to learn, first. I have nothing else to do.

[*She goes up the steps to the porch, but turns for a final word, almost of warning.*]

And nowhere to go.

[*And presently she moves into the house to the others, as the lights dim down and out, except for the small circle upon* HELEN *solitary at the pump, which ends the act.*]

READING FOR DETAILS

Annie Accepts a Challenge

A skillful playwright strives to end each act of a play at a point of such high interest that the audience is eager to find out what happens next. As Act I ends, Annie realizes, with both humor and awe, that in Helen she has a devilish little adversary who feels she "has won the first round."

Earlier in this first act, Mr. Gibson laid the groundwork for understanding why Helen is the problem she is and how Annie Sullivan had come to her as a teacher.

1. What frightening discovery did Kate Keller make about the one-and-one-half-year-old Helen in the first scene of the play? How old is Helen when she is next introduced?

2. Why does Captain Keller stubbornly refuse, for a long time, to write to the doctor in Baltimore? How does each member of the household feel about Helen? Through whom are the Kellers put in touch with Anagnos and in turn with Annie Sullivan?

3. What do you learn of Annie Sullivan's background in her conversation with Anagnos? What does she say Perkins Institution has done for her? What is the attitude of Anagnos and the children of Perkins Institution toward Annie? What is the gift the children send to Helen?

4. When do you have the first indication that Annie believes that a child handicapped as Helen should be treated as an ordinary child?

5. Identify the characters who speak the following lines and briefly outline the situation in which the words are spoken:
   a. . . . I'm as shaky inside as a baby's rattle!
   b. Great improvement. Now we have two of them to look after.
   c. All right, Miss O'Sullivan. Let's begin with doll.
   d. Don't worry. They'll find you, you're not lost. Only out of place. And toothless.

READING FOR MEANING

Cite evidence from Act I that supports or refutes the following statements:

1. We are most sympathetic or understanding toward those with problems closest to our own.

2. One small grievance can often ruin a lifetime.

READING FOR APPRECIATION

Characterization

The opening stage directions in Act I tell you only that Kate Keller is a "young gentlewoman with a sweet girlish face," while Captain Keller is "a hearty gentleman in his forties with chin whiskers."

1. Captain Keller's first speech reveals a bluff heartiness which carries with it the impression that he is used to imposing his opinions on others without being sensitive to their feelings. How is this trait of his reflected in other situations throughout Act I?

2. In his dialogue, particularly with Annie, the Captain emerges as an almost comically pompous figure. What ideas does he have about proper behavior for "ladies"? Find lines in which Annie's Irish wit makes him look rather ludicrous. Discuss those lines on page 208 which indicate that sometimes the Captain feels he is not as important as he would like to believe.

3. Although Kate Keller is a "gentlewoman," her gentleness overlays a strength of purpose which is brought out plainly after Helen's tragic illness. In what instances does she demonstrate both strength of character and persistence? While she shows strength of character, she could also be considered "weak." Explain why this is true.

4. Helen is an unrestrained, spoiled, strong-willed child, desperate with the frustration of being unable to communicate. This is evident from the first scene in which she appears. Discuss those incidents in Act I which show that Helen wishes to talk and have eyes that see. Describe her physical appearance. What indicates to Annie that Helen is a "bright" child and has a good mind that needs only to be reached?

5. Find lines from Act I which show that Annie understands her own nature. What does Anagnos say that Annie lacks? What does Annie say about her ability to love other people? Discuss those qualities which equip her best for her struggle with Helen.

6. Why do you think there is no description of Aunt Ev? How would you characterize her?

Significant Detail

1. What is the importance of the battered volume which Annie is carrying under her arm when she gets off the train?

2. Locate the line in Act I in which Annie tells Kate that she will try to teach Helen language. Upon whose words is she basing her plan?

3. What does Helen's gesture of touching her cheek mean?

Staging

As the play progressed, it undoubtedly became apparent to the reader why Mr. Gibson specified that the stage should be divided into two areas.

1. What does the area behind the diagonal represent? Describe how this space is divided up. Why is the area in front of the diagonal called "neutral" ground? Discuss the meaning of the author's direction that "locales should be only skeletal suggestions, and the movement from one to another should be accomplishable by little more than lights."

2. Although the stage is kept as uncluttered as possible, certain stage properties are used to indicate where action is taking place. How is the audience made aware that action has shifted (a) to the Perkins Institution in Boston, (b) to the railroad station?

3. What device is used to indicate the passing of five years early in Act I?

4. If *The Miracle Worker* had been planned for conventional scene changing, how many separate scenes would have been necessary for Act I?

TECHNIQUES: THE PLAYWRIGHT'S ART

CHARACTERIZATION

In a novel, authors have the opportunity to provide detailed descriptions of the characters and their actions. In a drama, the playwright must reveal and develop characters primarily through costuming, action, and dialogue on the stage. Generally, the main characters in a drama will undergo change as a result of the action of the play while the minor characters will not. The minor characters serve to further the action of the play and provide increased possibility for giving the audience more insight into the main characters. Think back over Act I. Discuss how this concept can be illustrated in the character of Aunt Ev.

For Annie Sullivan, things have never been easy. Had she not had a lot of fighting spirit, she very likely would not have survived the horrors of her early childhood and adolescence. Playwright Gibson describes her face as grave and rather obstinate in repose but impudent, combative, and twinkling with life when she is active.

Aunt Ev, Viney, and James all help give insight into the characters of Helen, Kate, and Captain Keller. Discuss the minor characters introduced in Act I who help to establish Annie's character.

SIGNIFICANT DETAIL

Pantomime is one of the oldest forms of drama. For such performances the performers express themselves by mute gestures. The entire personality of Helen must be revealed through statements from other characters about her or their reactions to her, and through her pantomime. Unless one reads the detailed stage directions carefully, much of what is significant in this play would be overlooked.

Why would one have missed a great deal of the dramatic impact at the end of Act I by not reading the stage direction on page 217?

STAGING

The staging of a play must be consistent with mood of the action. The setting not only provides the atmosphere for the play but helps foreshadow the drama that follows the opening scene. Notice the opening scenes of each act of *The Miracle Worker*. Consider how each one is consistent with the act it opens.

Act II

It is evening.

The only room visible in the KELLER *house is* ANNIE'S, *where by lamplight* ANNIE *in a shawl is at a desk writing a letter; at her bureau* HELEN *in her customary unkempt state is tucking her doll in the bottom drawer as a cradle, the contents of which she has dumped out, creating as usual a fine disorder.*

ANNIE *mutters each word as she writes her letter, slowly, her eyes close to and almost touching the page, to follow with difficulty her penwork.*

ANNIE. ". . . and, nobody, here, has, attempted, to, control, her. The, greatest, problem, I, have, is, how, to, discipline, her, without, breaking, her, spirit."

[*Resolute voice*]

"But, I, shall, insist, on, reasonable, obedience, from, the, start—"

[*At which point* HELEN, *groping about on the desk, knocks over the inkwell.* ANNIE *jumps up, rescues her letter, rights the inkwell, grabs a towel to stem the spillage, and then wipes at* HELEN'S *hands;* HELEN *as always pulls free, but not until* ANNIE *first gets three letters into her palm.*]

Ink.

[HELEN *is enough interested in and puzzled by this spelling that she proffers her hand again; so* ANNIE *spells and impassively dunks it back into the spillage.*]

Ink. It has a name.

[*She wipes the hand clean, and leads* HELEN *to her bureau, where she looks for something to engage her. She finds a sewing card, with needle and thread, and going to her knees, shows* HELEN'S *hand how to connect one row of holes.*]

Down. Under. Up. And be careful of the needle—

[HELEN *gets it, and* ANNIE *rises.*]

Fine. You keep out of the ink and perhaps I can keep out of—the soup.

[*She returns to the desk, tidies it, and resumes writing her letter, bent close to the page.*]

"These, blots, are, her, handiwork. I—"

[*She is interrupted by a gasp:* HELEN *has stuck her finger, and sits sucking at it, darkly. Then with vengeful resolve she seizes her doll, and is about to dash its brains out on the floor when* ANNIE *diving catches it in one hand, which she at once shakes with hopping pain but otherwise ignores patiently.*]

All right, let's try temperance.

[*Taking the doll, she kneels, goes through the motion of knocking its head to the floor, spells into* HELEN'S *hand:*]

Bad, girl.

[*She lets* HELEN *feel the grieved expression on her face.* HELEN *imitates it. Next she makes* HELEN *caress the doll and kiss the hurt spot and hold it gently in her arms, then spells into her hand:*]

Good, girl.

[*She lets* HELEN *feel the smile on her face.* HELEN *sits with a scowl, which suddenly clears; she pats the doll, kisses it, wreathes her face in a large artificial smile, and bears the doll to the washstand, where she carefully sits it.* ANNIE *watches, pleased.*]

Very good girl—

[*Whereupon* HELEN *elevates the pitcher and dashes it on the floor instead.* ANNIE *leaps to her feet, and stands inarticulate;* HELEN *calmly gropes back to sit to the sewing card and needle.*

ANNIE *manages to achieve self-control. She picks up a fragment or two of the pitcher, sees* HELEN *is puzzling over the card, and resolutely kneels to demonstrate it again. She spells into* HELEN'S *hand.*

KATE *meanwhile coming around the corner with folded sheets on her arm, halts at the doorway and watches them for a moment in silence; she is moved, but level.*]

KATE (*presently*). What are you saying to her?

[ANNIE *glancing up is a bit embarrassed, and rises from the spelling, to find her company manners.*]

ANNIE. Oh, I was just making conversation. Saying it was a sewing card.

KATE. But does that—

[*She imitates with her fingers.*]

—mean that to her?

ANNIE. No. No, she won't know what spelling is till she knows what a word is.

KATE. Yet you keep spelling to her. Why?

ANNIE (*cheerily*). I like to hear myself talk!

KATE. The Captain says it's like spelling to the fence post.

ANNIE (*a pause*). Does he, now.

KATE. Is it?

ANNIE. No, it's how I watch you talk to Mildred.

KATE. Mildred.

ANNIE. Any baby. Gibberish, grown-up gibberish, baby-talk gibberish, do they understand one word of it to start? Somehow they begin to. If they hear it, I'm letting Helen hear it.

KATE. Other children are not—impaired.

ANNIE. Ho, there's nothing impaired in that head, it works like a mousetrap!

KATE (*smiles*). But after a child hears how many words, Miss Annie, a million?

ANNIE. I guess no mother's ever minded enough to count.

[*She drops her eyes to spell into* HELEN'S *hand, again indicating the card;* HELEN *spells back, and* ANNIE *is amused.*]

KATE (*too quickly*). What did she spell?

ANNIE. I spelt card. She spelt cake!

[*She takes in* KATE'S *quickness, and shakes her head, gently.*]

No, it's only a finger-game to her, Mrs. Keller. What she has to learn first is that things have names.

KATE. And when will she learn?

ANNIE. Maybe after a million and one words.

[*They hold each other's gaze;* KATE *then speaks quietly.*]

KATE. I should like to learn those letters, Miss Annie.

ANNIE (*pleased*). I'll teach you tomorrow morning. That makes only a half million each!

KATE (*then*). It's her bedtime.

[ANNIE *reaches for the sewing card,* HELEN *objects,* ANNIE *insists, and* HELEN *gets rid of* ANNIE'S *hand by jabbing it with the needle.* ANNIE *gasps, and moves to grip* HELEN'S *wrist; but* KATE *intervenes with a proffered sweet, and* HELEN *drops the card, crams the sweet into her mouth, and scrambles up to search her mother's hands for more.* ANNIE *nurses her wound, staring after the sweet.*]

I'm sorry, Miss Annie.

ANNIE (*indignantly*). Why does she get a reward? For stabbing me?

KATE. Well—

[*Then, tiredly*]

We catch our flies with honey, I'm afraid. We haven't the heart for much else, and so many times she simply cannot be compelled.

ANNIE (*ominous*). Yes. I'm the same way myself.

[KATE *smiles, and leads* HELEN *off around the corner.* ANNIE *alone in her room picks up things and in the act of removing* HELEN'S *doll gives way to unmannerly temptation: she throttles it. She drops it on her bed, and stands pondering. Then she turns back, sits decisively, and writes again, as the lights dim on her.*]

[*Grimly*]

"The, more, I, think, the, more, certain, I, am, that, obedience, is, the, gateway, through, which, knowledge, enters, the, mind, of, the, child—"

[*On the word "obedience" a shaft of sunlight hits the water pump outside, while* ANNIE'S *voice ends in the dark, followed by a distant cockcrow; daylight comes up over another corner of the sky, with* VINEY'S *voice heard at once.*]

VINEY. Breakfast ready!

[VINEY *comes down into the sunlight beam, and pumps a pitcherful of water. While the pitcher is brimming we hear conversation from the dark; the light grows to the family room of the house where all are either entering or already seated at breakfast, with* KELLER *and* JAMES *arguing the war.* HELEN *is wandering around the table to explore the contents of the other plates. When* ANNIE *is in her chair, she watches* HELEN. VINEY *reenters, sets the pitcher on the table;* KATE *lifts the almost empty biscuit plate with an inquiring look,* VINEY *nods and bears it off back, neither of them interrupting the men.* ANNIE *meanwhile sits with fork quiet, watching* HELEN, *who at her mother's plate pokes her hand among some scrambled eggs.* KATE *catches* ANNIE'S *eyes on her, smiles with a wry gesture.* HELEN *moves on to* JAMES'S *plate, the male talk continuing,* JAMES *deferential and* KELLER *overriding.*]

JAMES. —no, but shouldn't we give the devil his due, father? The fact is we lost the South two years earlier when he outthought us behind Vicksburg.[1]

KELLER. Outthought is a peculiar word for a butcher.

JAMES. Harness maker, wasn't he?

KELLER. I said butcher, his only virtue as a soldier was numbers and he led them to slaughter with no more regard than for so many sheep.

JAMES. But even if in that sense he was a butcher, the fact is he—

KELLER. And a drunken one, half the war.

JAMES. Agreed, father. If his own people said he was I can't argue he—

KELLER. Well, what is it you find to admire in such a man, Jimmie, the butchery or the drunkenness?

JAMES. Neither, father, only the fact that he beat us.

KELLER. He didn't.

JAMES. Is it your contention we won the war, sir?

KELLER. He didn't beat us at Vicksburg. We lost Vicksburg because Pemberton gave Bragg five thousand of his cavalry and Loring,[2] whom I knew personally for a nincompoop before you were born, marched away from Champion's Hill with enough men to have held them, we lost Vicksburg by stupidity verging on treason.

JAMES. I would have said we lost Vicksburg because Grant was one thing no Yankee general was before him—

KELLER. Drunk? I doubt it.

JAMES. Obstinate.

KELLER. Obstinate. Could any of them compare even in that with old Stonewall? If

---

1. James is referring to General U. S. Grant, whose Union troops captured Vicksburg on July 4, 1863.
2. **Pemberton, Bragg,** and **Loring,** mentioned by Captain Keller, were Confederate officers.

he'd been there we would still have Vicks-burg.

JAMES. Well, the butcher simply wouldn't give up, he tried four ways of getting around Vicksburg and on the fifth try he got around. Anyone else would have pulled north and—

KELLER. He wouldn't have got around if we'd had a Southerner in command, instead of a half-breed Yankee traitor like Pember-ton—

[*While this background talk is in progress,* HELEN *is working around the table, ultimately toward* ANNIE'S *plate. She messes with her hands in* JAMES'S *plate, then in* KELLER'S, *both men taking it so for granted they hardly notice. Then* HELEN *comes groping with soiled hands past her own plate, to* ANNIE'S; *her hand goes to it, and* ANNIE, *who has been waiting, deliberately lifts and removes her hand.* HELEN *gropes again,* ANNIE *firmly pins her by the wrist, and removes her hand from the table.* HELEN *thrusts her hands again,* ANNIE *catches them, and* HELEN *begins to flail and make noises; the interruption brings* KELLER'S *gaze upon them.*]

What's the matter there?

KATE. Miss Annie. You see, she's accustomed to helping herself from our plates to any-thing she—

ANNIE (*evenly*). Yes, but *I'm* not accustomed to it.

KELLER. No, of course not. Viney!

KATE. Give her something, Jimmie, to quiet her.

JAMES (*blandly*). But her table manners are the best she has. Well.

[*He pokes across with a chunk of bacon at* HELEN'S *hand, which* ANNIE *releases; but* HELEN *knocks the bacon away and stubbornly thrusts at* ANNIE'S *plate,* ANNIE *grips her wrists again, the struggle mounts.*]

KELLER. Let her this time, Miss Sullivan, it's

the only way we get any adult conversation. If my son's half merits that description.

[*He rises.*]

I'll get you another plate.

ANNIE (*gripping* HELEN). I have a plate, thank you.

KATE (*calling*). Viney! I'm afraid what Captain Keller says is only too true, she'll persist in this until she gets her own way.

KELLER (*at the door*). Viney, bring Miss Sulli-van another plate—

ANNIE (*stonily*). I have a plate, nothing's wrong with the *plate*, I intend to keep it.

[*Silence for a moment, except for* HELEN'S *noises as she struggles to get loose; the* KELLERS *are a bit nonplussed, and* ANNIE *is too darkly intent on* HELEN'S *manners to have any thoughts now of her own.*]

JAMES. Ha. You see why they took Vicksburg?

KELLER (*uncertainly*). Miss Sullivan. One plate or another is hardly a matter to struggle with a deprived child about.

ANNIE. Oh, I'd sooner have a more—

[HELEN *begins to kick,* ANNIE *moves her ankles to the opposite side of the chair.*]

—heroic issue myself, I—

KELLER. No, I really must insist you—

[HELEN *bangs her toe on the chair and sinks to the floor, crying with rage and feigned injury;* ANNIE *keeps hold of her wrists, gazing down, while* KATE *rises.*]

Now she's hurt herself.

ANNIE (*grimly*). No, she hasn't.

KELLER. Will you please let her hands go?

KATE. Miss Annie, you don't know the child well enough yet, she'll keep—

ANNIE. I know an ordinary tantrum well enough, when I see one, and a badly spoiled child—

JAMES. Hear, hear.

KELLER (*very annoyed*). Miss Sullivan! You would have more understanding of your pupil if you had some pity in you. Now kindly do as I—

ANNIE. Pity?

[*She releases* HELEN *to turn equally annoyed on* KELLER *across the table; instantly* HELEN *scrambles up and dives at* ANNIE'S *plate. This time* ANNIE *intercepts her by pouncing on her wrists like a hawk, and her temper boils.*]

For this *tyrant?* The whole house turns on her whims, is there anything she wants she doesn't get? I'll tell you what I pity, that the sun won't rise and set for her all her life, and every day you're telling her it will, what good will your pity do her when you're under the strawberries, Captain Keller?

KELLER (*outraged*). Kate, for the love of heaven will you—

KATE. Miss Annie, please, I don't think it serves to lose our—

ANNIE. It does you good, that's all. It's less trouble to feel sorry for her than to teach her anything better, isn't it?

KELLER. I fail to see where you have taught her anything yet, Miss Sullivan!

ANNIE. I'll begin this minute, if you'll leave the room, Captain Keller!

KELLER (*astonished*). Leave the—

ANNIE. Everyone, please.

[*She struggles with* HELEN, *while* KELLER *endeavors to control his voice.*]

KELLER. Miss Sullivan, you are here only as a paid teacher. Nothing more, and not to lecture—

ANNIE. I can't *un*teach her six years of pity if you can't stand up to one tantrum! Old Stonewall, indeed. Mrs. Keller, you promised me help.

KATE. Indeed I did, we truly want to—

ANNIE. Then leave me alone with her. Now!

KELLER (*in a wrath*). Katie, will you come outside with me? At once, please.

Annie and Helen struggle during the wild breakfast room scene.

[*He marches to the front door.* KATE *and* JAMES *follow him. Simultaneously* ANNIE *releases* HELEN'S *wrists, and the child again sinks to the floor, kicking and crying her weird noises;* ANNIE *steps over her to meet* VINEY *coming in the rear doorway with biscuits and a clean plate, surprised at the general commotion.*]

VINEY. Heaven sakes—

ANNIE. Out, please.

[*She backs* VINEY *out with one hand, closes the door on her astonished mouth, locks it, and removes the key.* KELLER *meanwhile snatches his hat from a rack, and* KATE *follows him down the porch steps.* JAMES *lingers in the doorway to address* ANNIE *across the room with a bow.*]

JAMES. If it takes all summer, general.

[ANNIE *comes over to his door in turn, removing her glasses grimly; as* KELLER *outside begins speaking,* ANNIE *closes the door on* JAMES, *locks it, removes the key, and turns with her back against the door to stare ominously at* HELEN, *kicking on the floor.*

JAMES *takes his hat from the rack, and going down the porch steps joins* KATE *and* KELLER *talking in the yard,* KELLER *in a sputter of ire.*]

KELLER. This girl, this—cub of a girl—*presumes!* I tell you, I'm of half a mind to ship her back to Boston before the week is out. You can inform her so from me!

KATE (*eyebrows up*). I, Captain?

KELLER. She's a *hireling!* Now I want it clear, unless there's an apology and complete change of manner she goes back on the next train! Will you make that quite clear?

KATE. Where will you be, Captain, while I am making it quite—

KELLER. At the office!

[*He begins off left, finds his napkin still in his irate hand, is uncertain with it, dabs his lips with dignity, gets rid of it in a toss to* JAMES, *and marches off.* JAMES *turns to eye* KATE.]

JAMES. Will you?

[KATE'S *mouth is set, and* JAMES *studies it lightly.*]

I thought what she said was exceptionally intelligent. I've been saying it for years.

KATE (*not without scorn*). To his face?

[*She comes to relieve him of the white napkin, but reverts again with it.*]

Or will you take it, Jimmie? As a flag?

[JAMES *stalks out, much offended, and* KATE *turning stares across the yard at the house; the lights narrowing down to the following pantomime in the family room leave her motionless in the dark.*

ANNIE *meanwhile has begun by slapping both keys down on a shelf out of* HELEN'S *reach; she returns to the table, upstage.* HELEN'S *kicking has subsided, and when from the floor her hand finds* ANNIE'S *chair empty she pauses.* ANNIE *clears the table of* KATE'S, JAMES'S, *and* KELLER'S *plates; she gets back to her own across the table just in time to slide it deftly away from* HELEN'S *pouncing hand. She lifts the hand and moves it to* HELEN'S *plate, and after an instant's exploration,* HELEN *sits again on the floor and drums her heels.* ANNIE *comes around the table and resumes her chair. When* HELEN *feels her skirt again, she ceases kicking, waits for whatever is to come, renews some kicking, waits again.* ANNIE *retrieving her plate takes up a forkful of food, stops it halfway to her mouth, gazes at it devoid of appetite, and half-lowers it; but after a look at* HELEN *she sighs, dips the forkful toward* HELEN *in a for-your-sake toast, and puts it in her own mouth to chew, not without an effort.*

HELEN *now gets hold of the chair leg, and half-succeeds in pulling the chair out from under her.* ANNIE *bangs it down with her rear, heavily, and sits with all her weight.* HELEN'S *next attempt to topple it is unavailing, so her fingers dive in a pinch at* ANNIE'S *flank.* ANNIE *in the middle of her mouthful almost loses it with startle, and she slaps down her fork to round on* HELEN. *The child comes up with curiosity to feel what* ANNIE *is doing, so* ANNIE *resumes eating, letting* HELEN'S *hand follow the movement of her fork to her mouth; whereupon* HELEN *at once reaches into* ANNIE'S *plate.* ANNIE *firmly removes her hand to her own plate.* HELEN *in reply pinches* ANNIE'S *thigh, a good mean pinchful that makes* ANNIE *jump.* ANNIE *sets the fork down, and sits with her mouth tight.* HELEN *digs another pinch into her thigh, and this time* ANNIE *slaps her hand smartly away;* HELEN *retaliates with a roundhouse fist that catches* ANNIE *on the ear, and* ANNIE'S *hand leaps at once in a forceful slap across* HELEN'S *cheek;* HELEN *is the startled one now.* ANNIE'S *hand in compunction falters to her own face, but when* HELEN *hits at her again,* ANNIE *deliberately slaps her again.* HELEN *lifts her fist irresolute for another roundhouse,* ANNIE *lifts her hand resolute for*

A lull before the continuing storm——
Annie and Helen in breakfast room battle.

another slap, and they freeze in this posture, while HELEN *mulls it over. She thinks better of it, drops her fist, and giving* ANNIE *a wide berth, gropes around to her mother's chair, to find it empty; she blunders her way along the table, upstage, and encountering the empty chairs and missing plates, she looks bewildered; she gropes back to her mother's chair, again touches her cheek and indicates the chair, and waits for the world to answer.*

ANNIE *now reaches over to spell into her hand, but* HELEN *yanks it away; she gropes to the front door, tries the knob, and finds the door locked, with no key. She gropes to the rear door, and finds it locked, with no key. She commences to bang on it.* ANNIE *rises, crosses, takes her wrists, draws her resisting back to the table, seats her, and releases her hands upon her plate; as* ANNIE *herself begins to sit,* HELEN *writhes out of her chair, runs to the front door, and tugs and kicks at it.* ANNIE *rises again, crosses, draws her by one wrist back to the table, seats her, and sits;* HELEN *escapes back to the door, knocking over her mother's chair en route.* ANNIE *rises again*

in pursuit, and this time lifts HELEN *bodily from behind and bears her kicking to her chair. She deposits her, and once more turns to sit.* HELEN *scrambles out, but as she passes* ANNIE *catches her up again from behind and deposits her in the chair;* HELEN *scrambles out on the other side, for the rear door, but* ANNIE *at her heels catches her up and deposits her again in the chair. She stands behind it.* HELEN *scrambles out to her right, and the instant her feet hit the floor* ANNIE *lifts and deposits her back; she scrambles out to her left, and is at once lifted and deposited back. She tries right again and is deposited back, and tries left again and is deposited back, and now feints* ANNIE *to the right but is off to her left, and is promptly deposited back. She sits a moment, and then starts straight over the tabletop, dishware notwithstanding;* ANNIE *hauls her in and deposits her back, with her plate spilling in her lap, and she melts to the floor and crawls under the table, laborious among its legs and chairs; but* ANNIE *is swift around the table and waiting on the other side when she surfaces, immediately bearing her aloft;* HELEN *clutches at* JAMES'S *chair for anchorage, but it comes with her, and halfway back she abandons it to the floor.* ANNIE *deposits her in her chair, and waits,* HELEN *sits tensed motionless. Then she tentatively puts out her left foot and hand,* ANNIE *interposes her own hand, and at the contact* HELEN *jerks hers in. She tries her right foot,* ANNIE *blocks it with her own, and* HELEN *jerks hers in. Finally, leaning back, she slumps down in her chair, in a sullen biding.*

ANNIE *backs off a step, and watches;* HELEN *offers no move.* ANNIE *takes a deep breath. Both of them and the room are in considerable disorder, two chairs down and the table a mess, but* ANNIE *makes no effort to tidy it; she only sits on her own chair, and lets her energy refill. Then she takes up knife and fork, and resolutely addresses her food.* HELEN'S *hand comes out to explore, and seeing it* ANNIE *sits without moving; the child's hand goes over her hand and* *fork, pauses—*ANNIE *still does not move—and withdraws. Presently it moves for her own plate, slaps about for it, and stops, thwarted. At this,* ANNIE *again rises, recovers* HELEN'S *plate from the floor and a handful of scattered food from the deranged tablecloth, drops it on the plate, and pushes the plate into contact with* HELEN'S *fist. Neither of them now moves for a pregnant moment—until* HELEN *suddenly takes a grab of food and wolfs it down.* ANNIE *permits herself the humor of a minor bow and warming of her hands together; she wanders off a step or two, watching.* HELEN *cleans up the plate.*

After a glower of indecision, she holds the empty plate out for more. ANNIE *accepts it, and crossing to the removed plates, spoons food from them onto it; she stands debating the spoon, tapping it a few times on* HELEN'S *plate; and when she returns with the plate she brings the spoon, too. She puts the spoon first into* HELEN'S *hand, then sets the plate down.* HELEN *discarding the spoon reaches with her hand, and* ANNIE *stops it by the wrist; she replaces the spoon in it.* HELEN *impatiently discards it again, and again* ANNIE *stops her hand, to replace the spoon in it. This time* HELEN *throws the spoon on the floor.* ANNIE *after considering it lifts* HELEN *bodily out of the chair, and in a wrestling match on the floor closes her fingers upon the spoon, and returns her with it to the chair.* HELEN *again throws the spoon on the floor.* ANNIE *lifts her out of the chair again; but in the struggle over the spoon* HELEN *with* ANNIE *on her back sends her sliding over her head;* HELEN *flees back to her chair and scrambles into it. When* ANNIE *comes after her she clutches it for dear life;* ANNIE *pries one hand loose, then the other, then the first again, then the other again, and then lifts* HELEN *by the waist, chair and all, and shakes the chair loose.* HELEN *wrestles to get free, but* ANNIE *pins her to the floor, closes her fingers upon the spoon, and lifts her kicking under one arm; with her*

other hand she gets the chair in place again, and plunks HELEN *back on it. When she releases her hand,* HELEN *throws the spoon at her.*

ANNIE *now removes the plate of food.* HELEN *grabbing finds it missing, and commences to bang with her fists on the table.* ANNIE *collects a fistful of spoons and descends with them and the plate on* HELEN; *she lets her smell the plate, at which* HELEN *ceases banging, and* ANNIE *puts the plate down and a spoon in* HELEN'S *hand.* HELEN *throws it on the floor.* ANNIE *puts another spoon in her hand.* HELEN *throws it on the floor.* ANNIE *puts another spoon in her hand.* HELEN *throws it on the floor. When* ANNIE *comes to her last spoon she sits next to* HELEN, *and gripping the spoon in* HELEN'S *hand compels her to take food in it up to her mouth.* HELEN *sits with lips shut.* ANNIE *waits a stolid moment, then lowers* HELEN'S *hand. She tries again;* HELEN'S *lips remain shut.* ANNIE *waits, lowers* HELEN'S *hand. She tries again; this time* HELEN *suddenly opens her mouth and accepts the food.* ANNIE *lowers the spoon with a sigh of relief, and* HELEN *spews the mouthful out at her face.* ANNIE *sits a moment with eyes closed, then takes the pitcher and dashes its water into* HELEN'S *face, who gasps astonished.* ANNIE *with* HELEN'S *hand takes up another spoonful, and shoves it into her open mouth.* HELEN *swallows involuntarily, and while she is catching her breath* ANNIE *forces her palm open, throws four swift letters into it, then another four, and bows toward her with devastating pleasantness.*]

ANNIE. Good girl.

[ANNIE *lifts* HELEN'S *hand to feel her face nodding;* HELEN *grabs a fistful of her hair, and yanks. The pain brings* ANNIE *to her knees, and* HELEN *pummels her; they roll under the table, and the lights commence to dim out on them.*

Simultaneously the light at left has been rising, slowly, so slowly that it seems at first we only imagine what is intimated in the yard: a few ghostlike figures, in silence, motionless, waiting. Now the distant belfry chimes commence to toll the hour, also very slowly, almost—it is twelve—interminably; the sense is that of a long time passing. We can identify the figures before the twelfth stroke, all facing the house in a kind of watch: KATE *is standing exactly as before, but now with the baby Mildred sleeping in her arms, and placed here and there, unmoving, are* AUNT EV *in her hat with a hanky to her nose, and the two Negro children,* PERCY *and* MARTHA *with necks outstretched eagerly, and* VINEY *with a knotted kerchief on her head and a feather duster in her hand.*

The chimes cease, and there is silence. For a long moment none of the group moves.]

VINEY (*presently*). What am I gone do, Miss Kate? It's noontime, dinner's comin', I didn't get them breakfast dishes out of there yet.

[KATE *says nothing, stares at the house.* MARTHA *shifts* HELEN'S *doll in her clutch, and it plaintively says momma.*]

KATE (*presently*). You run along, Martha.

[AUNT EV *blows her nose.*]

AUNT EV (*wretchedly*). I can't wait out here a minute longer, Kate, why, this could go on all afternoon, too.

KATE. I'll tell the Captain you called.

VINEY (*to the children*). You hear what Miss Kate say? Never you mind what's going on here.

[*Still no one moves.*]

You run along tend your own bizness.

[*Finally* VINEY *turns on the children with the feather duster.*]

Shoo!

[*The two children divide before her. She chases them off.* AUNT EV *comes to* KATE, *on her dignity.*]

AUNT EV. Say what you like, Kate, but that child is a *Keller.*

[*She opens her parasol, preparatory to leaving.*]

I needn't remind you that all the Kellers are cousins to General Robert E. Lee. I don't know *who* that girl is.

[*She waits; but* KATE *staring at the house is without response.*]

The only Sullivan I've heard of—from Boston too, and I'd think twice before locking her up with that kind—is that man John L.[3]

[*And* AUNT EV *departs, with head high. Presently* VINEY *comes to* KATE, *her arms out for the baby.*]

VINEY. You give me her, Miss Kate, I'll sneak her in back, to her crib.

[*But* KATE *is moveless, until* VINEY *starts to take the baby;* KATE *looks down at her before relinquishing her.*]

KATE (*slowly*). This child never gives me a minute's worry.

VINEY. Oh yes, this one's the angel of the family, no question bout *that.*

[*She begins off rear with the baby, heading around the house; and* KATE *now turns her back on it, her hand to her eyes. At this moment there is the slamming of a door, and when* KATE *wheels* HELEN *is blundering down the porch steps into the light like a ruined bat out of hell.* VINEY *halts, and* KATE *runs in;* HELEN *collides with her mother's knees, and reels off and back to clutch them as her savior.* ANNIE *with smoked*

---

3. **John L. Sullivan** (1858–1918), of Boston, was heavyweight boxing champion from 1882 to 1892.

glasses in hand stands on the porch, also much undone, looking as though she had indeed just taken Vicksburg. KATE *taking in* HELEN'S *ravaged state becomes steely in her gaze up at* ANNIE.]

KATE. What happened?

[ANNIE *meets* KATE'S *gaze, and gives a factual report, too exhausted for anything but a flat voice.*]

ANNIE. She ate from her own plate.

[*She thinks a moment.*]

She ate with a spoon. Herself.

[KATE *frowns, uncertain with thought, and glances down at* HELEN.]

And she folded her napkin.

[KATE'S *gaze now wavers, from* HELEN *to* ANNIE, *and back.*]

KATE (*softly*). Folded—her napkin?
ANNIE. The room's a wreck, but her napkin is folded.

[*She pauses, then:*]

I'll be in my room, Mrs. Keller.

[*She moves to reenter the house; but she stops at* VINEY'S *voice.*]

VINEY (*cheery*). Don't be long, Miss Annie. Dinner be ready right away!

[VINEY *carries Mildred around the back of the house.* ANNIE *stands unmoving, takes a deep breath, stares over her shoulder at* KATE *and* HELEN, *then inclines her head graciously, and goes with a slight stagger into the house. The lights in her room above steal up in readiness for her.*

KATE *remains alone with* HELEN *in the yard, standing protectively over her, in a kind of wonder.*]

KATE (*slowly*). Folded her napkin.

[*She contemplates the wild head at her thighs, and moves her fingertips over it, with such a tenderness, and something like a fear of its strangeness, that her own eyes close; she whispers, bending to it:*]

My Helen—folded her napkin—

[*And still erect, with only her head in surrender,* KATE *for the first time that we see loses her protracted war with grief; but she will not let a sound escape her, only the grimace of tears comes, and sobs that shake her in a grip of silence. But* HELEN *feels them, and her hand comes up in its own wondering, to interrogate her mother's face, until* KATE *buries her lips in the child's palm.*

Upstairs, ANNIE *enters her room, closes the door, and stands back against it; the lights, growing on her with their special color, commence to fade on* KATE *and* HELEN. *Then* ANNIE *goes wearily to her suitcase, and lifts it to take it toward the bed. But it knocks an object to the floor, and she turns back to regard it. A new voice comes in a cultured murmur, hesitant as with the effort of remembering a text:*]

MAN'S VOICE.[4] This—soul—

[ANNIE *puts the suitcase down, and kneels to the object: it is the battered Perkins report, and she stands with it in her hand, letting memory try to speak:*]

This—blind, deaf, mute—woman—

[ANNIE *sits on her bed, opens the book, and finding the passage, brings it up an inch from her eyes to read, her face and lips following the overheard words, the voice quite factual now:*]

Can nothing be done to disinter this human soul? The whole neighborhood

---

4. This voice represents that of Dr. Howe reading his report on Laura Bridgman.

would rush to save this woman if she were buried alive by the caving in of a pit, and labor with zeal until she were dug out. Now if there were one who had as much patience as zeal, he might awaken her to a consciousness of her immortal—

[*When the boy's voice comes,* ANNIE *closes her eyes, in pain.*]

BOY'S VOICE. Annie? Annie, you there?
ANNIE. Hush.
BOY'S VOICE. Annie, what's that noise?

[ANNIE *tries not to answer; her own voice is drawn out of her, unwilling.*]

ANNIE. Just a cot, Jimmie.
BOY'S VOICE. Where they pushin' it?
ANNIE. To the deadhouse.
BOY'S VOICE. Annie. Does it hurt, to be dead?

[ANNIE *escapes by opening her eyes, her hand works restlessly over her cheek; she retreats into the book again, but the cracked old crones interrupt, whispering.* ANNIE *slowly lowers the book.*]

FIRST CRONE'S VOICE. There is schools.
SECOND CRONE'S VOICE. There is schools outside—
THIRD CRONE'S VOICE. —schools where they teach blind ones, worse'n you—
FIRST CRONE'S VOICE. To read—
SECOND CRONE'S VOICE. To read and write—
THIRD CRONE'S VOICE. There is schools outside where they—
FIRST CRONE'S VOICE. There is schools—

[*Silence.* ANNIE *sits with her eyes shining, her hand almost in a caress over the book. Then:*]

BOY'S VOICE. You ain't goin' to school, are you, Annie?
ANNIE (*whispering*). When I grow up.
BOY'S VOICE. You ain't either, Annie. You're goin' to stay here take care of me.
ANNIE. I'm goin' to school when I grow up.

BOY'S VOICE. You said we'll be together, forever and ever and ever—
ANNIE (*fierce*). I'm goin' to school when I grow up!
DOCTOR'S VOICE (*slowly*). Little girl. Little girl, I must tell you. Your brother will be going on a journey, soon.

[ANNIE *sits rigid, in silence. Then the boy's voice pierces it, a shriek of terror.*]

BOY'S VOICE. Annie!

[*It goes into* ANNIE *like a sword, she doubles onto it; the book falls to the floor. It takes her a racked moment to find herself and what she was engaged in here; when she sees the suitcase she remembers, and lifts it once again toward the bed. But the voices are with her, as she halts with suitcase in hand.*]

FIRST CRONE'S VOICE. Good-bye, Annie.
DOCTOR'S VOICE. Write me when you learn how.
SECOND CRONE'S VOICE. Don't tell anyone you came from here. Don't tell anyone—
THIRD CRONE'S VOICE. Yeah, don't tell anyone you came from—
FIRST CRONE'S VOICE. Yeah, don't tell anyone—
SECOND CRONE'S VOICE. Don't tell any—

[*The echoing voices fade. After a moment* ANNIE *lays the suitcase on the bed; and the last voice comes faintly, from far away.*]

BOY'S VOICE. Annie. It hurts, to be dead. Forever.

[ANNIE *falls to her knees by the bed, stifling her mouth in it. When at last she rolls blindly away from it, her palm comes down on the open report; she opens her eyes, regards it dully, and then, still on her knees, takes in the print.*]

MAN'S VOICE (*factual*). —might awaken her to a consciousness of her immortal nature. The chance is small indeed; but with a

BOY'S VOICE: *"You said we'll be together, forever and ever and ever———"*

smaller chance they would have dug desperately for her in the pit; and is the life of the soul of less import than that of the body?

[ANNIE *gets to her feet. She drops the book on the bed, and pauses over her suitcase; after a moment she unclasps and opens it. Standing before it, she comes to her decision; she at once turns to the bureau, and taking her things out of its drawers, commences to throw them into the open suitcase.*

In the darkness down left a hand strikes a match, and lights a hanging oil lamp. It is KELLER'S *hand, and his voice accompanies it, very angry; the lights rising here before they fade on* ANNIE

show KELLER *and* KATE *inside a suggestion of a garden house, with a bay-window seat towards center and a door at back.*]

KELLER. Katie, I will not *have* it! Now you did not see when that girl after supper tonight went to look for Helen in her room—

KATE. No.

KELLER. The child practically climbed out of her window to escape from her! What kind of teacher *is* she? I thought I had seen her at her worst this morning, shouting at me, but I come home to find the entire house disorganized by her—Helen won't stay one second in the same room, won't come to the table with her, won't let herself be bathed or undressed or put to bed by her, or even by Viney now, and the end result is that *you* have to do more for the child than before we hired this girl's services! From the moment she stepped off the train she's been nothing but a burden, incompetent, impertinent, ineffectual, immodest—

KATE. She folded her napkin, Captain.

KELLER. What?

KATE. Not ineffectual. Helen did fold her napkin.

KELLER. What in heaven's name is so extraordinary about folding a napkin?

KATE (*with some humor*). Well. It's more than you did, Captain.

KELLER. Katie. I did not bring you all the way out here to the garden house to be frivolous. Now, how does Miss Sullivan propose to teach a deaf-blind pupil who won't let her even touch her?

KATE (*a pause*). I don't know.

KELLER. The fact is, today she scuttled any chance she ever had of getting along with the child. If you can see any point or purpose to her staying on here longer, it's more than—

KATE. What do you wish me to do?

KELLER. I want you to give her notice.

KATE. I can't.

KELLER. Then if you won't, I must. I simply will not—

[*He is interrupted by a knock at the back door.* KELLER *after a glance at* KATE *moves to open the door;* ANNIE *in her smoked glasses is standing outside.* KELLER *comtemplates her, heavily.*]

Miss Sullivan.

ANNIE. Captain Keller.

[*She is nervous, keyed up to seizing the bull by the horns again, and she assumes a cheeriness which is not unshaky.*]

Viney said I'd find you both over here in the garden house. I thought we should— have a talk?

KELLER (*reluctantly*). Yes, I— Well, come in.

[ANNIE *enters, and is interested in this room; she rounds on her heel, anxiously, studying it.* KELLER *turns the matter over to* KATE, *sotto voce.*]

Katie.

KATE (*turning it back, courteously*). Captain.

[KELLER *clears his throat, makes ready.*]

KELLER. I, ah—wanted first to make my position clear to Mrs. Keller, in private. I have decided I—am not satisfied—in fact, am deeply dissatisfied—with the manner in which—

ANNIE (*intent*). Excuse me, is this little house ever in use?

KELLER (*with patience*). In the hunting season. If you will give me your attention, Miss Sullivan.

[ANNIE *turns her smoked glasses upon him; they hold his unwilling stare.*]

I have tried to make allowances for you because you come from a part of the country where people are—women, I should say— come from who—well, for whom—

[*It begins to elude him.*]

—allowances must—be made. I have decided, nevertheless, to—that is, decided I—

[*Vexedly*]

Miss Sullivan, I find it difficult to talk through those glasses.

ANNIE (*eagerly, removing them*). Oh, of course.

KELLER (*dourly*). Why do you wear them, the sun has been down for an hour.

ANNIE (*pleasantly, at the lamp*). Any kind of light hurts my eyes.

[*A silence;* KELLER *ponders her, heavily.*]

KELLER. Put them on. Miss Sullivan, I have decided to—give you another chance.

ANNIE (*cheerfully*). To do what?

KELLER. To—remain in our employ.

[ANNIE'S *eyes widen.*]

But on two conditions. I am not accustomed to rudeness in servants or women, and that is the first. If you are to stay, there must be a radical change of manner.

ANNIE (*a pause*). Whose?

KELLER (*exploding*). Yours, young lady, isn't it obvious? And the second is that you persuade me there's the slightest hope of your teaching a child who flees from you now like the plague, to anyone else she can find in this house.

ANNIE (*a pause*). There isn't.

[KATE *stops sewing, and fixes her eyes upon* ANNIE.]

KATE. What, Miss Annie?

ANNIE. It's hopeless here. I can't teach a child who runs away.

KELLER (*nonplussed*). Then—do I understand you—propose—

ANNIE. Well, if we all agree it's hopeless, the next question is what—

KATE. Miss Annie.

[*She is leaning toward* ANNIE, *in deadly earnest; it commands both* ANNIE *and* KELLER.]

I am not agreed. I think perhaps you—underestimate Helen.

ANNIE. I think everybody else here does.

KATE. She did fold her napkin. She learns, she learns, do you know she began talking when she was six months old? She could say "water." Not really—"wahwah." "Wahwah," but she meant water, she knew what it meant, and only six months old, I never saw a child so—bright, or outgoing—

[*Her voice is unsteady, but she gets it level.*]

It's still in her, somewhere, isn't it? You should have seen her before her illness, such a good-tempered child—

ANNIE (*agreeably*). She's changed.

[*A pause,* KATE *not letting her eyes go; her appeal at last is unconditional, and very quiet.*]

KATE. Miss Annie, put up with it. And with us.

KELLER. Us!

KATE. Please? Like the lost lamb in the parable, I love her all the more.

ANNIE. Mrs. Keller, I don't think Helen's worst handicap is deafness or blindness. I think it's your love. And pity.

KELLER. Now what does that mean?

ANNIE. All of you here are so sorry for her you've kept her—like a pet, why, even a dog you housebreak. No wonder she won't let me come near her. It's useless for me to try to teach her language or anything else here. I might as well—

KATE (*cuts in*). Miss Annie, before you came we spoke of putting her in an asylum.

[ANNIE *turns back to regard her. A pause.*]

ANNIE. What kind of asylum?

KELLER. For mental defectives.

KATE. I visited there. I can't tell you what I saw, people like—animals, with—*rats*, in the halls, and—

[*She shakes her head on her vision.*]

What else are we to do, if you give up?

ANNIE. Give up?

KATE. You said it was hopeless.

ANNIE. Here. Give up, why, I only today saw what has to be done, to begin!

[*She glances from* KATE *to* KELLER, *who stare, waiting; and she makes it as plain and simple as her nervousness permits.*]

I—want complete charge of her.

KELLER. You already have that. It has resulted in—

ANNIE. No, I mean day and night. She has to be dependent on me.

KATE. For what?

ANNIE. Everything. The food she eats, the clothes she wears, fresh—

[*She is amused at herself, though very serious.*]

—air, yes, the air she breathes, whatever her body needs is a—primer, to teach her out of. It's the only way, the one who lets her have it should be her teacher.

[*She considers them in turn; they digest it,* KELLER *frowning,* KATE *perplexed.*]

Not anyone who *loves* her, you have so many feelings they fall over each other like feet, you won't use your chances and you won't let me.

KATE. But if she runs from you—*to* us—

ANNIE. Yes, that's the point. I'll have to live with her somewhere else.

KELLER. What!

ANNIE. Till she learns to depend on and listen to me.

KATE (*not without alarm*). For how long?

ANNIE. As long as it takes.

[*A pause. She takes a breath.*]

I packed half my things already.

KELLER. Miss—Sullivan!

[*But when* ANNIE *attends upon him he is speechless, and she is merely earnest.*]

ANNIE. Captain Keller, it meets both your conditions. It's the one way I can get back in touch with Helen, and I don't see how I can be rude to you again if you're not around to interfere with me.

KELLER (*red-faced*). And what is your intention if I say no? Pack the other half, for home, and abandon your charge to—to—

ANNIE. The asylum?

[*She waits, appraises* KELLER'S *glare and* KATE'S *uncertainty, and decides to use her weapons.*]

I grew up in such an asylum. The state almshouse.

[KATE'S *head comes up on this, and* KELLER *stares hard;* ANNIE'S *tone is cheerful enough, albeit level as gunfire.*]

Rats—why, my brother Jimmie and I used to play with the rats because we didn't have toys. Maybe you'd like to know what Helen will find there, not on visiting days? One ward was full of the—old women, crippled, blind, most of them dying, but even if what they had was catching there was nowhere else to move them, and that's where they put us. There were younger ones across the hall, . . . mostly with T.B., and epileptic fits, . . . and some insane. Some just had the D.T.'s.[5] . . . The room Jimmie and I played in was the deadhouse, where they kept the bodies till they could dig—

KATE (*closes her eyes*). Oh, my dear—

ANNIE. —the graves.

[*She is immune to* KATE'S *compassion.*]

No, it made me strong. But I don't think you need send Helen there. She's strong enough.

[*She waits again; but when neither offers her a word, she simply concludes.*]

No, I have no conditions, Captain Keller.

KATE (*not looking up*). Miss Annie.

ANNIE. Yes.

KATE (*a pause*). Where would you—take Helen?

ANNIE. Ohh—

[*Brightly*]

Italy?

KELLER (*wheeling*). What?

ANNIE. Can't have everything, how would this garden house do? Furnish it, bring Helen here after a long ride so she won't recognize it, and you can see her every day. If she doesn't know. Well?

KATE (*a sigh of relief*). Is that all?

ANNIE. That's all.

KATE. Captain.

[KELLER *turns his head; and* KATE'S *request is quiet but firm.*]

With your permission?

KELLER (*teeth in cigar*). Why must she depend on you for the food she eats?

ANNIE (*a pause*). I want control of it.

KELLER. Why?

ANNIE. It's a way to reach her.

KELLER (*stares*). You intend to *starve* her into letting you touch her?

ANNIE. She won't starve, she'll learn. All's fair in love and war, Captain Keller, you never cut supplies?

KELLER. This is hardly a war!

---

5. **D.T.'s** (dē'tēz'), an abbreviation for *delirium tremens* (di lir'ē əm trē'mənz), a violent trembling of the body, often accompanied by visual hallucinations, due to excessive use of alcohol.

ANNIE. Well, it's not love. A siege is a siege.

KELLER (*heavily*). Miss Sullivan. Do you *like* the child?

ANNIE (*straight in his eyes*). Do you?

[*A long pause.*]

KATE. You could have a servant here—

ANNIE (*amused*). I'll have enough work without looking after a servant! But that boy Percy could sleep here, run errands—

KATE (*also amused*). We can let Percy sleep here, I think, Captain?

ANNIE (*eagerly*). And some old furniture, all our own—

KATE (*also eager*). Captain? Do you think that walnut bedstead in the barn would be too—

KELLER. I have not yet consented to Percy! Or to the house, or to the proposal! Or to Miss Sullivan's—staying on when I—

[*But he erupts in an irate surrender.*]

Very well, I consent to everything!

[*He shakes the cigar at* ANNIE.]

For two weeks. I'll give you two weeks in this place, and it will be a miracle if you get the child to tolerate you.

KATE. Two weeks? Miss Annie, can you accomplish anything in two weeks?

KELLER. Anything or not, two weeks, then the child comes back to us. Make up your mind, Miss Sullivan, yes or no?

ANNIE. Two weeks. For only one miracle?

[*She nods at him, nervously.*]

I'll get her to tolerate me.

[KELLER *marches out, and slams the door.* KATE *on her feet regards* ANNIE, *who is facing the door.*]

KATE (*then*). You can't think as little of love as you said.

[ANNIE *glances questioning.*]

Or you wouldn't stay.

ANNIE (*a pause*). I didn't come here for love. I came for money!

[KATE *shakes her head to this, with a smile; after a moment she extends her open hand.* ANNIE *looks at it, but when she puts hers out it is not to shake hands, it is to set her fist in* KATE'S *palm.*]

KATE (*puzzled*). Hm?

ANNIE. A. It's the first of many. Twenty-six!

[KATE *squeezes her fist, squeezes it hard, and hastens out after* KELLER. ANNIE *stands as the door closes behind her, her manner so apprehensive that finally she slaps her brow, holds it, sighs, and, with her eyes closed, crosses herself for luck.*

The lights dim into a cool silhouette scene around her, the lamp paling out, and now, in formal entrances, persons appear around ANNIE *with furniture for the room:* PERCY *crosses the stage with a rocking chair and waits;* MARTHA *from another direction bears in a stool,* VINEY *bears in a small table, and the other Negro servant rolls in a bed partway from left; and* ANNIE, *opening her eyes to put her glasses back on, sees them. She turns around in the room once, and goes into action, pointing out locations for each article; the servants place them and leave, and* ANNIE *then darts around, interchanging them. In the midst of this—while* PERCY *and* MARTHA *reappear with a tray of food and a chair, respectively—*JAMES *comes down from the house with* ANNIE'S *suitcase, and stands viewing the room and her quizzically;* ANNIE *halts abruptly under his eye, embarrassed, then seizes the suitcase from his hand, explaining herself brightly.*]

ANNIE. I always wanted to live in a doll's house!

[*She sets the suitcase out of the way, and continues;* VINEY *at left appears to position a rod with drapes for a doorway, and the other servant at center pushes in a wheelbarrow loaded with a couple of boxes of* HELEN'S *toys and clothes.* ANNIE *helps lift them into the room, and the servant pushes the wheelbarrow off. In none of this is any heed taken of the imaginary walls of the garden house, the furniture is moved in from every side and itself defines the walls.*

ANNIE *now drags the box of toys into center, props up the doll conspicuously on top; with the people melted away, except for* JAMES, *all is again still. The lights turn again without pause, rising warmer.*]

JAMES. You don't let go of things easily, do you? How will you—win her hand now, in this place?

ANNIE (*curtly*). Do I know? I lost my temper, and here we are!

JAMES (*lightly*). No touching, no teaching. Of course, you *are bigger*—

ANNIE. I'm not counting on force, I'm counting on her. That little imp is dying to know.

JAMES. Know what?

ANNIE. Anything. Any and every crumb in God's creation. I'll have to use that appetite too.

[*She gives the room a final survey, straightens the bed, arranges the curtains.*]

JAMES (*a pause*). Maybe she'll teach you.

ANNIE. Of course.

JAMES. That she isn't. That there's such a thing as—dullness of heart. Acceptance. And letting go. Sooner or later we all give up, don't we?

ANNIE. Maybe you all do. It's my idea of the original sin.

JAMES. What is?

ANNIE (*witheringly*). Giving up.

JAMES (*nettled*). You won't open her. Why can't you let her be? Have some—pity on her, for being what she is—

ANNIE. If I'd ever once thought like that, I'd be dead!

ANNIE: *"Now all I have to teach you is——one word. Everything."*

JAMES (*pleasantly*). You will be. Why trouble?

[ANNIE *turns to glare at him; he is mocking.*]

Or will you teach me?

[*And with a bow, he drifts off.*

Now in the distance there comes the clopping of hoofs, drawing near, and nearer, up to the door; and they halt. ANNIE *wheels to face the door. When it opens this time, the* KELLERS—KATE *in travelling bonnet,* KELLER *also hatted—are standing there with* HELEN *between them; she is in a cloak.* KATE *gently cues her into the room.* HELEN *comes in groping, baffled, but interested in the new surroundings;* ANNIE *evades her exploring hand, her gaze not leaving the child.*]

ANNIE. Does she know where she is?

KATE (*shakes her head*). We rode her out in the country for two hours.

KELLER. For all she knows she could be in another town—

[HELEN *stumbles over the box on the floor and in it discovers her doll and other battered toys, is pleased, sits to them, then becomes puzzled and suddenly very wary. She scrambles up and back to her mother's thighs, but* ANNIE *steps in, and it is hers that* HELEN *embraces.* HELEN *recoils, gropes, and touches her cheek instantly.*]

KATE. That's her sign for me.
ANNIE. I know.

[HELEN *waits, then recommences her groping, more urgently.* KATE *stands indecisive, and takes an abrupt step toward her, but* ANNIE'S *hand is a barrier.*]

In two weeks.
KATE. Miss Annie, I—Please be good to her. These two weeks, try to be very good to her—
ANNIE. I will.

[KATE, *turning then, hurries out. The* KELLERS *cross back of the main house.*

ANNIE *closes the door.* HELEN *starts at the door jar, and rushes it.* ANNIE *holds her off.* HELEN *kicks her, breaks free, and careens around the room like an imprisoned bird, colliding with furniture, groping wildly, repeatedly touching her cheek in a growing panic. When she has covered the room, she commences her weird screaming.* ANNIE *moves to comfort her, but her touch sends* HELEN *into a paroxysm of rage: she tears away, falls over her box of toys, flings its contents in handfuls in* ANNIE'S *direction, flings the box too, reels to her feet, rips curtains from the window, bangs and kicks at the door, sweeps objects off the mantelpiece and shelf, a little tornado incarnate, all destruction, until she comes upon her doll and, in the act of hurling it, freezes. Then she clutches it to herself, and in*

exhaustion sinks sobbing to the floor. ANNIE *stands contemplating her, in some awe.*]

Two weeks.

[*She shakes her head, not without a touch of disgusted bewilderment.*]

What did I get into now?

[*The lights have been dimming throughout, and the garden house is lit only by moonlight now, with* ANNIE *lost in the patches of dark.*

KATE, *now hatless and coatless, enters the family room by the rear door, carrying a lamp.* KELLER, *also hatless, wanders simultaneously around the back of the main house to where* JAMES *has been waiting, in the rising moonlight, on the porch.*]

KELLER. I can't understand it. I had every intention of dismissing that girl, not setting her up like an empress.
JAMES. Yes, what's her secret, sir?
KELLER. Secret?
JAMES (*pleasantly*). That enables her to get anything she wants out of you? When I can't.

[JAMES *turns to go into the house, but* KELLER *grasps his wrist, twisting him half to his knees.* KATE *comes from the porch.*]

KELLER (*angrily*). She does *not* get anything she—
JAMES (*in pain*). Don't—don't—
KATE. Captain.
KELLER. He's afraid.

[*He throws* JAMES *away from him, with contempt.*]

What *does* he want out of me?
JAMES (*an outcry*). My God, don't you know?

[*He gazes from* KELLER *to* KATE.]

Everything you forgot, when you forgot my mother.

KELLER. What!

[JAMES *wheels into the house.* KELLER *takes a stride to the porch, to roar after him.*]

One thing that girl's secret is not, she doesn't fire one shot and disappear!

[KATE *stands rigid, and* KELLER *comes back to her.*]

Katie. Don't mind what he—
KATE. Captain, *I* am proud of you.
KELLER. For what?
KATE. For letting this girl have what she needs.
KELLER. Why can't my son be? He can't bear me, you'd think I treat him as hard as this girl does Helen—

[*He breaks off, as it dawns in him.*]

KATE (*gently*). Perhaps you do.
KELLER. But he has to learn some respect!
KATE (*a pause, wryly*). Do you like the child?

[*She turns again to the porch, but pauses, reluctant.*]

How empty the house is, tonight.

[*After a moment she continues on in.* KELLER *stands moveless, as the moonlight dies on him. The distant belfry chimes toll, two o'clock, and with them, a moment later, comes the boy's voice on the wind, in a whisper:*]

BOY'S VOICE. Annie. Annie.

[*In her patch of dark* ANNIE, *now in her nightgown, hurls a cup into a corner as though it were her grief, getting rid of its taste through her teeth.*]

ANNIE. No! No pity, I won't have it.

[*She comes to* HELEN, *prone on the floor.*]

On either of us.

[*She goes to her knees, but when she touches*

HELEN'S *hand the child starts up awake, recoils, and scrambles away from her under the bed.* ANNIE *stares after her. She strikes her palm on the floor, with passion.*]

I *will* touch you!

[*She gets to her feet, and paces in a kind of anger around the bed, her hand in her hair, and confronting* HELEN *at each turn.*]

How, how? How do I—

[ANNIE *stops. Then she calls out urgently, loudly.*]

Percy! Percy!

[*She moves swiftly to the drapes, at left.*]

Percy, wake up!

[PERCY'S *voice comes in a thick sleepy mumble, unintelligible.*]

Get out of bed and come in here, I need you.

[ANNIE *darts away, finds and strikes a match, and touches it to the hanging lamp; the lights come up dimly in the room, and* PERCY *stands bare to the waist in torn overalls between the drapes, with eyes closed, swaying.* ANNIE *goes to him, pats his cheeks vigorously.*]

Percy. You awake?
PERCY. No'm.
ANNIE. How would you like to play a nice game?
PERCY. Whah?
ANNIE. With Helen. She's under the bed. Touch her hand.

[*She kneels* PERCY *down at the bed, thrusting his hand under it to contact* HELEN'S; HELEN *emits an animal sound and crawls to the opposite side, but commences sniffing.* ANNIE *rounds the bed with* PERCY *and thrusts his hand again at* HELEN; *this time* HELEN *clutches it, sniffs in recognition, and comes scrambling out after*

PERCY, *to hug him with delight.* PERCY *alarmed struggles, and* HELEN'S *fingers go to his mouth.*]

PERCY. Lemme go. Lemme go—

[HELEN *fingers her own lips, as before, moving them in dumb imitation.*]

She tryin' talk. She gonna hit me—
ANNIE (*grimly*). She *can* talk. If she only knew, I'll show you how. She makes letters.

[*She opens* PERCY'S *other hand, and spells into it:*]

This one is C. C.

[*She hits his palm with it a couple of times, her eyes upon* HELEN *across him;* HELEN *gropes to feel what* PERCY'S *hand is doing, and when she encounters* ANNIE'S *she falls back from them.*]

She's mad at me now, though, she won't play. But she knows lots of letters. Here's another, A. C, a. C, a.

[*But she is watching* HELEN, *who comes groping, consumed with curiosity;* ANNIE *makes the letters in* PERCY'S *hand, and* HELEN *pokes to question what they are up to. Then* HELEN *snatches* PERCY'S *other hand, and quickly spells four letters into it.* ANNIE *follows them aloud.*]

C, a, k, e! She spells cake, she gets cake.

[*She is swiftly over to the tray of food, to fetch cake and a jug of milk.*]

She doesn't know yet it means this. Isn't it funny she knows how to spell it and doesn't *know* she knows?

[*She breaks the cake in two pieces, and extends one to each;* HELEN *rolls away from her offer.*]

Well, if she won't play it with me, I'll play it with you. Would you like to learn one she doesn't know?
PERCY. No'm.

[*But* ANNIE *seizes his wrist, and spells to him.*]

ANNIE. M, i, l, k. M is this. I, that's an easy one, just the little finger. L is this—

[*And* HELEN *comes back with her hand, to feel the new word.* ANNIE *brushes her away, and continues spelling aloud to* PERCY. HELEN'S *hand comes back again, and tries to get in;* ANNIE *brushes it away again.* HELEN'S *hand insists, and* ANNIE *puts it away rudely.*]

No, why should I talk to you? I'm teaching Percy a new word. L. K is this—

[HELEN *now yanks their hands apart; she butts* PERCY *away, and thrusts her palm out insistently.* ANNIE'S *eyes are bright, with glee.*]

Ho, you're *jealous,* are you!

[HELEN'S *hand waits, intractably waits.*]

All *right.*

[ANNIE *spells into it, milk; and* HELEN *after a moment spells it back to* ANNIE. ANNIE *takes her hand, with her whole face shining. She gives a great sigh.*]

Good! So I'm finally back to where I can touch you, hm? Touch and go! No love lost, but here we go.

[*She puts the jug of milk into* HELEN'S *hand and squeezes* PERCY'S *shoulder.*]

You can go to bed now, you've earned your sleep. Thank you.

[PERCY *stumbling up weaves his way out through the drapes.* HELEN *finishes drinking, and holds the jug out, for* ANNIE; *when* ANNIE *takes it,* HELEN *crawls onto the bed, and makes for sleep.* ANNIE *stands, looks down at her.*]

Now all I have to teach you is—one word. Everything.

[*She sets the jug down. On the floor now* ANNIE *spies the doll, stoops to pick it up, and with it dangling in her hand, turns off the lamp. A shaft of moonlight is left on* HELEN *in the bed, and a second shaft on the rocking chair; and* ANNIE, *after putting off her smoked glasses, sits in the rocker with the doll. She is rather happy, and dangles the doll on her knee, and it makes its momma sound.* ANNIE *whispers to it in mock solicitude.*]

Hush, little baby. Don't—say a word—

[*She lays it against her shoulder, and begins rocking with it, patting its diminutive behind; she talks the lullaby to it, humorously at first.*]

*Momma's gonna buy you—a mockingbird:
If that—mockingbird don't sing—*

[*The rhythm of the rocking takes her into the tune, softly, and more tenderly.*]

*Momma's gonna buy you a diamond ring:
If that diamond ring turns to brass—*

[*A third shaft of moonlight outside now rises to pick out* JAMES *at the main house, with one foot on the porch step; he turns his body, as if hearing the song.*]

*Momma's gonna buy you a looking-glass:
If that looking-glass gets broke—*

[*In the family room a fourth shaft picks out* KELLER, *seated at the table, in thought; and he, too, lifts his head, as if hearing.*]

*Momma's gonna buy you a billy goat:
If that billy goat won't pull—*

[*The fifth shaft is upstairs in* ANNIE'S *room, and picks out* KATE, *pacing there; and she halts, turning her head, too, as if hearing.*]

*Momma's gonna buy you a cart and bull:
If that cart and bull turns over,
Momma's gonna buy you a dog named
    Rover;
If that dog named Rover won't bark—*

[*With the shafts of moonlight on* HELEN, *and* JAMES, *and* KELLER, *and* KATE, *all moveless,* and ANNIE *rocking the doll, the curtain ends the act.*]

READING FOR DETAILS

A General Decides Upon Her Strategy

No one who reads or sees *The Miracle Worker* will soon forget the exhausting breakfast battle which Annie and Helen wage with only two words spoken—those of Annie when she says "Good girl" to Helen. To thank her for the compliment, Helen grabs a fistful of Annie's hair and yanks her to her knees. But in this memorable clash of wills, Annie comes out the victor. Helen *folds* her napkin!

1. Even though Annie has won a battle, she is so weary from it that she starts packing her suitcase to leave the Keller household. Whose voice causes her to stop and reconsider her decision? From what text are the words coming? In her conference with the Kellers, what demand does she make and how is it received? What is the outcome of this interview?

2. Identify the characters who speak the following lines and briefly outline the situation in which the words are spoken:
   a. The, more, I, think, the, more, certain, I, am, that, obedience, is, the, gateway, through, which, knowledge, enters, the, mind, of, the, child—
   b. Yes, but *I'm* not accustomed to it.
   c. It's the first of many. Twenty-six!
   d. Maybe you all do. It's my idea of the original sin.
   e. . . . don't you know? Everything you forgot, when you forgot my mother.
   f. Now all I have to teach you is—one word. Everything.

READING FOR MEANING

Cite evidence from Act II that supports or refutes the following statements:

1. Intelligence can be recognized by those who understand it even though it is not demonstrated in the usual ways.

2. Pity is a very destructive emotion.
3. There are occasions when it is necessary to be "cruel in order to be kind."

READING FOR APPRECIATION

Characterization
Annie understood Helen through her own experiences and through her own intelligence. Kate understood Helen with her heart and from watching her closely over the years. Why did Captain Keller misinterpret Helen's needs and capabilities so thoroughly?

Significant Detail
Since readers of a play must interpret the lines themselves rather than having them interpreted for them by an actor, they must be alert to notice the significance of the punctuation. Why did playwright Gibson place a comma after every word written by Miss Sullivan at the beginning of Act II?

Staging
The ability to visualize the stage and the action on it is most essential to get the full dramatic effect of the ending of Act II.
1. Why is lighting of key importance in this closing scene?
2. Briefly discuss the significance of lighting in the staging of the entire play.

Understanding the Play

Just as for a good story, a drama depends on conflict for interest and action. In Act I we have begun to see the tension within the Keller family, and the conflict between Annie and Helen is begun. In Act II this last conflict is acted out wildly but not resolved. Before the breakfast room battle, which other conflicts are carried forward? What are the issues in these minor conflicts?

Act III

The stage is totally dark, until we see ANNIE *and* HELEN *silhouetted on the bed in the garden house.* ANNIE'S *voice is audible, very patient, and worn; it has been saying this for a long time.*

ANNIE. Water, Helen. This is water. W, a, t, e, r. It has a *name.*

[*A silence. Then:*]

Egg, e, g, g. It has a *name,* the name stands for the thing. Oh, it's so simple, simple as birth, to explain.

[*The lights have commenced to rise, not on the garden house but on the homestead. Then:*]

Helen, Helen, the chick *has* to come out of its shell, sometime. You come out, too.

[*In the bedroom upstairs, we see* VINEY *unhurriedly washing the window, dusting, turning the mattress, readying the room for use again; then in the family room a diminished group at one end of the table—*KATE, KELLER, JAMES—*finishing up a quiet breakfast; then outside, down right, the other Negro servant on his knees, assisted by* MARTHA, *working with a trowel around a new trellis and wheelbarrow. The scene is one of everyday calm, and all are oblivious to* ANNIE'S *voice.*]

There's only one way out, for you, and it's language. To learn that your fingers can talk. And say anything, anything you can name. This is mug. Mug, m, u, g. Helen, it has a *name.* It—has—a—*name—*

[KATE *rises from the table.*]

KELLER (*gently*). You haven't eaten, Katie.
KATE (*smiles, shakes her head*). I haven't the appetite I'm too—restless, I can't sit to it.
KELLER. You should eat, my dear. It will be a long day, waiting.

JAMES (*lightly*). But it's been a short two weeks. I never thought life could be so—noiseless, went much too quickly for me.

[KATE *and* KELLER *gaze at him, in silence.* JAMES *becomes uncomfortable.*]

ANNIE. C, a, r, d. Card. C, a—

JAMES. Well, the house has been practically normal, hasn't it?

KELLER (*harshly*). Jimmie.

JAMES. Is it wrong to enjoy a quiet breakfast, after five years? And you two even seem to enjoy each other—

KELLER. It could be even more noiseless, Jimmie, without your tongue running every minute. Haven't you enough feeling to imagine what Katie has been undergoing, ever since—

[KATE *stops him, with her hand on his arm.*]

KATE. Captain.

[*To* JAMES.]

It's true. The two weeks have been normal, quiet, all you say. But not short. Interminable.

[*She rises, and wanders out; she pauses on the porch steps, gazing toward the garden house.*]

ANNIE (*fading*). W, a, t, e, r. But it means *this*. W, a, t, e, r. *This*. W, a, t—

JAMES. I only meant that Miss Sullivan is a boon. Of contention, though, it seems.

KELLER (*heavily*). If and when you're a parent, Jimmie, you will understand what separation means. A mother loses a—protector.

JAMES (*baffled*). Hm?

KELLER. You'll learn, we don't just keep our children safe. They keep us safe.

[*He rises, with his empty coffee cup and saucer.*]

There are of course all kinds of separation, Katie has lived with one kind for five years. And another is disappointment. In a child.

[*He goes with the cup out the rear door.* JAMES *sits for a long moment of stillness. In the garden house the lights commence to come up;* ANNIE, *haggard at the table, is writing a letter, her face again almost in contact with the stationery;* HELEN, *apart on the stool, and for the first time as clean and neat as a button, is quietly crocheting an endless chain of wool, which snakes all around the room.*]

ANNIE. "I, feel, every, day, more, and, more, in—"

[*She pauses, and turns the pages of a dictionary before her; her finger descends the words to a full stop. She elevates her eyebrows, then copies the word.*]

"—adequate."

[*In the main house* JAMES *pushes up, and goes to the front doorway, after* KATE.]

JAMES. Kate?

[KATE *turns her glance.* JAMES *is rather weary.*]

I'm sorry. Open my mouth, like that fairy tale, frogs jump out.

KATE. No. It has been better. For everyone.

[*She starts away, up center.*]

ANNIE (*writing*). "If, only, there, were, someone, to, help, me, I, need, a, teacher, as, much, as, Helen—"

JAMES. Kate.

[KATE *halts, waits.*]

What does he want from me?

KATE. That's not the question. Stand up to the world, Jimmie, that comes first.

JAMES (*a pause, wryly*). But the world is him.

KATE. Yes. And no one can do it for you.

JAMES. Kate.

[*His voice is humble.*]

At least we—Could you—be my friend?

KATE. I am.

[KATE *turns to wander, up back of the garden house.* ANNIE'S *murmur comes at once; the lights begin to die on the main house.*]

ANNIE. "—my, mind, is, undisciplined, full, of, skips, and, jumps, and—"

[*She halts, rereads, frowns.*]

Hm.

[ANNIE *puts her nose again in the dictionary, flips back to an earlier page, and fingers down the words;* KATE *presently comes down toward the bay window with a trayful of food.*]

Disinter—disinterested—disjoin—dis—

[*She backtracks, indignant.*]

Disinterested, disjoin—Where's disipline?

[*She goes a page or two back, searching with her finger, muttering.*]

What a dictionary, have to know how to spell it before you can look up how to spell it, disciple, *discipline!* Diskipline.

[*She corrects the word in her letter.*]

Undisciplined.

[*But her eyes are bothering her, she closes them in exhaustion and gently fingers the eyelids.* KATE *watches her through the window.*]

KATE. What are you doing to your eyes?

[ANNIE *glances around; she puts her smoked glasses on, and gets up to come over, assuming a cheerful energy.*]

ANNIE. It's worse on my vanity! I'm learning to spell. It's like a surprise party, the most unexpected characters turn up.

KATE. You're not to overwork your eyes, Miss Annie.

ANNIE. Well.

[*She takes the tray, sets it on her chair, and carries chair and tray to* HELEN.]

Whatever I spell to Helen I'd better spell right.

KATE (*almost wistful*): How—serene she is.

ANNIE. She learned this stitch yesterday. Now I can't get her to stop!

[*She disentangles one foot from the wool chain, and sets the chair before* HELEN. HELEN *at its contact with her knee feels the plate, promptly sets her crocheting down, and tucks the napkin in at her neck, but* ANNIE *withholds the spoon; when* HELEN *finds it missing, she folds her hands in her lap, and quietly waits.* ANNIE *twinkles at* KATE *with mock devoutness.*]

Such a little lady, she'd sooner starve than eat with her fingers.

[*She gives* HELEN *the spoon, and* HELEN *begins to eat, neatly.*]

KATE. You've taught her so much, these two weeks. I would never have—

ANNIE. Not enough.

[*She is suddenly gloomy, shakes her head.*]

Obedience isn't enough. Well, she learned two nouns this morning, key and water, brings her up to eighteen nouns and three verbs.

KATE (*hesitant*): But—not—

ANNIE. No. Not that they mean things. It's still a finger-game, no meaning.

[*She turns to* KATE, *abruptly.*]

Mrs. Keller—

[*But she defers it; she comes back, to sit in the bay and lift her hand.*]

Shall we play our finger-game?

KATE. How will she learn it?

ANNIE. It will come.

[*She spells a word;* KATE *does not respond.*]

KATE. How?

ANNIE (*a pause*). How does a bird learn to fly?

[*She spells again.*]

We're born to use words, like wings, it has to come.

KATE. How?

ANNIE (*another pause, wearily*). All right. I don't know how.

[*She pushes up her glasses, to rub her eyes.*]

I've done everything I could think of. Whatever she's learned here—keeping herself clean, knitting, stringing beads, meals, setting-up exercises each morning, we climb trees, hunt eggs, yesterday a chick was born in her hands—all of it I spell, everything we do, we never stop spelling. I go to bed with—writer's cramp from talking so much!

KATE. I worry about you, Miss Annie. You must rest.

ANNIE. Now? She spells back in her *sleep*, her fingers make letters when she doesn't know! In her bones those five fingers know, that hand aches to—speak out, and something in her mind is asleep, how do I—nudge that awake? That's the one question.

KATE. With no answer.

ANNIE (*long pause*). Except keep at it. Like this.

[*She again begins spelling—I, need—and* KATE'S *brows gather, following the words.*]

KATE. More—time?

[*She glances at* ANNIE, *who looks her in the eyes, silent.*]

Here?

ANNIE. Spell it.

[KATE *spells a word—no—shaking her head;* ANNIE *spells two words—why, not—back, with an impatient question in her eyes; and* KATE *moves her head in pain to answer it.*]

KATE. Because I can't—

ANNIE. Spell it! If she ever learns, you'll have a lot to tell each other, start now.

[KATE *painstakingly spells in air. In the midst of this the rear door opens, and* KELLER *enters with the setter Belle in tow.*]

KELLER. Miss Sullivan? On my way to the office, I brought Helen a playmate—

ANNIE. Outside please, Captain Keller.

KELLER. My dear child, the two weeks are up today, surely you don't object to—

ANNIE (*rising*). They're not up till six o'clock.

KELLER (*indulgent*). Oh, now. What difference can a fraction of one day—

ANNIE. An agreement is an agreement. Now you've been very good, I'm sure you can keep it up for a few more hours.

[*She escorts* KELLER *by the arm over the threshold; he obeys, leaving Belle.*]

KELLER. Miss Sullivan, you are a tyrant.

ANNIE. Likewise, I'm sure. You can stand there, and close the door if she comes.

KATE. I don't think you know how eager we are to have her back in our arms—

ANNIE. I do know, it's my main worry.

KELLER. It's like expecting a new child in the house. Well, she *is*, so—composed, so—

[*Gently*]

Attractive. You've done wonders for her, Miss Sullivan.

ANNIE (*not a question*). Have I.

KELLER. If there's anything you want from us in repayment tell us, it will be a privilege to—

ANNIE. I just told Mrs. Keller. I want more time.

KATE. Miss Annie—

ANNIE. Another week.

[HELEN *lifts her head, and begins to sniff.*]

KELLER. We miss the child. *I* miss her, I'm glad to say, that's a different debt I owe you—

ANNIE. Pay it to Helen. Give *her* another week.

KATE (*gently*). Doesn't she miss us?

KELLER. Of course she does. What a wrench this unexplainable—exile must be to her, can you say it's not?

ANNIE. No. But I—

[HELEN *is off the stool, to grope about the room; when she encounters Belle, she throws her arms around the dog's neck in delight.*]

KATE. Doesn't she need affection too, Miss Annie?

ANNIE (*wavering*). She—never shows me she needs it, she won't have any—caressing or—

KATE. But you're not her mother.

KELLER. And what would another week accomplish? We are more than satisfied, you've done more than we ever thought possible, taught her constructive—

ANNIE. I can't promise anything. All I can—

KELLER (*no break*).—things to do, to behave like—even look like—a human child, so manageable, contented, cleaner, more—

ANNIE (*withering*). Cleaner.

KELLER. Well. We say cleanliness is next to godliness, Miss—

ANNIE. Cleanliness is next to nothing, she has to learn that everything has its name! That words can be her *eyes*, to everything in the world outside her, and inside too, what is she without words? With them she can think, have ideas, be reached, there's not a thought or fact in the world that can't be hers. You publish a newspaper, Captain Keller, do I have to tell you what words are? And she has them already—

KELLER. Miss Sullivan.

ANNIE. —eighteen nouns and three verbs, they're in her fingers now, I need only time to push *one* of them into her mind! One, and everything under the sun will follow. Don't you see what she's learned here is only clearing the way for that? I can't risk her unlearning it, give me more time alone with her, another week to—

KELLER. Look.

[*He points, and* ANNIE *turns.* HELEN *is playing with Belle's claws; she makes letters with her fingers, shows them to Belle, waits with her palm, then manipulates the dog's claws.*]

What is she spelling?

[*A silence.*]

KATE. Water?

[ANNIE *nods.*]

KELLER. Teaching a dog to spell.

[*A pause*]

The dog doesn't know what she means, any more than she knows what you mean, Miss Sullivan. I think you ask too much, of her and yourself. God may not have meant Helen to have the—eyes you speak of.

ANNIE (*toneless*). I mean her to.

KELLER (*curiously*). What is it to you?

[ANNIE'S *head comes slowly up.*]

You make us see how we indulge her for our sake. Is the opposite true, for you?

ANNIE (*then*). Half a week?

KELLER. An agreement *is* an agreement.

ANNIE. Mrs. Keller?

KATE (*simply*). I want her back.

[*A wait;* ANNIE *then lets her hands drop in surrender, and nods.*]

KELLER. I'll send Viney over to help you pack.

ANNIE. Not until six o'clock. I have her till six o'clock.

KELLER (*consenting*). Six o'clock. Come, Katie.

[KATE *leaving the window joins him around back, while* KELLER *closes the door; they are shut out.*

Only the garden house is daylit now, and the light on it is narrowing down. ANNIE *stands watching* HELEN *work Belle's claws. Then she settles beside them on her knees, and stops* HELEN'S *hand.*]

ANNIE (*gently*). No.

[*She shakes her head, with* HELEN'S *hand to her face, then spells.*]

Dog. D, o, g. Dog.

[*She touches* HELEN'S *hand to Belle.* HELEN *dutifully pats the dog's head, and resumes spelling to its paw.*]

Not water.

[ANNIE *rolls to her feet, brings a tumbler of water back from the tray, and kneels with it, to seize* HELEN'S *hand and spell.*]

Here. Water. *Water.*

[*She thrusts* HELEN'S *hand into the tumbler.* HELEN *lifts her hand out dripping, wipes it daintily on Belle's hide, and taking the tumbler from* ANNIE, *endeavors to thrust Belle's paw into it.* ANNIE *sits watching, wearily.*]

I don't know how to tell you. Not a soul in the world knows how to tell you. Helen, Helen.

[*She bends in compassion to touch her lips to* HELEN'S *temple, and instantly* HELEN *pauses, her hands off the dog, her head slightly averted. The lights are still narrowing, and Belle slinks off. After a moment* ANNIE *sits back.*]

Yes, what's it to me? They're satisfied. Give them back their child and dog, both house-broken, everyone's satisfied. But me, and you.

[HELEN'S *hand comes out into the light, groping.*]

Reach. *Reach!*

[ANNIE *extending her own hand grips* HELEN'S; *the two hands are clasped, tense in the light, the rest of the room changing in shadow.*]

I wanted to teach you—oh, everything the earth is full of, Helen, everything on it that's ours for a wink and it's gone, and what we are on it, the—light we bring to it and leave behind in—words, why, you can see five thousand years back in a light of words, everything we feel, think, know—and share, in words, so not a soul is in darkness, or done with, even in the grave. And I know, I *know*, one word and I can—put the world in your hand—and whatever it is to me, I won't take less! How, how, how do I tell you that *this*—

[*She spells.*]

—means a *word*, and the word means this *thing*, wool?

[*She thrusts the wool at* HELEN'S *hand;* HELEN *sits, puzzled.* ANNIE *puts the crocheting aside.*]

Or this—s, t, o, o, l—means this *thing*, stool?

[*She claps* HELEN'S *palm to the stool.* HELEN

waits, uncomprehending. ANNIE *snatches up her napkin, spells:*]

Napkin!

[*She forces it on* HELEN'S *hand, waits, discards it, lifts a fold of the child's dress, spells:*]

Dress!

[*She lets it drop, spells:*]

F, a, c, e, face!

[*She draws* HELEN'S *hand to her cheek, and pressing it there, staring into the child's responseless eyes, hears the distant belfry begin to toll, slowly: one, two, three, four, five, six.*

On the third stroke the lights stealing in around the garden house show us figures waiting: VINEY, *the other servant,* MARTHA, PERCY *at the drapes, and* JAMES *on the dim porch.* ANNIE *and* HELEN *remain, frozen. The chimes die away. Silently* PERCY *moves the drape-rod back out of sight;* VINEY *steps into the room—not using the door—and unmakes the bed; the other servant brings the wheelbarrow over, leaves it handy, rolls the bed off;* VINEY *puts the bed linens on top of a waiting boxful of* HELEN'S *toys, and loads the box on the wheelbarrow;* MARTHA *and* PERCY *take out the chairs, with the trayful, then the table; and* JAMES, *coming down and into the room, lifts* ANNIE'S *suitcase from its corner.* VINEY *and the other servant load the remaining odds and ends on the wheelbarrow, and the servant wheels it off.* VINEY *and the children departing leave only* JAMES *in the room with* ANNIE *and* HELEN. JAMES *studies the two of them, without mockery, and then, quietly going to the door and opening it, bears the suitcase out, and housewards. He leaves the door open.*

KATE *steps into the doorway, and stands.* ANNIE *lifting her gaze from* HELEN *sees her; she takes* HELEN'S *hand from her cheek, and returns it to*

the child's own, stroking it there twice, in her mother-sign, before spelling slowly into it:]

M, o, t, h, e, r. Mother.

[HELEN *with her hand free strokes her cheek, suddenly forlorn.* ANNIE *takes her hand again.*]

M, o, t, h—

[*But* KATE *is trembling with such impatience that her voice breaks from her, harsh.*]

KATE. Let her *come!*

[ANNIE *lifts* HELEN *to her feet, with a turn, and gives her a little push. Now* HELEN *begins groping, sensing something, trembling herself; and* KATE *falling one step in onto her knees clasps her, kissing her.* HELEN *clutches her, tight as she can.* KATE *is inarticulate, choked, repeating* HELEN'S *name again and again. She wheels with her in her arms, to stumble away out the doorway;* ANNIE *stands unmoving, while* KATE *in a blind walk carries* HELEN *like a baby behind the main house, out of view.* ANNIE *is now alone on the stage. She turns, gazing around at the stripped room, bidding it silently farewell, impassively, like a defeated general on the deserted battlefield. All that remains is a stand with a basin of water; and here* ANNIE *takes up an eyecup, bathes each of her eyes, empties the eyecup, drops it in her purse, and tiredly locates her smoked glasses on the floor. The lights alter subtly; in the act of putting on her glasses* ANNIE *hears something that stops her, with head lifted. We hear it too, the voices out of the past, including her own now, in a whisper:*]

BOY'S VOICE. You said we'd be together, forever— You promised, forever and—*Annie!*
ANAGNOS'S VOICE. But that battle is dead and
done with, why not let it stay buried?
ANNIE'S VOICE (*whispering*). I think God must
owe me a resurrection.
ANAGNOS'S VOICE. What?

[*A pause; and* ANNIE *answers it herself, heavily.*]

ANNIE. And I owe God one.

BOY'S VOICE. Forever and ever—

[ANNIE *shakes her head.*]

—forever, and ever, and—

[ANNIE *covers her ears.*]

—forever, and ever, and ever—

[*It pursues* ANNIE; *she flees to snatch up her purse, wheels to the doorway, and* KELLER *is standing in it. The lights have lost their special color.*]

KELLER. Miss—Annie.

[*He has an envelope in his fingers.*]

I've been waiting to give you this.

ANNIE (*after a breath*). What?

KELLER. Your first month's salary.

[*He puts it in her hand.*]

With many more to come, I trust. It doesn't express what we feel, it doesn't pay our debt. For what you've done.

ANNIE. What have I done?

KELLER. Taken a wild thing, and given us back a child.

ANNIE (*presently*). I taught her one thing, no. Don't do this, don't do that—

KELLER. It's more than all of us could, in all the years we—

ANNIE. I wanted to teach her what language is. I wanted to teach her yes.

KELLER. You will have time.

ANNIE. I don't know how. I know without it to do nothing but obey is—no gift, obedience without understanding is a—blindness, too. Is that all I've wished on her?

KELLER (*gently*). No, no—

ANNIE. Maybe. I don't know what else to do. Simply go on, keep doing what I've done, and have—faith that inside she's— That inside it's waiting. Like water, underground. All I can do is keep on.

KELLER. It's enough. For us.

ANNIE. You can help, Captain Keller.

KELLER. How?

ANNIE. Even learning no has been at a cost. Of much trouble and pain. Don't undo it.

KELLER. Why should we wish to—

ANNIE (*abruptly*). The world isn't an easy place for anyone, I don't want her just to obey but to let her have her way in everything is a lie, to *her*, I can't—

[*Her eyes fill, it takes her by surprise, and she laughs through it.*]

And I don't even love her, she's not my child! Well, you've got to stand between that lie and her.

KELLER. We'll try.

ANNIE. Because *I* will. As long as you let me stay, that's one promise I'll keep.

KELLER. Agreed. We've learned something too, I hope.

[*A pause*]

Won't you come now, to supper?

ANNIE. Yes.

[*She wags the envelope, ruefully.*]

Why doesn't God pay His debts each month?

KELLER. I beg your pardon?

ANNIE. Nothing. I used to wonder how I could—

[*The lights are fading on them, simultaneously rising on the family room of the main house, where* VINEY *is polishing glassware at the table set for dinner.*]

—earn a living.

KELLER. Oh, you do.

ANNIE. I really do. Now the question is, can I survive it!

[KELLER *smiles, offers his arm.*]

KELLER. May I?

[ANNIE *takes it, and the lights lose them as he escorts her out.*

Now in the family room the rear door opens, and HELEN *steps in. She stands a moment, then sniffs in one deep grateful breath, and her hands go out vigorously to familiar things, over the door panels, and to the chairs around the table, and over the silverware on the table, until she meets* VINEY; *she pats her flank approvingly.*]

VINEY. Oh, we glad to have you back, too, prob'ly.

[HELEN *hurries groping to the front door, opens and closes it, removes its key, opens and closes it again to be sure it is unlocked, gropes back to the rear door and repeats the procedure, removing its key and hugging herself gleefully.*

AUNT EV *is next in by the rear door, with a relish tray; she bends to kiss* HELEN'S *cheek.* HELEN *finds* KATE *behind her, and thrusts the keys at her.*]

KATE. What? Oh.

[*To* EV]

Keys.

[*She pockets them, lets* HELEN *feel them.*]

Yes, *I'll* keep the keys. I think we've had enough of locked doors, too.

[JAMES, *having earlier put* ANNIE'S *suitcase inside her door upstairs and taken himself out of view around the corner, now reappears and comes down the stairs as* ANNIE *and* KELLER *mount the porch steps. Following them into the family room, he pats* ANNIE'S *hair in passing, rather to her surprise.*]

JAMES. Evening, general.

[*He takes his own chair opposite.*]

VINEY *bears the empty water pitcher out to the porch. The remaining suggestion of garden house is gone now, and the water pump is unobstructed;* VINEY *pumps water into the pitcher.*

KATE *surveying the table breaks the silence.*]

KATE. Will you say the grace, Jimmie?

[*They bow their heads, except for* HELEN, *who palms her empty plate and then reaches to be sure her mother is there.* JAMES *considers a moment, glances across at* ANNIE, *lowers his head again, and obliges.*]

JAMES (*lightly*). And Jacob was left alone, and wrestled with an angel until the breaking of the day; and the hollow of Jacob's thigh was out of joint, as he wrestled with him; and the angel said, Let me go, for the day breaketh. And Jacob said, I will not let thee go, except thou bless me. Amen.[1]

[ANNIE *has lifted her eyes suspiciously at* JAMES, *who winks expressionlessly and inclines his head to* HELEN.]

Oh, you angel.

[*The others lift their faces;* VINEY *returns with the pitcher, setting it down near* KATE, *then goes out the rear door; and* ANNIE *puts a napkin around* HELEN.]

AUNT EV. That's a very strange grace, James.
KELLER. Will you start the muffins, Ev?
JAMES. It's from the Good Book, isn't it?
AUNT EV (*passing a plate*). Well, of course it is. Didn't you know?
JAMES. Yes. I knew.
KELLER (*serving*). Ham, Miss Annie?
ANNIE. Please.
AUNT EV. Then why ask?

---

1. James gives a shortened version of the King James translation of Genesis 32: 24–26.

JAMES. I meant it *is* from the Good Book, and therefore a fitting grace.

AUNT EV. Well. I don't know about *that.*

KATE (*with the pitcher*). Miss Annie?

ANNIE. Thank you.

AUNT EV. There's an awful *lot* of things in the Good Book that I wouldn't care to hear just before eating.

[*When* ANNIE *reaches for the pitcher,* HELEN *removes her napkin and drops it to the floor.* ANNIE *is filling* HELEN'S *glass when she notices it; she considers* HELEN'S *bland expression a moment, then bends, retrieves it, and tucks it around* HELEN'S *neck again.*]

JAMES. Well, fitting in the sense that Jacob's thigh was out of joint, and so is this piggie's.

AUNT EV. I declare, James—

KATE. Pickles, Aunt Ev?

AUNT EV. Oh, I should say so, you know my opinion of your pickles—

KATE. This is the end of them, I'm afraid. I didn't put up nearly enough last summer, this year I intend to—

[*She interrupts herself, seeing* HELEN *deliberately lift off her napkin and drop it again to the floor. She bends to retrieve it, but* ANNIE *stops her arm.*]

KELLER (*not noticing*). Reverend looked in at the office today to complain his hens have stopped laying. Poor fellow, *he* was out of joint, all he could—

[*He stops too, to frown down the table at* KATE, HELEN, *and* ANNIE *in turn, all suspended in midmotion.*]

JAMES (*not noticing*). I've always suspected those hens.

AUNT EV. Of what?

JAMES. I think they're Papists. Has he tried—

[*He stops, too, following* KELLER'S *eyes.* ANNIE *now stoops to pick the napkin up.*]

Helen clinging to her mother to escape Annie's discipline.

AUNT EV. James, now you're pulling my lower extremity, the first thing you know we'll be—

[*She stops, too, hearing herself in the silence.* ANNIE, *with everyone now watching, for the third time puts the napkin on* HELEN. HELEN *yanks it off, and throws it down.* ANNIE *rises, lifts* HELEN'S *plate, and bears it away.* HELEN, *feeling it gone, slides down and commences to kick up under the table; the dishes jump.* ANNIE *contemplates this for a moment, then coming back takes* HELEN'S *wrists firmly and swings her off the chair.* HELEN *struggling gets one hand free, and catches at her mother's skirt; when* KATE *takes her by the shoulders,* HELEN *hangs quiet.*]

KATE. Miss Annie.

ANNIE. No.

KATE (*a pause*). It's a very special day.

ANNIE (*grimly*). It will be, when I give in to that.

[*She tries to disengage* HELEN'S *hand;* KATE *lays hers on* ANNIE'S.]

KATE. Please. I've hardly had a chance to welcome her home—

ANNIE. Captain Keller.

KELLER (*embarrassed*). Oh. Katie, we—had a little talk, Miss Annie feels that if we indulge Helen in these—

AUNT EV. But what's the child done?

ANNIE. She's learned not to throw things on the floor and kick. It took us the best part of two weeks and—

AUNT EV. But only a napkin, it's not as if it were breakable!

ANNIE. And everything she's learned *is?* Mrs. Keller, I don't think we should—play tug-of-war for her, either give her to me or you keep her from kicking.

KATE. What do you wish to do?

ANNIE. Let me take her from the table.

AUNT EV. Oh, let her stay, my goodness, she's only a child, she doesn't have to wear a napkin if she doesn't want to her first evening—

ANNIE (*level*). And ask outsiders not to interfere.

AUNT EV (*astonished*). Out—outsi—I'm the child's *aunt!*

KATE (*distressed*). Will once hurt so much, Miss Annie? I've—made all Helen's favorite foods, tonight.

[*A pause*]

KELLER (*gently*). It's a homecoming party, Miss Annie.

[ANNIE *after a moment releases* HELEN. *But she cannot accept it, at her own chair she shakes her head and turns back, intent on* KATE.]

ANNIE. She's testing you. You realize?

JAMES (*to* ANNIE). She's testing you.

KELLER. Jimmie, be quiet.

[JAMES *sits, tense.*]

Now she's home, naturally she—

ANNIE. And she wants to see what will happen. At your hands. I said it was my main worry, is this what you promised me not half an hour ago?

KELLER (*reasonably*). But she's *not* kicking, now—

ANNIE. And not learning not to. Mrs. Keller, teaching her is bound to be painful, to everyone. I know it hurts to watch, but she'll live up to just what you demand of her, and no more.

JAMES (*palely*). She's testing *you.*

KELLER (*testily*). Jimmie.

JAMES. I have an opinion, I think I should—

KELLER. No one's interested in hearing your opinion.

ANNIE. *I'm* interested, of course she's testing me. Let me keep her to what she's learned and she'll go on learning from me. Take her out of my hands and it all comes apart.

[KATE *closes her eyes, digesting it;* ANNIE *sits again, with a brief comment for her.*]

Be bountiful, it's at her expense.

[*She turns to* JAMES, *flatly.*]

Please pass me more of—her favorite foods.

[*Then* KATE *lifts* HELEN'S *hand, and turning her toward* ANNIE, *surrenders her;* HELEN *makes for her own chair.*]

KATE (*low*). Take her, Miss Annie.

ANNIE (*then*). Thank you.

[*But the moment* ANNIE *rising reaches for her hand,* HELEN *begins to fight and kick, clutching to the tablecloth, and uttering laments.* ANNIE *again tries to loosen her hand, and* KELLER *rises.*]

KELLER (*tolerant*). I'm afraid you're the difficulty, Miss Annie. Now I'll keep her to what she's learned, you're quite right there—

[*He takes* HELEN'S *hands from* ANNIE, *pats them;* HELEN *quiets down.*]

—but I don't see that we need send her from the table, after all, she's the guest of honor. Bring her plate back.

ANNIE. If she was a seeing child, none of you would tolerate one—

KELLER. Well, she's not, I think some compromise is called for. Bring her plate, please.

[ANNIE'S *jaw sets, but she restores the plate, while* KELLER *fastens the napkin around* HELEN'S *neck; she permits it.*]

There. It's not unnatural, most of us take some aversion to our teachers, and occasionally another hand can smooth things out.

[*He puts a fork in* HELEN'S *hand;* HELEN *takes it. Genially:*]

Now. Shall we start all over?

[*He goes back around the table, and sits.* ANNIE *stands watching.* HELEN *is motionless, thinking things through, until with a wicked glee she deliberately flings the fork on the floor. After another moment she plunges her hand into her food, and crams a fistful into her mouth.*]

JAMES (*wearily*). I think we've started all over—

[KELLER *shoots a glare at him, as* HELEN *plunges her other hand into* ANNIE'S *plate.* ANNIE *at once moves in, to grasp her wrist, and* HELEN *flinging out a hand encounters the pitcher; she swings with it at* ANNIE; ANNIE *falling back blocks it with an elbow, but the water flies over her dress.* ANNIE *gets her breath, then snatches the pitcher away in one hand, hoists* HELEN *up bodily under the other arm, and starts to carry her out, kicking.* KELLER *stands.*]

ANNIE (*savagely polite*). Don't get up!

KELLER. Where are you going?

ANNIE. Don't smooth anything else out for me, don't interfere in any way! I treat her like a seeing child because I *ask* her to see, I *expect* her to see, don't undo what I do!

KELLER. Where are you taking her?

ANNIE. To make her fill this pitcher again!

[*She thrusts out with* HELEN *under her arm, but* HELEN *escapes up the stairs and* ANNIE *runs after her.* KELLER *stands rigid.* AUNT EV *is astounded.*]

AUNT EV. You let her speak to you like that, Arthur? A creature who *works* for you?

KELLER (*angrily*). No, I don't.

[*He is starting after* ANNIE *when* JAMES, *on his feet with shaky resolve, interposes his chair between them in* KELLER'S *path.*]

JAMES. Let her go.

KELLER. What!

JAMES (*a swallow*). I said—let her go. She's right.

[KELLER *glares at the chair and him.* JAMES *takes a deep breath, then headlong:*]

She's right. Kate's right, I'm right, and you're wrong. If you drive her away from here it will be over my dead—chair, has it never occurred to you that on one occasion you might be consummately wrong?

[KELLER'S *stare is unbelieving, even a little fascinated.* KATE *rises in trepidation, to mediate.*]

KATE. Captain.

[KELLER *stops her with his raised hand; his eyes stay on* JAMES'S *pale face, for a long hold. When he finally finds his voice, it is gruff.*]

KELLER. Sit down, everyone.

[*He sits.* KATE *sits.* JAMES *holds onto his chair.* KELLER *speaks mildly.*]

Helen being dragged to the well to refill the spilled pitcher.

Please sit down, Jimmie.

[JAMES *sits, and a moveless silence prevails;* KELLER'S *eyes do not leave him.*
ANNIE *has pulled* HELEN *downstairs again by one hand, the pitcher in her other hand, down the porch steps, and across the yard to the pump. She puts* HELEN'S *hand on the pump handle, grimly.*]

ANNIE. All right. Pump.

[HELEN *touches her cheek, waits uncertainly.*]

No, she's not here. Pump!

[*She forces* HELEN'S *hand to work the handle, then lets go. And* HELEN *obeys. She pumps till the water comes, then* ANNIE *puts the pitcher in her other hand and guides it under the spout, and the water tumbling half into and half around the pitcher douses* HELEN'S *hand.* ANNIE *takes over the handle to keep water*

coming, and does automatically what she has done so many times before, spells into* HELEN'S *free palm:*]

Water. W, a, t, e, r. *Water.* It has a—*name*—

[*And now the miracle happens.* HELEN *drops the pitcher on the slab under the spout, it shatters. She stands transfixed.* ANNIE *freezes on the pump handle: there is a change in* HELEN'S *face, some light coming into it we have never seen there, some struggle in the depths behind it; and her lips tremble, trying to remember something the muscles around them once knew, till at last it finds its way out, painfully, a baby sound buried under the debris of years of dumbness.*]

HELEN. Wah. Wah.

[*And again, with great effort*]

Wah. Wah.

[HELEN *plunges her hand into the dwindling water, spells into her own palm. Then she gropes frantically,* ANNIE *reaches for her hand, and* HELEN *spells into* ANNIE'S *hand.*]

ANNIE (*whispering*). Yes.

[HELEN *spells into it again.*]

Yes!

[HELEN *grabs at the handle, pumps for more water, plunges her hand into its spurt and grabs* ANNIE'S *to spell it again.*]

Yes! Oh, my dear—

[*She falls to her knees to clasp* HELEN'S *hand, but* HELEN *pulls it free, stands almost bewildered, then drops to the ground, pats it swiftly, holds up her palm, imperious.* ANNIE *spells into it:*]

Ground.

[HELEN *spells it back.*]

Yes!

[HELEN *whirls to the pump, pats it, holds up her palm, and* ANNIE *spells into it.*]

Pump.

[HELEN *spells it back.*]

Yes! Yes!

[*Now* HELEN *is in such an excitement she is possessed, wild, trembling, cannot be still, turns, runs, falls on the porch step, claps it, reaches out her palm, and* ANNIE *is at it instantly to spell:*]

Step.

[HELEN *has no time to spell back now, she whirls groping, to touch anything, encounters the trellis, shakes it, thrusts out her palm, and* ANNIE *while spelling to her cries wildly at the house.*]

Trellis. Mrs. Keller! *Mrs. Keller!*

[*Inside,* KATE *starts to her feet.* HELEN *scrambles back onto the porch, groping, and finds the bell string, tugs it; the bell rings, the distant chimes begin tolling the hour, all the bells in town seem to break into speech while* HELEN *reaches out and* ANNIE *spells feverishly into her hand.* KATE *hurries out, with* KELLER *after her;* AUNT EV *is on her feet, to peer out the window; only* JAMES *remains at the table, and with a napkin wipes his damp brow. From up right and left the servants—*VINEY, *the two Negro children, the other servant—run in, and stand watching from a distance as* HELEN, *ringing the bell, with her other hand encounters her mother's skirt; when she throws a hand out,* ANNIE *spells into it:*]

Mother.

[KELLER *now seizes* HELEN'S *hand, she touches him, gestures a hand, and* ANNIE *again spells:*]

Helen Keller in the dramatic last minutes of The Miracle Worker——*Water!*

Papa—She *knows!*

[KATE *and* KELLER *go to their knees, stammering, clutching* HELEN *to them, and* ANNIE *steps unsteadily back to watch the threesome,* HELEN *spelling wildly into* KATE'S *hand, then into* KELLER'S, KATE *spelling back into* HELEN'S; *they cannot keep their hands off her, and rock her in their clasp.*

Then HELEN *gropes, feels nothing, turns all around, pulls free, and comes with both hands groping, to find* ANNIE. *She encounters* ANNIE'S *thighs,* ANNIE *kneels to her,* HELEN'S *hand pats* ANNIE'S *cheek impatiently, points a finger, and waits; and* ANNIE *spells into it:*]

Teacher.

[HELEN *spells it back, slowly;* ANNIE *nods.*]

Teacher.

[*She holds* HELEN'S *hand to her cheek. Presently* HELEN *withdraws it, not jerkily, only with reserve, and retreats a step. She stands thinking it over, then turns again and stumbles back to her parents. They try to embrace her, but she has something else in mind, it is to get the keys, and she hits* KATE'S *pocket until* KATE *digs them out for her.*

ANNIE *with her own load of emotion has retreated, her back turned, toward the pump, to sit;* KATE *moves to* HELEN, *touches her hand questioningly, and* HELEN *spells a word to her.* KATE *comprehends it, their first act of verbal communication, and she can hardly utter the word aloud, in wonder, gratitude, and deprivation; it is a moment in which she simultaneously finds and loses a child.*]

KATE. Teacher?

[ANNIE *turns; and* KATE, *facing* HELEN *in her direction by the shoulders, holds her back, holds her back, and then relinquishes her.* HELEN *feels her way across the yard, rather shyly, and when her moving hands touch* ANNIE'S *skirt she stops. Then she holds out the keys and places them in* ANNIE'S *hand. For a moment neither of them moves. Then* HELEN *slides into* ANNIE'S *arms, and lifting away her smoked glasses, kisses her on the cheek.* ANNIE *gathers her in.*

KATE *torn both ways turns from this, gestures the servants off, and makes her way into the house, on* KELLER'S *arm. The servants go, in separate directions.*

The lights are half down now, except over the pump. ANNIE *and* HELEN *are here, alone in the yard.* ANNIE *has found* HELEN'S *hand, almost without knowing it, and she spells slowly into it, her voice unsteady, whispering:*]

ANNIE. I, love, Helen.

[*She clutches the child to her, tight this time, not spelling, whispering into her hair.*]

Forever, and—

[*She stops. The lights over the pump are taking on the color of the past, and it brings* ANNIE'S *head up, her eyes opening, in fear; and as slowly as though drawn she rises, to listen, with her hands on* HELEN'S *shoulders. She waits, waits, listening with ears and eyes both, slowly here, slowly there: and hears only silence. There are no voices. The color passes on, and when her eyes come back to* HELEN *she can breathe the end of her phrase without fear:*]

—ever.

[*In the family room* KATE *has stood over the table, staring at* HELEN'S *plate, with* KELLER *at her shoulder; now* JAMES *takes a step to move her chair in, and* KATE *sits, with head erect, and* KELLER *inclines his head to* JAMES; *so it is* AUNT EV, *hesitant, and rather humble, who moves to the door.*

Outside HELEN *tugs at* ANNIE'S *hand, and* ANNIE *comes with it.* HELEN *pulls her toward the house; and hand in hand, they cross the yard, and ascend the porch steps, in the rising lights, to where* AUNT EV *is holding the door open for them.*

The curtain ends the play.]

READING FOR DETAILS

Everything Has Its Name

In finally bringing Helen to understand language, Annie achieves a "miracle" which allows Helen to come to know ". . . everything the earth is full of. . . ." A woman of lesser spirit and determination would have given up long before such dramatic victory, but Annie felt she couldn't settle for less.

1. Act III opens on the final day of the two weeks Annie has had with Helen in the garden house. How have Helen's behavior and appearance changed in the two weeks she has been away from the family?

2. Describe Helen's homecoming meal. Why does Helen act as she does? What had Annie told Kate earlier in the play that she considered to be Helen's greatest handicap? Why do you think Kate finally decides to let Annie discipline Helen?

3. Identify the characters who speak the following lines and briefly outline the situation in which the words are spoken:

   a. I go to bed with—writer's cramp from talking so much!

   b. The dog doesn't know what she means, any more than she knows what you mean, Miss Sullivan.

   c. . . . obedience without understanding is a—blindness, too.

   d. . . . she'll live up to just what you demand of her, and no more.

   e. Papa—She *knows!*

READING FOR MEANING

Consider the following statement in light of the entire play:

By devoting your life to helping others you help yourself too.

READING FOR APPRECIATION

Characterization

1. How do Kate and James differ as to how long the two weeks have seemed?

2. Described in Act I as "an indolent young man," James seems weak, cynical, and vacillating through much of the play. What in James's situation gives him an excuse to feel abused and left out?

   When does James finally stand up to his father and oppose him? How do you think this display of courage might change him and his father's attitude toward him?

3. Throughout the play, Annie hears off-stage voices which have a great deal to do with understanding her character and the action in the play. Whose is the boy's voice she hears? Where, in her memories, are the crones' voices coming from? What man's voice is responsible for her decision to keep on trying to help Helen even after the battle in the breakfast room? What is the significance of the fact that she no longer can hear the voices as the play ends?

Significant Detail

1. What word is Annie teaching Helen when Act III begins? Why is it necessary that the reader or audience understand that Helen has learned the manual alphabet symbols for this particular word?

2. When Helen returns to the big house, Viney greets her with, "Oh, we glad to have you back, too, prob'ly." What does this humorous detail contribute to the tension of the scene?

3. Explain the significance of the business about the keys.

Staging

1. After Captain Keller exits following the opening breakfast scene, James asks Kate to be his friend. Very briefly, she replies, "I am," and leaves. Several different interpretations are possible about her response depending on her gestures and tone of voice. Suggest several of these possibilities and explain how the actress might have conveyed them.

2. In this play, we repeatedly find the Keller family at mealtime. What function does this setting serve for the drama?

LANGUAGE AND VOCABULARY

A. We may be given good clues to the meanings of words when they are contrasted with familiar elements. If we read "his ideas were clear and definite rather than nebulous," we may safely guess that *nebulous* in this sentence may mean *vague, cloudy,* or *ill-formed.* Of course, elements joined by *and* and similar connectives must be compatible with each other, able to fit together without confusion in meaning. If we read "the Asians were dressed in the strange and exotic costumes of their home countries," *exotic* must be at least compatible with *strange* so that there is no contradiction between them. Check over the following for these context clues as you try to guess the meanings of the italicized words:

1. This discussion is at an end! I'll thank you not to *broach* it again.
2. We hear a boy's voice whispering; perhaps we see shadowy *intimations* of these speakers in the background.
3. Keller then *irately* flings his newspaper on the porch floor, stamps into the house past Viney and disappears.
4. KELLER: I intend to carry you. Climb onto my shoulder and hold tight.
   ANNIE: Oh, no. It's—very *chivalrous* of you, but . . .
5. Is it your *contention* we won the war, sir?
6. Helen is working around the table, *ultimately* toward Annie's plate . . . .
7. Annie slaps her hand smartly away; Helen *retaliates* with a roundhouse fist that catches Annie on the ear.

B. *Ab-, ad-, com-,* etc., have been mentioned as situational prefixes. Other similar prefixes include *inter-,* with the general meaning of *among, between; intro-,* or *intra-,* which may mean *inwardly, to the inside, within; ob-,* suggesting *over, against, toward; per-,* often, but not always, meaning *through; pro-,* indicating *forward, forth, favoring; re-,* which is likely to mean *back, away* when it does not mean *again;* and *sub-,* often meaning *under, beneath, down.* Using your dictionary, check the meanings of the prefixes in the following words: *protrude, permission, reproachful, intercept, oblivious, proffer, object* (vb.)*, intervene, persist, revert, subside, retaliate, interpose, relinquish, perplex, proposal, opposite.* Write the meaning of the prefix after each word. Underline those that agree with the meanings given above.

C. What are the companion nouns for the following verbs from the first two acts of the play: *divide, designate, emit, approach, restrain, annoy, seize, commence, retrieve, conceal, collide, gratify, maintain, dismay, evade, descend, acquire, manage, remove, perceive?* How many different patterns show up in your list?

COMPOSITION

In Act I (see page 204) Annie expresses to her teacher, Mr. Anagnos, the thought that her childhood at Tewksbury had been so horrible that she believed that God must owe her a "resurrection," that is, a chance to be reborn.

With this in mind, write a short essay in which you compare Annie's childhood with Helen's. Defend your point of view as to which of these two individuals should be considered the more remarkable in view of their respective upbringings.

BIOGRAPHICAL NOTE

William Gibson (1914–   ), American poet, short story writer, novelist, and playwright, was born and educated in New York City, which serves as the setting for his first stories. Gibson has also lived in both the Midwest and the Rockies, locales for a number of his poems. His most popular works are *Two for the Seesaw* and *The Miracle Worker.*

At the end of *The Miracle Worker* we see Helen wild with joy and quivering with the desire to learn, as quickly as possible, everything about this new world into which she has been drawn. This dramatic moment of awakening provided a natural climax for *The Miracle Worker*. But a play can only show us Helen Keller from the *outside*. Now compare an account of the incident at the pump, written from the *inside*, by Helen herself. The following selection from *The Story of My Life* begins at exactly the moment when *The Miracle Worker* ended. Miss Keller goes on to tell of what happened after that—now that she had this "strange, new sight that had come to me."

HOW I LEARNED TO SEE
Helen Keller

My teacher placed my hand under the spout. As the cool stream gushed over one hand she spelled into the other the word *water*, first slowly, then rapidly. I stood still, my whole attention fixed upon the motions of her fingers. Suddenly I felt a misty consciousness as of something forgotten—a thrill of returning thought; and somehow the mystery of language was revealed to me. I knew then that "w-a-t-e-r" meant the wonderful cool something that was flowing over my hand. That living word awakened my soul, gave it light, hope, joy, set it free! There were barriers still, it is true, but barriers that could in time be swept away.

I left the well-house eager to learn. Everything had a name, and each name gave birth to a new thought. As we returned to the house every object which I touched seemed to quiver with life. That was because I saw everything with the strange, new sight that had come to me. On entering the door I remembered the doll I had broken. I felt my way to the hearth and picked up the pieces. I tried vainly to put them together. Then my eyes filled with tears; for I realized what I had done, and for the first time I felt repentance and sorrow.

I learned a great many new words that day. I do not remember what they all were; but I do know that *mother, father, sister, teacher* were among them—words that were to make the world blossom for me, "like Aaron's rod, with flowers."* It would have been difficult to find a happier child than I was as I lay in my crib at the close of that eventful day and lived over the joys it had brought me, and for the first time longed for a new day to come . . .

I recall many incidents of the summer of 1887 that followed my soul's sudden awakening. I did nothing but explore with my hands and learn the name of every object that I touched; and the more I handled things and learned their names and uses, the more joyous and confident grew my sense of kinship with the rest of the world . . .

---

*Aaron's rod or wand blossomed miraculously and bore almonds in the Biblical story told in Numbers 17:8.

When the time of daisies and buttercups came Miss Sullivan took me by the hand across the fields, where men were preparing the earth for the seed, to the banks of the Tennessee River, and there, sitting on the warm grass, I had my first lessons in the beneficence of nature. I learned how the sun and the rain make to grow out of the ground every tree that is pleasant to the sight and good for food, how birds build their nests and live and thrive from land to land, how the squirrel, the deer, the lion and every other creature finds food and shelter. As my knowledge of things grew I felt more and more the delight of the world I was in. Long before I learned to do a sum in arithmetic or describe the shape of the earth, Miss Sullivan had taught me to find beauty in the fragrant woods, in every blade of grass, and in the curves and dimples of my baby sister's hand. She linked my earliest thoughts with nature, and made me feel that "birds and flowers and I were happy peers."

But about this time I had an experience which taught me that nature is not always kind. One day my teacher and I were returning from a long ramble. The morning had been fine, but it was growing warm and sultry when at last we turned our faces homeward. Two or three times we stopped to rest under a tree by the wayside. Our last halt was under a wild cherry tree a short distance from the house. The shade was grateful, and the tree was so easy to climb that with my teacher's assistance I was able to scramble to a seat in the branches. It was so cool up in the tree that Miss Sullivan proposed that we have our luncheon there. I promised to keep still while she went to the house to fetch it.

Suddenly a change passed over the tree. All the sun's warmth left the air. I knew the sky was black, because all the heat, which meant light to me, had died out of the atmosphere. A strange odor came up from the earth. I knew it, it was the odor that always precedes a thunderstorm, and a nameless fear clutched at my heart. I felt absolutely alone, cut off from my friends and the firm earth. The immense, the unknown, enfolded me. I remained still and expectant; a chilling terror crept over me. I longed for my teacher's return; but above all things I wanted to get down from that tree.

There was a moment of sinister silence, then a multitudinous stirring of the leaves. A shiver ran through the tree, and the wind sent forth a blast that would have knocked me off had I not clung to the branch with might and main. The tree swayed and strained. The small twigs snapped and fell about me in showers. A wild impulse to jump seized me, but terror held me fast. I crouched down in the fork of the tree. The branches lashed about me. I felt the intermittent jarring that came now and then, as if something heavy had fallen and the shock had traveled up till it reached the limb I sat on. It worked my suspense up to the highest point, and just as I was thinking the tree and I should fall together, my teacher seized my hand and helped me down. I clung to her, trembling with joy to feel the earth under my feet once more. I had learned a new lesson—that nature "wages open war against her children, and under softest touch hides treacherous claws."

After this experience it was a long time before I climbed another tree. The mere thought filled me with terror . . .

Helen Keller, age seven

Annie Sullivan and Helen Keller on the lawn of Dr. Alexander Graham Bell's home.

I had now the key to all language, and I was eager to learn to use it. Children who hear acquire language without any particular effort; the words that fall from others' lips they catch on the wing, as it were, delightedly, while the little deaf child must trap them by a slow and often painful process. But whatever the process, the result is wonderful. Gradually from naming an object we advance step by step until we have traversed the vast distance between our first stammered syllable and the sweep of thought in a line of Shakespeare.

At first, when my teacher told me about a new thing I asked very few questions. My ideas were vague, and my vocabulary was inadequate; but as my knowledge of things grew, and I learned more and more words, my field of inquiry broadened, and I would return again and again to the same subject, eager for further information. Sometimes a new word revived an image that some earlier experience had engraved on my brain.

I remember the morning that I first asked the meaning of the word, "love." This was before I knew many words. I had found a few early violets in the garden and brought them to my teacher. Miss Sullivan put her arm gently round me and spelled into my hand, "I love Helen."

"What is love?" I asked.

She drew me closer to her and said, "It is here," pointing to my heart, whose beats I was conscious of for the first time. Her words puzzled me very much because I did not then understand anything unless I touched it.

I smelt the violets in her hand and asked, half in words, half in signs, a question which meant, "Is love the sweetness of flowers?"

"No," said my teacher.

Again I thought. The warm sun was shining on us.

"Is this not love?" I asked, pointing in the direction from which the heat came, "Is this not love?"

It seemed to me that there could be nothing more beautiful than the sun, whose warmth makes all things grow. But Miss Sullivan shook her head, and I was greatly puzzled and disappointed. I thought it strange that my teacher could not show me love.

A day or two afterward I was stringing beads of different sizes in symmetrical groups—two large beads, three small ones, and so on. I had made many mistakes, and Miss Sullivan had pointed them out again and again with gentle patience. Finally I noticed a very obvious error in the sequence and for an instant I concentrated my attention on the lesson and tried to think how I should have arranged the beads. Miss Sullivan touched my forehead and spelled with decided emphasis, "Think."

In a flash I knew that the word was the name of the process that was going on in my head. This was my first conscious perception of an abstract idea.

For a long time I was still—I was not thinking of the beads in my lap, but trying to find a meaning for "love" in the light of this new idea. The sun had been under a cloud all day, and there had been brief showers; but suddenly the sun broke forth in all its southern splendor.

Again I asked my teacher, "Is this not love?"

"Love is something like the clouds that were in the sky before the sun came out," she replied. Then in simpler words than these, which at that time I could not have understood, she explained: "You cannot touch the clouds, you know; but you feel the rain and know how glad the flowers and the thirsty earth are to have it after a hot day. You cannot touch love either; but you feel the sweetness that it pours into everything. Without love you would not be happy or want to play."

The beautiful truth burst upon my mind—I felt that there were invisible lines stretched between my spirit and the spirits of others.

From the beginning of my education Miss Sullivan made it a practice to speak to me as she would speak to any hearing child; the only difference was that she spelled the sentences into my hand instead of speaking them. If I did not know the words and idioms necessary to express my thoughts she supplied them, even suggesting conversation when I was unable to keep up my end of the dialogue.

This process was continued for several years; for the deaf child does not learn in a month, or even in two or three years, the numberless idioms and expressions used in the simplest daily intercourse. The little hearing child learns these from constant repetition and imitation. The conversation he hears in his home stimulates his mind and suggests topics and calls forth the spontaneous expression of his own thoughts. This natural exchange of ideas is denied to the deaf child. My teacher, realizing this, determined to supply the kinds of stimulus I lacked. This she did by repeating to me as far as possible, verbatim, what she heard, and by showing me how I could take part in the conversation. But it was a long time before I ventured to take the initiative, and still longer before I could find something appropriate to say at the right time.

The deaf and the blind find it very difficult to acquire the amenities of conversation. How much more this difficulty must be augmented in the case of those who are both deaf and blind! They cannot distinguish the tone of the voice or, without assistance, go up and down the gamut of tones that give significance to words; nor can they watch the expression of the speaker's face, and a look is often the very soul of what one says . . .

Thus I learned from life itself. At the beginning I was only a little mass of possibilities. It was my teacher who unfolded and developed them. When she came, everything about me breathed of love and joy and was full of meaning. She has never since let pass an opportunity to point out the beauty that is in everything, nor has she ceased trying in thought and action and example to make my life sweet and useful.

Postscript

Destined to become a celebrity before she was ten because of her astounding accomplishments, Helen Keller went on to learn not only to read, to write, to ride a toboggan, to swim, to ride a horse, but also she learned to speak. After only a dozen lessons from a special teacher, she had mastered simple sentences. The one she repeated over and over during the first few days of her triumph was, "I am not dumb now."

So great was her determination to use her voice, rather than the manual alphabet, that she had Miss Sullivan tape her fingers together so that she could not give in to the impulse to use them in communicating. Learning to speak was one of the most difficult of her achievements.

After graduating from college, Miss Keller, accompanied by Anne Sullivan, went on a series of successful lecture tours across the United States. Though her voice and intonation were not like those of a hearing person, she was as easily understood as people who speak with a foreign accent.

For two years she traveled with the Orpheum Circuit (vaudeville) and once played in an early silent Hollywood film entitled *Deliverance*. Her task, as she saw it, was to awaken public interest in helping the handicapped.

She traveled to many parts of the world at the invitation of various governments and private organizations. Many times she went of her own accord to visit hospitals, asylums, and institutions for the physically afflicted, in this country and abroad. Her plea to people everywhere was for help to liberate, as she was liberated, the blind, the deaf, the mute, from their lonely cells of isolation. One of the founders of the American Foundation of the Blind in 1923, she helped that organization raise millions of dollars.

How does one act toward a person who is physically handicapped? The physically handicapped wish simply to be treated like other people—without pity. All of her life, Miss Keller resented those who pitied her.

When someone remarked that Helen Keller's life must be terribly dull with night the same as day, Mark Twain, a close friend, retorted, "Blindness is an exciting business, I tell you. If you don't believe it, get up on some dark night on the wrong side of your bed when the house is on fire, and try to find the door!"

Although Anne Sullivan was often in ill health and underwent several operations trying to save her poor eyesight, Helen's beloved Teacher was, except for brief periods, always with her pupil. Even after Miss Sullivan married the literary critic and writer, John Macy, the Macys at once brought Helen to live with them.

When Anne Sullivan Macy died in 1936, Helen Keller felt that part of herself had died, too. In her diary she wrote, "Always I shall look about, despite myself, for the sparkle with which she charmed the dullest person into a new appreciation of beauty or justice or human rights."

All of the many honors that were bestowed upon her, and all of the achievements she made, Helen Keller credited to Teacher. Thus it is appropriate that one of her latest books is the one Miss Keller wanted to write most of her life—*Teacher: Anne Sullivan Macy*.

In addition to *The Story of My Life*, *Midstream* and *Helen Keller's Journal* are especially fascinating reading.

READING FOR DETAILS

Breaking the Barrier

One of the interesting things to think about in "How I Learned to See" is the way Helen Keller tried to find meanings for words that referred to things she could not touch or taste or smell. For example, she tells us that at that time "light" to her meant "heat," like that coming from the sun.

1. Recall her experience in the storm and explain how she knew the sky was *black*.
2. Discuss the way Miss Sullivan explained to Helen what the abstraction "love" meant. Is this different from the way it could be explained to a seeing and hearing child?

READING FOR MEANING

Consider and discuss the following statements in light of Helen Keller's life:

1. Blindness is an exciting business, I tell you.
2. Nature "wages open war against her children."

READING FOR APPRECIATION

Significant Detail

Helen Keller had no access to the visible forms of nature and yet she has communicated a spring storm (paragraphs 7 and 8) and her response to it with wonderful clarity. Through the senses of smell and touch she sets a scene filled with atmosphere and emotion. List the details which affected each of these two senses.

LANGUAGE AND VOCABULARY

After "How I Learned to See," there is a postscript in which comments are made about Miss Keller. The prefix *post-* means "after," and *script* means "written." A postscript, therefore, is anything that is written after the main body of material. The meaning "after" can be seen in the words *posterity* and *postgraduate*. When a person leaves something to *posterity*, he is leaving it to those who come after him, that is, future generations. A *postgraduate* is a student who pursues further studies after he has graduated. The very opposite of *post* is the prefix *ante-*, "before," as in *anteroom* and *antecedent*. An anteroom is a room that is placed before another room and often serves as an entrance or, sometimes, as a waiting room. In English grammar, an antecedent is the word to which a pronoun refers; it comes before the pronoun. In the sentence "William lost his book," *William* is the antecedent of *his*. Remembering the meanings of the two prefixes *post-* and *ante-* and using your dictionary, try to answer the following questions:

1. When were *antebellum* homes built?
2. What is a *postmortem* examination?
3. If a person *postdated* a letter, what would he have done?
4. What is the *posterior* side of an insect?
5. What time of the day is referred to by *ante meridiem*?
6. What is an *antechamber*?

BIOGRAPHICAL NOTE

Helen Keller (1880–1968) was born in Tuscumbia, Alabama. After graduation from Radcliffe College in 1904, Miss Keller dedicated her life to working for the blind through lectures, writings, and the Helen Keller Endowment Foundation. Her best-known books are *The Story of My Life*, *Out of the Dark*, and *Teacher*. She was awarded many honorary degrees because of her work in behalf of the handicapped. The Medal of Freedom, the highest honor a President of the United States can bestow on a civilian, was given to her in 1964.

The Inner Circle

The Father and His Sons

A father had a family of seven sons who were constantly quarreling among themselves. When he saw that he could not persuade them to change their quarrelsome ways by anything he said, the father determined to give them a practical illustration. For this purpose, he told them one day to bring him a bundle of sticks. When they had done so, he placed the bound bundle into the hands of each son in succession, and ordered him to break it in pieces. Each tried with all his strength, and was not able to do it. He next unbound the bundle, took the sticks separately and, one by one, put them into their hands again; now they broke them easily. Then he addressed them in these words: "My sons, if you are of one mind, and unite to assist each other, you will be as this bundle of sticks, uninjured by all the attempts of your enemies; but if you are divided among yourselves, you will be broken as easily as these separate twigs."

AESOP FABLE

THE BANJO LESSON
Henry O. Tanner
Hampton Institute Archival & Museum Collection
Hampton, Va.

In the sixth century B.C., Aesop told this fable about a father who brought his sons together in order to counsel them against quarreling among themselves. Although this family formed an inner circle of shared lives, the father felt it necessary to give the sons a practical lesson on what happens when family members are not loyal and united.

Aesop's fable has survived through the centuries because its theme has always been relevant. At present, beset by tensions resulting from rapidly shifting economic, social, and environmental conditions, family members find it difficult to maintain stable relationships. Families continue to be torn apart by jealousy, frustration, and a myriad of other emotions. Some sociologists think family patterns may change in the future, but being part of an inner circle will be a continuing need unless the essential nature of people changes also. For within us all is the fundamental need to love and be loved—a need that manifests itself very early in life and continues until death.

In the diverse selections in this unit there are many inner circles that feel the frustrations, pain, laughter, satisfactions, and tragedy that result from the desire of most people to form close ties with one another.

The major selection is a play that has had an almost unbroken record of performances on the stage for nearly four centuries. What could make this play so popular? There are many answers to this question, but the most generally accepted one is that the story *Romeo and Juliet* tells never grows old. Here is the kind of once-in-a-lifetime romantic love that, ideally, is the beginning of so many inner circles. Here is a lack of understanding and communication between parents and children, a problem of the past as well as the present. Here is the kind of pressure that prevents people from making decisions that are carefully thought through. Here is a tragedy that might easily have been avoided. And here, also, is a beauty of language combined with dramatic action that holds a fascination for either the reader or the audience.

UNIT TECHNIQUES

Elements of the Short Story

Edgar Allan Poe (1809–1849), an American author whose stories and poems you will read later in this book, and Guy de Maupassant (1850–1893), a famous French writer, were recognized leaders in determining the structure of the modern short story as an art form.

EFFECT

Poe is given credit for first formulating certain principles of short story writing. In setting forth these principles, he said he always began by considering the *effect*, or impression, he wished to make upon the reader. He then used the three ingredients of a story—*characters, action,* and *setting*—to "construct" the desired effect.

It was de Maupassant later in the century who said that readers are divided into various groups, each saying to the writer:

"Comfort me."   "Make me laugh."
"Amuse me."   "Make me shudder."
"Touch me."   "Make me weep."
"Make me dream."   "Make me think."

Within a limited number of pages, this is really what the short story strives to do—to comfort, to amuse, to touch the reader in some way, leaving a single overall effect.

How the story ingredients of character, action, and setting are combined has limitless variations. In simple definition, the *characters* are the figures who are in the story. *Characterization* (see Unit Techniques, Unit II, p. 135) is most important when writers depend primarily upon the development of a certain character or characters for their effects. The *action* is what the characters do or what happens to them. The *plot* (see Unit Techniques, Unit I, p. 3) is of primary importance if the action is tightly organized but the characterization is sketchy. The *setting* is the background or surroundings in which the story takes place. Setting is not often the most important element, but it may be very significant when it influences both characters and action.

Action is the catalyst or "combiner" of the three ingredients and emerges as *conflict* (see Unit Techniques, Unit I, p. 3), which may or may not be organized by the author into a tightly woven plot.

Toward the end of the century it was another American, William Sydney Porter, writing under the pseudonym of O. Henry, who also made a recognized contribution to the development of the structured short story. In the previous unit you read his well-known story "The Gift of the Magi." To O. Henry's way of thinking, it was the way a story ended that left its effect upon the reader.

With the opening of the present century, variations of the structured short story of plot began to appear. These are sometimes called "slice of life" stories and depend for their effect upon the very real or natural segment of life they present.

THEME

When authors write stories, they usually have a *theme*, or basic idea, that they wish to set forth. For example, the theme for the short story "The Most Dangerous Game" in CALL TO ADVENTURE might be said to be that a person's judgment of good or evil is influenced by his or her circumstances. The theme of a story may not be easy for the reader to see and put into words. In deciding upon the theme of a story, it is helpful to use the following formula: "In this story, the author is trying to show that . . ." When the theme is most significant, authors achieve their effects through setting forth the basic idea in a memorable way.

NARRATIVE VIEWPOINT

One problem that always confronts authors is the matter of deciding upon *narrative viewpoint*. The authors, of course, are always the ones who really tell their stories, but they must decide from what viewpoint it would be of advantage to tell them. They must choose whether to tell them in first or third person. If they tell stories in first person, the pronoun "I" indicates the narrator. If "I" is understood to be the author, the author appears to be sharing a true experience.

However, the writer may decide to write in third person, thus speaking of the characters as "he" or "she" or using their names. When telling a story in third person, writers may limit the reader's information to the observations, thoughts, and actions of the one character; but they are free to range from one character to another as *omniscient*, or "all-knowing, all-seeing," observers. It is from this omniscient viewpoint that Morley Callaghan presents the story you are about to read, even though he is primarily concerned with revealing how Alfred thinks and feels about things.

SYMBOLISM

Sometimes authors will use a concrete thing to stand for a difficult-to-describe idea necessary to a story. Their representation of an invisible element by something visible is called *symbolism*. The symbolism may be a very simple illustration of an idea, such as that in the opening fable. You recall that the father used a bundle of sticks as an effective symbol of the unity he wished to teach his sons. Here, the sticks carried the father's meaning much more vividly than all his lectures. Symbolism is an important part of *imaginative language*. (see Unit Techniques, Unit I, p. 3).

Ever since Alfred had left school
he had been getting into trouble wherever he worked.

ALL THE YEARS OF HER LIFE

Morley Callaghan

They were closing the drugstore, and Alfred Higgins, who had just taken off his white jacket, was putting on his coat and getting ready to go home. The little gray-haired man, Sam Carr, who owned the drugstore, was bending down behind the cash register, and when Alfred Higgins passed him, he looked up and said softly, "Just a moment, Alfred. One moment before you go."

The soft, confident, quiet way in which Sam Carr spoke made Alfred start to button his coat nervously. He felt sure his face was white. Sam Carr usually said, "Good night," brusquely, without looking up. In the six months he had been working in the drugstore Alfred had never heard his employer speak softly like that. His heart began to beat so loud it was hard for him to get his breath. "What is it, Mr. Carr?" he asked.

"Maybe you'd be good enough to take a few things out of your pocket and leave them here before you go," Sam Carr said.

"What things? What are you talking about?"

"You've got a compact and a lipstick and at least two tubes of toothpaste in your pockets, Alfred."

"What do you mean? Do you think I'm crazy?" Alfred blustered. His face got red and he knew he looked fierce with indignation. But Sam Carr, standing by the door with his blue eyes shining bright behind his glasses and his lips moving underneath his gray mustache, only nodded his head a few times, and then Alfred grew very frightened and he didn't know what to say. Slowly he raised his hand and dipped it into his pocket, and with his eyes never meeting Sam Carr's eyes, he took out a blue compact and two tubes of toothpaste and lipstick, and he laid them one by one on the counter.

"Petty thieving, eh, Alfred?" Sam Carr said. "And maybe you'd be good enough to tell me how long this has been going on."

"This is the first time I ever took anything."

"So now you think you'll tell me a lie, eh? What kind of a sap do I look like, huh? I don't know what goes on in my own store, eh? I tell you you've been doing this pretty steady," Sam Carr said as he went over and stood behind the cash register.

Ever since Alfred had left school he had been getting into trouble wherever he worked. He lived at home with his mother and his father, who was a printer. His two older brothers were married and his sister had got married last year, and it would have been all right for his parents now if Alfred had only been able to keep a job.

While Sam Carr smiled and stroked the side of his face very delicately with the tips of his fingers, Alfred began to feel that familiar terror growing in him that had been in him every time he had got into such trouble.

"I liked you," Sam Carr was saying. "I liked you and would have trusted you, and now look what I got to do." While Alfred watched with his alert, frightened blue eyes, Sam Carr drummed with his fingers on the counter. "I don't like to call a cop in point-blank," he was saying as he looked very worried. "You're a fool, and maybe I should call your father and tell him you're a fool. Maybe I should let them know I'm going to have you locked up."

"My father's not at home. He's a printer. He works nights," Alfred said.

"Who's at home?"

"My mother, I guess."

"Then we'll see what she says." Sam Carr went to the phone and dialed the number. Alfred was not so much ashamed, but there was that deep fright growing in him, and he blurted out arrogantly, like a strong, full-grown man, "Just a minute. You don't need to draw anybody else in. You don't need to tell her." He wanted to sound like a swaggering, big guy who could look after himself, yet the old, childish hope was in him, the longing that someone at home would come and help him. "Yeah, that's right, he's in trouble," Mr. Carr was saying. "Yeah, your boy works for me. You'd better come down in a hurry." And when he was finished Mr. Carr went over to the door and looked out at the street and watched the people passing in the late summer night. "I'll keep my eye out for a cop," was all he said.

Alfred knew how his mother would come rushing in; she would rush in with her eyes blazing, or maybe she would be crying, and she would push him away when he tried to talk to her, and make him feel her dreadful contempt; yet he longed that she might come before Mr. Carr saw the cop on the beat passing the door.

While they waited—and it seemed a long time—they did not speak, and when at last they heard someone tapping on the closed door, Mr. Carr, turning the latch, said crisply, "Come in, Mrs. Higgins." He looked hard-faced and stern.

Mrs. Higgins must have been going to bed when he telephoned, for her hair was tucked in loosely under her hat, and her hand at her throat held her light coat tight across her chest so her dress would not show. She came in, large and plump, with a little smile on her friendly face. Most of the store lights had been turned out and at first she did not see Alfred, who was standing in the shadow at the end of the counter. Yet as soon as she saw him she did not look as Alfred thought she would look: she smiled, her blue eyes never wavered, and with a calmness and dignity that made them forget that her clothes seemed to have been thrown on her, she put out her hand to Mr. Carr and said politely, "I'm Mrs. Higgins. I'm Alfred's mother."

Mr. Carr was a bit embarrassed by her lack of terror and her simplicity, and he hardly knew what to say to her, so she asked, "Is Alfred in trouble?"

"He is. He's been taking things from the store. I caught him redhanded. Little things like compacts and toothpaste and lipsticks. Stuff he can sell easily," the proprietor said.

As she listened Mrs. Higgins looked

at Alfred sometimes and nodded her head sadly, and when Sam Carr had finished she said gravely, "Is it so, Alfred?"

"Yes."

"Why have you been doing it?"

"I been spending money, I guess."

"On what?"

"Going around with the guys, I guess," Alfred said.

Mrs. Higgins put out her hand and touched Sam Carr's arm with an understanding gentleness, and speaking as though afraid of disturbing him, she said, "If you would only listen to me before doing anything." Her simple earnestness made her shy; her humility made her falter and look away, but in a moment she was smiling gravely again, and she said with a kind of patient dignity, "What did you intend to do, Mr. Carr?"

"I was going to get a cop. That's what I ought to do."

"Yes, I suppose so. It's not for me to say, because he's my son. Yet I sometimes think a little good advice is the best thing for a boy when he's at a certain period in his life," she said.

Alfred couldn't understand his mother's quiet composure, for if they had been at home and someone had suggested that he was going to be arrested,

he knew she would be in a rage and would cry out against him. Yet now she was standing there with that gentle, pleading smile on her face, saying, "I wonder if you don't think it would be better just to let him come home with me. He looks a big fellow, doesn't he? It takes some of them a long time to get any sense," and they both stared at Alfred, who shifted away with a bit of light shining for a moment on his thin face and the tiny pimples over his cheekbone.

But even while he was turning away uneasily Alfred was realizing that Mr. Carr had become aware that his mother was really a fine woman; he knew that Sam Carr was puzzled by his mother, as if he had expected her to come in and plead with him tearfully, and instead he was being made to feel a bit ashamed by her vast tolerance. While there was only the sound of the mother's soft, assured voice in the store, Mr. Carr began to nod his head encouragingly at her. Without being alarmed, while being just large and still and simple and hopeful, she was becoming dominant there in the dimly lit store. "Of course, I don't want to be harsh," Mr. Carr was saying. "I'll tell you what I'll do. I'll just fire him and let it go at that. How's that?" and he got up and shook hands with Mrs. Higgins, bowing low to her in deep respect.

There was such warmth and gratitude in the way she said, "I'll never forget your kindness," that Mr. Carr began to feel warm and genial himself.

"Sorry we had to meet this way," he said. "But I'm glad I got in touch with you. Just wanted to do the right thing, that's all," he said.

"It's better to meet like this than never, isn't it?" she said. Suddenly they clasped hands as if they liked each other, as if they had known each other a long time. "Good night, sir," she said.

"Good night, Mrs. Higgins. I'm truly sorry," he said.

The mother and son walked along the street together, and the mother was taking a long, firm stride as she looked ahead with her stern face full of worry. Alfred was afraid to speak to her, he was afraid of the silence that was between them, so he only looked ahead too, for the excitement and relief were still pretty strong in him; but in a little while, going along like that in silence made him terribly aware of the strength and the sternness in her; he began to wonder what she was thinking of as she stared ahead so grimly; she seemed to have forgotten that he walked beside her; so when they were passing under the Sixth Avenue elevated and the rumble of the train seemed to break the silence, he said in his old, blustering way, "Thank God it turned out like that. I certainly won't get in a jam like that again."

"Be quiet. Don't speak to me. You've disgraced me again and again," she said bitterly.

"That's the last time. That's all I'm saying."

"Have the decency to be quiet," she snapped. They kept on their way, looking straight ahead.

When they were at home and his mother took off her coat, Alfred saw that she was really only half-dressed, and she made him feel afraid again when she said, without even looking at him, "You're a bad lot. God forgive you. It's one thing after another and always has been. Why do you stand there stupidly? Go to bed, why don't you?" When he was going, she said, "I'm going to make myself a cup of tea. Mind, now, not a word about tonight to your father."

While Alfred was undressing in his bedroom, he heard his mother moving around the kitchen. She filled the kettle and put it on the stove. She moved a chair. And as he listened there was no shame in him, just wonder and a kind of admiration of her strength and repose. He could still see Sam Carr nodding his head encouragingly to her; he could hear her talking simply and earnestly, and as he sat on his bed he felt a pride in her strength. "She certainly was smooth," he thought. "Gee, I'd like to tell her she sounded swell."

And at last he got up and went along to the kitchen, and when he was at the door he saw his mother pouring herself a cup of tea. He watched and he didn't move. Her face, as she sat there, was a frightened, broken face utterly unlike the face of the woman who had been so assured a little while ago in the drugstore. When she reached out and lifted the kettle to pour hot water in her cup, her hand trembled and the water splashed on the stove. Leaning back in the chair, she sighed and lifted the cup to her lips, and her lips were groping loosely as if they would never reach the cup. She swallowed the hot tea eagerly, and then she straightened up in relief, though her hand holding the cup still trembled. She looked very old.

It seemed to Alfred that this was the way it had been every time he had been in trouble before, that this trembling had really been in her as she hurried out half-dressed to the drugstore. He understood why she had sat alone in the kitchen the night his young sister had

kept repeating doggedly that she was getting married. Now he felt all that his mother had been thinking of as they walked along the street together a little while ago. He watched his mother, and he never spoke, but at that moment his youth seemed to be over; he knew all the years of her life by the way her hand trembled as she raised the cup to her lips. It seemed to him that this was the first time he had ever looked upon his mother.

READING FOR DETAILS

A Boy Gains Insight

Alfred does some growing up as he watches his mother drinking the cup of tea in the kitchen. Suddenly, he sees her not as a pillar of strength and courage, but as an individual beset by uncertainties and feeling old.

1. What is Alfred's first reaction when Mr. Carr accuses him of stealing?
2. How does Mrs. Higgins gain Mr. Carr's sympathy and understanding? Does this seem realistic? What evidence is there that Mrs. Higgins really did not feel the tolerance she pretended?
3. What lines tell the reader that the parents in this household do not work together in helping the children with their problems?

READING FOR MEANING

Consider and discuss these ideas as they relate to the story:

1. Parents serve as role models for their children.
2. Few people ever really understand one another.

READING FOR APPRECIATION

Characterization

If a character remains the same throughout a story or drama, that character is called *static*.

If the character changes, the term used is *dynamic*. When authors are skilled in the use of characterization techniques, they show their readers how characters change and develop into different personalities under stress. In the last three paragraphs of this story the author deepens the characterizations of both Alfred and his mother and determines the reader's feelings toward them.

1. Analyze your feelings toward this mother and son. Do you: (a) pity them, (b) understand them, (c) detest them, (d) condemn them, or (e) admire them?
2. How would the characterizations have been changed if Alfred had seen his mother smiling, seemingly pleased with herself, as she sat alone in the kitchen?

Conflict

As you recall, conflict is the struggle between opposing forces. In this story, although you do not see two enemies actively fighting one another as you did in "The Most Dangerous Game," conflict is very much present. Look back to page 3 where the four kinds of conflicting action are listed.

1. Which is the only kind of conflict *not* involved in this story?
2. Discuss in what way Alfred was in conflict with society. How was he in conflict with himself?

COMPOSITION

The incidents making up the plot structure of a story should fit together to bring the story to a successful conclusion. If an incident or situation within a story had been developed differently, the story's effect would have been changed.

Write a new incident for the story, beginning at the point where Sam Carr goes to the phone. This time have him dial the police first, then Alfred's mother. Develop the incident with a specific description of the police officer, a different personality for Alfred's mother, and action on Mr. Carr's part that shows whether he really wants Alfred punished. You need not take your version of the story through to a new conclusion, but you should be aware of the *effect* you want to achieve with the incident you write.

If you choose not to rewrite an incident from "All the Years of Her Life," select one from any of the other stories in the previous unit and develop it in a new direction, adding a character or characters and any appropriate details.

BIOGRAPHICAL NOTE

Morley Callaghan (1903–   ), Canadian novelist and short story writer, was born in Toronto. After graduating from the University of Toronto in 1925, Callaghan became a reporter on the *Toronto Daily Star*. While working on the *Star,* he met Ernest Hemingway, who both encouraged him and introduced him to most of the literary giants and editors of the era. His writing style, which is reminiscent of Hemingway's, is stark and to the point.

"You're going to the game, aren't you, Dad?
You and Mother?" Wild horses couldn't have kept
Mr. Whalen away.

THE HERO
Margaret Weymouth Jackson

Mr. Whalen came into the kitchen by the back door and closed it softly behind him. He looked anxiously at his wife.

"Is Marv in?" he asked.

"He's resting," she whispered. Mr. Whalen nodded. He tiptoed through the dining room and went into the front hall as quiet as a mouse, and hung his hat and coat away. But he could not resist peeking into the darkened living room. A fire burned on the hearth, and on the couch lay a boy, or young man, who looked, at first glance, as though he were at least seven feet tall. He had a throw[1] pulled up around his neck, and his stocking feet stuck out from the cuffs of his corduroy trousers over the end of the sofa.

"Dad?" a husky young voice said.

"Yes. Did I waken you? I'm sorry."

"I wasn't sleeping. I'm just resting."

Mr. Whalen went over to the couch and looked down at the long figure with deep concern.

"How do you feel?" he asked tenderly.

"Swell, Dad. I feel fine. I feel as though I'm going to be lucky tonight."

"That's fine! That's wonderful!" said his father fervently.

"What time is it, Dad?"

"Quarter to six."

"About time for me to get up and have my supper. Is it ready? I ought to stretch a bit."

"You lie still now, Marv. I'll see about your supper."

Mr. Whalen hurried back into the kitchen.

"He's awake," he informed his wife. "Is his supper ready?"

"In a minute, dear. I'm just making his tea."

Mr. Whalen went back into the living room with his anxious, bustling air.

The young man was up from the couch. He had turned on the light in a table lamp. He was putting on his shoes. He looked very young, not more than sixteen. His hair was thick as taffy and about the same color. He was thin, with a nose a little too big, and with clear blue eyes and a pleasant mouth and chin. He was not especially handsome, except to his father, who thought him the finest-looking boy in the whole wide world. The boy looked up a little shyly and smiled, and somehow his father's opinion was justified.

"I couldn't hit a thing in short practice yesterday," Marvin said. "That means I'll be hot tonight. Red-hot!"

1. **throw,** a small rug or blanket.

"I hope so. I certainly hope so."

"You're going to the game, aren't you, Dad? You and Mother?"

Wild horses couldn't have kept Mr. Whalen away.

Marvin rose from his chair. He went up and up and up. Six feet four in his stocking feet, a hundred and seventy-six pounds, and sixteen years of age. Marvin flexed his muscles, crouched a little, and made a twisting leap into the air, one arm going up over his head in a swinging circle, his hand brushing the ceiling. He landed lightly as a cat. His father watched him, appearing neither astonished nor amused. There was nothing but the most profound respect and admiration in Mr. Whalen's eyes.

"We've been timing that pivot. Mr. Leach had two guards on me yesterday and they couldn't hold me, but I couldn't hit. Well, Dad, let's eat. I ought to be getting up to the gym."

They went into the kitchen, where the supper was laid on a clean cloth at a small round table. There was steak and potatoes and salad and chocolate cake for his parents, toast and tea and coddled eggs for the boy.

"I don't think you ought to put the cake out where Marv can see it, when he can't have any," fussed Mr. Whalen.

Marvin grinned. "It's okay, Dad. I don't mind. I'll eat some when I get home."

"Did you take your shower? Dry yourself good?"

"Sure, Dad. Of course."

"Was the doctor at school today? This was the day he was to check the team, wasn't it?"

"Yes. He was there. I'm okay. The arch supports Mr. Leach sent for came. You know, my left foot's been getting a little flat. Doc thought I ought to have something while I'm still growing."

"It's a good thing. Have you got them here?"

"Yes. I'll get them."

"No. Just tell me where they are. I'll look at them."

"In my room. In my gym shoes."

Mr. Whalen wasn't eating a bite of supper. It just gave him indigestion to eat on game nights. He got too excited. He couldn't stand it. The boy was eating calmly. He ate four coddled eggs. He ate six pieces of toast. He drank four cups of tea with lemon and sugar. In the boy's room Mr. Whalen checked the things in his bag—the white woolen socks, the clean folded towel, the shoes with their arch supports, and so on. The insets looked all right, his father thought. The fine, heavy satin playing suits would be packed in the box in which they came from the dry cleaner's, to keep them from getting wrinkled before the game.

There, alone in Marvin's room, with Marvin's ties hanging on his dresser, with his windbreaker thrown down in a chair and his high school books on the table, Mr. Whalen felt a little ill. He pressed his hand over his heart. He mustn't show his anxiety, he thought. The boy was calm.

He felt lucky. Mustn't break that feeling. Mr. Whalen went back into the kitchen with an air of cheer, a plump, middle-aged man with a retreating hairline and kind, anxious, brown eyes. Mr. Whalen was a few inches shorter than his wife. But he had never regretted marrying a tall woman. Look at his boy!

Marv was looking at the funnies in the evening paper. Mr. Whalen resisted the temptation to look at the kitchen clock. The boy would know when to go. He took the front part of the paper and sat down and tried to put his mind on the news. Mrs. Whalen quietly washed the supper dishes. Marvin finished the funnies in the local paper and handed it to his father. Mr. Whalen took it and read the news that Hilltown High was to play Sunset High, of Stone City, at the local gym that evening. The Stone City team hadn't lost a game. They were grooming for the state championship. Mr. Whalen felt weak. He hoped Marvin hadn't read this. Indignation grew in the father, as he read on down the column, that the odds were against the local team. How dare Mr. Minton print such nonsense for the boys to read—to discourage them? It was outrageous. Mr. Whalen would certainly give the editor a piece of his mind. Perhaps Marvin had read it and believed it! Everything was so important—the psychology wasn't good.

Marvin had finished the funnies in the city paper, and he put it down and rose. He said a little ruefully, "I'm still hungry, but I can't eat more now."

"I'll have something ready for you when you get home," his mother said.

Marvin went into his room and came back in his windbreaker, his hair combed smoothly on his head.

"I'll see you at the gym," he said. "Sit where you always do, will you, Dad?"

"Yes. Yes. We'll be there."

"Okay. I'll be seeing you."

"Don't you want me to take you down in the car?"

"No. Thanks, Dad, but no. It'll do me good to run down there. It won't take me but a minute."

A shrill whistle sounded from the street.

"There's Johnny." Marvin left at once.

Mr. Whalen looked at his watch. "Better hurry, Mother. The first game starts at seven. We won't get our regular seats if we're late."

"I'm not going to the gym at half-past six," said Mrs. Whalen definitely. "We'll be there in time, and no one will take our seats. If you don't calm down, you are going to have a stroke at one of these games."

"I'm perfectly calm," said Mr. Whalen indignantly; "I'm as calm as—as calm as a June day. That's how calm I am. You know I'm not of a nervous temperament. Just because I want to get to the game on time, you say I am excited. You're as up in the air as I am."

"I am not," said Mrs. Whalen. She sat down at the cleared table and looked at the advertisements in the paper. Mr. Whalen looked at his watch again. He fidgeted.

"You can go ahead, if you like," she said. "I'll come alone."

"No, no," he protested, "I'll wait for you. Do you think we had better take the car? I put it up, but I can get it out again."

"We'll walk," she said. "It will do you good—quiet your nerves."

"I'm not nervous," he almost shouted. Then he subsided again, muttered a little, pretended to read the paper, checked his watch against the kitchen clock to see if it had stopped.

"If we're going to walk . . ." he said in a minute.

Mrs. Whalen looked at him with pity. He couldn't help it, she knew. She folded the papers and put them away, took off her white apron, smoothed her hair, and went to get her wraps. Mr. Whalen was at the front door, his overcoat on, his hat in his hand. She deliberately pottered, getting the cat off the piano and putting him out-of-doors, locking the kitchen door, turning out lights, hunting for her gloves. Mr. Whalen was almost frantic by the time she joined him on the front porch. They went down the walk together, and when they reached the sidewalk they met neighbors also bound for the gym.

"How's Marv?" asked the man next door. "Is he all right?"

"Marv's fine, just fine. He couldn't be better."

"Boy, oh, boy," said the other enthusiastically, "would I like to see the boys whip Stone City! It would be worth a million dollars—a cool million. Stone City thinks no one can beat them. We'd burn the town down."

"Oh, this game doesn't matter so much," said Mr. Whalen deprecatingly. "The team is working toward the tournaments. Be a shame to show all their stuff tonight."

"Well, we'll see. We'll see."

They went ahead. At the next corner they met other friends.

"How's Marv? How's the big boy?"

"He's fine. He's all right." Mr. Whalen's chest expansion increased. Cars were parked all along the sidewalk before the group of township school buildings—the grade school and the high school, with the fine brick gymnasium between them. The walks were crowded now, for the whole town, except those in wheel chairs or just born, went to the games, and this was an important game with Hilltown's hereditary foe. Mr. Whalen grew very anxious about their seats. If Marvin looked around for them and didn't find them . . . He hurried his wife a little. They went into the outer hall of the gymnasium. The school principal was standing there talking to the coach, Mr. Leach. Mr. Whalen's heart plummeted. Had anything gone wrong? Had something happened to Marvin? He looked at them anxiously, but they spoke in normal tones.

"Good evening, Mrs. Whalen. Good evening, Tom."

Several small boys were running up and down the stairs, and the school principal turned and spoke to them severely. The Whalens had to make room for a young married couple, he carrying a small baby, she holding the hand of a little boy. Then they reached the window where the typing teacher was tearing off ticket stubs. Mr. Whalen paid his half dollar and they went inside the iron bar and up the steps to the gym proper.

The gymnasium wasn't half full. The bleachers which rose on either side of the shining, sacred floor with its cabalistic[2] markings were spotted with people. The Hilltown eighth grade was playing the Sugar Ridge eighth grade. The boys scrambled, fell down, got up, and threw the ball, panted and heaved and struggled on the floor. A basketball flew about. A group of smaller children were seated in a tight knot, and two little girls whose only ambition in life was to become high school cheerleaders led a piercing yell:

> *Hit 'em high,*
> *Hit 'em low:*
> *Come on, eighth grade,*
> *Let's go!*

The voices of the junior high were almost piping. Mr. Whalen remembered how he had suffered when Marvin was in the eighth grade and they had to go to the games at six o'clock to watch him play. The junior-high games were very abbreviated, with six-minute quarters, which was all the state athletic association would let them play. Marvin had been five feet ten at thirteen, but too thin. He had put on a little weight in proportion to this height since then, but his father thought he should be heavier. The present eighth-grade team could not compare with Marvin's, Mr. Whalen decided.

But the boys did try hard. They were winning. The gun sounded, the junior high went to pieces with wild cheering, and the teams trotted off the floor, panting, sweating, happy.

Almost at once another group came on in secondhand white wool tops and the old blue satin trunks from last year. This was the second team. The boys were pretty good. They practiced, throwing the ball from far out, running in under the basket, passing to one another. Mr. and Mrs. Whalen had found their regular seats unoccupied, halfway between the third and fourth uprights which supported the lofty gymnasium ceiling. Mr.

---

2. **cabalistic,** having a secret or mystical meaning.

Whalen sat down a little weakly and wiped his forehead. Mrs. Whalen began at once to visit with a friend sitting behind her, but Mr. Whalen could not hear what anyone said.

The Stone City reserves came out on the floor to warm up. They looked like first-string men.

Mr. Leach was talking to the timekeeper. He was a good coach—a mighty good coach. They were lucky to keep him here at Hilltown. The luckiest thing that had ever happened to the town was when Mr. Leach had married a Hilltown girl who didn't want to move away. They'd never have been able to hold him otherwise. It meant so much to the boys to have a decent, kindly man to coach them. Some of the high school coaches felt that their teams had to win, no matter how. It would be very bad to have his boy under such an influence, thought Mr. Whalen, who simply could not bear to see the team defeated, and who was always first to yell "Thief!" and "Robber!"

The officials came out in their green shirts, and Mr. Whalen almost had heart failure. There was that tall, thin man who had fouled Marvin every time he had moved in the tournaments last year. He was always against Hilltown. He had been so unfair that Mr. Leach had complained about him to the state association. The only time Mr. Leach had ever done such a thing. Oh, this was awful. Mr. Whalen twisted his hat in his hands. The other official he had seen often. He was fair—very fair. Sugar Ridge had complained about him for favoring Hilltown, but Mr. Whalen thought him an excellent referee.

The gymnasium was filling fast now. All the high school students—two hundred of them—were packed in the cheering section. The junior high was swallowed up, lost. The cheering section looked as though not one more could get into it, and yet youngsters kept climbing up, squeezing in. The rest of the space was filled with townspeople, from toddlers in snowsuits to graybearded dodderers. On the opposite side of the gymnasium, the visiting fans were filling their seats. Big crowd from Stone City. Businessmen and quarrymen and stone carvers and their wives and children. They must feel confident of winning, Mr. Whalen thought. Their cheerleaders were out on the floor. Where were Hilltown's? Ah, there they were—Beth and Mary. Hilltown's cheerleaders were extremely pretty adolescents dressed in blue satin slacks with white satin shirts, the word "Yell" in blue letters over their shoulders—a true gilding of the lily. Mary was Marvin's girl. She was the prettiest girl in town. And she had personality, too, and vigor.

Now the two girls leaped into position, spun their hands, spread out their arms, catapulted their bodies into the air in perfect synchronization, and the breathless cheering section came out in a long roll.

> *Hello, Stone City,*
> *Hello, Stone City,*
> *Hilltown says,*
> *Hello-o-o-o!*

Not to be outdone, the Stone City leaders, in crimson-and-gold uniforms, returned the compliment:

> *Hello, Hilltown . . .*

and the sound came nicely across the big gym. Mr. Whalen got a hard knot in his throat, and the bright lights and colors of the gymnasium swam in a mist. He couldn't help it. They were so young. Their voices were so young!

The whistle blew. The reserves were at it.

Mr. Whalen closed his eyes and sat still. It would be so long; the cheering wouldn't really start, the evening wouldn't begin until the team came out. He remembered when Marvin was born. He had been tall then—twenty-two inches. Mr. Whalen prayed, his lips moving a little, that Marvin wouldn't get hurt tonight. Suppose he had a heart attack and fell dead, like that boy at Capital City years ago. Suppose he got knocked against one of the steel uprights and hurt his head—damaged his brain? Suppose he got his knee injured? Mr. Whalen opened his eyes. He must not think of those things. He had promised his wife he would not worry so. He felt her hand, light but firm, on his arm.

"Here are the Lanes," she said.

Mr. Whalen spoke to them. Johnny's parents crowded in behind the Whalens. Johnny's father's hand fell on Mr. Whalen's shoulder.

"How's Marv tonight?"

"Fine, fine. How's Johnny?"

"Couldn't be better. I believe the boys are going to take them."

The two fathers looked at each other and away. Mr. Whalen felt a little better.

"How's business?" asked Johnny's father, and they talked about business a moment or two, but they were not interested.

There was a crisis of some kind on the floor. Several players were down in a pile. Someone was hurt. Mr. Whalen bit the edge of his felt hat. The boy was up

now. The Stone City coach was out on the floor, but the boy shook his head. He was all right. The game was resumed.

At last it was over. The reserves had won. Mr. Whalen thought that was a bad omen. The eighth grade had won. The reserves had won. No, it was too much. The big team would lose. If the others had lost, he would have considered that a bad omen too. Every omen was bad to Mr. Whalen at this stage. The floor was empty. The high school band played "Indiana," and "Onward, Hilltown," and everyone stood up and sang.

There was a breathless pause, and then a crashing cheer hit the ceiling of the big gym and bounced back. The Team was out. Out there on the floor in their blue satin suits, with jackets over their white tops, warming up, throwing the ball deftly about. What caused the change? Mr. Whalen never knew, but everything was quick now, almost professional in tone and quality. Self-confidence, authority, had come into the gymnasium. Ten or twelve boys out there warming up. But there was really only one boy on the floor for Mr. Whalen, a tall, thin, fair boy with limber legs still faintly brown from summer swimming. Mr. Whalen did not even attempt to tear his eyes from Marvin.

The Stone City team came out. Mr. Whalen looked away from Marvin for a moment to study them. Two or three of them were as tall as Marvin, maybe taller. He felt indignant. They must be seniors, all of them. Or five-year men. He studied the boys. He liked to see if he could pick out the first-string men from the lot. He could almost always do it—not by their skill or their height, but by their faces. That little fellow with the pug nose—he was a first-string man. And the two big ones—the other tall man Mr. Whalen discarded correctly. And the boy with the thick chest. What it was, he wasn't sure —some carelessness, some ease that marked the first-string men. The others were always a little self-conscious, a little too eager.

The referee blew the whistle. The substitutes left the floor, carrying extra jackets. The boy with the pug nose came forward for Stone City. So he was captain? Mr. Whalen felt gratified in his judgment. Marvin came forward for his team. He was captain too. There was a Number 1 in blue on the sleeveless white satin shirt he wore. The referee talked to them. The boys took their positions, the umpire his along the edge of the floor. The cheering section roared:

We may be rough,
We may be tough,
But we're the team
That's got the stuff!
Fight! Fight! Fight!

Mary turned a complete somersault, her lithe young body going over backward, her heels in the air, then hitting the floor to bounce her straight up in a spread eagle. Her pretty mouth was open in a square. The rooting swelled. The substitutes sat down with their coaches. Marvin stood back out of the center ring until the referee, ball in hand, waved him in. The ball went into the air as the whistle blew, and the game was on.

Marvin got the tip-off straight to Johnny. Marv ran down into the corner, where he circled to confuse his guard. Johnny brought the ball down over the line, faked a pass and drew out Marvin's guard, bounced the ball to Perk, who carried it almost to the foul line and passed to Marvin, who threw the ball into the basket. Stone City leaped outside, threw the ball in, a long pass. Perk leaped for it, but missed. The tall Stone City forward dribbled, dodging skillfully. The guards were smothering him, but he pivoted, flung the ball over his head and into the basket. A basket each in the first minute of play!

Mr. Whalen had stopped breathing. He was in a state of suspended animation.[3] The game was very fast—too fast. Stone City scored a second and a third time. Marvin called time out. Someone threw a wet towel from the bench, and it slid along the floor. The boys wiped their faces with it, threw it back. They whispered together. The referee blew the whistle. Yes, they were going to try the new trick play they had been practicing. It worked. Marvin's pivot was wonderful. The score was four to six.

Marvin played with a happy romping abandon. He was skillful, deft, acute. The youngsters screamed his name. Mr. Whalen saw Mary's rapt, adoring look. Marvin romped down the floor like a young colt.

At the end of the quarter, the score was fourteen to ten in Stone City's favor. At the end of the half, it was still in Stone City's favor, but only fourteen to thirteen. Stone City didn't score in the second quarter.

Mr. Whalen felt a deep disquietude. He had been watching the tall center on the other team, the pivot man. He had thick, black, curly hair and black eyes. Mr. Whalen thought he looked tough.

---

3. **. . . suspended animation.** He was so still his vital functions seemed temporarily suspended.

He had fouled Marvin twice in the first half. That is, he had been called for two fouls, but he had fouled him oftener. Mr. Whalen was sure he had tripped Marvin that time Marvin fell on the floor and cracked his elbow. Marvin had jumped up again at once. The Stone City center was a dirty player and ought to be taken off the floor. The school band was playing, but Mr. Whalen couldn't hear it. He was very upset. If the referees were going to let Stone City foul Hilltown and get away with it . . . He felt hot under the collar. He felt desperate.

"Why don't you go out and smoke?" his wife asked. Mr. Whalen folded his overcoat to mark his place and went out of the gym. He smoked two cigarettes as fast as he could. He would stay out here. The stars were cool and calm above his head. The night air was fresh. He couldn't stand it in the gymnasium. He would wait here until the game was over. If Marvin was hurt, he wouldn't see it. He resolved this firmly. But when the whistle blew and he heard the burst of cheering, he rushed back into the gymnasium like a man going to a fire.

The second half had begun. Again the big center fouled Marvin. Marvin got two free throws and made both good.

Fifteen to fourteen now! The crowd went wild. The game got very fast again. Mr. Whalen watched Marvin and his opponent like a hawk. There! It happened.

Mr. Whalen was on his feet, yelling, "Watch him! Watch him!"

The Stone City center had driven his elbow into Marvin's stomach. Marvin was doubled up. Marvin was down on the floor. A groan went up from the bleachers. Mr. Whalen started out on the floor.

Something held him. He looked around blindly. His wife had a firm grip on his coattails. She gave him a smart yank and pulled him unexpectedly down on the bench beside her.

"He doesn't want you on the floor," she said fiercely.

Mr. Whalen was very angry, but he controlled himself. He sat still. Marvin was up again. Mary led a cheer for him. Marvin was all right. He got two more free throws. Now Hilltown was three points ahead. Marvin was fouled again, got two more free throws and missed them both. He was hurt! He never missed free throws—well, hardly ever. What was the matter with the referee? Was he crazy? Was he bribed? Mr. Whalen groaned.

Stone City took time out, and in the last minute of the third quarter they made three quick baskets. It put them ahead again, three points. A foul was called on Marvin—for pushing.

"Why, he never did at all!" yelled Mr. Whalen. "He couldn't stop fast enough—that's not a foul! Just give them the ball, boys! Don't try to touch it!"

"Will you hush?" demanded his wife.

The Stone City forward made one of the two throws allowed. It was the quarter.

The game was tied three times in the last quarter. With five minutes to play, the big center fouled Marvin again. His last personal. He was out of the game. The Hilltown crowd booed him. None so loud as Mr. Whalen, who often talked long and seriously to Marvin about sportsmanship.

Then Marvin got hot. He couldn't miss. Everyone on the team fed him the ball, and he could throw it from anywhere and it went, plop, right into the basket. Marvin pivoted. His height, his spring, carried him away from his guards. Marvin pranced. His long legs carried him where he would. He threw the ball over his head and from impossible angles. Once he was knocked down on the floor, and he threw from there and made the basket. His joy, his perfection, his luck, caused the crowd to burst into continuous wild cheering. Stone City took time out. They ran in substitutes, but they couldn't stop Marvin. Perk would recover the ball; he and Johnny fed it skillfully to Marvin, and Marvin laid it in. The gun went off with Hilltown twelve points ahead.

Mr. Whalen was a wreck. He could hardly stand up. Mrs. Whalen took his arm and half supported him toward the stairs that led down to the school grounds. The Stone City fans were angry. A big, broad-shouldered man with fierce black eyes complained in a loud, quarrelsome voice:

"That skinny kid—that Whalen boy—he fouled my boy! Who cares? But when my boy protects himself, what happens? They put him off the floor. They put my Guido[4] out, so Hilltown wins. I get my hands on that tall monkey and I'll fix him."

"Be careful. That's my son you're talking about." The strength had returned to Mr. Whalen. He was strong as a lion. Mrs. Whalen pulled at his arm, but he jerked away. He turned on the crowded stairs. "Before you do anything to Marvin," he said, his voice loud and high, "you'd better do something to me. Your son fouled repeatedly."

"That's a lie!" yelled the other, and Mr. Whalen hit him. He hit him right in the stomach as hard as he could punch him. Instantly there was a melee. Johnny's father was punching somebody, and for a moment the crowd heaved and milled on the stairs. Someone screamed. Something like a bolt of lightning hit Mr. Whalen in the eye, and he struck back.

Friends were pulling him away. The town marshal shouldered good-naturedly between the combatants. The big man was in the grip of others from Stone City, who dragged him back up the stairs. Mr. Whalen struggled with his captors, fellow townsmen, who sympathized with him but had no intention of letting him fight. Johnny's mother and Marvin's mother hustled their men out into the cold night air.

"Really!" the high school principal was saying anxiously. "Really, we mustn't have any trouble. The boys don't fight. If we could just keep the fathers away from the games! Really, Mrs. Whalen, this won't do."

"I've got a good notion to take a poke at him too," said Mr. Whalen, who was clear above himself.

In the kitchen, Mr. Whalen looked in a small mirror at his reflection. He felt wonderful. He felt marvelous. He was going to have a black eye. He grabbed his wife and kissed her soundly.

"They beat them!" he said. "They beat Stone City!"

"You old fool!" cried Mrs. Whalen. "I declare I'd be ashamed of Marvin if he acted like that. You and Johnny's father—fighting like hoodlums."

"I don't care!" said Mr. Whalen. "I'm glad I hit him. Teach him a lesson. I feel

4. **Guido** (gē′dō′) or (gwē′dō′).

great. I'm hungry. Make some coffee, Mother."

Marvin wouldn't be in for another hour. He would have a date with Mary at the soda parlor, to which the whole high school would repair.[5] They heard the siren blowing, they looked out of the window and saw the reflection of the bonfire on the courthouse lawn. They heard the fire engine. The team was having a ride on the fire engine. Mr. Whalen stood on his front porch and cheered. The town was wild with joy. Not a citizen that wasn't up in the air tonight.

At last Marvin came in. He was cheerful, practical.

"Did you really have a fight, Dad? Someone told me you popped Guido's father. . . . Boy, are you going to have a shiner!" Marvin was greatly amused. He examined his father's eye, recommended an ice pack.

"I want it to get black," said Mr. Whalen stubbornly.

"We sure fixed Guido," said Marvin, and laughed.

"Did you have a fight?" asked his father eagerly.

"Heck, no! I'm going to get him a date with Betty. He noticed her. He's

5. **repair,** go.

coming up next Sunday. Their team went downtown for sodas because Guido wanted to meet Betty. I wasn't sore at him. I only mean he was easy to handle. I saw right away that I could make him foul me, give me extra shots, get him off the floor. It's very easy to do with a big clumsy guy like that."

Mr. Whalen fingered his swelling eye and watched Marvin eat two hot ham sandwiches and a big slab of chocolate cake and drink a quart of milk. Marvin had already had a soda.

"You must sleep late in the morning," Mr. Whalen said. "Maybe you got too tired tonight. Now, don't eat too much cake."

Mr. Whalen's eye hurt. Mrs. Whalen got him to bed and put a cold compress on it.

"Old ninny," she murmured, and stooped and kissed him. Mr. Whalen sighed. He was exhausted. He was getting too old to play basketball, he thought confusedly.

READING FOR DETAILS

Who's the Hero?
Mr. Whalen is almost too much involved in his son's life.

1. What "heroic" efforts are performed by Mr. Whalen?
2. How does Mr. Whalen's behavior affect this inner circle?
3. What is Mrs. Whalen's influence on the family?

READING FOR MEANING

Consider these statements and discuss the evidence for or against them.

1. There is evidence of real "inner circle" feeling among the members of this family.
2. Marv conceals his tensions and inner-most thoughts while his father expresses his.
3. Marv is the "hero" referred to in the title.
4. Mr. Whalen is the "hero" referred to in the title.
5. Mr. Whalen's desire to have his son excel comes from his own self-centeredness.

READING FOR APPRECIATION

Characterization
Although Mr. Whalen seems like an individual, he is actually more of a *type character*. Think what *type* would mean when it is used to refer to a person, and then explain what you think a *type character* would be.

Theme
Do you think the author was trying to tell you that most fathers desire to live through their sons the glories they never achieved themselves? If you believe that this theme is insufficient, compose a statement of your own which you feel is more satisfactory.

Narrative Viewpoint
"The Hero" is an example of a story told in third person. Most of the action is viewed through the eyes of (choose one):

1. a central character.
2. a minor character.
3. a disinterested spectator.

Effect
How has the author pointed out that something is reversed in the attitudes of Marvin and his father?

BIOGRAPHICAL NOTE

Margaret Weymouth Jackson (1895–1974) was born in Eureka, Arkansas. After attending Hillsdale College in Michigan, she began her writing career. She was on the editorial staff of two magazines and wrote several widely acclaimed novels: *Elizabeth's Tower, Kindy's Crossing,* and *First Fiddle.*

When she sat back on her heels to smile up at her
father she felt her throat constrict with a smothering fear.

FROM MOTHER . . . WITH LOVE
Zoa Sherburne

The day that Minta Hawley grew up was
a crisp golden day in early September.

Afterwards she was to remember
everything about that day with poignant
clarity. She remembered the slapping
sound the waves made, the pungent
smell of the logs burning, even the gulls
that soared and swooped overhead; but
most of all she remembered her father's
face when he told her.

It began like any other Saturday, with
Minta lying in bed an extra hour. Breakfast was always lazy and unhurried on
Saturday mornings. The three of them in
the breakfast room—Minta's father engrossed in his paper; her mother flying
around in a gayly colored housecoat,
mixing waffles and frying bacon; Minta
setting the table.

They talked, the casual happy talk of
people who love each other and don't
have to make conversation. About neighborhood doings . . . about items in the
paper . . . about the clothes Minta would
need when she went away to school in a
couple of weeks.

It was after the dishes were finished
that Minta's father asked her if she would
like to go down to the beach for a little
while.

"Low tide," he said. "Might get a few
clams."

Reprinted by permission of Zoa Sherburne and The Ann Elmo Agency, Inc.

Minta nodded agreement, but her
mother made a little face.

"Horrors, clam chowder for another
week!"

"Sure you wouldn't like to go, Mary?"
Minta's father asked. "The salt air might
help your headache."

"No. You two run along. I'll curl up
with an apple and a television program."
She yawned and stretched, looking almost as young as Minta.

Minta ran upstairs and got into her
heavy shoes and jeans. "Shall I call Sally
and ask her if she wants to go?" she
yelled, leaning far over the bannister.

"Let's just go by ourselves this time,"
her father answered rather shortly.

He was silent as they drove toward
the beach, but it wasn't the companion-
able silence that Minta had come to expect from him. There was something
grim about it.

"He's going to talk to me about
school," Minta told herself. "He's going
to try to talk me out of it again."

It was funny the way her father had
acted when she announced her intention
of going to MaryHill this term. It had
always been such an accepted thing; her
mother had graduated from MaryHill
and it followed that Minta should be enrolled there as a matter of course.

Last year was different. With Mother
just recovering from that operation it was

natural that he should expect Minta to stay home; she had even *wanted* to stay. But now going to MaryHill was something special. She would live in a dormitory and be part of all the campus fun. It wasn't as if MaryHill were clear across the country, either, she'd probably be getting home every month or so . . . and there were the Christmas holidays . . . and then spring vacation.

Minta's chin was lifted in a stubborn line as her father parked the car and went around to get the shovels and pail from the trunk.

It wasn't like him to be so stubborn; usually he was jolly and easygoing and inclined to leave such matters entirely up to Minta's mother.

She followed him down to the beach, her boots squishing in the wet sand. The tide was far out and farther up the beach she could see bent figures busily digging along the water's edge.

A scattered beach fire smoldered near the bank and Minta poked it into place and revived it with splinters of driftwood until she had coaxed back a steady warming blaze. When she sat back on her heels to smile up at her father she felt her throat constrict with a smothering fear. His eyes looked the way they had when . . .

When?

Suddenly she remembered. He was looking at her and trying to smile, just the way he had looked at her the time her appendix burst and they were taking her to the hospital. She could almost hear the wail of the ambulance siren and feel the way he had held her hands tightly, trying to make it easier. His eyes had told her then, as they told her now, that he would a thousand times rather bear the pain than watch her suffer.

It seemed like a long time that she knelt there by the beach fire, afraid to move, childishly willing herself to wake from the nightmarish feeling that gripped her.

He took her hand and pulled her to her feet and they started walking up the beach slowly, not toward the group of people digging clams, but in the other direction, toward the jagged pile of rocks that jutted out into the bay.

She heard a strange voice, her own voice.

"I thought . . . I thought you wanted to talk to me about school, but it isn't that, is it, Father?"

Father.

She never called him Father. It was always "Dad" or "Pops" or, when she was feeling especially gay, "John Henry."

His fingers tightened around hers. "In a way it is . . . about school."

And then, before the feeling of relief could erase the fear he went on. "I went to see Dr. Morton last week, Minta. I've been seeing him pretty regularly these last few months."

She flashed a quick frightened look up at him. "You aren't ill?"

"No." He sighed and it was a heartbreaking sound. "No. It isn't me. It's your mother. That's why I don't want you to go to MaryHill this year."

"But . . . but she's feeling so much better, Dad. Except for these headaches once in a while. She's even taking on a little weight—" She broke off and stopped walking and her hand was steady on his arm. "Tell me," she said quietly.

The look was back in his eyes again but this time Minta scarcely noticed it, she was aware only of his words, the dreadful echoing finality of his words.

Her mother was going to die.

To die.

Her mother.

To die, the doctor said. Three months, perhaps less. . . .

Her mother who was gay and scatter-brained and more fun than anyone else in the world. Her mother who could be counted on to announce in the spring that she was going to do her Christmas shopping early *this* year, and then left everything until the week before Christmas.

No one was worse about forgetting anniversaries and birthdays and things like that; but the easy-to-remember dates, like Valentine's Day and St. Patrick's Day and Halloween were always gala affairs complete with table favors and three-decker cakes.

Minta's mother wore the highest heels and the maddest hats of any mother on the block. She was so pretty. And she always had time for things like listening to new records and helping paste pictures in Minta's scrapbook.

She wasn't ever sick—except for the headaches and the operation last year which she had laughingly dismissed as a rest cure.

"I shouldn't have told you." Her father was speaking in a voice that Minta had never heard from him before. A voice that held loneliness and fear and a sort of angry pain. "I was afraid I couldn't make you understand, why you had to stay home . . . why you'd have to forget about MaryHill for this year." His eyes begged her to forgive him and for some reason she wanted to put her arms around him, as if she were much older and stronger.

"Of course you had to tell me," she said steadily. "Of course I had to know." And then—"Three months, but Dad, that's *Christmas*."

He took her hand and tucked it under his arm and they started walking again.

It was like walking through a nightmare. The steady squish-squish of the wet sand and the little hollows their feet made filling up almost as soon as they passed.

He talked quietly, explaining, telling her everything the doctor had said, and Minta listened without tears, without comment.

She watched his face as though it were the face of a stranger.

She thought about a thousand unrelated things.

Last winter when he had chased her and her mother around the back yard to wash their faces in the new snow. She could still see the bright red jacket her mother had worn . . . the kerchief that came off in the struggle . . . the way the neighbors had watched from their windows, laughing and shaking their heads.

She remembered all the times they had gone swimming this past summer. Minta and her father loved to swim but her mother had preferred to curl up on a beach blanket and watch them.

"You have the disposition of a Siamese cat," Minta had accused her mother laughingly. "A cushion by the fire in the winter and a cushion in the sun in the summer. . . ."

"And a bowl of cream nearby," her mother had agreed instantly.

She was always good-natured about their teasing.

But in spite of her apparent frailty

and her admitted laziness she managed to accomplish an astounding amount of work. Girl Scouts, PTA, Church bazaars, Red Cross. People were always calling her to head a committee or organize a drive. Young people congregated in her home. Not just Minta's gang, but the neighborhood youngsters. She had Easter egg hunts for them; she bought their raffle tickets and bandaged their skinned knees.

It was like coming back from a long journey when her father stopped talking and they turned back toward the car.

"So that's why I can't let you go away, Midge." Her father's voice was very low and he didn't seem to realize that he had called her by the babyish name she had discarded when she started to first grade. "It isn't just your mother I'm thinking about . . . it's me. I need you."

She looked at him quickly and her heart twisted with pity. He did need her. He would need her more than ever.

In the car she sat very close to him.

"We didn't get the clams," she reminded him once, but he only nodded.

Just before they reached home he reached over and took her hand in a tight hurting grip.

"We can't tell her, Minta. The doctor left it up to me and I said not to tell her. We have to let her have this last time . . . this last little time . . . without that hanging over her. We have to go on as if everything were exactly the same."

She nodded to show that she understood. After a moment she spoke past the ache in her throat. "About school. I'll . . . I'll tell her that I decided to wait until next year. Or that I'm afraid I'd be lonesome without the gang. I've been sort of

. . . sort of seesawing back and forth, anyway."

It seemed impossible that life could go on exactly as before.

The small private world peopled by the three of them was as snug and warm and happy as though no shadow had touched them.

They watched television and argued good-naturedly about the programs. Minta's friends came and went and there was the usual round of parties and dances and games. Her father continued to bowl two evenings a week and her mother became involved in various pre-holiday pursuits.

"I really must get at my Christmas shopping," she mentioned the day she was wrapping trick-or-treat candy for Halloween.

Minta shook her head and sighed gustily.

Her mother started this "I-must-get-at-my-Christmas-shopping" routine by every spring and followed it up until after Thanksgiving but she never actually got around to it until two or three days before Christmas.

It was amazing that Minta could laugh and say, "Oh, *you* . . ." the way she did year after year.

It was a knife turning in her heart when her mother straightened up from the gay cellophane-wrapped candies and brushed a stray wisp of taffy-colored hair back from one flushed cheek.

"Don't laugh," she said, pretending to be stern. "You know you're just exactly like me."

It was a warming thought. She *was* like her mother. Inside, where it really mattered she was like her mother, even though she had her father's dark eyes and straight black hair, even though she had his build and the firm chin of all the Hawleys.

She wanted to put her arm around her mother and hug her, hard. She wanted to say, "I hope I am like you. I want to be."

But instead she got up and stretched and wrinkled her nose.

"Perish forbid," she said, "that I should be such a scatterbrain."

She was rewarded by the flash of a dimple in her mother's cheek.

It seemed to Minta, as week followed week, that the day at the beach had been something out of a nightmare: something that she could push away from her and forget about. Sometimes she looked at her father, laughing, teasing them, or howling about the month-end bills and she thought, "It didn't happen . . . it isn't true."

And then at night she would lie sleepless in her room, the pretty room that had been reconverted from her nursery. She watched the moonlight drift patterns across the yellow bedspread and the breeze billow the curtains that her mother had made by hand, because that was the only way she could be sure of an absolute match.

"Yellow is such a difficult color to match," she had explained around a mouthful of pins.

And in the dark hours of the night Minta had known it wasn't a nightmare. It was true. It was true.

One windy November day she hurried home from school and found her mother in the yard raking leaves. She wore a bright kerchief over her head and she had Minta's old polo coat belted around her. She looked young and gay and carefree and her eyes were shining.

"Hi!" She waved the rake invitingly. "Change your clothes and come help. We'll have a smudge party in the alley."

Minta stopped and leaned on the gate. She saw with a new awareness that there were dark circles under her mother's eyes and that the flags of color in her cheeks were too bright. But she managed a chuckle.

"I wish you could see yourself, Mom. For two cents I'd get my camera and take a picture of you."

She ran into the house and got her camera and they took a whole roll of pictures.

"Good," her mother said complacently. "Now we can show them to your father the next time he accuses me of being a Sally-Sit-by-the-Fire."

They piled the leaves into a huge damp stack, with the help of half a dozen neighborhood children. It wouldn't burn properly but gave out with clouds of thick, black, wonderfully pungent smoke.

Her mother was tired that night. She lay on the davenport and made out her Christmas card list while Minta and her father watched the wrestling matches. It was like a thousand other such evenings but in some unaccountable way it was different.

"Because it's the last time," Minta told herself. "The last time we'll ever rake the leaves and make a bonfire in the alley. The last time I'll snap a picture of her with her arms around the Kelly kids. The last time . . . the last time. . . ."

She got up quickly and went out into the kitchen and made popcorn in the electric popper, bringing a bowl to her mother first, remembering just the way she liked it, salt and not too much butter.

But that night she wakened in the chilly darkness of her room and began to cry, softly, her head buried in the curve of her arm. At first it helped, loosening the tight bands about her heart, washing away the fear and the loneliness, but when she tried to stop she found that she couldn't. Great wracking sobs shook her until she could no longer smother them against her pillow. And then the light was on and her mother was there bending over her, her face concerned, her voice soothing.

"Darling, what is it? Wake up, baby, you're having a bad dream."

"No . . . no, it isn't a dream," Minta choked. "It's true . . . it's true."

The thin hand kept smoothing back her tumbled hair and her mother went on talking in the tone she had always used to comfort a much smaller Minta.

She was aware that her father had come to the doorway. He said nothing, just stood there watching them while Minta's sobs diminished into hiccupy sighs.

Her mother pulled the blanket up over Minta's shoulder and gave her a little spank. "The idea! Gollywogs, at your age," she said reprovingly. "Want me to leave the light on in case your spook comes back?"

Minta shook her head, blinking against the tears that crowded against her eyelids, even managing a wobbly smile.

She never cried again.

Not even when the ambulance came a week later to take her mother to the hospital. Not even when she was standing beside her mother's high white hospital bed, holding her hand tightly, forcing herself to chatter of inconsequential things.

"Be sure that your father takes his vitamin pills, won't you, Minta? He's so careless unless I'm there to keep an eye on him."

"I'll watch him like a beagle," Minta promised lightly. "Now you behave yourself and get out of here in a hurry, you hear?"

Not even at the funeral. . . .

The friends and relatives came and went and it was as if she stood on the sidelines watching the Minta who talked with them and answered their questions. As if her heart were encased in a shell that kept it from breaking.

She went to school and came home afterwards to the empty house. She tried to do the things her mother had done but even with the help of well-meaning friends and neighbors it was hard. She tried not to hate the people who urged her to cry.

"You'll feel better, dear," her Aunt Grace had insisted and then had lifted her handkerchief to her eyes and walked away when Minta had only stared at her with chilling indifference.

She overheard people talking about her mother.

"She never knew, did she?" they asked.

And always Minta's father answered, "No, she never knew. Even at the very last, when she was waiting for the ambulance to come she looked around the bedroom and said, 'I must get these curtains done up before Christmas.'"

Minta knew that her father was worried about her and she was sorry, but it was as if there were a wall between them, a wall that she was too tired to surmount.

One night he came to the door of her room where she was studying.

"I wonder if you'd like to go through those clothes before your Aunt Grace takes them to the church bazaar," he began haltingly. And then when she looked up at him, not understanding, he went on gently, "Your mother's clothes. We thought someone might as well get some good out of them."

She stood up and closed the book and went past him without another word, but she closed the door behind her when she went into her mother's room.

There were some suit boxes by the closet door and Minta vaguely remembered that the women from the bazaar committee had called several times.

Her hands felt slightly unsteady as she pulled open the top dresser drawer and looked down at the stacks of clean handkerchiefs, the stockings in their quilted satin case, the gloves folded into tissue wrappings.

"I can't do it," she told herself, but she got a box and started putting the things into it, trying not to look at them, trying to forget how delighted her mother had been with the pale green slip, trying not to remember.

Once she hesitated and almost lifted a soft wool sweater from the pile that was growing in the suit box. She had borrowed it so often that her mother used to complain that she felt like a criminal every time she borrowed it back again. She didn't mean it though . . . she loved having Minta borrow her things.

Minta put the sweater with the other things and closed the box firmly.

Now, the things in the closet—

Opening the door was almost like feeling her mother in the room beside her. A faint perfume clung to most of her garments. The housecoat . . . the woolly robe . . . the tan polo coat . . . the scarlet jacket . . . her new blue wool with the pegtop skirt.

Minta started folding the things with almost frantic haste, stuffing them into boxes, cramming the lids on and then starting on another box.

At the very back of the closet were the two pieces of matched luggage that had been her mother's last birthday gift from her father. They were heavy when she tried to move them—too heavy.

She brought them out into the room and put them side by side on her mother's bed. Her breath caught in her throat when she opened them.

Dozens and dozens of boxes, all tied with bright red ribbon, the gift tags written out in her mother's careful script. Gayly colored Christmas stickers, sprigs of holly.

To Minta from Mother and Dad . . . to Grace from Mary . . . to John from Mary . . . to the Kelly Gremlins from Aunt Mary . . . to Uncle Art from the Hawley family . . .

"So you knew," Minta whispered the words. "You knew all the time."

She looked down in surprise as a hot tear dropped on her hand and she dashed it away almost impatiently.

She picked up another package and read the tag. To Minta from Mother . . . with love.

Without opening it she knew that it was a picture frame and she remembered the way she had teased her mother to have a good photograph taken.

"The only one I have of you looks like a fugitive from a chain gang," she had pointed out. "I can't very well go away to school next year with *that*."

She put the package back in the suitcase with all the others and carried the cases back into the closet.

Poor Dad, she thought.

"She never knew," she could hear him saying. "Not even at the last."

Minta opened the box beside the bed and took out the sweater and the pale green slip.

"You know perfectly well that you're just exactly like me," she remembered her mother saying.

She brushed the tears away and went down the stairs and out into the cheerless living room.

"I'd like to keep these things, Dad," she said in her most matter-of-fact voice, and she showed him the sweater and slip. "The slip is a little big but I'll grow into it. It . . . it looks like her, I think."

She went around the room, snapping on the lamps, turning on the television that had been silent for so long. She was aware that his eyes followed her, that he could hardly avoid noticing the tear stains on her cheeks.

"I think I'll have an apple," she said. "Want one?"

He nodded. "Sure. Bring me one as long as you're making the trip."

It was natural. It was almost like old times, except that the blue chair by the fireplace was vacant.

She went out into the kitchen hurriedly.

"I'll tell him that I pestered mother to do her shopping early this year," she told herself as she got the apples from the refrigerator. "I'll tell him that it was my idea about the photographs. She wanted him to believe that she didn't know."

The vitamin pills were pushed back on a shelf. She took them out of the refrigerator and put them on the window sill where she would be sure to see them in the morning.

When she came back into the living room she noticed that a light in a Christmas wreath was winking on and off in the Kelly's window across the street.

"I guess we should start thinking about Christmas, Dad." She tossed him an apple as she spoke and he caught it deftly.

She hesitated for just a moment and then walked over and sat down in the blue chair by the fire, as if she belonged there, and looked across at her father, and smiled.

READING FOR DETAILS

The Empty Chair

Minta's story seems a complicated one. First, she had to accept the knowledge that her mother was to die; then, learn to live with this aching fear; and in the end, accept the reality of her mother's death. Many "inner circles" are broken apart temporarily or permanently under circumstances as heartbreaking.

Discuss these statements in relation to their significance in the story:

1. They talked, the casual happy talk of people who love each other and don't have to make conversation.
2. She never cried again. . . . Not even when the ambulance came . . . to take her mother to the hospital. . . . Not even at the funeral.
3. The mother's statement, "You know you're just exactly like me," helped Minta face reality.

READING FOR MEANING

Consider and discuss the merits of these statements in light of the story:

1. The members of this family did the wise thing to pretend to each other that the mother was going to be all right.
2. Actually, whether it is death or some other problem, the best course of action is a frank discussion among those concerned.

READING FOR APPRECIATION

Effect

Tone or atmosphere in writing is achieved much as it is in music. The composer combines musical sounds in a particular way and with a particular rhythm to arouse specific feelings in the listener. Similarly, writers use descriptive words and phrases to fit a certain pattern and tempo. In this way, they may arouse predetermined feelings such as foreboding and sadness, amusement, seriousness, or even gaiety.

1. "From Mother . . . with Love" definitely has a unity of tone. What emotional response did you get from reading the story? Do you think your response was the kind the author intended?

2. Has the author created her atmosphere in a cheap and sentimental fashion or did she use restraint? Discuss.

COMPOSITION

Write a brief narrative about a person who has a character trait you would like to have. Use at least one incident that illustrates this trait.

Make your opening an interest-catcher. Catapult the reader immediately into the center of the incident you imagine.

In your incident be sure to use description of character and setting, dialogue, and details made vivid by the use of imaginative language, such as simile and metaphor.

BIOGRAPHICAL NOTE

Zoa Morin Sherburne (1912–   ), American short story writer and novelist, was born in Seattle, Washington, and attended Seattle public schools. Chosen Woman of the Year by Phi Delta Nu, Miss Sherburne has been writing professionally since 1947. *Almost April, The High White Wall*, and *Ballerina on Skates* are her most widely read books.

It was bad enough having an invalid brother, but having one who possibly was not all there was unbearable.

THE SCARLET IBIS

James Hurst

It was in the clove of seasons, summer was dead but autumn had not yet been born, that the ibis lit in the bleeding tree. The flower garden was stained with rotting brown magnolia petals and ironweeds grew rank amid the purple phlox. The five o'clocks by the chimney still marked time, but the oriole nest in the elm was untenanted and rocked back and forth like an empty cradle. The last graveyard flowers were blooming, and their smell drifted across the cotton field and through every room of our house, speaking softly the names of our dead.

It's strange that all this is still so clear to me, now that that summer has long since fled and time has had its way. A grindstone stands where the bleeding tree stood, just outside the kitchen door, and now if an oriole sings in the elm, its song seems to die up in the leaves, a silvery dust. The flower garden is prim, the house a gleaming white, and the pale fence across the yard stands straight and spruce. But sometimes (like right now), as I sit in the cool, green-draped parlor, the grindstone begins to turn, and time with all its changes is ground away—and I remember Doodle.

Doodle was just about the craziest brother a boy ever had. Of course, he wasn't a crazy crazy like old Miss Leedie, who was in love with President Wilson[1] and wrote him a letter every day, but was a nice crazy, like someone you meet in your dreams. He was born when I was six and was, from the outset, a disappointment. He seemed all head, with a tiny body which was red and shriveled like an old man's. Everybody thought he was going to die—everybody except Aunt Nicey, who had delivered him. She said he would live because he was born in a caul[2] and cauls were made from Jesus' nightgown. Daddy had Mr. Heath, the carpenter, build a little mahogany coffin for him. But he didn't die, and when he was three months old Mama and Daddy decided they might as well name him. They named him William Armstrong, which was like tying a big tail on a small kite. Such a name sounds good only on a tombstone.

I thought myself pretty smart at many things, like holding my breath, running, jumping, or climbing the vines in Old Woman Swamp, and I wanted more than anything else someone to race to Horsehead Landing, someone to box with, and someone to perch with in the top fork of the great pine behind the

---

1. **Woodrow Wilson** (1856–1924), president of the United States from 1913 to 1921.
2. **caul** (kôl), a portion of the membrane enclosing a child in the womb that is sometimes found clinging to the head at birth. It was supposed to bring good luck.

barn, where across the fields and swamps you could see the sea. I wanted a brother. But Mama, crying, told me that even if William Armstrong lived, he would never do these things with me. He might not, she sobbed, even be "all there." He might, as long as he lived, lie on the rubber sheet in the center of the bed in the front bedroom where the white marquisette curtains billowed out in the afternoon sea breeze, rustling like palmetto fronds.

It was bad enough having an invalid brother, but having one who possibly was not all there was unbearable, so I began to make plans to kill him by smothering him with a pillow. However, one afternoon as I watched him, my head poked between the iron posts of the foot of the bed, he looked straight at me and grinned. I skipped through the rooms, down the echoing halls, shouting, "Mama, he smiled. He's all there! He's all there!" and he was.

When he was two, if you laid him on his stomach, he began to try to move himself, straining terribly. The doctor said that with his weak heart this strain would probably kill him, but it didn't. Trembling, he'd push himself up, turning first red, then a soft purple, and finally collapse back onto the bed like an old worn-out doll. I can still see Mama watching him, her hand pressed tight across her mouth, her eyes wide and unblinking. But he learned to crawl (it was his third winter), and we brought him out of the front bedroom, putting him on the rug before the fireplace. For the first time he became one of us.

As long as he lay all the time in bed, we called him William Armstrong, even though it was formal and sounded as if we were referring to one of our ancestors, but with his creeping around on the deerskin rug and beginning to talk, something had to be done about his name. It was I who renamed him. When he crawled, he crawled backwards, as if he were in reverse and couldn't change gears. If you called him, he'd turn around as if he were going in the other direction, then he'd back right up to you to be picked up. Crawling backward made him look like a doodlebug, so I began to call him Doodle, and in time even Mama and Daddy thought it was a better name than William Armstrong. Only Aunt Nicey disagreed. She said caul babies should be treated with special respect since they might turn out to be saints. Renaming my brother was perhaps the kindest thing I ever did for him, because nobody expects much from someone called Doodle.

Although Doodle learned to crawl, he showed no signs of walking, but he wasn't idle. He talked so much that we all quit listening to what he said. It was about this time that Daddy built him a go-cart and I had to pull him around. At first I just paraded him up and down the piazza, but then he started crying to be taken out into the yard and it ended up by my having to lug him wherever I went. If I so much as picked up my cap, he'd start crying to go with me and Mama would call from wherever she was, "Take Doodle with you."

He was a burden in many ways. The doctor had said that he mustn't get too excited, too hot, too cold, or too tired and that he must always be treated gently. A long list of dont's went with him, all of which I ignored once we got out of the house. To discourage his coming with

THE CLIMBING PATH AT THE HERMITAGE, PONTOISE
Camille Pissaro
The Brooklyn Museum, Brooklyn, New York

me, I'd run with him across the ends of the cotton rows and careen him around corners on two wheels. Sometimes I accidentally turned him over, but he never told Mama. His skin was very sensitive, and he had to wear a big straw hat whenever he went out. When the going got rough and he had to cling to the sides of the go-cart, the hat slipped all the way down over his ears. He was a sight. Finally, I could see I was licked. Doodle was my brother and he was going to cling to me forever, no matter what I did, so I dragged him across the burning cotton field to share with him the only beauty I knew, Old Woman Swamp. I pulled the go-cart through the saw-tooth fern, down into the green dimness where the palmetto fronds whispered by the stream. I lifted him out and set him down in the soft rubber grass beside a tall pine. His eyes were round with wonder as he gazed about him, and his little hands began to stroke the rubber grass. Then he began to cry.

"For heaven's sake, what's the matter?" I asked, annoyed.

"It's so pretty," he said. "So pretty, pretty, pretty."

After that day Doodle and I often went down into Old Woman Swamp. I would gather wildflowers, wild violets, honeysuckle, yellow jasmine, snakeflowers, and water lilies, and with wire grass we'd weave them into necklaces and crowns. We'd bedeck ourselves with our handiwork and loll about thus beautified, beyond the touch of the everyday world. Then when the slanted rays of the sun burned orange in the tops of the pines, we'd drop our jewels into the stream and watch them float away toward the sea.

There is within me (and with sadness I have watched it in others) a knot of cruelty borne by the stream of love, much as our blood sometimes bears the seed of our destruction, and at times I was mean to Doodle. One day I took him up to the barn loft and showed him his casket, telling him how we all had believed he would die. It was covered with a film of Paris green sprinkled to kill the rats, and screech owls had built a nest inside it.

Doodle studied the mahogany box for a long time, then said, "It's not mine."

"It is," I said. "And before I'll help you down from the loft, you're going to have to touch it."

"I won't touch it," he said sullenly.

"Then I'll leave you here by yourself," I threatened, and made as if I were going down.

Doodle was frightened of being left. "Don't go leave me, Brother," he cried, and he leaned toward the coffin. His hand, trembling, reached out, and when he touched the casket he screamed. A screech owl flapped out of the box into our faces, scaring us and covering us with Paris green. Doodle was paralyzed, so I put him on my shoulder and carried him down the ladder, and even when we were outside in the bright sunshine, he clung to me, crying, "Don't leave me. Don't leave me."

When Doodle was five years old, I was embarrassed at having a brother of that age who couldn't walk, so I set out to teach him. We were down in Old Woman Swamp and it was spring and the sick-sweet smell of bay flowers hung everywhere like a mournful song. "I'm going to teach you to walk, Doodle," I said.

He was sitting comfortably on the soft grass, leaning back against the pine. "Why?" he asked.

I hadn't expected such an answer. "So I won't have to haul you around all the time."

"I can't walk, Brother," he said.

"Who says so?" I demanded.

"Mama, the doctor—everybody."

"Oh, you can walk," I said, and I took him by the arms and stood him up. He collapsed onto the grass like a half-empty flour sack. It was as if he had no bones in his little legs.

"Don't hurt me, Brother," he warned.

"Shut up. I'm not going to hurt you. I'm going to teach you to walk." I heaved him up again, and again he collapsed.

This time he did not lift his face up out of the rubber grass. "I just can't do it. Let's make honeysuckle wreaths."

"Oh yes you can, Doodle," I said. "All

you got to do is try. Now come on," and I hauled him up once more.

It seemed so hopeless from the beginning that it's a miracle I didn't give up. But all of us must have something or someone to be proud of, and Doodle had become mine. I did not know then that pride is a wonderful, terrible thing, a seed that bears two vines, life and death. Every day that summer we went to the pine beside the stream of Old Woman Swamp, and I put him on his feet at least a hundred times each afternoon. Occasionally I too became discouraged because it didn't seem as if he was trying, and I would say, "Doodle, don't you *want* to learn to walk?"

He'd nod his head, and I'd say, "Well, if you don't keep trying, you'll never learn." Then I'd paint for him a picture of us as old men, whitehaired, him with a long white beard and me still pulling him around in the go-cart. This never failed to make him try again.

Finally one day, after many weeks of practicing, he stood alone for a few seconds. When he fell, I grabbed him in my arms and hugged him, our laughter pealing through the swamp like a ringing bell. Now we knew it could be done. Hope no longer hid in the dark palmetto thicket but perched like a cardinal in the lacy toothbrush tree, brilliantly visible. "Yes, yes," I cried, and he cried it too, and the grass beneath us was soft and the smell of the swamp was sweet.

With success so imminent, we decided not to tell anyone until he could actually walk. Each day, barring rain, we sneaked into Old Woman Swamp, and by cotton-picking time Doodle was ready to show what he could do. He still wasn't able to walk far, but we could wait no longer. Keeping a nice secret is very hard to do,

like holding your breath. We chose to reveal all on October eighth, Doodle's sixth birthday, and for weeks ahead we mooned around the house, promising everybody a most spectacular surprise. Aunt Nicey said that, after so much talk, if we produced anything less tremendous than the Resurrection,[3] she was going to be disappointed.

At breakfast on our chosen day, when Mama, Daddy, and Aunt Nicey were in the dining room, I brought Doodle to the door in the go-cart just as usual and had them turn their backs, making them cross their hearts and hope to die if they peeked. I helped Doodle up, and when he was standing alone I let them look. There wasn't a sound as Doodle walked slowly across the room and sat down at his place at the table. Then Mama began to cry and ran over to him, hugging him and kissing him. Daddy hugged him too, so I went to Aunt Nicey, who was thanks praying in the doorway, and began to waltz her around. We danced together quite well until she came down on my big toe with her brogans,[4] hurting me so badly I thought I was crippled for life.

Doodle told them it was I who had taught him to walk, so everyone wanted to hug me, and I began to cry.

"What are you crying for?" asked Daddy, but I couldn't answer. They did not know that I did it for myself; that pride, whose slave I was, spoke to me louder than all their voices, and that Doodle walked only because I was ashamed of having a crippled brother.

Within a few months Doodle had learned to walk well and his go-cart was

---

3. **Resurrection,** the rising again of Christ after His death and burial.
4. **brogans,** strong work shoes made of heavy leather.

put up in the barn loft (it's still there) beside his little mahogany coffin. Now, when we roamed off together, resting often, we never turned back until our destination had been reached, and to help pass the time, we took up lying. From the beginning Doodle was a terrible liar and he got me in the habit. Had anyone stopped to listen to us, we would have been sent off to Dix Hill.

My lies were scary, involved, and usually pointless, but Doodle's were twice as crazy. People in his stories all had wings and flew wherever they wanted to go. His favorite lie was about a boy named Peter who had a pet peacock with a ten-foot tail. Peter wore a golden robe that glittered so brightly that when he walked through the sunflowers they turned away from the sun to face him. When Peter was ready to go to sleep, the peacock spread his magnificent tail, enfolding the boy gently like a closing go-to-sleep flower, burying him in the gloriously iridescent, rustling vortex. Yes, I must admit it. Doodle could beat me lying.

Doodle and I spent lots of time thinking about our future. We decided that when we were grown we'd live in Old Woman Swamp and pick dog-tongue for a living. Beside the stream, he planned, we'd build us a house of whispering leaves and the swamp birds would be our chickens. All day long (when we weren't gathering dog-tongue) we'd swing through the cypresses on the rope vines, and if it rained we'd huddle beneath an umbrella tree and play stick-frog. Mama and Daddy could come and live with us if they wanted to. He even came up with the idea that he could marry Mama and I could marry Daddy. Of course, I was old enough to know this wouldn't work out, but the picture he painted was so beautiful and serene that all I could do was whisper Yes, yes.

Once I had succeeded in teaching Doodle to walk, I began to believe in my own infallibility and I prepared a terrific development program for him, unknown to Mama and Daddy, of course. I would teach him to run, to swim, to climb trees, and to fight. He, too, now believed in my infallibility, so we set the deadline for these accomplishments less than a year away, when, it had been decided, Doodle could start to school.

That winter we didn't make much progress, for I was in school and Doodle suffered from one bad cold after another. But when spring came, rich and warm, we raised our sights again. Success lay at the end of summer like a pot of gold,[5] and our campaign got off to a good start. On hot days, Doodle and I went down to Horsehead Landing and I gave him swimming lessons or showed him how to row a boat. Sometimes we descended into the cool greenness of Old Woman Swamp and climbed the rope vines or boxed scientifically beneath the pine where he had learned to walk. Promise hung about us like the leaves, and wherever we looked, ferns unfurled and birds broke into song.

That summer, the summer of 1918, was blighted. In May and June there was no rain and the crops withered, curled up, then died under the thirsty sun. One morning in July a hurricane came out of the east, tipping over the oaks in the yard

---

5. The author is comparing success at the end of summer to the pot of gold that is said to lie at the end of the rainbow.

and splitting the limbs of the elm trees. That afternoon it roared back out of the west, blew the fallen oaks around, snapping their roots and tearing them out of the earth like a hawk at the entrails of a chicken. Cotton bolls were wrenched from the stalks and lay like green walnuts in the valleys between the rows, while the cornfield leaned over uniformly so that the tassels touched the ground. Doodle and I followed Daddy out into the cotton field, where he stood, shoulders sagging, surveying the ruin. When his chin sank down onto his chest, we were frightened, and Doodle slipped his hand into mine. Suddenly Daddy straightened his shoulders, raised a giant knuckly fist, and with a voice that seemed to rumble out of the earth itself began cursing heaven, hell, the weather, and the Republican Party. Doodle and I, prodding each other and giggling, went back to the house, knowing that everything would be all right.

And during that summer, strange names were heard through the house: Château Thierry, Amiens, Soissons, and in her blessing at the supper table, Mama once said, "And bless the Pearsons, whose boy Joe was lost at Belleau Wood."[6]

So we came to that clove of seasons. School was only a few weeks away, and Doodle was far behind schedule. He could barely clear the ground when climbing the rope vines and his swimming was certainly not passable. We decided to double our efforts, to make that last drive and reach our pot of gold. I made him swim until he turned blue and row until he couldn't lift an oar. Wherever we went, I purposely walked fast, and although he kept up, his face turned red and his eyes became glazed. Once, he

could go no further, so he collapsed on the ground and began to cry.

"Aw, come on, Doodle," I urged. "You can do it. Do you want to be different from everybody else when you start school?"

"Does it make any difference?"

"It certainly does," I said. "Now, come on," and I helped him up.

As we slipped through dog days, Doodle began to look feverish, and Mama felt his forehead, asking him if he felt ill. At night he didn't sleep well, and sometimes he had nightmares, crying out until I touched him and said, "Wake up, Doodle. Wake up."

It was Saturday noon, just a few days before school was to start. I should have already admitted defeat, but my pride wouldn't let me. The excitement of our program had now been gone for weeks, but still we kept on with a tired doggedness. It was too late to turn back, for we had both wandered too far into a net of expectations and had left no crumbs behind.[7]

Daddy, Mama, Doodle, and I were seated at the dining-room table having lunch. It was a hot day, with all the windows and doors open in case a breeze should come. In the kitchen Aunt Nicey

6. **Château Thierry** (sha tō', tye rē), **Amiens** (am yan'), **Soissons** (swa son'), and **Belleau** (bel'ō) **Wood** were scenes of World War I battles in which U.S. troops took part in 1918.
7. **"It was too late to turn back, for we had both wandered too far into a net of expectations and had left no crumbs behind."** This is an allusion to the situation in the well-known fairy tale "Hansel and Gretel." The brother and sister know they are being led into the dense forest to perish. Thinking to mark the path so they can find their way back home, Hansel drops bread crumbs behind them. His plan fails because hungry birds eat the crumbs.

was humming softly. After a long silence, Daddy spoke. "It's so calm, I wouldn't be surprised if we had a storm this afternoon."

"I haven't heard a rain frog," said Mama, who believed in signs, as she served the bread around the table.

"I did," declared Doodle. "Down in the swamp."

"He didn't," I said contrarily.

"You did, eh?" said Daddy, ignoring my denial.

"I certainly did," Doodle reiterated, scowling at me over the top of his iced-tea glass, and we were quiet again.

Suddenly, from out in the yard, came a strange croaking noise. Doodle stopped eating, with a piece of bread poised ready for his mouth, his eyes popped round like two blue buttons. "What's that?" he whispered.

I jumped up, knocking over my chair, and had reached the door when Mama called, "Pick up the chair, sit down again, and say excuse me."

By the time I had done this, Doodle had excused himself and had slipped out into the yard. He was looking up into the bleeding tree. "It's a great big red bird!" he called.

The bird croaked loudly again, and Mama and Daddy came out into the yard. We shaded our eyes with our hands against the hazy glare of the sun and peered up through the still leaves. On the topmost branch a bird the size of a chicken, with scarlet feathers and long legs, was perched precariously. Its wings hung down loosely, and as we watched, a feather dropped away and floated slowly down through the green leaves.

"It's not even frightened of us," Mama said.

"It looks tired," Daddy added. "Or maybe sick."

Doodle's hands were clasped at his throat, and I had never seen him stand still so long. "What is it?" he asked.

Daddy shook his head. "I don't know, maybe it's—"

At that moment the bird began to flutter, but the wings were uncoordinated, and amid much flapping and a spray of flying feathers, it tumbled down, bumping through the limbs of the bleeding tree and landing at our feet with a thud. Its long, graceful neck jerked twice into an S, then straightened out, and the bird was still. A white veil came over the eyes and the long white beak unhinged. Its legs were crossed and its clawlike feet were delicately curved at rest. Even death did not mar its grace, for it lay on the earth like a broken vase of red flowers, and we stood around it, awed by its exotic beauty.

"It's dead," Mama said.

"What is it?" Doodle repeated.

"Go bring me the bird book," said Daddy.

I ran into the house and brought back the bird book. As we watched, Daddy thumbed through its pages. "It's a scarlet ibis," he said, pointing to a picture. "It lives in the tropics—South America to Florida. A storm must have brought it here."

Sadly, we all looked back at the bird. A scarlet ibis! How many miles it had traveled to die like this, in *our* yard, beneath the bleeding tree.

"Let's finish lunch," Mama said, nudging us back toward the dining room.

"I'm not hungry," said Doodle, and he knelt down beside the ibis.

"We've got peach cobbler for dessert," Mama tempted from the doorway.

Doodle remained kneeling. "I'm going to bury him."

"Don't you dare touch him," Mama warned. "There's no telling what disease he might have had."

"All right," said Doodle. "I won't."

Daddy, Mama, and I went back to the diningroom table, but we watched Doodle through the open door. He took out a piece of string from his pocket and, without touching the ibis, looped one end around its neck. Slowly, while singing softly *Shall We Gather at the River,* he carried the bird around to the front yard and dug a hole in the flower garden, next to the petunia bed. Now we were watching him through the front window, but he didn't know it. His awkwardness at digging the hole with a shovel whose handle was twice as long as he was made us laugh, and we covered our mouths with our hands so he wouldn't hear.

When Doodle came into the dining room, he found us seriously eating our cobbler. He was pale and lingered just inside the screen door. "Did you get the scarlet ibis buried?" asked Daddy.

Doodle didn't speak but nodded his head.

"Go wash your hands, and then you can have some peach cobbler," said Mama.

"I'm not hungry," he said.

"Dead birds is bad luck," said Aunt Nicey, poking her head from the kitchen door. "Specially *red* dead birds!"

As soon as I had finished eating, Doodle and I hurried off to Horsehead Landing. Time was short, and Doodle still had a long way to go if he was going to keep up with the other boys when he started school. The sun, gilded with the yellow cast of autumn, still burned fiercely, but the dark green woods through which we passed were shady and cool. When we reached the landing, Doodle said he was too tired to swim, so we got into a skiff and floated down the creek with the tide. Far off in the marsh a rail was scolding, and over on the beach locusts were singing in the myrtle trees. Doodle did not speak and kept his head turned away, letting one hand trail limply in the water.

After we had drifted a long way, I put the oars in place and made Doodle row back against the tide. Black clouds began to gather in the southwest, and he kept watching them, trying to pull the oars a little faster. When we reached Horsehead Landing, lightning was playing across half the sky and thunder roared out, hiding even the sound of the sea. The sun disappeared and darkness descended, almost like night. Flocks of marsh crows flew by, heading inland to their roosting trees, and two egrets, squawking, arose from the oyster-rock shallows and careened away.

Doodle was both tired and frightened, and when he stepped from the skiff he collapsed onto the mud, sending an armada of fiddler crabs rustling off into the marsh grass. I helped him up, and as he wiped the mud off his trousers, he smiled at me ashamedly. He had failed and we both knew it, so we started back home, racing the storm. We never spoke (What are the words that can solder cracked pride?), but I knew he was watching me, watching for a sign of mercy. The lightning was near now, and from fear he walked so close behind me he kept stepping on my heels. The faster I walked, the faster he walked, so I began to run. The rain was coming, roaring through the pines, and then, like a bursting Roman candle, a gum tree ahead of us was shattered by a bolt of lightning. When the deafening peal of thunder had died, and in the moment before the rain arrived, I heard Doodle, who had fallen behind, cry out, "Brother, Brother, don't leave me! Don't leave me!"

The knowledge that Doodle's and my plans had come to naught was bitter, and that streak of cruelty within me awakened. I ran as fast as I could, leaving him far behind with a wall of rain dividing us. The drops stung my face like nettles, and the wind flared the wet glistening leaves of the bordering trees. Soon I could hear his voice no more.

I hadn't run too far before I became tired, and the flood of childish spite evanesced as well. I stopped and waited for Doodle. The sound of rain was everywhere, but the wind had died and it fell straight down in parallel paths like ropes hanging from the sky. As I waited, I peered through the downpour, but no one came. Finally I went back and found him huddled beneath a red nightshade bush beside the road. He was sitting on the ground, his face buried in his arms, which were resting on his drawn-up knees. "Let's go, Doodle," I said.

He didn't answer, so I placed my hand on his forehead and lifted his head. Limply, he fell backwards onto the earth. He had been bleeding from the mouth, and his neck and the front of his shirt were stained a brilliant red.

"Doodle! Doodle!" I cried, shaking him, but there was no answer but the ropy rain. He lay very awkwardly, with his head thrown far back, making his vermillion neck appear unusually long and slim. His little legs, bent sharply at the knees, had never before seemed so fragile, so thin.

I began to weep, and the tear-blurred vision in red before me looked very familiar. "Doodle!" I screamed above the pounding storm and threw my body to the earth above his. For a long long time, it seemed forever, I lay there crying, sheltering my fallen scarlet ibis from the heresy of rain.

READING FOR DETAILS

Little Boy with a Big Heart

Pride has many ways of showing itself. Unlike Mr. Whalen, who had such pride in Marvin that he was willing to punch anyone who dared suggest that Marvin was less than perfect, Doodle's brother was too proud to accept a handicapped member into his inner circle.

Consider and discuss:

1. Why was it such a disappointment to the older boy when the baby was born strange-looking and sickly?
2. What was the first indication that "William Armstrong" had a great deal of courage despite his weak heart? Why was he a burden to his older brother? What was Doodle's reaction when he was first taken to Old Woman Swamp? How did this affect the relationship between the two brothers? Was his older brother unnaturally cruel to Doodle? How did Doodle regard his older brother?
3. What is the relationship of the mother and father with the two boys? What place does Aunt Nicey have in the circle?

READING FOR MEANING

Consider and discuss the following quotations in light of the story:

1. . . . pride is a wonderful, terrible thing, a seed that bears two vines, life and death.

2. There is within me (and with sadness I have watched it in others) a knot of cruelty borne by the stream of love, . . .

READING FOR APPRECIATION

Theme

Either of the two quotations given in Reading for Meaning could be considered the theme, or basic idea, for "The Scarlet Ibis." Select the one you believe to be better and explain why.

Effect

This is a story written with sensitivity and beautiful language. The atmosphere of haunting sadness which unifies the narrative is established in the first paragraph and is felt throughout the story. Amidst this atmosphere, the author makes the relationship between the two brothers seem natural and believable.

In creating his atmosphere, James Hurst uses unusual words and expressions, *imaginative language, symbolism,* and *foreshadowing.*

Consider and discuss:

1. Three unusual words or expressions. Note specifically the identification of the time when the story opens, and the indication of something strange about the baby's birth.
2. Three examples of symbolism, in particular:
   a. the many direct and indirect references to a certain color
   b. what the fall season symbolizes
   c. what is symbolic about the coming of the great red bird
3. Two of the most vivid examples of simile and metaphor.
4. The foreshadowing of the ending.

Narrative Viewpoint

From whose viewpoint does the author narrate his story? Discuss the advantage of telling it in first person.

COMPOSITION

In a brief paper, compare the final effect, or impression, of this story with that of "The Hero."

BIOGRAPHICAL NOTE

James Hurst (1922–   ) was born on a North Carolina farm. After studying to be a chemical engineer at North Carolina State College, Hurst turned to the world of opera and began studying voice in New York at the Juilliard School of Music and in Rome. When his operatic career failed, he took a job as a bank clerk during the day and wrote at night. After publishing a number of stories in little-known magazines, he made his first appearance in a national magazine, *The Atlantic,* in 1960 with "The Scarlet Ibis."

Although this poem is not very long,
it tells you a great deal about what the narrator thought was
important within the inner circle of her home when she was
growing up.

Nikki-Rosa

childhood remembrances are always a drag
if you're Black
you always remember things like living in Woodlawn
with no inside toilet
and if you become famous or something   5
they never talk about how happy you were to have your mother
all to yourself and
how good the water felt when you got your bath from one of those
big tubs that folk in chicago barbecue in
and somehow when you talk about home   10
it never gets across how much you
understood their feelings
as the whole family attended meetings about Hollydale
and even though you remember
your biographers never understand   15
your father's pain as he sells his stock
and another dream goes
and though you're poor it isn't poverty that
concerns you
and though they fought a lot   20
it isn't your father's drinking that makes any difference
but only that everybody is together and you
and your sister have happy birthdays and very good christmasses
and I really hope no white person ever has cause to write about me
because they never understand Black love is Black wealth and they'll   25
probably talk about my hard childhood and never understand that
all the while I was quite happy

NIKKI GIOVANNI

Reprinted with permission from Broadside/Crummell Press, "Nikki Rosa,"
from *Black Judgement* by Nikki Giovanni. (Detroit, Michigan, 1968.)

The narrator prefers her home to
"the houses straight as dead men."

in the inner city

in the inner city
or
like we call it
home
we think a lot about uptown   5
and the silent nights
and the houses straight as
dead men
and the pastel lights
and we hang on to our no place   10
happy to be alive
and in the inner city
or
like we call it
home   15

LUCILLE CLIFTON

From GOOD TIMES, by Lucille Clifton, Copyright © 1969 by Lucille Clifton. Reprinted by permission of Random House, Inc.

NARRATIVE VIEWPOINT

1. In "Nikki-Rosa," why wouldn't the narrator want a white biographer writing
   about her childhood?
2. What are some of the happy memories?
3. Why did the narrator consider such
   things as the family's fighting and the
   father's drinking unimportant?
4. In "in the inner city," why does the
   narrator prefer "home" to the houses
   uptown?

5. How do you think the narrator would
   react to the old adage "Home is where
   the heart is"?

COMPOSITION

Whether people have moved frequently from
place to place or stayed for years in one location, they at some time experience a strong
feeling of "homeness," a sense of "this is the
right place."

Each poet has set forth for us her sense of
what makes a home. Now write a brief essay
or a poem in which you set down your ideas
on this subject.

BIOGRAPHICAL NOTES

Nikki Giovanni (1943–   ) was born in
Knoxville, Tennessee. She attended Fisk University and the University of Pennsylvania
and is now teaching literature at Rutgers University. Her prose and poetry have been published in *Negro Digest* (now *Black World*) and
other periodicals. One collection of her poetry, *Black Judgment*, was printed in 1968. She
has recently published a book of poetry for
children called *Vacation Time*.

Lucille Clifton (1936–   ), a poet who lives
and writes in Baltimore, grew up in Depew,
New York, and attended Howard University
and Fredonia State Teachers College. She
was a YMHA grantee in 1969 and a National
Endowment for the Arts grantee in 1970. She
is a member of the Authors League and
Authors Guild. Clifton's books include *Good
News About the Earth*, *Generations*, and *Sonora
Beautiful*. She is coauthor of *Free to Be You and
Me*, which won an Emmy (television) award in
1974.

Gallery

There is an inner circle that embraces us rather than confines us. Within it, we're comfortable; outside of it, we feel exiled and alienated. The very shape of this circle makes it an appropriate and popular subject for artists. Notice the circles formed by the clustering figures in all but one of the paintings in this gallery. Be aware of the feeling this creates in you.

Thomas Hart Benton, **THE MUSIC LESSON**
Mrs. Fred Chase Koch Collection

These two paintings from two different worlds are united by their circles of sharing. In Benton's depiction of a father giving an impromptu guitar lesson to his entranced daughter, the bond of family, of concentration, of a shared interest all combine to form a circle that excludes everything else—including the abandoned doll on the floor. In the scroll print by the famous Japanese artist Hokusai, at the right, the five feminine virtues form a circle of nineteenth-century Oriental womanliness. Taken together, they form a pattern of completion. Violated, they break the circle, and the person—at least in that culture—becomes a fragment of a person.

Hokusai, **FIVE BEAUTIES**
Seattle Art Museum

Edward Hopper, **ROOM IN NEW YORK**
Sheldon Memorial Art Gallery
University of Nebraska

There is a moment in every human relationship when the circle can either be renewed or broken. The two figures in Edward Hopper's painting above have reached that moment. The artist deliberately faces them outward to convey this.

George Seurat, **SUNDAY AFTERNOON ON THE ISLE OF LA GRANDE JATTE**
Art Institute of Chicago

Henry Moore, **FAMILY GROUP,** 1948-49
Collection, Museum of Modern Art, New York, A. Conger Goodyear Fund

The people in Seurat's painting are grouped in many circles of companionship. Note how the elongated shadows emphasize both the privacy and the intimacy of these inner circles. Above, Henry Moore has dealt with a more orthodox family circle. Form and space work together in this unified, massive sculpture.

Two dreamy studies by two American artists illustrate yet another interpretation of the inner circle of human relationships. Mother and son in Daniel Garber's sundrenched painting at the right speak across a chessboard. Yet, the form of the painting informs us that this is more a bond than a barrier. Floating in a sea of green, the nineteenth-century ladies of Thomas Dewing's *La Pêche* (named after the lady with the fishing rod) are playing another sort of game. Will the others be caught by the fisherwoman and complete the circle? Or won't they? The artist lets your imagination answer the question and finish the story.

Daniel Garber, **MOTHER AND SON**
Courtesy of Pennsylvania Academy of Fine Arts

Thomas W. Dewing
LA PÊCHE, Courtesy of Kennedy Galleries, New York City

Mary Cassatt, **THE BOATING PARTY**
National Gallery of Art, Washington, D.C., A. Conger Goodyear Fund

In American Impressionist Mary Cassatt's depiction of a family group, the bold contrasts, bright colors, and sweeping lines are an uplifting use of the form of the circle. Sail and oar, boat and body, the looks in the eyes and the attitudes of the bodies, the contrast and clash of color, all combine to tell the tale of love and attachment and the sharing of a soft summer day. The inner circle is rendered gloriously outward.

SUMMING UP: THE INNER CIRCLE

The inner circles found in the selections you have read are of many kinds. In the first inner circle you saw tense, worried Alfred Higgins and his heartsick, uncertain mother; and you were aware of his uninvolved father. In other inner circles, real and fictional, you saw such people as the reminiscing poet Nikki Giovanni, the slightly foolish Mr. Whalen, and the gallant and tragic Doodle. Each person was different, but all were in need of the love and security found most abundantly in a close inner circle of family or friends.

READING FOR MEANING

Discuss how each of the following quotations applies to ideas expressed in one or more of the preceding selections.

1. All happy families resemble one another; every unhappy family is unhappy in its own fashion.—Leo Tolstoy, nineteenth century.
2. If a house be divided against itself, that house cannot stand.—Mark 3:25.
3. There is nothing more tragic in life than the utter impossibility of changing what you have done.—John Galsworthy, twentieth century.

READING FOR APPRECIATION

The fable, ancestor of the short story, is ordinarily quite short and written with the purpose of teaching a useful lesson, or moral. Its lesson is summed up in a final statement called a maxim or proverb. See if you can recall the maxim with which the Aesop fable on the opening page of THE INNER CIRCLE concluded. Check yourself to see how nearly you remembered the exact wording.

Theme and Effect

The modern short story, if it follows the pattern established by such well-known authors as the French writer de Maupassant and the American writer Edgar Allan Poe, has a basic idea, or *theme*, and strives for a single *effect*.

1. Discuss in what ways you think a short story presenting a basic idea, or theme, would differ from a fable.
2. Some of the selections in this section depended heavily upon their appeal to the emotions to achieve the final *effect*. Recall the ways de Maupassant stated (page 269) that the reader wished to be reached. Opposite each category below, list one or more selections from THE INNER CIRCLE which affected you emotionally in that particular way:
   a. "Amused me."
   b. "Made me weep."
   c. "Made me think."

Narrative Viewpoint

The point of view from which a story is told is a matter to be considered carefully for both short and long stories. Discuss the possible viewpoints from which an author can narrate a story. What advantages or disadvantages go with each viewpoint?

Symbolism

When authors use a concrete thing to stand for an idea difficult to describe, they are using symbolism. How did James Hurst use the scarlet ibis as a symbol to convey meaning in his story about the little boy, Doodle?

COMPOSITION WORKSHOP

THE BRIEF NARRATIVE

All of the short stories that you have read in this unit are examples of a kind of writing called narration. In fictional narration an author tells what could happen or what might happen. A series of imaginary events are presented to tell a story that sheds some light upon human beings and how they feel and act.

Practical writers also use narration to tell a story. But a practical writer uses a type of narration that is best called factual narration. The purpose of factual narration is to tell what really happened as exactly as possible.

Like all practical writers, the writer of a factual narrative must gather information together. The writer can sometimes collect the raw material through direct observation. For a great many topics, however, personal observation is impossible. When this is the case, a writer must turn to printed sources or to eyewitnesses.

A brief narrative report often deals with an event that takes place over a relatively short period of time. The following narrative tells about Charles A. Lindbergh's final approach to Paris and his landing at the city's Le Bourget Airport. It covers a time period of a little more than an hour. Notice how the writer groups the related incidents that describe the event.

It was still daylight when he saw the coast of France. Now Paris was only a little more than an hour away. He was three hours ahead of schedule. That would surprise the people all right! He thought of what he would do after he arrived. He had no visa; that might be a problem. He had to buy a suit; he had only the flying clothes he was wearing. Maybe he should take his plane on a tour of Europe—even fly on around the world. It would demean the *Spirit of St. Louis* to return to the United States aboard a ship.

As he passed the 3,500-mile mark, he knew he had broken the world's record for nonstop airplane flight. In a kind of celebration, he ate a sandwich. It didn't taste very good, but he chewed it down, following each mouthful with a swig of water. He certainly did not have to conserve his supply of water any longer. He crumpled the paper wrapping and started to throw it out the window. Instead, he stuffed it into the bag. He didn't want his first contact with France to be litter.

As he angled in toward Paris at 4,000 feet, he thought how wonderful a plane the *Spirit of St. Louis* was—"Like a living creature, gliding along smoothly, happily, as though a successful flight means as much to it as to me . . . *We* have made this flight across the ocean, not *I* or *it*."

Soon he picked up the patterned lights of the Paris streets, the Eiffel Tower—he circled it, naturally—then headed northeast toward Le Bourget. He thought he saw the airport, but it seemed terribly close to the city, so he flew past to make sure there wasn't another field farther along. He returned to Le Bourget—it was Le Bourget, all right—and wondered why they had all those floodlights lit, but no beacons, no approach lights, no warning lights. He banked over the field to get an idea what he was landing in, then circled lower. The wind sock showed a gentle breeze.

He came in lower. He could see what seemed like a lot of automobiles on a road nearby. What were they doing there? The plane felt funny, he was coming in as slowly as he dared, almost stalling, yet he might very well overshoot the field. He was flying out of the lighted area into unknown, unseen hazards. He sideslipped, held the nose up, finally felt his wheels touch. Should he stay on the ground and possibly run into a building? Or should he gun the engine and take off again for another landing? He chose the earth. The plane rolled more slowly, but it was rolling into darkness. He couldn't see a thing. At least he could turn, and began to taxi over toward the hangars. It was 10:22 P.M. Paris time, thirty-three and a half hours after he left Roosevelt Field.

Le Bourget had been empty a moment before. Now, suddenly, out of the darkness burst an avalanche, a flood, a torrent of running figures. People. They were spreading all over the field; they would engulf the plane; they might get hurt by the propellor. He cut the engine, hoping the propellor would not be turning over when they reached him. The *Spirit of St. Louis* was resting in the center of Le Bourget Airport.

—from Walter S. Ross,
The Last Hero: Charles
A. Lindbergh (Harper & Row, 1964)

The selection that you have just read contains two features that are typical of a brief factual narrative. First of all, notice how the narrative is structured. The entire event is presented in six paragraphs. Each of the paragraphs includes the things that Lindbergh does and thinks during one part of the overall event. The following rough outline shows the structure clearly:

TOPIC: The Landing in Paris

I. At the coastline
II. Passing the 3,500-mile mark
III. Toward Paris at 4,000 feet
IV. Spotting the lights of Paris
V. The final approach
VI. On the ground at Le Bourget

Note that each of the paragraphs does not begin with the usual main-idea sentence. As is often the case in narrative writing, the first sentence in each paragraph merely identifies the single stage in the overall event that the paragraph will cover.

The second typical feature of the factual narrative is found in the order in which the main parts of the total event are presented. Each of the six paragraphs in the narrative occurs in strict time order, beginning from the point where Lindbergh's plane crosses the French coastline and ending at the point when it comes to rest at the Paris airport. Notice also that the individual incidents and thoughts that make up each paragraph are also presented in strict time order. In a fictional narrative, an author will sometimes break the time sequence and flash back to recount a prior event. But a factual narrative will almost always follow a strict time order so that the reader can follow the action as it advances.

Finally, notice that Walter Ross in the passage from *The Last Hero* had to collect information from outside sources in order to write his factual narrative. Since he was not in the cockpit with Lindbergh, he could not rely upon personal observation. The practical writer must always be prepared to dig out needed raw material before the writing begins.

ACTIVITY 1

Find a historical event that interests you. You might, for example, select the sinking of the steamship *Titanic,* Hannibal's crossing of the Alps, the invention of the telephone, the first landing on the moon, or the voyage of the first submarine. Zero in on a relatively brief time period for the event you choose. In the case of the sinking *Titanic,* for example, concentrate on the incidents that took place just before and during the actual sinking. Do not try to relate too many incidents that make up the entire event. Narrow down the time period that you will cover.

ACTIVITY 2

Gather information in the form of notes for the event that you selected in Activity 1. Consult at least two printed sources for factual information about the event, for no two sources ever provide exactly the same information. Make a rough outline that identifies the time periods that each of the paragraphs in the report will cover, and arrange the notes into four or five groupings of incidents that are related to the time periods. Make sure that the rough outline follows a strict time order.

ACTIVITY 3

Write the brief factual report that you have been preparing in Activities 1 and 2. Make sure that all of the incidents included in each of the paragraphs that make up the report are in strict time order.

INTRODUCTION TO
Romeo and Juliet

Perhaps the best-known story in western literature on the theme of tragic young love is *Romeo and Juliet.* When he wrote his drama on this popular theme in 1595, the thirty-one-year-old William Shakespeare could not possibly have known he was creating a masterpiece that would still be appearing on the stage more than three and one-half centuries later. Also, he might have scoffed at the suggestion that his play would have such appeal that it would influence the ideas of millions of young persons about romantic love and inspire the creation of paintings, music, opera, ballet, musicals, and film.

Shakespeare and His Times

No poet and playwright in the history of English literature has a greater reputation than William Shakespeare. That he was an actor undoubtedly helped him to write plays that have real audience appeal.

To fully appreciate a Shakespearean play when reading it, one needs to have some knowledge of what the theater was like in Shakespeare's time. There were none of the elaborate stage sets seen in much present-day theater. For a long time plays had been performed only in inns or taverns. Most of these had an inner courtyard and rooms opening onto balconies overlooking the yard. The performers set up their stage at one end of the yard, and those in the audience who could afford it sat in the balconies, protected from the weather by the balcony roofs. The poorer spectators stood on the ground around the stage. Much of the clowning and buffoonery that was common to stage productions was to keep these "groundlings" from becoming restless.

When theaters began to be built, they generally followed the layout of the inns—roofed rows of seats along all the walls except the one from which the stage extended. The center area was left open to the sky so that action on the stage could be seen plainly. In the beginning there was no artificial lighting, and plays were performed in the afternoon.

The stage was a large platform, at the back of which there were two doors, at the right and the left, with a room or recessed space, sometimes curtained, in between. Action such as that for a street scene or a ball would take place out on the open platform. Action set in a smaller area or room, such as that in Friar Laurence's cell, would take place in the recessed space. Above this space was a raised platform, or balcony, to be remembered as the place where Juliet stood for two of the most famous scenes in the play you are about to read.

The "groundlings," who stood around the stage in the regular theater buildings as they had at the inns or taverns, were the noisy section of the audience. They ate lunch, cracked nuts, threw garbage, and heckled the performers if they didn't like the action on the stage.

Most of the stories dramatized at this time were stories the audience already knew. The audience's familiarity with the story, however, detracted nothing from their enjoyment of, or enthusiasm for, the play.

Another point of interest about the theater of Shakespeare's time is that it used no actresses. The usual theatrical troupe consisted of about fifteen men. With each com-

The Globe Theater, Bankside, in the days of Shakespeare

pany of adults there were two or three young boys who played the female roles in the plays while they learned the art of acting. All members of a company had to be versatile performers because among them they had to handle all the different roles that would be required in doing a variety of plays.

The Playwright's Art

Staging

All of the entrances and exits of the actors in Shakespeare's time had to be made in full view of the audience since there were no outside curtains for the stage. A playwright could not depend on realistic sets or even on very many "props" (stage properties) to create an illusion. Information had to be woven into the actors' lines to help the audi-

ence understand the scenes on the stage. A common practice was to use an introductory speech, or prologue, at the beginning of the play and/or at the beginning of separate acts to give the audience a summary of the story or to call attention to the theme. This prologue was usually spoken by a single narrator, or chorus.

As you will note in *Romeo and Juliet*, the chorus enters first to give in the prologue a brief summary of the story. The action begins in Verona, Italy, where two influential families have been feuding for years. From these bitterly feuding households come a boy and a girl who fall in love. Their love is star-crossed, or ill-fated, from the beginning. Only the deaths of the two young people force their parents to realize the folly of their feud.

In the action of the play Shakespeare demonstrates his mastery of the staging techniques necessary to keep the audience's interest. The play moves rapidly. The entire drama spans less than one week in the lives of the characters. In this brief time the two central characters meet, fall in love, and die. In the two dozen short, action-packed scenes, Shakespeare makes the audience feel the pressure of time and the inevitability of the tragic end.

In addition to fast-paced action to hold his audience, Shakespeare uses contrast— contrast in characters, contrast in mood, contrast in setting. For example, the servants who open the play amuse the audience with their foolish prattle. When Tybalt enters, however, the deadly depth of the hatred between the families is revealed. Shortly after, with the entrance of old Capulet in his nightgown, calling for his sword, humor is again introduced when Lady Capulet suggests he would do better to call for a crutch.

With the entrance of Prince Escalus, Shakespeare introduces the heavy element of authority. Prince Escalus' decree of death to those who disturb the peace of the streets again creates a feeling of foreboding about what lies ahead. Contrast is offered again in the purity of feeling the young lovers have for each other and the coarse and more matter-of-fact views toward romance offered by Juliet's nurse and Romeo's friend Mercutio.

As you read the play, try to visualize the characters as they would have appeared on Shakespeare's stage and note the fast pace of the action and the way the tragic and comic elements are woven together to keep the drama interesting to the very end.

Language

To playgoers of Shakespeare's time, a successful drama was one that combined variety of action with variety of language. Audiences expected to hear passages of great poetic beauty, dramatic speeches filled with bom-

bast, and coarse, boisterous wordplay. Shakespeare gave them all of these.

Within the play there are a notable amount of rhyme, many extended conceits (farfetched ideas expressed in fanciful language), and a number of musically beautiful passages such as those in the first balcony scene and in the farewell of the lovers at dawn.

Act I, Scene 1 opens with *punning*, a type of wordplay that delighted Shakespeare's audiences. A pun may be defined as a play on words based on the similarity of sound between two words with different meanings. The opening conversation of the play between Sampson and Gregory, the two servants of the Capulet family, is an example of punning. The meanings of many of the expressions are strange to you but would be familiar to people living in Shakespeare's day. The marginal notes will help you quickly understand strange words and expressions.

ROMEO AND JULIET William Shakespeare

CHARACTERS

ESCALUS (es′kə ləs), *Prince of Verona.*

MONTAGUE (mont′ə gyü), } *heads of two feuding households.*
CAPULET (kap′yə lət),

LADY MONTAGUE, } *their wives.*
LADY CAPULET,

ROMEO, *the son of the Montagues.*

JULIET, *the daughter of the Capulets.*

MERCUTIO (mər kyü′shē ō), *kinsman of Prince Escalus and friend of Romeo.*

BENVOLIO (ben vō′lē ō), *nephew of Montague and friend of Romeo.*

TYBALT (ti bəlt′), *nephew of Lady Capulet.*

PARIS (par′is), *kinsman of Prince Escalus and suitor of Juliet.*

FRIAR LAURENCE, *Franciscan priest.*

FRIAR JOHN, *messenger of Friar Laurence.*

NURSE, *servant and friend of Juliet.*

SAMPSON, } *servants of Capulet.*
GREGORY,

BALTHASAR, *servant of Romeo.*

ABRAHAM, *servant of Montague.*

PETER, *servant of Juliet's nurse.*

APOTHECARY, *druggist, pharmacist.*

MUSICIANS, MASKERS, WATCHMEN, PAGES, OFFICERS, CITIZENS, *and* **ATTENDANTS.**

Scene: Verona, Italy; Mantua, Italy.
Time: the fourteenth century.

Edited for high school readers.

Prologue

CHORUS. Two households, both alike in dignity,[1]
  In fair Verona, where we lay our scene,
  From ancient grudge break to new mutiny,[2]
  Where civil blood makes civil hands unclean,[3]
  From forth the fatal loins of these two foes
  A pair of star-crossed[4] lovers take their life;
  Whose misadventured piteous overthrows
  Doth with their death bury their parents' strife.
  The fearful passage of their death-marked love,
  And the continuance of their parents' rage,
  Which, but[5] their children's end, naught could remove,
  Is now the two hours' traffic of our stage;
  The which if you with patient ears attend,
  What here shall miss, our toil shall strive to mend.

1. **dignity,** rank.

2. **mutiny,** rioting.
3. **Where . . . unclean,** where citizens' hands are soiled with one another's blood.
4. **star-crossed,** fated for disaster. In Shakespeare's time it was a common belief that the stars controlled people's lives.

5. **but,** with the exception of.

Act I
Scene 1

A summer morning in a public square in Verona, Italy.
SAMPSON *and* GREGORY, *servants of the Capulet family, come into the square, armed with swords and small shields. They carry*

*weapons because in a bloody feud such as that between the
Capulets and the Montagues, even the servants must be
prepared to fight at any moment.*

SAMPSON. Gregory, on my word, we'll not carry coals.[1]

GREGORY. No, for then we should be colliers.[2]

SAMPSON. I mean, an[3] we be in choler,[4] we'll draw.

GREGORY. Ay, while you live, draw your neck out of collar.[5]

SAMPSON. I strike quickly, being moved. 5

GREGORY. But thou art not quickly moved to strike.

SAMPSON. A dog of the house of Montague moves me.

GREGORY. To move is to stir; and to be valiant is to stand; therefore, if thou art moved, thou run'st away.

SAMPSON. A dog of that house shall move me to stand. 10
I will take the wall of[6] any man of Montague's.

GREGORY. The quarrel is between our masters and us their
men.

SAMPSON. 'Tis all one. I will show myself a tyrant.

GREGORY. (*In warning.*) Draw thy sword! Here comes two of the 15
house of Montague.

[*Enter* ABRAHAM *and* BALTHASAR, *servants of the
Montagues.*]

SAMPSON. My naked weapon is out; quarrel, I will back thee.

GREGORY. How? Turn thy back and run?

SAMPSON. Fear me not.

GREGORY. No, marry.[7] I fear thee! 20

SAMPSON. Let us take the law of our sides;[8] let them begin.

GREGORY. I will frown as I pass by, and let them take it as they
list.[9]

SAMPSON. Nay, as they dare. I will bite my thumb[10] at them,
which is disgrace to them if they bear it. 25

ABRAHAM. Do you bite your thumb at us, sir?

SAMPSON. I do bite my thumb, sir.

ABRAHAM. Do you bite your thumb at us, sir?

SAMPSON. (*Aside to* GREGORY.) Is the law of our side if I say ay?

GREGORY. (*Aside to* SAMPSON.) No. 30

SAMPSON. No, sir, I do not bite my thumb at you, sir; but I bite
my thumb, sir.

GREGORY. Do you quarrel, sir?

ABRAHAM. Quarrel, sir? No, sir.

SAMPSON. But if you do, sir, I am for you. I serve as good a man 35
as you.

ABRAHAM. No better.

SAMPSON. Well, sir.

1. **carry coals,** submit to insults.
2. **colliers** (kol′yərs), coal
merchants.
3. **an,** if.
4. **in choler** (kol′ər), angry.
5. **collar,** hangman's noose.

6. **take . . . wall of,** get the better of.

7. **marry,** by the Virgin Mary,
a mild oath.
8. **take . . . sides,** keep on the
right side of the law.
9. **list,** please.
10. **bite my thumb,** make an
insulting gesture.

[*Enter* BENVOLIO.]

GREGORY. (*Aside to* SAMPSON.) Say "better." Here comes one of   **40**
my master's kinsmen.

SAMPSON. Yes, better, sir.

ABRAHAM. You lie.

SAMPSON. Draw, if you be men. Gregory, remember thy swashing[11] blow.

11. **swashing,** smashing.

[*The four servants fight.*]

BENVOLIO. Part, fools! (*Beats down their swords.*)   **45**
Put up your swords. You know not what you do.

[*Enter* TYBALT.]

TYBALT. (*Contemptuously.*) What, art thou drawn among these
heartless hinds?[12]
Turn thee Benvolio, look upon thy death.

12. **heartless hinds,** cowardly
servants.

BENVOLIO. I do but keep the peace. Put up thy sword,
Or manage it to part these men with me.   **50**

TYBALT. What, drawn, and talk of peace? I hate the word
As I hate hell, all Montagues, and thee.
Have at thee, coward! (*They fight.*)

[*Enter an* OFFICER *and three or four* CITIZENS *with clubs or
partisans.*]

OFFICER. Clubs, bills, and partisans![13] Strike, beat them
down.

13. **bills . . . partisans,** long-
handled weapons tipped with
sharp blades.

CITIZENS. Down with the Capulets! Down with the Montagues!·   **55**

[*Enter old* CAPULET *in his gown.*[14] LADY CAPULET *is trying
to hold him back.*]

14. **gown,** a dressing gown.

CAPULET. What noise is this? Give me my long sword, ho!

LADY CAPULET. A crutch,[15] a crutch! Why call you for a
sword?

15. **crutch.** Lady Capulet suggests a crutch is a better weapon
for him at his age.

CAPULET. My sword, I say! Old Montague is come
And flourishes his blade in spite[16] of me.

16. **spite,** defiance.

[*Enter old* MONTAGUE *and* LADY MONTAGUE.]

MONTAGUE. Thou villain Capulet!—Hold me not; let me go.   **60**

LADY MONTAGUE. Thou shalt not stir one foot to seek a foe.

[*Enter* PRINCE ESCALUS *and his* ATTENDANTS.]

"Throw your mistempered weapons to the ground
And hear the sentence of your movèd prince."

PRINCE. Rebellious subjects, enemies to peace,
Profaners of this neighbor-stainèd steel—
Will they not hear? What, ho! You men, you beasts,
That quench the fire of your pernicious rage   65
With purple fountains issuing from your veins!
On pain of torture, from those bloody hands
Throw your mistempered weapons to the ground
And hear the sentence of your movèd prince.
Three civil brawls, bred of an airy word   70
By thee, old Capulet, and Montague,
Have thrice disturbed the quiet of our streets
And made Verona's ancient citizens
Cast by their grave beseeming ornaments
To wield old partisans, in hands as old,   75
Cank'red with peace, to part your cank'red hate.
If ever you disturb our streets again,
Your lives shall pay the forfeit of the peace.[17]
For this time all the rest depart away.
You, Capulet, shall go along with me;   80
And, Montague, come you this afternoon,
To know our farther pleasure in this case,
To old Freetown, our common judgment place.
Once more, on pain of death, all men depart.

[*Exeunt*[18] *all but* MONTAGUE, LADY MONTAGUE, *and*
BENVOLIO.]

MONTAGUE. Who set this ancient quarrel new abroach?[19]   85
Speak, nephew, were you by when it began?
BENVOLIO. Here were the servants of your adversary
And yours, close fighting ere I did approach.
I drew to part them. In the instant came
The fiery Tybalt, with his sword prepared,   90
Which, as he breathed defiance to my ears,
He swung about his head and cut the winds,
Who, nothing hurt withal,[20] hissed him in scorn.
While we were interchanging thrusts and blows,
Came more and more, and fought on part and part,   95
Till the Prince came, who parted either part.
LADY MONTAGUE. O, where is Romeo? Saw you him today?
Right glad I am he was not at this fray.
BENVOLIO. Madam, an hour before the worshiped sun
Peered forth the golden window of the east,   100
A troubled mind drave me to walk abroad,
Where underneath the grove of sycamore
That westward rooteth from this city side,

17. **forfeit . . . peace,** penalty for creating a disturbance.

18. **Exeunt** (ek′sē ənt), plural form of *exit.*

19. **set . . . abroach,** started this old quarrel again.

20. **withal,** with this.

So early walking did I see your son.
Towards him I made, but he was ware of me   105
And stole into the covert of the wood.
I, measuring his affections[21] by my own,
That most are busied when they're most alone,
Pursued my humor[22] not pursuing his,
And gladly shunned who gladly fled from me.   110
MONTAGUE. Many a morning hath he there been seen,
With tears augmenting the fresh morning's dew,
Adding to clouds more clouds with his deep sighs.
But all so soon as the all-cheering sun
Should in the farthest east begin to draw   115
The shady curtains from Aurora's[23] bed,
Away from light steals home my heavy[24] son
And private in his chamber pens himself,
Shuts up his windows, locks fair daylight out,
And makes himself an artificial night.   120
Black and portentous must this humor prove,
Unless good counsel may the cause remove.
BENVOLIO. My noble uncle, do you know the cause?
MONTAGUE. I neither know it nor can learn of him.
BENVOLIO. Have you importuned him by any means?   125
MONTAGUE. Both by myself and many other friends.
But he, his own affections' counsellor,
Is to himself—I will not say how true—
But to himself so secret and so close,[25]
So far from sounding and discovery,[26]   130
As is the bud bit with an envious worm,
Ere he can spread his sweet leaves to the air,
Or dedicate his beauty to the sun.
Could we but learn from whence his sorrows grow,
We would as willingly give cure as know.   135

[*Enter* ROMEO *lost in thought.*]

BENVOLIO. See where he comes, so please you step aside.
I'll know his grievance or be much denied.[27]
MONTAGUE. I would thou wert so happy by thy stay[28]
To hear true shrift.[29] Come madam, let's away.

[*Exeunt* MONTAGUE *and* LADY MONTAGUE.]

BENVOLIO. Good morrow, cousin.
ROMEO.   Is the day so young?   140
BENVOLIO. But new struck nine.
ROMEO.   Ay me! Sad hours seem
long.

21. **affections,** inclinations.

22. **humor,** mood.

23. **Aurora,** goddess of the dawn.
24. **heavy,** depressed.

25. **close,** not inclined to talk.
26. **sounding and discovery,** responding to efforts to understand his views.

27. **be much denied.** He will find it difficult to refuse me an answer.
28. **happy . . . stay,** fortunate in waiting.
29. **To hear . . . shrift,** as to hear a true confession.

Was that my father that went hence so fast?

BENVOLIO. It was. What sadness lengthens Romeo's hours?

ROMEO. Not having that which having makes them short.

BENVOLIO. In love?   **145**

ROMEO. Out——

BENVOLIO. Of love?

ROMEO. Out of her favor where I am in love.

BENVOLIO. Alas that love, so gentle in his view,
  Should be so tyrannous and rough in proof![30]   **150**

ROMEO. Alas that love, whose view is muffled still,[31]
  Should without eyes see pathways to his will!
  Where shall we dine? O me! What fray was here?
  Yet tell me not, for I have heard it all.
  Here's much to do with hate, but more with love.   **155**
  Why then, O brawling love, O loving hate,
  O anything, of nothing first create!
  O heavy lightness, serious vanity,
  Misshapen chaos of well-seeming forms,
  Feather of lead, bright smoke, cold fire, sick health,   **160**
  Still-waking[32] sleep, that is not what it is!
  This love feel I, that feel no love in this.[33]
  Dost thou not laugh?

BENVOLIO.   No, coz,[34] I rather weep.

ROMEO. Good heart, at what?

BENVOLIO.   At thy good heart's oppression.

ROMEO. Why, such is love's transgression.   **165**
  Griefs of mine own lie heavy in my breast,
  Which thou wilt propagate, to have it pressed
  With more of thine; this love that thou hast shown
  Doth add more grief to too much of mine own.
  Love is a smoke made with the fume of sighs;   **170**
  Being purged, a fire sparkling in lovers' eyes;
  Being vexed, a sea nourished with lover's tears.
  What is it else? A madness most discreet,
  A choking gall, and a preserving sweet.
  Farewell, my coz.

BENVOLIO.   Soft![35] I will go along.   **175**
  And if you leave me so, you do me wrong.

ROMEO. Tut! I have lost myself; I am not here.
  This is not Romeo, he's some other where.

BENVOLIO. Tell me in sadness,[36] who is that you love?

ROMEO. What, shall I groan and tell thee?

BENVOLIO.   Groan? Why, no;   **180**
  But sadly tell me who.

30. **in proof,** in experiencing.
31. **view . . . still,** sight is blind-folded. Cupid was often pictured with a blindfold.

32. **Still-waking,** always wake-ful.
33. **that feel . . . this,** that can take no pleasure in this love.
34. **coz** (kuz), cousin.

35. **Soft!,** wait a moment.

36. **sadness,** seriousness.

ROMEO. Bid a sick man in sadness make his will!
　Ah, word ill urged to one that is so ill!
　In sadness, cousin, I do love a woman.
BENVOLIO. I aimed so near when I supposed you loved. 185
ROMEO. A right good markman. And she's fair I love.
BENVOLIO. A right fair mark, fair coz, is soonest hit.
ROMEO. Well in that hit you miss. She'll not be hit
　With Cupid's arrow. She hath Dian's wit,[37] 190
　And in strong proof of chastity well armed,
　From love's weak childish bow she lives uncharmed.
　She hath forsworn to love, and in that vow
　Do I live dead that live to tell it now.
BENVOLIO. Be ruled by me; forget to think of her.
ROMEO. O, teach me how I should forget to think! 195
BENVOLIO. By giving liberty unto thine eyes.
　Examine other beauties.
ROMEO. 　　　　　　　　'Tis the way
　To call hers, exquisite, in question more.
　Farewell. Thou canst not teach me to forget.
BENVOLIO. I'll pay that doctrine, or else die in debt.[38] 200

　[*They exit.*]

37. **Dian's wit,** wisdom of the goddess Diana.

38. **I'll . . . debt.** I'll teach you or die trying.

Tying the Scenes Together: Scene 1

There has been a street brawl. An uneasy peace has been declared. Romeo has made an appearance to moan about an unhappy love affair. From what you have learned thus far about Benvolio, Tybalt, and Romeo, which one would you expect to start the fight again?

Scene 2

A street near the Capulet house. Enter CAPULET, PARIS, *and* SERVANT.

CAPULET. (*Addressing* PARIS.) But Montague is bound as well
　as I,
　In penalty alike; and 'tis not hard, I think,
　For men so old as we to keep the peace.
PARIS. Of honorable reckoning[1] are you both,
　And pity 'tis you lived at odds so long. 5
　But now, my lord, what say you to my suit?
CAPULET. But saying o'er what I have said before:
　My child is yet a stranger in the world,
　She hath not seen the change of fourteen years;
　Let two more summers wither in their pride 10

1. **reckoning,** reputation.

Ere we may think her ripe to be a bride.
Earth hath swallowed all my hopes but she:
She is the hopeful lady of my earth.[2]
But woo her, gentle Paris, get her heart;
My will to her consent is but a part.[3]   15
And she agree, within her scope of choice
Lies my consent and fair according voice.
This night I hold an old accustomed feast,
Whereto I have invited many a guest,
Such as I love; and you among the store,   20
One more, most welcome, makes my number more.
At my poor house look to behold this night
Earth-treading stars that make dark heaven light.
Such comfort as do lusty young men feel
When well-apparelled April on the heel   25
Of limping Winter treads, even such delight
Among fresh female buds shall you this night
Inherit[4] at my house. Hear all, all see,
And like her most whose merit most shall be.
Come, go with me. (*To* SERVANT, *giving him a paper*.) Go,
   sirrah,[5] trudge about   30
Through fair Verona; find those persons out
Whose names are written there, and to them say
My house and welcome on their pleasure stay.

[CAPULET *and* PARIS *exit*.]

SERVANT. Find them out whose names are written here! It is
written that the shoemaker should meddle with his yard,   35
and the tailor with his last, the fisher with his pencil, and the
painter with his nets.[6] But I am sent to find those persons
whose names are here writ, and can never find what names
the writing person hath here writ. I must to the learned.[7] In
good time![8]   40

[*Enter* BENVOLIO *and* ROMEO.]

BENVOLIO. Tut man, one fire burns out another's burning;
   One pain is lessened by another's anguish;
   Turn giddy, and be holp by backward turning;
   One desperate grief cures with another's languish.
   Take thou some new infection to thy eye,   45
   And the rank poison of the old will die.
ROMEO. Your plantain leaf[9] is excellent for that.
BENVOLIO. For what, I pray thee?
ROMEO.   For your broken shin.
BENVOLIO. Why Romeo, art thou mad?

---

2. **hopeful . . . earth.** She is his only living child.

3. **My will . . . part.** Her consent is more important than my wishes.

4. **Inherit,** enjoy.

5. **sirrah,** a term of familiar address.

6. **It . . . nets.** Confusing tradesmen and their tools was a stock comic routine on the stage at this time.
7. **learned,** someone who can read.
8. **In good time!** The servant exclaims at his good fortune that Benvolio and Romeo approach.

9. **plantain leaf,** considered effective in stopping the flow of blood.

ROMEO. Not mad, but bound more than a madman is;   50
    Shut up in prison, kept without my food,
    Whipped and tormented and—God-den,[10] good fellow.

SERVANT. God gi' god-den. I pray, sir, can you read?

ROMEO. Ay, mine own fortune in my misery.

SERVANT. Perhaps you have learned it without book. But, I   55
    pray, can you read anything you see?

ROMEO. Ay, if I know the letters and the language.

SERVANT. Ye say honestly,[11] rest you merry.[12]

ROMEO. Stay fellow; I can read. (*He reads the letter.*) "Signior
    Martino and his wife and daughters; County Anselme and   60
    his beauteous sisters; the lady widow of Vitruvio; Signior
    Placentio and his lovely nieces; Mercutio and his brother
    Valentine; mine uncle Capulet, his wife and daughters; my
    fair niece Rosaline; Livia; Signior Valentio and his cousin
    Tybalt; Lucio and the lively Helena." (*He returns the paper to*   65
    the SERVANT.)
    A fair assembly. Whither should they come?

SERVANT. Up.

ROMEO. Whither? To supper?

SERVANT. To our house.

ROMEO. Whose house?   70

SERVANT. My master's.

ROMEO. Indeed I should have asked you that before.

SERVANT. Now I'll tell you without asking. My master is the
    great rich Capulet, and if you be not of the house of
    Montagues, I pray come and crush a cup[13] of wine. Rest you   75
    merry. (*He exits.*)

BENVOLIO. At this same ancient[14] feast of Capulet's
    Sups the fair Rosaline whom thou so loves,
    With all the admirèd beauties of Verona.
    Go thither, and with unattainted eye,   80
    Compare her face with some that I shall show,
    And I will make thee think thy swan a crow.

ROMEO. One fairer than my love? The all-seeing sun
    Ne'er saw her match since first the world begun.

BENVOLIO. Tut, you saw her fair, none else being by,   85
    Herself poised[15] with herself in either eye.
    But in that crystal scales[16] let there be weighed
    Your lady's love against some other maid
    That I will show you shining at this feast,
    And she shall scant show well that now shows best.   90

ROMEO. I'll go along, no such sight to be shown.
    But to rejoice in splendor of mine own.[17]

[*Exit* ROMEO *and* BENVOLIO.]

---

10. **God-den,** good evening.

11. **honestly.** He thinks Romeo is joking and starts to leave.
12. **rest you merry,** may you be merry.

13. **crush a cup,** have a drink.

14. **ancient,** traditional.

15. **poised,** balanced.
16. **crystal scales,** Romeo's eyes.

17. **splendor . . . own,** my own lady's splendor.

Tying the Scenes Together: Scene 2

Paris has asked Capulet for Juliet's hand. Capulet has sent out invitations for a masked ball. Romeo and Benvolio have learned about this party and plan to attend uninvited. What do you expect will happen at the masked ball?

Scene 3

A room in Capulet's house. LADY CAPULET *and* NURSE *enter.*

LADY CAPULET. Nurse, where's my daughter? Call her forth to
  me.
NURSE. I bade her come. What, lamb! What, ladybird!
  God forbid, where's this girl? What, Juliet!

[*Enter* JULIET.]

JULIET. How now? Who calls?   5
NURSE. Your mother.
JULIET. Madam, I am here. What is your will?
LADY CAPULET. This is the matter—Nurse, give leave awhile,
  We must talk in secret. Nurse, come back again;
  I have remembered me, thou's[1] hear our counsel.   10   1. **thou's,** thou shalt.
  Thou knowest my daughter's of a pretty age.
NURSE. Faith, I can tell her age unto an hour.
LADY CAPULET. She's not fourteen.
NURSE. I'll lay fourteen of my teeth, and yet, to my teen[2] be it   2. **teen,** sorrow.
  spoken, I have but four, she's not fourteen. How long is it   15
  now to Lammastide?[3]   3. **Lammastide,** August 1.
LADY CAPULET. A fortnight and odd days.
NURSE. Even or odd, of all days in the year,
  Come Lammas Eve at night shall she be fourteen.
  Susan and she—God rest all Christian souls—   20
  Were of an age. Well, Susan is with God,
  She was too good for me. But, as I said,
  On Lammas Eve at night shall she be fourteen;
  That shall she, marry, I remember it well.
  'Tis since the earthquake now eleven years;   25
  And she was weaned—I never shall forget it—
  Of all the days of the year, upon that day.
LADY CAPULET. Enough of this. I pray thee hold thy peace.
NURSE. Peace, I have done. God mark thee to His grace!
  Thou wast the prettiest babe that e'er I nursed.   30
  And I might live to see thee married once,
  I have my wish.

LADY CAPULET. Marry, that "marry" is the very theme
   I came to talk of. Tell me, daughter Juliet,
   How stands your dispositions to be married?   35
JULIET. It is an honor that I dream not of.
LADY CAPULET. Well, think of marriage now. Younger than
   you,
   Here in Verona, ladies of esteem,
   Are made already mothers. By my count,
   I was your mother much upon these years[4]   40
   That you are now a maid. Thus then in brief—
   The valiant Paris seeks you for his love.
NURSE. A man, young lady! Lady, such a man
   As all the world—why he's a man of wax.[5]
LADY CAPULET. Verona's summer hath not such a flower.   45
NURSE. Nay he's a flower, in faith a very flower.
LADY CAPULET. What say you? Can you love the gentleman?
   This night you shall behold him at our feast.
   Read o'er the volume of young Paris' face,
   And find delight writ there with beauty's pen;   50
   Examine every married lineament,[6]
   And see how one another lends content;[7]
   And what obscured in this fair volume lies
   Find written in the margent of his eyes.
   Speak briefly, can you like of Paris' love?   55
JULIET. I'll look to like, if looking liking move.[8]
   But no more deep will I endart mine eye
   Than your consent gives strength to make it fly.

   [*Enter a* SERVANT.]

SERVANT. Madam, the guests are come, supper served up, you
   called, my young lady asked for, the nurse cursed in the   60
   pantry, and everything in extremity. I must hence to wait. I
   beseech you follow straight.[9]
LADY CAPULET. We follow thee. (*Exit* SERVANT.) Juliet, the
   County stays.[10]
NURSE. Go girl, seek happy days.

   [*They exit.*]

4. **much . . . years,** almost at the same age.

5. **a man of wax,** a man of perfect figure.

6. **married lineament,** harmonious feature.
7. **one . . . content,** all enhance one another.

8. **I'll . . . move.** I agree to look favorably on him, if mere eyesight can produce affection.

9. **straight,** at once.

10. **the County stays,** Count Paris waits for you.

Tying the Scenes Together: Scene 3

Juliet and her nurse have made an appearance. Juliet has been told that Paris seeks her love. The nurse is in favor of such a match. What is the nurse's character like?

Scene 4

A street near the Capulet house that same evening. Enter
ROMEO, MERCUTIO, *and* BENVOLIO *along with other*
MASKERS *and* TORCHBEARERS. *Although they have not been
invited, they are on their way to the Capulet masquerade party,
confident that their costumes and masks will keep them from
being recognized.*

ROMEO. What, shall this speech be spoke for our excuse? Or
  shall we on without apology?[1]

BENVOLIO. Let them measure us by what they will,
  We'll measure[2] them a measure, and be gone.

ROMEO. Give me a torch, I am not for this ambling;[3]
  Being but heavy, I will bear the light.

MERCUTIO. Nay, gentle Romeo, we must have you dance.

ROMEO. Not I, believe me. You have dancing shoes
  With nimble soles; I have a soul of lead
  So stakes me to the ground I cannot move.

MERCUTIO. You are a lover, borrow Cupid's wings
  And soar with them above a common bound.[4]

ROMEO. I am too sore enpierced with his shaft
  To soar with his light feathers; and so bound,
  I cannot bound a pitch[5] above dull woe.
  Under love's heavy burden do I sink.

MERCUTIO. And—to sink in it, should you burden love—
  Too great oppression for a tender thing.

ROMEO. Is love a tender thing? It is too rough,
  Too rude, too boisterous, and it pricks like thorn.

MERCUTIO. If love be rough with you, be rough with love;
  Give me a case[6] to put my visage in.
  A visor for a visor![7] (*Puts on a mask.*) What care I
  What curious eye doth quote[8] deformities?
  Here are the beetle brows shall blush for me.

BENVOLIO. Come, knock and enter; and no sooner in
  But every man betake him to his legs.

ROMEO. A torch for me! Let wantons light of heart
  Tickle the senseless rushes[9] with their heels;
  For I am proverbed with a grandsire phrase,[10]
  I'll be a candle-holder[11] and look on.

MERCUTIO. Come, we burn daylight, ho!

ROMEO. Nay, that's not so.

MERCUTIO.   I mean sir, in delay
  We waste our lights in vain, like lights by day.

ROMEO. We mean well in going to this masque,
  But 'tis no wit to go.

1. **without apology,** without the prepared speech with which visiting maskers usually introduce themselves.
2. **measure,** dance.
3. **ambling,** courtly dancing.

4. **bound,** leap made in some dances.

5. **a pitch,** any height.

6. **case,** mask.
7. **A visor . . . visor,** a mask for an ugly masklike face.
8. **quote,** take notice of.

9. **senseless rushes,** unfeeling fibers used as floor coverings.
10. **proverbed . . . phrase,** taught by an old saying.
11. **candle-holder,** a spectator.

Mercutio and Romeo

MERCUTIO.   Why, may one ask?

ROMEO. I dreamt a dream tonight.

MERCUTIO.   And so did I.

ROMEO. Well, what was yours?

MERCUTIO.   That dreamers often lie.

ROMEO. In bed asleep, while they do dream things true.

MERCUTIO. O, then I see Queen Mab[12] hath been with you. 40
    She is the fairies' midwife, and she comes
    In shape no bigger than an agate stone
    On the forefinger of an alderman,
    Drawn with a team of little atomies[13]
    Over men's noses as they lie asleep. 45
    Her wagon spokes made of long spinners'[14] legs,
    The cover, of the wings of grasshoppers;
    Her traces,[15] of the smallest spider web;
    Her collars,[16] of the moonshine's watery beams;
    Her whip, of cricket's bone; the lash, of film; 50
    Her wagoner, a small gray-coated gnat,
    Not half so big as a round little worm,

12. **Queen Mab** (mab), queen of the fairies.

13. **atomies,** tiny creatures.

14. **spinners',** spiders'.

15. **traces,** harnesses.

16. **collars,** harness collars.

Pricked from the lazy finger of a maid.
Her chariot is an empty hazelnut,
Made by the joiner squirrel or old grub,[17]
Time out o' mind the fairies' coachmakers.
And in this state she gallops night by night
Through lovers' brains, and then they dream of love;
On courtiers' knees, that dream on curtsies straight;
O'er lawyers' fingers, who straight dream on fees;
O'er ladies' lips, who straight on kisses dream,
Which oft the angry Mab with blisters plagues,
Because their breath with sweetmeats tainted are.
Sometime she gallops o'er a courtier's nose,
And then dreams he of smelling out a suit;[18]
And sometime comes she with a tithe pig's[19] tail
Tickling a parson's nose as 'a lies asleep,
Then he dreams of another benefice.[20]
Sometime she driveth o'er a soldier's neck,
And then dreams he of cutting foreign throats,
Of breaches, ambuscadoes,[21] Spanish blades,
Of healths five fathom deep; and then anon
Drums in his ear, at which he starts and wakes;
And being thus frighted, swears a prayer or two,
And sleeps again. This is that very Mab
That plats the manes of horses in the night
And bakes the elflocks[22] in foul sluttish hairs,
Which once untangled much misfortune bodes.
This is she—
ROMEO.   Peace, peace, Mercutio, peace!
Thou talk'st of nothing.
MERCUTIO.   True, I talk of dreams;
Which are the children of an idle brain,
Begot of nothing but vain fantasy;
Which is as thin of substance as the air,
And more inconstant than the wind, who woos
Even now the frozen bosom of the north
And, being angered, puffs away from thence,
Turning his side to the dew-dropping south.
BENVOLIO. This wind you talk of blows us from ourselves.
Supper is done, and we shall come too late.
ROMEO. I fear, too early; for my mind misgives
Some consequence yet hanging in the stars,
Shall bitterly begin his fearful date
With this night's revels, and expire the term
Of a despisèd life closed in my breast,
By some vile forfeit of untimely death.

55

17. **joiner . . . old grub,** both woodworkers and adept at hollowing out nuts.

60

65

18. **smelling out a suit,** finding someone who will pay for a favor granted.
19. **tithe pig,** a pig due the parson as part of a parishioner's contribution.
20. **benefice** (ben'ə fis), another assured source of income.

70

21. **ambuscadoes** (am'bə skā'-dōz), surprise attacks with swords made of fine steel from Toledo in Spain.

75

22. **elflocks,** matted hair.

80

85

90

95

But he that hath the steerage of my course
Direct my sail. On, lusty gentlemen!
BENVOLIO. Strike, drum.

[*They march about the stage and then exit.*]

Tying the Scenes Together: Scene 4
Romeo, Benvolio, and Mercutio have come masked to the Capulets' door. Romeo, though, has said that he has misgivings about crashing this party of their enemies. He feels something terrible is going to happen. Why do you think Shakespeare has Romeo say this?

Scene 5

The ballroom in Capulet's house where dancing is about to begin. ROMEO, *costumed as a pilgrim returned from the Holy Land, and his friends are among the guests.* CAPULET, LADY CAPULET, *and* JULIET *are welcoming the revelers to the dancing.*

Masquerade party in Capulet ballroom.

CAPULET. Welcome, gentlemen! Ladies that have their toes
  Unplagued with corns will walk a bout with you.
  Ah ha, my mistresses, which of you all
  Will now deny to dance? She that makes dainty,
  She I'll swear hath corns. Am I come near ye now?   5
  Welcome, gentlemen! I have seen the day
  That I have worn a visor[1] and could tell
  A whispering tale in a fair lady's ear,
  Such as would please. 'Tis gone, 'tis gone, 'tis gone.
  You are welcome, gentlemen! Come, musicians, play.   10

[MUSICIANS *play and guests dance.*]

  A hall, a hall,[2] give room, and foot it, girls.
  (*To* SERVANTS.) More light you knaves, and turn the tables
    up,[3]
  And quench the fire, the room is grown too hot.
  (*To an elderly kinsman.*) Nay sit, nay sit, good cousin Capulet,
  For you and I are past our dancing days.   15
  How long is't now since last yourself and I
  Were in a mask?
SECOND CAPULET. By'r lady, thirty years.
CAPULET. What man, 'tis not so much, 'tis not so much;
  'Tis since the nuptial of Lucentio,
  Come Pentecost as quickly as it will,   20
  Some five and twenty years, and then we masked.
SECOND CAPULET. 'Tis more, 'tis more, his son is elder sir;
  His son is thirty.
CAPULET.   Will you tell me that?
  His son was but a ward two years ago.

[ROMEO, *looking about for* ROSALINE, *sees* JULIET *among the dancers, and he instantly falls in love with her.*]

ROMEO. (*To a* SERVANT.) What lady's that which doth enrich
  the hand   25
  Of yonder knight?
SERVANT. I know not sir.
ROMEO. O, she doth teach the torches to burn bright!
  It seems she hangs upon the cheek of night
  As a rich jewel in an Ethiop's ear;   30
  Beauty too rich for use, for earth too dear.
  So shows a snowy dove trooping with crows,
  As yonder lady o'er her fellows shows.
  The measure done, I'll watch her place of stand,
  And, touching hers, make blessèd my rude hand.   35

1. **visor,** mask.

2. **A hall, a hall,** clear the room for dancing.

3. **turn the tables up.** The tables were flat leaves hinged together and placed on trestles. When they were folded, they took up little space.

Did my heart love till now? Forswear it sight,
For I ne'er saw true beauty till this night.

TYBALT. (*Who has overheard* ROMEO.) This by his voice, should
    be a Montague.
    Fetch me my rapier, boy. What, dares the slave
    Come hither covered with an antic face,[4]   40
    To fleer and scorn at our solemnity?[5]
    Now by the stock and honor of my kin,
    To strike him dead I hold it not a sin.

CAPULET. (*Overhearing* TYBALT.) Why, how now, kinsman?
    Wherefore storm you so?

TYBALT. Uncle, this is a Montague, our foe,   45
    A villain that is hither come in spite
    To scorn at our solemnity this night.

CAPULET. Young Romeo is it?

TYBALT.   'Tis he, that villain Romeo.

CAPULET. Content thee, gentle coz, let him alone.
    'A bears him like a portly gentleman,   50
    And, to say truth, Verona brags of him
    To be a virtuous and well-governed youth.
    I would not for the wealth of all this town
    Here in my house do him disparagement.
    Therefore be patient; take no note of him.   55
    It is my will, the which if thou respect,
    Show a fair presence and put off these frowns,
    An ill-beseeming semblance for a feast.

TYBALT. It fits when such a villain is a guest.
    I'll not endure him.

CAPULET.   He shall be endured.   60
    What, goodman boy![6] I say he shall. Go to![7]
    Am I the master here, or you? Go to!
    You'll not endure him, God shall mend my soul!
    You'll make a mutiny among my guests!
    You will set cock-a-hoop.[8] You'll be the man!   65

TYBALT. Why, uncle, 'tis a shame.

CAPULET.   Go to, go to!
    You are a saucy boy. Is't so, indeed?
    This trick may chance to scathe you. I know what.
    You must contrary me! Marry, 'tis time.

TYBALT. I will withdraw, but this intrusion shall,   70
    Now seeming sweet, convert to bitt'rest gall. (*He exits.*)

[*As* TYBALT *exits,* ROMEO *approaches* JULIET *and takes her
hand. His words are like those of a pilgrim who has found the
shrine that he is seeking.*]

4. **antic face,** grotesque mask.

5. **To fleer . . . solemnity,** to
mock our festivities.

6. **goodman boy,** a scornful
term.
7. **Go to!** That's enough!

8. **set cock-a-hoop,** throw off all
restraint.

ROMEO. If I profane with my unworthiest hand
   This holy shrine,[9] the gentle sin is this:
   My lips, two blushing pilgrims, ready stand
   To smooth that rough touch with a tender kiss.   75
JULIET. Good pilgrim, you do wrong your hand too much,
   Which mannerly devotion shows in this;
   For saints have hands that pilgrims' hands do touch,
   And palm to palm is holy palmers' kiss.[10]
ROMEO. Have not saints lips, and holy palmers too?   80
JULIET. Ay, pilgrim, lips that they must use in prayer.
ROMEO. O, then, dear saint, let lips do what hands do.
   They pray; grant thou, lest faith turn to despair.
JULIET. Saints do not move, though grant for prayers' sake.[11]
ROMEO. Then move not while my prayer's effect I take. Thus   85
   from my lips, by thine, my sin is purged. (*Kisses her.*)
JULIET. Then have my lips the sin that they have took.
ROMEO. Sin from my lips? O trespass sweetly urged.
   Give me my sin again. (*Kisses her.*)
JULIET.   You kiss by th' book.[12]
NURSE. Madam, your mother craves a word with you.   90

   [JULIET *goes to her mother.*]

ROMEO. What is her mother?
NURSE.   Marry, bachelor,
   Her mother is the lady of the house,
   And a good lady, and a wise and virtuous.
   I nursed her daughter that you talked withal.
   I tell you, he that can lay hold of her   95
   Shall have the chinks.[13]
ROMEO.   Is she a Capulet?
   O dear account, my life is my foe's debt.[14]
BENVOLIO. Away, be gone; the sport is at the best.
ROMEO. Ay, so I fear, the more is my unrest.
CAPULET. Nay, gentlemen, prepare not to be gone;   100
   We have a trifling foolish banquet towards.[15]
   Is it e'en so? Why then, I thank you all.
   I thank you, honest gentlemen. Good night.
   More torches here! Come on then; let's to bed.
   Ah, sirrah, by my fay,[16] it waxes late;   105
   I'll to my rest.

   [*All exit except for* JULIET *and* NURSE.]

JULIET. Come hither, nurse. What is yond gentleman?
NURSE. The son and heir of old Tiberio.
JULIET. What's he that now is going out of door?

---

9. **shrine,** Juliet's hand.

10. **holy palmers' kiss.** Juliet suggests that pilgrims usually kiss by touching palms.

11. **Saints . . . sake.** Saints do not interfere in human affairs, they only answer prayers.

12. **by th' book,** by formal rules.

13. **chinks,** money.

14. **my life . . . debt.** My life is owed to my foe.

15. **foolish banquet towards,** light refreshments in preparation.

16. **fay,** faith.

NURSE. Marry, that, I think, be young Petruchio.   110
JULIET. What's he that follows here, that would not dance?
NURSE. I know not.
JULIET. Go ask his name—if he is married,
  My grave is like to be my wedding bed.
NURSE. His name is Romeo, and a Montague,   115
  The only son of your great enemy.
JULIET. My only love sprung from my only hate,
  Too early seen unknown, and known too late!
  Prodigious[17] birth of love it is to me
  That I must love a loathèd enemy.   120
NURSE. What's this? What's this?
JULIET.   A rhyme I learnt even now
  Of one I danced withal. (*A call off-stage: "Juliet."*)
NURSE.   Anon, anon!
  Come, let's away; the strangers all are gone.

[JULIET *and* NURSE *leave.*]

17. **Prodigious** (prə dij′əs), monstrous: promising misfortune.

Tying the Scenes Together: Scene 5

Capulet has made everyone welcome at the party but has had to restrain Tybalt from fighting Romeo. Romeo and Juliet have met briefly and have fallen desperately in love. What do they learn about one another that gives them cause for grief?

READING FOR DETAILS

Enemies Fall in Love

1. What penalty does Prince Escalus set for the next Capulet or Montague who breaks the peace?
2. What is Capulet's attitude toward Paris as a future son-in-law?
3. At the masked ball, what is the argument between Tybalt and Capulet?

READING FOR MEANING

Discuss the following statements in light of the play:

1. Young people are in love with the idea of being in love.
2. An inner circle is often held together by dislike or ill-feeling toward another inner circle.
3. People who lack formal education tend to be laughed at or made fun of by those who have education.

READING FOR APPRECIATION

Staging

1. Why would the "groundlings" be amused in Scene 2 by the speech of the servant told to distribute invitations to the Capulets' ball? What kind of actions would you visualize for him?
2. Why would a masked ball be particularly pleasing to Shakespeare's audiences? How does Benvolio taunt Romeo into going?

Language

There is much fanciful language and wordplay in *Romeo and Juliet.* One of the most famous passages in the play is Mercutio's "Queen Mab" speech in Act I, Scene 4. What imaginative pictures does he draw of Queen Mab? Why would Mercutio's description of the fairy queen's activities amuse many in the audience?

Act II

Prologue

CHORUS. Now old desire doth in his deathbed lie,
  And young affection gapes to be his heir;
  That fair for which love groaned for and would die,
  With tender Juliet matched, is now not fair.
  Now Romeo is beloved, and loves again,   5
  Alike bewitchèd by the charm of looks;
  But to his foe supposed he must complain,
  And she steal love's sweet bait from fearful hooks.
  Being held a foe, he may not have access
  To breathe such vows as lovers use to swear;   10
  And she as much in love, her means much less
  To meet her new belovèd anywhere;
  But passion lends them power, time means, to meet,
  Temp'ring extremities with extreme sweet.

Scene 1

*A lane outside the wall of Capulet's orchard, shortly after the
party.* ROMEO *enters alone.*

ROMEO. Can I go forward when my heart is here?
  Turn back, dull earth,[1] and find thy center[2] out.

1. **earth,** his own body.
2. **center,** heart, or, figuratively, Juliet.

[ROMEO *climbs the wall and leaps down into the orchard as*
BENVOLIO *and* MERCUTIO *enter.*]

BENVOLIO. Romeo! My cousin Romeo! Romeo!
MERCUTIO.   He is wise
  And, on my life, hath stolen him home to bed.
BENVOLIO. He ran this way and leaped this orchard wall.   5
  Call, good Mercutio.
MERCUTIO.   Nay, I'll conjure[3] too.

3. **conjure,** call him up by magic.

  Romeo! Humors! Madman! Passion! Lover!
  Appear thou in the likeness of a sigh,
  Speak but one rhyme and I am satisfied;
  Cry but "Ay me"; pronounce but "love" and "dove."   10
  He heareth not, he stirreth not, he moveth not;
  The ape[4] is dead, and I must conjure him.

4. **ape.** Romeo, hiding, is compared to a trained ape that plays dead until his master says a special word.

  I conjure thee by Rosaline's bright eyes,
  By her high forehead and her scarlet lip,
  That in thy likeness thou appear to us.   15

BENVOLIO. Come, he hath hid himself among these trees
　　To be consorted with[5] the humorous night.
　　Blind is his love and best befits the dark.
MERCUTIO. If love be blind, love cannot hit the mark.
　　Romeo, good night, I'll to my truckle bed;[6]
　　This field bed is too cold for me to sleep.
　　Come, shall we go?
BENVOLIO.　　　　　　Go then, for 'tis in vain
　　To seek him here that means not to be found.

[BENVOLIO *and* MERCUTIO *exit.*]

5. **be consorted with,** harmonize with or blend into.

20　6. **truckle bed,** trundle bed.

Tying the Scenes Together: Scene 1

After the party, Romeo has slipped away from his friends and leaped over the wall surrounding Capulet's orchard. Benvolio and Mercutio have tried to find him as they joked about his love affairs. What do you notice about Mercutio's personality that could get him into trouble easily?

Scene 2

Inside Capulet's orchard. There is a balcony directly outside of Juliet's bedroom. ROMEO *is standing in the shadows.*

JULIET: "Deny thy father and refuse thy name."

ROMEO. (*Moving toward the house.*) He jests at scars that never
    felt a wound.

[JULIET *comes out on the balcony. She is unaware of* ROMEO
standing below.]

But soft, what light through yonder window breaks?
It is the East, and Juliet is the sun.
Arise, fair sun, and kill[1] the envious moon,
Who is already sick and pale with grief,   5
That thou her maid[2] art far more fair than she.
Be not her maid, since she is envious.
Her vestal livery[3] is but sick and green,
And none but fools do wear it. Cast it off.
It is my lady. O, it is my love!   10
O, that she knew she were!
She speaks, yet she says nothing. What of that?
Her eye discourses; I will answer it.
I am too bold, 'tis not to me she speaks.
Two of the fairest stars in all the heaven,   15
Having some business, do entreat her eyes
To twinkle in their spheres[4] till they return.
What if her eyes were there, they in her head?
The brightness of her cheek would shame those stars
As daylight doth a lamp; her eyes in heaven   20
Would through the airy region stream so bright
That birds would sing and think it were not night.
See how she leans her cheek upon her hand.
O, that I were a glove upon that hand,
That I might touch that cheek!

JULIET.   Ay me!

ROMEO.   She speaks.   25
O, speak again, bright angel, for thou art
As glorious to this night, being o'er my head,
As is a wingèd messenger of heaven
Unto the white-upturnèd wond'ring eyes
Of mortals that fall back to gaze on him   30
When he bestrides the lazy pacing clouds
And sails upon the bosom of the air.

JULIET. O Romeo, Romeo, wherefore art thou Romeo?
Deny thy father and refuse thy name;
Or, if thou wilt not, be but sworn my love,   35
And I'll no longer be a Capulet.

ROMEO. (*Aside.*) Shall I hear more, or shall I speak at this?

JULIET. 'Tis but thy name that is my enemy.
Thou art thyself, though not a Montague.

1. **kill,** make disappear.

2. **maid.** Juliet, as an unmarried girl, would be under supervision of Diana, goddess of the moon and patroness of the unmarried.
3. **vestal livery,** virgin dress.

4. **spheres,** the hollow, transparent globes in which, it was believed, the stars and planets were set.

What's Montague? It is nor hand, nor foot,   40
Nor arm, nor face, nor any other part
Belonging to a man. O, be some other name.
What's in a name? That which we call a rose
By any other name would smell as sweet;
So Romeo would, were he not Romeo called,   45
Retain that dear perfection which he owes[5]
Without that title. Romeo, doff thy name,
And for thy name, which is no part of thee,
Take all myself.

ROMEO. (*Speaking loudly enough to be heard by* JULIET.)
     I take thee at thy word.
Call me but love, and I'll be new baptized;   50
Henceforth I never will be Romeo.

JULIET. What man art thou, that, thus bescreened in night,
So stumblest on my counsel?

ROMEO.   By a name
I know not how to tell thee who I am.
My name, dear saint, is hateful to myself   55
Because it is an enemy to thee.
Had I it written, I would tear the word.

JULIET. My ears have yet not drunk a hundred words
Of thy tongue's uttering, yet I know the sound.
Art thou not Romeo, and a Montague?   60

ROMEO. Neither, fair maid, if either thee dislike.

JULIET. How camest thou hither, tell me, and wherefore?
The orchard walls are high and hard to climb,
And the place death, considering who thou art,
If any of my kinsmen find thee here.   65

ROMEO. With love's light wings did I o'erperch[6] these walls;
For stony limits cannot hold love out,
And what love can do, that dares love attempt.
Therefore thy kinsmen are no stop to me.

JULIET. If they do see thee, they will murder thee. 70

ROMEO. Alack, there lies more peril in thine eye
Than twenty of their swords; look thou but sweet,
And I am proof[7] against their enmity.

JULIET. I would not for the world they saw thee here.

ROMEO. I have night's cloak to hide me from their eyes; 75
And but thou love me, let them find me here.
My life were better ended by their hate
Than death proroguèd,[8] wanting of thy love.

JULIET. By whose direction found'st thou out this place?

ROMEO. By love, that first did prompt me to inquire. 80
He lent me counsel, and I lent him eyes.

5. **owes,** owns.

6. **o'erperch,** fly over.

7. **proof,** protected.

8. **proroguèd** (prō rō′ged), postponed.

I am no pilot; yet, wert thou as far
As that vast shore washed with the farthest sea,
I should adventure for such merchandise.

JULIET. Thou knowest the mask of night is on my face,   85
    Else would a maiden blush bepaint my cheek
    For that which thou hast heard me speak tonight.
    Fain would I dwell on form,[9] fain, fain deny
    What I have spoke; but farewell compliment.[10]
    Dost thou love me? I know thou wilt say "Ay,"   90
    And I will take thy word. Yet, if thou swear'st,
    Thou mayst prove false; at lovers' perjuries,
    They say Jove laughs. O gentle Romeo,
    If thou dost love, pronounce it faithfully.
    Or if thou thinkest I am too quickly won,   95
    I'll frown and be perverse and say thee nay,
    So thou wilt woo; but else, not for the world.
    In truth, fair Montague, I am too fond,
    And therefore thou mayst think my havior[11] light.
    But trust me, gentleman, I'll prove more true   100
    Than those that have more cunning to be strange.[12]
    I should have been more strange, I must confess,
    But that thou overheard'st, ere I was ware,
    My true love's passion; therefore pardon me,
    And not impute this yielding to light love,   105
    Which the dark night hath so discoverèd.

ROMEO. Lady, by yonder blessèd moon I vow,
    That tips with silver all these fruit tree tops—

JULIET. O, swear not by the moon, th' inconstant moon,
    That monthly changes in her circled orb,   110
    Lest that thy love prove likewise variable.

ROMEO. What shall I swear by?

JULIET.   Do not swear at all;
    Or if thou wilt, swear by thy gracious self,
    Which is the god of my idolatry,
    And I'll believe thee.

ROMEO.   If my heart's dear love—   115

JULIET. Well, do not swear. Although I joy in thee,
    I have no joy of this contract tonight;
    It is too rash, too unadvised,[13] too sudden,
    Too like the lightning, which doth cease to be
    Ere one can say "It lightens." Sweet, good night!   120
    This bud of love, by summer's ripening breath,
    May prove a beauteous flower when next we meet.
    Good night, good night! As sweet repose and rest
    Come to thy heart as that within my breast.

9. **Fain ... form.** Happily would I follow the usual rules of courtship.

10. **compliment,** niceties of etiquette.

11. **havior,** behavior.

12. **strange,** shy, reserved.

13. **unadvised,** heedless.

ROMEO. O, wilt thou leave me so unsatisfied?   125
JULIET. What satisfaction canst thou have tonight?
ROMEO. Th' exchange of thy love's faithful vow for mine.
JULIET. I gave thee mine before thou didst request it.
    And yet I would it were to give again.
ROMEO. Wouldst thou withdraw it? For what purpose, love?   130
JULIET. But to be frank[14] and give it thee again.
    And yet I wish but for the thing I have.
    My bounty is as boundless as the sea,
    My love as deep; the more I give to thee,
    The more I have, for both are infinite.   135

[NURSE *calls within.*]

    I hear some noise within. Dear love, adieu!
    Anon, good nurse! Sweet Montague, be true.
    Stay but a little, I will come again.

[JULIET *goes into her room.*]

ROMEO. O blessèd, blessèd night! I am afeard,
    Being in night, all this is but a dream,   140
    Too flattering-sweet to be substantial.

[JULIET *returns to the balcony.*]

JULIET. Three words, dear Romeo, and good night indeed.
    If that thy bent of love be honorable,
    Thy purpose marriage, send me word tomorrow,
    By one that I'll procure to come to thee,   145
    Where and what time thou wilt perform the rite;
    And all my fortunes at thy foot I'll lay
    And follow thee my lord throughout the world.
NURSE. (*Within.*) Madam!
JULIET. I come anon.—But if thou meanest not well, I do be-   150
    seech thee—
NURSE. (*Within.*) Madam!
JULIET.   By and by I come.—
    To cease thy strife and leave me to my grief.
    Tomorrow will I send.
ROMEO.   So thrive my soul—
JULIET. A thousand times good night! (*She exits.*)   155
ROMEO. A thousand times the worse, to want thy light!
    Love goes toward love as schoolboys from their books;
    But love from love, toward school with heavy looks.

[JULIET *reappears on the balcony.*]

14. **frank,** generous.

JULIET. Hist! Romeo, hist! O for a falconer's voice
    To lure this tassel-gentle[15] back again.   160
    Bondage is hoarse and may not speak aloud,[16]
    Else would I tear the cave where Echo[17] lies
    And make her airy tongue more hoarse than mine
    With repetition of my Romeo's name.
    Romeo!   165
ROMEO. It is my soul that calls upon my name.
    How silver-sweet sound lovers' tongues by night,
    Like softest music to attending ears.
JULIET. Romeo!
ROMEO.   My sweet?
JULIET.   At what o'clock tomorrow
    Shall I send to thee?
ROMEO.   By the hour of nine.   170
JULIET. I will not fail; 'tis twenty years till then.
    I have forgot why I did call thee back.
ROMEO. Let me stand here till thou remember it.
JULIET. I shall forget, to have thee still stand there,
    Remembering how I love thy company.   175
ROMEO. And I'll still stay, to have thee still forget,
    Forgetting any other home but this.
JULIET. 'Tis almost morning; I would have thee gone,
    And yet no farther than a wanton's[18] bird,
    That lets it hop a little from her hand,   180
    Like a poor prisoner in his twisted gyves,[19]
    And with a silken thread plucks it back again,
    So loving-jealous of his liberty.
ROMEO. I would I were thy bird.
JULIET.   Sweet, so would I;
    Yet I should kill thee with much cherishing.   185
    Good night, good night! Parting is such sweet sorrow
    That I shall say good night till it be morrow.[20] (*Exit.*)
ROMEO. Sleep dwell upon thine eyes, peace in thy breast.
    Would I were sleep and peace, so sweet to rest.
    Hence will I to my ghostly[21] father's cell,   190
    His help to crave, and my dear hap[22] to tell. (*Exit.*)

15. **tassel-gentle,** male falcon.
16. **Bondage . . . aloud.** She is held prisoner by the nearness of her parents so she must speak softly.
17. **Echo,** in classical mythology, a mountain nymph who pined away for love of Narcissus until only her voice remained.
18. **wanton's,** pampered child's.
19. **gyves** (jīvs), bonds, fetters.
20. **morrow,** morning.
21. **ghostly,** spiritual.
22. **dear hap,** good fortune.

Tying the Scenes Together: Scene 2

Romeo and Juliet have exchanged vows of love. Juliet has agreed to send a messenger to Romeo the next morning to learn what plan he has made for their wedding. What character traits do you see revealed in this scene in both Romeo and Juliet?

Scene 3

Early morning in a small room in a Franciscan monastery.
Enter FRIAR LAURENCE, *carrying a basket of plants and herbs.*

FRIAR LAURENCE. The gray-eyed morn smiles on the frown-
    ing night,
Check'ring the eastern clouds with streaks of light;
And fleckèd darkness like a drunkard reels
From forth day's path and Titan's fiery wheels.[1]
Now, ere the sun advance his burning eye   5
The day to cheer, and night's dank dew to dry,
I must up-fill this osier cage[2] of ours
With baleful weeds and precious-juicèd flowers,
Many for many virtues excellent,
None but for some, and yet all different.   10
O, mickle[3] is the powerful grace that lies
In plants, herbs, stones, and their true qualities;
For naught so vile that on the earth doth live,
But to the earth some special good doth give;
Nor aught so good but, strained from that fair use,   15
Revolts from true birth,[4] stumbling on abuse.
Virtue itself turns vice, being misapplied,
And vice sometimes by action dignified.

[ROMEO *enters and stands, unseen, by the door.*]

Within the infant rind of this weak flower
Poison hath residence and medicine power;   20
For this, being smelt, with that part cheers each part;[5]
Being tasted, slays all senses with the heart.[6]
Two such opposèd kings encamp them still
In man as well as herbs—grace[7] and rude will;[8]
And where the worser is predominant,   25
Full soon the canker[9] death eats up that plant.
ROMEO. Good morrow, Father.
FRIAR LAURENCE.   Benedicite![10]
What early tongue so sweet saluteth me?
Young son, it argues a distempered head[11]
So soon to bid good morrow to thy bed.   30
Care keeps his watch in every old man's eye,
And where care lodges, sleep will never lie;
But where unbruisèd youth with unstuffed brain
Doth couch his limbs, there golden sleep doth reign.

1. **Titan's fiery wheels,** the chariot wheels of the Titan sun god.

2. **osier** (ō′zhər) **cage,** willow basket.

3. **mickle,** much.

4. **true birth,** its true nature.

5. **being smelt . . . each part.** Its odor is a stimulant.
6. **slays . . . heart,** by stopping the heart.
7. **grace,** goodness.
8. **rude will,** lust or evil.

9. **canker,** cankerworm, eater of plants.

10. **Benedicite** (ben′ə dik′tā), God bless you.

11. **distempered head,** troubled mind.

Therefore thy earliness doth me assure   35
Thou art up-roused with some distemperature;
Or if not so, then here I hit it right,
Our Romeo hath not been in bed tonight.

ROMEO. That last is true; the sweeter rest was mine.

FRIAR LAURENCE. God pardon sin! Wast thou with Rosaline?   40

ROMEO. With Rosaline, my ghostly father? No.
I have forgot that name and that name's woe.

FRIAR LAURENCE. That's my good son; but where hast thou
been then?

ROMEO. I'll tell thee ere thou ask it me again.
I have been feasting with mine enemy,   45
Where on a sudden one hath wounded me,
That's by me wounded; both our remedies
Within thy help and holy physic[12] lies.   12. **physic,** healing medicine.
I bear no hatred, blessèd man, for, lo,
My intercession likewise steads my foe.   50

FRIAR LAURENCE. Be plain, good son, and homely in thy
drift.[13]   13. **homely ... drift,** simple
                                                               and direct in your speech.
Riddling[14] confession finds but riddling shrift.[15]   14. **Riddling,** misleading.
                                                               15. **shrift,** forgiveness.

ROMEO. Then plainly know my heart's dear love is set
On the fair daughter of rich Capulet.
As mine on hers, so hers is set on mine,   55
And all combined,[16] save what thou must combine   16. **all combined.** The arrange-
By holy marriage. When, and where, and how,   ment is complete.
We met, we wooed, and made exchange of vow,
I'll tell thee as we pass; but this I pray,
That thou consent to marry us today.   60

FRIAR LAURENCE. Holy Saint Francis, what a change is here!
Is Rosaline that thou didst love so dear,
So soon forsaken? Young men's love then lies
Not truly in their hearts, but in their eyes.
Jesu Maria, what a deal of brine   65
Hath washed thy sallow cheeks for Rosaline!
How much salt water thrown away in waste
To season love, that of it doth not taste!
The sun not yet thy sighs from heaven clears,
Thy old groans ring yet in mine ancient ears.   70
Lo, here upon thy cheek the stain doth sit
Of an old tear that is not washed off yet.
If e'er thou wast thyself, and these woes thine,
Thou and these woes were all for Rosaline.
And art thou changed? Pronounce this sentence then: 75
Women may fall when there's no strength in men.

ROMEO. Thou chid'st[17] me oft for loving Rosaline.   17. **chid'st,** scolded.

FRIAR LAURENCE. For doting, not for loving, pupil mine.

ROMEO. And bad'st me bury love.

FRIAR LAURENCE. Not in a grave,
   To lay one in, another out to have. 80

ROMEO. I pray thee chide me not, her I love now
   Doth grace for grace, and love for love allow.
   The other did not so.

FRIAR LAURENCE. O she knew well
   Thy love did read by rote, that could not spell.
   But come, young waverer, come go with me, 85
   In one respect I'll thy assistant be;
   For this alliance may so happy prove,
   To turn your households' rancor to pure love.

ROMEO. O let us hence! I stand on sudden haste.

FRIAR LAURENCE. Wisely and slow, they stumble that run 90
   fast.

[ROMEO *and* FRIAR LAURENCE *exit.*]

Tying the Scenes Together: Scene 3

Romeo has talked Friar Laurence into performing the marriage rites that very day. How does the Friar show himself very human in his reactions to Romeo's sudden switch in sweethearts?

Scene 4

A street, later in the morning. Enter BENVOLIO *and*
MERCUTIO.

MERCUTIO. Where the devil should this Romeo be?
   Came he not home tonight?

BENVOLIO. Not to his father's; I spoke with his man.

MERCUTIO. Why that same pale hard-hearted wench, that
      Rosaline,
   Torments him so that he will sure run mad. 5

BENVOLIO. Tybalt, the kinsman to old Capulet,
   Hath sent a letter to his father's house.

MERCUTIO. A challenge,[1] on my life.

BENVOLIO. Romeo will answer it.

MERCUTIO. Any man that can write may answer a letter. 10

BENVOLIO. Nay, he will answer the letter's master, how he
   dares, being dared.

MERCUTIO. Alas, poor Romeo, he is already dead, stabbed
   with a white wench's black eye, run through the ear with a
   love song, the very pin[2] of his heart cleft with the blind 15
   bow-boy's butt-shaft;[3] and is he a man to encounter Tybalt?

1. **challenge,** that is, challenge to a duel.

2. **pin,** the center of a target.
3. **bow-boy's butt-shaft,** Cupid's blunt arrow. Mercutio suggests that Cupid needed only the least powerful weapon to overwhelm Romeo.

BENVOLIO. Why, what is Tybalt?

MERCUTIO. More than Prince of Cats.[4] O, he's the courageous captain of compliments.[5] He fights as you sing, keeps time, distance, and proportion; he rests his minim rests,[6] one, two, and the third in your bosom! The very butcher of a silk button,[7] a duelist, a duelist; a gentleman of the very first house,[8] of the first and second cause.[9] Ah, the immortal passado![10] The punto reverso![11] The hay![12]

[ROMEO *enters in a good mood.*]

BENVOLIO. Here comes Romeo, here comes Romeo!

MERCUTIO. Signior Romeo, bon jour![13] There's a French salutation to your French slop.[14] You gave us the counterfeit[15] fairly last night.

ROMEO. Good morrow to you both. What counterfeit did I give you?

MERCUTIO. The slip,[16] sir, the slip; can you not conceive?

ROMEO. Pardon, good Mercutio, my business was great, and in such a case as mine a man may strain courtesy.

MERCUTIO. That's as much as to say, such a case as yours constrains a man to bow in the hams.[17]

ROMEO. Meaning, to curtsy.

MERCUTIO. Thou hast most kindly hit it.

ROMEO. A most courteous exposition.

MERCUTIO. Nay, I am the very pink of courtesy.

ROMEO. Pink for flower.

MERCUTIO. Right.

ROMEO. Why, then is my pump[18] well flowered.

MERCUTIO. Sure wit, follow me this jest now till thou hast worn out thy pump, that, when the single sole of it is worn, the jest may remain, after the wearing, solely singular.[19]

ROMEO. O single-soled jest, solely singular for the singleness![20]

MERCUTIO. Come between us, good Benvolio! My wits faints.

ROMEO. Swits and spurs,[21] swits and spurs, or I'll cry a match.[22]

MERCUTIO. Why, is not this better now than groaning for love? Now art thou sociable, now art thou Romeo; now art thou what thou art, by art as well as by nature.

BENVOLIO. Stop there, stop there!

ROMEO. Here's goodly gear![23] A sail, a sail!

[*Enter* NURSE *and* PETER, *her servant.*]

MERCUTIO. Two, two; a shirt and a smock.[24]

NURSE. Peter.

PETER. Anon.

NURSE. My fan, Peter.

---

4. **Prince of Cats,** a play on Tybalt's name. In a collection of fables, the name of the Prince of Cats was Tibert or Tibalt.

5. **captain of compliments,** maker of rules of ceremony in dueling.

6. **minim rests,** half rests in music.

7. **butcher . . . button,** one who can select and cut off any button of his adversary's dress.

8. **of . . . house,** of the first rank as a duelist.

9. **of . . . cause,** ready to quarrel over anything or nothing.

10. **passado** (pə sod′ō), a step forward or aside in thrusting.

11. **punto reverso** (pun′tō re ver′sō), a backward thrust from the left side of the body.

12. **hay,** a home thrust.

13. **Signior** (sē′nyôr) **. . . bon jour** (bōn zhür′), Sir Romeo, good day.

14. **slop,** full trousers, cut French style.

15. **gave. . .counterfeit,** played us a trick.

16. **slip,** escape; counterfeit coin.

17. **hams,** hips.

18. **pump,** shoe; "well flowered" refers to an ornamental flower design punched into the leather.

19. **solely singular,** all alone.

20. **single-soled . . . singleness,** weak joke, outstanding for its feebleness.

21. **Swits and spurs,** switch and spurs; that is, keep your horse running.

22. **cry a match,** claim a victory.

23. **goodly gear,** handsome merchandise (spoken here facetiously).

24. **smock,** lady's blouse.

MERCUTIO. Good Peter, to hide her face, for her fan's the fairer face.

NURSE. God ye good morrow, gentlemen. Can any of you tell me where I may find the young Romeo?

ROMEO. I can tell you; but young Romeo will be older when you have found him than he was when you sought him. I am the youngest of that name, for fault of a worse.

NURSE. You say well.

MERCUTIO. Yea, is the worst well? Very well took i' faith, wisely, wisely.

NURSE. If you be he, sir, I desire some confidence with you.

MERCUTIO. Romeo, will you come to your father's?
We'll to dinner thither.

ROMEO. I will follow you.

MERCUTIO. Farewell, ancient lady, farewell. (*Singing.*) "Lady, lady, lady."

[MERCUTIO *and* BENVOLIO *exit.*]

NURSE. I pray you, sir, what saucy merchant was this that was so full of his ropery?[25]

25. **ropery,** joking.

ROMEO. A gentleman, Nurse, that loves to hear himself talk and will speak more in a minute than he will stand to in a month.

NURSE. And 'a speak anything against me, I'll take him down, and 'a were lustier than he is, and twenty such Jacks;[26] and if I cannot, I'll find those that shall. Scurvy knave! I am none of his flirt-gills.[27] (*To* PETER.) And thou must stand by, too, and suffer every knave to use me at his pleasure!

26. **Jacks,** rascals.

27. **flirt-gills,** flirtatious women.

PETER. I saw no man use you at his pleasure. If I had, my weapon should quickly have been out, I warrant you. I dare draw as soon as another man, if I see occasion in a good quarrel, and the law on my side.

NURSE. Now, afore God, I am so vexed that every part about me quivers. Scurvy knave! Pray you, sir, a word; and, as I told you, my young lady bid me inquire you out. What she bid me say, I will keep to myself; but first let me tell ye, if ye should lead her in a fool's paradise,[28] as they say, it were a very gross kind of behavior, as they say; for the gentlewoman is young; and therefore, if you should deal double with her, truly it were an ill thing to be offered to any gentlewoman, and very weak dealing.

28. **lead . . . paradise,** let her think you wish to marry her when you do not.

ROMEO. Nurse, commend[29] me to thy lady and mistress. I protest[30] unto thee——

29. **commend,** recommend.
30. **protest,** vow.

NURSE. Good heart, and i' faith I will tell her as much. Lord, lord, she will be a joyful woman.

ROMEO. What wilt thou tell her, Nurse? Thou dost not mark
me.

NURSE. I will tell her, sir, that you do protest, which, as I take it,
is a gentlemanlike offer.

ROMEO. Bid her devise   105
Some means to come to shrift this afternoon;
And there she shall at Friar Laurence' cell
Be shrived³¹ and married. Here is for thy pains.   31. **shrived,** cleansed of sin.

NURSE. No, truly, sir, not a penny.

ROMEO. Go to! I say you shall.   110

NURSE. This afternoon, sir? Well, she shall be there.

ROMEO. And stay, good Nurse, behind the abbey wall.
Within this hour my man shall be with thee
And bring thee cords made like a tackled stair,³²   32. **tackled stair,** rope ladder.
Which to the high topgallant³³ of my joy   115   33. **topgallant,** summit, height.
Must be my convoy in the secret night.
Farewell. Be trusty, and I'll quit thy pains.
Farewell. Commend me to thy mistress.

NURSE. Now God in heaven bless thee. Hark you, sir.

ROMEO. What say'st thou, my dear Nurse?   120

NURSE. Is your man secret? Did you ne'er hear say,
Two may keep counsel, putting one away?

ROMEO. Warrant thee my man's as true as steel.

NURSE. Well, sir, my mistress is the sweetest lady. Lord, lord,
when 'twas a little prating thing. O, there is a nobleman in 125
town, one Paris, that would fain lay knife aboard;³⁴ but she,   34. **fain . . . aboard,** gladly
good soul, had as lief see a toad, a very toad, as see him. I   seize, in the manner of a pirate,
anger her sometimes, and tell her that Paris is the properer   what he desires.
man, but I'll warrant you, when I say so, she looks as pale as
any clout³⁵ in the versal³⁶ world.   130   35. **clout,** rag.
                                                                      36. **versal,** universal.

ROMEO. Commend me to thy lady.

NURSE. Ay, a thousand times. (*Exit* ROMEO.) Peter!

PETER. Anon.

NURSE. Before, and apace.

[NURSE *and* PETER *exit*.]

Tying the Scenes Together: Scene 4

Mercutio and Benvolio have met Romeo in the street that morning and found that he seems to have recovered his senses. He no
longer moans over Rosaline. Juliet has sent her nurse to learn the
wedding plans from Romeo. How does Mercutio's encounter with
the nurse bear out the judgment you have already made about his
character?

Scene 5

Capulet's orchard. JULIET *enters.*

JULIET. The clock struck nine when I did send the Nurse;
  In half an hour she promised to return.
  Perchance she cannot meet him—that's not so.
  O, she is lame! Love's heralds should be thoughts,
  Which ten times faster glides than the sun's beams,   5
  Driving back shadows over low'ring hills.
  Therefore do nimble-pinioned[1] doves draw love,[2]
  And therefore hath the wind-swift Cupid wings.
  Now is the sun upon the highmost hill
  Of this day's journey, and from nine till twelve   10
  Is three long hours, yet she is not come.
  Had she affections and warm youthful blood,
  She would be as swift in motion as a ball;
  My words would bandy[3] her to my sweet love,
  And his to me.   15
  But old folks, many feign[4] as they were dead,
  Unwieldy, slow, heavy, and pale as lead.

[*Enter* NURSE *and* PETER.]

  O God, she comes! O honey Nurse, what news?
  Hast thou met with him? Send thy man away.
NURSE. Peter, stay at the gate. (PETER *exits.*)   20
JULIET. Now, good sweet Nurse—O Lord, why look'st thou sad?
  Though news be sad, yet tell them merrily;
  If good, thou shamest the music of sweet news
  By playing it to me with so sour a face.
NURSE. I am aweary, give me leave[5] awhile.   25
  Fie, how my bones ache! What a jaunce[6] have I had!
JULIET. I would thou hadst my bones, and I thy news.
  Nay, come, I pray thee speak; good, good Nurse, speak.
NURSE. Jesu, what haste! Can you not stay awhile?
  Do you not see that I am out of breath?   30
JULIET. How art thou out of breath when thou hast breath
  To say to me that thou art out of breath?
  The excuse that thou dost make in this delay
  Is longer than the tale thou dost excuse.
  Is thy news good or bad? Answer to that.   35
  Say either, and I'll stay the circumstance.[7]
  Let me be satisfied, is't good or bad?

---

1. **nimble-pinioned,** swift-winged.
2. **love,** Venus, the goddess whose chariot was drawn by doves.

3. **bandy,** speed.

4. **feign** (fān), appear.

5. **give me leave,** let me alone.
6. **jaunce,** jolting, rough journey.

7. **stay the circumstance,** wait to hear the details.

NURSE. Well, you have made a simple[8] choice; you know not how to choose a man. Romeo? No, not he; though his face be better than any man's, yet his leg excels all men's; and for a hand and a foot, and a body, though they be not to be talked on, yet they are past compare. He is not the flower of courtesy, but I'll warrant him, as gentle as a lamb. Go thy ways, wench; serve God. What, have you dined at home?

JULIET. No, no. But all this did I know before. What says he of our marriage? What of that?

NURSE. Lord, how my head aches! What a head have I! It beats as it would fall in twenty pieces. My back o' t' other side—ah, my back, my back! Beshrew[9] your heart for sending me about To catch my death with jaucing up and down!

JULIET. I' faith, I am sorry that thou art not well. Sweet, sweet, sweet Nurse, tell me, what says my love?

NURSE. Your love says, like an honest gentleman, and a courteous, and a kind, and a handsome, and, I warrant, a virtuous——— Where is your mother?

JULIET. Where is my mother? Why, she is within. Where should she be? How oddly thou repliest! "Your love says, like an honest gentleman, Where is your mother?"

NURSE.   O God's lady dear, Are you so hot?[10] Marry come up, I trow.[11] Is this the poultice[12] for my aching bones? Henceforward do your messages yourself.

JULIET. Here's such a coil![13] Come, what says Romeo?

NURSE. Have you got leave to go to shrift today?

JULIET. I have.

NURSE. Then hie you hence to Friar Laurence' cell; There stays a husband to make you a wife. Now comes the wanton blood up in your cheeks; They'll be in scarlet straight at any news. Hie you to church; I must another way, To fetch a ladder, by the which your love Must climb a bird's nest soon when it is dark. I am the drudge, and toil in your delight. Go; I'll to dinner; hie you to the cell.

JULIET. Hie to high fortune! Honest Nurse, farewell.

[*They exit in opposite directions.*]

Tying the Scenes Together: Scene 5

The impatient Juliet has finally managed to get the talkative nurse to tell her the wedding plans. How does the nurse add humor to this scene?

8. **simple,** foolish.

9. **Beshrew,** shame upon.

10. **hot,** angry.
11. **trow,** declare.
12. **poultice** (pōl'tis), ointment.

13. **coil,** fuss.

ROMEO: "Do thou but close our hands with holy words."

Scene 6

It is afternoon in Friar Laurence's cell. Enter FRIAR
LAURENCE *and* ROMEO.

FRIAR LAURENCE. So smile the heavens upon this holy act
That after hours with sorrow chide us not!
ROMEO. Amen, amen! But come what sorrow can,
It cannot countervail[1] the exchange of joy
That one short minute gives me in her sight.   5
Do thou but close our hands with holy words,
Then love-devouring death do what he dare;
It is enough I may but call her mine.
FRIAR LAURENCE. These violent delights have violent ends
And in their triumph die, like fire and powder,   10
Which, as they kiss, consume. The sweetest honey
Is loathsome in his own deliciousness
And in the taste confounds[2] the appetite.
Therefore love moderately: long love doth so;
Too swift arrives as tardy as too slow.   15

[*Enter* JULIET.]

Here comes the lady. O, so light a foot
Will ne'er wear out the everlasting flint.[3]
A lover may bestride the gossamers[4]
That idles in the wanton summer air,
And yet not fall; so light is vanity.[5]   20
JULIET. Good even to my ghostly confessor.
FRIAR LAURENCE. Romeo shall thank thee, daughter, for us
both.
JULIET. As much to him, else is his thanks too much.
ROMEO. Ah, Juliet, if the measure of thy joy
Be heaped like mine, and that thy skill be more   25
To blazon[6] it, then sweeten with thy breath
This neighbor air, and let rich music's tongue
Unfold the imagined happiness that both
Receive in either by this dear encounter.
JULIET. Conceit, more rich in matter than in words,   30
Brags of his substance, not of ornament.[7]
They are but beggars that can count their worth.
But my true love is grown to such excess,
I cannot sum up sum of half my wealth.
FRIAR LAURENCE. Come, come with me, and we will make
short work;   35

1. **countervail,** outweigh.

2. **confounds,** destroys.

3. **wear . . . flint,** referring to an old proverb: "Small water drops will eventually wear away the stone."
4. **gossamers** (gos′ə mərz), spider's web.
5. **vanity,** earthly love.

6. **blazon,** describe.

7. **Conceit . . . ornament.** Juliet's love is more important than fancy words.

For, by your leaves, you shall not stay alone
Till holy Church incorporate two in one.

[*They exit to perform the simple wedding ceremony.*]

Tying the Scenes Together: Scene 6
What has just taken place in Friar Laurence's cell?

READING FOR DETAILS

The Lovers Marry
1. How does Romeo happen to find out that Juliet wishes he had a different name?
2. How does Juliet ask Romeo to prove that he is sincere in his love?
3. Although Friar Laurence is scandalized at the shallowness of Romeo's love for Rosaline, what good does the Friar think might come of Romeo's love for Juliet?
4. By whom does Romeo send word to Juliet?
5. What do you think is the most important single event that occurs in this act?

READING FOR MEANING

Identify the following generalizations with the characters who express these beliefs in Act II.
1. A man in love makes a poor fighter.
2. Moderate love is more lasting than love that is sudden and violent.
3. Sincerity of intention and action is more important than fancy language.

READING FOR APPRECIATION

Staging
1. Why do you think Shakespeare opened Act II with the scene between Benvolio and Mercutio?

2. The balcony scene is one of the most famous in stage history. As you visualize it, what is there about its staging that makes it memorable?
3. In Scene 4, how does Mercutio's presence on the stage add interest when Juliet's nurse comes to see Romeo?

Language
Many of the lines spoken by Romeo and Juliet in the famous balcony scene have been memorized and repeated so often that they are universally recognized whenever they are quoted. What lines did you recognize as you read this scene?

COMPOSITION

The second act of *Romeo and Juliet* is filled with lines that reveal the personalities of Mercutio, Friar Laurence, Juliet's nurse, and Juliet and Romeo. Choose one of these characters and reread his or her lines as preparation for writing a brief composition on one of the following topics:
1. A "Mercutio" would be popular in any time.
2. Juliet's nurse has great audience appeal.
3. Friar Laurence is an understanding counselor.
4. Juliet is an admirable combination of girlish fancy and mature opinion.
5. Romeo is a young man of continuing romantic appeal.

Be careful to substantiate your judgments with lines or line references from the play.

Act III

Scene 1

The public square. Enter BENVOLIO, MERCUTIO, *and some of their men.*

BENVOLIO. I pray thee, good Mercutio, let's retire.
 The day is hot, the Capulets are abroad,
 And, if we meet, we shall not 'scape a brawl,
 For now, these hot days, is the mad blood stirring.

[*Enter* TYBALT *with other men of the Capulet family.*]

BENVOLIO. By my head, here come the Capulets.   5
MERCUTIO. By my heel, I care not.
TYBALT. Follow me close, for I will speak to them. Gentlemen,
 good den. A word with one of you.
MERCUTIO. And but one word with one of us? Couple it with
 something; make it a word and a blow.   10
TYBALT. You shall find me apt enough to that, sir, and you will
 give me occasion.
MERCUTIO. Could you not take some occasion without giving?
TYBALT. Mercutio, thou consortest with Romeo.
MERCUTIO. Consort?[1] What, dost thou make us minstrels?   15
 And thou make minstrels of us, look to hear nothing but
 discords. Here's my fiddlestick;[2] here's that shall make you
 dance. Zounds,[3] consort!
BENVOLIO. We talk here in the public haunt of men.
 Either withdraw unto some private place,   20
 Or reason coldly of your grievances,
 Or else depart. Here all eyes gaze on us.
MERCUTIO. Men's eyes were made to look, and let them gaze.
 I will not budge for no man's pleasure, I.

[ROMEO *enters.*]

TYBALT. Well, peace be with you, sir. Here comes my man.   25
MERCUTIO. But I'll be hanged, sir, if he wear your livery.[4]
 Marry, go before to field,[5] he'll be your follower!
 Your worship in that sense may call him man.
TYBALT. Romeo, the love I bear thee can afford
 No better term than this—thou art a villain.[6]   30
ROMEO. Tybalt, the reason that I have to love thee
 Doth much excuse the appertaining[7] rage
 To such a greeting—villain am I none.
 Therefore farewell. I see thou knowest me not.

1. **Consort,** associate with, also term for a musical group.

2. **fiddlestick,** rapier.
3. **Zounds,** by God's wounds.

4. **livery,** servant's uniform.
5. **field,** dueling place.

6. **villain,** one of low birth.

7. **appertaining,** suitable.

TYBALT. Boy, this shall not excuse the injuries   35
  That thou hast done me; therefore turn and draw.
ROMEO. I do protest I never injured thee,
  But love thee better than thou canst devise
  Till thou shalt know the reason of my love.
  And so, good Capulet, which name I tender[8]   40   8. **tender,** cherish.
  As dearly as mine own, be satisfied.
MERCUTIO. O calm, dishonorable, vile submission!
  Alla stoccata[9] carries it away.[10] (*Draws his sword.*)   9. **Alla stoccata** (ä'lo sto ka′ta), at the thrust, a fencing term.
  Tybalt, you rat catcher,[11] will you walk?   10. **carries it away.** Tybalt's fencing skill has intimidated Romeo.
TYBALT. What wouldst thou have with me?   45
MERCUTIO. Good King of Cats, nothing but one of your nine   11. **rat catcher,** a cat.
  lives. That I mean to make bold withal, and as you shall use
  me hereafter, dry-beat[12] the rest of the eight. Will you pluck   12. **dry-beat,** bruise.
  your sword out of his pilcher[13] by the ears? Make haste, lest   13. **pilcher,** scabbard.
  mine be about your ears ere it be out.   50
TYBALT. I am for you. (*Draws his sword.*)
ROMEO. Gentle Mercutio, put thy rapier up.
MERCUTIO. Come, sir, your passado!

  [TYBALT *and* MERCUTIO *fight.*]

ROMEO. Draw, Benvolio, beat down their weapons.
  Gentlemen, for shame! Forbear this outrage!   55
  Tybalt, Mercutio, the Prince expressly hath
  Forbid this bandying in Verona streets.
  Hold, Tybalt! Good Mercutio!

  [ROMEO *tries to separate* MERCUTIO *and* TYBALT *and in
  doing so he blocks* MERCUTIO *from using his rapier.* TYBALT
  stabs MERCUTIO *and exits with his followers.*]

MERCUTIO.   I am hurt.
  A plague a both your houses![14] I am sped.[15]   14. **houses,** the houses of Capulet and Montague.
  Is he gone and hath nothing?   15. **sped,** fatally injured.
BENVOLIO.   What, art thou hurt?   60
MERCUTIO. Ay, ay, a scratch, a scratch. Marry, 'tis enough.
  Where is my page? Go, villain, fetch a surgeon.

  [*Exit* PAGE.]

ROMEO. Courage man, the hurt cannot be much.
MERCUTIO. No, 'tis not so deep as a well, nor so wide as a
  church door, but 'tis enough, 'twill serve. Ask for me tomor-   65
  row, and you shall find me a grave[16] man. I am peppered,[17]   16. **grave,** double meaning of "serious" and "in the grave."
  I warrant, for this world. A plague a both your houses!   17. **peppered,** finished.
  Zounds, a dog, a rat, a mouse, a cat, to scratch a man to
  death! A braggart, a rogue, a villain, that fights by the book

or arithmetic![18] Why the devil came you between us? I was   70   18. **arithmetic,** counting his
hurt under your arm.   strokes.

ROMEO. I thought all for the best.

MERCUTIO. Help me into some house Benvolio,
Or I shall faint. A plague a both your houses!
They have made worms' meat of me. I have it,[19]   75   19. **I have it.** I am wounded.
And soundly too. Your houses!

[*Exit* MERCUTIO *supported by* BENVOLIO.]

ROMEO. This gentleman, the Prince's near ally,
My very friend, hath got this mortal hurt
In my behalf; my reputation stained
With Tybalt's slander, Tybalt, that an hour   80
Hath been my cousin. O sweet Juliet,
Thy beauty hath made me effeminate
And in my temper softened valor's steel!

[*Enter* BENVOLIO.]

BENVOLIO. O Romeo, Romeo, brave Mercutio is dead!
That gallant spirit hath aspired[20] the clouds,   85   20. **aspired,** risen to.
Which too untimely here did scorn the earth.

ROMEO. This day's black fate on moe[21] days doth depend;[22]   21. **moe,** more.
This but begins the woe others must end.   22. **depend,** cast a frightening
                                                                           shadow.

[*Enter* TYBALT.]

BENVOLIO. Here comes the furious Tybalt back again.

ROMEO. Alive in triumph, and Mercutio slain?   90
Away to heaven respective lenity,[23]   23. **lenity,** mercy.
And fire-eyed fury be my conduct now!
Now, Tybalt, take the villain back again
That late thou gavest me, for Mercutio's soul
Is but a little way above our heads,   95
Staying for thine to keep him company.
Either thou or I, or both, must go with him.

TYBALT. Thou, wretched boy, that didst consort him here,
Shalt with him hence.

ROMEO.   This shall determine that.

[*They fight.* TYBALT *falls.*]

BENVOLIO. Romeo, away, be gone!   100
The citizens are up, and Tybalt slain.
Stand not amazed; the Prince will doom thee death
If thou art taken. Hence, be gone, away!

ROMEO. O, I am fortune's fool!

BENVOLIO.   Why dost thou stay?

[ROMEO *exits and* CITIZENS *enter.*]

CITIZEN. Which way ran he that killed Mercutio?   105
 Tybalt, that murderer, which way ran he?

BENVOLIO. There lies that Tybalt.

CITIZEN.   Up, sir, go with me.
 I charge thee in the Prince's name obey.

[*Enter* PRINCE, *old* MONTAGUE, CAPULET, *their wives, and
all.*]

PRINCE. Where are the vile beginners of this fray?

BENVOLIO. O noble Prince, I can discover[24] all   110 24. **discover,** reveal.
 The unlucky manage[25] of this fatal brawl.   25. **manage,** conduct.
 There lies the man, slain by young Romeo,
 That slew thy kinsman, brave Mercutio.

LADY CAPULET. Tybalt, my cousin! O my brother's child!
 O Prince! O cousin! Husband! O, the blood is spilt   115
 Of my dear kinsman! Prince, as thou art true,
 For blood of ours shed blood of Montague.
 O cousin, cousin!

PRINCE. Benvolio, who began this bloody fray?

BENVOLIO. Tybalt, here slain, whom Romeo's hand did slay. 120
 Romeo, that spoke him fair, bid him bethink
 How nice[26] the quarrel was, and urged withal   26. **nice,** trivial.
 Your high displeasure. All this, uttered
 With gentle breath, calm look, knees humbly bowed,
 Could not take truce with the unruly spleen[27]   125 27. **spleen,** temper.
 Of Tybalt deaf to peace, but that he tilts[28]   28. **tilts,** strikes.
 With piercing steel at bold Mercutio's breast;
 Who, all as hot, turns deadly point to point,
 And, with a martial scorn, with one hand beats
 Cold death aside, and with the other sends   130
 It back to Tybalt, whose dexterity
 Retorts it. Romeo he cries aloud,
 "Hold, friends; friends, part," and swifter than his tongue,
 His agile arm beats down their fatal points,
 And 'twixt them rushes; underneath whose arm   135
 An envious thrust from Tybalt hit the life
 Of stout Mercutio, and then Tybalt fled;
 But by and by comes back to Romeo,
 Who had but newly entertained revenge,
 And to't they go like lightning; for, ere I   140

Could draw to part them, was stout Tybalt slain;
And, as he fell, did Romeo turn and fly.
This is the truth, or let Benvolio die.
LADY CAPULET. He is a kinsman to the Montague;
Affection makes him false, he speaks not true.   145
Some twenty of them fought in this black strife,
And all those twenty could but kill one life.
I beg for justice, which thou, Prince, must give.
Romeo slew Tybalt, Romeo must not live.
PRINCE. Romeo slew him, he slew Mercutio.   150
Who now the price of his dear blood doth owe?[29]

29. **Who . . . owe?** Who now should give his life?

MONTAGUE. Not Romeo, Prince; he was Mercutio's friend.
His fault concludes but what the law should end,
The life of Tybalt.
PRINCE.   And for that offense
Immediately we do exile him hence.   155
I have an interest in your hate's proceeding,
My blood for your rude brawls doth lie a-bleeding;
But I'll amerce[30] you with so strong a fine

30. **amerce,** punish.

That you shall all repent the loss of mine.
I will be deaf to pleading and excuses;   160
Nor tears nor prayers shall purchase out abuses.[31]

31. **purchase . . . abuses,** buy pardons for crimes.

Therefore use none. Let Romeo hence in haste,
Else, when he is found, that hour is his last.
Bear hence this body and attend our will.
Mercy but murders, pardoning those that kill.   165

[*They all exit.*]

Tying the Scenes Together: Scene 1

Tybalt has killed Mercutio, and Romeo in revenge has killed Tybalt. The Prince has decreed that Romeo is to be banished rather than put to death. Discuss whether the actions of Mercutio and Tybalt are what you would have expected of them. Which of the two characters do you think is the audience's favorite?

Scene 2

Capulet's orchard, a short time after the street fight. JULIET *enters.*

JULIET. Gallop apace, you fiery-footed steeds,
Towards Phoebus'[1] lodging; such a wagoner
As Phaëthon[2] would whip you to the west
And bring in cloudy night immediately.
Spread thy close curtain, love-performing night,   5

1. **Phoebus** (fē′bəs), the sun god.
2. **Phaëthon** (fā′a thon), son of Phoebus. He was allowed to drive the chariot of the sun for a day. Too weak to control the horses, he nearly destroyed the universe.

That runaways' eyes[3] may wink, and Romeo
Leap to these arms untalked of and unseen.
Come night, come Romeo, come thou day in night;
For thou wilt lie upon the wings of night
Whiter than new snow upon a raven's back. 10
Come gentle night, come loving, black-browed night;
Give me my Romeo, and when he shall die,
Take him and cut him out in little stars,
And he will make the face of heaven so fine
That all the world will be in love with night 15
And pay no worship to the garish sun.
O, here comes my nurse,

[NURSE *enters with a rope ladder.*]

And she brings news; and every tongue that speaks
But Romeo's name speaks heavenly eloquence.
Now, Nurse, what news? What hast thou there, the cords 20
That Romeo bid thee fetch?
NURSE.   Ay, ay, the cords.
JULIET. Ay me! What news? Why dost thou wring thy hands?
NURSE. Ah, weladay! He's dead, he's dead, he's dead!
We are undone, lady, we are undone!
Alack the day! He's gone, he's killed, he's dead! 25
JULIET. Can heaven be so envious?
NURSE.   Romeo can,
Though heaven cannot. O Romeo, Romeo,
Who ever would have thought it? Romeo!
JULIET. What devil art thou that dost torment me thus?
This torture should be roared in dismal hell. 30
Hath Romeo slain himself? Say thou but "Ay,"
And that bare vowel "I"[4] shall poison more
Than the death-darting eye of cockatrice.[5]
I am not I, if there be such an I,
Or those eyes' shut[6] that makes thee answer "Ay." 35
If he be slain, say "Ay"; or if not, "No."
Brief sounds determine of my weal or woe.
NURSE. I saw the wound, I saw it with mine eyes,
God save the mark[7]—here on his manly breast.
A piteous corse,[8] a bloody piteous corse; 40
Pale, pale as ashes, all bedaubed in blood,
All in gore-blood. I swounded[9] at the sight.
JULIET. O, break, my heart! Poor bankrupt, break at once!
To prison, eyes; ne'er look on liberty.
Vile earth, to earth resign; end motion here, 45
And thou and Romeo press one heavy bier!

3. **runaways' eyes,** eyes of the sun's horses.

4. **I,** used in word play here with "ay" (yes) or "eye."
5. **cockatrice** (kok′ə tris), fabled creature that could kill with a glance of its eyes.
6. **those eyes' shut,** that is, the nurse's eyes.

7. **God . . . mark.** God have pity on us.
8. **corse,** corpse.

9. **swounded,** swooned.

NURSE. O Tybalt, Tybalt, the best friend I had!
  O courteous Tybalt; honest gentleman!
  That ever I should live to see thee dead!
JULIET. What storm is this that blows so contrary?   50
  Is Romeo slaughtered, and is Tybalt dead?
  My dearest cousin, and my dearer lord?
  Then, dreadful trumpet, sound the general doom,
  For who is living, if those two are gone?
NURSE. Tybalt is gone, and Romeo banished;   55
  Romeo that killed him, he is banished.
JULIET. O God! Did Romeo's hand shed Tybalt's blood?
NURSE. It did, it did, alas the day, it did!
JULIET. O serpent heart, hid with a flowering face!
  Did ever dragon keep so fair a cave?   60
  Beautiful tyrant, fiend angelical,
  Dove-feathered raven, wolvish-ravening lamb,
  Despisèd substance of divinest show,
  Just opposite to what thou justly seem'st—
  A damned saint, an honorable villain!   65
  O nature, what hadst thou to do in hell
  When thou didst bower the spirit of a fiend
  In mortal paradise of such sweet flesh?
  Was ever book containing such vile matter
  So fairly bound? O, that deceit should dwell   70
  In such a gorgeous palace!
NURSE.   There's no trust,
  No faith, no honesty in men; all perjured,
  All forsworn,[10] all naught, all dissemblers.
  Ah, where's my man? Give me some aqua vitae.[11]
  These griefs, these woes, these sorrows make me old.   75
  Shame come to Romeo!
JULIET.   Blistered be thy tongue
  For such a wish! He was not born to shame.
  Upon his brow shame is ashamed to sit;
  For 'tis a throne where honor may be crowned
  Sole monarch of the universal earth.   80
  O, what a beast was I to chide at him!
NURSE. Will you speak well of him that killed your cousin?
JULIET. Shall I speak ill of him that is my husband?
  Ah, poor my lord, what tongue shall smooth thy name
  When I, thy three-hours wife, have mangled it?   85
  But wherefore, villain, didst thou kill my cousin?
  That villain cousin would have killed my husband.
  Back, foolish tears, back to your native spring,
  Your tributary drops belong to woe,

10. **forsworn,** faithless.
11. **aqua vitae** (ak′wə vīt′ē), brandy.

Which you, mistaking, offer up to joy.   90
My husband lives, that Tybalt would have slain;
And Tybalt's dead, that would have slain my husband.
All this is comfort, wherefore weep I then?
Some word there was, worser than Tybalt's death,
That murdered me. I would forget it fain;   95
But O, it presses to my memory
Like damnèd guilty deeds to sinners' minds:
"Tybalt is dead, and Romeo—banishèd."
That "banishèd," that one word "banishèd,"
Hath slain ten thousand Tybalts. Tybalt's death   100
Was woe enough, if it had ended there.
Or, if sour woe delights in fellowship,
And needly will be ranked with other griefs,
Why followed not, when she said "Tybalt's dead,"
Thy father, or thy mother, nay, or both,   105
Which modern lamentation might have moved?
But with a rearward following Tybalt's death,
"Romeo is banishèd"—to speak that word
Is father, mother, Tybalt, Romeo, Juliet,
All slain, all dead. "Romeo is banishèd"—   110
There is no end, no limit, measure, bound,
In that word's death; no words can that woe sound.
Where is my father and my mother, Nurse?
NURSE. Weeping and wailing over Tybalt's corse.[12]   12. **corse,** corpse.
Will you go to them? I will bring you thither.   115
JULIET. Wash they his wounds with tears? Mine shall be
    spent,
When theirs are dry, for Romeo's banishment.
Take up those cords. Poor ropes, you are beguiled,
Both you and I, for Romeo is exiled.
NURSE. Hie to your chamber. I'll find Romeo   120
To comfort you. I wot[13] well where he is.   13. **wot,** know.
Hark ye, your Romeo will be here at night.
I'll to him; he is hid at Laurence' cell.
JULIET. O, find him! Give this ring to my true knight
And bid him come to take his last farewell.   125

[JULIET *and* NURSE *exit.*]

Tying the Scenes Together: Scene 2

Juliet, waiting for her husband, has been told by the nurse that
Romeo has killed Tybalt. Her grief for her cousin Tybalt was less
than her joy over the fact that Romeo still lives. The nurse has
promised to find Romeo and bring him to Juliet before he leaves
the city. What is revealed about Juliet's character in this scene?

Scene 3

FRIAR LAURENCE *enters his cell.*

FRIAR LAURENCE. Romeo, come forth; come forth, thou
   fearful man.
  Affliction is enamored of thy parts,
  And thou art wedded to calamity.

[ROMEO *enters.*]

ROMEO. Father, what news? What is the Prince's doom?
  What sorrow craves acquaintance at my hand   5
  That I yet know not?
FRIAR LAURENCE.   Too familiar
  Is my dear son with such sour company.
  I bring thee tidings of the Prince's doom.
ROMEO. What less than doomsday[1] is the Prince's doom?
FRIAR LAURENCE. A gentler judgment vanished[2] from his
   lips;   10
  Not body's death, but body's banishment.
ROMEO. Ha, banishment? Be merciful, say "death";
  For exile hath more terror in his look,
  Much more than death. Do not say "banishment."
FRIAR LAURENCE. Hence from Verona art thou banishèd.   15
  Be patient, for the world is broad and wide.
ROMEO. There is no world without Verona walls,
  But purgatory, torture, hell itself.
  Hence banishèd is banished from the world,
  And world's exile is death. Then "banishèd"   20
  Is death mistermed. Calling death "banishèd,"
  Thou cut'st my head off with a golden axe,
  And smilest upon the stroke that murders me.
FRIAR LAURENCE. O deadly sin! O rude unthankfulness!
  Thy fault our law calls death, but the kind Prince,   25
  Taking thy part, hath rushed aside the law,
  And turned that black word "death" to "banishment."
  This is dear mercy, and thou seest it not.
ROMEO. 'Tis torture, and not mercy. Heaven is here,
  Where Juliet lives; and every cat and dog   30
  And little mouse, every unworthy thing,
  Live here in heaven and may look on her;
  But Romeo may not, he is banishèd.
  And sayest thou yet that exile is not death?
  Hadst thou no poison mixed, no sharp-ground knife,   35
  No sudden mean of death, though ne'er so mean,

1. **doomsday,** death.
2. **vanished,** issued.

But "banishèd" to kill me—"banishèd"?
O Friar, the damnèd use that word in hell;
Howling attends it! How hast thou the heart,
Being a divine, a ghostly confessor,   40
A sin-absolver, and my friend professed,
To mangle me with that word "banishèd"?

FRIAR LAURENCE. Thou fond mad man, hear me a little
  speak.

ROMEO. O, thou wilt speak again of banishment.

FRIAR LAURENCE. I'll give thee armor to keep off that word; 45
  Adversity's sweet milk, philosophy,
  To comfort thee, though thou art banishèd.

ROMEO. Yet "banishèd"? Hang up philosophy!
  Unless philosophy can make a Juliet,
  Displant a town, reverse a prince's doom,   50
  It helps not, it prevails not. Talk no more.

FRIAR LAURENCE. O, then I see that madmen have no ears.

ROMEO. How should they, when that wise men have no eyes?

FRIAR LAURENCE. Let me dispute with thee of thy estate.[3]

ROMEO. Thou canst not speak of that thou dost not feel. 55
  Wert thou as young as I, Juliet thy love,
  An hour but married, Tybalt murdered,
  Doting like me, and like me banishèd,
  Then mightst thou speak, then mightst thou tear thy hair,
  And fall upon the ground, as I do now,   60
  Taking the measure of an unmade grave.

3. **estate,** situation.

[NURSE *knocks on the door.*]

FRIAR LAURENCE. Arise, one knocks. Good Romeo, hide thyself.

ROMEO. Not I; unless the breath of heart-sick groans
  Mistlike infold me from the search of eyes.

[NURSE *knocks again.*]

FRIAR LAURENCE. Hark, how they knock! Who's there?   65
  Romeo, arise;
  Thou wilt be taken.—Stay awhile!—Stand up;

[*Knocking grows louder.*]

Run to my study.—By and by!—God's will,
What simpleness is this.—I come, I come!
Who knocks so hard? Whence come you? What's your will?

[NURSE *enters.*]

NURSE. Let me come in, and you shall know my errand.　　　　70
　　I come from Lady Juliet.
FRIAR LAURENCE.　　　　Welcome then.
NURSE. O holy Friar, O, tell me, holy Friar,
　　Where is my lady's lord, where's Romeo?
FRIAR LAURENCE. There on the ground, with his own tears
　　made drunk.
NURSE. O, he is even in my mistress' case,[4]　　　　75
　　Just in her case! O woeful sympathy!
　　Piteous predicament! Even so lies she,
　　Blubbering and weeping, weeping and blubbering.
　　Stand up, stand up; stand, and you be a man.
　　For Juliet's sake, for her sake, rise and stand!　　　　80
　　Why should you fall into so deep an O?[5]
ROMEO. (*Rises.*) Nurse—.
NURSE. Ah sir, ah sir! Death's the end of all.
ROMEO. Spakest thou of Juliet? How is it with her?
　　Doth not she think me an old[6] murderer,　　　　85
　　Now I have stained the childhood of our joy
　　With blood removed but little from her own?
　　Where is she? And how doth she! And what says
　　My concealed lady to our cancelled love?
NURSE. O, she says nothing, sir, but weeps and weeps,　　　　90
　　And now falls on her bed, and then starts up,
　　And Tybalt calls, and then on Romeo cries,
　　And then down falls again.
ROMEO.　　　　　　　As if that name,
　　Shot from the deadly level[7] of a gun,
　　Did murder her; as that name's cursèd hand　　　　95
　　Murdered her kinsman. O, tell me, Friar, tell me,
　　In what vile part of this anatomy
　　Doth my name lodge? Tell me, that I may sack
　　The hateful mansion.

[ROMEO *draws his dagger and offers to stab himself.* NURSE
snatches it away.]

FRIAR LAURENCE. Hold thy desperate hand.
　　Art thou a man? Thy form cries out thou art;　　　　100
　　Thy tears are womanish, thy wild acts denote
　　The unreasonable fury of a beast.
　　Unseemly woman in a seeming man!
　　And ill-beseeming beast in seeming both!
　　Thou hast amazed me. By my holy order,　　　　105
　　I thought thy disposition better tempered.
　　Hast thou slain Tybalt? Wilt thou slay thyself,
　　And slay thy lady that in thy life lives,

4. **O . . . case.** Romeo is in the
same state as Juliet.

5. **O,** fit of grief.

6. **old,** calloused.

7. **level,** aim.

By doing damnèd hate upon thyself?
Why railest[8] thou on thy birth, the heaven, and earth,
Since birth, and heaven, and earth, all three do meet
In thee at once; which thou at once wouldst lose?
What, rouse thee, man! Thy Juliet is alive,
For whose dear sake thou wast but lately dead.
There art thou happy. Tybalt would kill thee,
But thou slewest Tybalt; there art thou happy too.
The law, that threatened death, becomes thy friend
And turns it to exile; there art thou happy.
A pack of blessings light upon thy back,
Happiness courts thee in her best array;
But like a misbehaved and sullen wench,
Thou pouts up thy fortune and thy love.
Take heed, take heed, for such die miserable.
Go get thee to thy love, as was decreed,
Ascend her chamber, hence and comfort her.
But look thou stay not till the watch be set,[9]
For then thou canst not pass to Mantua,
Where thou shalt live till we can find a time
To blaze[10] your marriage, reconcile your friends,[11]
Beg pardon of the Prince, and call thee back
With twenty hundred thousand times more joy
Than thou went'st forth in lamentation.
Go before, Nurse. Commend me to thy lady,
And bid her hasten all the house to bed,
Which heavy sorrow makes them apt unto.
Romeo is coming.

NURSE. O Lord, I could have stayed here all the night
To hear good counsel. O, what learning is!
My lord, I'll tell my lady you will come.

ROMEO. Do so, and bid my sweet prepare to chide.

NURSE. Here, sir, a ring she bid me give you, sir.
Hie you, make haste, for it grows very late.

[NURSE *exits.*]

ROMEO. How well my comfort is revived by this!

FRIAR LAURENCE. Go hence; good night; and here stands all
    your state—
Either be gone before the watch be set,
Or by the break of day disguised from hence.
Sojourn in Mantua; I'll find out your man,
And he shall signify from time to time
Every good hap to you that chances here.
Give me thy hand; 'tis late. Farewell; good night.

110

115

120

125

130

135

140

145

150

8. **railest,** complain.

9. **watch be set,** the night watch takes up its post at the city gates.

10. **blaze,** announce.
11. **friends,** families.

ROMEO. But that a joy past joy calls out on me,
   It were a grief so brief to part with thee.
   Farewell.

   [ROMEO *exits.*]

Tying the Scenes Together: Scene 3

Romeo has learned from the Friar that the Prince has ordered
banishment rather than death. The Friar has comforted Romeo
when he despaired and has suggested he go to Mantua to live
until the Prince grants a pardon. The nurse has told Romeo to
hurry to comfort Juliet. The Friar has warned him he must leave
Verona before daybreak. Does Romeo show himself to be weak or
strong in this scene? Is Juliet any stronger emotionally?

Scene 4

Capulet's house, later that night. Enter CAPULET, LADY
CAPULET, *and* PARIS.

CAPULET. Things have fallen out, sir, so unluckily
   That we have had no time to move[1] our daughter.
   Look you, she loved her kinsman Tybalt dearly,
   And so did I. Well, we were born to die.
   'Tis very late; she'll not come down tonight.   5
   I promise you, but for your company,
   I would have been abed an hour ago.
PARIS. These times of woe afford no times to woo.
   Madam, good night. Commend me to your daughter.
LADY CAPULET. I will, and know her mind early tomorrow;   10
   Tonight she's mewed up to her heaviness.[2]
CAPULET. Sir Paris, I will make a desperate tender[3]
   Of my child's love. I think she will be ruled
   In all respects by me; nay more, I doubt it not.
   Wife, go you to her ere you go to bed;   15
   Acquaint her here of my son Paris' love
   And bid her, mark you me, on Wednesday next—
   But soft! What day is this?
PARIS.   Monday, my lord.
CAPULET. Monday? Ha, ha! Well, Wednesday is too soon.
   A Thursday let it be, a Thursday, tell her,   20
   She shall be married to this noble earl.
   Will you be ready? Do you like this haste?
   We'll keep no great ado—a friend or two;
   For hark you, Tybalt being slain so late,
   It may be thought we held him carelessly,   25

1. **move,** talk with.

2. **mewed . . . heaviness,** shut
up with her grief.
3. **desperate tender,** rash offer.

Being our kinsman, if we revel much.
Therefore we'll have some half a dozen friends,
And there an end. But what say you to Thursday?
PARIS. My lord, I would that Thursday were tomorrow.
CAPULET. Well, get you gone. A Thursday be it then.   30
Go you to Juliet ere you go to bed;
Prepare her, wife, against this wedding day.
Farewell, my lord. Light to my chamber, ho!
Afore me, it is so very late that we
May call it early by and by. Good night.   35

Tying the Scenes Together: Scene 4

Capulet decides that Paris and Juliet will marry in three days.
What does this show about him as a father?

Scene 5

Capulet's orchard. ROMEO *and* JULIET *enter from her room to
the balcony.*

JULIET. Wilt thou be gone? It is not yet near day.
It was the nightingale, and not the lark,[1]
That pierced the fearful hollow of thine ear;
Nightly she sings on yond pomegranate tree.
Believe me, love, it was the nightingale.   5
ROMEO. It was the lark, the herald of the morn,
No nightingale. Look, love, what envious streaks
Do lace the severing clouds in yonder east.
Night's candles[2] are burnt out, and jocund[3] day   10
Stands tiptoe on the misty mountaintops.
I must be gone and live, or stay and die.
JULIET. Yond light is not daylight, I know it, I.
It is some meteor that the sun exhales,
To be to thee this night a torchbearer,
And light thee on thy way to Mantua.   15
Therefore stay yet; thou need'st not to be gone.
ROMEO. Let me be ta'en, let me be put to death.
I am content, so thou wilt have it so.
I'll say yon gray is not the morning's eye,
'Tis but the pale reflex of Cynthia's[4] brow;   20
Nor that is not the lark whose notes do beat
The vaulty heaven so high above our heads.
I have more care to stay than will to go.
Come, death, and welcome, Juliet wills it so.
How is't, my soul? Let's talk; it is not day.   25

1. **nightingale . . . lark.** The nightingale is a night songster, while the lark sings at daybreak.

2. **Night's candles,** the stars.
3. **jocund** (jok'ənd), cheery.

4. **Cynthia,** another name for the moon goddess, Diana.

JULIET. It is, it is; hie hence, be gone, away!
  It is the lark that sings so out of tune,
  Straining harsh discords and unpleasing sharps.
  Some say the lark makes sweet division;[5]
  This doth not so, for she divideth us.   30
  Some say the lark and loathèd toad change eyes;[6]
  O, now I would they had changed voices too,
  Since arm from arm that voice doth us affray,[7]
  Hunting thee hence with hunt's-up[8] to the day.
  O, now be gone! More light and light it grows.   35
ROMEO. More light and light, more dark and dark our woes.

[NURSE *enters*.]

NURSE. Madam!
JULIET. Nurse?
NURSE. Your lady mother is coming to your chamber.
  The day is broke; be wary, look about. (*She exits.*)   40
JULIET. Then, window, let day in, and let life out.
ROMEO. Farewell, farewell! One kiss, and I'll descend.

[*He descends the rope ladder.*]

JULIET. Art thou gone so, love, lord, ay husband, friend?
  I must hear from thee every day in the hour,
  For in a minute there are many days.   45
  O, by this count I shall be much in years
  Ere I again behold my Romeo!
ROMEO. Farewell!
  I will omit no opportunity
  That may convey my greetings, love, to thee.   50
JULIET. O, think'st thou we shall ever meet again?
ROMEO. I doubt it not; and all these woes shall serve
  For sweet discourses in our times to come.
JULIET. O God, I have an ill-divining soul![9]
  Methinks I see thee, now thou art so low,[10]   55
  As one dead in the bottom of a tomb.
  Either my eyesight fails, or thou lookest pale.
ROMEO. And trust me, love, in my eye so do you.
  Dry sorrow drinks our blood.[11] Adieu, adieu!

[ROMEO *exits*.]

JULIET. O fortune, fortune! All men call thee fickle;   60
  If thou art fickle, what dost thou with him
  That is renowned for faith? Be fickle, fortune,
  For then I hope thou wilt not keep him long,
  But send him back.

5. **division,** melody.

6. **change eyes,** a folk tale.

7. **affray,** frighten.
8. **hunt's-up,** morning call to awaken hunters.

9. **ill-divining soul,** one that foresees evil.
10. **low.** Romeo now stands on the ground.

11. **Dry . . . blood.** Sorrow was believed to dry up the blood.

LADY CAPULET. (*Off-stage.*) Ho, daughter! Are you up?   65
JULIET. Who is't that calls? It is my lady mother.
  Is she not down[12] so late, or up so early?
  What unaccustomed cause procures[13] her hither?

12. **down,** in bed.
13. **procures,** brings.

[LADY CAPULET *enters.*]

LADY CAPULET. Why, how now, Juliet?
JULIET.   Madam, I am not
  well.
LADY CAPULET. Evermore weeping for your cousin's death?   70
  What, wilt thou wash him from his grave with tears?
  And if thou couldst, thou couldst not make him live.
  Therefore have done. Some grief shows much of love;
  But much of grief shows still some want of wit.
JULIET. Yet let me weep for such a feeling loss.   75
LADY CAPULET. So shall you feel the loss, but not the friend
  Which you weep for.
JULIET.   Feeling so the loss,
  I cannot choose but ever weep the friend.
LADY CAPULET. Well, girl, thou weep'st not so much for his
  death
  As that the villain lives which slaughtered him.   80
JULIET. What villain, madam?
LADY CAPULET.   That same villain Romeo.
JULIET. (*Aside.*) Villain and he be many miles asunder.—
  God pardon him; I do with all my heart.
  And yet no man like he doth grieve my heart.
LADY CAPULET. That is because the traitor murderer lives.   85
JULIET. Ay, madam, from the reach of these my hands.
  Would none but I might venge my cousin's death!
LADY CAPULET. We will have vengeance for it, fear thou not.
  Then weep no more. I'll send to one in Mantua,
  Where that same banished runagate doth live,   90
  Shall give him such an unaccustomed dram,[14]
  That he shall soon keep Tybalt company.
  And then I hope thou wilt be satisfied.

14. **dram,** drink; here, poisoned.

JULIET. Indeed I never shall be satisfied
  With Romeo till I behold him—dead[15]—   95
  Is my poor heart so for a kinsman vexed.
  Madam, if you could find out but a man
  To bear a poison, I would temper it,
  That Romeo should, upon receipt thereof,
  Soon sleep in quiet. O, how my heart abhors   100
  To hear him named, and cannot come to him,

15. **dead.** Juliet arranges her words in such a way that Lady Capulet will mistakenly think that Juliet wishes to see Romeo dead.

To wreak the love I bore my cousin
Upon his body that hath slaughtered him!

LADY CAPULET. Find thou the means, and I'll find such a
man.

But now I'll tell thee joyful tidings, girl. 105

JULIET. And joy comes well in such a needy time.
What are they, beseech your ladyship?

LADY CAPULET. Well, well, thou hast a careful father, child,
One who, to put thee from thy heaviness,
Hath sorted out a sudden day of joy, 110
That thou expects not nor I looked not for.

JULIET. Madam, in happy time! What day is that?

LADY CAPULET. Marry, my child, early next Thursday morn
The gallant, young, and noble gentleman,
The County Paris, at Saint Peter's Church, 115
Shall happily make thee there a joyful bride.

JULIET. Now by Saint Peter's Church, and Peter too,
He shall not make me there a joyful bride!
I wonder at this haste, that I must wed
Ere he that should be husband comes to woo. 120
I pray you tell my lord and father, madam,
I will not marry yet, and when I do, I swear
It shall be Romeo, whom you know I hate,
Rather than Paris. These are news indeed!

LADY CAPULET. Here comes your father, tell him so yourself, 125
And see how he will take it at your hands.

[*Enter* CAPULET *and* NURSE.]

CAPULET. When the sun sets, the earth doth drizzle dew;
But for the sunset of my brother's son
It rains downright.
How now? A conduit,[16] girl? What, still in tears? 130   16. **conduit,** fountain.
Evermore showering? In one little body
Thou counterfeits a bark, a sea, a wind;
For still thy eyes, which I may call the sea,
Do ebb and flow with tears; the bark thy body is,
Sailing in this salt flood; the winds, thy sighs, 135
Who, raging with thy tears and they with them,
Without a sudden calm will overset
Thy tempest-tossèd body. How now, wife?
Have you delivered to her our decree?

LADY CAPULET. Ay, sir, but she will none,[17] she gives you 140   17. **will none,** refuses "our de-
thanks.   cree."
I would the fool were married to her grave!

CAPULET. Soft! Take me with you, take me with you, wife.
How will she none? Doth she not give us thanks?
Is she not proud? Doth she not count her blest,
Unworthy as she is, that we have wrought   145
So worthy a gentleman to be her bridgegroom?

JULIET. Not proud you have, but thankful that you have.
Proud can I never be of what I hate,
But thankful even for hate that is meant love.

CAPULET. How, how, how, how, chop-logic?[18] What is this?   150   18. **chop-logic,** quibbling.
"Proud," and "I thank you," and "I thank you not;"
And yet "not proud." Mistress minion[19] you,   19. **minion,** spoiled darling.
Thank me no thankings, nor proud me no prouds,
But fettle[20] your fine joints 'gainst Thursday next   20. **fettle,** prepare.
To go with Paris to Saint Peter's Church,   155
Or I will drag thee on a hurdle[21] thither.   21. **hurdle,** sled on which criminals were carried to execution.
Out, you green-sickness carrion![22] Out, you baggage![23]   22. **you green-sickness carrion,** pale and sickly creature.
You tallow-face![24]   23. **baggage,** worthless woman.
   24. **tallow-face,** pale face.

LADY CAPULET. Fie, fie! What, are you mad?

JULIET. Good father, I beseech you on my knees,   160
Hear me with patience but to speak a word.

CAPULET. Hang thee, young baggage! Disobedient wretch!
I tell thee what—get thee to church a Thursday
Or never after look me in the face.
Speak not, reply not, do not answer me!
My fingers itch.[25] Wife, we scarce thought us blest   165   25. **itch,** to strike her.
That God had lent us but this only child;
But now I see this one is one too much.
And that we have a curse in having her.
Out on her, hilding![26]   26. **hilding,** worthless being.

NURSE.   God in heaven bless her!
You are to blame, my lord, to rate[27] her so.   170   27. **rate,** abuse.

CAPULET. And why, my lady wisdom? Hold your tongue,
Good prudence. Smatter with your gossips, go!

NURSE. I speak no treason.

CAPULET.   O, God ye god-den.

NURSE. May not one speak?

CAPULET.   Peace, you mumbling fool!
Utter your gravity o'er a gossip's bowl,   175
For here we need it not.

LADY CAPULET.   You are too hot.

CAPULET. God's bread![28] It makes me mad.   28. **God's bread,** by the sacrament; a mild oath.
Day, night, hour; tide, time; work, play;
Alone, in company; still my care hath been
To have her matched; and having now provided   180

Juliet, Lady Capulet, and Nurse

A gentleman of noble parentage,
Of fair demesnes,[29] youthful, and nobly trained,
Stuffed, as they say, with honorable parts,
Proportioned as one's thought would wish a man—
And then to have a wretched puling[30] fool,
A whining mammet,[31] in her fortune's tender,[32]
To answer "I'll not wed, I cannot love;
I am too young, I pray you pardon me"
But, and you will not wed, I'll pardon you!
Graze where you will, you shall not house with me.
Look to't, think on't; I do not use to jest.
Thursday is near; lay hand on heart, advise.
An you be mine, I'll give you to my friend;
An you be not, hang, beg, starve, die in the streets,
For, by my soul, I'll ne'er acknowledge thee,
Nor what is mine shall never do thee good.
Trust to't. Bethink you. I'll not be forsworn.

[CAPULET *exits.*]

29. **demesnes** (di mānz′),   demeanor.

185

30. **puling,** whimpering.

31. **mammet,** doll.
32. **in . . . tender,** in response to her good fortune.

190

195

JULIET. Is there no pity sitting in the clouds,
That sees into the bottom of my grief?
O sweet my mother, cast me not away!   200
Delay this marriage for a month, a week;
Or if you do not, make the bridal bed
In that dim monument where Tybalt lies.
LADY CAPULET. Talk not to me, for I'll not speak a word.
Do as thou wilt, for I have done with thee.   205

[*She exits leaving* JULIET *and* NURSE *alone.*]

JULIET. O God! O Nurse, how shall this be prevented?
My husband is on earth, my faith in heaven;
How shall that faith return again to earth
Unless that husband send it me from heaven
By leaving earth? Comfort me, counsel me.   210
Alack, alack, that heaven should practice stratagems
Upon so soft a subject as myself!
What say'st thou? Hast thou not a word of joy?
Some comfort, Nurse.
NURSE.   Faith, here it is.
Romeo is banished; and all the world to nothing   215
That he dares ne'er come back to challenge you;
Or if he do, it needs must be by stealth.
Then, since the case so stands as now it doth,
I think it best you married with the County.
O, he's a lovely gentleman!   220
Romeo's a dishclout[33] to him. An eagle, madam,
Hath not so green, so quick, so fair an eye
As Paris hath. Beshrew[34] my very heart,
I think you are happy in this second match,
For it excels your first; or if it did not,   225
Your first is dead, or 'twere as good he were
As living here and you no use of him.
JULIET. Speak'st thou from thy heart?
NURSE. And from my soul too; else beshrew them both.
JULIET. Amen!   230
NURSE. What?
JULIET. Well, thou hast comforted me marvelous much.
Go in, and tell my lady I am gone,
Having displeased my father, to Laurence' cell,
To make confession and to be absolved.   235
NURSE. Marry, I will; and this is wisely done. (*Exit.*)
JULIET. Ancient damnation![35] O most wicked fiend!
Is it more sin to wish me thus forsworn,[36]
Or to dispraise my lord with that same tongue

33. **dishclout,** dishcloth.

34. **Beshrew,** a curse on.

35. **damnation,** devilish old woman.
36. **forsworn,** guilty of breaking her marriage vow to Romeo.

Which she hath praised him with above compare   **240**
So many thousand times? Go, counselor!
Thou and my bosom[37] henceforth shall be twain.   37. **bosom,** confidence.
I'll to the Friar to know his remedy.
If all else fail, myself have power to die.

[JULIET *exits*.]

Tying the Scenes Together: Scene 5

Romeo and Juliet have parted at daybreak. Juliet's parents have
told her she is to be married to Paris in three days. If she does not
consent, they will disown her. The nurse has advised Juliet to go
ahead and marry Paris. Juliet has decided to go to Friar Laurence
for help. Do you think Capulet's rage at Juliet's "ingratitude" is
the natural reaction of a father living in his time?

READING FOR DETAILS

Romeo Is Banished

1. Why does Mercutio fight with Tybalt, and how does it happen that Mercutio is killed?
2. What causes the Prince to banish Romeo?
3. What sensible advice does Friar Laurence give when Romeo threatens to kill himself?
4. Before Juliet can recover from the shock of Romeo's banishment, what ultimatum is she given by her father?
5. What advice does the nurse give to Juliet?
6. Why does Juliet go to Friar Laurence as the act ends?

READING FOR MEANING

Identify happenings in Scene 1 of Act III that might justify each of the following statements:

1. A great deal of what seems to be bravery is really vanity.
2. The best of intentions often result in tragedy.
3. Some persons are victims of fate and cannot help themselves.

READING FOR APPRECIATION

Staging

A dramatic bit of "stage business" occurs with the nurse in Act III, just as it does in Act II. In the previous act, the nurse held Juliet in suspense and complained about her aches and pains before finally giving Juliet the information she desired. In Act III, Scene 2, when the nurse comes in bringing the ladder Romeo is to use to get to Juliet's room, how does she throw Juliet into immediate panic?

Act III is long, but Shakespeare displays great skill in sustaining audience interest. One technique he uses is to shift the action around so that all parts and levels of the stage are used. He also opens the act with slashing swordplay that results in the deaths of two important characters and the banishment of the hero. To increase the tension, he introduces the pressure of time. Discuss in which scenes and in what way the pressure of time is revealed to the audience.

Act IV

Scene 1

The cell of Friar Laurence, Tuesday forenoon. Enter FRIAR
LAURENCE *with* PARIS.

FRIAR LAURENCE. On Thursday, sir? The time is very short.
PARIS. My father Capulet will have it so,
  And I am nothing slow to slack his haste.
FRIAR LAURENCE. You say you do not know the lady's mind.
  Uneven is the course; I like it not.   5
PARIS. Immoderately she weeps for Tybalt's death,
  And therefore have I little talked of love;
  For Venus smiles not in a house of tears.
  Now, sir, her father counts it dangerous
  That she do give her sorrow so much sway,   10
  And in his wisdom hastes our marriage
  To stop the inundation of her tears,
  Which, too much minded by herself alone,
  May be put from her by society.
  Now do you know the reason of this haste.   15
FRIAR LAURENCE. (*Aside.*) I would I knew not why it should
  be slowed.
  Look, sir, here comes the lady toward my cell.

[JULIET *enters.*]

PARIS. Happily met, my lady and my wife!
JULIET. That may be, sir, when I may be a wife.
PARIS. That may be, must be, love, on Thursday next.   20
JULIET. What must be shall be.
FRIAR LAURENCE.   That's a certain text.[1]
PARIS. Come you to make confession to this Father?
JULIET. To answer that, I should confess to you.
PARIS. Do not deny to him that you love me.
JULIET. I will confess to you that I love him.   25
PARIS. So will ye, I am sure, that you love me.
JULIET. If I do so, it will be of more price,[2]
  Being spoke behind your back, than to your face.
PARIS. Poor soul, thy face is much abused with tears.
JULIET. The tears have got small victory by that,   30
  For it was bad enough before their spite.
PARIS. Thou wrong'st it more than tears with that report.
JULIET. That is no slander, sir, which is a truth;
  And what I spake, I spake it to my face.

1. **text,** truth.

2. **price,** value.

PARIS: "Do not deny to him that you love me."

PARIS. Thy face is mine, and thou hast sland'red it.   35
JULIET. It may be so, for it is not mine own.
   Are you at leisure, holy Father, now,
   Or shall I come to you at evening mass?
FRIAR LAURENCE. My leisure serves me, pensive daughter,
     now.
   My lord, we must entreat the time alone.   40
PARIS. God shield I should disturb devotion!
   Juliet, on Thursday early will I rouse ye.
   Till then, adieu, and keep this holy kiss.

   [PARIS *exits.*]

JULIET. O, shut the door, and when thou hast done so,
   Come weep with me, past hope, past cure, past help!   45
FRIAR LAURENCE. O Juliet, I already know thy grief;
   It strains me past the compass of my wits.[3]
   I hear thou must, and nothing may prorogue it,
   On Thursday next be married to this County.
JULIET. Tell me not, Friar, that thou hearest of this,   50
   Unless thou tell me how I may prevent it.
   If in thy wisdom thou canst give no help,
   Do thou but call my resolution wise
   And with this knife I'll help it presently.[4]
   God joined my heart and Romeo's, thou our hands;   55
   And ere this hand, by thee to Romeo's sealed,
   Shall be the label to another deed,

3. **the compass . . . wits,** my wit's end.

4. **presently,** at once.

Or my true heart with treacherous revolt
Turn to another, this shall slay them both.
Therefore, out of thy long-experienced time, 60
Give me some present counsel; or, behold,
'Twixt my extremes and me this bloody knife
Shall play the umpire, arbitrating that
Which the commission of thy years and art
Could to no issue of true honor bring. 65
Be not so long to speak. I long to die
If what thou speak'st speak not of remedy.

FRIAR LAURENCE. Hold, daughter. I do spy a kind of hope,
Which craves as desperate an execution
As that is desperate which we would prevent. 70
If, rather than to marry County Paris,
Thou hast the strength of will to slay thyself,
Then is it likely thou wilt undertake
A thing like death to chide away this shame,
That cop'st with[5] death himself to scape from it; 75
And, if thou darest, I'll give thee remedy.

JULIET. O, bid me leap, rather than marry Paris,
From off the battlements of any tower,
Or walk in thievish ways, or bid me lurk
Where serpents are; chain me with roaring bears, 80
Or hide me nightly in a charnel house,[6]
O'ercovered quite with dead men's rattling bones,
With reeky[7] shanks and yellow chapless[8] skulls;
Or bid me go into a new-made grave
And hide me with a dead man in his shroud— 85
Things that, to hear them told, have made me tremble—
And I will do it without fear or doubt,
To live an unstained wife to my sweet love.

FRIAR LAURENCE. Hold, then. Go home, be merry, give consent
To marry Paris. Wednesday is tomorrow. 90
Tomorrow night look that thou lie alone;
Let not thy nurse lie with thee in thy chamber.
Take thou this vial, being then in bed,
And this distilling liquor drink thou off;
When presently through all thy veins shall run 95
A cold and drowsy humor;[9] for no pulse
Shall keep his native progress, but surcease;[10]
No warmth, no breath, shall testify thou livest;
The roses in thy lips and cheeks shall fade
To waned ashes, thy eyes' windows fall 100
Like death when he shuts up the day of life;
Each part, deprived of supple government,[11]

5. **cop'st with,** deals.

6. **charnel house,** vault where the bodies of the dead were placed.
7. **reeky,** reeking.
8. **chapless,** jawless.

9. **humor,** bodily fluid.

10. **surcease,** cease.

11. **supple government,** ease of movement.

Shall, stiff and stark and cold, appear like death;
And in this borrowed likeness of shrunk death
Thou shalt continue two-and-forty hours,   105
And then awake as from a pleasant sleep.
Now, when the bridegroom in the morning comes
To rouse thee from thy bed, there art thou dead,
Then, as the manner of our country is,
In thy best robes uncovered, on the bier,   110
Thou shalt be borne to that same ancient vault
Where all the kindred of the Capulets lie.
In the meantime, against thou shalt awake,[12]
Shall Romeo by my letters know our drift,[13]
And hither shall he come; and he and I   115
Will watch thy waking, and that very night
Shall Romeo bear thee hence to Mantua.
And this shall free thee from this present shame,
If no inconstant toy[14] nor womanish fear
Abate thy valor in the acting it.   120

JULIET. Give me, give me! O, tell not me of fear!

FRIAR LAURENCE. Hold! Get you gone, be strong and pros-
    perous
    In this resolve. I'll send a friar with speed
    To Mantua, with my letters to thy lord.

JULIET. Love give me strength, and strength shall help afford.   125
    Farewell, dear father.

[*They exit together.*]

12. **against . . . awake,** in preparation for your waking.
13. **drift,** intention.

14. **toy,** whim.

Tying the Scenes Together: Scene 1
Paris has made arrangements with the Friar to marry him to Juliet
on Thursday. Juliet has come to the Friar for counsel. He has
given her a drug to take the night before the wedding. This drug
will put her into a death-like trance. She is to be placed in the
family burial vault, from which she will be rescued by Romeo and
taken to Mantua. What does Juliet's willingness to take this powerful drug show about her character?

Scene 2

A hall in the house of Capulet. Enter CAPULET, LADY
CAPULET, NURSE, *and* SERVANTS. CAPULET *hands* SERVANT
a list of guests to be invited to the wedding.

CAPULET. So many guests invite as here are writ.

[*Exit* FIRST SERVANT.]

Sirrah, go hire me twenty cunning cooks.

SECOND SERVANT. You shall have none ill, sir; for I'll try if they
can lick their fingers.

CAPULET. How canst thou try them so?   5

SECOND SERVANT. Marry, sir, 'tis an ill cook that cannot lick his
own fingers; therefore he that cannot lick his fingers goes
not with me.

CAPULET. Go, begone.

[*Exit* SECOND SERVANT.]

We shall be much unfurnished for this time.   10
What, is my daughter gone to Friar Laurence?

NURSE. Ay, forsooth.

CAPULET. Well, he may chance to do some good on her.

[JULIET *enters in good spirits.*]

NURSE. See where she comes from shrift with merry look.

CAPULET. How now, my headstrong? Where have you been
gadding?   15

JULIET. Where I have learnt me to repent the sin
Of disobedient opposition
To you and your behests,[1] and am enjoined   1. **behests,** orders.
By holy Laurence to fall prostrate here
And beg your pardon. Pardon, I beseech you!   20
Henceforward I am ever ruled by you.

CAPULET. Send for the County; go tell him of this.
I'll have this knot knit up tomorrow morning.

JULIET. I met the youthful lord at Laurence' cell
And gave him what becomèd[2] love I might,   25   2. **becomèd,** suitable.
Not stepping o'er the bounds of modesty.

CAPULET. Why, I am glad on't; this is well. Stand up.
This is as't should be. Let me see the County.
Ay, marry, go, I say, and fetch him hither.
Now, afore God, this reverend holy Friar,   30
All our whole city is much bound to him.

JULIET. Nurse, will you go with me into my closet[3]   3. **closet,** private room.
To help me sort such needful ornaments
As you think fit to furnish me tomorrow?

LADY CAPULET. No, not till Thursday. There is time enough. 35

CAPULET. Go, Nurse, go with her. We'll to church tomorrow.

[JULIET *and* NURSE *exit.*]

LADY CAPULET. We shall be short in our provision;
'Tis now near night.

CAPULET. Tush, I will stir about,
And all things shall be well, I warrant thee, wife.
Go thou to Juliet, help to deck up her.   40
I'll not to bed tonight; let me alone.
I'll play the housewife for this once. What, ho!
They are all forth. Well, I will walk myself
To County Paris to prepare up him
Against tomorrow. My heart is wondrous light,   45
Since this same wayward girl is so reclaimed.

[CAPULET *and* LADY CAPULET *exit.*]

Tying the Scenes Together: Scene 2

The Capulet household has begun preparations for the wedding.
Juliet has pretended a willingness to obey her father's wishes. In
his joy, her father has decided to set the wedding ahead a day.
Why is this decision characteristic of the father?

Scene 3

Juliet's room. JULIET *and* NURSE *enter.*

JULIET. Ay, those attires are best; but, gentle Nurse,
I pray thee leave me to myself tonight,
For I have need of many orisons[1]   1. **orisons** (ôr'ə zənz), prayers.
To move the heavens to smile upon my state,
Which, well thou knowest, is cross[2] and full of sin.   5   2. **cross,** irregular.

[*Enter* LADY CAPULET.]

LADY CAPULET. What, are you busy, ho? Need you my help?
JULIET. No, madam, we have culled[3] such necessaries   3. **culled,** chosen.
As are behoveful[4] for our state tomorrow.   4. **behoveful,** necessary.
So please you, let me now be left alone,
And let the nurse this night sit up with you;   10
For I am sure you have your hands full all
In this so sudden business.
LADY CAPULET.   Good night.
Get thee to bed, and rest, for thou hast need.

[*Exit* LADY CAPULET *and* NURSE.]

JULIET. Farewell! God knows when we shall meet again.
I have a faint cold fear thrills through my veins
That almost freezes up the heat of life.   15
I'll call them back again to comfort me.
Nurse! What should she do here?

My dismal scene I needs must act alone.
Come, vial. 20
What if this mixture do not work at all?
Shall I be married then tomorrow morning?
No, no! This shall forbid it. Lie thou there.

[*She lays down her dagger.*]

What if it be a poison which the Friar
Subtly hath ministered to have me dead, 25
Lest in this marriage he should be dishonored
Because he married me before to Romeo?
I fear it is, and yet methinks it should not,
For he hath still been tried a holy man.
How if, when I am laid into the tomb, 30
I wake before the time that Romeo
Come to redeem me? There's a fearful point!
Shall I not then be stifled in the vault,
To whose foul mouth no healthsome air breathes in,
And there die strangled ere my Romeo comes? 35
Or, if I live, is it not very like
The horrible conceit⁵ of death and night,
Together with the terror of the place—
As in a vault, an ancient receptacle
Where, for this many hundred years the bones 40
Of all my buried ancestors are packed;
Where bloody Tybalt, yet but green in earth,
Lies festering in his shroud; where, as they say,
At some hours in the night spirits resort.
Alack, alack, is it not like that I, 45
So early waking, what with loathsome smells,
And shrieks like mandrakes⁶ torn out of the earth,
That living mortals, hearing them, run mad:—
O, if I wake, shall I not be distraught,
Environed with all these hideous fears, 50
And madly play with my forefathers' joints,
And pluck the mangled Tybalt from his shroud,
And, in this rage, with some great kinsman's bone
As with a club dash out my desperate brains?
O, look! Methinks I see my cousin's ghost 55
Seeking out Romeo, that did spit his body
Upon a rapier's point. Stay, Tybalt, stay!
Romeo, Romeo, Romeo, I drink to thee.

[*She drinks and falls upon her curtained bed.*]

5. **conceit,** imagination.

6. **mandrake,** plant with a forked root. It resembles a human figure and is believed to shriek when pulled from the ground.

Tying the Scenes Together: Scene 3
Juliet has dismissed her mother and the nurse for the night and, after thinking of the many things that might go wrong, has drunk the potion. Why might she have good cause to fear that the Friar might really have given her a poison?

Scene 4

A hall in the house of Capulet on Wednesday morning. Enter LADY CAPULET *and* NURSE. *They are busy with wedding feast preparations.*

LADY CAPULET. Hold, take these keys and fetch more spices, Nurse.
NURSE. They call for dates and quinces in the pastry.[1]

> 1. **pastry,** baking room.

[*Enter* CAPULET.]

CAPULET. Come, stir, stir, stir! The second cock hath crowed,
The curfew bell hath rung, 'tis three o'clock.
The County will be here with music straight   5
For so he said he would. (*Music plays.*)
                I hear him near.
Nurse! Wife! What, ho! What, Nurse, I say!
Go waken Juliet; go and trim her up.
I'll go and chat with Paris. Hie, make haste,
Make haste; the bridegroom he is come already;   10
Make haste, I say.

[*They exit.*]

Tying the Scenes Together: Scene 4
All but the very last-minute wedding preparations have been completed in the Capulet household. The nurse has been sent to help the bride dress. What do you know the nurse is going to discover?

Scene 5

Juliet's room, moments later. NURSE *enters.*

NURSE. Mistress! What, mistress! Juliet! Fast,[1] I warrant her.
   She——
Why, lamb! Why, lady! Fie, you slugabed.
Why, love, I say! Madam! Sweetheart! Why, bride!
I needs must wake her, Madam, madam, madam!

> 1. **Fast,** fast asleep.

[*She pulls back the curtains around the bed.*]

What, dressed, and in your clothes, and down again?   5
I must needs wake her. Lady! Lady! Lady!
Alas, alas! Help, help! My lady's dead!
O weladay[2] that ever I was born!   2. **O weladay,** alas.
Some aqua vitae, ho! My lord! My lady!

[*Enter* LADY CAPULET.]

LADY CAPULET. What noise is here?
NURSE.   O lamentable day!   10
LADY CAPULET. What is the matter?
NURSE.   Look, look! O heavy
  day!
LADY CAPULET. O me, O me! My child, my only life!
  Revive, look up, or I will die with thee!
  Help, help! Call help.

[*Enter* CAPULET.]

CAPULET. For shame, bring Juliet forth; her lord is come.   15
NURSE. She's dead, deceased; she's dead, alack the day!
LADY CAPULET. Alack the day, she's dead, she's dead, she's
  dead!
CAPULET. Ha! Let me see her. Out alas! She's cold,
  Her blood is settled, and her joints are stiff;
  Life and these lips have long been separated.   20
  Death lies on her like an untimely frost
  Upon the sweetest flower of all the field.
NURSE. O lamentable day!
LADY CAPULET.   O woeful time!
CAPULET. Death, that hath ta'en her hence to make me wail,
  Ties up my tongue and will not let me speak.   25

[*Enter* FRIAR LAURENCE *and* PARIS.]

FRIAR LAURENCE. Come, is the bride ready to go to church?
CAPULET. Ready to go, but never to return.
  Death is my son-in-law, Death is my heir;
  My daughter he hath wedded. I will die
  And leave him all. Life, living,[3] all is Death's.   30   3. **living,** worldly goods.
PARIS. Have I thought, love, to see this morning's face,
  And doth it give me such a sight as this?
LADY CAPULET. Accursed, unhappy, wretched, hateful day!
  Most miserable hour that e'er time saw
  In lasting labor of his pilgrimage!   35
  But one, poor one, one poor and loving child,
  But one thing to rejoice and solace in,
  And cruel Death hath catched it from my sight.

NURSE. O woe! O woeful, woeful, woeful day!
  Most lamentable day, most woeful day   40
  That ever, ever I did yet behold!
  O day, O day, O day! O hateful day!
  Never was seen so black a day as this.
  O woeful day! O woeful day!

PARIS. Beguiled, divorced, wronged, spited, slain!   45
  Most detestable Death, by thee beguiled,
  By cruel, cruel thee, quite overthrown.
  O love! O life; not life, but love in death!

CAPULET. Despised, distressed, hated, martyred, killed!
  Uncomfortable time, why cam'st thou now   50
  To murder, murder our solemnity?[4]
  O child, O child! My soul, and not my child!
  Dead art thou! Alack, my child is dead,
  And with my child my joys are buried!

4. **To murder . . . solemnity,** to ruin our ceremony.

FRIAR LAURENCE. Peace, ho, for shame! Confusion's[5] cure lives
    not   55
  In these confusions. Heaven and yourself
  Had part in this fair maid, now heaven hath all,
  And all the better is it for the maid.
  Your part in her you could not keep from death,
  But heaven keeps his part in eternal life.   60
  The most you sought was her promotion,
  For 'twas your heaven she should be advanced;
  And weep ye now, seeing she is advanced
  Above the clouds, as high as heaven itself?
  O, in this love, you love your child so ill   65
  That you run mad, seeing that she is well.
  She's not well married that lives married long,
  But she's best married that dies married young.
  Dry up your tears and stick your rosemary[6]
  On this fair corse, and, as the custom is,   70
  And in her best array bear her to church;
  For though fond nature bids us all lament,
  Yet nature's tears are reason's merriment.

5. **Confusion's,** disaster's.

6. **rosemary,** a symbol of immortality and enduring love, used at both funerals and weddings.

CAPULET. All things that we ordained festival
  Turn from their office to black funeral;   75
  Our instruments to melancholy bells,
  Our wedding cheer to a sad burial feast;
  Our solemn hymns to sullen dirges change;
  Our bridal flowers serve for a buried corse;
  And all things change them to the contrary.   80

FRIAR LAURENCE. Sir, go you in; and, madam, go with him;
And go, Sir Paris; everyone prepare
To follow this fair corse unto her grave.
The heavens do lower upon you for some ill;
Move them no more by crossing their high will.   85

[*They exit.*]

Tying the Scenes Together: Scene 5

The nurse has discovered Juliet in her bed. Everyone thinks she is
dead. The Friar urges the family to put aside its grief and prepare
Juliet for burial. The wedding has turned into a funeral.

READING FOR DETAILS

A Desperate Course Is Taken

1. What brings Paris to Friar Laurence's cell?
2. Briefly outline the desperate plan the Friar proposes to Juliet.
3. What change does Capulet make in the wedding plans?
4. What fears beset Juliet before she drinks the potion?

READING FOR MEANING

Consider and discuss the following ideas in light of the play:

1. One act of deception leads to another.
2. Persons who wish to believe something is true are easily deceived into thinking that it is.
3. Most grief is self-pity.

READING FOR APPRECIATION

Staging

1. What does the playwright accomplish by having Capulet suddenly decide to set the wedding a day ahead?
2. At the end of Scene 1, the audience is left tense and fearful from the desperate session they have just witnessed in Friar Laurence's cell. Why do you think it was good theater for Shakespeare to open Scene 2 with the gay atmosphere of wedding preparations? What comedy is introduced before Juliet's entrance?

Language

1. The conversation between Paris and Juliet in the Friar's cell is filled with word play and double meanings. The audience finds it particularly interesting because they know what Juliet means when she answers Paris, though he is ignorant of what she is really saying. Reread this brief conversation (Scene 1, lines 18–43) and discuss.
2. What horrors does Juliet describe that she would endure rather than be married to another man?

Act V

Scene 1

A street in Mantua on the following day. ROMEO *enters.*

ROMEO. If I may trust the flattering truth of sleep,
    My dreams presage[1] some joyful news at hand.
    My bosom's lord[2] sits lightly in his throne,
    And all this day an unaccustomed spirit
    Lifts me above the ground with cheerful thoughts.   5
    I dreamt my lady came and found me dead—
    Strange dream that gives a dead man leave to think—
    And breathed such life with kisses in my lips
    That I revived and was an emperor.
    Ah me, how sweet is love itself possessed,   10
    When but love's shadows[3] are so rich in joy.

[*Enter* BALTHASAR.]

    News from Verona! How now, Balthasar?
    Dost thou not bring me letters from the Friar?
    How doth my lady? Is my father well?
    How fares my Juliet? That I ask again,   15
    For nothing can be ill if she be well.
BALTHASAR. Then she is well, and nothing can be ill.
    Her body sleeps in Capels' monument,
    And her immortal part with angels lives.
    I saw her laid low in her kindred's vault,   20
    And presently took post[4] to tell it you.
    O, pardon me for bringing these ill news,
    Since you did leave it for my office, sir.
ROMEO. Is it even so? Then I defy you, stars!
    Thou knowest my lodging. Get me ink and paper   25
    And hire post horses; I will hence tonight.
BALTHASAR. I do beseech you, sir, have patience.
    Your looks are pale and wild and do import
    Some misadventure.
ROMEO.   Tush, thou art deceived.
    Leave me and do the thing I bid thee do.   30
    Hast thou no letters to me from the Friar?
BALTHASAR. No, my good lord.
ROMEO.   No matter. Get thee gone.
    And hire those horses; I'll be with thee straight.

[*Exit* BALTHASAR.]

1. **presage,** foretell.
2. **bosom's lord,** heart.
3. **shadows,** dreams.
4. **took post,** rode in haste.

Well, Juliet, I will lie with thee tonight.
Let's see for means. O mischief, thou art swift   35
To enter in the thoughts of desperate men.
I do remember an apothecary—
And hereabouts 'a dwells—which late I noted
In tattered weeds, with overwhelming[5] brows,   5. **overwhelming,** overhanging.
Culling of simples;[6] meager with his looks,   40   6. **simples,** herbs.
Sharp misery had worn him to the bones;
And in his needy shop a tortoise hung,
An alligator stuffed, and other skins
Of ill-shaped fishes; and about his shelves
A beggarly account of empty boxes,   45
Green earthen pots, bladders, and musty seeds,
Remnants of packthread,[7] and old cakes of roses,[8]   7. **packthread,** wrapping string.
Were thinly scattered, to make up a show.   8. **cakes of roses,** pressed rose
Noting this penury,[9] to myself I said,   petals used in cosmetics.
"An if a man did need a poison now   9. **penury** (pen'yə rē), poverty.
Whose sale is present death in Mantua,   50
Here lives a caitiff[10] wretch would sell it him."
O, this same thought did but forerun my need,   10. **caitiff** (kā'tif), miserable.
And this same needy man must sell it me.
As I remember, this should be the house.   55
Being holiday, the beggar's shop is shut.
What, ho, apothecary!

[*Enter* APOTHECARY.]

APOTHECARY.   Who calls so loud?
ROMEO. Come hither, man. I see that thou art poor.
Hold, there is forty ducats.[11] Let me have   11. **ducats** (duk'ətz), gold coins.
A dram[12] of poison, such soon-speeding gear[13]   60   12. **dram,** fluid measure.
As will disperse itself through all the veins   13. **gear,** stuff.
That the life-weary taker may fall dead,
And that the trunk[14] may be discharged of breath   14. **trunk,** body.
As violently as hasty powder fired
Doth hurry from the fatal cannon's womb.[15]   65   15. **womb,** barrel.
APOTHECARY. Such mortal drugs I have; but Mantua's law
Is death to any he that utters[16] them.   16. **utters,** distributes.
ROMEO. Art thou so bare and full of wretchedness
And fearest to die? Famine is in thy cheeks,
Need and oppression starveth in thy eyes,   70
Contempt and beggary hangs upon thy back.
The world is not thy friend, nor the world's law;
The world affords no law to make thee rich;
Then be not poor, but break it and take this.

APOTHECARY. My poverty but not my will consents.   75

ROMEO. I pay thy poverty and not thy will.

APOTHECARY. Put this in any liquid thing you will
  And drink it off, and if you had the strength
  Of twenty men, it would dispatch you straight.

ROMEO. There is thy gold, worse poison to men's souls, 80
  Doing more murder in this loathsome world,
  Than these poor compounds that thou mayst not sell.
  I sell thee poison; thou hast sold me none.
  Farewell. Buy food and get thyself in flesh.
  Come, cordial[17] and not poison, go with me 85 **17. cordial,** reviving liquid.
  To Juliet's grave; for there must I use thee.

[*He exits.*]

Tying the Scenes Together: Scene 1

Romeo has learned of Juliet's supposed death and after buying
poison to kill himself, has set out for Verona. How does his conversation with the apothecary show you that Romeo feels there is
a great deal wrong with the social conditions of his time?

Scene 2

Friar Laurence's cell, that night. FRIAR JOHN *enters.*

FRIAR JOHN. Holy Franciscan Friar, brother, ho!

[*Enter* FRIAR LAURENCE.]

FRIAR LAURENCE. This same should be the voice of Friar
  John.
  Welcome from Mantua. What says Romeo?
  Or, if his mind be writ, give me his letter.

FRIAR JOHN. Going to find a barefoot brother[1] out, 5 **1. barefoot brother,** another friar.
  One of our order, to associate[2] me   **2. associate,** accompany.
  Here in this city visiting the sick,
  And finding him, the searchers[3] of the town,   **3. searchers,** health officials.
  Suspecting that we both were in a house
  Where the infectious pestilence[4] did reign, 10 **4. pestilence,** plague.
  Sealed up the doors, and would not let us forth,
  So that my speed to Mantua there was stayed.

FRIAR LAURENCE. Who bare my letter, then, to Romeo?

FRIAR JOHN. I could not send it—here it is again—
  Nor get a messenger to bring it thee, 15
  So fearful were they of infection.

FRIAR LAURENCE. Unhappy fortune! By my brotherhood,
　The letter was not nice,[5] but full of charge,[6]
　Of dear import;[7] and the neglecting it
　May do much danger. Friar John, go hence,　　　　20
　Get me an iron crow[8] and bring it straight
　Unto my cell.
FRIAR JOHN. Brother, I'll go and bring it thee. (*Exit.*)
FRIAR LAURENCE. Now must I to the monument[9] alone.
　Within this three hours will fair Juliet wake.　　　25
　She will beshrew me much that Romeo
　Hath had no notice of these accidents;
　But I will write again to Mantua,
　And keep her at my cell till Romeo come—
　Poor living corse, closed in a dead man's tomb! (*Exit.*)　　30

5. **nice,** trifling.
6. **charge,** information.
7. **dear import,** great importance.
8. **crow,** crowbar.

9. **monument,** tomb.

Tying the Scenes Together: Scene 2

Friar Laurence learns that his letter to Romeo has not been delivered, so he hurries to Juliet's tomb to be there when she awakens. Is the Friar's reaction to Friar John's news what you would have expected of him? Explain.

Scene 3

A church graveyard where the Capulets' burial vault is located, late that night. Enter PARIS *and* PAGE *who is carrying a torch, flowers, and perfumed water.*

PARIS. Give me thy torch, boy. Hence, and stand aloof.
　Yet put it out, for I would not be seen.
　Under yond yew trees lay thee all along,
　Holding thy ear close to the hollow ground.
　So shall no foot upon the churchyard tread—　　　5
　Being loose, unfirm, with digging up of graves—
　But thou shalt hear it. Whistle then to me,
　As signal that thou hearest something approach.
　Give me those flowers. Do as I bid thee, go.
PAGE. (*Aside.*) I am almost afraid to stand alone　　　10
　Here in the churchyard; yet I will adventure.

[*He retires.*]

PARIS. Sweet flower, with flowers thy bridal bed I strew,
　O woe! Thy canopy is dust and stones
　Which with sweet water nightly I will dew;

Or, wanting that, with tears distilled by moans.   15
The obsequies[1] that I for thee will keep
Nightly shall be to strew thy grave and weep.

1. **obsequies** (ob'sə kwēz), funeral rites.

[PAGE *whistles off-stage.*]

The boy gives warning something doth approach.
What cursèd foot wanders this way tonight
To cross my obsequies and true love's rite?   20
What, with a torch? Muffle me, night, awhile.

[PARIS *retires as* ROMEO *and* BALTHASAR *enter carrying a torch, a mattock, and a crow of iron.*]

ROMEO. Give me that mattock[2] and the wrenching iron.
  Hold, take this letter; early in the morning
  See thou deliver it to my lord and father.
  Give me the light. Upon thy life I charge thee,   25
  Whate'er thou hearest or seest, stand all aloof,
  And do not interrupt me in my course.
  Why I descend into this bed of death
  Is partly to behold my lady's face,
  But chiefly to take thence from her dead finger   30
  A precious ring[3]—a ring that I must use
  In dear employment. Therefore hence, be gone.
  But if thou, jealous,[4] dost return to pry
  In what I farther shall intend to do,
  By heaven, I will tear thee joint by joint   35
  And strew this hungry churchyard with thy limbs.
  The time and my intents are savage-wild,
  More fierce and more inexorable far,
  Than empty tigers or the roaring sea.
BALTHASAR. I will be gone, sir, and not trouble ye.   40
ROMEO. So shalt thou show me friendship. (*Offering money.*)
    Take thou that.
  Live, and be prosperous, and farewell, good fellow.
BALTHASAR. (*Aside.*) For all this same, I'll hide me hereabout.
  His looks I fear, and his intents I doubt. (*He retires.*)
ROMEO. Thou detestable maw,[5] thou womb of death,   45
  Gorged with the dearest morsel of the earth,
  Thus I enforce thy rotten jaws to open,
  And in despite I'll cram thee with more food.

[ROMEO *opens the tomb.*]

PARIS. This is that banished haughty Montague
  That murdered my love's cousin, with which grief   50

2. **mattock,** pickaxe.

3. **precious ring.** A false excuse to keep Balthasar from interfering.
4. **jealous,** curious.

5. **maw,** stomach.

"Thus with a kiss I die."

It is supposed the fair creature died,
And here is come to do some villainous shame
To the dead bodies. I will apprehend him.
Stop thy unhallowèd toil, vile Montague!
Can vengeance be pursued further than death?   55
Condemnèd villain, I do apprehend thee.
Obey, and go with me, for thou must die.
ROMEO. I must indeed; and therefore came I hither.
Good gentle youth, tempt not a desperate man;
Fly hence and leave me. Think upon these gone;   60
Let them affright thee. I beseech thee, youth,
Put not another sin upon my head
By urging me to fury. O, be gone!
By heaven, I love thee better than myself,
For I come hither armed against myself.   65
Stay not, be gone. Live, and hereafter say
A madman's mercy bid thee run away.
PARIS. I do defy thy conjurations.[6]
And apprehend thee for a felon[7] here.
ROMEO. Wilt thou provoke me? Then have at thee, boy!   70
PAGE. O Lord, they fight! I will go call the watch. (*Exits.*)

6. **conjurations,** appeals.
7. **felon,** criminal.

PARIS. (*Falls.*) O, I am slain! If thou be merciful,
  Open the tomb, lay me with Juliet. (*Dies.*)
ROMEO. In faith, I will. Let me peruse this face.
  Mercutio's kinsman, noble County Paris!   75
  What said my man when my betossèd soul
  Did not attend him as we rode? I think
  He told me Paris should have married Juliet.
  Said he not so, or did I dream it so?
  Or am I mad, hearing him talk of Juliet,   80
  To think it was so? O, give me thy hand,
  One writ with me in sour misfortune's book!
  I'll bury thee in a triumphant grave.
  A grave? O, no, a lanthorn,[8] slaughtered youth,
  For here lies Juliet, and her beauty makes   85
  This vault a feasting presence[9] full of light.
  Death, lie thou there, by a dead man interred.

[*He places* PARIS *in the tomb.*]

  How oft when men are at the point of death
  Have they been merry! Which their keepers call
  A lightning before death. O, how may I   90
  Call this a lightning? O my love, my wife!
  Death, that hath sucked the honey of thy breath,
  Hath had no power yet upon thy beauty.
  Thou art not conquered. Beauty's ensign[10] yet
  Is crimson in thy lips and in thy cheeks,   95
  And death's pale flag is not advancèd there.
  Tybalt, liest thou there in thy bloody sheet?
  O, what more favor can I do to thee
  Than with that hand that cut thy youth in twain
  To sunder his that was thine enemy?   100
  Forgive me, cousin! Ah, dear Juliet,
  Why art thou yet so fair? Shall I believe
  That unsubstantial Death is amorous,
  And the lean abhorrèd monster keeps
  Thee here in dark to be his paramour?[11]   105
  For fear of that I still will stay with thee
  And never from this pallet of dim night
  Depart again. Here, here will I remain
  With worms that are thy chambermaids. O, here
  Will I set up my everlasting rest   110
  And shake the yoke of inauspicious stars[12]
  From this world-wearied flesh. Eyes, look your last!
  Arms, take your last embrace! And, lips, O you

8. **lanthorn,** here, a many windowed tower, as atop a cathedral.

9. **feasting presence,** festive room for royalty.

10. **ensign,** banner.

11. **paramour,** lover.

12. **inauspicious stars,** ill luck.

The doors of breath, seal with a righteous kiss
A dateless bargain to engrossing death!   115
Come, bitter conduct, come, unsavory guide!
Thou desperate pilot, now at once run on
The dashing rocks thy seasick weary bark!
Here's to my love! (*He drinks the poison.*) O true apothecary!
Thy drugs are quick. Thus with a kiss I die.   120

[*He kisses* JULIET *and falls. Enter* FRIAR LAURENCE *with
lantern, crowbar, mattock, and spade.*]

FRIAR LAURENCE. Saint Francis be my speed! How oft to-
   night
  Have my old feet stumbled at graves! Who's there?
BALTHASAR. Here's one, a friend, and one that knows you
   well.
FRIAR LAURENCE. Bliss be upon you! Tell me, good my
   friend,
  What torch is yond that vainly lends his light   125
  To grubs and eyeless skulls? As I discern,
  It burneth in the Capels' monument.
BALTHASAR. It doth so, holy sir; and there's my master,
  One that you love.
FRIAR LAURENCE.   Who is it?
BALTHASAR.   Romeo.
FRIAR LAURENCE. How long hath he been there?
BALTHASAR.   Full half
  an hour.   130
FRIAR LAURENCE. Go with me to the vault.
BALTHASAR.   I dare not, sir.
  My master knows not but I am gone hence,
  And fearfully did menace me with death
  If I did stay to look on his intents.
FRIAR LAURENCE. Stay then; I'll go alone. Fear comes upon
   me.   135
  O, much I fear some ill unthrifty[13] thing.   13. **unthrifty,** unlucky.
BALTHASAR. As I did sleep under this yew tree here,
  I dreamt my master and another fought,
  And that my master slew him.
FRIAR LAURENCE.   Romeo!
  Alack, alack, what blood is this which stains   140
  The stony entrance of this sepulcher?
  What mean these masterless and gory swords
  To lie discolored by this place of peace?

[*He enters the tomb.*]

Romeo! O, pale! Who else? What, Paris too?
And steeped in blood? Ah, what an unkind hour   145
Is guilty of this lamentable chance!
The lady stirs.

[JULIET *slowly rises*.]

JULIET. O comfortable[14] Friar! Where is my lord?   **14. comfortable,** comforting.
 I do remember well where I should be,
 And there I am. Where is my Romeo?   150
FRIAR LAURENCE. I hear some noise. Lady, come from that
   nest
 Of death, contagion, and unnatural sleep.
 A greater power than we can contradict
 Hath thwarted our intents. Come, come away.
 Thy husband in thy bosom there lies dead;   155
 And Paris too. Come, I'll dispose of thee
 Among a sisterhood of holy nuns.
 Stay not to question, for the watch is coming.
 Come, go, good Juliet. I dare no longer stay.

[*He leaves* JULIET *alone*.]

JULIET. Go, get thee hence, for I will not away.   160
 What's here? A cup, closed in my truelove's hand?
 Poison, I see, hath been his timeless[15] end.   **15. timeless,** untimely.
 O churl![16] Drunk all, and left no friendly drop   **16. churl,** miser.
 To help me after? I will kiss thy lips.
 Haply some poison yet doth hang on them   165
 To make me die with a restorative.
 Thy lips are warm!
CHIEF WATCHMAN. (*Off-stage*.) Lead, boy. Which way?
JULIET. Yea, noise? Then I'll be brief. O happy[17] dagger! **17. happy,** opportune.

[*Snatches Romeo's dagger*.]

This is thy sheath; (*Stabs herself and falls*.) there rust, and
   let me die.   170

[*Enter* WATCH *with the* PAGE *of* PARIS.]

PAGE. This is the place. There, where the torch doth burn.
CHIEF WATCHMAN. The ground is bloody. Search about the
   churchyard.
 Go, some of you; whoe'er you find attach.[18]   **18. attach,** arrest.
 Pitiful sight! Here lies the County slain;
 And Juliet bleeding, warm, and newly dead,   175

Who here hath lain this two days buried.
Go, tell the Prince; run to the Capulets';
Raise up the Montagues; some others search.
We see the ground whereon these woes do lie,
But the true ground of all these piteous woes   180
We cannot without circumstance descry.[19]

19. **without . . . descry,** without details discern.

[*Enter some members of the* WATCH *with* BALTHASAR.]

SECOND WATCHMAN. Here's Romeo's man. We found him in
  the churchyard.
CHIEF WATCHMAN. Hold him in safety till the Prince come
  hither.

[*Enter* FRIAR LAURENCE *with another* WATCHMAN.]

THIRD WATCHMAN. Here is a friar that trembles, sighs, and
  weeps.
  We took this mattock and this spade from him   185
  As he was coming from this churchyard's side.
CHIEF WATCHMAN. A great suspicion! Stay the friar too.

[*Enter* PRINCE ESCALUS *and* ATTENDANTS.]

PRINCE. What misadventure is so early up,
  That calls our person from our morning rest?

[*Enter* CAPULET *and* LADY CAPULET.]

CAPULET. What should it be, that is so shrieked abroad?   190
LADY CAPULET. O, the people in the street cry "Romeo,"
  Some "Juliet," and some "Paris"; and all run
  With open outcry toward our monument.
PRINCE. What fear is this which startles in your ears?
CHIEF WATCHMAN. Sovereign, here lies the County Paris
  slain;   195
  And Romeo dead; and Juliet, dead before,
  Warm and new killed.
PRINCE. Search, seek, and know how this foul murder comes.
CHIEF WATCHMAN. Here is a friar, and slaughtered Romeo's
  man.
  With instruments upon them fit to open   200
  These dead men's tombs.
CAPULET. O heavens! O wife, look how our daughter bleeds!
  This dagger hath mista'en, for, lo, his house[20]

20. **his house,** its scabbard.

  Is empty on the back of Montague,
  And it missheathèd in my daughter's bosom!   205

LADY CAPULET. O me, this sight of death is as a bell
    That warns[21] my old age to a sepulcher.

21. **warns,** summons.

[*Enter* MONTAGUE *and others.*]

PRINCE. Come, Montague; for thou art early up
    To see thy son and heir more early down.
MONTAGUE. Alas, my liege, my wife is dead tonight;   240
    Grief of my son's exile hath stopped her breath.
    What further woe conspires against mine age?
PRINCE. Look, and thou shalt see.
MONTAGUE. O thou untaught! What manners is in this,
    To press before thy father to a grave?   215
PRINCE. Seal up the mouth of outrage[22] for a while,
    Till we can clear these ambiguities[23]

22. **mouth of outrage,** loud out-cries.
23. **ambiguities** (am'bə gyü'ə tēz), mysteries.

    And know their spring, their head, their true descent;
    And then will I be general of your woes
    And lead you even to death. Meantime forbear,   220
    And let mischance be slave to patience.
    Bring forth the parties of suspicion.
FRIAR LAURENCE. I am the greatest, able to do least,
    Yet most suspected, as the time and place
    Doth make against me, of this direful murder;   225
    And here I stand, both to impeach and purge[24]

24. **impeach and purge,** accuse and clear.

    Myself condemned and myself excused.
PRINCE. Then say at once what thou dost know in this.
FRIAR LAURENCE. I will be brief, for my short date of
      breath[25]

25. **date of breath,** years to live.

    Is not so long as is a tedious tale.   230
    Romeo, there dead, was husband to that Juliet,
    And she, there dead, that's Romeo's faithful wife.
    I married them, and their stol'n marriage day
    Was Tybalt's doomsday, whose untimely death
    Banished the new-made bridegroom from this city,   235
    For whom, and not for Tybalt, Juliet pined.
    You, to remove that siege of grief from her,
    Betrothed and would have married her perforce
    To County Paris. Then comes she to me
    And with wild looks bid me devise some mean   240
    To rid her from this second marriage,
    Or in my cell there would she kill herself.
    Then gave I her, so tutored by my art,
    A sleeping potion; which so took effect
    As I intended, for it wrought on her   245
    The form of death. Meantime I writ to Romeo
    That he should hither come as this dire night

To help to take her from her borrowed[26] grave,
Being the time the potion's force should cease.
But he which bore my letter, Friar John,   250
Was stayed by accident, and yesternight
Returned my letter back. Then all alone
At the prefixèd hour of her waking
Came I to take her from her kindred's vault;
Meaning to keep her closely[27] at my cell   255
Till I conveniently could send to Romeo.
But when I came, some minute ere the time
Of her awakening, here untimely lay
The noble Paris and true Romeo dead.
She wakes; and I entreated her come forth   260
And bear this work of heaven with patience;
But then a noise did scare me from the tomb,
And she, too desperate, would not go with me,
But, as it seems, did violence on herself.
All this I know, and to the marriage   265
Her nurse is privy;[28] and if aught in this
Miscarried by my fault, let my old life
Be sacrificed some hour before his time
Unto the rigor of severest law.
PRINCE. We still have known thee for a holy man.   270
Where's Romeo's man? What can he say to this?
BALTHASAR. I brought my master news of Juliet's death;
And then in post[29] he came from Mantua
To this same place, to this same monument.
This letter he early bid me give his father,   275
And threatened me with death, going in the vault,
If I departed not and left him there.
PRINCE. Give me the letter. I will look on it.
Where is the County's page that raised the watch?
Sirrah, what made your master in this place?   280
PAGE. He came with flowers to strew his lady's grave;
And bid me stand aloof, and so I did.
Anon comes one with light to ope the tomb;
And by and by my master drew on him;
And then I ran away to call the watch.   285
PRINCE. This letter doth make good the Friar's words,
Their course of love, the tidings of her death;
And here he writes that he did buy a poison
Of a poor 'pothecary and therewithal
Came to this vault to die and lie with Juliet.   290
Where be these enemies? Capulet, Montague,
See what a scourge[30] is laid upon your hate,

26. **borrowed,** temporary.

27. **closely,** secretly.

28. **privy** (priv′ē), in on the secret.

29. **in post,** in haste.

30. **scourge,** punishment.

That heaven finds means to kill your joys with love.
And I, for winking at your discords too,
Have lost a brace of kinsmen. All are punished.   **295**

CAPULET. O brother Montague, give me thy hand.
This is my daughter's jointure,[31] for no more   31. **jointure,** dowry.
Can I demand.

MONTAGUE.   But I can give thee more;
For I will raise her statue in pure gold,
That whiles Verona by that name is known,   **300**
There shall no figure at such rate[32] be set   32. **rate,** value.
As that of true and faithful Juliet.

CAPULET. As rich shall Romeo's by his lady's lie,
Poor sacrifices of our enmity.

PRINCE. A glooming peace this morning with it brings.   **305**
The sun for sorrow will not show his head.
Go hence, to have more talk of these sad things;
Some shall be pardoned, and some punishèd;
For never was a story of more woe
Than this of Juliet and her Romeo.   **310**

Tying the Scenes Together: Scene 3

Romeo has killed Paris at the Capulet tomb and has drunk poison
himself before the Friar arrives. Juliet has stabbed herself upon
discovering Romeo dead. The Prince, the Capulets, and the
Montagues have come to the Capulet tomb. Friar Laurence has
explained why Romeo and Juliet are dead, and the families have
agreed to put an end to their senseless feud.

READING FOR DETAILS

A Tragic Tale Is Ended

1. In Scene 1, what desperate course of
   action does Romeo take after Balthasar
   brings him the news about Juliet?
2. Why had Friar John been unable to deliver Friar Laurence's letter to Romeo?
   What does Friar Laurence decide he
   must do immediately?
3. Explain the presence of Paris at the
   tomb. What does he think when he sees
   Romeo come into the burial vault?
4. What dreadful sight meets the eyes of
   Friar Laurence when he enters the
   Capulet tomb? Why does he leave the
   tomb even though Juliet has awakened?

5. Why does Juliet kill herself? Which two
   people are caught by the watchmen?
6. What causes the Capulets and the Montagues to end their feud? What do the
   fathers decide to do to commemorate
   their children's love?

READING FOR MEANING

Many people argue about the central theme,
or what Shakespeare was trying to show in
Romeo and Juliet. Perhaps he had more than
one theme. Or he may have had one central
theme and a number of less important ones.
Discuss the following statements and decide
whether you can find support for all of them
in the play and which one or ones you would
consider important enough to be themes.

1. The road to disaster is paved with good intentions.
2. A person's destiny is determined in the stars or by fate.
3. Grief is a common cause of death.
4. Love triumphs over hate.
5. Youth often must suffer for parents' mistakes.
6. Haste and lack of wise forethought bring about disaster.
7. There is a close connection between the characters of men and the misfortunes they suffer.
8. The force of overwhelming love is bound to result in good.
9. The only way some people learn is through suffering.
10. Most of life's misfortunes are the result of accidental happenings.

BIOGRAPHICAL NOTE

William Shakespeare (1564–1616) was one of the greatest dramatists and poets in Western literature. By the time he wrote *Romeo and Juliet,* it is believed that he had already written more than a half dozen of the thirty-seven plays that were to make him world famous. Very little is actually known about his boyhood, his schooling, or how he happened to become a writer and an actor. One story is that he got started as a dramatist by holding the horses of playgoers outside a theater in London. Eventually an opportunity presented itself, and he was given employment within. But this may be just folklore.

Although many details of his life are obscure, it is known that Shakespeare was born in the town of Stratford-on-Avon, England, in April of 1564, the son of a prosperous shopkeeper and glovemaker. His father held a number of city offices, including those of alderman and mayor. Because of his father's importance in the community, William would have been entitled to go to grammar school free. Many Shakespeare scholars believe that this is what happened. In the grammar school of that time, he would have received all the learning necessary to become a writer. Many cultivated men of Shakespeare's time received all their formal education in grammar school.

The one record of his youth that is undisputed is a marriage license, issued by the Bishop of Worcester in 1582, permitting him to marry Anne Hathaway. He was then eighteen and Anne some seven or eight years older. They had three children, a girl first and twins about two years later.

What Shakespeare first did to make a living is not certain. Some believe he may have been a teacher for a short period in Stratford, but there is no proof that this is true.

It is known that by 1592, he was one of the best-established and most important dramatists in London. As well as being a successful actor and playwright, Shakespeare was a good businessman. Acting troupes were then organized on a business basis and shared the profits they made in producing plays. Shakespeare was a member of a company made up of the greatest actors in England which was known as the King's Men after 1603, when King James I of England became its patron.

The members of the King's Men had their own building, the Globe, one of the handsomest theaters of the time. In the cold English winters, however, its open-air center discouraged many people from attending the plays. To overcome this difficulty, Shakespeare's company took over a roomy hall located within the walls of an old monastery building. This hall, protected from the weather, with a stage artificially lighted by candle chandeliers, became a very popular winter playhouse known as the Second Blackfriars Theater.

During his career in London, Shakespeare made enough money to buy a home for his family in Stratford as well as a good deal of other property. He retired to Stratford about five years before his death to live as a "gentleman," a title which meant he was by that time the possessor of a royal coat of arms.

The Ways of a Poet

What Is Poetry?

What is poetry? Who knows?
Not a rose, but the scent of the rose;
Not the sky, but the light in the sky;
Not the fly, but the gleam of the fly;
Not the sea, but the sound of the sea;
Not myself, but what makes me
See, hear, and feel something that prose
Cannot: and what it is, who knows?

ELEANOR FARJEON

Bivalve

The pearl is a disease of the oyster,
A poem is a disease of the spirit
Caused by the irritation
Of a granule of Truth
Fallen into that soft gray bivalve
We call the mind.

CHRISTOPHER MORLEY

ABSTRACTION ON SPECTRUM
Stanton MacDonald-Wright
Des Moines Art Center
Coffin Fine Arts Trust Fund

On Poetry

If I read a book and it makes my whole
        body so cold no fire can warm me,
I know that is poetry.
If I feel physically as if the top of my head
        were taken off,
I know that is poetry.
These are the only ways I know it.
Is there any other way?

EMILY DICKINSON

When we read a poem or hear one read, we are seeing for a moment through the poet's eyes. It is almost as if the poet had said to us simply, "Look, I have seen something interesting; I have felt a certain way about it; I would like to share my experience with you."

If we accept the poet's invitation, if we try to understand her or his response to life, we may discover new, exciting ways of seeing the world around us. We may increase our understanding of other people and even of ourselves. The poet's purpose is to make the reader see and feel through skillful use of language. The sculptor fashions clay or stone; the painter mixes colors and transfers them to canvas; the poet works with words, arranging and rearranging them to convey meaning.

An effective poem concentrates much thought and feeling into a short space. Consider, for example, the vivid impression the poet Louis MacNeice suggests with the title and first two lines of this poem:

Sunday Morning
Down the road someone is practicing scales,
The notes like little fishes vanish with a wink of tails. . . .

Both the title and the lines at once appeal to our senses of time and place, seeing and hearing. We react to the words "Sunday Morning" in terms of our own Sunday mornings, usually a time of quiet. We are reminded of all the times we have heard someone practicing a musical instrument in the distance. We see the black shapes of the notes with their "tails" squirming across a sheet of music. We hear the runs of musical scales as each note dashes through the air of the quiet street like a tiny fish darting in a stream.

MacNeice has made his twenty words count. He calls to mind the reader's own experience in order to create a sharp sense of Sunday morning. The comparison of musical notes to little fishes strikes us with a sense of surprise. Here lies the true test of all poets—*what their poetry does to us.*

Obviously, if a poem is going to have any effect upon us, we must cooperate with the poet. We must allow the poet's words to shape our imaginations. In the poems printed on

"Sunday Morning" from COLLECTED POEMS, by Louis MacNeice. Reprinted by permission of Oxford University Press.

the next few pages, one poet asks us to see a hungry child staring through a train window; another asks us to see an orange-haired old woman feeding pigeons by the public library. We must be willing to see with these poets, feel with them, laugh with them, listen to their stories.

Poetry is usually printed in a pattern of short, rhythmical lines surrounded by more than the usual amount of white space on the page. Sometimes it is in rhyme, sometimes not. Often it even springs at us from a page of prose, as when, in *The Red Badge of Courage,* Stephen Crane writes: "The red sun was pasted in the sky like a wafer." Poetry, finally, is as much a part of the rhythm of living as is breathing or the beat of the heart.

Although poetry often comes to us through our eyes, it will not give us the greatest pleasure if it does not also strike our ears. In all likelihood, you will read the verses on the following pages silently. However, read some of them *aloud,* not once but two or three times. As you do so, observe carefully the way each poem is punctuated. Failure to do this is like driving through traffic ignoring the traffic signals.

The practice of voicing the rhythm and sound of the lines will help you get more enjoyment from the poems. Studying the poems will also stimulate you to look about you with new eyes and to listen with new ears.

UNIT TECHNIQUES

The poet Coleridge declared that poetry is "the best words in their best order." Other people before and after him have said so many other things that, finally, it is not easy to say exactly what poetry is. Certainly it isn't just rhyme or meter, because acceptable poetry has been written without one or the other of these. *Blank verse* lacks rhyme and *free verse* lacks a formal beat. However, while no one can say what it is that any one poem must have, there are general characteristics that can be discovered from a study of a large body of poetry. Some of these are imagery, rhyme and rhythm, and technique and type.

IMAGERY

Poetry is usually rich in *imagery* or *figurative language* involving some form of comparison. Of the varied forms of comparison, *simile* and *metaphor* are most often used. In brief review, the simile uses connectives such as *like* or *as* to compare dissimilar things. In Louis Mac-Neice's poem, "Sunday Morning," for example, (p. 410) the poet compares musical notes to swimming fish: "Down the road someone is practicing scales,/The notes like little fishes vanish with a wink of tails. . . ."

Metaphor makes a direct comparison without the use of a connective. An example of this is found in Carl Wendell Hines, Jr.'s poem "Jazz Poem Two," lines 36–39, (p. 189): ". . . he/is no longer a man. no not even/a Black man. but (yeah!)/a Bird!—"

Symbolism, another form of comparison, generally uses a tangible (real, concrete) object to represent something that is intangible (cannot be seen, heard, or felt). Thus, in Aesop's fable about the father and his sons, (p. 267) the bundle of sticks represents unity.

Personification, in which nonhuman things or ideas are given human qualities or shape, is still another kind of comparison. In *Romeo and Juliet* (Act I, Scene 2, lines 25–26, p. 332), Shakespeare wrote: "When well-apparelled April on the heel/Of limping Winter treads, . . ." Here he personified April and Winter as human—April, well-dressed and eager; Winter, tired and limping.

Because, in poetry, every word must count, figurative language is an indispensable aid to writers who must concisely and imaginatively picture the things they want the reader to see.

RHYME AND RHYTHM

Rhyme may be defined as the repetition of similar or identical sounds in the middle or at the ends of lines of poetry. *Rhythm* is the pattern of stressed and unstressed syllables in the lines. Rhyme and rhythm so delight the ear and appeal to the senses that they have always been tools of poets to use or not to use as they desire.

Poetry which has *meter,* that is, a generally *regular* pattern of stressed and unstressed syllables, is divided into units called *feet.* In English, a foot most often consists of one stressed and one or more unstressed syllables.

"Ĭ méant/tŏ dó/mý wórk/tŏdáy."

There are four *iambic* (an unstressed syllable followed by a stressed syllable) feet in the line above, taken from a poem you will be reading. (p. 434) In English, the standard poetic feet are: iambic (˘ ′), trochaic (′ ˘), anapestic (˘ ˘ ′), dactylic (′ ˘ ˘), spondaic (′ ′), and pyrrhic (˘ ˘).

The standard English lines are: monometer, one foot; dimeter, two feet; trimeter, three feet; tetrameter, four feet; pentameter, five feet; hexameter, six feet; heptameter, seven feet; and octameter, eight feet.

Iambic pentameter appears more frequently in English verse than any other metrical line. It may be rhymed or unrhymed. *Blank verse* is usually defined as unrhymed iambic pentameter. It is the closest of the metrical forms to casual English speech and was often used masterfully by Shakespeare in his plays.

"H̆e jésts/ăt scárs/thăt né/vĕr félt/ă wóund.

Bŭt sóft,/whăt líght/thr̆ough yón/dĕr wín/dŏw breáks?"

In the above lines selected at random from *Romeo and Juliet,* (Act II, Scene 2, lines 1–2, p. 346), Romeo first comments about his jesting friend Mercutio before beginning his famous balcony speech. You will note in checking the rest of his speech in your text that the words definitely follow blank verse patterning, although they have been spoken with such variety of expression by actors over the years.

Now glance back at the Prologue opening Act II. You quickly realize that *lie* rhymes with *die* and *heir* with *fair,* and that the alternate rhyme continues down to the last two lines which rhyme as a *couplet.*

It is obvious that the *Prologue,* as a poem in itself, follows a definite *rhyme scheme,* or rhyme pattern. A rhyme scheme is designated by a new letter of the alphabet for each new rhyme. Thus the rhyme pattern of the *Prologue* is abab cdcd efef gg. The rhythm is iambic pentameter, made up of three *quatrains* (four-line stanzas) and a final couplet. This is known as Shakespearean, or English, *sonnet* form.

Free verse, as distinguished from blank verse, does not follow any metered pattern. Most literary critics agree, however, that good free verse has what is termed "poetic rhythm," or word flow that carries the reader along in emotional response to the poem's thought. For an example of free verse, see "The Term," page 422.

Just as prose writing has paragraph divisions, so poetry is divided into stanzas. The *stanza,* a grouping of two or more lines, may be determined by the need to separate thoughts or by the rhyme or rhythm pattern.

SOUND EFFECTS

Poets have special ways of using words and rhymes. *Alliteration* is the repetition of beginning sounds. These beginning sounds, most often consonants or consonant clusters, can be heard in the example, "The tall, tanned Texan." In *tall* and *tanned* there is also the repetition of the vowel sound *a*. Repetition of similar vowel sounds in close proximity is called *assonance.* The very *repetition,* or repeating of words, sounds, lines, or stanzas in poetry, is in itself a technique that can add much musicality and rhythm to poetry. Another effective poetic device is *onomatopoeia,* the use of words whose sounds suggest their meanings. You can hear it in "the *buzz* of a bee."

POETIC FORMS

Some of the special types of poetry are lyric, light and satiric verse, haiku, ballads, and epics. *Lyric* verse speaks of the poet's feelings. The name reminds us that such poetry was once sung to the accompaniment of a small, harplike instrument called a lyre. *Ballads,* also, were originally for singing. These traditional story-poems were common during the Middle Ages and survived by word of mouth for hundreds of years before they were written down. In general, their language is simple: they contain refrains and they celebrate love, bravery, or treachery. *Epics* like the *Odyssey* are longer and more heroic than ballads, but they, too, are narrative, storytelling poetry.

Humorous verse and *light* verse are playful poetry, while *satiric* verse holds its subject up to ridicule.

THE POET SEES

In this section, "The Poet Sees," each writer has tried to present sharp-edged pictures. The sense of sight—the shapes, the sizes, the colors of things—is dominant in these poems. But the poets may appeal to the other senses as well. They call to mind the smell, the taste, the sound, the touch of the world around us.

Mechanical things often seem to have a life of their own. This poem lets us see a steam shovel as a prehistoric beast.

Steam Shovel

The dinosaurs are not all dead.
I saw one raise its iron head
To watch me walking down the road
Beyond our house today.
Its jaws were dripping with a load   5
Of earth and grass that it had cropped.
It must have heard me where I stopped,
Snorted white steam my way,
And stretched its long neck out to see,
And chewed, and grinned quite amiably.   10

CHARLES MALAM

Ogden Nash's glimpses of
creatures are quick and comic.

The Hippopotamus

Behold the hippopotamus!
We laugh at how he looks to us,
And yet in moments dank and grim
I wonder how we look to him.
Peace, peace, thou hippopotamus!   5
We really look all right to us,
As you no doubt delight the eye
Of other hippopotami.

OGDEN NASH

The Camel

The camel has a single hump;
The dromedary, two;
Or else the other way around.
I'm never sure. Are you?

OGDEN NASH

The Ostrich

The ostrich roams the great Sahara.*
Its mouth is wide, its neck is narra.
It has such long and lofty legs,
I'm glad it sits to lay its eggs.

OGDEN NASH

* **The Sahara** (sə har′ə, sə här′ə) is the great desert of
North Africa.

A chance glimpse of a face
you may never see again—why does it haunt you?

Through a Train Window

Hunger-eyed and sallow-cheeked
The child stared in at me, and
I stared back, full-bellied,
A vintage wine beside my plate.
No despair showed on her face,   5
None at least that I could see.
Just a trace of disbelief
That I ate there instead of she.

GORDON PARKS

These poems by Richard Wright follow a pattern
developed by the Japanese centuries ago. Called a hokku, or
haiku, each poem captures a complete picture or mood in
seventeen syllables, with five syllables in the first line, seven
in the second line, and five in the third.

Hokku Poems

I am nobody
A red sinking autumn sun
Took my name away

In the falling snow
A laughing boy holds out his palms
Until they are white

The crow flew so fast
That he left his lonely caw
Behind in the fields

RICHARD WRIGHT

How do the following two poems
suggest that the pigeon and the eagle
resemble human beings?

Pigeon Woman
May Swenson

Slate, or dirty-marble-colored,
or rusty-iron-colored, the pigeons
on the flagstones in front of the
Public Library make a sharp lake

into which the pigeon woman wades   5
at exactly 1:30. She wears a
plastic pink raincoat with a round
collar (looking like a little

girl, so gay) and flat gym shoes,
her hair square-cut orange.   10
Wide-apart feet carefully enter
the spinning, crooning waves

(as if she'd just learned how
to walk, each step conscious,
an accomplishment) blue knots in the   15
calves of her bare legs (uglied marble),

age in angled cords of jaw
and neck, her pimento-colored hair,
hanging in thin tassels, is gray
around a balding crown.   20

The day-old bread drops down
from her veined hand dipping out
of a paper sack. Choppy, shadowy ripples,
the pigeons strike around her legs.

Sack empty, she squats and seems to rinse   25
her hands in them—the rainy greens and
oily purples of their necks. Almost
they let her wet her thirsty fingertips—

but drain away in an untouchable tide.
A make-believe trade   30
she has come to, in her lostness
or illness or age—to treat the motley

city pigeons at 1:30 every day, in all
weathers. It is for them she colors
her own feathers. Ruddy-footed   35
on the lime-stained paving,

purling to meet her when she comes,
they are a lake of love. Retreating
from her hands as soon as empty,
they are the flints of love.   40

The Eagle

He clasps the crag with crooked hands;
Close to the sun in lonely lands,
Ring'd with the azure world, he stands.

The wrinkled sea beneath him crawls;
He watches from his mountain walls,   5
And like a thunderbolt he falls.

ALFRED, LORD TENNYSON

What tells the wild geese when to fly south?

Something Told the Wild Geese

a	Something told the wild geese
b	It was time to go.
c	Though the fields lay golden
b	Something whispered, "Snow."
d	Leaves were green and stirring, 5
e	Berries, luster-glossed,
f	But beneath warm feathers
e	Something cautioned, "Frost."
g	All the sagging orchards
h	Steamed with amber spice, 10
i	But each wild breast stiffened
h	At remembered ice.
a	Something told the wild geese
j	It was time to fly—
k	Summer sun was on their wings, 15
j	Winter in their cry.

RACHEL FIELD

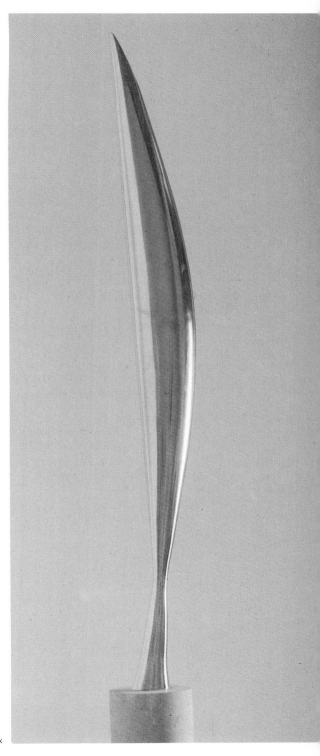

BIRD IN SPACE
Constantin Brancusi
Constantin Brancusi Collection
The Museum of Modern Art, New York

Is there life after war?

There Will Come Soft Rains

War Time

There will come soft rains and the smell of the ground,
And swallows circling with their shimmering sound;

And frogs in the pools singing at night,
And wild plum-trees in tremulous* white.

Robins will wear their feathery fire   5
Whistling their whims on a low-fence-wire;

And not one will know of the war, not one
Will care at last when it is done.

Not one would mind, neither bird nor tree,
If mankind perished utterly;   10

And Spring herself, when she woke at dawn
Would scarcely know that we were gone.

SARA TEASDALE

* **tremulous,** trembling.

On which of these ships
would you care to sail?

Cargoes

Quinquireme[1] of Nineveh[2] from distant Ophir,[3]
Rowing home to haven in sunny Palestine,
With a cargo of ivory,
And apes and peacocks,
Sandalwood, cedarwood, and sweet white wine.   5

Stately Spanish galleon coming from the Isthmus,[4]
Dipping through the Tropics by the palm-green shores,
With a cargo of diamonds,
Emeralds, amethysts,
Topazes, and cinnamon, and gold moidores.[5]   10

Dirty British coaster with a salt-caked smokestack,
Butting through the Channel in the mad March days,
With a cargo of Tyne coal,[6]
Road rails, pig lead,
Firewood, ironware, and cheap tin trays.   15

JOHN MASEFIELD

1. **Quinquireme** (kwink'kwə'rēm), an ancient galley propelled by five banks of oars.
2. **Nineveh** (nin'ə və), ancient city on the Tigris River, in Asia Minor.
3. **Ophir** (o'fər), ancient country rich in gold.
4. **Isthmus** (is'məs), Panama.
5. **moidores** (moi'dôrz'), Portuguese gold coins.
6. **Tyne coal,** coal from the British mining center, Newcastle-upon-Tyne.

See the picture this poet
is painting with words. Is it more than just
a picture?

The Term

A rumpled sheet
of brown paper
about the length

and apparent bulk
of a man was   5
rolling with the

wind slowly over
and over in
the street as

a car drove down   10
upon it and
crushed it to

the ground. Unlike
a man it rose
again rolling   15

with the wind over
and over to be as
it was before.

WILLIAM CARLOS WILLIAMS

The next two verses tell us humorously of human foibles. Reading the first one is like rapidly flipping a TV channel selector. The second reveals that at times even birds seem to act like people.

Reflections Dental

How pure, how beautiful, how fine
Do teeth on television shine!
No flutist flutes, no dancer twirls,
But comes equipped with matching pearls.
Gleeful announcers all are born   5
With sets like rows of hybrid corn.
Clowns, critics, clergy, commentators,
Ventriloquists and roller skaters,
M.C.s who beat their palms together,
The girl who diagrams the weather,   10
The crooner crooning for his supper—
All flash white treasures, lower and upper.
With miles of smiles the airwaves teem,
And each an orthodontist's* dream.

'Twould please my eye as gold a miser's—   15
One charmer with uncapped incisors.

PHYLLIS McGINLEY

"Reflections Dental" from TIMES THREE by Phyllis McGinley. Copyright © 1957 by Phyllis McGinley. Originally appeared in *The New Yorker*. Reprinted by permission of Viking Penguin, Inc.

* **orthodontist** (ôr′thə don′tist), a dentist who specializes in straightening teeth.

Seagulls

Two medicos, immaculate in gray
Hold converse on the pilings of the quay.
Each eyes the other with a chilly glance,
As rivals will, of deep malevolence;
Each then propounds his learned diagnosis: 5
"Ulcer," screams one; the other shrieks, "Cirrhosis!"

Then, since the conferees will not agree,
Professionally cool, they fly away.

FRANCES HIGGINSON SAVAGE

Reprinted by permission of The Golden Quill Press.

It's all in how you look at it.

Point of View

Thanksgiving dinner's sad and thankless
Christmas dinner's dark and blue
When you stop and try to see it
From the turkey's point of view.

Sunday dinner isn't sunny   5
Easter feasts are just bad luck
When you see it from the viewpoint
Of a chicken or a duck.

Oh how I once loved tuna salad
Pork and lobsters, lamb chops too   10
Till I stopped and looked at dinner
From the dinner's point of view.

SHEL SILVERSTEIN

How do *you* visualize spring rain? How does it
sound to *you*? When you have just the right picture
in your mind and just the right sound in your ears, read
the following poem.

Rain Music

On the dusty earth-drum
  Beats the falling rain;
Now a whispered murmur,
  Now a louder strain.

Slender, silvery drumsticks, 5
  On an ancient drum,
Beat the mellow music
  Bidding life to come.

Chords of earth awakened,
  Notes of greening spring, 10
Rise and fall triumphant
  Over every thing.

Slender, silvery drumsticks
  Beat the long tattoo—
God, the Great Musician, 15
  Calling life anew.

JOSEPH SEAMON COTTER, JR.

No pretense about this
poem, is there? Do you like it? Why?

Soup

I saw a famous man eating soup.
I say he was lifting a fat broth
Into his mouth with a spoon.
His name was in the newspapers that day
Spelled out in tall black headlines 5
And thousands of people were talking about him.

  When I saw him,
He sat bending his head over a plate
Putting soup in his mouth with a spoon.

CARL SANDBURG

From SMOKE AND STEEL by Carl Sandburg, copyright, 1920, by Harcourt Brace Jovanovich, Inc.; copyright, 1948, by Carl Sandburg. Reprinted
by permission of the publishers.

The poet of the following sketch has given you such exacting facts to observe that you might not be aware that he has included some ideas for you to consider.

The Runaway

Once when the snow of the year was beginning to fall,
We stopped by a mountain pasture to say, "Whose colt?"
A little Morgan* had one forefoot on the wall,
The other curled at his breast. He dipped his head
And snorted at us. And then he had to bolt.   5
We heard the miniature thunder where he fled,
And we saw him, or thought we saw him, dim and gray,
Like a shadow against the curtain of falling flakes.
"I think the little fellow's afraid of the snow.
He isn't winter-broken. It isn't play   10
With the little fellow at all. He's running away.
I doubt if even his mother could tell him, 'Sakes,
It's only weather.' He'd think she didn't know!
Where is his mother? He can't be out alone."
And now he comes again with a clatter of stone,   15
And mounts the wall again with whited eyes
And all his tail that isn't hair up straight.
He shudders his coat as if to throw off flies.
"Whoever it is that leaves him out so late,
When other creatures have gone to stall and bin,   20
Ought to be told to come and take him in."

ROBERT FROST

* **Morgan,** one of a famous small, sturdy breed of horses.

Many people have the mistaken idea
that poetry is always about nature, flowers, love,
and generally vague topics. "The Base Stealer,"
like "Soup," shows that a real poet can find
something of interest in the most common event.
The subject of this poem is no farther away
than your local ball park.

The Base Stealer

Poised between going on and back, pulled
Both ways taut like a tightrope-walker,
Fingertips pointing the opposites,
Now bouncing tiptoe like a dropped ball
Or a kid skipping rope, come on, come on,   5

Running a scattering of steps sidewise,
How he teeters, skitters, tingles, teases,
Taunts them, hovers like an ecstatic bird,
He's only flirting, crowd him, crowd him,
Delicate, delicate, delicate, delicate—now!   10

ROBERT FRANCIS

THE POET SEES

Steam Shovel

The poet observes a common sight—an earth-moving machine in action. His reaction is far from ordinary. What has he done to transform an ordinary subject into a delightful picture?

Explain how the poet uses *metaphor* in the poem. For a review of this term, see Unit Techniques, page 412.

At the time this poem was written, most steam shovels were actually powered by steam, as the name implies. Now, however, these machines have either diesel or gasoline engines. What mythical monster does the poet suggest when he says the machine "snorted white steam"?

Three Poems by Ogden Nash

Ogden Nash was one of America's most popular writers of humorous verse. To make us laugh, he tried to take us by surprise, to catch us off guard. With his unexpected endings and his unusual, even fantastic, rhymes he gives a whimsical view of everyday subjects. Incidentally, how many humps does a dromedary have?

From these verses by Ogden Nash, select an example to show how the poet has stretched the shapes of words to make a rhyme. Discuss how this affects the humor. Consider and discuss this statement: Beauty is in the eye of the beholder.

Through a Train Window

Gordon Parks is a well-known photographer as well as a writer. In his book *A Poet and His Camera,* from which this poem comes, there is a photograph of the little girl he saw through the window. Other people looking out at her might not have seen what Parks saw. They might have been more interested in the way she was dressed or perhaps wondered why she was standing so near the train.

1. What does the fact that he had a "vin-

tage wine" beside his plate indicate about the cost of the meal?

2. What does this poem tell you about the poet?

Hokku Poems

Discuss the picture or momentary observation you find in each of Richard Wright's poems. Which of the three do you find most vivid? Why?

Pigeon Woman; The Eagle

May Swenson uses imagery combined with colors to paint her picture of the pigeon woman.

1. What detailed metaphor does she use to describe the way the woman approaches and feeds the birds?

2. What colors does she use in making the word picture vivid?

3. What is the woman seeking in her feeding of the birds? Do they give it to her?

4. Why do you think Tennyson uses the word *hands* in line one? Why not *claws,* which would be more accurate and more in tune with the *c* sounds?

Something Told the Wild Geese

If all poetry were written in regular, rhymed patterns, the reader would soon cry out for relief—for something to break the monotonous beat. But the experienced poet knows when to use a regular, controlled verse pattern to make a strong impression on the reader's senses and help convey the feeling she or he intends. In her poem, Rachel Field expresses the idea that wild creatures feel the rhythms of the changing seasons and somehow know when to do what they are supposed to do.

1. What were those things that should have misled the geese into staying longer in the region where they were "summering"?

2. In the final two lines why does the poet say the geese have "Summer . . . on their wings . . ." and "Winter in their cry"?

3. Lines 2 and 4 rhyme. What other pairs of lines rhyme to make this verse form regular?

There Will Come Soft Rains

The poet questions the relative importance of mankind in the eternal cycle of nature.

1. Describe the images and the tone of the first three stanzas. How is the tone affected by the rhyme and alliteration?

2. What kind of imagery is found in the last three stanzas? Describe the change in tone.

3. Why do you think the poet included the subtitle?

Cargoes

From ancient times to modern times, ships have sailed the seven seas carrying every kind of cargo imaginable.

1. The first two ships in the poem carry cargoes that are magnificent, exotic, and colorful. What kind of cargo does the third ship carry? How does the poet use language to convey his feelings about the three ships?

2. When read carefully, the first two parts of "Cargoes" proceed smoothly word to word. The rhythm of the third part is characterized by several jolting stops and starts. How does this change in rhythm reflect the poet's attitude toward the third ship and its cargo?

What does the poem imply about the differences between past times and modern times?

The Term

1. Do you think William Carlos Williams intended his poem to amuse you, to make you angry, to make you think?

2. Discuss whether the experience described is one common to many persons.

3. Why did the paper look like a man? How did it show it was different from a man?

4. If it had been a man, what would very likely have happened to the term, or period of life, he had to live?

Reflections Dental; Seagulls

To help us see more than surface situations in their verses, these poets use a gentle form of *satire*.

1. What human trait is being satirized in each of these poems?

2. Some poets employ what is called near-rhyme. Look up the pronunciation of *quay*, found in the poem "Seagulls." Does it rhyme with *gray*? What other examples of near-rhyme do you find in this poem?

3. Give the rhyme scheme for "Reflections Dental." If you are a bit uncertain about marking rhyme scheme, turn back to Unit Techniques, page 413, then study the rhyme scheme marked for "Something Told the Wild Geese," page 419.

Point of View

Shel Silverstein's poetry is considered both funny and profound.

1. The rhyme scheme in "Point of View" seems to signal to the reader: "I'm being funny." What is the rhyme scheme? In what manner would you read the poem aloud?

2. In the poem Silverstein could be promoting a serious idea. What might it be?

Rain Music

Now that you have read the poem "Rain Music," in what ways did Cotter's impressions of spring rain differ from yours? Was the mood of the poem different from yours? Explain.

The poet's purpose was certainly to create a colorful word picture of sight and sound—the rising symphony of rain. His images, "dusty earth-drum," "slender, silvery drumsticks," "mellow music," "greening spring," appeal to the senses and stir the imagination. But the poet also had something else in mind. What does he suggest about the cycle of life and seasons?

Read the last four lines again. Without

this last verse, what idea would have been omitted?

Soup

A famous man looks just like any other man when he's eating a bowl of soup, according to Carl Sandburg.

1. Is the poet's choice of language realistic or imaginative? Why does the title fit the poem so well?
2. Discuss whether you think readers see what Sandburg wanted them to see when they have finished reading the poem.

The Runaway

1. Anyone who has observed the ways of colts knows that Robert Frost's description of the little Morgan is true to life. Read the poem again, carefully. Do you think Frost means to suggest a similarity between the behavior of the colt and that of another kind of young animal?
2. Discuss the effects that the poet achieves with the following: "curled at his breast," "miniature thunder," "winter-broken," "whited eyes," "shudders his coat," "stall and bin."

The Base Stealer

Understanding this poem requires some knowledge of baseball. If you have ever tried to steal a base or have watched someone try it, you know that base stealing is an art. It requires nerve, speed, timing, and the ability to make a split-second decision. It requires, too, the ability to rattle the players on the opposing team so they will be caught off balance when the base stealer finally streaks toward the coveted base.

1. In this lively, one-sentence look at the player's antics, the poet interjects directions and comments to the players. Find these interjections and discuss what effect the poet gains by using them.
2. Look again at the words in the last line.

To whom do you think they are spoken? They are spoken in response to what kind of action taking place on the field?

COMPOSITION

The haiku, or hokku, with its seventeen syllables is short enough to be spoken in one breath. It is one tiny scene, one observation that is almost like a photograph.

In composing haiku, writers make an observation, recording their impression through a careful choice and placement of words. Usually each haiku answers three questions: what the main topic of interest is, where it is, and when. Some writers choose to rhyme the first and third lines in order to make each verse seem a complete unit. Finally, the writer must choose words carefully so that they make up the exact syllabic count for each line: five syllables in line one, seven syllables in line two, and five syllables in line three.

The following are two examples of haiku written by students. Note that the first one rhymes.

Through the greening earth
The purple crocus lifts up
Arms in sudden birth.

Across the desert
Wagons keep moving westward.
The red man watches.

Now try your hand at writing a haiku—or two or three or four. You will find it challenging fun.

A SUMMING UP

The Poet Sees

Think back over some of the poems you have read in this section. *Do not turn back to the poems.* Think of each poem in turn. Let the images from each poem come before your eyes like a series of paintings hung in a row. Which images remain sharp in your mind?

Which is the most vivid? Here, for your reference, are the titles of some of the poems to consider:

"Through a Train Window"
"Hokku Poems"
"Cargoes"
"Soup"
"The Term"
"Seagulls"
"Pigeon Woman"
"The Base Stealer"

When you have decided which is the most vivid image for you, turn back to the poem in which it occurs. Study the poem and the image. Then write a paragraph of a few sentences explaining why this particular word picture stayed with you.

If possible, exchange papers with others and read them aloud to compare reasons for making choices. It should be interesting, and you will find out that there are many ways of seeing a poem.

BIOGRAPHICAL NOTES

Joseph Seamon Cotter, Jr. (1895–1919) was born in Louisville, Kentucky. He attended Fisk University but developed tuberculosis in his eighteenth year and was forced to leave school. His poetry, most of which he wrote during the last six years of his illness, is ranked among the best produced by black poets in the period during World War I.

Rachel Field (1894–1942) often wrote of the New England countryside where she spent her early years. She was the first woman to win the Newbery Medal and was a successful writer of adult fiction and biography in addition to poetry.

Robert Francis (1901–   ), poet, lecturer, and teacher, was born in Upland, Pennsylvania. A graduate of Harvard University, he was the Harvard Phi Beta Kappa poet in 1960. His chief interests are writing, reading, music, and gardening.

Robert Frost (1874–1963) was born in San Francisco. When he was ten years old his father died, and the family moved to Lawrence, Massachusetts, the home of several generations of his family. After attending Dartmouth College for a short time, Frost left to work at a variety of jobs—mill hand, schoolteacher, and farmer. Following his marriage, he entered Harvard University, but left after two years to become a farmer in New Hampshire. When he failed in this, he took his family to England and devoted three years to writing. His first two books of poetry, *A Boy's Will* and *North of Boston,* were immediately successful, and he returned to the United States.

In New England he continued to write volume after volume of fine poetry, in addition to giving lectures, teaching in various colleges and universities, and farming. Four times Frost was awarded the Pulitzer Prize for poetry and long before his death was regarded as one of the world's foremost modern poets. While most of his verses have a New England setting, Frost was not concerned mainly with this particular section of the country. His basic concern was the drama of people engaged in everyday affairs.

At the ceremony following the inauguration of President John F. Kennedy in January, 1961, Frost became the first poet ever honored on such an occasion by being invited to read one of his poems.

Charles Malam (1906–   ) is an American poet, born in South Reygate, Vermont. When he was 21 years old, he won a $200 prize at a writer's conference for producing the most promising work. He studied in Europe and from 1929 to 1931 was a Rhodes scholar. His poems, like "Steam Shovel," often treat everyday objects and happenings with a light, whimsical touch. He has also written one-act plays.

John Masefield (1878–1967), chosen as the Poet Laureate of England in 1930, went to sea as a cabin boy when he was fourteen and continued his wanderings for several years. He returned to England in 1897, where he lived for a while with the Irish poet and playwright, Synge. His early works, based on his wanderings, tended to overemphasize passion and brutality. However, when he turned to narrative verse, his poetry seemed to bloom, because he tempered the rough physical world with the exalted spiritual one.

Phyllis McGinley (1905–1978) was born in Oregon and grew up in both Colorado and Utah. At one time she and her brother attended a rural Colorado school in which they were the only pupils. A writer of light verse and stories for children, she wrote about day-to-day happenings with much penetrating insight. She was awarded a Pulitzer Prize in 1961.

Ogden Nash (1902–1971), whose hundreds of rib-tickling rhymes have appeared in many magazines and have been collected in several books, was considered the leading American writer of humorous verse. Born in Rye, New York, Nash attended Harvard, then worked in a publishing firm before devoting full time to writing, lecturing, and giving readings.

Gordon Parks (1912–   ) was born in Fort Scott, Kansas. Recognized as one of the most creative photographic journalists in the United States, this black writer has many other talents. He plays piano well, has composed symphonies that have been performed in the United States and abroad, and has written, produced, and directed motion pictures. Among his books are the novels *The Learning Tree* and *Shannon* and an autobiography, *A Choice of Weapons*. His book *A Poet and His Camera* combines many of Parks's world famous color photographs with his poetry.

Carl Sandburg (1878–1967), "poet of the people," was born in Galesburg, Illinois.

After "riding the rails" as a hobo and trying his hand at a variety of odd jobs—newspaper reporter, advertising writer, farmhand, and foreign correspondent—Sandburg first tasted fame in 1916 with the publication of *Chicago Poems*. He was known as the "voice of the common man," writing in the vernacular and frequently using both contemporary slang and colloquialisms. Winner of two Pulitzer Prizes, Sandburg is famed for his voluminous and popular biography of Abraham Lincoln.

Frances Higginson Savage (1898–   ) was born in New York City and educated at Bryn Mawr College. She taught English for several years. She has won several prizes for her poetry, has published many books of verse, and has been published in such magazines as *Ladies' Home Journal*, *The New Yorker*, *Atlantic*, and *Lyric*.

Shel Silverstein (1923–   ), a native of Chicago, is a poet, cartoonist, folksinger, and composer of country and western songs. He has been published in several magazines and has written several popular books. *Light in the Attic*, his most current book of poems, was a best seller and is popular with both adults and children.

May Swenson (1919–   ) was born in Utah and attended Utah State University. After graduation she went to New York to write. Her poetry, which is widely read, has been praised especially for its sharp imagery. One of her popular poetry collections is *To Mix with Time*.

Sara Teasdale (1884–1933) was a Missouri-born poet who was educated at home and in private school. While still quite young, she toured Europe and the Near East. At one time she was enthusiastically courted by the poet Vachel Lindsay, whose overwhelming exuberance fascinated and frightened her. In

1914 she married Ernst Filsinger and moved to New York City. Unfortunately, she was essentially a lone spirit, and the marriage ended in divorce. Her last years were spent in seclusion . . . almost friendless. She drowned in the bath tub of her New York apartment. During her lifetime she published seven books of poetry, of which *Love Songs* (1917) won a Pulitzer Prize. Her poetry, direct and almost barren of imagery and metaphor, strives to communicate a mood rather than to state universal truths.

Alfred, Lord Tennyson (1809–1892) was a living embodiment of Victorian virtues and the perfect "bard" of his age. He was born at Somersby Rectory, Lincolnshire, into the family of a minister. In 1828, Tennyson entered Cambridge but left without achieving a degree. He joined the Spanish insurgents, and when he was twenty-four published a volume of poetry. His efforts were so derided by critics that Tennyson published nothing more for nine years. Having fallen in love with Emily Sellwood, he was rejected by her family because he lacked money to support a wife. Fourteen years later, when he was forty-one and successful, he and Emily were married. In this same year, he celebrated the enthusiastic public reception of *In Memoriam* and his appointment as Poet Laureate of England. *Idylls of the King*, a collection of verse stories about King Arthur and his knights of the round table, is one of his best-known works.

William Carlos Williams (1883–1963) was born in New Jersey where he grew up and practiced medicine. His poems and stories are popular in the United States and around the English-speaking world. For his writings Dr. Williams drew from the everyday, the commonplace. Although his verses seem at first to be simple statements, they generally yield a deeper meaning when examined carefully. His major work of poetry is *Paterson*, completed in 1958. Williams received the National Book Award for poetry in 1950. After his death he was awarded the Pulitzer Prize (1963) for poetry.

Richard Wright (1908–1960) was born on a farm near Natchez, Mississippi, and was taken to Memphis, Tennessee, in his early youth. After his father deserted his family, his partially paralyzed mother was forced first to put Wright in an orphanage and later to send him to live with various relatives. At the age of nineteen, in 1927, he went to Chicago where he worked as a street cleaner, dishwasher, post-office clerk, porter, and at other odd jobs. During this period he was writing in fictional form about his childhood in the South and his experiences in Chicago. In 1937, Wright joined the Federal Writer's Project, and his first book of four novellas, *Uncle Tom's Children*, was published in 1938. His novel *Native Son*, published in 1940, was to make him world famous. Wright lived in Paris from 1947 until his death.

THE POET FEELS

The first group of poems in THE WAYS OF A POET is titled "The Poet Sees," because the emphasis is upon external things: sights and sounds. In each of the next poems the emphasis comes from the poet's internal world. The central theme is the poet's own feelings. Note, however, that even here poets cannot express their feelings unless they refer to specific things in the world about them. It is not very interesting merely to hear someone say "I am sad" or "I am happy." Good poets express themselves in terms of particular places (as in "I Meant to Do My Work Today"), particular persons (as in "John Doe, Jr."), or particular things. Note the specific objects mentioned in "Days."

Days

Some days my thoughts are just cocoons—all cold, and dull, and blind,
They hang from dripping branches in the gray woods of my mind;
And other days they drift and shine—such free and flying things!
I find the gold dust in my hair, left by their brushing wings.

KARLE WILSON BAKER

"I Meant to Do My Work Today"

I meant to do my work today,
But a brown bird sang in the apple tree,
And a butterfly flitted across the field,
And all the leaves were calling me.

And the wind went sighing over the land,   5
Tossing the grasses to and fro,
And a rainbow held out its shining hand—
So what could I do but laugh and go?

RICHARD LE GALLIENNE

EAST WIND OVER WEEHAWKEN
Edward Hopper
Philadelphia Academy of Fine Arts
Philadelphia, Pennsylvania

How do *you* feel when you see a rainbow?

My Heart Leaps Up

My heart leaps up when I behold
A rainbow in the sky.
So was it when my life began;
So is it now I am a man,
So be it when I shall grow old,   5
  Or let me die!
The child is father of the man;
And I could wish my days to be
Bound each to each by natural piety.*

WILLIAM WORDSWORTH

*natural piety, a feeling of profound respect for nature.

Have you ever felt like this?

Empty

No, nothing
passes
through my mind;
it is like a wide sky
empty and white.   5

Yet I am here,
quiet, before you,
and looking at you,
yet I do not see you.

No, nothing   10
passes
through my mind;
it is like a wide sky
empty and white.

MARÍA NÚÑEZ
Reprinted by permission of the author.

The speaker in the next poem is also looking
back and expressing a strong feeling about what happened to
an individual, but the narrative viewpoint has shifted.

John Doe, Jr.

Among the Missing . . .
              I think he always was—
Only no one thought to mention it before. . . .
He was the boy who didn't make the team
although, God knows, he tried: his were the fingers,   5
always too eager, that always fumbled the ball.
He was the fellow
people forgot to invite when they planned a party.
After the party, once in a while, they would say,
"We should have invited John." But that was after;   10
and most of the time they did not think about it.
John thought about it: thought of the laughter and music.
He was the chap who dreamed that his loneliness
might somehow find in words a redemptive beauty:
the yearning youth who sent his poems and stories,   15
bundled in hope, to editors—and found them,
paired to rejection slips,* in his mail-box, later.
He was the man, defeated by diffidence,
who waited in line—and who did not get the job. . . .

Only war had use for him, and only   20
long enough to lose him. . . .
              Among the missing. . . .

BONARO W. OVERSTREET

"John Doe, Jr." is reprinted from HANDS LAID UPON THE WIND, by
Bonaro W. Overstreet, with the permission of W. W. Norton & Company,
Inc. Copyright 1955 by W. W. Norton & Company, Inc.

Rejection slips, notes from editors or publishers to an
author rejecting his or her product.

Do you feel the rhyme and rhythm
rocking your cares away?

The Day Is Done

The day is done, and the darkness
   Falls from the wings of night,
As a feather is wafted downward
   From an eagle in his flight.

I see the lights of the village   5
   Gleam through the rain and the mist,
And a feeling of sadness comes o'er me.
   That my soul cannot resist:

A feeling of sadness and longing,
   That is not akin to pain,   10
And resembles sorrow only
   As the mist resembles the rain.

Come, read to me some poem,
   Some simple and heartfelt lay,[1]
That shall soothe this restless feeling,   15
   And banish the thoughts of day.

Not from the grand old masters,
   Not from the bards sublime,[2]
Whose distant footsteps echo
   Through the corridors of time.   20

For, like strains of martial music,
   Their mighty thoughts suggest
Life's endless toil and endeavor;
   And tonight I long for rest.

Read from some humbler poet,   25
   Whose songs gushed from his heart,
As showers from the clouds of summer,
   Or tears from the eyelids start;

Who, through long days of labor,
   And nights devoid of ease,   30
Still heard in his soul the music
   Of wonderful melodies.

Such songs have power to quiet
   The restless pulse of care,
And come like the benediction[3]   35
   That follows after prayer.

Then read from the treasured volume
   The poem of thy choice,
And lend to the rhyme of the poet
   The beauty of thy voice.   40

And the night shall be filled with music,
   And the cares, that infest the day,
Shall fold their tents, like the Arabs,
   And as silently steal away.

HENRY WADSWORTH LONGFELLOW

1. **lay,** a ballad or story poem.
2. **bards sublime,** poets who wrote lofty, exalted poems.
3. **benediction,** state of blessedness or grace.

Here is a song of praise
dating from about the tenth century B.C.

The Twenty-third Psalm

The Lord is my shepherd; I shall not want.
He maketh me to lie down in green pastures;
    he leadeth me beside the still waters.
He restoreth my soul; he leadeth me in the paths
    of righteousness for his name's sake.   5
Yea, though I walk through the valley of the shadow
    of death, I will fear no evil; for thou art with
    me; thy rod and thy staff,[1] they comfort me.
Thou preparest a table before me in the presence
    of mine enemies; thou anointest my head with   10
    oil;[2] my cup runneth over.
Surely goodness and mercy shall follow me all the
    days of my life; and I will dwell in the house
    of the Lord for ever.

THE BIBLE

1. **thy rod and thy staff,** of a shepherd.
2. **oil,** an ointment used ceremonially by the Hebrews
to dedicate a person or a thing to God.

THE POET FEELS

Two Poems of Changing Mood

1. In "Days" Baker tells us how the world of her thoughts and emotions seems on different days. Le Gallienne tells us how his mood changed on a certain day and why. Make a list of the things Le Gallienne says called him away from his work and explain whether you think his decision was really difficult.

2. Think what cocoons eventually become, then explain why the poet makes a logical development of this metaphor in "Days."

My Heart Leaps Up

This lyric verse sings out the poet's reverent response to nature—to its beauty and to its ability to teach people about both God and human beings. The poet spent much of his long life writing and teaching that poetry should be the spontaneous outpouring of feelings.

1. Does one's heart actually "leap up" when one beholds beauty? Discuss.

2. What does the poet wish to keep always?

3. Line 7: "The child is father of the man; . . ." is known as a *paradox*, or a seeming contradiction, because it appears to be contrary to common sense, yet is significant when viewed from a certain angle, or point of view. In Wordsworth's view a child is much better able to appreciate the teachings and the beauty of nature than the adult who gradually loses reverence for the natural world through the demeaning exercise of "getting and spending." According to the poet what should the adult have learned from childhood? In what way, then, is the child the father of the man he becomes?

Empty

Do you sometimes find yourself looking at a person, apparently listening to what is being said, yet not really hearing? Your mind is empty. Why do you think the first and third stanzas in this poem are the same?

John Doe, Jr.

1. John Doe is an imaginary name used in certain legal procedures and has come to mean generally any fictitious person. Discuss reasons why the poet chose to use John Doe, Jr., instead of the boy's real name.

2. The first two lines of the poem suggest that the poet has been stirred to remember John. What news has she obviously just heard?

3. Since the poet refers to John's contemporaries as "they," discuss the way she appears to view her own part in the boy's life.

The Day Is Done

It might be said of this poem that it does not offer any profound insight or inspirational message. Longfellow's humble task was to write a song "to quiet / The restless pulse of care."

1. Describe the tone established in the opening quatrain of the poem. Why is this an effective beginning?

2. Longfellow uses several striking similes throughout "The Day Is Done." Note at least three of these similes and explain the comparison made in each.

The Twenty-third Psalm

This psalm is one of the best-known poems in all literature. One of the many songs of praise thought to have been written by the shepherd David, it is found in the Old Testament of the Bible.

1. Explain the metaphor of the shepherd.

2. What images in line 2 give the reader or listener a feeling of comfort and security?

COMPOSITION

Look over the humorous verse in THE WAYS OF A POET (for examples, see the poems by Nash and Silverstein in "The Poet Sees"). Decide what ingredients make them humorous. Is there outlandish rhyme, silly situation, cutting satire, what?

Think of a situation that you believe is humorous; then put it into an appropriate verse form. You may wish to pattern your poem on one of the humorous selections in the unit, or you may wish simply to strike out on your own.

If you are having trouble zeroing in on an idea, perhaps the following questions will suggest a humorous poetical situation to you:

If you have delivered newspapers, how is your aim?

Do you get confused in making introductions?

Have you seen animals and birds act as people do?

Who is the most miserly person you know?

In what ways do people show that they are conceited?

How do people act after they have just missed catching a bus, plane, or train?

A SUMMING UP

The Poet Feels

1. Review the poems in "The Poet Feels" with an eye to answering this question: Do most of the poets speak of their feelings in general, abstract terms, or do they express emotion through telling of specific objects, places, people, and events? Discuss with examples.
2. Select the poem in this group which seems to you to express the greatest depth of feeling. Explain your choice.

LANGUAGE AND VOCABULARY

A. In "The Twenty-third Psalm" there are verb endings that are archaic, that is, no longer used in English: *-eth* as in *maketh* and *-est* as in *preparest*. In Old English (449–1100) and in Middle English (1100–1500), *-eth* was used to form the third person singular (he) present tense as in *he leadeth,* and *-est* was used for the second person singular (thou) present tense as in *thou anointest. Thou,* of course, is *you* in modern English. The possessive form of *thou* is *thy,* as in *thy rod.* In contemporary English, *thy* is *your.* Suffixes, then, are not the only archaic forms in the poem. What do *yea, art,* and *mine* mean?

B. A good dictionary not only defines a word but also briefly sketches its derivation, that is, its origin and historical development. For example, if you looked up the word *natural,* which appears in "My Heart Leaps Up," you would find it stems from a Latin word meaning "Nature." We generally think of something natural as being healthy, produced by nature, not artificial. Related to *natural* are such words as *naturalist, naturalize,* and *naturally.* For each of the following words from the unit "The Poet Feels," find background information in the dictionary: *diffidence, redemptive, rejection, groping,* and *cocoon.*

C. To inform the reader of the status of a word, a good dictionary uses various labels, including *archaic, informal, British, regional,* and *foreign language.* An archaic word is one that once was widely used but now is rarely used, such as *thou* in "The Twenty-third Psalm." The label *informal* is applied to a word that is appropriate for everyday, ordinary conversations but not suitable for more formal situations. *Chap* in "John Doe, Jr." is an informal word meaning "a man or boy." Although in a conversation you might refer to someone as a *chap,* in a serious speech you probably would refer to him as a *person*. If the meaning of a word differs in British English from American English, that word is labeled *chiefly British*. In British English, for example, *tin* means "a container for preserved foodstuff; a can." And a *lift* is an "elevator." A word that is popular in one region of the country but virtually unknown elsewhere is labeled *regional*, and the area where it is common is specified, for example, *Southern U.S., New England,* and *Southwestern U.S.* The word *bayou*, when it means "a marshy, sluggish body of water that is tributary to a river or other body of water," is labeled *Southern U.S.* Foreign words that have not been fully integrated into English—though they may be fairly common—and are regarded by native speakers to be non-English are given the label of the language to which they belong. *Répondez s'il vous plaît*, which is commonly abbreviated R.S.V.P., is used on formal invitations; it means "Please reply." It is labeled *French*. When using your dictionary for the various exercises in this book, be sure to pay attention to the five labels discussed above.

BIOGRAPHICAL NOTES

Karle Wilson Baker (1878–1960), poet, short story writer, novelist, and essayist, was born in Little Rock, Arkansas. She attended the University of Chicago. A college professor, Ms. Baker was awarded the Southern Prize by the Poetry Society of South Carolina in 1925.

Richard Le Gallienne (1866–1947), British poet and essayist, was born in Liverpool, England. He was educated at Liverpool College and then went to work for an accounting firm. In 1891 he became literary critic of the *London Star*. He moved to the United States in 1898.

Henry Wadsworth Longfellow (1807–1882) achieved great popularity during his life both as a poet and a professor of modern European literature at Harvard. His first poem, published when he was thirteen, showed no great promise but did indicate his early eagerness to write. At fourteen he entered Bowdoin College and after graduation was invited by Bowdoin to fill a chair in modern languages and literature especially created for him. He was only nineteen when he felt the need to prepare for this position, so he went abroad where he remained for almost four years. When he was twenty-seven, he left Bowdoin and became professor of languages and belles-lettres at Harvard. Though he claimed that he never liked teaching, he taught for twenty-four years. In 1854, he retired to devote full time to his writing. Longfellow's poetry is direct, easy to read, melodious, and filled with appealing ideas.

María Núñez (1934–   ), originally from Almuñécar, Granada, Spain, is now a Canadian citizen and lives in Toronto. Her poetry has been published in magazines in Spain and Argentina. Only recently she began writing poems in English.

Bonaro W. Overstreet (1902–   ), American poet, teacher, lecturer, was born in Geyserville, California. She has published a number of books including a collection of poems entitled *Footsteps on the Earth*. Ms. Overstreet uses Bonaro Wilkinson as her pen name. In addition to her own writing, she has collaborated with her husband, Harry Allen Overstreet, on many books.

William Wordsworth (1770–1850), one of England's major poets, grew up in the countryside and for most of his long life lectured and wrote on the importance of nature. He argued that poetry should treat "incidents and situations from common life," and be written in language used by most people. Poetry, he said, should be "the spontaneous overflow of powerful feelings." Thus, much of his poetry is intensely lyrical.

The ways of the poet aren't always the ways of the world. The world is interested in facts, in tangibility, in what you can touch and turn into a profit. But the poet sees beyond and beneath reality, and creates worlds in words. And sometimes, these worlds are more real than the real world of facts.

The Poet Sees:

L. C. Tiffany
MAGNOLIA AND IRISES
Metropolitan Museum of Art
New York City
Anonymous Gift

Wassily Kandinsky, **LANDSCAPE NEAR MURNAU**
Guggenheim Museum, New York City

Two artists: two landscapes; two visions. To L.C. Tiffany, the often imitated but rarely equalled artist of stained glass, the world is recognizable and factual. Yet, the mere act of putting this world on glass transforms it, for glass can assume only certain colors and certain textures, and can become a world in itself. Wassily Kandinsky, on the other hand, turns his landscape into a storm of color, a whirlwind of motion, a circus of shapes. By personalizing his scene in such an abstract way, he allows you, the viewer, to re-create or remember your own personal landscape.

Juan Gris, **BREAKFAST**
Collection, Museum of Modern Art, Acquired through the Lillie P. Bliss Bequest

Edvard Munch, **THE VOICE**
Courtesy, Museum of Fine Arts, Boston
Ernest Wadsworth Longfellow Fund

The Poet Feels:

Two other poets of the palette give us two more opportunities to experience their worlds. On the left, Spanish painter Juan Gris sets a breakfast table of the mind. It's complete, right down to the morning paper, except that it's shattered. It is a unique vision, expressed in a special way. And the way you put the shattered pieces together makes it special and particular and personal to *you.* Above, the Norwegian artist Edvard Munch enters your senses directly. The girl is in a forest of the mind. Her body glows with controlled agony, and the upthrust, sinister trees fill us—and her—with dark foreboding. The scene, like a poem, not only creates, but *becomes* a mood.

The Poet Tells A Story:

The poet and the painter often just suggest: with a roof, some swirls of hills, a punctuation of trees. A few brush strokes are all the Japanese print-maker Korin needs to evoke a summer day for us.

Sometimes, the poet and the painter set the scene for a story. In Pissarro's painting, Paris is just moving into morning. From your window, you can see people begin-ning a day. What will the day hold for them?

Nicolas Lancret, **THE PICNIC AFTER THE HUNT** National Gallery of Art Washington, D.C. Samuel H. Kress Collection

Although the hunt is over, there is a great deal of action in the painting by French artist Nicolas Lancret. What do you think the people are discussing? The hunt? Perhaps more personal matters?

Fantasy and mystery and poetry always leave unanswered questions. If life is really a racetrack, as Ryder seems to suggest in his painting at the left, why is death the only rider? Your answer will complete your interpretation of the painting.

Albert Pinkham Ryder **THE RACETRACK, OR DEATH ON A PALE HORSE** Cleveland Museum of Art, Purchase from the J. H. Wade Fund

THE POET TELLS A STORY

We have read poems which put an emphasis on external sights and sounds and poems which put an emphasis on emotion and ways of feeling. Now we turn to narrative poems—poems that tell tales. Some of these stories are full of emotion, some have rapid action, some are mysterious, some humorous, and some historical. The emphasis here is on the narration of an event. But note that the elements we have studied already—sharp imagery and emotion—are still present.

This short Greek legend tells one of the best-known stories of the ancient world. According to the myth, King Minos of the island of Crete wished to have a secret labyrinth built. He sent for the master craftsman Daedalus, who brought his son, Icarus, with him. After Daedalus built the maze, the king, fearful that his secret would be revealed, held the father and son prisoners.

The Story of Daedalus and Icarus

Ovid

Homesick for homeland, Daedalus hated Crete
And his long exile there, but the sea held him.
"Though Minos blocks escape by land or water,"
Daedalus said, "surely the sky is open,
And that's the way we'll go. Minos' dominion   5
Does not include the air." He turned his thinking
Toward unknown arts, changing the laws of nature.
He laid out feathers in order, first the smallest,
A little larger next it, and so continued,
The way that pan-pipes rise in gradual sequence.   10
He fastened them with twine and wax, at middle,
At bottom, so, and bent them, gently curving,
So that they looked like wings of birds, most surely.
And Icarus, his son, stood by and watched him,
Not knowing he was dealing with his downfall,   15

Stood by and watched, and raised his shiny face
To let a feather, light as down, fall on it,
Or stuck his thumb into the yellow wax,
Fooling around, the way a boy will, always,
Whenever a father tries to get some work done.   20
Still, it was done at last, and the father hovered,
Poised, in the moving air, and taught his son:
"I warn you, Icarus, fly a middle course:
Don't go too low, or water will weigh the wings down;
Don't go too high, or the sun's fire will burn them.   25
Keep to the middle way. And one more thing,
No fancy steering by star or constellation,
Follow my lead!" That was the flying lesson,
And now to fit the wings to the boy's shoulders.
Between the work and warning the father found   30
His cheeks were wet with tears, and his hands trembled.
He kissed his son (*Good-bye,* if he had known it),
Rose on his wings, flew on ahead, as fearful
As any bird launching the little nestlings
Out of high nest into thin air. *Keep on,*   35
Keep on, he signals, *follow me!* He guides him
In flight—O fatal art!—and the wings move
And the father looks back to see the son's wings moving.
Far off, far down, some fisherman is watching
As the rod dips and trembles over the water,   40
Some shepherd rests his weight upon his crook,
Some ploughman on the handles of the ploughshare,
And all look up, in absolute amazement,
At those air-borne above. They must be gods!
They were over Samos, Juno's sacred island,   45
Delos and Paros toward the left, Lebinthus
Visible to the right, and another island,
Calymne, rich in honey. And the boy
Thought *This is wonderful!* and left his father,
Soared higher, higher, drawn to the vast heaven,   50
Nearer the sun, and the wax that held the wings
Melted in that fierce heat, and the bare arms
Beat up and down in air, and lacking oarage
Took hold of nothing. *Father!* he cried, and *Father!*
Until the blue sea hushed him, the dark water   55
Men call the Icarian now. And Daedalus,
Father no more, called "Icarus, where are you!

Where are you, Icarus? Tell me where to find you!"
And saw the wings on the waves, and cursed his talents,
Buried the body in a tomb, and the land   60
Was named for Icarus.

Born in the woods and cradled on pine,
was William Sycamore a real man or a symbol of all the men
who created the Western frontier?

The Ballad of William Sycamore (1790–1871)

Stephen Vincent Benét

My father, he was a mountaineer,
His fist was a knotty hammer;
He was quick on his feet as a running deer,
And he spoke with a Yankee stammer.

My mother, she was merry and brave,   5
And so she came to her labor,
With a tall green fir for her doctor grave
And a stream for her comforting neighbor.

And some are wrapped in the linen fine,
And some like a godling's scion;[1]   10
But I was cradled on twigs of pine
In the skin of a mountain lion.

And some remember a white, starched lap
And a ewer with silver handles;
But I remember a coonskin cap   15
And the smell of bayberry candles!

1. **godling's scion** (sī'ən), descendant of a god.

FLAX SKUTCHING BEE
Linton Park
National Gallery of Art, Washington, D.C.
Gift of Edgar William and Bernice Chrysler Garbisch

The cabin logs, with the bark still rough,
And my mother who laughed at trifles,
And the tall, lank visitors, brown as snuff,
With their long, straight squirrel rifles.   **20**

I can hear them dance, like a foggy song,
Through the deepest one of my slumbers,
The fiddle squeaking the boots along
And my father calling the numbers.[2]

The quick feet shaking the puncheon[3] floor,   **25**
And the fiddle squeaking and squealing,
Till the dried herbs rattled above the door
And the dust went up to the ceiling.

2. His father called out the numbers that directed various steps in square dances.
3. **puncheon,** made of smooth-faced timber.

There are children lucky from dawn till dusk,
But never a child so lucky!   30
For I cut my teeth on "Money Musk"[4]
In the Bloody Ground of Kentucky![5]

When I grew tall as the Indian corn,
My father had little to lend me,
But he gave me his great, old powder horn   35
And his woodsman's skill to befriend me.

With a leather shirt to cover my back,
And a redskin nose to unravel
Each forest sign,[6] I carried my pack
As far as a scout could travel.   40

Till I lost my boyhood and found my wife,
A girl like a Salem clipper![7]
A woman straight as a hunting knife
With eyes as bright as the Dipper!

We cleared our camp where the buffalo feed,   45
Unheard-of streams were our flagons;
And I sowed my sons like the apple seed
On the trail of the Western wagons.

They were right, tight boys, never sulky or slow,
A fruitful, a goodly muster.   50
The eldest died at the Alamo.[8]
The youngest fell with Custer.[9]

4. **"Money Musk"** (musk), was a square-dance tune.
5. **The Bloody Ground of Kentucky** was so named because of the bitter battles there between American Indians and settlers.
6. **redskin nose . . . sign,** the forest knowledge of an American Indian.
7. Fast, tall-masted sailing ships from Salem (sā′ləm) Massachusetts, famous in the mid-nineteenth century.
8. **The Alamo** (al′ə mō) is a fort at San Antonio, Texas, at which a garrison of 187 Texans was killed by Mexican forces in 1836.
9. **George Custer** (1839–1876) and all his men were killed in a battle with Sioux Indians in Montana in 1876.

The letter that told it burned my hand.
Yet we smiled and said, "So be it!"
But I could not live when they fenced the land,   55
For it broke my heart to see it.

I saddled a red, unbroken colt
And rode him into the day there;
And he threw me down like a thunderbolt
And rolled on me as I lay there.   60

The hunter's whistle hummed in my ear
As the city men tried to move me,
And I died in my boots like a pioneer
With the whole wide sky above me.

Now I lie in the heart of the fat, black soil,   65
Like the seed of a prairie thistle;
It has washed my bones with honey and oil
And picked them clean as a whistle.

And my youth returns, like the rains of spring,
And my sons, like the wild geese flying;   70
And I lie and hear the meadow lark sing
And have much content in my dying.

Go play with the towns you have built of blocks,
The towns where you would have bound me!
I sleep in my earth like a tired fox,   75
And my buffalo have found me.

454 THE WAYS OF A POET

Naturally a poem can tell a comic story as well as a serious
one. The first two poems below are as brief and to the point as
a joke or wisecrack. The third poem is a longer, more leisurely
"yarn"—such as those told by Mark Twain and other American
humorists. No poem could be more typically American than
"Casey at the Bat." Celebrating "the great American game,"
these verses are perhaps the most popular ever written about
a sports event.

The Termite

Some primal termite knocked on wood
And tasted it, and found it good,
And that is why your Cousin May
Fell through the parlor floor today.

OGDEN NASH

The Purist

I give you now Professor Twist,
A conscientious scientist.
Trustees exclaimed, "He never bungles!"
And sent him off to distant jungles.
Camped on a tropic riverside,   5
One day he missed his loving bride.
She had, the guide informed him later,
Been eaten by an alligator.
Professor Twist could not but smile.
"You mean," he said, "a crocodile."   10

OGDEN NASH

Casey at the Bat

Ernest Lawrence Thayer

The outlook wasn't brilliant for the Mudville nine that day;
The score stood four to two, with but one inning more to play;
And so, when Cooney died at first, and Burrows did the same,
A sickly silence fell upon the patrons of the game.

A straggling few got up to go in deep despair. The rest   5
Clung to the hope which springs eternal in the human breast;
They thought, if only Casey could but get a whack at that,
They'd put up even money now, with Casey at the bat.

But Flynn preceded Casey, as did also Jimmy Blake,
And the former was a pudding, and the latter was a fake;   10
So upon that stricken multitude grim melancholy sat,
For there seemed but little chance of Casey's getting to the bat.

But Flynn let drive a single, to the wonderment of all,
And Blake, the much despised, tore the cover off the ball;
And when the dust had lifted, and they saw what had occurred,   15
There was Jimmy safe on second, and Flynn a-hugging third.

Then from the gladdened multitude went up a joyous yell,
It bounded from the mountaintop, and rattled in the dell;
It struck upon the hillside, and recoiled upon the flat;
For Casey, mighty Casey, was advancing to the bat.   20

There was ease in Casey's manner as he stepped into his place,
There was pride in Casey's bearing, and a smile on Casey's face;
And when, responding to the cheers, he lightly doffed his hat,
No stranger in the crowd could doubt 'twas Casey at the bat.

Ten thousand eyes were on him as he rubbed his hands with dirt,   25
Five thousand tongues applauded when he wiped them on his shirt;
Then while the writhing pitcher ground the ball into his hip,
Defiance gleamed in Casey's eye, a sneer curled Casey's lip.

And now the leather-covered sphere came hurtling through the air,
And Casey stood a-watching it in haughty grandeur there;   30
Close by the sturdy batsman the ball unheeded sped.
"That ain't my style," said Casey. "Strike one," the umpire said.

From the benches, black with people, there went up a muffled roar,
Like the beating of the storm-waves on a stern and distant shore;
"Kill him! kill the umpire!" shouted someone on the stand,   35
And it's likely they'd have killed him had not Casey raised his hand.

With a smile of Christian charity great Casey's visage shone;
He stilled the rising tumult; he bade the game go on;
He signaled to the pitcher, and once more the spheroid flew,
But Casey still ignored it, and the umpire said, "Strike two."   40

"Fraud!" cried the maddened thousands, and the echo answered, "Fraud!"
But a scornful look from Casey, and the audience was awed;
They saw his face grow stern and cold, they saw his muscles strain,
And they knew that Casey wouldn't let that ball go by again.

The sneer is gone from Casey's lips, his teeth are clenched in hate,   45
He pounds with cruel violence his bat upon the plate;
And now the pitcher holds the ball, and now he lets it go,
And now the air is shattered by the force of Casey's blow.

Oh! somewhere in this favored land the sun is shining bright,
The band is playing somewhere, and somewhere hearts are light;
And somewhere men are laughing, and somewhere children shout,   50
But there is no joy in Mudville—mighty Casey has struck out!

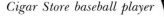

Cigar Store baseball player

In a quiet and undramatic way this narrative poem relates
an experience that had great meaning for a boy who was

Fifteen

South of the Bridge on Seventeenth
I found back of the willows one summer
day a motorcycle with engine running
as it lay on its side, ticking over
slowly in the high grass. I was fifteen.   5

I admired all that pulsing gleam, the
shiny flanks, the demure headlights
fringed where it lay; I led it gently
to the road and stood with that
companion, ready and friendly. I was fifteen.   10

We could find the end of a road, meet
the sky on out Seventeenth. I thought about
hills, and patting the handle got back a
confident opinion. On the bridge we indulged
a forward feeling, a tremble. I was fifteen.   15

Thinking, back farther in the grass I found
the owner, just coming to, where he had flipped
over the rail. He had blood on his hand, was pale—
I helped him walk to his machine. He ran his hand
over it, called me good man, roared away.   20

I stood there, fifteen.

WILLIAM STAFFORD

Pay particular attention to the punctuation in the next poem. Many of the lines have no end punctuation. Thus, both sound and the sense depend upon alert reading. What actually happens and what does the poet think about this episode at the zoo?

At Woodward's Gardens
Robert Frost

A boy, presuming on his intellect,
Once showed two little monkeys in a cage
A burning-glass they could not understand.
And never could be made to understand.
Words are no good: to say it was a lens   5
For gathering solar rays would not have helped.
But let him show them how the weapon worked.
He made the sun a pinpoint on the nose
Of first one then the other till it brought
A look of puzzled dimness to their eyes   10
That blinking could not seem to blink away.
They stood arms laced together at the bars,
And exchanged troubled glances over life.
One put a thoughtful hand up to his nose
As if reminded—or as if perhaps   15
Within a million years of an idea.
He got his purple little knuckles stung.
The already known had once more been confirmed
By psychological experiment,
And that were all the finding to announce   20

SIX PANEL SCREEN; JAPANESE MACAQUES (detail)
Mori Sosen
Metropolitan Museum of Art, New York City
Charles Stewart Smith Collection

Had the boy not presumed too close and long.
There was a sudden flash of arm, a snatch,
And the glass was the monkeys', not the boy's.
Precipitately they retired back-cage
And instituted an investigation   25
On their part, though without the needed insight.
They bit the glass and listened for the flavor.
They broke the handle and the binding off it.
Then none the wiser, frankly gave it up,
And having hid it in their bedding straw   30
Against the day of prisoners' ennui,
Came dryly forward to the bars again
To answer for themselves: Who said it mattered
What monkeys did or didn't understand?
They might not understand a burning-glass.   35
They might not understand the sun itself.
It's knowing what to do with things that counts.

THE POET TELLS A STORY

The Story of Daedalus and Icarus

In the opening lines of this poem you are
given a natural picture of a father and son.

1. What important project is the father
   working on? What does the boy do while
   his father works?
2. Discuss the advice the father gives his
   son before they begin the flight. Although the father scolds, how does he
   feel about his son?
3. What happens to Icarus? How does this
   make the father feel?

   An idea to consider:

   What older people say, young people dis-
regard.

The Ballad of William Sycamore

1. By placing the dates under the title, the
   poet suggests that William Sycamore was
   a real person. However, the details given
   in the ballad indicate that Will Sycamore
   is probably a symbol of the American
   pioneer. Look back through the poem
   and select lines which support this symbolism.
2. The following are often found in ballads. Find an example in this poem of:
   a. a tragic incident
   b. an act of physical courage
   c. the supernatural
3. One of the earliest forms of literature, the ballad, usually set to music,
   was used to tell a historic or exciting

story. The poet has written this modern American ballad with a rhythm and a beat like that found in square-dance music. Why is this appropriate? Experiment with reading this poem aloud as you tap your toe to a square-dance rhythm.

Discuss whether or not this ballad would have been more effective had it ended with line 64.

The Termite; The Purist

These are "just for fun" by one of the masters of humorous verse. Try to decide just what it is that makes these two verses funny.

Casey at the Bat

1. Part of the humor of this poem comes from the author's use of unexpected words and expressions. These expressions seem a bit "fancy" or formal for the situation: for example, "gladdened multitude" (l. 17) or "spheroid" (l. 39). Find two more such examples and discuss how they contribute to the humor of the poem.
2. It can be fun to dramatize this poem. The characters are Casey, Blake, Flynn, a catcher, a pitcher, an umpire, and the fans. One of the most expressive readers in the class should narrate the poem, while the cast goes through the action. Any speeches are said by the characters themselves at the appropriate points. Then the narrator picks up the thread of the story.

Fifteen

The dream of owning a motorcycle is very real to many young persons—a dream shared by numbers of adults. Why do you think the motorcycle has such appeal?

1. What happens in the first stanza of the poem?
2. How does the boy feel about his "find"?
3. What happens in the final stanza?
4. How do you know that the boy and the owner of the motorcycle understand each other?
5. What verse form does the poet use? Why do you think he uses the refrain: "I was fifteen"?

At Woodward's Gardens

1. The poet lets us know how he feels about this incident in the first line of the poem. He says that the boy was "presuming on his intellect." (Look up this meaning of *presume* in the dictionary.) Does this mean that the poet really thought the boy was very bright? What attitude is suggested in line 7 when the poet refers to the lens as a *weapon*?
2. What level of intelligence does the poet assign to the monkeys? What lines show this?
3. There is strong satire in lines 18 and 19. Explain.
4. Explain the last line of the poem. Who really knew "what to do" with the burning-glass? The monkeys or the boy?
5. Discuss the meaning of the poet's statement: "It's knowing what to do with things that counts" (l. 37).

COMPOSITION

Perhaps the nearest thing in contemporary life to the ballad of times past is the country-western song. However, only a few of these tell a story in such detail as "The Ballad of William Sycamore." You will recall that the following are often found in the ballad:

a. a tragic incident
b. an act of physical courage
c. the supernatural

Benét's poem contains all three.

Do you have someone in your family who you think is strong enough or different enough to make a good central character in a ballad? Do you know of a tragic incident into which you could weave your own characters and details? Or perhaps you can think of another intriguing subject for a ballad. At any rate, try writing a ballad. Use the rhyme scheme of the four-line stanza, rhyming the first and third and the second and fourth lines, as found in "The Ballad of William Sycamore."

A SUMMING UP

The Poet Tells a Story

The poems in this group do more than tell a story. Each depends on the use of imagery and on the expression of emotions. Explain how this is done in each poem.

Moreover, each story-poem expresses an idea, or a theme, as well. Identify the poems that contain any of these ideas:

1. Overconfidence may bring disaster.
2. People who think themselves intelligent are often made to look silly.
3. What is important to us changes with the passage of years.

BIOGRAPHICAL NOTES

Stephen Vincent Benét (1898–1943), poet, short story writer, and playwright, was born in Bethlehem, Pennsylvania. He received both his B.A. and his M.A. from Yale University and did further graduate work at the Sorbonne. His epic poem, *John Brown's Body*, was awarded a Pulitzer Prize.

Robert Frost (For biographical note see page 431.)

Ogden Nash (For biographical note see page 432.)

Ovid (43 B.C.–A.D. 17), Roman poet, was born in Sulmona, Italy. After training for a legal career, Ovid abandoned law and politics and turned to the literary life. Although a great favorite in Augustan Age society, Ovid was suddenly banished by Augustus to Tomi, a town on the Black Sea. He spent the rest of his life in exile.

William Stafford (1914–   ), a native of Kansas, has taught English in several colleges and has published many books of poetry. Like the poem "Fifteen," most of his verse is informal, filled with simple imagery, and approximates spoken language. He won the National Book Award for Poetry in 1963.

Ernest Lawrence Thayer (1863–1940), ballad writer and journalist, was born in Lawrence, Massachusetts. After graduating from Harvard University, where he edited the *Harvard Crimson,* the school paper, he worked for a number of newspapers.

SUMMING UP: THE WAYS OF A POET

Poetry, like all forms of art, is a shared experience. Through our involvement with the poet's experience we learn new ways of using our senses.

The ways of poets are not easy. They must be able to recognize truth and let others see it through their eyes. To do this, they must be acute observers of life. They must incorporate their observations in imagery so vivid that we experience a shock of surprise when we recognize the familiar and the believable in what they have written.

Consider and discuss these quotations and statements about poetry:

1. The impact of good poetry does not come from the subject of the poem; it comes from the style and metaphor.
2. Robert Frost said that a poem "begins in delight and ends in wisdom."
3. A poem that expresses strong feeling is quite personal.
4. Simply because a poet writes in the first person, we should not conclude that the poem is autobiographical.
5. An old poem is probably better than a new one.
6. "All slang is metaphor, and all metaphor is poetry."—Chesterton.
7. "All poets are mad."—Burton.
8. "Poetry is certainly something more than good sense, but it must be good sense at all events; just as a palace is more than a house, but it must be a house at least."—Coleridge.

LANGUAGE AND VOCABULARY

A. In several other sections on language and vocabulary, you learned that there are various processes by which new words are formed. In addition to those you learned about before, there is the combining of words to make self-explaining compounds. *Tightrope* (in "The Base Stealer"), *headlines* (in "Soup"), and *homeland* (in "The Story of Daedalus and Icarus") are good examples of compound words that explain themselves. This kind of compound word must be distinguished from an idiomatic compound, which is not self-explanatory. The words *egghead* and *Molotov cocktail* do not explain themselves, for an egghead has nothing to do with an egg, and a Molotov cocktail is not something to drink. Today, self-explaining compounds make up about eight percent of all new word formations in our language. Some further examples of these compounds are *atomic bomb, appointment book, supermarket, jack-in-the-box, sharpshooter,* and *ingroup.* What compounds can you add to this list?

B. As you may remember, one way of creating new words is by adding suffixes to existing words or roots. Two of the common suffixes added to words to make them into verbs are *-en* and *-ize.* Both of these suffixes have the meaning "to cause to be" or "to come to be."

Which of the two endings would you add to each of the following words to make it into a verb? Use each of the words in a sentence: *white, deep, dead, dark, patron, eternal*

COMPOSITION WORKSHOP

SUMMARIZING A POEM

Students are often asked to write brief reports about literature. One common type of assignment asks students to write about a poem. This kind of assignment usually demands two things. First of all, the writer must summarize and make clear what the surface message of the poem is. The poem's surface message is what the poet is actually saying. Secondly, the writer must identify the deeper meaning the poet might have had in mind.

As you make the poet's message as clear as possible in the first part of the report, you gain some practice in the important skill of summarizing. In writing about what you believe the poem's deeper message to be, you gain some valuable practice in the important skill of interpretation. Let's look at how a writer might go about planning and writing a report on a poem, using the Roman poet Ovid's "The Story of Daedalus and Icarus" as the topic.

The writer's first task in the brief report on Ovid's poem will be to summarize the story the poet tells. When you summarize something, you present the most important points. You do not translate everything that someone else has written into your own words. If you read Ovid's poem carefully two or three times, you will see that the story is divided into three parts. First, the poet tells about Daedalus's preparations for the escape from Crete. Second, the poet tells about how Daedalus tries to prepare his son for the coming flight. Finally, the poet tells what happens during the flight. The discovery that the story has three separate parts should suggest to you that the part of the report that summarizes the story might sensibly appear in three paragraphs, one paragraph for each of the three parts. The following rough outline sketches out the plan for the first section of the report:

I. Preparations for the flight
II. Preparing Icarus for the flight
III. The flight itself

The writer's second task in the brief report will be to identify the poem's deeper meaning. Since many interpretations of a poem are possible, you are not trying in this part of the report to discover the correct interpretation. What you are looking for is a sensible interpretation, one that you as the writer can make a case for. As you read and study the poem, two possible interpretations occur to you. You feel that the poet might be making a statement about the rashness and love of adventure that all young people possess. You also feel that the poet might be saying something about the danger of human beings going too far with their advances and discoveries. Since both of these deeper meanings occur to you, you decide to include both in your brief report about the poem. The following rough outline sketches out the plan for the second section of the poem:

IV. Rashness of youth
V. Limits of human talent

The study of Ovid's poem suggests a body of a report made up of five paragraphs. Only an introductory paragraph remains to be planned. Most experienced writers assemble the introductory paragraph after the body of the report has been written. The writer can study the body of the report carefully, making sure that the introductory paragraph contains a thesis sentence that introduces both sections of the report.

Here is a sample brief report on "The Story of Daedalus and Icarus."

In "The Story of Daedalus and Icarus," the Roman poet Ovid tells an interesting story with a couple of timely messages. The poet told the tale about two thousand years ago. But there are messages in the poem that are as valuable today as they were twenty centuries ago.

Daedalus and his son Icarus had grown tired of their long imprisonment on the island of Crete. Unable to escape by land or water, Daedalus decides that only the air offers them a chance for freedom. But in order to fly, he must alter the laws of nature. He rises to the challenge by gathering feathers of various sizes together. He arranges the feathers in the order of their size, from the shortest to the longest. He fastens them together with twine and wax and curves them until they resemble the wings of a bird. While Daedalus goes about his task with great seriousness, his inexperienced son plays with the feathers and the fastening wax.

Daedalus finally completes the four wings and tests two of them by hovering in the air. As any father would, he tries very hard to teach his son how to make proper use of the wings. He explains to Icarus that if the boy flies too low, the mists from the sea will weigh the wings down. If he flies too high, the heat from the sun will melt the wax and dislodge the feathers from their frameworks. He warns him to stay on a middle course. He tells him also that he should not attempt to do his own navigating. Instead, he should follow and be led by his more experienced father. Having done what he could to prepare the boy for flight, Daedalus fits the wings to Icarus's shoulders. He cries as he does so.

Daedalus takes to the air and signals his son to follow. He is like the adult bird who watches carefully as the newly hatched take their first flights. Before long Icarus is blinded by the thrill of flying. He decides not to follow his father and strikes out on his own. He abandons the middle course and soars higher and higher. As he gets nearer to the sun, the wax that binds the feathers to the frame melts. The feathers fall free. His wingless arms beat uselessly against the air. He falls into the sea and drowns. Daedalus sees the ruined wings floating upon the surface of the sea and curses his talent that made the tragedy possible.

One of the poem's timeless messages has to do with the rashness of youth. Daedalus knows that young people often find it hard to listen to those who have already profited from experience. He cautions his son and tries to tell him what he himself has learned. The middle course is best. It is always better to avoid extremes. But he knows how hard it will be for Icarus to accept the voice of experience, so he cries as he straps the wings on his son's arms. Modern parents feel the same concern. They caution their children to approach new experiences slowly. They ask them to stay with the middle course until they become more familiar with what they have not known before. The parent who hands the car keys to a son or daughter hopes that the message is accepted. Sometimes it is not.

Another of the poem's timeless messages has to do with the limits of human talent and ingenuity. Daedalus curses his own talent and ability when he sees that it has resulted in the death of his son. He wishes that he had never made flight possible. Many people have similar thoughts about some of the technological advances of the modern world. For example, we have learned to harness nuclear energy and to use it to heat and light our homes. But improperly used and carelessly controlled, that same nuclear energy can be a destructive force.

ACTIVITY 1

Find a poem in this unit that can serve as a topic for a brief report. Poems like May Swenson's "Pigeon Woman," Bonaro Overstreet's "John Doe, Jr.," and Shel Silverstein's "Point of View" would be excellent choices. Determine what deeper meaning or meanings the poem has.

ACTIVITY 2

Study your chosen poem carefully. Determine how many paragraphs you will need to summarize the surface message in the poem, and do a rough outline of that section of the report. Determine how many paragraphs you will need to interpret the poem's deeper meaning or meanings, and do a rough outline of that section of the report.

ACTIVITY 3

Write the body of the brief report that you outlined in Activity 2. Then prepare an introductory paragraph that includes a thesis statement that will tell a reader what the report will cover.

Identity

Who Am I?

The trees ask me,
And the sky,
And the sea asks me

Who am I?

The grass asks me,   5
And the sand,
And the rocks ask me
Who am I?

The wind tells me
At nightfall,   10
And the rain tells me
Someone small.

Someone small
Someone small
    But a piece   15
        of
        it
        all.

FELICE HOLMAN

I Am

impossible to explain
remote from old and new interpretations
and yet
not exactly

JUNE JORDAN

GIRL READING
Auguste Renoir
Frankfurt, Städlesches
Kunstinstitut/Artothek

I am different. I am also very much like other people. Whether I am young or very old, I still feel the need for a separate identity, to be recognized as an individual or person, a need to let other persons know who I am.

The people in the following pages establish their identities through a variety of means, ranging from wearing a snappy uniform to kicking over a bucket of apricots. As the inner feelings of these individuals are revealed, each of us may understand a little more clearly why we feel hurt if someone we know passes us in the hall without speaking or if we are overlooked when nominations are being made for student council or if someone we'd like for a friend snubs us instead of smiling.

Our feelings are just as complex as the many parts that go into our physical makeup. Each of us wants to be recognized as a person who is in some way different from others.

EVENING ON KARL JOHAN STREET
Edvard Munch
Bergen Billedgalleri
Rasmus Meyers Sandlinger

UNIT TECHNIQUES

STYLE

One of the most interesting things to look for in a piece of writing is the author's style. Actually, most of the elements that have already been discussed in this section are parts of style. The word choice of authors—simple and direct or unusual and complicated—their imagery and the things they select for description, the arrangement of sentences, and the spirit and outlook of the authors themselves expressed in their writings all figure in the totality of their style.

To understand the nature of a writing style, it is best to examine the writing of two authors whose styles are in strong contrast to each other. For illustration, read a page of Richard Connell's "The Most Dangerous Game" in CALL TO ADVENTURE. Note the expressive imagery of his similes and metaphors, the vivid description of Zaroff, Ivan, and the tropical island. Now read several of the opening paragraphs of "The Hero" by Margaret Weymouth Jackson in THE INNER CIRCLE. Are there any words that are not familiar? What sort of things are described? What is the attitude of the characters toward each other?

Both of these authors, Connell and Jackson, have highly individual styles. One is very descriptive, the other very simple. Both writing styles are good in that they create a particular effect. Readers are conscious of the writers' individual styles without analyzing the styles.

The use of words that are exactly right is of great importance in setting forth an idea, arousing emotions, or creating images. Word choice varies according to the effect the writer wants to achieve. Look at the sentence "She hung up her clothes," and substitute another word—*apparel, rags, raiment, gowns, garments, weeds*—for the word *clothes*. Note how the use of a word that is formal or informal, slangy or humorous can change the effect of the sentence. Each may be appropriate in a particular situation.

GIVING INSIGHT

Insight may be defined as "seeing into inner character or underlying truth." Each of the selections in this anthology was chosen to give the reader insights into life. However, the selections in IDENTITY deal particularly with the inner self, the way persons see themselves, their desire for recognition as individuals. For this reason, in the Reading for Appreciation section of the study notes, attention will be drawn to the ways the authors give insight into character.

For example, in the story you will read next, Tango is a fellow who has come to accept the idea that he doesn't amount to much. The author establishes this very early by his statement, "If they had given Tango a tail, he would have put it between his legs when Mireault spoke." A dog that tucks its tail between its legs is one that is timid, one that is afraid. Through the use of imaginative language, the author very quickly gives an idea of Tango's feelings about himself.

As is true with an author's style, the way an author gives insight is not confined to the use of one specific literary technique. Rather, an author employs many techniques. Observing how the various writers reveal character will serve to reemphasize many of the literary considerations discussed earlier in the text.

Are clothes very important to people?
Does it make much difference how they look?
When you find out what a handsome police uniform did for
Tango, you may have an answer to the above questions!

CLOTHES MAKE THE MAN

Henri Duvernois

"I don't like it," Tango complained again. "I won't feel right, walking up and down in that."

"Shut up and put it on," Mireault[1] told him, and so, of course, Tango obeyed. Mireault was half the size but he was clever. If they had given Tango a tail, he would have put it between his legs when Mireault spoke.

"Now, see?" Mireault said. "What did I tell you? Looks good, doesn't it? See, you've even got a whistle."

"Not bad," Tango had to admit, surveying himself in the mirror. He pushed out his mighty chest and threw back his broad shoulders. Even the Eel, the quick silent one who was Mireault's working partner and who rarely opened his mouth, was stirred to speech. "Boy, ain't he handsome!" he said.

No doubt about it, Tango made a noble sight. The policeman's uniform might have been cut to his measure by the best tailor in Paris. His little eyes looked brighter beneath the visor of the jaunty cap; they almost looked intelligent.

"Stop gawking at yourself and wipe that dumb grin off your face," Mireault said impatiently, "and listen. This is so simple a halfwit could do it, so maybe if you try hard you can too."

With regret Tango turned away from the mirror. His broad forehead wrinkled in the painful expression that meant he was concentrating.

"All you do is walk up and down the street," Mireault said. "Easy and slow, like a real cop on his beat. Then if anyone hears us working in the house they won't get suspicious, seeing you. Keep walking until we come out, then hang around a few minutes covering us. That's all there is to it. We'll meet back here. Now you understand?"

"Sure," Tango said, his eyes straying to the mirror.

"Then get going!" Mireault snapped.

Tango was a little nervous walking to the street Mireault and the Eel had picked out, but nothing happened. It was a prosperous section, and in the dim glow of the shaded corner light Tango could see what handsome houses they were—sober, solid, well cared for. The house where the job was to be pulled was in the middle of the block, behind a garden wall. Mireault and the Eel had cased it thoroughly; there was a tin-can wall safe upstairs with a very comfortable load in-

1. **Mireault** (mĕr ō′).

side. Apparently the old-fashioned family didn't believe in banks. Maybe they would, Mireault had said, after tonight.

Tango wondered what it would be like to live in so fine a house, but the effort of imagination was beyond him. He had seldom ever seen a street such as this one. He worked in the shabby quarters of Paris—a little purse-snatching, a little shoplifting; he even panhandled. Yes, he was good at panhandling. Timid businessmen usually came right across when Tango's huge shoulders towered over them; they looked fearfully at the massive hands and dug for whatever change they had.

He sauntered down the pavement, turned at the corner and came back. Halfway, he saw the two shadowy figures slip over the garden wall and disappear. Mireault and the Eel were at work.

Tango fell to thinking of how he had looked in the mirror. With the impressive image vivid in his mind, he straightened his shoulders and threw out his chest again. Standing erect, he tried a salute. It felt good. He grinned, oddly pleased, and walked on.

It was while he was turning at the other corner that he saw the police lieutenant.

Such a sight was usually enough to send him traveling as rapidly as his feet would move. He stared in horror. He fancied that the lieutenant, approaching, was gazing at him curiously. Tango's body was rigid; his palms were sweating. With a tremendous effort he restrained

the wild impulse to plunge away. He shuddered. Then, stiffly, with the lieutenant no more than a few feet from him, he raised his arm and saluted.

The lieutenant casually acknowledged the salute and passed by.

Tango stood peering after him. After a moment, he felt a peculiar gratification. "Say!" he said to himself. "Say, you see that? I salute, and he salutes right back. Say, that—that's pretty fine!"

It was extraordinary, the pleasure it gave him. He almost wanted to run up to the lieutenant and salute again. He threw back his shoulders straighter than ever and, erect and proud, walked down the pavement. At the corner he paused and rocked on his heels a moment as all policemen do.

"I guess I looked good to him," he told himself. "I guess he don't see many cops looking so good."

After a few more trips, he found an old lady hesitating on the corner. He saw her make two or three false starts to get across and each time nervously come back.

Tango did not even notice the plump-looking purse in her hand. He poised in front of her, saluted, and offered his arm. She looked at him with a sweet smile. "Oh, thank you, officer!" she said.

There was no traffic visible, but Tango held up his other arm majestically, as if halting a horde of roaring trucks. With infinite dignity they crossed to the other side. It was a pretty picture indeed.

"Thank you so much, officer!" she said.

"Please, madam," Tango said, "don't mention it." He paused. "That's what we're here for, you know," he added. And, gallantly, he saluted again.

He stood proudly watching her retreating figure. Before she had quite disappeared, she glanced back to regard him with another smile. Tango stood so straight the cloth strained across his chest. With a flourish, he saluted once more.

He went down the block, saluting at intervals. An indefinable emotion was stirring in him. In all Paris there could have been no more perfect an example of the calm, strong, resourceful guardian of law and order.

A disheveled figure came weaving toward him out of the shadows. It was a man, waving his arms aggressively, shuffling his feet and muttering savage but unintelligible epithets.[2] His glazed eyes fell upon Tango and he scowled. "Yea!" he cried. "Lousy cop!"

A deep sense of shock ran through Tango. "Here! Here!" he said. "Get along, get along."

"Big cowardly cop!" the drunk yelled. "Big bag of wind in a uniform! Beat up the little fellow and let the big crooks go! Thass all y' good for—beat up the little fellows an'—"

A mingled emotion of outrage and anger grew in Tango. A flush rose to his face.

"I spit on you!" the drunk declared scornfully. "Bah! There!" And he suited the action to the words.

Something popped in Tango's head. His face was purple. He seized the other with one mighty hand, shook him ferociously, and, without any clear idea of what he was going to do with him, dragged him off down the street.

Overawed, shaken out of his wits, the drunk was now passive and silent. But

---

2. **epithets** (ep′ə thets), uncomplimentary names.

Tango was beside himself, and when, halfway down the block, two figures came skimming over the garden wall and landed on the pavement near him, he was in no mood to stop.

"You fool, what are you doing?" Mireault said in a furious whisper. "You want to ruin the whole job? Let go of him, Blockhead!" And he struck Tango across the cheek.

Indescribable emotions swirled in Tango's head. He remembered the lieutenant answering his salute; he remembered the old lady's look of gratitude and admiration; he remembered the splendid figure of himself in the mirror. And he remembered what the drunk had said.

He arose to the full pitch of a mighty fury. While Mireault and the Eel stared at him in sheer paralyzed horror, he stuffed the shiny whistle in his mouth and blew a salvo[3] of blasts loud and long enough to bring all the police in Paris.

"Crooks, robbers!" he bellowed. "I arrest you! I arrest you in the name of the law!"

READING FOR DETAILS

A Man Transformed
Mireault and the Eel give Tango the job of lookout to make sure they are uninterrupted in their burglary attempt.
  1. Why doesn't Tango arouse suspicion as he paces back and forth on the street in front of the house?
  2. Describe Tango's meeting with the police lieutenant.
  3. How does he help the old lady?
  4. Why does he become furious with the drunk?
  5. How does the story end? What do you suppose happened after this?

READING FOR MEANING

Consider and discuss these statements in light of the story:
  1. Fine clothing makes fine persons.
  2. A weak-minded person is most easily led.
  3. All persons wish to feel important.

READING FOR APPRECIATION

Style
Henri Duvernois's writing style is lively and vivid. His choice of words is especially colorful and expressive. For example, in paragraph four, Tango is described as "*surveying* himself in the mirror." This gives the impression of his turning this way and that to inspect himself in great detail. A less vivid word choice would have been "*looking* at himself in the mirror."
  1. In paragraph six, find a similar example of a more expressive word being used in a place where *looking* might have been used.
  2. The following lines from the story all exemplify Duvernois's choice of expressive words where commonplace ones would have served. List the word he uses and give the more ordinary synonym for each:
     a. . . . he saw the two shadowy figures _____ over the garden wall. . . .
     b. He _____ down the pavement. . . .
     c. He _____ in front of her, saluted. . . .
     d. A disheveled figure came _____ toward him. . . .
     e. . . . two figures came _____ over the garden wall. . . .

Giving Insight
Although the story is lightly and humorously told, Tango is actually a pathetic figure, considered almost a half-wit by his accomplices.

---

3. **salvo** (sal'vō), a series; here, a round of whistle blasts.

This is, no doubt, one reason why the reader enjoys the way the story ends. There is the feeling that the crooks, who are simply using poor Tango, have managed to outsmart themselves.

1. Find three statements in the first twelve paragraphs of the story with which the author gives insight concerning Tango's lack of intelligence.
2. How does Tango feel when the lieutenant returns his salute?
3. What feelings swirl through Tango's head after Mireault strikes him? Why is Tango's blowing his whistle consistent with the insight about his character that has been given?

LANGUAGE AND VOCABULARY

Read the following sentences from "Clothes Make the Man," focusing your attention on the *italicized* words:

"I don't like it," Tango *complained*. . . .

"Then get going!" Mireault *snapped*.

"Big cowardly cop!" the drunk *yelled*.

The words *complained, snapped,* and *yelled* serve the same purpose as the more general word *said,* but they are more specific and more vivid. They convey the attitude or the tone of the speaker; in other words, they tell in what manner he is speaking. The speaker's state of mind may also be expressed by *said* coupled with a modifier, as in this example:

"Stop gawking at yourself and wipe that dumb grin off your face," Mireault *said impatiently*. . . .

Yet, a single word like *snapped* is more forceful than *said impatiently;* it is also more economical. In each of the following sentences, *said* is used with an *ly* modifier. In each sentence, substitute a single vivid word for the two *italicized* ones.

1. "Please don't go now," she *said pleadingly*.
2. "I will not compromise!" she *said angrily*.
3. *Bitterly*, he *said*, "And to think that I trusted you."
4. "We must prepare ourselves," he *said urgently*.
5. "Our team has won!" Ralph *said happily*.

COMPOSITION

Why does designer clothing, much of it with eye-catching logos or labels, now have such widespread appeal? Are these garments, shoes, and accessories an indication of a person's merit?

In a personal essay express your views, both *pro* and *con,* on the often-heard criticism that wearing designer items is an act of snobbery.

BIOGRAPHICAL NOTE

Henri Duvernois (1875–1937), a Frenchman, wrote under the pen name of Henri Simon Schwabacher. His novels, stories, and plays have been translated into several languages. His writings in translation were popular in American magazines in the first quarter of this century.

In this autobiographical account,
Richard Wright said the first test in a new school comes
"not in books but in how one's fellows took one. . . ."

THE FIGHT
Richard Wright

After breakfast, Uncle Clark took me to school, introduced me to the principal. The first half of the school day passed without incident. I sat looking at the strange reading book, following the lessons. The subjects seemed simple, and I felt that I could keep up. My anxiety was still in me; I was wondering how I would get on with the boys. Each new school meant a new area of life to be conquered. Were the boys tough? How hard did they fight? I took it for granted that they fought.

At noon recess I went into the school grounds, and a group of boys sauntered up to me, looked at me from my head to my feet, whispering among themselves. I leaned against a wall, trying to conceal my uneasiness.

"Where you from?" a boy asked abruptly.

"Jackson," I answered.

"How come they make you people so ugly in Jackson?" he demanded.

There was loud laughter.

"You're not any too good-looking yourself," I countered instantly.

"Oh!"

"Aw!"

"You hear what he told 'im?"

"You think you're smart, don't you?" the boy asked, sneering.

"Listen, I ain't picking a fight," I said. "But if you want to fight, I'll fight."

"Hunh, hard guy, ain't you?"

"As hard as you."

"Do you know who you can tell that to?" he asked me.

"And you know who you can tell it back to?" I asked.

"Are you talking about my mama?" he asked, edging forward.

"If you want it that way," I said.

This was my test. If I failed now, I would have failed at school, for the first trial came not in books but in how one's fellows took one, what value they placed upon one's willingness to fight.

"Take back what you said," the boy challenged me.

"Make me," I said.

The crowd howled, sensing a fight. The boy hesitated, weighing his chances of beating me.

"You ain't gonna take what that new boy said, is you?" someone taunted the boy.

The boy came close. I stood my ground. Our faces were four inches apart.

"You think I'm scared of you, don't you?" he asked.

"I told you what I think," I said.

Somebody, eager and afraid that we would not fight, pushed the boy, and he bumped into me. I shoved him away violently.

"Don't push me!" the boy said.

"Then keep off me!" I said.

He was pushed again, and I struck out with my right and caught him in the mouth. The crowd yelled, milled, surging so close that I could barely lift my arm to land a blow. When either of us tried to strike the other, we would be thrown off balance by the screaming boys. Every blow landed elicited shouts of delight. Knowing that if I did not win or make a good showing, I would have to fight a new boy each day, I fought tigerishly, trying to leave a scar, seeking to draw blood as proof that I was not a coward, that I could take care of myself. The bell rang, and the crowd pulled us apart. The fight seemed a draw.

"I ain't through with you!" the boy shouted.

In the classroom the boys asked me questions about myself; I was someone worth knowing. When the bell rang for school to be dismissed, I was set to fight again, but the boy was not in sight.

On my way home I found a cheap ring in the streets, and at once I knew what I was going to do with it. The ring had a red stone held by tiny prongs which I loosened, took the stone out, leaving the sharp tiny prongs jutting up. I slid the ring on to my finger and shadow-boxed. Now let a bully come, and I would show him how to fight; I would leave a crimson streak on his face with every blow.

But I never had to use the ring. After I had exhibited my new weapon at school, a description of it spread among the boys. I challenged my enemy to another fight, but he would not respond. Fighting was now not necessary. I had been accepted.

READING FOR DETAILS

He Passed the Test
1. Why did Richard Wright fight so ferociously when he was challenged by the boy at the new school?
2. How did he know he had "passed the test" when class resumed?
3. What weapon did Wright fashion for himself that he never had to use?

READING FOR MEANING

Find evidence in the selection to support the following statements:
1. Human relations are more important than scholastic achievement.
2. Most people are eager to fight only when they feel they can win.

READING FOR APPRECIATION

Style
Wright's style of writing is straightforward and realistic. What do you think makes the scene on the school grounds at noon recess seem so real and the action move so rapidly?

Giving Insight
The final sentence of the first paragraph gives insight into the way Richard Wright thinks. He has no false notions that what is ahead will be easy. What is this matter-of-fact statement that lets the reader know his attitude?

BIOGRAPHICAL NOTE

Richard Wright (For biographical note see page 433.)

The two men, centered in a huge
ring of red-ringed eyes, glared at each other.

THE CONFRONTATION
Raymond Barrio

No matter which way he turned, he was trapped in an endless maze of apricot trees, as though forever, neat rows of them, neatly planted, row after row, just like the blackest bars on a jail. There had to be an end. There had to be. There—trapped. There had to be a way out. Locked. There had to be a respite.[1] Animal. The buckets and the crates kept piling up higher. Brute. He felt alone. Though surrounded by other pickers. Beast. Though he was perspiring heavily, his shirt was powder dry. Savage. The hot dry air. The hot dry air sucking every drop of living moisture from his brute body. Wreck. He stopped and walked to the farthest end of the first row for some water, raised the dented dipper from the brute tank, drank the holy water in great brute gulps so he wouldn't have to savor its tastelessness, letting it spill down his torn shirt to cool his exhausted body, to replenish his brute cells and animal pores and stinking follicles[2] and pig gristle, a truly refined wreck of an animal, pleased to meetcha. Predator.

Lunch.

Almost too exhausted to eat, he munched his cheese with tortillas,[3] smoked on ashes, then lay back on the cool ground for half an hour. That short rest in the hot shade replenished some of his humor and resolve. He felt his spirit swell out again like a thirsty sponge in water. Then up again. The trees. The branches again. The briary branches. The scratching leaves. The twigs tearing at his shirt sleeves. The ladder. The rough bark. The endlessly unending piling up of bucket upon box upon crate upon stack upon rack upon mound upon mountain. He picked a mountain of cots[4] automatically. An automaton. A beast. A ray of enemy sun penetrated the tree that was hiding him and split his forehead open. His mind whirred. He blacked out. Luckily he'd been leaning against a heavy branch. His feet hooked to the ladder's rung. His half-filled bucket slipped from his grasp and fell in slow motion, splattering the fruit he'd so laboriously picked. To the ground. Roberto happened by and shook his head. "Whatsamatter, can't you see straight." Manuel was too tired even to curse. He should have had some salt pills.

Midafternoon.

The summer's fierce zenith[5] passed overhead. It passed. Then dropped. It started to light the ocean behind him, back of the hills. Sandy dreams. Cool

1. **respite** (res′pit), an interval of relief or rest.
2. **follicle** (fol′ə kəl), small anatomical cavity.
3. **tortillas** (tôr tē′yəs), flat, unleavened cakes.
4. **cots,** apricots.
5. **zenith,** the point at which a celestial body, in this case the sun, is directly above the observer.

From THE PLUM PLUM PICKERS by Raymond Barrio. Copyright © Ventura Press, P.O. Box 1076, Guerneville, California 95446.

TWIN HEADS
Alfred H. Maurer
Collection of Whitney Museum of
American Art, New York City

nights. Cold drinks. Soft guitar music with Lupe sitting beside him. All wafting through his feverish moments. Tiredness drained his spirit of will. Exhaustion drained his mind. His fingers burned. His arms flailed the innocent trees. He was slowing down. He could hardly fill his last bucket. Suddenly the whistle blew. The day's work was at last ended.

Ended!

The contratista[6] Roberto Morales[7] stood there.

6. **contratista** (kōn tra tēs′tə), a labor contractor.
7. **Morales** (mō ra′les).

His feet straddled. Mexican style. A real robber. A Mexican general. A gentlemanly, friendly, polite, grinning, vicious, thieving brute. The worst kind. To his own people. Despite his being a fellow Mexican, despite his torn, old clothing, everyone knew what kind of clever criminal he was. Despite his crude, ignorant manner, showing that he was one of them, that he'd started with them, that he grew up with them, that he'd suffered all the sordid deprivations with them, he was actually the shrewdest, smartest, richest cannibal in forty counties around. They sure couldn't blame the güeros[8] for this miscarriage.[9] He was a crew chief. How could anyone know what he did to his own people? And what did the güeros care? So the anglo[10] growers and güero executives, smiling in their cool filtered offices, puffing their elegant thin cigars, washed their clean blond bloodless dirtless hands of the whole matter. All they did was hire Roberto Morales. Firm, fair, and square. For an agreed-upon price. Good. How he got his people down to the pickings was no concern of theirs. They were honest, those güeros. They could sleep at night. They fulfilled their end of the bargain, and cheated no one. Their only crime; their only soul crime indeed was that they just didn't care how that migratory scum lived. It was no concern of theirs. Their religion said it was no concern of theirs. Their wives said it was no concern of theirs. Their aldermen[11] said it was no concern of theirs. Their——

Whenever Roberto Morales spoke, Manuel had to force himself not to answer. He had to keep his temper from flaring.

"Now," announced Morales at last, in his friendliest tone. "Now. I must take two cents from every bucket. I am sorry. There was a miscalculation. Everybody understands. Everybody?" He slid his eyes around, smiling, palms up.

The tired, exhausted pickers gasped as one.

Yes. Everyone understood. Freezing in place. After all that hard work.

"Any questions, men?"

Morales grinned, knowing everyone realized that he had the upper hand, that that would mean a loss of two or three dollars out of each picker's pay that day, a huge windfall for Morales.

"You promised to take nothing!" Manuel heard himself saying. Everyone turned in astonishment to stare at Manuel.

"I said two cents, hombre. You got a problem or what?"

"You promised."

The two men, centered in a huge ring of red-ringed eyes, glared at each other. Reaching for each other's jugular. The other exhausted animals studied the tableau[12] through widening eyes. It was so unequal. Morales remained calm, confident, studying Manuel. As though memorizing his features. He had the whole advantage. Then, with his last remaining energy, Manuel lifted his foot and clumsily tipped over his own last bucket of cots. They rolled away in all directions around everyone's feet.

---

8. **güeros** (gue'rōs), a Mexican word meaning persons with fair hair.

9. **miscarriage,** a failure in the administration of justice.

10. **anglo,** an English speaking resident of the United States.

11. **aldermen,** members of a governing body.

12. **tableau** (tab'lō), scene.

Roberto Morales' eyes blazed. His fists clenched. "You pick them up, Gutierrez."

So. He knew his name. After all. For answer, Manuel kicked over another bucket, and again the fruit rolled away in all directions.

Then an astonishing thing happened.

All the other pickers moved toward their own buckets still standing beside them on the ground awaiting the truck gatherer, and took an ominous position over them, straddling their feet over them. Without looking around, without taking his eyes off Manuel, Roberto Morales said sharply, "All right. All right, men. I shall take nothing this time."

Manuel felt a thrill of power course through his nerves.

He had never won anything before. He would have to pay for this, for his defiance, somehow, again, later. But he had shown defiance. He had salvaged his money savagely and he had earned respect from his fellow slaves. The big bosses would never know of this little incident, and would probably be surprised, and perhaps even a little mortified, for a few minutes. But they wouldn't care. It was bread, pan y[13] tortillas out of his children's mouths. But they still wouldn't give a single hoot. Manuel had wrenched Morales' greedy fingers away and removed a fat slug of a purse from his sticky grasp. And in his slow way, in his stupid, accidental, dangerous way, Manuel had made an extravagant discovery, as Don Gaspar had also made two centuries before, in almost exactly the same spot. And that was—that a man counted for something. For men, Manuel dimly suspected, are built for something more important and less trifling than the mere gathering of prunes and apricots, hour upon hour, decade upon decade, insensibly, mechanically, antlike. Men are built to experience a certain sense of honor and pride.

Or else they are dead before they die.

READING FOR DETAILS

A Leader Is Born

The contratista, or labor contractor, Morales, is a traitor to his own people, willing to rob them for personal gain.

1. What demand does he make of the fruit pickers after they have finished their day's work?
2. How does Manuel surprise himself?
3. What action does he take in defiance of Morales?
4. How do the other pickers support him?
5. How does Manuel feel about what he has done?

READING FOR MEANING

Consider these propositions in light of the selection:

1. Desire for money will corrupt most people.
2. It is more contemptible to rob your own people than to rob others.
3. People become much braver when they have a leader.

READING FOR APPRECIATION

Style

When individuals are working under nearly intolerable conditions—as, for example, in extreme heat—and they push their bodies almost past the limit of their endurance, their thoughts become chaotic and disorganized. Raymond Barrio's writing style in "The Confrontation" is choppy and sometimes hard to understand. Why is this style an effective way of revealing Manuel's thoughts?

13. **pan y** (pän′ē), Spanish for "bread and . . ."

Giving Insight

1. How are Manuel's feelings about Morales first revealed?
2. How does the reader know that Morales had realized that Manuel was a potential threat to him?
3. Why is Manuel's victory so important to him?

3. On page 479 Manuel expresses the thought that the white farmers and business executives just don't care how the "migratory scum lived." What is the related word that defines workers who travel from one area to another in search of work?

LANGUAGE AND VOCABULARY

It is sometimes possible to tell at a glance that two or more words are related in some way. The words *automatically* and *automaton*, from "The Confrontation," are obviously related; both are derived from the Greek forms *auto*, "self," and *matos*, "willing." Both words, therefore, refer to self-willed or self-controlled action. In the context of the story, *automatically* means "mechanically," and *automaton* means "machine or robot." Manuel, the writer says, performed his monotonous, back-breaking job mechanically, as if he were a robot, not a human being. Also from the story are two other look-alike words—*cents* and *century*. Both words come from the Latin word *centum*, meaning "hundred." In the United States, a *cent* is one one-hundredth of a dollar, the basic monetary unit. And a *century*, of course, is a hundred years. Keeping in mind what you have just learned, use your dictionary to try to answer the following questions:

1. Does *automation* increase or decrease jobs in a factory? Explain.
2. What is the adjective commonly used to define a 100-year celebration or observation?

COMPOSITION

From a personal point of view, write a brief paper about a person you feel does not have a strong identity—someone who is just a face in a crowd. This may be a real or imaginary individual, but before you begin to write have a clear picture in your mind. Included in your composition should be an illustrative incident that has some action, a detailed description of the person's appearance, and the necessary exposition for the reader to see clearly the picture you paint. You might begin: "I really felt sorry for _____ when _____ didn't recognize him that day. . . ."

BIOGRAPHICAL NOTE

Raymond Barrio (1921–   ) was born in New Jersey but has lived in California most of his life. A combat veteran of World War II, he attended various colleges in New York, Connecticut, and California. He now teaches at West Valley Junior College in California. His works include numerous articles in art and travel magazines and short fiction in literary periodicals. He has written several novels and is looked upon by some critics as one of the leading Mexican-American writers.

To the artist, a portrait is more than a rendering of a face. It's a frozen, moment in that person's life, the sum and substance of his or her identity captured on canvas.

George Catlin, **WHITE CLOUD, HEAD CHIEF OF THE IOWAS**
National Gallery of Art, Washington, D.C.
Paul Mellon Collection

Charles Sheeler, **ARTIST LOOKS AT NATURE**
Art Institute of Chicago
Gift of the Society for Contemporary American Art

George Catlin's White Cloud, at the left, wears not only a dignified and determined expression, but the badges of his office, identifying him as the proud leader of a great nation. Charles Sheeler says more about his creative identity than about his actual life by showing us a landscape both as it is and as it becomes after it has filtered through his vision and senses.

Salvador Dali, PORTRAIT OF GALA
Collection, Museum of Modern Art
New York
Gift of Abby Aldrich Rockefeller

The artists on these pages are all concerned with the identity of themselves and those close to them. The portrait above of Gala, Salvador Dali's wife, deals with an age-old problem of identity: How many people inhabit us? How many personalities does each of us have? Gala surveys herself, maybe in a mirror, maybe not, and we wonder: who is the real Gala?

The self-portrait of Malvin Gray Johnson at the left contains the long history of his race. In shape and texture and abundance, the masks and drums reflect the man himself.

Malvin Gray Johnson, **SELF-PORTRAIT**
National Museum of American Art, Washington, D.C.
Gift of the Harmon Foundation

James MacNeill Whistler, **THE ARTIST IN HIS STUDIO**
Courtesy of the Art Institute of Chicago

Roberto Montenegro, **SELF-PORTRAIT**
Brooks Memorial Art Gallery
Memphis, Tenn.
Gift of Isaac L. Meyers

Whistler (above) and Montenegro (left) see themselves as parts of something larger, too. Whistler is only a part of the life of his studio. Montenegro appears as a reflection in a globe that could be the world, held aloft by two hands that could belong to God, or a friend, or you.

485

Edgar Degas, **CAFE SINGER WEARING A GLOVE**
Fogg Art Museum, Harvard University
Collection of Maurice Wertheim, Class of 1906

Max Beckmann, **SELF-PORTRAIT**
Art Institute of Chicago

There is pride in these two paintings. Degas' delightful cafe singer at the left knows that her every gesture, every movement is watched with rapt attention by the audience. She is practiced and professional. But what is real, and what is counterfeit? How much of the actress is the actual woman, and how can we—or she—tell? Max Beckmann, in his haughty and disdainful self-portrait at the right, seems to have no trouble in either finding or stating his opinion of his identity. He clothes himself and poses himself with arrogant self-assurance, balancing his figure with the brightness of a joyful background. Note the two huge, oversized hands. A man who would admit to these hands is a man who has nothing to hide.

487

"I only regret that I have but one life to lose for my country."

NATHAN HALE
Nancy Hale

"The boy was only a couple of years out of New Haven[1] when he joined up. He'd hardly got started. He'd been teaching school, you know, up at East Haddam and then down in New London, and it looked as if he was shaping up into a fine teacher. He'd made a lot of friends everywhere he went, and the girls always liked him. They say he was a good-looking boy.

"Then the war came. Things had looked bad to us Americans for a long time, but when the first gun was fired on that April day[2] it seemed to light a sudden strong fire in everyone's heart. It seemed to call out—'Americans!' The boy's brothers, John and Joseph, volunteered first off. It was a patriotic family—the father'd been a Deputy in the old Connecticut Assembly. The boy himself had signed up with the school for a year. He wasn't the kind to let people down, but he did write and ask to be released from his contract two weeks early. He joined up in July, as a Lieutenant in Webb's Seventh Connecticut.

"Well, you know how things went after that. The boy was in camp up near Boston all winter. It wasn't an exciting siege. But there was a lot to do getting the men to reenlist. Most of their terms of enlistment ran out in December. The General was worried about it. Our boy offered the men in his company his own pay for a month if they'd stay that much longer. Anyway the siege was maintained.

"He got a leave in the winter and went home. Maybe that was when he got engaged. Alicia Adams. A lovely girl; they would have made a handsome couple. When Spring came the enemy evacuated Boston and our army went down to New York, where real trouble was threatening. The boy'd been made a captain by that time. He was twenty-one years old.

"Our Long Island campaign was just this side of disastrous. Morale was none too good, afterwards. I don't suppose the General was in a worse spot in the whole war than he was for those three weeks right after the Battle of Long Island. There we lay, facing the enemy across the East River, and no way of knowing what they had up their sleeve. Surprise was what we feared. The answer to that was companies of rangers, to scout around and find out what was up. Knowlton's Rangers was organized, and our boy switched over to it. He wanted action, you see.

"But the rangers weren't enough.

From THERE WERE GIANTS IN THE LAND. Copyright 1942, © 1970 by Holt, Rinehart and Winston. Reprinted by permission of Holt, Rinehart and Winston, Publishers.

1. **New Haven,** location of Yale University in Connecticut.
2. **April day,** April 19, 1775, when the American troops fought the British redcoats around Lexington, Massachusetts.

The General wanted to know two things: when the enemy was planning to attack, and where. Nobody could tell him. The General let it be known that he'd welcome volunteers to spy.

"Now, people didn't take kindly to the word 'spy' around these parts. It didn't mean excitement or glamour or any of those things. It meant something degrading. It was a job they gave to bums, who didn't care. But the General said he wanted a spy. Well, our boy volunteered. His friends tried to talk him out of it. They spoke of the indignity; they also told him he'd make a terrible spy—frank, open boy like him.

"But his idea was, the job was necessary. That was the great thing. Its being necessary seemed to him to make it honorable. He was sent through the enemy lines dressed up like a Dutch schoolmaster.

"He didn't make such a bad spy, after all. He got what he went after, and hid the drawings in his shoes. He was on his way back, crossing their lines, when they caught him. They found the information on him. He admitted he was over there to spy. You know what a spy gets. They hanged him in the morning. He wrote some letters to the family at home, but they were destroyed before his eyes, they say. But in his last moment, they let him say what he wanted to. And later one of their officers told one of our officers what he'd said.

"There he was, with the noose around his neck. He hadn't got much done. He'd got caught on the first big job of his life. He wasn't going to marry Alicia Adams, nor to have any children, nor to do any more teaching, nor to finish fighting this war. He stood there in the morning air, and he spoke and said who he was, his commission and all. And then he added, 'I only regret that I have but one life to lose for my country.'"

You could tell the story like that, simply, because it is a simple story, and when you'd finished you'd have told about all there is to tell about Nathan Hale. There isn't even a contemporary picture of him. Most of the friends to whom he wrote didn't keep his letters. He was just a young American who'd gone to war, who'd lived for twenty-one ordinary enough years before—in the day's work—he died for his country.

One of his brothers, Enoch, was my great-great-grandfather.

When I was a child there was a small bronze statue, about four feet high, that stood in the corner of the living room at home. It was just about my height, but it wasn't another child. It was a young man, with his wrists tied behind him and his ankles bound. I passed it several times a day every day of my childhood. Sometimes I used to touch the bronze face. It was a small-scale replica of the Nathan Hale statue at Yale.

I must have been told his story, because I always knew it. But my father never went on about it, if you know what I mean. There his story was, for what it might mean to you. Some of my other ancestors were the kind of characters that have a whole legend of anecdotes surrounding them, pointed, stirring, or up-roarious. But the young man with his hands bound had died at twenty-one, a patriot, as stark and all alone and anecdoteless as young men of twenty-one must be.

Once I was set upon the knees of an old gentleman whose grandmother had been Alicia Adams. She had married and had children, and lived to be eighty-eight, a pretty, sparkling old lady. And when she died she said, "Where is Nathan?" But about the young man himself there were no family reminiscences, no odd little jokes, no tales beyond the short, plain story of his life and death. He had had no time to do anything memorable but die.

Nevertheless . . . It was my job as a child to fill the kitchen scuttle with coal from the cellar. I was not a brave child, and to me the long corners of the cellar seemed menacing and full of queer, moving shadows—wolves? robbers? I cannot remember when I first started taking the thought of Nathan Hale down cellar with me, for a sword and buckler.[3] I thought, "If he could be hanged, I can go down cellar." The thing was, he was no impossible hero; he was a member of the family, and he was young too. He was a hero you could take along with you into the cellar of a New England farmhouse. You felt he'd be likely to say, "Aren't any wolves or robbers back there that I can see."

Well, I am grown up now and I know very little more about Nathan Hale than I did then. There are, of course, a mass of details about his short life. A devoted scholar named George Dudley Seymour has spent years in collecting all that can

3. **buckler,** a small, round shield.

be collected about him. There's a war-time diary. They know his friends. He played football and checkers at camp. He drank wine at Brown's Tavern and cider at Stone's. But when you add all these little things you only affirm the peculiar simplicity of the story.

Hale is a symbol of all the young American men who fight and who die for us. Partly he is a symbol because he was the first of our heroes in the first of our own wars. He was the first to show the world what Americans are made of. The reason they destroyed his letters home at the time of his death was, they said, so that "the rebels should not know they have a man who can die so firmly." He showed them.

He is no Washington or Jefferson although he ranks with the heroes. Washington was a great general and Jefferson was a genius. All of our nation's heroes are great men who are great by their minds and by their deeds and by their careers. All except Hale. His special gift to his country, and to us who love that country, was the manner of his death.

He is the young American. He is the patron of all the young Americans who have grown up as he did in quiet self-respecting families; who have gone to college and done well, and had fun too; who have started out along their life's careers, well spoken of, promising; and then broken off to join their country's forces in time of war without an instant's hesitation; knowing what must be done and who must do it. He was no different than they. He was an American boy. Everything that can be said of them can be said of him. In the letters of his friends written about him after his death, certain words keep cropping up. They sound oddly familiar. "Promising . . . patriotic . . . generous . . . modest . . . high-spirited . . . devoted . . ." His friends fitted the words to Hale. They fit Americans.

Nothing was more American in Hale than his taking on the duties that led to his death. It was a dirty job, spying. Nobody wanted it. He took it. There's something about that, taking on a dirty job that's got to be done, that rings a bell. It's an American custom of American heroes. He wasn't a remarkably articulate boy. His letters are nothing special. He just jotted things in his diary. But he became the spokesman for young American fighting men who have to die for their country. He chanced to say the thing they think; the thing they mean, when there's not even a split second to think. He stood there at Turtle Bay on Manhattan Island. Don't think he declaimed.[4] He wasn't that kind. He had those few moments, and he was thinking about all the different things that were ending for him. He said and I think it was more like a remark:

"I only regret . . ."

READING FOR DETAILS

A Spokesman for Young Americans
1. What was Nathan Hale doing before he joined the Army?
2. Why did he take the job of spying?
3. Describe the scene when he was hanged.
4. In what way did Nathan Hale help Nancy when she was a child?

READING FOR MEANING

Consider and discuss the following statements in light of the selection:
1. Spying is a dishonorable job.

---

4. **declaimed,** made a formal speech.

2. "All of our nation's heroes are great men who are great by their minds and by their deeds and by their careers."

3. Nathan Hale was a typical American boy.

READING FOR APPRECIATION

Style

1. How do you know where the storyteller breaks off the straight narrative and begins to include personal reminiscences?

2. What words at the beginning of the third paragraph are particularly characteristic of the oral storyteller?

COMPOSITION

Choose one or more of the following composition exercises:

1. In your own words, condense this rambling account of Nancy Hale's into a more structured pattern of four or five paragraphs in which you place the thesis statement—Hale as a typical young American is the symbol of all young American men who fight and die for their country—in the first or second paragraph.

2. Nancy Hale tells that the reason the British destroyed Nathan's letters home was so that "the rebels should not know they have a man who can die so firmly."

On that last evening, young Hale undoubtedly wrote a letter to his fiancée, Alicia Adams, and to his parents and family and some valued friends. Place yourself back in time and circumstances and assume his identity. Write a letter to a loved one, knowing you are to be hanged at dawn. Try to include as many details as you can imagine that give insight into Nathan Hale's character.

3. In a few brief paragraphs write the thoughts you imagine may have passed through Nathan Hale's mind before he spoke those memorable words: "I only regret . . ."

BIOGRAPHICAL NOTE

Nancy Hale (1908–   ) was born in Boston. Her stories and novels have been published widely both here and abroad. She is from a New England family famous in American life and letters. In addition to Nathan Hale, her relatives include Edward Everett Hale, who wrote *The Man Without a Country*, Harriet Beecher Stowe, author of *Uncle Tom's Cabin*, and Lucretia Hale, author of *The Peterkin Papers*.

You have something that is yours alone.

Thumbprint

In the heel of my thumb
are whorls, whirls, wheels
in a unique design:
mine alone.
What a treasure to own!   5
My own flesh, my own feelings.
No other, however grand or base,
can ever contain the same.
My signature,
thumbing the pages of my time.   10

My universe key,
my singularity.
Impress, implant,
I am myself,
of all my atom parts I am the sum.   15
And out of my blood and my brain
I make my own interior weather,
my own sun and rain.
Imprint my mark upon the world,
whatever I shall become.   20

EVE MERRIAM

A REPEATED SIGNATURE

The poet voices a rather startling thought with the lines: "My signature,/thumbing the pages of my time." Some persons might feel dismay that each time they leaf through a magazine or open a car or refrigerator door they are leaving evidence of their identity behind as clearly as though they had signed their names.

1. What feeling does the poet express about the individuality of her thumbprint?
2. This poem is as individual in verse form as in subject and does not have a set rhythm or rhyme scheme. Nevertheless, it has some rhyming lines. Where are they?

BIOGRAPHICAL NOTE

Eve Merriam (1916–   ), whose poetry for youth centers largely on the pleasures of word play, was born in Philadelphia, but has spent most of her life in New York. A teacher at both the City University of New York and New York University, she has written radio and TV scripts, short stories, and poetry. Her main books include *It Doesn't Always Have to Rhyme, Out Loud, A Word or Two with You,* and *Nitty Gritty City.* She has received the Excellence in Poetry for Children Award of the National Council of Teachers of English.

Here is shared identity.

Grandma

If you dig that hole deep enough
you'll reach China, they used to tell me,
a child in a backyard, Allentown, Pa.
Not strong enough to dig that hole,
I waited twenty years   5
then sailed back
half way around the world

In Taiwan I first met Grandma.
Before she came to view I heard
her slippered feet softly measure   10
the tatami* floor with even step.
The aqua paper door slid open
and there, breathless, I faced
my five foot height, my sturdy legs and feet,
my square forehead, high cheeks, and wide-set eyes.   15
My image stood before me
acted on by fifty years;
here in my past was my future.

She smiled, stretched her arms
to take to heart the eldest daughter   20
of her youngest son a quarter century away.
She spoke a tongue I knew no word of
and I was sad I could not understand,
but I could hug her.

AMY LING

Appeared in *BRIDGE*, Spring/Summer 1980. By permission of the author, Amy Ling.

*__tatami,__ a matting that is woven from rice straw and bound with cloth.

A LOOK INTO THE FUTURE

"You look just like . . ." Whenever there are family gatherings, this bit of conversation is almost sure to be heard.

1. When and where did Amy Ling first see her grandmother?
2. What is the meaning of the last line of the second stanza: "here in my past was my future"?
3. What is Amy's regret when she sees her grandmother?

BIOGRAPHICAL NOTE

Amy Ling (1939–   ) was born in Peking, China, and brought to the United States at age six. She received degrees from Queens College, the University of California at Davis, and a Ph.D. in comparative literature from New York University. Her poems have appeared in several magazines, including *Critique* and *Straight Ahead International*. Ms. Ling teaches American literature and writing at Rutgers University.

SUMMING UP: IDENTITY

A UNIVERSAL DESIRE

What is it that causes a person to want to establish an identity? It would appear that one's nationality or race makes little difference. Whether a person is a crook, a schoolboy, a schoolteacher, or a fruit-picker, that person feels the need to establish an identity.

As people grow up, they know that they are changing, that they are not what they were nor yet what they will become. They want to be themselves and to let others know who they are. To do this, they often must do something out of the ordinary. Manuel in "The Confrontation" was probably the first fruit-picker ever to stand up to Morales, the labor contractor. In "The Fight" Richard Wright's establishment of his identity at school was unquestionably a matter of simple survival.

Establishing an identity must be a continuing process. Discuss why this is true.

READING FOR MEANING

Which selections in the unit seem to support the following statements? Discuss.

1. Who a person "is" depends on the situation.
2. Identity is usually established by accident.
3. Establishing an identity is pointless for people unless it is of benefit to them.
4. Everyone has an identity.

READING FOR APPRECIATION

Style

Style includes a writer's choice of words, sentence structure, point of view, use of imagery, and attitude toward the subject. Think back over the selections you have read in this unit. Combinations of descriptive terms follow. Each combination applies more directly to the style of one specific selection than to the others. See if you can match the selection with the appropriate set of terms.

1. Choppy, disorganized, obvious sympathy for the main character
2. Factual, conversational, storytelling manner
3. Realistic, hard-hitting, autobiographical
4. Light, humorous, tongue-in-cheek attitude

Giving Insight

Giving insight is managed by a writer through the use of a variety of techniques. In each of the sentences that follow there are words that triggered individuals to assert their identity. Without looking back through the unit, see how well you can reconstruct the circumstances in which the following lines were spoken and how they made the character feel.

1. "Now. I must take two cents from every bucket."
2. "How come they make you people so ugly in Jackson?"
3. "Let go of him, Blockhead!" And he struck Tango across the cheek.

COMPOSITION

Write an illustrative story about a character who devises a scheme to get rid of a habit or problem that gives him or her an unwanted identity. Pattern your story after the fable and use a person, animal, bird, or insect as the central character. Your fable may be intentionally humorous or serious and the outcome successful or unsuccessful. You may reiterate the teaching, or moral, of your fable at the end if you desire. Some ideas:

A man thought greedy because he eats so rapidly.

A woman judged bad-tempered because she speaks so loudly.

A cat thought crazy because it is kind to mice.

COMPOSITION WORKSHOP

DEVELOPING AN OUTLINE

Like the careful traveler, the careful writer prepares a plan before beginning any piece of writing longer than a single paragraph. The plan, or outline, allows the writer to sketch out the route that will be followed in developing the topic. The outline also allows the writer to rework easily the overall structure of the piece of writing if necessary. The reader benefits from the outline as well, for the outline helps to insure that the piece of writing is organized and easy to follow.

There are many kinds of outlines. Two kinds of outlines—the *rough outline* and the *paragraph outline*—are usually used to sketch out the brief reports that most students are called upon to write.

Let's examine how both the rough outline and the paragraph outline help the writer. Let's say that a writer becomes interested in the Ute Indian tribe while reading Hal Borland's novel *When the Legends Die*. The writer gathers information on the tribe by consulting a number of sources. The writer studies all of the gathered information and decides to eliminate some pieces that turn out to be unrelated to the topic. Using the information that remains, the writer sorts it into categories. The writer notes that some of the information has to do with the area that the tribe originally inhabited. The writer notes that other pieces of information relate to the tribe's earliest way of life, the important changes that came to the tribe when it obtained the use of the horse, and the tribe's later and current problems brought about by unfair government policies.

Once the writer has arranged the collected information into the four groupings described above, the writer is ready to construct a rough outline for the report. The rough outline may be made up of single-word descriptions of each category or of phrases or clauses that identify each category. It is never made up of complete sentences. The rough outline is always temporary, since one of its main purposes is to allow the writer to shift the items in it around until the best order for the presentation is found. The rough outline usually begins with the identification of the topic, followed by a brief description of each paragraph in the report. In front of each description stands an Arabic numeral. At the rough outline stage, the first numeral merely notes the report's introduction, which is always best planned after the writer has made a final decision about the paragraphs that will make up the body of the report. Look at the following rough outline. It could very well be the fourth or fifth that the writer prepared.

TOPIC: The Ute Tribe

1. Introduction
2. Area inhabited
3. Early way of life
4. Horse brings changes
5. More recent history

Once a final rough outline has been completed, a writer may prepare a paragraph outline, which is a more detailed plan for the report. The writer begins this stage by examining each of the four groups of collected information that make up the body of the report and writes a main-idea sentence for each. The writer then examines all of the main-idea sentences and writes a thesis sentence which covers all of the main-idea sentences. In the report's paragraph outline, this thesis sentence appears next to the first Arabic numeral. Here is a paragraph outline for a brief report on the Ute Indian tribe.

TOPIC: The Ute Tribe

1. THESIS STATEMENT: The Ute tribe, from whom the state of Utah takes its name, has always been one of the most important of the Great Basin tribes.

2. The Utes once occupied a large area of the Great Basin.
3. Before the white settlers arrived in the Great Basin, the Utes were hunters and seed gatherers.
4. The horse changed the Utes' way of life.
5. Like many other tribes, the Utes suffered a great deal as a result of the shortsighted government policy toward America's Indians.

Study the following brief report on the Ute tribe. Notice that it follows the plan of both the rough outline and the paragraph outline.

The Ute tribe, from whom the state of Utah takes its name, has always been one of the most important of the Great Basin tribes. The Great Basin is also the home of five other tribes that, like the Utes, speak a dialect of the Shoshonean Indian language. The Great Basin covers an area 600 miles wide between the Wasatch Mountains in Utah and the Sierra Nevada Mountains in California. Nine hundred miles in length, it stretches from Oregon into Mexico.

The Utes once occupied a large area of the Great Basin. The tribe's hunting grounds extended northward into Wyoming, eastward into Kansas, and southward into the Oklahoma panhandle, northern Texas, and central New Mexico.

Before the white settlers arrived in the Great Basin, the Utes were hunters and seed gatherers. They were never farmers. They were famous for their ability to obtain food from the largest game available. During the summer, they occupied the mountain valleys in small family groups, seeking berries, fish, and a wide variety of game. During the cold and snowy winters, they abandoned the mountains in favor of the plateaus to the south. In these warmer regions they hunted the antelope, deer, and buffalo that also wintered there.

The horse changed the Utes' way of life. They were the first Indians in the Great Basin to get horses from the Spanish colonizers of New Mexico. The Utes probably secured their first horses through raids upon Spanish settlements halfway through the seventeenth century. They immediately became expert and courageous riders. They used the horse to hunt buffalo over the Plains to the east of their homeland. The horse also allowed the tribe to range over a wider area. They used the horse to do battle with powerful Plains tribes such as the Arapaho and the Cheyenne. The Utes also used the horse to raid Spanish settlements that they believed were threatening their homeland.

Like many other tribes, the Utes suffered a great deal as a result of the shortsighted government policy toward America's Indians. The tribe signed a treaty with the United States government in 1868. According to the treaty's provisions, the tribe was granted reservations in Colorado and Utah. The original Colorado reservation occupied a little less than one-half of that state's territory. The Utah reservation was located in the northeast corner of the state and included about one-eighth of the state. The Utah reservation is about the same size today as it was in 1868. The Colorado reservation, however, has shriveled to an area of a little over 500,000 acres in the southwest corner of the state. Deprived of its lands and separated from its old ways, the tribe struggles to survive intact in an unfamiliar, industrialized world.

ACTIVITY 1

Choose a topic that could be developed in a brief report. Collect information for your topic from as many sources as possible. Eliminate any items that do not belong. Then arrange the remaining information into categories for the body of your report.

ACTIVITY 2

Using the information that you have collected and sorted in Activity 1, write a rough outline for your report. Then write a topic sentence for each of the paragraphs that will make up the report's body. Study the topic sentences and write a thesis statement. Then prepare a paragraph outline for your report.

ACTIVITY 3

Prepare a final draft of your report by writing the paragraphs that make up the report's body. Then write an introductory paragraph that includes the report's thesis statement.

INTRODUCTION TO
When the Legends Die

The last selection on the theme of identity is the short novel *When the Legends Die*. In this absorbing story Tom Black Bull, a Ute Indian, is trapped between two ways of life—the Utes' way and the white people's way—and he searches desperately for answers to the questions of who he is and where he belongs.

On thin strips of land in southwestern Colorado, northwestern New Mexico, and southeastern Utah are clustered Ute and Navaho reservations. On these reservations, which are administered by the Bureau of Indian Affairs of the Department of the Interior, thousands of American Indians live nearly totally managed lives—the result of the white people's attempt to "civilize" them, to force them to stop being what they were. As a young man, the author, Hal Borland, knew many Utes and spent considerable time in their homeland.

It is no secret that the reservation system has been far from successful in achieving assimilation. Turned away by the hostile barriers of bigotry that keep most American Indians out of the mainstream of life in the United States, the American Indian clings precariously to the lowest rung of the economic ladder.

Before the white people herded the last American Indians onto reservations, the latter's lifestyle reflected rhythms and rituals that were already ancient at the time of Columbus's discovery of the New World. Never a wanton destroyer of the land and the life upon it, the American Indians maintained a balance between themselves and their surroundings, a precious balance that has been lost.

This novel is divided into four sections, or chapters, and each chapter can be read much as you would read a short story. However, a novel allows for greater development of character, situations, and theme.

Three Levels of Meaning in a Novel

Readers of a novel must allow the words to create pictures and feelings in their minds; they must let the words create characters so vividly that they actually live their experience through the words. The duty of the writer, then, is to select words and incidents that will create these pictures, telling just enough, but not too much, to let readers project themselves into the action. As you read *When the Legends Die*, try to share the experience as though you lived it too. Put yourself in the place of Tom Black Bull. Imagine his surroundings. This "substitute experience" is the first level of reading.

However, a well-written novel like *When the Legends Die* does more than simply tell a story or take a reader through an experience. The events usually show something worth knowing about human beings and the ways in which they live. This significant comment about people in general is the second level of reading in a novel.

Sometimes in a novel the words are so exactly right that the reader takes pleasure in their remarkable clarity. Sometimes the story itself is arranged so beautifully that the reader can enjoy the sheer skill of the storyteller. Recognizing the beauty of an author's skill is the third level of reading.

WHEN THE LEGENDS DIE Hal Borland

1 Bessie

He came home in midafternoon, hurrying through the alley. Bessie was sitting on the back step of the unpainted two-room house, peeling willow twigs with her teeth and watching the boy chase butterflies among the tall horseweeds. She looked up and saw her man come toward her. His face was bloody, his shirt torn and bloody down the front. She clapped a hand to her mouth to stifle her cry, and followed him into the house. He whispered, in the Ute[1] tongue, "They will come after me. Bring water to wash. Get the other shirt."

She filled the tin basin and brought it to him. There was a cut over his left eye and a darkening bruise beside his mouth. She got the other shirt while he washed; then she took the pan of red-stained water outside and poured it on the ground among the weeds. It sank into the dry soil and left only a dark, wet spot. When she went inside again he was pulling the clean shirt over his head. He wrapped the torn shirt into a bundle, the bloody places hidden, and said, still in Ute, "I shall go to the stream with black-stem ferns on Horse Mountain. Come to me there." He tucked the bundle under his arm, took his rifle, went to the door and looked, waited. Then he touched her face with his free hand and hurried through the scrub oak toward the river. The magpies screamed for a moment, then were silent.

She searched the floor for spots of blood and dried the basin; then she went to sit on the step again.

The boy, who was five years old and only an inch or so taller than the horseweeds, came and stood at her knee, asking questions with his eyes.

She smiled at him. "Nobody came. Nothing happened. Remember, if they ask." He nodded. She handed him a willow twig. He peeled the bark with his teeth, as she had done, and chewed it, tasting the green bitterness. "Go catch a grasshopper," she said. He went back among the weeds.

She waited half an hour.

Then they came up the street and stood in front of her, the tall sheriff, the short, fat man from the sawmill, and Blue Elk, with his squeaky shoes, black coat and derby hat, his wool-bound braids, his air of importance.

She clapped her hand to her mouth and began to wail. "You bring trouble!" Then, to Blue Elk, in the Ute tongue, "My man is hurt?"

The sheriff said to Blue Elk, "See what she knows."

Blue Elk rubbed his soft hands together. He said in Ute, "Bessie! Stop the wailing. Let the other woman mourn. Your man is not hurt. Where have you hidden him?"

"He is not here. Why do you come here for him?"

"He was here. He came here."

"If you know this, find him." She gestured toward the house.

"What does she say?" the sheriff asked.

"She says he is not here. She says we should look."

The sheriff and the sawmill man went inside. She asked Blue Elk, "Why do you want my man? What happened?"

1. **Ute** (yüt).

"He killed a man. He killed Frank No Deer."

"That one." Scorn was in her eyes.

"I know. A thief, a no-good. But George killed him. Where did George go?"

She shrugged.

"Where is the boy?"

She glanced at the weed patch and then waved her hand vaguely. "Boys play, go where they will."

The men came back. "No sign of him."

"They will watch you," Blue Elk said, still in the tongue.

"If they want me, I am here."

The sheriff said, "Tell her we'll find him if we have to run down every little Ute fishing and berry camp in the mountains. He covered his tracks, or she did. But we'll find him."

Blue Elk said to her, "You heard. For the cost of two horses I could settle this."

"I have not the cost of two horses."

"One horse," Blue Elk offered.

She shook her head. "I have not the cost of one goat."

"What does she say?" the sheriff asked.

"She says she has not seen him."

"I think she's lying."

"My people," Blue Elk said in English, "do not lie."

The sheriff grunted. "They just kill each other over a lunch pail. Some day one of them is going to kill you, Blue Elk." He turned to the sawmill man. "Let's go find Frank's squaw. You better tell her you'll pay for the funeral."

"Fifty dollars for a coffin. That's all," the other said.

The woman said scornfully in Ute, "The cost of two ponies!"

"What does she say?" the sheriff asked.

"She says she is glad it was not her man who was killed."

"You know where to find Frank's squaw?"

Blue Elk nodded, and they left.

She sat on the steps another ten minutes. Then she said, "Come now," and there was a movement among the horseweeds. The boy stood up and came to her and they went indoors. She praised him. She walked about the house, choosing things, not yet taking them from their places. Ammunition. Fishhooks and line. The axe. Knives. Spare moccasins. The boy's coat. Two blankets.

She started a fire in the stove and put meat on to boil. She neatened up the house, to leave it clean, and to occupy the time. It was a company house. For two years, the sawmill had taken money from her man's pay for rent and for the old iron bed, the dresser with the broken leg, the four chairs, the table, the stove. By now, they owned the two blankets, and that was all she was taking. The knives and axe were hers, and she had made the moccasins and the coat. When it was dark, they would pack these things and go. Two summers ago Blue Elk had brought them here from Horse Mountain. Now he was sending them back.

She sat on the step with the boy and thought of that summer of 1910.

They had lived near Arboles on the Southern Ute reservation in southwestern Colorado, and her man had a cornfield. The drought came and the corn burned up. One evening her man said, "We are going fishing. Our friends are going, Charley Huckleberry too, so it is all right." Charley was a member of the council.

The next morning, in six wagons, they went up the Piedra River to the reservation line and camped. All summer they caught and ate fish and picked berries and there were no cornfields to worry about.

It was like the old days. In the evening the men wrestled and ran races and the children threw stones at the magpies and the women sat and talked. It was a happy time.

The day they broke camp someone said

they should go into Piedra Town and buy candy for the children. Charley Huckleberry said it was all right to go. So they went to the store and spent all the money they had on the candy.

Then someone said, "Let us go farther up the river and camp and catch more fish." Charley Huckleberry said he guessed that would be all right, too.

There were plenty of fish and service-berries were ripe. The women and children picked them, and set up racks and smoked the fish they didn't eat. Then the men killed two fat deer which had come to the river to drink. The venison tasted good after so much fish, and the women told the men to go up on Horse Mountain and get more deer and they would dry it, the old way, for winter.

Nobody remembered how long they were there because it didn't matter. When they had made enough meat, they said, and had smoked fish and dried berries for the winter, they would go back to the reservation.

Then Blue Elk came and told them the police were after them because they had no fishing and hunting permit. Charley said there couldn't be any trouble because he was in charge and he was a member of the council. But Blue Elk said the council had sent him to find them.

Charley said, "Somebody always pays you to come to tell of trouble. The council didn't pay you. Who did?" But everybody knew that Charley was worried.

"I came to warn you," Blue Elk said, "and to tell you that this trouble can be taken care of."

Johnny Sour Water said, "Maybe we should let our women put you on the drying rack, like a fat fish, and smoke you too."

Everybody laughed, because Blue Elk did look like a big, fat fish. But they didn't laugh much. They didn't know how this would come out. Bessie's man, George Black Bull, said, "We dried fish and berries; we made deer meat for the winter. We did not kill

sheep or cows. Nobody can make trouble of this." Bessie was proud of him.

But Blue Elk said, "You did it without permits. There will be a fine for that. You are not so foolish as to think you can keep that meat?"

Then he said, "Your cornfields are burned. Your blankets are thin. Your women need new skirts. You already owe money to the trader. But I can get work for you and you will not have to worry about the winter."

"What do the sawmill men in Pagosa pay for you making this talk to us?" Charley Huckleberry asked.

Blue Elk said, "I worry for my people. That is why I tell you now that the sawmill man will give you jobs. He needs more men to work. He will pay two dollars a day, silver."

There was talk at that. Two dollars a day, silver!

Then Charley Huckleberry said Blue Elk was probably right about the fine because they had come too far off the reservation and stayed too long. That was not big trouble, and that was all the trouble there would be, Charley said.

But there still was this matter of two dollars a day, silver. The women said this might be a good thing, and the men said that if all of them went together to Pagosa it would be a happy time, maybe. And they did not have to stay long. In two months, they would have more than a hundred dollars, all silver. . . . So they went back to the reservation, the council took the meat and smoked fish for a fine, and Blue Elk got permits for them to go to work in the sawmill so they would not be hungry that winter.

In Pagosa Blue Elk helped the men to make their sign on the papers that said so much would be kept out of their pay to pay rent and buy furniture. And they could buy what they needed at the company store. The papers said they could not go away while they owed money for these things.

Then, one day, Blue Elk came to the

house and told Bessie that she and George must get married.

Bessie said, "George is my man. That is enough. That is married as it always was."

Blue Elk said, "There is the boy. You must be married for the boy, and the preacher must baptize him with holy water and give him a name."

"I wash him with water when he is dirty," Bessie said. "I have given him his name. Can the preacher do more than this?"

"It must be done. It will cost five dollars."

"I do not have five dollars," Bessie told him. "They take my man's money and do not pay it to him."

"I will see that he gets five dollars this week," Blue Elk said, and he did. George gave the money to Blue Elk and he took them to the preacher. The preacher said words and wrote on a paper and they were married. Then he asked what they wanted to name the boy. Bessie said, "He is Little Black Bull. He will choose when he needs another name." The preacher said he must have another name now, and that Thomas was a good name. Bessie said it didn't matter because Little Black Bull would pick his own name when the time came. So the preacher sprinkled water on the boy's head and George got no pay at all the next week because of that five dollars.

When the aspens came to leaf the next spring, George told the sawmill man he was going back to the reservation. The man looked in the book and said George owed forty-two dollars at the company store and must work four more weeks. But the next week the man gave George only seven dollars and kept the rest of his wages for rent and furniture. And the next week it was only five because one day the sawmill broke down and didn't run.

In four weeks George had saved only fifteen dollars. He hid the money in his lunch pail, but someone stole his lunch pail. Nobody saw the thief; but Frank No Deer, who was a mixed-blood Apache from the Jicarilla reservation in New Mexico, bought a new hat and boots that cost exactly fifteen dollars. George accused him of stealing his money and Frank laughed and said he had won that money in a dice game. Nobody knew of such a dice game, but George could not prove this thing. So he started again to save his money.

It was August before he had fifteen dollars again. He put it in a bean can and buried it, and when he found someone had dug it up, he told Frank No Deer he had stolen it. Frank only laughed. But he bought a suit of clothes, and the man at the store said it cost exactly fifteen dollars.

They did not go back to the reservation that fall either because now they owed fifty dollars at the store. All that winter George saved money again, this time in paper money which he kept in his pocket. He saved forty dollars, and two days ago he had told Bessie that in two weeks they would go back even if they were hungry next winter. Bessie said that would be a happy time.

Then yesterday, when he had quit work for lunch, someone had taken his lunch pail. He went out to where the other men were eating and Frank No Deer had that lunch pail. George said, "You are a thief. But this time you did not steal my money because it was not in my lunch pail. It is here in my pocket."

Then George tried to take his lunch pail and Frank No Deer tried to take it back and they had a fight. George sat on Frank No Deer and pounded his head on the ground. Then he let him up and Frank No Deer went away and did not come back to work all afternoon. After he had gone, George felt in his pocket. Frank No Deer had stolen his money while they wrestled.

George told Bessie last night, "Three times Frank No Deer has stolen my money and tomorrow I am going to kill him. . . ."

Bessie remembered all these things. She looked at the boy and thought it would be good to go away from here. The boy should know the old ways.

In her mind was one of the old songs that her mother had sung, a song about the roundness of things, of grass stems and aspens and the sun and the days and the years. Bessie sang it now, softly, and added words of her own about the roundness of a little boy's eyes and arms and legs, and the roundness of a bird's nest and a basket, coiled and complete, a part of the roundness of the whole.

The boy smiled as he heard it.

And then it was sunset, and they ate the meat. She put the boy to bed and he put his head against her and touched her cheek with his hand. Then he went to sleep and she waited for the deep darkness, saying thanks that there would be no moon.

The star that is a hunter with a pack on his back[2] was halfway down the sky in the northwest when she went out on the step and listened. Everything was quiet. She had made no light in the house, so she could see in this darkness. She went down the path to the alley, and nobody was there. She went around the house. Nobody was in the street. Nobody was watching. She knew this.

She wakened the boy, and whispered, "Do not talk. Stay close to me. Hold to my skirt and walk where I walk. We will make a game." They went out and she picked up the pack and the axe.

They went to the alley and turned left, not the way her man had gone, and followed a path to the top of the hill. In the starlight Bessie could see the road that led west toward Piedra Town. If she followed that road seventeen miles she would come to the road to Arboles, and there she would turn north. But half that far would be as far as the boy should walk tonight. In the starlight her eyes also saw an owl, two rabbits, a striped cat from town, a jay sleeping on a branch. She wanted to tell the boy how to see these things in the starlight. But tonight they were not talking.

She felt the boy's tiredness as he walked behind her, and she put down the pack and held him in her arms while they rested. They went on again. The hunter star was down near the horizon, making the big circle the stars made every night. It was good to know the roundness, the completeness, again; not the sharp squareness of houses and streets. They came to a stream and drank and then found a grove of spruces. She pushed the drooping branches aside and went into that green spruce lodge and spread the blankets and they slept.

She wakened soon after sunrise and lay listening. The jays were scolding. A squirrel cried at them and she knew it was only jays and squirrels. She tucked the blankets around the sleeping boy, and took a fishhook and line and a knife and went to a grassy place beside the stream. She caught four grasshoppers, stiff with the night chill, put one on the hook and tossed it into a quiet pool. She caught four fish and went back past the grassy place and thanked the grasshoppers before she cleaned the fish. She gathered wood and built a fire near the stream, so the thin smoke would not be seen in the morning mist from the water, and she put green sticks inside the fish to hold them open and set them beside the fire to cook.

Then she wakened the boy and they ate. They washed themselves in the pool and sat naked on a rock, clean and rested and fed, and watched the sun rise over the mountain. Softly she sang the old song for washing yourself when the sun is rising, and the boy sang a part of it with her. He did not yet know all the words. After that, they put on their clothes and went on again.

---

2. **The star . . . back,** actually the constellation of Orion.

That afternoon they came to the place where the two roads met. They sat in the scrub oak on the hillside and watched. Nobody came along either road. Then they went north where there was no road but only the game trails, to the east branch of the Piedra. She found a cave in which to spend the night, and the next afternoon they came to the foot of Horse Mountain.

She turned away from the place where the black-stem ferns grow, and they climbed the mountain till she found a place to watch the valley. They watched until the sun sank. Nobody came.

They stayed there two days, eating berries, building no fire to make smoke or smell; and nobody came. Then they went back down and around the mountain to the place where the black-stem ferns grow. At the spring beyond the ferns, she found his sign, a leafless willow twig that stood in a mossy place. She pulled it out; it had been peeled at the bottom. She put it back, peeled two more twigs and thrust them into the moss beside it. Then she and the boy climbed to a sheltered place from which she could see the spring.

He came that evening. He stepped out of the deep shadows and took the twigs from the moss, and then he was gone. She said her thanks to the earth and sky and the quarters of the earth, and then she and the boy slept. He knew they had come.

It was not until the second day afterward that he came for them. He held her hand and smiled at the boy. He said, "They have not yet come here." And she knew he had gone back the way she came and made sure nobody had followed her.

That afternoon they went over the shoulder of Horse Mountain. They saw four spruce grouse sitting on a low branch, and while she walked in front of them to keep them watching her he went around behind them and killed two with a stick. When it was

dark he built a fire inside an old bear den and she cooked the grouse. They were together. It was a happy time.

The next day they followed the big fork of the Piedra to Bald Mountain. At the far side of the mountain, he built a shelter close beside a spring. It was the first week of August.

They heard a mountain lion's kill-cry in the night and next morning he went up the mountain to look for the deer carcass. He found it in a patch of brush where the lion had dragged it after eating a forequarter. He butchered out the meat and took what was left of the skin and packed them down to the shelter. She built a drying rack, sliced the meat thin to cure; now she had skin to make leather and sinew for sewing. And that night he kept a fire going and sat watching for the lion, which prowled the nearby darkness, growling but fire-wary.

She said that if he would get more deer she could make meat for the winter. He said, "The rifle makes too big a noise. But when I was a boy I killed birds with arrows." And the next day he cut a strip of scrub oak and shaped it and cured it by fire and sun. He made pine shafts and feathered them with grouse feathers and hardened their points in the fire. He hid where the deer came to a pool at dusk to drink and shot all his arrows. But he did not kill one deer.

She said, "We did not sing the song for hunting deer." He said that a rifle was better than a song for killing deer, but he didn't dare use the rifle yet. So she taught him the song for hunting deer, and that night he killed a fat doe. She made meat. She made leather leggings and shirts. It was like the old days.

One morning they saw that Pagosa Peak to the east was white with snow. They moved to the south side of the mountain where the sun would shine when the short days came.

He found a place where an old slide had taken down a whole grove of lodgepole pines. He said, "I will make a house of those poles."

She said, "I do not want a house. I want a lodge that is round, like the path of the stars, like good things that have no end." So he cut poles and made a lodge, and piled other poles and brush around it, and when the aspen leaves littered the earth with gold you could not see that lodge. It was a part of the earth itself.

She and the boy gathered wild pea seeds and dug roots of the elk thistle. They gathered acorns and pine nuts. She shaped a grinding stone and ground acorn meal and she wove a willow basket and filled it with water-leached meal.[3] They caught fish and dried them on a rack set over the fire.

The aspen leaves fell and the wind sang a song of wide skies and far mountaintops. The first snow came, fluffy as cotton grass in bloom. He looked about the lodge, stocked with food, snug and safe, and he said, "This is not like having a cornfield on the reservation or the company store at the sawmill." She smiled; this was the way it should be. She sang the song of the lodge safe for the winter. The boy sang most of the words with her. He was learning the old ways.

Winter is long in the high country and the white days can bring black hunger. But the Utes have lived many generations, many grandmothers, in that land. They speak its language.

Before ice locked the valleys, Bessie and the boy gathered willow shoots and inner bark and ripe grasses for her winter basketry. She made rawhide, and her man shaped ironwood frames on which she wove snowshoes. He took deer while they still had their fat and taught the boy to set snares for rabbits. Then, when the cold shrank the days, she kept the stewpot full and simmering.

Winter passed, and came again. They lived as their people had always lived. And no one came looking for them.

The third time the aspens turned to gold, he looked at the boy, now almost as tall as his mother. "Soon the boy can go with me and kill deer in the thickets," he said. But that was a winter of much snow. When it was half over, the deer had been driven to lower valleys, and there was little meat in the lodge. One day he said, "I must go and find the deer," and he put on his snowshoes. He said he was going over the ridge into the valley beyond, and he went up the slope to cross the gully, an hour's travel from the lodge. It was a hot-sun morning after a brittle cold night.

He had been gone an hour when she heard the thunder sound, the voice of an avalanche. She went outside and saw a plume of fine snow like a cloud over a big snowslide, and she saw where the slide had come lunging down the mountain. She cried out once in horror, and the boy came and stood beside her, watching, as the snow plume floated away and the thunder echoed into silence down the gully.

She moaned with grief, knowing as clearly as though she had seen it happen. She said to the boy, "We must make mourning. But first we must find him."

They put on snowshoes, and went up the slope, following her man's tracks to the gully. It was swept clean, not one tree left standing. Far down the valley they saw the heap of snow and rocks and broken trees where the slide had piled upon itself. They crossed to the other side of the gully. There were no tracks. He had not crossed the gully.

They went down to the foot of the slide, looking along its jumbled face. Then the boy shouted and pointed to something in the snow. It was the shaft of an arrow. They dug in the snow, and finally they found his body

---

3. **water-leached meal,** acorn meal that has been washed in water.

and stood beside it, crying for him; and the boy sang the wailing song for the dead. She had not taught him that; he had it in his heart. Then she got the broken body over her shoulders and, step by heavy step, she carried him home to the lodge. And all that night they made mourning.

The next day she dressed him in new leggings and shirt and wrapped him in blanket and deerskin. She filled baskets with food and looped long thongs to a deerskin, and they hauled him up the mountain to a cave. They set the food beside him, that he might eat on his long journey. Then they sang the death songs for him, with the stars watching them, and they went down the mountain and back to the lodge.

She said to the boy, "Now you are the man."

It was a long winter. Some days the boy's snares had no rabbits and they went hungry. Each day she told him the old tales and sang the old songs, and he watched the way she wove baskets. Each day he strung the bow and drew the bowstring as far as he could. When there were leaves on the aspens again he could draw an arrow almost to the point. Then the deer came back up the valleys and he made his first big meat.

She said, "Soon you will know a name for yourself." He said, "This morning I met a she-bear, a grizzly, and she was not afraid of me. We talked to each other. When I killed the deer I left part of the meat for that she-bear. I shall call myself Bear's Brother."

And that was his name.

Summer passed like a white cloud drifting over the mountain. One day when she was cutting wood the axehead broke. She said to the boy, "We must go to Pagosa for a new axe. They cannot want him now for killing Frank No Deer."

She was not sure this was true, but she knew she had to go. So she took two of her best baskets and they went down to Pagosa, to Jim Thatcher's store. People turned to look, because they wore deerskin clothes. But nobody said, "Where is your man?"

Jim Thatcher had been in that store many years, and his father there before him. He traded salt and sugar and knives and axes and cans of beans for Indian robes and leatherwork and baskets. She set the two baskets on his counter. He looked at them, then at her. "You used to live here, didn't you?" he said.

She made the sign that she did not understand. "How much?" she said, pointing to the baskets.

"Do you want cash or trade?" he asked.

Without answering, she chose an axe and put it on the counter beside the baskets. Then she beckoned to the boy, and together they looked eagerly about the store. The boy stopped at a case of hunting knives. She asked what he would like. He said, in the tongue, "There is nothing." But his eye went back to the knives. Jim Thatcher saw this. He took out a knife and laid it on the counter. "This one?" he asked. The boy closed his eyes. He said again to his mother, "There is nothing."

She turned to Jim and said, "Candy." Jim filled a small bag and set it on the counter. He started to put the knife back in the case, but she made a quick gesture. So Jim Thatcher mentally added up the prices: two dollars for the axe, a dollar and a half for the knife, a nickel for the candy. . . . But the baskets were the best Ute work he had ever seen. He might get three or four dollars apiece for them. He put the knife back on the counter, and she nodded, satisfied. He asked, "Where is your man?" She looked at him, a flash of fear in her eyes. "I remember you," he said. "Your man is George Black Bull."

She put the things in her pack and started to leave. "No need to run," he said. "That case is all cleared up. Self-defense, they called it. Do you understand?" She stared at him, searching his face. "You understand English. Tell George he can come back. They're not looking for him anymore."

She shook her head, and spoke to the boy in Ute, and they left the store.

Nobody spoke to them. Nobody followed. . . . But it could have been a trick, what Thatcher had said. Maybe they wanted the boy. They left the road and sat hidden in the brush, watching, for an hour. But there was nobody. They went on, following the game trails, walking carefully to leave no track.

One day in the spring when he went to catch fish, he met the she-bear again. He said to her, "I am Bear's Brother and we are friends." She listened as he sang a song of friendship that came to him. Then she went away, but he followed her and saw her uproot an old stump and catch three chipmunks and lick up the swarming ants. He left half the fish he caught for her.

When he told his mother of this, she said, "It is good to have a friend." She told him that the Utes had been friends of everything in the mountains in the old days—bears, deer, mountain lions, jays, ravens. Then she was silent. She could not tell him the things that were in her mind, the things Jim Thatcher had said about her man. She had been so afraid that she hadn't really heard what he said. She wanted to hear these things again. She told the boy she must go on a journey alone. If they took her, she could get away, somehow; but the boy might not know how.

She took two baskets to trade, and Jim liked them, as before. She chose calico for herself in trade and a blue coat with brass buttons for the boy. It was more than he would like to give her for the baskets, but she wanted him to talk. They haggled, taking away, putting back. Finally he said, "Bessie, you didn't tell your man what I said. He hasn't been to town."

"There is this thing about Frank No Deer," she said. Unconsciously, she fell into English.

"I told you that was settled. You didn't believe me? Well, it is. Now where is George?" She made the gesture, "Cut off, finished."

"That's too bad. What happened?"

"The snowslide. Two winters gone."

"I'm sorry, Bessie. And the boy?"

She smiled. Then she held out a hand, high as her head. She put her hand on the blue jacket. "For him," she said. He let her take the calico and jacket, and when she left the store with them she met Blue Elk. He stopped in surprise. "I have waited a long time to see you."

"I am here. You see me." Her voice was cold.

"We must talk," Blue Elk said, and he took her to a vacant lot near the bridge. They sat down and he glanced at her clothes. "You are living in the old way. Where?" She didn't answer.

"Your man can come back," he said. "I settled that thing for the cost of two horses. You owe me the cost of two horses."

"I told you I did not have the cost of one goat."

"I told them he killed Frank No Deer because Frank tried to kill him. That is the way it was settled. Your man owes me for this. Where is your man?" She made the cut-off sign. "Dead?" he asked. She nodded. "And the boy?" She did not answer. "The boy should be in the school at Ignacio."[4]

"No! . . . No!"

He grabbed her pack, pulling it open. The calico and the coat with brass buttons fell out. She caught the coat up and held it away from him. He took the cloth. "You owe me for settling this thing. Give me the coat."

---

4. **Ignacio** (ig na'syō).

He was on his knees, holding to the pack and her cloth. She turned and ran up the street. She went back to Bald Mountain with no food, no cloth, but with the blue coat with brass buttons. And with the knowledge that it was settled, this thing about Frank No Deer.

The next summer she went alone to Pagosa again. This time she took four baskets and traded them for a red blanket. When she had put it in her pack, Jim said, "Watch out for Blue Elk, Bessie."

"That one!" She said it like a curse.

"He tried to sell your cloth back to me last summer. He made quite a fuss when I wouldn't take it. What happened?"

"He stole that cloth from me. He said I owed him the cost of two horses. For settling that thing about my man."

"Why, the old scoundrel! He wasn't even a witness at the inquest. Well, he's out of town today."

So she went back and gave the blanket to the boy for his bed. He knew that red is the rainbow color for protection.

He had begun to fill out, with the stocky frame of the Utes. He could drive an arrow all the way through a deer and carry its hind-quarters on his shoulders. He had braids almost as long as his mother's, and he wore a breechclout[5] and moccasins in the summer, and in the winter, leggings and the winter shirt.

That was a bad winter. Their meat was gone before the days began to lengthen, though Bessie ate little, saving it for the boy. "You must be strong," she said. "When these storms end we must go to the lower valleys for meat."

At last the storms eased and they prepared to get meat. She went with him, though he said she should not, for she remembered what had happened to her man.

She was weak from lack of food and the cold made her cough. When he took a deer, they ate the liver and those parts that make

strength. They made packs of the meat and went back to the lodge. It was a long journey and when they returned she was so weak she could scarcely stand. He made her lie on her bed and cooked soup for her. She had a pain in her chest.

She said, "Help me to sit up," and he helped her. She tried to work at a basket, but her hands would not do what she told them to do. He sat beside her and made the basket for her. He said, "My hands have watched your hands many times. My hands are your hands now."

The pain became worse. She was so hot she could not have even one robe around her shoulders, then so cold that he put his red blanket around her and still she shivered. She said, "I am sick." He said, "I am singing the songs for making you well." She said, "I do not hear these songs." He said, "I am singing them inside." She said, "Sing them outside. I am very sick."

He sang the songs all that night. She said, "I am not going to get over this sickness, my son." He said, "I will not sing the song for going away yet." She said, "No. Not yet."

That afternoon she talked about things he had not known, the sawmill and Blue Elk and Frank No Deer. Then she did not talk. It was night. She said, "Sing the song for going away, my son." She tried to reach up and touch his face, but her arm was too weak. He took her hand and held it to his face. Then she died.

He made mourning all that night, and when it was daylight he put her deerskin dress on her and wrapped her in the red blanket, then in a deerskin robe, so she would be warm on the long journey. He put dried berries and dried meat, the last there was in the lodge, in two baskets. And he took her up the mountains to the cave where they had

---

5. **breechclout** (brēch′klout), a cloth or animal skin worn to cover the loins.

buried his father. He buried his mother there, and he sang the old songs. Then he went back to the lodge and he was alone.

Spring came again. Strawberries made the grass white with blossom and red anemones were in bloom. The boy caught trout in the pools, and watched for his friend, the bear. Then he saw her one morning in a wild meadow, eating grass and strawberries. She had two cubs with her. He talked to her and she shook her head and growled. A she-bear with cubs is not friendly. Her cubs listened, curious about this boy, but she cuffed them and hurried them away into the brush.

For days he watched them. He found where she went for food, and where she slept. But she was no longer his friend. One day he said to the cubs, "I am Bear's Brother. You are my brother and my sister." But the she-bear growled to him to go away.

So he made friends of the squirrels that lived in a hollow pine tree near the lodge. They sat in his hand and talked to him. Then the chipmunks in the rocks asked to be friends. They came into the lodge and lived with him. A jay said it wanted to be his friend. It rode on his shoulder and pecked at the lobe of his ear. Serviceberries ripened and he dried them. He made meat and smoked it as he had learned from his mother.

Then the man came.

The boy was fishing when his friend the jay called an alarm from a nearby aspen. The boy drew in his line, covered his tracks, and sat in the brush to watch. The jay flew down the valley, screaming, and came back, tree by tree, telling the boy a stranger was coming. Then the man appeared, with his mouse-colored burro. He stopped at the pool, picked up a handful of sand and let the water from it trickle between his fingers. He shook his head and threw the sand back. Then he and the burro went on up the creek. The jay sat on the boy's shoulder and was silent.

The boy followed the man all afternoon. He went slowly, scooping a handful of sand from every pool. Toward evening he found some that pleased him. He took a pan from the pack on the burrow, put sand and water into it and slowly swished it out again, then rubbed his finger on the bottom of the pan. Then he unpacked the burro and made camp beside the stream.

The boy went back to his lodge. On the way, he met the she-bear and her cubs. He tried to tell her about the stranger, but she told her not to talk to her. He was going out to watch again the next morning when he heard the thunder of a gun. Three times. Then there was silence.

He did not hurry. What happened had happened and could not be changed. But soon he heard the man shouting angrily. Then he saw him at the creek, his left arm red with blood to his fingers. The man washed his arm, but could not stop the blood. And then the boy saw the she-bear, a grizzled brown heap beside the man's fire. The man walked around her, still afraid. He tore his shirt and tied a strip of cloth around his arm and twisted a stick in it, but the blood still ran from his fingers. His talk became fear-talk. He went to get his burro, but it was afraid of the bear and braced its legs, and the man was so weak he almost fell before he got on its back. He shouted and beat the burro with his gun and it went around the bear and down the valley at a trot.

The boy left his watching place. The female cub was dead beside the she-bear; he heard the other cub crying beyond the creek. He found it and talked to it and it went with him to the man's camp. It cried when it nosed at the dead she-bear. He talked to it again, and fed it the man's food. Then he told the cub to come with him to his lodge, and it came.

That is how the boy and the bear cub became brothers and friends. After that the boy was not alone.

Jim Thatcher was checking invoices on a warm July day when he heard the yelps of a dogfight in the street. Then someone shouted, "Get a gun! It's a bear!" Jim ran outside with his .30-30.[6] He couldn't believe his eyes. There was a grizzly cub, hunkered back in the dust, with three dogs yelping and dancing around it. A boy was shouting to the cub in Ute. He was ten or eleven years old, and dressed in the old way, with breechclout, moccasins, and braids. The cub started to go to him, only to be attacked by the dogs again. It snarled, and slapped a dog sprawling with a gash along its ribs.

Men were running up from all directions. Someone shouted, "Kill it, Jim, before it kills every dog in town!" The cub licked the boy's hand, then faced the crowd, frightened by the uproar, but ready to fight.

Jim called to the men, "Keep your shirts on. Can't you see it's a pet cub?" He turned to the boy. "Tell your friend to behave himself, son."

The boy looked at him, bewildered. He said something in Ute, caught the bear's scruff in one hand, and picked up his pack. Then he and the cub walked into Jim's store. Jim followed and closed the door behind him. The crowd clustered outside the door.

While the cub stood beside him, the boy set three baskets on the counter. Then he went to a pile of blankets, found a red one and brought it back to the counter.

Jim examined the baskets. They were identical with the last ones Bessie had brought in, though of even better workmanship. He looked at the boy. "Where is your mother?" There was no answer. The boy

---

6. **.30-30,** a hunting rifle referred to commonly as a "thirty-thirty."

pushed the baskets toward Jim and drew the blanket toward himself.

Jim shook his head. No use dickering. This boy was a throwback, right out of the old, old days. Jim asked, "Don't you know any English at all?"

The boy's blank look said, truthfully, that he didn't.

Jim went outside and found Blue Elk in the crowd, and Blue Elk came into the store, beaming at being singled out. Jim said, "This is Bessie Black Bull's boy. He doesn't savvy[7] English. Find out where his mother is."

Blue Elk spoke to the boy in the tongue. "We are of the people, we two. I am your friend. The man wants to know where is your mother, where you are living now."

The boy scowled. "My mother—" He made the cut-off sign. "I live in my lodge with my brother."

When Blue Elk said Bessie was dead, Jim exclaimed, "I don't believe it! She made these baskets. When did she die?"

Blue Elk asked the question, but the boy said, "I will not talk of this thing." He made the cut-off sign, sharply.

"Boys do not speak to the old men of their people in this way!" Blue Elk said impatiently.

But the boy folded the blanket into his pack, put his hand on the cub's scruff and went out through the crowd, the cub beside him. Nobody tried to stop them as they went back to the hills.

As Blue Elk went off, puzzling over this matter, the preacher caught up with him. "Who was that boy, Blue Elk?"

Blue Elk glanced at him. "Thomas Black Bull."

"Thomas Black Bull? Then that's the boy I baptized. Why is he running around in a clout like a savage? Where are his parents?"

"His parents are dead. He lives with his brother."

"I didn't know he had a brother. Does he mean an uncle?"

Blue Elk looked at him shrewdly. "I could find out."

"I wish you would. I baptized him. I feel responsible."

"I worry for my people," Blue Elk said. "But it is a hard trip, and I am old. I have no money for this trip."

The preacher felt in his pocket, and Blue Elk heard the clink of silver dollars. The preacher offered him one, but Blue Elk shook his head. "This will be a very hard trip. Ten dollars."

"All I have is the mission money, but I might make it five. And if you bring the boy in to the reservation school, the Indian agent might give you five more dollars of government money."

"I do this for my people." Blue Elk held out his hand.

Blue Elk tracked the boy and the bear into the mountains, and on the third day he rode into the hollow below the lodge. A jay screamed at him; a squirrel chattered. He waited, letting the jay and the squirrel say he was there, and soon the boy appeared. He said, "I did not ask you to come here."

"I have come to help you. I am tired and hungry."

The boy looked at him, the jay on his shoulder. Then he said, "You may rest and eat. Then you must go." He led the way to the lodge.

Inside, in the coolness and dimness, Blue Elk remembered his grandmother's lodge. The boy set dried meat in front of him, and it had the taste of meat he had eaten in his boyhood. He saw the bows and arrows, the venison on the drying rack, the tanned robes on

---

7. **savvy,** a slang term for "understand" or "know"; a corruption of the Spanish word "sabe."

the walls, the sewing basket with its coil of dry sinew and its bone awls.[8] He saw the willow twigs and ferns for baskets. There was a coil of strips in a bowl of water, pliant for weaving, and a partly finished basket. It was a lodge such as only the old people remembered.

He said, "When I was young I knew a lodge such as this. When the short white days came we were hungry."

"That is the way it is."

"That is the way it was. The old days are gone." The boy did not answer. "Your father was my friend," Blue Elk said. "Now your father is gone, I am a grandfather to you. I must tell you what to do."

The boy looked at Blue Elk and sang the beginning of the mourning song. He stopped. "If you are a grandfather," he said, "you will sing the mourning song." But Blue Elk was silent. The boy said, "How can you tell me what to do when you do not know the songs?"

"I sing the song inside."

"My mother and father will not know if you sing the song inside." He sang again, and Blue Elk closed his eyes and sang with him. His memory did not know the words, but his tongue remembered, and tears came to his eyes. It was a song for Blue Elk's own mother. Then Blue Elk opened his eyes, and forgot the old people. He said, "When did your mother go away?"

"In the winter before the winter that is past."

Blue Elk stared at him. "You have been alone too many days." The boy made no answer. "My ears are listening," Blue Elk said. "It is good to talk of what happened."

The boy looked into the ashes. It was a long time since he had talked to anyone except the bear cub, the jay, and the squirrels. He was a boy, with things to tell, not a man who can contain all the things that happen.

At last he said, "I will tell of these things." But there was a whine at the doorway. He said, "Come in, Brother. We have one of the grandfathers with us."

The bear cub came in, sniffing warily. Blue Elk sat quietly and let it know his smell. It bristled and turned to the boy. The boy said, "Come, I shall tell this grandfather about you." The cub went to him and lay down, and the boy told Blue Elk about the bear and about his father and mother. When he had done, Blue Elk said, "The old days are gone, ended."

"How can there be an end?" the boy asked. "There is the roundness." He made the gesture for the circle, the no-end.

"There is the roundness. But our people have forgotten it." He studied the boy's face. "Do you know the song for remembering?" The boy sang it. When he was through, Blue Elk said, "You will sing that song to our people who have forgotten, in Ignacio."

The boy sat silent for a long time. Then he said, "You will go and tell them of the songs. I will stay here."

"They should hear these songs," Blue Elk said. "It is good for a people to change but it is not good for them to forget."

He believed this as he said it. Then he remembered the Indian agent, who might give him five more dollars, and the preacher who felt responsible for this boy. He told himself he must do this thing. He said, "Tomorrow we will go to Ignacio."

The boy said, "Tomorrow I will talk of this."

The next morning they went down to the pool and bathed. Blue Elk gasped in the icy coldness, but he was warm inside as he had not been since he was a boy. When they had bathed, they sat on a rock that faced the ris-

---

8. **bone awls,** pointed tools of bone used for making holes in leather.

ing sun. The boy sang the song to the sun, and Blue Elk's tongue remembered. He said again, "Our people should hear these songs."

The boy thought. He asked, "How long is it to Ignacio?" and Blue Elk said, "Less than three days' journey."

After breakfast, still considering, the boy called the jay and the squirrels. When the jay sat on his shoulder and one of the squirrels in his hand, he whispered a question and they seemed to answer.

Blue Elk was looking around the lodge at all the things worth silver dollars. He could return. Even if the agent did not pay him five dollars, he could be well paid for the journey. Then he told himself: I came for the boy's good. This boy should not be here alone in the winter.

The boy turned from the doorway. "I will come. The jay and the squirrels will watch till I return." He turned to the bear cub. "But you will go with me, Brother."

That is how it happened.

DISCUSSION FOR UNDERSTANDING

1. Why do George Black Bull, Bessie, and the boy go back to living in the old ways?
2. Why does Bessie want a lodge that is round?
3. Describe the circumstances under which the boy is given a name by the white man. What name does he later choose for himself and why?
4. Why does Blue Elk follow the boy back to his lodge? How does he persuade the boy to go with him to Ignacio?

2 The School

When they came in sight of the agency Blue Elk wished he had left the bear on the mountain. The Utes respected bears, but the agency people did not understand these things.

There were many buildings at the agency: the headquarters and the school, the dormitory and the barns and stables. There was a flagpole, with a red, white, and blue flag at the top. The boy wondered what it meant. There were Indians hurrying from one building to another, but the men and boys had short hair, which was a strange thing to see. Blue Elk said, "We will talk to the head man. He will hear what you have to say, but first you must do as he says."

The boy understood Blue Elk's words, but he did not know what Blue Elk meant by those words. He said to the bear, "We will talk to the head man in this big lodge."

Inside the headquarters Blue Elk led the way to a white man at a desk. The man looked up. "Hello, Blue Elk," he said. Then he saw the boy and the bear. "What's that bear doing here?" he demanded sharply.

"The bear belongs to the boy," Blue Elk said uneasily. "The boy wouldn't come without him. He should be put in a strong pen." Then he added, "The boy does not understand your talk. He speaks only Ute. The preacher said he should be in school."

The man hurried out. He came back with a strong collar and a chain, and handed them to Blue Elk. The bear was wrinkling its nose as though it did not like the man's smell. But it stood quietly, the boy's hand on its neck.

Blue Elk turned to the boy. "The man wants you to put this collar on the bear. It is so he will not be hurt. These people are afraid of bears."

Reluctantly, the boy fastened the collar on the bear cub, and the man led them to a pen for breaking wild horses. The man fastened the chain to a post in the middle of the pen.

"My brother will not like this thing," the boy said.

"The head man cannot hear what you have to say if he is afraid of the bear. Come." The boy spoke into the bear's ear before he went with Blue Elk and the man to the agent's office.

The government agent was a fat, red-faced man with freckles, sandy hair, and eyes so light blue they looked milky. He said, "Well, Blue Elk, what have you got up your sleeve this time? I understand you brought a bear cub with you." He looked at the boy. "And why is this boy running around in a clout? Who is he?"

"The preacher christened him Thomas Black Bull. He has been living alone, in the old way. He has no English, and his father and mother are dead."

The agent frowned. "Go get Benny Grayback. You wait outside, Blue Elk. I want to talk to this boy alone."

Benny Grayback was a stocky Ute, perhaps thirty years old. He wore a white shirt and a blue necktie, like the agent. He was in charge of the carpentry shop.

The agent said, "Benny, I want to talk to this boy. Blue Elk says he speaks no English. Is that true?"

Benny asked the question. "It is true," he said, and then he questioned the boy in Ute.

"He says his name is Bear's Brother and he lives with his brother," Benny said finally. "His friends, a jay and the squirrels and chipmunks, also live with him." Benny smiled. "He has lived this way since his mother died, the winter before last. I think he must be wrong, but that is what he says."

"Tell him he will live here now, with other boys and girls. He will go to school and learn the things he should know."

"He says he did not come here to live, he came to tell us of the old ways." Benny smiled again. "Blue Elk told him we would want to know these things."

"Sounds like Blue Elk. Tell him we will hear about the old ways at a proper time. First he must learn the new ways."

"He says he will go back to his own lodge until you want to listen to him."

"No. He *must* stay here for a while."

Benny said this. The boy did not answer.

The agent sighed. "Go get him some clothes, Benny. And look after him a few days, get him started. He looks like a bright boy. And Benny, don't let him turn that bear cub loose. I'll hold you responsible. Now send Blue Elk in again."

Benny left with the boy and Blue Elk came in, all smiles and expectancy. "This Thomas Black Bull," the agent said, "is he George Black Bull's son? The one who hid back in the hills?"

"That is right."

"Who told you to bring him in?"

"The preacher in Pagosa. He said he should be in school. He said you would pay me for the trip. It was a hard trip and I am an old man."

"I haven't any funds for that kind of thing. If you had come and told me, I would have sent my own men after him. You would sell your own grandmother, wouldn't you, Blue Elk?"

"My grandmother," Blue Elk said, "is dead."

He waited, but the agent dismissed him, and Blue Elk went out, hurt and angry. Well, if the agent would not pay him, there were other ways. As he rode past the horse-breaking pen, he thought it was good that the bear was here, not loose on Bald Mountain guarding the lodge.

They put Thomas Black Bull in a room with Luther Spotted Dog, who was fourteen and had been at the school several years. Luther helped Thomas put on the stiff new agency pants and shirt. Thomas tried one shoe, threw it aside, and kept his moccasins. When Luther showed him how soft the cot was, Thomas tore the bed apart and arranged the blankets on the floor. When Luther began to praise the school and the teachers, Thomas looked out the window and ignored him.

The supper bell rang, and they went down to the dining room. Thomas made a face at the cooking smells and when he tasted the meat he spat it out.

"It stinks," he said to Luther, and got up and went out.

Benny Grayback had been watching. He followed Thomas to the horse-breaking pen. "Where are you going?"

Thomas didn't answer. He opened the gate and the bear cub ran toward him. It was snubbed by the chain and jerked from its feet. Benny caught the boy by the shoulder.

"I am going back to the lodge!" the boy shouted.

"No," Benny said, holding his arms. "You are staying here."

"I shall take my brother and go!" The boy bit Benny's hand. Benny slapped him, closed the gate and hauled him away. "You are an evil person!" the boy cried, trying to wrench free. "I hate you! My brother hates you!"

But Benny twisted his arms behind him and forced him back to his dormitory room. There Benny made him sit down and told him he must learn to live the new way. The boy sat in defiant silence, and when Luther Spotted Dog came from supper Benny said, "Thomas is to stay here until breakfast time. I will hold you responsible."

Luther looked at Thomas dubiously, but he nodded.

Then Benny told Neil Swanson, the man in charge of livestock, to secure the bear. Neil lassoed the bear cub, choked it into submission, and padlocked the chain around its neck and to the snubbing post. Benny pocketed the keys.

The next morning Luther's face was scratched and his right eye almost closed. Thomas limped and his wrists were raw. After breakfast, which Thomas pushed away, Benny said to Luther, "You had a hard time last night."

"He would have killed me. I had to tie him up."

"Bring him to my class," Benny ordered.

When Benny introduced Thomas to the fifteen boys in the carpentry class, he stared at them coldly, then went to a window and stood with his back to the room. Two boys whispered, in Ute, about his braids. One of them took two long shavings and hung them behind his ears. All the boys laughed except Luther Spotted Dog. Benny told them to be quiet. Then a boy near Thomas whined like a bear and said in falsetto, "My name is Bear Meat." Without a word Thomas picked up a wooden mallet from the nearest bench and flung it at him. The boy dodged and the mallet clattered the length of the room.

"Stop it!" Benny ordered. "All of you! Get back to work." He took Thomas by the arm, led him to his desk. "Why did you do that?" he demanded in Ute. "These boys want to be your friends."

"I have no friends here," Thomas said.

So Benny took Thomas to Miss Rowena Ellis, who taught English. A plump woman who spoke several Indian tongues, she was unofficial mother to every homesick child in the school. To Thomas she said, in Ute, "We

should know each other. This place is full of strangeness. I will tell you about it."

"I came here," he said, "to tell them of the old ways."

"I want to hear," she said, "but first I will tell you of the new ways." She started to tell him about the school.

He cut her off. "I do not need these things."

She was a patient woman. She smiled, and as her class filed into the room, she said: "We have a new boy, Thomas Black Bull. He will tell us about his interesting life, but first we must teach him some English. We will start today with oral review." The boys groaned, but she kept them at vocabulary drill while Thomas stood by the window. When it was over, Miss Ellis went to him. "You see, it is not so hard to learn new things. You learned something today. I know this."

"I do not need these things," Thomas said. "You do not understand."

He left the room and ran outside to the breaking pen. The bear whined, and he tore angrily at the padlocks with his fingers. At last he gave up and stood silent while the bear licked his hands. Then he saw Benny Grayback waiting at the gate. "I will do these things you tell me to do if you will let my brother live with me."

Benny said, "Luther Spotted Dog would not be happy with a bear living in his room."

"Luther Spotted Dog can live in another place."

Benny said, "I am busy; but if you will go to your room after lunch, we will talk later."

Luther did not return to the room until after his last class. He opened the door and saw all his belongings piled in one corner. Thomas said, "Take your things and go." He threw Luther's things into the hall and closed the door. Luther ran for Benny Grayback, and together they forced the door. "What does this mean?" Benny demanded.

"Now there is room here for my brother," Thomas said.

Benny took Thomas by the arm. "Come with me. There is another room where you are going to live."

"First we will talk."

"We will go to this other room. Then we will talk."

He took Thomas downstairs to a room so small there was space for only a cot and a washstand. It had one small window, with bars on the outside, and it had a heavy door with a lock. Thomas said, "My brother will not like this place."

"We will not talk about the bear today," Benny said. He went out, and locked the door. The boy beat on the door with his fists, and then began to chant. It was a sorrow song, a song that Benny had never heard because it was the boy's own song. Benny did not want to listen but he heard, and although he wanted to go away he stayed there. He began to say the words softly, and to sway with the rhythm. It was a song from far back, not only in the boy but in Benny's own people. Its rhythm was his own heartbeat.

Then he heard his own voice, and forced himself to stop. This was nonsense. The old ways were gone. He hurried away and went to see the agent.

The agent was annoyed and said, "It is all because of that bear cub. We'll have to shoot it."

Benny Grayback gasped. "No!" he exclaimed. "You cannot kill the bear!" Then he clapped his hand over his mouth.

The agent frowned. He had tried to understand these people for twenty-five years, but there still were things that he could not fathom, emotions and superstitions that he

couldn't reach, even in someone like Benny Grayback, who was civilized and educated.

"I know the feeling about bears," he said, carefully. "But when one is a troublemaker you kill it, don't you?" Benny nodded. "And this one is making trouble, isn't it?"

Benny hesitated. "There is trouble, yes."

"Because of the bear."

"I do not know this," Benny said, falling into the old speech pattern even though he spoke English. He paused. "If you kill the bear," he said, "then you will kill the boy."

"What makes you think that, Benny?"

"My grandmother—" Benny broke off. The boy's sorrow chant had beaten at him again. He shrugged away his grandmother and the old ways. "I know it," he said. "That is all."

The agent sighed. "Very well, Benny. Do the best you can for a day or two. And find Blue Elk; I think he can help us."

"Where have you been?" the agent asked when Blue Elk at last arrived. "I sent for you three days ago."

Blue Elk looked smug. "I have been busy," he said.

"I want you to take that bear back to the mountains."

Blue Elk shook his head. "I cannot do this. It is not my bear. It does not know me."

The agent smiled grimly. "The boy will take the bear. You will go along and bring the boy back without the bear."

Blue Elk seemed to be worrying something in his mind. "I cannot take the bear back to Bald Mountain," he said.

"The other side of Horse Mountain will be far enough."

Blue Elk seemed to relax somewhat. "That is a long journey."

"I will pay you ten dollars, silver."

Blue Elk sighed. "I do not like this job, but I need this money."

After supper he went to see the boy. "I have come to take you back to the mountains," he said. "Your brother will go with us."

"I do not need you to take us back. I can find the way."

"The agent says I go with you because I brought you here."

"Your mouth," the boy said bitterly, "is like Benny Grayback's. It is full of lies." And he began to chant his sorrow song.

"Be quiet," Blue Elk ordered. But the boy went on chanting, and before long Blue Elk was swaying to the rhythms and saying words that he remembered. Then darkness came, and the boy's hoarse voice died away, and Blue Elk fell asleep on the cot.

They started at dawn the next day, the bear dragging the chain still locked around its neck. They traveled two days, and each night Blue Elk padlocked the bear to a tree. The third morning they came to the foot of Horse Mountain. Again Blue Elk chained the bear to a tree. Then he said, "We will leave the bear here."

"My brother wants to go with me to my lodge."

"The bear can go," Blue Elk said. "But you must come back to the school with me."

Then the boy knew what they had done to him. Without a word, he came at Blue Elk, kicking, clawing, trying to take the keys from him. But Blue Elk was too strong for him. He took a rope and tied the boy's arms and ankles. "Let us have no more trouble," he said, when he had caught his breath. "The bear must go away. You must go back with me."

"No."

Blue Elk shrugged. "If you do not tell the bear to go, we will leave him chained to that tree. If that is the way you want it to be—" He waited, but the boy did not answer. Finally Blue Elk untied the boy's ankles. "We

will go back now," he said. He took the end of the rope that bound the boy's arms, tied it to his pony's saddle horn and got into the saddle.

The boy looked at the bear, and he looked at Blue Elk. He said, "I will tell my brother to go home."

Blue Elk freed the boy's hands and gave him the keys, but he held on to the end of the rope. The boy said to the bear, "They have made me do this, Brother." He took off the chain, hugged the cub's head to him and buried his face in its neck. Then he stepped back. "Go home," he ordered. "Go!" And he turned away.

The bear stood for a moment, then took a step toward him. The boy cried, "Go—before they put the chain on you again!" And the bear turned, uncertain, and walked away from him. The boy said to Blue Elk, "I wish you were dead for this thing you have done."

Back at school, Thomas seemed finally to accept the routine. He ate the food and went back to a regular room in the dormitory. Rowena Ellis thought he had learned more than he let on in everything; but he was useless in the stables, and the slowest in the class in carpentry. He did better in the cobbler's shop, where the teacher noticed his unusual skill with his fingers and suggested that he might be a basketmaker. So Thomas was sent to the basketry class of Dolly Beaverfoot, a Paiute[1] from Utah.

Dolly gave Thomas the conventional basket materials, but he pushed the coarse reeds aside and said, "These are no good." He went outside and came back with an armful of willow stems. Dolly smiled with pleasure as he began stripping the bark from

---

1. **Paiute** (pī yüt′), an American Indian tribe.

them with his teeth, in the old way. When he had the material to suit him he wove a basket that not even Dolly could match.

The girls in the basketry class—Thomas was the only boy—had whispered that he was handsome; and the boys, of course, heard about this. They began talking about "the new girl" and saying, "She makes better baskets than the teacher," and "Her name is really Bear's Sister."

Thomas ignored these things until one afternoon when he and Luther and two other boys were cleaning the horse barn. One of the boys said to Luther, "Was Bear's Sister nice to you, Luther, when she lived in your room?"

Luther grinned broadly. "No. She was a very poor squaw." He pretended to trip on his pitchfork and threw a forkful of dirty straw at Thomas.

Thomas said, "Don't do that again."

Luther laughed. "Bear's Sister is getting mad."

Thomas knocked Luther down, but another boy leaped on his back. He caught that boy by the hair and threw him to the floor. The fourth boy ran to find Neil Swanson, but when Neil got there Thomas had backed both his tormentors into a corner and was pounding their faces in turn.

Neil dragged him off, and ordered the other boys to their rooms. Then he asked, "Why did you start this fight?"

Thomas was silent.

"All right," Neil said, "I'll have to teach you a lesson." He got a harness strap and flogged him, and Thomas took it tight-lipped, without a sound. Neil said, "Now go to your room."

Thomas went to the basketry room instead and tore his baskets to shreds. Then he went to his room and locked the door. Neither Benny nor Rowena could make him unlock it. The agent said, "Leave him alone. He'll starve out in a day or two."

He didn't starve out. The second night he put on his breechclout, took a blanket and climbed out the window. He slid down a drain spout to the ground, forced his way into the kitchen and took a knife, a ball of strong cord and a two-pound remnant of pot roast. Then he started north, eating the meat as he traveled.

He went first to Horse Mountain. There he looked for bear sign and sang the bear song, but there was no sign and no answer, so he went on to their lodge on Bald Mountain.

He drank at his stream, and washed in his pool, and started up the path his moccasins had helped to make. Bushes already were overgrowing it. He called to the jay, but it screamed and flew off. The chipmunks ran and hid among the rocks. The squirrels scurried up the pines, scolding at his intrusion.

He came to the last turn in the path, and he put a hand to his mouth to stop the cry of pain. There was no lodge. Where it had been was a charred place, a circle of ashes.

He poked among the ashes. Nothing, not even a knife blade.

And then he knew. It was no accident. Someone had come and taken everything, even the battered cooking pot, and burned the lodge. He stood among the ashes and whispered his sorrow chant, not even saying it aloud. For small griefs you shout, but the big griefs must be borne alone, inside.

When he had finished he looked up the mountainside for a long time, thinking of his father and his mother. Then he sang his bear song as loud as he could sing. There was no answer. At dusk he sang it again. There was no answer.

It was as though he had never been here.

He lay in his blanket and slept, and the next morning clouds hung low over the mountain and the valley was filled with mist as cold as sleet. He bathed at the pool, but he sang no song for a new day. He did not even whisper the sorrow song.

There was no song in him. Only a numbness, a nothing. . .

The next day, he met them at the foot of Horse Mountain. There were only two of them, Benny Grayback and an old tracker called Fish. Benny said, "We came to take you back to the reservation."

"I will go back," Thomas said, in English.

The day after he returned to school, Thomas had his braids cut off. The next morning he put on shoes. And after his return, he spoke only in English. He worked in the cobbler's shop, designing and plaiting quirts[2] and bridles. He was as skillful at this as he had been at basketry. He still made no friends, though several girls would have liked to be his friends. The boys who had taunted him left him alone, for he often carried one of the quirts he made.

Winter passed, and late March came. There were catkins[3] on the willows and tassels on the aspens. Thomas knew the bears would soon be leaving their winter dens to claim their old ranges.

A moonlit night came and he sat in his room and knew what was going to happen. He hoped it would happen, and he wished it would not. He waited, and the cattle bawled in their pens. The horses snorted and raced about their corrals. He opened his window, and in the moonlight he saw the bear beside the horse-breaking pen. It stood there nosing the air, then shuffled its feet like a great shaggy dog. It whined softly.

Other windows opened. . . . Someone shouted an alarm.

Thomas picked up a quirt and ran through the moonlight to the corral, singing the bear song. The bear came to meet him. He stopped singing and shouted warning words, then angry words. The bear stopped and growled, then came on, whining again. He went up to it, swished the quirt in its face and screamed in Ute, "Go away! Go home to the mountains!"

The bear rose on its hind legs and spread its forepaws as though to tear him to pieces. Its teeth were white in the moonlight. It was a two-year-old now and stood taller than the boy. The boy lashed it across the face with the quirt, again and again, screaming, "Go! Go! Go!" The bear dropped to all fours, whimpering. It nosed the boy's hands, and it cried like a child. And the boy put an arm around its neck, buried his face in its fur and wept. He wept until the bear drew away and licked his face and whimpered again.

The boy backed away. "You are no longer my brother," he cried. "When I went to find my brother and sang my song he would not listen. Now there is nobody."

He stood silent in the moonlight, his head bowed, and the bear swayed from side to side, from foot to foot, moaning.

"Go, or they will kill you," the boy said. "They do not need guns to kill. They kill without guns." He put a hand on the bear's neck and he said, "Come. I will go a little way with you." And they walked slowly across the grounds in the moonlight, toward the aspens with catkins like chipmunk tails. They walked among the trees and into the shadows, and after a little while there was the sound of a song so desolate that the coyotes answered it from the gullies beyond.

After another little while the boy came back out of the shadows of the trees, walking alone. Men and boys were standing beside the doorway. They stepped aside, making way for him, and later they said it was like seeing a remote and terrible man, not a boy.

The next day he went to his classes as though nothing had happened, but in his eyes people saw something that made them afraid. Nobody spoke of what had happened in the moonlight.

---

2. **quirts,** riding whips with short handles and lashes of braided leather.
3. **catkins,** dense, drooping clusters of small, scalelike flowers.

That spring Neil Swanson tried to make a farmer out of him. He learned, readily enough, to hitch a team to a plow, but plowing seemed senseless to him. Why should anyone rip up grass and make the earth grow something else? If left to itself, the earth would grow grass and many other things. When you plowed up the grass you were making the earth into something it did not want to be.

After two weeks of crooked furrows, Swanson said, "Since you won't learn to plow, you'll have to learn to milk."

The smell of warm milk made him feel sick, but he learned to milk a cow. And that summer Neil sent him out with the horse herd each day. He learned to ride the old herd horse, and the long hours in the open were a relief. There was sunshine, sky, distance and a degree of freedom.

Soon Thomas began to wonder what it would be like to ride an unbroken horse. One day he roped a two-year-old colt and got on its back. He was thrown after the first two jumps. He caught the colt and tried again. That time he landed in a bed of cactus and spent the rest of the afternoon pulling out thorns. But the next day he rode another colt for several minutes before it bucked him off. He soon learned that each horse has its own rhythm—not only in its gaits,[4] but in the way it bucks and pitches. If he rode the horse with its own rhythm, gripped with his knees and thighs and kept his balance, he could ride every horse in the herd. He began to feel a sense of mastery, something he had not felt since the day he stood in front of his burned lodge and knew that everything that had ever mattered to him was gone.

Toward the end of August he was riding a particularly mean two-year-old pinto when Benny Grayback rode out to the grazing ground. He was so intent on the pinto that he rode it to a standstill before he knew that Benny was there.

Benny glared at him. "How long have you been riding the colts? They are supposed to graze. Neil says they are all too thin, and I came to find out why."

"The grass is poor," Thomas said.

"You give them no time to eat it. It is not for you to tame them. When they are needed, they will be tamed by those who know how to break horses." Which was true. Each spring the horses were driven into the breaking pen, beaten, choked and water-starved until there was no fight in them. In the old days the Utes had respected their horses and tamed them. Now they broke the horses, broke their spirit.

Thomas gathered the herd, and he and Benny took them back to the agency. And that was the end of his horse-herding.

Classes started and Thomas went back to leatherwork and the hated cow barn. When the winter began to thin away, Benny said, "Albert Left Hand needs a helper for the lambing season, and Thomas Black Bull isn't good for anything else; he might make a sheep-herder."

The agent said, "It's worth a try."

So they took him to Albert Left Hand out at the edge of the reservation. Albert was a short, fat man who smelled of rancid mutton tallow. When he was not napping or sitting in silence beside his tent, he spent his time hunting prairie dogs, and he seemed to eat nothing but prairie dog stew. He was a surly old man of few words, and those usually were abusive.

Despite this, Thomas found a degree of peace and contentment with Albert Left Hand. It was spring and the arid sage flats came to life in purple ground plum, starry cactus, white lilies and larkspur, the gold of pucker-petaled sundrops and the fragrant moonglow of primroses. Meadowlarks greeted the sunrise and cheered the evening.

---

4. **gaits,** a series of foot movements such as walk, trot, pace, or canter by which a horse moves forward.

Horned larks spilled song all day in their spiraling flight. In the prairie dog towns, burrowing owls tilted on their long, slim legs and hissed and screeched.

When the ewes[5] began to drop their lambs, Albert Left Hand showed Thomas how to help a ewe in the birth struggle, how to get a lamb on its feet and sucking. When a lamb or ewe failed to survive, Albert skinned it. "Pelt's worth a quarter," he said. Then, when all the lambs were born, Albert went back to hunting prairie dogs.

But Thomas was busier than ever, for the lambs had even less sense than their foolish mothers. They strayed, they fell into canyons, they thrust stupid noses at buzzing rattlesnakes. And at dusk, the coyotes got one now and then.

July came and they had saved forty-five out of sixty lambs. The ewes had put on fat and were showing prime fleeces when Thomas helped Albert herd them to the shearing pens near the agency. After they were penned, Albert said, "Now we will go to Bayfield. I will sell the skins. I will buy you a bottle of pop."

Drowsy Bayfield had its Saturday afternoon crowd. A dozen horses were hitched at the long rack in front of the general store; the two saloons spilled loud talk and laughter onto the board sidewalk. When they had unloaded the stinking pelts Albert gave Thomas a nickel, but Thomas didn't know where to get pop. Looking, he came to the saddlery shop. In the window was the most beautiful saddle he had ever seen, polished and ornately tooled. He stared at it, admiring with all his heart.

Then he saw the black-and-white bridle hanging from the saddle horn. It was one he had made, with a pattern he had thought up. He read the price tag and gasped. Five dollars! He hadn't got anything for it because the money went to pay for his keep. If he could

sell bridles for five dollars, then some day he could buy that saddle.

He was still staring at it when two cowhands came out of the nearest saloon. The tall, slim one jabbed a thumb into Thomas's ribs and said, "You know how to ride a horse—all Indian kids do. Look, you go get my horse and ride it back here and I'll give you this quarter."

Tom looked at the man wide-eyed. A quarter just to ride a horse! "Get the black gelding down there in the cottonwoods," the cowhand said. "And *ride* him. He don't lead very well." His companion laughed.

Thomas found the horse, hitched by a neck rope. It was so skittish he had to drive it around the tree until the rope was wound tight. Then he snubbed the reins to the saddle horn, so it couldn't get its head down, untied the rope, got his foot in the stirrup and swung into the saddle as the horse began buckjumping. When he had its rhythm and his own balance, he gave it a little slack in the reins and it bucked viciously a time or two before he got it headed up the street. Holding its head high with the snubbed reins, he rode it to the waiting cowhand, got off and handed the reins to its owner.

The cowhand growled, "You snubbed the reins."

"He brought the horse, didn't he?" his companion said. "Pay up, Slim. And let's see *you* ride him. Unless you're afraid."

"I can ride anything with hair and four legs," Slim said, giving Tom the quarter. He swung into the saddle, but before he hit the seat the horse had ducked its head and begun to buck. Three jumps and Slim was loose. The fourth jump sent him sprawling. He got to his feet, cursing, and someone in the crowd that had gathered caught the horse and brought it back.

---

5. **ewes** (yūz), female sheep.

The other cowhand turned to Thomas. "I'll give you a dollar if you ride that horse again—without snubbing the reins."

Thomas hesitated. But a dollar, a whole dollar!

He took the reins, gave them one turn around his left hand, and swung up. He held the horse's head up for one jump while he settled himself, then tightened his knees, let the reins go slack and rode with the buck. The horse came down stiff-legged, went into a series of twisting bucks, and side-lunged halfway up the block. Tom kept his seat and put it to a stiff-legged trot. It tossed its head and wanted to run, but he held it in to the end of the block, then came back in a series of short, jolting jumps.

A moment later, proud and embarrassed, he was squirming away through the crowd with his silver dollar when an unshaven red-haired man in levis and worn, fancy-stitched boots stopped him.

"You're quite a rider, son," he began. Then, edging down the street with Thomas, he asked many questions, and Thomas told him his name and why he was herding sheep.

The man grinned. "A boy like you herding sheep! You just throw in with Red Dillon and we'll *both* go places. How'd you like to be a real bronc twister? I got a place down in New Mexico, the other side of the reservation, with a whole string of bad horses you can ride."

Thomas hesitated. "I haven't got a permit."

"I'll tend to that. The agency's right on our way."

They found Albert Left Hand in the café and Red told him he was taking Thomas home with him. Albert Left Hand didn't even look up. He took a bite of raisin pie, chewed for a moment, then growled, "Boys come, boys go. That one's no good."

Red grinned as they turned away. "We ought to eat before we go," he said to Thomas. "Me giving you a job, you ought to treat. Money's no good in your pocket."

So they found stools at the other end of the counter, and Red ordered chili and coffee for both of them, until they had an even dollar's worth. Then Thomas gave Red his dollar and Red paid.

Red's horses, a black and a sorrel,[6] were waiting. Both were saddled, but the saddle on the black had no horn. Red saw Thomas puzzling. "This here's a bronc saddle, for rodeoing," he said. "If a bronc comes over backwards onto you, there's no horn to punch a hole in your guts. If you get throwed frontwards by a mean bucker there's no horn to hang you up by your chap strings. You're going to see a lot of this saddle, Tom." He swung onto the sorrel and Tom mounted the black, and they headed for the agency.

---

6. **sorrel,** a horse with a reddish-brown colored coat.

DISCUSSION FOR UNDERSTANDING

1. What makes Blue Elk decide to return to the lodge on Bald Mountain?
2. How do the agent and Blue Elk trick Tom into parting with the bear?
3. How does Tom change when he returns to school after running away to Bald Mountain? How is he different after his second parting with the bear?

3 The Arena

Red got the permit without any trouble. For the agent, it solved the whole problem of Thomas Black Bull.

Tom and Red Dillon rode south to New Mexico. The second day they rode across rolling flats, mirages shimmering and vanishing ahead of them, and Red made a sweeping gesture. "Now we're on my range. Grass enough here for a thousand head of horses. But help eats up all the profits, so I keep my layout small. Me and old Meo handle it. You'll like Meo. Used to be quite a rider himself, till a bronc fell on him eight, ten years ago. Broke something in his back. Ever seen a rodeo, Tom?"

"No."

"Things go right, we'll go to the show in Aztec next month. And we'll get paid for it, Tom. We'll *make* them pay." He laughed. "I've got a feeling my luck's turned."

In the midafternoon they came to the sharp-walled canyon of the San Juan,[1] which swept in a great arc down through a corner of New Mexico before it swung north again into Utah and the incredible canyons of the Colorado.[2] They rode down a trail where the river twisted like a silver snake in its canyon, and came to a weathered cabin, a log barn and some corrals among huge old cottonwoods. A man was hoeing a patch of beans and pepper plants beyond the cabin, and when they had taken care of their horses he came to meet them. He was a gnomish,[3] leather-faced old Mexican with a hump on his shoulders.

"This is Tom, Meo," Red said. "We're going to teach him to be a bronc twister."

Meo looked at Tom. Then he asked Red, "You win at Mancos?"

Red shook his head. "Cleaned out. But my luck's changed. Me and Tom are going to Aztec and take their shirts."

"Maybe," Meo said, and he went back to the garden.

The cabin was one long room with bunks against one wall and assorted riding gear on pegs on the other. A string of red chilies hung from a beam, and on the ashes in the fireplace stood a coffeepot and a simmering iron kettle. Red filled two bowls with beans and chili from the kettle.

"Well, Tom," he said, "the agent asked would I see to it that you had a home and learned a trade. I don't know what he'd say about this place, but you won't starve. As for a trade, well, I never been in the poorhouse, and I don't plan to be. You stick with me and we'll both make out. Now eat up. Put some gristle in your gut. You'll need it, because you're going to start learning that trade tomorrow."

The next morning Tom got his first lesson as a bronc rider. Red had nine horses out on the range, all buckers and outlaws.[4] "You learn to ride my string of outlaws, you can ride any horse you'll draw in the kind of shows we'll work," Red said.

He told Tom to put on a pair of chaps[5] he had soaked in the horse trough to make them cling, and then they roped a horse, cinched[6] on a bronc saddle and Tom mounted. He rode only four jumps before he was thrown.

"Too much rein," Red said. "Try again." Tom rode a few jumps longer that time. "Not enough rein," Red announced. "Now do it right."

---

1. **San Juan,** a river.
2. **Colorado,** a river.
3. **gnomish,** dwarflike, shriveled.
4. **outlaws,** horses that are vicious.
5. **chaps,** heavy leather trousers without a seat that are worn over ordinary trousers to protect the legs from brush and cacti.
6. **cinched,** secured the saddle to the horse. Cinches are the straps on a saddle that are secured around the belly of a horse.

Tom got into the saddle again, bruised and angry. He was loosened in the saddle twice, but the wet chaps clung and he rode the horse to a standstill. "That's better," Red said grudgingly, and Meo brought a fresh horse.

Tom was thrown five times the first day, but he began to learn how to fall as well as how to ride. The second day he found his timing, began to gauge a horse's pattern in its first few jumps. At the end of the week he rode two horses in succession to a standstill.

Then they built a rodeo chute in the corral; a plank pen with walls just wide enough to take a horse, gates at each end that crowded a horse so it could neither lunge nor buck, and a narrow runway on each side from which to saddle the horse and mount. The first horse Tom rode out of the chute was a big roan[7] as mean as a tomcat with its tail on fire. When Meo opened the gate, it lunged out, fighting like a fiend. The rein slipped in Tom's sweaty hands; he lost a stirrup and went head over heels onto the hard-packed corral. Red caught the roan and shouted, "Come back in and ride him right this time!"

Tom dried his hands on his shirt, straddled the chute and lowered himself into the saddle again. The roan went out just as viciously as before, rearing and coming down with jolts that made Tom's teeth hurt. But Tom rode him, for ages it seemed, though once he had to grab the saddle with his free right hand. When the horse, gasping, slowed to a crowhop, he eased out of the saddle, his legs quivering, his belly drum-tight. "You pulled leather," Red accused. "You didn't ride him clean."

"I rode him." Tom started for the corral fence but couldn't make it before he threw up.

Red said, "You've done your puking. Now you ride like I tell you to." He had a fresh horse in the chute.

Two more weeks and Tom had ridden every horse in Red's string to a standstill. "We're almost ready for Aztec," Red said. "But there's still a thing or two you've got to learn."

The next morning they put a gray mare in the chute. She was a ducker and a dodger but Tom knew her tricks. He was buckling on his chaps when Red asked unexpectedly, "How does the saddle suit you? Cinches tight enough?"

Tom shook the saddle. It seemed right—front cinch tight, back cinch just snug. "It'll do," he said. He mounted and set his spurs at the base of the horse's neck, and Meo swung the gate open. The gray lunged out. She bucked twice and the saddle began to turn. Tom kicked free of the stirrups just in time to be thrown clear as the saddle fell.

He landed hard, and as he got up he saw Red laughing. Tom looked at the saddle and saw that both straps that held the cinches were broken. They had been cut halfway through with a knife. He looked at Red. "You did that!" he said.

"Sure I did," Red said, still laughing.

Tom was thirty pounds lighter than Red Dillon, but he lunged at him with both fists. Red dodged, hit him one quick blow, knocked him down and held him down by the shoulders. "Cool off," he said. "I told you yesterday you still had to learn a thing or two. First one is, don't trust anybody when it comes to your saddle and your gear. Not even me. Check everything."

He let go, and Tom got to his feet, still glowering.

"Second thing you just learned," Red said, "is not to jump somebody bigger than you. When you get mad like that, take it out

---

7. **roan,** a horse with a reddish-brown or brown coat thickly sprinkled with white or gray.

on a horse, where you've got a chance to win."
He turned and walked away.

Tom caught the gray mare, tied a rope around for a surcingle,[8] mounted her and rode her to a standstill. When she finally came to a stop, snorting bloody foam, he got off and went to the house.

Red was at the table, drinking coffee. "Get it out of your system?" he asked.

"I rode her," Tom said.

"Sure. I knew you could." Red stirred his coffee and watched him for a moment. "You can ride the horses they'll have at Aztec, too. But you're going to lose, just the same."

"No, I'm not."

"I say you are. They'll figure you're just another Indian kid who thinks he can ride; and that's what I'll tell them you are. So you enter the saddle bronc riding, and you score high in the first two go-rounds. But you lose the final. Understand?"

"No."

"You better understand, because that's what you're going to do. You lose the final go-round. After that you ride again. Never mind how come. You ride again, and you ride that horse right into the ground."

"But—"

"Don't but me! You didn't think I just wanted to make a hero out of you, did you? Not with that Aztec bunch just aching to bet. *Now* do you understand?" Tom hesitated, and Red rubbed his knuckles. "You got one beauty of a shiner. No need getting another one like it. Now, you're going to do what I say, aren't you?"

Tom nodded. "Yes," he said.

Aztec was just a wide place in the road, but its rodeo drew ranch folk from the whole area. The contestants were mostly ranch hands; purses were small, but betting free-handed. It was a two-day show with the preliminary rounds the first afternoon, the semifinals and finals the next day. The main event

was the bronc riding, man against horse, the historic reason for rodeo itself.

Red had ridden there the year before, but he told people he'd just come this time to see the show. "And to see if the boy, here, can ride. He thinks he can, and I guess this is a good time to find out."

His listeners looked at Tom, just another Indian boy in faded levis, with hair that looked as though it had been cut with dull sheep shears. Several men grinned and asked Red if he'd like to lay a few bets on the kid.

Red laughed. "I said he *thinks* he can ride. Let's wait for the first go-round."

According to rodeo rules, Tom would have to ride holding the rein in one hand, not touching saddle or horse with the other. He must rake with his spurs, keep his feet moving, and ride ten full seconds. Then the horn would blow, a mounted pickup man would come alongside, take his rein and let him pivot out of the saddle to the ground.

The ride was scored on points based on skill in the saddle and the difficulty of the horse. If a rider was thrown or committed a foul he lost the go-round. At Aztec, as in most small rodeos, each go-round was an elimination contest, leaving only the five top riders for the finals. "So start right out riding rough and tough," Red told Tom.

The first day Tom drew a snaky, wide-winding black that bucked in a tight circle. He had no special trouble and was surprised to realize that the crowd was applauding him. He placed second.

That evening there was a good deal of talk about this Indian kid who didn't look more than twelve or thirteen but rode like a man. Red made a few small bets for the second go-round in the morning, but refused to bet on the finals. "Tom's luck may run out," he said.

---

8. **surcingle,** cinch.

Next morning Tom drew a big roan that went out of the chute in a series of spectacular lunges that brought an instant roar from the crowd. After two jumps Tom knew he could ride him, so he raked and gouged with his spurs, the roan bellowed and fought, and Tom punished him every legal way he knew. When the horn blew, the crowd was in an uproar. Tom won the round.

At lunchtime Red had several drinks and began to brag as though he'd had one too many. The betting crowd winked at each other. A few of them placed bets with him on the finals, but again Red kept the bets low. The minute he and Tom started back to the rodeo grounds Red sobered up. "Well, Tom," he said, "you've been a hero. Like it?"

"Yes," Tom said.

"I thought so. Well, you're going to be a bum in the finals. I've got the deadfall all set up. You're going to give your horse slack in the rein after the first few jumps and look for a soft place to land."

"No I'm not. I can—"

"You do like I say, or I'll break your neck! But then you're going to ride again. A special event. And then you'd *better* be a hero or start running. Now do you understand?"

"I guess so," Tom said reluctantly.

Back in the arena Red played the drunken braggart again, but as Tom mounted the big black he had drawn, there was threat in Red's eyes. Then the announcer bellowed, "Coming out of Chute Number Three, on Tar Baby, Tom Black Bull!" and the crowd began to roar. The black lunged out bucking. It side-jumped and Tom raked with his spurs. He knew he could ride this horse, but after a few bucks he let the rein slip as the black ducked its head. It got six inches of slack, came up in another buck, and Tom kicked his feet free and went sprawling hard.

The crowd groaned. Tom lay for a moment, gasping, aching with pain, and hurting inside because he could have ridden that horse to a standstill. He hunched to his knees

till the pain eased and then got slowly to his feet. He limped back to the chutes, head bowed.

Red came to meet him. He put an arm around Tom's shoulders and said loudly, "Tough luck, kid! What happened?"

Tom looked at him, hating him, and didn't answer. They went back to the chutes. Tom sat down in the shade, head in his hands, and heard the chute open and the last rider's horse go out squealing. A few minutes later the announcer was bellowing the final results. Tom Black Bull, because of his spectacular rides in the first two go-rounds, placed fourth.

The men who had bets with Red came to collect, and he paid them off. "You took me," he said. "But I still say the boy is the best rider here. He just had bad luck with that big black." When the others laughed, he added, "I say Tom can ride any horse here—*any* of them."

"That's big talk, Dillon," a stocky black-haired ranchman said. "Maybe we could set up a special event for him. What odds would you give?"

"Odds?" Red laughed derisively. "The boy just got thrown and you want me to give odds!"

The announcer had come over to see what was happening. Now he bellowed to the crowd, "Don't hurry off, folks! We may have a special event in the making. Stick around!"

Red turned to Tom. "Want to make another ride, Tom?"

Tom knew the answer he had to make. Anyway, he wanted to ride again, to prove himself. "Yes," he said.

Red turned to the men around him. "You heard him. Give me two-to-one odds and the boy'll ride any horse you pick, not just to the ten-second horn, but all the way. Now what do you say?"

"That," the black-haired man said, "I want to see."

Red covered the bets, using his saddle

and two horses as collateral, and the bettors went to the corral and picked out a big bay horse which had thrown its first rider in six seconds.

The announcer bellowed to the crowd, "Well, folks, we've got us a special event. Tom Black Bull is going to ride that big bay they're bringing to the chutes right now. And listen to this, folks! Tom is going to try to ride this horse to a standstill!" There was a roar of approval from the crowd.

Red and Tom checked everything from stirrups to reins. Then the bay was put in the chute and saddled. Tom dried his hands, jammed his hat tight and mounted, and the gate swung open.

The bay took two steps and went into the air; it zigzagged, bucked, reared and spun. Tom felt as though his head were being driven down between his shoulders; his left arm seemed about to be torn from its socket. But he rode, and he rode clean.

The ten-second horn blew. The crowd was in an uproar, but Tom heard nothing. He was riding for himself now. The blood drummed in his ears, his teeth ached with the pounding. He gouged the horse with his spurs, shifted his weight, brought it down with every jump, punishing the horse; he snapped the rein as though trying to break the horse's neck. The bay was grunting with every leap. Finally it bellowed and came up in a pawing, dancing leap of fury, and then it came down with a jolt that jarred the earth and began to buck in a tight circle. But the bellows became gasps of pain. It bucked again, came down spraddlelegged, staggered, began to cough, took a few steps and stood trembling. It tried to buck once more and failed.

The crowd was yelling, and a pickup man was alongside, shouting to Tom. "Get clear! He's going down!" Tom felt the horse sagging; he grabbed the pickup man's shoulder and kicked free just as the bay fell from under him. His feet struck the ground and

his knees buckled. He went down, and looked around to see the fallen horse jerking convulsively. There was a gush of blood from its mouth, and its head fell down. Tom heard the crowd gasp. He got to his feet and walked to the chute, clung to the planks and began to retch.

"Give him air!" Red ordered. "All right?" he asked Tom. Tom nodded, clinging to the chute, and Red went to collect his winnings. A man brought Tom's saddle over, staring at Tom in awe. "Bay's dead," he said. "Ruptured its lungs."

Red came back stuffing money into his pockets. "Come on, Tom," he said. "Let's get out of here." They started toward the corrals and their own saddle horses, but the black-haired ranchman followed them. "Just a minute, Dillon," he said. "That was a setup!" He was flushed with anger.

"You picked the horse, and the boy rode him, didn't he?"

"He did. But he could have ridden the black in the final go-round, too. Only he had orders not to. Didn't you, son?"

"Leave him alone!" Red snapped. "He made his ride!"

The man turned to Tom. "You had your orders, didn't you?"

Red cocked his fist. "I said leave him alone!"

The man stepped back. "All right, Dillon. You took us. But don't you ever show up at an Aztec rodeo again!"

"Aztec!" Red laughed derisively. "Why, you two-bit tinhorn! We're going where there's *real* money! . . . Come on, Tom."

They rode at a lope the first five miles and Red kept watching the road behind them. Then, since nobody was following them, they slowed to a trot and Red began gloating. Tom heard his braggart voice, his jeering laugh, and remembered the way he had ridden the bay to death, punishing not the horse but something that Red Dillon represented. He had killed the horse, but Red's grating laughter was still right here beside him. He felt queasy again, got off his horse and began to retch.

Red grinned. "You're kind of shook-up, I guess."

Just at dark they rode up to a trading post and Red went in. He came back with three bottles, stowed two of them in his bedroll, opened the third and took a long drink. After that he drank as he rode, talking and laughing to himself. Tom would fall asleep in the saddle, then wake up feeling the queasiness again, as Red's voice rasped at his ears.

It was almost midnight when they reached home. Red bellowed for Meo, and when the old man appeared, lantern in hand, he said, "Meo, you old chili-eater, I took 'em!" His words were slurred. Meo steadied him as he dismounted, and he wove his way to the cabin. Then Tom himself almost fell as he pulled his saddle off.

"I'll finish," Meo said. "Go get food and coffee."

Red was sprawled in his bunk, already asleep, and Tom was sitting at the table, staring at his beans and coffee, when Meo came in. "You won?" Meo said.

Tom shook his head. "I lost."

"And then you rode again?"

"Yes." Tom wondered how he knew. "I killed a horse."

"Ah-h-h." Meo nodded. He glanced toward Red, snoring in his bunk, and pointed with his chin. "*He* won." Tom nodded, and Meo went over to Red. He took the money from his pockets, counted it, then put back a few bills. He thrust the rest into his own pocket. Then he sat down opposite Tom with a cup of coffee. "Tell me about it," he said.

Tom told him, and at last Meo said, "Some day they will kill that one. Or he will kill himself." He sipped his coffee. "Why did you come here, Tom?" he asked.

"One must live somewhere. I lived in the mountains in the old way. They took me away."

"The mountains are still there," Meo said after a time.

"The old way is finished." Unconsciously Tom made the cut-off sign. "I have no one. So I came to be a rider."

Meo grunted. "Why?" he asked again.

Tom wondered how to tell him what he had felt when he was riding the big bay at Aztec, but it was deeper than words. At last he said, knowing it was not the whole truth, but still a part of it, "To be the boss. I am the boss, on the horse."

"Sometimes. When *he* tells you to be." Meo finished his coffee.

"Tomorrow," he said, "we will harvest the frijoles,[9] you and I. Go to bed now."

They harvested the beans in the old way, piling the vines on a tarp, flailing them with a stick. Then they picked the chilies. On the fourth afternoon Red came out of the cabin, pale, weak-kneed, but sober. The next morning he told Meo to bring the horses in.

"Week after next we're going to hit the road," he said to Tom. "But before we go you're going to learn how to lose a go-around without getting thrown. Let a horse throw you, you may break an arm or something. Then we're out of business for a month." Tom was staring at him, his mouth set angrily. "You got ideas?" Red flared. "If you have, get rid of them. Heroes are a dime a dozen, little two-bit heroes everywhere you go. And they all wind up broke, especially Indians and Mexes. Meo was a hero once." He laughed. "Now take a look at him. Just another broken down old chili-eater."

Tom made no comment.

---

9. **frijoles** (fri hō′lēz),   beans.

Red said, "There's a dozen ways to lose a go-round. You're going to learn them all. And you're going to learn how to look like you're doing your best *not* to lose." He saw the look in Tom's eyes, and added, "And if you try double-crossing me, I'll break your neck."

So Tom entered the world of small-time rodeo, a world of hot, dusty little cow-country towns, vicious, unpredictable horses, ambitious country riders and jealous third-rate professionals, and, with Red Dillon, a world of noisy saloons, smoky pool halls, ratty hotels and flyspecked chili parlors.

The night before a rodeo opened Red would give Tom his orders. Then, with variations, it would be the same story as that first time at Aztec. And when Red had collected his winnings, they would get out of town before the bettors knew what hit them.

The system wasn't foolproof. Red got jumped occasionally by irate bettors, and once they were chased out of town by a posse. Now and then a horse outguessed Tom and he was thrown when Red had ordered him to win, and twice he was so badly hurt that they had to call it quits until Meo could nurse him back to health at home. But, as Red said, things averaged out pretty well.

For two years they worked the rodeos in eastern New Mexico and the Oklahoma Panhandle and northern Texas, and then Red bought a pickup truck with a two-horse trailer so they could cover more ground. Wherever they went, Tom drifted through the routine and didn't even think; what he really lived for were the winning top-form rides that Red eventually ordered. The other riders paid him little attention. In fact, time after time, some gay-shirted, arrogant rider mistook him for a stable boy and ordered him out of the arena. Tom had grown a couple of inches, put on twenty pounds of muscle and sinew, and was almost as big as Red, but he

still played the part of a backcountry Indian kid with ragged hair and shabby work clothes.

In the fall season of their third year, Red struck north into Colorado and Wyoming. But now bettors were suspicious. Red wouldn't admit it, but Tom had outgrown his role. On foot, he might look like a novice, but once in the saddle, his skill and experience couldn't be hidden. The next spring Red headed for southern Arizona where he said there was more sucker money. But except for one good cleanup, he couldn't raise a bet, and even Tom's luck seemed to be running out. He couldn't seem to win even when Red ordered him to. Sometimes he knew he was going to lose as soon as he got in the saddle.

"I'm getting tired," he said. "My timing's off. Let's go home, Red."

"We're not going home broke! You can still ride when you want to. There's a show in Uvalde County next week. If we win, we go home. But if you lose—" Red rubbed his fist and laughed, a short, ugly laugh.

So they drove north, to Uvalde County. They took a room at the hotel and Red went out to set things up. It was after midnight when he came back, stumbling drunk. He was still sleeping the next morning when Tom got up and went out to the arena to look at the horses and listen to the old, familiar talk about horses and women. Finally he climbed into the empty stands and sat in the sun. And the questions came: Who am I? Where do I belong?

As in a dream, he saw a boy he once knew who lived in the old way, a boy called Bear's Brother. Then there was another boy, Thomas Black Bull, who lived on the reservation, herded sheep and braided hair ropes and bridles. He remembered those boys. But he wasn't Bear's Brother and he wasn't Thomas Black Bull. Then he saw another boy, at Red Dillon's place, learning how to ride clean or dirty, how to do what he was told. That boy was partly himself but still a stranger. That was the boy who had told old Meo he rode so he could be the boss.

He sat there, remembering, and he saw a little whirlwind pick up a puff of dust down in the arena and swirl it past the loafers beside the empty chutes. The dust hid them for a moment and in their place he saw a crowd of riders, shouting, swearing at the horses, laughing. He heard the horses grunting, squealing, heard the crowd cheering. He felt the tightness in his belly as he sat in the saddle, braced, just before the gate opened, the quiver in his legs. The feel of the horse you got through the rein; the feel of his ribs beneath your calves. The feel of the stirrups, the rake of the spurs, the rhythm. The exhilaration, the sense of mastery. The contest won, not over the other riders but over the horse, the violence, the elemental force. The sense of triumph.

He left the stands and went back to the hotel.

Red was up and dressed, bleary-eyed with a hangover. "Where have you been?" he demanded truculently.[10] Tom didn't answer. "Get over being tired? You'd better. I'm setting up the deadfall,[11] so start figuring how to lose the first go-round and make it look good."

Tom shook his head. "No, Red. Bet it straight."

Red gasped. "Don't you say no to me!"

"I'm going to ride this one clean and for keeps, Red."

"Why, you dirty, double-crossing, lousy little Indian!" Red made a lunge at him. Tom sidestepped and knocked Red down. He scrambled to his feet, and Tom knocked him down again, then quickly left the room. He went out onto the street and walked for half an hour, letting his anger cool.

Red wasn't there when he went back. He waited ten minutes, then went out to the rodeo grounds, got his gear, checked his saddle and took it out to the chutes. There was still no sign of Red when the announcer bellowed, "Coming out of Chute Number Three, on Black Star—Tom Black!"

The bronc lunged out, and for the first few jumps Tom didn't know whether he could make it or not. Then something happened inside. He was riding a hurt, a hate. He had walked away from Red this morning because, though he hated him, he didn't want to kill him. Now he wanted to hurt and maim. His timing came back, all his skill. He gouged and fought, and the horse fought back. The stands roared, but Tom didn't hear them. He didn't hear the ten-second horn. The pickup man yelled, "Time! Time, you fool!" He grabbed the rein, and Tom automatically pivoted to the ground. He left the arena, not waiting for the score. He had made his ride. The score didn't matter.

Red was back at the hotel, deep in drunken sleep. Tom went through his pockets, and found more than seven hundred dollars. He took all but ten, then went out again. He walked along the street until he came to a clothing store and caught sight of himself in a mirror in the window. He stared, unbelieving. With his beat-up old hat, his long, ragged hair, his faded work shirt and worn levis, he looked like an overgrown reservation kid.

He went inside and bought a whole new outfit: cream-colored hat, pink-striped silk shirt, purple neckerchief, copper-riveted levis, fancy-stitched boots. He put everything on and left his old clothes in the fitting room, except for his boots. They are the one thing a bronc rider never throws away, for he feels the horse, senses every move it makes, through his feet in the stirrups, through his old, soft, worn boots.

10. **truculently** (truk′yə lənt lē), in a threatening manner.
11. **deadfall,** a trap, in this instance for unwary bettors.

Then Tom sat in a barber chair for the first time in his life, and when the barber had finished he stared at himself in the mirror. He was no longer a boy. He looked like a ranch hand fresh in town, with two months' wages on his back. He looked to be eighteen or nineteen years.

Still marveling, he went to a restaurant for supper. The waitress smiled at him, though waitresses usually gave him one look and turned away, sniffing. As he walked back in the dusk to the hotel he saw two girls watching him. One of them came up to him, smiling. "Don't I know you? Isn't your name—" She paused, her eyes inviting. "What *is* your name?" she asked.

He wanted to run, and yet he wanted to stay. "Tom," he said. "Tom Black."

She put a hand on his arm. "My," she said softly, "you are sure good-looking. I'll bet you're here with the rodeo." He nodded. "I just love rodeo men!" She smiled. "And I'm not busy tonight." She pressed against him, and his sensitive nose caught a musky smell. His pulse throbbed in his temples. Then he saw the crow's-feet, the blotches beneath her makeup and the hard look in her eyes. And he knew what she was. He pushed her away and hurried on, hoping Red would still be there. But the room was empty.

He stood at the window a long time, letting his pulse ebb. He was sure now that there was only one thing that mattered to him—the arena, the battle with the broncs. Today it had been a good ride. Tomorrow his draw was a leggy bay called Sleepwalker. A big horse, mean as they come. Which suited him right down to the ground. "The devil with them!" he said aloud. "Red, and the women and . . . all of them!"

Red had not reappeared by morning, and he was not at the arena. An old man helped Tom saddle Sleepwalker, and he went out of the chute to make one of the best, most brutal rides of his life—vicious, hard, su-

perbly skillful. When the day's totals were announced, Tom Black was top man again. He was packing his gear when the head judge, a gaunt old-timer with a white mustache, came over. He said, "You must have a crawful of cockleburs, son. What are you trying to do? Kill yourself, or kill every horse you straddle?"

"I rode clean, didn't I?" Tom demanded.

The judge sucked his teeth a moment. "Look, son, forget it, whatever it is. Yes, you rode clean. You could be a champion. But if you keep on this way you won't live to see the day."

"Does it matter?" Tom asked.

The judge saw the look in his eyes and walked away.

Late that night there was a banging at the door. It was the old man who had helped Tom saddle up. "Your redheaded partner," he said, "is in the hoosegow.[12] Dead drunk."

"Thanks."

"You going to leave him there?"

"Yes," Tom said.

The next morning Tom drove the truck to a garage and traded it in on a secondhand Buick convertible, paying the difference with some of Red's money. He drove the Buick to the livery stable and had the horse trailer hitched to it. Then he went to the arena.

He won the finals with another horse-killing ride and gave the old man who had helped him twenty-five dollars from his purse money. Then he went to the livery stable for the Buick-trailer outfit, drove it to the jail, paid Red's fine and loaded him, still in a stupor, into the back seat and headed for home. It was the second day before Red came to. He licked his dry lips, and asked, eyes shut, "Where are we?"

"On the way home."

Red opened his eyes and looked at Tom. His mouth fell open; then he grinned, a silly

12. **hoosegow,** slang for jail.

grin. "A haircut. A pink shirt. You stinking dude!" Tom drove in silence, and Red looked around, felt the Buick upholstery. "Where did you get this? Did you sell the horses and the trailer?"

"No, they're hitched on. I didn't even sell your saddle."

"Good." Then Red felt in his pockets. "Somebody rolled me."

"I did."

Red was silent a long time. At last he said, "Meo used to roll me." He covered his eyes with his hands. "I never could save a dime. Somebody always took it off of me. Now it's you." He wasn't complaining. He was stating sad, unemotional fact.

They were beyond Pecos when Red spoke again. "We'd have made a fortune, back there in Uvalde County, if you hadn't got so stiffnecked, Tom. We could still clean up, out in California."

"No, Red. I'm through with that. I'm riding for keeps now."

"What you got in mind, Tom? The big time?"

"Yes."

Red sighed. "Always wanted to see that Odessa show." He reached for the big names. "And Calgary, Denver, Albuquerque . . . I'm glad you didn't sell my saddle, Tom. Fellow sells his saddle, he's just about at the end of his rope."

In October Tom brought the horses into the corral and began working with them alone. Red had become mean as a rabid coyote, wanting excitement, riding away and returning with a hangover. Meo said he was *malo*, meaning either sick or mean, or both.

Then one day Red rode off and didn't come back. A week later a Mexican rode down to the cabin. Red, he said, was sick, very sick, in the hotel in Aztec.

The road was only a trail, but Tom made the thirty miles in less than an hour. He found Red lying gaunt and listless in a chipped iron bed.

Red caught a shallow breath at sight of him. "I'm sick, Tom. Doc Wilson—" He gasped. "Take me home. Don't let me die in this rathole."

Tom took one of Red's hands. The hot fingers gripped his. "Take me home," Red said again.

"Pretty soon," Tom said. "After I see the doctor."

Tom found Doc Wilson's house and went in the door marked OFFICE without knocking. He said, "I'm Tom Black. I want to know how sick Red Dillon is."

The doctor's voice was a tired growl. "Dillon," he said, "has a bad heart, his kidneys are riddled, and his liver is shot. I saw him three hours ago and figured he'd be dead by dark. He's still alive, I take it."

"Yes. I'm going to take him home."

"Don't, son. He'll be dead before you get there."

Only Red's eyes moved when Tom came back into his room. He watched Tom a moment, his expression vague, then he rasped, "Tell Meo to make a fresh pot of coffee. Got an awful hangover." Then his eyes seemed to clear. "Take me home, Tom."

He tried to sit up, and Tom put an arm around him. Red stared at him and whispered, "Better luck next time." His lips moved and Tom leaned close. "Game's over," Red gasped. Then the breath seemed to ease out of him, and Tom let him back gently onto the pillow.

Two days later he and Meo buried Red in a dusty little graveyard in Aztec, and Meo paid all the expenses with money that was really Red's. When they got home, Meo said, "Now it is my place."

"Yes," Tom said. "It's your place now, Meo."

Meo seemed surprised at having no argument about it. "When my time comes," he said, "then it is your place."

"Don't worry about that, Meo. I won't be

here long. I'm riding at Odessa in a few weeks. Do you want to come along?"

Meo shook his head. "I rode my horses. I am an old man."

It didn't matter to Tom whether Meo went along or not. You have to ride your own furies.

"You come, you go, just like him," Meo said.

Odessa was just a small southwest Texas town, but its show opened the season for the big rodeos. Veteran riders went there to test their reflexes, newcomers to see if youth and hunger for glory could outweigh experience in the arena. Many newcomers were weeded out at Odessa; a fortunate few rode to glory. Tom's hands were sweating as he sat in his saddle awaiting the signal for his first ride, and he made a mediocre showing. He did better in the second go-round, but he was still too tense, and he knew it.

Then in the finals he drew a horse so mean and full of fight that he had no time to think of anything, and for the first time he rode the way he knew he could ride. He placed second in the final round, won enough place money to pay his hotel bill. The money mattered little. He had begun to find himself. That *did* matter.

From Odessa he went on to the next show, and the next. The newcomers began to drop out, but at the end of the season Tom was named the best first-year man on the circuit, and the next season, after some time home with Meo, he took up where he had left off.

For three months he was in the money in every show; the crowd began to know him by name, and rodeo people said Tom Black was on his way to the championship, something practically unheard of for a second-year man.

It was hot, sweaty June when a horse went crazy under him, lunged back into an empty chute, and impaled itself, screaming, on a splintered gate. Tom was thrown heavily against the chute, his left shoulder crushed.

The doctor said it would be two months before he could ride again.

Four days later, driving with one arm, he headed west, for home, for Meo. But when he got to the cabin he had the uneasy feeling that something was wrong. He pushed open the door; no one was there. The barn was empty, too, and Meo's saddle missing.

At Doc Wilson's house in Aztec, he banged on the office door and walked in. "Where's Meo?" he asked.

The doctor said, "Meo is dead."

"When?" Tom asked. "What happened?"

"About a month ago. He rode in to see me one afternoon and said, 'I am going to die.' He didn't look sick to me, and his pulse and blood pressure were normal. I told him he'd live another twenty years. But he just said, 'No. Tonight,' as if he knew all about it. And he gave me a roll of bills and said I should see that he was buried right, with a coffin and a priest." The doctor paused. "He died that night, in his sleep." He looked at Tom, frowning. "I've known some of these people to *wish* themselves to death, but that was when they were dying anyway. I swear there wasn't anything wrong with Meo."

"He just knew," Tom said.

"What do you mean, he knew?"

Tom shrugged and made no comment.

Dr. Wilson shifted uneasily in his chair. . . . "Now, let's have a look at that shoulder of yours."

He examined it gently. "Young bones knit fast. What are you going to do now?"

"Go out to the place till this is all right. Then rodeo."

The doctor looked at him, speculating. "I'd think you'd want to settle down. Put a little herd of sheep out there, or a few cattle—" Tom was shaking his head. "Look, I know you're a reservation boy, but you're smart; you could make something of yourself. Dillon was a tinhorn gambler and Meo illiterate, but you've got a chance, if you'll take it."

He stopped. Time after time he had seen an Indian just draw the curtains and retreat into a kind of pride that was all mixed up with hurt and resentment. Tom Black was doing it now. The doctor shrugged again. "Well," he said, "I suppose . . ." He got to his feet, and Tom thanked him and left. The doctor had reminded him of the Indian agent. He didn't want to think about those things.

He went back to the cabin and tried to settle in, but for all its familiar corners, it was a strange place, alien. He thought: I do not belong here.

He walked on the flats to keep his legs strong. He saw falcons and a few jackrabbits, and once he saw four of Red's broncs, wild as deer. Cobwebbed memories of Albert Left Hand, of Benny Grayback and Blue Elk drifted through his mind, like shadows, leaving a dull ache.

He was a stranger on Red's land. All he had here was a hatful of memories. Scars of old hurts.

He looked at the empty corral. He saw himself there, learning to fight a bronc, learning to punish. The moon rose and the corral became a breaking pen with a bear cub chained to a snubbing post. And the barn became a barn where a tormented boy was flogged for turning on his tormentors.

He got to his feet and went into the cabin for an axe and matches. He cut the rails of the corral and piled them against the barn. Then he set fires in the litter of old hay inside it. Within minutes, flames leaped through the roof; it fell in with a roar and a great billowing of embers. Tom loaded his car. Then he split kindling and lit it on the cabin floor. He sat in his car almost an hour, watching the flames consume the cabin, seeing Meo's garden turn into a patch of charred ground. When the fire had subsided into smoldering ashes, Tom looked at the circuit schedule. The next show was at Wolf Point, on the Missouri River, up in Montana. He had four days to get there.

Before Tom's ride in the first go-round at Wolf Point, the announcer said, "The next man out is just back in business. A bronc put him in the hospital, and could be he's out for revenge! Here he comes, out of Chute Number Two, on High Tension—the old devil-killer himself, Tom Black!"

The crowd roared as he came out. Three jumps and he was dizzy with pain from his arm. Every jolt drove the pain deeper, but he fought it down with raking spurs. His shoulder was healed but so stiff that he couldn't trust the rein in his left hand; from now on he would be an unorthodox right-handed rider. At Wolf Point this put him off balance at first. But in anger and pain, he rode each go-round like a fiend, and he kept the crowd in turmoil.

He rode every remaining show on the circuit. The pain eased, and as he got used to riding right-handed, his balance and timing came back.

But his whole riding style had changed. He was still a slick, skillful rider who could pile up points when he wanted to, but now he wasn't riding for points. He was riding for the ride, for the punishment he could give a horse, and he was riding that way consistently. He still won enough purse money to pay his expenses but he would not make a clean, high-scoring ride if he could choose a rule-defying one that brought out the worst in a horse. And he knew a dozen ways to drive a bronc into a frenzy.

He didn't even come close to the championship that year. But he left no doubt that he rode for revenge, though nobody was quite sure why. He was the devil-killer, and no one seemed to wonder who the real devil was whom he was trying to kill. The crowds went wild when Killer Tom Black was announced, and when he rode, the silence was so tense, so profound, that some even said they could hear Devil Tom cursing his horse. That wasn't true. Tom rode tight-lipped, even more quietly venomous in the saddle than he was on foot. And he was known as a hostile, silent man who had no friends.

As the seasons went by, Tom Black became a living legend. Whenever rodeo folk gathered to swap stories they would talk of the great broncs—Steamboat, Midnight, War Paint, Iron Mountain, Tipperary. Then they would mention the great riders. And almost at once someone would say, "Well, for my money, Tom Black . . ." And there would be a pause. The name was always spoken with respect that verged on awe.

A first-year man, brash in his ignorance, might ask, "What year did Black win the championship?" And one of the veterans would say with rebuke in his voice, "Tom never won the championship. He never went after it." And if the first-year man persisted, "Why not, if he's so good?" the answer would be: "Old Man Satan never had to win a title to prove how good *he* was."

"How long has Tom Black been up?"

"I couldn't say. He was here when I came up, six years ago."

"Why, I saw him ride at Odessa eight years ago!"

If anyone had asked Tom Black himself, he would have had to stop and figure to know how long he had been riding on the big circuit. Time no longer mattered to him. Between shows he merely went through the motions of living. Nothing but the rodeo mattered because there *was* nothing else. Ride three times, pack, go. . . . Ride three times, pack, go. . . . It was a rhythm, almost like the rhythm of a bronc. He was stomped by horses; he was thrown. He was stuck together with tape and catgut. But still he rode.

Time had no meaning.

That's the way the years passed.

It was almost noon when he wakened, and for a few minutes he didn't know where he was. All cities sounded pretty much alike. Then he remembered: this was New York. He stared at the ceiling. It was sky-blue. Blue,

the female color. He was surprised to be thinking in the old way. Blue for the south, the gentle, the female. Black for the north, the harsh, the male.

He put the thought away. Blue was blue. He yawned and stretched, and felt the deep, old aches. His right knee throbbed, the knee that was smashed in Denver. There was a dull ache in his left shoulder, the stiff one. The aches you live with. He dressed, went downstairs and bought a paper. He found the feature story on an inside page. The photograph of a scowling face with a slit mouth, crooked nose, wide cheekbones, the scar across the chin. And the headline read: THE KILLER RIDES AGAIN.

The first few lines, written by the show publicity man, were so familiar he could have read them with his eyes shut:

> Tom Black is back in the Garden[13] with the rodeo, and the crowds are waiting for him to kill another horse. Black, a full-blooded Indian, is known to rodeo buffs as Killer Tom, Devil Tom, and an assortment of other grim nicknames. He has earned them all. A veteran bronc rider, Tom Black has ridden nine horses to death in the rodeo arena. . . .

The story was full of vivid detail, only half true. Actually, he had been involved in the death of only six broncs, including that first one at Aztec. But he had to admit, to himself at least, that several others had been retired, wind or spirit broken, after he rode them.

The bull riding was going on when he got to the Garden. After that came the girls, who might just as well have been Broadway show girls except that they had learned to ride a horse and do stunts on a special saddle. The bronc riding was next.

13. **Garden,** Madison Square Garden, a huge enclosed arena in New York City for sporting events and other large gatherings.

Tom had drawn tonight's number-three ride. He went over to the chute as the number-one rider was announced. A helper was there, holding a big roan's head. Tom stepped up onto the chute runway, saddle in hand, and let it down easily, cinches dangling. The roan flinched, but didn't even hunch its back. Some broncs tried to fight the saddle. Others saved their fight for the rider.

The crowd was roaring. Number one, a newcomer who had made a spectacular ride last night, was doing all right for himself again. Tom didn't look up from snugging the cinches, but he could hear the stomp of hoofs, the grunting wheezes. Then the horn blew and the crowd cheered and whistled. Tom glanced up and saw the rider grin at the crowd and wave his hat. He was good, and he knew it, a boy on his way up.

Tom let himself down into the saddle, sensed the taut muscles of the bronc beneath his calves. The crowd groaned as the number-two rider was thrown. A moment later, the announcer was bellowing, "And now, ladies and gentlemen, here comes a rider you all know. Some call him Devil Tom, some call him Black Death—he has a whole string of names like that." The crowd had begun to cheer. The announcer waited for the cheers to ease off. "I don't have to tell you any more about him, I see. Anyway, here he is, coming out of Chute Number Three—I give you Tom Black, on Sky Rocket!"

The crowd roared again, then tensed into silence.

Sky Rocket went out with a bellow. Rein taut, spurs raking, Tom Black began his ride. He had made that ride a thousand times. Sky Rocket was a pattern bucker: three lunges, a side jump, a half spin, then three lunges again.

Tom rode with the rhythm, punishing with spurs, brutal with rein. Three times the roan followed the pattern: lunge, lunge, lunge, side jump, spin. Then, frantic, it tried to duck left. Tom shifted his weight for lever-

age, and a stab of pain shot through his right knee and streaked to his ankle. To keep from losing the stirrup he jabbed his spur deeper. The roan squealed and bunched, neck bowed for another lunge. Tom powered its head around as it left the ground. Off-balance, it seemed to tangle its feet in the air, and Tom felt it begin to fall. He tried to thrust himself clear, but his numb right foot didn't respond. He was still in the saddle as the roan came down with a crash on its right side. . . .

Tom felt one crushing blow across his hips before his head struck the arena. Then the whole world seemed to explode in a burst of light and pain. Then darkness, nothing. . . .

In the hospital, most of the first week Tom existed in the half-world of the critically hurt where there is neither night nor day, but only overlapping periods of confused consciousness and dreams, and always for Tom, the chilling nightmare of falling, trapped in the saddle on a bronc that was forever falling but never landing. His body fought its battles quite apart from his mind, with the help of transfusions, injections, surgery.

Then slowly his vitality reasserted itself. The first morning of his second week, he wakened at dawn and saw the flame of sunrise in his window. The memory of another dawn came to him, the dawn when he and his mother, fleeing from Pagosa, bathed in an icy brook, then sat naked on the rocks and sang the chant to a new day. The rhythm of that chant throbbed in his memory. He tried to move, but pain stabbed at his chest and hips, and bitterness rose in him at his helplessness.

He was still rankling when a nurse came in. She had coppery hair and blue eyes, and when she said, "Good morning! How are we today?" he immediately resented her ready smile and bubbly air. She set down a tray, lowered the window shade and started to put a thermometer into his mouth. "Put up that shade," he ordered.

"But the sun is right in your eyes."

"I like the sun. Put it up!"

She laughed at him, raised the shade, then took his pulse and temperature. She put the breakfast tray on the bed table, saw that he took two capsules—"Happy pills, to sweeten your disposition"—and went away. The coffee tasted the way burning hay smelled, and he remembered the strong, bitter coffee Meo used to make; but he ate hungrily.

"What's your name?" he asked the nurse next morning.

"Mary Redmond." She moved to lower the window shade.

"Leave that shade alone! Where are you from?"

"Massachusetts." She came back to his bedside.

"That's New England." It was an accusation. "I used to have a mealymouthed schoolteacher who talked like you. She was from New England."

She laughed. "You're talkative this morning. You must be feeling better." She took his temperature and then asked, "Where did you know this charming teacher from New England?"

"In Colorado, on the reservation."

"Oh?" She poured him fresh water.

He repeated sharply, "On the reservation."

"I heard you the first time. Look, Chief, put away your tomahawk and take the feathers out of your hair. You're just another man to me. . . . Anything else I can do for you?"

"No. Leave me alone."

That afternoon Dr. Ferguson, the surgeon, came in to see him. "How many ribs?" Tom asked as Ferguson checked him.

"Several—plus a lung puncture, a deep concussion, a broken femur[14] and a broken pelvis."

"How long will I be laid up?"

"We've pinned your femur—that's the big bone in your thigh. You can walk as soon as your pelvis knits. I'd say six weeks."

"How soon can I ride again?"

"Never, if you take my advice."

"I didn't ask for advice. And I'll ride again."

"It's up to you." Dr. Ferguson shrugged and left.

He watched Mary Redmond every morning with rising resentment. Her gentle efficiency emphasized his helplessness, his need for care.

"I hear it's beautiful out in Colorado," she said one day.

"You wouldn't like it. It's all mountains and trees."

"I like mountains and trees." Most men, she was thinking, were grumpy when they were sick. Then they began to get well and appreciated what you did for them. She filled his water glass and made his bed, humming softly. "Now, what more can I do for you?"

"Get me a glass of fresh water."

"I just filled your glass. See?"

He drank the water and held out the glass. "I said fresh water." His voice was testy. "Don't you know who I am?"

She filled the glass. "Of course I do. You're the man who rode ten horses to death. Aren't you proud of that?"

"So they say it's ten, now?"

"Yes, ten, counting the one that put you in here."

"So that one's dead too? I didn't know."

"Well, now you know." She said it sharply. He didn't seem to be sorry at all, and suddenly she was angry at him.

He wasn't listening. He was thinking about the big roan, though he didn't want to think about it—or the others.

That night he had the nightmare again, of being trapped in the saddle and the big roan falling, falling, never coming down. He wakened and, lying in the darkness, he was able, for the first time, to remember the ride from the moment the chute gate opened

---

14. **femur,** thighbone.

right through to the end. He remembered his anger; then his fear, the fear that made him so desperate that he jerked the roan off balance.

And now he knew why he hadn't been able to remember anything but that sensation of falling. He had refused to face the fact that fear had caused the fall. *Fear.* According to the code of the arena, a bronc rider isn't afraid of man, beast, or devil. You don't admit fear, even to yourself. Instead, you get up off the ground and back in the saddle, and you ride the bronc to a standstill, and the fear with it. Tom had known he had to ride again, but he hadn't known why. Now he did, and he slept, free of the nightmare at last.

Mary Redmond did not appear the next day, or the next. He wondered why, but it wasn't important. He had plans to make. He would get out of here, go somewhere for a while, get back in shape, then catch up with the circuit by the end of the summer.

Mary was back the third morning; she had simply taken her regular two days off. "Where have you been?" he demanded.

"Why, Chief!" she exclaimed. "Don't tell me you missed me. The last time I saw you, you hated everybody in sight."

"I still do."

"Some folks," she said as she began to make the bed, "are just too mean to die. You'll live a long, long time." He's mad at life, she was thinking, not at me.

That afternoon Dr. Ferguson took the stitches out of his thigh, and a morning came when Mary triumphantly brought a wheelchair. He managed it so well that a few days later she said, "Doctor may let you try the walker in a week."

When she had left him in the sun porch, Tom wheeled himself to a window frame and pulled himself onto his feet. He took a few tentative steps, almost fell, and sweated with the effort. But the next morning he managed a dozen steps, balancing carefully on his weak legs. He could walk again.

He was halfway down the room when Mary came in.

"What are you doing!" she exclaimed, running toward him. "Suppose you had fallen!" He let her help him back to the chair, and she ran for Dr. Ferguson.

"So," said the surgeon, "you pulled a Lazarus."[15] He smiled. "All right, let's see you do it again. If you've damaged those bones, a few more steps won't matter."

Carefully, Tom crossed to the window, turned, and came back. His forehead was beaded but there was triumph in his eyes. "How soon can I get out of here?" he demanded.

"That depends. You're walking on sheer will power now." Dr. Ferguson considered. "I want some X rays and I want to run a few tests. Meanwhile you get those muscles toughened up. Maybe next Tuesday or Wednesday. But you'll need a few weeks in some place where you can be taken care of. I'll send you a list of convalescent homes." He held out his hand. "Stout fellow."

Next morning, Tom was looking at the list when Mary came in. He didn't like the sound of any of them. "Well, stout fellow!" she said. "I thought you'd be up and have your bed made."

"Where is White Plains?" he asked.

"Out in Westchester. Why?" She looked over his shoulder and saw the list. "Oh, those homes—most of them are pretty terrible. What you need is just a quiet place and somebody to see that you get good meals and plenty of rest." He was silent and Mary went on. "I wish you had a place like my apartment! It's just two blocks from the Drive. You could walk along the river." Her hands seemed even more deft and gentle than usual as she gave him an alcohol rub.

The next day she said triumphantly, "I've

---

15. **Lazarus** (laz′ər əs), a biblical character whom Jesus raised from the dead.

found just the place for you. It's near Nyack, just up the Hudson. You'll love it. I called the woman who runs it last night and she'll save a room for you. Isn't that wonderful?"

"I'll have to think about it." Something in this situation added up wrong. Tom tried to puzzle it out, forgot to concentrate on his walking, and almost fell. Mary ran to take his arm. He snapped, "Leave me alone." He was angry at himself, not at her; but when she said, "You'd better rest," he flared again. "Leave me alone!"

That afternoon she came into his room before she went off duty. "I have to call my friend in Nyack," she said. "Shall I tell her to hold that room?" When he didn't answer, she said, "I'm not trying to talk you into anything." She hesitated, then hurried on. "When I mentioned my apartment yesterday I didn't mean a thing. I was just thinking you would have a nice place to walk. So don't get any wrong ideas. If you go to Nyack I may go up there on a day off to see that you are doing all right. But beyond that—"

Then the whole pattern fell into place. Blue Elk, Benny, Red, Rowena Ellis—they had trapped him, every one of them. And now Mary Redmond. "Tell your friend," he said, "I've made other plans."

"Oh . . . Well, I hope the place is what you need."

When she had gone, he got a pencil and set down figures and added them up. He had never saved his money; he had lived it up, and, in the past few years, spent a lot on hospitals. There wasn't much left but he figured that after he had sold his car, settled with the surgeon and the hospital, paid train fare and bus fare, he would have maybe two hundred dollars. Enough for a while. "Heroes die broke," he could hear Red say. Well, he wasn't dead, and he wasn't broke. Not quite.

Mary was almost as gay as ever the next morning. She chattered and hummed to herself as she made his bed. She seemed as impersonal as though he were someone who had just walked in off the street. She made him feel like an absolute stranger.

When she left, he was tempted to tell her that he would go to the place in Nyack, that he wanted to be taken care of, comforted. Then he said to himself angrily, You big fool! You've been taken care of for almost six weeks.

That afternoon, just before going off duty, she came to his room again. "I just stopped in to say good-by. I do with all my patients before they go."

"I'm not leaving till tomorrow."

"I'm off duty then. Well . . ." She hesitated. "Well, good-by. And good luck."

He was still listening to her footsteps down the hall when Dr. Ferguson came in to say that the X rays and tests were all right. "Where did you decide to go, by the way?" he asked.

"I'm going back home," Tom said.

"Good!" said the doctor.

After he left, Tom went out into the corridor and walked toward the sun porch, without the wheelchair and with no one at his elbow. He almost wished someone would try to stop him. But nobody did.

DISCUSSION FOR UNDERSTANDING

1. In addition to fine points of bronc riding, what two lessons does Dillon teach Tom?
2. What reasons does Tom give Meo for having come to Red Dillon's place? Why?
3. How does Tom change significantly while he and Red are at the Uvalde County Rodeo? What happens to Red shortly after they return home?
4. Why does Tom burn Meo's cabin? How does he acquire fame as Killer Tom Black?
5. Why is he hospitalized in New York City? Why does he reject Mary Redmond's offer of friendship?

4 The Mountains

He was the only passenger to get off at Pagosa. As the bus roared on toward Bayfield, he looked up and down the street. It had stores on only one side, above a slope and the tumbling mountain stream of the upper San Juan River. He wondered why he had come. It was only vaguely familiar, like a place in a long-forgotten dream. It wasn't home. But he had to come somewhere.

The few passersby, men in work clothes, stared at him, and he was conscious of his tan sport jacket, striped shirt, fancy-stitched boots. For years he had been stared at, but that was a part of being what he was. Now he felt self-conscious.

Two Indians were sitting on the curb in front of the hardware store. They, too, stared at him; and he had walked on past before he thought that he knew one of them. He reached back, found a name. Luther . . . Luther Spotted Dog. The boy he had thrown out of the room. Luther Spotted Dog, looking like a skid-row character!

He came to a market, Thatcher's Market, the sign said. He stared through the new, big window. The place was changed, but he was tempted to go in, to see if Jim Thatcher was still there. But even if he were, he probably wouldn't remember Bessie and little Tom.

Tom crossed the street, went down the slope to the San Juan and sat down. A startled magpie flew squawking from a nearby aspen. He watched the stream glinting in the sun.

He had wondered all the way from Denver to Wolf Creek Pass what it would be like. Then, as the road wound steeply down from the pass through the pines and aspens, the smells began to touch the quick of his being, the resinous pine smell, the damp woods smell, the clean smell of fast water. It was almost painful, the way it cut down through the layers of the years. He had finally had to close his eyes and make himself aware of the bus smells to ease it.

After half an hour he climbed back up the slope. He must find a cheap room somewhere. But first he had to get some other clothes. In these he looked like a millionaire dude.

In the clothing store, a clerk showed him a pair of tight-cut, fancy-stitched denim pants. "No. Work clothes," Tom said. He glanced down at himself and smiled. "I've got the dude kind."

Another man came in, a man in dusty levis and a sweat-stained black hat. He waited while the clerk showed Tom some levis cut for ease not style. Tom nodded. "And a couple of shirts, work boots and a brush jacket."

While he was trying on the boots, the clerk asked, "You staying around here?" It was only a conversational question.

"I used to live around here." Then, with a smile, "I used to herd sheep, over near Bayfield."

The clerk chuckled, knowing it was a joke. He knew the dress boots Tom had just taken off cost eighty-five dollars a pair.

When Tom paid his bill and turned to leave, the man in the dusty levis stopped him. "Did I hear you say you used to herd sheep? You wouldn't know where I could find a good herder?"

Tom shook his head. Then, trying to make contact with someone, something, here, he asked, "Why do you need a herder this time of year? Your flocks must be out on grass."

"They are. Up on summer range. But I lost one of my herders, name of Manuel, last week—fool shot himself in the foot. His flock's on the Piedra, up Horse Mountain. Know that country?"

"I've been there."

"Your face looks familiar," the man said. "Do I know you? My name's Jim Woodward."

"I'm Tom Black Bull." He said the name without thinking.

Woodward shook his head. "No, I guess not."

Tom started out of the store. Then, on impulse, he turned back. "I'll take that flock for you," he said.

Woodward stared at him, unbelieving. "You mean that?"

"Yes."

"Well, I'll be doggoned!" Woodward laughed. "I was thinking you were probably an actor from that movie crowd at Durango. If you don't mind my asking, what do you want to herd sheep for?"

"I broke a leg; doctor says it's all right to walk on, but I want something that's not too hard work for a while now."

"Well, come on! I've got a man from the home ranch up there holding the flock, but I need him in the hayfield. Throw your things in the jeep over there. I'll be right with you."

They headed west on the highway, and Woodward answered Tom's questions. He said the home ranch was in the San Luis Valley, over near Antonito. He ran twelve to fifteen thousand head of sheep, parceled out in flocks of two thousand head, and sent them out into the high country for summer range. He sold the lambs, after they were fattened, in the fall, wintered the ewes at the home ranch. "My supply man makes the rounds once a week," Woodward said. "If you know that Horse Mountain country, you'll make out."

At Piedra Town the jeep turned north into the hills on a track that couldn't even be called a wagon trail. Before Tom could believe it, remembering his trips on foot, they were making their way around Horse Mountain. They found the flock grazing at the far end of a big natural meadow edged by aspens and scattered pines.

Woodward drove past a tent beside a small creek, and across the meadow toward the sheep. A tall, sinewy youngster got to his feet and waved. Two dogs barked, and a saddle horse lifted its head.

"Dave," Woodward shouted, "this is Tom. He's going to take the flock. Come on in to camp and show him where things are."

Dave kept a neat camp. The Dutch oven beside the cooking fireplace was clean, the coffeepot airing, the skillet scoured. Dave showed Tom the tin-covered grub box, the cooler in the creek with meat and butter, the kerosene can for the lantern. He flipped open the tent flaps, pointed to the blankets neatly drawn up on the canvas cot. . . . "No bugs. Anything I hate is a lousy bed." He turned to the dogs. "Shep and Spot know the hand signals. And old Mac"—nodding toward the bay gelding—"is a lazy old plug, but he doesn't wander. You don't have to hobble him."

Woodward was getting restless. He handed Tom his clothes bag from the jeep, then picked up two boxes of .30-30 shells. "Almost forgot these. You may need them."

Dave nodded. "Manuel said there's a bear or two around. The rifle's in the saddle boot. She's sighted in at a hundred yards and shoots good and flat."

Dave and Woodward got into the jeep. "Anything comes up, ask Charley, the supply man. He'll be around Thursday," Woodward said. "Or is it Wednesday up here?"

"Thursday," Dave said.

Woodward was gunning the motor. Dave shouted, "Good luck!" as the jeep swung toward the valley.

Tom watched them out of sight, heard the motor a few minutes longer. Then he just stood and listened to the silence. It was unbelievable. He had forgotten. He heard the burbling of the creek, the whispering of the aspens, but those sounds were like a part of the silence, the peace.

One of the dogs nosed his hand. He rubbed its ear, then looked at the flock, be-

ginning to scatter into the edge of the timber. He ordered the dogs to go pull the flock together, but they were baffled by his words. Without thinking, he made the hand signals Albert Left Hand had used so long ago, and the dogs raced across the meadow.

He walked after them, leading the horse, and the grass underfoot felt strangely soft. It had been a long time since he walked on grass. His legs were stiff, but he walked all the way to the flock; then he let the horse graze.

He sat down, savoring the thin, pine-scented air, resting his eyes on the nearby green, the distant blue. He heard lambs bleating, ewes blatting their answers, and he smiled. He had come to rest, to work his way back to the arena. But he hadn't expected to go all the way back to his beginnings. He was

a sheepherder again, right back where he started.

The sun slipped down beyond the peaks to the west; he watered the sheep, then unsaddled the horse and hung the saddle from a rope over a low branch of a pine to keep it out of reach of porcupines.[1] When he had eaten a can of beans and fed the dogs, he walked around the flock. The stars glinted, the aspens whispered to the night. The sheep were quiet. He went back to the tent and was asleep in five minutes.

It was dawn when he wakened. The dogs, curled up beside the fireplace, stretched and

---

1. **to keep . . . porcupines,** attracted by the salt from the horse's sweat in the leather, the porcupines would chew on the saddle.

whined a greeting. He went to the creek, washed in the icy water and noticed the dew dripping from the bushes. He had forgotten how wet everything was in a mountain dawn, and how chilly. He built a fire, cooked bacon and pancakes. Jays screamed and one came close, expecting a handout. He tossed it a piece of pancake. Then he fried the last of the batter and flipped it out for the birds and chipmunks.

He got the stew meat from the cooler and set it to cook with onions and potatoes in the Dutch oven. Then, with old Mac and the dogs, he gathered the scattered sheep. Afterward he circled the meadow, orienting himself.

He couldn't remember this particular meadow, but he was sure he had been in the valley just below. He would recognize many places once he let the layers of time slip off. Time, he thought, was like the onions he had just peeled. Layer on layer, and to get down to the heart of things, you let the layers peel off, one by one.

He came to a place where the timbered slope fell away steeply and a wide vista opened to the northwest. The mountains in the distance seemed to stand in ranks, but two peaks loomed above the others. He smiled, knowing them: Granite Peak and Bald Mountain. He felt another layer of time peeling off.

The gossipy, friendly supply man, Charley, came and went. Tom put the fresh meat and butter in the cooler, stowed the groceries, and was glad to be alone. But that night he dreamed about Blue Elk. In the dream Tom was no longer a boy. He was a man, come back after the long years, but Blue Elk, wearing his derby and squeaky shoes, talked as though Tom were still a boy. "The old ways are gone," Blue Elk said. "You must learn the white man's reading and writing. You must learn to plow and plant." And Tom asked, "Did you learn to plow and plant, Blue Elk? Did you learn to read and write?"

"I am old," Blue Elk said. "I speak for your own good."

Tom said to him, "I learned. Don't you know who I am? I am Devil Tom, the Killer. I killed you, Blue Elk, and I would have killed Red Dillon, but he killed himself. Do you know that, Blue Elk?"

And the man in his dream wasn't Blue Elk at all. It was Red Dillon, laughing at him. "When you feel that way," Red said, "take it out on the horses."

"I took it out on the horses!" Tom cried.

Then there was Blue Elk again, and Tom was a boy chanting a song long forgotten of the rhythm of the earth and the days and the seasons. He chanted and Blue Elk began to sway and chant, humming the words he couldn't remember. His voice rose to a mournful howl that swelled and then faded. And Tom wakened to hear one of the dogs howling outside the tent.

At dawn next morning, Tom bathed in the icy creek, wondering why he did not wait, as usual, until the air was warm. But as he rubbed warmth into his body, he felt a glow that made him glad he had done it.

Riding out to the flock, he thought out why he had had that dream. The supply man reminded him of Red, and Red reminded him of Blue Elk. Nothing mysterious about that. This was just another day, he told himself sensibly, another day of getting ready to go back to the arena. Suddenly he smelled the arena, heard the sounds. He remembered the jolt of a bronc, sensed the pattern: lunge, lunge, lunge; half spin, side jump, lunge, lunge, lunge.

And caught himself. No need to go over that ride in the Garden again. He got to his feet, walked along the edge of the flock. He laughed to himself. Killer Tom herding sheep!

Weeks passed, marked only by Charley's visits. Jays came to share Tom's breakfast each morning, and chipmunks sat on his knee and ate crumbs from his hand. He plucked grass stems and wove a basket half the size of his fist, his fingers remembering a forgotten skill. Then he knew it was childish. But he hung it on a bush where a field mouse looking for a winter haven might find it.

One day he realized that the fawns he saw at the creek were losing their spots; the season was passing. A few mornings later he saw a white cap of snow on Pagosa Peak, far off to the northeast.

Then Woodward arrived again, alone in his jeep. After he had had a look at the sheep, he said, "Found some rodeo pictures the other day in an old magazine." Tom said nothing. "One bronc rider," Woodward said, "was a dead ringer for you. His name was Tom Black. Ever know him?"

"Yes."

"Quite a rider, I judge." Woodward smiled. "What ever happened to him?"

"He's still around."

Woodward seemed pleased with his discovery and didn't press Tom further. "We'll move the sheep down in a couple of weeks," he said. "I keep good herders on for the winter. Want to stay?"

"I've got other plans."

"So you think you're ready to ride again. Well, you've done a good job here. See you in a couple of weeks."

Now that he had committed himself, Tom studied the rodeo schedule. He decided Albuquerque was the place to start. He'd always had good luck there, and it was close by.

Two more weeks. He wished he had a string of horses to tune up with. But he hadn't, so he would have to start cold. You don't forget, though. It would all come back, just as soon as he straddled a bronc.

The final week he took the flock to a small north meadow from which he could see Granite Peak and Bald Mountain. Another month and they would be beautiful, with aspen gold and scrub-oak red. Then the leaves would fall and you would see forty miles on those perfect days when you felt that the whole world was yours, and you had been here forever. Mountains did that to you, these mountains. Then winter would come, snow and silence, and the deep, deep green of pine and spruce. He'd like to know winter here again. But he'd be in California then, getting ready to open the circuit in January.

He was looking at the sheep, not really seeing them, when old Mac snorted, and began to dance sideways, watching a tongue of brush that spilled out into the meadow from the uphill side. The dogs leaped up, bristling and growling.

Tom started to get to his feet, but he was still on his knees when the bear lunged out of the brush, moving with deceptive speed, into a little band of sheep. It slapped with one big paw. The herd blatted and ran in every direction, but a lamb lay there quivering, its neck broken.

Tom was on his feet now, shouting. The bear lifted its head, heaved itself up onto its hind legs for a better look, then dropped to all four again and nosed the lamb. Tom ran toward it, the dogs just ahead of him. The bear hesitated, then picked up the lamb in its jaws, and turned back into the brush.

Tom shouted to the dogs, "Gather them! Bring them in!" They hesitated and he gave the hand signals, and the dogs raced to try to pull the panicky flock together.

Tom hurried on after the bear, now crashing through the underbrush. The trail up the slope was easy to follow. In a hundred yards he came to a little opening in the timber, and there, not fifty yards away, he saw the bear. It stopped, the lamb in its jaw, and faced him across the clearing.

He stepped into the open and paused. The bear dropped the lamb, rumbled a deep growl, and took a few steps toward him. He shouted, "Stop that! Get out of here!" The bear stopped and seemed to bunch its muscles for a rush. It swung its head from side to side, backed away a few steps. Then it picked up the lamb, turned and went on up the mountain.

Tom watched it go, then wiped his face. He felt sweat flowing down his neck. His actions had been incredible. Following a bear that had just made a kill, into brush, without even a belt knife! Then walking out into the open with the bear not fifty yards away and hollering at it! What a fool he had been.

When he went back down the slope, the blatting sheep were still charging about, running from their own shadows, and the dogs were trying desperately to bunch them, almost as frantic as the sheep themselves. It was an hour before he had the flock back on the home meadow.

That evening, as he drank his coffee, the meadow shimmered peacefully in the moonlight with rolling puffs of mist, white as smoke, in the hollows, and the quivering aspen leaves reflecting the moonlight like spangles. But something nagged at Tom. It had been a big bear, high in the shoulders. Its head was broad and he was sure its face was dished. It had a grizzled look, almost frosty. Then he thought maybe it was the light that made it look grizzled. And he thought: You're telling yourself crazy stories. Forget it.

He rolled up in a blanket beside the fire, rifle at hand, and he told himself that if the bear came back he would shoot it.

Next morning, watching the sheep, he realized that he had been putting off something he had to do, something he had to know before he left here. And finally he rode old Mac to the little meadow of the afternoon before.

He went on foot into the brush, taking the rifle this time, and searched for tracks. In the little clearing he found it, the mark of a bear's hind paw. There was the long triangular sole print, the mark of five toes, but only four claw marks. The print was six inches across and at least ten inches long. He looked at it a long time. Then he rode back to the flock.

That evening, sitting beside the fire, he wished he hadn't found the track. Things kept coming back, and he knew why he hadn't gone into Thatcher's Market. Why rake up the old memories?

Sure, he was an Indian, a Ute. But he wasn't a clout Indian or a reservation Indian. He'd made something of himself, forced them to accept him. They would remember Killer Tom Black a long time.

Well, he had found the bear track, and he had gone over the memories, and that was that. He put the whole thing out of his head, and went to bed. And dreamed about his mother, and chanted the death chant and waked himself up. He went outside and looked at the peaceful night till the chill got to him.

Woodward arrived in the jeep with two men. The men would herd the flock on foot to the valley. There the jeep would meet them with the horse trailer and mounts for the herders. They'd camp that night and Woodward would drive Tom to Pagosa in the morning.

So Tom took one last look at Granite Peak and Bald Mountain and helped the others herd the flock down the valley, keeping the drags moving while the others, on the flanks of the flock, kept strays out of the deep timber. That night Woodward brought his plate and sat beside Tom at supper. "Meant to ask, did you have any bear trouble up there?"

"No trouble. I only saw one bear. It got a lamb—I didn't even get a shot—but it never came back."

"Probably the one Manuel saw. A big old cinnamon?"

"It could have been, maybe."

"It *had* to be," Woodward said. "There aren't any grizzlies left. Jim Boon shot the last one years ago over near Granite Peak."

"A big devil," Charley, the supply man, said. "Old as the hills. Scared the daylights out of me, just looking at the hide."

"Every now and then," Woodward said, "somebody still reports a grizzly. Always turns out to be a big cinnamon. See one in the right light, though, he can fool you. You ever see a grizzly?"

"Years ago."

"Dish-faced, high in the shoulder. Leaves tracks that long." He held his hands a foot apart.

Then the talk turned to wild game in general, but Tom was almost unaware of it. Everything had changed. He didn't know why. All he knew was that he had no choice. It was clear what he had to do now to end that last, nagging hurt.

The next morning he told Woodward he would go only as far as Piedra Town. Woodward paid him off there and said, "Well, good luck. I'll plan on watching you ride in Denver."

Woodward headed east toward Antonita, and Tom looked around for the grocery and the hardware store. Half an hour later, shouldering a pack, he picked up his rifle, and took the trail back to Horse Mountain.

He tried the old campsite but had to move to the little meadow because, even with the sheep gone, their smell persisted. He had been so used to it all summer that he hadn't noticed, but now it seemed to taint the air. He thought wryly that a good many things were like the sheep. You thought you got free of them, but the smell kept coming back. Well, that's why he was here. He had to get rid of the last memory smell before he went back to the arena. He was going to run that bear down, and if it was a grizzly, he was going to kill it.

The next morning he climbed the old trail. Half a mile beyond the clearing where he'd seen the bear, he found the remains of the lamb; two hoofs, a scattering of bones. He went on and in early afternoon found a big pine with claw marks as high on the trunk as he could reach. But the bear had rolled a rock away to get at ants and grubs; it could have stood on that rock first to make its claw marks. Tom circled the mountain without finding another sign.

He tried to figure it. A big cinnamon would have left more signs, for a cinnamon is just a black bear in a cinnamon color phase. All bears are wanderers, but blacks and cinnamons keep to a smaller range than grizzlies. If this had been a cinnamon, it would have come back for another lamb, or at least stayed around for a few days, hopeful. But an old grizzly will travel until it makes a big kill, like a deer. Then it eats, hides its kill, sleeps, and gorges again before moving on. It didn't add up either way.

In spite of Woodward, there might still be a wise old grizzly around that had outwitted the hunters; but the chance that it was the cub Tom had known was less than one in a hundred. A grizzly cub doesn't reach full growth till it is six or seven years old, and there would be special hazards for a cub that had been a pet. Some grizzlies live to be thirty, or more, but the chances of survival this long were slim, between hunters and bear-hating ranchmen.

All the odds said that the bear Tom saw was a big cinnamon. But he was going to run it down anyway.

Late the next day Tom found a place where a bear had rolled two rotting logs aside looking for beetles, then had dug out a den of marmots or chipmunks. It must have been a big bear to have moved those big logs. But it had been there several days before and its tracks were smudged.

Up West Fork a little way, he found a rotten stump that had been ripped apart, more of the bear's work. But again, no recognizable tracks. By all the signs, the bear was going northwest, away from Horse Mountain. Tom was already two hours from his camp, and as he worked his way wearily back there, he thought that if he were doing this the old way he would forget about camp, take his rifle and knife and stay with the trail till he caught up with the bear. And, he thought, sing the bear chant! But that's why he had come back—to be free at last of such things.

He took his gear down to West Fork, but during the next two or three days all he found was a place where the bear had dug camas[2] roots. Then a chill wind blew up and a cold rain began. He rigged his small tarp under a clump of spruces and sat there miserably, before a smoky, wet-wood fire, trying to make sense of what he was doing. He had hunted for a week and was no closer to the bear than when he started. Why, if it was a cinnamon, didn't it stay in one place? And why, if it was a grizzly, didn't it either move out or make a big kill? There were deer tracks around.

Thinking of deer, he was suddenly hungry for venison.[3] He was sick of soggy pancakes, bacon and trout. He would take a deer tomorrow. Butcher out a loin; one loin, that's all he needed. . . .

Then something deep inside said that it wasn't right to waste meat. "Waste meat, and what you take to use will soon begin to stink," said the grandmothers. He shook his head angrily. Superstition! What was he anyway? A clout Indian?

He felt the damp under him and moved to a drier place. He put more wet wood on the smoldering fire. No, he decided wryly, he wasn't a clout Indian or he would have picked

2. **camas** (kam'əs), a plant of the lily family that has edible roots.
3. **venison,** deer meat.

a better campsite and watched the weather signs. All right, so he had made a mistake. Another mistake. His first mistake was in coming back here.

Why had he come back, anyway? Because he saw a bear that might be a grizzly and he had to kill it. Why? Because he was Killer Tom Black and wanted to forget that he was an Indian, that's why!

He laughed at that, in derision. Devil-Killer Tom was just newspaper stuff. All right, so he had a grudge and took it out on the broncs. He lived up to his reputation, gave the crowds what they wanted. But he had got that out of his system now. He was going back to ride for points, for money. He would wind up his career with a record they would be shooting at for a long time to come.

The more he thought about what he was doing here in the woods, the more he felt like a fool. He had lived with everything that bear represented for a long time. He could go on living with it. As soon as this rain stopped he would pack up and get out.

Next day the sky cleared, and as Tom started out he saw a doe and two fawns come out of the brush to the stream. He raised his rifle, fired, and killed the doe with one clean shot while the fawns whirled back into the brush.

He butchered out a loin and took it back to his camp, exulting. He cooked a slice of venison. The first few mouthfuls tasted wonderful. Then the taste began to change, he didn't know why. Something was bothering him, and he was angry at himself for being bothered. He exclaimed aloud, "I didn't sing the deer chant, either!" Then he was silent, abashed.[4]

He cooked enough slices to last him on the trip back to Pagosa, stowed them in his pack, and left the rest of the loin on the ground, where the carrion eaters would soon dispose of it. Then he started down the trail beside the creek through crisp, almost frosty air.

He came to a place where the creek made a small mud flat, and his eyes caught something: bear tracks, big ones, full of water. They must have been made during the rain yesterday. One track was clean and plain; it was identical with the print he had seen on Horse Mountain.

He climbed the mountainside, away from the creek, finding signs here and there. A quarter of a mile up the slope he found a stump that had been ripped apart. Beside it was the mark of a forepaw, the rough half-moon of the palm, the round heel print, the round toe and claw prints. There was no doubt now. No cinnamon ever had such paws, such claws.

The trail wasn't more than thirty-six hours old. He forgot time until it was midafternoon and he was hungry and the pack straps were cutting into his shoulders. He went to a nearby rise and took his bearings.

To the southeast he saw Horse Mountain; to the northeast, Bald Mountain. He must be on the first bench of Granite Peak. He worked his way along the bench till he came to a place where a small creek bubbled across an opening with a thicket of lodgepole pines at the back, the kind of campsite he should have chosen in the first place. He cut poles and slung his tarp, made a fireplace, built a fire and warmed some venison. It didn't taste fresh, but it was food. That night he slept soundly, dog-tired.

The sun wakened him the next morning. After breakfast, he stowed everything except his knife and rifle and a small pack of venison under the tarp, and went back to where he had left the trail yesterday.

It was a cold trail now, but his eyes were sharpening and he saw little signs he had missed the day before: a broken bush here, a scuffed patch of gravel there. By afternoon he was able to lay out a line to follow; the bear had stopped wandering and was going some-

---

4. **abashed,** uneasy and somewhat ashamed.

where. He forced himself to stop thinking like a man and began to think the way a bear would. It hadn't made a big kill since he had been on the trail, and it was getting hungry for something more than grubs and camas roots and chipmunks. It would go down into the valley where the deer were. He laid out a line and followed it, and knew he was right, for down the slope he came to a pine tree where the bear had stopped to scratch its back. A few white-tipped hairs were still caught in the bark of a low branch. He would have missed that sign yesterday.

Then it was dusk, and he made a cold camp and ate some of the venison, though he didn't like the smell of it. Next morning he ate more of it before he went on. Then, following the bear's trail up Los Pinos Creek, he began to have cramps. He vomited, and felt better, but before he went on he opened the packet of meat. It had begun to stink. He threw the meat away, found a serviceberry bush and chewed a few twigs. The taste cleaned out his mouth and cleared his nose so that he could go on, following the bear tracks to the lower reaches of Bald Mountain.

The next morning he found where the bear had slept, beside a deer run, and that afternoon he found the place where the bear had made a kill. It had hidden in the brush until four deer came along—two does and two fawns. The bear had struck down a doe. The whole story was written unmistakably in frantic hoofprints, drying blood, broken brush, and in blood and deer hair on the brush through which the bear had dragged its kill up the mountainside.

He followed the trail, wary now, every sense alert. It was only a few hours old. Less than a hundred yards up the mountainside he found a cache. The bear had eaten its fill, then hidden the rest of the carcass under a heap of scratched-up dirt and leaves.

Cautiously he made his way around the edge of the clearing. The bear, gorged, would be sleeping nearby, but later it would return and eat again. Halfway around the clearing he found a tumbled heap of boulders. Moving like a shadow, he searched among them to make sure the bear wasn't there, then settled down, hidden in the rocks, to wait. The cache was in clear sight, not thirty yards away. His rifle would be deadly at that range.

At first the sun felt comfortably warm, but as the rocks caught and reflected the heat his head ached and his mouth was parched with thirst. He was hungry, too, but he could fast; thirst was the torture. He sucked a few pebbles, but that was little help.

His muscles were cramped from lying in one position, and he tried to stretch his legs; but that made a noise among the dry twigs lodged in the rocks, so he lay still again, enduring the aches. Nothing came to the cache but a squawking magpie. Then the sun slid down behind the shoulder of the mountain and he felt the quick chill of early autumn evening.

As the first stars appeared, a cold breeze flowed down the mountainside. He edged closer to the rocks to share the warmth they still held.

Night came. He tried to remember where the moon stood in its cycle, and knew that he hadn't really seen the moon in a long time. And knew that was wrong, since a man should have a friendship with the moon, the sun, the earth. He looked up and saw familiar stars. At least he hadn't forgotten the stars he once knew.

He waited, staring at the dark mound of the cache. Nothing moved, and his eyes wearied, lost their focus. He was tired. He dozed, jerked himself awake, then drifted into sleep.

He didn't know how long he slept, but when he wakened, a starved half-moon was in the sky and he could see the cache clearly through the moon shadows. It was undisturbed. He waited, but nothing came, and he drifted into weary half-sleep again.

Then something was there, just beyond

him in the moonlight. He tensed, gripped his rifle—and knew it was not the bear. It was a woman.

He couldn't see her features, but something deep inside him knew who she was. She was the mother; not his own mother but the All-Mother, the mothers and grandmothers all the way back to the beginning. She was chanting in a sad and pleading voice, and before he knew it, he was chanting with her. But time after time he forgot the words before he came to the meaningful parts. He was singing softly, as she sang, and at last he knew he was singing the bear chant. He closed his eyes and chanted, his voice remembering now, and when he had finished he opened his eyes and she was gone.

Only the moon was there, directly overhead. And his voice went on singing as though apart from him.

Then he saw the bear.

It came out of the shadows and crossed the opening, pausing to look and listen and nose the air. It was frosty in the moonlight, and its face was dished, not long and straight like a cinnamon bear's. It came slowly toward the cache, then stopped and stared at the rocks where he was hidden. It lifted its massive head and uttered a throaty growl and shifted its forefeet, lifting one, then the other.

He paused in his humming song and the bear's ears stiffened, alert. It rumbled the deep growl again, took two steps toward the rocks. He sang the low, humming song again, came to the meaningful part, sang it. The bear stopped, waited.

Still humming the bear chant, he carefully raised the rifle, resting it on the rocks. His eyes tried to sight it, but the light was dim. Wait, he told himself. Wait for more light.

And, the beat of the chant in his pulse, he waited, and the bear turned away and went to the cache. It tossed leaves and dirt aside with

sweeps of its powerful paws and, dragging the carcass into the open, it began to eat.

He watched, and his humming slowly died away, but the beat was still in him. The bear paused in its eating from time to time and looked at the rocks, now accepting his silence as a part of the night. His pulse drummed the beat of the chant and time passed. At last, first light of dawn dimmed the stars overhead, and the moon began to fade. He could see the rifle's sights clearly. It was time to kill.

He pressed his cheek to the rifle's stock, aimed low in the shoulder where the heart lay. He tried to squeeze the trigger, but his finger refused.

He closed his eyes, fighting with himself. "I came to kill the bear!" His throbbing pulse asked, "Why?" He answered, "I must!" And again his pulse beat, "Why?" He answered, "To be myself!" And the pulse asked, "Who—are—you?" He had no answer. Angrily he said, "This bear has made trouble!" The question beat back, "To—whom?" And his own bitter answer, "To me!" Then the question, as before, "Who—are—you?" And he, having no answer he could face, said, whispering the words aloud, "This bear did not make trouble. The trouble is in me." And he lowered the rifle.

It was almost sunrise. The bear nosed the carcass, looked at the rocks, lifted its lip and sniffed the air. Then it turned and crossed the clearing to the trees whence it had come in the moonlight.

He watched it go, and when it was gone he asked himself if he had seen a bear at all. He looked at the rocks and trees and sky and he felt a stranger here. He waited, expecting the feeling to pass, but when he touched the rocks with his hand they were cold and unfriendly. When he moved his cramped legs the dry twigs made a harsh, rasping sound. When he got to his feet a jay screamed at him, saying he did not belong here.

He rubbed life into his numb legs and went down the slope. The bushes resented him and the rocks bruised his knees as he knelt at the creek to drink. The water made him feel sick. I am weak from hunger, he told himself.

He watched beside the deer run for a time but nothing came, so he stumbled noisily, like a drunken man, across the valley. He found nothing to eat, not even dried berries, and the twigs he chewed were bitter in his mouth.

Darkness came, and the stars appeared. He tried to find one to guide him to his camp, but they wavered in the sky. As he waited for them to settle into place again, he heard the All-Mother singing the star chant, the chant to the night. He began to sing with her and after a little while the stars were steady again. He chose one to guide by, and at last he was going up the long slope of Granite Peak, climbing through aspens and pines which still said silently that he was a stranger there.

But he hoarsely whispered the star chant, and the stars stayed in their places.

It was almost morning when he came to his camp. He drank from the creek, lay down, wrapped his blanket around him and dozed. Then, when dawn lightened the sky he sat up, knowing what he must do. He stripped himself naked and went to a rocky pool in the creek.

The cold, black water drove fiery needles into his legs. He splashed it on his belly and chest as he sat in the knee-deep pool. The cold was like knives; pain sliced at his very vitals. Then it eased, and he scrubbed himself with handfuls of sand. As the sun was about to rise he got out and rubbed life back into his legs. Then he sat on a rock facing the east. He chanted the song to a new day, to the sun and the earth and everything between. Then, naked and unarmed, he started up the mountain.

All morning he made his way through brush and timber, over rocks and gravelly slopes. Noon came and he stopped to rest, and he looked up at the sun and thought how round it is and how round is the path it follows. He looked at the blue roundness of the sky and the roundness of the aspen trunks. He closed his eyes and sang a silent chant to the great roundness of life. When he had finished he lay close to the earth and let the sun beat on his back. He lay there a long time, the earth and the sun holding him between them. Then he went on.

The last part was a difficult climb. It was already deep dusk in the valleys when he reached the top. He stood there and watched the sun sink behind a cloud on the horizon and send flaming colors racing across the sky, gold, then pink, then purple. But he sang no song. He had come to listen, not to talk.

When the first stars appeared he went down the mountainside till he came to a clump of junipers with a mat of prickly needles beneath them. He crawled in and lay down, weak with fasting and fatigue. His muscles ached, and chill bit at his flesh. The prickles in his bed bit into his skin. But he slept.

Dreams came—first, unwanted ones. He was in the corral at the agency, riding a huge, frosty bear, and he lashed it with a rawhide quirt. It lunged three times and side-jumped, and now it was a big roan bronc. It fell and he was trapped; but he crawled free, and there was Red Dillon, saying, "You do like I say, or I'll break your neck!" He struck Red with his fist, and Red was not there. A bronc was struggling on the ground; it sighed and was dead.

He wakened, so tense his muscles screamed with pain. Then he felt the cold and the fiery bite of the needles and he drew his knees up to his chest to feel his own warmth and slept again, and dreamed.

And now he was alone, walking over the earth in the night. He came to a mountain and he said, "I have forgotten who I am." There was no answer. He said, "I was the boy who did what Blue Elk said I must do." Again there was no answer. "I went with Red Dillon and did what he said I must do." Still there was no answer.

"I killed as they taught me to kill!" he cried.

And at last the mountain's voice asked, "Why?"

He was silent a long time. Then he said, "I had to kill the past. I had to be myself. And now there is nothing left to kill except myself, for I did not kill the bear."

And the mountain asked, "Who are you?"

He could not answer, but a voice answered for him. "He is my son." It was the voice of the All-Mother.

Then he wakened and the white light of truth and understanding was all around him. And he saw frost on all the juniper branches, shining in the light of dawn.

He lay there, at first not knowing where he was, then remembering. He crept out from the junipers, too stiff with cold to stand until he had rubbed his legs with handfuls of frosty needles. He washed himself with the needles, and when the sun rose he stared at it till his eyes were blinded, and then sang the chant to the new day. Then he went back down the mountain, so weak from fasting that he had to stop often and rest.

At his camp he opened his pack of supplies, but he did not eat. He took a handful of flour and went down the creek to a place where deer might come to drink. He smoothed a patch of sand with his palm, then took a stick and drew a picture of a deer. He spoke to the picture, calling it by name, and said he needed its help. He said he had killed its sister and wasted her parts because he had forgotten who he was. He said that a man's memory is a faltering thing, but that he had

purified himself and now he remembered. He scattered the flour over the picture, his offering to it, and he sang the deer chant.

He said, "I will be quick and merciful, Brother Deer, and I will use your parts as I should."

He slept till late afternoon, still fasting. Then he put on a breechclout, took the rifle and the knife and returned to the place where he had drawn the picture in the sand. He sat down in the brush and made himself a part of the earth and the evening.

Just before the light was too dim to see the rifle's sights they came to drink, two does and a buck. His hands were quivering, but he forced himself to steadiness, and the shot shook the earth. The does were gone in one quick rush, but the buck went to its knees and fell with a long sigh of expended breath. Then there was a silence.

He crossed the stream and slit the buck's throat, and he whispered, "Earth, drink this blood that now belongs to you." He butchered the buck the old way and carried every part back to his camp. Then he broke his fast. He cooked and ate, and he slept.

He built his lodge on Granite Peak, but first he set up a drying rack, sliced the venison into thin strips and hung it to cure in the smoke of a smudged fire. He fleshed the hide and started the tanning with a mixture of liver and brains. He put aside sinews for sewing, saved antlers and bones from which to make awls, scrapers and other tools, boiled out and saved marrow fat.

Then he cut lodgepoles in the pine thicket, leaving no obvious gaps. He built the lodge and banked it with brush and earth and leaves to make it winter-warm and to mask it on the mountainside. Then he took another deer, cured more meat for the winter; and he made rawhide for moccasin soles and snowshoe webbing, leather for winter moccasins and leggings. He caught trout and smoked them. He gathered sweet acorns and piñon nuts[5] and wild white pea seeds and elk-thistle roots. He cut and trimmed ironwood for snowshoe frames. He stowed firewood in the lodge.

Aspen leaves fell and the dark flame of the scrub oaks faded to the brown of their bitter little acorns. The season turned to that pause when the mountains rest between summer and winter and a man knows, if there is any understanding in him, the truth of his own being.

And one afternoon, sitting in the sun, sewing the sole on a moccasin, he thought again of the bear. He began examining why he was driven to the hunt in the first place, why he had acted as he did.

Searching for the whys, he reached back to beginnings. To the cub, to Blue Elk, to the school, to the quirting and the denial in the moonlight.[6] That was where the hunt began. That was when he began hunting down all the painful things of the past, to kill them.

And one by one, over the years, he did kill them. All except the bear. All except his childhood, his own heritage. Blue Elk, Benny Grayback, Neil Swanson, Red Dillon, Meo—he paused, considering Meo; then nodded, knowing he killed Meo too when he burned his garden patch.

No, he didn't shoot or knife any of them to death. There are other ways to kill. He killed them, the memory of them, in the arena, when he became Killer Tom Black.

And then he had come back to the mountains, come back to heal his body so he could go on trying to kill the one thing left—the bear, his own boyhood. And he met the bear, and tried to go away again thinking he could forget the bear; and had to come back knowing he couldn't forget.

He had thought he could make an end to his childhood with a bullet, only to find, when the moment came, that he had done his kill-ing. He had killed so many memories that there was nothing left to kill except himself. And not knowing who he was, forgetting even his own identity, he didn't kill the bear. He went in search of himself.

He sewed to the end of the sinew and took another strand, remembering the penance trip up the mountain. He had been so weak from fasting that he had done what he had to do by instinct, knowing that this was the answer, the ultimate hunt. And he had accomplished on that trip what he had set out to accomplish, unknowing, on the bear hunt. He had killed the self he had been for so long. He had killed Tom Black.

And now he remembered a chipmunk he had had as a small boy. He had asked his mother the meaning of the stripes on the chipmunk's back. Those stripes, she said, were the paths from its eyes, with which it sees now and tomorrow, to its tail, which is always behind it and a part of yesterday.

He had laughed at that and said he wished he, too, had a tail. His mother had said, "When you are a man you will have a tail, though you will never see it. You will always have something behind you."

Now he understood. Time lays scars on a man like the chipmunk's stripes, paths that lead from where he is now back to where he came from, from the eyes of his knowing to the tail of his remembering.

He had had a long journey; the long and lonely journey a man must make when he denies his own past, refuses to face his own identity. There was no question now who he was. The All-Mother's words, in his vision, stated it beyond denial: "He is my son." He

---

5. **piñon** (pin′yən) **nuts,** refers to the edible seeds of various low-growing nut pines.
6. **denial . . . moonlight,** refers to the time when Tom had used the quirt and chased away the bear when it came back to him at the school in Ignacio.

was a Ute, an Indian, and nothing would ever change that. Blue Elk's way and Red Dillon's way could not erase the simple truth of the chipmunk's stripes, the ties that bind a man to his own small part of the enduring roundness.

He finished the moccasin and examined it, satisfied because his hands remembered and his mind had begun to accept. The moccasin was a part of the acceptance. He could never again be a clout Indian, but for a time he had to go back to the old ways, to make his peace with himself. He had begun to feel that peace, at last. In time, he would go down to Pagosa, talk with Jim Thatcher, if he was still alive, learn what happened to Blue Elk, and try to understand why he sold his own people as he did. He would go to the school eventually, and see what was happening there now, try to understand that, too.

But never again would he go back to the arena. He was no longer Tom Black. He was Tom Black Bull, a man who knew and was proud of his own inheritance, who had come to the end of his long hunt.

He went into the lodge, put the moccasin carefully with its mate. Then he went out into the evening and up the slope a little way to a big rock where he could see Horse Mountain and Bald Mountain and the whole tumbled range. He sat there and watched the shadows darken in the valleys; when the sun had set he whispered the chant to the evening. It was an old chant, a very old one, and he sang it not to the evening but to himself, to be sure he would never again forget.

DISCUSSION FOR UNDERSTANDING

1. Why does Tom return to Pagosa? What work does he find there? Describe his feelings and dreams at the sheep camp.
2. Why doesn't he leave the area after he turns down Woodward's job offer?
3. Why can't Tom bring himself to shoot the bear? What admission does he make to himself at this time?
4. Who or what finally answers Tom's question as to his identity?
5. What did Tom decide was his reason for becoming a horse killer? What did the bear symbolize? What did the penance trip up the mountain accomplish?
6. What do you suppose are Tom's plans for the future?

READING FOR DETAILS

Back to His Beginnings

It was from his mother, Bessie, that Tom Black Bull learned the old ways of his people. She gave him his birthright by teaching him the songs and rituals that were in the tradition of the Ute. Tricked by Blue Elk, a member of his own tribe, into leaving his home, Tom loses his sense of identity. After years of being spiritually lost, he regains his identity in a dream, when the All-Mother claims him by saying, "He is my son."

When The Legends Die is a story filled with symbolic meaning. It is an odyssey in that Tom Black Bull travels far from the land of his beginnings and then returns. In his early years, those who influence him most are his mother and father. Later on, Blue Elk and Red Dillon both play major roles in shaping his attitudes. In addition to these two people, Tom Black Bull encounters a number of others who contribute to the shaping of his life. Identify the following characters and discuss their significance in Tom Black Bull's life:

1. Charley Huckleberry
2. Jim Thatcher
3. Benny Grayback
4. Luther Spotted Dog
5. Miss Rowena Ellis
6. Albert Left Hand
7. Doc Wilson
8. Meo
9. Dr. Ferguson
10. Jim Woodward

READING FOR MEANING

Discuss the following as they relate to the novel:

1. The white person is by nature more deceitful than the American Indian.
2. American Indians should be encouraged to live in the "old ways" on reservations.
3. The surest way for anyone from a minority group to achieve success in the world is in professional sports or entertainment.
4. People become lost when they reject the spiritual side of their nature.
5. A period of questioning and unrest is necessary to confirm any individual's belief in his or her own identity.

READING FOR APPRECIATION

Style

A number of qualities are obvious in Hal Borland's writing. He has a deep knowledge of the people and the country he writes about. The vivid imagery he uses particularly demonstrates his familiarity with the locale. He knows the terrain, the plant life, and the seasonal changes. His attitude toward his subject matter is almost immediately obvious, too. He presents his story from the point of view of the American Indian, and does so with compassion.

1. In writing from the American Indian point of view, Hal Borland adopts a style that the reader accepts as being Indian-like. Quickly skim the opening scene with George and Bessie. How does the dialogue strike you as being typically Indian?
2. Look at the last line of part 1 (p. 514). How does this support the conclusions you reached in your answer to question 1?
3. From what source are almost all of Hal Borland's images drawn? Discuss one example that you find particularly vivid.

4. Explain how the author's attitude is revealed in the following passages:
   a. For two years, the sawmill had taken money from her man's pay for rent and for the old iron bed, the dresser with the broken leg, the four chairs, the table, the stove. By now, they owned the two blankets, and that was all she was taking. (p. 501)
   b. George gave the money to Blue Elk and he took them to the preacher. The preacher said words and wrote on a paper and they were married. Then he asked what they wanted to name the boy. Bessie said, "He is Little Black Bull. He will choose when he needs another name." The preacher said he must have another name now, and that Thomas was a good name. Bessie said it didn't matter because Little Black Bull would pick his own name when the time came. So the preacher sprinkled water on the boy's head and George got no pay at all the next week because of that five dollars. (p. 503)
   c. "I came here," he said, "to tell them of the old ways."
      "I want to hear," she said, "but first I will tell you of the new ways." She started to tell him about the school.
      He cut her off. "I do not need these things."
      She was a patient woman. She smiled, and as her class filed into the room, she said: "We have a new boy, Thomas Black Bull. He will tell us about his interesting life, but first we must teach him some English. We will start today with oral review." The boys groaned, but she kept them at vocabulary drill while Thomas stood by the window. When it was over, Miss Ellis went to him. "You see, it is not so hard to learn new things. You learned something today. I know this." (p. 517)

Gaining Insight

To review, insight is defined as "seeing into inner character or underlying truth." Discuss what the following excerpts tell you about American Indian character and beliefs:

1. It was good to know the roundness, the completeness, again; not the sharp squareness of houses and streets. (p. 504)
2. She caught four fish and went back past the grassy place and thanked the grasshoppers before she cleaned the fish. (p. 504)
3. He said, "This morning I met a she-bear, a grizzly. . . . We talked to each other. When I killed the deer I left part of the meat for that she-bear. I shall call myself Bear's Brother." (p. 507)
4. For small griefs you shout, but the big griefs must be borne alone, inside. (p. 520)
5. Why should anyone rip up grass and make the earth grow something else? . . . When you plowed up the grass you were making the earth into something it did not want to be. (p. 522)
6. "He lay there a long time, the earth and the sun holding him between them." (p. 553)
7. "He came to a mountain and he said, 'I have forgotten who I am.'" (p. 553)

LANGUAGE AND VOCABULARY

A. In the following sentences, the italicized words are slang:

> Why, you dirty, double-crossing, *lousy* little Indian.
>
> Your redheaded partner, he said, is in the *hoosegow*.
>
> Dillon was a *tinhorn* gambler. . . .

Slang refers to a nonstandard vocabulary consisting largely of coined words, arbitrarily changed words, and extravagant, forced, or humorous figures of speech. Generally speaking, slang develops from the attempt to find fresh, catchy, vigorous, vivid, or funny expressions. Frequently, a slang expression has only temporary circulation, possibly because of overuse. But sometimes it gains formal status and enters into the standard vocabulary. However, some slang words retain their nonstandard position even though they are frequently used. Language scholars generally agree that slang has a rightful place in English. They point out that whether or not slang is appropriate depends on several factors, including the following:

   a. the occasion
   b. the person who is spoken to
   c. the person who is speaking
   d. the circumstances under which one is speaking

As a general rule, slang is used in casual, everyday situations rather than in more formal ones. Keeping the above information in mind, see whether you can answer these questions: What popular slang words do you currently use? What other examples of slang can you find in *When the Legends Die*? How are argot, cant, shoptalk, and jargon related to slang?

B. As you may have learned from previously reading in this book, Spanish has contributed to the word stockpile of English. The Spanish word may be integrated into English in its original form or it may be changed somewhat to make it more English-sounding. In *When the Legends Die*, there are several words of Spanish origin, for example, *canyon, cinch, rodeo, corral,* and *bronc[o]*. Most of these words, as you can see, are related to ranch life. Some other Spanish loanwords in this category are *buckaroo, lariat, lasso, wrangler, ranch, stampede,* and *quirt* ("riding whip"). Try to determine the meaning of the italicized Spanish loanword in each of the following sentences:

1. In the old West, *vigilantes* often did more harm than good.
2. The posse tracked down the *desperado*.

3. Held *incommunicado,* the suspect refused to talk to the authorities.
4. For breaking the law, he was detained in the *calaboose.*
5. He had just been released from the *hoosegow* in another town.

C. Like other ethnic groups—for example, the Spanish, as you saw earlier—American Indians have enriched American English through numerous loanwords. These words, many of which have been changed from their original form, come from a variety of American-Indian languages. Some examples may be cited from *When the Legends Die: moccasin, tomahawk, Ute, chipmunk,* and *squaw.* Some other Indian words are *papoose, persimmon, moose, raccoon, pone, hickory,* and *wigwam.* Using your dictionary, try to answer the following questions which involve Indian words:

1. In what state(s) would you be most likely to find a *sequoia?*
2. What is a *mackinaw* used for?
3. What kind of activity goes on in a *caucus?*

COMPOSITION

As mentioned in Reading for Details, page 556, Thomas Black Bull undertakes an odyssey, traveling far from the land of his beginnings and then returning. As you recall, Odysseus goes on a similar journey in Homer's timeless epic the *Odyssey,* which you read in the unit CALL TO ADVENTURE. In the ancient Greek epic, the gods take part in the story, deciding the successes and failures of human beings. For example, in the *Odyssey,* Poseidon, god of the sea, works against Odysseus while Athene, goddess of wisdom, comes to his rescue when he needs help. The many gods and goddesses who dwelt on Mt. Olympus were of great importance to the ancient Greeks.

Because Thomas Black Bull is deeply religious in the way of his people, his temporary alienation from his tribal beliefs and his rejection of the spiritual side of his being cause him to suffer.

The seven excerpts from the story listed under Gaining Insight, page 558, reveal much of this contemporary Indian hero's spiritual relationship to the Great Mystery of his universe. Using these story excerpts as an aid, write a short paper in which you compare Tom Black Bull's religious beliefs to those of the ancient Greeks.

BIOGRAPHICAL NOTE

Hal Borland (1900–1978) was born in Sterling, Nebraska, and moved with his family when he was nine years old to a homestead farm on the prairie of eastern Colorado. As a result of his life in this environment he became interested in wildlife, conservation, and the history of the West. He often used the pen name Ward West. A regular contributor to magazines and newspapers, he wrote many books, several in collaboration with his wife, Barbara Dodge Borland. Among the books they wrote together are *The Dog Who Came to Stay, The Seventh Winter,* and *The Amulet.* He recounted his own early days in *High, Wide, and Lonesome.* He also wrote a book of essays, *Homelands: A Report from the Country.* For the last several years of his life, Borland lived with his wife on a farm in Connecticut.

The Strange
and Eerie

The Coming of the Plague

September was when it began.
Locusts dying in the fields; our dogs
Silent, moving like shadows on a wall;
And strange worms crawling; flies of a kind
We had never seen before; huge vineyard
    moths;   5
Badgers and snakes, abandoning
Their holes in the field; the fruit gone rotten;
Queer fungi sprouting; the woods
Covered with spiderwebs; black vapors
Rising from the earth—all these,   10
And more, began that fall. Ravens flew
    round
The hospital in pairs. Where there was water,
We could hear the sound of beating clothes
All through the night. We could not count
All the miscarriages, the quarrels, the
    jealousies.   15
And one day in a field I saw
A swarm of frogs, swollen and hideous.
Hundreds upon hundreds, sitting on each
    other,
Huddled together, silent, ominous,
And heard the sound of rushing wind.   20

WELDON KEES

Reprinted from COLLECTED POEMS OF WELDON KEES, Revised Ed.,
1975 by permission of University of Nebraska Press. © 1962, 1975 by University of Nebraska Press.

CHURCH BELLS RINGING, RAINY WINTER NIGHT
Charles Burchfield
Cleveland Museum of Art

The eyes grow wide! Breathing almost stops! But the eyes continue to move across that first page and to the next. This is a picture of self-torture, a torture enjoyed by all who like to read stories of the unknown, the mystifying, the terrifying, the strange and eerie.

Weldon Kees tells of unusual things happening in "The Coming of the Plague"—dying locusts, black vapors rising from the earth, a swarm of hideous, bloated frogs; everywhere omens of horror to come. Beginning with this poem, the selections in THE STRANGE AND EERIE have been chosen deliberately for the effect they will have upon readers. For this reason, the unit concludes with a group of selections by Edgar Allan Poe, an author who believed the most important consideration when writing a story or poem was the effect it would have upon readers. And the effect he was a master at achieving was that of horror.

But lest readers be too horrified—before they reach the Poe section, "Once Upon a Midnight"—they will find a number of selections that will leave them wondering: Could this be? Will this ever happen? What lies in the unknown?

UNIT TECHNIQUES

The techniques emphasized in this first section of THE STRANGE AND EERIE are ones with which you are already familiar. They are introduced and explained near the beginning of the text (p. 3) with the selections in CALL TO ADVENTURE.

SUSPENSE

Exploring the strange and eerie is a form of adventure. In writing stories on this theme, authors must build *suspense*, "a state of excited uncertainty." In "August Heat," the first story in this unit, the main character, Withencroft, states his purpose to be a straightforward accounting of events as they had taken place on a certain day. However, the opening line deliberately sets a trap to catch the reader's interest by describing that day as having been "the most remarkable" in his life. Because readers feel this statement promises that something truly unusual is to be told, they are interested in learning more about the character telling the story.

FORESHADOWING

In maintaining suspense as the story progresses, the author makes use of the technique of *foreshadowing*, "planting hints of dangers and perils that lie ahead." Even before Withencroft begins to describe the man he has drawn, for example, he classifies the man as a criminal. The mere use of the word "criminal" deepens interest, even though this is too early for the reader to understand the significance the term will later have.

"August Heat" demonstrates the use of foreshadowing to an extraordinary extent. Even the explanation the mason gives as to the effect weather has upon flawed marble foreshadows the effect weather may have upon a person less than perfect "beneath the surface" with regard to emotional stability. After you read the story, discuss those things about the gravestone and its inscription that make it an excellent example of foreshadowing.

IMAGINATIVE LANGUAGE

In most stories that have appeal because they are about things which are haunting, fearsome, or unexplainable, there is *imaginative language*, "words used so that they arouse the reader's feelings." This is exemplified in "August Heat" when the author describes the awful heat that came up from the dusty asphalt pavement as "an almost palpable wave." Many persons have experienced the sensation of being drowned in waves of heat. For this reason, the author's comparison helps the reader *feel* what the character feels.

In the same paragraph that the author describes the heat as rising from the pavement as an almost palpable wave, he also uses imaginative language to help his reader *see* the clouds. After you read the story, try to recall how he described them. Discuss.

THE TEMPTATION OF SAINT ANTHONY (detail)
Pieter Bruegel the Elder
National Gallery of Art, Washington, D.C.
Samuel H. Kress Collection

For some time I sat in silence.
Then a cold shudder ran down my spine.

AUGUST HEAT
W. F. Harvey

Phenistone Road, Clapham, August 20th, 190—. I have had what I believe to be the most remarkable day in my life, and while the events are still fresh in my mind, I wish to put them down on paper as clearly as possible.

Let me say at the outset that my name is James Clarence Withencroft.

I am forty years old, in perfect health, never having known a day's illness.

By profession I am an artist, not a very successful one, but I earn enough money by my black-and-white work to satisfy my necessary wants.

My only near relative, a sister, died five years ago, so that I am independent.

I breakfasted this morning at nine, and after glancing through the morning paper I lighted my pipe and proceeded to let my mind wander in the hope that I might chance upon some subject for my pencil.

The room, though door and windows were open, was oppressively hot, and I had just made up my mind that the coolest and most comfortable place in the neighborhood would be the deep end of the public swimming bath, when the idea came.

I began to draw. So intent was I on my work that I left my lunch untouched, only stopping work when the clock of St. Jude's struck four.

The final result, for a hurried sketch, was, I felt sure, the best thing I had done.

It showed a criminal in the dock immediately after the judge had pronounced sentence. The man was fat—enormously fat. The flesh hung in rolls about his chin; it creased his huge, stumpy neck. He was clean shaven (perhaps I should say a few days before he must have been clean shaven) and almost bald. He stood in the dock, his short, clumsy fingers clasping the rail, looking straight in front of him. The feeling that his expression conveyed was not so much one of horror as of utter, absolute collapse.

There seemed nothing in the man strong enough to sustain that mountain of flesh.

I rolled up the sketch, and without quite knowing why, placed it in my pocket. Then with the rare sense of happiness which the knowledge of a good thing well done gives, I left the house.

I believe that I set out with the idea of calling upon Trenton, for I remember walking along Lytton Street and turning to the right along Gilchrist Road.

From there onward I have only the vaguest recollections of where I went. The one thing of which I was fully conscious was the awful heat that came up from the dusty asphalt pavement as an

SACRED TO THE MEMORY
OF
JAMES CLARENCE WITHENCROFT
BORN JAN. 18TH 1860
HE PASSED AWAY VERY SUDDENLY
ON AUGUST 20TH, 190—
"IN THE MIDST OF LIFE WE ARE IN DEATH"

almost palpable wave. I longed for the thunder promised by the great banks of clouds that hung low over the western sky.

I must have walked five or six miles, when a small boy roused me from my reverie by asking the time.

It was twenty minutes to seven.

When he left me I began to take stock of my bearings. I found myself standing before a gate that led into a yard bordered by a strip of thirsty earth, where there were flowers, purple stock and scarlet geranium. Above the entrance was a board with the inscription—

CHAS. ATKINSON
MONUMENTAL MASON
WORKER IN ENGLISH AND
ITALIAN MARBLES

From the yard itself came a cheery whistle, the noise of hammer blows, and the cold sound of steel meeting stone.

A sudden impulse made me enter.

A man was sitting with his back toward me, busy at work on a slab of curiously veined marble. He turned round as he heard my steps and stopped short.

It was the man I had been drawing, whose portrait lay in my pocket.

He sat there, huge and elephantine, the sweat pouring from his scalp, which he wiped with a red silk handkerchief. But though the face was the same, the expression was absolutely different.

He greeted me smiling, as if we were old friends, and shook my hand.

I apologized for my intrusion.

"Everything is hot and glary outside," I said. "This seems an oasis in the wilderness."

"I don't know about the oasis," he replied, "but it certainly is hot. Take a seat, sir!"

He pointed to the end of the gravestone on which he was at work, and I sat down.

"That's a beautiful piece of stone you've got hold of," I said.

He shook his head. "In a way it is," he answered; "the surface here is as fine as anything you could wish, but there's a big flaw at the back, though I don't expect you'd ever notice it. I could never make really a good job of a bit of marble like that. It would be all right in the summer like this; it wouldn't mind the blasted heat. But wait till the winter comes. There's nothing quite like frost to find out the weak points in stone."

"Then what's it for?" I asked.

The man burst out laughing.

"You'd hardly believe me if I was to tell you it's for an exhibition, but it's the truth. Artists have exhibitions, so do grocers and butchers; we have them too. All the latest little things in headstones, you know."

He went on to talk of marbles, which sort best withstood wind and rain, and which were easiest to work; then of his garden and a new sort of carnation he had bought. At the end of every other minute he would drop his tools, wipe his shining head, and curse the heat.

I said little, for I felt uneasy. There was something unnatural, uncanny, in meeting this man.

I tried at first to persuade myself that I had seen him before, that his face, unknown to me, had found a place in some out-of-the-way corner of my memory, but I knew that I was practicing little more than a plausible piece of self-deception.

Mr. Atkinson finished his work, spat on the ground, and got up with a sigh of relief.

"There! what do you think of that?" he said, with an air of evident pride.

The inscription which I read for the first time was this—

SACRED TO THE MEMORY
OF
JAMES CLARENCE WITHENCROFT.
BORN JAN. 18TH, 1860.
HE PASSED AWAY VERY SUDDENLY
ON AUGUST 20TH, 190–

"In the midst of life we are in death."

For some time I sat in silence. Then a cold shudder ran down my spine. I asked him where he had seen the name.

"Oh, I didn't see it anywhere," replied Mr. Atkinson. "I wanted some name, and I put down the first that came into my head. Why do you want to know?"

"It's a strange coincidence, but it happens to be mine."

He gave a long, low whistle.

"And the dates?"

"I can only answer for one of them, and that's correct."

"It's a rum go!" he said.

But he knew less than I did. I told him of my morning's work. I took the sketch from my pocket and showed it to him. As he looked, the expression of his face altered until it became more and more like that of the man I had drawn.

"And it was only the day before yesterday," he said, "that I told Maria there were no such things as ghosts!"

Neither of us had seen a ghost, but I knew what he meant.

"You probably heard my name," I said.

"And you must have seen me somewhere and have forgotten it! Were you at Clacton-on-Sea last July?"

I had never been to Clacton in my life. We were silent for some time. We were both looking at the same thing, the two dates on the gravestone, and one was right.

"Come inside and have some supper," said Mr. Atkinson.

His wife is a cheerful little woman, with the flaky red cheeks of the country-bred. Her husband introduced me as a friend of his who was an artist. The result was unfortunate, for after the sardines and watercress had been removed, she brought me out a Doré Bible,* and I had to sit and express my admiration for nearly half an hour.

I went outside and found Atkinson sitting on the gravestone smoking.

We resumed the conversation at the point we had left off.

"You must excuse my asking," I said, "but do you know of anything you've done for which you could be put on trial?"

He shook his head.

"I'm not a bankrupt, the business is prosperous enough. Three years ago I gave turkeys to some of the guardians at Christmas, but that's all I can think of. And they were small ones, too," he added as an afterthought.

He got up, fetched a can from the porch, and began to water the flowers. "Twice a day regular in the hot weather," he said, "and then the heat sometimes gets the better of the delicate ones. And ferns, they could never stand it. Where do you live?"

I told him my address. It would take an hour's quick walk to get back home.

"It's like this," he said. "We'll look at the matter straight. If you go back home

---

*Doré Bible, a Bible illustrated by Paul Gustave Doré (1833–1883), the French artist.

tonight, you take your chance of accidents. A cart may run over you, and there's always banana skins and orange peel, to say nothing of fallen ladders."

He spoke of the improbable with an intense seriousness that would have been laughable six hours before. But I did not laugh.

"The best thing we can do," he continued, "is for you to stay here till twelve o'clock. We'll go upstairs and smoke; it may be cooler inside."

To my surprise I agreed.

We are sitting in a long, low room beneath the eaves. Atkinson has sent his wife to bed. He himself is busy sharpening some tools at a little oilstone, smoking one of my cigars the while.

The air seems charged with thunder. I am writing this at a shaky table before the open window. The leg is cracked, and Atkinson, who seems a handy man with his tools, is going to mend it as soon as he has finished putting an edge on his chisel.

It is after eleven now. I shall be gone in less than an hour.

But the heat is stifling.

It is enough to send a man mad.

READING FOR DETAILS

A Most Remarkable Day

When this story opens, James Clarence Withencroft is writing down what has happened during what he calls the most remarkable day of his life.

1. Where is he when he is writing this account?
2. Describe the picture he had drawn that morning.
3. How did he discover the identity of the man he had drawn?
4. What is inscribed on the gravestone that Atkinson was finishing?
5. What is Atkinson doing as Withencroft writes?

READING FOR MEANING

Discuss the following statements in light of the story:

1. It is useless to struggle against fate.
2. The human mind is capable of sending and receiving mental images without conscious effort.

READING FOR APPRECIATION

Foreshadowing

1. Beginning with the title and continuing throughout this account, the reader is constantly reminded of the thing that is to bring about tragedy at the story's end. With what two lines does the author foreshadow what must have happened in the short time before Withencroft was to have left to return home?
2. When did you first feel certain that there was something uncanny or unnatural about the way things were happening in this story?

BIOGRAPHICAL NOTE

William Fryer Harvey (1885–1937) was a British physician whose hobby was writing horror stories. He also wrote essays on the Quakers. During World War I he served in the British Navy and was decorated for bravery when he risked his life to save a fellow sailor trapped in the flooded engine room of a destroyer. Twenty of his best tales have been collected in the book, *The Beast With Five Fingers*.

"It had a spell put on it by an old fakir," said the sergeant major, "a very holy man. He wanted to show that fate ruled people's lives, and that those who interfered with it did so to their sorrow."

THE MONKEY'S PAW
W. W. Jacobs

Without, the night was cold and wet; but in the small parlor of Lakesman Villa the blinds were drawn and the fire burned brightly. Father and son were at chess, the former, who possessed ideas about the game involving radical changes, putting his king into such sharp and unnecessary perils that it even provoked comment from the white-haired old lady knitting placidly by the fire.

"Hark at the wind," said Mr. White, who, having seen a fatal mistake after it was too late, was amiably desirous of preventing his son from seeing it.

"I'm listening," said the latter, grimly surveying the board as he stretched out his hand. "Check."[1]

"I should hardly think that he'd come tonight," said his father, with his hand poised over the board.

"Mate,"[2] replied the son.

"That's the worst of living so far out," bawled Mr. White, with sudden and unlooked-for violence; "of all the beastly, slushy, out-of-the-way places to live in, this is the worst. Pathway's a bog, and the road's a torrent. I don't know what people are thinking about. I suppose because only two houses on the road are let they think it doesn't matter."

"Never mind, dear," said his wife soothingly; "perhaps you'll win the next one."

Mr. White looked up sharply, just in time to intercept a knowing glance between mother and son. The words died away on his lips, and he hid a guilty grin in his thin gray beard.

"There he is," said Herbert White as the gate banged loudly and heavy footsteps came toward the door.

The old man rose with hospitable haste and, opening the door, was heard condoling[3] with the new arrival. The new arrival also condoled with himself, so that Mrs. White said, "Tut, tut!" and coughed gently as her husband entered the room, followed by a tall burly man, beady of eye and rubicund[4] of visage.

"Sergeant Major Morris," he said, introducing him.

The sergeant major shook hands and, taking the proffered seat by the fire, watched contentedly while his host got out whiskey and tumblers and stood a small copper kettle on the fire.

At the third glass his eyes got brighter

"The Monkey's Paw" from LADY OF THE BARGE by W. W. Jacobs. Permission courtesy of Dodd, Mead & Company.

1. **Check,** a move that directly attacks the opponent's king but does not result in a checkmate.
2. **Mate,** a shortened form of *checkmate* that ends the game.
3. **condoling** (kən dōl′ing), expressing sympathy for.
4. **rubicund** (rü′bə kund), rosy complexioned.

and he began to talk, the little family circle regarding with eager interest this visitor from distant parts as he squared his broad shoulders in the chair and spoke of strange scenes and doughty deeds, of wars and plagues and strange peoples.

"Twenty-one years of it," said Mr. White, nodding at his wife and son. "When he went away, he was a slip of a youth in the warehouse. Now look at him."

"He don't look to have taken much harm," said Mrs. White politely.

"I'd like to go to India myself," said the old man, "just to look around a bit, you know."

"Better where you are," said the sergeant major, shaking his head. He put down the empty glass and, sighing softly, shook it again.

"I should like to see those old temples and fakirs⁵ and jugglers," said the old man. "What was that you started telling me the other day about a monkey's paw or something, Morris?"

"Nothing," said the soldier hastily. "Leastways, nothing worth hearing."

"Monkey's paw?" said Mrs. White curiously.

"Well, it's just a bit of what you might call magic, perhaps," said the sergeant major offhandedly.

His three listeners leaned forward eagerly. The visitor absent-mindedly put his empty glass to his lips and then set it down again. His host filled it for him.

"To look at," said the sergeant major, fumbling in his pocket, "it's just an ordinary little paw, dried to a mummy."

He took something out of his pocket and proffered it. Mrs. White drew back with a grimace, but her son, taking it, examined it curiously.

"And what is there special about it?" inquired Mr. White as he took it from his son and, having examined it, placed it upon the table.

"It had a spell put on it by an old fakir," said the sergeant major, "a very holy man. He wanted to show that fate ruled people's lives, and that those who interfered with it did so to their sorrow. He put a spell on it so that three separate men could each have three wishes from it."

His manner was so impressive that his hearers were conscious that their light laughter jarred somewhat.

"Well, why don't you have three, sir?" said Herbert White cleverly.

The soldier regarded him in the way that middle age is wont to regard presumptuous youth. "I have," he said quietly, and his blotchy face whitened.

"And did you really have the three wishes granted?" asked Mrs. White.

"I did," said the sergeant major, and his glass tapped against his strong teeth.

"And has anybody else wished?" inquired the old lady.

"The first man had his three wishes, yes," was the reply. "I don't know what the first two were, but the third was for death. That's how I got the paw."

His tones were so grave that a hush fell upon the group.

"If you've had your three wishes, it's no good to you now, then, Morris," said the old man at last. "What do you keep it for?"

The soldier shook his head. "Fancy, I suppose," he said slowly. "I did have

---

5. **fakirs** (fā′kərz), Hindu religious beggars who perform feats of magic and endurance.

some idea of selling it, but I don't think I will. It has caused enough mischief already. Besides, people won't buy. They think it's a fairy tale, some of them, and those who do think anything of it want to try it first and pay me afterward."

"If you could have another three wishes," said the old man, eying him keenly, "would you have them?"

"I don't know," said the other. "I don't know."

He took the paw and, dangling it between his front finger and thumb, suddenly threw it upon the fire. White, with a slight cry, stooped down and snatched it off.

"Better let it burn," said the soldier solemnly.

"If you don't want it, Morris," said the old man, "give it to me."

"I won't," said his friend doggedly. "I threw it on the fire. If you keep it, don't blame me for what happens. Pitch it on the fire again, like a sensible man."

The other shook his head and examined his new possession closely. "How do you do it?" he inquired.

"Hold it up in your right hand and wish aloud," said the sergeant major, "but I warn you of the consequences."

"Sounds like the *Arabian Nights*," said Mrs. White as she rose and began to set

the supper. "Don't you think you might wish for four pairs of hands for me?"

Her husband drew the talisman[6] from his pocket, and then all three burst into laughter as the sergeant major, with a look of alarm on his face, caught him by the arm.

"If you must wish," he said gruffly, "wish for something sensible."

Mr. White dropped it back into his pocket and, placing chairs, motioned his friend to the table. In the business of supper the talisman was partly forgotten, and afterward the three sat listening in an enthralled fashion to a second installment of the soldier's adventures in India.

"If the tale about the monkey paw is not more truthful than those he has been telling us," said Herbert as the door closed behind their guest, just in time for him to catch the last train, "we shan't make much out of it."

"Did you give him anything for it, father?" inquired Mrs. White, regarding her husband closely.

"A trifle," said he, coloring slightly. "He didn't want it, but I made him take it. And he pressed me again to throw it away."

"Likely," said Herbert, with pretended horror. "Why, we're going to be rich, and famous, and happy. Wish to be an emperor, father, to begin with; then you can't be henpecked."

He darted round the table, pursued by the maligned Mrs. White armed with an antimacassar.[7]

Mr. White took the paw from his pocket and eyed it dubiously. "I don't know what to wish for, and that's a fact," he said slowly. "It seems to me I've got all I want."

"If you only cleared[8] the house, you'd be quite happy, wouldn't you," said Her-

bert, with his hand on his shoulder. "Well, wish for two hundred pounds, then; that'll just do it."

His father, smiling shamefacedly at his own credulity, held up the talisman as his son, with a solemn face somewhat marred by a wink at his mother, sat down at the piano and struck a few impressive chords.

"I wish for two hundred pounds," said the old man distinctly.

A fine crash from the piano greeted the words, interrupted by a shuddering cry from the old man. His wife and son ran toward him.

"It moved," he cried, with a glance of disgust at the object as it lay on the floor. "As I wished, it twisted in my hands like a snake."

"Well, I don't see the money," said his son as he picked it up and placed it on the table, "and I bet I never shall."

"It must have been your fancy, father," said his wife, regarding him anxiously.

He shook his head. "Never mind, though; there's no harm done, but it gave me a shock all the same."

They sat down by the fire again while the two men finished their pipes. Outside, the wind was higher than ever, and the old man started nervously at the sound of a door banging upstairs. A silence unusual and depressing settled upon all three, which lasted until the old couple rose to retire for the night.

"I expect you'll find the cash tied up in a big bag in the middle of your bed,"

6. **talisman** (tal′i smən), an object presumed to have magical powers.

7. **antimacassar** (an′ti mə kas′ər), a small covering to protect the back or arms of a chair, sofa, etc., against soiling.

8. **cleared,** here, paid off the mortgage.

said Herbert as he bade them good night, "and something horrible squatting up on top of the wardrobe watching you as you pocket your ill-gotten gains."

In the brightness of the wintry sun next morning as it streamed over the breakfast table, Herbert laughed at his fears. There was an air of prosaic wholesomeness about the room which it had lacked on the previous night, and the dirty, shriveled little paw was pitched on the sideboard with a carelessness which betokened no great belief in its virtues.

"I suppose all old soldiers are the same," said Mrs. White. "The idea of our listening to such nonsense! How could wishes be granted in these days? And if they could, how could two hundred pounds hurt you, father?"

"Might drop on his head from the sky," said the frivolous Herbert.

"Morris said the things happened so naturally," said his father, "that you might if you so wished attribute it to coincidence."

"Well, don't break into the money before I come back," said Herbert as he rose from the table. "I'm afraid it'll turn you into a mean, avaricious man, and we shall have to disown you."

His mother laughed and, following him to the door, watched him down the road and, returning to the breakfast table, was very happy at the expense of her husband's credulity. All of which did not prevent her from scurrying to the door at the postman's knock, nor prevent her from referring somewhat shortly to retired sergeant majors of bibulous[9] habits when she found that the post brought a tailor's bill.

"Herbert will have some more of his funny remarks, I expect, when he comes home," she said as they sat at dinner.

"I dare say," said Mr. White, pouring himself out some beer; "but for all that, the thing moved in my hand; that I'll swear to."

"You thought it did," said the old lady soothingly.

"I say it did," replied the other. "There was no thought about it; I had just—What's the matter?"

His wife made no reply. She was watching the mysterious movements of a man outside, who, peering in an undecided fashion at the house, appeared to be trying to make up his mind to enter. In mental connection with the two hundred pounds, she noticed that the stranger was well dressed and wore a silk hat of glossy newness. Three times he paused at the gate, and then walked on again. The fourth time he stood with his hand upon it, and then with sudden resolution flung it open and walked up the path. Mrs. White at the same moment placed her hands behind her and, hurriedly unfastening the strings of her apron, put that useful article of apparel beneath the cushion of her chair.

She brought the stranger, who seemed ill at ease, into the room. He gazed furtively at Mrs. White and listened in a preoccupied fashion as the old lady apologized for the appearance of the room and her husband's coat, a garment which he usually reserved for the garden. She then waited as patiently as her sex would permit for him to broach his business, but he was at first strangely silent.

"I—was asked to call," he said at last, and stooped and picked a piece of cotton

---

9. **bibulous** (bib′yə ləs), drinking.

from his trousers. "I come from Maw and Meggins."

The old lady started. "Is anything the matter?" she asked breathlessly. "Has anything happened to Herbert? What is it? What is it?"

Her husband interposed. "There, there, mother," he said hastily. "Sit down, and don't jump to conclusions. You've not brought bad news, I'm sure, sir," and he eyed the other wistfully.

"I'm sorry—" began the visitor.

"Is he hurt?" demanded the mother.

The visitor bowed in assent. "Badly hurt," he said quietly, "but he is not in any pain."

"Oh, thank God!" said the old woman, clasping her hands. "Thank God for that! Thank—"

She broke off suddenly as the sinister meaning of assurance dawned upon her and she saw the awful confirmation of her fears in the other's averted face. She caught her breath and, turning to her slower-witted husband, laid her trembling old hand upon his. There was a long silence.

"He was caught in the machinery," said the visitor at length, in a low voice.

"Caught in the machinery," repeated Mr. White, in a dazed fashion, "yes."

He sat staring blankly out at the window and, taking his wife's hand between his own, pressed it as he had been wont to do in their old courting days nearly forty years back.

"He was the only one left to us," he said, turning gently to the visitor. "It is hard."

The other coughed and, rising, walked slowly to the window. "The firm wished me to convey their sincere sympathy with you in your great loss," he said,

without looking round. "I beg that you will understand I am only their servant and merely obeying orders."

There was no reply; the old woman's face was white, her eyes staring, and her breath inaudible; on her husband's face was a look such as his friend the sergeant might have carried into his first action.

"I was to say that Maw and Meggins disclaim all responsibility," continued the other. "They admit no liability at all, but in consideration of your son's services they wish to present you with a certain sum as compensation."

Mr. White dropped his wife's hand and, rising to his feet, gazed with a look of horror at his visitor. His dry lips shaped the words, "How much?"

"Two hundred pounds," was the answer.

Unconscious of his wife's shriek, the old man smiled faintly, put out his hands like a sightless man, and dropped, a senseless heap, to the floor.

In the huge new cemetery, some two miles distant, the old people buried their dead, and came back to a house steeped in shadow and silence. It was all over so quickly that at first they could hardly realize it, and remained in a state of expectation as though of something else to happen—something else which was to lighten this load, too heavy for old hearts to bear. But the days passed, and expectation gave place to resignation—the hopeless resignation of the old, sometimes miscalled apathy. Sometimes they hardly exchanged a word, for now they had nothing to talk about and their days were long to weariness.

It was about a week after that that the old man, waking suddenly in the night, stretched out his hand and found himself alone. The room was in darkness, and the sound of subdued weeping came from the window. He raised himself in bed and listened.

"Come back," he said tenderly. "You will be cold."

"It is colder for my son," said the old woman, and wept afresh.

The sound of her sobs died away on his ears. The bed was warm, and his eyes heavy with sleep. He dozed fitfully, and then slept until a sudden wild cry from his wife awoke him with a start.

"The monkey's paw!" she cried wildly. "The monkey's paw!"

He started up in alarm. "Where? Where is it? What's the matter?"

She came stumbling across the room toward him. "I want it," she said quietly. "You've not destroyed it?"

"It's in the parlor, on the bracket," he replied, marveling. "Why?"

She cried and laughed together and, bending over, kissed his cheek.

"I only just thought of it," she said hysterically. "Why didn't I think of it before? Why didn't you think of it?"

"Think of what?" he questioned.

"The other two wishes," she replied rapidly. "We've only had one."

"Was not that enough?" he demanded fiercely.

"No," she cried triumphantly; "we'll have one more. Go down and get it quickly, and wish our boy alive again."

The man sat up in bed and flung the bedclothes from his quaking limbs. "Good God, you are mad!" he cried, aghast.

"Get it," she panted; "get it quickly, and wish—Oh, my boy, my boy!"

Her husband struck a match and lit the candle. "Get back to bed," he said unsteadily. "You don't know what you are saying."

"We had the first wish granted," said the old woman feverishly. "Why not the second?"

"A coincidence," stammered the old man.

"Go and get it and wish," cried the old woman, and dragged him toward the door.

He went down in the darkness, and felt his way to the parlor and then to the mantelpiece. The talisman was in its place, and a horrible fear that the unspoken wish might bring his mutilated son before him ere he could escape from the room seized upon him, and he caught his breath as he found that he had lost the direction of the door. His brow cold with sweat, he felt his way round the table and groped along the wall until he found himself in the small passage with the unwholesome thing in his hand.

Even his wife's face seemed changed as he entered the room. It was white and expectant, and to his fears seemed to have an unnatural look upon it. He was afraid of her.

"Wish!" she cried, in a strong voice.

"It is foolish and wicked," he faltered.

"Wish!" repeated his wife.

He raised his hand. "I wish my son alive again."

The talisman fell to the floor, and he regarded it shudderingly. Then he sank trembling into a chair as the old woman, with burning eyes, walked to the window and raised the blind.

He sat until he was chilled with the cold, glancing occasionally at the figure of the old woman peering through the window. The candle end, which had burnt below the rim of the china candle-

stick, was throwing pulsating shadows on the ceiling and walls, until, with a flicker larger than the rest, it expired. The old man, with an unspeakable sense of relief at the failure of the talisman, crept back to his bed, and a minute or two afterward the old woman came silently and apathetically beside him.

Neither spoke, but both lay silently listening to the ticking of the clock. A stair creaked, and a squeaky mouse scurried noisily through the wall. The darkness was oppressive and, after lying for some time screwing up his courage, the husband took the box of matches and, striking one, went downstairs for a candle.

At the foot of the stairs the match went out, and he paused to strike an- other, and at the same moment a knock, so quiet and stealthy as to be scarcely audible, sounded on the front door.

The matches fell from his hand. He stood motionless, his breath suspended until the knock was repeated. Then he turned and fled swiftly back to his room, and closed the door behind him. A third knock sounded through the house.

"What's that?" cried the old woman, starting up.

"A rat," said the old man, in shaking tones, "a rat. It passed me on the stairs."

His wife sat up in bed listening. A loud knock resounded through the house.

"It's Herbert!" she screamed. "It's Herbert!"

She ran to the door, but her husband

was before her and, catching her by the arm, held her tightly.

"What are you going to do?" he whispered hoarsely.

"It's my boy; it's Herbert!" she cried, struggling mechanically. "I forgot it was two miles away. What are you holding me for? Let go. I must open the door."

"For God's sake, don't let it in," cried the old man, trembling.

"You're afraid of your own son!" she cried, struggling. "Let me go. I'm coming, Herbert; I'm coming."

There was another knock, and another. The old woman with a sudden wrench broke free and ran from the room. Her husband followed to the landing, and called after her appealingly as she hurried downstairs. He heard the chain rattle back and the bottom bolt drawn slowly and stiffly from the socket. Then the old woman's voice, strained and panting.

"The bolt!" she cried loudly. "Come down. I can't reach it."

But her husband was on his hands and knees groping wildly on the floor in search of the paw. If he could only find it before the thing outside got in. A perfect fusillade of knocks reverberated through the house, and he heard the scraping of a chair as his wife put it down in the passage against the door. He heard the creaking of the bolt as it came slowly back, and at the same moment he found the monkey's paw and frantically breathed his third and last wish.

The knocking ceased suddenly, although the echoes of it were still in the house. He heard the chair drawn back and the door opened. A cold wind rushed up the staircase, and a long loud wail of disappointment and misery from his wife gave him courage to run down to her side and then to the gate beyond. The street lamp flickering opposite shone on a quiet and deserted road.

READING FOR DETAILS

Should One Tempt Fate?

That there is a warm relationship between the parents and their son, Herbert, is revealed in the opening paragraphs of "The Monkey's Paw." When a knowing glance passes between mother and son as Mr. White blusters loudly about the weather and the location of their home, the reader realizes that the father is trying to distract Herbert's attention from the chess game and that mother and son are amused by this. It adds to the fun of the chess playing. It is into this close-knit family situation that the sergeant major comes with his tales from years of experience in the military.

1. In what country had the sergeant major obtained the monkey's paw? According to the spell, how many men could have wishes on the paw? What feeling do you have about the wishes the sergeant major had made?

2. Why does Mr. White wish for the sum of 200 pounds? What does he feel as soon as he has made the wish?

3. What news does the man from Maw and Meggins bring to the Whites? What amount of compensation was the company willing to pay?

4. What idea comes to Mrs. White about a week after Herbert's funeral? Why does Mr. White oppose the idea?

5. How is the third and final wish used?

READING FOR MEANING

Do you find support for all these concepts in the story? Discuss the soundness of each.

1. Fate rules people's lives and those who interfere with it do so to their sorrow.

2. Most people associate money with achieving the greatest happiness.
3. If people are reasonably happy, they should not challenge fate by asking for more.

READING FOR APPRECIATION

Foreshadowing

The story opens with the words "Without, the night was cold and wet. . . ." The author goes on to picture the cozy family scene within the house. Storm and wind are often associated with fearsome happenings in stories of horror and suspense; they serve to foreshadow events to come. In addition to setting the beginning events of the story in a storm, W. W. Jacobs foreshadows horror to come with the details he gives about the mummified paw.

1. How does Sergeant Major Morris look when asked about the wishes he had made? What had happened to the first man who wished on the paw? What does this foreshadow for the Whites?
2. When Mr. White retrieves the paw from the fire, what words of Sergeant Major Morris foreshadow ill luck if White keeps it?
3. Discuss whether the reader feels the compensation will be 200 pounds before the man from Maw and Meggins reveals the amount.

Irony

Irony occurs when what would appear to be true isn't actually true at all (see Reading for Appreciation, page 120). For example, one would think that when the Whites had three wishes granted to them and each wish came true, they would benefit.

What actually was the result of their three wishes?

COMPOSITION

Select one of the three statements in Reading for Meaning, pages 577–578, and argue *for* or *against* the statement in a brief essay. Make certain to include sufficient details to support your point of view.

BIOGRAPHICAL NOTE

W. W. (William Wymark) **Jacobs** (1866–1943) was born in London. His father was employed as a stevedore, and it was from this background that the son gathered ideas and situations for many of his stories and plays. Although he wrote many stories, his best known is "The Monkey's Paw."

No one ever knew why Ivan, moistening his lips,
said suddenly: "Yes, Lieutenant, I'll cross the cemetery!"

CEMETERY PATH

Leo Rosten

Ivan was a timid little man—so timid that the villagers called him "Pigeon" or mocked him with the title, "Ivan the Terrible." Every night Ivan stopped in at the saloon which was on the edge of the village cemetery. Ivan never crossed the cemetery to get to his lonely shack on the other side. The path through the cemetery would save him many minutes, but he had never taken it—not even in the full light of noon.

Late one winter's night, when bitter wind and snow beat against the saloon, the customers took up the familiar mockery. "Ivan's mother was scared by a canary when she carried him in her womb." "Ivan the Terrible—Ivan the Terribly Timid One."

Ivan's sickly protest only fed their taunts, and they jeered cruelly when the young Cossack lieutenant flung his horrid challenge at their quarry.

"You are a pigeon, Ivan. You'll walk all around the cemetery in this fiendish cold—but you dare not cross the cemetery."

Ivan murmured, "The cemetery is nothing to cross, Lieutenant. It is nothing but earth, like all the other earth."

The lieutenant cried, "A challenge, then! Cross the cemetery tonight, Ivan, and I'll give you five rubles—five gold rubles!"

Perhaps it was the vodka. Perhaps it was the temptation of the five gold rubles. No one ever knew why Ivan, moistening his lips, said suddenly: "Yes, Lieutenant, I'll cross the cemetery!"

The saloon echoed with their disbelief. The lieutenant winked to the men and unbuckled his saber. "Here, Ivan. When you get to the center of the cemetery, in front of the biggest tomb, stick the saber into the ground. In the morning we shall go there. And if the saber is in the ground—five gold rubles to you!"

Ivan took the saber. The men drank a toast: "To Ivan the Terrible!" They roared with laughter.

The wind howled around Ivan as he closed the door of the saloon behind him. The cold was knife-sharp. He buttoned his long coat and crossed the dirt road. He could hear the lieutenant's voice, louder than the rest, yelling after him, "Five rubles, pigeon! *If you live!*"

Ivan pushed the cemetery gate open. He walked fast. "Earth, just earth . . . like any other earth." But the darkness was a massive dread. "Five gold rubles . . ." The wind was cruel and the saber was like ice in his hands. Ivan shivered under the long, thick coat and broke into a limping run.

He recognized the large tomb. He must have sobbed—that was the sound

ONE YEAR THE MILKWEED
Arshile Gorky
National Gallery of Art, Washington, D.C.
Ailsa Mellon Bruce Fund

that was drowned in the wind. And he kneeled, cold and terrified, and drove the saber into the hard ground. With his fist, he beat it down to the hilt. It was done. The cemetery . . . the challenge . . . five gold rubles.

Ivan started to rise from his knees. But he could not move. Something held him. Something gripped him in an unyielding and implacable hold. Ivan tugged and lurched and pulled—gasping in his panic, shaken by a monstrous fear. But something held Ivan. He cried out in terror, then made senseless gurgling noises.

They found Ivan, next morning, on the ground in front of the tomb that was in the center of the cemetery. His face was not that of a frozen man's, but of a man killed by some nameless horror.

And the lieutenant's saber was in the ground where Ivan had pounded it—through the dragging folds of his long coat.

READING FOR DETAILS

A Senseless Challenge

1. What caused Ivan to cross the cemetery?
2. What killed Ivan?

READING FOR MEANING

Find evidence in the story to support the following statements:

1. Fear or panic is stronger than reason.
2. Some persons are doomed by their own natures or dispositions.

READING FOR APPRECIATION

Foreshadowing

Brief as this account is, with what italicized words does the author foreshadow the ending? Discuss.

Suspense

Suspense builds from the moment Ivan accepts the young lieutenant's dare, but it is felt even more strongly after he pushes open the gate to the cemetery. Where do you think the suspense ends? Why?

COMPOSITION

Many are the tales of terror told about cemeteries and burial grounds. Numerous television and movie scripts recount the fate of the hapless wayfarer who knowingly or unknowingly travels through a sacred burial place.

Write a short composition in which you describe, as a story setting, a graveyard or burial ground in detail. Set your description in the fall, winter, or summer, making sure that the season of the year contributes to the effectiveness of your prose. Fall, of course, is a time of decaying vegetation, of falling leaves, and crying wind; winter brings the cold and snow, when life lies buried beneath a frozen surface; and summer brings the tangle of overgrown shrubbery that casts fearful shadows. As you write your composition, give your senses free rein and let your eyes *see*, your ears *hear*, your nose *smell*, and your fingers *feel* the ghostly qualities of the burial ground you describe.

BIOGRAPHICAL NOTE

Leo Rosten (1908–   ) was born in Poland and brought to the United States when he was two years old. Growing up in a poor neighborhood in Chicago, he worked at odd jobs to help defray school expenses, and earned his Ph.D. from the University of Chicago in 1937. His series of humorous stories about Hyman Kaplan, a student in a night school for adults, was published in book form in 1937 with the title *The Education of Hyman Kaplan,* under the pseudonym Leonard Q. Ross. Later, this book was combined with *The Return of Hyman Kaplan* to form a new version, *O Kaplan! My Kaplan!*

Gallery The Strange and Eerie

The mood of a painting is defined and determined by the intertwined imaginations of the painter and the viewer. This mood can be benign and beautiful, peaceful and pleasant, charged and exciting, or strange and eerie. In the works on these two pages, two artists suspend our disbelief by suspending their subjects in midair. Piazetta's Elijah, eerily floating on a bed of fire, is seen by us from below as he ascends into realms above. The Surrealist René Magritte suspends a massive rock, crowned by a castle, above a seascape. No real rock remains aloft for long, but he paints it so convincingly that he easily disengages and destroys our disbelief.

Giovanni Battista Piazetta, **ELIJAH TAKEN UP IN A CHARIOT OF FIRE**
National Gallery of Art, Washington, D.C.
Samuel H. Kress Collection

René Magritte, **THE CASTLE OF THE PYRENEES**
Private Collection, N.Y.
© ADAGP

Ibo Tribe, **AFRICAN MASK**
Manu Sassonian/Art Resource, Inc.

Look long enough at the African tribal mask at the left and a weird feeling will creep up on you—which is just what its maker intended. These masks were never meant to represent gods. They were designed either to summon them up or frighten them away. For which purpose do you think *this* mask was designed?

Elihu Vedder, **THE QUESTIONER OF THE SPHINX**
Courtesy, Museum of Fine Arts, Boston
Bequest of Mrs. Martin Brimmer

Eugene Berman, **PROSERPINA**
St. Louis Art Museum

The American painter Elihu Vedder strews his imaginary landscape with skulls and ruins and mystery. He asks our imagination to accept the surroundings and our natural inquisitiveness to guess the answer the Sphinx is whispering to the rapt listener. Eugene Berman, on the other hand, is intent only upon creating a mood. All is ominous bleakness in his rendering of the plight of Proserpina, who was condemned by the gods to live half her life in the underworld.

Odilon Redon, **EVOCATION OF ROUSSEL**
National Gallery of Art, Washington, D.C.
Chester Dale Collection

Hans Memling, **CHALICE OF ST. JOHN**
National Gallery of Art, Washington, D.C.
Samuel H. Kress Collection

Impressionist composer Albert Roussel once wrote a misty piece of music called *Evocations*. In the painting at the left, French Symbolist artist Odilon Redon evokes not only the composer, but the eerie, flowerlike fragileness of the music itself. The fifteenth-century Flemish painter Hans Memling, in his moody painting above, presents us with impending doom in the shape of a poisoned cup. His chalice becomes, not a comely container for wine, but a sinister repository for a snake.

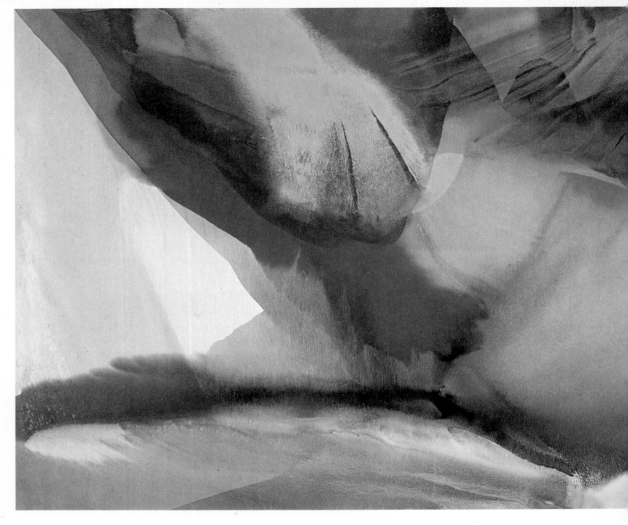

The Arctic trails have their secret tales/That would make your blood run cold.

The Cremation of Sam McGee
Robert W. Service

There are strange things done in the midnight sun
By the men who moil[1] for gold;
The Arctic trails have their secret tales
That would make your blood run cold;
The Northern Lights have seen queer sights,   5
But the queerest they ever did see
Was that night on the marge[2] of Lake Lebarge
I cremated Sam McGee.

1. **moil** (moil), work hard in the dirt.
2. **marge** (marj), shore.

"The Cremation of Sam McGee," by Robert W. Service, from COLLECTED POEMS OF ROBERT SERVICE.

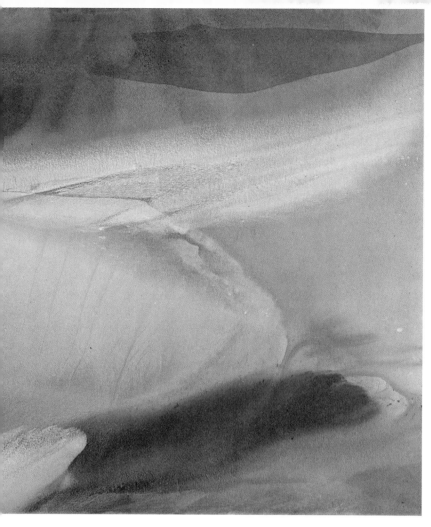

PHENOMENA SOUND OF SUNDIALS
Paul Jenkins
National Gallery of Art, Washington, D.C.
Gift of Vincent Melzac

Now Sam McGee was from Tennessee, where the cotton blooms and blows.
Why he left his home in the South to roam 'round the Pole, God only knows.   10
He was always cold, but the land of gold seemed to hold him like a spell;
Though he'd often say in his homely way that "he'd sooner live in hell."

On a Christmas Day we were mushing our way over the Dawson trail.
Talk of your cold! through the parka's fold it stabbed like a driven nail.
If our eyes we'd close, then the lashes froze till sometimes we couldn't see;   15
It wasn't much fun, but the only one to whimper was Sam McGee.

And that very night, as we lay packed tight in our robes beneath the snow,
And the dogs were fed, and the stars o'erhead were dancing heel and toe,
He turned to me, and "Cap," says he, "I'll cash in this trip, I guess;
And if I do, I'm asking that you won't refuse my last request."   20

Well, he seemed so low that I couldn't say no; then he says with a sort of moan:
"It's the cursed cold, and it's got right hold till I'm chilled clean through to the bone.
Yet 'taint being dead—it's my awful dread of the icy grave that pains;
So I want you to swear that, foul or fair, you'll cremate my last remains."

A pal's last need is a thing to heed, so I swore I would not fail;   25
And we started on at the streak of dawn; but God! he looked ghastly pale.
He crouched on the sleigh, and he raved all day of his home in Tennessee;
And before nightfall a corpse was all that was left of Sam McGee.

There wasn't a breath in that land of death, and I hurried, horror-driven,
With a corpse half-hid that I couldn't get rid, because of a promise given;   30
It was lashed to the sleigh, and it seemed to say: "You may tax your brawn and brains.
But you promised true, and it's up to you to cremate these last remains."

Now a promise made is a debt unpaid, and the trail has its own stern code.
In the days to come, though my lips were dumb, in my heart how I cursed that load.
In the long, long night, by the lone firelight, while the Huskies, round in a ring,
Howled out their woes to the homeless snows—O God! how I loathed the thing.

And every day that quiet clay[3] seemed to heavy and heavier grow;
And on I went, though the dogs were spent and the grub was getting low;
The trail was bad, and I felt half mad, but I swore I would not give in;
And I'd often sing to the hateful thing, and it harkened with a grin.   40

Till I came to the marge of Lake Lebarge, and a derelict[4] there lay;
It was jammed in the ice, but I saw in a trice it was called the *Alice May*.
And I looked at it, and I thought a bit, and I looked at my frozen chum;
Then "Here," said I, with a sudden cry, "is my cre-ma-to-re-um."[5]

Some planks I tore from the cabin floor, and I lit the boiler fire;   45
Some coal I found that was lying around, and I heaped the fuel higher;
The flames just soared, and the furnace roared—such a blaze you seldom see;
And I burrowed a hole in the glowing coal, and I stuffed in Sam McGee.

Then I made a hike, for I didn't like to hear him sizzle so;
And the heavens scowled, and the Huskies howled, and the wind began to blow.

---

3. **quiet clay,** Sam's body.
4. **derelict,** a ship abandoned and afloat at sea.
5. **crematorium** (krē′mə tôr′ē əm), a building or other
place in which bodies are cremated.

It was icy cold, but the hot sweat rolled down my cheeks, and I don't know why;
And the greasy smoke in an inky cloak went streaking down the sky.

I do not know how long in the snow I wrestled with grisly fear;
But the stars came out and they danced about ere again I ventured near;
I was sick with dread, but I bravely said: "I'll just take a peep inside.   55
I guess he's cooked, and it's time I looked"; . . . then the door I opened wide.

And there sat Sam, looking cool and calm, in the heart of the furnace roar;
And he wore a smile you could see a mile, and he said: "Please close that door.
It's fine in here, but I greatly fear you'll let in the cold and storm—
Since I left Plumtree down in Tennessee, it's the first time I've been warm."   60

There are strange things done in the midnight sun
By the men who moil for gold;
The Arctic trails have their secret tales
That would make your blood run cold;
The Northern Lights have seen queer sights,   65
But the queerest they ever did see
Was that night on the marge of Lake Lebarge
I cremated Sam McGee.

READING FOR APPRECIATION

Foreshadowing and Suspense

While working in a bank in the Yukon during the gold rush at the end of the last century, Robert W. Service began turning out rhymes in a half-jesting manner about the life of the sourdoughs (gold miners). These poems struck "pay dirt" immediately and he became famous. This poem was a great favorite with the men and women who went to Alaska to "moil for gold."

1. The poem builds awesome suspense. In the first forty lines we have visions of the storyteller going stark, raving mad. However, from line forty-one on, the poet lets us know that events will take a grimly humorous turn. He does this by such words and phrases as "frozen chum" and "stuffed in Sam McGee."

Find two other such cues. Explain how these are used to change the tone of the poem from one of horror to one of gruesome comedy.

2. Give your feelings about this poem. Explain why it does or does not have an appeal for you. Remember that such an explanation is more interesting if you refer to specific words and phrases.

BIOGRAPHICAL NOTE

Robert W. Service (1876–1958), Canadian poet and novelist, was born in Preston, England. After attending Glasgow University and training for a career in banking, Service emigrated to Canada in 1897. His travels for the Canadian Bank of Commerce to the Yukon and Vancouver served as background for many of his verses.

NIGHT AND CLOUDS (detail)
Albert Pinkham Ryder
City Art Museum, St. Louis

Whom does the Traveler
expect to answer his knock on the moonlit door?

The Listeners

"Is there anybody there?" said the Traveler,
   Knocking on the moonlit door;
And his horse in the silence champed the grasses
   Of the forest's ferny floor;
And a bird flew up out of the turret,   5
   Above the Traveler's head:
And he smote upon the door again a second time;
   "Is there anybody there?" he said.
But no one descended to the Traveler;
   No head from the leaf-fringed sill   10
Leaned over and looked into his gray eyes,
   Where he stood perplexed and still.
But only a host of phantom listeners
   That dwelt in the lone house then
Stood listening in the quiet of the moonlight   15
   To that voice from the world of men:
Stood thronging the faint moonbeams on the dark stair
   That goes down to the empty hall,

Hearkening* in an air stirred and shaken
    By the lonely Traveler's call.   20
And he felt in his heart their strangeness,
    Their stillness answering his cry,
While his horse moved, cropping the dark turf,
    'Neath the starred and leafy sky;
For he suddenly smote on the door, even   25
    Louder, and lifted his head:—
"Tell them I came, and no one answered,
    That I kept my word," he said.
Never the least stir made the listeners,
    Though every word he spake   30
Fell echoing through the shadowiness of the still house
    From the one man left awake:
Aye, they heard his foot upon the stirrup,
    And the sound of iron on stone,
And how the silence surged softly backward,   35
    When the plunging hoofs were gone.

*__Hearkening__ (här′kən ing), listening attentively.

WALTER DE LA MARE

READING FOR APPRECIATION

Suspense and Imaginative Language

There is something about an empty house that captures the imagination. How many people have lived there? If the old house could talk, what strange tales could it tell about its occupants? De la Mare capitalizes on this almost universal interest in deserted houses by having a traveler come to the door of one, knocking and calling. Suspense is immediately aroused. Will anyone hear or answer?

1. With what word does he characterize the listeners?
2. Discuss whether you are relieved or disappointed that the Traveler does not enter the house or challenge the silent listeners with intrusion.

3. A poetic device to create effect is alliteration (p. 413), the repetition of consonant sounds, usually at the beginning of words. What examples of this do you find in lines 4 and 35 of the poem? Why is that in line 35 particularly effective?

BIOGRAPHICAL NOTE

Walter de la Mare (1873–1956) was born in Kent, England, but spent most of his life in London. He worked for an oil company for several years and during this time turned out many stories and poems that won high acclaim. Later, able to devote all of his time to writing, he became one of the best-known poets writing in English in the first half of the present century.

SUMMING UP: THE STRANGE AND EERIE

Two subjects that fascinate people and arouse terror in them at the same time are death and the unfamiliar. These topics are both repugnant and enthralling. For this reason, reading strange and eerie stories involves a victory of mind over emotions. Most people go ahead and read what they know was expressly written to frighten them.

It is true that not everyone is afraid of the unfamiliar or of death under ordinary circumstances. Scientists constantly seek answers to the unknown or unfamiliar, and many people accept the fact of death with courage and composure. But in stories written expressly to thrill and chill readers, the unfamiliar is introduced or the threat of death appears when readers are totally unprepared to cope with either. Thus they become involved in an enjoyable form of self-torture as they share the fears and apprehensions of the characters in such stories.

READING FOR DETAILS

Think back over the selections "August Heat," "The Monkey's Paw," "Cemetery Path," and "The Cremation of Sam McGee." Which treated death in a humorous way? Which was the only selection that did not actually involve the unfamiliar, or supernatural? Which story depended most heavily upon a principle sometimes referred to as ESP, or extrasensory perception? Which story dealt with the horror aroused by the possibility of a person's returning from the dead?

READING FOR MEANING

Consider and discuss the following statements:

1. It's fun to be scared.
2. We tend to value strange experiences as worthy of being told again and again.
3. There are more things to be frightened of in people than in their environment.

READING FOR APPRECIATION

Suspense

Suspense may be defined as "a state of excited uncertainty." Leo Rosten begins to build suspense in the very beginning of his story, "Cemetery Path." What words or phrases in the first paragraph work especially well to help create suspense?

Foreshadowing

Sometimes we see the shadow of a being or an object before we see that which casts the shadow. This often happens in literature. The author, depending upon the effect he or she intends, suggests the shadow of a coming event so that the reader may be partially prepared for that event. At the same time, too, the author is increasing reader believability in that the foreshadowing makes the event seem plausible. For example, what is foreshadowed for members of the White family if they make a wish on the monkey's paw? In "August Heat," what is foreshadowed when the writer discovers what is on the tombstone?

COMPOSITION

You awaken at midnight to see a frightening creature from the unknown creeping toward your bed. Write three or more paragraphs in which you use imaginative language and foreshadowing to create suspense. The *effect* you wish to leave upon your reader is one of horror.

COMPOSITION WORKSHOP

SUMMARIZING STORIES

The novelist usually writes in what might be called a leisurely manner. For example, she or he often goes into great detail in recounting an action or describing a scene. In recounting an event, the novelist may note the smallest movement and will sometimes furnish a moment-by-moment account of exactly what occurred.

The practical writer must also provide a wealth of detail in many writing situations. But in some writing situations, the practical writer is called upon to summarize, or restate briefly, what would otherwise be a lengthy and detailed message. For example, the writer of a magazine article that explains the importance of a historical event will usually not have space to relate the event in detail. As an aid to the reader, the writer will provide a brief summary of the event, so that the reader can better understand the explanation that will follow it.

As is the case with all forms of practical writing, the writer of a summary must begin by gathering information. Since the kind of summary that the writer is most often called upon to do is the kind that briefly restates something already written, the raw material for the summary is readily at hand. The writer therefore begins with a careful study of whatever is to be summarized. A writer who wants to prepare a summary of W. F. Harvey's short story "August Heat" in this unit, for example, might read the story very carefully and slowly and then might reread it once or twice more at a more normal rate of speed. The slow and thoughtful reading allows the writer to take in everything in the story. The additional readings help the writer to a deeper understanding of what the author had to say.

Once the writer has a firm understanding of what is to be summarized, the next step is to look for natural divisions in the selection to be summarized. These divisions will become the individual paragraphs in the summary. The writer can then develop a rough outline that shows these divisions. A rough outline for "August Heat" might look like this:

1. Preliminary events at Withencroft's home
2. The meeting with Atkinson and the discovery of the tombstone's inscription
3. The events in the evening at Atkinson's home to the story's end

Once the writer has developed a rough outline, the next sensible step would be to note the key events that would be covered in each of the outline's three parts. In choosing the events to be included in the summary, the writer will select only those that are absolutely necessary for the reader to grasp the main story line. The writer will overlook all minor details. Here is an example of the first section of the outline with major events briefly noted:

1. Preliminary events at Withencroft's home
   —James Clarence Withencroft, the artist, is writing about the events of a most remarkable day
   —heat is oppressive; he casts about for an idea for a sketch, gets one, and begins to draw
   —over six hours later he admires his sketch of an enormously fat man in the criminal's section of a court
   —he rolls up sketch and without knowing why, places it in jacket pocket, and leaves home

Since the paragraphs in narrative writing are

usually structured according to the events being related and not by main-idea sentences, a paragraph outline would not be necessary. If the writer were summarizing a factual piece of writing, however, a paragraph outline would be most desirable and useful.

Once the writer has developed the rough outline for the summary of "August Heat," and noted the major events that will be included in each part, the actual writing may begin. Keep in mind when preparing any summary that your job is not to quote sentences from the original. Your job, instead, is to state briefly and in your own words what the author presented in more detail. It is impossible to say exactly how long a summary should be. Its exact length will depend upon what is being summarized.

Study the following summary of "August Heat." Notice that it presents the main story line of the original. While the summary does not develop the sense of horror and suspense found in the original story, it does tell the reader in a nutshell what the story is about.

As the story opens, James Clarence Withencroft, a not very successful artist, is writing about the events that have occurred on this very remarkable August day. He notes that after breakfast on that oppressively hot day he began to cast about for an idea for a sketch. Something comes to him and he starts to draw. Over six hours later he admiringly examines the sketch he had created of an enormously fat man standing in the section of a courtroom reserved for those accused of a crime. He rolls up the sketch and without knowing why places it in his pocket. He then leaves the house, apparently intending to visit a friend.

Withencroft can't recall why he walked where he did, but after about two hours he is standing in front of the gate of Charles Atkinson, a stonemason and maker of monuments. On an impulse, Withencroft enters and finds himself standing in front of the man that he had sketched that morning. Atkinson welcomes his unexpected visitor and continues to work on a marble gravestone. He asks Withencroft what he thinks of the work, and Withencroft notices that the stone contains his own name and birthdate. The date of death is this very August day. He tells Atkinson of these things and the man is amazed by the coincidence. Withencroft then shows Atkinson the sketch he had drawn that morning. Atkinson begins to look even more like the man in the sketch as he stares at it.

Atkinson invites Withencroft to dinner, and after the meal they continue to talk about the amazing coincidence. Withencroft asks if his host has ever been in difficulty with the law and receives a negative answer. Noting the lateness of the hour, Atkinson invites his guest to stay until after midnight to avoid the possibility of suffering an accidental death trying to return home in the dark. Withencroft notes that the two are alone in a room at the top of the house. Withencroft writes that it is approaching midnight. Atkinson is sharpening some tools as the two wait for the next day.

ACTIVITY 1

Choose another short story in this unit to summarize. Familiarize yourself with it by reading it very carefully once. Then read it two or more times at a more normal rate.

ACTIVITY 2

Develop a rough outline for the story that you prepared in Activity 1. Be sure that your rough outline reflects the natural divisions of the story. For each division, list the major events that occur.

ACTIVITY 3

Prepare a summary of the story that you have chosen. Read it carefully to be sure that the reader can easily understand what takes place in the story.

ONCE UPON A MIDNIGHT
AN INTRODUCTION TO Edgar Allan Poe

Over a hundred years ago a strange, darkly handsome, tormented man wrote a body of stories and poems that have haunted people ever since. This man, Edgar Allan Poe (1809–1849), never seemed able to find success or happiness. He was two years old when his actor parents died. A wealthy tobacco exporter of Richmond, Virginia, took him into his home, although he never really adopted the boy.

Poe was sent to the University of Virginia where, symbolically enough, his room assignment was number 13. Because of gambling debts, however, he was forced to leave before the year was over. He published a small volume of verse in 1827, tried the Army for a few years, and then was admitted to West Point. After a few months there, he was discharged for neglect of duty and disobedience. He worked tirelessly at his writing, but he lost a series of jobs on magazines because of his compulsive drinking.

His cousin, fourteen-year-old Virginia Clemm, a pale-skinned, dark-haired, fragile beauty, became his bride, but she eventually died from tuberculosis. During her life Poe did his most inspired writing and was probably as happy as he ever was. Virginia's death plus financial problems wore at his mind until he went through periods of mental imbalance. He died at a comparatively young age, ending a life of anguished suffering.

The writing Edgar Allan Poe left behind has made him one of the best-known American authors outside the United States. He is read and admired throughout the world for the weird and terrifying visions that he managed to trap in words.

PORTRAIT OF POE
James Hill

A mind like Poe's, brilliant and sensitive though distorted by drinking, failure, and despair, was fascinated by the devices and dark elements of human nature. Such facets of life attracted him as a moth is attracted by light or a mouse by the cobra's eye. Poe was a master at finding the combination of words and events to send shudders up the spine of the reader. Most of us enjoy toying with possibilities of things just beyond the edge of reality. We like to imagine monsters that are distortions of human beings or to horrify ourselves with frightening, terrifying events. Poe does these things for us with an artistry and skill that can be found in few other writers.

Join with him as a madman creeps down a dark passageway, mysterious subterranean catacombs open up in flickering lights, or a strange bird croaks mournfully, once upon a midnight.

TECHNIQUES: THE ART OF EDGAR ALLAN POE

Edgar Allan Poe believed that in writing a short story authors should decide upon the emotional *effect* that they wished to produce in their readers (see Unit Techniques, p. 269) and deliberately set out to put together a tale that would produce that effect. Thus if a writer wished the effect to be that of terror, as is the case with "The Tell-Tale Heart," care would be taken to choose every detail of setting, characterization, and action so that they blended to give a feeling of terror. Such a general feeling, or mood, which pervades a story from beginning to end is called *atmosphere*.

We might think of the atmosphere in a literary selection as being much like the atmosphere in a restaurant in which the proprietor has installed fortune tellers, serenading musicians, special lighting, and costumed waiters. Each touch has been deliberately chosen to create certain attitudes and expectations in the patrons. Similarly, the writer builds atmosphere to achieve a particular emotional response from the readers.

Poe knew that people are fascinated by the horrible, the terrible, and the fantastic. Because he wished his stories to have popular appeal, he skillfully developed an atmosphere of terror or horror in many of them.

To create his popular stories, Poe took deliberate advantage of *narrative viewpoint, significant detail, imaginative language, diction* (word choice), and *irony*. These terms, already familiar to you, will be reemphasized in the discussions for this section. In the study notes following the poetry selections, *alliteration, onomatopoeia, rhyme scheme*, and *rhythm* will be discussed again.

THE DREAM OF REASON PRODUCES MONSTERS (detail)
Francisco Goya
National Gallery of Art, Washington, D.C.

You fancy me mad. Madmen know nothing. But you should have seen me. You should have seen how wisely I proceeded—

THE TELL-TALE HEART

True!—nervous—very, very dreadfully nervous I had been and am! but why *will* you say that I am mad? The disease had sharpened my senses—not destroyed—not dulled them. Above all was the sense of hearing acute. I heard all things in the heaven and in the earth. I heard many things in hell. How, then, am I mad? Hearken! and observe how healthily—how calmly I can tell you the whole story.

It is impossible to say how first the idea entered my brain; but once conceived, it haunted me day and night. Object there was none. Passion there was none. I loved the old man. He had never wronged me. He had never given me insult. For his gold I had no desire. I think it was his eye! yes, it was this! One of his eyes resembled that of a vulture—a pale blue eye, with a film over it. Whenever it fell upon me, my blood ran cold; and so by degrees—very gradually—I made up my mind to take the life of the old man, and thus rid myself of the eye for ever.

Now this is the point. You fancy me mad. Madmen know nothing. But you should have seen *me*. You should have seen how wisely I proceeded—with what caution—with what foresight—with what dissimulation I went to work! I was never kinder to the old man than during the whole week before I killed him. And every night, about midnight, I turned the latch of his door and opened it—oh, so gently! And then, when I had made an opening sufficient for my head, I put in a dark lantern, all closed, closed, so that no light shone out, and then I thrust in my head. Oh, you would have laughed to see how cunningly I thrust it in! I moved it slowly—very, very slowly, so that I might not disturb the old man's sleep. It took me an hour to place my whole head within the opening so far that I could see him as he lay upon his bed. Ha!—would a madman have been so wise as this? And then, when my head was well in the room, I undid the lantern cautiously—oh, so cautiously—cautiously (for the hinges creaked)—I undid it just so much that a single thin ray fell upon the vulture eye. And this I did for seven long nights—every night just at midnight—but I found the eye always closed; and so it was impossible to do the work; for it was not the old man who vexed me, but his Evil Eye. And every morning, when the day broke, I went boldly into the chamber, and spoke courageously to him, calling him by name in a hearty tone, and inquiring how he had passed the night. So you see he would have been a very profound old man, indeed, to suspect that every night, just at twelve, I looked in upon him while he slept.

Upon the eighth night I was more than usually cautious in opening the door. A watch's minute hand moves more quickly than did mine. Never before that night had I *felt* the extent of my own powers—of my sagacity. I could scarcely contain my feelings of triumph. To think that there I was, opening the door, little by little, and he not even to dream of my secret deeds or thoughts. I fairly chuckled at the idea; and perhaps he heard me; for he moved on the bed suddenly, as if startled. Now you may think that I drew back—but no. His room was as black as pitch with the thick darkness, (for the shutters were close fastened, through fear of robbers), and so I knew that he could not see the opening of the door, and I kept pushing it on steadily, steadily.

I had my head in, and was about to open the lantern, when my thumb slipped upon the tin fastening, and the old man sprang up in the bed, crying out—"Who's there?"

I kept quite still and said nothing. For a whole hour I did not move a muscle, and in the meantime I did not hear him lie down. He was still sitting up in the bed listening—just as I have done, night after night, hearkening to the death watches in the wall.

Presently I heard a slight groan, and I knew it was the groan of mortal terror. It was not a groan of pain or of grief—oh, no!—it was the low stifled sound that arises from the bottom of the soul when overcharged with awe. I knew the sound well. Many a night, just at midnight, when all the world slept, it has welled up from my own bosom, deepening, with its dreadful echo, the terrors that distracted me. I say I knew it well. I knew what the old man felt, and pitied him, although I chuckled at heart. I knew that he had been lying awake ever since the first slight noise, when he had turned in the bed. His fears had been ever since growing upon him. He had been trying to fancy them causeless, but could not. He had been saying to himself—"It is nothing but the wind in the chimney—it is only a mouse crossing the floor," or "It is merely a cricket which has made a single chirp." Yes, he had been trying to comfort himself with these suppositions; but he had found all in vain. *All in vain;* because Death, in approaching him, had stalked with his black shadow before him, and enveloped the victim. And it was the mournful influence of the unperceived shadow that caused him to feel—although he neither saw nor heard—to *feel* the presence of my head within the room.

When I had waited a long time, very patiently, without hearing him lie down, I resolved to open a little—a very, very little crevice in the lantern. So I opened it—you cannot imagine how stealthily, stealthily—until, at length, a single dim ray, like the thread of the spider, shot from out the crevice and fell upon the vulture eye.

It was open—wide, wide open—and I grew furious as I gazed upon it. I saw it with perfect distinctness—all a dull blue, with a hideous veil over it that chilled the very marrow in my bones; but I could see nothing else of the old man's face or person: for I had directed the ray, as if by instinct, precisely upon the damned spot.

And now have I not told you that what you mistake for madness is but over-acuteness of the senses?—now, I say, there came to my ears a low, dull, quick sound, such as a watch makes when enveloped in cotton. I knew *that* sound well, too. It was the beating of the old man's heart. It increased my fury, as the beating of a drum stimulates the soldier into courage.

But even yet I refrained and kept still. I scarcely breathed. I held the lantern motionless. I tried how steadily I could maintain the ray upon the eye.

Meantime the hellish tattoo of the heart increased. It grew quicker and quicker, and louder and louder every instant. The old man's terror *must* have been extreme! It grew louder, I say, louder every moment!—do you mark me well? I have told you that I am nervous: so I am. And now at the dead hour of the night, amid the dreadful silence of that old house, so strange a noise as this excited me to uncontrollable terror. Yet, for some minutes longer I refrained and stood still. But the beating grew louder, louder! I thought the heart must burst. And now a new anxiety seized me—the sound would be heard by a neighbor! The old man's hour had come! With a loud yell, I threw open the lantern and leaped into the room. He shrieked once—once only. In an instant I dragged him to the floor, and pulled the heavy bed over him. I then smiled gaily, to find the deed so far done. But, for many minutes, the heart beat on with a muffled sound. This, however, did not vex me; it would not be heard through the wall. At length it ceased. The old man was dead. I removed the bed and examined the corpse. Yes, he was stone, stone dead. I placed my hand upon the heart and held it there many minutes. There was no pulsation. He was stone dead. His eye would trouble me no more.

If still you think me mad, you will think so no longer when I describe the wise precautions I took for the concealment of the body. The night waned, and I worked hastily, but in silence. First of all I dismembered the corpse. I cut off the head and the arms and the legs.

I then took up three planks from the flooring of the chamber, and deposited all between the scantlings. I then replaced the boards so cleverly, so cunningly, that no human eye—not even *his*—could have detected anything wrong. There was nothing to wash out—no stain of any kind—no blood-spot whatever. I had been too wary for that. A tub had caught all—ha! ha!

When I had made an end of these labors, it was four o'clock—still dark as midnight. As the bell sounded the hour, there came a knocking at the street door. I went down to open it with a light heart—for what had I *now* to fear? There entered three men, who introduced themselves, with perfect suavity, as officers of the police. A shriek had been heard by a neighbor during the night; suspicion of foul play had been aroused; information had been lodged at the police office, and they (the officers) had been deputed to search the premises.

I smiled—for *what* had I to fear? I bade the gentlemen welcome. The shriek, I said, was my own in a dream. The old man, I mentioned, was absent in the country. I took my visitors all over the house. I bade them search—search *well*. I led them, at length, to *his* chamber. I showed them his treasures, secure, undisturbed. In the enthusiasm of my confidence, I brought chairs into the room, and desired them *here* to rest from their fatigues, while I myself, in the wild audacity of my perfect triumph, placed my own seat upon the very spot beneath which reposed the corpse of the victim.

The officers were satisfied. My *manner* had convinced them. I was singularly at ease. They sat, and while I answered cheerily, they chatted familiar things. But, ere long, I felt myself getting pale and wished them gone. My head ached, and I fancied a ringing in my ears: but still they sat and still chatted. The ringing became more distinct: it continued and became more distinct: I talked more freely to get rid of the feeling: but it continued and gained definitiveness—until, at length, I found that the noise was *not* within my ears.

No doubt I now grew *very* pale; but I talked more fluently, and with a heightened voice. Yet the sound increased—and what could I do? It was *a low, dull, quick sound—much such a sound as a watch makes when enveloped in cotton.* I gasped for breath—and yet the officers heard it not. I talked more quickly—more vehemently; but the noise steadily increased. I arose and argued about trifles, in a high key and with violent gesticulations, but the noise steadily increased. Why *would* they not be gone? I paced the floor to and fro with heavy strides, as if excited to fury by the observation of the men—but the noise steadily increased. O God! what *could* I do? I foamed—I raved—I swore! I swung the chair upon which I had been sitting, and grated it upon the boards, but the noise arose over all and continually increased. It grew louder—louder—*louder!* And still the men chatted pleasantly, and smiled. Was it possible they heard not? Almighty God!—no, no! They heard!—they suspected! they *knew!*—they were making a *mockery* of my horror!—this I thought, and this I think. But anything was better than this agony! Anything was more tolerable than this derision! I could bear those hypocritical smiles no longer! I felt that I must scream or die!—and now—again—hark! louder! louder! louder! *louder!*—"Villains!" I shrieked, "dissemble no more! I admit the deed!—tear up the planks!—here, here!—it is the beating of his hideous heart!"

READING FOR DETAILS

Murder at Midnight

Although this account is actually of a brutal, premeditated murder, the madman telling the story seems concerned mainly with convincing his listeners of his sanity.

Discuss the "reasons" the murderer gives for the following:

1. his heightened sense of hearing
2. his decision to kill the old man
3. his manner toward the old man each morning
4. his understanding of the old man's terror
5. his invitation to the police officers to sit and visit with him

READING FOR MEANING

Consider and discuss these statements in light of the story:

1. Insane people think that they are sane.
2. The senses of an insane person are more acute than are those of a normal person.

READING FOR APPRECIATION

Atmosphere

Reread the opening lines of "The Tell-Tale Heart," and consider the details which have an effect of creating atmosphere and inspiring terror.

1. Who appears to be telling the story? What is the advantage to using first person as the narrative viewpoint?
2. What is there about the way the words are put together which makes the reader feel that this is truly the raving of a madman? What is the reaction of most persons toward anyone who seems dangerously insane?

   As the story unfolds, Poe uses imaginative language to deepen the atmosphere of terror. Discuss:

   a. Poe's personification of death
   b. the figure of speech used to describe the sound of the old man's heart

Although the dwarf, Hop-Frog, was a jester,
his final "joke" leaves the reader overcome with horror.

HOP-FROG

I never knew anyone so keenly alive to a joke as the king was. He seemed to live only for joking. To tell a good story of the joke kind and to tell it well, was the surest road to his favor. Thus it happened that his seven ministers were all noted for their accomplishments as jokers. They all took after the king, too, in being large, corpulent, oily men, as well as inimitable jokers. Whether people grow fat by joking, or whether there is something in fat itself which predisposes to a joke, I have never been quite able to determine; but certain it is that a lean joker is a *rara avis in terris.*[1]

About the refinement, or, as he called them, the "ghosts" of wit, the king troubled himself very little. He had an especial admiration for *breadth* in a jest, and would often put up with *length,* for the sake of it. Overniceties wearied him. He would have preferred Rabelais' *Gargantua,* to the *Zadig* of Voltaire:[2] and, upon the whole, practical jokes suited his taste far better than verbal ones.

At the date of my narrative, professing jesters had not altogether gone out of fashion at court. Several of the great continental "powers" still retained their "fools," who wore motley, with caps and bells,[3] and who were expected to be always ready with sharp witticisms, at a moment's notice, in consideration of the crumbs that fell from the royal table.

Our king, as a matter of course, retained his "fool." The fact is, he *required* something in the way of folly—if only to counterbalance the heavy wisdom of the seven wise men who were his ministers—not to mention himself.

His fool, or professional jester, was not *only* a fool, however. His value was trebled in the eyes of the king, by the fact of his being also a dwarf and a cripple. Dwarfs were as common at court, in those days, as fools; and many monarchs would have found it difficult to get through their days (days are rather longer at court than elsewhere) without both a jester to laugh *with,* and a dwarf to laugh *at.* But, as I have already observed, your jesters, in ninety-nine cases out of a hundred, are fat, round, and unwieldy—so that it was no small source of self-gratulation with our king that, in Hop-Frog (this was the fool's name), he possessed a triplicate treasure in one person.

I believe the name "Hop-Frog" was *not* that given to the dwarf by his sponsors at baptism, but it was conferred upon him, by general consent of the seven ministers, on account of his inability to walk as other men do. In fact,

---

1. **rara avis in terris** (rer′ə ā′vis in ter′is), "a rare bird in the land."
2. **Rabelais** (rab′ə lā), French satirist (d. 1553) who wrote a coarse and extreme book in which the giant king **Gargantua** (gär gan′chü ə) figured. The character **Zadig** (za′dig) in the work of **Voltaire** (vol ter′) (1694–1778) is very polished.
3. **motley, with cap and bells,** the traditional costume of the jester.

Hop-Frog could only get along by a sort of interjectional gait—something between a leap and a wriggle—a movement that afforded illimitable amusement, and of consolation, to the king, for (notwithstanding the protuberance of his stomach and a constitutional swelling of the head) the king, by his whole court, was accounted a capital figure.

But although Hop-Frog, through the distortion of his legs, could move only with great pain and difficulty along a road or floor, the prodigious muscular power which nature seemed to have bestowed upon his arms, by way of compensation for deficiency in the lower limbs, enabled him to perform many feats of wonderful dexterity, where trees or ropes were in question, or anything else to climb. At such exercises he certainly much more resembled a squirrel, or a small monkey, than a frog.

I am not able to say, with precision, from what country Hop-Frog originally came. It was from some barbarous region, however, that no person ever heard of—a vast distance from the court of our king. Hop-Frog, and a young girl very little less dwarfish than himself (although of exquisite proportions, and a marvelous dancer), had been forcibly carried off from their respective homes in adjoining provinces, and sent as presents to the king, by one of his ever-victorious generals.

Under these circumstances, it is not to be wondered at that a close intimacy arose between the two little captives. Indeed, they soon became sworn friends. Hop-Frog, who, although he made a great deal of sport, was by no means popular, had it not in his power to render Trippetta many services; but *she,* on account of her grace and exquisite beauty (although a dwarf), was universally admired and petted; so she possessed much influence; and never failed to use it, whenever she could, for the benefit of Hop-Frog.

On some grand state occasion—I forget what—the king determined to have a masquerade; and whenever a masquerade, or anything of that kind, occurred at our court, then the talents both of Hop-Frog and Trippetta were sure to be called in play. Hop-Frog, in especial, was so inventive in the way of getting up pageants, suggesting novel characters and arranging costume, for masked balls, that nothing could be done, it seems, without his assistance.

The night appointed for the *fête*[4] had arrived. A gorgeous hall had been fitted up, under Trippetta's eye, with every kind of device which could possibly give *éclat*[5] to a masquerade. The whole court was in a fever of expectation. As for costumes and characters,. it might well be supposed that everybody had come to a decision on such points. Many had made up their minds (as to what *rôles* they should assume) a week, or even a month, in advance; and, in fact, there was not a particle of indecision anywhere—except in the case of the king and his seven ministers. Why *they* hesitated I never could tell, unless they did it by way of a joke. More probably, they found it difficult, on account of being so fat, to make up their minds. At all events, time flew; and, as a last resource, they sent for Trippetta and Hop-Frog.

---

4. **fête** (fāt), festival or party.
5. **éclat** (ā klä′), renown, splendor.

When the two little friends obeyed the summons of the king, they found him sitting at his wine with the seven members of his cabinet council; but the monarch appeared to be in very ill humor. He knew that Hop-Frog was not fond of wine; for it excited the poor cripple almost to madness; and madness is no comfortable feeling. But the king loved his practical jokes, and took pleasure in forcing Hop-Frog to drink and (as the king called it) "to be merry."

"Come here, Hop-Frog," said he, as the jester and his friend entered the room; "swallow this bumper to the health of your absent friends [here Hop-Frog sighed] and then let us have the benefit of your invention. We want characters—*characters,* man—something novel—out of the way. We are wearied with this everlasting sameness. Come, drink! the wine will brighten your wits."

Hop-Frog endeavored, as usual, to get up a jest in reply to these advances from the king; but the effort was too much. It happened to be the poor dwarf's birthday, and the command to drink to his "absent friends" forced the tears to his eyes. Many large, bitter drops fell into the goblet as he took it, humbly, from the hand of the tyrant.

"Ah! ha! ha! ha!" roared the latter, as the dwarf reluctantly drained the beaker. "See what a glass of good wine can do! Why, your eyes are shining already!"

Poor fellow! his large eyes *gleamed,* rather than shone; for the effect of wine on his excitable brain was not more powerful than instantaneous. He placed the goblet nervously on the table, and looked round upon the company with a half-insane stare. They all seemed highly amused at the success of the king's *"joke."*

"And now to business," said the prime minister, a *very* fat man.

"Yes," said the king. "Come, Hop-Frog, lend us your assistance. Characters, my fine fellow; we stand in need of characters—all of us—ha! ha! ha!" and as this was seriously meant for a joke, his laugh was chorused by the seven.

Hop-Frog also laughed, although feebly and somewhat vacantly.

"Come, come," said the king, impatiently, "have you nothing to suggest?"

"I am endeavoring to think of something *novel,*" replied the dwarf, abstractedly, for he was quite bewildered by the wine.

"Endeavoring!" cried the tyrant, fiercely; "what do you mean by *that?* Ah, I perceive. You are sulky, and want more wine. Here, drink this!" and he poured out another goblet full and offered it to the cripple, who merely gazed at it, gasping for breath.

"Drink, I say!" shouted the monster, "or by the fiends——"

The dwarf hesitated. The king grew purple with rage. The courtiers smirked. Trippetta, pale as a corpse, advanced to the monarch's seat, and, falling on her knees before him, implored him to spare her friend.

The tyrant regarded her, for some moments, in evident wonder at her audacity. He seemed quite at a loss what to do or say—how most becomingly to express his indignation. At last, without uttering a syllable, he pushed her violently from him, and threw the contents of the brimming goblet in her face.

The poor girl got up as best she could, and, not daring even to sigh, resumed her position at the foot of the table.

There was a dead silence for about half a minute, during which the falling of a leaf, or of a feather, might have been heard. It was interrupted by a low, but harsh and protracted *grating* sound which seemed to come at once from every corner of the room.

"What—what—*what* are you making that noise for?" demanded the king, turning furiously to the dwarf.

The latter seemed to have recovered, in great measure, from his intoxication, and looking fixedly but quietly into the tyrant's face, merely ejaculated:

"I—I? How could it have been me?"

"The sound appeared to come from without," observed one of the courtiers. "I fancy it was the parrot at the window, whetting his bill upon his cage-wires."

"True," replied the monarch, as if much relieved by the suggestion; "but, on the honor of a knight, I could have sworn that it was the gritting of this vagabond's teeth."

Hereupon the dwarf laughed (the king was too confirmed a joker to object to any one's laughing), and displayed a set of large, powerful, and very repulsive teeth. Moreover, he avowed his perfect willingness to swallow as much wine as desired. The monarch was pacified; and having drained another bumper with no very perceptible ill effect, Hop-Frog entered at once, and with spirit, into the plans for the masquerade.

"I cannot tell what was the association of idea," observed he, very tranquilly, and as if he had never tasted wine in his life, "but *just after* your majesty had struck the girl and thrown the wine in her face—*just after* your majesty had done this, and while the parrot was making that odd noise outside the window, there came into my mind a capital diversion—one of my own country frolics—often enacted among us, at our masquerades: but here it will be new altogether. Unfortunately, however, it requires a company of eight persons, and——"

"Here we *are!*" cried the king, laughing at his acute discovery of the coincidence; "eight to a fraction—I and my seven ministers. Come! what is the diversion?"

"We call it," replied the cripple, "the Eight Chained Ourang-Outangs, and it really is excellent sport if well enacted."

"*We* will enact it," remarked the king, drawing himself up, and lowering his eyelids.

"The beauty of the game," continued Hop-Frog, "lies in the fright it occasions among the women."

"Capital!" roared in chorus the monarch and his ministry.

"I will equip you as ourang-outangs,"[6] proceeded the dwarf; "leave all that to me. The resemblance shall be so striking, that the company of masqueraders will take you for real beasts—and of course, they will be as much terrified as astonished."

"Oh, this is exquisite!" exclaimed the king. "Hop-Frog! I will make a man of you."

"The chains are for the purpose of increasing the confusion by their jangling. You are supposed to have escaped, *en masse,* from your keepers. Your majesty cannot conceive the *effect* produced, at a masquerade, by eight chained ourang-outangs, imagined to be real ones

6. **ourang-outangs,** large apes of the forests of Borneo and Sumatra.

by most of the company; and rushing in with savage cries, among the crowd of delicately and gorgeously habited men and women. The *contrast* is inimitable."

"It *must* be," said the king: and the council arose hurriedly (as it was growing late), to put in execution the scheme of Hop-Frog.

His mode of equipping the party as ourang-outangs was very simple, but effective enough for his purposes. The animals in question had, at the epoch of my story, very rarely been seen in any part of the civilized world; and as the imitations made by the dwarf were sufficiently beast-like and more than sufficiently hideous, their truthfulness to nature was thus thought to be secured.

The king and his ministers were first encased in tight-fitting stockinet[7] shirts and drawers. They were then saturated with tar. At this stage of the process, some one of the party suggested feathers; but the suggestion was at once overruled by the dwarf, who soon convinced the eight, by ocular demonstration, that the hair of such a brute as the ourang-outang was much more efficiently represented by *flax*. A thick coating of the latter was accordingly plastered upon the coating of tar. A long chain was now procured. First, it was passed about the waist of the king, *and tied;* then about another of the party, and also tied; then about all successively, in the same manner. When this chaining arrangement was complete, and the party stood as far apart from each other as possible, they formed a circle; and to make all things appear natural, Hop-Frog passed the residue of the chain, in two diameters, at right angles, across the circle, after the fashion adopted, at the present day, by those who

capture chimpanzees, or other large apes, in Borneo.[8]

The grand saloon in which the masquerade was to take place, was a circular room, very lofty, and receiving the light of the sun only through a single window at top. At night (the season for which the apartment was especially designed) it was illuminated principally by a large chandelier, depending by a chain from the centre of the sky-light, and lowered, or elevated, by means of a counterbalance as usual; but (in order not to look unsightly) this latter passed outside the cupola and over the roof.

The arrangements of the room had been left to Trippetta's superintendence; but, in some particulars, it seems, she had been guided by the calmer judgment of her friend the dwarf. At his suggestion it was that, on this occasion, the chandelier was removed. Its waxen drippings (which, in weather so warm, it was quite impossible to prevent) would have been seriously detrimental to the rich dresses of the guests, who, on account of the crowded state of the saloon, could not *all* be expected to keep from out its centre—that is to say, from under the chandelier. Additional sconces were set in various parts of the hall, out of the way; and a flambeau, emitting sweet odor, was placed in the right hand of each of the Caryatides[9] that stood against the wall—some fifty or sixty all together.

The eight ourang-outangs, taking Hop-Frog's advice, waited patiently until midnight (when the room was thor-

---

7. **stockinet,** an elastic knitted fabric.
8. **Borneo** (bôr'nē ō), a large tropical island in the East Indies.
9. **flambeau** (flam'bō) **. . . Caryatides** (kar'ē at'idz), a torch; a pillar designed in the form of a draped female figure.

oughly filled with masqueraders) before making their appearance. No sooner had the clock ceased striking, however, than they rushed, or rather rolled in, all together—for the impediments of their chains caused most of the party to fall, and all to stumble as they entered.

The excitement among the masqueraders was prodigious, and filled the heart of the king with glee. As had been anticipated, there were not a few of the guests who supposed the ferocious-looking creatures to be beasts of *some* kind in reality, if not precisely ourang-outangs. Many of the women swooned with affright; and had not the king taken the precaution to exclude all weapons from the saloon, his party might soon have expiated their frolic in their blood. As it was, a general rush was made for the doors; but the king had ordered them to be locked immediately upon his entrance; and, at the dwarf's suggestion, the keys had been deposited with *him*.

While the tumult was at its height, and each masquerader attentive only to his own safety (for, in fact, there was much *real* danger from the pressure of the excited crowd), the chain by which the chandelier ordinarily hung, and which had been drawn up on its removal, might have been seen very gradually to descend, until its hooked extremity came within three feet of the floor.

Soon after this, the king and his seven friends having reeled about the hall in all directions, found themselves, at length, in its centre, and, of course, in immediate contact with the chain. While they were thus situated, the dwarf, who had followed noiselessly at their heels, inciting them to keep up the commotion, took hold of their own chain at the intersec-tion of the two portions which crossed the circle diametrically and at right angles. Here, with the rapidity of thought, he inserted the hook from which the chandelier had been wont to depend; and, in an instant, by some unseen agency, the chandelier-chain was drawn so far upward as to take the hook out of reach, and, as an inevitable consequence, to drag the ourang-outangs together in close connection, and face to face.

The masqueraders, by this time, had recovered, in some measure, from their alarm; and, beginning to regard the whole matter as a well-contrived pleasantry, set up a loud shout of laughter at the predicament of the apes.

"Leave them to *me!*" now screamed Hop-Frog, his shrill voice making itself easily heard through all the din. "Leave them to *me*. I fancy *I* know them. If I can only get a good look at them, *I* can soon tell who they are."

Here, scrambling over the heads of the crowd, he managed to get to the wall; when, seizing a flambeau from one of the Caryatides, he returned, as he went, to the centre of the room—leaped, with the agility of a monkey, upon the king's head—and thence clambered a few feet up the chain—holding down the torch to examine the group of ourang-outangs, and still screaming, "*I* shall soon find out who they are!"

And now, while the whole assembly (the apes included) were convulsed with laughter, the jester suddenly uttered a shrill whistle; when the chain flew violently up for about thirty feet—dragging with it the dismayed and struggling ourang-outangs, and leaving them suspended in mid-air between the sky-light and the floor. Hop-Frog, clinging to the

THE VENGEANCE OF HOP-FROG
James Ensor Collection
Museum of Modern Art, New York
Gift of Victor S. Riesenfeld

chain as it rose, still maintained his relative position in respect to the eight maskers, and still (as if nothing were the matter) continued to thrust his torch down toward them, as though endeavoring to discover who they were.

So thoroughly astonished were the whole company at this ascent, that a dead silence, of about a minute's duration, ensued. It was broken by just such a low, harsh, *grating* sound, as had before attracted the attention of the king and his councillors when the former threw the wine in the face of Trippetta. But, on the present occasion, there could be no question as to *whence* the sound issued. It came from the fang-like teeth of the dwarf, who ground them and gnashed them as he foamed at the mouth, and glared, with an expression of maniacal rage, into the upturned countenances of the king and his seven companions.

"Ah, ha!" said at length the infuriated jester. "Ah, ha! I begin to see who these people *are,* now!" Here, pretending to scrutinize the king more closely, he held the flambeau to the flaxen coat which enveloped him, and which instantly burst into a sheet of vivid flame. In less than half a minute the whole eight ourang-outangs were blazing fiercely, amid the shrieks of the multitude who gazed at them from below, horror-stricken, and without the power to render them the slightest assistance.

At length the flames, suddenly increasing in virulence, forced the jester to climb higher up the chain, to be out of their reach; and, as he made this movement, the crowd again sank, for a brief instant, into silence. The dwarf seized his opportunity, and once more spoke:

"I now see *distinctly,*" he said, "what manner of people these maskers are. They are a great king and his seven privy-councillors,—a king who does not scruple to strike a defenseless girl, and his seven councillors who abet him in the outrage. As for myself, I am simply Hop-Frog, the jester—and *this is my last jest.*"

Owing to the high combustibility of both the flax and the tar to which it adhered, the dwarf had scarcely made an end of his brief speech before the work of vengeance was complete. The eight corpses swung in their chains, a fetid, blackened, hideous, and indistinguishable mass. The cripple hurled his torch at them, clambered leisurely to the ceiling, and disappeared through the sky-light.

It is supposed that Trippetta, stationed on the roof of the saloon, had been the accomplice of her friend in his fiery revenge, and that, together, they effected their escape to their own country: for neither was seen again.

READING FOR DETAILS

A Fiery Revenge

As a poor unfortunate creature whose duty it was to amuse the court, Hop-Frog was denied the right to express the feelings and emotions of a man. He could stand the abuse heaped upon himself, but when the king mistreated Trippetta, the cunning mind of the "fool" conceived a daring scheme of revenge. Actually, of course, the slave was much more intelligent than the master.

1. How does the reader come to realize that the king is really a very stupid person? For what qualities had the king chosen his ministers?
2. How and why had the lighting been changed in the great room where the masquerade was held?
3. Although Hop-Frog was unable to walk as most men do, he had great strength in his arms and shoulders. Why does Poe mention this detail early in the story?
4. When does it become evident that the "low, harsh, *grating* sound" is made by the dwarf?

READING FOR MEANING

Find evidence in the story that supports the following ideas:

1. A loud laugh usually covers a vacant mind.
2. Revenge may be sweet, but each time

people gain revenge they lose some part of their own humanity.

READING FOR APPRECIATION

Foreshadowing Atmosphere

This story of Poe's is based upon the theme of revenge. In creating an atmosphere which carries the reader along to a final reaction of horror, Poe's first sentence is significant. He opens his story with the statement: "I never knew anyone so keenly alive to a joke as the king was."

What word here foreshadows the fact that all is no longer well with the king—that something has happened either to him or to his sense of humor?

Irony

Review the study notes for Part IV of the *Odyssey*. Ironic statements which reverse the known facts or pretend to ignorance have many variations.

1. A crude or biting kind of irony is called sarcasm. Poe carefully employs both irony and sarcasm to make the king seem contemptible.

Discuss the irony and sarcasm in the quotations below:

a. *Our* king . . . *required* something in the way of folly—if only to counterbalance the heavy wisdom of the seven wise men who were his ministers—not to mention himself.

b. "Oh, this is exquisite!" exclaimed the king. "Hop-Frog! I will make a man of you."

c. "I now see *distinctly*," he said, "what manner of people these maskers are. They are a great king and his seven privy-councillors. . . ."

2. With the corpses of the king and his ministers hanging ". . . a fetid, blackened, hideous, and indistinguishable mass," Poe leaves the reader with a last horrible image in mind. However, it is grimly satisfying. Discuss why this should be so.

The dark mysteries of death intrigued Poe in his poetry as well as in his stories. In an article for *Graham's Magazine*, April, 1846, he wrote, "The death, then, of a beautiful woman is, unquestionably, the most poetical topic in the world—and equally is it beyond doubt that the lips best suited for such a topic are those of a bereaved lover."

Two of Poe's most famous poems, "The Raven" and "Annabel Lee," are based upon this theme. "The Raven" was written about two years before his young wife's death, during the time when she was so frail and sickly that Poe, who loved her very much, probably suffered her death in his imagination many times. A playing back and forth of sounds in the poem creates the atmosphere, a feeling of dark shadows moving in from the corners.

Poe felt that poetry was not only truth or emotions, but also music. "The Raven" is a poem to be accompanied by the even, pounding rhythm of a bass drum and the wailing notes of a bassoon. At midnight, we look into the study of a man whose sweetheart has died.

The Raven

Once upon a midnight dreary, while I pondered, weak and weary,
Over many a quaint and curious volume of forgotten lore—
While I nodded, nearly napping, suddenly there came a tapping,
As of someone gently rapping, rapping at my chamber door.
"'Tis some visitor," I muttered, "tapping at my chamber door—   5
   Only this and nothing more."

Ah, distinctly I remember it was in the bleak December;
And each separate dying ember wrought its ghost upon the floor.
Eagerly I wished the morrow;—vainly I had sought to borrow
From my books surcease of sorrow—sorrow for the lost Lenore—   10
For the rare and radiant maiden whom the angels name Lenore—
   Nameless here for evermore.

And the silken, sad, uncertain rustling of each purple curtain
Thrilled me—filled me with fantastic terrors never felt before;
So that now, to still the beating of my heart, I stood repeating   15
"'Tis some visitor entreating entrance at my chamber door,
Some late visitor entreating entrance at my chamber door:
   This it is and nothing more."

Presently my soul grew stronger; hesitating then no longer,
"Sir," said I, "or Madam, truly your forgiveness I implore: 20
But the fact is I was napping, and so gently you came rapping,
And so faintly you came tapping, tapping at my chamber door,
That I scarce was sure I heard you"—here I opened wide the door;—
   Darkness there and nothing more.

Deep into that darkness peering, long I stood there wondering, fearing,   25
Doubting, dreaming dreams no mortals ever dared to dream before:
But the silence was unbroken, and the stillness gave no token,
And the only word there spoken was the whispered word, "Lenore?"
This I whispered, and an echo murmured back the word, "Lenore!"
    Merely this and nothing more.   30

Back into the chamber turning, all my soul within me burning,
Soon again I heard a tapping somewhat louder than before.
"Surely," said I, "surely that is something at my window lattice;
Let me see, then, what thereat is, and this mystery explore;
Let my heart be still a moment and this mystery explore: 35
    'Tis the wind and nothing more!"

Open here I flung the shutter, when, with many a flirt and flutter,
In there stepped a stately Raven of the saintly days of yore;
Not the least obeisance made he; not a minute stopped or stayed he;
But with mien of lord or lady, perched above my chamber door,   40
Perched upon a bust of Pallas[1] just above my chamber door:
    Perched, and sat, and nothing more.

Then this ebon[2] bird beguiling my sad fancy into smiling
By the grave and stern decorum of the countenance it wore,
"Though thy crest be shorn and shaven, thou," I said, "art sure no craven,   45
Ghastly grim and ancient Raven wandering from the Nightly shore—
Tell me what thy lordly name is on the Night's Plutonian[3] shore!"
    Quoth the Raven, "Nevermore."

Much I marveled this ungainly fowl to hear discourse so plainly,
Though its answer little meaning—little relevancy bore;   50
For we cannot help agreeing that no living human being
Ever yet was blessed with seeing bird above his chamber door,
Bird or beast upon the sculptured bust above his chamber door,
    With such name as "Nevermore."

But the Raven, sitting lonely on the placid bust, spoke only   55
That one word, as if his soul in that one word he did outpour.

1. **Pallas** (pal′əs), or **Pallas Athene,** was goddess of the
arts and industry in classical Greek mythology.
2. **ebon** (eb′ən), old form of ebony: black, dark.
3. **Plutonian** (plü tō′nē ən), pertaining to the realm of
Pluto, or Hades, the god of the underworld, the gloomy
abode of the ghosts of the dead.

*"Prophet!" said I,
"thing of evil!"
prophet still,
if bird or devil!*

Nothing further then he uttered, not a feather then he fluttered,
Till I scarcely more than muttered,—"Other friends have flown before;
On the morrow *he* will leave me, as my Hopes have flown before."
   Then the bird said, "Nevermore." 60

Startled at the stillness broken by reply so aptly spoken,
"Doubtless," said I, "what it utters is its only stock and store,
Caught from some unhappy master whom unmerciful Disaster
Followed fast and followed faster till his songs one burden bore—
Till the dirges of his Hope that melancholy burden bore 65
   Of 'Never—nevermore.'"

But the Raven still beguiling all my fancy into smiling,
Straight I wheeled a cushioned seat in front of bird and bust and door;
Then, upon the velvet sinking, I betook myself to linking
Fancy unto fancy, thinking what this ominous bird of yore,   70
What this grim, ungainly, ghastly, gaunt, and ominous bird of yore
   Meant in croaking, "Nevermore."

This I sat engaged in guessing, but no syllable expressing
To the fowl whose fiery eyes now burned into my bosom's core;
This and more I sat divining, with my head at ease reclining   75
On the cushion's velvet lining that the lamplight gloated o'er,
But whose velvet violet lining with the lamplight gloating o'er
   She shall press, ah, nevermore!

Then, methought, the air grew denser, perfumed from an unseen censer
Swung by Seraphim[4] whose footfalls tinkled on the tufted floor.   80
"Wretch," I cried, "thy God hath lent thee—by these angels he hath sent thee
Respite—respite and nepenthe[5] from thy memories of Lenore,
Quaff,[6] oh, quaff this kind nepenthe, and forget this lost Lenore!"
   Quoth the Raven, "Nevermore."

"Prophet!" said I, "thing of evil! prophet still, if bird or devil!   85
Whether Tempter sent, or whether tempest tossed thee here ashore,
Desolate yet all undaunted, on this desert land enchanted—
On this home by Horror haunted—tell me truly, I implore:
Is there—*is* there balm in Gilead?[7]—tell me—tell me, I implore!"
   Quoth the Raven, "Nevermore."   90

"Prophet!" said I, "thing of evil—prophet still, if bird or devil!
By that Heaven that bends above us, by that God we both adore,
Tell this soul with sorrow laden if, within the distant Aidenn,[8]
It shall clasp a sainted maiden whom the angels name Lenore—
Clasp a rare and radiant maiden whom the angels name Lenore!"   95
   Quoth the Raven, "Nevermore."

4. **Seraphim** (ser′ə fim), plural of seraph, the highest ranking angels.
5. **nepenthe** (ni pen′thē), a drink or drug supposed to bring forgetfulness of sorrow or trouble, according to an old legend.
6. **Quaff,** drink in large swallows.
7. **Is there balm in Gilead?,** is there cure or healing? Balm is a soothing oil, an ancient product of the Biblical land Gilead. Jeremiah 8:22, in the Old Testament.
8. **Aidenn** (ā′din), paradise; a variant spelling of the Arabic word for Eden.

"Be that word our sign of parting, bird or fiend!" I shrieked, upstarting:
"Get thee back into the tempest and the Night's Plutonian shore!
Leave no black plume as a token of that lie thy soul hath spoken!
Leave my loneliness unbroken—quit the bust above my door!   100
Take thy beak from out my heart, and take thy form from off my door!"
    Quoth the Raven, "Nevermore."

And the Raven, never flitting, still is sitting, *still* is sitting
On the pallid bust of Pallas just above my chamber door;
And his eyes have all the seeming of a demon's that is dreaming,   105
And the lamplight o'er him streaming throws his shadow on the floor;
And my soul from out that shadow that lies floating on the floor
    Shall be lifted—nevermore!

READING FOR DETAILS

A Midnight Visitor
It is a dark and gloomy midnight. A man who has lost his beloved Lenore is trying to forget her by burying himself in his books. Suddenly he hears a mysterious tapping at the door. Did you follow the story from there? What happens:

1. When he opens the door?
2. When he returns to his books?
3. When he opens the window and the lattice?
4. When the Raven comes in?
5. When he asks the Raven its name?
6. When he asks the Raven to leave?

READING FOR MEANING

Consider these statements in light of "The Raven":

1. The man discovers that the bird has been trained to say one word. So when he asks questions, he really knows what the answer will be. Thus he is asking things that really increase his unhappiness.
2. The compulsive desire to suffer is a common one, and many people find pleasure in thus punishing themselves.

READING FOR APPRECIATION

Imaginative Language
Poe apparently felt that the word *nevermore* had as melancholy a sound as any in the English language. Thus, he uses the word as the sound of gloom and despair. What other words in the poem seem to have been chosen to give a quality of gloom?

1. This poem is rich in the use of *alliteration,* a term you have used before. Find examples of alliteration and explain what effect they have in the poem.
2. a. When two or more poetic lines or portions of lines near one another have a similar structure and express a similar meaning, they are considered *parallel.* Find examples of such parallelism in "The Raven."
   b. What words repeated in the refrain are often quoted because once people have read them they find the words hard to forget?
3. Read through the poem again, noting the imagery chosen for light, color, and texture. List the descriptive words for each group in separate columns. Discuss what each group contributes to the atmosphere of the poem.

Like the singing of violins, the rhythms of "Annabel Lee" pulse through the reader's heart. Though the poem may have been inspired by the death of his wife, Poe did not give it the dark, somber quality of "The Raven." But, like "The Raven," this poem is built on Poe's contention that the most suitable subject for poetry is the grief of a man over the death of a beautiful woman.

Annabel Lee

It was many and many a year ago,
   In a kingdom by the sea,
That a maiden there lived whom you may know
   By the name of Annabel Lee;
And this maiden she lived with no other thought   5
   Than to love and be loved by me.

I was a child and *She* was a child,
   In the kingdom by the sea,
But we loved with a love that was more than love,
   I and my Annabel Lee;   10
With a love that the wingéd seraphs of heaven
   Coveted her and me.

And this was the reason that, long ago,
   In this kingdom by the sea,
A wind blew out of a cloud, chilling   15
   My beautiful Annabel Lee;
So that her highborn kinsmen came
   And bore her away from me,
To shut her up in a sepulcher
   In this kingdom by the sea.   20

The angels, not half so happy in heaven,
   Went envying her and me;
Yes! That was the reason (as all men know,
   In this kingdom by the sea)
That the wind came out of the cloud by night,   25
   Chilling and killing my Annabel Lee.

But our love was stronger by far than the love
   Of those who were older than we,
   Of many far wiser than we;

For the moon never beams without bringing me dreams
  Of the beautiful Annabel Lee.

And neither the angels in heaven above,   30
    Nor the demons down under the sea,
Can ever dissever my soul from the soul
    Of the beautiful Annabel Lee:

For the moon never beams without bringing me dreams
    Of the beautiful Annabel Lee;   35
And the stars never rise, but I feel the bright eyes
    Of the beautiful Annabel Lee;
And so, all the night-tide, I lie down by the side
Of my darling—my darling—my life and my bride,
    In the sepulcher there by the sea,   40
    In her tomb by the sounding sea.

READING FOR APPRECIATION

Mood and Pattern

"Annabel Lee" is one of the favorite poems of the English language. Its lines are so melodic that people have memorized them almost without trying. The shadowy outline of a story teases the imagination of readers, urging them to try filling in details. But the poem is interesting mainly because words are used to create a mood almost the way sound is used in music. The rhythm imitates the melancholy sound of quiet breakers rolling gently upon the seashore, an effect achieved by the pattern of repetition and variation.

What do you discover about the following?

1. the number of lines in the stanzas
2. the regularity of the rhyme scheme
3. the repetition of rhyming words from one stanza to the next
4. the variation in the length of lines
5. the repetition of the rhythm of lines

A town is enveloped in the madness that is carnival. Raucous laughter, flickering light of torches, gayly costumed and masked figures are contrasted with the bitter hate and horrible thoughts in the mind of one man. Slowly, slowly, the plot unravels. Prepare for a chill as penetrating as that of the cold, dank earth in the catacombs.

THE CASK OF AMONTILLADO

The thousand injuries of Fortunato I had borne as best I could, but when he ventured upon insult, I vowed revenge. You, who so well know the nature of my soul, will not suppose, however, that I gave utterance to a threat. *At length* I would be avenged; this was a point definitely settled—but the very definiteness with which it was resolved precluded the idea of risk. I must not only punish, but punish with impunity. A wrong is unredressed when retribution overtakes its redresser. It is equally unredressed when the avenger fails to make himself felt as such to him who has done the wrong.

It must be understood that neither by word nor deed had I given Fortunato cause to doubt my good will. I continued, as was my wont, to smile in his face, and he did not perceive that my smile *now* was at the thought of his immolation.

He had a weak point—this Fortunato—although in other regards he was a man to be respected and even feared. He prided himself on his connoisseurship in wine. Few Italians have the true virtuoso spirit. For the most part their enthusiasm is adopted to suit the time and opportunity, to practice imposture upon the British and Austrian millionaires. In painting and gemmary,[1] Fortunato, like his countrymen, was a quack, but in the matter of old wines he was sincere. In this respect I did not differ from him materially. I was skillful in the Italian vintages myself and bought largely whenever I could.

It was about dusk, one evening during the supreme madness of the carnival season, that I encountered my friend. He accosted me with excessive warmth, for he had been drinking much. The man wore motley. He had on a tight-fitting parti-striped dress, and his head was surmounted by the conical cap and bells. I was so pleased to see him that I thought I should never have done wringing his hand.

I said to him, "My dear Fortunato, you are luckily met. How remarkably well you are looking today! But I have received a pipe[2] of what passes for Amontillado,[3] and I have my doubts."

"How?" said he. "Amontillado? A pipe? Impossible! And in the middle of the carnival!"

"I have my doubts," I replied; "and I was silly enough to pay the full Amontillado price without consulting you in the

---

1. **gemmary,** the science of gems.
2. **pipe,** a large barrel.
3. **Amontillado** (ə mon'tə lä'dō), a fine Spanish sherry wine.

matter. You were not to be found, and I was fearful of losing a bargain."

"Amontillado!"

"I have my doubts."

"Amontillado!"

"And I must satisfy them."

"Amontillado!"

"As you are engaged, I am on my way to Luchesi. If anyone has a critical turn,[4] it is he. He will tell me—"

"Luchesi cannot tell Amontillado from Sherry."

"And yet some fools will have it that his taste is a match for your own."

"Come, let us go."

"Whither?"

"To your vaults."

"My friend, no; I will not impose upon your good nature. I perceive you have an engagement. Luchesi—"

"I have no engagement—come."

"My friend, no. It is not the engagement, but the severe cold with which I perceive you are afflicted. The vaults are insufferably damp. They are incrusted with niter."[5]

"Let us go nevertheless. The cold is merely nothing. Amontillado! You have been imposed upon. And as for Luchesi, he cannot distinguish Sherry from Amontillado."

Thus speaking, Fortunato possessed himself of my arm. Putting on a mask of black silk, and drawing a *roquelaure*[6] closely about my person, I suffered him to hurry me to my palazzo.[7]

There were no attendants at home; they had absconded to make merry in honor of the time. I had told them that I should not return until the morning, and had given them explicit orders not to stir from the house. These orders were sufficient, I well knew, to insure their imme-diate disappearance, one and all, as soon as my back was turned.

I took from their sconces[8] two flambeaux, and giving one to Fortunato, bowed him through several suites of rooms to the archway that led into the vaults. I passed down a long and winding staircase, requesting him to be cautious as he followed. We came at length to the foot of the descent and stood together on the damp ground of the catacombs of the Montresors.

The gait of my friend was unsteady, and the bells upon his cap jingled as he strode.

"The pipe," said he.

"It is farther on," said I; "but observe the white webwork which gleams from these cavern walls."

He turned toward me, and looked into my eyes with two filmy orbs that distilled the rheum[9] of intoxication.

"Niter?" he asked at length.

"Niter," I replied. "How long have you had that cough?"

"Ugh! ugh! ugh!—ugh! ugh! ugh!— ugh! ugh! ugh!—ugh! ugh! ugh!—ugh! ugh! ugh!"

My poor friend found it impossible to reply for many minutes.

"It is nothing," he said at last.

"Come," I said, with decision, "we will go back; your health is precious. You are rich, respected, admired, beloved; you are happy, as once I was. You are a man

---

4. **If anyone has a critical turn,** if anyone is able to criticize.
5. **niter** (nī′tər), the white webbing was a potassium or sodium salt—saltpeter—commonly collected on the walls of wet, dark places.
6. **roquelaure** (rō′kə lōr′), cloak.
7. **palazzo** (pä lät′sō), a palace.
8. **sconces,** brackets projecting from a wall, used to hold candles or other lights.
9. **rheum** (rüm), tears.

to be missed. For me it is no matter. We will go back; you will be ill, and I cannot be responsible. Besides, there is Luchesi—"

"Enough," he said; "the cough is a mere nothing; it will not kill me. I shall not die of a cough."

"True—true," I replied; "and, indeed, I had no intention of alarming you unnecessarily—but you should use all proper caution. A draught of this Médoc[10] will defend us from the damps."

Here I knocked off the neck of a bottle which I drew from a long row of its fellows that lay upon the mold.

"Drink," I said, presenting him the wine.

He raised it to his lips with a leer. He paused and nodded to me familiarly, while his bells jingled.

"I drink," he said, "to the buried that repose around us."

"And I to your long life."

He again took my arm, and we proceeded.

"These vaults," he said, "are extensive."

"The Montresors," I replied, "were a great and numerous family."

"I forget your arms."

"A huge human foot *d'or*,[11] in a field azure; the foot crushes a serpent rampant whose fangs are embedded in the heel."

"And the motto?"

"Nemo me impune lacessit."[12]

"Good!" he said.

The wine sparkled in his eyes and the bells jingled. My own fancy grew warm with the Médoc. We had passed through walls of piled bones, with casks and puncheons intermingling, into the inmost recesses of the catacombs. I paused

again, and this time I made bold to seize Fortunato by an arm above the elbow.

"The niter!" I said. "See, it increases. It hangs like moss upon the vaults. We are below the river's bed. The drops of moisture trickle among the bones. Come, we will go back ere it is too late. Your cough—"

"It is nothing," he said; "let us go on. But first, another draft of the Médoc."

I broke and reached him a flagon of De Grâve.[13] He emptied it at a breath. His eyes flashed with a fierce light. He laughed, and threw the bottle upward with a gesticulation I did not understand.

I looked at him in surprise. He repeated the movement—a grotesque one.

"You do not comprehend?" he said.

"Not I," I replied.

"Then you are not of the brotherhood."

"How?"

"You are not of the masons."

"Yes, yes," I said. "Yes, yes."

"You? Impossible! A mason?"

"A mason," I replied.

"A sign," he said.

"It is this," I answered, producing a trowel from beneath the folds of my *roquelaure*.

"You jest," he exclaimed, recoiling a few paces. "But let us proceed to the Amontillado."

"Be it so," I said, replacing the tool beneath the cloak and again offering him my arm. He leaned upon it heavily. We

---

10. **Médoc** (mā'dok), a French wine.
11. **d'or** (dōr), golden, of gold. This describes the coat of arms of Montresor's family.
12. **Nemo me impune lacessit** (ne'mō mā im'pū ne la ke'set), "No one attacks me without being punished for it."
13. **De Grâve** (də grav'), wine.

"For the love of God, Montresor!"

continued our route in search of the Amontillado. We passed through a range of low arches, descended, passed on, and, descending again, arrived at a deep crypt, in which the foulness of the air caused our flambeaux rather to glow than flame.

At the most remote end of the crypt there appeared another, less spacious. Its walls had been lined with human remains, piled to the vault overhead, in the fashion of the great catacombs of Paris. Three sides of this interior crypt were still ornamented in this manner. From the fourth the bones had been thrown down, and lay promiscuously upon the earth, forming at one point a mound of some size. Within the wall thus exposed by the displacing of the bones we perceived a still interior crypt or recess, in depth about four feet, in width three, in height six or seven. It seemed to have been constructed for no especial use within itself, but formed merely the interval between two of the colossal supports of the roof of the catacombs, and was backed by one of their circumscribing walls of solid granite.

It was in vain that Fortunato, uplifting his dull torch, endeavored to pry into the depth of the recess. Its termination the feeble light did not enable us to see.

"Proceed," I said; "herein is the Amontillado. As for Luchesi—"

"He is an ignoramus," interrupted my friend, as he stepped unsteadily forward, while I followed immediately at his heels. In an instant he had reached the extremity of the niche, and finding his progress arrested by the rock, stood stupidly bewildered. A moment more, and I had fettered him to the granite. In its surface were two iron staples, distant from each other about two feet, horizontally. From one of these depended a short chain, from the other a padlock. Throwing the links about his waist, it was but the work of a few seconds to secure it. He was too much astounded to resist. Withdrawing the key, I stepped back from the recess.

"Pass your hand," I said, "over the wall; you cannot help feeling the niter. Indeed it is *very* damp. Once more let me *implore* you to return. No? Then I must positively leave you. But I must first render you all the little attentions in my power."

"The Amontillado!' ejaculated my friend, not yet recovered from his astonishment.

"True," I replied. "The Amontillado."

As I said these words I busied myself among the pile of bones of which I have before spoken. Throwing them aside, I soon uncovered a quantity of building stone and mortar. With these materials and with the aid of my trowel, I began vigorously to wall up the entrance of the niche.

I had scarcely laid the first tier of the masonry when I discovered that the intoxication of Fortunato had in a great measure worn off. The earliest indication I had of this was a low moaning cry from the depth of the recess. It was *not* the cry of a drunken man. There was then a long and obstinate silence. I laid the second tier, and the third, and the fourth; and then I heard the furious vibrations of the chain. The noise lasted for several minutes, during which, that I might hearken to it with the more satisfaction, I ceased my labors and sat down upon the bones. When at last the clanking subsided, I resumed the trowel, and finished without interruption the fifth, the sixth, and the seventh tier. The wall was now nearly upon a level with my breast. I again paused, and holding the flambeaux over the masonwork, threw a few feeble rays upon the figure within.

A succession of loud and shrill screams, bursting suddenly from the throat of the chained form, seemed to thrust me violently back. For a brief moment I hesitated, I trembled. Unsheathing my rapier, I began to grope with it about the recess; but the thought of an instant reassured me. I placed my hand upon the solid fabric of the catacombs, and felt satisfied. I re-approached the wall; I replied to the yells of him who clamored. I re-echoed—I aided—I surpassed them in volume and in strength. I did this, and the clamorer grew still.

It was now midnight, and my task was drawing to a close. I had completed the eighth, the ninth, and the tenth tier. I had finished a portion of the last and the eleventh; there remained but a single stone to be fitted and plastered in. I struggled with its weight; I placed it partially in its destined position. But now there came from out the niche a low laugh that erected the hairs upon my head. It was succeeded by a sad voice, which I had difficulty in recognizing as that of the noble Fortunato. The voice said:

"Ha! ha! ha!—he! he! he!—a very good joke indeed—an excellent jest. We will have many a rich laugh about it at the palazzo—he! he! he!—over our wine—he! he! he!"

"The Amontillado!" I said.

"He! he! he!—he! he! he!—yes, the Amontillado. But is it not getting late?

Will not they be awaiting us at the palazzo—the Lady Fortunato and the rest? Let us be gone."

"Yes," I said, "let us be gone."

"For the love of God, Montresor!"

"Yes," I said, "for the love of God!"

But to these words I hearkened in vain for a reply. I grew impatient. I called aloud,—

"Fortunato!"

No answer. I called again,—

"Fortunato!"

No answer still. I thrust a torch through the remaining aperture and let it fall within. There came forth in return only the jingling of the bells. My heart grew sick—on account of the dampness of the catacombs. I hastened to make an end of my labor. I forced the last stone into its position; I plastered it up. Against the new masonry I re-erected the old rampart of bones. For the half of a century no mortal has disturbed them. *In pace requiescat.*[14]

READING FOR DETAILS

An Unsuspecting Victim

The story leads the reader along just as Fortunato is led along. Neither the reader nor Fortunato is aware of the horrible plan being unwound. The final horror is so shocking that the reader's mind rejects the truth just as Fortunato tries to believe it is all a joke.

Consider the following:

1. Why is carnival season a good time for Montresor to carry out his diabolical plot?
2. How does Montresor work on Fortunato's vanity to lure him into the trap?

---

14. *In pace requiescat* (in pä′kə re′kwē es′kät), "May he rest in peace."

3. What details are given of the catacombs which make them seem particularly depressing?

4. How does Montresor keep Fortunato from any suspicion of his intention?

READING FOR MEANING

The two statements below are quotations from the story. Discuss the meaning in each.

1. A wrong is unredressed when retribution overtakes its redresser.

2. It is equally unredressed when the avenger fails to make himself felt as such to him who has done the wrong.

READING FOR APPRECIATION

Atmosphere

Poe manages a fiendish irony throughout the story, making it grimly humorous in places and adding to the final impact of horror. Discuss why each of the following is ironic:

a. the victim's name, Fortunato

b. Montresor's apparent concern for Fortunato's health

c. Montresor's toast to Fortunato's long life

d. Fortunato's wearing a cap with bells that tinkle as he walks

e. Montresor's urging the chained Fortunato to return to the street with him

f. Montresor's saying in the final paragraph: "My heart grew sick—on account of the dampness of the catacombs."

g. *In pace requiescat.*

LANGUAGE AND VOCABULARY

Edgar Allan Poe was a nineteenth-century literary figure, and, naturally, he wrote in the literary language of his time. His choice of words may seem bookish and rather formal to you, especially when compared to other selections in this book. Find a number of examples to back up your own ideas on this subject.

COMPOSITION

"Hop Frog" and "The Cask of Amontillado" have in common the theme of revenge. Write a brief paper in which you compare the magnitude of the insult or insults being revenged in these two stories, and, as a conclusion, express your feelings about the motives of the avengers.

SUMMING UP: ONCE UPON A MIDNIGHT

READING FOR DETAILS

What are the major topics or subjects with which authors who write of the strange and eerie seem preoccupied? Which of these do you think held the greatest fascination for Poe?

READING FOR MEANING

Consider and discuss the following statements:

1. A creative writer usually has an unhappy, searching nature.
2. People are fearful, superstitious creatures.
3. One reason people are so fascinated by the strange, the eerie, and the unreal is that deep down they believe such things could happen.

READING FOR APPRECIATION

It was through his control of *atmosphere* that Poe usually made the strong single effect in his stories.

Consider the atmospheres of the three Poe stories in "Once Upon a Midnight." What do they have in common? In which way is the atmosphere of each story distinct from that of the other stories?

COMPOSITION

Maurice Sagoff has written a popular paperback entitled *ShrinkLits*, in which he reduces to the absurd many of the revered classics in literature. His theory is that within every fat selection there is a skinny one trying to get out through all the wrappings of unnecessary words. Tongue-in-cheek, this author suggests that summarizing such as he has done in the following example could radically conserve space needed for the home library.

The Raven*

Raven lurches
In, perches
    Over door.
Poet's bleary
Query—
    "Where's Lenore?"
Creepy bird
Knows one word:
    "Nevermore."

EDGAR ALLAN POE

This is but one example of his "absurd shrinking." In reducing other classics, Sagoff has used less terse wording, assorted rhythm patterns and rhyme schemes, but his final products are consistently very brief. A "ShrinkLit" quickly done for "The Cask of Amontillado" *might* read:

To get revenge on Fortunato
Montresor sealed him in a grotto,
Ha, ha, ho, ho—Is this a joke?
Yes, very funny, eh? Choke, Choke!

Have fun and write some "ShrinkLits" for any of the Poe selections or stories from THE STRANGE AND EERIE. Or, if you think of another selection or selections from other units that you wish to reduce, do not confine yourself to the one unit.

* From SHRINKLITS by Maurice Sagoff, Workman Publishing Co. Copyright 1980 Maurice Sagoff.

Moments
of Decision

The Road Not Taken

Two roads diverged in a yellow wood,
And sorry I could not travel both
And be one traveler, long I stood
And looked down one as far as I could
To where it bent in the undergrowth;   5

Then took the other, as just as fair,
And having perhaps the better claim,
Because it was grassy and wanted wear;
Though as for that the passing there
Had worn them really about the same,   10

And both that morning equally lay
In leaves no step had trodden black.
Oh, I kept the first for another day!
Yet knowing how way leads on to way,
I doubted if I should ever come back.   15

I shall be telling this with a sigh
Somewhere ages and ages hence:
Two roads diverged in a wood, and I—
I took the one less traveled by,
And that has made all the difference.   20

ROBERT FROST

From THE POETRY OF ROBERT FROST edited by Edward Connery
Lathem. Copyright 1916, © 1969 by Holt, Rinehart and Winston, Copyright
1944 by Robert Frost. Reprinted by permission of Holt, Rinehart and Winston, Publishers.

CONVERSATION AMONG THE RUINS
Giorgio de Chirico
National Gallery of Art, Washington, D.C.
Chester Dale Collection

There are many decisions people feel ambivalent about—everyday choices such as: Should I have my hair cut or let it grow? Should I order a hamburger or some pizza? Should I watch television or get my homework done? But sometimes people are ambivalent when they have important decisions to make, and they have very little to guide them. This is the kind of decision Robert Frost was thinking about when he wrote that sometimes it may be "the road not taken" that makes an important difference in the way a person's life turns out.

How are decisions made? Is there any sort of magic formula or pattern that could help a person who is trying to make a difficult choice?

In the selections that follow, you will meet a great variety of people faced with difficult decisions. John Bagley in the short story "The Decision" believes that a scientific appraisal of a situation is necessary before a decision can be made. In the short story "Number One Son," Ming must decide between doing what's best for himself and assuming the traditional responsibilities of his cultural heritage. And in the classic novel of Charles Dickens, *A Tale of Two Cities,* the main characters must all face great moments of decision, which test to the limit their personal values of morality and courage.

As a reflection of life, literature naturally contains much that shows people wavering between courses of action, feeling the anguish of being unable to decide. In sharing their moments of decision, we may discover some of the general patterns of decision making.

UNIT TECHNIQUES

Attention is centered in this group of selections upon *beginnings* and *endings*. Unless a story begins in a fashion that catches our interest, we often do not bother to continue; and unless it ends in a satisfying, dramatic, or interesting way, it leaves us with a disappointed feeling. In some respects, reading a story is like becoming acquainted with a person. First impressions and last ones are of great importance.

BEGINNINGS

There are two common methods for beginning a story. One interest-catching way is to start with some of the characters engaged in a conversation. If authors begin in this fashion, they must, without being obvious or awkward, give the reader exposition, or information, that cues the reader to *who* is talking and *why*.

In the story you are about to read, for example, author Tom Burnam catches the reader's attention by beginning with conversation. In the first few paragraphs, he skillfully lets you know that the characters are a woman named Myra; her husband, whose name is not given until later; and their son, Kit. They are traveling through Montana in a car, tired, and looking for a place to camp. *What* they say and *how* they say it tells you much about their personalities.

A second method commonly used is for the writers to begin by simply telling the reader what is happening. They introduce the characters and the background information without conversation. This type of opening may discourage the reader if it is dull or uninteresting, but it need not be that. Edgar Allan Poe made little use of conversation, but by presenting many of his straight narrative accounts as personal experiences, he made them interesting from the beginning.

ENDINGS

There are two common methods for ending stories also. One closes the story at the highest point of emotional interest. The *conflict* is settled and *suspense* ended at the same time that the story concludes. The way "The Most Dangerous Game" (p. 22) ends exemplifies this very well. Here the last line is: "He had never slept in a better bed, Rainsford decided." These few words tell you the outcome of the life-and-death struggle between General Zaroff and Rainsford, release you from the strain of sustained suspense, and, at the same time, end the story.

The second type of ending occurs when authors continue their narratives past the high point and "round them off." They tell you what happened after the climax passed and suspense lessened. If, for example, Richard Connell had gone on to tell how Rainsford managed to leave the island and get home, he would have given his story this kind of conclusion. The "rounded-off," rather than abrupt, ending may be very brief or may take up much of the story.

To give readers a satisfied feeling when they finish a story, the ending must be as carefully planned as the beginning.

Since this unit includes short stories, fables, and a novel, many literary terms discussed earlier are reviewed in this unit.

He would need to proceed calmly,
efficiently, exploring every possibility. Don't
lose your head, he said to himself, don't, don't.

THE DECISION
Tom Burnam

"That looks like a nice spot," said Myra Bagley hopefully. She was tired, and the boy Kit was irritable; the day's ride had been long and dusty.

"Well, I don't know," said her husband, slowing the car as they studied the grassy meadow ahead. "Maybe we're not supposed to camp there."

"For heaven's sake, we're in *Montana*," said Myra. "They told us we could camp anywhere that wasn't posted. You know that." She had not meant to sound quite so sharp.

"We'll flip a nickel," said John Bagley, but then Kit wailed, "Oh, Dad, make up your mind."

John set his lips and stepped on the gas; and though it was too late now, Myra wanted to say, "Kit, *keep quiet!*"

Then a miracle happened. A mile farther, beyond a curve, was a Forest Service marker, "Camp Ground Ahead," and then a triangular sign with an arrow pointing down a narrow winding road which led from the highway to the bank of the stream below.

John slowed the car.

"Will this do?" he asked. Myra bit her lip and didn't answer. The trouble with being married to a scientist, she had long ago decided, was that everything had to

be so scientific. First the Hypothesis: This camp ground will serve us well. Then the Examination of the Facts: Is there water? Do poisonous snakes abound? Are there adequate toilet facilities? Will the slope provide surface drainage in case of rain?

Sometimes she protested while they were trying to buy a new car (this one has a good transmission, he would say, but that one has better brakes) or new furniture (will foam rubber stand up?)—or even a new can opener for the kitchen (the consumer people say it drops metal shavings into the soup). Then John would withdraw in offended silence after pointing out that he had been *trained* to think on all sides of a question before making a decision.

But for once she had no cause for alarm. "We'll camp here," John said, and both Myra and Kit sighed in relief.

Somewhat downstream from the Bagleys' camp ground, though on the other side of the large creek, a huge rock had for uncounted years squatted on the brow of the narrow defile at the bottom of the canyon where now the railroad ran. The train crews sometimes used it as a kind of informal checkpoint: "There's the rock. Two minutes behind today."

Near the point where the rock hung over the tracks was a small fault.[1] Over

1. **fault,** a deep crack in the earth's crust.

the years, this fault had resulted in a slight slippage and settling, so that the rock began to tip just a trifle more toward the tracks some sixty feet below. None of the train crews noticed the almost imperceptible increase in the angle of the rock's inclination; and certainly none of them knew that the rock was now very precariously balanced, so that the slightest further movement in the fault—indeed, perhaps just the right vibration set up by a passing truck on the highway or a locomotive on the tracks—might send it hurtling down.

At such locations as this small canyon where the rock was, the railroad maintained protective fences; any slides or falling chunks would break one or more of the electric wires, setting into operation certain warning devices. An hour or two before the Bagleys found their camp ground, a boy who lived on a nearby backwoods ranch had aimed his new .22 rifle at an insulator atop the electric fence. The bullet shattered the insulator but did not sever the wire, which merely hung an inch or two lower, the electric circuit remaining unbroken.

"Let's not try to push on too fast tomorrow," Myra said after they had pitched the umbrella tent and Kit had set up his own pup tent close by. "I'm tired."

"But—" John started to say. Then he grinned. "Suits me," he said. "I'm tired too. And maybe tomorrow Kit and I can get in a little fishing. This *is* a nice spot."

The camp ground—they were a little surprised to have it all to themselves—was secluded from the highway. Close by tumbled the large creek which rushed through the canyon; on the opposite side were the railroad tracks, and the rock above them.

"Come on, son," said John the next morning. "Let's cross the bridge and see if we can stir up a trout or two."

The bridge was of heavy but ancient timbers; once used by logging trucks, it was now placarded "Unsafe for Vehicles."

"Be careful," said Myra Bagley. "Don't get run over by a train."

"Oh, Mom," said Kit, but he saw that she was joking, or at least mostly joking.

The man and his son picked up their fishing rods and set off.

"Did you hear that old train go past last night, Dad?" said Kit. "*I* thought it was going right through my pup tent."

John Bagley grimaced. "I think it did go through our tent," he said. "It woke your mother up in fine fashion, I can tell you."

"I bet it did," said Kit, and they grinned together, sharing companionably their masculine delight at the way the noise of the train had alarmed Mother.

"I'll bet that's why we had the camp ground to ourselves," said Kit. "Probably all the natives around here know about the trains."

"Probably," agreed his father.

They had reached the other side. The old truck crossing was barricaded now, though a footpath remained, and a sign said "NOTICE. Property of Montana & Pacific Railway. Permission to Cross Revocable at Any Time."

"What's that mean?" said Kit.

"It means the railroad doesn't want to lose its legal title to the right-of-way," said John.

"Oh," said Kit, who was willing to accept his father's explanation even though he did not wholly understand it. "Can we walk up the tracks?"

"I guess the railroad won't care," said his father, laughing. "It's certainly easier than scrambling along the bank."

"Let's go toward that big rock," said Kit. "See? The one above the tracks, there. I'll bet there's some good fishing right about there."

"Why?" said his father.

"Well," said Kit, "well, that rock makes a shadow on the water, and the trouts like to stay there."

"Trout," said his father. "It's the same, singular or plural."

"O.K.," said Kit, who secretly could not see that it mattered much.

Together father and son walked up the track. It was straight only for a short distance; at either end of the straight stretch the tracks curved away, following the S sweep of the stream and the canyon.

"Better keep our eyes open," said Kit, proud of remembering caution like an adult. "If a train came roaring along, we wouldn't see it."

John looked ahead and behind. For only a quarter mile or so, until the tracks curved around rock cliffs at either end, did one have a clear view. He smiled at his son. "We'd hear it in plenty of time," he said. The thought of the shattering, surrounding roar the train had made last night caused him only half-consciously to prick up his ears a little. Evidently the trains came through here fast, faster than one would think for mountain country. On a sudden impulse he stopped, went down on one knee, and placed his ear on one of the rails.

"What are you doing?" asked Kit, astonished.

"An old trick I learned when I was about your age," his father said. "Didn't you ever try it?" Then he realized that of course Kit, raised in the city, had never learned how to listen for the trains. Kit at once laid his own ear to a rail. "I don't hear nothing."

"Good heavens," said his father. "*Anything.*"

"Anything," said Kit. "What are you supposed to listen for?"

"It's a kind of humming," his father said. "I didn't hear anything either, as a matter of fact. But if a train were coming, maybe even five miles or so away, you'd hear it."

"Gee," said Kit. "Five miles?"

"Maybe even more," said his father.

"Here's that old rock," said Kit, pointing up. It did indeed cast a shadow on the stream; John noted that there was a small indentation in the bank, and the water looked quite deep. There just might be trout, at that.

"Hey, Dad," said Kit. "What's that fence for?"

John looked where Kit was pointing. "Why, I don't know," he said. "It must be electric, from the look of those insulators. Maybe to keep animals off the track."

"Like bears?" said Kit.

"More likely cows," said his father. "Montana's an open-range state. Though I don't know what a cow would be doing on this side of the creek, or what good a fence would do there, between the canyon wall and the track. Anyway, don't touch it."

"O.K., Dad," said Kit. "Let's put some bait on." He pulled out of his pocket the tin of worms he had dug from the bank of the stream before they started. They were standing in the middle of the track directly beneath the rock, Kit intent on impaling a wriggling worm on his hook, his father tying on a Black Gnat.[2]

At that moment a huge truck with M.A.D. on its side, for "Montana and Dakota"—the "mad trucks" were a regional joke—hit a sizable chuckhole in the road across the stream out of sight behind the tall thick pines on the opposite bank. The driver swore and slammed into a lower gear.

John Bagley felt, or thought he felt, the slightest tremor in the cross-tie under his feet. And something, in a brief split second, struck him as odd about the shadow in which they stood. It was—it was moving, and Kit's scream and John Bagley's instinctive leap as he tried to grab Kit but instead, because his foot hit a small pebble, he got only empty air, were all a part of a kaleidoscopic nightmare of confusion, alarm, and incoherent noise as the great boulder above crashed mightily down, splitting in two with a great cracking sound as it did so, one large chunk stopping inches short of the electric fence in such position that the other and larger piece falling immediately behind struck it, hurtled into the air, and cleared the fence by the merest fraction of an inch.

Had the bottom chunk not stopped where it did, had the other half not happened to strike it exactly as it did, or had the shattered insulator not permitted just enough slack in the electric wire to enable the rock to leap it without touching it, the electric fence would have flashed its warning.

For a confused moment John Bagley stared wildly around. Rock dust hung in the air and he had fallen as he slipped on the pebble and *where was* Kit?

"Dad! Dad!" he heard, and he whirled around. Kit was half-lying on the track. The great split-off chunk of rock, resting partly on one rail, was across his leg.

John Bagley moved swiftly to his son. With horror in his eyes, he knelt down and took Kit's hand.

"I can't move, Dad!" cried Kit. "I can't move."

John looked at the boulder. Maybe, maybe it had not crushed or broken his son's leg; it appeared to be resting on the rail and a cross-tie.

"Does it hurt much?" he asked softly, but Kit was weeping hysterically and could not answer.

"Kit!" He was ashamed of speaking so sharply, but it did what he hoped: Kit stopped crying.

"It doesn't hurt," Kit said. "Not much, anyway. But I can't pull loose. Move the rock, Dad. Please move it!"

John Bagley looked at the rock. "Move it, Dad," Kit whimpered. John put his shoulder to the rock, knowing the futility of it, knowing that no one man could budge it, but knowing too that for his son he had to try. He pushed until his heart pounded and his eyes misted. The rock did not budge, and John hated it for its stolid resistance to his human muscles.

He realized that he must not succumb to hysteria. What he could see of Kit's leg showed no obvious deformation, and thank God there was no blood. He would need to proceed calmly, efficiently, exploring every possibility. Don't lose your head, he said to himself, don't, don't.

Again he knelt beside his son. Appar-

2. **a Black Gnat,** a fishing lure made from feathers and colored silk, and meant to resemble an insect.

ently the boulder was resting on a rail and the firm ballast beneath the ties, or on a tie itself. The lower part of Kit's leg disappeared beneath the boulder in the small space between the bottom of the boulder, the rail, and the ground.

"I think it's my foot, Dad," whispered Kit. "My leg's all right, but I can't move my foot, I can't pull it out."

Then the horror struck his father, and his face turned white as he thought, Oh, God, let me keep Kit from thinking of it.

"Dad!" cried Kit. "Oh, Dad, what if—what if—"

It was too late. Kit had thought of it too.

"Come on, son," said John. "Let's pull you loose." He seized Kit by the shoulders.

"You're hurting me," said Kit, sobbing again.

It was no use. Only if help could be found, enough help to take the weight of the rock off the rail and open up what (thank the good Lord for this, at least) must be the small pocket in which Kit's foot was caught, would Kit be free.

"Dad," Kit said, "what are you going to do?" He had stopped crying, but he was shaking, shaking all over, violently.

At that moment they both heard, from some indeterminate distance and direction, the faint hoarse blat of a diesel locomotive's air-horn.

"It's a train," whispered Kit, his eyes wide with terror. "Oh, Daddy, it's a train." He had not called his father "Daddy" for a long time.

Get control of yourself, thought John Bagley. Don't throw yourself at the rock, don't try to move it, you can't move it.

You can't pull him loose, you've tried to the limit of your strength, and more. You haven't even got a knife, or a hatchet. . . . But he could not pursue this thought further.

"Kit," said John, "I'm going to have to leave you here and run up the track and stop the train." He spoke as rapidly as he could, knowing at the same time that he must not communicate the full extent of his fear to the boy. "Then we'll get help from the trainmen and push the rock off."

The hoarse blat of the horn came again. It seemed noticeably closer.

"Dad!" cried Kit. "Where's it coming from? What if you run the wrong way?" He twisted and wriggled as he spoke, pushing and crying as he tried to free himself. *"Where's it coming from?"* Faintly, in the distance, they could hear now a dull rumbling clattering roar, echoing and reechoing through the canyon.

"It's from that way," said John, and he started swiftly to run toward the direction from which the sound seemed to come when his son's cry stopped him.

"No, Dad, no! From there, from there!" Kit pointed in the opposite direction. If only they could see! If only the tracks did not curve out of sight in either direction! If only every rock and tree did not twist and distort and bounce the sound, now seeming much louder, of the train approaching fast and invisible, approaching—but from where? If only diesels made smoke. . . . Now he could not tell at all where the sound originated, and he was afraid his son knew he could not tell, and no matter what happened this, at least, his son must not know.

Sweating, John Bagley put his ear to

the rail, and fought down his fear as the loud humming sounded so close by his head.

"You can tell that way, Daddy, can't you?" said Kit. "You can tell where it's coming from?"

John straightened and looked at his son. All his life he had dreaded some such moment as this. He knew—had always known—how to make decisions in the laboratory. Always there was something to go on, a collection of data to assess, or a logical corollary to what had gone before, or a table of figures which, even though capable of misinterpretation, was nevertheless *there*. But always he had feared that the time might come when the data or the corollary or the figures simply did not exist, and yet a step had to be taken even though taking it meant plunging ahead in darkness.

"You *can* tell, Daddy?" Kit was nearly hysterical again. John Bagley had tried never to lie, to himself or others.

"Yes, Kit," said John. "Now I know. Don't worry." Then he was running desperately up the track, as fast as he could in the direction from which he and Kit had come, and he prayed incoherently as he ran.

Another bleat of the horn. Was it louder? Less loud? And the rising-fading-rising rumble . . . it seemed farther away. John Bagley almost stopped, but it was too late now, too late: his course was set, the step in the dark had been taken, and for the first time in his life he knew fully what it was to be committed irrevocably to action without evidence, without the slightest shred of proof that the decision was correct. Yet he knew he must go on. There flashed into his mind a crazy picture of himself running frantically first one way, then the other, betrayed by the mountain echoes, like a foolish base-runner trapped between second and third.

His feet pounded on the cinders between the ties, which he cursed for being so spaced that now and then he stumbled. Once he fell, tearing the knees out of his trousers, then scrambling to his feet, pounding on. Again the horn, and his heart almost stopped, for it seemed much less loud. But he forced himself on. The decision had been made. Right or wrong, it had been made.

He reached the curve somewhere beyond which—if he was right—would be the train. Would have to be the train. Over his shoulder he caught a last quick look at Kit, pinned by the rock, seeming much too close behind (surely he had covered more ground than that!) and he ran faster, blood-pounding, heart-pounding, sweat-streaming faster. He had hoped that once into the curve he would be able to see (and be seen) a long distance. But the curve was sharp enough, or the walls of the cut through which it ran were close enough to the tracks, so that still he could see nothing.

He stopped, sobbing with exhaustion. He could run no farther. Here he must stand if he was to have enough strength to wave his arms. But there was no train at which to wave. The train tracks, shining in the sun, curved mockingly away until they disappeared behind the canyon wall, and they were empty. He strained with terrible intensity to hear something, to hear anything, but only the pounding rush of exhaustion filled his ears. He felt himself waver at the edge of consciousness; and for the first time, trying to fight it off but losing ground, he knew that futility and despair were beginning at last utterly to overwhelm him.

Then suddenly above the roaring in his ears sounded a tremendous alien noise, the rasping blast of an air-horn, very close, and three hundred yards away, its great steel snout roaring into view, he saw the train bearing down, and standing squarely in the middle of the track he mustered his final reserves to wave and, foolishly, yell, and he stayed where he was as he heard the increasing roar of the horn, jumping aside so late that for a fright-filled moment he was afraid he himself would be the one to be ground beneath the wheels.

Thank God, now, that it *was* a diesel, for that meant a clear view ahead for both engineer and fireman: they *must* have seen him. Then he heard the grinding squeal of brakes, and he saw the sparks fly as wheel after wheel locked and slid on the rails, and before he fainted he thought dimly: I got through to them, they're going to flatten every wheel. Thank God they saw me, they saw me, and they're stopping.

He returned to consciousness as the last of the cars ground to a shuddering halt and a trainman, leaping down, ran to him.

"My son," he gasped, pointing. "My son . . . down there."

Later, after the train crew had pried the rock up enough so that Kit could be pulled free, and the brakeman had put a small splint on Kit's ankle, though it seemed only to be bruised, and they were all back at the camp ground together (the burly brakeman had insisted on carrying Kit all the way), Myra Bagley looked at her husband and whispered, "Oh, John, how could you tell which direction the train was coming from? How could you tell, in mountains like these where everything echoes so?"

"Myra," John started to say, "I—"

Then he stopped. How could he tell her? The imponderable brooding fact of chance, of Fate, the dark reminder that beyond the shining realm of the controlled experiment, the offer of proof, the calculated risk, lay something incalculable—it was too much now for her. Later, maybe, later. Let Myra (and Kit) think now that he *had* known.

"I used an old Boy Scout trick," he said, smiling a little, feeling his strength return. "I put my ear to the rail."

"And you could tell the *direction?*" Myra asked.

"Sure," he lied. "Sure, if you know how."

"I'm so relieved," Myra said. "Oh, John, if you'd had to *guess.* . . ."

He knew then that he could never tell her.

READING FOR DETAILS

A Blind Choice

No matter what processes people normally go through before making a decision, there are times when they seem to have nothing to indicate which direction to take. John Bagley found himself deserted by all the formulas that he had grown accustomed to using, yet his decision *had* to be the right one.

Consider and discuss the significance of the following details:

1. the location of the rock
2. the locomotive's being a diesel

3. the railroad track's winding through a narrow canyon
4. the father's placing his ear to the rails
5. the untruth John Bagley tells his wife

READING FOR MEANING

Consider and discuss in light of the selection:
1. The best decisions are those made in emergency situations.
2. The greatest mistake is being afraid to make a mistake.
3. Thoughtlessness often brings as much damage to society as deliberate, malicious action.

READING FOR APPRECIATION

Suspense

From the point in the story where the thought enters the minds of the father and son that a train *might* come before they can move the huge rock from the boy's leg, the author carefully includes details to increase the anxiety of the reader. Discuss three of these details.

Endings

When the train grinds to a halt in the exciting climax to an agony of suspense, readers feel intense relief. "Now," they think, "they'll rescue Kit and everything will be all right."

Why do you think the author goes beyond this point in drawing the story to its conclusion? Think back to the title of the story when you answer.

COMPOSITION

It is unlikely that you have been forced to make a decision in a situation as life-threatening as the one posed in this story. You can probably recall, however, several occasions in which the decisions you made were important to you—for example, deciding what to do when you were temporarily lost on a camping trip, in a strange city, or in an unfamiliar building.

Write about such a situation in your life, what you decided to do, and the outcome of your decision. Strive for an interesting opening sentence and for an ending that indicates clearly how you felt about the course of action you took.

BIOGRAPHICAL NOTE

Tom Burnam (1913–   ), short story writer and English professor, was born in Montana. After doing undergraduate work at the University of Idaho, he received his Ph.D. from the University of Washington. Burnam, who was a Visiting Professor of American Literature at the University of Helsinki in Finland in 1961, has taught literature and writing at Colorado State College.

Even his mother was to abide
by his decisions now. He looked around at his
brothers and sisters and felt the circle closing in about
his life, tying it in chains of traditional responsibility.

NUMBER ONE SON
Monfoon Leong

In a few minutes Ming would be home. Slumped in his seat, he glared out of the window as the suburban bus jerked and shook its way through the downtown traffic. The usual hurrying shoppers pushed along, arms filled with packages. The usual harried policemen watched over the intersections. The usual drivers inched through the crowds to make their turns. All were preoccupied with the business of shopping for Christmas.

Ming wondered, and reproached himself even as he wondered, if he really cared any more than those strangers did that his father had died. This father of his had been little more than an old man with iron-gray hair that he saw occasionally on his Sunday trips home. Then it was nearly always only, "Hello, Pa," answered by an almost inaudible grunt as the old man hurried in from the restaurant to spend his two-hour rest period in bed. The dishwashing was bad for his rheumatism, Ming had heard him say many times, but you had to work when there were six children and a woman to feed. Really, there were only five since Ming was out working as a houseboy, but Ming had never corrected him. Now he was dead.

Ming braced himself against the window ledge as the bus turned a corner and headed toward Chinatown. He wondered if Mrs. Warner would be able to take care of the house and the twins without him. The twins, a pair of hellions,* were only eight, but they were nearly as tall as Ming, and he was fifteen. He had planned to teach them to play football. There was always a time right after school before he had to start helping with the preparation of dinner. He saw again the three square boxes already under their Christmas tree. Two helmets and a football, probably. He caught himself wishing that his father could buy him a football helmet and he shut the Warners from his mind. His father could never buy him anything. He should be grieving, but all he could feel was a harsh resentment against the man who had been hardly aware of his existence and who had just left him with a family to support.

He deposited a dime in the coin box and got off the bus to walk the one block to his home. Passing the two "hotels" just around the corner from his home, he couldn't resist glancing up at the second story windows. A woman sat at one of them, the hard beauty of her much too

*__hellions__ (hel′yənz), mischievous persons.

heavily made up face apparent even through the curtains. Catching Ming's glance, she winked at him. He jerked his eyes quickly back to the street, walked a little faster, and turned the corner.

A half dozen of the neighborhood boys were playing football in the street. They stopped their playing to let a car go by and saw Ming.

One of the boys yelled, "Come on—" but stopped short when one of the others whispered fiercely into his ear. Ming raised his hand in greeting, but said nothing. They very carefully ignored him and started playing again.

"Home" for Ming was in a long, one-story building running the entire length of the block. Set at regular intervals in the once-whitewashed plaster wall that faced the street were screen doors, each flanked by a large, screened window. Most of the screens were brown with rust and sagging gently in their frames. Ming stopped at the third door from the corner and pulled it open. He stepped directly into his front room, for the heavy inner door was open.

The entire family was in the small room. He knew that his mother must have gathered them together to await his coming. On the worn, faded couch that squatted in front of the window sat his brothers, the three youngest of the family. All three turned identically serious faces toward him as he walked in, faces whose subdued quality was strained and unfamiliar, almost ludicrous. The younger of his sisters, sitting near the end of the couch in a straight-backed chair with her thin, brown legs wrapped around those of the chair, looked as if she were about to burst into tears. The other was

seated with their mother opposite the boys. She held her mother's hand in both of hers and was looking anxiously up into her face.

His mother's eyes were dull with a lifeless opaqueness, their lids red and puffy. Her fleshless cheeks were tightly drawn, her lips set in a line of resignation. Ming wanted to run to his mother, to throw his arms around her to ease the pain of her grief, but his Chinese childhood and years of working as a houseboy had taught him to restrain his impulses. If he did hold her in his arms, he would not know what to say to console her. He did not know the proper Chinese words. He took a few steps toward her and stood mute for a few moments, searching for something to say. Then he said quietly and deliberately in his mother's Cantonese dialect, "Papa . . . when die?"

She opened her mouth, closed it again and swallowed hard, then said hoarsely, "Last night. I wait till morning to call you. Not want to wake up your boss."

Poor mother, Ming thought. Afraid he'd lose his job? The pay wouldn't be enough to take care of the family. He said, "Papa is where now?"

"At funeral parlor. Last night they took him there."

"Did you not call doctor?"

"Papa died before he came. Doctor said, heart had something wrong." She paused, then added, "Papa gone now, Ming. You are number one son, now head of family."

She needn't have told Ming that. He had heard often of the old custom. Even his mother was to abide by his decisions now. He looked around at his brothers

THE CHINESE MERCHANTS
Childe Hassam
Freer Gallery of Art
Smithsonian Institution, Washington, D.C.

and sisters and felt the circle closing in about his life, tying it in chains of traditional responsibility. He felt his jaw tighten.

It was his father who had begotten this big brood, his father who could earn barely enough to keep them alive, his father who had left the empty rice bowls for him to fill, his father who had given him nothing. He wanted to curse his father and did not dare. There would be no more school for him. He would have to work full time now to support his father's children. He had been told in school that his I.Q. was high. What good was a high I.Q. when he would not be able to finish high school, much less even dream of college? Curse the Chinese custom. He was an American. He had the right to leave the family and pursue his own happiness.

"Ming?" The voice at the door was a familiar one.

"Come in, Grandfather Choak," he said, trying to hide the tremor in his voice.

The door opened with a creak and a short, round man entered. He looked like nothing more or less than a Buddha in an American business suit. Ming had always called the man "Grandfather" although they were not actually related in any way. It was customary because he was of the same clan as Ming's mother and had come from the same village in China. To Ming, he had always been no less than a real grandfather.

The old man glanced quickly at all the family, but addressed himself only to Ming in his mother's dialect. "Ming," he said very solemnly, "your father leave no money. We must get money from friends for funeral. You come with me."

"I must go?" Ming started to turn toward his mother as he said it.

"You are head of family," Grandfather Choak said.

Ming started to frame a denial, but under Grandfather Choak's placid gaze, he stopped himself and said, "Yes, I go with you." He followed the old man to the door, but stopped and said, "My Chinese not very good. I won't know what to say to people."

"I talk for you."

They stopped first at Kwon Kim's herb store. Kwon Kim was weighing out some bear gall for a customer. Ming watched the wizened old herbalist behind the counter as he carefully placed a whole gall bladder on the pan of his balance and peered over his glasses to read the weight. Ming remembered that Kwon Kim had always grumbled when the kids had come in the store to beg for the sweet prunes that were kept in a huge jar on the counter. They were only to be used by his customers to take the bitter taste of his herb teas from their mouths, Kwon Kim had said. The memory of the man's miserliness made Ming very uneasy and he found himself wishing that Grandfather Choak had decided to start with someone else.

When Kwon Kim had finished with his customer, he turned to Ming and Grandfather Choak. He clucked his tongue and said, "Very sorry your father pass beyond, Ming. Leave big family for you."

Ming strained for the words to reply. Grandfather Choak cleared his throat and said, "Father of Ming leave no money, Kim."

The herbalist cocked his head over to one side for a moment as if to let the statement drain from his ear to his mind. Then, without a word, he pulled out a drawer behind the counter, picked up a bill, and dropped it on the counter, shaking his head and muttering, "Too bad. Too bad."

While Grandfather Choak pulled a pencil and a tablet of rice paper from his coat pocket and started writing some characters in the tablet, Ming stared at the bill on the counter. It was a twenty. And Grandfather Choak had not even asked Kwon Kim for money. Kwon Kim was speaking.

"Father of Ming was good father," he said. "Every day I saw him go by carrying bag of cakes for children."

It was true. Ming had forgotten. His father had unfailingly brought home a bag of cakes from the restaurant when he returned for his afternoon nap. But they couldn't live on those cakes now.

He thanked Kwon Kim and followed Grandfather Choak out. The Buddha-like man waddled down the street with Ming at his side and turned into a new, self-service grocery. Flaunting its modernity, shiny gold letters on the big front window announced, "Chung's Super Market." Grandfather Choak went directly to the well-fed-looking young man who was presiding over the cash register. There was no mistaking the Mr. Chung of "Chung's Super Market."

Before Grandfather Choak had finished telling of the need of Ming's family, Mr. Chung snorted, "Man is fool to have such big family when cannot make enough money for them." He looked hard at Ming. "Young man must face truth about father. He was failure as father and failure as man. Must depend on others even when he is dead. I would be fool to give money."

Ming felt his heart pounding in his throat and choking him and his fists doubled up, ready to lash out at the face with its upper lip curled over white teeth in a self-righteous grimace. He sucked in his breath with a sob when Grandfather Choak took his arm and said, "Come."

As they turned to go, Chung said, "Wait," rang up a "No Sale" on the register and drew out a five-dollar bill which he tossed on the counter. "Here."

Grandfather Choak picked it up without a word and made a note in his tablet.

"Don't take it, Grandfather Choak," Ming forced out through his clenched teeth.

"Must pay for funeral, Ming." He put a hand on Ming's shoulder before he could say anything more and urged him out of the store.

On the sidewalk, the anger oozed quickly out of Ming, leaving him weighted with a great weariness. He unclenched his fists. "He was right, Grandfather Choak," he said. "My father was a failure."

"Do not talk that way about your father."

"But he was. Family lives in hole in wall, goes without so many things other people have. Mother washes all our clothes with washboard and tub. You know I have worked since I was nine years old." All the resentment of years began to boil out of Ming. He stuttered and stumbled over the words that had to be torn up from his Chinese vocabulary, but they had to come out. "Father had no love for me. Hardly knew he had eldest son."

Grandfather Choak again put his hand on Ming's shoulder and stopped him. "Your father did best he could, Ming. Came from China without education, without English. What could he do? Raised fine, healthy family. Loved his children."

Ming's lips squeezed together. "Father loved children? He did not know what love is."

They glared into each other's eyes for a long time. Then Grandfather Choak said gently. "You go home, Ming. Perhaps it will be better if I go see others by self." He patted Ming's arm and waddled off. Ming watched him go up the street, then he turned and started homeward.

From babyhood he had been taught to respect the words of his elders. Always he had had an especially profound respect for the wisdom of Grandfather Choak, but he felt sure that Grandfather Choak was dead wrong now. Perhaps his father had tried, but trying wasn't enough. He thought of Mr. Warner's home, the football helmets. His father had not given him even the love of a father. And now he was expected to revere his memory, to take his place, to give up his chance for an education, to struggle and go down as had his father. They had no right to ask it of him.

He was about to pass the Widow Loo without speaking when she gripped his arm. "Ming Kwong!" she said. "How tall you are now." She was a dumpy woman of about forty, several inches shorter than Ming. The note of surprise dropped from her voice as she continued, "I heard about your father. Am so very sorry. Your father fine man."

She released Ming's arm to fish in a well-worn purse she was carrying. "Many times your father helped me and children. He had little money but much heart." She pulled two crumpled bills from her purse and put them into Ming's hand. "I know he did not leave you much," she said. "Maybe this will help a little."

Ming whispered a "Thank you," and she bustled away. He looked at the two one-dollar bills in his hand for a long while.

His mother was anxiously waiting at the door for him. "Ming, your father's watch. They took it with them last night. We must get it back."

"Watch? Of what importance is watch? We can get it back at any time."

"No. It is gold watch your father had for many years. Undertakers will keep it. He told me many times that he wanted to give it to you when he was ready to go."

Ming could not believe his father had actually said that, but he said, "OK," then continued in Chinese, "We go now."

The young man in the office of the undertaker greeted them cordially. He listened politely while Ming explained that they had come for the gold watch that his father had been wearing when they had taken him away. The man said that he would check on it and glided into another office. He returned and said with a smile, "I'm sorry, but your father had no watch when he was brought in."

Ming interpreted for his mother. She looked sharply at the man and said to Ming, "He lies. Your father always wore watch. They try to steal it." Only the knowledge that his mother's eyes were filling with tears kept Ming from hurrying her out of the office. He turned to the man, who was listening curiously.

"My mother says that she is sure that he had it on," he said.

"I'm sorry," the man said with a shrug of his shoulders.

The condescension on the man's face struck deep into Ming and his anger began to rise within him. Did this man think that he was talking to a child? He spoke deliberately, trying to keep the tremor out of his voice. "I suggest that you check on it again."

"But I'm sure it is not here."

Ming used his deepest tones to say, "If the watch isn't found, we will go to the police."

A slight twitch passed over the man's face, but he recovered quickly and said, "Of course, we may have overlooked it. I'll check again." He disappeared into the inner office. It was not long before he strode back in, waving his fist triumphantly. "We did find it in a pocket we had overlooked," he said. He put the watch into Ming's outstretched hand.

Closing his fingers over the watch without looking at it, Ming muttered, "Thank you," and, taking his mother's arm, walked out.

Ming blinked at the sudden wintry sunlight. He stopped with his mother in the shadow of the building and looked at the watch in his hand. It was large and heavy, attached to a massive-looking chain. It must have been many years old for it was of the type whose face was protected by a snap cover. He squeezed down the stem and the cover flipped open. Inside the cover, he saw several words engraved in ornate script. Squinting his eyes against the brightness he read, "For Ming, my son." His mouth was suddenly dry and he had difficulty swallowing as he tried to moisten it.

His mother was watching him. "Only last year, your father had something put in cover," she said.

Ming couldn't speak. They started walking homeward.

"You are number one son, head of family now, but after funeral, you must go back to Mrs. Warner and to school," his mother said.

"But the family——"

"Many things a woman can do at home to earn money."

"No," Ming said firmly. "I will work and go to night school."

His mother started to say something further, but Ming stopped her with, "Remember, I am number one son, head of family."

He took her arm to help her across the street.

READING FOR DETAILS

A Young Man Makes His Decision

Ming's decision was not a matter of choice but a matter of custom.

1. What did Ming's father do for a living? Where does Ming work? How does Ming feel upon learning of his father's death?
2. Why hadn't Ming's mother called him as soon as his father died? Why do Ming and Grandfather Choak go to see neighbors and business people?
3. How do the opinions of Kwon Kim, Mr. Chung, and the Widow Loo contrast with regard to Ming's father?
4. Why do Ming and his mother return to the undertaker's? How does Ming get his father's watch back?
5. What surprise awaits Ming when he opens the cover of the watch? How does this change his attitude toward his father and the family?

READING FOR MEANING

Discuss whether the story directly or indirectly supports all of the following statements:

1. The oldest son *should* assume responsibility for his father's family.
2. Individuals should be allowed to make their own decisions.
3. Love can be measured by surface behavior.
4. The opinion of neighbors is a reliable indicator of an individual's worth.
5. Oriental family customs are un-American.

READING FOR APPRECIATION

Beginnings

Within the opening two paragraphs, Monfoon Leong gives the reader a total picture of Ming's situation and an indication of how Ming feels about it.

1. What verbs in sentence two tell you of the way Ming feels?
2. For what does Ming reproach himself in the first sentence of paragraph two?

Endings

Ming's decision to accept the responsibility for his family comes as a climax to the story.

1. When does Ming first show that he is thinking of himself as the man of the family?
2. What is the value of the final sentence of the story?

BIOGRAPHICAL NOTE

Monfoon Leong (1916–1964) was born in San Diego's Chinatown, the eldest in a family of four brothers and two sisters. When he was fourteen years old his father died and, in the Chinese tradition, he assumed the role of head of the household. He worked as a houseboy to support the family but managed to graduate from high school. When he was no longer the sole support of the family, he went to college and developed his talent for writing. Disturbed by the stereotyped portrayal of Chinese Americans, he wrote of his own people's humanity, values, and conflicts. His stories were collected for the book *Number One Son*.

It was just a "lousy snapper." Did it have a right to live?

THE TURTLE
George Vukelich

They were driving up to fish the White Creek for German Browns[1] and the false dawn was purpling the Wisconsin countryside when they spotted the huge hump-backed object in the middle of the sandroad and Jimmy coasted the station wagon to a stop.

"Pa," he said. "Turtle. Lousy snapper."

Old Tony sat up.

"Is he dead?"

"Not yet," Jimmy said. "Not yet he isn't." He shifted into neutral and pulled the handbrake. The snapper lay large and dark green in the headlight beams, and they got out and went around to look at it closely. The turtle moved a little and left razorlike clawmarks in the wet sand, and it waited.

"Probably heading for the creek," Jimmy said. "They kill trout like crazy."

They stood staring down.

"I'd run the wagon over him," Jimmy said. "Only he's too big."

He looked around and walked to the ditchway, and came back with a long finger-thick pine branch. He jabbed it into the turtle's face and the snakehead lashed out and struck like springsteel and the branch snapped like a stick of macaroni, and it all happened fast as a match-flare.

"Looka that!" Tony whistled.

"You bet, Pa. I bet he goes sixty pounds. Seventy maybe."

The turtle was darting its head around now in long stretching movements.

"I think he got some branch stuck in his craw," Jimmy said. He got out a cigaret and lighted it, and flipped the match at the rock-green shell.

"I wish now I'd brought the twenty-two," he said. "The pistol."

"You going to kill him?"

"Why not?" Jimmy asked. "They kill trout, don't they?"

They stood there smoking and not talking, and looking down at the unmoving shell.

"I could use the lug wrench on him," Jimmy said. "Only I don't think it's long enough. I don't want my hands near him."

Tony didn't say anything.

"You watch him," Jimmy said. "I'll go find something in the wagon."

Slowly Tony squatted down onto his haunches and smoked and stared at the turtle. Poor Old One, he thought. You had the misfortune to be caught in the middle of a sandroad, and you are very vulnerable on the sandroads, and now you are going to get the holy life beaten out of you.

"The Turtle." First printed in the University of Kansas City *Review*. © 1959 by the University of Kansas City *Review*.

1. **German Browns,** trout having yellow-brown sides with reddish spots.

The turtle stopped its stretching movements and was still. Tony looked at the full webbed feet and the nail claws and he knew the truth.

"It would be different in the water, turtle," he said. "In the water you could cut down anybody."

He thought about this snapper in the water and how it would move like a torpedo and bring down trout, and nobody would monkey with it in the water—and here it was in the middle of a sandroad, vulnerable as a baby and waiting to get its brains beaten out.

He finished his cigaret and field-stripped[2] it, and got to his feet and walked to the wagon and reached into the glove compartment for the thermos of coffee. What was he getting all worked up about a turtle for? He was an old man and he was acting like a kid, and they were going up to the White for German Browns, and he was getting worked up about a turtle in the middle of a sandroad. He walked back to the turtle and hunched down and sipped at the strong black coffee and watched the old snapper watching him.

Jimmy came up to him holding the bumper jack.

"I want to play it safe," he said. "I don't think the lug wrench is long enough." He squatted beside Tony. "What do you think?"

"He waits," Tony said. "What difference what I think?"

Jimmy squinted at him.

"I can tell something's eating you. What are you thinking, Pa?"

"I am thinking this is not a brave thing."

"What?"

"This turtle—he does not have a chance."

Jimmy lit a cigaret and hefted the bumper jack. The turtle moved ever so slightly.

"You talk like an old woman. An old tired woman."

"I can understand this turtle's position."

"He doesn't have a chance?"

"That's right."

"And that bothers you?"

Tony looked into Jimmy's face.

"That is right," he said. "That bothers me."

"Well of all the dumb, stupid things," Jimmy said. "What do you want me to do? Get down on all fours and fight with him?"

"No," Tony said. "Not on all fours. Not on all fours." He looked at Jimmy. "In the water. Fight this turtle in the water. That would be a brave thing, my son."

Jimmy put down the bumper jack and reached for the thermos jug and didn't say anything. He drank his coffee and smoked his cigaret, and he stared at the turtle and didn't say anything.

"You're crazy," he said finally.

"It is a thought, my son. A thought. This helpless, plodding old one like a little baby in this sandroad, eh? But in the water, his home . . ." Tony snapped his fingers with the suddenness of a switchblade. "In the water he could cut down anyone, anything . . . any man. Fight him in the water, Jimmy. Use your bumper jack in the water . . ."

---

2. **fieldstripped,** peeled off the remaining cigaret paper and scattered the tobacco.

"I think you're nuts," Jimmy said. "I think you're honest to goodness nuts."

Tony shrugged. "This does not seem fair for you, eh? To be in the water with this one." He motioned at the turtle. "This seems nuts to you. Crazy to you. Because in the water he could cripple you. Drown you. Because in the water you are not a match."

"What are you trying to prove, Pa?"

"Jimmy. This turtle is putting up his life. In the road here you are putting up nothing. You have nothing to lose at all. Not a finger or a hand or your life. Nothing. You smash him with a long steel bumper jack and he cannot get to you. He has as much chance as a ripe watermelon."

"So?"

"So I want you to put up something also. You should have something to lose or it is no match."

Jimmy looked at the old man and then at the turtle.

"Any fool can smash a watermelon," Tony said. "It does not take a brave man."

"Pa. It's only a turtle. You're making a federal case."

Old Tony looked at his son. "All right," he said. "Finish your coffee now and do what you are going to do. I say nothing more. Only for the next five minutes put yourself into this turtle's place. Put yourself into his shell and watch through his eyes. And try to think what he is thinking when he sees a coward coming to kill him with a long steel bumper jack."

Jimmy got to his feet and ground out his cigaret.

"All right, Pa," he said. "All right. You win."

Tony rose slowly from his crouch.

"No," he said. "Not me. You. You win."

"But Pa, they do kill trout."

"So," Tony said. "They kill trout. Nature put them here, and they kill trout. To survive. The trout are not extinct, eh? We kill trout also, we men. To survive? No, for sport. This old one, he takes what he needs. I do not kill him for being in nature's plan. I do not play God."

Jimmy walked to the rear of the wagon then and flung down the bumper jack and closed up the door and came back.

"Pa," he said. "Honest to goodness you got the nuttiest ideas I ever heard."

Old Tony walked around behind the snapper and gently prodded it with his boot toe, and the turtle went waddling forward across the road and toppled over the sand shoulder and disappeared in the brushy growth of the creek bank. Tony and his son climbed into the wagon and sat looking at each other. The sun was coming up strong now and the sky was cracking open like a shell and spilling reds and golds and blues, and Jimmy started the engine.

Tony put the thermos away and got out his cigarets and stuck one in his son's mouth.

"So?" he said.

They sat smoking for a full minute watching each other, and then Jimmy released the emergency and they rolled slowly along the drying sandroad and down past the huge cleansing dawn coming, and the pine forests growing tall in the rising mists, and the quickly quiet waters of the eternal creek.

READING FOR DETAILS

A Debated Decision

Tony felt compassion for the old turtle. He thought his son should fight him fairly.

1. Why does Jimmy feel that he should kill the turtle?
2. What ways to kill the old snapper does Jimmy consider?
3. How does the father suggest that his son should fight the turtle? Why?

READING FOR MEANING

Discuss the following statements in light of the story:

1. The old feel sympathy for the old; the young feel impatience.
2. People have no right to play God.
3. Wisdom comes with age.

READING FOR APPRECIATION

Beginnings

Although "The Turtle" is short, it tells a story clearly and forcefully. The author uses only one long sentence to let the reader know what the situation is before he introduces conversation. Careful consideration of this beginning conversation shows that it serves a definite purpose.

1. What does the reader learn from Jimmy's first speech?
2. Describe the incident near the beginning of the story that shows that the turtle could be a dangerous fighter.

Endings

"The Turtle" is an excellent illustration of the second type of ending described on page 631.

1. Where does the climax occur and the suspense lessen?
2. What does the reader learn about Tony and the relationship between him and his son in the last paragraphs of the story after the climax has occurred?

COMPOSITION

When Jimmy says that turtles kill trout, Old Tony says, "We kill trout also, we men. To survive? No, for sport. This old one, he takes what he needs. I do not kill him for being in nature's plan. I do not play God."

Write a brief paper in which you compare and discuss Old Tony's philosophy about nature and life with that of some other person you have read about in the text. You could use either Rainsford or General Zaroff from "The Most Dangerous Game," the boy Nathan from "The Woods-Devil," Tom Black Bull from *When The Legends Die*, or some other character whose philosophy intrigues you.

BIOGRAPHICAL NOTE

George Vukelich (1927–   ), who is a native of Wisconsin, has published poetry and short stories in several national magazines. In addition, he has written scripts for National Educational Television and for other broadcasting systems. He is a radio announcer as well as an assistant editor for a state magazine.

The moment of decision is a little like a high peak to a mountain climber: It's the supreme climax to a supreme effort, and everything afterward seems small by comparison. No wonder, then, that it's one of the artist's favorite subjects.

Jacob Lawrence, **DAYBREAK—A TIME TO REST**
National Gallery of Art, Washington, D.C.
Gift of an Anonymous Donor

John Trumbull, **DECLARATION OF INDEPENDENCE**
Courtesy Yale University Art Gallery

The two widely contrasting artists on these two pages have captured the moment before and the moment of decision. Jacob Lawrence, a contemporary black painter, uses a deceptively primitive style to view the instant of daybreak. There is anticipation in the painting, for all of its surface tranquility. Something will occur, but not quite yet. It's waiting, just beyond the rim of the painting. John Trumbull's famous recording of the signing of the Declaration of Independence is an example of painting-as-journalism. Done while the signers were still alive, it's a true copy of the scene, with portraits drawn from life. The attitudes of the bodies inform us that this is a monumental moment of decision.

Juan de Flandes, **ANNUNCIATION**
National Gallery of Art, Washington, D.C.
Samuel H. Kress Collection

The devout Virgin in the Rennaisance painting at the left has already made her decision, and the angel and the bird of heaven are poised to affirm it. The coy couple at the right, on the other hand, tremble on the brink of *in*decision, providing some mirth for their friends.

George Caleb Bingham captures a frontier moment in his famous canvas at the left. Stumping for a vote, the politician tries to influence the decisions of three somewhat skeptical voters.

Pablo Picasso, **BULLFIGHT: DEATH OF THE TOREADOR**
Musée Picasso, Paris

Pablo Picasso was probably the most influential artist of the twentieth century. Leader of the Cubist style, master of imagination and inventiveness, there is hardly a subject with which he didn't experiment. His vitality, humor, and originality can well be seen in the painting above. The gay colors and the general festive air mock the imminent death of the toreador.

Lucas Von Leyden
CHESS GAME

The sixteenth-century lady trying to concentrate on her chess game is hardly different from the park chess player of today. There is always an abundance of advice in public places; there are more suggesters of decisions than makers of them. In the lovely and delicate painting from the same century at the right, St. Anthony affirms his sainthood by acting upon his decision to share his wealth with the poor and the needy.

Sassetta and Assistant, **SAINT ANTHONY DISTRIBUTING HIS WEALTH TO THE POOR**
National Gallery of Art, Washington, D.C.
Samuel H. Kress Collection

Here are two stories to be read one immediately following the other. Each concerns a beautiful princess faced with a momentous decision. After you have read the first selection, long considered a classic, you will understand why it became the subject for so much conjecture and controversy. With James Thurber as the author of the second story, of course you can expect anything, so don't be surprised. Remember, however, that Thurber used humor as a way of saying something serious.

THE LADY, OR THE TIGER?
Frank R. Stockton

In the very olden times, there lived a semi-barbaric king, whose ideas, though somewhat polished and sharpened by the progressiveness of distant Latin neighbors, were still large, florid, and untrammeled, as became the half of him which was barbaric. He was a man of exuberant fancy, and, withal, of an authority so irresistible that, at his will, he turned his fancies into facts. He was greatly given to self-communing; and, when he and himself agreed upon anything, the thing was done. When every member of his domestic and political systems moved smoothly in its appointed course, his nature was bland and genial; but whenever there was a little hitch, and some of his orbs got out of their orbits, he was blander and more genial still, for nothing pleased him so much as to make the crooked straight, and crush down uneven places.

Among the borrowed notions by which his barbarism had become semified[1] was that of the public arena, in which, by exhibitions of manly and beastly valor, the minds of his subjects were refined and cultured.

But even here the exuberant and bar-baric fancy asserted itself. The arena of the king was built, not to give the people an opportunity of hearing the rhapsodies of dying gladiators, nor to enable them to view the inevitable conclusion of a conflict between religious opinions and hungry jaws, but for purposes far better adapted to widen and develop the mental energies of the people. This vast amphitheater, with its encircling galleries, its mysterious vaults, and its unseen passages, was an agent of poetic justice, in which crime was punished, or virtue rewarded, by the decrees of an impartial and incorruptible chance.

When a subject was accused of a crime of sufficient importance to interest the king, public notice was given that on an appointed day the fate of the accused person would be decided in the king's arena—a structure which well deserved its name; for, although its form and plan were borrowed from afar, its purpose emanated solely from the brain of this

---

1. **semified,** cut in half. The reference is to "semi-barbaric" in the opening sentence.

man, who, every barleycorn[2] a king, knew no tradition to which he owed more allegiance than pleased his fancy, and who ingrafted on every adopted form of human thought and action the rich growth of his barbaric idealism.

When all the people had assembled in the galleries, and the king, surrounded by his court, sat high up on his throne of royal state on one side of the arena, he gave a signal, a door beneath him opened, and the accused subject stepped out into the amphitheater. Directly opposite him, on the other side of the enclosed space, were two doors, exactly alike and side by side. It was the duty and the privilege of the person on trial to walk directly to these doors and open one of them. He could open either door he pleased; he was subject to no guidance or influence but that of the aforementioned impartial and incorruptible chance. If he opened the one, there came out of it a hungry tiger, the fiercest and most cruel that could be found, which immediately

2. **barleycorn,** an ancient measure equal to one third of an inch. The phrase is a mockery of "every inch a king," and means that this particular king was very small-minded.

sprang upon him and tore him to pieces as a punishment for his guilt. The moment that the case of the criminal was thus decided, doleful iron bells were clanged, great wails went up from the hired mourners posted on the outer rim of the arena, and the vast audience, with bowed heads and downcast hearts, wended slowly their homeward way, mourning greatly that one so young and fair, or so old and respected, should have merited so dire a fate.

But, if the accused person opened the other door, there came forth from it a lady, the most suitable to his years and station that His Majesty could select among his fair subjects; and to this lady he was immediately married, as a reward of his innocence. It mattered not that he might already possess a wife and family, or that his affections might be engaged upon an object of his own selection; the king allowed no such subordinate arrangements to interfere with his great scheme of retribution and reward. The exercise, as in the other instance, took place immediately and in the arena. Another door opened beneath the king, and a priest, followed by a band of choristers, and dancing maidens blowing joyous airs on golden horns and treading an epithalamic measure[3] advanced to where the pair stood, side by side; and the wedding was promptly and cheerily solemnized. Then the gay brass bells rang forth their merry peals, the people shouted glad hurrahs, and the innocent man, preceded by children strewing flowers on his path, led his bride to his home.

This was the king's semi-barbaric method of administering justice. Its perfect fairness is obvious. The criminal could not know out of which door would come the lady; he opened either he pleased, without having the slightest idea whether, in the next instant, he was to be devoured or married. On some occasions the tiger came out one door; and on some, out of the other. The decisions of this tribunal were not only fair, they were positively determinate; the accused person was instantly punished if he found himself guilty; and, if innocent, he was rewarded on the spot, whether he liked it or not. There was no escape from the judgments of the king's arena.

The institution was a very popular one. When the people gathered together on one of the great trial days, they never knew whether they were to witness a bloody slaughter or a hilarious wedding. This element of uncertainty lent an interest to the occasion which it could not otherwise have attained. Thus, the masses were entertained and pleased; and the thinking part of the community could bring no charge of unfairness against this plan, for did not the accused person have the whole matter in his own hands?

This semi-barbaric king had a daughter as blooming as his most florid fancies and with a soul as fervent and impervious as his own. As is usual in such cases, she was the apple of his eye and was loved by him above all humanity. Among his courtiers was a young man of that firmness of blood and lowness of station common to the conventional heroes of romance who love royal maidens. This royal maiden was well satisfied with her lover, for he was handsome and brave to a degree unsurpassed in all this kingdom; and she

---

3. **epithalamic** (ep′ə thə lā′mik) **measure,** a wedding song.

loved him with an ardor that had enough of barbarism in it to make it exceedingly warm and strong. This love affair moved on happily for many months, until one day the king happened to discover its existence. (He did not hesitate nor waver in regard to his duty in the premises. The youth was immediately cast into prison, and a day was appointed for his trial in the king's arena. This, of course, was an especially important occasion; and His Majesty, as well as all the people, was greatly interested in the workings and development of this trial. Never before had such a case occurred; never before had a subject dared to love the daughter of a king. In after years such things became commonplace enough; but then they were, in no slight degree, novel and startling.

The tiger cages of the kingdom were searched for the most savage and relentless beasts, from which the fiercest monster might be selected for the arena; and the ranks of maiden youth and beauty throughout the land were carefully surveyed by competent judges in order that the young man might have a fitting bride in case fate did not determine for him a different destiny. Of course, everybody knew that the deed with which the accused was charged had been done. He had loved the princess, and neither he, she, nor anyone else thought of denying the fact; but the king would not think of allowing any fact of this kind to interfere with the working of the tribunal, in which he took such great delight and satisfaction. No matter how the affair turned out, the youth would be disposed of; and the king would take an aesthetic pleasure in watching the course of events, which would determine whether or not the young man had done wrong in allowing himself to love the princess.

The appointed day arrived. From far and near the people gathered and thronged the great galleries of the arena; and crowds, unable to gain admittance, massed themselves against its outside walls. The king and his court were in their places, opposite the twin doors—those fateful portals, so terrible in their similarity.

All was ready. The signal was given. A door beneath the royal party opened, and the lover of the princess walked into the arena. Tall, beautiful, fair, his appearance was greeted with a low hum of admiration and anxiety. Half the audience had not known so grand a youth had lived among them. No wonder the princess loved him! What a terrible thing for him to be there!

As the youth advanced into the arena, he turned, as the custom was, to bow to the king; but he did not think at all of that royal personage; his eyes were fixed upon the princess who sat to the right of her father. Had it not been for the moiety[4] of barbarism in her nature, it is probable that lady would not have been there; but her intense and fervid soul would not allow her to be absent on an occasion in which she was so terribly interested. From the moment that the decree had gone forth, that her lover should decide his fate in the king's arena, she had thought of nothing, night or day, but this great event and the various subjects connected with it. Possessed of more power, influence, and force of character than anyone who had ever before been interested in such a case, she had done what

4. **moiety** (moi′ə tē), half portion.

no other person had done—she had possessed herself of the secret of the doors. She knew in which of the two rooms that lay behind those doors stood the cage of the tiger, with its open front, and in which waited the lady. Through these thick doors, heavily curtained with skins on the inside, it was impossible that any noise or suggestion should come from within to the person who should approach to raise the latch of one of them; but gold, and the power of a woman's will, had brought the secret to the princess.

And not only did she know in which room stood the lady ready to emerge, all blushing and radiant, should her door be opened, but she knew who the lady was. It was one of the fairest and loveliest of the damsels of the court who had been selected as the reward of the accused youth, should he be proved innocent of the crime of aspiring to one so far above him; and the princess hated her. Often had she seen, or imagined that she had seen, this fair creature throwing glances of admiration upon the person of her lover; and sometimes she thought these glances were perceived and even returned. Now and then she had seen them talking together; it was but for a moment or two, but much can be said in a brief space; it may have been on most unimportant topics, but how could she know that? The girl was lovely, but she had dared to raise her eyes to the loved one of the princess; and, with all the intensity of the savage blood transmitted to her through long lines of wholly barbaric ancestors, she hated the woman who blushed and trembled behind the silent door.

When her lover turned and looked at her, and his eyes met hers as she sat there paler and whiter than anyone in the vast ocean of anxious faces about her, he saw, by that power of quick perception which is given to those whose souls are one, that she knew behind which door crouched the tiger and behind which stood the lady. He had expected her to know it. He understood her nature; and his soul was assured that she would never rest until she had made plain to herself this thing, hidden to all other lookers-on, even to the king. The only hope for the youth in which there was any element of certainty was based upon the success of the princess in discovering this mystery; and the moment he looked upon her, he saw she had succeeded, as in his soul he knew she would succeed.

Then it was his quick and anxious glance asked the question: "Which?" It was as plain to her as if he shouted it from where he stood. There was not an instant to be lost. The question was asked in a flash; it must be answered in another.

Her right arm lay on the cushioned parapet before her. She raised her hand, and made a slight, quick movement toward the right. No one but her lover saw her. Every eye but his was fixed on the man in the arena.

He turned, and with a firm and rapid step he walked across the empty space. Every heart stopped beating, every breath was held, every eye was fixed immovable upon that man. Without the slightest hesitation, he went to the door on the right and opened it.

Now, the point of the story is this: Did the tiger come out of that door, or did the lady?

The more we reflect upon this question the harder it is to answer. It involves a study of the human heart which leads us through devious mazes of passion, out of which it is difficult to find our way. Think of it, fair reader, not as if the decision of the question depended upon yourself, but upon that hot-blooded, semi-barbaric princess, her soul at a white heat beneath the combined fires of despair and jealousy. She had lost him, but who should have him?

How often, in her waking hours and in her dreams, had she started in wild horror and covered her face with her hands as she thought of her lover opening the door on the other side of which waited the cruel fangs of the tiger!

But how much oftener had she seen him at the other door! How in her grievous reveries had she gnashed her teeth and torn her hair when she saw his start of rapturous delight as he opened the door of the lady! How her soul had burned in agony when she had seen him rush to meet that woman, with her flushing cheek and sparkling eye of triumph; when she had seen him lead her forth, his whole frame kindled with the joy of recovered life; when she had heard the loud shouts from the multitude and the wild ringing of the happy bells; when she had seen the priest with his joyous followers advance to the couple and make them man and wife before her very eyes; and when she had seen them walk away together upon their path of flowers, followed by the tremendous shouts of the hilarious multitude, in which her one despairing shriek was lost and drowned!

Would it not be better for him to die at once and go to wait for her in the blessed regions of semi-barbaric futurity?

And yet, that awful tiger, those shrieks, that blood!

Her decision had been indicated in an instant, but it had been made after days and nights of anguished deliberation. She had known she would be asked; she had decided what she would answer; and without the slightest hesitation, she had moved her hand to the right.

The question of her decision is not one to be lightly considered, and it is not for me to presume to set myself up as the one person able to answer it. And so I leave it all with you: Which came out of the opened door—the lady, or the tiger?

". . . it is the most valuable of all the gifts. . . ."

THE PRINCESS AND THE TIN BOX
James Thurber

Once upon a time, in a far country, there lived a king whose daughter was the prettiest princess in the world. Her eyes were like the cornflower, her hair was sweeter than the hyacinth, and her throat made the swan look dusty.

From the time she was a year old, the princess had been showered with presents. Her nursery looked like Cartier's window.* Her toys were all made of gold or platinum or diamonds or emeralds. She was not permitted to have wooden blocks or china dolls or rubber dogs or linen books, because such materials were considered cheap for the daughter of a king.

When she was seven, she was allowed to attend the wedding of her brother and throw real pearls at the bride instead of rice. Only the nightingale, with his lyre of gold, was permitted to sing for the princess. The common blackbird, with his boxwood flute, was kept out of the palace grounds. She walked in silver-and-samite slippers to a sapphire-and-topaz bathroom and slept in an ivory bed inlaid with rubies.

On the day the princess was eighteen, the king sent a royal ambassador to the courts of five neighboring kingdoms to announce that he would give his daughter's hand in marriage to the prince who brought her the gift she liked the most.

The first prince to arrive at the palace rode a swift white stallion and laid at the feet of the princess an enormous apple made of solid gold which he had taken from a dragon who had guarded it for a thousand years. It was placed on a long ebony table set up to hold the gifts of the princess's suitors. The second prince, who came on a gray charger, brought her a nightingale made of a thousand diamonds, and it was placed beside the golden apple. The third prince, riding on a black horse, carried a great jewel box made of platinum and sapphires, and it was placed next to the diamond nightingale. The fourth prince, astride a fiery yellow horse, gave the princess a gigantic heart made of rubies and pierced by an emerald arrow. It was placed next to the platinum-and-sapphire jewel box.

Now the fifth prince was the strongest and handsomest of all the five suitors, but he was the son of a poor king whose realm had been overrun by mice and locusts and wizards and mining engineers so that there was nothing much of value left in it. He came plodding up to the palace of the princess on a plow horse, and he brought her a small tin box filled with mica and feldspar and hornblende which he had picked up on the way.

*__Cartier's__ (kär′tē āz), a famous jeweler in New York.

The other princes roared with disdainful laughter when they saw the tawdry gift the fifth prince had brought to the princess. But she examined it with great interest and squealed with delight, for all her life she had been glutted with precious stones and priceless metals, but she had never seen tin before or mica or feldspar or hornblende. The tin box was placed next to the ruby heart pierced with an emerald arrow.

"Now," the king said to his daughter, "you must select the gift you like best and marry the prince that brought it."

The princess smiled and walked up to the table and picked up the present she liked the most. It was the platinum-and-sapphire jewel box, the gift of the third prince.

"The way I figure it," she said, "is this. It is a very large and expensive box, and when I am married, I will meet many admirers who will give me precious gems with which to fill it to the top. Therefore, it is the most valuable of all the gifts my suitors have brought me and I like it the best."

The princess married the third prince that very day in the midst of great merriment and high revelry. More than a hundred thousand pearls were thrown at her and she loved it.

Moral: All those who thought the princess was going to select the tin box filled with worthless stones instead of one of the other gifts will kindly stay after class and write one hundred times on the blackboard "I would rather have a hunk of aluminum silicate than a diamond necklace."

READING FOR DETAILS

Two Girls Make Up Their Minds

By far the most popular thing Frank Stockton ever wrote was the short story first titled "In the King's Arena." Originally, it was intended to be read as part of an evening's entertainment at a party for friends. However, the party turned out to be one of gay confusion, and Stockton decided not to read his story. Later, he reworked it a bit and sent it to *Century Magazine,* which bought it for $50.

Eventually his story was published under the title, "The Lady, or the Tiger?" Almost immediately it became a literary sensation, with the solution to the problem it presented being discussed all over the country.

Robert Browning, a famous British writer, after being asked to read the story and give his opinion, decided without hesitation that the princess directed her lover to the tiger's door.

1. There are many who believe that Stockton himself suggested the decision the princess made. In debating whether or not you believe this to be true, consider and discuss:

a. Stockton's repeated reference to the girl as hot-blooded and semi-barbaric

b. lines which indicate that the princess was uncertain that her love was fully returned

c. the feeling the princess had for the damsel who was behind the closed door

d. the fact that Stockton was regarded as

a realist who used his fairy tales to put across truths which he felt he could not do otherwise

2. Find any passages that seem to support the opposite theory—that the princess would choose to let her lover live, even though she lost him. Discuss.

3. Discuss the ways in which Stockton's description of the king and his methods of dispensing justice are slyly humorous or satirical.

4. What was the decision which Thurber's princess had to make? How did she explain her choice? With what moral did Thurber conclude his fable? What does he suggest is all-important to most people at the present time?

READING FOR MEANING

Consider and discuss:

The tremendous popularity of "The Lady, or the Tiger?" stemmed almost entirely from the unanswered, perhaps unanswerable, human problems which Stockton set forth. He was deluged with so many thousands of letters begging a solution that he finally answered with a puzzling statement which brought satisfaction to very few: "If you decide which it was—the lady, or the tiger—you find out what kind of a person you are yourself."

1. Consider Stockton's statement carefully and discuss whether you agree that when you decide whether jealousy or love was the stronger influence on the princess, you reveal your own character.

2. The young man knew from the princess's gesture what he would find behind the door he chose.

READING FOR APPRECIATION

Beginnings and Endings

Thurber's aim in "The Princess and the Tin Box" is to make readers *think* at the same time that they are being entertained. How does the author accomplish his purpose?

In the first place, Thurber knew quite a bit about the ways people think and act. He knew that human beings are most comfortable doing things that fall into certain familiar patterns.

1. Explain why the four familiar words at the very beginning of Thurber's story lead the reader to assume that the tale will end with four other equally well-known words.

2. Thurber describes how the princess had been reared in great and exaggerated luxury, yet the reader is not prepared to accept the rather logical decision the princess finally makes. Why?

3. Stockton's story has been said to have no ending. Discuss. Which of the two stories do you believe you will remember longer? Why?

BIOGRAPHICAL NOTES

Frank R. Stockton (1834–1902), short story writer, was born in Philadelphia, Pennsylvania. After graduating from high school, he learned the trade of woodcarving, a skill he later utilized when he used his own engravings as illustrations for some of his writings. After turning to writing as a full-time career, he worked for his brother's newspaper and for several magazines, eventually rising to the position of assistant editor of *St. Nicholas* magazine.

James Thurber (1894–1961), American novelist and illustrator, was born in Columbus, Ohio. Educated at Ohio State University, Thurber worked on both the *Columbus Dispatch* and the Paris edition of the *Chicago Tribune*. He also served as managing editor and staff writer for *The New Yorker*. One of the great American humorists, Thurber is best known for his classic short story, "The Secret Life of Walter Mitty." In 1960, Thurber acted in a dramatic revue *(The Thurber Carnival)* of several of his essays and short stories.

SUMMING UP: MOMENTS OF DECISION

The decisions read about in MOMENTS OF DECISION are as varied as the personalities of the individuals who made them. Yet in looking back over the selections, one can discover some of the general patterns into which decisions fall.

By far the greatest number of decisions are *routine* and are made without much thought; many are *planned* and take a great deal of thought; some are *emergency* decisions and arise from the need for immediate action with no time for the lengthy consideration of various possibilities. Choices made under any of these conditions, of course, might be thought of as either morally good or morally bad, and might win approval or disapproval.

Whether, like Robert Frost, persons must decide which road to take, or whether, like John Bagley, they are suddenly thrust into a position where they must make many critical decisions quickly, their background of experience will determine to a large extent the kinds of choices they will make and the ease with which they will make them.

READING FOR MEANING

Summary Statements

One of the following should be selected as a topic for a short class talk. You will probably want to expand on the subject chosen by using ideas gained from the unit selections, the study materials, outside research, and personal experience.

1. The most miserable human beings are those who cannot make up their minds about what they want to do.
2. Most decisions are forced upon us.
3. Most people would make a better decision if given a second chance.
4. Since what is to be will be, any decision an individual makes is of little consequence.
5. Persons in official positions should be held responsible for the decisions they make.
6. Most people have a set of values established early in life that determine the kinds of decisions they make.

READING FOR APPRECIATION

1. Compare Aesop's fable "The Father and His Sons" (THE INNER CIRCLE, page 267) with Thurber's fable "The Princess and the Tin Box." In what ways do they differ with respect to: (a) purpose, (b) language, (c) ending?
2. Decide which character from the selections in this unit is most memorable for you. Discuss why this is true, keeping in mind the author's skill and your own background of experience.

COMPOSITION

One reason you will likely never forget "The Lady, or the Tiger?" is that you are left to imagine the ending.

Write a definite ending to this story. Do not feel constrained to have it conform to what might be expected. Perhaps, this time, something other than the expected two alternatives may lie behind the doors. Or in view of the fact that this young man was of such outstanding bravery, perhaps he vanquished the tiger. Would the king then relent and allow him to marry his daughter? Give your imagination free rein to write an ending that satisfies you. Try for a concluding sentence that leaves the reader with the *effect* you wish to achieve.

COMPOSITION WORKSHOP

THE BOOK REPORT

No one can possibly read even a small percentage of all the books that have been published. The book review performs a very useful service by bringing important and useful books to the attention of readers.

The writer of a book report usually has three purposes in mind:

1. *The writer will want to give the reader a good idea of what the book is about.* The writer will accomplish this purpose by providing a brief summary of the book. This summary will not be as detailed as a complete summary and will usually not be any longer than two paragraphs. A more complete summary would tell too much of the story and might deprive the reader of the pleasure of reading the book.

2. *The writer will want to present his or her personal view of the book.* The readers of a book report expect the writer's personal opinion about the book. But the opinion that the writer presents must be supported. It is not enough to say that the book was interesting or boring, good or bad. The reader wants to know why the writer has come to the opinion.

3. *The writer will want to include some information about the book's author.* A reader likes to know that the author of a nonfiction book has some experience and knowledge of the topic explored in the book. A reader likes to know if the author of a work of fiction has written other books that the reader might already know about or be interested in.

With these three purposes in mind, the writer can begin to plan the report. Let's say a writer wants to report on Mari Sandoz's *Winter Thunder,* a suspense-filled novel enjoyed especially by young teen-agers. The writer might begin by developing a rough outline. Since the writer already knows that an introductory paragraph should precede the three

purposes stated above, he or she might concentrate first upon the section of the report that will summarize the story.

In deciding how to best summarize the story, the writer might decide to follow the same pattern that Mari Sandoz follows. She devotes the first few pages of *Winter Thunder* to setting the scene and introducing the characters. The balance of the story focuses on the frightening events and how the brave teacher deals with those events as best she can. The rough outline might look like this:

I. Introduction
II. Summary (opening events)
III. Summary (balance of story)
IV. Opinion
V. Author

Using the rough outline as a guide, the report writer begins to list the supporting material for the paragraphs that will make up the report, leaving the introductory paragraph until the others have been fleshed out. For the last paragraph, the writer goes to standard reference material to gather information about the author's life. Once supporting notes have been assembled for each paragraph in the body of the report, the writer can write a topic sentence for each. The writer can then examine the topic sentences and from them develop a thesis sentence that will be the report's opening sentence. The writer might then develop the following paragraph outline:

I. *Winter Thunder* is a short novel that captures a reader's attention at once.
II. From the very beginning, the novel sets the stage for the characters' battle against nature.
III. *Winter Thunder* tells the courageous story of Lecia Terry.
IV. *Winter Thunder* is an exciting book, but it is much more than an adventure story.

V. In *Winter Thunder* Mari Sandoz captures the frontier spirit that has played
such an important role in much of her
writing.

Study the following book report based on
the paragraph outline above. Notice that it
begins with a special heading that includes
some basic information about the subject of
the report.

Title: **Winter Thunder**
Author: **Mari Sandoz**
Publisher: **Westminster Press, 1951**
Pages: **87**

Winter Thunder **is a short novel that captures a reader's attention at once and holds it
until the book's final line.**

**From the very beginning, the novel sets
the stage for the characters' battle against nature. It opens on a bleak and snowy morning
on the plains of Nebraska. An old school bus
picks its way carefully along a road that is
barely visible in the blinding storm. Inside the
bus are nine people. The oldest is Lecia Terry,
a twenty-three-year-old school teacher. The bus
is driven by Chuck, a boy of sixteen who is
substituting for his ailing father. The seven
remaining passengers are children who range
in age from six to twelve. The passengers are
on their way to a rural school that they will
never get to. As the blizzard that surrounds
them intensifies, the bus falters and overturns.
Shortly after the frightened passengers climb
out of the bus, it bursts into flames and is destroyed.**

Winter Thunder **tells the courageous story
of Lecia Terry. She is a young teacher who
conquers her own fear and manages to lead her
young charges through the terrors of a howling
blizzard that lasts for eight horrible days. Accepting the responsibility that is suddenly
thrust upon her, Lecia remains calm enough to
remember important survival skills taught to
her by her ancestors who first settled on these
often violent plains. She carefully rations the
skimpy supply of food that the children were
traveling to school with. She constructs a life-
preserving structure, using the few raw materials that are at hand. She builds and maintains a
fire. She manages through strength of will to
gain the cooperation of Chuck, whose strength**

**she needs. As the increasingly ill children need
more and more of her support, she somehow
finds the strength to supply it. Against all
odds, her heroism outlasts the storm. As the
novel ends, the survivors cling to each other as
they walk to safety. They are together at the
end because she has taught them to work together from the beginning of their ordeal.**

Winter Thunder **is an exciting book, but it
is much more than an adventure story. It has
something to say about genuine courage. The
reader learns that real courage is not made up
of deeds that are larger than life and almost
superhuman. It comes instead from devotion
and selflessness. The teacher in the novel does
not want what is thrust upon her. But she accepts the responsibility that is hers. She is not
a person of great physical strength. In fact she
has to force herself to continue to care for the
children. The unforgettable Lecia Terry brings
the children through the terrible storm by developing in them, through her own example,
the courage and sense of caring that they need
to survive.**

In *Winter Thunder* **Mari Sandoz captures
the frontier spirit that has played such an important role in much of her writing. She first
brought this spirit to the attention of readers in
1935 with the publication of** *Old Jules,* **an
award-winning biography of her pioneer father. Her appreciation of the plains and the
people who have lived on them are shown as
well in her nonfiction books** *Crazy Horse, Cheyenne Autumn, Love Song to the Plains,* **and** *These
Were the Sioux.* **Mari Sandoz was always able to
make real people come alive for the reader.
She did this job very well in this exciting story
of simple courage.**

ACTIVITY

Choose a book upon which to write a report.
Be sure you are completely familiar with the
book on which you are reporting. Develop a
plan for your report in the form of a rough
outline. Gather supporting material for the
parts of the outline. Then develop a paragraph outline for your report. Finally, write a
report of no more than five paragraphs on
the book you selected. Make sure that each
paragraph begins with a topic sentence.

INTRODUCTION TO
A Tale of Two Cities

The British novelist Charles Dickens (1812–1870) experienced a harsh childhood. After his father was arrested and imprisoned for debt, the boy went to work at the age of twelve to help support his family. Dickens was thus largely deprived of a formal education. But through his powers of perseverance and imagination he succeeded in becoming one of the world's greatest storytellers. His writing career made him an international celebrity, and he died a wealthy man.

Most of Dickens's novels vividly re-create for us the world of nineteenth-century England, then the most powerful country on earth. Dickens was one of the first novelists to portray all classes of society, from the noble to the very humble. Many of his best-known books, such as *Oliver Twist, A Christmas Carol, David Copperfield,* and *Great Expectations* are familiar to modern audiences through stage and screen adaptations. Dickens explored several fundamental themes in these works: the growth of the individual from youth to adulthood, the cruelty of social injustice, and the true meaning of love for our fellow human beings. You will recognize the importance of the latter two themes in the selection that follows.

A Tale of Two Cities, published in 1859, introduces us to the historical novel, a form in which some characters and details are invented by the author, but the setting, historical personages, and other details are accurately re-created from a period in the past. The two cities of the title are London and Paris. The period is the age leading up to the French Revolution, which began in 1789. We know that Dickens painstakingly researched this novel. The geography of Paris and the social customs of the French are based on factual information which Dickens found in historical sources, and which he then included in his imaginative tale.

The French Revolution was years in the making. The cruel oppression of the peasants by the nobility, the abuses of justice, and the misery of the people made violent rebellion almost inevitable. When the Revolution finally came, and the monarchy of King Louis XVI and his queen, Marie Antoinette, was overthrown, France endured years of chaotic, random violence. You will note how vividly Dickens conveys the atmosphere of suspicion and terror of this period.

In *A Tale of Two Cities,* the main characters are caught up in events they cannot control. Dr. Manette, Charles Darnay, and Sydney Carton must all face great moments of decision, which test to the limit their personal values of morality and courage. The backdrop of their lives is the great drama of a nation in turmoil.

A Tale of Two Cities is a novel of plot, in which the structure of the story is very carefully designed. Almost all of the incidents are interconnected and essential to the story's development. Dickens makes extensive use of the techniques of foreshadowing and suspense. When you read this selection, be alert to the ways in which the author withholds certain information at critical points in the story in order to intensify the excitement of the outcome.

Siege of the Bastille. Vive la Révolution!

A TALE OF TWO CITIES Charles Dickens

Part One

Chapter 1
The Preparation

It was the best of times, it was the worst of times, it was the age of wisdom, it was the age of foolishness, it was the epoch of belief, it was the epoch of incredulity, it was the season of Light, it was the season of Darkness, it was the spring of hope, it was the winter of despair, we had everything before us, we had nothing before us, we were all going direct to Heaven, we were all going direct the other way—in short, the period was so far like the present period, that some of its noisiest authorities insisted on its being received, for good or for evil, in the superlative degree of comparison only.

There were a king with a large jaw and a queen with a plain face, on the throne of England; there were a king with a large jaw and a queen with a fair face, on the throne of France.[1] In both countries it was clearer than crystal to the lords of the State preserves of loaves and fishes, that things in general were settled for ever.

It was the year of Our Lord one thousand seven hundred and seventy-five. It was the Dover[2] road that lay, on a Friday night late in November, before the first of the persons with whom this history has business. The Dover road lay, as to him, beyond the Dover mail, as it lumbered up Shooter's Hill. He walked uphill in the mire by the side of the mail, as the rest of the passengers did; not because they had the least relish for walking exercise, under the circumstances, but because the hill, and the harness, and the mud, and the mail, were all so heavy, that the horses had three times already come to a stop.

Two other passengers, besides the one, were plodding up the hill by the side of the mail. All three were wrapped to the cheekbones and over the ears, and wore jack-boots. Not one of the three could have said, from anything he saw, what either of the other two was like. In those days, travellers were very shy of being confidential on a short notice, for anybody on the road might be a robber or in league with robbers. Once more, the Dover mail struggled on, with the jack-boots of its passengers squashing along by its side. They had stopped when the coach stopped, and they kept close company with it. If any one of the three had had the hardihood to propose to another to walk on a little ahead into the mist and darkness, he would have put himself in a fair way of getting shot instantly as a highwayman.[3]

The sound of a horse at a gallop came fast and furiously up the hill.

"So-ho!" the guard sang out, as loud as he could roar. "Yo there! Stand! I shall fire!"

The pace was suddenly checked, and, with much splashing and floundering, a man's voice called from the mist, "Is that the Dover mail?"

1. King George III (reigned 1760–1820) and Queen Charlotte of England; King Louis XVI (reigned 1774–1792) and Queen Marie Antoinette of France.
2. The road to **Dover,** a small port town about 70 miles southeast of London.
3. **highwayman,** robber.

"Never you mind what it is!" the guard retorted. "What are you?"

"*Is* that the Dover mail?"

"Why do you want to know?"

"I want a passenger, if it is."

"What passenger?"

"Mr. Jarvis Lorry."

"What is the matter?" asked the passenger, then, with mildly quavering speech, "Who wants me? Is it Jerry?"

"Yes, Mr. Lorry."

"What is the matter?"

"A dispatch sent after you from over yonder. T. and Co."

"I know this messenger, guard," said Mr. Lorry, getting down into the road. "He may come close; there's nothing wrong."

The figures of a horse and rider came slowly through the eddying mist, and came to the side of the mail, where the passenger stood. The rider stooped, and, casting up his eyes at the guard, handed the passenger a small folded paper.

"Guard!" said the passenger, in a tone of quiet business confidence.

The watchful guard, with his right hand at the stock of his raised blunderbuss, his left at the barrel, and his eye on the horseman, answered curtly, "Sir."

"There is nothing to apprehend. I belong to Tellson's Bank. You must know Tellson's Bank in London. I am going to Paris on business. I may read this?"

"If so be as you're quick, sir."

He opened it in the light of the coach-lamp on that side, and read—first to himself and then aloud: "'Wait at Dover for Mam'selle.' It's not long, you see, guard. Jerry, say that my answer was, RECALLED TO LIFE."

Jerry started in his saddle. "That's a Blazing strange answer, too," said he.

"Take that message back, and they will know that I received this, as well as if I wrote. Make the best of your way. Good night."

With those words the passenger opened the coach door and got in; not at all assisted by his fellow-passengers, who had expeditiously secreted their watches and purses in their boots, and were now making a general pretense of being asleep.

When the mail got successfully to Dover, in the course of the forenoon, the head drawer[4] at the Royal George Hotel opened the coach-door as his custom was. He did it with some flourish of ceremony, for a mail journey from London in winter was an achievement to congratulate an adventurous traveller upon.

By that time, there was only one adventurous traveller left to be congratulated; for the two others had been set down at their respective roadside destinations. The mildewy inside of the coach, with its damp and dirty straw, its disagreeable smell, and its obscurity, was rather like a larger dog-kennel. Mr. Lorry, the passenger, shaking himself out of it in chains of straw, a tangle of shaggy wrapper, flapping hat, and muddy legs, was rather like a larger sort of dog.

"There will be a packet to Calais,[5] tomorrow, drawer?"

"Yes, sir, if the weather holds and the wind sets tolerable fair. The tide will serve pretty nicely at about two in the afternoon, sir. Bed, sir?"

"I shall not go to bed till night; but I want a bedroom, and a barber."

"And then breakfast, sir? Yes, sir."

The coffee-room had no other occupant, that forenoon, than the gentleman in brown. His breakfast-table was drawn before the fire, and as he sat, with its light shining on him, waiting for the meal, he sat so still, that he might have been sitting for his portrait.

Very orderly and methodical he looked,

---

4. **drawer,** a waiter.
5. **packet,** a fast boat. **Calais** (ka lā′), port city of Northern France, across the English Channel from Dover.

with a hand on each knee, and a loud watch ticking a sonorous sermon under his flapped waistcoat, as though it pitted its gravity and longevity against the levity and evanescence of the brisk fire. He had a good leg, and was a little vain of it, for his brown stockings fitted sleek and close, and were of a fine texture; his shoes and buckles, too, though plain, were trim. He wore an odd little sleek crisp flaxen wig, setting very close to his head: which wig, it is to be presumed, was made of hair, but which looked far more as though it were spun from filaments of silk or glass. His linen,[6] though not of a fineness in accordance with his stockings, was as white as the tops of the waves that broke upon the neighboring beach, or the specks of sail that glinted in the sunlight far at sea. A face, habitually suppressed and quieted, was still lighted up under the quaint wig by a pair of moist bright eyes that it must have cost their owner, in years gone by, some pains to drill to the composed and reserved expression of Tellson's Bank. He had a healthy color in his cheeks, and his face, though lined, bore few traces of anxiety. But, perhaps the confidential bachelor clerks in Tellson's Bank were principally occupied with the cares of other people; and perhaps second-hand cares, like second-hand clothes, come easily off and on.

Completing his resemblance to a man who was sitting for his portrait, Mr. Lorry dropped off to sleep. The arrival of his breakfast roused him, and he said to the drawer, as he moved his chair to it:

"I wish accommodation prepared for a young lady who may come here at any time today. She may ask for Mr. Jarvis Lorry, or she may only ask for a gentleman from Tellson's Bank. Please to let me know."

"Yes, sir. Tellson's Bank in London, sir?"

"Yes."

"Yes, sir. We have oftentimes the honor to entertain your gentlemen in their travelling backwards and forwards betwixt London and Paris, sir. A vast deal of travelling, sir, in Tellson and Company's House."

"Yes. We are quite a French House, as well as an English one."

"Yes, sir. Not much in the habit of such travelling yourself, I think, sir?"

"Not of late years. It is fifteen years since we—since I—came last from France."

"Indeed, sir? That was before my time here, sir. Before our people's time here, sir. The George was in other hands at that time, sir."

"I believe so."

"But I would hold a pretty wager, sir, that a House like Tellson and Company was flourishing, a matter of fifty, not to speak of fifteen years ago?"

"You might treble that, and say a hundred and fifty, yet not be far from the truth."

"Indeed, sir!"

When Mr. Lorry had finished his breakfast, he went out for a stroll on the beach. As the day declined into the afternoon, the air, which had been at intervals clear enough to allow the French coast to be seen, became again charged with mist and vapor. When it was dark, he sat before the coffee-room fire, awaiting his dinner as he had awaited his breakfast.

He had just poured out his last glassful of wine when a rattling of wheels came up the narrow street, and rumbled into the inn-yard.

He set down his glass untouched. "This is Mam'selle!" said he.

In a very few minutes the waiter came in to announce that Miss Manette had arrived from London, and would be happy to see the gentleman from Tellson's.

"So soon?"

Miss Manette had taken some refreshment on the road, and required none then, and was extremely anxious to see the gentle-

---

6. **linen,** an old term for men's shirts and handkerchiefs.

man from Tellson's immediately, if it suited his pleasure and convenience.

The gentleman from Tellson's had nothing left for it but to empty his glass with an air of stolid desperation, settle his odd little flaxen wig at the ears, and follow the waiter to Miss Manette's apartment. It was a large, dark room. The obscurity was so difficult to penetrate that Mr. Lorry, picking his way over the well-worn Turkey carpet, supposed Miss Manette to be, for the moment, in some adjacent room, until he saw standing to receive him, a young lady of not more than seventeen, in a riding-cloak, and still holding her straw travelling-hat by its ribbon, in her hand. As his eyes rested on a short, slight, pretty figure, a quantity of golden hair, a pair of blue eyes that met his own with an inquiring look, and a forehead with a singular capacity (remembering how young and smooth it was), of lifting and knitting itself into an expression that was not quite one of perplexity, or wonder, or alarm, or merely of a bright fixed attention, though it included all the four expressions—as his eyes rested on these things, a sudden vivid likeness passed before him, of a child whom he had held in his arms on the passage across that very Channel, one cold time, when the hail drifted heavily and the sea ran high. The likeness passed away, say, like a breath along the surface of the gaunt pier glass[7] behind her, and he made his formal bow to Miss Manette.

"Pray take a seat, sir." In a very clear and pleasant young voice; a little foreign in its accent, but a very little indeed.

"I kiss your hand, miss," said Mr. Lorry, with the manners of an earlier date, as he made his formal bow again, and took his seat.

"I received a letter from the Bank, sir, yesterday, informing me that some intelligence—or discovery—"

"The word is not material, miss; either word will do."

"—respecting the small property of my poor father, whom I never saw—so long dead—rendered it necessary that I should go to Paris, there to communicate with a gentleman of the Bank, so good as to be dispatched to Paris for the purpose."

"Myself."

"As I was prepared to hear, sir."

She curtsyed to him (young ladies made curtsys in those days), with a pretty desire to convey to him that she felt how much older and wiser he was than she. He made her another bow.

"I replied to the Bank, sir, that as it was considered necessary, by those who know, and who are so kind as to advise me, that I should go to France, and that as I am an orphan and have no friend who could go with me, I should esteem it highly if I might be permitted to place myself, during the journey, under that worthy gentleman's protection. The gentleman had left London, but I think a messenger was sent after him to beg the favor of his waiting for me here."

"I was happy," said Mr. Lorry, "to be entrusted with the charge. I shall be more happy to execute it."

"Sir, I thank you indeed. I thank you very gratefully. It was told me by the Bank that the gentleman would explain to me the details of the business, and that I must prepare myself to find them of a surprising nature. I have done my best to prepare myself, and I naturally have a strong and eager interest to know what they are."

"Naturally," said Mr. Lorry. "Yes—I—"

After a pause, he added, again settling the crisp flaxen wig at the ears:

"It is very difficult to begin."

He did not begin, but, in his indecision, met her glance. The young forehead lifted itself into that singular expression—but it was pretty and characteristic, besides being singu-

---

7. **pier glass,** a tall, narrow mirror.

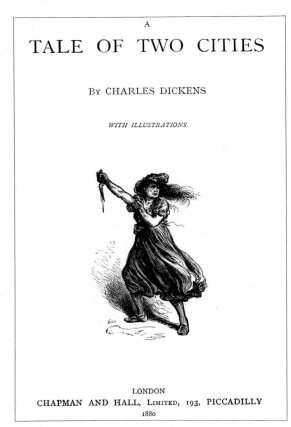
Title page of an old English edition.

lar—and she raised her hand, as if with an involuntary action she caught at, or stayed, some passing shadow.

"Are you quite a stranger to me, sir?"

"Am I not?" Mr. Lorry opened his hands, and extended them outwards with an argumentative smile.

Between the eyebrows and just over the little feminine nose, the line of which was as delicate and fine as it was possible to be, the expression deepened itself as she took her seat thoughtfully in the chair by which she had hitherto remained standing. He watched her as she mused, and the moment she raised her eyes again, went on:

"In your adopted country, I presume, I cannot do better than address you as a young English lady, Miss Manette?"

"If you please, sir."

"Miss Manette, I am a man of business. I have a business charge to acquit myself of. In your reception of it, don't heed me any more than if I was a speaking machine—truly, I am not much else. I will, with your leave, relate to you, miss, the story of one of our customers."

"Story!"

He seemed wilfully to mistake the word she had repeated, when he added, in a hurry, "Yes, customers; in the banking business we usually call our connection our customers. He was a French gentleman; a scientific gentleman; a man of great acquirements—a Doctor."

"Not of Beauvais?"[8]

"Why, yes, of Beauvais. Like Monsieur Manette, your father, the gentleman was of Beauvais. Like Monsieur[9] Manette, your father, the gentleman was of repute in Paris. I had the honor of knowing him there. Our relations were business relations, but confidential. I was at that time in our French House, and had been—oh! twenty years."

"At that time—I may ask, at what time, sir?"

"I speak, miss, of twenty years ago. He married—an English lady—and I was one of the trustees. His affairs, like the affairs of many other French gentleman and French families, were entirely in Tellson's hands. In a similar way I am, or I have been, trustee of one kind or other for scores of our customers. These are mere business relations, miss; there is no friendship in them, no particular interest, nothing like sentiment. I have passed from one to another, in the course of my business life, just as I pass from one of our customers to another in the course of my business day; in short, I have no feelings; I am a mere machine. To go on—"

"But this is my father's story, sir; and I begin to think"—the curiously roughened

8. **Beauvais** (bō′vā), a cathedral city 40 miles from Paris, noted for its medical college.
9. **Monsieur** (mə syoe′), French word for "Mr."

forehead was very intent upon him—"that when I was left an orphan through my mother's surviving my father only two years, it was you who brought me to England. I am almost sure it was you."

Mr. Lorry took the hesitating little hand that confidingly advanced to take his, and he put it with some ceremony to his lips. He then conducted the young lady straightway to her chair again, and, holding the chair-back with his left hand, and using his right by turns to rub his chin, pull his wig at the ears, or point what he said, stood looking down into her face while she sat looking up into his.

"Miss Manette, it *was* I. And you will see how truly I spoke of myself just now, in saying I had no feelings, and that all the relations I hold with my fellow-creatures are mere business relations, when you reflect that I have never seen you since. No; you have been the ward of Tellson's House since, and I have been busy with the other business of Tellson's House since. Feelings! I have no time for them, no chance of them. I pass my whole life, miss, in turning an immense pecuniary Mangle."[10]

After this odd description of his daily routine of employment, Mr. Lorry flattened his flaxen wig upon his head with both hands (which was most unnecessary, for nothing could be flatter than its shining surface was before), and resumed his former attitude.

"So far, miss (as you have remarked), this is the story of your regretted father. Now comes the difference. If your father had not died when he did—Don't be frightened! How you start!"

She did, indeed, start. And she caught his wrist with both her hands.

"Pray," said Mr. Lorry, in a soothing tone, bringing his left hand from the back of the chair to lay it on the supplicatory fingers that clasped him in so violent a tremble: "pray control your agitation—a matter of business. As I was saying—"

Her look so discomposed him that he stopped, wandered, and began anew:

"As I was saying; if Monsieur Manette had not died; if he had suddenly and silently disappeared; if he had been spirited away; if it had not been difficult to guess to what dreadful place, though no art could trace him; if he had an enemy in some compatriot who could exercise a privilege that I in my own time have known the boldest people afraid to speak of in a whisper, across the water, there; for instance, the privilege of filling up blank forms[11] for the consignment of any one to the oblivion of a prison for any length of time; if his wife had implored the king, the queen, the court, the clergy, for any tidings of him, and all quite in vain;—then the history of your father would have been the history of this unfortunate gentleman, the Doctor of Beauvais. Now if this doctor's wife, though a lady of great courage and spirit, had suffered so intensely from this cause before her little child was born—"

"The little child was a daughter, sir?"

"A daughter. A—a—matter of business—don't be distressed. Miss, if the poor lady had suffered so intensely before her little child was born, that she came to the determination of sparing the poor child the inheritance of any part of the agony she had known the pains of, by rearing her in the belief that her father was dead—No, don't kneel! In Heaven's name why should you kneel to me?"

Without directly answering to this appeal, she sat so still when he had very gently raised her, and the hands that had not ceased

---

10. The image here is based on a machine which uses rollers to press and smooth flat laundry items such as sheets and towels. In Dickens's day, the rollers of a mangle were turned by a hand crank.

11. **blank forms,** a reference to *lettres de cachet*, forms issued by the king, and given to his nobility or other favorites. The holder of a *lettre de cachet* could fill in the name of an enemy and have that person imprisoned for an indefinite time without a trial or hearing.

to clasp his wrists were so much more steady than they had been, that she communicated some reassurance to Mr. Jarvis Lorry.

"That's right, that's right. Courage! Business! You have business before you; useful business. Miss Manette, your mother took this course with you. And when she died—I believe brokenhearted—having never slackened her unavailing search for your father, she left you, at two years old, to grow to be blooming, beautiful, and happy, without the dark cloud upon you of living in uncertainty whether your father soon wore his heart out in prison, or wasted there through many lingering years."

As he said the words he looked down, with an admiring pity, on the flowing golden hair; as if he pictured to himself that it might have been already tinged with grey.

"You know that your parents had no great possession, and that what they had was secured to your mother and to you. There has been no new discovery, of money, or of any other property; but—"

He felt his wrist held closer, and he stopped. The expression in the forehead, which had so particularly attracted his notice, and which was now immovable, had deepened into one of pain and horror.

"But he has been—been found. He is alive. Greatly changed, it is too probable; almost a wreck, it is possible; though we will hope the best. Still, alive. Your father has been taken to the house of an old servant in Paris, and we are going there: I, to identify him if I can: you, to restore him to life, love, duty, rest, comfort."

A shiver ran through her frame, and from it through his. She said, in a low, distinct, awe-stricken voice, as if she were saying it in a dream,

"I am going to see his Ghost! It will be his Ghost—not him!"

Mr. Lorry quietly chafed the hands that held his arm. "There, there, there! See now,

see now! The best and the worst are known to you, now. You are well on your way to the poor wronged gentleman, and, with a fair sea voyage, and a fair land journey, you will be soon at his dear side."

She repeated in the same tone, sunk to a whisper, "I have been free, I have been happy, yet his Ghost has never haunted me!"

"Only one thing more," said Mr. Lorry, laying stress upon it as a wholesome means of enforcing her attention: "he has been found under another name; his own, long forgotten or long concealed. It would be worse than useless now to inquire which; worse than useless to seek to know whether he has been for years overlooked, or always designedly held prisoner. It would be worse than useless now to make any inquiries, because it would be dangerous. Better not to mention the subject, anywhere or in any way, and to remove him—for a while at all events—out of France. Even I, safe as an Englishman, and even Tellson's, important as they are to French credit, avoid all naming of the matter. I carry about me not a scrap of writing openly referring to it. This is a secret service altogether. My credentials, entries, and memoranda, are all comprehended in the one line, 'Recalled to Life'; which may mean anything. But what is the matter? She doesn't notice a word! Miss Manette!"

Perfectly still and silent, and not even fallen back in her chair, she sat under his hand, utterly insensible; with her eyes open and fixed upon him, and with that last expression looking as if it were carved or branded into her forehead. So close was her hold upon his arm, that he feared to detach himself lest he should hurt her; therefore he called out loudly for assistance without moving.

A wild-looking woman,[12] whom even in his agitation, Mr. Lorry observed to be all of a

---

12. The woman is later identified by Dickens as Miss Pross, Lucie's devoted servant.

red color, and to have red hair, and to be dressed in some extraordinary tight-fitting fashion, and to have on her head a most wonderful bonnet like a Grenadier wooden measure, and good measure too, or a great Stilton cheese, came running into the room in advance of the inn servants, and soon settled the question of his detachment from the poor young lady, by laying a brawny hand upon his chest, and sending him flying back against the nearest wall.

("I really think this must be a man!" was Mr. Lorry's breathless reflection, simultaneously with his coming against the wall.)

"Why, look at you all!" bawled this figure, addressing the inn servants. "Why don't you go and fetch things, instead of standing there staring at me? I am not so much to look at, am I? Why don't you go and fetch things? I'll let you know, if you don't bring smelling-salts, cold water, and vinegar, quick, I will."

There was an immediate dispersal for these restoratives, and she softly laid the patient on a sofa, and tended her with great skill and gentleness: calling her "my precious!" and "my bird!" and spreading her golden hair aside over her shoulders with great pride and care.

"And you in brown!" she said, indignantly turning to Mr. Lorry; "couldn't you tell her what you had to tell her, without frightening her to death? Look at her, with her pretty pale face and her cold hands. Do you call *that* being a Banker?"

Mr. Lorry was so exceedingly disconcerted by a question so hard to answer, that he could only look on, at a distance, with much feebler sympathy and humility, while the strong woman, having banished the inn servants under the mysterious penalty of "letting them know" something not mentioned if they stayed there, staring, recovered her charge by a regular series of gradations, and coaxed her to lay her drooping head upon her shoulder.

"I hope she will do well now," said Mr. Lorry.

"No thanks to you in brown, if she does. My darling pretty!"

"I hope," said Mr. Lorry, after another pause of feeble sympathy and humility, "that you accompany Miss Manette to France?"

"A likely thing, too!" replied the strong woman. "If it was ever intended that I should go across salt water, do you suppose Providence would have cast my lot in an island?"

This being another question hard to answer, Mr. Jarvis Lorry withdrew to consider it.

Chapter 2
The Wine-shop

A large cask of wine had been dropped and broken, in the street. The accident had happened in getting it out of a cart; the cask had tumbled out with a run, the hoops had burst, and it lay on the stones just outside the door of the wine-shop, shattered like a walnut-shell.

All the people within reach had suspended their business, or their idleness, to run to the spot and drink the wine. The rough, irregular stones of the street, pointing every way, and designed, one might have thought, expressly to lame all living creatures that approached them, had dammed it into little pools; these were surrounded, each by its own jostling group or crowd, according to its size. Some men kneeled down, made scoops of their two hands joined, and sipped, or tried to help women, who bent over their shoulders, to sip, before the wine had all run out between their fingers. Others, men and women, dipped in the puddles with little mugs of mutilated earthenware, or even with handkerchiefs from women's heads, which were squeezed dry into infants' mouths; others made small mud embankments, to stem the wine as it ran; others, directed by lookers-on up at high windows, darted here and there, to cut off little streams of wine that started away in new directions; others devoted themselves to the sodden and lee-dyed pieces of the cask, licking, and even champing the moister wine-rotted fragments with eager relish. There was no drainage to carry off the wine, and not only did it all get taken up, but so much mud got taken up along with it, that there might have been a scavenger in the street, if anybody acquainted with it could have believed in such a miraculous presence.

The wine was red wine, and had stained the ground of the narrow street in the suburb of Saint Antoine, in Paris, where it was spilled. Those who had been greedy with the staves of the cask, had acquired a tigerish smear about the mouth; and one tall joker so besmirched, his head more out of a long squalid bag of a night-cap than in it, scrawled upon a wall with his finger dipped in muddy wine—BLOOD.

The time was to come, when that wine too would be spilled on the street-stones, and when the stain of it would be red upon many there.

The wine-shop was a corner shop, better than most others in its appearance and degree, and the master of the wine-shop had stood outside it, in a yellow waistcoat and green breeches, looking on at the struggle for the lost wine. "It's not my affair," said he, with a final shrug of the shoulders. "The people from the market did it. Let them bring another."

There, his eyes happening to catch the tall joker writing up his joke, he called to him across the way:

"Say, then, my Gaspard, what do you do there?"

The fellow pointed to his joke with immense significance.

"What now? Are you a subject for the mad hospital?" said the wine-shop keeper, crossing the road, and obliterating the jest with a handful of mud, picked up for the purpose, and smeared over it. "Why do you write in the public streets? Is there—tell me thou—is there no other place to write such words in?"

This wine-shop keeper was a bull-necked, martial-looking man of thirty, and he should have been of a hot temperament, for, although it was a bitter day, he wore no coat, but carried one slung over his shoulder. His shirt-sleeves were rolled up, too, and his brown arms were bare to the elbows. Neither did he wear anything more on his head than his own crisply-curling short dark hair. He was a dark man altogether, with good eyes and a good bold breadth between them. Good-humored-looking on the whole, but implacable-looking, too; evidently a man of a strong resolution and a set purpose; a man not desirable to be met, rushing down a narrow path with a gulf on either side, for nothing would turn the man.

Madame Defarge, his wife, sat in the shop behind the counter as he came in. Madame Defarge was a stout woman of about his own age, with a watchful eye that seldom seemed to look at anything, a large hand heavily ringed, a steady face, strong features, and great composure of manner. There was a character about Madame Defarge, from which one might have predicated that she did not often make mistakes against herself in any of the reckonings over which she presided. Madame Defarge being sensitive to cold, was wrapped in fur, and had a quantity of bright shawl twined about her head, though not to the concealment of her large earrings. Her knitting was before her, but she had laid it down to pick her teeth with a toothpick. Thus engaged, with her right elbow supported by her left hand, Madame Defarge said nothing when her lord came in, but coughed just one grain of cough. This, in combination with the lifting of her darkly defined eyebrows over her toothpick by the breadth of a line, suggested to her husband that he would do well to look around the shop among the customers, for any new customer who had dropped in while he stepped over the way.

The wine-shop keeper accordingly rolled his eyes about, until they rested upon an elderly gentleman and a young lady, who were seated in a corner. Other company were there: two playing cards, two playing dominoes, three standing by the counter lengthening out a short supply of wine. As he passed behind the counter, he took notice that the elderly gentleman said in a look to the young lady, "This is our man."

"What the devil do *you* do in that galley there?" said Monsieur Defarge to himself; "I don't know you."

But, he feigned not to notice the two strangers, and fell into discourse with the triumvirate of customers who were drinking at the counter.

"How goes it, Jacques?" said one of these three to Monsieur Defarge. "Is all the spilt wine swallowed?"

"Every drop, Jacques," answered Monsieur Defarge.

When this interchange of christian name was effected, Madame Defarge, picking her teeth with her toothpick, coughed another grain of cough, and raised her eyebrows by the breadth of another line.

"It is not often," said the second of the three, addressing Monsieur Defarge, "that many of these miserable beasts know the taste of wine, or of anything but black bread and death. Is it not so, Jacques?"

"It is so, Jacques," Monsieur Defarge returned.

At this second interchange of the christian name, Madame Defarge, still using her toothpick with profound composure,

During the Revolution, the guillotine was the instrument of "Justice."

coughed another grain of cough, and raised her eyebrows by the breadth of another line.

The last of the three now said his say, as he put down his empty drinking vessel and smacked his lips.

"Ah! So much the worse! A bitter taste it is that such poor cattle always have in their mouths, and hard lives they live, Jacques. Am I right, Jacques?"

"You are right, Jacques," was the response of Monsieur Defarge.

This third interchange of the christian name was completed at the moment when Madame Defarge put her toothpick by, kept her eyebrows up, and slightly rustled in her seat.

"Hold then! True!" muttered her husband."Gentlemen—my wife!"

The three customers pulled off their hats to Madame Defarge, with three flourishes. She acknowledged their homage by bending her head, and giving them a quick look. Then she glanced in a casual manner round the wine-shop, took up her knitting with great apparent calmness and repose of spirit, and became absorbed in it.

"Gentlemen," said her husband, who had kept his bright eye observantly upon her, "good day. The chamber, furnished bachelor-fashion, that you wished to see, and were inquiring for when I stepped out, is on the fifth floor. The doorway of the staircase gives on the little court-yard close to the left here," pointing with his hand, "near to the window of my establishment. But, now that I remember, one of you has already been there, and can show the way. Gentlemen, adieu!"

They paid for their wine, and left the place. The eyes of Monsieur Defarge were studying his wife at her knitting when the elderly gentleman advanced from his corner, and begged the favor of a word.

"Willingly, sir," said Monsieur Defarge, and quietly stepped with him to the door.

Their conference was very short, but very decided. Almost at the first word, Monsieur Defarge started and became deeply attentive. It had not lasted a minute, when he nodded and went out. The gentleman then beckoned to the young lady, and they, too, went out. Madame Defarge knitted with nimble fingers and steady eyebrows, and saw nothing.

Mr. Jarvis Lorry and Miss Manette, emerging from the wine-shop thus, joined Monsieur Defarge in the doorway to which he had directed his other company just before. It opened from a stinking little black court-yard, and was the general public entrance to a great pile of houses, inhabited by a great number of people. In the gloomy tile-paved entry to the gloomy tile-paved staircase, Monsieur Defarge bent down on one knee to the child of his old master, and put her hand to his lips. It was a gentle action, but not at all gently done; a very remarkable transformation had come over him in a few seconds. He had no good-humor in his face, nor any openness of aspect left, but had become a secret, angry, dangerous man.

"It is very high; it is a little difficult. Better to begin slowly." Thus, Monsieur Defarge, in a stern voice, to Mr. Lorry, as they began ascending the stairs.

At last, the top of the staircase was gained. There was yet an upper staircase, of a steeper inclination and of contracted dimensions, to be ascended, before the garret story was reached. The keeper of the wine-shop, always going a little in advance, and always going on the side which Mr. Lorry took, as though he dreaded to be asked any question by the young lady, turned himself about here, and, carefully feeling in the pockets of the coat he carried over his shoulder, took out a key.

They went up slowly and softly. The staircase was short, and they were soon at the top. There, as it had an abrupt turn in it, they came all at once in sight of three men, whose heads were bent down close together at the side of a door, and who were intently looking into the room to which the door belonged, through some chinks or holes in the wall. On hearing footsteps close at hand, these three turned, and rose, and showed themselves to be the three of one name who had been drinking in the wine-shop.

"I forgot them in the surprise of your visit," explained Monsieur Defarge. "Leave us, good boys; we have business here."

The three glided by, and went silently down.

There appearing to be no other door on that floor, and the keeper of the wine-shop going straight to this one when they were left alone, Mr. Lorry asked him in a whisper, with a little anger:

"Do you make a show of Monsieur Manette?"

"I show him, in the way you have seen, to a chosen few."

"Is that well?"

"*I* think it is well."

"Who are the few? How do you choose them?"

"I choose them as real men, of my name—Jacques is my name—to whom the sight is likely to do good. Enough; you are English; that is another thing. Stay there, if you please, a little moment."

With an admonitory gesture to keep them back, he stooped, and looked in through the crevice in the wall. Soon raising his head again, he struck twice or thrice upon the door—evidently with no other object than to make a noise there. With the same intention, he drew the key across it, three or four times, before he put it clumsily into the lock, and turned it as heavily as he could.

The door slowly opened inward under his hand, and he looked into the room and said something. A faint voice answered something. Little more than a single syllable could have been spoken on either side.

He looked back over his shoulder, and beckoned them to enter. Mr. Lorry got his arm securely round the daughter's waist, and held her; for he felt that she was sinking.

"A—a—a—business, business!" he urged, with a moisture that was not of business shining on his cheek. "Come in, come in!"

"I am afraid of it," she answered, shuddering.

"Of it? What?"

"I mean of him. Of my father."

Rendered in a manner desperate, by her state and by the beckoning of their conductor, he drew over his neck the arm that shook upon his shoulder, lifted her a little, and hur-

ried her into the room. He set her down just within the door, and held her, clinging to him.

Defarge drew out the key, closed the door, locked it on the inside, took out the key again, and held it in his hand. All this he did, methodically, and with as loud and harsh an accompaniment of noise as he could make. Finally, he walked across the room with a measured tread to where the window was. He stopped there, and faced round.

The garret, built to be a depository for firewood and the like, was dim and dark: for, the window of dormer shape, was in truth a door in the roof, with a little crane over it for the hoisting up of stores from the street: unglazed, and closing up the middle in two pieces, like any other door of French construction. To exclude the cold, one half of this door was fast closed, and the other was opened but a very little way. Such a scanty portion of light was admitted through these means, that it was difficult, on first coming in, to see anything; and long habit alone could have slowly formed in any one the ability to do any work requiring nicety in such obscurity. Yet, work of that kind was being done in the garret; for, with his back towards the door, and his face towards the window where the keeper of the wine-shop stood looking at him, a white-haired man sat on a low bench, stooping forward and very busy, making shoes.

Chapter 3
The Shoemaker

"GOOD DAY!" said Monsieur Defarge, looking down at the white head that bent low over the shoemaking.

It was raised for a moment, and a very faint voice responded to the salutation, as if it were at a distance:

"Good day!"

"You are still hard at work, I see?"

After a long silence, the head was lifted for another moment, and the voice replied, "Yes—I am working." This time, a pair of haggard eyes had looked at the questioner, before the face had dropped again.

"I want," said Defarge, who had not removed his gaze from the shoemaker, "to let in a little more light here. You can bear a little more?"

The shoemaker stopped his work; looked with a vacant air of listening, at the floor on one side of him; then similarly, at the floor on the other side of him; then, upward at the speaker.

"What did you say?"

"You can bear a little more light?"

"I must bear it, if you let it in." (Laying the palest shadow of a stress upon the second word.)

The opened half-door was opened a little further, and secured at that angle for the time. A broad ray of light fell into the garret, and showed the workman with an unfinished shoe upon his lap, pausing in his labor. His few common tools and various scraps of leather were at his feet and on his bench. He had a white beard, raggedly cut, but not very long, a hollow face, and exceedingly bright eyes. The hollowness and thinness of his face would have caused them to look large, under his yet dark eyebrows and his confused white hair, though they had been really otherwise; but, they were naturally large, and looked unnaturally so. His yellow rags of shirt lay open at the throat, and showed his body to be withered and worn. He, and his old canvas frock, and his loose stockings, and all his poor tatters of clothes, had, in a long seclusion from direct light and air, faded down to such a dull uniformity of parchment-yellow, that it would have been hard to say which was which.

He had put up a hand between his eyes and the light, and the very bones of it seemed transparent. So he sat, with a steadfastly vacant gaze, pausing in his work. He never looked at the figure before him, without first looking down on this side of himself, then on that, as if he had lost the habit of associating place with sound; he never spoke, without first wandering in this manner, and forgetting to speak.

"Are you going to finish that pair of shoes to-day?" asked Defarge, motioning to Mr. Lorry to come forward.

"What did you say?"

"Do you mean to finish that pair of shoes to-day?"

"I can't say that I mean to. I suppose so. I don't know."

But, the question reminded him of his work, and he bent over it again.

Mr. Lorry came silently forward, leaving the daughter by the door. When he had stood, for a minute or two, by the side of Defarge, the shoemaker looked up. He showed no surprise at seeing another figure, but the unsteady fingers of one of his hands strayed to his lips as he looked at it (his lips and his nails were of the same pale lead-color), and then the hand dropped to his work, and he once more bent over the shoe. The look and the action had occupied but an instant.

"You have a visitor, you see," said Monsieur Defarge.

"What did you say?"

"Here is a visitor."

The shoemaker looked up as before, but without removing a hand from his work.

"Come!" said Defarge. "Here is monsieur, who knows a well-made shoe when he sees one. Show him that shoe you are working at. Take it, monsieur."

Mr. Lorry took it in his hand.

"Tell monsieur what kind of shoe it is, and the maker's name."

There was a longer pause than usual, before the shoemaker replied:

"I forgot what it was you asked me. What did you say?"

"I said, couldn't you describe the kind of shoe, for monsieur's information?"

"It is a lady's shoe. It is a young lady's walking-shoe. It is in the present mode. I never saw the mode. I have had a pattern in my hand." He glanced at the shoe with some little passing touch of pride.

"And the maker's name?" said Defarge.

Now that he had no work to hold, he laid the knuckles of the right hand in the hollow of the left, and then the knuckles of the left hand in the hollow of the right, and then passed a hand across his bearded chin, and so on in regular changes, without a moment's intermission. The task of recalling him from the vacancy into which he always sank when he had spoken, was like recalling some very weak person from a swoon, or endeavoring, in the hope of some disclosure, to stay the spirit of a fast-dying man.

"Did you ask me for my name?"

"Assuredly I did."

"One Hundred and Five, North Tower."

"Is that all?"

"One Hundred and Five, North Tower."

With a weary sound that was not a sigh, nor a groan, he bent to work again, until the silence was again broken.

"You are not a shoemaker by trade?" said Mr. Lorry, looking steadfastly at him.

His haggard eyes turned to Defarge as if he would have transferred the question to him; but as no help came from that quarter, they turned back on the questioner when they had sought the ground.

"I am not a shoemaker by trade? No, I was not a shoemaker by trade. I—I learnt it here. I taught myself. I asked leave to—"

He lapsed away, even for minutes, ringing those measured changes on his hands the whole time. His eyes came slowly back, at last, to the face from which they had wandered; when they rested on it, he started, and resumed, in the manner of a sleeper that moment awake, reverting to a subject of last night.

"I asked leave to teach myself, and I got it with much difficulty after a long while, and I have made shoes ever since."

As he held out his hand for the shoe that had been taken from him, Mr. Lorry said, still looking steadfastly in his face:

"Monsieur Manette, do you remember nothing of me?"

The shoe dropped to the ground, and he sat looking fixedly at the questioner.

"Monsieur Manette," Mr. Lorry laid his hand upon Defarge's arm; "do you remember nothing of this man? Look at him. Look at me. Is there no old banker, no old business, no old servant, no old time, rising in your mind, Monsieur Manette?"

As the captive of many years sat looking fixedly, by turns, at Mr. Lorry and at Defarge, some long obliterated marks of an actively intent intelligence in the middle of the forehead, gradually forced themselves through the black mist that had fallen on him. They were overclouded again, they were fainter, they were gone; but they had been there. And so exactly was the expression repeated on the fair young face of her who had crept along the wall to a point where she could see him, and where she now stood looking at him, with hands which at first had been only raised in frightened compassion, if not even to keep him off and shut out the sight of him, but which were now extending towards him, trembling with eagerness to lay the spectral face upon her warm young breast, and love it back to life and hope—so exactly was the expression repeated (though in stronger characters) on her fair young face, that it looked as though it had passed like a moving light, from him to her.

Darkness had fallen on him in its place.

The Bastille, where Dr. Manette was imprisoned for so many years, was a symbol of the French people's oppression.

He looked at the two, less and less attentively, and his eyes in gloomy abstraction sought the ground and looked about him in the old way. Finally, with a deep long sigh, he took the shoe up, and resumed his work.

"Have you recognized him, monsieur?" asked Defarge in a whisper.

"Yes; for a moment. At first I thought it quite hopeless, but I have unquestionably seen, for a single moment, the face that I once knew so well. Hush! Let us draw further back. Hush!"

She had moved from the wall of the garret, very near to the bench on which he sat. There was something awful in his unconsciousness of the figure that could have put out its hand and touched him as he stooped over his labor.

Not a word was spoken, not a sound was made. She stood, like a spirit, beside him, and he bent over his work.

It happened, at length, that he had occasion to change the instrument in his hand, for his shoemaker's knife. It lay on that side of him which was not the side on which she stood. He had taken it up, and was stooping to work again, when his eyes caught the skirt of her dress. He raised them, and saw her face. The two spectators started forward, but she stayed them with a motion of her hand. She had no fear of his striking at her with the knife, though they had.

He stared at her with a fearful look, and after a while his lips began to form some words, though no sound proceeded from them. By degrees, in the pauses of his quick and labored breathing, he was heard to say:

"What is this?"

With the tears streaming down her face, she put her two hands to her lips, and kissed them to him; then clasped them on her breast, as if she laid his ruined head there.

"You are not the gaoler's[1] daughter?"

She sighed "No."

"Who are you?"

Not yet trusting the tones of her voice, she sat down on the bench beside him. He recoiled, but she laid her hand upon his arm. A strange thrill struck him when she did so, and visibly passed over his frame; he laid the knife down softly, as he sat staring at her.

Her golden hair, which she wore in long curls, had been hurriedly pushed aside, and fell down over her neck. Advancing his hand by little and little, he took it up and looked at it. In the midst of the action he went astray, and, with another deep sigh, fell to work at his shoemaking.

But not for long. Releasing his arm, she laid her hand upon his shoulder. After looking doubtfully at it, two or three times, as if to be sure that it was really there, he laid down his work, put his hand to his neck, and took off a blackened string with a scrap of folded rag attached to it. He opened this, carefully, on his knee, and it contained a very little quantity of hair: not more than one or two long golden hairs, which he had, in some old day, wound off upon his finger.

He took her hair into his hand again, and looked closely at it. "It is the same. How can it be! When was it! How was it!"

As the concentrating expression returned to his forehead, he seemed to become conscious that it was in hers too. He turned her full to the light, and looked at her.

"She had laid her head upon my shoulder, that night when I was summoned out—she had a fear of my going, though I had none—and when I was brought to the North Tower they found these upon my sleeve. 'You will leave me them? They can never help me to escape in the body, though they may in the spirit.' Those were the words I said. I remember them very well."

He formed this speech with his lips many times before he could utter it. But when he did find spoken words for it, they came to him coherently, though slowly.

"How was this?—*Was it you?*"

Once more, the two spectators started, as he turned upon her with a frightful suddenness. But she sat perfectly still in his grasp, and only said, in a low voice, "I entreat you, good gentlemen, do not come near us, do not speak, do not move!"

"Hark!" he exclaimed. "Whose voice was that?"

His hands released her as he uttered this cry, and went up to his white hair, which they tore in a frenzy. It died out, as everything but his shoemaking did die out of him, and he refolded his little packet and tried to secure it in his breast; but he still looked at her, and gloomily shook his head.

"No, no, no; you are too young, too blooming. It can't be. See what the prisoner is. These are not the hands she knew, this is not the face she knew, this is not a voice she ever heard. No, no. She was—and He was—before the slow years of the North Tower—ages ago. What is your name, my gentle angel?"

Hailing his softened tone and manner, his daughter fell upon her knees before him, with her appealing hands upon his breast.

"O, sir, at another time you shall know my name and who my mother was, and who my father, and how I never knew their hard, hard history. But I cannot tell you at this time, and I cannot tell you here. All that I

---

1. **gaoler** (jā′lər), British spelling of jailer.

may tell you, here and now, is, that I pray to you to touch me and to bless me."

His cold white head mingled with her radiant hair, which warmed and lighted it as though it were the light of Freedom shining on him.

"If you hear in my voice—I don't know that it is so, but I hope it is—if you hear in my voice any resemblance to a voice that once was sweet music in your ears, weep for it, weep for it! If you touch, in touching my hair, anything that recalls a beloved head that lay in your breast when you were young and free, weep for it, weep for it! If, when I hint to you of a Home there is before us, where I will be true to you with all my duty and with all my faithful service, I bring back the remembrance of a Home long desolate, while your poor heart pined away, weep for it, weep for it!"

She held him closer round the neck, and rocked him on her breast like a child.

"If, when I tell you, dearest dear, that your agony is over, and that I have come here to take you from it, and that we go to England to be at peace and at rest, I cause you to think of your useful life laid waste, and of our native France so wicked to you, weep for it, weep for it! And if, when I shall tell you of my name, and of my father who is living, and of my mother who is dead, you learn that I have to kneel to my honored father, and implore his pardon for having never for his sake striven all day and lain awake and wept all night, because the love of my poor mother hid his torture from me, weep for it, weep for it! Weep for her, then, and for me! Good gentlemen, thank God! I feel his tears upon my face, and his sobs strike against my heart. O, see! Thank God for us, thank God!"

He had sunk in her arms, and his face dropped on her breast: a sight so touching, yet so terrible in the tremendous wrong and suffering which had gone before it, that the two beholders covered their faces.

Jarvis Lorry and Lucie Manette return with Dr. Manette to England, where Lucie's father slowly recovers from the ordeal of his long imprisonment. Five years pass. At the opening of the next chapter, a clerk of Tellson's Bank in London sends Jerry Cruncher, the bank messenger, on an important errand.

Chapter 4
A Sight

"You know the Old Bailey[1] well, no doubt?" said one of the oldest of clerks to Jerry the messenger.

"Ye-es, sir," returned Jerry, in something of a dogged manner. "I *do* know the Bailey."

"Just so. And you know Mr. Lorry."

"I know Mr. Lorry, sir, much better than I know the Bailey. Much better," said Jerry, not unlike a reluctant witness at the establishment in question, "than I, as a honest tradesman, wish to know the Bailey."

"Very well. Find the door where the witnesses go in, and show the door-keeper this note for Mr. Lorry. He will then let you in."

"Into the court, sir?"

"Into the court."

Mr. Cruncher's eyes seemed to get a little closer to one another, and to interchange the inquiry, "What do you think of this?"

"Am I to wait in the court, sir?" he asked, as the result of that conference.

"I am going to tell you. The door-keeper will pass the note to Mr. Lorry, and do you make any gesture that will attract Mr. Lorry's attention, and show him where you stand. Then what you have to do, is, to remain there until he wants you."

"Is that all, sir?"

"That's all. He wishes to have a messenger at hand. This is to tell him you are there."

---

1. **Old Bailey,** London's principal court at the time.

As the ancient clerk deliberately folded and superscribed the note, Mr. Cruncher, after surveying him in silence until he came to the blotting-paper stage, remarked:

"I suppose they'll be trying Forgeries this morning?"

"Treason!"

"That's quartering," said Jerry. "Barbarous!"

"It is the law," remarked the ancient clerk, turning his surprised spectacles upon him. "It is the law."

"It's hard in the law to spile a man, I think. It's hard enough to kill him, but it's wery hard to spile[2] him, sir."

"Not at all," returned the ancient clerk. "Speak well of the law. Take care of your chest and voice, my good friend, and leave the law to take care of itself. I give you that advice."

"It's the damp, sir, what settles on my chest and voice," said Jerry. "I leave you to judge what a damp way of earning a living mine is."

"Well, well," said the old clerk; "we all have our various ways of gaining a livelihood. Some of us have damp ways, and some of us have dry ways. Here is the letter. Go along."

Jerry took the letter, made his bow, and went his way.

Making his way through the tainted crowd, with the skill of a man accustomed to make his way quietly, the messenger found out the door he sought, and handed in his letter through a trap in it.

After some delay and demur, the door grudgingly turned on its hinges a very little way, and allowed Mr. Jerry Cruncher to squeeze himself into court.

"What's on?" he asked, in a whisper, of the man he found himself next to.

"Nothing yet."

"What's coming on?"

"The Treason case."

"The quartering one, eh?"

"Ah!" returned the man, with a relish; "he'll be drawn on a hurdle[3] to be half hanged, and then he'll be taken down and sliced before his own face, and then his inside will be taken out and burnt while he looks on, and then his head will be chopped off, and he'll be cut into quarters. That's the sentence."

"If he's found Guilty, you mean to say?" Jerry added, by way of proviso.

"Oh! they'll find him guilty," said the other. "Don't you be afraid of that."

Mr. Cruncher's attention was here diverted to the door-keeper, whom he saw making his way to Mr. Lorry, with the note in his hand. Mr. Lorry sat at a table, among the gentlemen in wigs: not far from a wigged gentleman, the prisoner's counsel, who had a great bundle of papers before him: and nearly opposite another wigged gentleman with his hands in his pockets, whose whole attention, when Mr. Cruncher looked at him then or afterwards, seemed to be concentrated on the ceiling of the court. After some gruff coughing and rubbing of his chin and signing with his hand, Jerry attracted the notice of Mr. Lorry, who had stood up to look for him, and who quietly nodded and sat down again.

"What's *he* got to do with the case?" asked the man he had spoken with.

"Blest if I know," said Jerry.

"What have *you* got to do with it, then, if a person may inquire?"

"Blest if I know that either," said Jerry.

The entrance of the Judge, and a consequent great stir and settling down in the court, stopped the dialogue. Presently, the dock[4] became the central point of interest. Two gaolers, who had been standing there,

2. **wery** = very; **spile** = spoil (mutilate).
3. **hurdle,** a sled used to drag the condemned to execution.
4. **dock,** the place in the courtroom where the prisoner stands during the trial.

went out, and the prisoner was brought in, and put to the bar.

Everybody present, except the one wigged gentleman who looked at the ceiling, stared at him. The object of all this staring, was a young man of about five-and-twenty, well-grown and well-looking, with a sunburnt cheek and a dark eye. His condition was that of a young gentleman. He was plainly dressed in black, or very dark grey, and his hair, which was long and dark, was gathered in a ribbon at the back of his neck; more to be out of his way than for ornament. As an emotion of the mind will express itself through any covering of the body, so the paleness which his situation engendered came through the brown upon his cheek, showing the soul to be stronger than the sun. He was otherwise quite self-possessed, bowed to the Judge, and stood quiet.

Silence in the court! Charles Darnay had yesterday pleaded Not Guilty to an indictment denouncing him (with infinite jingle and jangle) for that he was a false traitor to our serene, illustrious, excellent, and so forth, prince, our Lord the King, by reason of his having, on divers occasions, and by divers means and ways, assisted Lewis, the French King, in his wars against our said serene, illustrious, excellent, and so forth; that was to say, by coming and going, between the dominions of our said serene, illustrious, excellent, and so forth, and those of the said French Lewis, and wickedly, falsely, traitorously, and otherwise evil-adverbiously, revealing to the said French Lewis what forces our said serene, illustrious, excellent, and so forth, had in preparation to send to Canada and North America.[5] This much, Jerry, with his head becoming more and more spiky as the law terms bristled it, made out with huge satisfaction, and so arrived circuitously at the understanding that the aforesaid, and over and over again aforesaid, Charles Darnay, stood there before him upon his trial; that the

jury were swearing in; and that Mr. Attorney-General was making ready to speak.

The accused, who was (and who knew he was) being mentally hanged, beheaded, and quartered, by everybody there, neither flinched from the situation, nor assumed any theatrical air in it. He was quiet and attentive; watched the opening proceeding with a grave interest; and stood with his hands resting on the slab of wood before him, so composedly, that they had not displaced a leaf of the herbs with which it was strewn. The court was all bestrewn with herbs and sprinkled with vinegar, as a precaution against gaol[6] air and gaol fever.

Over the prisoner's head there was a mirror, to throw the light down upon him. A change in his position making him conscious of a bar of light across his face, he looked up; and when he saw the glass his face flushed, and his right hand pushed the herbs away.

It happened, that the action turned his face to that side of the court which was on his left. About on a level with his eyes, there sat, in that corner of the Judge's bench, two persons upon whom his look immediately rested; so immediately, and so much to the changing of his aspect, that all the eyes that were turned upon him, turned to them.

The spectators saw in the two figures, a young lady of little more than twenty, and a gentleman who was evidently her father; a man of very remarkable appearance in respect of the absolute whiteness of his hair, and a certain indescribable intensity of face: not of an active kind, but pondering and self-communing. When this expression was upon him, he looked as if he were old; but when it was stirred and broken up—as it was now, in a moment, on his speaking to his

---

5. Charles is accused of being a traitor to England during the American Revolution, then in progress. The French actively aided the American cause.
6. **gaol** (jāl), British spelling of *jail*.

Trial of Charles Darnay.

daughter—he became a handsome man, not past the prime of life.

His daughter had one of her hands drawn through his arm, as she sat by him, and the other pressed upon it. She had drawn close to him, in her dread of the scene, and in her pity for the prisoner. Her forehead had been strikingly expressive of an engrossing terror and compassion that saw nothing but the peril of the accused. This had been so very noticeable, so very powerfully and naturally shown, that starers who had had no pity for him were touched by her; and the whisper went about, "Who are they?"

Jerry, the messenger, who had made his own observations, in his own manner, and who had been sucking the rust off his fingers in his absorption, stretched his neck to hear who they were. The crowd about him had pressed and passed the inquiry on to the nearest attendant, and from him it had been more slowly pressed and passed back; at last it got to Jerry:

"Witnesses."

"For which side?"

"Against."

"Against what side?"

"The prisoner's."

The Judge, whose eyes had gone in the general direction, recalled them, leaned back in his seat, and looked steadily at the man whose life was in his hand, as Mr. Attorney-General rose to spin the rope, grind the axe, and hammer the nails into the scaffold.

Chapter 5
A Disappointment

Mr. Attorney-General called Mr. Jarvis Lorry.

"Mr. Jarvis Lorry, are you a clerk in Tellson's bank?"

"I am."

"On a certain Friday night in November one thousand seven hundred and seventy-five, did business occasion you to travel between London and Dover by the mail?"

"It did."

"Were there any other passengers in the mail?"

"Two."

"Did they alight on the road in the course of the night?"

"They did."

"Mr. Lorry, look upon the prisoner. Was he one of those two passengers?"

"I cannot undertake to say that he was."

"Does he resemble either of these two passengers?"

"Both were so wrapped up, and the night was so dark, and we were all so reserved, that I cannot undertake to say even that."

"Mr. Lorry, look again upon the prisoner. Supposing him wrapped up as those two passengers were, is there anything in his bulk and stature to render it unlikely that he was one of them?"

"No."

"You will not swear, Mr. Lorry, that he was not one of them?"

"No."

"So at least you say he may have been one of them?"

"Yes. Except that I remember them both to have been—like myself—timorous of highwaymen, and the prisoner has not a timorous air."

"Did you ever see a counterfeit of timidity, Mr. Lorry?"

"I certainly have seen that."

"Mr. Lorry, look once more upon the prisoner. Have you seen him, to your certain knowledge, before?"

"I have."

"When?"

"I was returning from France a few days afterwards, and, at Calais, the prisoner came on board the packet-ship in which I returned, and made the voyage with me."

"At what hour did he come on board?"

"At a little after midnight."

"In the dead of the night. Was he the only passenger who came on board at that untimely hour?"

"He happened to be the only one."

"Never mind about 'happening,' Mr. Lorry. He was the only passenger who came on board in the dead of the night?"

"He was."

"Were you travelling alone, Mr. Lorry, or with any companion?"

"With two companions. A gentleman and lady. They are here."

"They are here. Had you any conversation with the prisoner?"

"Hardly any. The weather was stormy, and the passage long and rough, and I lay on a sofa, almost from shore to shore."

"Miss Manette!"

The young lady, to whom all eyes had been turned before, and were now turned again, stood up where she had sat. Her father rose with her, and kept her hand drawn through his arm.

"Miss Manette, look upon the prisoner."

To be confronted with such pity, and such earnest youth and beauty, was far more trying to the accused than to be confronted with all the crowd. Standing, as it were, apart with her on the edge of his grave, not all the staring curiosity that looked on, could, for the moment, nerve him to remain quite still. His hurried right hand parcelled out the herbs before him into imaginary beds of flowers in a garden; and his efforts to control and steady his breathing shook the lips from which the color rushed to his heart.

"Miss Manette, have you seen the prisoner before?"

"Yes, sir."

"Where?"

"On board of the packet-ship just now referred to, sir, and on the same occasion."

"You are the young lady now referred to?"

"O! most unhappily, I am!"

The plaintive tone of her compassion merged into the less musical voice of the Judge, as he said something fiercely: "Answer the questions put to you, and make no remark upon them."

"Miss Manette, had you any conversation with the prisoner on that passage across the Channel?"

"Yes, sir."

"Recall it."

In the midst of a profound stillness, she faintly began:

"When the gentleman came on board—"

"Do you mean the prisoner?" inquired the Judge, knitting his brows.

"Yes, my Lord."

"Then say the prisoner."

"When the prisoner came on board, he noticed that my father," turning her eyes lovingly to him as he stood beside her, "was much fatigued and in a very weak state of health. My father was so reduced, that I was afraid to take him out of the air, and I had made a bed for him on the deck near the cabin steps, and I sat on the deck at his side to take care of him. There were no other passengers that night, but we four. The prisoner was so good as to beg permission to advise me how I could shelter my father from the wind and weather, better than I had done. I had not known how to do it well, not understanding how the wind would set when we were out of the harbor. He did it for me. He expressed great gentleness and kindness for my father's state, and I am sure he felt it. That was the manner of our beginning to speak together."

"Let me interrupt you for a moment. Had he come on board alone?"

"No."

"How many were with him?"

"Two French gentlemen."

"Had they conferred together?"

"They had conferred together until the last moment, when it was necessary for the French gentlemen to be landed in their boat."

"Had any papers been handed about among them, similar to these lists?"

"Some papers had been handed about among them, but I don't know what papers."

"Like these in shape and size?"

"Possibly, but indeed I don't know, although they stood whispering very near to me: because they stood at the top of the cabin steps to have the light of the lamp that was hanging there; it was a dull lamp, and they spoke very low, and I did not hear what they said, and saw only that they looked at papers."

"Now, to the prisoner's conversation, Miss Manette."

"The prisoner was as open in his confidence with me—which arose out of my helpless situation—as he was kind, and good, and useful to my father. I hope," bursting into tears, "I may not repay him by doing him harm to-day."

"Miss Manette, if the prisoner does not perfectly understand that you give the evidence which it is your duty to give—which you must give—and which you cannot escape from giving—with great unwillingness, he is the only person present in that condition. Please to go on."

"He told me that he was travelling on business of a delicate and difficult nature, which might get people into trouble, and that he was therefore travelling under an assumed name. He said that this business had, within a few days, taken him to France, and might, at intervals, take him backwards and forwards between France and England for a long time to come."

"Did he say anything about America, Miss Manette? Be particular."

"He tried to explain to me how that quarrel had arisen, and he said that, so far as he could judge, it was a wrong and foolish one on England's part. He added, in a jesting way, that perhaps George Washington might gain almost as great a name in history as George the Third. But there was no harm in his way of saying this: it was said laughingly, and to beguile the time."

Any strongly marked expression of face on the part of a chief actor in a scene of great interest to whom many eyes are directed, will be unconsciously imitated by the spectators. Her forehead was painfully anxious and intent as she gave this evidence, and, in the pauses when she stopped for the Judge to write it down, watched its effect upon the Counsel for and against. Among the lookers-on there was the same expression in all quarters of the court; insomuch, that a great majority of the foreheads there, might have been mirrors reflecting the witness, when the Judge looked up from his notes to glare at that tremendous heresy about George Washington.

Mr. Attorney-General now signified to my Lord, that he deemed it necessary, as a matter of precaution and form, to call the young lady's father, Doctor Manette. Who was called accordingly.

"Doctor Manette, look upon the prisoner. Have you ever seen him before?"

"Once. When he called at my lodgings in London. Some three years, or three years and a half ago."

"Can you identify him as your fellow-passenger on board the packet, or speak to his conversation with your daughter?"

"Sir, I can do neither."

"Is there any particular and special reason for your being unable to do either?"

He answered, in a low voice, "There is."

"Has it been your misfortune to undergo a long imprisonment, without trial, or even accusation, in your native country, Doctor Manette?"

He answered, in a tone that went to every heart, "A long imprisonment."

"Were you newly released on the occasion in question?"

"They tell me so."

"Have you no remembrance of the occasion?"

"None. My mind is a blank, from some time—I cannot even say what time—when I employed myself, in my captivity, in making shoes, to the time when I found myself living in London with my dear daughter here. She had become familiar to me, when a gracious God restored my faculties; but I am quite unable even to say how she had become familiar. I have no remembrance of the process."

Mr. Attorney-General sat down, and the father and daughter sat down together.

A singular circumstance then arose in the case. The object in hand, being, to show that the prisoner went down, with some fellow-plotter untracked, in the Dover mail on that Friday night in November five years ago, and got out of the mail in the night, as a blind, at a place where he did not remain, but from which he travelled back some dozen miles or more, to a garrison and dockyard, and there collected information; a witness was called to identify him as having been at the precise time required, in the coffee-room of an hotel in that garrison-and-dockyard town, waiting for another person. The prisoner's counsel was cross-examining this witness with no result, except that he had never seen the prisoner on any other occasion, when the wigged gentleman who had all this time been looking at the ceiling of the court, wrote a word or two on a little piece of paper, screwed it up, and tossed it to him. Opening this piece of paper in the next pause, the counsel looked with great attention and curiosity at the prisoner.

"You say again you are quite sure that it *was* the prisoner?"

The witness was quite sure.

"Did you ever see anybody very like the prisoner?"

Not so like (the witness said) as that he could be mistaken.

"Look well upon that gentleman, my learned friend there," pointing to him who had tossed the paper over, "and then look well upon the prisoner. How say you? Are they very like each other?"

Allowing for my learned friend's appearance being careless and slovenly if not debauched, they were sufficiently like each other to surprise, not only the witness, but everybody present, when they were thus brought into comparison. My Lord being prayed to bid my learned friend lay aside his wig, and giving no very gracious consent, the likeness became much more remarkable. My Lord inquired of Mr. Stryver (the prisoner's counsel), whether they were next to try Mr. Carton (name of my learned friend) for treason? But, Mr. Stryver replied to my Lord, no; but he would ask the witness to tell him whether what happened once, might happen twice; whether he would have been so confident if he had seen this illustration of his rashness sooner, whether he would be so confident, having seen it; and more. The upshot of which was, to smash this witness like a crockery vessel, and shiver his part of the case to useless lumber.

And now, the jury turned to consider.

Mr. Carton, who had so long sat looking at the ceiling of the court, changed neither his place nor his attitude, even in this excitement. While his learned friend, Mr. Stryver, massing his papers before him, whispered with those who sat near, and from time to time glanced anxiously at the jury; while all the spectators moved more or less, and grouped themselves anew; while even my Lord himself arose from his seat, and slowly paced up and down his platform, not unattended by a suspicion in the minds of the audience that his state was feverish; this one man sat leaning back, with his torn gown half off him, his untidy wig put on just as it had happened to light on his head after its removal, his hands in his pockets, and his eyes on the ceiling as they had been all day. Something especially reckless in his demeanor, not only gave him a disreputable look, but so diminished the strong resemblance he undoubtedly bore to the prisoner (which his momentary earnestness, when they were compared together, had strengthened), that many of the lookers-on, taking note of him now, said to one another they would hardly have thought the two were so alike.

Yet, this Mr. Carton took in more of the details of the scene than he appeared to take in; for now, when Miss Manette's head dropped upon her father's breast, he was the first to see it, and to say audibly: "Officer! look to that young lady. Help the gentleman to take her out. Don't you see she will fall!"

There was much commiseration for her as she was removed, and much sympathy with her father. It had evidently been a great distress to him, to have the days of his imprisonment recalled. He had shown strong internal agitation when he was questioned, and that pondering or brooding look which made him old, had been upon him, like a heavy cloud, ever since. As he passed out, the jury, who had turned back and paused a moment, spoke, through their foreman.

They were not agreed, and wished to retire. My Lord (perhaps with George Washington on his mind) showed some surprise that they were not agreed, but signified his pleasure that they should retire under watch and

French patriots volunteer to serve the Revolution.

ward,[1] and retired himself. The trial had lasted all day, and the lamps in the court were now being lighted. It began to be rumored that the jury would be out a long while. The spectators dropped off to get refreshment, and the prisoner withdrew to the back of the dock, and sat down.

Mr. Lorry, who had gone out when the young lady and her father went out, now reappeared, and beckoned to Jerry: who, in the slackened interest, could easily get near him.

"Jerry, if you wish to take something to eat, you can. But, keep in the way. You will be sure to hear when the jury come in. Don't be a moment behind them, for I want you to take the verdict back to the bank. You are the quickest messenger I know, and will get to Temple Bar[2] long before I can."

Jerry had just enough forehead to knuckle, and he knuckled it in acknowledgement of this communication and a shilling. Mr. Carton came up at the moment, and touched Mr. Lorry on the arm.

"How is the young lady?"

"She is greatly distressed; but her father is comforting her, and she feels the better for being out of court."

"I'll tell the prisoner so. It won't do for a

1. **watch and ward,** under guard.
2. **Temple Bar,** street in London noted for its banks and courts.

respectable bank gentleman like you, to be seen speaking to him publicly, you know."

Mr. Lorry reddened as if he were conscious of having debated the point in his mind, and Mr. Carton made his way to the outside of the bar. The way out of court lay in that direction, and Jerry followed him, all eyes, ears, and spikes.

"Mr. Darnay!"

The prisoner came forward directly.

"You will naturally be anxious to hear of the witness, Miss Manette. She will do very well. You have seen the worst of her agitation."

"I am deeply sorry to have been the cause of it. Could you tell her so for me, with my fervent acknowledgements?"

"Yes, I could. I will, if you ask it."

Mr. Carton's manner was so careless as to be almost insolent. He stood, half turned from the prisoner, lounging with his elbow against the bar.

"I do ask it. Accept my cordial thanks."

"What," said Carton, still only half turned towards him, "do you expect, Mr. Darnay?"

"The worst."

"It's the wisest thing to expect, and the likeliest. But I think their withdrawing is in your favor."

Loitering on the way out of the court not being allowed, Jerry heard no more: but left them—so like each other in feature, so unlike each other in manner—standing side by side, both reflected in the glass above them.

An hour and a half limped heavily away in the thief-and-rascal crowded passages below, even though assisted off with mutton pies and ale. The hoarse messenger, uncomfortably seated on a form after taking that refection, had dropped into a doze, when a loud murmur and a rapid tide of people setting up the stairs that led to the court, carried him along with them.

"Jerry! Jerry!" Mr. Lorry was already calling at the door when he got there.

"Here, sir! It's a fight to get back again. Here I am, sir!"

Mr. Lorry handed him a paper through the throng. "Quick! Have you got it?"

"Yes, sir!"

Hastily written on the paper was the word "ACQUITTED."[3]

3. **acquitted** (ə kwit′id), declared not guilty.

Chapter 6
Congratulatory

From the dimly-lighted passages of the court, the last sediment of the human stew that had been boiling there all day, was straining off, when Doctor Manette, Lucie Manette his daughter, Mr. Lorry, the solicitor for the defense, and its counsel Mr. Stryver, stood gathered round Mr. Charles Darnay—just released—congratulating him on his escape from death.

It would have been difficult by a far brighter light, to recognize in Doctor Manette, intellectual of face and upright of bearing, the shoemaker of the garret in Paris. Yet, no one could have looked at him twice, without looking again: even though the opportunity of observation had not extended to the mournful cadence of his low grave voice, and to the abstraction that overclouded him fitfully, without any apparent reason. While one external cause, and that a reference to his long lingering agony, would always—as on the trial—evoke this condition from the depths of his soul, it was also in its nature to arise of itself, and to draw a gloom over him, as incomprehensible to those unacquainted with his story as if they had seen the shadow of the actual Bastille[1] thrown upon him by a

1. **Bastille** (ba stēl′), one of the main prisons of Paris. The Revolution began with the people's storming of the Bastille on July 14, 1789.

summer sun, when the substance was three hundred miles away.

Only his daughter had the power of charming this black brooding from his mind. She was the golden thread that united him to a Past beyond his misery, and to a Present beyond his misery: and the sound of her voice, the light of her face, the touch of her hand, had a strong beneficial influence with him almost always. Not absolutely always, for she could recall some occasions on which her power had failed; but they were few and slight, and she believed them over.

Mr. Darnay had kissed her hand fervently and gratefully, and had turned to Mr. Stryver, whom he warmly thanked. Mr. Stryver, a man of little more than thirty, but looking twenty years older than he was, stout, loud, red, bluff, and free from any drawback of delicacy, had a pushing way of shouldering himself (morally and physically) into companies and conversations, that argued well for his shouldering his way up in life.

He still had his wig and gown on, and he said, squaring himself at his late client to that degree that he squeezed the innocent Mr. Lorry clean out of the group: "I am glad to have brought you off with honor, Mr. Darnay. It was an infamous prosecution, grossly infamous; but not the less likely to succeed on that account."

"You have laid me under an obligation to you for life—in two senses," said his late client, taking his hand.

"I have done my best for you, Mr. Darnay; and my best is as good as another man's, I believe."

It clearly being incumbent on some one to say, "Much better," Mr. Lorry said it; perhaps not quite disinterestedly, but with the interested object of squeezing himself back again.

"You think so?" said Mr. Stryver. "Well! you have been present all day, and you ought to know. You are a man of business, too."

"And as such," quoth Mr. Lorry, whom the counsel learned in the law had now shouldered back into the group, just as he had previously shouldered him out of it—"as such I will appeal to Doctor Manette, to break up this conference and order us all to our homes. Miss Lucie looks ill, Mr. Darnay has had a terrible day, we are worn out."

"Speak for yourself, Mr. Lorry," said Stryver; "I have a night's work to do yet. Speak for yourself."

"I speak for myself," answered Mr. Lorry, "and for Mr. Darnay, and for Miss Lucie, and—Miss Lucie, do you not think I may speak for us all?" He asked her the question pointedly, and with a glance at her father.

His face had become frozen, as it were, in a very curious look at Darnay: an intent look, deepening into a frown of dislike and distrust, not even unmixed with fear. With this strange expression on him his thoughts had wandered away.

"My father," said Lucie, softly laying her hand on his.

He slowly shook the shadow off, and turned to her.

"Shall we go home, my father?"

With a long breath, he answered "Yes."

The friends of the acquitted prisoner had dispersed, under the impression—which he himself had originated—that he would not be released that night. The lights were nearly all extinguished in the passages, the iron gates were being closed with a jar and a rattle, and the dismal place was deserted until tomorrow morning's interest of gallows, pillory, whipping-post, and branding-iron, should re-people it. Walking between her father and Mr. Darnay, Lucie Manette passed into the open air. A hackney-coach[2] was called, and the father and daughter departed in it.

Mr. Stryver had left them in the passages, to shoulder his way back to the robing-room.

---

2. **hackney-coach,** a four-wheeled carriage.

Another person, who had not joined the group, or interchanged a word with any one of them, but who had been leaning against the wall where its shadow was darkest, had silently strolled out after the rest, and had looked on until the coach drove away. He now stepped up to where Mr. Lorry and Mr. Darnay stood upon the pavement.

"So, Mr. Lorry! Men of business may speak to Mr. Darnay now?"

Nobody had made any acknowledgement of Mr. Carton's part in the day's proceedings; nobody had known of it. He was unrobed, and was none the better for it in appearance.

"If you knew what a conflict goes on in the business mind, when the business mind is divided between good-natured impulse and business appearances, you would be amused, Mr. Darnay."

Mr. Lorry reddened, and said, warmly, "You have mentioned that before, sir. We men of business, who serve a House, are not our own masters. We have to think of the House more than ourselves."

"*I* know, *I* know," rejoined Mr. Carton, carelessly. "Don't be nettled, Mr. Lorry. You are as good as another, I have no doubt: better, I dare say."

"And indeed, sir," pursued Mr. Lorry, not minding him, "I really don't know what you have to do with the matter. If you'll excuse me, as very much your elder, for saying so, I really don't know that it is your business."

"Business! Bless you, *I* have no business," said Mr. Carton.

"It is a pity you have not, sir."

"I think so, too."

"If you had," pursued Mr. Lorry, "perhaps you would attend to it."

"Lord love you, no!—I shouldn't," said Mr. Carton.

"Well, sir!" cried Mr. Lorry, thoroughly heated by his indifference, "business is a very good thing, and a very respectable thing. And, sir, if business imposes its restraints and

its silences and impediments, Mr. Darnay as a young gentleman of generosity knows how to make allowance for that circumstance. Mr. Darnay, good-night, God bless you, sir! I hope you have been this day preserved for a prosperous and happy life.—Chair there!"

Perhaps a little angry with himself, as well as with the barrister, Mr. Lorry bustled into the chair, and was carried off to Tellson's. Carton, who smelt of port wine, and did not appear to be quite sober, laughed then, and turned to Darnay:

"This is a strange chance that throws you and me together. This must be a strange night to you, standing alone here with your counterpart on these street stones?"

"I hardly seem yet," returned Charles Darnay, "to belong to this world again."

"I don't wonder at it; it's not so long since you were pretty far advanced on your way to another. You speak faintly."

"I begin to think I *am* faint."

"Then why the devil don't you dine? I dined, myself, while those numskulls were deliberating which world you should belong to—this, or some other. Let me show you the nearest tavern to dine well at."

Drawing his arm through his own, he took him down Ludgatehill to Fleet-street, and so, up a covered way, into a tavern. Here, they were shown into a little room, where Charles Darnay was soon recruiting his strength with a good plain dinner and good wine: while Carton sat opposite to him at the same table, with his separate bottle of port before him, and his fully half-insolent manner upon him.

"Do you feel, yet, that you belong to this terrestrial scheme again, Mr. Darnay?"

"I am frightfully confused regarding time and place; but I am so far mended as to feel that."

"It must be an immense satisfaction!"

He said it bitterly, and filled up his glass again: which was a large one.

"As to me, the greatest desire I have, is to

forget that I belong to it. It has no good in it for me—except wine like this—nor I for it. So we are not much alike in that particular. Indeed, I begin to think we are not much alike in any particular, you and I."

Confused by the emotion of the day, and feeling his being there with this Double of coarse deportment, to be like a dream, Charles Darnay was at a loss how to answer; finally, answered not at all.

"Now your dinner is done," Carton presently said, "why don't you call a health, Mr. Darnay; why don't you give your toast?"

"What health? What toast?"

"Why, it's on the tip of your tongue. It ought to be, it must be, I'll swear it's there."

"Miss Manette, then!"

"Miss Manette, then!"

Looking his companion full in the face while he drank the toast, Carton flung his glass over his shoulder against the wall, where it shivered to pieces; then, rang the bell, and ordered in another.

"That's a fair young lady to hand to a coach in the dark, Mr. Darnay!" he said, filling his new goblet.

A slight frown and a laconic "Yes," were the answer.

"That's a fair young lady to be pitied by and wept for by! How does it feel? Is it worth being tried for one's life, to be the object of such sympathy and compassion, Mr. Darnay?"

Again Darnay answered not a word.

"She was mightily pleased to have your message, when I gave it her. Not that she showed she was pleased, but I suppose she was."

The allusion served as a timely reminder to Darnay that this disagreeable companion had, of his own free will, assisted him in the strait of the day. He turned the dialogue to that point, and thanked him for it.

"I neither want any thanks, nor merit any," was the careless rejoinder. "It was nothing to do, in the first place; and I don't know

why I did it, in the second. Mr. Darnay, let me ask you a question."

"Willingly, and a small return for your good offices."

"Do you think I particularly like you?"

"Really, Mr. Carton," returned the other, oddly disconcerted, "I have not asked myself the question."

"But ask yourself the question now."

"You have acted as if you do; but I don't think you do."

"*I* don't think I do," said Carton. "I begin to have a very good opinion of your understanding."

"Nevertheless," pursued Darnay, rising to ring the bell, "there is nothing in that, I hope, to prevent my calling the reckoning,[3] and our parting without ill-blood on either side."

Carton rejoining, "Nothing in life!" Darnay rang. "Do you call the whole reckoning?" said Carton. On his answering in the affirmative, "Then bring me another pint of this same wine, drawer, and come and wake me at ten."

The bill being paid, Charles Darnay rose and wished him good-night. Without returning the wish, Carton rose too, with something of a threat of defiance in his manner, and said, "A last word, Mr. Darnay: you think I am drunk?"

"I think you have been drinking, Mr. Carton."

"Think? You know I have been drinking."

"Since I must say so, I know it."

"Then you shall likewise know why. I am a disappointed drudge, sir. I care for no man on earth, and no man on earth cares for me."

"Much to be regretted. You might have used your talents better."

"May be so, Mr. Darnay; may be not. Don't let your sober face elate you, however;

---

3. **reckoning,** the bill.

you don't know what it may come to. Good-night!"

When he was left alone, this strange being took up a candle, went to a glass that hung against the wall, and surveyed himself minutely in it.

"Do you particularly like the man?" he muttered, at his own image; "why should you particularly like a man who resembles you? There is nothing in you to like; you know that. Ah, confound you! What a change you have made in yourself! A good reason for taking to a man, that he shows you what you have fallen away from, and what you might have been! Change places with him, and would you have been looked at by those blue eyes as he was, and commiserated by that agitated face as he was? Come on, and have it out in plain words! You hate the fellow."

He resorted to his pint of wine for consolation, drank it all in a few minutes, and fell asleep on his arms, with his hair straggling over the table, and a long winding-sheet[4] in the candle dripping down upon him.

4. **winding sheet,** a sheetlike formation of wax around a candle, often regarded as an omen of death.

READING FOR DETAILS

Recalled to Life
In Part One of *A Tale of Two Cities*, two men are recalled to life: Dr. Manette, who is released after his long imprisonment, and Charles Darnay, who is acquitted of charges of treason. The opening chapters of Dickens's novel show how a coincidence has intertwined the destinies of these two characters.

1. Why does Jarvis Lorry journey from London to Dover?
2. What does Lorry tell Lucie Manette about her long-lost father?
3. What is the occupation of Monsieur and Madame Defarge?
4. What was Monsieur Defarge's relationship with Dr. Manette before the doctor was imprisoned?
5. From what delusion does Dr. Manette suffer after his release?
6. How does Dr. Manette recognize his daughter Lucie?
7. For what offense is Charles Darnay tried at the Old Bailey?
8. Why are Dr. Manette and Lucie present at the trial?
9. How does Charles come to be acquitted?
10. Who is Jerry Cruncher?
11. Who is Mr. Stryver? How is he characterized?
12. What is Dr. Manette's first reaction when he has a close look at Charles?

READING FOR MEANING

Find evidence in the novel to support the following statements:

1. The French people were ready for the Revolution.
2. Sydney Carton is a mixed bag of virtue and vice.

READING FOR APPRECIATION

Beginnings
Dickens is a well-known master of plot and suspense. In the opening chapters of *A Tale of Two Cities*, he deliberately withholds specific information from the reader, leading the reader to ask certain important questions, the answers to which will be revealed only later. See if you can name at least three of these questions.

LANGUAGE AND VOCABULARY

Check the definitions of the following words in the dictionary. Select *ten* words, and write a sentence for each word, making sure you use it correctly.

stolid	barrister	gradations
longevity	endeavor	timorous
perplexity	deference	spectral
implacable	notoriety	slovenly
feign	abominable	disreputable

Part Two

Monsieur the Marquis ran his eyes over them all, as if they had been mere rats come out of their holes.

Dr. Manette's curious reaction to Charles makes us suspect that he knows some mysterious secret about the young man's true identity. The scene changes to France, where this secret will be disclosed to the reader. The cruel and proud aristocrats increase their oppression of the people. One of these nobles, the Marquis Saint Evrémonde, returns from the capital city of Paris to his country château (or castle). His utter contempt for the people is revealed when his carriage strikes and kills the small child of the peasant Gaspard. The Marquis flings a gold coin to the child's father and drives on. Gaspard, momentarily restrained by Ernest Defarge, the wine-shop keeper, decides upon vengeance. Frantic with grief, he manages to enter the grounds of the château by concealing himself under the nobleman's carriage.

That very evening, the Marquis receives a visitor from England. It is none other than Charles Darnay, whose true family name is Saint Evrémonde; he is the nephew of the Marquis. Charles sorrowfully protests to his uncle against the injustices the family has committed, but the Marquis refuses to acknowledge any wrongdoing. Charles renounces his claim to the family property, saying that he will continue to live as a voluntary exile in England, and the Marquis coldly bids him good night. But Gaspard has his revenge: in the morning, the Marquis is found in his bed, stabbed through the heart.

Chapter 7
Two Promises

More months, to the number of twelve, had come and gone, and Mr. Charles Darnay was established in England as a higher teacher of the French language who was conversant with French literature. In this age, he would have been a Professor; in that age, he was a Tutor.

In London, he had expected neither to walk on pavements of gold, nor to lie on beds of roses: if he had had any such exalted expectation, he would not have prospered. He had expected labor, and he found it, and did it, and made the best of it. In this, his prosperity consisted.

Now, from the days when it was always summer in Eden, to these days when it is mostly winter in fallen latitudes, the world of a man has invariably gone one way—Charles Darnay's way—the way of the love of a woman.

He had loved Lucie Manette from the hour of his danger. He had never heard a sound so sweet and dear as the sound of her compassionate voice; he had never seen a face so tenderly beautiful, as hers when it was confronted with his own on the edge of the grave that had been dug for him. But, he had not yet spoken to her on the subject; the assassination at the deserted château far away beyond the heaving water and the long, long, dusty roads—the solid stone château which had itself become the mere mist of a dream—had been done a year, and he had never yet, by so much as a single spoken word, disclosed to her the state of his heart.

That he had his reasons for this, he knew full well. It was again a summer day when, lately arrived in London from his college occupation, he turned into the quiet corner in Soho,[1] bent on seeking an opportunity of opening his mind to Doctor Manette. It was the close of the summer day, and he knew Lucie to be out with Miss Pross.

He found the Doctor reading in his arm-chair at a window. The energy which had at once supported him under his old sufferings and aggravated their sharpness, had been gradually restored to him. He was now a very energetic man indeed, with great firmness of purpose, strength of resolution, and vigor of action. In his recovered energy he was sometimes a little fitful and sudden, as he had at first been in the exercise of his other recovered faculties; but, this had never been frequently observable, and had grown more and more rare.

He studied much, slept little, sustained a great deal of fatigue with ease, and was equally cheerful. To him, now entered Charles Darnay, at sight of whom he laid aside his book and held out his hand.

"Charles Darnay! I rejoice to see you. We have been counting on your return these three or four days past. Mr. Stryver and Sydney Carton were both here yesterday, and both made you out to be more than due."

"I am obliged to them for their interest in the matter," he answered, a little coldly as to them, though very warmly as to the Doctor. "Miss Manette—"

"Is well," said the Doctor, as he stopped short, "and your return will delight us all. She has gone out on some household matters, but will soon be home."

"Doctor Manette, I knew she was from home. I took the opportunity of her being from home, to beg to speak to you."

There was a blank silence.

"Yes?" said the Doctor, with evident constraint. "Bring your chair here, and speak on."

He complied as to the chair, but appeared to find the speaking on less easy.

"I have had the happiness, Doctor

1. **Soho,** a district in London.

Manette, of being so intimate here," so he at length began, "for some year and a half, that I hope the topic on which I am about to touch may not—"

He was stayed by the Doctor's putting out his hand to stop him. When he had kept it so a little while, he said, drawing it back:

"Is Lucie the topic?"

"She is."

"It is hard for me to speak of her, at any time. It is very hard for me to hear her spoken of in that tone of yours, Charles Darnay."

"It is a tone of fervent admiration, true homage, and deep love, Doctor Manette!" he said deferentially.

There was another blank silence before her father rejoined:

"I believe it. I do you justice; I believe it."

His constraint was so manifest, and it was so manifest, too, that it originated in an unwillingness to approach the subject, that Charles Darnay hesitated.

"Shall I go on, sir?"

Another blank.

"Yes, go on."

"You anticipate what I would say, though you cannot know how earnestly I say it, how earnestly I feel it, without knowing my secret heart, and the hopes and fears and anxieties with which it has long been laden. Dear Doctor Manette, I love your daughter fondly, dearly, disinterestedly, devotedly. If ever there were love in the world, I love her. You have loved yourself; let your old love speak for me!"

The Doctor sat with his face turned away, and his eyes bent on the ground. At the last words, he stretched out his hand again, hurriedly, and cried:

"Not that, sir! Let that be! I adjure you, do not recall that!"

His cry was so like a cry of actual pain, that it rang in Charles Darnay's ears long after he had ceased. He motioned with the hand he had extended, and it seemed to be an appeal to Darnay to pause. The latter so received it, and remained silent.

"I ask your pardon," said the Doctor, in a subdued tone, after some moments. "I do not doubt your loving Lucie; you may be satisfied of it."

He turned towards him in his chair, but did not look at him, or raise his eyes. His chin dropped upon his hand, and his white hair overshadowed his face:

"Have you spoken to Lucie?"

"No."

"Nor written?"

"Never."

"It would be ungenerous to affect not to know that your self-denial is to be referred to your consideration for her father. Her father thanks you."

He offered his hand; but his eyes did not go with it.

"I know," said Darnay, respectfully, "how can I fail to know, Doctor Manette, I who have seen you together from day to day, that between you and Miss Manette there is an affection so unusual, so touching, so belonging to the circumstances in which it has been nurtured, and that it can have few parallels, even in the tenderness between a father and child. I know, Dr. Manette—how can I fail to know—that, mingled with the affection and duty of a daughter who has become a woman, there is, in her heart, towards you, all the love and reliance of infancy itself. I know that, as in her childhood she had no parent, so she is now devoted to you with all the constancy and fervor of her present years and character, united to the trustfulness and attachment of the early days in which you were lost to her. I know perfectly well that if you had been restored to her from the world beyond this life, you could hardly be invested, in her sight, with a more sacred character than that in which you are always with her. I know that when she is clinging to you, the hands of baby, girl, and woman, all in one, are round your neck. I know that in loving you she sees and loves her mother at her own age, sees and loves you at my age, loves her mother broken-hearted, loves you through your dreadful trial and in your blessed restoration. I have known this, night and day, since I have known you in your home."

Her father sat silent, with his face bent down. His breathing was a little quickened; but he repressed all other signs of agitation.

"Dear Doctor Manette, always knowing this, always seeing her and you with this hallowed light about you, I have forborne, and forborne, as long as it was in the nature of man to do it. I have felt, and do even now feel, that to bring my love—even mine—between you, is to touch your history with something not quite so good as itself. But I love her. Heaven is my witness that I love her!"

"I believe it," answered her father, mournfully. "I have thought so before now. I believe it."

"But, do not believe," said Darnay, upon whose ear the mournful voice struck with a reproachful sound, "that if my fortune were so cast as that, being one day so happy as to make her my wife, I must at any time put any separation between her and you, I could or would breathe a word of what I now say. Besides that I should know it to be hopeless, I should know it to be a baseness. If I had any such possibility, even at a remote distance of years, harbored in my thoughts, and hidden in my heart—if it ever had been there—if it ever could be there—I could not now touch this honored hand."

He laid his own upon it as he spoke.

"No, dear Doctor Manette. Like you, a voluntary exile from France; like you, driven from it by its distractions, oppressions, and miseries; like you, striving to live away from it by my own exertions, and trusting in a happier future; I look only to sharing your fortunes, sharing your life and home, and being faithful to you to the death. Not to divide with Lucie her privilege as your child, companion, and friend; but to come in aid of it, and bind her closer to you, if such a thing can be."

His touch still lingered on her father's hand. Answering the touch for a moment, but not coldly, her father rested his hands upon the arms of his chair, and looked up for the first time since the beginning of the conference. A struggle was evidently in his face; a struggle with that occasional look which had a tendency in it to dark doubt and dread.

"You speak so feelingly and so manfully, Charles Darnay, that I thank you with all my heart, and will open all my heart—or nearly so. Have you any reason to believe that Lucie loves you?"

"None. As yet, none."

"Is it the immediate object of this confidence, that you may at once ascertain that, with my knowledge?"

"Not even so. I might not have the hopefulness to do it for weeks; I might (mistaken or not mistaken) have that hopefulness to-morrow."

"Do you seek any guidance from me?"

"I ask none, sir. But I have thought it possible that you might have it in your power, if you should deem it right, to give me some."

"Do you seek any promise from me?"

"I do seek that."

"What is it?"

"I well understand that, without you, I could have no hope. I well understand that, even if Miss Manette held me at this moment in her innocent heart—do not think I have the presumption to assume so much—I could retain no place in it against her love for her father."

"If that be so, do you see what, on the other hand, is involved in it?"

"I understand equally well, that a word from her father in any suitor's favor, would outweigh herself and all the world. For which reason, Doctor Manette," said Darnay, modestly but firmly, "I would not ask that word, to save my life."

"I am sure of it. Charles Darnay, mysteries arise out of close love, as well as out of wide division; in the former case, they are subtle and delicate, and difficult to penetrate. My daughter Lucie is, in this one respect, such a mystery to me; I can make no guess at the state of her heart."

"May I ask, sir, if you think she is—" As he hesitated, her father supplied the rest.

"Is sought by any other suitor?"

"It is what I meant to say."

Her father considered a little before he answered:

"You have seen Mr. Carton here, yourself. Mr. Stryver is here too, occasionally. If it be at all, it can only be by one of these."

"Or both," said Darnay.

"I had no thought of both; I should not think either, likely. You want a promise from me. Tell me what it is."

"It is, that if Miss Manette should bring to you at any time, on her own part, such a confidence as I have ventured to lay before you, you will bear testimony to what I have said, and to your belief in it. I hope you may be able to think so well of me, as to urge no influence against me. I say nothing more of my stake in this; this is what I ask. The condition on which I ask it, and which you have an undoubted right to require, I will observe immediately."

"I give the promise," said the Doctor, "without any condition. I believe your object to be, purely and truthfully, as you have stated it. I believe your intention is to perpetuate, and not to weaken, the ties between me and my other and far dearer self. If she should ever tell me that you are essential to her perfect happiness, I will give her to you. If there were—Charles Darnay, if there were—"

The young man had taken his hand gratefully; their hands were joined as the Doctor spoke:

"—any fancies, any reasons, any apprehensions, anything whatsoever, new or old, against the man she really loved—the direct responsibility thereof not lying on his head—they should all be obliterated for her sake. She is everything to me; more to me than suffering, more to me than wrong, more to me—Well! This is idle talk."

So strange was the way in which he faded into silence, and so strange his fixed look when he had ceased to speak, that Darnay felt his own hand turn cold in the hand that slowly released and dropped it.

"You said something to me," said Doctor Manette, breaking into a smile. "What was it you said to me?"

He was at a loss how to answer, until he remembered having spoken of a condition. Relieved as his mind reverted to that, he answered:

"Your confidence in me ought to be returned with full confidence on my part. My present name, though but slightly changed from my mother's, is not, as you will remember, my own. I wish to tell you what that is, and why I am in England."

"Stop!" said the Doctor of Beauvais.

"I wish it, that I may the better deserve your confidence, and have no secret from you."

"Stop!"

For an instant, the Doctor even had his two hands at his ears; for another instant, even had his two hands laid on Darnay's lips.

"Tell me when I ask you, not now. If your suit should prosper, if Lucie should love you, you shall tell me on your marriage morning. Do you promise?"

"Willingly."

"Give me your hand. She will be home directly, and it is better she should not see us together tonight. Go! God bless you!"

Chapter 8
The Fellow of No Delicacy

If Sydney Carton ever shone anywhere, he certainly never shone in the house of Doctor Manette. He had been there often, during a whole year, and had always been the same moody and morose lounger there. When he cared to talk, he talked well; but, the cloud of caring for nothing, which overshadowed him with such a fatal darkness, was very rarely pierced by the light within him.

And yet he did care something for the streets that environed that house, and for the senseless stones that made their pavements. Many a night he vaguely and unhappily wandered there, when wine had brought no transitory gladness to him; many a dreary daybreak revealed his solitary figure lingering there, and still lingering there when the first beams of the sun brought into strong relief, removed beauties of architecture in spires of churches and lofty buildings, as perhaps the quiet time brought some sense of better things, else forgotten and unattainable, into his mind. Of late, the neglected bed in the Temple Court had known him more scantily than ever; and often when he had thrown himself upon it no longer than a few minutes, he had got up again, and haunted that neighborhood.

On a day in August, when the sight and scent of flowers in the City streets had some waifs of goodness in them for the worst, of health for the sickliest, and of youth for the oldest, Sydney's feet still trod those stones. From being irresolute and purposeless, his feet became animated by an intention, and, in the working out of that intention, they took him to the Doctor's door.

He was shown upstairs, and found Lucie at her work, alone. She had never been quite at her ease with him, and received him with some little embarrassment as he seated himself near her table. But, looking up at his face in the interchange of the first few commonplaces, she observed a change in it.

"I fear you are not well, Mr. Carton!"

"No. But the life I lead, Miss Manette, is not conducive to health. What is to be expected of, or by, such profligates?"

"Is it not—forgive me; I have begun the question on my lips—a pity to live no better life?"

"God knows it is a shame!"

"Then why not change it?"

Looking gently at him again, she was surprised and saddened to see that there were tears in his eyes. There were tears in his voice too, as he answered.

"It is too late for that. I shall never be better than I am. I shall sink lower, and be worse."

He leaned an elbow on her table, and covered his eyes with his hand. The table trembled in the silence that followed.

She had never seen him softened, and was much distressed. He knew her to be so, without looking at her, and said:

"Pray forgive me, Miss Manette. I break down before the knowledge of what I want to say to you. Will you hear me?"

"If it will do you any good, Mr. Carton, if it would make you happier, it would make me very glad!"

"God bless you for your sweet compassion!"

He unshaded his face after a little while, and spoke steadily.

"Don't be afraid to hear me. Don't shrink from anything I say. I am like one who died young. All my life might have been."

"No, Mr. Carton. I am sure that the best part of it might still be; I am sure that you might be much, much worthier of yourself."

"Say of you, Miss Manette, and although I know better—although in the mystery of my own wretched heart I know better—I shall never forget it!"

She was pale and trembling. He came to her relief with a fixed despair of himself which made the interview unlike any other that could have been holden.

"If it had been possible, Miss Manette, that you could have returned the love of the man you see before you—self-flung away, wasted, drunken, poor creature of misuse as you know him to be—he would have been conscious this day and hour, in spite of his happiness, that he would bring you to misery, bring you to sorrow and repentance, blight you, disgrace you, pull you down with him. I know very well that you can have no tenderness for me; I ask for none; I am even thankful that it cannot be."

"Without it, can I not save you, Mr. Carton? Can I not recall you—forgive me again!—to a better course? Can I in no way repay your confidence? I know this is a confidence," she modestly said, after a little hesitation, and in earnest tears, "I know you would say this to no one else. Can I turn it to no good account for yourself, Mr. Carton?"

He shook his head.

"To none. No, Miss Manette, to none. If you will hear me through a very little more, all you can ever do for me is done. I wish you to know that you have been the last dream of my soul. In my degradation I have not been so degraded but that the sight of you with your father, and of this home made such a home by you, has stirred old shadows that I thought had died out of me. Since I knew you, I have been troubled by a remorse that I thought would never reproach me again, and have heard whispers from old voices impelling me upward, that I thought were silent for ever. I have had unformed ideas of striving afresh, beginning anew, shaking off sloth and sensuality and fighting out the abandoned fight. A dream, all a dream, that ends in nothing, and leaves the sleeper where he lay down, but I wish you to know that you inspired it."

"Will nothing of it remain? O Mr. Carton, think again! Try again!"

"No, Miss Manette; all through it, I have known myself to be quite undeserving. And yet I have had the weakness, and have still the weakness, to wish you to know with what a sudden mastery you kindled me, heap of ashes that I am, into fire—a fire, however, inseparable in its nature from myself, quickening nothing, lighting nothing, doing no service, idly burning away."

"Since it is my misfortune, Mr. Carton, to have made you more unhappy than you were before you knew me—"

"Don't say that, Miss Manette, for you would have reclaimed me, if anything could. You will not be the cause of my becoming worse."

"Since the state of your mind that you describe, is, at all events, attributable to some influence of mine—this is what I mean, if I can make it plain—can I use no influence to serve you? Have I no power for good, with you, at all?"

"The utmost good that I am capable of now, Miss Manette, I have come here to realize. Let me carry through the rest of my misdirected life, the remembrance that I opened my heart to you, last of all the world; and that there was something left in me at this time which you could deplore and pity."

"Which I entreated you to believe, again and again, most fervently, with all my heart, was capable of better things, Mr. Carton!"

"Entreat me to believe it no more, Miss Manette. I have proved myself, and I know better. I distress you; I draw fast to an end. Will you let me believe, when I recall this day, that the last confidence of my life was reposed in your pure and innocent breast, and that it lies there alone, and will be shared by no one?"

"If that will be a consolation to you, yes."

French patriots take the Revolution to the Royal gardens.

"Not even by the dearest one ever to be known to you?"

"Mr. Carton," she answered, after an agitated pause, "the secret is yours, not mine; and I promise to respect it."

"Thank you. And again, God bless you."

He put her hand to his lips, and moved towards the door.

"Be under no apprehension, Miss Manette, of my ever resuming this conversation by so much as a passing word. I will never refer to it again. If I were dead, that could not be surer than it is henceforth. In the hour of my death, I shall hold sacred the one good remembrance—and shall thank and bless you for it—that my last avowal of myself was made to you, and that my name, and faults, and miseries were gently carried in your heart. May it otherwise be light and happy!"

He was so unlike what he had ever shown himself to be, and it was so sad to think how much he had thrown away, and how much he every day kept down and perverted, that Lucie Manette wept mournfully for him as he stood looking back at her.

"Be comforted!" he said, "I am not worth such feeling, Miss Manette. An hour or two hence, and the low companions and low habits that I scorn but yield to, will render me less worth such tears as those, than any wretch who creeps along the streets. Be comforted! But, within myself, I shall always be, towards you, what I am now, though outwardly I shall be what you have heretofore seen me. The last supplication but one I make to you, is, that you will believe this of me."

"I will, Mr. Carton."

"My last supplication of all, is this; and with it, I will relieve you of a visitor with whom I well know you have nothing in unison, and between whom and you there is an impassable space. It is useless to say it, I know, but it rises out of my soul. For you, and for any dear to you, I would do anything. If my career were of that better kind that there was any opportunity or capacity of sacrifice in it, I would embrace any sacrifice for you and for those dear to you. Try to hold me in your mind, at some quiet times, as ardent and sincere in this one thing. The time will come, the time will not be long in coming, when new ties will be formed about you—ties that will bind you yet more tenderly and strongly to the home you so adorn—the dearest ties that will ever grace and gladden you. O Miss Manette, when the little picture of a happy father's face looks up in yours, when you see your own bright beauty springing up anew at your feet, think now and then that there is a man who would give his life, to keep a life you love beside you!"

He said, "Farewell!" said "A last God bless you!" and left her.

In the quarter of Saint Antoine, at the wine-shop, a road-mender from the country comes to tell Defarge and his wife of the arrest and execution of Gaspard for the Marquis's murder. Madame Defarge vows that the entire family of the Marquis will be "registered" for execution when the Revolution comes. She keeps a record of all who will be killed by knitting their names and descriptions in a secret code. The Defarges recruit the road-mender to the Revolutionary cause, and take him to view the splendor of the King's court at Versailles, outside Paris. As the next chapter opens, the wine-shop keeper and his wife return to the city.

Chapter 9
Still Knitting

The Defarges, husband and wife, came lumbering under the starlight, in their public vehicle, to that gate of Paris whereunto their journey naturally tended. There was the usual stoppage at the barrier guard-house, and the usual lanterns came glancing forth for the usual examination and inquiry. Monsieur Defarge alighted: knowing one or two of the soldiery there, and one of the police. The latter he was intimate with, and affectionately embraced.

When Saint Antoine[1] had again enfolded the Defarges in his dusky wings, and they, having finally alighted near the Saint's boundaries, were picking their way on foot through the black mud and offal of his streets, Madame Defarge spoke to her husband:

"Say then, my friend; what did Jacques of the police tell thee?"

"Very little tonight, but all he knows. There is another spy commissioned for our quarter. There may be many more, for all that he can say, but he knows of one."

"Eh well!" said Madame Defarge, raising her eyebrows with a cool business air. "It is necessary to register him. How do they call that man?"

"He is English."

"So much the better. His name?"

"Barsad," said Defarge, making it French by pronunciation. But, he had been so careful to get it accurately, that he then spelt it with perfect correctness.

---

1. The author is ironically comparing the Saint Antoine suburb to Saint Anthony (the saint for whom the suburb was named).

"Barsad," repeated madame. "Good. Christian name?"

"John."

"John Barsad," repeated madame, after murmuring it once to herself. "Good. His appearance; is it known?"

"Age, about forty years; height, about five feet nine; black hair; complexion dark; generally, rather handsome visage; eyes dark, face thin, long, and sallow; nose aquiline, but not straight, having a peculiar inclination towards the left cheek; expression, therefore, sinister."

"Eh my faith. It is a portrait!" said madame, laughing. "He shall be registered to-morrow."

Next noontide saw the admirable woman in her usual place in the wine-shop, knitting away assiduously. A rose lay beside her, and if she now and then glanced at the flower, it was with no infraction of her usual preoccupied air. There were a few customers, drinking or not drinking, standing or seated, sprinkled about.

A figure entering at the door threw a shadow on Madame Defarge which she felt to be a new one. She laid down her knitting, and began to pin her rose in her head-dress, before she looked at the figure.

It was curious. The moment Madame Defarge took up the rose, the customers ceased talking, and began gradually to drop out of the wine-shop.

"Good day, madame," said the new comer.

"Good day, monsieur."

She said it aloud, but added to herself, as she resumed her knitting: "Hah! Good day, age about forty, height about five feet nine, black hair, generally rather handsome visage, complexion dark, eyes dark, thin long and sallow face, aquiline nose but not straight, having a peculiar inclination towards the left

cheek which imparts a sinister expression! Good day, one and all!"

"Have the goodness to give me a little glass of old cognac, and a mouthful of cool fresh water, madame."

Madame complied with a polite air.

"Marvellous cognac this, madame!"

It was the first time it had ever been so complimented, and Madame Defarge knew enough of its antecedents to know better. She said, however, that the cognac was flattered, and took up her knitting. The visitor watched her fingers for a few moments, and took the opportunity of observing the place in general.

"You knit with great skill, madame."

"I am accustomed to it."

"A pretty pattern too!"

"*You* think so?" said madame, looking at him with a smile.

"Decidedly. May one ask what it is for?"

"Pastime," said madame, still looking at him with a smile, while her fingers moved nimbly.

"Not for use?"

"That depends. I may find a use for it one day. If I do—well," said madame, drawing a breath and nodding her head with a stern kind of coquetry, "I'll use it!"

It was remarkable; but the taste of Saint Antoine seemed to be decidedly opposed to a rose on the head-dress of Madame Defarge. Two men had entered separately, and had been about to order drink, when, catching sight of that novelty, they faltered, made a pretense of looking about as if for some friend who was not there, and went away. Nor, of those who had been there when this visitor entered, was there one left. They had all dropped off. The spy had kept his eyes open, but had been able to detect no sign. They had lounged away in a poverty-stricken, purposeless, accidental manner, quite natural and unimpeachable.

"John," thought madame, checking off her work as her fingers knitted, and her eyes looked at the stranger. "Stay long enough, and I shall knit 'Barsad' before you go."

"You have a husband, madame?"

"I have."

"Children?"

"No children."

"Business seems bad?"

"Business is very bad; the people are so poor."

"Ah, the unfortunate, miserable people! So oppressed, too—as you say."

"As *you* say," madame retorted, correcting him, and deftly knitting an extra something into his name that boded him no good.

"Pardon me; certainly it was I who said so, but you naturally think so. Of course."

"*I* think?" returned madame, in a high voice. "I and my husband have enough to do to keep this wine-shop open, without thinking. All we think, here, is how to live. That is the subject *we* think of, and it gives us, from morning to night, enough to think about, without embarrassing our heads concerning others. *I* think for others? No, no."

The spy, who was there to pick up any crumbs he could find or make, did not allow his baffled state to express itself in his sinister face; but, stood with an air of gossiping gallantry, leaning his elbow on Madame Defarge's little counter, and occasionally sipping his cognac.

"A bad business this, madame, of Gaspard's execution. Ah! the poor Gaspard!" With a sigh of great compassion.

"My faith!" returned madame, coolly and lightly, "if people use knives for such purposes, they have to pay for it. He knew beforehand what the price of his luxury was; he has paid the price."

"I believe," said the spy, dropping his soft voice to a tone that invited confidence, and expressing an injured revolutionary susceptibility in every muscle of his wicked face: "I

believe there is much compassion and anger in this neighborhood, touching the poor fellow? Between ourselves."

"Is there?" asked madame, vacantly.

"Is there not?"

"—Here is my husband!" said Madame Defarge.

As the keeper of the wine-shop entered at the door, the spy saluted him by touching his hat, and saying, with an engaging smile, "Good day, Jacques!" Defarge stopped short, and stared at him.

"Good day, Jacques!" the spy repeated; with not quite so much confidence, or quite so easy a smile under the stare.

"You deceive yourself, monsieur," returned the keeper of the wine-shop. "You mistake me for another. That is not my name. I am Ernest Defarge."

"It is all the same," said the spy, airily, but discomfited too: "good day!"

"Good day!" answered Defarge, drily.

"I was saying to madame, with whom I had the pleasure of chatting when you entered, that they tell me there is—and no wonder!—much sympathy and anger in Saint Antoine, touching the unhappy fate of poor Gaspard."

"No one has told me so," said Defarge, shaking his head. "I know nothing of it."

Having said it, he passed behind the little counter, and stood with his hand on the back of his wife's chair, looking over that barrier at the person to whom they were both opposed, and whom either of them would have shot with the greatest satisfaction.

The spy, well used to his business, did not change his unconscious attitude, but drained his little glass of cognac, took a sip of fresh water, and asked for another glass of cognac. Madame Defarge poured it out for him, took to her knitting again, and hummed a little song over it.

"You seem to know this quarter well; that is to say, better than I do?" observed Defarge.

"Not at all, but I hope to know it better. I am so profoundly interested in its miserable inhabitants."

"Hah!" muttered Defarge.

"The pleasure of conversing with you, Monsieur Defarge, recalls to me," pursued the spy, "that I have the honor of cherishing some interesting associations with your name."

"Indeed!" said Defarge, with much indifference.

"Yes, indeed. When Dr. Manette was released, you, his old domestic, had the charge of him, I know. He was delivered to you. You see I am informed of the circumstances?"

"Such is the fact, certainly," said Defarge. He had had it conveyed to him, in an accidental touch of his wife's elbow as she knitted and warbled, that he would do best to answer, but always with brevity.

"It was to you," said the spy, "that his daughter came; and it was from your care that his daughter took him, accompanied by a neat brown monsieur; how is he called?—in a little wig—Lorry—of the bank of Tellson and Company—over to England."

"Such is the fact," repeated Defarge.

"Very interesting remembrances!" said the spy. "I have known Dr. Manette and his daughter, in England."

"Yes?" said Defarge.

"You don't hear much about them now?" said the spy.

"No," said Defarge.

"In effect," madame struck in, looking up from her work and her little song, "we never hear about them. We received the news of their safe arrival, and perhaps another letter, or perhaps two; but, since then, they have gradually taken their road in life—we, ours—and we have held no correspondence."

"Perfectly so, madame," replied the spy. "She is going to be married."

"Going?" echoed madame. "She was pretty enough to have been married long ago. You English are cold, it seems to me."

"Oh! You know I am English."

"I perceive your tongue is," returned madame; "and what the tongue is, I suppose the man is."

He did not take the identification as a compliment; but he made the best of it, and turned it off with a laugh. After sipping his cognac to the end, he added:

"Yes, Miss Manette is going to be married. But not to an Englishman; to one who, like herself, is French by birth. And speaking of Gaspard (ah, poor Gaspard! It was cruel, cruel!), it is a curious thing that she is going to marry the nephew of Monsieur the Marquis, for whom Gaspard was exalted to that height of so many feet; in other words, the present Marquis. But he lives unknown in England, he is no Marquis there; he is Mr. Charles Darnay. D'Aulnais is the name of his mother's family."

Madame Defarge knitted steadily, but the intelligence had a palpable effect upon her husband. Do what he would, behind the little counter, as to the striking of a light and the lighting of his pipe, he was troubled, and his hand was not trustworthy. The spy would have been no spy if he had failed to see it, or to record it in his mind.

Having made, at least, this one hit, whatever it might prove to be worth, and no customers coming in to help him to any other, Mr. Barsad paid for what he had drunk, and took his leave: taking occasion to say, in a genteel manner, before he departed, that he looked forward to the pleasure of seeing Monsieur and Madame Defarge again. For some minutes after he had emerged into the outer presence of Saint Antoine, the husband and wife remained exactly as he had left them, lest he should come back.

"Can it be true," said Defarge, in a low voice, looking down at his wife as he stood smoking with his hand on the back of her chair: "what he has said of Mam'selle Manette?"

"As he said it," returned madame, lifting her eyebrows a little, "it is probably false. But it may be true."

"If it is—" Defarge began, and stopped.

"If it is?" repeated his wife.

"—And if it does come, while we live to see it triumph—I hope, for her sake, Destiny will keep her husband out of France."

"Her husband's destiny," said Madame Defarge, with her usual composure, "will take him where he is to go, and will lead him to the end that is to end him. That is all I know."

"But it is very strange—now, at least, is it not very strange"—said Defarge, rather pleading with his wife to induce her to admit it, "that, after all our sympathy for Monsieur her father, and herself, her husband's name should be proscribed under your hand at this moment, by the side of that infernal dog's who has just left us?"

"Stranger things than that will happen when it does come," answered madame. "I have them both here, of a certainty; and they are both here for their merits; that is enough."

Chapter 10
One Night

Never did the sun go down with a brighter glory on the quiet corner in Soho, than one memorable evening when the Doctor and his daughter sat under the plane-tree together. Never did the moon rise with a milder radiance over great London, than on that night when it found them still seated under the tree, and shone upon their faces through its leaves.

Lucie was to be married tomorrow. She had reserved this last evening for her father, and they sat alone under the plane-tree.

"You are happy, my dear father?"

"Quite, my child."

They had said little, though they had been there a long time. When it was yet light enough to work and read, she had neither engaged herself in her usual work nor had she read to him. She had employed herself in both ways, at his side under the tree, many and many a time; but, this time was not quite like any other, and nothing could make it so.

"And I am very happy tonight, dear father. I am deeply happy in the love that Heaven has so blessed—my love for Charles, and Charles's love for me. But, if my life were not to be still consecrated to you, or if my marriage were so arranged as that it would part us, even by the length of a few of these streets, I should be more unhappy and self-reproachful now than I can tell you. Even as it is—"

Even as it was, she could not command her voice.

In the sad moonlight, she clasped him by the neck, and laid her face upon his breast. In the moonlight which is always sad, as the light of the sun itself is—as the light called human life is—at its coming and its going.

"Dearest dear! Can you tell me, this last time, that you feel quite, quite sure, no new affections of mine, and no new duties of mine, will ever interpose between us? *I* know it well, but do you know it? In your own heart, do you feel quite certain?"

Her father answered, with a cheerful firmness of conviction he could scarcely have assumed, "Quite sure, my darling! More than that," he added, as he tenderly kissed her: "my future is far brighter, Lucie, seen through your marriage, than it could have been—nay, than it ever was—without it."

"If I could hope *that,* my father!—"

"Believe it, love! Indeed it is so. Consider how natural and how plain it is, my dear, that it should be so. You, devoted and young, cannot fully appreciate the anxiety I have felt that your life should not be wasted—"

She moved her hand towards his lips, but he took it in his, and repeated the word.

"—wasted, my child—should not be wasted, struck aside from the natural order of things—for my sake. Your unselfishness cannot entirely comprehend how much my mind has gone on this; but, only ask yourself, how could my happiness be perfect, while yours was incomplete?"

"If I had never seen Charles, my father, I should have been quite happy with you."

He smiled at her unconscious admission that she would have been unhappy without Charles, having seen him, and replied:

"My child, you did see him, and it is Charles. If it had not been Charles, it would have been another. Or, if it had been no other, I should have been the cause, and then the dark part of my life would have cast its shadow beyond myself, and would have fallen on you."

It was the first time, except at the trial, of her ever hearing him refer to the period of his suffering. It gave her a strange and new sensation while his words were in her ears; and she remembered it long afterwards.

"See!" said the Doctor of Beauvais, raising his hand towards the moon. "I have looked at her from my prison-window, when I could not bear her light. I have looked at her when it has been such torture to me to think of her shining upon what I had lost, that I have beaten my head against my prison-walls. I have looked at her, in a state so dull and lethargic, that I have thought of nothing but the number of horizontal lines I could draw across her at the full, the number of perpendicular lines with which I could intersect them." He added in his inward and pondering manner, as he looked at the moon, "It was twenty either way, I remember, and the twentieth was difficult to squeeze in."

The strange thrill with which she heard him go back to that time, deepened as he dwelt upon it; but, there was nothing to shock her in the manner of his reference. He only seemed to contrast his present cheerfulness and felicity with the dire endurance that was over.

"I have looked at her, speculating thousands of times upon the unborn child from whom I had been rent. Whether it was alive. Whether it had been born alive, or the poor mother's shock had killed it. Whether it was a son who would some day avenge his father. (There was a time in my imprisonment, when my desire for vengeance was unbearable.) Whether it was a son who would never know his father's story; who might even live to weigh the possibility of his father's having disappeared of his own will and act. Whether it was a daughter who would grow to be a woman."

She drew closer to him, and kissed his cheek and his hand.

"I have pictured my daughter, to myself, as perfectly forgetful of me—rather, altogether ignorant of me, and unconscious of me. I have cast up the years of her age, year after year. I have seen her married to a man who knew nothing of my fate. I have altogether perished from the remembrance of the living, and in the next generation my place was a blank."

"My father! Even to hear that you had such thoughts of a daughter who never existed, strikes to my heart as if I had been that child."

"You, Lucie? It is out of the consolation and restoration you have brought to me, that these remembrances arise, and pass between us and the moon on this last night.—What did I say just now?"

"She knew nothing of you. She cared nothing for you."

"So! But on other moonlight nights, when the sadness and the silence have touched me in a different way—have affected me with something as like a sorrowful sense of peace, as any emotion that had pain for its foundations could—I have imagined her as coming to me in my cell, and leading me out into the freedom beyond the fortress. I have seen her image in the moonlight often, as I now see you; except that I never held her in my arms; it stood between the little grated window and the door. But, you understand that that was not the child I am speaking of?"

"The figure was not; the—the—image; the fancy?"

"No. That was another thing. It stood before my disturbed sense of sight, but it never moved. The phantom that my mind pursued, was another and more real child. Of her outward appearance I know no more than that she was like her mother. The other had that likeness too—as you have—but was not the same. Can you follow me, Lucie? Hardly, I think? I doubt you must have been a solitary prisoner to understand these perplexed distinctions."

His collected and calm manner could not prevent her blood from running cold, as he thus tried to anatomize his old condition.

"In that more peaceful state, I have imagined her, in the moonlight, coming to me and taking me out to show me that the home of her married life was full of her loving remembrance of her lost father. My picture was in her room, and I was in her prayers. Her life was active, cheerful, useful; but my poor history pervaded it all."

"I was that child, my father. I was not half so good, but in my love that was I."

"And she showed me her children," said the Doctor of Beauvais, "and they had heard of me, and had been taught to pity me. When they passed a prison of the State, they kept far from its frowning walls, and looked up at its bars, and spoke in whispers. She could never deliver me; I imagined that she always brought me back after showing me such things. But then, blessed with the relief of tears, I fell upon my knees, and blessed her."

"I am that child, I hope, my father. O my dear, my dear, will you bless me as fervently tomorrow?"

"Lucie, I recall these old troubles in the reason that I have to-night for loving you better than words can tell, and thanking God for my great happiness. My thoughts, when they were wildest, never rose near the happiness that I have known with you, and that we have before us."

He embraced her, solemnly commended her to Heaven, and humbly thanked Heaven for having bestowed her on him. By-and-by, they went into the house.

There was no one bidden to the marriage but Mr. Lorry; there was even to be no bridesmaid but the gaunt Miss Pross. The marriage was to make no change in their place of residence; they had been able to extend it, by taking to themselves the upper rooms formerly belonging to a lodger, and they desired nothing more.

Doctor Manette was very cheerful at the little supper. They were only three at table, and Miss Pross made the third. He regretted that Charles was not there; was more than half disposed to object to the loving little plot that kept him away; and drank to him affectionately.

So, the time came for him to bid Lucie good night, and they separated. But, in the stillness of the third hour of the morning, Lucie came downstairs again, and stole into his room: not free from unshaped fears, beforehand.

All things, however, were in their places; all was quiet; and he lay asleep, his white hair picturesque on the untroubled pillow, and his hands lying quiet on the coverlet. She put her needless candle in the shadow at a distance, crept up to his bed, and put her lips to his; then, leaned over him, and looked at him.

Into his handsome face, the bitter waters of captivity had worn; but, he covered up their tracks with a determination so strong, that he held the mastery of them, even in his sleep. A more remarkable face in its quiet, resolute, and guarded struggle with an unseen assailant, was not to be beheld in all the wide dominions of sleep, that night.

She timidly laid her hand on his dear breast, and put up a prayer that she might ever be as true to him as her love aspired to be, and as his sorrows deserved. Then, she withdrew her hand, and kissed his lips once more, and went away. So, the sunrise came, and the shadows of the leaves of the plane-tree moved upon his face, as softly as her lips had moved in praying for him.

On the wedding day, Charles confides the secret of his identity to Dr. Manette. The doctor is so shaken that, immediately after the departure of Charles and Lucie for their honeymoon, his delusion that he is a shoemaker in prison returns. After nine days of anxious observation, Jarvis Lorry gently coaxes Dr. Manette back to sanity. The doctor now believes himself to be permanently cured. Although he does not reveal the connection with the Saint Evrémonde family that has so deeply disturbed him, he permits Lorry and Miss Pross to destroy his shoemaking tools. His illness is kept secret from Charles and Lucie.

Chapter 11
A Plea

When the newly-married pair came home, the first person who appeared, to offer his congratulations, was Sydney Carton. They had not been at home many hours, when he presented himself. He was not improved in habits, or in looks, or in manner; but there was a certain rugged air of fidelity about him, which was new to the observation of Charles Darnay.

He watched his opportunity of taking Darnay aside into a window, and of speaking to him when no one overheard.

"Mr. Darnay," said Carton, "I wish we might be friends."

"We are already friends, I hope."

"You are good enough to say so, as a fashion of speech; but, I don't mean any fashion of speech. Indeed, when I say I wish we might be friends, I scarcely mean quite that, either."

Charles Darnay—as was natural—asked him, in all good-humor and good-fellowship, what he did mean?

"Upon my life," said Carton, smiling, "I find that easier to comprehend in my own mind, than to convey to yours. However, let me try. You remember a certain famous occasion when I was more drunk than—than usual?"

"I remember a certain famous occasion when you forced me to confess that you had been drinking."

"I remember it too. The curse of those occasions is heavy upon me, for I always remember them. I hope it may be taken into account one day, when all days are at an end for me!—Don't be alarmed; I am not going to preach."

"I am not at all alarmed. Earnestness in you, is anything but alarming to me."

"Ah!" said Carton, with a careless wave of his hand, as if he waved that away. "On the drunken occasion in question (one of a large number, as you know), I was insufferable about liking you, and not liking you. I wish you would forget it."

"I forgot it long ago."

"Fashion of speech again! But, Mr. Darnay, oblivion is not so easy to me, as you represent it to be to you. I have by no means forgotten it, and a light answer does not help me to forget it."

"If it was a light answer," returned Darnay, "I beg your forgiveness for it. I had no other object than to turn a slight thing, which, to my surprise, seems to trouble you too much, aside. I declare to you on the faith of a gentleman, that I have long dismissed it from my mind. Good Heaven, what was there to dismiss! Have I had nothing more important to remember, in the great service you rendered me that day?"

"As to the great service," said Carton, "I am bound to avow to you, when you speak of it in that way, that it was mere professional claptrap. I don't know that I cared what became of you, when I rendered it.—Mind! I say when I rendered it; I am speaking of the past."

"You make light of the obligation," returned Darnay, "but I will not quarrel with *your* light answer."

"Genuine truth, Mr. Darnay, trust me! I have gone aside from my purpose; I was speaking about our being friends. Now, you know me; you know I am incapable of all the higher and better flights of men. If you doubt it, ask Stryver, and he'll tell you so."

"I prefer to form my own opinion, without the aid of his."

"Well! At any rate you know me as a dissolute dog who has never done any good, and never will."

"I don't know that you 'never will.'"

"But I do, and you must take my word for it. Well! If you could endure to have such a worthless fellow, and a fellow of such indifferent reputation, coming and going at odd times, I should ask that I might be permitted to come and go as a privileged person here; that I might be regarded as an useless (and I would add, if it were not for the resemblance I detected between you and me, an unornamental), piece of furniture, tolerated for its old service, and taken no notice of. I doubt if I should abuse the permission. It is a hundred to one if I should avail myself of it four times in a year. It would satisfy me, I dare say, to know that I had it."

"Will you try?"

"That is another way of saying that I am placed on the footing I have indicated. I thank you, Darnay. I may use that freedom with your name?"

"I think so, Carton, by this time."

They shook hands upon it, and Sydney turned away. Within a minute afterwards, he was, to all outward appearance, as unsubstantial as ever.

When he was gone, and in the course of an evening passed with Miss Pross, the Doctor, and Mr. Lorry, Charles Darnay made some mention of this conversation in general terms, and spoke of Sydney Carton as a problem of carelessness and recklessness. He spoke of him, in short, not bitterly or meaning to bear hard upon him, but as anybody might who saw him as he showed himself.

He had no idea that this could dwell in the thoughts of his fair young wife; but, when he afterwards joined her in their own rooms, he found her waiting for him with the old pretty lifting of the forehead strongly marked.

"We are thoughtful tonight!" said Darnay, drawing his arm about her.

"Yes, dearest Charles," with her hands on his breast, and the inquiring and attentive expression fixed upon him; "we are rather thoughtful tonight, for we have something on our mind tonight."

"What is it, my Lucie?"

"Will you promise not to press one question on me, if I beg you not to ask it?"

"Will I promise? What will I not promise to my Love?"

What, indeed, with his hand putting aside the golden hair from the cheek, and his other hand against the heart that beat for him!

"I think, Charles, poor Mr. Carton deserves more consideration and respect than you expressed for him tonight."

"Indeed, my own? Why so?"

"That is what you are not to ask me. But I think—I know—he does."

"If you know it, it is enough. What would you have me do, my Life?"

"I would ask you, dearest, to be very generous with him always, and very lenient on his faults when he is not by. I would ask you to believe that he has a heart he very, very seldom reveals, and that there are deep wounds in it. My dear, I have seen it bleeding."

"It is a painful reflection to me," said Charles Darnay, quite astounded, "that I should have done him any wrong. I never thought this of him."

"My husband, it is so. I fear he is not to be reclaimed; there is scarcely a hope that anything in his character or fortunes is reparable now. But, I am sure that he is capable of good things, gentle things, even magnanimous things."

She looked so beautiful in the purity of her faith in this lost man, that her husband could have looked at her as she was for hours.

"And, O my dearest Love!" she urged, clinging nearer to him, laying her head upon his breast, and raising her eyes to his, "remember how strong we are in our happiness, and how weak he is in his misery!"

The supplication touched him home. "I will always remember it, dear Heart! I will remember it as long as I live."

He bent over the golden head, and put the rosy lips to his, and folded her in his arms. If one forlorn wanderer then pacing the dark streets, could have heard her innocent disclosure, and could have seen the drops of pity kissed away by her husband from the soft blue eyes so loving of that husband, he might have cried to the night—and the words would not have parted from his lips for the first time—

"God bless her for her sweet compassion!"

Over six years pass. It is now July, 1789. In England, Charles and Lucie have become the glad parents of a daughter. Sydney Carton pays them rare but affectionate visits. In France, the Revolution finally begins with the people storming the Bastille, one of Paris's most notorious prisons. Ernest Defarge searches Dr. Manette's former cell, and retrieves a diary. The angry crowd lynches the governor of the prison, and Madame Defarge cuts off his head with her knife. She is joined in the violence by another bloodthirsty woman, a grocer's wife who is known as "The Vengeance."

In the countryside, the château of the Marquis Saint Evrémonde is burned to the ground. One of the servants, Gabelle, fears for his life, and barricades his house; for the moment, he escapes from harm.

At the opening of the following chapter, three more years have passed: it is now August, 1792. Many French aristocrats have taken refuge in England.

Chapter 12
Drawn to the Loadstone Rock

The August of the year one thousand seven hundred and ninety-two was come, and Monseigneur[1] was by this time scattered far and wide.

As was natural, the head-quarters and great gathering-place of Monseigneur, in London, was Tellson's Bank. Spirits are supposed to haunt the places where their bodies most resorted, and Monseigneur without a guinea haunted the spot where his guineas

---

1. **Monseigneur** (mon se nyoer′), French for "my lord." Dickens uses the word as a general term for the whole class of French aristocrats.

used to be. Moreover, it was the spot to which such French intelligence as was most to be relied upon, came quickest. Again: Tellson's was a munificent house, and extended great liberality to old customers who had fallen from their high estate. Again: those nobles who had seen the coming storm in time, and anticipating plunder or confiscation, had made provident remittances to Tellson's, were always to be heard of there by their needy brethren. To which it must be added that every new comer from France reported himself and his tidings at Tellson's, almost as a matter of course. For such variety of reasons, Tellson's was at that time, as to French intelligence, a kind of High Exchange; and this was so well known to the public, and the inquiries made there were in consequences so numerous, that Tellson's sometimes wrote the latest news out in a line or so and posted it in the Bank windows, for all who ran through Temple Bar to read.

On a steaming, misty afternoon, Mr. Lorry sat at his desk, and Charles Darnay stood leaning on it, talking with him in a low voice. The penitential den once set apart for interviews with the House, was now the news-Exchange, and was filled to overflowing. It was within half an hour or so of the time of closing.

"But, although you are the youngest man that ever lived," said Charles Darnay, rather hesitating, "I must still suggest to you—"

"I understand. That I am too old?" said Mr. Lorry.

"Unsettled weather, a long journey, uncertain means of travelling, a disorganized country, a city that may not be even safe for you."

"My dear Charles," said Mr. Lorry, with cheerful confidence, "you touch some of the reasons for my going: not for my staying away. It is safe enough for me; nobody will care to interfere with an old fellow of hard upon four-score[2] when there are so many people there much better worth interfering with. As to its being a disorganized city, if it were not a disorganized city there would be no occasion to send somebody from our House here to our House there, who knows the city and the business, of old, and is in Tellson's confidence. As to the uncertain travelling, the long journey, and the winter weather, if I were not prepared to submit myself to a few inconveniences for the sake of Tellson's, after all these years, who ought to be?"

"I wish I were going myself," said Charles Darnay, somewhat restlessly, and like one thinking aloud.

"Indeed! You are a pretty fellow to object and advise!" exclaimed Mr. Lorry. "You wish you were going yourself? And you a Frenchman born? You are a wise counsellor."

"My dear Mr. Lorry, it is because I am a Frenchman born, that the thought (which I did not mean to utter here, however) has passed through my mind often. One cannot help thinking, having had some sympathy for the miserable people, and having abandoned something to them," he spoke here in his former thoughtful manner, "that one might be listened to, and might have the power to persuade to some restraint. Only last night, after you had left us, when I was talking to Lucie—"

"When you were talking to Lucie," Mr. Lorry repeated. "Yes. I wonder you are not ashamed to mention the name of Lucie! Wishing you were going to France at this time of day!"

"However, I am not going," said Charles Darnay, with a smile. "It is more to the purpose that you say you are."

"And I am, in plain reality. The truth is, my dear Charles," Mr. Lorry glanced at the distant House, and lowered his voice, "you

2. **four-score,** eighty.

The people arm themselves. The Reign of Terror has begun!

can have no conception of the difficulty with which our business is transacted, and of the peril in which our books and papers over yonder are involved. The Lord above knows what the compromising consequences would be to numbers of people, if some of our documents were seized or destroyed; and they might be, at any time, you know, for who can say that Paris is not set a-fire to-day, or sacked tomorrow! Now, a judicious selection from these with the least possible delay, and the burying of them, or otherwise getting of them out of harm's way, is within the power (without loss of precious time) of scarcely any one but myself, if any one. And shall I hang back, when Tellson's knows this and says this—Tellson's, whose bread I have eaten these sixty years—because I am a little stiff about the joints? Why, I am a boy, sir, to half a dozen old codgers here!"

"How I admire the gallantry of your youthful spirit, Mr. Lorry."

"Tut! Nonsense, sir—And, my dear Charles," said Mr. Lorry, glancing at the House again, "you are to remember, that getting things out of Paris at this present time, no matter what things, is next to an impossibility. Papers and precious matters were this very day brought to us here (I speak in strict confidence; it is not business-like to whisper it, even to you), by the strangest bearers you can imagine, every one of whom had his head hanging on by a single hair as he passed the Barriers. At another time, our parcels would come and go, as easily as in business-like Old England; but now, everything is stopped."

"And do you really go tonight?"

"I really go tonight, for the case has become too pressing to admit of delay."

"And do you take no one with you?"

"All sorts of people have been proposed to me, but I will have nothing to say to any of them. I intend to take Jerry. Jerry has been my body-guard on Sunday nights for a long time past, and I am used to him. Nobody will suspect Jerry of being anything but an English bull-dog, or of having any design in his head but to fly at anybody who touches his master."

"I must say again that I heartily admire your gallantry and youthfulness."

"I must say again, nonsense, nonsense! When I have executed this little commission, I shall, perhaps, accept Tellson's proposal to retire and live at my ease. Time enough, then, to think about growing old."

This dialogue had taken place at Mr. Lorry's usual desk, with Monseigneur swarming within a yard or two of it, boastful of what he would do to avenge himself on the rascal-people before long. It was too much the way of Monseigneur under his reverses as a refugee, and it was much too much the way of native British orthodoxy, to talk of this terrible Revolution as if it were the one only harvest ever known under the skies that had not been sown—as if nothing had ever been done, or omitted to be done, that had led to it—as if observers of the wretched millions in France, and of the misused and perverted resources that should have made them prosperous, had not seen it inevitably coming, years before, and had not in plain words recorded what they saw. Such vaporing, combined with the extravagant plots of Monseigneur for the restoration of a state of things that had utterly exhausted itself, and worn out Heaven and earth as well as itself, was hard to be endured without some remonstrance by any sane man who knew the truth. And it was such vaporing all about his ears, like a troublesome confusion of blood in his own head, added to a latent uneasiness in his mind, which had already made Charles Darnay restless, and which still kept him so.

Among the talkers, was Stryver, of the King's Bench Bar, far on his way to state promotion, and, therefore, loud on the theme: broaching to Monseigneur his devices for blowing the people up and exterminating them from the face of the earth and doing without them: and for accomplishing many similar objects akin in their nature to the abolition of eagles by sprinkling salt on the tails of the race. Him, Darnay heard with a particular feeling of objection; and Darnay stood divided between going away that he might hear no more, and remaining to interpose his word, when the thing that was to be went on to shape itself out.

The House approached Mr. Lorry, and laying a soiled and unopened letter before him, asked if he had yet discovered any traces of the person to whom it was addressed? The House laid the letter down so close to Darnay that he saw the direction—the more quickly because it was his own right name. The address, turned into English, ran: "Very pressing. To Monsieur heretofore the Marquis St. Evrémonde, of France, Confided to the cares of Messrs. Tellson and Co., Bankers, London, England."

On the marriage morning, Dr. Manette had made it his one urgent and express request to Charles Darnay, that the secret of this name should be—unless he, the Doctor, dissolved the obligation—kept inviolate between them. Nobody else knew it to be his name; his own wife had no suspicion of the fact; Mr. Lorry could have none.

"No," said Mr. Lorry, in reply to the House; "I have referred it, I think, to everybody now here, and no one can tell me where this gentleman is to be found."

The hands of the clock verging upon the hour of closing the Bank, there was a general set of the current of talkers past Mr. Lorry's desk. He held the letter out inquiringly; and Monseigneur looked at it, in the person of this plotting and indignant refugee; and This, That, and The Other, all had something disparaging to say, in French or in English, concerning the Marquis who was not to be found.

"Nephew, I believe—but in any case de-

generate successor—of the polished Marquis who was murdered," said one. "Happy to say, I never knew him."

"A craven who abandoned his post," said another—this Monseigneur had been got out of Paris, legs uppermost and half suffocated, in a load of hay—"some years ago."

"Infected with the new doctrines," said a third, eyeing the direction through his glass in passing; "set himself in opposition to the last Marquis, abandoned the estates when he inherited them, and left them to the ruffian herd. They will recompense him now, I hope, as he deserves."

"Hey?" cried the blatant Stryver. "Did he though? Is that the sort of fellow? Let us look at his infamous name. D—n the fellow!"

Darnay, unable to restrain himself any longer, touched Mr. Stryver on the shoulder, and said:

"I know the fellow."

"Do you, by Jupiter?" said Stryver. "I am sorry for it."

"Why?"

"Why, Mr. Darnay? D'ye hear what he did? Don't ask, why, in these times."

"But I do ask why."

"Then I tell you again, Mr. Darnay, I am sorry for it. I am sorry to hear you putting any such extraordinary questions. Here is a fellow, who, infected by the most pestilent and blasphemous code of devilry that ever was known, abandoned his property to the vilest scum of the earth that ever did murder by wholesale, and you ask me why I am sorry that a man who instructs youth knows him? Well, but I'll answer you. I am sorry because I believe there is contamination in such a scoundrel. That's why."

Mindful of the secret, Darnay with great difficulty checked himself, and said: "You may not understand the gentleman."

"I understand how to put *you* in a corner, Mr. Darnay," said Bully Stryver, "and I'll do it. If this fellow is a gentleman, I *don't* understand him. You may tell him so, with my compliments. You may also tell him, from me, that after abandoning his worldly goods and position to this butcherly mob, I wonder he is not at the head of them. But, no, gentlemen," said Stryver, looking all round, and snapping his fingers, "I know something of human nature, and I tell you that you'll never find a fellow like this fellow, trusting himself to the mercies of such precious *protégés*.[3] No, gentlemen; he'll always show 'em a clean pair of heels very early in the scuffle, and sneak away."

With those words, and a final snap of his fingers, Mr. Stryver shouldered himself into Fleet-street, amidst the general approbation of his hearers. Mr. Lorry and Charles Darnay were left alone at the desk, in the general departure from the Bank.

"Will you take charge of the letter?" said Mr. Lorry. "You know where to deliver it?"

"I do."

"Will you undertake to explain, that we suppose it to have been addressed here, on the chance of our knowing where to forward it, and that it has been here some time?"

"I will do so. Do you start for Paris from here?"

"From here, at eight."

"I will come back, to see you off."

Very ill at ease with himself, and with Stryver and most other men, Darnay made the best of his way into the quiet of the Temple, opened the letter, and read it. These were its contents:

"Prison of the Abbaye, Paris.
June 21, 1792.

"Monsieur heretofore the Marquis,

"After having long been in danger of my life at the hands of the village, I have been seized, with great violence and indignity, and brought a long journey on foot to Paris. On the road I have suffered a great deal. Nor is that all; my house has been destroyed—razed to the ground.

"The crime for which I am imprisoned, Monsieur heretofore the Marquis, and for which I shall be summoned before the tribunal, and shall lose my life (without your so generous help), is, they tell me, treason against the majesty of the people, in that I have acted against them for an emigrant. It is in vain I represent that I have acted for them, and not against, according to your commands. It is in vain I represent that, before the sequestration of emigrant property, I have remitted the imposts they had ceased to pay; that I had collected no rent; that I had had recourse to no process. The only response is, that I have acted for an emigrant, and where is that emigrant?

"Ah! most gracious Monsieur heretofore the Marquis, where is that emigrant? I cry in my sleep where is he? I demand of Heaven, will he not come to deliver me? No answer. Ah, Monsieur heretofore the Marquis, I send my desolate cry across the sea, hoping it may perhaps reach your ears through the great bank of Tilson[4] known at Paris!

"For the love of Heaven, of justice, of generosity, of the honor of your noble name, I supplicate you, Monsieur heretofore the Marquis, to succor and release me. My fault is, that I have been true to you. Oh Monsieur heretofore the Marquis, I pray you be you true to me!

"From this prison here of horror, whence I every hour tend nearer and nearer to destruction, I send you, Mon-

---

3. **protégé,** a person taken under the wing of a powerful protector or teacher.
4. **Tilson,** Gabelle's spelling of Tellson.

sieur heretofore the Marquis, the assurance of my dolorous and unhappy service.

"Your afflicted
"GABELLE."

The latent uneasiness in Darnay's mind was roused to vigorous life by this letter. The peril of an old servant and a good one, whose only crime was fidelity to himself and his family, stared him so reproachfully in the face, that, as he walked to and fro in the Temple considering what to do, he almost hid his face from the passers-by.

He knew very well, that in his horror of the deed which had culminated the bad deeds and bad reputation of the old family house, in his resentful suspicions of his uncle, and in the aversion with which his conscience regarded the crumbling fabric that he was supposed to uphold, he had acted imperfectly. He knew very well, that in his love for Lucie, his renunciation of his social place, though by no means new to his own mind, had been hurried and incomplete. He knew that he ought to have systematically worked it out and supervised it, and that he had meant to do it, and that it had never been done.

The happiness of his own chosen English home, the necessity of being always actively employed, the swift changes and troubles of the time which had followed on one another so fast, that the events of this week annihilated the immature plans of last week, and the events of the week following made all new again; he knew very well, that to the force of these circumstances he had yielded:—not without disquiet, but still without continuous and accumulating resistance. That he had watched the times for a time of action, and that they had shifted and struggled until the time had gone by, and the nobility were trooping from France by every highway and byway, and their property was in course of confiscation and destruction, and their very names were blotting out, was as well known to himself as it could be to any new authority in France that might impeach him for it.

But, he had oppressed no man, he had imprisoned no man; he was so far from having harshly exacted payment of his dues, that he had relinquished them of his own will, thrown himself on a world with no favor in it, won his own private place there, and earned his own bread. Monsieur Gabelle had held the impoverished and involved estate on written instructions, to spare the people, to give them what little there was to give—such fuel as the heavy creditors would let them have in the winter, and such produce as could be saved from the same grip in the summer—and no doubt he had put the fact in plea and proof, for his own safety, so that it could not but appear now.

This favored the desperate resolution Charles Darnay had begun to make, that he would go to Paris.

Yes. Like the mariner in the old story, the winds and streams had driven him within the influence of the Loadstone Rock,[5] and it was drawing him to itself, and he must go. Everything that arose before his mind drifted him on, faster and faster, more and more steadily, to the terrible attraction. His latent uneasiness had been, that bad aims were being worked out in his own unhappy land by bad instruments, and that he who could not fail to know that he was better than they, was not there, trying to do something to stay bloodshed, and assert the claims of mercy and humanity. With this uneasiness half stifled, and half reproaching him, he had been brought to the pointed comparison of himself with the brave old gentleman in whom duty was so strong; upon that comparison (injuri-

5. **Loadstone Rock,** in folklore, a rock which possessed a mysterious magnetic power, attracting ships to their doom.

ous to himself) had instantly followed the sneers of Monseigneur, which had stung him bitterly, and those of Stryver, which above all were coarse and galling, for old reasons. Upon those, had followed Gabelle's letter: the appeal of an innocent prisoner, in danger of death, to his justice, honor, and good name.

His resolution was made. He must go to Paris.

Yes. The Loadstone Rock was drawing him, and he must sail on, until he struck. He knew of no rock; he saw hardly any danger. The intention with which he had done what he had done, even although he had left it incomplete, presented it before him in an aspect that would be gratefully acknowledged in France on his presenting himself to assert it. Then, that glorious vision of doing good, which is so often the sanguine mirage of so many good minds, arose before him, and he even saw himself in the illusion with some influence to guide this raging Revolution that was running so fearfully wild.

As he walked to and fro with his resolution made, he considered that neither Lucie nor her father must know of it until he was gone. Lucie should be spared the pain of separation; and her father, always reluctant to turn his thoughts towards the dangerous ground of old, should come to the knowledge of the step, as a step taken, and not in the balance of suspense and doubt. How much of the incompleteness of his situation was referable to her father, through the painful anxiety to avoid reviving old associations of France in his mind, he did not discuss with himself. But, that circumstance too, had had its influence in his course.

He walked to and fro, with thoughts very busy, until it was time to return to Tellson's and take leave of Mr. Lorry. As soon as he arrived in Paris he would present himself to this old friend, but he must say nothing of his intention now.

A carriage with post-horses was ready at the Bank door, and Jerry was booted and equipped.

"I have delivered that letter," said Charles Darnay to Mr. Lorry. "I would not consent to your being charged with any written answer, but perhaps you will take a verbal one?"

"That I will, and readily," said Mr. Lorry, "if it is not dangerous."

"Not at all. Though it is to a prisoner in the Abbaye."

"What is his name?" said Mr. Lorry, with his open pocketbook in his hand.

"Gabelle."

"Gabelle. And what is the message to the unfortunate Gabelle in prison?"

"Simply, 'that he had received the letter, and will come.'"

"Any time mentioned?"

"He will start upon his journey tomorrow night."

"Any person mentioned?"

"No."

He helped Mr. Lorry to wrap himself in a number of coats and cloaks, and went out with him from the warm atmosphere of the old Bank into the misty air of Fleet-street. "My love to Lucie, and to little Lucie," said Mr. Lorry at parting, "and take precious care of them till I come back." Charles Darnay shook his head and doubtfully smiled, as the carriage rolled away.

That night—it was the fourteenth of August—he sat up late, and wrote two fervent letters; one was to Lucie, explaining the strong obligation he was under to go to Paris, and showing her, at length, the reasons that he had, for feeling confident that he could become involved in no personal danger there; the other was to the Doctor, confiding Lucie and their dear child to his care, and dwelling on the same topics with the strongest assurances. To both, he wrote that he would dispatch letters in proof of his safety, immediately after his arrival.

It was a hard day, that day of being among them, with the first reservation of their joint lives on his mind. It was a hard matter to preserve the innocent deceit of which they were profoundly unsuspicious. But, an affectionate glance at his wife, so happy and busy, made him resolute not to tell her what impended (he had been half moved to do it, so strange it was to him to act in anything without her quiet aid), and the day passed quickly away. Early in the evening he embraced her, and her scarcely less dear namesake, pretending that he would return by-and-by (an imaginary engagement took him out, and he had secreted a valise of clothes ready), and so he emerged into the heavy mist of the heavy streets, with a heavier heart.

The unseen force was drawing him fast to itself, now, and all the tides and winds were setting straight and strong towards it. He left his two letters with a trusty porter, to be delivered half an hour before midnight, and no sooner; took horse for Dover; and began his journey. "For the love of Heaven, of justice, of generosity, of the honor of your noble name!" was the poor prisoner's cry with which he strengthened his sinking heart, as he left all that was dear on earth behind him, and floated away for the Loadstone Rock.

READING FOR DETAILS

Decisions

1. How much time passes between the end of Chapter 6 and the beginning of Chapter 7?
2. What is Charles Darnay's new occupation in England?
3. What are the "two promises" referred to in the title of Chapter 7?
4. What is Sydney Carton's request of Lucie?
5. How does Madame Defarge register those who will be executed in the Revolution?
6. Who is John Barsad? What information does he give the Defarges? How do the Defarges react?
7. On the night before her marriage, what does Lucie tell Dr. Manette?
8. After the wedding, what two things does Sydney Carton ask of Charles?
9. What great event began in July of 1789?
10. Why does Jarvis Lorry undertake another trip to France in Chapter 12?
11. Who is Gabelle? Why is the letter that he writes so important to the plot?
12. Why does Charles Darnay decide to travel to France?

READING FOR MEANING

1. The relatively minor character of Gaspard underlines the cruelty of the French aristocracy and the violent reactions of the French people. Discuss.
2. In Part Two of *A Tale of Two Cities*, we become more knowledgeable about the relationships of the principal characters. Discuss the relationships of the following:
   a. Dr. Manette and Charles Darnay
   b. Dr. Manette and his daughter Lucie
   c. Sydney Carton and Lucie Manette
   d. Monsieur and Madame Defarge

READING FOR APPRECIATION

Irony is the device in writing in which there is a reversal of meaning, or a telling difference between what is said on the surface and what is actually meant. Irony can be humorous, or it can convey a serious, even threatening, tone. Consider the following phrases and passages from Part Two of *A Tale of Two Cities*, and identify what is ironic about them:

1. the title of Chapter 8, "The Fellow of No Delicacy"
2. the conversation between the Defarges and John Barsad in Chapter 9
3. the portrait of "Monseigneur" in Chapter 12

Part Three

Ernest Defarge assigns Charles Darnay to the prison of La Force.

Once inside France, Charles is arrested as an emigrant aristocrat and an enemy of the people. He is sent to Paris under escort. At the gates of the capital, he is handed over to Ernest Defarge, now an official of the Revolutionary government. Charles is assigned to solitary confinement in the prison of La Force, with Defarge stubbornly refusing to aid him.

Chapter 13
The Grindstone

Tellson's bank, established in the Saint Germain Quarter of Paris, was in a wing of a large house, approached by a court-yard and shut off from the street by a high wall and a strong gate. The house belonged to a great nobleman who had lived in it until he made a flight from the troubles, in his own cook's dress, and got across the borders.

What money would be drawn out of Tellson's henceforth, and what would lie there, lost and forgotten; what plate[1] and jewels would tarnish in Tellson's hiding-places, while the depositors rusted in prisons, and when they should have violently perished; how many accounts with Tellson's never to be balanced in this world, must be carried over into the next; no man could have

---

1. **plate,** silver tableware.

said, that night, any more than Mr. Jarvis Lorry could, though he thought heavily of these questions. He sat by a newly-lighted wood fire (the blighted and unfruitful year was prematurely cold), and on his honest and courageous face there was a deeper shade than the pendent lamp could throw, or any object in the room distortedly reflect—a shade of horror.

He occupied rooms in the Bank, in his fidelity to the House of which he had grown to be a part, like a strong root-ivy. It chanced that they derived a kind of security from the patriotic occupation of the main building, but the true-hearted old gentleman never calculated about that. All such circumstances were indifferent to him, so that he did his duty. On the opposite side of the court-yard, under a colonnade, was extensive standing for carriages—where, indeed, some carriages of Monseigneur yet stood. Against two of the pillars were fastened two great flaring flambeaux,[2] and in the light of these, standing out in the open air, was a large grindstone: a roughly mounted thing which appeared to have hurriedly been brought there from some neighboring smithy, or other workshop. Rising and looking out of window at these harmless objects, Mr. Lorry shivered, and retired to his seat by the fire. He had opened, not only the glass window, but the lattice blind outside it, and he had closed both again, and he shivered through his frame.

From the streets beyond the high wall and the strong gate, there came the usual night hum of the city, with now and then an indescribable ring in it, weird and unearthly, as if some unwonted sounds of a terrible nature were going up to Heaven.

"Thank God," said Mr. Lorry, clasping his hands, "that no one near and dear to me is in this dreadful town tonight. May He have mercy on all who are in danger!"

Soon afterwards, the bell at the great gate sounded, and he thought, "They have come back!" and sat listening. But, there was no loud eruption into the court-yard, as he had expected, and he heard the gate clash again, and all was quiet.

The nervousness and dread that were upon him inspired that vague uneasiness respecting the Bank, which a great change would naturally awaken, with such feelings roused. It was well guarded, and he got up to go among the trusty people who were watching it, when his door suddenly opened, and two figures rushed in, at sight of which he fell back in amazement.

Lucie and her father! Lucie with her arms stretched out to him, and with that old look of earnestness so concentrated and intensified, that it seemed as though it had been stamped upon her face expressly to give force and power to it in this one passage of her life.

"What is this?" cried Mr. Lorry, breathless and confused. "What is the matter? Lucie! Manette! What has happened? What has brought you here? What is it?"

With the look fixed upon him, in her paleness and wildness, she panted out in his arms, imploringly, "O my dear friend! My husband!"

"Your husband, Lucie?"

"Charles."

"What of Charles?"

"Here."

"Here, in Paris?"

"Has been here some days—three or four—I don't know how many—I can't collect my thoughts. An errand of generosity brought him here unknown to us; he was stopped at the barrier, and sent to prison."

The old man uttered an irrepressible cry. Almost at the same moment, the bell of the great gate rang again, and a loud noise of feet and voices came pouring into the court-yard.

"What is that noise?" said the Doctor, turning towards the window.

2. **flambeaux** (flam′bōz), ornamental candlesticks.

"Don't look!" cried Mr. Lorry. "Don't look out! Manette, for your life, don't touch the blind!"

The Doctor turned, with his hand upon the fastening of the window, and said, with a cool bold smile:

"My dear friend, I have a charmed life in this city. I have been a Bastille prisoner. There is no patriot in Paris—in Paris? In France—who, knowing me to have been a prisoner in the Bastille, would touch me, except to overwhelm me with embraces, or carry me in triumph. My old pain has given me a power that has brought us through the barrier, and gained us news of Charles there, and brought us here. I knew it would be so; I knew I could help Charles out of all danger; I told Lucie so.—What is that noise?" His hand was again upon the window.

"Don't look!" cried Mr. Lorry, absolutely desperate. "No, Lucie, my dear, nor you!" He got his arm round her, and held her. "Don't be so terrified, my love. I solemnly swear to you that I know of no harm having happened to Charles; that I had no suspicion even of his being in this fatal place. What prison is he in?"

"La Force!"

"La Force! Lucie, my child, if ever you were brave and serviceable in your life—and you were always both—you will compose yourself now, to do exactly as I bid you; for more depends upon it than you can think, or I can say. There is no help for you in any action on your part tonight; you cannot possibly stir out. I say this, because what I must bid you to do for Charles's sake, is the hardest thing to do of all. You must instantly be obedient, still, and quiet. You must let me put you in a room at the back here. You must leave your father and me alone for two minutes, and as there are Life and Death in the world you must not delay."

"I will be submissive to you. I see in your face that you know I can do nothing else than this. I know you are true."

The old man kissed her, and hurried her into his room, and turned the key; then, came hurrying back to the Doctor, and opened the window and partly opened the blind, and put his hand upon the Doctor's arm, and looked out with him into the court-yard.

Looked out upon a throng of men and women: not enough in number, or near enough, to fill the court-yard: not more than forty or fifty in all. The people in possession of the house had let them in at the gate, and they had rushed in to work at the grindstone; it had evidently been set up there for their purpose, as in a convenient and retired spot.

But, such awful workers, and such awful work!

The grindstone had a double handle, and, turning at it madly were two men, whose faces, as their long hair flapped back when the whirlings of the grindstone brought their faces up, were more horrible and cruel than the visages of the wildest savages in their most barbarous disguise. False eyebrows and false moustaches were stuck upon them, and their hideous countenances were all bloody and sweaty, and all awry with howling, and all staring and glaring with beastly excitement and want of sleep. As these ruffians turned and turned, their matted locks now flung forward over their eyes, now flung backward over their necks, some women held wine to their mouths that they might drink; and what with dropping blood, and what with dropping wine, and what with the stream of sparks struck out of the stone, all their wicked atmosphere seemed gore and fire. The eye could not detect one creature in the group free from the smear of blood. Shouldering one another to get next at the sharpening-stone, were men stripped to the waist, with the stain all over their limbs and bodies; men in all sorts of rags, with the stain upon those rags; men devilishly set off with spoils of women's lace and silk and ribbon, with the stain dyeing those trifles through and through. Hatchets, knives, bayonets, swords,

The streets of Paris, wild with Revolution.

all brought to be sharpened, were all red with it. Some of the hacked swords were tied to the wrists of those who carried them, with strips of linen and fragments of dress: ligatures various in kind, but all deep of the one colour. And as the frantic wielders of these weapons snatched them from the stream of sparks and tore away into the streets, the same red hue was red in their frenzied eyes;—eyes which any unbrutalized beholder would have given twenty years of life, to petrify with a well-directed gun.

All this was seen in a moment, as the vision of a drowning man, or of any human creature at any very great pass, could see a world if it were there. They drew back from

the window, and the Doctor looked for explanation in his friend's ashy face.

"They are," Mr. Lorry whispered the words, glancing fearfully round at the locked room, "murdering the prisoners. If you are sure of what you say; if you really have the power you think you have—as I believe you have—make yourself known to these devils, and get taken to La Force. It may be too late, I don't know, but let it not be a minute later!"

Doctor Manette pressed his hand, hastened bareheaded out of the room, and was in the court-yard when Mr. Lorry regained the blind.

His streaming white hair, his remarkable face, and the impetuous confidence of his manner, as he put the weapons aside like water, carried him in an instant to the heart of the concourse at the stone. For a few moments there was a pause, and a hurry, and a murmur, and the unintelligible sound of his voice; and then Mr. Lorry saw him, surrounded by all, and in the midst of a line of twenty men long, all linked shoulder to shoulder, and hand to shoulder, hurried out with cries of—"Live the Bastille prisoner! Help for the Bastille prisoner's kindred in La Force! Room for the Bastille prisoner in front there! Save the prisoner Evrémonde at La Force!" and a thousand answering shouts.

He closed the lattice again with a fluttering heart, closed the window and the curtain, hastened to Lucie, and told her that her father was assisted by the people, and gone in search of her husband. He found her child and Miss Pross with her; but, it never occurred to him to be surprised by their appearance until a long time afterwards, when he sat watching them in such quiet as the night knew.

Lucie had, by that time, fallen into a stupor on the floor at his feet, clinging to his hand. Miss Pross had laid the child down on his own bed, and her head had gradually fallen on the pillow beside her pretty charge. O the long, long night, with the moans of the poor wife! And O the long, long night, with no return of her father and no tidings!

Twice more in the darkness the bell at the great gate sounded, and the eruption was repeated, and the grindstone whirled and spluttered. "What is it?" cried Lucie, affrighted. "Hush! The soldiers' swords are sharpened there," said Mr. Lorry. "The place is national property now, and used as a kind of armory, my love."

The great grindstone, Earth, had turned when Mr. Lorry looked out again, and the sun was red on the court-yard. But, the lesser grindstone stood alone there in the calm morning air, with a red upon it that the sun had never given, and would never take away.

Jarvis Lorry arranges to remove Lucie, her child, and Miss Pross to separate lodgings. Defarge arrives as a messenger from Dr. Manette. He brings a note from Charles, assuring Lucie that he is well. But Madame Defarge's menacing hostility causes Lucie to shudder in fear.

Fifteen months pass. Dr. Manette manages to protect Charles from harm in prison, and arranges for Lucie to walk to a certain street corner every afternoon, so that Charles can see her and their child from the prison window.

In December, 1793, Charles is finally summoned before the prison tribunal. Gabelle and Dr. Manette support his case, and the court acquits him of the charge of crimes against the people. But shortly afterwards, officers re-arrest him, explaining that he has been denounced by the Defarges. Charles is returned to prison, despite the protests of Dr. Manette.

Meanwhile, Sydney Carton arrives in Paris. He recognizes Miss Pross's long-lost brother Solomon as the disreputable spy John Barsad, now an agent for the Revolutionary government. As if playing at a game of cards (compare the title of the next chapter), Carton threatens Barsad with exposure and denunciation if he fails to cooperate with a plan to gain access to the prison where Charles is held. Barsad is forced to agree.

Chapter 14
The Game Made

Sydney Carton and the spy returned from the dark room. "Adieu,[1] Mr. Barsad," said the former; "our arrangement thus made, you have nothing to fear from me."

---

1. **adieu** (ə dü'), French for "goodbye." Since *adieu* literally means "to God," it differs from *au revoir*, which means "till we meet again."

He sat down in a chair on the hearth, over against Mr. Lorry. When they were alone, Mr. Lorry asked him what he had done?

"Not much. If it should go ill with the prisoner, I have ensured access to him, once."

Mr. Lorry's countenance fell.

"It is all I could do," said Carton. "To propose too much, would be to put this man's head under the axe, and, as he himself said, nothing worse could happen to him if he were denounced. It was obviously the weakness of the position. There is no help for it."

"But access to him," said Mr. Lorry, "if it should go ill before the Tribunal, will not save him."

"I never said it would."

Mr. Lorry's eyes gradually sought the fire; his sympathy with his darling, and the heavy disappointment of this second arrest, gradually weakened them; he was an old man now, overborne with anxiety of late, and his tears fell.

"You are a good man and a true friend," said Carton, in an altered voice. "Forgive me if I notice that you are affected. I could not see my father weep, and sit by, careless. And I could not respect your sorrow more, if you were my father. You are free from that misfortune, however."

Though he said the last words, with a slip into his usual manner, there was a true feeling and respect both in his tone and in his touch, that Mr. Lorry, who had never seen the better side of him, was wholly unprepared for. He gave him his hand, and Carton gently pressed it.

"To return to poor Darnay," said Carton. "Don't tell Her of this interview, or this arrangement. It would not enable Her to go to see him. She might think it was contrived, in case of the worst, to convey to him the means of anticipating the sentence."

Mr. Lorry had not thought of that, and he looked quickly at Carton to see if it were in

his mind. It seemed to be; he returned the look, and evidently understood it.

"She might think a thousand things," Carton said, "and any of them would only add to her trouble. Don't speak of me to her. As I said to you when I first came, I had better not see her. I can put my hand out, to do any little helpful work for her that my hand can find to do, without that. You are going to her, I hope? She must be very desolate tonight."

"I am going now, directly."

"I am glad of that. She has such a strong attachment to you and reliance on you. How does she look?"

"Anxious and unhappy, but very beautiful."

"Ah!"

It was a long, grieving sound, like a sigh—almost like a sob. It attracted Mr. Lorry's eyes to Carton's face, which was turned to the fire. A light, or a shade (the old gentleman could not have said which), passed from it as swiftly as a change will sweep over a hill-side on a wild bright day, and he lifted his foot to put back one of the little flaming logs, which was tumbling forward. He wore the white riding-coat and top-boots, then in vogue, and the light of the fire touching their light surfaces made him look very pale, with his long brown hair, all untrimmed, hanging loose about him. His indifference to fire was sufficiently remarkable to elicit a word of remonstrance of Mr. Lorry; his boot was still upon the hot embers of the flaming log, when it had broken under the weight of his foot.

"I forgot it," he said.

Mr. Lorry's eyes were again attracted to his face. Taking note of the wasted air which clouded the naturally handsome features, and having the expression of prisoners' faces fresh in his mind, he was strongly reminded of that expression.

"And your duties here have drawn to an end, sir?" said Carton, turning to him.

"Yes. As I was telling you last night when

Lucie came in so unexpectedly, I have at length done all that I can do here. I hoped to have left them in perfect safety, and then to have quitted Paris. I have my Leave to Pass. I was ready to go."

They were both silent.

"Yours is a long life to look back upon, sir?" said Carton, wistfully.

"I am in my seventy-eighth year."

"You have been useful all your life; steadily and constantly occupied; trusted, respected, and looked up to?"

"I have been a man of business, ever since I have been a man. Indeed, I may say that I was a man of business when a boy."

"See what a place you fill at seventy-eight. How many people will miss you when you leave it empty!"

"A solitary old bachelor," answered Mr. Lorry, shaking his head. "There is nobody to weep for me."

"How can you say that? Wouldn't She weep for you? Wouldn't her child?"

"Yes, yes, thank God. I didn't quite mean what I said."

"It *is* a thing to thank God for; is it not?"

"Surely, surely."

"If you could say, with truth, to your own solitary heart, to-night, 'I have secured to myself the love and attachment, the gratitude or respect, of no human creature; I have won myself a tender place in no regard; I have done nothing good or serviceable to be remembered by!' your seventy-eight years would be seventy-eight heavy curses; would they not?"

"You say truly, Mr. Carton; I think they would be."

Sydney turned his eyes again upon the fire, and, after a silence of a few moments, said:

"I should like to ask you:—Does your childhood seem far off? Do the days when you sat at your mother's knee, seem days of very long ago?"

Responding to his softened manner, Mr. Lorry answered:

"Twenty years back, yes; at this time of my life, no. For, as I draw closer and closer to the end, I travel in the circle, nearer and nearer to the beginning. It seems to be one of the kind smoothings and preparings of the way. My heart is touched now, by many remembrances that had long fallen asleep, of my pretty young mother (and I so old!), and by many associations of the days when what we call the World was not so real with me, and my faults were not confirmed in me."

"I understand the feeling!" exclaimed Carton, with a bright flush. "And you are the better for it?"

"I hope so."

Carton terminated the conversation here, by rising to help him on with his outer coat; "but you," said Mr. Lorry, reverting to the theme, "you are young."

"Yes," said Carton. "I am not old, but my young way was never the way to age. Enough of me."

"And of me, I am sure," said Mr. Lorry. "Are you going out?"

"I'll walk with you to her gate. You know my vagabond and restless habits. If I should prowl about the streets a long time, don't be uneasy; I shall reappear in the morning. You go to the Court tomorrow?"

"Yes, unhappily."

"I shall be there, but only as one of the crowd. My Spy[2] will find a place for me. Take my arm, sir."

Mr. Lorry did so, and they went downstairs and out in the streets. A few minutes brought them to Mr. Lorry's destination. Carton left him there; but lingered at a little distance, and turned back to the gate again when it was shut, and touched it. He had heard of her going to the prison every day. "She came out here," he said, looking about

---

2. **My Spy,** John Barsad.

him, "turned this way, must have trod on these stones often. Let me follow in her steps."

It was ten o'clock at night when he stood before the prison of La Force, where she had stood hundreds of times. A little wood-sawyer, having closed his shop, was smoking his pipe at his shop-door.

"Good night, citizen," said Sydney Carton, pausing in going by; for, the man eyed him inquisitively.

"Good night, citizen."

"How goes the Republic?"

"You mean the Guillotine. Not ill. Sixty-three today. We shall mount to a hundred soon. Samson[3] and his men complain sometimes, of being exhausted. Ha, ha, ha! He is so droll, that Samson. Such a Barber!"

"Do you often go to see him—"

"Shave? Always. Every day. What a barber! You have seen him at work?"

"Never."

"Go and see him when he has a good batch. Figure this to yourself, citizen; he shaved the sixty-three today, in less than two pipes! Less than two pipes. Word of honor!"

As the grinning little man held out the pipe he was smoking, to explain how he timed the executioner, Carton was so sensible of a rising desire to strike the life out of him, that he turned away.

"But you are not English," said the wood-sawyer, "though you wear English dress?"

"Yes," said Carton, pausing again, and answering over his shoulder.

"You speak like a Frenchman."

"I am an old student here."

"Aha, a perfect Frenchman! Good night, Englishman."

"Good night, citizen."

"But go and see that droll dog," the little man persisted, calling after him. "And take a pipe with you!"

Sydney had not gone far out of sight, when he stopped in the middle of the street under a glimmering lamp, and wrote with his pencil on a scrap of paper. Then, traversing with the decided step of one who remembered the way well, several dark and dirty streets—much dirtier than usual, for the best public thoroughfares remained uncleansed in those times of terror—he stopped at a chemist's shop, which the owner was closing with his own hands. A small, dim, crooked shop, kept in a tortuous, up-hill thoroughfare, by a small, dim, crooked man.

Giving this citizen, too, good night, as he confronted him at his counter, he laid the scrap of paper before him. "Whew!" the chemist whistled softly, as he read it. "Hi! hi! hi!"

Sydney Carton took no heed, and the chemist said:

"For you, citizen?"

"For me."

"You will be careful to keep them separate, citizen? You know the consequences of mixing them?"

"Perfectly."

Certain small packets were made and given to him. He put them, one by one, in the breast of his inner coat, counted out the money for them, and deliberately left the shop. "There is nothing more to do," said he, glancing upward at the moon, "until tomorrow. I can't sleep."

It was not a reckless manner, the manner in which he said these words aloud under the fast-sailing clouds, nor was it more expressive of negligence than defiance. It was the settled manner of a tired man, who had wandered and struggled and got lost, but who at length struck into his road and saw its end.

Long ago, when he had been famous among his earliest competitors as a youth of great promise, he had followed his father to the grave. His mother had died, years before.

---

3. **Samson,** the executioner.

These solemn words, which had been read at his father's grave, arose in his mind as he went down the dark streets, among the heavy shadows, with the moon and the clouds sailing on high above him. "I am the resurrection and the life, saith the Lord: he that believeth in me, though he were dead, yet shall he live: and whosoever liveth and believeth in me, shall never die."[4]

In a city dominated by the axe, alone at night, with natural sorrow rising in him for the sixty-three who had been that day put to death, and for tomorrow's victims then awaiting their doom in the prisons, and still of tomorrow's and tomorrow's, the chain of association that brought the words home, like a rusty old ship's anchor from the deep, might have been easily found. He did not seek it, but repeated them and went on.

With a solemn interest in the lighted windows where the people were going to rest, forgetful through a few calm hours of the horrors surrounding them; in the towers of the churches, where no prayers were said, for the popular revulsion had even travelled that length of self-destruction from years of priestly impostors, plunderers, and profligates; in the distant burial-places, reserved, as they wrote upon the gates, for Eternal Sleep; in the abounding gaols; and in the streets along which the sixties rolled to a death which had become so common and material, that no sorrowful story of a haunting Spirit ever arose among the people out of all the working of the Guillotine; with a solemn interest in the whole life and death of the city settling down to its short nightly pause in fury; Sydney Carton crossed the Seine again for the lighter streets.

Few coaches were abroad, for riders in coaches were liable to be suspected, and gentility hid its head in red nightcaps, and put on heavy shoes, and trudged. But, the theaters were all well filled, and the people poured cheerfully out as he passed, and went chatting home. At one of the theater doors, there was a little girl with a mother, looking for a way across the street through the mud. He carried the child over, and before the timid arm was loosed from his neck asked her for a kiss.

"I am the resurrection and the life, saith the Lord: he that believeth in me, though he were dead, yet shall he live: and whosoever liveth and believeth in me, shall never die."

Now, that the streets were quiet, and the night wore on, the words were in the echoes of his feet, and were in the air. Perfectly calm and steady, he sometimes repeated them to himself as he walked; but, he heard them always.

The night wore out, and, as he stood upon the bridge listening to the water as it splashed the river-walls of the Island of Paris, where the picturesque confusion of houses and cathedral[5] shone bright in the light of the moon, the day came coldly, looking like a dead face out of the sky. Then, the night, with the moon and the stars, turned pale and died, and for a little while it seemed as if Creation were delivered over to Death's dominion.

But, the glorious sun, rising, seemed to strike those words, that burden of the night, straight and warm to his heart in its long bright rays. And looking along them, with reverently shaded eyes, a bridge of light appeared to span the air between him and the sun, while the river sparkled under it.

The strong tide, so swift, so deep, and certain, was like a congenial friend, in the morning stillness. He walked by the stream, far from the houses, and in the light and warmth of the sun fell asleep on the bank. When he awoke and was afoot again, he lingered there yet a little longer, watching an

---

4. **"I am the resurrection . . . shall never die,"** from the New Testament, John 11:25–26.
5. **cathedral,** the cathedral of Notre Dame.

Revolution before the cathedral of Notre Dame.
"I am the resurrection and the life, saith the Lord."

eddy that turned and turned purposeless, until the stream absorbed it, and carried it on to the sea.—"Like me!"

A trading-boat, with a sail of the softened color of a dead leaf, then glided into his view, floated by him, and died away. As its silent track in the water disappeared, the prayer that had broken up out of his heart for a merciful consideration of all his poor blindnesses and errors, ended in the words, "I am the resurrection and the life."

Charles is brought before the tribunal again. Defarge testifies that the diary of Dr. Manette, which was found in the Bastille, will furnish sufficient evidence to convict the prisoner. The diary is read to the court. Written years before by Dr. Manette, it concerns events of the year 1757. At last we learn the mysterious connection between Dr. Manette and Charles's family. It was Charles's father and uncle who condemned Manette to prison, because he dared to protest their brutal treatment of a poor peasant family. At the end of his diary, Dr. Manette cursed the Saint Evrémondes and all their descendants. With a roar from the crowd, the court sentences Charles to the guillotine. He must die the following day.

Charles embraces Lucie and is returned to his cell. Lucie faints from the shock, and Dr. Manette rushes off, declaring that he will make a last-minute plea to the authorities for Charles's life. Sydney Carton—although he seems to agree gloomily with Jarvis Lorry that there is no hope—arranges to meet Lorry later that evening. In the wine-shop, Carton overhears Madame Defarge swear eternal vengeance against the Evrémondes: it turns out that she is the surviving sister of one of the old Marquis's victims. In a hurried conversation with Lorry, Carton explains that Lucie and the child are in grave danger. He

concludes the final arrangements for their escape from Paris. Carton walks to the courtyard of the house where Lucie is staying, and looks at her lighted window as he bids her a silent farewell.

Chapter 15
Fifty-two

In the black prison of the Conciergerie,[1] the doomed of the day awaited their fate. They were in number as the weeks of the year. Fifty-two were to roll that afternoon on the life-tide of the city to the boundless everlasting sea. Before their cells were quit of them, new occupants were appointed; before their blood ran into the blood spilled yesterday, the blood that was to mingle with theirs tomorrow was already set apart.

Two score and twelve were told off. From the farmer-general of seventy, whose riches could not buy his life, to the seamstress of twenty, whose poverty and obscurity could not save her. Physical diseases, engendered in the vices and neglects of men, will seize on victims of all degrees; and the frightful moral disorder, born of unspeakable suffering, intolerable oppression, and heartless indifference, smote equally without distinction.

Charles Darnay, alone in a cell, had sustained himself with no flattering delusion since he came to it from the Tribunal. In every line of the narrative he had heard, he had heard his condemnation. He had fully comprehended that no personal influence could possibly save him, that he was virtually sentenced by the millions, and that units could avail him nothing.

Nevertheless, it was not easy, with the face of his beloved wife fresh before him, to

---

1. **Conciergerie,** literally a porter's lodge, this was the building where the condemned awaited execution.

compose his mind to what it must bear. His hold on life was strong, and it was very, very hard to loosen; by gradual efforts and degrees unclosed a little here, it clenched the tighter there; and when he brought his strength to bear on that hand and it yielded, this was closed again. There was a hurry, too, in all his thoughts, a turbulent and heated working of his heart, that contended against resignation. If, for a moment, he did feel resigned, then his wife and child who had to live after him, seemed to protest and to make it a selfish thing.

But, all this was at first. Before long, the consideration that there was no disgrace in the fate he must meet, and that numbers went the same road wrongfully, and trod it firmly every day, sprang up to stimulate him. Next followed the thought that much of the future peace of mind enjoyable by the dear ones, depended on his quiet fortitude. So, by degrees he calmed into the better state, when he could raise his thoughts much higher, and draw comfort down.

Before it had set in dark on the night of his condemnation, he had travelled thus far on his last way. Being allowed to purchase the means of writing, and a light, he sat down to write until such time as the prison lamps should be extinguished.

He wrote a long letter to Lucie, showing her that he had known nothing of her father's imprisonment, until he had heard of it from herself, and that he had been as ignorant as she of his father's and uncle's responsibility for that misery, until the paper had been read. He had already explained to her that his concealment from herself of the name he had relinquished, was the one condition—fully intelligible now—that her father had attached to their betrothal, and was the one promise he had still exacted on the morning of their marriage. He entreated her, for her father's sake, never to seek to know whether her father had become oblivious of

the existence of the paper, or had had it recalled to him (for the moment, or for good), by the story of the Tower, on that old Sunday under the dear old plane-tree in the garden. If he had preserved any definite remembrance of it, there could be no doubt that he had supposed it destroyed with the Bastille, when he had found no mention of it among the relics of prisoners which the populace had discovered there, and which had been described to all the world. He besought her—though he added that he knew it was needless—to console her father, by impressing him through every tender means she could think of, with the truth that he had done nothing for which he could justly reproach himself, but had uniformly forgotten himself for their joint sakes. Next to her preservation of his own last grateful love and blessing, and her overcoming of her sorrow, to devote herself to their dear child, he adjured her, as they would meet in Heaven, to comfort her father.

To her father himself, he wrote in the same strain; but, he told her father that he expressly confided his wife and child to his care. And he told him this, very strongly, with the hope of rousing him from any despondency or dangerous retrospect towards which he foresaw he might be tending.

To Mr. Lorry, he commended them all, and explained his worldly affairs. That done, with many added sentences of grateful friendship and warm attachment, all was done. He never thought of Carton. His mind was so full of the others, that he never once thought of him.

He had time to finish these letters before the lights were put out. When he lay down on his straw bed, he thought he had done with this world.

But, it beckoned him back in his sleep, and showed itself in shining forms. Free and happy, back in the old house in Soho (though it had nothing in it like the real house), unaccountably released and light of heart, he was with Lucie again, and she told him it was all a dream, and he had never gone away. A pause of forgetfulness, and then he had even suffered, and had come back to her, dead and at peace, and yet there was no difference in him. Another pause of oblivion, and he awoke in the somber morning, unconscious where he was or what had happened, until it flashed upon his mind, "This is the day of my death!"

Thus, had he come through the hours, to the day when the fifty-two heads were to fall. And now, while he was composed, and hoped that he could meet the end with quiet heroism, a new action began in his waking thoughts, which was very difficult to master.

He had never seen the instrument that was to terminate his life. How high it was from the ground, how many steps it had, where he would be stood, how he would be touched, whether the touching hands would be dyed red, which way his face would be turned, whether he would be the first, or might be the last: these and many similar questions, in no wise directed by his will, obtruded themselves over and over again, countless times. Neither were they connected with fear: he was conscious of no fear. Rather, they originated in a strange besetting desire to know what to do when the time came; a desire gigantically disproportionate to the few swift moments to which it referred; a wondering that was more like the wondering of some other spirit within his, than his own.

The hours went on as he walked to and fro, and the clocks struck the numbers he would never hear again. Nine gone for ever, ten gone for ever, eleven gone for ever, twelve coming on to pass away. After a hard contest with that eccentric action of thought which had last perplexed him, he had got the better of it. He walked up and down, softly repeating their names to himself. The worst

of the strife was over. He could walk up and down, free from distracting fancies, praying for himself and for them.

Twelve gone for ever.

He had been apprised that the final hour was Three, and he knew he would be summoned some time earlier, inasmuch as the tumbrils[2] jolted heavily and slowly through the streets. Therefore, he resolved to keep Two before his mind, as the hour, and so to strengthen himself in the interval that he might be able, after that time, to strengthen others.

Walking regularly to and fro with his arms folded on his breast, a very different man from the prisoner, who had walked to and fro at La Force, he heard One struck away from him, without surprise. The hour had measured like most other hours. Devoutly thankful to Heaven for his recovered self-possession, he thought, "There is but another now," and turned to walk again.

Footsteps in the stone passage outside the door. He stopped.

The key was put in the lock, and turned. Before the door was opened, or as it opened, a man said in a low voice, in English: "He has never seen me here; I have kept out of his way. Go you in alone; I wait near. Lose no time!"

The door was quickly opened and closed, and there stood before him face to face, quiet, intent upon him, with the light of a smile on his features, and a cautionary finger on his lip, Sydney Carton.

There was something so bright and remarkable in his look, that, for the first moment, the prisoner misdoubted him to be an apparition of his own imagining. But, he spoke, and it was his voice; he took the prisoner's hand, and it was his real grasp.

---

2. **tumbrils,** the wagons which carried the condemned to the guillotine.

"Of all the people upon earth, you least expected to see me?" he said.

"I could not believe it to be you. I can scarcely believe it now. You are not"—the apprehension came suddenly into his mind—"a prisoner?"

"No. I am accidentally possessed of a power over one of the keepers here, and in virtue of it I stand before you. I come from her—your wife, dear Darnay."

The prisoner wrung his hand.

"I bring you a request from her."

"What is it?"

"A most earnest, pressing, and emphatic entreaty, addressed to you in the most pathetic tones of the voice so dear to you, that you well remember."

The prisoner turned his face partly aside.

"You have no time to ask me why I bring it, or what it means; I have no time to tell you. You must comply with it—take off those boots you wear, and draw on these of mine."

There was a chair against the wall of the cell, behind the prisoner. Carton, pressing forward, had already, with the speed of lightning, got him down into it, and stood over him, barefoot.

"Draw on these boots of mine. Put your hands to them; put your will to them. Quick!"

"Carton, there is no escaping from this place; it never can be done. You will only die with me. It is madness."

"It would be madness if I asked you to escape; but do I? When I ask you to pass out at that door, tell me it is madness and remain here. Change that cravat[3] for this of mine, that coat for this of mine. While you do it, let me take this ribbon from your hair, and shake out your hair like this of mine!"

With wonderful quickness, and with a strength both of will and action, that appeared quite supernatural, he forced all these changes upon him. The prisoner was like a young child in his hands.

"Carton! Dear Carton! It is madness. It

cannot be accomplished, it never can be done, it has been attempted, and has always failed. I implore you not to add your death to the bitterness of mine."

"Do I ask you, my dear Darnay, to pass the door? When I ask that, refuse. There are pen and ink and paper on this table. Is your hand steady enough to write?"

"It was when you came in."

"Steady it again, and write what I shall dictate. Quick, friend, quick!"

Pressing his hand to his bewildered head, Darnay sat down at the table. Carton, with his right hand in his breast, stood close beside him.

"Write exactly as I speak."

"To whom do I address it?"

"To no one." Carton still had his hand in his breast.

"Do I date it?"

"No."

The prisoner looked up, at each question. Carton, standing over him with his hand in his breast, looked down.

"'If you remember,'" said Carton, dictating, "'the words that passed between us, long ago, you will readily comprehend this when you see it. You do remember them, I know. It is not in your nature to forget them.'"

He was drawing his hand from his breast; the prisoner chancing to look up in his hurried wonder as he wrote, the hand stopped, closing upon something.

"Have you written 'forget them'!" Carton asked.

"I have. Is that a weapon in your hand?"

"No; I am not armed."

"What is it in your hand?"

"You shall know directly. Write on; there are but a few words more." He dictated again. "'I am thankful that the time has come, when I can prove them. That I do so is not subject

---

3. **cravat,** scarf worn knotted around the neck.

for regret or grief.'" As he said these words with his eyes fixed on the writer, his hand slowly and softly moved down close to the writer's face.

The pen dropped from Darnay's fingers on the table, and he looked about him vacantly.

"What vapor is that?" he asked.

"Vapor?"

"Something that crossed me?"

"I am conscious of nothing; there can be nothing here. Take up the pen and finish. Hurry, hurry!"

As if his memory were impaired, or his faculties disordered, the prisoner made an effort to rally his attention. As he looked at Carton with clouded eyes and with an altered manner of breathing, Carton—his hand again in his breast—looked steadily at him.

"Hurry, hurry!"

The prisoner bent over the paper, once more.

"'If it had been otherwise,'" Carton's hand was again watchfully and softly stealing down; "'I never should have used the longer opportunity. If it had been otherwise';" the hand was at the prisoner's face; "'I should but have had so much the more to answer for. If it had been otherwise—'" Carton looked at the pen and saw it was trailing off into unintelligible signs.

Carton's hand moved back to his breast no more. The prisoner sprang up with a reproachful look, but Carton's hand was close and firm at his nostrils, and Carton's left arm caught him round the waist. For a few seconds he faintly struggled with the man who had come to lay down his life for him; but, within a minute or so, he was stretched insensible on the ground.

Quickly, but with hands as true to the purpose as his heart was, Carton dressed himself in the clothes the prisoner had laid aside, combed back his hair, and tied it with the ribbon the prisoner had worn. Then, he softly called, "Enter there! Come in!" and the Spy presented himself.

"You see?" said Carton, looking up, as he kneeled on one knee beside the insensible figure, putting the paper in the breast: "is your hazard very great?"

"Mr. Carton," the Spy answered, with a timid snap of his fingers, "my hazard is not *that*, in the thick of business here, if you are true to the whole of your bargain."

"Don't fear me. I will be true to the death."

"You must be, Mr. Carton, if the tale[4] of fifty-two is to be right. Being made right by you in that dress, I shall have no fear."

"Have no fear! I shall soon be out of the way of harming you, and the rest will soon be far from here, please God! Now, get assistance and take me to the coach."

"You?" said the Spy nervously.

"Him, man, with whom I have exchanged. You go out at the gate by which you brought me in?"

"Of course."

"I was weak and faint when you brought me in, and I am fainter now you take me out. The parting interview has overpowered me. Such a thing has happened here, often, and too often. Your life is in your own hands. Quick! Call assistance!"

"You swear not to betray me?" said the trembling Spy, as he paused for a last moment.

"Man, man!" returned Carton, stamping his foot; "have I sworn by no solemn vow already, to go through with this, that you waste the precious moments now? Take him yourself to the court-yard you know of, place him yourself in the carriage, show him yourself to Mr. Lorry, tell him yourself to give him no restorative but air, and to remember my words of last night, and his promise of last night, and drive away!"

---

4. **tale,** total count, tally.

The Spy withdrew, and Carton seated himself at the table, resting his forehead on his hands. The Spy returned immediately, with two men.

"How, then?" said one of them, contemplating the fallen figure. "So afflicted to find that his friend has drawn a prize in the lottery of Sainte Guillotine?"[5]

"A good patriot," said the other, "could hardly have been more afflicted if the Aristocrat had drawn a blank."

They raised the unconscious figure, placed it on a litter they had brought to the door and bent to carry it away.

"The time is short, Evrémonde," said the Spy, in a warning voice.

"I know it well," answered Carton. "Be careful of my friend, I entreat you, and leave me."

"Come, then, my children," said Barsad. "Lift him, and come away!"

The door closed, and Carton was left alone. Straining his powers of listening to the utmost, he listened for any sound that might denote suspicion or alarm. There was none. Keys turned, doors clashed, footsteps passed along distant passages: no cry was raised, or hurry made, that seemed unusual. Breathing more freely in a little while, he sat down at the table, and listened again until the clock struck Two.

Sounds that he was not afraid of, for he divined their meaning, then began to be audible. Several doors were opened in succession and finally his own. A gaoler, with a list in his hand, looked in, merely saying, "Follow me, Evrémonde!" and he followed into a large dark room, at a distance. It was a dark winter day, and what with the shadows within, and what with the shadows without, he could but dimly discern the others who were brought there to have their arms bound. Some were standing; some seated. Some were lamenting, and in restless motion; but, these were few.

The great majority were silent and still, looking fixedly at the ground.

As he stood by the wall in a dim corner, while some of the fifty-two were brought in after him, one man stopped in passing, to embrace him, as having a knowledge of him. It thrilled him with a great dread of discovery; but the man went on. A very few moments after that, a young woman, with a slight girlish form, a sweet spare face in which there was no vestige of color, and large widely opened patient eyes, rose from the seat where he had observed her sitting, and came to speak to him.

"Citizen Evrémonde," she said, touching him with her cold hand. "I am a poor little seamstress, who was with you in La Force."

He murmured for answer: "True. I forget what you were accused of?"

"Plots. Though the just Heaven knows I am innocent of any. Is it likely? Who would think of plotting with a poor little weak creature like me?"

The forlorn smile with which she said it, so touched him, that tears started from his eyes.

"I am not afraid to die, Citizen Evrémonde, but I have done nothing. I am not unwilling to die, if the Republic which is to do so much good to us poor, will profit by my death; but I do not know how that can be, Citizen Evrémonde. Such a poor weak little creature!"

As the last thing on earth that his heart was to warm and soften to, it warmed and softened to this pitiable girl.

"I heard you were released, Citizen Evrémonde. I hoped it was true?"

"It was. But, I was again taken and condemned."

"If I may ride with you, Citizen Evré-

---

monde, will you let me hold your hand? I am not afraid, but I am little and weak, and it will give me more courage."

As the patient eyes were lifted to his face, he saw a sudden doubt in them, and then astonishment. He pressed the work-worn, hunger-worn young fingers, and touched his lips.

"Are you dying for him?" she whispered.

"And his wife and child. Hush! Yes."

"O you will let me hold your brave hand, stranger?"

"Hush! Yes, my poor sister; to the last."

The same shadows that are falling on the prison, are falling, in that same hour of the early afternoon, on the Barrier with the crowd about it, when a coach going out of Paris drives up to be examined.

"Who goes here? Whom have we within? Papers!"

The papers are handed out, and read.

"Alexandre Manette. Physician. French. Which is he?"

This is he; this helpless inarticulately murmuring, wandering old man pointed out.

"Apparently the Citizen-Doctor is not in his right mind? The Revolution-fever will have been too much for him?"

Greatly too much for him.

"Hah! Many suffer with it. Lucie. His daughter. French. Which is she?"

This is she.

"Apparently it must be. Lucie, the wife of Evrémonde; is it not?"

It is.

"Hah! Evrémonde has an assignation elsewhere. Lucie, her child. English. This is she?"

She and no other.

"Kiss me, child of Evrémonde. Now, thou hast kissed a good Republican; something new in thy family; remember it! Sydney Carton. Advocate. English. Which is he?"

He lies here, in this corner of the carriage. He, too, is pointed out.

"Apparently the English advocate is in a swoon?"

It is hoped he will recover in the fresher air. It is represented that he is not in strong health, and has separated sadly from a friend who is under the displeasure of the Republic.

"Is that all? It is not a great deal, that! Many are under the displeasure of the Republic, and must look out at the little window. Jarvis Lorry. Banker. English. Which is he?"

"I am he. Necessarily, being the last."

It is Jarvis Lorry who has replied to all the previous questions. It is Jarvis Lorry who has alighted and stands with his hand on the coach door, replying to a group of officials. They leisurely walk round the carriage and leisurely mount the box, to look at what little luggage it carries on the roof; the country-people hanging about, press nearer to the coach doors and greedily stare in; a little child, carried by its mother, has its short arm held out for it, that it may touch the wife of an aristocrat who has gone to the Guillotine.

"Behold your papers, Jarvis Lorry, countersigned."

"One can depart, citizen?"

"One can depart. Forward, my postilions![6] A good journey!"

"I salute you, citizens.—And the first danger passed!"

These are again the words of Jarvis Lorry, as he clasps his hands, and looks upward. There is terror in the carriage, there is weeping, there is the heavy breathing of the insensible traveller.

"Are we not going too slowly? Can they not be induced to go faster?" asks Lucie, clinging to the old man.

"It would seem like flight, my darling. I must not urge them too much; it would rouse suspicion."

"Look back, look back, and see if we are pursued!"

"The road is clear, my dearest. So far, we are not pursued."

Houses in twos and threes pass by us, soli-

---

6. **postilions,** mounted escorts for a coach.

Everywhere shots echoed. Everywhere blood flowed.

tary farms, ruinous buildings, dye-works, tanneries, and the like, open country, avenues of leafless trees. The hard uneven pavement is under us, the soft deep mud is on either side. Sometimes, we strike into the skirting mud, to avoid the stones that clatter us and shake us; sometimes we stick in ruts and sloughs there. The agony of our impatience is then so great, that in our wild alarm and hurry we are for getting out and running—hiding—doing anything but stopping.

Out of the open country, in again among ruinous buildings, solitary farms, dye-works, tanneries, and the like, cottages in twos and threes, avenues of leafless trees. Have these men deceived us, and taken us back by another road? Is not this the same place twice over? Thank Heaven, no. A village. Look back, look back, and see if we are pursued! Hush! the posting-house.

Leisurely, our four horses are taken out; leisurely, the coach stands in the little street, bereft of horses, and with no likelihood upon it of ever moving again; leisurely, the new horses come into visible existence, one by one; leisurely, the new postilions follow, sucking and plaiting the lashes of their whips; leisurely, the old postilions count their money, make wrong additions, and arrive at dissatisfied results. All the time, our overfraught hearts are beating at a rate that would far outstrip the fastest gallop of the fastest horses ever foaled.

At length the new postilions are in their saddles, and the old are left behind. We are through the village, up the hill, and down the hill, and on the low watery grounds. Suddenly, the postilions exchange speech with animated gesticulation, and the horses are pulled up, almost on their haunches. We are pursued?

"Ho! Within the carriage there. Speak then!"

"What is it?" asks Mr. Lorry, looking out a window.

"How many did they say?"

"I do not understand you."

"—At the last post. How many to the Guillotine to-day?"

"Fifty-two."

"I said so! A brave number! My fellow-citizen here would have it forty-two; ten more heads are worth having. The Guillotine goes handsomely. I love it. Hi forward. Whoop!"

The night comes on dark. He moves more; he is beginning to revive, and to speak intelligibly; he thinks they are still together; he asks him, by his name, what he has in his hand. O pity us, kind Heaven, and help us! Look out, look out, and see if we are pursued.

The wind is rushing after us, and the clouds are flying after us, and the moon is plunging after us, and the whole wild night is in pursuit of us; but, so far we are pursued by nothing else.

Madame Defarge does not waver in her plan to exterminate all the Evrémondes, and she resolves to denounce Lucie and the child immediately. Setting out for their house, she entrusts her knitting to The Vengeance, and says that she will join her in her usual seat to watch the executions that afternoon.

Jarvis Lorry has left Miss Pross and Jerry Cruncher behind in Paris. They are to follow in another coach. In order to avoid suspicion, Miss Pross tells Jerry to arrange a different departure-point for the coach. Left alone, she is suddenly confronted by Madame Defarge.

Chapter 16
The Knitting Done

Afraid, in her extreme perturbation, of the loneliness of the deserted rooms, and of half-imagined faces peeping from behind every open door in them, Miss Pross got a basin of cold water and began laving[1] her eyes, which were swollen and red. Haunted by her feverish apprehensions, she could not bear to have her sight obscured for a minute at a time by the dripping water, but constantly paused and looked round to see that there was no one watching her. In one of those pauses she recoiled and cried out, for she saw a figure standing in the room.

The basin fell to the ground broken, and the water flowed to the feet of Madame Defarge. By strange stern ways, and through much stained blood, those feet had come to meet that water.

Madame Defarge looked coldly at her, and said, "The wife of Evrémonde; where is she?"

It flashed upon Miss Pross's mind that the doors were all standing open, and would suggest the flight. Her first act was to shut them. There were four in the room, and she shut them all. She then placed herself before the door of the chamber which Lucie had occupied.

Madame Defarge's dark eyes followed her through this rapid movement, and rested on her when it was finished. Miss Pross had nothing beautiful about her; years had not tamed the wildness, or softened the grimness, of her appearance; but, she too was a determined woman in her different way, and she measured Madame Defarge with her eyes, every inch.

"You might, from your appearance, be the wife of Lucifer," said Miss Pross, in her breathing. "Nevertheless, you shall not get the better of me. I am an Englishwoman."

Madame Defarge looked at her scornfully, but still with something of Miss Pross's own perception that they two were at bay. She saw a tight, hard, wiry woman before her, as Mr. Lorry had seen in the same figure a woman with a strong hand, in the years gone by. She knew full well that Miss Pross was the family's devoted friend; Miss Pross knew full well that Madame Defarge was the family's malevolent enemy.

"On my way yonder," said Madame Defarge, with a slight movement of her hand towards the fatal spot, "where they reserve my chair and my knitting for me, I am come to make my compliments to her in passing. I wish to see her."

"I know that your intentions are evil," said Miss Pross, "and you may depend upon it, I'll hold my own against them."

Each spoke in her own language; neither understood the other's words; both were very watchful, and intent to deduce from look and manner, what the unintelligible words meant.

"It will do her no good to keep herself concealed from me at this moment," said Madame Defarge. "Good patriots will know what that means. Let me see her. Go tell her that I wish to see her. Do you hear?"

"If those eyes of yours were bed-winches," returned Miss Pross, "and I was an English four-poster, they shouldn't loose a splinter of me. No, you wicked foreign woman; I am your match."

Madame Defarge was not likely to follow these idiomatic remarks in detail; but, she so far understood them as to perceive that she was set at naught.

"Woman imbecile and pig-like!" said Madame Defarge, frowning. "I take no answer from you. I demand to see her. Either tell her that I demand to see her, or stand out of the way of the door and let me go to her!" This, with an angry explanatory wave of her right arm.

"I little thought," said Miss Pross, "that I should ever want to understand your nonsensical language; but I would give all I have, except the clothes I wear, to know whether you suspect the truth, or any part of it."

---

1. **laving** (lāv'ing), washing.

Neither of them for a single moment released the other's eyes. Madame Defarge had not moved from the spot where she stood when Miss Pross first became aware of her; but she now advanced one step.

"I am a Briton," said Miss Pross, "I am desperate. I don't care an English Twopence for myself. I know that the longer I keep you here, the greater hope there is for my Lady-bird. I'll not leave a handful of that dark hair upon your head, if you lay a finger on me!"

Thus Miss Pross, with a shake of her head and a flash of her eyes between every rapid sentence, and every rapid sentence a whole breath. Thus Miss Pross, who had never struck a blow in her life.

But, her courage was of that emotional nature that it brought the irrepressible tears into her eyes. This was a courage that Madame Defarge so little comprehended as to mistake for weakness. "Ha, ha!" she laughed, "you poor wretch! What are you worth! I address myself to that Doctor." Then she raised her voice and called out, "Citizen Doctor! Wife of Evrémonde! Child of Evrémonde! Any person but this miserable fool, answer the Citizeness Defarge!"

Perhaps the following silence, perhaps some latent disclosure in the expression of Miss Pross's face, perhaps a sudden misgiving apart from either suggestion, whispered to Madame Defarge that they were gone. Three of the doors she opened swiftly, and looked in.

"Those rooms are all in disorder, there has been hurried packing, there are odds and ends upon the ground. There is no one in that room behind you! Let me look."

"Never!" said Miss Pross, who understood the request as perfectly as Madame Defarge understood the answer.

"If they are not in that room, they are gone, and can be pursued and brought back," said Madame Defarge to herself.

"As long as you don't know whether they are in that room or not, you are uncertain what to do," said Miss Pross to herself; "and you shall not know that, if I can prevent your knowing it; and know that, or not know that, you shall not leave here while I can hold you."

"I have been in the streets from the first, nothing has stopped me, I will tear you to pieces, but I will have you from that door," said Madame Defarge.

"We are alone at the top of a high house in a solitary court-yard, we are not likely to be heard, and I pray for bodily strength to keep you here, while every minute you are here is worth a hundred thousand guineas to my darling," said Miss Pross.

Madame Defarge made at the door. Miss Pross, on the instinct of the moment, seized her round the waist in both her arms, and held her tight. It was in vain for Madame Defarge to struggle and strike; Miss Pross, with the vigorous tenacity of love, always so much stronger than hate, clasped her tight, and even lifted her from the floor in the struggle that they had. The two hands of Madame Defarge buffeted and tore her face; but, Miss Pross, with her head down, held her round the waist, and clung to her with more than the hold of a drowning woman.

Soon, Madame Defarge's hands ceased to strike, and felt at her encircled waist. "It[2] is under my arm," said Miss Pross, in smothered tones, "you shall not draw it. I am stronger than you, I bless Heaven for it. I'll hold you till one or other of us faints or dies!"

Madame Defarge's hands were at her bosom. Miss Pross looked up, saw what it was, struck at it, struck out a flash and a crash, and stood alone—blinded with smoke.

All this was in a second. As the smoke cleared, leaving an awful stillness, it passed out on the air, like the soul of the furious woman whose body lay lifeless on the ground.

2. Miss Pross has felt a weapon concealed in Madame Defarge's clothing.

In the first fright and horror of her situation, Miss Pross passed the body as far from it as she could, and ran down the stairs to call for fruitless help. Happily, she bethought herself of the consequences of what she did, in time to check herself and go back. It was dreadful to go in at the door again; but, she did go in, and even went near it, to get the bonnet and other things that she must wear. These she put on, out on the staircase, first shutting and locking the door and taking away the key. She then sat down on the stairs a few moments to breathe and to cry, and then got up and hurried away.

By good fortune she had a veil on her bonnet, or she could hardly have gone along the streets without being stopped. By good fortune, too, she was naturally so peculiar in appearance as not to show disfigurement like any other woman. She needed both advantages, for the marks of gripping fingers were deep in her face, and her hair was torn, and her dress (hastily composed with unsteady hands) was clutched and dragged a hundred ways.

In crossing the bridge, she dropped the door key in the river. Arriving at the cathedral some few minutes before her escort, and waiting there, she thought, what if the key were already taken in a net, what if it were identified, what if the door were opened and the remains discovered, what if she were stopped at the gate, sent to prison, and charged with murder! In the midst of these fluttering thoughts, the escort appeared, took her in, and took her away.

"Is there any noise in the streets?" she asked him.

"The usual noises," Mr. Cruncher replied; and looked surprised by the question and by her aspect.

"I don't hear you," said Miss Pross. "What do you say?"

It was in vain for Mr. Cruncher to repeat what he said; Miss Pross could not hear him.

"So I'll nod my head," thought Mr. Cruncher, amazed, "at all events she'll see that." And she did.

"Is there any noise in the streets now?" asked Miss Pross again, presently.

Again Mr. Cruncher nodded his head.

"I don't hear it."

"Gone deaf in a hour?" said Mr. Cruncher, ruminating, with his mind much disturbed; "wot's come to her?"

"I feel," said Miss Pross, "as if there had been a flash and a crash, and that crash was the last thing I should ever hear in this life."

"Blest if she ain't in a queer condition!" said Mr. Cruncher, more and more disturbed. "Wot can she have been a takin', to keep her courage up? Hark! There's the roll of them dreadful carts! You can hear that, miss?"

"I can hear," said Miss Pross, seeing that he spoke to her, "nothing. O, my good man, there was first a great crash, and then a great stillness, and that stillness seems to be fixed and unchangeable, never to be broken any more as long as my life lasts."

"If she don't hear the roll of those dreadful carts, now very nigh their journey's end," said Mr. Cruncher, glancing over his shoulder, "it's my opinion that indeed she never will hear anything else in this world."

And indeed she never did.

Chapter 17
The Footsteps Die Out for Ever

Along the Paris streets, the death-carts rumble, hollow and harsh. Six tumbrils carry the day's wine to La Guillotine. All the devouring and insatiate Monsters imagined since imagination could record itself, are fused in the one realization, Guillotine. And yet there is not in France, with its rich variety of soil and climate, a blade, a leaf, a root, a sprig, a peppercorn, which will grow to maturity under conditions more certain than those that have produced this horror. Crush humanity out of shape once more, under similar hammers, and it will twist itself into the same tortured forms. Sow the same seed of rapacious license and oppression over again, and it will surely yield the same fruit according to its kind.

As the somber wheels of the six carts go round, they seem to plough up a long crooked furrow among the populace in the streets. Ridges of faces are thrown to this side and to that, and the ploughs go steadily onward. So used are the regular inhabitants of the houses to the spectacle, that in many windows there are no people, and in some the occupation of the hands is not so much as suspended, while the eyes survey the faces in the tumbrils. Here and there, the inmate has visitors to see the sight; then he points his finger, with something of the complacency of a curator or authorized exponent, to this cart and to this, and seems to tell who sat here yesterday, and who there the day before.

Of the riders in the tumbrils, some observe these things, and all things on their last roadside, with an impassive stare; others, with a lingering interest in the ways of life and men. Some, seated with drooping heads, are sunk in silent despair; again, there are some so heedful of their looks that they cast upon the multitude such glances as they have seen in theaters, and in pictures. Several close their eyes, and think, or try to get their straying thoughts together. Only one, and he a miserable creature, of a crazed aspect, is so shattered and made drunk by horror, that he sings, and tries to dance. Not one of the whole number appeals by look or gesture, to the pity of the people.

There is a guard of sundry horsemen riding abreast of the tumbrils, and faces are often turned up to some of them, and they are asked some question. It would seem to be always the same question, for, it is always followed by a press of people towards the third cart. The horsemen abreast of that cart, frequently point out one man in it with their swords. The leading curiosity is, to know which is he; he stands at the back of the tumbril with his head bent down, to converse with a mere girl who sits on the side of the cart, and holds his hand. He has no curiosity or care for the scene about him, and always speaks to the girl. Here and there in the long street of St. Honoré, cries are raised against him. If they move him at all, it is only to a quiet smile, as he shakes his hair a little more loosely about his face. He cannot easily touch his face, his arms being bound.

The clocks are on the stroke of three, and the furrow ploughed among the populace is turning round, to come on into the place of execution, and end. The ridges thrown to this side and to that, now crumble in and close behind the last plough as it passes on, for all are following to the Guillotine. In front of it, seated in chairs, as in a garden of public diversion, are a number of women, busily knitting. On one of the foremost chairs, stands The Vengeance, looking about for her friend.

"Thérèse!" she cries, in her shrill tones. "Who has seen her? Thérèse Defarge!"

"She never missed before," says a knitting-woman of the sisterhood.

"No; nor will she miss now," cries The Vengeance, petulantly. "Thérèse!"

"Louder," the woman recommends.

Ay! Louder, Vengeance, much louder, and still she will scarcely hear thee. Louder yet, Vengeance, with a little oath or so added, and yet it will hardly bring her. Send other women up and down to seek her, lingering somewhere; and yet, although the messengers have done dread deeds, it is questionable whether of their own wills they will go far enough to find her!

"Bad Fortune!" cries The Vengeance, stamping her foot in the chair, "and here are

"It is a far, far better thing that I do, than I have ever done . . ."

the tumbrils! And Evrémonde will be dispatched in a wink, and she not here! See her knitting in my hand, and her empty chair ready for her. I cry with vexation and disappointment!"

As The Vengeance descends from her elevation to do it, the tumbrils begin to discharge their loads. The ministers of Sainte Guillotine are robed and ready. Crash!—A head is held up, and the knitting-women who scarcely lifted their eyes to look at it a moment ago when it could think and speak, count One.

The second tumbril empties and moves on; the third comes up. Crash!—And the knitting-women, never faltering or pausing in their work, count Two.

The supposed Evrémonde descends, and the seamstress is lifted out next after him. He has not relinquished her patient hand in getting out, but still holds it as he promised. He gently places her with her back to the crash engine that constantly whirs up and falls, and she looks into his face and thanks him.

"But for you, dear stranger, I should not be so composed, for I am naturally a poor little thing, faint of heart; nor should I have been able to raise my thoughts to Him who was put to death, that we might have hope and comfort here today. I think you were sent to me by Heaven."

"Or you to me," says Sydney Carton. "Keep your eyes upon me, dear child, and mind no other object."

"I mind nothing while I hold your hand. I shall mind nothing when I let it go, if they are rapid."

"They will be rapid. Fear not!"

The two stand in the fast-thinning throng of victims, but they speak as if they were alone. Eye to eye, voice to voice, hand to hand, heart to heart, these two children of the Universal Mother, else so wide apart and differing, have come together on the dark highway, to repair home together, and to rest in her bosom.

"Brave and generous friend, will you let me ask you one last question? I am very ignorant, and it troubles me—just a little."

"Tell me what it is."

"I have a cousin, an only relative and an orphan, like myself, whom I love very dearly. She is five years younger than I, and she lives in a farmer's house in the south country. Poverty parted us, and she knows nothing of my fate—for I cannot write—and if I could, how should I tell her! It is better as it is."

"Yes, yes; better as it is."

"What I have been thinking as we came along, and what I am still thinking now, as I look into your kind strong face which gives me so much support, is this:—If the Republic really does good to the poor, and they come to be less hungry, and in all ways to suffer less, she may live a long time: she may even live to be old."

"What then, my gentle sister?"

"Do you think:" the uncomplaining eyes in which there is so much endurance, fill with tears, and the lips part a little more and tremble: "that it will seem long to me, while I wait for her in the better land where I trust both you and I will be mercifully sheltered?"

"It cannot be, my child; there is no Time there, and no trouble there."

"You comfort me so much! I am so ignorant. Am I to kiss you now? Is the moment come?"

"Yes."

She kisses his lips; he kisses hers; they solemnly bless each other. The spare hand does not tremble as he releases it; nothing worse than a sweet, bright constancy is in the patient face. She goes next before him—is gone; the knitting-women count Twenty-Two.

"I am the Resurrection and the Life, saith the Lord: he that believeth in me, though he were dead, yet shall he live: and whosoever liveth and believeth in me shall never die."

The murmuring of many voices, the up-turning of many faces, the pressing on of many footsteps in the outskirts of the crowd, so that it swells forward in a mass, like one great heave of water, all flashes away. Twenty-Three.

* * *

They said of him, about the city that night, that it was the peacefullest man's face ever beheld there. Many added that he looked sublime and prophetic.

One of the most remarkable sufferers by the same axe—a woman—had asked at the foot of the same scaffold, not long before, to be allowed to write down the thoughts that were inspiring her. If he had given an utterance to his, and they were prophetic, they would have been these:

"I see Defarge, The Vengeance, the Jury-man, the Judge, long ranks of the new oppressors who have risen on the destruction of the old, perishing by this retributive instrument, before it shall cease out of its present use. I see a beautiful city and a brilliant people rising from this abyss, and, in their struggles to be truly free, in their triumphs and defeats, through long years to come, I see the evil of this time and of the previous time of which this is the natural birth, gradually making expiation for itself and wearing out.

"I see the lives for which I lay down my life, peaceful, useful, prosperous and happy, in that England which I shall see no more. I see Her[1] with a child upon her bosom, who bears my name. I see her father, aged and bent, but otherwise restored, and faithful to all men in his healing office, and at peace. I see the good old man, so long their friend, in ten years' time enriching them with all he has, and passing tranquilly to his reward.

"I see that I hold a sanctuary in their hearts, and in the hearts of their descendants, generations hence. I see her, an old woman, weeping for me on the anniversary of this day. I see her and her husband, their course done, lying side by side in their last earthly bed, and I know that each was not more honored and held sacred in the other's soul, than I was in the souls of both.

"I see that child who lay upon her bosom and who bore my name, a man winning his way up in that path of life which once was mine. I see him winning it so well, that my name is made illustrious there by the light of his. I see the blots I threw upon it, faded away. I see him, foremost of just judges and honored men, bringing a boy of my name, with a forehead that I know and golden hair, to this place—then fair to look upon, with not a trace of this day's disfigurement—and I hear him tell the child my story, with a tender and faltering voice.

"It is a far, far better thing that I do, than I have ever done; it is a far, far better rest that I go to than I have ever known."

1. **Her,** Lucie.

READING FOR DETAILS

The Track of a Storm

1. Why is Charles arrested in France?
2. Why does Dr. Manette believe that he can help Charles?
3. What piece of evidence finally convicts Charles? Why is this ironic?
4. How does Sydney Carton arrange to gain access to the prison where Charles is held?
5. Why does Carton fear Madame Defarge?
6. What trick does Carton use to substitute himself for Charles Darnay?
7. How does Madame Defarge meet her end?

8. Who accompanies Sydney Carton to the guillotine?

9. According to the author, what will happen to the main characters after the close of the novel?

READING FOR MEANING

1. Consider the following sentences from the novel, and discuss the ways in which they sum up some of Dickens's principal themes in *A Tale of Two Cities:*

   a. "It is a far, far better thing that I do, than I have ever done; it is a far, far better rest that I go to than I have ever known."

   b. It was in vain for Madame Defarge to struggle and strike; Miss Pross, with the vigorous tenacity of love, always so much stronger than hate, clasped her tight, and even lifted her from the floor in the struggle that they had.

   c. Sow the same seed of rapacious license and oppression over again, and it will surely yield the same fruit according to its kind.

2. Comment on how each of these characters faces a great moment of decision in the course of the novel. In which chapters do these decisions take place?

   a. Dr. Manette
   b. Charles Darnay
   c. Sydney Carton
   d. Miss Pross

3. Many readers have thought that Sydney Carton and Dr. Manette are more complex and more believable than Charles and Lucie. Do you agree or disagree?

READING FOR APPRECIATION

Beginnings

Analyze very carefully the first chapter of the novel. Dickens begins by focusing on a relatively minor character, Jarvis Lorry. Yet notice how many intriguing questions are raised in his conversation with Lucie Manette. Why was Dr. Manette originally imprisoned? How has he changed, now that he has been released? What happened to Lucie's mother? Discuss the effectiveness of these questions in terms of narrative technique.

Endings

The closing scene of *A Tale of Two Cities* is one of the memorable portraits in world literature. Reread the last chapter carefully, noting how Dickens employs an almost cinematic technique. Upon whom does he focus his lens? What is the effect of his descriptions of the crowd, of the knitting women, and of the brief conversation between Sydney Carton and the young girl who is also to be executed? What device does the writer use to look far into the future, in order to tell us what will happen to the other main characters?

COMPOSITION

In the last section of *A Tale of Two Cities*, we see Sydney Carton make a momentous decision: to die in place of his friend Charles Darnay. Write a short composition explaining the factors that lead to this decision.

BIOGRAPHICAL NOTE

Charles Dickens (1812–1870) was born in Portsmouth, England. By the time he was twenty-four, Dickens found fame and financial success with the episodic group of narrative sketches, *The Pickwick Papers* (1836), and he gave up his job as a reporter of debates in the House of Commons for a full-time career in the writing of fiction. Most of Dickens's fifteen novels were published in serial form, with regular installments appearing in magazines over a period of many months. With such works as *Oliver Twist* (1838), *David Copperfield* (1850), *Bleak House* (1853), and *Great Expectations* (1861), he became internationally famous. *A Tale of Two Cities*, his best-known historical novel, was published in 1859. Dickens died while working on a novel called *The Mystery of Edwin Drood.*

HANDBOOK OF LITERARY TERMS

Alliteration: The repetition of the beginning sound in closely associated words or syllables. For example, Act I, Scene 2, line 21 of *Romeo and Juliet* (p. 332) is alliterative: "One **m**ore, **m**ost welcome, **m**akes **m**y nu**m**ber **m**ore." (See **Assonance, Consonance.**)

Allusion: A reference, usually brief, to a person or thing the writer expects the reader to recognize. For example, in Act III, Scene 5, line 20 (p. 375) of *Romeo and Juliet*, Romeo alludes to the moon when he says, "'Tis but the pale reflex of Cynthia's brow. . . ." (Cynthia was goddess of the moon.)

Ambiguity: When applied to literature, refers to the use of words or actions that have two or more interpretations. These are intended to be blended in the reader's mind.

Anecdote: A brief account of some interesting or humorous happening, many times biographical in nature. It is more important that an anecdote be entertaining or informative than of superior literary quality. In "The Most Dangerous Game" (p. 5) General Zaroff tells Rainsford a series of brief anecdotes of his hunting exploits.

Assonance: The repetition of similar vowel sounds having different consonants. For example, in the poem "The Term" the poet uses words repeating the **o** vowel sound in the following: ". . . r**o**lling with the wind sl**o**wly **o**ver and **o**ver . . ." (p. 422). (See **Alliteration, Consonance, Onomatopoeia.**)

Atmosphere: The overall tone or mood of a literary selection. Often the mood is established in part by the setting. For example, the atmosphere in the story "August Heat" builds to one of suffocation, possibly madness and murder, through the remarkable series of coincidences and the unusual weather (p. 564). In the poem "The Raven" the atmosphere is established quickly as one of dark shadows, of hopelessness and mourning (p. 612). (See **Mood, Tone.**)

See also pages 298, 598.

Autobiography: The story of a person's life written by that person. "Why Don't You Wear Shoes?" is a brief chapter in the life of Senator Daniel Inouye (p. 136). (See **Biography, Nonfiction.**)

See also page 135.

Ballad: One of the oldest verse forms, originally composed for singing or recitation. The ballad told a simple tale, had a refrain, and was handed down through generations. Often the original words and story were varied. Authors of a true ballad are usually unknown. The modern ballad, however, imitates the old form and usually has a known author. See "The Ballad of William Sycamore" (p. 450). (See **Narrative.**)

See also page 413.

Biography: The account of a person's life written by another person. Some biographies suggest that they are entirely factual; others, like "Woman of Iron" (p. 64), are made more interesting by the author's imaginary details. (See **Autobiography, Nonfiction.**)

See also pages 135, 192.

Blank verse: A poetic line, usually of ten syllables, with the odd-numbered syllables usually unstressed and the even ones stressed. This basic line (unrhymed iambic pentameter) has been used more than any other for serious English verse. Most of *Romeo and Juliet* (p. 324) is written in blank verse. (See **Rhythm.**)

Characterization: The ways a writer shows what a character is like. This includes telling what the character says, does, thinks, and feels, as well as how the character looks or dresses. It also includes telling what others say about the character. Note how deftly James Hurst sketches the character of Doodle in the third paragraph (p. 299) of "The Scarlet Ibis": "Doodle was about the craziest brother a boy ever had. Of course, he wasn't crazy crazy like old Miss Leedie. . . ." Thus he begins to establish a memorable person in your mind. (See **Point of view.**)

See also pages 135, 191, 220, 275.

Chronological: A pattern of organization in writing in which events are presented in the order in which they happen. "The Woods-Devil" (p. 24) uses this kind of organization. (See **Flashback.**)

Climax: The item of greatest importance in a literary work, the point of highest reader interest and emotional response. At this point the conflict must turn toward a solution. In "Through the Tunnel" the climax comes near the end of the story (p. 33) when the boy struggles desperately to swim through the tunnel. (See **Conflict, Plot.**)

Conflict: The struggle between opposing forces in a literary selection. Without conflict there is no drama, interest, suspense. Conflict is of several kinds: that between individual and individual, between an individual and the forces of nature, between an individual and a group, and within the individual. Most stories have more than one kind of conflict. For example, in *The Miracle Worker* (p. 196) Helen Keller is in conflict not only with Annie Sullivan but also with members of her family, herself, and the forces of nature. (See **Plot.**)

See also pages 3, 126.

Connotation: The emotional associations a word may arouse. (See **Denotation.**)

Connote: To suggest or imply a meaning beyond the dictionary definition.

Consonance: The close repetition of identical consonant sounds before and after different vowels; for example, the words *flip: flop* or *pitter: patter.* Poets often use words at the ends of their verses in which the final consonants in the stressed syllables agree, but the vowels that come before them differ. For example, Emily Dickinson used consonance instead of rhyme in the following quatrain:

'T was later when the summer went
Than when the cricket *came,*
And yet we knew that gentle clock
Meant nought but going *home.*

The linking of *came* and *home* is an example of consonance.

Denotation: The specific or literal meaning of a word without its emotional coloration or association. For example, the denotation of *gorilla* is a large anthropoid ape having a stocky body and coarse, dark hair. If the word, however, suggests to the listener or reader a brutish or thuglike person, the word has acquired connotations. (See **Connotation.**)

Denote: To reveal or indicate.

Dialogue: Conversation among characters in a play, story, poem, or essay.

Drama or play: A prose or verse composition written for performance by actors.

See pages 195, 220, 321.

Effect: The overall impression the writer strives to create in a literary selection. Edgar Allan Poe wrote that he always began a writing by considering the effect he wished to make on his readers. In his

"The Tell-Tale Heart" (p. 599), for example, he produces the effect of terror by very carefully blending the details of setting, characterization, and action. (See **Mood.**)

See also pages 269, 598.

Epic: One of the oldest known literary forms, in which a great hero performs feats that require superhuman daring and skill. One of the best-known epics in the world's literature is Homer's *Odyssey* (p. 83).

See page 78.

Epithet: Name or description in a literary work applied to a person or thing over and over again. This ancient literary device was used by Homer in the *Odyssey*. For example, Ithaca is referred to several times as "a sun-bright land" (Part I, line 104, p. 84) and daybreak as "rosy-fingered dawn" (line 158, p. 86). To the listeners the minstrel's use of these epithets had a familiar and somehow reassuring ring.

See page 94.

Essay: A short literary composition on a single subject, usually presenting views of the writer or writers. See "Nathan Hale" (p. 488). Newspaper editorials and book and film reviews are called essays. Any list, however, that tried to name all the kinds of essays would be impossibly long and still incomplete. The majority of essays tend to be *persuasive*, since they try to bring the reader to the writer's point of view. Some essays are principally *expository* (to present information) or *narrative* (to tell a story). Others are a combination of all three. One common differentiation made is between the formal and informal essay. The Declaration of Independence, in which Thomas Jefferson enumerated the reasons why the American colonies should separate themselves from England, is a good example of the *formal* essay.

In contrast, the *informal* essay is generally more personal, more casual in language and subject, and more flexible in structure. The bulk of essay writing would be classified as informal or *familiar*. (See **Nonfiction.**)

See also page 23.

Exaggeration or overstatement: Deliberate exaggeration or overstatement is frequently used to achieve humor. James Thurber was a master of hyperbole (exaggeration). In the third paragraph of "The Princess and the Tin Box" (p. 664), note how Thurber has the princess throwing, not rice, but pearls at her brother's wedding, and how "Only the nightingale, with his lyre of gold, was permitted to sing for the princess. The common blackbird, with his boxwood flute, was kept out of the palace grounds."

Exposition: Explanatory material placed in a story or drama to give the necessary information about characters, setting, and action. In general, exposition in writing explains something. In Act I of *The Miracle Worker*, the playwright uses scenes that give the audience the necessary insight into who the main characters are and what has happened to bring them together. The playwright must do this before a believable series of events can be created on stage. (See **Plot.**)

See also page 631.

Fable: A brief story that illustrates a moral. The characters are often animals that speak and act like people. Compare Aesop's fable "The Father and His Sons" (p. 267) with the modern, humorous fable "The Princess and the Tin Box" (p. 664). Compare the moral of each.

See page 318.

Fantasy: Any literary work that has in it impossible characters and happenings. Much of what happens in "The Cremation of Sam McGee" (p. 588) occurs in the realm of fantasy.

Fiction: Anything made up or imagined, such as a short story or novel.

Figurative language: Language using "figures of speech," such as the simile, the metaphor, or other forms of imagery. For example, the title "Woman of Iron" is figurative, since no one is literally made of iron. Note the figurative language in "Pigeon Woman" (p. 417). Here the poet describes the pigeons surrounding the woman as forming "a lake of love." (See **Metaphor, Personification, Simile.**)

See also page 3.

Flashback: An interlude in a story in which an event that took place at an earlier time interrupts the story's action momentarily. In *The Miracle Worker* (p. 196), the dramatization of Annie Sullivan's memories (of her childhood, of Dr. Anagnos, etc.) provides several poignant and haunting flashbacks.

Foreshadowing: The hint or suggestion of a coming event. In the Prologue to the *Odyssey,* lines 21–26 (p. 83) foreshadow trouble for the hero:

Not when the day came when the gods
Granted, as circling seasons passed,
That he might once again return
To Ithaca—not even then,
With those that loved him, might he find
A rest from strife.

(See **Suspense.**)

See also pages 3, 563, 594.

Form: The design, structure, or pattern of a piece of literature.

See page 413.

Free verse: Poetry without a formal beat and with an irregular metrical pattern. One of the arguments for use of free verse form over the formal rhymed patterns is that free verse frees the poet to gain spontaneity and life in a poem. Robert Frost's "The Runaway" (p. 426) is a good example of free verse. Note the irregular rhyme pattern. (See **Poetry, Rhythm.**)

See also page 413.

Haiku: A seventeen-syllable poem that is purposely short enough to be spoken in one breath. The subject is one scene or observation. Some writers prefer to rhyme the first and third lines:

Night that ends so soon
in the ford there is still held
one slice of the moon. (Buson)

Other writers, like Richard Wright (p. 416), use no rhyme.

See page 430.

Hero or protagonist: The character, male or female, in a story on whom the reader's interest centers. If such a person is weak or despicable, he or she is referred to as the anti-hero. Animals may also be protagonists. The rival of a protagonist is an antagonist.

Hexameter: A line of poetry of six metrical feet. This was the metrical line of Greek and Latin poetry; however, it translates clumsily into English, and in the Bates translation of the *Odyssey* a shorter line of four measures is used. Poets writing in English rarely use the hexameter line.

Hyperbole: See **Exaggeration or overstatement.**

Imagery: The images, or pictures, in a literary work. Generally imagery is achieved through use of metaphor and simile. For example, note the picture in the poem "The Base Stealer" (p. 427) in which the base runner ". . . hovers like an ecstatic bird. . . ."

See page 412.

Internal rhyme: Rhyme that occurs within a single line of poetry, as in Robert W. Service's "The Cremation of Sam McGee":

There are strange things *done* in the midnight *sun* (p. 588)

One of the best-known internal rhymes is that in Poe's "The Raven":

Once upon a midnight *dreary,* while I pondered weak and *weary* (p. 612)

Irony: Contrast between what appears to be true and what is really true. In the *Odyssey,* Part IV, lines 1920–1930 (p. 116), Penelope assures the suitors that they should not fear that the stranger (Odysseus in disguise), even though he should manage to string the great bow, would ever think of making Penelope his wife!

See pages 120, 727.

Legend: An unverified, popular story handed down from earlier days, often with roots in an actual happening. Sometimes events or persons are romanticized and become legends in their own periods.

Lyric: A poem with a single speaker who expresses her or his feeling on a subject. The plural, *lyrics,* refers to the words of a song. One of the best examples of a lyric in the text is "I Meant to Do My Work Today" (p. 434). (See **Sonnet.**)

See also page 413.

Metaphor: A figure of speech in which two unlike things are compared. For example, in line 37 (p. 590) of "The Cremation of Sam McGee," the poet refers to the corpse as "that quiet clay." (See **Figurative language, Simile.**)

See also page 23.

Mood: The tone that prevails in a literary work. The mood that Poe establishes in "Annabel Lee" (p. 617) is one of melancholy or sorrow. (See **Atmosphere, Tone.**)

Moral: A lesson or truth about life that concludes a fable. (See **Fable.**)

Myth and legend: Ancient myths are folk stories, added to and changed by many storytellers before being finally written down. These deal with supernatural beings, heroes, and ancestors. The *Odyssey* (p. 83) is a good example of a story based on myth and legend.

Narrative: A story or description of actual or fictional events.

See page 319.

Narrator: The person in a work of literature who is telling the story or experience. Sometimes it is a character in the story. Although at times it may seem to be the author speaking, she or he is usually only "role playing." (See **Point of view.**)

See also page 181.

Nonfiction: A factual report of events. In most biography and autobiography, the author is forced to do some fictionalizing to add interest, but the writing is still classified as nonfiction. An example is "A Boy Who Was Traded for a Horse" (p. 153). (See **Essay.**)

See also page 48.

Novel: An extended piece of narrative prose fiction with a wide range of characters and experiences. The possibilities of subject matter and the ways these are handled are endless, making it almost impossible to spell out precisely what a novel is or to catalogue its parts. (See **Short story.**)

See also pages 498, 670.

Onomatopoeia: The use of words whose sounds suggest their meanings. The "buzz of a bee" is an example of the use of onomatopoeia. (See **Alliteration, Assonance, Figurative language.**)

Paradox: A statement that at first seems absurd or contrary to common sense, but really is not, as in Wordsworth's line from "My Heart Leaps Up" (p. 435):

The child is father of the man . . .

Parallelism: The use of phrases, clauses, or sentences that have a similar structure and express a similar meaning. These lines from Edgar Allan Poe's "Annabel Lee" (p. 617) include parallel phrases, sentence structures, and meanings:

For the moon never beams without
> bringing me dreams
Of the beautiful Annabel Lee;
And the stars never rise, but I feel the
> bright eyes
Of the beautiful Annabel Lee;

See page 616.

Personification: A figure of speech in which inanimate objects or abstract ideas are given human qualities or actions, as in Romeo's lines in *Romeo and Juliet* (Act I, Scene 4, page 336):

Is love a tender thing? It is too rough,
Too rude, too boisterous, and it pricks like
> thorn.

(See **Figurative language, Metaphor.**)

Plot: The arrangement of happenings in a story or drama that lead to a climax, or turning point, in the action. (See **Conflict, Exposition.**)

See also pages 3, 670.

Poetry: The term used for the many rhythmic forms people use to give written or oral expression to their most imaginative and insightful views of their world, themselves, and the ways these two are related. The definition is inadequate, of course, because the appeal of poetic form and subject is unique to the individual. Perhaps Emily Dickinson's definition comes as close to the mark as any: "If I read a book and it makes my whole / body so cold no fire can warm me, / I know that is poetry. / If I feel physically as if the top of my head were taken off, / I know that is poetry." (p. 409).

See pages 410, 412, 463, 464.

Point of view: The person through whose eyes the reader sees the story. In the first person, the storyteller is "I," usually a character in the story telling what she or he sees and thinks. For a first-person narrative see "The Cask of Amontillado" (p. 620). Many stories are written from the author's point of view, which is called *omniscient,* or all-knowing. This allows the writer to reveal the thoughts and actions of any and all of the characters. (See **Narrator.**)

See also page 270.

Psalm: A sacred song.

Pun: A play on words, in which a word or phrase has two or more meanings. Shakespeare uses several puns in the opening lines (Act I, Scene 1) of *Romeo and Juliet.* (See footnotes, p. 325.)

Quatrain: A poem or stanza of four lines. "The Ballad of William Sycamore" (p. 450) and "Casey at the Bat" (p. 455) are poems made up of quatrains.

Refrain: A group of words, usually a phrase or sentence, repeated at intervals in a poem and usually at the end of a stanza. A refrain in the poem "The Raven" (p. 615) is: Quoth the Raven, "Nevermore."

Rhyme: Repetition of similar or identical sounds in the middle or at the ends of lines of poetry. The rhymes in "Reflections Dental" (p. 423) are *fine/shine, twirls/pearls, born/corn,* etc.

See page 412.

Rhythm: The sense of movement coming from the arrangement of strong and weak sounds in speech and writing. In poetry, rhythm is the measured flow of sound in a pattern of stressed and unstressed syllables. The *meter* is the more or less regular pattern of stressed (accented ´) and unstressed (unaccented ˘) syllables in a line of poetry. Meter, or metrical pattern, is seldom constant throughout a poem but is determined by the metrical *foot* that appears most frequently in the lines.

A foot, the basic unit of measurement, must always have one stressed or accented syllable.

See page 412.

Satire: A literary work that uses wit or humor to make fun of human behavior. This can run from gentle scoffing to severe mockery aimed at arousing contempt and bringing about reform. Thurber's "The Princess and the Tin Box" (p. 664) is satirical because he pokes fun at people who are not realistic. (See **Irony.**)

Science fiction: A piece of fiction that draws imaginatively on scientific knowledge and speculation. Often these stories involve future scientific possibilities.

Setting: The when and where something takes place in a literary work. Setting can be significant when it influences both characters and action. For example, the tropical island setting for the short story "The Most Dangerous Game" (p. 5) is vitally important to the action. (See **Plot, Theme.**)

See also page 269.

Short story: A relatively brief fictional narrative in prose. Ancient Egyptian writings, Old Testament tales, Greek and Roman myths and fables, the beast fables of the Middle Ages, and later collections of tales such as the stories of King Arthur are all forerunners of the short story, which came into being as a literary form in the 19th century.

The "short-short story" usually runs about 500 words. The bulk of short stories fall between the "short-short" and the "short-long," which is sometimes called the *novelette,* or if longer than this, the *novella.* The chief difference between the short story and the full-length novel is that in the novel the author has greater length in which to develop plot, characterization, and setting.

See pages 4, 269.

Simile: A comparison of two different things by using connectives such as *like, as, resembles,* etc. In "The Most Dangerous Game" (p. 5) Rainsford uses simile in the sixth paragraph when he says that the night is "like moist black velvet." Romeo uses simile in *Romeo and Juliet* (Act II, Scene 2, lines 26–28, p. 346): ". . . for thou art/ As glorious to this night, being o'er my head,/ As is a winged messenger of heaven." (See **Figurative language, Metaphor.**)

See also page 23.

Soliloquy: A speech, usually in a play, wherein a character who is alone, or who believes he or she is alone, speaks thoughts aloud. Examples of well-known soliloquies are those of both Romeo and Juliet at the outset of the balcony scene (Act II, Scene 2, pp. 346–347).

Sonnet: A poem of 14 lines in one of several rhyme schemes.

See page 413.

Stanza: A subdivision of a poem set off by extra white space before and after, often having a certain number of lines and a fixed length, meter, and rhyme scheme. (See **Quatrain.**)

Style: Refers to the way something is written—the devices an author uses, such as word choice, figurative language, and the relationship of words and sentences.

See page 469.

Suspense: Curiosity aroused in the reader as to what will happen next. The boy's frightening underwater passage in "Through the Tunnel" (p. 39) is suspenseful. (See **Foreshadowing, Plot.**)

See also page 3.

Symbol: A thing that stands for or represents something else. In James Hurst's story, the scarlet ibis is a symbol of Doodle's fate (p. 299).

See pages 270, 563.

Theme: The main idea or concept of a literary work. Usually the theme is not stated directly. However, after reading a selection, the reader can usually determine the theme by completing the following: "In this selection, the writer is trying to show us that . . . ."

The selections in this book are grouped under headings that identify the major theme that runs through each unit.

See page 269.

Tone: The mood of anger, joy, melancholy, grief, and so on that the author conveys in the story she or he is telling. (See **Atmosphere, Mood.**)

See also page 298.

Tragedy: Any literary work with a serious theme carried to a disastrous conclusion. *Romeo and Juliet* (p. 324) is one of Shakespeare's most famous tragedies.

Understatement: A form of irony that states less than it indirectly suggests. In *Romeo and Juliet* (Act III, Scene 1, p. 363) Mercutio has been mortally wounded by Tybalt. The dying man, asked by Benvolio if he is hurt, responds:

Ay, ay, a scratch, a scratch. . . .

GLOSSARY

This Glossary contains those relatively common yet difficult words used in the selections contained in this book. Many of the words occur two or more times in the book. The definitions are in accord with how the words are used in the selections.

Technical, archaic, obscure, and foreign words are footnoted with the selections as they occur.

The pronunciation symbols used in both the Glossary and the footnotes follow the system used in the *Thorndike/Barnhart Advanced Dictionary* (1979). For words having more than one pronunciation, the first pronunciation is the one used here; regional pronunciations may therefore vary from some of the pronunciations provided in this Glossary.

Syllable divisions and stress marks for primary and secondary accent marks used in the pronunciations also follow the system used in the *Advanced Dictionary*, including the practice of putting stress marks after the syllables stressed.

The following abbreviations are used to indicate parts of speech:

n. noun   *v.* verb   *conj.* conjunction
adj. adjective   *adv.* adverb

abashed (ə basht′) *v.* Somewhat ashamed; made uneasy.

abhors (ab hôrz′) *v.* Hates completely; detests.

abominable (ə bom′ə nə bəl) *adj.* Arousing disgust and hatred; detestable.

abrupt (ə brupt′) *adj.* Sudden; unexpected.

absconded (ab skond′əd) *v.* Gone off and hid.

absorbed (ab sôrbd′) *adj.* Very much interested in.

abstract (ab′strakt) *adj.* Expressing or naming a quality, idea, etc., rather than a particular object or concrete thing.

acclaimed (ə klāmd′) *v.* Praised highly.

accosted (ə kôst′əd) *v.* Approached and spoke to first.

accusation (ak′yə zā′shən) *n.* A charge of wrongdoing.

adhered (ad hird′) *v.* Stuck fast.

Pronunciation Key

hat, āge, fär; let, ēqual, tėrm;
it, īce; hot, ōpen, ôrder;
oil, out; cup, pút, rüle;
ch, child; ng, long; sh, she;
th, thin; ŦH, then; zh, measure;
ə represents *a* in about, *e* in taken,
i in pencil, *o* in lemon, *u* in circus.

adjourned (ə jėrnd′) *v.* Transferred the meeting place.

admonitory (ad mon′ə tôr′ē) *adj.* Gently scolding; warning against something.

advocate (ad′və kit) *n.* Supporter; a person who publicly recommends a theory, policy, belief, etc.

aesthetic (es thet′ik) *adj.* Showing good taste; artistic.

affable (af′ə bəl) *adj.* Courteous and pleasant; gracious.

affront (ə frunt′) *n.* Open insult.

agile (aj′əl) *adj.* Lively; nimble.

agility (ə jil′ə tē) *n.* Movement with speed and ease; nimbleness.

albeit (ôl bē′it) *conj.* Although; even though.

alien (ā′lyən) *adj.* Strange; entirely different from one's usual circumstances.

allegiance (ə lē′jəns) *n.* Loyalty; faithfulness to a person, cause, etc.

alliance (ə lī′əns) *n.* A joining of family interests through marriage.

amenities (ə men′ə tēz) *n.* Things that make life easier and more pleasant; polite ways; pleasant features.

amiably (ā′mē ə blē) *adv.* In a good-natured and friendly manner.

analytical (an′l it′ə kəl) *adj.* Concerned with studying all the parts of anything complex.

ancestors (an′ses′tərz) *n.* Forefathers.

anecdotes (an′ik dōts) *n.* Brief stories about single events, usually in a person's life.

anguished (ang′gwisht) *adj.* Distressed by extreme mental pain or suffering; tormented.

animated (an′ə mā′tid) *adj.* Lively; vigorous.

animates (an′ə māts) *v.* Inspires; moves to action; encourages.

animosity (an′ə mos′ə tē) *n.* Strong hostile feelings; active dislike; ill will.

annoyances (ə noi′əns əs) *n.* Troubles; things that irritate or vex a person.

anonymous (ə non′ə məs) *adj.* Having no name; nameless.

antagonistic (an tag′ə nis′tik) *adj.* Having an opposing view or opinion; hostile.

apathetically (ap′ə thet′i kəl ē) *adv.* Unemotionally; in a manner indicating lack of feeling or interest.

apathy (ap′ə thē) *n.* Lack of interest in or desire for activity; indifference.

aperture (ap′ər chúr) *n.* An opening; a hole.

appalled (ə pôld′) *v.* Filled with consternation and horror.

appalling (ə pô′ling) *adj.* Causing consternation and horror; terrifying.

apparition (ap′ə rish′ən) *n.* Ghost or phantom.

appendages (ə pen′di jəz) *n.* Arms and legs.

appertaining (ap′ər tān′ing) *v.* Relating to; belonging as a part of.

appraisal (ə prā′zəl) *n.* An evaluation of the quality or worth of something.

appraising (ə prāz′ing) *v.* Judging; estimating the make-up of a person or thing.

apprehensive (ap′ri hen′siv) *adj.* Fearful that some misfortune is about to occur; anxious about the future.

apprentice (ə pren′tis) *n.* Person learning a trade; beginner; learner.

approbation (ap′rə bā′shən) *n.* Favorable opinion; approval.

ardent (ärd′nt) *adj.* Passionate.

arid (ar′id) *adj.* Barren.

armada (är mä′də) *n.* A large group of moving things; usually used to mean a fleet of ships.

arrogance (ar′ə gəns) *n.* Excessive pride with contempt of others; haughtiness.

articulate (är tik′yə lit) *adj.* Being able to put one's thoughts into words easily and clearly.

ascension (ə sen′shən) *n.* The moving upward of something, such as a balloon.

ascertain (as′ər tān′) *v.* Make sure of; determine.

asperity (a sper′ə tē) *n.* Harshness or sharpness of temper, especially as shown in tone or manner.

asphyxiation (a sfik′sē ā′shən) *n.* Suffocation; death due to stopping of the breath.

assemblage (ə sem′blij) *n.* A group or collection of things.

assertion (ə sèr′shən) *n.* A positive statement; firm declaration.

assignation (as′ig nā′shən) *n.* Appointment.

astuteness (ə stüt′nəs) *n.* Shrewdness; being hard to fool.

audaciously (ô dā′shəs lē) *adv.* Boldly.

audacity (ô das′ə tē) *n.* Reckless daring; boldness.

auger (ô′gər) *n.* A tool for boring holes in wood.

authoritarian (ə thôr′ə ter′ē ən) *adj.* Based on power and demanding blind acceptance of principles, rules, etc.

authorized (ô′thə rīzd′) *v.* Allowed by; enforced by.

automaton (ô tom′ə ton) *n.* Person whose actions are entirely mechanical.

avail (ə vāl′) *v.* Help; be of use or value.

avaricious (av′ə rish′əs) *adj.* Greedy for wealth.

aversion (ə vèr′zhən) *n.* A strong or fixed dislike.

averted (ə vèrt′əd) *v.* and *adj.* Turned away or aside.

averting (ə vèrt′ing) *v.* Turning away or aside.

baleful (bāl′fəl) *adj.* Harmful.

bane (bān) *n.* Destruction of any kind; ruin; harm.

baronial (bə rō′nē əl) *adj.* Splendid, stately, and grand.

barricaded (bar′ə kād′əd) *v.* Blocked or obstructed.

bedeck (bi dek′) *v.* Adorn; decorate.

beguiling (bi gīl′ing) *v.* Behaving charmingly; pleasantly misleading.

bemusedly (bi myüz′əd lē) *adv.* With confusion and bewilderment.

benediction (ben′ə dik′shən) *n.* Blessing.

benefactor (ben′ə fak′tər) *n.* A person who has helped someone either by gifts of money or by some kind act.

beneficence (bə nef′ə səns) *n.* Kindness; gift.

bereft (bi reft′) *adj.* Left alone and desolate.

beseeching (bi sēch′ing) *v.* Asking earnestly; begging.

bizarre (bə zär′) *adj.* Fantastic; very odd in appearance or style.

blanched (blancht) *v.* Turned white or pale.

blurted (blèrt′əd) *v.* Said suddenly, without thinking.

blustered (blus′tərd) *v.* Said noisily and violently.

brazen (brā′zn) *adj.* Like brass in color and strength.

briary (brī′ər ē) *adj.* Thorny.

broach (brōch) *v.* Begin conversation or discussion about.

brusquely (brusk′lē) *adv.* In an abrupt manner; bluntly.

buoyant (boi′ənt) *adj.* Able to keep things afloat.

burrowing (bėr′ō ing) *v.* Digging.

cache (kash) *n.* A hiding place, especially of goods, treasure, food, etc.

cadence (kād′ns) *n.* Any movement regularly repeating itself; modulation.

calibrated (kal′ə brāt′əd) *v.* Measured; determined.

candid (kan′did) *adj.* Frank and outspoken; saying openly what one really thinks.

cantle (kan′tl) *n.* The part of a saddle that sticks up in back.

capital (kap′ə təl) *adj.* Excellent.

capricious (kə prish′əs) *adj.* Likely to change suddenly without reason; fickle.

careening (kə rēn′ing) *v.* Swaying sharply; leaning or tilting.

carnivorous (kär niv′ər əs) *adj.* Flesh-eating; using other animals as food.

carrion (kar′ē ən) *n.* Dead and decaying flesh.

cataclysmic (kat′ə kliz′mik) *adj.* Extremely sudden and violent.

catacomb (kat′ə kōm) *n.* An underground burial place.

catapulted (kat′ə pult əd) *v.* Hurled; threw.

catastrophe (kə tas′trə fē) *n.* Great misfortune.

cavalcade (kav′əl kād′) *n.* Procession of persons riding on horses, in carriages, or in automobiles.

censer (sen′sər) *n.* Container in which incense is burned, especially during religious ceremonies.

chagrin (shə grin′) *n.* A feeling of disappointment, failure, or humiliation.

chaperones (shap′ə rōnz′) *n.* Persons, especially married or older women, who are present at a party or other social activity of younger people to see that good taste is observed.

chivalrous (shiv′əl rəs) *adj.* Being graciously courteous and considerate, especially of women.

chivalry (shiv′əl rē) *n.* Respect and courtesy, especially toward women.

chronicle (kron′ə kəl) *v.* Write the story of; put on record.

circumscribing (sėr′kəm skrīb′ing) *v.* Surrounding; moving to encircle.

cirrhosis (sə rō′sis) *n.* A chronic disease of the liver.

citadel (sit′ə dəl) *n.* Fortress.

client (klī′ənt) *n.* Person, company, etc., for whom a lawyer, accountant, or other professional person acts.

Pronunciation Key

hat, āge, fär; let, ēqual, tėrm;
it, īce; hot, ōpen, ôrder;
oil, out; cup, pùt, rüle;
ch, child; ng, long; sh, she;
th, thin; ̴FH, then; zh, measure;
ə represents *a* in about, *e* in taken,
i in pencil, *o* in lemon, *u* in circus.

---

cocoons (kə künz′) *n.* Protective cases or coverings, such as those spun by insect larvae to live in.

coerced (kō ėrst′) *v.* Compelled; forced.

collateral (kə lat′ər əl) *n.* Something pledged as security for a loan.

colossus (kə los′əs) *n.* Gigantic person or thing; anything huge.

combustibility (kəm bus′tə bil′ə tē) *n.* Quality of being easily set on fire.

commences (kə mens′əs) *v.* Begins; starts.

commiseration (kə miz′ə rā′shən) *n.* Expression of sorrow for another's suffering or trouble.

commotion (kə mō′shən) *n.* Violent movement; great confusion and disturbance.

compassion (kəm pash′ən) *n.* Feeling for another's sorrow or hardship, with a strong desire to help; sympathy.

compensation (kom′pən sā′shən) *n.* Increased size or activity of one part to make up for loss or weakness of another part; something given to make up for a loss, an injury, etc.

complacently (kəm plā′snt lē) *adv.* In a self-satisfied manner.

composite (kəm poz′it) *n.* All of the individuals making up a group.

composure (kəm pō′zhər) *n.* Self-control; calmness; quietness.

compressed (kom prest′) *v.* Squeezed together.

compulsive (kəm pul′siv) *adj.* Forceful; compelling.

concentration (kon′sən trā′shən) *n.* Close attention.

condescending (kon′di sen′ding) *adj.* Lowering oneself; granting a favor in a haughty manner.

condescension (kon′di sen′shən) *n.* A haughty or patronizing manner.

condone (kən dōn′) *v.* Forgive or overlook.

conducive (kən dü′siv) *adj.* Favorable; helpful.

conferees (kon'fə rēz') *n.* Persons who consult together or exchange ideas.

conferred (kən fėrd') *v.* Given; awarded; bestowed.

congenial (kən jē'nyəl) *adj.* Agreeable; suitable.

congestion (kən jes'chən) *n.* Too much blood or mucus in one part of the body.

conniving (kə nīv'ing) *v.* Secretly cooperating or planning; conspiring; plotting.

connoisseurship (kon'ə sėr'ship) *n.* Expertness, especially in making a judgment of something fine.

conscientious (kon'shē en'shəs) *adj.* Careful to get things right; painstaking.

conscientiously (kon'shē en'shəs lē) *adv.* Carefully, in order to do what is right.

consequences (kon'sə kwens əs) *n.* Results or outcome.

consequential (kon'sə kwen'shəl) *adj.* Self-important; pompous.

consolingly (kən sōl'ing lē) *adv.* In a comforting manner.

conspicuously (kən spik' yü əs lē) *adv.* In an easily seen manner; prominently; noticeably.

constellation (kon'stə lā'shən) *n.* Group of stars usually having a geometric shape, such as the Big Dipper.

consternation (kon'stər nā'shən) *n.* Great dismay; paralyzing horror.

constraint (kən strānt) *n.* Restraint; something that hinders.

constrict (kən strikt') *v.* Draw together; contract.

constricted (kən strikt'əd) *v.* Drew together; contracted.

consummately (kən sum'it lē) *adv.* Completely; absolutely.

contemplated (kon'təm plāt'əd) *v.* Studied and thought about for a long time; looked at for a long time.

contemporaries (kən tem'pə rer'ēz) *n.* Persons of the same age or date.

contemporary (kən tem'pə rer'ē) *adj.* Belonging to or living in the same period of time; of the same age or date.

contempt (kən tempt') *n.* A feeling that a person, act, or thing is worthless; scorn; disdain.

contemptuously (kən temp'chü əs lē) *adv.* Scornfully.

contention (kən ten'shən) *n.* Statement maintained as true; point that one has argued for.

contrition (kən trish'ən) *n.* Sense or feeling of guilt.

convalescent (kon'və les'ənt) *adj.* Having to do with recovering health and strength after illness.

conversant (kən vėr'sənt) *adj.* Familiar by use or study.

convey (kən vā') *v.* Carry.

conveyed (kən vād') *v.* Expressed; communicated.

convulsive (kən vul'siv) *adj.* Being violent, sudden, and spasmodic.

coping (kōp'ing) *v.* Struggling to deal with.

coquetry (kō'kə trē) *n.* Flirting.

corollary (kôr'ə ler'ē) *n.* Something proved by inference from something else already proved; something that follows naturally.

corpulent (kôr'pyə lənt) *adj.* Large or bulky of body; fat.

corrugated (kôr'ə gāt əd) *adj.* Bent into wavy folds or ridges.

cosmonaut (koz'mə nôt) *n.* Pilot or member of the crew of a spaceship.

covet (kuv'it) *v.* Desire eagerly something that belongs to someone else.

coveted (kuv'it əd) *adj.* Greatly desired.

credulity (krə dü'lə tē) *n.* A too great readiness to believe.

crescendo (krə shen'dō) *n.* A gradual increase in loudness or in force.

crevice (krev'is) *n.* A narrow split, crack, or opening.

crooner (krün'ər) *n.* A person who sings in a low, sentimental voice.

crouched (kroucht) *v.* Stooped low, bending the legs.

crypt (kript) *n.* An underground room or vault.

crystallized (kris'tl īzd) *v.* Formed into a definite shape.

cultivate (kul'tə vāt) *v.* Give time, thought, and effort to; practice.

cultivated (kul'tə vā'tid) *adj.* Cultured; refined.

cunningly (kun'ing lē) *adv.* Cleverly; slyly.

cupola (kyü'pə lə) *n.* A rounded roof; a small dome or tower on a roof.

curator (kyü rā'tər) *n.* Person in charge of all or part of a museum, library, art gallery, etc.

custody (kus'tə dē) *n.* Care; keeping.

dank (dangk) *adj.* Unpleasantly damp or moist.

deceitful (di sēt'fəl) *adj.* Misleading; meant to deceive.

decisively (di sī′siv lē) *adv.* Firmly; in a manner indicating that something is true beyond question or doubt.

decorum (di kôr′əm) *n.* Proper behavior; seemliness.

decrepit (di krep′it) *adj.* Old and feeble; broken down or weakened by old age.

deference (def′ər əns) *n.* Great respect; a yielding to the judgment or wishes of another.

deferential (def′ə ren′shəl) *adj.* Respectful.

defiance (di fī′əns) *n.* Challenge to meet in a contest, to do something or prove something; standing up against authority and refusing to recognize or obey it.

defiantly (di fī′ənt lē) *adv.* In an openly resistant manner.

deficiency (di fish′ən sē) *n.* Lack of something needed or required; incompleteness.

defile (di fīl′) *n.* A steep and narrow valley.

definitiveness (di fin′ə tiv nəs) *n.* Finality; the condition of being completely finished or settled; something final.

deflated (di flāt′əd) *adj.* Injured; having one's confidence destroyed.

deft (deft) *adj.* Quick and skillful in actions.

deftly (deft′lē) *adv.* Quickly and skillfully.

delegation (del′ə gā′shən) *n.* Representatives to a meeting.

deliberately (di lib′ər it lē) *adv.* On purpose.

delicacies (del′ə kə sēz) *n.* Choice kinds of food.

delicately (del′ə kit lē) *adv.* Lightly; with a light touch.

delirious (di lir′ē əs) *adj.* Irrational, as if out of one's senses.

demeanor (di mē′nər) *n.* Way a person looks and acts.

demoralizing (di môr′ə līz ing) *adj.* Weakening the spirit of; disheartening.

demure (di myūr′) *adj.* Modest and serious.

deprecatingly (dep′rə kāt′ing lē) *adv.* In a strongly disapproving manner.

depreciate (di prē′shē āt) *v.* Lessen the value of; belittle.

deprivations (dep′rə vā′shənz) *n.* Lack of comforts or of the necessities of life.

deranged (di rānjd′) *adj.* Disordered; having the parts of something displaced or out of order.

derision (di rizh′ən) *n.* Ridicule.

derisively (di rī′siv lē) *adv.* Mockingly; in a manner indicating ridicule.

descent (di sent′) *n.* A way down; a downward slope; the act of going down from a higher place to a lower place.

desiccated (des′ə kāt′əd) *adj.* Dried up.

designated (dez′ig nāt əd) *adj.* Selected or appointed.

desolation (des′ə lā′shən) *n.* A ruined, lonely, or deserted condition.

despair (di sper′) *n.* Loss of hope; helplessness.

desperation (des′pə rā′shən) *n.* A hopeless and reckless feeling; readiness to run any risk.

despoiler (di spoil′ər) *n.* A person who robs and otherwise ruins something.

despondency (di spon′dən sē) *n.* Discouragement; dejection.

destination (des′tə nā′shən) *n.* Place to which a person is going.

detrimental (det′rə men′tl) *adj.* Harmful; injurious.

devious (dē′vē əs) *adj.* Not straightforward; roundabout; winding.

devoid (di void′) *adj.* Entirely without; empty; lacking.

dexterity (dek ster′ə tē) *n.* Skill in using the hands or body.

diagnosis (dī′əg nō′sis) *n.* The process of identifying a disease.

diffidence (dif′ə dəns) *n.* Lack of self-confidence; shyness.

diligence (dil′ə jəns) *n.* Constant and earnest effort to accomplish whatever is undertaken; industry.

diligently (dil′ə jənt lē) *adv.* In a hard-working manner.

diluted (də lüt′əd) *adj.* Weakened; lessened.

dimensions (də men′shənz) *n.* Elements making up a personality.

dire (dīr) *adj.* Dreadful; causing great fear or suffering.

dirge (dèrj) *n.* A funeral song or tune.

disarming (dis ärm'ing) v. Removing anger and suspicion; making oneself appear friendly.

disastrously (də zas'trəs lē) adv. In a manner causing much suffering and loss; ruinously.

discerned (də zėrnd') v. Saw clearly; recognized.

discernible (də zėr'nə bəl) adj. Capable of being seen or understood.

discipline (dis'ə plin) n. Trained order of obedience. v. Punish; bring under control; train.

discomfiture (dis kum'fi chùr) n. A complete defeat.

disconcerted (dis'kən sėrt'əd) adj. Confused; upset; disturbed enough to momentarily lose control of a situation.

discreet (dis krēt') adj. Very careful and sensible in speech and action; having or showing good judgment; wisely cautious.

disdain (dis dān') n. Feeling of scorn.

disheveled (də shev'əld) adj. Not neat; rumpled; untidy.

dismay (dis mā') n. Loss of ability to face or handle something upsetting; lack of confidence because of unexpected difficulty; sudden feeling of fear or anxiety.

dismembered (dis mem'bərd) v. Cut or tore the limbs from; tore into pieces.

disparagement (dis par'ij mənt) n. A lowering of the reputation; belittling; discrediting.

disposition (dis'pə zish'ən) n. One's habitual way of thinking and doing.

disqualify (dis kwol'ə fī) v. Make unfit or declare unfit to do something.

disquietude (dis kwī'ə tüd) n. Uneasiness; anxiety.

dissemble (di sem'bəl) v. Pretend; put on a false appearance.

dissemblers (di sem'blerz) n. Persons who hide their true feelings, thoughts, etc.; pretenders.

dissever (di sev'ər) v. Separate.

dissimulation (di sim'ə lā'shən) n. A hiding of the truth under a false appearance; pretending.

dissolution (dis'ə lü'shən) n. Ruin; destruction.

distinguish (dis ting'gwish) v. Tell apart; recognize.

distortion (dis tôr'shən) n. A twisting out of shape.

distracted (dis trakt'əd) adj. Having one's attention turned in another direction.

distraught (dis trôt') adj. In a state of mental conflict and confusion; crazed.

diversity (də vėr'sə tē) n. Variety; complete difference.

divert (də vėrt') v. Distract; turn the attention of; amuse.

dodderers (dod'ər ərz) n. Old people.

doggedness (dô'gid nəs) n. Stubborness; persistence.

dominant (dom'ə nənt) adj. Most powerful; controlling.

dominating (dom'ə nāt ing) v. Controlling by strength or power.

dominion (də min'yən) n. Rule or control over; territory under the control of one ruler or government.

dormitory (dôr'mə tôr'ē) n. A sleeping room containing many beds; a building with many sleeping rooms.

doughty (dou'tē) adj. Strong and bold; brave.

droll (drōl) adj. Odd and amusing; quaint and laughable.

dubiously (dü'bē əs lē) adv. Doubtfully; uncertainly.

eccentric (ek sen'trik) adj. Odd; peculiar.

ecstasy (ek'stə sē) n. Being overwhelmed or carried away by strong emotion.

ecstatic (ek stat'ik) adj. Filled with great joy; overwhelmed with delight.

eddy (ed'ē) n. Small whirlpool.

efficient (ə fish'ənt) adj. Able to produce the effect wanted without waste of time, energy, etc.

eking (ēk'ing) v. Barely managing to make a living.

elephantine (el'ə fan'tēn) adj. Clumsy and unwieldy; having enormous size or strength; massive.

elicited (i lis'it əd) v. Drew forth; brought out.

eloquence (el'ə kwəns) n. Art of using language so as to stir the feelings.

eloquent (el'ə kwənt) adj. Very expressive.

eludes (i lüdz') v. Escapes by cleverness, quickness, etc.

emanated (em'ə nāt əd) v. Came from; originated from.

embark (em bärk') v. Go on board a ship.

embellish (em bel'ish) v. Make more interesting by adding real or imaginary details; elaborate.

eminently (em'ə nənt lē) adv. Outstandingly.

emissaries (em'ə ser'ēz) n. Persons sent on a specific errand.

emphatic (em fat'ik) adj. Strongly expressed.

encumbrance (en kum'brəns) n. Something useless or in the way.

ennui (än'wē) *n.* Boredom; a feeling of weariness and discontent from lack of interest.

enormous (i nôr'məs) *adj.* Very large; huge.

enshrouded (en shroud'əd) *v.* Covered or hid.

enthralled (en thrôld') *adj.* Fascinated; charmed; held spellbound.

entreating (en trēt'ing) *v.* Begging; asking earnestly.

episode (ep'ə sōd) *n.* An outstanding incident or experience in a person's life, in the history of a country, etc.

epitome (i pit'ə mē) *n.* Typical or ideal example.

epoch (ep'ək) *n.* A period of time.

essence (es'ns) *n.* Important or necessary part.

etched (echt) *adj.* Having deep lines or furrows.

eternal (i tèr'nl) *adj.* Lasting throughout all time; without beginning or ending; always and forever the same.

evacuated (i vak'yü āt əd) *v.* Withdrawn from.

evanesced (ev'ə nest') *v.* Disappeared gradually; faded away.

ewer (yü'ər) *n.* A wide-mouthed water pitcher.

exasperated (eg zas'pə rāt'əd) *adj.* Very much irritated; annoyed.

exasperating (eg zas'pə rāt'ing) *adj.* Very irritating; very annoying.

excruciating (ek skrü'shē ā'ting) *adj.* Very painful; extreme.

exhibitionist (ek'sə bish'ə nist) *n.* Person with an excessive tendency to seek attention and show off his or her abilities.

exhilarated (eg zil'ə rāt'əd) *adj.* Filled with great joy; in high spirits.

exigencies (ek'sə jən sēz) *n.* Situations demanding prompt action or attention; emergencies.

exotic (eg zot'ik) *adj.* Fascinating or interesting because strange or different.

expended (ek spend'əd) *adj.* Used up.

expiated (ek'spē āt əd) *v.* Paid the penalty of.

explicit (ek splis'it) *adj.* Clearly expressed; definite.

exploit (ek'sploit) *n.* A bold, unusual act.

expulsion (ek spul'shən) *n.* A being expelled; being forced out.

extinct (ek stingkt') *adj.* No longer existing.

extravagant (ek strav'ə gənt) *adj.* Excessive; beyond the bounds of reason.

extremity (ek strem'ə tē) *n.* An extreme degree.

exuberant (eg zü'bər ənt) *adj.* Joyously unrestrained and enthusiastic; extreme or excessive.

Pronunciation Key

hat, āge, fär; let, ēqual, tèrm;
it, īce; hot, ōpen, ôrder;
oil, out; cup, pu̇t, rüle;
ch, child; ng, long; sh, she;
th, thin; ₮н, then; zh, measure;
ə represents *a* in about, *e* in taken,
i in pencil, *o* in lemon, *u* in circus.

---

exultation (eg'zul tā'shən) *n.* Great rejoicing; triumph.

facetiously (fə sē'shəs lē) *adv.* Jokingly; said in a slyly humorous manner.

facility (fə sil'ə tē) *n.* Absence of difficulty; ease.

faculties (fak'əl tēz) *n.* A person's mental and physical abilities.

faltered (fôl'tərd) *v.* Stammered; spoke in hesitating and broken words.

fanaticism (fə nat'ə siz'əm) *n.* Excessive or unreasonable enthusiasm, especially in matters of religion.

fantastic (fan tas'tik) *adj.* Very odd or queer; very fanciful and imaginative.

fastidiously (fa stid'ē əs lē) *adv.* In a manner showing that one is difficult and hard to please; in an excessively dainty manner.

feasible (fē'zə bəl) *adj.* Easy to carry out; possible without difficulty or damage.

feigned (fānd) *v.* Pretended.

ferociously (fə rō'shəs lē) *adv.* Fiercely; savagely.

ferreted (fer'it id) *v.* Hunted and driven out of a place.

fervent (fèr'vənt) *adj.* Ardent; intense.

fervently (fèr'vənt lē) *adv.* Earnestly; intensely.

fervid (fèr'vid) *adj.* Intensely emotional; ardent.

fetid (fet'id) *adj.* Smelling very bad.

fettered (fet'ərd) *v.* Chained the feet of.

feverishly (fē'vər ish lē) *adv.* Excitedly.

fiasco (fē as'kō) *n.* A complete or ridiculous failure.

fidgeted (fij'it əd) *v.* Moved about restlessly.

flagons (flag'ənz) *n.* Large bottles; containers for holding liquids, usually with a handle, spout, and cover.

flagrant (flā'grənt) *adj.* Outrageous; scandalous.

flailed (flāld) *v.* Beat; thrashed.

flailing (flāl'ing) *v.* and *adj.* Swinging and beating about.

flamboyant (flam boi′ənt) *adj.* Gorgeously brilliant; very ornate; very showy.

flaunting (flônt′ing) *v.* Displaying ostentatiously; showing off to impress others.

flax (flaks) *n.* Threadlike fibers from the flax plant.

floundered (floun′dərd) *v.* Struggled awkwardly without making much progress; plunged about.

fluently (flü′ənt lē) *adv.* Speaking in an easy, rapid manner.

forfeit (fôr′fit) *v.* Lose; give up something by one's own fault.

former (fôr′mər) *adj.* The first mentioned of two.

formidable (fôr′mə də bəl) *adj.* Hard to overcome; to be dreaded.

fortitude (fôr′tə tüd) *n.* Courage in facing pain, danger, trouble, etc.; firmness of spirit; strength of character.

frantically (fran′tik əl ē) *adv.* Very excitedly; wildly.

frenzy (fren′zē) *n.* A state of near madness; a frantic condition.

frivolous (friv′ə ləs) *adj.* Lacking in seriousness or sense; light-hearted; carefree.

furtive (fėr′tiv) *adj.* Done quickly and with stealth to avoid being noticed.

furtively (fėr′tiv lē) *adv.* Stealthily.

fusillade (fyü′zə lād) *n.* A rapid or continuous discharge of many firearms at the same time; any rapid and continuous sound, action, etc.

futile (fyü′tl) *adj.* Useless.

futility (fyü til′ə tē) *n.* A useless act; ineffectiveness.

gallantly (gal′ənt lē) *adv.* In a polite and attentive manner.

gamut (gam′ət) *n.* The whole series of notes on the musical scale.

gangrene (gang′grēn′) *n.* Death and decay of tissue when the blood supply of a part of a living person or animal is cut off by injury, infection, or freezing.

gargoyle (gär′goil) *n.* A protruding ornament in the shape of a fantastic animal.

garrote (gə rot′) *n.* Any device used to strangle.

gaunt (gônt) *adj.* Very thin and bony.

genial (jē′nyəl) *adj.* Kindly; cheerful and friendly.

genteel (jen tēl′) *adj.* Polite; well-bred.

gesticulations (je stik′yə lā′shəns) *n.* Lively or excited gestures.

ghastly (gast′lē) *adj.* Horrible; causing terror.

glancing (glans′ing) *adj.* Hitting or striking on a slant.

glibly (glib′lē) *adv.* In a smooth, easy, not very believable manner.

glower (glou′ər) *n.* An angry stare; a fierce scowl.

glowering (glou′ər ing) *v.* Staring angrily; scowling fiercely.

gout (gout) *n.* A drop, splash, or clot.

gracious (grā′shəs) *adj.* Pleasant and courteous.

grandeur (gran′jər) *n.* A magnificent or splendid appearance.

granule (gran′yül) *n.* A small bit, like a small grain.

grappling (grap′ling) *v.* Struggling to overcome.

gratification (grat′ə fə kā′shən) *n.* Satisfaction and pleasure.

gravity (grav′ə tē) *n.* Seriousness.

grimace (grə mās′) *n.* A twisting of the face; an ugly or funny smile.

grimaced (grə māst′) *v.* Said with a funny, twisted smile.

groping (grōp′ing) *v.* Searching blindly and uncertainly.

grotesque (grō tesk′) *adj.* Odd or unnatural in shape, appearance, manner, etc.; queer.

haggard (hag′ərd) *adj.* Looking worn from pain, fatigue, worry, hunger, etc.

hallowed (hal′ōd) *adj.* Made holy; sacred.

hapless (hap′lis) *adj.* Unlucky; unfortunate.

harangues (hə rangz′) *n.* Long, pompous speeches.

harbors (här′bərz) *v.* Has and keeps in mind.

harried (har′ēd) *adj.* Worried; troubled.

haven (hā′vən) *n.* Harbor or port; place of shelter and safety.

hereditary (hə red′ə ter′ē) *adj.* Passed on from earlier generations.

heresy (her′ə sē) *n.* Opinion or doctrine opposed to what is generally accepted as authoritative.

hoax (hōks) *n.* A mischievous trick, especially a made-up story passed off as true.

homage (hom′ij) *n.* Dutiful respect.

hostile (hos′tl) *adj.* Unfriendly; having to do with an enemy or enemies.

humiliation (hyü mil′ē ā′shən) *n.* A lowering of pride, dignity.

humility (hyü mil′ə tē) *n.* Feeling of humbleness; meekness.

hurtling (hėr′tling) *v.* Rushing violently.

hypocritical (hip′ə krit′ə kəl) *adj.* Insincere; false.

hypothesis (hī poth′ə sis) *n.* Something assumed

because it seems likely to be a true explanation; a theory.

hysteria (hi stir′ē ə) *n.* Unrestrained emotional excitement, often characterized by wild movements.

ibis (ī′bis) *n.* A large, long-legged wading bird of warm regions having a long, downward-curving bill.

idioms (id′ē əmz) *n.* Phrases or expressions whose meaning cannot be understood from the ordinary meanings of the words in them.

ignominiously (ig′nə min′ē əs lē) *adv.* Disgracefully; shamefully; humiliatingly; in a manner as to lose one's dignity.

illimitable (i lim′ə tə bəl) *adj.* Boundless; measureless.

illiterate (i lit′ər it) *adj.* Unable to read or write.

imbecile (im′bə səl) *n.* A very stupid or foolish person.

immaculate (i mak′yə lit) *adj.* Absolutely clean; without a spot or stain.

imminent (im′ə nənt) *adj.* Likely to happen soon; about to occur.

immoderately (i mod′ər it lē) *adv.* Excessively; in an extreme manner.

immolation (im′ə lā′shən) *n.* Being killed as a sacrifice.

impediments (im ped′ə mənts) *n.* Hindrances; obstructions.

imperative (im per′ə tiv) *adj.* Not to be avoided; urgent.

imperceptible (im′pər sep′tə bəl) *adj.* Very slight, gradual, subtle, or indistinct.

imperceptibly (im′pər sep′tə blē) *adv.* Gradually; in a manner so slight as not to be noticed.

imperiled (im per′əld) *v.* Put in danger; endangered.

imperious (im pir′ē əs) *adj.* Arrogant; overbearing; demanding.

imperiously (im pir′ē əs lē) *adv.* Arrogantly; haughtily.

impertinent (im pèrt′n ənt) *adj.* Disrespectful, as shown by meddling in other people's business or taking too many liberties with others; rude.

imperturbable (im′pər tèr′bə bəl) *adj.* Not easily excited, disturbed, or upset; calm.

impervious (im pèr′vē əs) *adj.* Not open to argument, suggestions, etc.; not capable of being disturbed by anything.

impetuous (im pech′ü əs) *adj.* Acting with sudden or rash energy.

implacable (im plak′ə bəl) *adj.* Unyielding; refusing to give up or release.

imponderable (im pon′dər ə bəl) *adj.* Incapable of being understood or evaluated.

imposture (im pos′chər) *n.* Deception; fraud.

imprudent (im prüd′nt) *adj.* Rash; unwise.

impudence (im′pyə dəns) *n.* Great rudeness; insolence.

impudently (im′pyə dənt lē) *adv.* In a shamelessly bold or rude manner.

impulsive (im pul′siv) *adj.* With a sudden inclination to act.

impunity (im pyü′nə tē) *n.* Freedom from punishment, injury, or other bad consequences.

inaccessible (in′ək ses′ə bəl) *adj.* Hard to reach or enter.

inadequacy (in ad′ə kwə sē) *n.* Not enough; not as much as is needed.

inadvertently (in′əd vèrt′nt lē) *adv.* Accidentally.

inarticulate (in är tik′yə lit) *adj.* Not said in distinct syllables or words; not able to put one's thoughts or feelings into words; speechless with amazement, fear, etc.

inaudible (in ô′də bəl) *adj.* That cannot be heard.

inaudibly (in ô′də blē) *adv.* So softly or quietly as not to be heard.

incalculable (in kal′kyə lə bəl) *adj.* Impossible to foretell or reckon beforehand; uncertain.

incarnate (in kär′nit) *adj.* Personified; typified.

incensed (in senst′) *v.* Very angry; filled with rage.

incessantly (in ses′nt lē) *adv.* Continuously; repeatedly, without interruption.

incidental (in′sə den′tl) *adj.* Happening along with something else more important.

inclination (in′klə nā′shən) *n.* Slope; slant.

incoherent (in′kō hir′ənt) *adj.* Having no logical connection; disconnected; confused.

incoherently (in'kō hir'ənt lē) *adv.* In a confused, illogical manner.

incompatible (in'kəm pat'ə bəl) *adj.* Incapable of existing together peaceably.

incompetent (in kom'pə tənt) *adj.* Lacking ability.

incomprehensible (in'kom pri hen'sə bəl) *adj.* Impossible to understand.

inconsequential (in'kon sə kwen'shəl) *adj.* Unimportant; trifling.

incorruptible (in'kə rup'tə bəl) *adj.* Not subject to bribery or other dishonest acts; lasting forever.

incredible (in kred'ə bəl) *adj.* Hard to believe; seeming too extraordinary to be possible.

incredibly (in kred'ə blē) *adv.* Unbelievably.

incredulous (in krej'ə ləs) *adj.* Showing lack of belief; not ready to believe; doubting; skeptical.

incumbent (in kum'bənt) *adj.* Resting on a person as a duty or obligation.

indefinable (in'di fī'nə bəl) *adj.* Unexplainable; that cannot be described exactly.

indignant (in dig'nənt) *adj.* Angry at something unworthy, unjust, or unfair.

indignation (in'dig nā'shən) *n.* Anger at something unworthy, unjust, unfair, or mean; righteous anger.

indignity (in dig'nə tē) *n.* Injury to one's self-respect; insult.

indolent (in'dl ənt) *adj.* Lazy; idle; fond of ease and not liking work.

indolently (in'dl ənt lē) *adv.* Lazily; idly.

indomitability (in dom'ə tə bil'ə tē) *n.* State of being unconquerable or unyielding.

indubitably (in dü'bə tə blē) *adv.* Certainly; unquestionably.

induce (in düs') *v.* Influence; persuade.

indulged (in duljd') *v.* Gave into; let oneself do what one wanted to.

ineffectual (in'ə fek'chü əl) *adj.* Not having the means to accomplish a purpose; useless.

ineptitude (in ep'tə tüd) *n.* Lack of ability; unfitness.

inestimable (in es'tə mə bəl) *adj.* Too great to be calculated; priceless.

inevitable (in ev'ə tə bəl) *adj.* Sure to happen; certain to come; not to be avoided.

inevitably (in ev'ə tə blē) *adv.* Surely; with certainty.

inexorable (in ek'sər ə bəl) *adj.* Relentless; unyielding.

inexorably (in ek'sər ə blē) *adv.* Relentlessly; in a way not to be influenced by pleading, etc.

infallibility (in fal'ə bil'ə tē) *n.* Inability to be mistaken; freedom from error.

ingenious (in jē'nyəs) *adj.* Cleverly planned and carried out; good at inventing.

inimitable (in im'ə tə bəl) *adj.* Impossible to imitate or copy; matchless.

initiative (i nish'ē ə tiv) *n.* Active part in taking the first steps in any undertaking; the lead.

innumerable (i nü'mər ə bəl) *adj.* Too many to count; countless.

inquest (in'kwest) *n.* A legal inquiry, especially before a jury, held to determine the cause of a death not clearly due to natural causes.

insensibly (in sen'sə blē) *adv.* Unfeelingly; indifferently; without being aware.

insinuatingly (in sin'yü āt'ing lē) *adv.* Suggesting in a sly, underhand, nasty manner.

insolence (in'sə ləns) *n.* Bold rudeness; insulting behavior or speech.

instigates (in'stə gāts) *v.* Stirs up; rouses.

instituted (in'stə tüt əd) *v.* Began; started.

insufferable (in suf'ər ə bəl) *adj.* Unbearable.

insufferably (in suf'ər ə blē) *adv.* Beyond endurance; unbearably.

intercept (in'tər sept') *v.* Take or seize on the way from one place to another.

interjected (in'tər jekt'əd) *v.* Thrown in between other things; inserted abruptly.

interjectional (in'tər jek'shə nəl) *adj.* Interrupted; jerky.

interlude (in'tər lüd) *n.* Pause; interval; a period of time between.

interminable (in tèr'mə nə bəl) *adj.* So long as to seem endless.

interminably (in tèr'mə nə blē) *adv.* Endlessly; unceasingly.

intermittent (in'tər mit'nt) *adj.* Stopping for a time and beginning again.

intermittently (in'tər mit'nt lē) *adv.* Starting and stopping; now and then.

interrogate (in ter'ə gāt) *v.* Ask questions of; examine.

intervals (in'tər vəlz) *n.* Spaces between or along something.

intervenes (in'tər vēnz') *v.* Comes between.

intimate (in'tə māt) *v.* Suggest; hint.

intimations (in'tə mā'shənz) *n.* Indirect suggestions; hints.

intimidation (in tim'ə dā'shən) *n.* Act of influencing by using force or fear.

intractably (in trak'tə blē) *adv.* Stubbornly.

intricate (in′trə kit) *adj.* Complicated; with many twists and turns; puzzling.

intriguing (in trē′ging) *adj.* Exciting the curiosity and interest.

intrusion (in trü′zhən) *n.* Act of forcing oneself in; coming unasked and unwanted.

invariable (in ver′ē ə bəl) *adj.* Unchanging; constant.

inviolate (in vī′ə lit) *adj.* Not violated; unbroken.

involuntarily (in vol′ən ter′ə lē) *adv.* Unintentionally; unwillingly.

irate (ī′rāt) *adj.* Angry; enraged.

irately (ī′rāt lē) *adv.* Angrily.

iridescent (ir′ə des′nt) *adj.* Changing color when moved or turned; displaying changing colors.

irrelevant (i rel′ə vənt) *adj.* Not to the point; off the subject.

irreparably (i rep′ər ə blē) *adv.* Beyond repair or the possibility of being righted or made good.

irresistible (ir′i zis′tə bəl) *adj.* Too great to be withstood; overwhelming.

irresolute (i rez′ə lüt) *adj.* Hesitating; not sure of what one wants.

irrevocably (i rev′ə kə blē) *adv.* Unalterably; in a manner impossible to change or call back.

jovial (jō′vē əl) *adj.* Good-hearted and full of fun; good-humored and merry.

jubilantly (jü′bə lənt lē) *adv.* Joyfully.

judgment (juj′mənt) *n.* Debt arising from the decision of a judge or court.

judicious (jü dish′əs) *adj.* Using good judgment; wise; sensible.

jugular (jug′yə lər) *adj.* Of the neck or throat. *n.* One of the two large veins in each side of the neck.

kaleidoscopic (kə lī′də skop′ik) *adj.* Continually changing.

keel (kēl) *n.* The main timber or steel piece that extends the whole length of the bottom of a ship or boat.

laboriously (lə bôr′ē əs lē) *adv.* Not easily; with much effort.

labyrinth (lab′ə rinth′) *n.* A complicated, confusing arrangement; a number of connecting passages so arranged that it is difficult to find one's way; a maze.

lacerated (las′ə rāt′əd) *adj.* Torn and mangled.

Pronunciation Key

hat, āge, fär; let, ēqual, tėrm;
it, īce; hot, ōpen, ôrder;
oil, out; cup, pủt, rüle;
ch, child; ng, long; sh, she;
th, thin; ₮H, then; zh, measure;
ə represents *a* in about, *e* in taken,
i in pencil, *o* in lemon, *u* in circus.

---

laconic (lə kon′ik) *adj.* Brief in speech or expression; concise.

lamentation (lam′ən tā′shən) *n.* Cries of sorrow, wailing.

lamented (lə ment′əd) *v.* Mourned for; wept.

lancing (lans′ing) *v.* Cutting or piercing.

languid (lang′gwid) *adj.* Without energy; not brisk or lively; listless.

languor (lang′gər) *n.* Indifference; weariness; quietness.

larded (lärd′əd) *v.* Interspersed with; given variety.

latent (lāt′nt) *adj.* Present but not active.

latter (lat′ər) *adj.* Second of two persons, things, etc.

layman (lā′mən) *n.* Person outside of a particular profession.

league (lēg) *n.* Measure of distance, usually about 3 miles.

liability (lī′ə bil′ə tē) *n.* State of being under obligation; a taking responsibility for something.

loathed (lō₮Hd) *v.* Hated; detested.

loathsome (lō₮H′səm) *adj.* Making one feel sick; disgusting.

longevity (lon jev′ə tē) *n.* Long life.

longitudinal (lon′jə tüd′n əl) *adj.* Running lengthwise.

lope (lōp) *n.* A long, easy stride; an easy, natural gait of a horse.

ludicrous (lü′də krəs) *adj.* Ridiculous; amusingly absurd.

luminous (lü′mə nəs) *adj.* Full of light; shining; bright.

lurid (lùr′id) *adj.* Glaring in brightness or color; lighted up by a red glare; sensational.

luxuriate (lug zhủr′ē āt) *v.* Indulge in; take great delight in.

magnanimous (mag nan′ə məs) *adj.* Noble in soul or mind.

majestically (mə jes′tə kəl ē) *adv.* Grandly; in a stately manner.

malevolence (mə lev′ə ləns) *n.* The wish that evil may happen to others; ill will; spite.

malice (mal′is) *n.* Wish to hurt or make suffer; spite.

maligned (mə līnd′) *adj.* Having evil spoken about one; injurious; slandered.

maneuvered (mə nü′vərd) *v.* Forced cleverly; caused to happen by a trick of some sort.

maneuvering (mə nü′vər ing) *v.* Planning skillfully; scheming.

maniacal (mə nī′ə kəl) *adj.* Insane.

manifest (man′ə fest) *adj.* Apparent to the eye or to the mind.

marquisette (mär′kə zet′) *n.* A very thin, sheer fabric made of cotton, silk, rayon, etc., and often used for curtains, dresses, etc.

marrow (mar′ō) *n.* A soft tissue that fills bone cavities.

martial (mär′shəl) *adj.* Warlike; given to fighting.

mediate (mē′dē āt) *v.* Help settle a dispute.

medieval (mē′dē ē′vəl) *adj.* Looking like something from the Middle Ages.

mediocre (mē′dē ō′kər) *adj.* Of average quality; ordinary; neither good nor bad.

melancholy (mel′ən kol′ē) *n.* Condition of sadness and low spirits; gloominess; dejection.

melee (mā′lā) *n.* A confused fight, often hand-to-hand, among a number of fighters.

menacing (men′is ing) *adj.* Threatening.

meteorological (mē′tē ər ə loj′ə kəl) *adj.* Relating to the study of weather.

mien (mēn) *n.* Way of acting and looking.

miniature (min′ē ə chùr) *adj.* Small-scale; tiny.

minute (mī nüt′) *adj.* Very small; tiny.

mirage (mə räzh′) *n.* Anything that does not exist; illusion; optical effect sometimes seen in the desert, at sea, or over a hot pavement that has the appearance of a pool of water or a mirror.

modicum (mod′ə kəm) *n.* A small or moderate quantity.

momentous (mō men′təs) *adj.* Very important; of great consequence.

momentum (mō men′təm) *n.* The force needed for movement.

monstrous (mon′strəs) *adj.* Huge; enormous.

morosely (mə rōs′lē) *adv.* Gloomily.

mortified (môr′tə fīd) *adj.* and *v.* Ashamed and humbled; humiliated.

motley (mot′lē) *n.* Suit of more than one color worn by clowns.

mottled (mot′ld) *v.* Marked with spots or streaks of different colors.

multitudinous (mul′tə tüd′n əs) *adj.* Very numerous; occurring in great numbers.

mutilated (myü′tl āt əd) *adj.* Being seriously injured by the cutting, tearing, or breaking off of some part; maimed; crippled.

mutinous (myüt′n əs) *adj.* Rebellious; unruly.

myriads (mir′ē ədz) *n.* Very great numbers.

naïve (nä ēv′) *adj.* Simple in nature; childlike.

negligence (neg′lə jəns) *n.* Lack of proper care or attention; carelessness.

neurotic (nù rot′ik) *adj.* Being emotionally disturbed.

nocturnal (nok tèr′nl) *adj.* Of the night; in the night.

nominal (nom′ə nəl) *adj.* Too small to be considered; almost nothing.

nonchalantly (non′shə lənt lē) *adv.* Unconcernedly; indifferently.

nonplussed (non plust′) *v.* Puzzled. *adj.* Unable to say or do anything.

novice (nov′is) *n.* One who is new to what she or he is doing; a beginner.

nymph (nimf) *n.* A lesser goddess of nature. Nymphs lived in seas, rivers, fountains, springs, hills, woods, or trees.

obeisance (ō bā′sns) *n.* Movement of the body expressing deep respect or reverence; action of bowing.

obese (ō bēs′) *adj.* Extremely fat.

oblivious (ə bliv′ē əs) *adj.* Not mindful; unaware of.

obscurity (əb skyùr′ə tē) *n.* Lack of light; dimness.

obstinate (ob′stə nit) *adj.* Stubborn; not willing to give in; persistent.

ocular (ok′yə lər) *adj.* Received by actual sight; seen.

offhandedly (ôf′han′did lē) *adv.* Without previous thought or preparation; in a free-and-easy manner; casually.

ominous (om′ə nəs) *adj.* Evil; unfavorable; threatening; of bad omen.

ominously (om′ə nəs lē) *adv.* Threateningly; unfavorably; with evil intent.

opaqueness (ō pāk′nəs) *n.* Something not letting light through; something not transparent; dull; lack of brightness.

opinionated (ə pin′yə nā′tid) *adj.* Obstinate or conceited with regard to one's opinions.

oppressed (ə prest′) *adj.* Burdened; weighed down by.

oppressively (ə pres′iv lē) *adv.* In a manner hard to bear; burdensomely; unbearably difficult.

option (op′shən) *n.* Right or freedom of choice; thing that is or can be chosen.

oratory (ôr′ə tôr′ē) *n.* Eloquent speaking and language; skill in public speaking.

ordained (ôr dānd′) *v.* Destined; caused by fate.

ornate (ôr nāt′) *adj.* Very fancy and decorative; elaborately done; greatly embellished.

ornately (ôr nāt′lē) *adv.* In a profusely decorative and ornamental manner.

orthodoxy (ôr′thə dok′sē) *n.* The holding of correct or generally accepted beliefs.

pacified (pas′ə fīd) *v.* Soothed; calmed; quieted.

palatial (pə lāt′shəl) *adj.* Magnificent.

pallid (pal′id) *adj.* Pale.

palpable (pal′pə bəl) *adj.* Obvious; that can be touched or felt; readily seen.

pantomime (pan′tə mīm) *n.* A play without words, in which the actors express themselves by gestures.

paralyzed (par′ə līzd) *adj.* Unable to move; motionless.

paroxysm (par′ək siz′əm) *n.* A sudden outburst of emotion or activity.

particulars (pər tik′yə lərz) *n.* Details; individual facts.

patent (pāt′nt) *adj.* Plain; evident.

pathetically (pə thet′ik lē) *adv.* Pitifully.

patron (pā′trən) *n.* A person chosen or named as a special guardian, supporter, or protector.

patronize (pā′trə nīz) *v.* Treat in a haughty, condescending way.

patronized (pā′trə nīzd) *v.* Was a regular customer of.

patronizing (pā′trə nīz ing) *v.* Treating in a condescending manner.

patrons (pā′trənz) *n.* Persons who regularly go to a store, hotel, athletic contest, etc.

pecuniary (pi kyü′nē er′ē) *adj.* Of or having to do with money.

pedestrianism (pə des′trē ə niz′əm) *n.* Practice of traveling on foot; walking.

peer (pir) *v.* Look.

pendant (pen′dənt) *adj.* Hanging; suspended.

pensive (pen′siv) *adj.* Melancholy; thoughtful in a serious or sad way.

perceptible (pər sep′tə bəl) *adj.* Noticeable; having the capacity for being seen.

perilous (per′ə ləs) *adj.* Dangerous.

pernicious (pər nish′əs) *adj.* Very injurious; causing great harm or damage.

perplexing (pər pleks′ing) *adj.* Puzzling; bewildering; confusing.

persistence (pər sis′təns) *n.* A holding firmly to one's purpose.

perturbation (pėr′tər bā′shən) *n.* Agitation.

petulant (pech′ə lənt) *adj.* Peevish; fretful; complaining; given to fits of bad temper.

phenomenon (fə nom′ə non) *n.* Something out of the ordinary, usually known through the senses rather than by thought.

piazza (pē az′ə) *n.* A large porch along one or more sides of a house.

picayune (pik′ə yün′) *n.* Any coin of small value.

placid (plas′id) *adj.* Pleasantly calm or peaceful; quiet; unexciting.

placidly (plas′id lē) *adv.* Peacefully; quietly; calmly.

plaintive (plān′tiv) *adj.* Expressive of sorrow; mournful.

plateau (pla tō′) *n.* A relatively level land surface that rises sharply above the surrounding land.

plausibility (plô′zə bil′ə tē) *n.* Appearance of being true or reasonable.

plausible (plô′zə bəl) *adj.* Appearing true, reasonable, or fair.

pliant (plī′ənt) *adj.* Flexible; supple.

plummeted (plum′it əd) *v.* Plunged; dropped.

poignant (poi′nyənt) *adj.* Very painful; piercing.

poised (poizd) *adj.* Held in a steady position; balanced.

pommel (pum′əl) *n.* The part of a saddle that sticks up in front.

pompous (pom′pəs) *adj.* Self-important; trying to seem very important.

pondered (pon′dərd) *v.* Considered carefully; thought over.

portentous (pôr ten′təs) *adj.* Indicating evil to come; ominous; threatening.

possessed (pə zest′) *adj.* Controlled or influenced by an evil spirit.

postern (pō′stərn) *adj.* Rear; lesser.

precariously (pri ker′ē əs lē) *adv.* Unsafely; uncertainly; dangerously; insecurely.

precaution (pri kô′shən) *n.* Care taken beforehand; thing done beforehand to secure good results.

precedents (pres′ə dənts) *n.* Examples; similar actions that occurred earlier.

precipitately (pri sip′ə tāt lē) *adv.* Suddenly; hastily; rashly.

precocious (pri kō′shəs) *adj.* Developed too early; occurring before the natural time.

predator (pred′ə tər) *n.* A person who injures or exploits others for his own gain.

predicated (pred′ə kāt əd) *v.* Declared to be an attribute or quality.

predisposes (prē′dis pōz′əz) *v.* Gives an inclination or tendency to.

premises (prem′is əz) *n.* A house or building with its grounds; matters previously stated, for example, laws governing certain actions.

premonition (prē′mə nish′ən) *n.* Feeling or warning of what is to come; forewarning.

preoccupation (prē ok′yə pā′shən) *n.* Being wholly absorbed by something to the exclusion of all else.

preoccupied (prē ok′yə pīd) *adj.* Engrossed; absorbed.

preposterously (pri pos′tər əs lē) *adv.* Unreasonably; absurdly; senselessly.

prerogatives (pri rog′ə tivz) *n.* Special superiority of rights or privileges.

presentable (pri zen′tə bəl) *adj.* Fit to be seen.

presuming (pri züm′ing) *v.* Taking for granted without proving; supposing.

presumptuous (pri zump′chü əs) *adj.* Too bold; forward; impudent.

primal (prī′məl) *adj.* Of early times; first.

primer (prim′ər) *n.* Something, such as a beginner's book, that equips a person with information, words, etc.

prodigious (prə dij′əs) *adj.* Very great; wonderful; marvelous.

profaners (prə fān′ərz) *n.* Persons who put something to wrong or unworthy use.

professing (prə fes′ing) *v.* Having as one's profession or business.

proffered (prof′ərd) *adj.* and *v.* Offered; presented.

prominent (prom′ə nənt) *adj.* Easy to see.

promiscuously (prə mis′kyü əs lē) *adv.* In a mixed and disorderly manner.

promontories (prom′ən tôr′ēz) *n.* High points of land extending from the coast into the water.

prone (prōn) *adj.* Lying face down; lying flat.

prophesy (prof′ə sī) *v.* Foretell; predict.

prosaic (prō zā′ik) *adj.* Ordinary; not exciting.

prospect (pros′peckt) *n.* Outlook for the future; thing expected to happen.

prospectors (pros′pek tərz) *n.* Persons who explore or examine a region, searching for gold, silver, etc.

protégé (prō′tə zhā) *n.* Person who has been taken under the protection or care of a friend or teacher.

protracted (prō trakt′əd) *adj.* Prolonged; extended.

protruded (prō trüd′əd) *v.* Stuck out.

protuberance (prō tü′bər əns) *n.* Bulge; part that sticks out.

prudent (prüd′nt) *adj.* Sensible; using good judgment.

puckered (puk′ərd) *adj.* Drawn into wrinkles or irregular folds. *v.* Drew into wrinkles or irregular folds.

pugilistic (pyü′jə lis′tik) *adj.* Having to do with boxing.

pungent (pun′jənt) *adj.* Sharply affecting the senses of taste and smell; sharp; spicy.

purling (pėrl′ing) *v.* Flowing with rippling motions and murmuring sounds.

quarry (kwôr′ē) *n.* Anything hunted or eagerly pursued.

quay (kē) *n.* A solid landing place where ships load and unload, often built of stone.

queasy (kwē′zē) *adj.* Suffering from nausea; tending to unsettle the stomach; uneasy.

queue (kyü) *n.* A line of people, automobiles, etc.

quizzically (kwiz′ə kəl ē) *adv.* Questioningly; in a baffled manner.

raiment (rā′mənt) *n.* Clothing; garments.

rancid (ran′sid) *adj.* Stale; spoiled.

rancor (rang′kər) *n.* Bitter ill will; extreme hatred or spite.

rank (rangk) *adj.* Having a strong, bad smell or taste.

rarity (rer′ə tē) *n.* Something very unusual.

ravaged (rav′ijd) *adj.* Greatly damaged.

recoil (rē′koil) *n.* A drawing or springing back.

recuperation (ri kyü′pə rā′shən) *n.* A recovering of one's health.

redemptive (ri demp′tiv) *adj.* Serving to save or rescue.

redresser (rē′dres ər) *n.* Person who sets to rights a wrong or offers a remedy, etc.; an avenger.

refrained (ri frānd′) *v.* Held back, especially from satisfying a momentary impulse.

rehabilitate (rē′hə bil′ə tāt) *v.* Restore to former standing, rank, etc.; restore to a good condition.

reiterated (rē it′ə rāt′əd) *v.* Repeated again and again; said several times.

relinquishes (ri ling′kwish əs) *v.* Lets go; releases.

relinquishing (ri ling′kwish ing) *v.* Letting go; releasing.

reluctantly (ri luk′tənt lē) *adv.* Unwillingly.

remarkable (ri mär′kə bəl) *adj.* Unusual; extraordinary.

reminiscences (rem′ə nis′ns əz) *n.* Accounts of something remembered; recollections.

repartee (rep′ər tē′) *n.* A witty reply or replies.

replenish (ri plen′ish) *v.* Fill again; renew; build up again.

reproached (ri prōcht′) *v.* Blamed; disapproved of.

repugnant (ri pug′nənt) *adj.* Disagreeable or offensive; objectionable.

resignation (rez′ig nā′shən) *n.* Patient acceptance; quiet submission.

resolutely (rez′ə lüt′lē) *adv.* In a firmly determined manner.

resolution (rez′ə lü′shən) *n.* Determination; decision.

respite (res′pit) *n.* Time of relief and rest; lull.

retaliates (ri tal′ē āts) *v.* Pays back wrong, injury, etc.; returns like for like.

retribution (ret′rə byü′shən) *n.* A deserved punishment; return for evil done.

retrospect (ret′rə spekt) *n.* Thinking about the past.

reverberated (ri vėr′bə rāt′əd) *v.* Echoed back; resounded.

revere (ri vir′) *v.* Honor greatly; love and respect deeply.

reverie (rev′ər ē) *n.* Dreamy thoughts, often of a pleasant nature.

revocable (rev′ə kə bəl) *adj.* Possible to be canceled or taken back.

rhapsodies (rap′sə dēz) *n.* Highly emotional utterances or cries.

righteous (rī′chəs) *adj.* Virtuous; proper.

roan (rōn) *n.* A horse having a yellowish- or reddish-brown color sprinkled with gray or white.

rogue (rōg) *n.* A dishonest person; a scoundrel or rascal.

rubicund (rü′bə kund) *adj.* Ruddy; having a rosy complexion.

rueful (rü′fəl) *adj.* Dejected; downcast; crestfallen; sorrowful; unhappy.

ruefully (rü′fəl ē) *adv.* Dejectedly; in an unhappy, crestfallen manner.

sagacity (sə gas′ə tē) *n.* Keen, sound judgment; mental acuteness.

sanctuary (sangk′chü er′ē) *n.* A sacred place.

sauntered (sôn′tərd) *v.* Strolled; walked slowly.

scoop (sküp) *n.* A hollow place.

scoundrel (skoun′drəl) *n.* Person without honor or good principles; rascal.

scrutinized (skrüt′n īzd) *v.* Examined carefully.

scrutinizing (skrü′tə nīz′ing) *v.* Examining carefully.

scuttle (skut′l) *n.* Kind of bucket for holding or carrying coal.

scuttled (skut′ld) *v.* Destroyed; ruined; sunk.

sensuous (sen'shü əs) *adj.* Having an effect on the bodily senses rather than on the mind; appealing strongly to the senses.

sepulcher (sep'əl kər) *n.* Tomb; grave.

seraphs (ser'əfs) *n.* Angels of the highest order.

serenely (sə rēn'lē) *adv.* Calmly; peacefully.

sextants (sek'stənts) *n.* Instruments used by navigators to determine latitude and longitude.

shambles (sham'bəlz) *n.* Great distruction; a mess.

silhouette (sil'ü et') *n.* A scene shown in outline.

silhouetted (sil'ü et'əd) *v.* Shown in outline.

simultaneously (sī'məl tā'nē əs lē) *adv.* At the same time.

singular (sing'gyə lər) *adj.* Extraordinary; unusual; strange; odd.

singularity (sing'gyə lar'ə tē) *n.* Condition of being one of its kind.

sinister (sin'ə stər) *adj.* Threatening; disastrous; unfortunate.

slithered (sliŦH'ərd) *v.* Slid along, especially unsteadily.

slough (sluf) *v.* Throw away; discard.

smoldering (smōl'dər ing) *v.* Suppressing heated emotion.

solemnized (sol'əm nīzd) *v.* Performed.

solicitor (sə lis'ə tər) *n.* A lawyer.

somber (som'bər) *adj.* Dark; gloomy; having deep shadows.

sonorous (sə nôr'əs) *adj.* Full and rich in sound.

sordid (sôr'did) *adj.* Dirty; filthy.

soughing (suf'ing) *n.* A rustling or murmuring sound.

spectacle (spek'tə kəl) *n.* A public show or display.

spectacular (spek tak'yə lər) *adj.* Making a great display or show; sensational.

speculating (spek'yə lāt ing) *v.* Guessing.

squandered (skwon'dərd) *v.* Wasted; spent foolishly.

squeamish (skwē'mish) *adj.* Easily shocked; easily affected by nausea.

staccato (stə kä'tō) *adj.* Abrupt; sharp and disconnected.

stimulus (stim'yə ləs) *n.* Something that stirs to action; incentive.

stolid (stol'id) *adj.* Unemotional; impassive; not easily excited.

stratagems (strat'ə jəmz) *n.* Schemes or tricks for deceiving an enemy; trickery.

stupor (stü'pər) *n.* A dazed condition; loss or lessening of the power to feel.

suavity (swä'və tē) *n.* Smooth politeness.

subdued (səb düd') *adj.* Toned down; suppressed.

submissive (səb mis'iv) *adj.* Yielding to the power, control, or authority of another.

subordinate (sə bôrd'n it) *adj.* Lower in importance; secondary.

subsequently (sub'sə kwənt lē) *adv.* At a later time.

subsided (səb sīd'əd) *v.* Grew less; died down.

subtle (sut'l) *adj.* Working unnoticeably; so fine as to escape observation.

succession (sək sesh'ən) *n.* The coming of one person or thing after another.

succulent (suk'yə lənt) *adj.* Having thick or fleshy and juicy leaves or stems.

succumb (sə kum') *v.* Give way to; yield.

sufficient (sə fish'ənt) *adj.* As much as is needed; enough.

sundry (sun'drē) *adj.* Several; various.

superstitions (sü'pər stish'ənz) *n.* Beliefs or practices founded on ignorant fear or mistaken reverence.

supple (sup'əl) *adj.* Moving easily and nimbly.

suppliant (sup'lē ənt) *n.* A person who asks humbly and earnestly.

supplication (sup'lə kā'shən) *n.* A humble prayer or plea.

suppositions (sup'ə zish'ənz) *n.* Possibilities; assumptions; beliefs; opinions.

suppurating (sup'yə rāt'ing) *v.* Forming or discharging pus; festering.

surcease (sər sēs') *n.* An end to; cessation, especially a temporary ceasing.

surmise (sər mīz') *n.* Formation of an idea with little or no evidence; a guessing.

surmount (sər mount') *v.* Overcome.

susceptible (se sep'tə bəl) *adj.* Very sensitive to.

symmetry (sim'ə trē) *n.* A well-balanced arrangement of parts.

synchronizing (sing'krə nīz ing) *v.* Taking place at the same rate and exactly together.

tableau (tab'lō) *n.* A scene; a picture.

talisman (tal'i smən) *n.* An object supposed to have magical powers; a charm.

tampering (tam'pər ing) *v.* Meddling improperly with.

tangible (tan'jə bəl) *adj.* Real; actual; able to be touched or felt by touch.

tattoo (ta tü') *n.* Series of raps, taps, beats, etc.; rapid rythmic beating or rapping.

taunted (tônt'əd) *v.* Jeered at; mocked.

taut (tôt) *adj.* Tightly drawn; tense.

tawdry (tô′drē) *adj.* Showy and cheap in appearance and quality.

temperance (tem′pər əns) *n.* Being moderate in action, speech, habits, etc.; moderation.

tenacious (ti nā′shəs) *adj.* Stubborn; persistent; holding fast.

tentacle (ten′tə kəl) *n.* A sensitive, hairlike growth on a plant.

tentatively (ten′tə tiv lē) *adv.* Experimentally; in a hesitating manner.

testy (tes′tē) *adj.* Easily irritated; impatient; peevish.

theoretical (thē′ə ret′ə kəl) *adj.* Based on observation and reasoning, not on fact.

thwarted (thwôrt′əd) *adj.* Prevented.

thwarts (thwôrts) *n.* Seats across a boat on which rowers sit.

timorous (tim′ər əs) *adj.* Easily frightened; timid.

tolerable (tol′ər ə bəl) *adj.* Fairly good; passable.

tolerance (tol′ər əns) *n.* A putting up with people whose opinions or ways differ from one's own.

tolerate (tol′ə rāt′) *v.* Put up with; endure; allow or permit.

tormentors (tôr men′tərz) *n.* Persons who worry or annoy another very much.

tranquilly (trang′kwəl ē) *adv.* Calmly; quietly.

transfixed (tran sfikst′) *v.* Made motionless or helpless.

transgression (trans gresh′ən) *n.* Breaking or going against a law, command, etc.; sin.

transitory (tran′sə tor′ē) *adj.* Lasting only a short time; fleeting.

transits (tran′sits) *n.* Instruments used in surveying to measure angles.

transpire (tran spīr′) *v.* Take place; happen; occur; become known.

traversed (trav′ərst) *v.* Passed across, over, or through.

treacherous (trech′ər əs) *adj.* Not to be trusted; not reliable; deceiving.

tremendous (tri men′dəs) *adj.* Very great; enormous.

tremor (trem′ər) *n.* A shaking or vibrating movement.

trepidation (trep′ə dā′shən) *n.* Nervous dread; fear; fright.

trial (trī′əl) *n.* A cause of trouble or hardship.

triumvirate (trī um′vər it) *n.* Any group of three.

truant (trü′ənt) *adj.* Staying away from school without permission.

Pronunciation Key

hat, āge, fär; let, ēqual, tėrm;
it, īce; hot, ōpen, ôrder;
oil, out; cup, pùt, rüle;
ch, child; ng, long; sh, she;
th, thin; ₮ℍ, then; zh, measure;
ə represents *a* in about, *e* in taken,
i in pencil, *o* in lemon, *u* in circus.

---

truculently (truk′yə lənt lē) *adv.* In a brutally harsh manner; fiercely.

tumult (tü′mult) *n.* Uproar; a violent disturbance or disorder; commotion.

turbulence (tėr′byə ləns) *n.* Violent up-and-down currents in the atmosphere.

turmoil (tėr′moil) *n.* An utterly confused or extremely agitated condition.

ultimate (ul′tə mit) *adj.* Last possible; final; beyond which there is nothing at all.

unaccountable (un′ə koun′tə bəl) *adj.* Unexplainable.

uncanny (un kan′ē) *adj.* Strange and mysterious; having some special power.

uncomprehending (un′kom pri hend′ing) *adj.* Not understanding something fully and correctly.

uncongenial (un′kən jē′nyəl) *adj.* Unfriendly; not agreeable.

uncoordinated (un′kō ôrd′n āt′əd) *adj.* Not acting together properly.

undismayed (un′dis mād′) *v.* Unafraid; untroubled.

undulated (un′jə lāt əd) *v.* Moved in waves.

unidentifiable (un′ī den′tə fī′ə bl) *adj.* Unrecognizable.

uniped (yü′nə ped) *n.* A person having only one foot or leg.

unkempt (un kempt′) *adj.* Untidy; not neat and clean.

unobtrusive (un′əb trü′siv) *adj.* Modest; inconspicuous.

unperceived (un′pər sēvd′) *adj.* Unseen; unobserved.

unplagued (un plāgd′) *adj.* Unbothered; not being annoyed.

unprovoked (un′prə vōkt′) *adj.* Not having cause or reason.

unredressed (un ri drest') *adj.* Not set right; not avenged.

unsavory (un sā'vər ē) *adj.* Unpleasant; distasteful.

untenanted (un ten'ənt əd) *adj.* Unoccupied; not lived in.

untrammeled (un tram'əld) *adj.* Not hindered; unrestrained; free.

uttering (ut'ər ing) *v.* Expressing; giving forth.

valedictorian (val'ə dik tôr'ē ən) *n.* Student who gives the farewell address at the graduating exercises, usually the one ranking highest in the class.

vanquished (vang'kwisht) *v.* Overcome by other than physical means; conquered; defeated.

vehemently (vē'ə mənt lē) *adv.* Forcefully; violently; very emphatically.

veneer (və nir') *n.* Surface appearance or show.

venomous (ven'ə məs) *adj.* Spiteful; malicious.

ventriloquists (ven tril'ə kwists) *n.* People who speak or utter sounds with the lips not moving so that the voice seems to come from some source other than the speaker.

verbatim (vər bā'tim) *adv.* and *adj.* Word for word; in exactly the same words.

verging (vėrj'ing) *v.* Tending toward; being on the brink of.

verified (ver'ə fīd) *v.* Confirmed; proved to be true.

vermilion (vər mil'yən) *n.* A bright red.

vestige (ves'tij) *n.* Trace, mark, sign, or other evidence.

vex (veks) *v.* Worry; trouble.

viciously (vish'əs lē) *adv.* Savagely; fiercely.

vigilance (vij'ə ləns) *n.* Watchfulness.

vigil (vij'əl) *n.* Careful observation; looking with care and attention.

vintages (vin'tij əz) *n.* Wines from certain crops of grapes.

virtuoso (vėr'chü ō'sō) *n.* A person who has a cultivated appreciation of something fine.

virulence (vir'yə ləns) *n.* Deadliness; quality of being very harmful.

visage (viz'ij) *n.* Face.

vivacious (vī vā'shəs) *adj.* Lively; sprightly; animated.

voluminous (və lü'mə nəs) *adj.* Of great size; large.

vortex (vôr'teks) *n.* A whirl of activity; whirlwind.

vouchsafe (vouch sāf') *v.* Be willing to grant or give.

vulnerable (vul'nər ə bəl) *adj.* Open to attack; easily hurt or wounded.

wanton (won'tən) *adj.* Reckless, heartless, or malicious.

warily (wer'ə lē) *adv.* Cautiously; carefully.

warrant (wôr'ənt) *v.* Give one's word for; promise; guarantee.

wary (wer'ē) *adj.* On one's guard against danger, deception, etc.; cautious or careful; being mistrustful and on the alert for danger or trouble.

wavered (wā'vərd) *v.* Became unsteady.

whetstone (hwet'stōn') *n.* Stone for sharpening knives or tools.

whimpered (hwim'pərd) *v.* Made low, mournful sounds.

wizened (wiz'nd) *adj.* Dried up; withered.

wont (wunt) *n.* Custom; habit.

wracking (rak'ing) *adj.* Destroying; utterly ruinous.

wretched (rech'id) *adj.* Miserable; very unfortunate or unhappy.

writhes (rīᴛʜz) *v.* Twists and turns.

writhing (rīᴛʜ'ing) *v.* Twisting and turning.

wryly (rī'lē) *adv.* In an ironic manner; with a grimly humorous intent.

zealous (zel'əs) *adj.* Very enthusiastic; earnest.

FINE ART INDEX

FINE ART SOURCES

PHOTO CREDITS

LITERARY TYPES INDEX

INDEX OF AUTHORS AND TITLES

Selection titles presented in the textbook are shown in italics. Numbers in italics refer to the pages on which the biographical notes of authors appear. Names of authors represented in the textbook and other references are shown in regular type.